The Great Pyramid

its Divine Message

AN ORIGINAL CO-ORDINATION OF HISTORICAL
DOCUMENTS AND ARCHAEOLOGICAL EVIDENCES

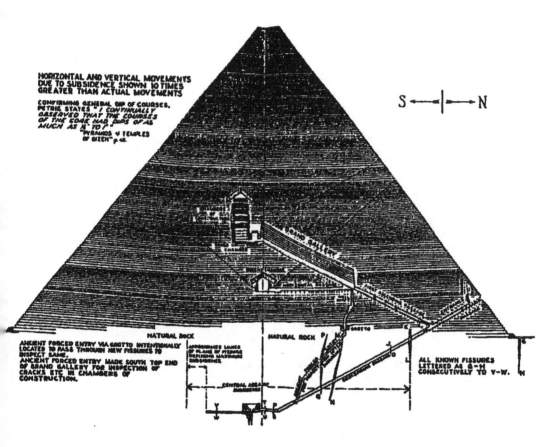

D. Davidson and H. Aldersmith

ISBN 1-56459-116-6

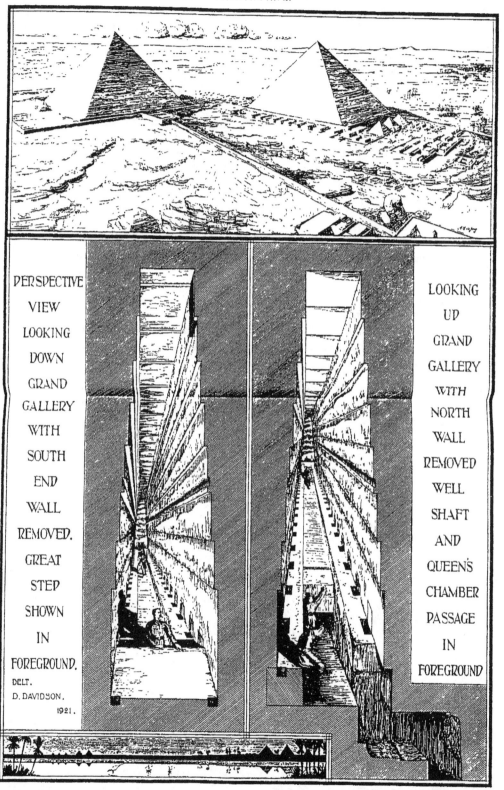

PERSPECTIVE VIEW LOOKING DOWN GRAND GALLERY WITH SOUTH END WALL REMOVED. GREAT STEP SHOWN IN FOREGROUND.

DELT. D. DAVIDSON. 1921.

LOOKING UP GRAND GALLERY WITH NORTH WALL REMOVED WELL SHAFT AND QUEEN'S CHAMBER PASSAGE IN FOREGROUND

The Edge of the Great Step—now badly broken and grooved, opposite the standing figure in the left-hand panel above—is here shown restored.

My elucidation of the various phases of the Great Pyramid's design has led me to perceive that it is an expression of the Truth in structural form.

I proclaim, with humility and yet with confidence, that the Pyramid's Message establishes the Bible as the Inspired Word of God, and testifies that Jesus Christ, by HIS DISPLACEMENT, paid the purchase price of mankind's Redemption, and effected the Salvation of all who truly believe in Him.

This Message concerns all mankind, to whom, in a humble spirit, this work is dedicated, in the hope that it may bring enlightenment and comfort to many.

D. D.

INTRODUCTION

It is very probable that the reader has already perused many other books dealing with the Great Pyramid, and professing to elucidate its mystery, and to demonstrate its connection with ancient astronomy and its supposed confirmation of Biblical prophecy. The history of modern Pyramid theory is not a long one, commencing only in the second half of the 18th century. During the latter half of this century, and at the beginning of the 19th century, several works were published containing the theory that the Pyramid's base measurements were an intentional representation of the number of days in the year. A considerable advance in Pyramid theory was made in the year 1859, when Mr. John Taylor, a London publisher of some repute as a literary man and mathematician, published a book advancing the hypothesis that the proportion of the Pyramid's height to its base circuit was that of the diameter of a circle to its circumference, that the Great Pyramid was built to convey a Divine Revelation, and that its unit of measure was the Polar Diameter inch.

Strong confirmation of Taylor's theories was furnished by the survey undertaken by Professor Piazzi Smyth in 1864–65. The interior of the Pyramid was carefully measured, and angular measurements were taken of the casing stones *in situ*, and of the slope of the passages. These measurements indicated the probability that the Polar Diameter inch was the unit of measure employed; that the base circuit was a representation of the solar year; and confirmed Taylor's theory relating to the proportion of height to base. This survey and the accurate survey made by Sir William M. F. Petrie are very fully discussed in the present work, and furnish the materials for the authors' reconstruction of the Great Pyramid.

In 1865 Mr. Robert Menzies advanced the theory that the Passage System was a chronological representation of prophecy; that the scale of the chronology was one Polar Diameter inch to a solar year, and that the Great Gallery symbolised the Christian Dispensation. Subsequent development of this theory indicated that the entrance doorway to the Antechamber symbolised the beginning of the final period of Great Wars and Tribulations prophesied in the Bible. It should be noted that these identifications were made long before any evidence had been obtained from Egyptian texts to show that this interpretation was correct, and before anything was known about the ancient Egyptian Messianic prophecy.

Menzies' theory was adopted by Piazzi Smyth, but, unfortunately, he also adopted Menzies' idea that the Christian Dispensation began at the Birth of Christ, and accepted the date of the Nativity as 1 A.D. The Christian Dispensation, of course, did not begin until the Resurrection, or until Pentecost of the Crucifixion year, and had this been realised by Smyth and his followers, and had they adopted a perpendicular co-ordinate instead of a vertical co-ordinate for the end of the Grand Gallery, they would have defined, fifty-nine years ago, the precise date of the beginning of the Great War.

Many Christian thinkers realised that it was incorrect to date the beginning of the Christian Dispensation from the Birth of Christ, and protest was first made in 1881–82 by the Rev. Commander L. G. A. Roberts, who took up the matter with Smyth's followers, but was unable to persuade them to accept his views. About the same time, Dr. H. Aldersmith and the Rev. Dr. Denis Hanan both agreed that if the Grand Gallery symbolised the Christian Dispensation, then the commencement of the Gallery must necessarily symbolise the date of the Crucifixion or that of the Pentecost of the Crucifixion year.

But it was not until 1905 that Col. J. Garnier, R.E., published a work entitled " The Great Pyramid, Its Builder and Prophecy," in which he identified the beginning of the Grand Gallery with the date of the Crucifixion. His system of chronology was invalidated, however, by his adoption of 31 A.D. as the date of the Crucifixion and by his use of a vertical instead of a perpendicular co-ordinate at the end of the Grand Gallery. Nevertheless, he obtained the date of 1913 A.D. for the beginning of the War Chaos.

Following this short history of the development of Pyramid theory, the writer desires to submit a brief epitome of the subjects discussed and the conclusions reached in the present work. It is demonstrated that—

(1) The Great Pyramid is a geometrical representation of the mathematical basis of the science of a former civilisation.

(2) This former civilisation had condensed its knowledge of natural law into a single general formula, and the application of this formula was analogous to the modern application of Einstein's Theory of Relativity.

(3) The universal application of this formula in the world of this former civilisation left its impress on every form of constructional expression, whether ethical, literary, or artistic.

(4) This civilisation was anterior to all other known civilisations of the ancient East. These civilisations were established by the former civilisation, firstly, by intercourse, and finally, by migration, and their various phases of ethical, literary, and artistic expression all bear the stamp of the original scientific principles of the former civilisation.

(5) The Egyptian Records define the geometrical dimensions and the unit of measure of a Standard Pyramid that constitutes the geometrical expression of the ancient Law of Relativity.

(6) The survey of Sir William M. F. Petrie shows that the Great Pyramid of Gizeh is the Standard Pyramid defined by the Egyptian Records.

(7) The Passage System forms the graphical representation of an elaborate system of prophetical chronology, intimately related to the Biblical prophecy, giving various essential datings for the Christian Dispensation and accurately predicting the precise dates of the beginning and ending of the Great War.

(8) The Pyramid symbolism, when considered in conjunction with Biblical prophecy, indicates that its message is addressed to the present era, and that the final Time of Tribulation, so often prophesied in the Bible, is now upon us.

The reader will realise that many new and startling interpretations are presented that will give ample scope for criticism to students of many and various branches of science. The authors do not claim to be experts in any particular science, but believe they have succeeded in co-ordinating the finished work of the best authorities in each particular branch of knowledge that is alluded to in this work.

It will be found that the work naturally divides itself into the following subjects :—

    I. The History of Geometry and Metrology.
    II. Gravitational Astronomy.
    III. Astronomical Chronology.
    IV. Archæology and History.
    V. Theology.

This range of deep and apparently unrelated subjects is necessary because it is found that the literary records of the ancient civilisations of the East—but particularly those of the Egyptians and Hebrews—indicate that the mathematical application of the ancient Law of Relativity governs the ancient form of presentation of each of the subjects enumerated.

A brief discussion of the scope of the present work under each of these headings will not be out of place.

I. THE HISTORY OF GEOMETRY AND METROLOGY.

It is shown that the system of ancient metrology was founded upon two functions of the earth and its orbit, the standard time unit being the solar year, and the standard distance unit a decimal sub-division of the earth's Polar Diameter. This standard distance unit is established independently from innumerable ancient metrological sources, from the Egyptian texts, and from the Great Pyramid itself, as the primitive or Pyramid inch, of the value of 1·0011 British inches. Twenty-five of such inches are one ten-millionth part of the earth's Polar Radius, and are also equal to the ancient Hebrew Sacred Cubit.

II. GRAVITATIONAL ASTRONOMY.

The numerical value of the extent of the hollowing-in of the casing of the Great Pyramid is an important function of the Pyramid's geometry of the year circle.   This particular function defines the horizontal displacement of the Passage System, the displacement of the Grand Gallery Roof above the first Ascending Passage Roof, and an important displacement relating to the Great Step in the Grand Gallery.   It is the principal factor of the geometrical expression of the ancient Law of Relativity, and in the present work has been termed the " Displacement Factor."

The Displacement Factor, in conjunction with the Pyramid's base circuit, of which it itself is a function, supplies nine different astronomical values defined with the accuracy of modern astronomy and represented by the external lines and surfaces of the Great Pyramid.   The Egyptian literary traditions state that the Great Pyramid was built for the purpose of handing on to a future race precisely such astronomical knowledge as is indicated by these nine values, and it would appear that the geometry of the Great Pyramid is a definition of gravitational astronomy as it was understood by a former civilisation.

III. ASTRONOMICAL CHRONOLOGY.

The External Geometrical System is the General Framework for the Internal Geometrical System of the Passages and Chambers.   The Internal System is a complete graphical exposition of Gravitational Astronomy of which the elements are furnished by the External System.   Ideas are dealt with and expressed without dependence upon any language, and presented entirely in the terms of natural science.

The Passage System is shown to contain a basic line of reference that forms an absolute scale of astronomical chronology.   Dates that are given by this scale are confirmed by references to variable astronomical values, such as the rate of Precession and the Longitude of Perihelion, the values for which, at the various dates referred to, are supplied by the geometry of the Passage System.   These values, in every case, agree with the values obtained by modern methods and formulæ.

It is a significant feature that this scale of astronomical chronology is the only scale—beginning at a definite zero date—that can form the arithmetical basis for the expression of every related function of Gravitational Law.   It is, therefore, the scale of the periodic law of astronomical motions and distances, and of the changes in these motions and distances, as they affect the earth, and the important Displacement Factor is employed in the definition of all changes in motion and distance.

IV. ARCHÆOLOGY AND HISTORY.

An examination of historical evidence shows that most of the ancient civilised peoples had adopted the astronomical chronology of the former civilisation, precisely as it is represented in the Great Pyramid, for their records are dated with reference to the Pyramid's ancient chronology. This has enabled the authors to synchronise the records of Egypt, Babylon, and Israel, and the reader will find that this synchronism, and the resulting solutions of ancient history and chronology, form one of the outstanding features of this book. The records of the Egyptians and ancestors of the Hebrews show that both these peoples originally possessed a highly scientific system of calendar year intercalation, with various related calendar and astronomical cycles, derived from the same original system represented by the Great Pyramid. This fact, established by different and independent sets of evidence in this book, throws an entirely new light upon the question of ancient history.

V. THEOLOGY.

Under this heading mention may be made of a striking solution of the true significance of the first eleven chapters of the Book of Genesis, and of the antediluvian genealogies.

In a discussion of the religious ceremonies performed by the ancient Egyptians, it is shown that the origin of these is identical with the origin of Hebrew ideas relating to the ancient cycles, and this leads to the demonstration that the ceremonies were related to the Messianic prophecies, both of the Ancient Egyptians and the Hebrews.

It is then shown that the Great Pyramid is defined by the ancient Egyptian Messianic texts as the symbolic representation of Messianic prophecy, its Passages and Chambers as allegorically picturing epochs and phases of history connected with the evolution of the Messianic kingdom ; and the astronomical datings of these Passages and Chambers as prophetically giving the dates of these epochs and phases of history.

The first important epoch indicated by the Egyptian Messianic texts, and by the Pyramid symbolism, is the turning-point in history, when the ascent began towards the conditions necessary for the first phase of Messianic prophecy. The date of the turning or beginning of the ascent, as defined by the Pyramid's chronology, is the date that is given by Egyptian, Hebrew, and Babylonian records for the Exodus of Israel.

The next two important epochs, similarly indicated, are those of the Birth and Passion of the Messiah. By a critical examination of contemporary history, and of the internal evidence of the Gospels, it is shown that the dates of the Nativity and Crucifixion are identical with the Pyramid datings for those points in its Passage System which are specified in the Egyptian Messianic texts as connected with these two epochs.

It is further demonstrated that the Pyramid imagery of the Egyptian Messianic texts was derived from the symbolism relating to Messianic prophecy in the Great Pyramid, and this throws a flood of light upon the Messianic prophecy of the Old and New Testaments. The time indications of these prophecies are seen to be identical with certain cycles and periods of remotely ancient prophecy, and with cycles and periods in the Great Pyramid's chronological representation. When studied in this light, it is seen that these prophecies give a predictive chronological continuation of the ancient system of astronomical chronology, and of the sequence of history presented by all the ancient records. Applied in this relation, they give the same epoch for the Messiah as is given by the ancient Egyptian Messianic prophecy and by the Pyramid's chronological indications. This accounts for the continual use of Pyramid symbolism in the predictive statements of the Old and New Testaments. The Pyramid, or " Stone Kingdom," represents the Messianic kingdom, of which Christ is the Apex Pyramid, or Head and Chief Corner Stone. All the spiritual entities in this state are in unity when the Messiah becomes the Appointed Head.

That the Message of the Pyramid is meant for the present time, or present civilisation, is indicated by all three systems of Messianic prophecy —the ancient Egyptian, the Pyramid, and the Hebrew prophecies. These unite in giving the date of December 1557 A.D. as the date of the beginning of the final phase of acceleration towards the establishing of the Messianic kingdom.

This date ushered in a period of development such as the world had never known, and that culminated in the great European War. The dates of the beginning and ending of the Great War are given to the day by the Pyramid's system of astronomical chronology, and the symbolism indicates that this is a period of chaos and oppression. Similarly, the period from 11th November 1918 to 29th May 1928 is symbolised as " Truce in Chaos," and the ancient Egyptian Messianic imagery defines the locality symbolising this period as the period of the " Triple Veil," a period in which something tangible is to be revealed concerning hidden things and purposes. After the " Truce in Chaos," it is indicated that a new period of chaos and oppression will begin which will continue until the 16th September 1936. What this date relates to, and what are the logical arguments leading up to the conclusions outlined above, can best be seen and understood by reading the book itself.

The question of Pyramid symbolism is very thoroughly dealt with, not only the symbolism relating to man's physical history and environment, but also its symbolism of his spiritual development and his spiritual necessities. It is impossible, within the limits of this introduction, to enlarge upon this subject, and the reader must refer to the concluding chapter of the book, where the Messianic symbolism of the Pyramid is elucidated. Suffice it to say that the all-important Displacement Factor is essential to this elucidation, as the Displacement Factor is the connecting geometrical link between the Apex Pyramid and the external and internal geometrical systems. The symbolism indicates that the Messiah was pre-elected before the creation of Man's Universe, for the purpose of effecting a reconciliation that would be necessary to establish eternal harmony in Creation ; that the Displacement of Man necessitated the displacement of the Messiah to restore man ; and that all the factors in the work of Creation were divinely co-ordinated with this pre-determined end in view.

The history of Pyramid prophecy in ancient times has been dealt with by the authors in an exhaustive manner, and the present writer has submitted, at the beginning of this Introduction, a brief statement of the modern development of Pyramid theory. It may not be out of place to add a short account of the genesis of this work. If the reader has already made a study of the various works that have been published dealing with the Pyramid and Pyramid theory, he will probably have realised that Pyramidology, for over sixty years, has consisted of intuitions, and theories based on these intuitions. In no case, however, has any one of the theories advanced been established, though certain elements common to all the theories have been presented in a manner that indicated the authors' opinion that their demonstration was merely a matter of time and fortuitous circumstance. The authors of the present work admit that it has been fortuitous circumstance alone that has placed in their hands the data for solution, and the solution itself, when—as they wish to have put on record—similar fortuitous circumstance would have been used to greater effect, and the resulting solution more ably demonstrated, by other more capable and more learned investigators.

In the early part of the present century, Mr. D. Davidson, who had been studying Egyptology as accessory to agnostic criticism of the Scriptures, was introduced to the study of the Great Pyramid by Mr. James Moncrieff of Glasgow, who forwarded him a small elementary book on the subject. Mr. Davidson's interest was aroused by discovering that it appeared certain that the Pyramid gave an intentional representation of the ratio, circumference of circle to radius of circle, and he was encouraged to continue his researches.

The results of his preliminary investigation, issued in serial form during 1910, were to the effect that the Pyramid contained a Divine Revelation, defined by a system of geometry connecting the exterior of the Pyramid with its internal Passage System, that, Petrie's measurements being correct, the outline of the geometrical system could be discovered by a study of the Pyramid's existing measures ; and that comparison of the Hebrew chronology with the Pyramid's geometrical chronology would indicate the identities postulated by Smyth and his school.

The publication of these results brought Mr. Davidson into a private controversy with the late Dr. H. Aldersmith, which eventually led to collaboration in further research work. Dr. Aldersmith concentrated upon prophecy interpretation and its fulfilment in history, and Mr. Davidson upon the mathematics of the Pyramid, its geometry in relation to gravitational astronomy, and the elucidation of astronomical chronology in Egypt, Babylon, and Israel.

The research work was interrupted by the war, and Dr. Aldersmith died in March 1918.   After the war Mr. Davidson found himself on the track of entirely new data that showed that the final solution of all the related problems was in sight.   The present volume embodies all the original and latest discoveries, covering the entire field already described.

There are two matters to which Mr. Davidson has asked the writer to make special allusion.   He wishes to lay stress upon the extreme reluctance he experienced in adopting a new horizontal scale for the Antechamber, King's Chamber, and connecting passage.   This horizontal scale was suggested by Mr. William Reeve of Toronto in 1904, and adopted by the Rev. Commander Roberts, who also discovered that the perpendicular from the sill of the Entrance Doorway of the first low Passage leading to the Antechamber indicated the date of the beginning of the Great War.   Mr. Davidson was hostile to the adoption of this scale, but, on investigating the matter, found that if the unit were taken as a month of thirty days (instead of one-twelfth of the solar year, as adopted by Commander Roberts) the theory actually agreed with the geometrical indications of the Antechamber, and also defined the dates of the beginning and ending of the Great War.

The other matter has reference to the Pyramid's representation of Natural Law and of the ancient Law of Relativity.   It is not intended that the reader should suppose that it is the authors' contention that the Pyramid is a precise representation of Natural Law as it was formulated by the Creator.   It is intended merely that the Pyramid's definition of this law should be understood as a Divine Revelation of certain aspects of this Law, which can be understood and appreciated by the men living during the era to which the message of the Pyramid is addressed.

It has not been an easy task to write this book ; it will not be an easy task to read it.   It will be realised that the exposition and the co-ordination of the mass of historical and scientific data that has been accumulated during many years of research has resulted in the composition of a work of such magnitude and importance as will prove difficult of assimilation even by the most careful reader.   The writer, indeed, cannot pretend to have thoroughly assimilated the work himself, but he is confident that its thorough understanding will well repay the necessary mental effort involved, for, if the authors' conclusions be accepted, the problems dealt with are of such a nature and of such importance as to affect the future welfare of all mankind.

Many, no doubt, will differ from the various conclusions presented by the authors, but all, he ventures to think, will award them due tribute for the sincerity and comprehensiveness of their efforts to unravel and to solve problems that have perplexed the world for countless generations.

J. CLEMISHAW.

PREFACE

THE title of this work is scarcely descriptive of the range of subjects dealt with. It more properly expresses the central idea towards which modern lines of research—when studied in co-ordinated relation—are seen to converge, and from which originated and diverged certain ancient conceptions and beliefs that have formed the bases of scholastic speculation from remote antiquity. This statement is warranted by a co-ordination of certain facts which have been public property for many centuries. This co-ordination, it is claimed, now appears in the present work in the original form from which these facts emerged, and is deemed to establish that the Great Pyramid monumentalises the science and philosophy of a past civilisation ; that it is a graphical (or geometrical) representation of a precise science, and that it contains a structural symbolism of the highest form of religious belief which man is capable of attaining. This result is due more to the work and researches of Sir William M. F. Petrie, Sir Ernest A. Wallis Budge, the late Sir Gaston Maspero, and Mr. Marsham Adams in Egyptology, and of Professors Oppolzer, Bauschinger, and Newcomb in Dynamical Astronomy, than to the researches of the authors of the present work.

It is the presentation of the several independent series of facts of different sciences, as these facts are established by reliable authorities, that constitutes the essential feature of the present work, and it is upon this presentation that the reader is asked to form his own conclusions. I believe that the *ultimate* consensus of opinion will be that this presentation is in itself the formulation of a new general science, and that the present work is a textbook upon the subject and a compendium relating to the data as these are understood at present.

It is usual to present a new exposition in technical form before a popular work on the subject is attempted. In the present volume the form of presentation has been designed to meet both requirements, as far as is possible in the circumstances. This explains the division of the chapters into three sections and the Summary and Conclusions relating to the data of each chapter being included under the first section. Section I of each chapter, with its Summary and Conclusions, forms the essential presentation of the thesis in the form most nearly approximating, under the conditions imposed, to the requirements of a popular exposition.

Briefly stated, the scope of the three sections of each chapter is as follows :—

Section I.—This is concerned with the development of the thesis with a minimum of technical and accessory detail. The central argument is maintained without digression. At the same time, Section I, in its " Summary and Conclusions," comprises the conclusions arrived at in the discussions under Sections II and III.

Section II.—This deals with the discussion of the principal accessory data bearing on Section I, but which, if dealt with under Section I. would break the continuity of presentation.

Section III.—This contains the detailed technical description of plates, charts, and diagrams, and the discussions of accessory data relating to the same. The latter data comprise data essential for reference in later chapters, or for amplification of the data in preceding chapters, but which, if included under Sections I and II, would appear to be digressions.

The reader—whatever his qualifications may be—is recommended to read the first sections of all five chapters in sequence before attempting the other sections.

Particular care has been taken in regard to the arrangement and preparation of the plates and tables to ensure that these should, generally, be self-explanatory to avoid frequent reference to the text. Accordingly, considerable detail has been concentrated into certain plates and tables. This is particularly the case in the plates of Chapter IV, and in the plates, tables, and attached annotations of Chapter V.

In a first reading too much attention should not be directed to this feature of the work. The reader is not recommended to attempt to master detail until he has grasped the general outline of the thesis. By proceeding in this manner the reader will find that difficulties encountered in the earlier chapters are cleared up in the later chapters. Difficulties thus disposed of in the preliminary reading recommended will enable the reader to proceed with confidence to the assimilation and the consequent criticism of Sections II and III and the details concentrated into the plates, tables, and annotations. It is the wide range of subjects dealt with that renders it necessary for me thus to presume to advise the reader, and that left me no other alternative than to arrange the work in this manner.

With the exception of a few pages in Section III of Chapter IV, the whole work has been written to be within the range of the mathematical attainments of the average reader. On this basis, tables and rules relating to all the chronological and astronomical calculations in this work have been prepared to enable the reader to check all the dates of the Egyptian, Babylonian, and Hebrew systems of chronology. These tables and rules are given in Section III of Chapter V.

An unusual feature of the work is provided by the particular series of chronological and historical tables and annotations inserted between Sections Iᴀ and Iʙ of Chapter V. These represent the result of fifteen years' work. They are the equivalent of my own MS. data that would have extended to an additional volume.

As now given in forty-four pages of tabulations and annotations, they create a context of comparative data, more easily assimilated than many hundreds of pages of analytical discussion, and certainly preferable to the usual process of proof by narrative and demonstration.

The original intention was to deal in the first volume only with my own particular researches in metrology, geometry, astronomy, and archæology relating to the Great Pyramid, and to deal in a second volume with the late Dr. Aldersmith's exposition of Old and New Testament prophecy and New Testament history, together with my own data relating to ancient history and chronology. The indication of this original intention is still preserved in the sub-title of this work. It was felt, however, as the work developed, that this intention scarcely expressed the high regard in which I held my late colleague and my indebtedness to him for many valuable suggestions, much sound criticism, and whole-hearted co-operation in the wearying task of exploring innumerable avenues of research in my own particular province of study prior to Dr. Aldersmith's death in March 1918. Bearing all this in mind, I eventually felt impelled to expand the scope of the present volume to include such part of Dr. Aldersmith's work as would not rob the second volume of its essential features of independent interest and importance. I have referred to such of his work as has been embodied in the text of Chapter V. I have also adopted in ¶¶ 331, 336, and 337 the essential data relating to his admirable exposition of the intention of the 70 weeks' prophecy of Daniel ix, and in many other cases of prophecy interpretations have been influenced to an undefinable extent by intimate knowledge of my late learned colleague's teaching and opinions concerning the interpretation of the Hebrew apocalyptic writings.

Since the date of Dr. Aldersmith's death the lines of study and research have led to the entirely new and complete form of presentation now developed in the present volume ; in one particular feature only have I departed from the opinions held by Dr. Aldersmith in relation to the application of his data. This concerns whether a particular allegory extends to the Church of the New Testament or to the nation Israel. It is a question one would like to see thoroughly investigated, and I have therefore presented it in the form in which I believe it will appeal to the largest number of readers.

The whole of the present volume has been written—or re-written in condensed form—during the fourteen months ending at the date of writing this preface.

Owing to the importance of the data contained in Section II of Chapter V, this section has been entirely re-written and re-arranged by Mr. J. Clemishaw, M.B.E., A.M.I.C.E., from the original MSS. Mr. Clemishaw has also read through the whole of the text of this volume with infinite care and patience, and my thanks are due to him for his kindly criticism and suggestions and for the invaluable assistance he has rendered throughout.   I am also under an obligation to him for preparing the Index.

I owe a debt of gratitude to my assistants, Mr. R. C. Dalley and Miss Hilda Sudbury, for the painstaking manner in which they have assisted me with the preparation of the work and for the keen and understanding interest they have taken in every phase and detail, as well as for many helpful suggestions and emendations both in preparing the plates and text and in the checking of all the proofs.   Mr. Dalley's assistance has been invaluable in connection with the preparation of the large number of technical plates, for the draughting of the majority of which, from the data supplied to him, he has been personally responsible.   Miss Sudbury has been most helpful in innumerable ways, and I gladly acknowledge the value of her services.

I must also acknowledge my indebtedness to my friends, Mr. James Moncrieff and Mr. R. Lendre-Ainslie, for their respective parts in inducing me to take up these studies and impelling me, by their interest and appreciation, to continue seriously with the solution of the problems encountered.   For appreciative interest and practical sympathy in my earlier efforts I am grateful to the Rt. Hon. Earl of Dysart, my late colleague Dr. H. Aldersmith, the late Mr. Douglas Onslow, J.P., A.K.C., and the late Mr. J. D. Reid, Messrs. J. G. Taylor and Herbert Garrison, F.R.G.S., the Rev. Commander L. G. A. Roberts, and innumerable kind and appreciative friends at home and abroad —in the British Colonies and in the United States of America.   Nor must I forget that I have been indebted to Mr. James Simpson of Edinburgh for much valuable data of an undefinable nature—due to an intimate knowledge of his lifelong work and the modesty wherewith he has mingled (unidentified) his own discoveries with the acknowledged work of others in the same field.

I must also express my profound gratitude to Mr. C. V. Stephens for his appreciation and generosity in making publication possible, and for his invaluable advice and suggestion concerning the organisation of the work.

Since I came into touch with Mr. Stephens the vital essentials of the presentation have developed in a manner altogether surprising to me, and I must acknowledge that it is chiefly due to his initiative, advice, and decision that the work has been presented in a form that far exceeds anything my late colleague and myself had ever hoped for.

D. DAVIDSON.

PREFACE TO THE SECOND EDITION

In this second edition some minor corrections have been made, and a few items of additional interest have been added. Since the first edition was published, a series of booklets explanatory of the larger work has been projected under the title " Talks on the Great Pyramid." These are designed to explain various outstanding features and applications of the Great Pyramid's scientific and prophetic symbolism, and at the same time to form a guide and narrative index (by means of footnote references) to the present volume. The first two booklets of this series have already been published, and are incorporated in the pages immediately following this preface. The reader new to the subject will find these explanatory pages a useful introduction to the work itself.[1]

One item of importance requires special comment. In the present volume, both in the text of the work itself and in the pages of the " Talks," attention is directed to the fact that the ancient Egyptian Messianic prophecies not only gave accurate details of our Lord's Life and Passion, but also represented the symbolism of the commencement of the Grand Gallery in the Great Pyramid as relating to the date and circumstances of the Passion of the promised Messiah. Now in the present volume (first and second editions) the discussion of the *scriptural* and *secular* evidences concerning our Lord's Life fixes the date of the Crucifixion as Friday, 15th Nisan, 7th April (Julian), 30 A.D., and the Pyramid's *astronomical* dating for the Grand Gallery commencement is shown to be the date corresponding to 4028.531789 Autumnal Equinoctial years of the Pyramid's chronology system. The latter dating was given in the first edition, on pages 301 and 302, as a date in A.D. 30, shortly after the Vernal Equinox. The corresponding Julian month date, however, was not given in the first edition because, at the time of publication, the Julian month date for the preceding Autumnal Equinox had not been determined by the writer. This has since been computed and has been checked by comparison with the accepted " Tables of the Sun " compiled by the Danish astronomer, Hansen. The result as now stated on page 302 of this edition, and on page 9 of No. 1 and page 7 of No. 2 of the " Talks," gives the date indicated by the commencement of the Grand Gallery as Friday, 15th Nisan, 7th April (Julian), A.D. 30, the precise day independently and previously fixed as the date of the Crucifixion.

All the evidences necessary to settle the day of the week, the day of the month, and the year of the Crucifixion are discussed in Chapter V, Section II, of this volume.

D. DAVIDSON.

18th March 1925.

[1] Further booklets will be incorporated at a later date.

TALKS ON THE GREAT PYRAMID

A New Series of Pyramid Booklets

BY

D. DAVIDSON, M.C., M.I.Struct.E.

(Joint Author of " The Great Pyramid : Its Divine Message ")

To the Reader :

A PROPHECY, 5,000 YEARS OLD, PROCLAIMS THAT THE PASSION OF THE MESSIAH WOULD BE ACCOMPLISHED ON FRIDAY, 7th APRIL, A.D. 30, A DATE CORRESPONDING TO THE 15th DAY OF THE HEBREW MONTH NISAN ON WHICH OUR LORD WAS CRUCIFIED.

From whatever standpoint we consider the Crucifixion, it must be conceded that it is the most important event that has taken place in the history of mankind. Without belief in the Atoning Sacrifice of our Lord, the Christian religion would mean little. It is a living Faith to many who already believe. It is, also, a matter of supreme importance to all who do not believe. Many of these would welcome any confirmation of the Gospel of Salvation that would appeal to them in terms acceptable to their understanding.

For nearly 5,000 years there have been in existence prophecies of the highest importance to mankind. For nearly 3,000 years before the Christian era these prophecies predicted the Advent of the Messiah, proclaimed the purpose of His coming, and gave the details of His life, mission, and death, and His victory over death and the grave. In the course of time these prophecies became paganised by the substitution of Osiris and other deities for the Messiah. From such perverted form emanated the traditions which led scholars to the conclusion that the essential basal elements of Christianity had been borrowed from previous religions. What has not hitherto been realised is that the great original prophecy, from which such traditions and pagan " anticipations " originated, gives the precise **day, month, and year** of the Passion of the Messiah. For nearly 3,000 years before the Advent of our Lord, the Egyptian Messianic prophecies associated the symbolism of the Great Pyramid with the advent of the promised Messiah, and defined a certain feature of that symbolism as the passing from " TRUTH IN DARKNESS " to " TRUTH IN LIGHT." This feature (the commencement of the Grand Gallery) was called also " THE CROSSING OF THE PURE WATERS OF LIFE," and was symbolically associated with the epoch of spiritual " REBIRTH " or "SECOND BIRTH."

Now the Pyramid's astronomical date (4028.531789 A.P.) for this particular feature falls on **the 15th of the Hebrew month Nisan, or Friday, 7th April (Julian), A.D. 30, 1-20 p.m., at Jerusalem, the time when our Lord was on the Cross.** The Great Pyramid's mathematical Displacement Factor also defines the 15th of Nisan (refer to Booklet No. 2, page 7) as the day of the Passion of our Lord, and in addition expresses the **spiritual uplift** accorded to mankind on that day by our Lord's Passion. That this was the actual date of the Crucifixion has been demonstrated by a comprehensive investigation of all the available literary evidence. One conclusion, and one only, can be drawn from the identity thus established : **that the Great Pyramid independently witnesses to the truth of Salvation through our Lord Jesus Christ.** The Great Pyramid of Gizeh is therefore the " sign and witness unto the Lord of Hosts " referred to by Isaiah as existing in Egypt.

TALKS ON THE GREAT PYRAMID

BY

D. DAVIDSON, M.C., M.I.Struct.E.

(Joint Author of "The Great Pyramid: Its Divine Message")

No. 1

THE SCIENCE OF THE PYRAMID'S REVELATION

The books of Jeremiah (xxxii, 18-20) and Isaiah (xix, 19 and 20) have long been supposed to refer to a Divine Revelation in structural form in Egypt. The ancient Egyptian texts represent that a Divine Revelation in such form exists in the Great Pyramid of Gizeh. These texts give us all the principal measurements of the exterior and interior of the Great Pyramid, and define the unit of measurement as a scientific inch-unit that is the 500 millionth part of the Earth's Polar diameter. The measurements thus given by the texts are in all cases simple geometrical functions of the year-circle, the latter being a circle whose circumference, in Polar diameter inches (or Pyramid inches), is 100 times the number of days in the solar year.

The form, arrangement and details of the Great Pyramid's exterior and of its Passages and Chambers can therefore be built up entirely from the geometry of the year-circle given in Polar diameter inches. Reduction of the resulting dimensions to British inches gives us the identical measurements of the Great Pyramid's exterior and interior obtained by the survey of Sir Flinders Petrie.

The literary traditions of the ancient Egyptians definitely claim that the Great Pyramid's Revelation consisted of a statement of prophecy given in geometrical and astronomical terms. Now there are six principal independent modern scientific methods whereby events can be geometrically symbolised and their dates astronomically indicated to the precise day, without reference to any calendar or civil system of reckoning days, months and years. Each of the six methods is found in operation in the Great Pyramid, and all of them agree in defining dates to the precise day. By such means the Pyramid gives the date of the prophesied Passion of the Messiah as 7th April (Julian) A.D. 30. This date occurred on a Friday, and on the 15th day of the Jewish month Nisan, thus coinciding with the Passover at which our Lord was crucified. The earliest and latest Egyptian Messianic texts—containing the elements of Pyramid prophecy—confirm the intention of this dating in the Great Pyramid. Other symbolised events are dated as relating to two periods of Chaos, the first period beginning 4-5 August, 1914 A.D. and ending 10-11 November, 1918 A.D., and the second beginning 29th May, 1928 A.D., and extending to 15-16 September 1936 A.D. The latter period is defined as associated with the events predicted as preceding the establishing of the Messianic Kingdom and as relating in particular to the history of the British Race.

PRICE 6^{D.}   (POSTAGE EXTRA)

D. DAVIDSON, 47, PARK SQUARE, LEEDS

THE SURVIVING FRAGMENTS OF ANCIENT EGYPTIAN MESSIANISM IN THE EGYPTIAN "BOOK OF THE DEAD"

COMPARED WITH THE MESSIANIC ALLEGORIES OF THE OLD AND NEW TESTAMENTS;

AND THE RELATION OF THE IMAGERY OF BOTH TO THE STRUCTURAL SYMBOLISM OF THE GREAT PYRAMID.

"The Pyramids and the 'Book of the Dead' reproduce the same original, the one in words, the other in stone" (*the late Sir Gaston Maspero, Director-General of Antiquities in Egypt.*)

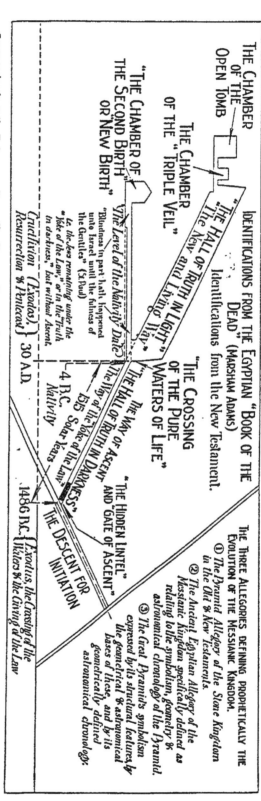

IDENTIFICATIONS FROM THE EGYPTIAN "BOOK OF THE DEAD" (MARSHAM ADAMS)

Identifications from the New Testament.

THE CHAMBER OF THE OPEN TOMB

THE CHAMBER OF THE "TRIPLE VEIL"

"THE CHAMBER OF THE "SECOND BIRTH" OR NEW BIRTH"

"THE HALL OF TRUTH IN LIGHT" The New and Living Way.

"The Level of the Nativity Date"

"Blindness in part hath happened unto Israel until the fulness of the Gentiles" (St. Paul)

i.e. the Jews remaining under the "Yoke of the Law," or in the "Truth in darkness," but without Ascent.

Crucifixion (Exodus), { Resurrection & Pentecost } 30 A.D.

4 B.C. Nativity

1515 Solar Years

The Way of the Yoke of the Law

THE HALL OF TRUTH IN ASCENT AND "GATE OF ASCENT"

THE CROSSING OF THE PURE WATERS OF LIFE"

THE WAY OF TRUTH IN DARKNESS"

"THE HIDDEN LINTEL" AND "GATE OF ASCENT"

THE DESCENT FOR INITIATION

1486 B.C. { Exodus, the Crossing of the Waters & the Giving of the Law

THE THREE ALLEGORIES DEFINING PROPHETICALLY THE EVOLUTION OF THE MESSIANIC KINGDOM.

① *The Pyramid Allegory of the Stone Kingdom in the Old & New Testaments.*

② *The Ancient Egyptian Allegory of the Messianic Kingdom specifically defined as relating to the symbolism, geometry & astronomical chronology of the Pyramid.*

③ *The Great Pyramid's symbolism expressed by its structural features, by the geometrical & astronomical bases of these, and by its geometrically defined astronomical chronology.*

Commencing from the Entrance or Descending Passage, the successive structural features are as follows :—

(1) The 1st Ascending Passage="The Hall of Truth in Darkness";

(2) The Horizontal Passage and Queen's Chamber ("The Chamber of Second—or New—Birth");

(3) The 2nd Ascending Passage or Grand Gallery="The Hall of Truth in Light"; its roof line being raised—"uplifted "—by the extent of the Pyramid's Displacement Factor, above the line of the roof of the 1st Ascending Passage. This is the symbolic equivalent of St. Paul's statement that Jesus Christ "will raise us up by His own Power" (1 Cor. vi, 14).

Then, following the horizontal floor from the Great Step at the upper end of the Grand Gallery (refer to Plate LXVc, as derived from Plates XLIII, LXVa, and LXVb in " The Great Pyramid ; Its Divine Message"):

(4) The 1st Low Passage ; 4-5 August, 1914, to 11 November, 1918.

(5) The Antechamber="The Chamber of the "Triple Veil"; 11 November, 1918 —29 May, 1928.

(6) The 2nd Low Passage; 29 May, 1928 to 16 Sept., 1936

(7) The King's Chamber=The Chamber of the Open Tomb, also called "The Hall of the Grand Orient."

The central Axial Plane of the Passages is displaced eastwards from the central North to South Vertical Central Plane of the Pyramid by the extent of the Pyramid's Displacement Factor. The Pyramid's Central North to South Vertical Plane cannot be reached within the structure until the King's Chamber is entered

TALKS ON THE GREAT PYRAMID

BY

D. DAVIDSON, M.C., M.I.Struct.E.

No. 1

THE SCIENCE OF THE PYRAMID'S REVELATION[1]

THE BASIS OF PYRAMID GEOMETRY.

The Divine Message of the Great Pyramid is conveyed by means of its scientific message. This scientific message is conveyed in terms of, and is defined by, the Great Pyramid's geometry of the year-circle, and the latter system of geometry is established (1) by ancient Egyptian literature ; (2) by the systems of measures of the ancient Egyptians ; and (3) by the dimensions of the Great Pyramid. The evidence from these three sources challenges contradiction. From ancient Egyptian literary sources we derive not only all the outstanding angles and linear dimensions of the Great Pyramid, but also the unit of these linear dimensions. This unit is defined as of the value of 1.0011 British inches,[2] and the dimensions are all simple linear functions of the geometry of a circle of 36,524.2(+) units (or Pyramid inches) in circumference.[3] Comparative analysis, again, of all the systems of linear and square measures of the ancient Egyptians shows that the units of these systems are in all cases simple functions of the geometry of a circle of circumference 3,652.42(+) Pyramid inches, of the value of 1.0011 British inches.[4] Examination of the best modern surveys of the Great Pyramid next establishes the fact that all the external and internal linear dimensions of that structure and its principal external and internal areas are simple functions of the geometry of circles of 36,524.2(+), 3,652.42(+), and 365.242(+) Pyramid inches circumference respectively ; the Pyramid inch being 1.0011 British inches.[5] Now the number of days in the solar year is 365.242(+), and the 500 millionth part of the Earth's polar diameter is 1.0011 British inches. These form the basal scientific elements of the Great Pyramid's system of geometrical representation.

Now there are three different years known to astronomers. These are the solar, sidereal and anomalistic years.[6] The geometry of the year-circle, which defines all the dimensions and features of the Great Pyramid, also defines these three different astronomical years by a single simple geometrical representation. This simple representation gives, in addition, the true mean Sun distance, the exact range of variation in the variable dimensions of the Earth's orbit, and a true geometrical definition of the Law of Gravitation.[7] The shaping of the Pyramid's external lines and surfaces to effect this geometrical definition has been the single factor that has baffled the leading Egyptological authorities who have made the Great Pyramid the subject of special study.[8]*

[1]Footnote references relate to " The Great Pyramid : Its Divine Message " as G.P.
[2]G.P., p. 78.   [3]G.P., pp. 75-80 and Plate XVI.   [4]G.P., pp. 65-75.
[5]G.P., pp. 81, 82, and Plates XVII, XLIIa, and XLIII.   [6]G.P., pp. 128, 131, 132.
[7]G.P., pp. 129-135 and Plates XXIII-XXV.
[8]G.P., pp. 81-83 120-124, 174-176, and Plates XVII, XVIII, XXI, and XXII.
*The four rock-cut sockets were laid down to define the *preliminary setting-out lines* for the base diagonal *alignments* prior to construction. The East Side of the S.E. socket was then taken as datum for the *preliminary* marking off of the base side of 9131 P″.=9141 B″. This distance was measured off from the selected datum and was found to overlap the West side of the S.W. socket by 17½″. The S.W. socket side was therefore extended 17½″ westwards, and its original place, defining by its S.W. corner the diagonal alignment, was marked by a chiselled line. This preliminary base line was measured by the Royal Engineers as 9140 B″, and by Petrie as 9141.4 B″ (Pyds. and Temples of Gizeh, p. 206 and footnote). The facts concerning this are clearly given on our G.P. Plate XX.
The next stage was to define the alignment of the central portion of each base side. Points defining these alignments would be marked off near the sockets, and vertical pillars erected for sighting purposes. The mark of one such bedded pillar has recently been discovered near the N.E. corner, and is within an inch of the alignment of the existing base casing stones, which exist now only near the centre of each side. The sockets were filled in with foundation deposits, as at the Lisht Pyramid, and covered over with the paving blocks before the corner casing stones were set in position (G.P., pp. 173-176).

THE CHRONOGRAPH OF CREATIVE SCIENCE.

The principal geometrical value operating in effecting this accurate definition of the Earth and its orbit, in time and distance, and of the Law of Gravitation, is an important function of the geometry of the year-circle. Its value is 286.1 Pyramid inches. This value the writer has termed " The Displacement Factor " since it is employed only in relation to displacements, eccentricities and variations in spiritual and physical conditions as expressed or interpreted in time and space. It is, in reality, the factor employed in the geometrical system to establish that the Pyramid's " Law of Relativity " is the Divine Law of Creative Science. The function of this displacement factor in the Passage System of the Pyramid is to represent the geometrical equivalent of the various formulæ for the annual values of astronomical motions.[1] The series of annual values selected for representation are such as cannot have the same annual values in any two years within a range of over 50,000 years.[2] By this means the Pyramid's Passage System is presented as an astronomical chronograph, with a zero year-point for chronological reckoning and with a chronological line geometrically divided into intervals representing successive periods of 1,000 solar years, indicated to the scale of 1 Pyramid inch to a solar year. The dates thus marked off by the 1,000 years' intervals are defined, by the associated astronomical data, as the Autumnal Equinoxes of 4000 B.C., 3000 B.C., 2000 B.C., 1000 B.C., 1 A.D., 1001 A.D., and 2001 A.D.[3] From this scientific conception originated, in early times, the belief concerning a period of 6,000 years set apart in the scheme of Creation for the tuition of man in the development and utilisation of various phases of civilisation.[4] Naturally enough the commencement of this period has been *mistakenly* identified as the date of the beginning of creation. The purely geometrical construction of the Pyramid's interior system of Passages, on the principles outlined, gives all the dimensions of these Passages and Chambers. Conversion of these dimensions into British inches gives the same measurements as were obtained by the survey of Sir Flinders Petrie.[5]

The remarkable feature of the Pyramid's scale of 1000 years' intervals is that the various geometrical formulæ for astronomical motions are framed upon this scale as geometrical basis, and could not be framed on the geometry of the year-circle in any other manner, nor for any other scale of 1000 years' intervals at any other position in time. This amounts to a scientific declaration that the chronological scale is the time scale of the Divine Law of Creation in relation to the Earth and its orbit. In other words, the Pyramid declares in scientific terms what ancient Egyptian literature and tradition proclaimed for 3,000 years of Egyptian history, namely, that the Great Pyramid contains a Divine Revelation.[6] This satisfactorily explains, as the writer has shown, the origin of the name *Pyramid* :[7] Greek *Pyramidos* derived from a composite Phrygian and Phœnician form, *Purim-middoh*, of the Chaldee-Hebrew *Urim-middin*, from *Urim* (Lights=Revelation) and *middin* (measures) ; thus denoting " Revelation-Measures." This derivation is confirmed by the Egyptian name for the Great Pyramid, namely, *Khuti*, " the Lights," also signifying " Glory."

[1] G.P., pp. 124, 126, 127, 196, 198, 203, 206, 210, 211, 221, 274, 275, 358, 367, 368, 381-383, 406, 419, 445-454.

[2] These are the values that define the difference between the three year-values given by the Pyramid's base circuit. The interval between (say) successive Autumnal Equinoxes defines the solar year. The interval between the earth's position, at any time in the year, in relation to the fixed stars, and its next return to that position defines the sidereal year. The interval between successive returns of the earth to the point (Perihelion) in its orbit nearest the sun defines the anomalistic year. The difference between the solar year and the sidereal year produces the " Precession of the Equinoxes." The annual rate of the movement is different for every year. The total separation of the Autumnal Equinox from Perihelion is defined as the Longitude of Perihelion. The annual rate of separation is different for every year.

[3] G.P., pp. 185-225.

[4] Man, however, has rejected the tuition of his Creator, and has devoted his energies to the misapplication of the riches and forces of Nature.

[5] G.P., Plates XXXVIII to XLIII with particular reference to Plate XLIa and page 276.

[6] G.P., pp. 230-232.   [7] G.P., pp. 8, 86, 87, and 233.

THE PYRAMID'S ASTRONOMICAL EPHEMERIS

The geometrical and astronomical indications of the Pyramid represent its day as beginning at midnight (Pyramid time), and its solar year as beginning at the Autumnal Equinox.[1] The geometrical representation of the formula for the annual rate of the movement known as the Precession of the Equinoxes defines the variable annual values for every year from 4699 B.C. to 2045 A.D., both dates being represented by specific points of the Pyramid's geometry. By this formula, the date for the central point of the Great Pyramid's geometrical system is defined as midnight ending 25th January 1844 A.D. This date is represented by the face of the Great Step at the end of the floor of the Passage known as the Grand Gallery. By the mathematical process known as integration, the Precessional formula gives a total motion of 90°—or one quarter of the complete " Precession " of the Equinoxes round the heavens—back from 25th January, 1844 A.D. to 4699 B.C.[2] This explains why these two dates are given by specific points of the Pyramid's geometry. We have therefore three proofs fixing, by the movement of precession and the Pyramid's geometry, the chronology of the Pyramid's Passage system *to the year and day*. Independently, the modern astronomical formula for precession gives 90° movement from 4699 B.C. to 1844 A.D.[3]

Again, the geometrical representation of the astronomical formula for the annual rate of change in the Longitude of Perihelion defines the variable annual values for every year from 4044 B.C. to 2045 A.D., both dates being represented by specific points of the Pyramid's geometry. By this formula, the Great Step date is again defined as midnight ending 25th January, 1844 A.D. Integration of the formula gives the Longitude of Perihelion 0° at 4044 B.C. and 103° 42' 28".6—the sum of the base angles of the Pyramid's section—at 2045 A.D. This, again, explains why these two dates are given by specific points of the Pyramid's geometry. We have, therefore, three proofs fixing, by the movement of Perihelion and the Pyramid's geometry, the chronology of the Pyramid's Passage System *to the year and day*. Independently, the modern astronomical tables for the Longitude of Perihelion agree with the table of values derived from the Pyramid's formula.[4]

There are, therefore, six independent proofs of the Pyramid's chronology system *to the year and day*. Six proofs agreeing to this degree of accuracy cannot be explained away by any mere assertion that the whole matter is due to accidental coincidence. A number of coincidences, of the precise nature encountered in this case, cannot happen accidentally. This statement may not be directly apparent to the average reader, but will be endorsed by any mathematician. The Pyramid's structural features and geometry, moreover, carefully define, stage by stage as the geometrical argument progresses, clear indications and conclusive test processes that depict, to the mathematician, as clearly as any language can, the proof of intention throughout.[5] This, however, is not all. Ancient Egyptian literature not only defines all the outstanding geometrical dimensions of the Great Pyramid, and specifies its unit, the Pyramid, or polar diameter inch, but it gives, connected therewith, all the principal cycles, periods and dated epochs that are fixed by the Pyramid's geometrical representation of astronomical chronology. These relate both to the Precession of the Equinoxes and to Perihelion,[6] thus constituting two additional proofs, or altogether **eight independent proofs of an accurate system of astronomical chronology that is also proved to be the time basis of Creative Science as applied to man, the Earth, and the Earth's orbit.**

The accompanying plate will serve to explain an additional matter of chronological importance. What is shown as " the Rhomboid of Displacement " (286.1) defines a date, December, 1557 A.D., 286.1 years back from the Great Step date.[7] Now the Precessional rate for December, 1557 A.D., is represented by a Precessional cycle of 25,826.54 years,[8] and 25826.54 Pyramid inches give the measurement of the Pyramid's " Precessional Circuit " (refer Plate), and of the sum of the Pyramid's base diagonals. The two values, 286.1 and 25826.54 comprise the data of formulation for the Pyramid's Precessional formula.

[1]G.P. pp. 213-216.   [2]G.P., pp. 189-217 and 264-270.   [3]G.P., pp. 212, 213.
[4]G.P., pp. 217-220 and 270-271.   [5]G.P., pp. 225-228.
[6]G.P., Plate XVI and pp. 185-189, 221-225, 229 and 230.
[7]G.P., pp. 203, 206, 210, 211, 221, 274, and 275.   [8]G.P., pp. 208, 211, and 212.

Once we realise that the literature of the ancient Egyptians supplies all the dimensions and the unit of measure of the Great Pyramid, and all its principal astronomical cycles, periods, and dated epochs, it is not surprising to find that these self-same cycles, periods and dated epochs also form the basis of the Egyptians' own chronology. This fact becomes apparent immediately the evidence is sifted and co-ordinated. The records of the ancient Egyptians, from the time of the XIIth Egyptian Dynasty to the end of Egyptian history are found to be dated with reference to the astronomical and calendar cycles framed upon the Pyramid's system of astronomical chronology and based upon its dated epochs. Recognition of this fact has enabled the problem of Egyptian chronology[1] and, by the same means, the problem of Babylonian chronology to be solved.[2] The result is an absolute synchronism of the histories of Egypt and Babylon with the history of Israel. The chronology of Israel, as given in the Old Testament is actually found to be based on the same system and to follow the same calendar and astronomical cycles.[3] One interesting feature of this side of the question is the scientific explanation of every item in the genealogies of the first eleven chapters of Genesis, and of what is shown to be the related problem of ancient Egyptian and ancient Chinese epochs and calendar festivals.[4]

A striking fact emerging from the mass of evidence fixing the scientific chronology of the Egyptians is that astronomical and calendar records, and even records of historical events, that have been discarded or ignored by certain eminent Egyptologists, as not agreeing with their theories of chronology, are now co-ordinated with the " accredited " records. The result has been to show that where a long period is deemed to have intervened between two Dynasties—the XIIth and the XVIIIth—no such long intervening period ever existed, and that a long period of 261 years did actually intervene between Dynasties XIX and XX, where no such gap had been suspected. Nevertheless, the two facts are in accordance with the Egyptians' own chronological lists, and are directly proclaimed by the records of the monuments and papyri.[5]

That such vital facts of Egyptian history have been overlooked or discarded is due to an utterly erroneous conception of the astronomical ideas of the Egyptians, and to an absurdly erroneous theory concerning astronomical chronology and the Egyptian calendar. Consideration of the evidence for the interval between the XIXth and XXth Dynasties alone shows how completely a theory of chronology can confuse a clear statement of fact. Apart from any archaeological or historical consideration, the chronological theory in question demands that Dynasty XIX should begin in 1322 B.C. As the XIXth Dynasty lasted for about a century, and the XXth Dynasty certainly began about 1200 B.C., the theory leaves no space for a long interval between Dynasties XIX and XX. An early XXth Dynasty record (the Harris Papyrus), however, states that a long period of anarchy, followed by a long period of famine and a period of foreign domination, intervened between the two Dynasties. *The King List of the Egyptian priest Manetho gives the interregnum as 182 years (i.e.*, 1050 years from the end of Dynasty XIX and 868 years from the beginning of Dynasty XX, to the end of native history), *and, in addition, gives a century excess for Dynasty XIX. The Old Chronicle of Egypt gives the interregnum as 178 years, and a century excess for Dynasty XIX.*[6] Now it is an easy matter to assert that these particular items in these two Lists are " obscure references." Such assertions, however, fail completely to explain the fact that these references confirm the long interregnum mentioned by the Harris Papyrus which was written soon after the events it describes. Another fact requiring emphasis is that it was the discovery of the scientific chronology of the Egyptians, and of the resulting 261 years' interregnum between the two Dynasties, that led the writer to the discovery of these confirmatory facts in the records. **The new chronology gives 480 years intervening between the date of the Israelitish record of the 5th year of Menephtah and the 4th year of Solomon, and this is confirmed by the 480 years of I Kings, vi, 1.** The date by the Egyptians' scientific chronology is 1486 B.C., and this is the date of the Exodus according to the chronology of the Old Testament.

Within the half-century preceding the discovery of the Israelitish record, Bunsen, Lenormant, George Rawlinson, and Sayce identified the 5th or 6th year of Menephtah as the year of the Exodus. Since the discovery of the record, Maspero, Sayce, Naville, and Hanbury Brown have all declared it to be the Egyptian " version " of the Exodus.[7]

[1]G.P., pp. 27-34, 43-51, 55-61, 79, 80, 84-86, 88-90, 185-189, 207, 221-224, 245-248, 263, 284-298, 303, 310-324, 332-339, 397, 398, 435-437, 439, 440, 488, 504-522, 527, and 531-556.
[2]G.P., pp. 291-293, 322-331, 344-347, 439, 441, and 455.
[3]G.P., pp. 35-38, 284, 309, 324, 332, 336, 340-353, 422-434, 438, 440-444, and 455.
[4]G.P., pp. 35-38, 422-434, and 438. [5]G.P., pp. 317-320, 325, 336, 337, and 538.
[6]G.P., Plate XVI, and pp. 114, 187, 224, 297, 313, 336, 337, 533, 534, 545, 552, 553, and 554.
[7]G.P., pp. 296, 297, 336, 337, 519-522.

EGYPTOLOGICAL SCHEMES OF CHRONOLOGY.

As was to be expected, this scientific synchronism of ancient chronology is denounced by certain theoretical schools of Egyptological chronology. It is as well, therefore, that the reader should know something concerning the facts. Egyptological critics have not attempted to deny the accuracy of the writer's astronomical calculations but have endeavoured to discredit the resulting statement of history by referring to their own empirical archæological methods as the standard basis for any test of trustworthiness. In this particular relation, and in connection with the historical period that has been specially selected for criticism, let us consider the facts of the critics' own experience and responsibility in dealing with this matter. This concerns the interval between the Egyptian XIIth and XVIIIth Dynasties. From 1894 to 1903, an eminent Egyptologist gave this interval as 978 years, with the accompanying assertion that the dates were correct within " about a generation." From 1904 to 1906, the same authority gave the interval as 1659 years (extended by him to 1779 years in 1911), with the assertion that the dates were " correct within a few years." Other Egyptologists—with the same theories and archæological premises—give the interval as 420 to 200 years. **When the purely archæological methods and theories can permit such latitude, these methods should not be postulated as the basis for testing the methods and calculations of an exact science.** It was certainly not ignorance of the data and methods of Egyptologists that led the writer to approach the solution of the problem along different lines. This much has been conceded by other Egyptologists than the critics mentioned.

Investigation along the lines referred to has shown that the Egyptians had a precise system of astronomical chronology, and that they dated their records and compiled their chronological lists on the basis of this system. All the datings of the records calculated on this basis give the interval between the XIIth and XVIIIth Dynasties as 25 years[1]—175 years less than the Berlin and American schools, and their followers in this country, and 1754 years less than the Petrie school of Egyptology (1911 datum). This is in agreement with the succession of XVIIIth Dynasty kings following directly the succession of XIIth Dynasty kings on the King Lists of Abydos and Sakkarah, compiled during the XIXth Dynasty.[2] The writer has also shown that the XVIIIth Dynasty Karnak List of Tahutmes III confirms the statement of the XIXth Dynasty Lists.[3] The Turin Papyrus List is, however, quoted against these because it gives the names of kings who were contemporary with the XIIth Dynasty. The general Egyptological assumption is that they were not contemporary, although the Egyptian priest Manetho distinctly states that the XVIIth Dynasty and *other Dynasties also* were contemporary with the Hyksos Dynasties XV and XVI.[4] The " others also " were obviously at least Dynasties XIII and XIV. The question then is, were these latter Dynasties contemporary with Dynasty XII? The Egyptians' own astronomical chronology proves they were contemporary, and this is confirmed by the Karnak List of Dynasty XVIII, and the Abydos and Sakkarah Lists of Dynasty XIX. Moreover, the late Sir Gaston Maspero, Director-General of Antiquities of Egypt, admitted that " the way in which the monuments of Sebekhotep Sekhem-khu-taui (Dynasty XIII) and his papyri are mingled with the monuments of Amenemhat III (Dynasty XII) at Semneh and in the Fayum show that it is difficult to separate him from that monarch."[5] The whole series of Egyptological theories in this connection have arisen from the fact that the Hyksos invaders certainly entered Egypt during Dynasty XIII, and from the consequent assumption that the Hyksos ruled as two successive dynasties *over the whole of Egypt* after the fall of Dynasty XIV. The certainty of the Hyksos entering Egypt during Dynasty XIII confirms that Dynasties XII and XIII were contemporaneous, since a record of the 6th year of Senusert II of Dynasty XII notes their coming into the country.[6] A record of Queen Hatshepsut (Dynasty XVIII) again informs us that the Hyksos ruled *in the Delta only.*[6]

[1]G.P., pp. 314-317, (Annotations D to p. 320), 321, and 284-290.
[2]G.P., p. 538.   [3]G.P., pp 318, 319, and 539-541.   [4]G.P., p. 317.
[5]For this and other confirmatory data refer G.P., pp. 318, 319.   [6]G.P., p. 317.

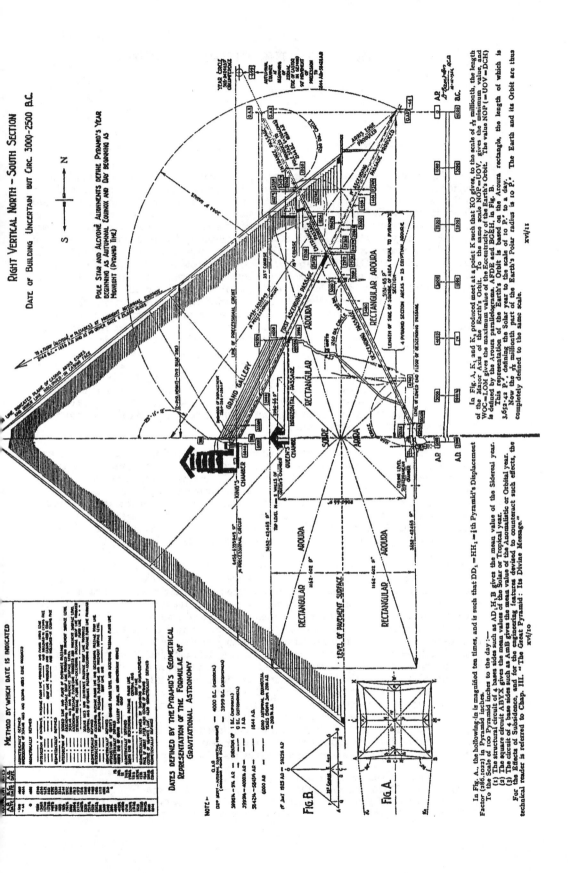

RIGHT VERTICAL NORTH – SOUTH SECTION

DATE OF BUILDING UNCERTAIN BUT CIRC. 3000-2500 B.C.

POLE STAR AND ALCYONE ALIGNMENTS DEFINE PYRAMID'S YEAR BEGINNING AS AUTUMNAL EQUINOX AND DAY BEGINNING AS MIDNIGHT (PYRAMID TIME)

In Fig. A., the hollowing-in is magnified ten times, and is such that $DD_1 = HH_1 = \frac{1}{9}$th Pyramid's Displacement Factor (286.1022) in Pyramid inches.

To the Scale of 100 Pyramid inches to the day:—

(1) The structural circuit of 4 bases sides such as AD, H₁B gives the mean value of the Sidereal year.
(2) The square circuit ABYX gives the mean values of the Solar or Tropical year.
(3) The circuit of 4 base sides such as AmB gives the mean value of the Anomalistic or Orbital year.

For the Effects of Subsidence, and for the engineering features devised to counteract such effects, the technical reader is referred to Chap. III. "The Great Pyramid: Its Divine Message."

xvi/10

In Fig. A., K, and K₁ produced meet at a point K such that KO gives, to the scale of $\frac{1}{9}$ millionth, the length of the Major Axis of the Earth's Orbit. To the same scale NOP=UOV, gives the minimum value, and WOC=LOM gives the maximum value of the Eccentricity of the Earth's Orbit. The value NOP (=UOV=DCH) is defined by the Aroura parallelogram, AFDE and BGEH, in Fig. B.

This representation of the Earth's Orbit is based on the Aroura rectangle, the length of which is 3,643·42 P., defining the Solar year to the scale of 10 P. to a day.

Now the $\frac{1}{9}$ millionth part of the Earth's Polar radius is to P.'. The Earth and its Orbit are thus completely defined to the same scale.

xvi/11

CHRONOLOGICAL ERRORS AND MISCONCEPTIONS.

Thus far we have considered the Egyptological schemes of chronology from the standpoint of the *historical* records. These schemes also claim to be based on a true appreciation of the *astronomical* facts of the Egyptian records. The essential basis of their astronomical theory is that the Egyptians had a calendar year of 365 days, with no Leap year or other method of intercalation. This statement is correct for the period from the XVIIIth Dynasty onwards to the 3rd century A.D. It is assumed, however, that an unbroken succession of such calendar years was observed from Dynasty I inclusive to the 3rd century A.D.[1] The records from Dynasty III to Dynasty XII inclusive, however, prove that the *calendar* month dates for the seasonal events of the *calendar* seasons of Sowing, Harvest, and Inundation agree with the solar year dates for the same seasonal events of the *actual* seasons of Sowing, Harvest, and Inundation respectively.[2] This is confirmed by a dated record of the heliacal rising of the star Sirius during Dynasty XII,[3] and serves to show that a fixed intercalated calendar year was observed from Dynasty III to Dynasty XII. The related facts prove that the *vague* or unintercalated calendar year of 365 days was instituted not many years before Dynasty XVIII began. The true astronomical chronology proves it began 31 years before Dynasty XVIII.[4] This is confirmed by the King List of Manetho,[5] by a traditional statement preserved by Syncellus, and agrees with the dated facts of the XVIIIth Dynasty records.[6] Now the question upon which the Petrie and the Berlin schools disagree, to the extent of 1460 (or 1580) years, in dating Dynasty XII, is precisely this question of the calendar year. **Both schools are now seen to disagree concerning the application of principles that did not exist at the time in question.**

Both schools, however, are agreed concerning the application of these principles and concerning the chronology during the period in which the unintercalated year is now known to have been observed—*i.e.*, from Dynasty XVIII onwards. Here, again, however, the contemporary records prove that the assumed continuity of unintercalated years was broken twice during the period. The records give the order for the month names during Dynasty XVIII different from that in use during Dynasty XX, and different again after the 22nd year of Uasarkon II of Dynasty XXII.[7] For this reason, the chronological basis of the two rival schools of Egyptological chronology is inapplicable prior to 874 B.C. The true astronomical chronology of the Egyptians, however, gives the precise dates and explains the reasons for the various calendar revisions. It was the elucidation of this matter that led to the discovery of the recorded facts concerning the various calendar alterations. It was from the recurrence of the cycles of astronomical chronology that the fact was first discovered that Uasarkon II, in his 22nd year, omitted a month from the current calendar year. Sir Isaac Newton saw the reason for this revision of the calendar and indicated its epoch 200 years ago. Recognition of this revision places Day 1, Month I of the Egyptian calendar coincident with the heliacal rising of Sirius in the 12th year of Ramessu III. The coincidence is noted in the 12th year dedication records of Ramessu III at Medinet Habu.[8] If we do not admit the calendar revision, we are compelled, as the Egyptological schools mentioned have been compelled, to place the High Nile dating at Thebes in the 3rd year of Uasarkon II a month earlier than the actual date of High Nile there, and to explain the dated harvest offerings of corn in the reign of Ramessu III as offerings of " green " corn *a month before the harvest.* In this connection, the eminent Egyptological authority already referred to invariably treats Julian month datings as if they were fixed seasonal datings, and has endeavoured to justify this by the statement that the solar year was "exactly" $365\frac{1}{4}$ days " within historic times." This must appear an astounding assertion to any astronomer.

---

[1]For a general statement of the facts refer G.P., pp. 43-51.
[2]G.P., Plates IX-XI and pp. 55-61.   [3]G.P., pp. 45 and 287-290.
[4]G.P., pp. 310 and 311.   [5]G.P., p. 310.   [6]G.P., pp. 49-51, 310, 311, 315, and 537.
[7]G.P., pp. 46, 311, and 338 ; refer also to Table XLV, facing p. 515.   [8]G.P., p. 311.

EGYPTIAN SYMBOLISM AND PYRAMID PROPHECY.

It is when we come to compare the dated periods of specific features of the Pyramid's passage system with the designations applied to those specific features by the ancient Egyptians that the modern mentality receives its greatest shock. Here the reader must understand that the two items of the identity we are about to consider were derived by independent investigators following lines of investigation in no way related. This concerns the identifications Marsham Adams made from " The Book of the Dead " as to the designations of specific features in the Pyramid, and the present writer's identifications of the astronomical datings attached to these features.[1]

Thus, to take two typical cases, there are the 1st Ascending Passage and the Grand Gallery. These are actually on the same unbroken line of ascent, but whereas the 1st Ascending Passage is so low as to compel a bent attitude in ascent, the Grand Gallery into which it leads is as high as a modern two storey house. These two passages, according to Marsham Adams, jointly formed what the ancient Egyptians called " The Double Hall of Truth." The 1st Ascending Passage was the " Hall of Truth in Darkness," and the Grand Gallery the " Hall of Truth in Light."[2] Now, what are the associated dates given by the Pyramid's geometrical astronomy ? The geometrically defined epoch for the commencement of the " Hall of Truth in Darkness " is April, 1486 B.C., the date obtained both from Egyptian chronology, and from Old Testament chronology, for the Exodus of Israel.[3] The date for the termination of the 1st Ascending Passage ("the Hall of Truth in Darkness") is 7th April, 30 A.D., a Friday, the date of the Passover at which our Lord was crucified.[4] The Pyramid's dating for the threshold of the Grand Gallery—the beginning of the " Hall of Truth in Light " and the ending of the " Hall of Truth in Darkness "—is therefore the date of the Crucifixion.* Appropriately enough, this threshold—the dividing line of " Darkness " and " Light "—was called by the Egyptians " the Crossing of the Pure Waters of Life."[5]

Reference to the accompanying Plates will show that the Egyptian designations have their appropriate equivalents in the symbolism of the New Testament. It will also be seen that the horizontal shallow passage from the beginning of the Grand Gallery leads into the Queen's Chamber, that the horizontal plane of the roof of this passage is the level of the termination of the 1st Ascending Passage, and that the horizontal plane of the floor of the Queen's Chamber cuts the floor of the 1st Ascending Passage at a point giving the dating of the Nativity in 4 B.C. The two horizontal planes connecting the Queen's Chamber with the chronological scale therefore define the duration of our Lord's life. Appropriately, the ancient Egyptian name for the Queen's Chamber, according to Marsham Adams, is " The Chamber of the Second Birth (or New Birth)."[6]

Now we come to the climax of the symbolism. At the upper end of the Grand Gallery the floor line is suddenly blocked by the Great Step. This lies precisely on the central vertical East to West plane of the Pyramid. At the top of this step the floor leading into the Antechamber and King's Chamber is horizontal. Before the Antechamber is reached, the Grand Gallery—the " Hall of Truth in Light "—suddenly ends, and access to the Antechamber is gained through a low narrow passage. Now the Antechamber is, according to Marsham Adams, the original " Chamber of the Triple Veil."[7] In this one can stand upright, but to enter it one has to walk in a crouching attitude through the 1st Low Passage, and to leave the Antechamber, one has again to assume a crouching attitude to proceed onwards to the King's Chamber.

[1]G.P., pp. 369-410. [2]G.P., p. 371. [3]G.P., pp. 300, 301, 371-374.
[4]G.P., pp. 301, 354-357, 461-503. [5]G.P., p. 370.
[6]G.P., pp. 370, 371. [7]G.P., p. 395.

*The Pyramid dating is 4028.531789 A.P. falling in the Spring of A.D 30. The preceding Autumnal Equinox (of A.D. 29=4028 A.P.) fell on 25th Sept (Julian), 7.45 a.m., at Jerusalem. The length of the Autumnal Equinoctial year was 365.2424 days at that time. The fraction of the year, 0.531789, therefore gives 194.232 days from Autumnal Equinox of 29 A.D. This gives 7th April (Julian), 1.20 p.m., at Jerusalem, at which time our Lord was on the Cross.

THE PREPARATION FOR THE FINAL MYSTERY

The Pyramid's astronomical dating for the Entrance Doorway of the 1st Low Passage leading into the Antechamber is the 4-5 August, 1914 A.D., and the dating for the termination of this passage on the threshold of the " Chamber of the Triple Veil " is 11th November, 1918 A.D.[1] Neither of these datings depends merely upon the measurement of the passages, but upon certain obvious geometrical dimensions that are *confirmed* by measurement. These geometrical dimensions are in all cases simple functions of the geometry of the Pyramid as a whole.[2]

The Pyramid therefore symbolises the period of the Great European War as a period of burden and tribulation. It symbolises also a second period of burden and tribulation (not necessarily beginning with war) from 29th May, 1928 A.D. to 16th September, 1936 A.D. Between the two periods of tribulation is the period represented by the " Chamber of the Triple Veil." This extends from 11th November, 1918 A.D. to 29th May, 1928 A.D. The symbolism of the " Triple Veil " is portrayed by a series of three parallel and vertical wall grooves on the West Wainscot of the chamber and a corresponding series exactly opposite on the East Wainscot. These have long been deemed to represent the positions of three portcullis slabs, but the true intent and meaning is now apparent. The symbolism of the historical passage through the period of the " Triple Veil " clearly relates to a period of " unveiling," or revealing, prior to the resumption of tribulation. Thereafter the 2nd Low Passage (symbolising the second period of burden and tribulation) continues to the threshold of the King's Chamber. The dating for this threshold is 16th September, 1936 A.D.—a date given by the chronological prophecies of the Old Testament as ending the last tribulation of Israel.[3]

Here the reader must understand that the general axis of the system of passages and chambers lies parallel to, but displaced 286.1 P. inches (the Displacement Factor) eastwards from, the central North to South vertical plane of the Great Pyramid. This is the vertical plane of the Pyramid's Apex—which, as the " head and chief corner stone " of Old and New Testament allegory, is symbolic of Christ. At no point within the Pyramid is it possible to come into this plane except in the King's Chamber. Entering this chamber—defined by Marsham Adams as the " Chamber of the Open Tomb " or the " Hall of the Grand Orient "[4]—we can proceed into the plane of the " Headstone," hitherto unattainable, by traversing the distance of the Displacement Factor. When this plane is reached, we find ourselves standing directly in front of, and looking down into the lidless coffer, the symbol of the " open tomb."[5] Here, in the words of Marsham Adams, is unfolded

> " the final mystery......when the tomb is opened and the body is raised in immortality. ' Hail thou, my Father of Light,' we read in the Chapter (cliv) which tells us how the body of the Holy One shall not see corruption. ' I come having this my flesh freed from decay; I am whole as my Father, the self-begotten God, whose image is in the incorruptible body. Do thou establish me. Do thou perfect me as the Master of the Grave. This ' so the chapter proceeds, ' is the mystery of the change, in the body, of the life that comes from the destruction of life.' And as we read, we cannot but recall the words of the Apostle : ' Behold, I show you a mystery, for the dead shall be raised incorruptible, and we shall be changed.' So, too, in the final chapter of this book we hear the resurrection proclaimed as with a trumpet blast, as in the innermost Chamber of the House (*i.e.*, the Great Pyramid) we find the Open Tomb. ' I have opened the doors........Well is the Great One who is in the coffin. For all the dead shall have passages made to Him through their embalming,' when their body in the flesh shall be raised in incorruption."

[1] G.P., pp. 385-390.

It should be explained that the Antechamber, King's Chamber, and connecting passages represent an enlarged scale of chronology, beginning from 4-5 August, 1914, with 1 inch to a month of 30 days in place of the general scale of 1 inch to a solar year.

[2] G.P., pp. 167 and 168, Plates XLIII and XLV a, b, and c.

[3] G.P., pp. 387-395.   [4] G.P., pp. 381-385.   [5] G.P., p. 167

THE SCIENCE OF THE PYRAMID'S EXTERIOR.

There are two facts that cannot be controverted. These are (1) that the ancient Egyptians have defined all the dimensions and units of the Great Pyramid, and (2) that the ancient Egyptian systems of measures were derived from the dimensions and units thus defined. The numerical values and units of the Great Pyramid supplied by the literary and metrological records of the ancient Egyptians are as follows :—

Height 5813; base circuit 36,524; base side 9131; sum of base diagonals 25,826 (accurately 25,826¼); a square circuit of 25,826 (accurately 25,826¼) at height 1702 (accurately 1702½) above the base; a square circuit 29,220 (accurately 29,219½) at height 1163 (accurately 1162.6) above the base. The Pyramid's base side, 9131, however, is also defined as 443, and the latter, being an independent mathematical number, 250 times the square root of π, or 443.1134627 – – etc. – –, completes the identification. For the Egyptian common cubit is definitely established by Sir Flinders Petrie as of the value 20.63 British inches, and a square of length of side 443.1134627 common cubits of 20.63 British inches, =9141.1 British inches, gives a square circuit of 36564.4 British inches, or 36524.2 units of 1.0011 British inches (refer note 8, p. 1 preceding). The latter defines the value of the solar year to a scale of 100 units (or Pyramid inches) to the day and the value of the Earth's Polar Diameter to the 1/500 millionth scale (G.P., pp. 65-95).

Professor Piazzi Smyth, late Astronomer-Royal for Scotland, without knowing the above data, stated that the Great Pyramid's base circuit defined the year to the scale and unit given. He also stated that the outstanding 35th course of the Great Pyramid defined the height 1162.6 Pyramid inches of the square circuit 29,219.36 Pyramid inches. Now the axis of this outstanding 35th course, as shown on the accompanying Plate (pp. 6 and 7), is actually at the height 1162.6 Pyramid inches, thus confirming the identification of the ancient Egyptians and Professor Smyth. The connected relations require an angle of face slope of 51° 51′ 14″.3, and this is the angle of face slope of the Great Pyramid.

Sir Flinders Petrie surveyed the Great Pyramid's exterior and measured its interior to test Professor Smyth's statements. He made the definite assertion that his survey disproved these statements. But what are the facts ? The facts are that Petrie found as follows :—

(1) That the masonry core escarpments, stepped to receive the casing, were hollowed inwards up the centre of each escarpment and at the centre of each base side, to an extent, on an average, of 36 inches, and that the average slope of the four escarpments gave Smyth's angle of 51° 51′.

(2) That the casing stones still existed *in situ* in the bottom course of the Pyramid, and near the centre of each base side, where the core is hollowed inwards, and that the angle of these casing stones did not disagree with Smyth's angle of 51° 51′.

(3) That the mean distance between the base edge of casing stones on opposite sides of the Pyramid was 9069 British inches (*i.e.*, 9059 P. inches) and therefore 36 inches *on each side* short of Smyth's 9141 British inches (*i.e.*, 9131 Pyramid inches.)

(4) That a uniform thickness of casing throughout would give a casing surface hollowed inwards up the centre of each face slope and at the centre of each base side, precisely as the core slopes are hollowed inwards, and, consequently, a corner to corner base side measurement of 9141 British inches, =9131 Pyramid inches, representing a square circuit of 36,524 Pyramid inches, as stated by the ancient Egyptians and Professor Smyth.

(5) That the *preliminary setting-out* marks and alignments of the Pyramid's builders confirmed the base side measurement of 9141 British inches, =9131 Pyramid inches (refer note 8, p. 1 preceding).

Sir Flinders Petrie adopted the first three of these items only, ignoring the fourth and fifth. He states in consequence that the Pyramid's base side measured 9069 British inches, and that *the casing up the centre of each side was double the thickness of the casing at the corners and up the arris edges !* The accompanying Plate (pp. 6 and 7), however, confirms the 36524.2 Pyramid inches circuit for the base. Here it is shown that the Egyptian unit of area, the *aroura*, as a rectangle, 3652.42 Pyramid inches long × 1162.6 Pyramid inches high, is defined by the 35th course axis, and as a square, 2060.66 Pyramid inches × 2060.66 Pyramid inches, =2063 British inches × 2063 British inches, is in agreement with the statements of Herodotus and Horapollo that its side consisted of 100 common cubits (of Petrie's stated value 20.63 British inches). Horapollo actually states that the ¼ *aroura* represented the value of the year, which it does, since its area is equal to the area of a circle of 3,652.42 Pyramid inches circumference. Fig. A (p. 6) indicates the hollowing in[1] of the Pyramid's base sides magnified ten times, and in conjunction with Fig. B geometrically defines the extent of the hollowing-in.

[1] The hollowing-in is perceptible only to special observations.

The Creative Law of Relativity and The Great Pyramid's Displacement Factor.

The Great Pyramid's Displacement Factor (286.1022) is proved by its various applications to be the MATHEMATICAL CONSTANT OF THE CREATIVE LAW OF RELATIVITY. All the astronomical values indicated by the Pyramid's dimensions are clearly determinate values that are simple functions of the year, the Earth's Polar Diameter, and the Mean Sun Distance. All variations in astronomical time rates and angular and linear distances and their respective rates of change are expressed in terms of the single mathematical constant defined by the Pyramid's "Displacement Factor." (G.P., pp. 445-448.)

The various applications of the Displacement Factor define as follows :—

(1) By means of the Pyramid's base plan,

    (a) the three astronomical forms of the year, i.e., the solar, sidereal, and anomalistic (G.P., pp. 128-131) ;

    (b) the mean sun distance, 92,996,085 miles (G.P., pp. 132-135) ;

    (c) the range of variation in the eccentricity of the Earth's orbit (G.P., pp. 132-135) ;

    (d) the Law of Gravitation as it affects motion in the Earth's orbit (G.P., pp. 133-135) ;

    (e) the general Law of Precessional Variation (G.P., pp. 444-448) ;

    (f) the general Law of Variations relating to the rate of change of the Longitude of Perihelion (G.P., pp. 446 and 447).

(2) By means of the geometrical framework of the Passages and Chambers,—the central vertical plane of which is itself displaced 286.1 Pyramid inches East from the Central Vertical North to South Plane of the Great Pyramid,

    (a) the formula giving the annual rate of Precession for every year from 4699 B.C. to 2045 A.D. (G.P., pp. 185-220) ;

    (b) the formula giving the annual rate of change in the Longitude of Perihelion for every year from 4699 B.C. to 2045 A.D. (G.P., pp. 185-220) ;

    (c) by (a) and (b) above—the precise scale of a system of astronomical chronology that formed the datum for the calendar cycles in use in ancient Egypt (G.P., pp. 186-189, 207, 221-225, 284-290, 310-340, and Appendix II) ;

    (d) the symbolism of spiritual uplift (286.1 Pyramid inches) commencing at the date coinciding with the date of the Crucifixion, 7th April, A.D. 30 (Accompanying Plate and G.P., pp. 201, 206, 210, 300-302, 354-356, and 367-371) ;

    (e) the precise dates of beginning and ending of the period to which the Pyramid's Message is addressed, together with the significance of that Message (G.P., pp. 221-225, 375-383, 405-407, and 453-458) ;

(3) By means of the direct geometrical relations between the Pyramid's apex, exterior, and interior (G.P., pp. 233, 301, 302, 367-371, 381-386, 405-410, 419-421, and 444-456),

    (a) that Jesus Christ—" the headstone and chief corner-stone "—" is before all things and by Him all things consist," " in whom are hid all the treasures of wisdom and knowledge " ;

    (b) that Jesus Christ, by His Displacement, paid the purchase price of mankind's Redemption, and effected the Salvation of all who truly believe in Him ;

    (c) that Jesus Christ, at a time appointed by God, and indicated by the Pyramid's expression of Divine Law, will effect " the restitution of all things" promised by the Apostle.

The reader's attention is particularly directed to the transcending significance of the data given above, comprising, as they do, an epitome of all the essential facts underlying the scientific presentation of the Pyramid's prophecy. Let him also reflect that it is **beyond the ingenuity of man** to devise a method of defining, by the application of a single factor, the governing physical, spiritual, and historical properties appertaining to the earth and mankind. **The Great Pyramid's Displacement Factor witnesses to the Divinity of Jesus Christ, "by whom all things were created."**

PYRAMID MESSIANISM.

"The Pyramids and the 'Book of the Dead' reproduce the same original, the one in words, the other in stone." This statement was made by the late Sir Gaston Maspero, Director-General of Antiquities in Egypt. It was made in relation to Mr. Marsham Adams' thesis that the symbolical passages and chambers of the allegory of the "Book of the Dead' refer to passages and chambers of the Great Pyramid of Gizeh. The allegorical names of the passages and chambers, and the prophetical significance attached to these names, are embodied in the beliefs of both the early and late periods of ancient Egyptian literature. In the earliest texts dealing with Pyramid allegory, we are brought into contact with prophecies concerning a Messiah **who was to come,** and in the late Egyptian literature we find it claimed that the promised Messiah **had come** in the person of Osiris. We find, moreover, that this latter identification was first made late in the XVIIIth or early in the XIXth Egyptian Dynasty, when the first *serious* attempt was made to identify the Egyptians as the Messianic Race of Pyramid prophecy. It was then represented that Osiris had reigned in Egypt and had accomplished the predicted Passion of the promised Messiah in pre-Pyramid times. Of these earlier times, however, there is no single text containing the identification, for the position of Osiris in these early texts is not Messianic. It is sufficient to say, in the words of Professor Breasted, that the Pyramid texts and the post-Pyramid texts of the Old Kingdom present us with a belief in "Messianism 1,000 years before the Hebrews." The later recensions of the 'Book of the Dead' interpret the allegory of the Great Pyramid's passages and chambers as applying to Osiris as the long predicted Messiah.

Two astronomically defined Pyramid Epochs, September, 348 B.C. and December, 1557 A.D., were given as Epochs of *European* civilisation ; the latter date being defined as the European Epoch of the Messianic Race, and the end of 5556¼ years of astronomical reckoning. Between the 16th century B.C. and the 3rd century B.C., the two Epochs were confused. One prominent Egyptian cult placed the termination of the 5556 years at the earlier Epoch in 348 B.C., thus anticipating history by 1904 years. To make the forgery convincing, it was necessary to add 1904 years to the recorded chronology of Egyptian history. The clumsily effected insertion of this number of years into the literary records of Egyptian history is apparent as soon as the astronomical methods and cycles of the ancient Egyptians are pointed out. **Other records do not contain the inserted period, but give intact the astronomical chronology of the Great Pyramid and of the ancient Messianic prophecy.** Refer to Plates XVI and XLII a and b in "The Great Pyramid : Its Divine Message."

The reason for the confusion of the Epochs is obvious. The original prophecy gave the earlier epoch, 348 B.C., associated with the end of native Egyptian history. A late cult asserted that this referred to the later epoch, 1557 A.D. When, therefore, native Egyptian history ended in 342 B.C.—a few years after the prophetic epoch—the exponents of the latter cult adopted 348 B.C. as the date of the later epoch, (*i.e.*, 1557 A.D.). The prophetic dating, 1557 A.D., marks the Epoch of Britain's "Extending Sphere of Sea-Power."

For 3,000 years the conception persisted in Egypt that the Great Pyramid enshrined a prophecy—that is a Divine Revelation. The form in which the traditional belief was received by the Copts is given in the Akbar-Ezzeman MS. This states that the Great Pyramid contained :—

> The wisdom and acquirements in the different arts and sciences . . . the sciences of arithmetic and geometry, that they might remain as records for the benefit of those who could afterwards comprehend them."
>
> " . . . the positions of the stars and their cycles ; together with the history and chronicle of time past, of that which is to come, and every future event which would take place in Egypt."

Similarly, Tohfat Alagaib states that the Great Pyramid contained " Plans of the stars and historical and prophetic records."

That the general statement of this tradition is shown to be correct by the scientific features of the Great Pyramid explains the statement in Jeremiah xxxii, 18-20 :—

> " The Great, the Mighty God, the Lord of Hosts is His name, Great in counsel and mighty in work . Which has set signs and wonders in the land of Egypt, even unto this day . . . "

It also explains the use of a Pyramid symbolism in the allegorical language of the Old and New Testaments, and the declaration of Isaiah xix, 19, 20 :—

> " In that day shall there be an altar to the Lord, in the midst of the land of Egypt, and a pillar at the border thereof to the Lord.
>
> " And IT shall be for a sign and a witness unto the Lord of Hosts in the land of Egypt ; for they shall cry unto the Lord because of the oppressors, and He shall send them a Saviour, and a great one, and He shall deliver them."

The concluding statement of the prophecy is fully dealt with in the last chapter of " The Great Pyramid : Its Divine Message."

TALKS ON THE GREAT PYRAMID

BY

D. DAVIDSON, M.C., M.I.Struct.E.

No. 2

THE SOLAR YEAR AND THE MESSIANIC YEAR.

PART I.

MESSIANIC PROPHECY AND THE CHRISTIAN YEAR.

EARLY MESSIANISM AND ITS PAGAN PERVERSION.

When the Gizeh Pyramids were built prophecies relating to the Messiah were already ancient. Before and after the Pyramids, the rites of the Lord's Supper were held—in one part or another of the world—not as a remembrance, but as an anticipation of the predicted Passion. This throws new light on our Lord's declaration, " Before Abraham was I AM." This subject has been exhaustively dealt with in the Vth Chapter (Sections IB and III) of " The Great Pyramid : Its Divine Message." Therein it is shown that the Messiah, in the earliest times, was associated with the manifestation of *Spiritual* LIGHT (" the Sun of righteousness," Mal. iv, 2), in contradistinction to *physical* LIGHT, as represented by the sun. The prophesied history of the Messiah, and the predicted purpose of His Passion, as portrayed in the earliest texts, are identical with the salient features and purpose of our Lord's life as described in the New Testament.* The anticipatory Sacrament of ancient times was debased, as the Sacrament of remembrance has since been debased, for identical reasons. The theory of transubstantiation is as old as history. The symbolic meaning, at an early date, was displaced by " *actuality*." Human sacrifices were ultimately provided, and a Sacrament of Cannibalism substituted for the Messianic Sacrament. The trial of Abraham's faith was actually the enactment of a parable, wherein the anticipatory Sacrament—by reason of its debasement—was displaced by the burnt offerings of Abraham and his seed.

THE PAGAN " RESURRECTION."

What happened in the case of the anticipatory Sacrament happened also in the depiction of the spiritual aspect of the predicted Messiah, His teaching, and the portrayal of His Passion and its purpose. *Spiritual* LIGHT was displaced by *physical* LIGHT. Physical LIGHT (the Sun) was mistakenly worshipped for " THE SUN OF RIGHTEOUSNESS." *Regeneration* was confounded with *reproduction*, and the elements of the Sacrament—the bread and the wine—were accepted as possessing the promised *virtue* in themselves ; with the result seen in the debaucheries of the Bacchanalian Festivals. The predicted *resurrection* was causally associated with the bread and wine and their virtues, and was actually deemed to be enacted in the annual decay and regrowth of vegetation, so that corn and wine were held to contain in themselves the literal elements of the resurrection. The Solar year and its vegetational " death and resurrection " therefore became the literal enactment of the cycle of the Passion of the solar deity. The original Egyptian corn-god Osiris therefore became the god of the dead, and the lord of the resurrection ; and by reason of the identification of the phenomena of vegetation with the cycle of the Solar year, ultimately absorbed the attributes of the composite solar god, Amen-Ra, by becoming Osiris-Ra

---

*" As He spake by the mouth of His holy prophets, which have been since the world began " Luke i, 70.

THE PAGAN SOLAR "MESSIANIC" YEAR.

As a result we find that the principal points of the solar year were identified with the Birth and Death or Resurrection of the promised Messiah. In the Pagan Roman calendar the principal points of the solar year were celebrated on 25 March, 24 June, 27 September, and 25 December. These were respectively the dates identified with the Vernal Equinox, the Summer Solstice, the Autumnal Equinox, and the Winter Solstice, in the 2nd century A.D. This pagan origin for the principal dates of the supposed Christian year has been dealt with by Sir Isaac Newton, on *Daniel*, p. 145. It will carry more weight, however, to quote modern authorities on the subject.

The Enc. Britt. (11th Ed.), Vol. vi, p. 293, states :—

> "Before the 5th century there was no general concensus of opinion as to when Christmas should come in the calendar, whether on the 6th of January, or the 25th of March, or the 25th of December."
>
> "The earliest identification of the 25th of December with the birthday of Christ is in a passage, otherwise unknown and probably spurious, of Theophilus of Antioch (A.D. 171-183), preserved in Latin by the Magdeburg centuriators (I, 3, 118), to the effect that the Gauls contended that as they celebrated the birth of the Lord on the 25th of December, whatever day of the week it might be, so they ought to celebrate the Pascha on the 25th of March *when the resurrection befell.*"

Light is thrown upon the last statement by the following account of the ceremonies of 24-25 March observed in *pagan* Rome at the Festival of Attis. The account is from Dr. Fraser's "Adonis, Osiris, Attis," p. 166 :—

> "When night (24 March) had fallen, the sorrow of the worshippers was turned to joy. For suddenly a light shone in the darkness : the tomb was opened : the god had risen from the dead : and as the priest touched the lips of the weeping mourners with balm, he softly whispered in their ears the glad tidings of salvation. On the morrow, the 25th day of March, the divine resurrection was celebrated with a wild outburst of glee, which at Rome, and probably elsewhere, took the form of a carnival. It was the Festival of Joy (Hilaria). A universal licence prevailed. Every man might say and do what he pleased . . ."

M. Alexandre Moret, in describing the ceremonies of "The Mysteries of Isis," in his "Gods and Kings of Egypt," quotes from Plutarch (*De Iside et Osiride*, 65, 70) :—

> "They say that Osiris is buried when they put the seed in the ground, and that he is born again and comes back to the earth when the seeds begin to sprout ; that is why Isis brings forth Horus-the-child (Harpocrates) about the time of the winter solstice ; after the spring equinox a festival is celebrated to commemorate the maternity of Isis."

Again the Enc. Britt. states :—

> "Certain Latins as early as 354 (A.D.) may have transferred the human birthday (of our Lord) from the 6th of January to the 25th of December, which was then a Mithraic feast, and is by the chronographer above referred to, but in another part of his compilation termed *Natalis Invicti Solis*, or the birthday of the unconquered sun. Cyprian calls Christ *Sol verus*, Ambrose *Sol novus noster*, and such rhetoric was widespread."

Such is the origin of the alleged Christian calendar whereby

The Annunciation	=	Vernal Equinox, 25 March (Julian),
Birth of John Baptist	=	Summer Solstice, 24 June (Julian),
Nativity of our Lord	=	Winter Solstice, 25 Dec. (Julian).

This is the form in which, by the time of the 3rd century, the Christian calendar was universally accepted by the Western Church. The identification first arose in Rome, where it was stated that the 25th December appeared as the Birthday of our Lord in the Bethlehem census roll in the Roman archives. The Eastern Church did not adopt this dating until it was received from Rome at the end of the 4th century. This is as stated on the title of a homily of St. Chrysostom preached at Antioch about 390 A.D.

PART II.

THE FIRST SIX MONTHS OF OUR LORD'S LIFE.*

THE NATIVITY NOT IN DECEMBER.

Let us assume, for the purpose of argument, that our Lord was born on 25th December (Julian), B.C. 4. The following Passover began on 31st March (Julian), B.C. 3, 98 days later. Herod died before this Passover. At the death of Herod our Lord was in Egypt. Now, Dr. Aldersmith and the present writer have shown that Josephus places the death of Herod at least seven or eight weeks before the Passover of B.C. 3, and that the Jewish Megillath Taanith gives the day of Herod's death as 1st Sebat. These two statements are substantially in agreement, since the latter statement places the death of Herod on the 18th January (Julian). This is 24 days after the Nativity date assumed. By this statement, Herod died 16 days before our Lord was presented in the Temple (Luke ii, 22, compared with Levit. xii, 2, 3, 4, and 6). But Matt. ii, 12-16, tells us that our Lord had been taken a 200 miles' journey into Egypt after this presentation in the Temple, and that He had been in Egypt for some time when Herod died.

If, however, Herod died on 18th January, as stated, Joseph and Mary could have returned to Nazareth (Matt. ii, 22, 23) long before the Passover on 31st March, and could, therefore, have been present at that Passover, mingling with the multitude unrecognised. This would explain the statement of Luke ii, 41, that "His parents went to Jerusalem *every* year at the Feast of the Passover." This also shows, however, that our Lord's presentation in the Temple was long before 18th January, and in consequence that our Lord was born long before 25th December. It also shows that our Lord was not born at the Feast of Dedication, which in that particular year fell, not on 25th December, but on 13th December (Julian). The Feast of Dedication was a feast of Maccabean origin, and not of Divine Institution. All the Feasts of Divine Institution typified one or other of the phases of our Lord's First Advent, or of His coming Second Advent. The Feasts of Tabernacles, Passover and Pentecost prefigured respectively, in type of circumstances and date, (1) our Lord's Birth on a journey ("when the Word became flesh and *tabernacled* among us," John i, 14) (2) our Lord's Passion (the Passing-over of death from mankind), and (3) the Descent of the Holy Spirit.** The Feast that prefigures in type of circumstances and date our Lord's Second Advent is the Feast of Trumpets on the 1st of Tisri—ranging generally from 6th September to 5th October *in the modern Jewish Calendar.*

---

* This is all fully discussed in "The Great Pyramid: Its Divine Message," pp. 461-503.

** In "The Great Pyramid: Its Divine Message," pp. 299-301, it is shown that (a) the Exodus, (b) the crossing of "the sea of reeds," and (c) the Giving of the Law fell upon the same days of the week, and the same days of the solar and lunar years, as (a) the Crucifixion (b) the Resurrection, and (c) Pentecost.
Joshua x, 13, and Ecclesiasticus xlvi, 4, contain the record of one particular week in 1446 B.C. being of the duration of 8 days by clock time. By this alteration the Sabbath (Day of Rest) was altered to the First Day of the week as reckoned by clock time. Prior to this revision, the original First Day of the week, when compared with the corresponding day of our week calculated back, should in all cases be our Saturday. In "The Great Pyramid: Its Divine Message," pp. 298-399, it is shown that the First Day of the initial year of the Pyramid's astronomical chronology, and of Hebrew, Egyptian and Babylonian chronology, was the day of the Autumnal Equinox and a Saturday, and therefore the original First Day of the week; on pp. 299-301, that the week as instituted amongst the Hebrews in the year of the Exodus also began with the First Day on our Saturday. After 1446 B.C., the week always began with the First Day on our Sunday.

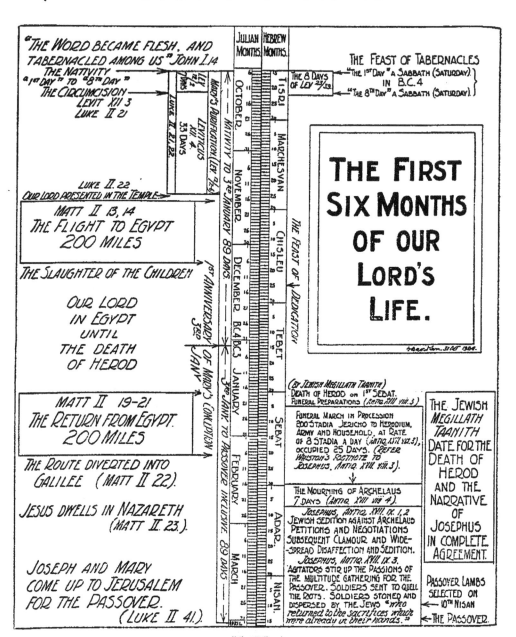

PLATE 1.

* BORN "THE LORD OF THE SABBATH":—Our Lord's "1st day" and His "8th day" of Circumcision (Levit. xii, 3; Luke ii, 21) coincided with "the 1st day" and "8th day" of Tabernacles respectively, which were both "holy Sabbaths" (Levit. xxiii, 39), regardless of the day of the week upon which they fell. In this particular year, these days fell upon the actual weekly Sabbath. Now the revision in 1446 B.C. at the time of Joshua's "long day" (Note ** to p. 3), had altered the weekly Sabbath from the original 7th day to the original 1st day of the week (i.e., to the 8th day) when reckoned by clock time. The circumstances of the Resurrection indicate what this prefigured (Note to p. 2)

THE FEAST OF TABERNACLES PREFIGURES THE NATIVITY.

The Feast of Tabernacles began on the 15th Tisri and continued for 7 days. FOURTEEN LAMBS were sacrificed on each of the 7 days. With the Nativity on the Feast of Tabernacles, these 7 days would be the initial 7 days of purification of Levit. xii, 2, prior to our Lord being circumcised on the 8th day (Levit. xii, 3 and Luke ii, 22). With this realised, the symbolical significance of the fourteen lambs of the Feast of Tabernacles becomes apparent as soon as we read Matt. i, 17. This deals with the generations prior to the Birth of our Lord. These are :—

Abraham to David	..	..	..	.. 14 generations.
David to Jewish Exile ..	..	..	..	14 generations.
The Jewish Exile to Christ	..	..	..	14 generations.

Moreover, at the Feast of Tabernacles beginning on the 15th of Tisri, the Divine Command in Levit. xxiii, 39, states " ye shall keep a feast unto the Lord 7 days : on the *first day* shall be a *Sabbath* and on the *eighth day* shall be a *Sabbath*."* Why ? Because our Lord was to be born at the Feast of Tabernacles, in a year divinely appointed in which the decreed 1st day should fall, in the natural course of events, upon a Sabbath. This occurred in B.C. 4, in the year that saw the Birth of our Lord. In that year the first day of the Feast—the 15th of Tisri—fell on the Sabbath, Saturday, 6th October (Julian) and the decreed 8th day fell on the Sabbath, Saturday, 13th October (Julian) when our Lord was circumcised.

Everything points to our Lord having been born at the Feast of Tabernacles, the Romans having arranged that the enrolling or census should be taken at the great gathering of the people for this Feast. In B.C. 4, the actual day of the Feast of Tabernacles fell on 6th October (Julian), a Sabbath (*i.e.*, Saturday). If we take this as the day of the Nativity, our Lord was taken up to the Temple on 15th November, and shortly afterwards taken to Egypt. He would arrive in Egypt at latest early in December, where He remained until after the death of Herod on the following 18th January. He returned to Nazareth some time in February, and His parents went up to Jerusalem to be present at the Passover on the following 31st March (refer to Plate I.)

THE COURSE OF ABIA CONFIRMS THE DATE.

The date of the Nativity at 6th October does not, therefore, depend upon our interpretation of the statement concerning the course of Abia. The two, however, are mutually confirmatory, it being admitted that the course of Abia (Luke i, 5) began fifteen months before our Lord's birth. Now there were 24 orders for "the governors of the sanctuary" (I Chron., xxiv), and Abia was the eighth. In the parallel cases of the twelve captains that served the king, and the twelve officers of the royal household, the courses began with the year (at 1st Nisan), and completed the year, a course for a month (I Chron., xxvii, 1-15 and I Kings, iv, 7). By the same sequence, the 24 orders of the priests above began on 1st Nisan and completed the year, two courses a month. This is not necessarily so, but if it gives the 6th October Nativity date, the two lines of evidence are in agreement. In such case, the 1st course would begin at 1st Nisan in B.C. 5, and the 8th course, that of Abia, on 15th Tammuz of the same year. The Nativity was fifteen months later. This gives the 15th Tisri in B.C. 4. Now, 15th Tisri is the date of the Feast of Tabernacles, and in B.C. 4, 15th Tisri coincided with the 6th October. The two items of evidence are therefore in agreement. Our Lord was born on 6th October, B.C. 4. This is all fully discussed in " The Great Pyramid : Its Divine Message," pages 463 and 471.

---

* RESURRECTED "THE LORD OF THE SABBATH."—In the year of the Crucifixion there were again a " 1st day " and an " 8th day." These fell not on the 7th day of the week but on the 1st day of the week. Our Lord was selected as God's Passover " Lamb ' on the 10th Nisan (John xii, 23-33 ; John i, 29 ; Rev. xiii, 8 ; I Cor. v, 7), when the Passover lambs were selected (Exod. xii, 13). This was on " Palm Sunday," the " 1st day " of the week. After His Crucifixion and burial, He rose again from the dead on the 1st day of the week, 17th Nisan, on " the 8th day." He rose as " The Sun of Righteousness." Born " the Lord of the Sabbath " (Mark ii, 28) under the Law, He was resurrected " the Lord of the Sabbath " bringing in the New Birth and the New Covenant, and consecrating His day of Resurrection as the Sabbath (Rest-day) of the New Covenant. What happened to the week in the time of Joshua again occurred at the Resurrection. Sunday is therefore the Christian's Sabbath (Rest) by the New Spiritual " Circumcision of Christ " (Col. ii 11-14), who is both " the minister of circumcision " (Rom. xv, 8) and " the Lord of the Sabbath " (Mark ii. 28). That is why circumcision was on " the 8th day.'

PART III.

THE TRUE CHRISTIAN YEAR.

THE GREAT PYRAMID'S DISPLACEMENT FACTOR AND THE MESSIANIC YEAR.

In " The Great Pyramid : Its Divine Message," it is shown that a certain numerical value (286.1022) defines God's Law of Relativity in relation to things *spiritual* and things *material*. This value is employed in the Great Pyramid to define all displacements, variations and eccentricities in astronomical time and space,* and in the prophetic elucidation of history concerning our Lord, His Church, and His Kingdom. In the work referred to, this value has not been applied to the elucidation of the Messianic year as distinct from the solar year : the year of *spiritual* LIGHT as distinct from the year of *physical* LIGHT : the year of " the Sun of Righteousness " as distinct from the year of the " Unconquered Sun " of pagan nomenclature. This application has only been suggested as a result of recent criticism of the datings of our Lord's life given in " The Great Pyramid : Its Divine Message."

In accordance with the Pyramid's representation of the Displacement Factor (286.1022), as seen in operation in other cases in the Pyramid, the principal points of the solar year should be negatively displaced from the corresponding principal points of the Messianic year. In other words, the former should precede the latter by 286.1022 days. The result is as shown on the accompanying diagram (Plate II), and may be stated in sequence as follows :—

(I) The Autumnal Equinox of B.C. 6 fell on 26th Sept. (Julian) 1.50 a.m. at Jerusalem, and forms the datum for the date of the conception of Elizabeth 286.1022 days later on 9th July (Julian) B.C. 5. This agrees with the date 5th July (Julian) given for the ending of the ministration of Zacharias (" The Great Pyramid : Its Divine Message," pp. 467-468), when compared with Luke i, 23, 24.

    The Autumnal Equinox is the original beginning of the solar year, and, analogously, here the conception of Elizabeth, in Luke i, forms the chronological beginning for the dating of our Lord's Birth.

(II). The Vernal Equinox of B.C. 5 fell on 22nd March (Julian) 9.40 p.m. at Jerusalem, and forms the datum for the date of Mary's Conception 286.1022 days later on 3rd January (Julian), B.C. 4. This, in conjunction with (I) above, agrees with the narrative of Luke i, 24-57. Compare the first anniversary of Mary's Conception—midway between the Feast of Tabernacles (15th Tisri) and the Feast of the Passover (15th Nisan) in the first six months of our Lord's Life (Plate I).

(III). The Winter Solstice of B.C. 5 fell on 23rd December (Julian), 0.20 a.m., at Jerusalem. From this datum, the interval of 286.1022 days terminates on 5th October (Julian). B.C. 4, at sunset of which day the Sabbath, 15th of Tisri, began. This was the first day of the Feast of Tabernacles and the day of our Lord's birth—sunset 5th Oct. to sunset 6th Oct.

(IV). The Summer Solstice of A.D. 29 fell on 24th June (Julian), 8.40 p.m. at Jerusalem. From this datum, the interval of 286.1022 days terminates at 11.10 p.m., 6th April (Julian), A.D. 30. This was the evening beginning the 15th Nisan, the day of our Lord's Last Supper, His Agony in Gethsemane, His Betrayal, Crucifixion and Burial. The precise hour agrees closely with the time of His Agony in Gethsemane.

The zero datum for the displacement of the Messianic year-beginning—as in (I) above—is the Autumnal Equinox of B.C. 6. This is two years before the Nativity, a fact that throws light upon the nature of the prophetical data possessed by the Magi, additional to that dealt with in " The Great Pyramid," pp. 468-470. " Two years old and under, according to the time which he (Herod) had diligently enquired of the wise men " (Matt. ii, 16).

*Gravitational Astronomy began with Kepler and Newton. Yet the Great Pyramid's geometrical system of astronomical representation is a complete exposition of gravitational astronomy, equalling, if not excelling, the latter in accuracy of definition. The Pyramid's Displacement Factor is the principal factor operating in this exposition. The various applications of the Displacement Factor are described in No. 1 of this Series, page 12.

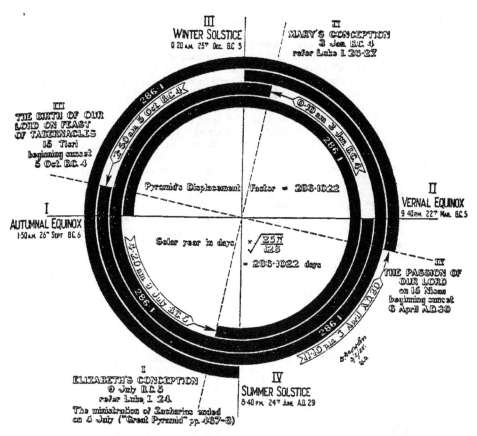

A recently discovered geometrical representation of the Pyramid formulæ for the Equinoxes and Solstices from 4429 B.C. to 2001 A.D. gives essentially the same results—within less than an hour of variation—as are to be derived from Hansen's solar tables. The Pyramid representation is given in terms of the Displacement Factor and other simple functions of the geometry of the solar year circle. Hansen's solar tables are confirmed by Newcomb's discussion of all recorded eclipses from 721 B.C. to 1750 A.D.

NOTE.—The Dates given above for the Solstices and Equinoxes are the exact Julian dates for the particular years stated The usual Julian dates given by Christian chronologers are for the 2nd Century A.D. This confirms the date of origin of the traditional Christian Calendar. For explanation of Gregorian Calendar dates refer page 8.

PLATE II.

The above diagram shows the Displacement Factor defining the 15th Nisan beginning Sunset 6th April, A.D. 30, as the day of the Passion of our Lord. This is confirmed by the Great Pyramid dating which is 4028·531789 A.P., i.e., 15th Nisan, 7th April, A.D. 30, 1-20 p.m. at Jerusalem, the time when our Lord was on the Cross.

The governing physical properties of the earth and its orbit (as given in Booklet No. 1 page 12), the Crucifixion date and the expression of SPIRITUAL UPLIFT accorded to man on that date are all defined by the same Displacement Factor. This constitutes a clear declaration—given in terms of God's Creative Law—proclaiming THE DIVINITY OF OUR LORD JESUS CHRIST, and confirming the words of the Apostle concerning "The mystery, which from the beginning of the world hath been hid in God, WHO CREATED ALL THINGS BY JESUS CHRIST," "In whom are hid all the treasures of wisdom and knowledge."

THE FUNCTIONING OF THE "STONE KINGDOM."

Another matter of additional interest is the date of the Conception. Here the reader must understand that the Julian year did not keep pace with the solar year, as the modern Gregorian year does. The Gregorian year was instituted in 1582 A.D., and if we carry the Gregorian method of Leap year intercalation back to the time of our Lord, we find that the Gregorian month dates are all numerically two days less than the Julian month dates. Thus, in B.C. 5, 3rd January (Julian), the date of the Conception, is 1st January (Gregorian), and the beginning of the calendar year of modern European and American civilisation. It is worth considering whether the accident of this identity having been effected in 1582 A.D. does not belong to the same category of accidents as that whereby the taking of the Census of Augustus coincided with the circumstances of our Lord's Birth. One fact seems to confirm that the identity is Divinely intentional This is that the central epoch of the Great Pyramid falls in the year 1844 A.D. This is the epoch of the Great Step, which lies in the central plane of the Apex, symbolic of our Lord enthroned as King. The centre of the Step, however, is displaced 286 P. inches (the Displacement Factor) East of the vertical line to the Apex. Now, in 1844 A.D.—and in no other year within a period of 21,000 years before or after—the Earth's longitude at noon of 1st January (Gregorian), the anniversary of the Conception, coincided with Perihelion. Now, Perihelion is a point on the major axis of the Earth's orbit, and this point lies nearest to the sun of all points in the Earth's orbit. Does this identity symbolise anything in relation to the "Perihelion" of the Divine "Orbit" of "The Sun of Righteousness"? If it does, it should refer to some date in the establishing of His Kingdom upon Earth, and this date should be related to the Displacement Factor.

Now the writer has already shown in "The Great Pyramid : Its Divine Message" that the Pyramid's geometry defines an interval of 286 years back from the Step date at 1844 A.D. to 1558 A.D. (actually given as December, 1557 A.D.), and that the Pyramid's symbolism defines this date for the beginning of the functioning of the Stone Kingdom of Biblical prophecy. Sir G. C. Doveton Sturdee, Admiral of the Fleet, in his Chairman's remarks at a lecture entitled "Cameos of Empire," at Central Hall, Westminster, on 15th October, 1924, referred to this date as the date of the beginning of Britain's Colonial Empire. Reference to Daniel ii, 34, 35, and 44, 45, and Matthew xxi, 42-44, will complete the identity. It should also be stated, however, that Mr. Harold Norris (the pupil and successor of Dr. H. Grattan Guinness) in his book "When will our Lord Return"? (4th Ed., 1918, pp. 121-125) gives the same date for the commencement of the 7th Gentile "Time" of 360 years. Dating this from the Pyramid's Stone Kingdom epoch, December, 1557, A.D., gives December, 1917, A.D., when the army of the Stone Kingdom delivered Jerusalem from "the desolator" (Luke xxi, 24 and Daniel ix, 27).

The latter event and its date were recognised by the late Rt. Rev. C. G. Handley Moule, D.D. (Lord Bishop of Durham) to mark the fulfilment of the indications of Scripture prophecy heralding the near approach of our Lord's Second Advent. In an address delivered on 8th June, 1919, Dr. Moule referred, gracefully and tactfully, to the fact that the books of Daniel and the Revelation of St. John have been explained by certain theological scholars as being, not inspired writings, but "hortatory rhapsodies," respectively given "to cheer sufferers under Antiochus Epiphanes" and "to cheer the victims of Nero and Domitian"; and reminded us that "forty years ago, in 1878, Guinness wrote that they who should see 1917, would probably see a great epoch for Jerusalem. The year came, and Allenby, *reverently victorious*, walked as liberator through the Jaffa Gate." The conclusions of Dr. Guinness, here mentioned, contained the following statement :—"THE DESTRUCTION OF THE POWER AND INDEPENDENCE OF THE OTTOMAN EMPIRE SHOULD BE AS A TRUMPET BLAST TO CHRISTENDOM PROCLAIMING THAT THE DAY OF CHRIST IS AT HAND." The emphasis in capitals is in the original—47 years ago. The TURKISH REPUBLIC has now displaced the OTTOMAN EMPIRE. The following number of this series will show what bearing this fact has upon the question of Scriptural and Pyramid prophecy.

PART IV.

THE ORBIT OF MESSIANIC CIVILISATION.

MESSIANIC CIVILISATION.

The evidence is complete that prophecies relating to the Messiah and a Messianic civilisation are older than the earliest historical records containing elements of these prophecies. The Messianic prophecies of the ancient Egyptians and of the Old and New Testaments not only identify our Lord Jesus Christ as the Messiah so long predicted and awaited, but also define and identify the British Race as the Stone (or Pyramid) Kingdom of Messianic Civilisation. Some few of the elements concerning this identification have been dealt with in the preceding pages. The whole subject, however, has been exhaustively treated in "The Great Pyramid: Its Divine Message." In that work it is proved to demonstration that the Divine Revelation of the Great Pyramid is clearly defined as addressed to the *Stone* Kingdom of the Messianic Civilisation, and therefore to the British Race in the British Empire and the United States of America. Dates are defined to the year and day for prophesied events in the *evolution* of the Messianic civilisation, and these dates, and the events that fulfil the predictions, are applicable only to the history of the British Race. The prophecies of the Old and New Testaments, however, define the same dates and events as relating to the history of Israel, as distinct from the people known as the Jews.[1] These prophecies represent the Jews as having no part in the development of the *higher constructive* elements of the Stone Kingdom, but do represent Israel as being destined to participate in all the prophesied functions of the Stone Kingdom. The evidence certainly suggests the necessity for the adoption of the working hypothesis that the British Race comprises the bulk of the dispersed of Israel—distinct from the Jews. The British Race thus constituted fulfils all the prophesied functions of the Stone Kingdom and all the prophesied functions of Israel.[2] The historical evidence confirms that Israelitish migrations into Britain via Greece and Phœnicia began from Egypt as early as the 16th-15th centuries B.C.—both before and during the period of the Egyptian bondage.[3] However this may be, it is sufficient to realise that the Egyptian Messianic prophecies and the Pyramid Messianic prophecies define the operations of the British Race, and the dates of the principal stages of these operations; that the Hebrew prophecies concerning the Stone Kingdom define the operations of the British Race, and the dates of the principal stages of these operations; and that the Hebrew prophecies concerning Israel—not the Jews—define Israel as employed in the same operations, and at the same dates. It is sufficient, therefore, for us to believe that, if the prophecies have been fulfilled in all other respects, they have certainly been fulfilled in regard to Israel.

In the Old Testament, Israel, under the Law, is figuratively referred to as the " wife " of Jehovah, and Jehovah is represented as the aspect of the Creator presented to Israel under the Law. Israel, failing to keep the Old Covenant of the Law, was given " a bill of divorcement," and became an " outcast " people,[4] with the promise that they would be restored under a new Covenant,[5] for " I am married unto you " said Jehovah.[6]

---

[1] G.P., Ch. V, Sect. Ic. "Israel" here refers to the ten tribed Northern kingdom of Samaria, which ceased at the *Assyrian* Captivity, and has never returned to Palestine. The "Jews" are that portion of the tribe of Judah that *returned* with the tribe of Benjamin and a portion of Levi, from the *Babylonian* Captivity. Refer Matt. x, 5-7 and Jeremiah iii, 14 and 18; Amos ix, 9; Hosea ix, 17; Jer. xxxi, 10; xxiii, 1-6

[2] For a general outline refer to Isa. xxix, 14; xli, 18-22; xliii, 21; liv. 17; lviii, 12; lix, 19; lx, 9; lxi, 4; lxv, 15. Deut. vii, 6. Gen. xvii, 6; xviii, 18; xxii, 17, 18; xlviii, 16, 19; xlix, 22. Ps. lxxxix, 25, 27; cxi. 5, 6 Jer. iii, 18; xxiii, 1, 2; li, 19, 21. Exod. xxiii, 27; xxxi, 16, 17. Num. xxiii, 22 and 24; xxiv, 7-9. Matt. xxi, 42-44. Dan. ii, 44

[3] G.P., p. 297 read in relation to pp. 5-7 and 65-75.

[4] Hosea i, 0-9; ii, 1-13; Jer. iii, 8.

[5] Hosea i, 10-11; ii, 14-23; Jer. iii. 12-18;   [6] Jer. iii, 14.

THE SPIRITUAL AND MATERIAL COUNTERPARTS.

To inaugurate the dispensation of the New Covenant the Godhead revealed ITSELF to man as " THE SON of Man," in fulfilment of the ancient Messianic prophecies. Our Lord therefore said " I and my Father are One," " before Abraham was, I AM," these expressions being clearly related to the words of Jehovah in Ex. iii, 14, " I AM THAT I AM—Thou shalt say unto the children of Israel, I AM hath sent me unto you." Our Lord therefore lived, suffered and conquered in fulfilment of the age-old prophecies. HE brought into being a new " BODY," the Church, of which He Himself is " the Head."[1] Through the Son of Man, individuals by the second or spiritual birth—brought into active operation by Him ; released by His conquest—could become " sons of God " and " partakers of the same body." This spiritual " Body "—allegorised in the New Testament as the " Bridegroom "—has its material counterpart, " the Bride " ; " the Spirit and the bride say, Come."[2] Similarly, in the parallel allegory, the *material* Stone Kingdom has its *spiritual* counterpart,[3] and is represented as failing to operate effectively until the two desire union and are joined.[4] The hand of God operates by Fatherly compulsion not only in things *spiritual* but in things *material*. It is essential therefore to realise that the British Race has derived the functions it has assumed, in accordance with all the prophecies, from its Israelitish elements. Israel, the " divorced wife " of Jehovah, was to be brought under the New Covenant. This means that Israel must be brought under the influence of the second or spiritual birth and be " born again " to become " the Bride " of the " New Covenant " or " New Testament." " I will yet be enquired of by the House of Israel to do it for them."[5] Circumstances are to compel Israel—and to compel the Stone Kingdom—to call upon God to fulfil this promise. This is the Message of the Old and New Testaments and it is the message of the Great Pyramid. The defined epoch of the compelling circumstances lies between 29th May, 1928, and 16th September, 1936 A.D.

Now the Messiah was to come of " the seed of Eve,"[6] of the seed of the race that was given dominion over the Earth.[7] Our Lord was born of this race and, by overcoming sin and death, and by His conquest of the " dragon,"[8] redeemed the forfeited gift of dominion over the Earth.[9] This gift was taken from the Jews and given *potentially* to the Stone Kingdom.[10] Our Lord therefore said " Who is My Mother, or My brethren ? And He looked round about on them which sat about Him and said, Behold My mother and My brethren ! For whosoever shall do the will of God, the same is my brother, and my sister, and mother." " Thy will be done on earth as it is in Heaven." The will of God on earth is that His elect should, by the power of His Son, have dominion over the earth. All this explains the figurative language of the 12th Chapter of Revelation. " The woman clothed with the sun "—*i.e.*, the symbol of Christ " the Sun of Righteousness "—is the " mother " of the " man-child who was to rule all nations with a rod of iron." The latter is the prophesied function of the Messiah,[11] and the declared future function of our Lord. The " woman " is clearly Israel under the Law, doing " the will of God " under the Old Covenant, and there-fore the " mother " of our Lord.[12] This identification is confirmed when we compare Dan. xii, 1 with Revelation xii, 6-17. In both, the arch-angel Michael appears as standing up against the opponent of Israel, and on behalf of Israel. That the Scriptures identify " the Father " with " the Son " (" the Lamb of God "), and that the " wife (Israel) of Jehovah " is " the mother " of " the Son " and is also to be spiritually reborn as " the Bride of the Lamb " explains many of the formulæ employed in the pagan perversion of the ancient original Messianic prophecies, wherein the pseudo-Messiah is described as " the son and husband of the mother."[13]

[1]I Cor. xii, 12-27 ; Col. i, 18 and 19 ; Eph. i, 22, 23 : ii, 19-22 ; iii, 6 ; iv, 4, 13-16 ; I Peter ii, 4-9.

[2]Rev. xxii, 17 ; xxi, 9-14 · Hos ii, 19-23 ; Jer iii, 14.

[3]Eph. ii, 19-22 : iii, 6, compared with I Peter ii, 4-10 : Hosea i, 10 ; ii, 23 ; Dan. ii, 34, 35, 45 : Matt. x, 5-7, 23 ; xii, 41 ; xxi, 42-44.

[4]Matt. xiii, 41-43 in relation to the other references above.

[5]Ezek. xxxvi, 37. Compare with Rev. xxii, 17, 20, and with Jer. xxiii, 6.

[6]Gen. iii, 15. [7]Gen. i, 26, 28. [8]Rev. xii, 7-12 ; Gen. iii, 15.

[9]Acts iii, 19-21. [10]Matt. xxi, 42-44.

[11]Psalm ii, 6-12 : cx, 1-7. [12]Rev. ii, 26, 27 ; xix, 15, 16.

[13]Mr. J. Clemishaw, on reading this, sends me the query :—" Is this the origin of the Greek legend of Oedipus ? "

I had not this legend in mind, but the evolution of the legend of Osiris and Isis and other older Oriental myths. Nevertheless, the legend of Oedipus has incorporated—obviously from Phœnician sources—many paganised elements of the original Messianic prophecies.—D. D.

We have seen what an important part the British Race has played in fulfilling the ancient Messianic prophecies concerning the Stone Kingdom (or its *material* elements) and concerning Israel. This brings us to the consideration of a remarkable book " The Phœnician Origin of Britons, Scots and Anglo-Saxons," by Col. L. A. Waddell, C.B., C.I.E., LL.D., Ex-Professor of Tibetan, London University. This book was published some two months after " The Great Pyramid ; Its Divine Message " and by the same firm of publishers. The present writer, however, had not read it until after the preceding parts of this booklet were written. Col. Waddell's book reaches the same conclusions—and from entirely different sources—concerning what we have termed " the ancient Messianic prophecies " relating to the Messianic race and civilisation, and the fulfilment of these prophecies in the British Race. Col. Waddell derives his data from Sumerian sources in the 3rd millenium B.C., from Hittite sources in the 2nd millenium B.C., and from Phœnician, Phrygian, Indian and pre-Roman British sources of the 1st millenium B.C. From all of these sources he shows the continuance of a prevailing belief in a Divinely guided race known by the name "Barats " or " Brits." This race is frequently represented symbolically as a woman, Barat-ana, ruling over the seas, and accompanied by the sign of the " Sun of Righteousness,"·a sun-circle encircling the St. George and St. Andrew crosses (i.e., the Union Jack). The allegory of St. George and the Dragon is shown to belong to Cappadocia in pre-Christian times, and to refer to " the Son of God " slaying the dragon. Andrew is of the same pre-Christian origin, being actually the Indo-Aryan *pagan* name, Indra, for Jehovah-Christ—the " I AM."

In the various representations, the dragon is pictured as being overcome by the Cross as a weapon, which fact, together with the identification of *Indra* as the Indo-Aryan *pagan* name for Jehovah-Messiah, gives significance to the words of the Vedic hymn :

" With thy Spiky Weapon, thy deadly bolt,
O Indra, thou smotest the Dragon in the face."

Waddell here shows by numerous examples that the " bolt " is the Cross, the original also of the " hammer " of Thor. In many of these ancient texts and representations, the arch-angel Michael (Mikel) is associated in the war against the dragon, and in upholding, or removing to safety, the *symbol* of the " Sun of Righteousness," borne in other cases by the woman " Barat-ana." Michael is pictured with eagle's wings and in other cases is symbolised by an eagle upholding the symbol of the " Sun of Righteousness " while transfixing the serpent with its talons. The representation appears on an early Briton pre-Christian coin, and is an almost exact representation of what now figures as the Eagle of the United States of America. On the obverse side of the Great Seal of the United States the Eagle is figured surmounted by the Sun, and on the reverse side of the original seal is figured the symbol of the Stone Kingdom—a Pyramid with its Apex Stone (symbolic of Christ), containing the Eye of Providence, suspended over it. These are shown on Plate LXVIII in " The Great Pyramid : Its Divine Message."

The Sun, Woman and Michael-Eagle symbols are, therefore, mythologically and heraldically attached to the British Race. Referring again to the 12th Chapter of Revelation, we see the significance of this. In verse 14 we are told " And to the woman were given two wings of a great *eagle*, that she might fly into the wilderness." Where is this wilderness ? The answer appears in the May 1922 " My Magazine "—" The Mighty Multitude of People " :

" In all the ages from the beginning of the earth down to 1760 the British Isles gained only 10 million people. Then, in only 160 years more, 37 millions more people were added. *That is so wonderful as to seem miraculous if we think about it.*

" And here is another thing just as wonderful. What we now call the United States of America was almost uninhabited down to quite recent times....In 1840....the United States had only 17 million people....America has grown from 17 to 106 millions in only 82 years, and has gained almost all her people in the last 100 years."

Extend the study to the colonies and dependencies of the British Empire, and we have the answer in full, even as it is given in Deut. xxxii. 8-17, 29 :

" When the Most High divided to the nations their inheritance....He set the bounds of the people according to the number of the children of Israel.

" For the Lord's portion is His people : Jacob is the lot (Hebrew—*the measuring cord*) of His inheritance.

" He found him in a desert land, and in the waste howling wilderness : He led him about, He instructed him, He kept him as the apple of His eye.

" As an *eagle* stirreth up her nest, fluttereth over her young, spreadeth abroad her wings, taketh them, *beareth them on her wings* :

" So the Lord did lead him......

" He made him ride on the high places of the earth........

" **Oh that they were wise, that they understood this, that they would consider their latter end.**"

"THE CHOSEN PEOPLE" OF THE VEDIC TEXTS

It must not be assumed by the reader that Col. Waddell claims any prophetic synchronism between the Hebrew prophecies and the traditional elements of the ancient Messianic prophecies contained in the Indian epics or in such other literary sources studied in relation. Col. Waddell does not appear to place the Hebrew scripture on any higher plane than his Vedic texts. This, however, makes his evidence and conclusions all the more striking, and of greater value when co-ordinated with the writer's own identical conclusions from the ancient Egyptian and ancient Hebrew Messianic prophecies, particularly when it is understood that Col. Waddell derives from the Indian epics that the race of " Barats," " Brits " or " Britons " are " the chosen people of God." Thus, referring to the various statements concerning this race, Col. Waddell quotes the ancient Indian epics as follows :

" His sources of subsistence are Arms and the Protection of the Earth.[1] The Guardianship of the Earth is his special province[2]....By intimidating the bad and cherishing the good, the ruler (of this race), who maintains the discipline of the different tribes, secures whatever region he desires " (p. 200).[3]

" The principal nations of the *Barats* are the Kurus (Syrians) and the able *Panch* (Phœnic-ians) " (p. 188).

" The able *Panch* setting out to invade the Earth, brought the whole World under their sway " (p. 1).

" The Brihat (' Brit-on ') singers belaud Indra (the pagan Indo-Aryan name of Jehovah) ....Indra hath raised the Sun on high in heaven....Indra leads us with single sway.... The *Panch* (*Phœnic*-ian Brihats) leaders of the Earth. Ours only and none others is He." (p.1).

It is important also to observe what Col. Waddell has to say concerning the civilisation of India that is responsible for the above identifications. He says :

" Nothing whatever of traces of civilisation, apart from rude Stone Circles, has ever been found by the scientifically equipped Indian archæological Survey Department, in their more or less exhaustive excavations on the oldest reputed sites down to the virgin soil during half a century, which can be specifically dated to before 600 B.C

" On the other hand, I observed, that historical India, like historic Greece, *suddenly* bursts into view about 600 B.C., in the pages of Buddhist literature, and in the Maha Barat epic...."*

"....I was led by numerous clues to trace these 'Aryan,' or as they called themselves 'Arya,' invaders of India back to Asia Minor and Syria-Phœnicia."

These identifications immediately led the present writer to remember certain long-forgotten passages of Sanchoniathon's " Phœnician History," " preserved " by Philo of Byblus in Phœnicia (B.C. 100). In relating the Phœnician traditions concerning origins " Sanchoniathon " states that there

" was one Elioun, called Hypsistus (*i.e.*, 'the Most High') ; and his wife named Beruth (Hebrew, Berith or Brith=Covenant), and they dwelt about Byblus," in Phœnicia. These were contemporary with " Sydyk " (*i.e.*, the Righteous One).

" Kronus or (Saturn) whom the Phœnicians call Israel, and who after his death was deified....when he was king, had by a nymph of the country called *A no-bret*, an only son, who, on that account is styled Jeoud ; for, so the Phœnicians still call an only son : and when great danger from war beset the land, he adorned the Altar, and invested this son with the emblems of royalty and sacrificed him."

All this merely means that the *Only Son*, Jeoud—the Only Son of the Most High—was to be of the seed of Israel, the seed of the people symbolised by the Israel-woman of Revelation, the Covenant One, or Brit-ana, here called Ano-Bret, by inversion in the account of Sanchoniathon. As to the explanation of the origin of the particular " Phœnicians " here mentioned, and of the Phœnician origin of certain early tribes in Britain, the reader is referred to page 197, in relation to pages 5 to 7 and 65 to 73 of " The Great Pyramid : Its Divine Message."

" They that shall be of thee shall build the old waste places : thou shalt raise up the foundations of many generations ; and thou shalt be called : The repairer of the breach, The restorer of the paths to dwell in." Isa. lviii, 12.[4]

[1] Jeremiah li, 20 ; Isa. liv, 17 :   [2] Deut. vii, 6 ; Isa. xliii, 21.
[3] Isa. xli, 18-22 ; lxi, 4 ; Gen. xlix, 22 : Deut. xxxii, 7-9, 29.
[4] Refer also to the whole of Isa. xlix.
* It is significant that the date of the migratory movement, here implied, coincides with the date of the fall of Assyria, and of the consequent release of the captive Israelites of the Ten-Tribed Kingdom of Samaria   This captivity must not be confused with the Babylonian captivity of Judah-Israel which took place soon after and as a result of the fall of the Assyrian Empire.

CONTENTS

CHAPTER V.

THE CHRONOGRAPH OF HISTORY.

APPENDIX I.

APPENDIX II.

LIST OF PLATES

LIST OF TABLES

APPENDIX I—THE EGYPTIAN KING LISTS.

TAILPIECES TO CHAPTERS

These are from the engravings of the drawings by Denon made during Napoleon's Egyptian Campaign, 1798–99.

TAILPIECE TO CHAPTER I.—View, at sunset, of the Island of Philæ, looking West. The island is now submerged by the impounded waters behind the Assouan Dam.

TAILPIECE TO CHAPTER II.—View of a small XVIIIth Dynasty peripteral temple on the Island of Elephantine. The temple was built by Amenhotep III and dedicated to the chief god of the 1st Cataract. It was destroyed by the Turkish governor in 1822. The temple shown is of interest as having been built during the early period of Semitic influence in the XVIIIth Dynasty, and as indicating a probable source for Greek architectural impulse (refer to Chapter V in this connection).

TAILPIECE TO CHAPTER III.—Another view of the Island of Philæ (North).

TAILPIECE TO CHAPTER IV.—View of the Temple of Thoth at Hermopolis. Maspero states that " The portico was destroyed about 1820 by the engineers who constructed the sugar refinery at Rodah, and now only a few shapeless fragments of it remain."

TAILPIECE TO CHAPTER V.—View of the 1st Cataract locality—looking South—with the Island of Elephantine shown in the foreground. This is now the site of the Assouan Dam.

PLATE I.

PLAN OF STONEHENGE. STONE CIRCLE AND OUTER EARTH CIRCLE.

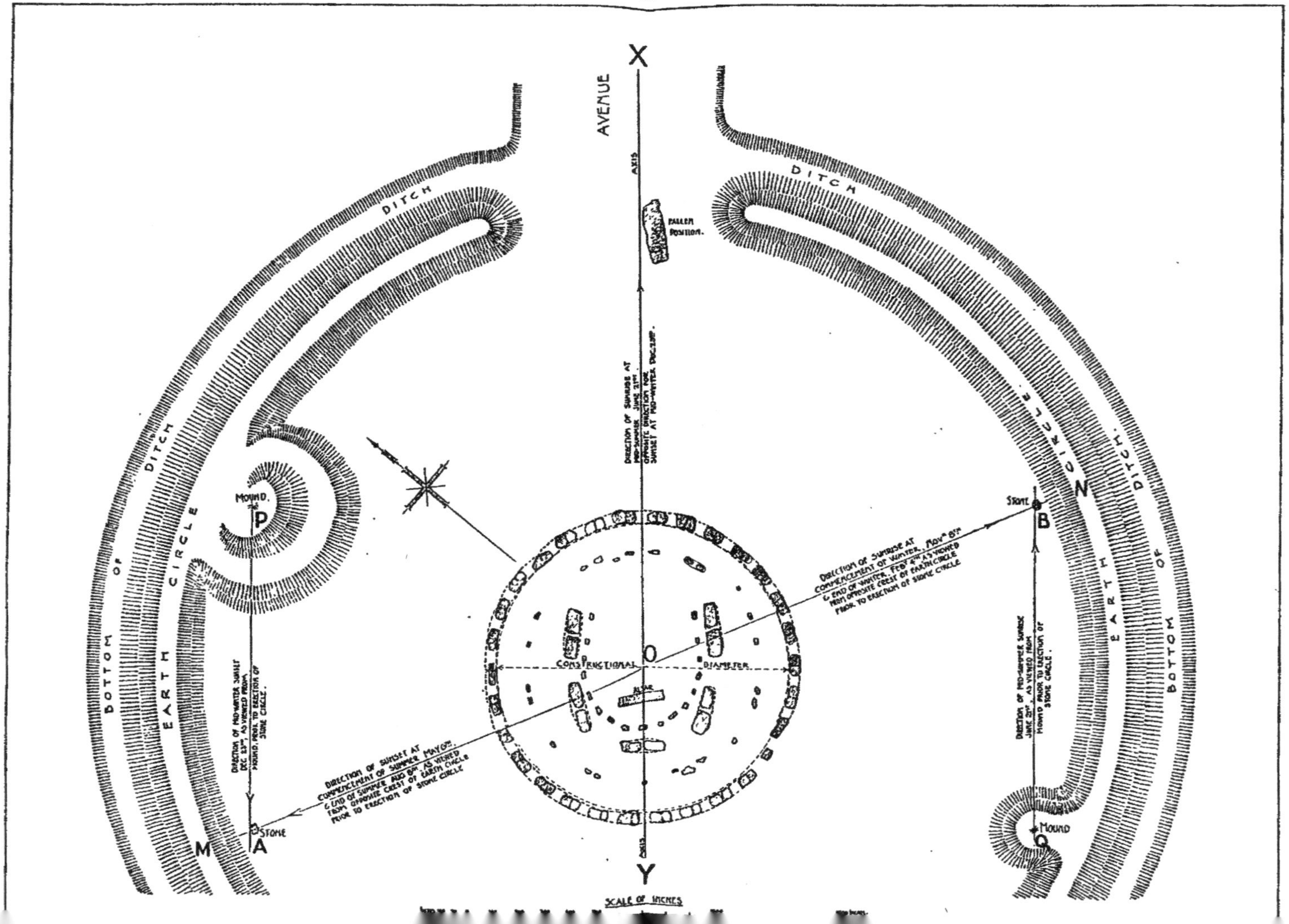

AVENUE

AXIS

X

Y

AXIS

DITCH

BOTTOM OF DITCH

EARTH CIRCLE

Stone B

FALLEN Position.

DIRECTION OF SUNRISE AT PRO-SUMMER JUNE 21st
OPPOSITE DIRECTION FOR SUNSET AT PRO-WINTER DEC 21st.

DIRECTION OF MID-WINTER SUNRISE
JUNE 21st., AS VIEWED FROM
MOUND PRIOR TO ERECTION OF
STONE CIRCLE.

Mound O

DIAMETER.

CONSTRUCTIONAL

Stone A

M

Mound O
P

DITCH

EARTH CIRCLE

BOTTOM OF DITCH

DIRECTION OF MID-WINTER SUNSET
DEC 21st., AS VIEWED FROM
MOUND, PREV. TO ERECTION OF
STONE CIRCLE.

SCALE OF INCHES

CHAPTER I.

ANCIENT ASTRONOMICAL OBSERVATORIES, ALMANAC DEVICES AND TRADITIONS.

SECTION I.—GENERAL.

¶ 1. ANCIENT KNOWLEDGE CONCERNING THE SOLAR YEAR.

It is evident that the civilised inhabitants of the Ancient East had precise knowledge of the duration of the Solar year. This is clear from every source of information, in archæology, literary tradition, and mythology, that is open to modern research. The Solar Year known in Earliest Times. Its Two Ancient Forms.

It was observed that the seasons were definitely fixed to the solar year, as defined by the astronomical phenomena accompanying the recurrence of the Solstices and Equinoxes.[1] From the knowledge of the recurrence of these, the four quarters of the agricultural year were observed to begin precisely mid-way between a Solstice and an Equinox. Astronomical (Solstices and Equinoxes): Vegetation (Astronomical Seasons).

The points of the Solar Astronomical Year and of the Solar Vegetation Year, as recognised in the earliest period of recorded ancient history are stated in terms of our modern (Gregorian) Calendar in Table I.

[1] Sir Norman Lockyer, "Dawn of Astronomy," pp. 12, 57, 62-66, 78-85, 89-93, 117-119, 244-245 (quotations from Ideler), 331 and 337.
Lockyer, "Stonehenge and Other British Stone Monuments," pp. 64-68, 96-106, 181-199, 308-315, 335 and 336.
The references are selected as, in our opinion, being free from elements that can be justifiably criticised on archæological grounds.
Prof. G. Forbes, "History of Astronomy," pp. 8-10.
W. G. Old, "The Chinese *Shu-King*," Introduction, Book I, Sect. I, and notes, Do. Sect. V, Book II, Sect. I, notes.
Encycl. Brit. (11th Edit.), Vol. I, pp. 224 and 317.

PLATE II.

PERSPECTIVE VIEW OF STONEHENGE AT TIME OF SUNRISE OF SUMMER SOLSTICE. 1680 B.C.

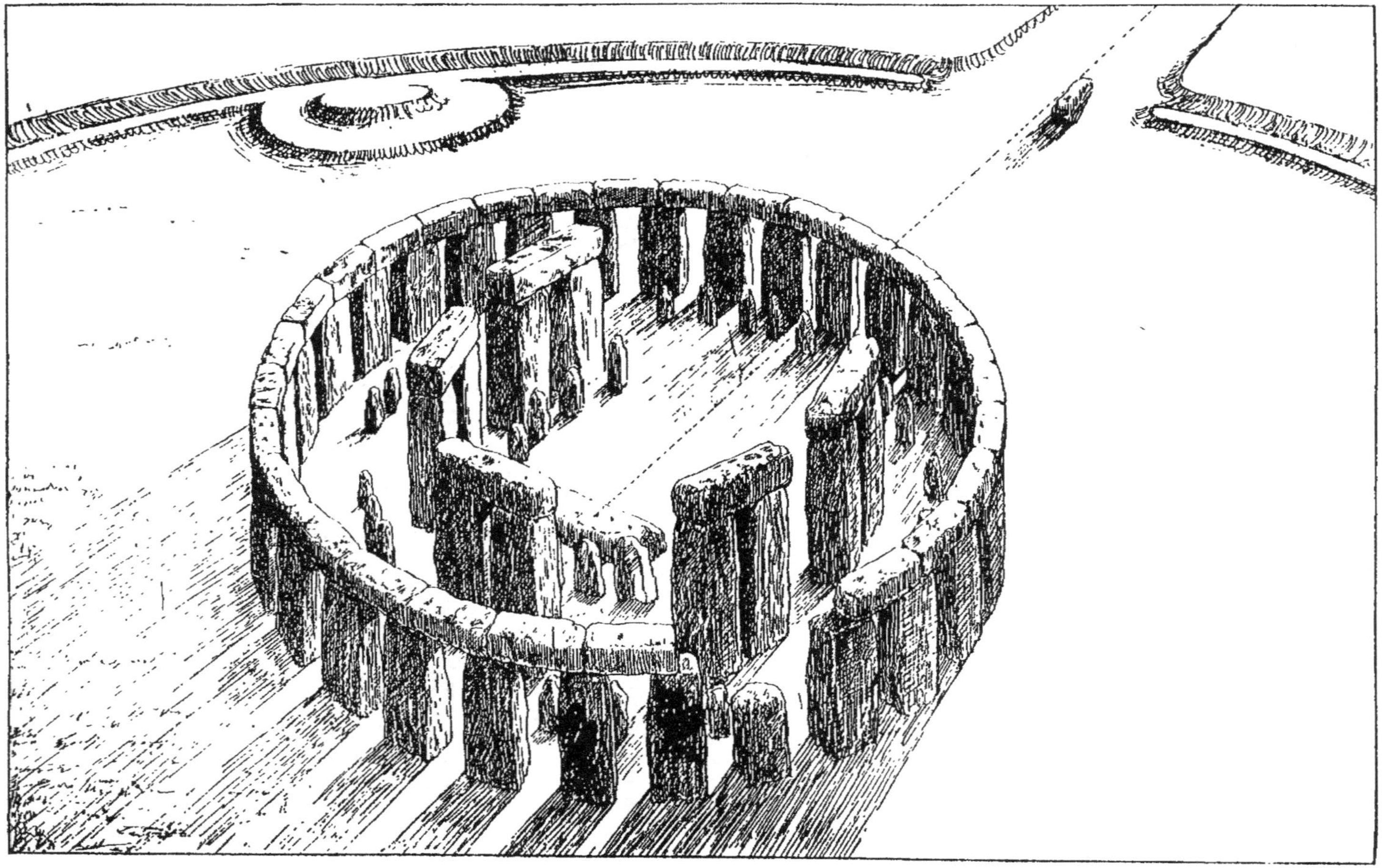

TABLE I.

THE TWO RECOGNISED FORMS OF SOLAR YEAR IN ANCIENT TIMES.

(STATED WITH REFERENCE TO MODERN CALENDAR YEAR FOR 1901 A.D.)

The Solar Astronomical Year.   *The Solar Vegetation Year.*

Early Semitic
Astronomical Year } 23 SEPT.
began at AUTUMNAL EQUINOX

WINTER BEGINS .. MID-WAY .. 8 Nov. { Ancient November Agricultural Year began.

WINTER SOLSTICE .. 23 DEC.

SPRING BEGINS .. MID-WAY .. 4 FEB. { Chinese Agricultural Year began, (B.C. 2448).[1]

Later Semitic
Astronomical Year } 21 MAR.
began at VERNAL EQUINOX

SUMMER BEGINS .. MID-WAY[2] .. 6 MAY { Ancient May Agricultural Year began.

SUMMER SOLSTICE .. 21 JUNE.
AUTUMN BEGINS .. MID-WAY[2] .. 8 AUG.
AUTUMNAL EQUINOX 23 SEPT.

¶ 2. STONEHENGE TEMPLE OBSERVATORY AND ALMANAC CIRCLE. (Plates I and II).

In our own country there exist hundreds of ancient structural devices for indicating the principal points of the two recognised forms of the Solar year. The best-known monument of this nature is that of the Stonehenge circle. This consists of the arrangement of upright stones and lintels contained within the earthwork circle, as figured restored, on Plates I and II. The Avenue Approach to the Circle cuts the Earthwork circle as shown on the Plates.

Stonehenge Alignments define the points of the Solar Astronomical and Solar Vegetation Years.

---

[1] "The Chinese *Shu-King*." W. G. Old, pp. 301-2, and note. Translation of Book I, Sect. I, pp. 1-2, and Translator's notes to same.
Encycl. Brit. (11th Edit.), Vol. VI, p. 317.
[2] By "Mid-Way" is intended 45° of *Right Ascension* from an Equinox or Solstice; not mid-way as defined by the interval in days.

Thanks to the admirable surveys of Sir William M. Flinders Petrie and Mr. Edgar Barclay, and Sir Norman Lockyer's[1] precise azimuth alignments, the purpose of the circle is now known with certainty.

As shown on Plate I, two separate alignments are directed to the horizon points of sunrise and sunset at the Summer Solstice and Winter Solstice respectively. Another alignment on Plate I gives the horizon point of Sunset at the beginning (May 6) and ending (August 8) of Summer, and of the horizon point of Sunrise at beginning (Nov. 8) and ending (February 4) of Winter.

Plate II shows the shadows thrown by the Stone Circle at Sunrise of Summer Solstice.

(Refer Section III Description of Plates ¶¶ 65 and 66).

¶ 3. OTHER BRITISH CIRCLES AND ALIGNMENTS.

Of equal astronomical importance to Stonehenge and its accessory alignments discussed by Lockyer and Barclay, are the circles and accessory alignments of Stenness, in Orkney.   Mr. Magnus Spence was the first to show that these were connected with the Solar year and its principal datings.   Investigations conducted by Sir Norman Lockyer confirm that the alignments were variously directed towards sunrise or sunset at the Solstitial and May and November points of the year.[2]   The data at Stenness in the Orkneys, then, agree with the data at Stonehenge.   Both define the principal points of the Solar Astronomical Year and of the Solar Vegetation year.

Stenness, Orkney, Alignments define the points of the Solar Astronomical and Solar Vegetation Years.

In this part of his subject Lockyer has some interesting evidence concerning the sighting purpose of the well-known perforated stones, met with in Britain and North-Western Europe, wherever similar astronomical alignments occur.[3]

Sixty-seven British Solar Astronomical and Vegetation Year Alignments.

Leaving out of consideration—as doubtful on archæological grounds— many of Lockyer's star rising and setting alignments in Britain, Lockyer discusses and tabulates twenty-five May alignments, eleven November alignments, and nineteen Summer, and twelve Winter Solstitial alignments in Great Britain and Ireland.[4]

¶ 4. ALIGNMENTS IN BRITTANY AND ELSEWHERE.

Thirty-four Solar Astronomical and Vegetation Year Alignments in Brittany.

Passing from Britain into Brittany, Lockyer finds eleven May alignments, three November alignments, six Summer and eleven Winter Solstitial alignments, and three Equinoctial alignments.[5]

[1]Petrie, " Stonehenge," Plates.
  Lockyer, " Stonehenge and other British Stone Monuments," pp 46 (Hoare's 1810 plan), 55-68 (Solstitial alignment), 88-95 (May-November alignment), 442-450 (The Welsh Gorsedd.— Solstitial and May-November alignments).
  Barclay, " Stonehenge and its Earthworks," pp. 63-66 (Solstitial alignment), 66-67 (Equinoctial alignment and altitude), 70, 99-110 (November, February, May, and August Festivals, and March, June, September, and December Festivals).   Barclay's Plates III and IV for alignments.
[2]Spence's " Standing Stones and Maeshowe of Stenness," *Scottish Review*, Oct., 1893.
[3]"Stonehenge and Other British Stone Monuments," pp. 37, 128, 282, 285, 286, 316, and 318.
[4]Ibid., Appendices, pp. 481 and 482.
[5]Ibid., Appendices, pp. 485-486.

As in parts of Britain, Lockyer[1]—quoting Baring-Gould—finds the May and August Festivals still celebrated in many parishes of Brittany. The same, however, is true of North-Western Europe, the reason being that, whereas Brittany lies on the Southern track of the megalithic builders from the East, the circles and alignments of North-Western Europe lie on the Northern track of the megalithic builders from Western Asia and Egypt.

Migratory Route indicated by Mediterranean and West European Megalithic Monuments.

" It must not be forgotten," says Lockyer, " that structures more or less similar to Stonehenge are found along a line from the East on both sides of the Mediterranean."[2]

Professor T. Eric Peet says that these " occupy a very remarkable position along a vast sea-board which includes the Mediterranean coast of Africa and the Atlantic coast of Europe. In other words, they lie entirely along a natural sea route."[3]

This confirms another statement by Lockyer that " the Druid culture (of Ancient Britain) had not passed through Gaul, and had therefore been water-borne to Britain."[4]

¶ 5. THE SEA ROUTE—WESTERN ASIA AND EGYPT TO BRITAIN.

As a matter of fact, the Libyo-Amorite route between Western Asia and the Atlantic coasts seems to have been almost entirely a sea route, rather than, as some have supposed, a North African Coast-Land route. The distribution of megalithic buildings along the coast of North-Western Africa and South-Western Europe is denser than along the coast of North-Eastern Africa. This undoubtedly points to the fact that these monuments were erected near colonized ports of call along the sea route to the ancient Portuguese, Spanish, British, and Baltic metal, amber, and jet deposits.

Megalithic Buildings near Ports of Call on Mediterranean Route.

The period for this earliest activity in maritime commerce between Britain and the East dates from before 2000 B.C. to 1200 B.C.[5]

Commercial Intercourse Circ. 2000 B.C. to 1200 B.C.

XVIIIth Dynasty Egyptian glazed beads (not made elsewhere, or by any other Egyptian dynasty than the XVIIIth and XIXth), were found at Stone-henge, together with beads of Baltic amber.[6] Similar beads of Baltic amber were also found in Egypt in XVIIIth and XIXth Dynasty remains.[7]

Stonehenge Egyptian Beads and Contemporary Amber in Egypt confirm Lockyer's Stonehenge date.

This identification of the period of Stonehenge confirms Lockyer's astrono-mical dating, 1680 B.C. ± 200 years, for the erection of the Stone Circle. Ancient British jet (from Whitby in Yorkshire) and worked pieces of Baltic amber have been found, in the deposits of the megalithic builders in Spain and Portugal, together with Egyptian ivory figures, a shell from the Red Sea, Egyptian alabaster and marble objects, and statuettes of a Babylonian type.[8]

[1] " Stonehenge and Other British Stone Monuments," pp. 198-199
[2] " Dawn of Astronomy," p. 90.
[3] " Rough Stone Monuments," (1912), pp. 147-8.
[4] " Stonehenge and Other British Stone Monuments," p. 323.
[5] Mr. Donald A. Mackenzie's " Ancient Man in Britain," pp. 91-108, 218-222.
[6] Sayce, in Journal of Egyptian Archæology, Vol. I, Pt. I., p. 18. H. R. Hall, p. 19.
[7] H. R. Hall, p. 19.
[8] D. A. Mackenzie, " Ancient Man in Britain," pp. 96, 97.

¶ 6. FOLKLORE AND TRADITION.

Long prior to the discovery of these evidences, Lockyer conducted an exhaustive inquiry into local Folklore and tradition for evidences concerning Druidic origins.[1] His conclusions are clearly and ably summed up in his comprehensive article, " The Uses and Dates of Ancient Temples," in *Nature*, May 20th, 1909, as follows :—

Summary of Lockyer's Conclusions.

" At the first blush there appears to be no resemblance between the Egyptian and Greek temples and the British stone monuments, but a careful study of both shows that this view is an erroneous one..........
In my inquiry I have not confined myself to the astronomical side of the question. I have tried to dip into the folklore and tradition already garnered in relation, not only to the sacred stones, but to the sacred wells and sacred trees.

Ancient British Astronomical Evidences indicate Egyptian influence.

" From what I have learned I am convinced that much light will be thrown on both when an attempt shall have been made to picture what the lives of the first British astronomer-priests must necessarily have been.

Local Folklore and Tradition indicate Semitic influence or origin.

" It is interesting to note that, while the astronomical side of the inquiry suggests a close connection with Egyptian thought, the folklore and traditions, when studied in relation with the monuments, indicate a close connection between ancient BRITISH and the SEMITIC civilisations.........The ' Druids ' of Cæsar's time were undoubtedly the descendants of the astronomer-priests, some of whose daily work has now perhaps at last been revealed."

In this connection a knowledge of the conclusions reached by the eminent Belgian Archæologist, M. Siret, is of more than ordinary interest. Mackenzie states that as a result of M. Siret's investigations concerning the Eastern origin of the megalithic builders and metal workers in Ancient Britain, Spain, and Portugal,

Modern Archæological Evidences indicate Eastern Origin of Megalithic Builders and identify them with Druids.

[2]" Siret has found evidence to show that the Tree Cult of the Easterners was connected with the early megalithic monuments. The testimony of tradition associates the stone circles, etc., with the Druids. ' We are now obliged,' he writes,[3] ' to go back to the theory of the archæologists of a hundred years ago who attributed the megalithic monuments to the Druids.   The instinct of our predecessors has been more penetrating than the scientific analysis which has taken its place.' In Gaelic, as will be shown, the words for a sacred grove, and the shrine within a grove are derived from the same root *nem*."

[1]" Stonehenge and Other British Stone Monuments," pp. 178-260.
[2]D. A. Mackenzie, " Ancient Man in Britain," pp. 155-6.
[3]*L'Anthropologie* (1921), pp. 268 *et seq.*

¶ 7. CONCLUSIONS FROM RECENT DISCOVERIES.

Mackenzie,[1] from the more recent evidences similarly sums up his inquiry, as follows :—

"The Celts appear to have embraced the Druidic system of the earlier Iberians in Western Europe, whose culture had been derived from that of the Oriental colonists." *(The Ancient Portuguese and Spanish Oriental Colonies.)*

"At an early period in the Early Agricultural Age and before bronze working was introduced, England and Wales, Scotland and Ireland, were influenced more directly than had hitherto been the case by the high civilizations of Egypt and Mesopotamia, and especially by their colonies in South-Western Europe." *(The Iberian Ports of Call on the Sea Route to Ancient Britain.)*

¶ 8. THE ORIGINAL IDEA ADOPTED BY THE MEGALITHIC BUILDERS.

Our inquiry is concerned chiefly with the origin of astronomical observatories and almanac devices employed to fix and portray the principal points of the solar astronomical and solar vegetation years. The astronomical evidences, and the evidences from folklore and tradition, and from archæological sources, have shown us that the origin is carried back to the valleys of the Euphrates and the Nile.

Lockyer has shown us that the Pyramid builders of the IVth and Vth Egyptian Dynasties, must, from their astronomical cult, have come from the region of the Euphrates. He shows also, that nearly all the ancient year cults of the Nile Delta are connected with the Euphratean equinoctial year.[2] Petrie, too, finds an Euphratean origin for the Vth Dynasty of Egypt.[3] *(The Egyptian Gizeh Pyramid Builders of Euphratean Origin.)*

Confirming our deductions from the data, we find at once that the idea of the IVth Dynasty Great Pyramid builders in Egypt was the original of the idea followed by all the megalithic builders from Egypt to Spain and Britain. The Great Pyramid was built, not alone as a Sundial of the day, but primarily, in its external features, as a Sundial of the Seasons. *(The external purpose of the Great Pyramid adopted by the Megalithic Builders in Northern Africa, Spain, and Britain.)*

¶ 9. THE ANCIENT SUNDIAL OF THE SEASONS.

One of the primary objects of early Pyramid *building* in ancient Egypt was undoubtedly to record and indicate automatically throughout the country the annual recurrence of the principal points of the two forms of solar year—the astronomical and the agricultural. No form of building, unless accurately and symmetrically built with proper reference to the North, South, East, and West, could be employed to effect this purpose. That the requisite *Sundial of the Seasons* should be a monument of public utility necessitated vast bulk, large external surfaces, the finest selected material, and extreme accuracy of workmanship. *(The Necessity for vast bulk, accurate orientation and perfection in workmanship.)*

[1] "Ancient Man in Britain," pp. 218 and 220.
[2] "Dawn of Astronomy," pp. 84, 85, 367-370.
[3] "History of Egypt," Vol. I, p. 85 (9th Ed.), p. 96 (10th Ed.).

All the necessary requirements are fulfilled by the gigantic proportions of the Pyramids of Gizeh, by their accurate orientation, and by their precision of workmanship. Then the site selected, on the elevated plateau of Gizeh, westward of the adjacent agricultural land,—the inhabited and cultivated strip of the Nile—and centrally south of the cultivated Delta, was the only possible site for the effective utilisation of the structural features. The admirable nature of the selected site, for the purpose indicated, is seen by reference to Plate III—Map of the Nile Delta—and Plate IV—Map of the Pyramids and Tombs on the Plateau of Gizeh—and by reference to the upper view of the frontispiece.

Conditions fulfilled by Gizeh Pyramids.

Ideal Site for Seasonal Sundial of the Delta.

¶ 10. THE REFLECTING SURFACES OF THE GREAT PYRAMID OF GIZEH.

Conceived and built the first of all the Pyramids of Gizeh, the Great Pyramid embodied in its external casing all the knowledge of the Ancients concerning the properties of the Sundial. Planned to effect its purpose primarily by means of reflected sunlight, and secondarily only by means of shadows, the casing of the Great Pyramid was selected from the whitest and best limestone from the quarries of Turra and Masara, on the opposite or Eastern side of the Nile.

The Great Pyramid's External Surfaces perfected for Reflections.

To ensure accuracy and continuity of unbroken plane, free from visible joints and beds, in the casing surface of each face slope of the Great Pyramid, the beds and joints, and the visible surfaces of all casing stones were worked as accurately as modern optician's work, but with this degree of accuracy extending to considerably larger surfaces. All joints and beds were so accurately fitted that even at this date a sheet of note-paper cannot be inserted between the stones still remaining unbroken and undisturbed *in situ*. Yet all these joints and beds were run with a fine film of cement.

The Refinement of Accuracy of Plane Surfaces of Beds, Joints, and Exposed Faces.

Another remarkable feature of constructional detail confirms the high degree of accuracy and smoothness of surface that was considered necessary. Flaws in the visible surfaces of the casing stones were cut out and refilled with accurately fitting pieces of limestone, invisibly cemented in. This indicates that the intention was to obtain the whole external visible surface so uniformly smooth and plane as to present a polished unbroken reflecting surface on all four casing sides of the Great Pyramid. It is obvious that it was from the brilliant reflexions from its casing slopes that the Great Pyramid is named, in the inscriptions of the Pyramid period, and in inscriptions of later times, *Khuti*, " the Lights."[1]

Flaws cut out and refilled without sign of restoration.

The Great Pyramid's Name in Ancient Egypt, "The Lights."

¶ 11. THE REFLECTED RAYS TRANSFORMED INTO VISIBLE EFFECT.

Name and Evidences imply that Reflexions were transformed into visible effect.

That the Pyramid's reflexions were transformed into visible effect, or were themselves rendered visible—at least around the hour of noon-day—is certain

[1]Brugsch, "Egypt under the Pharaohs," Vol. I, p. 73. Revised English Edit. (3rd). 1902, p. 35.

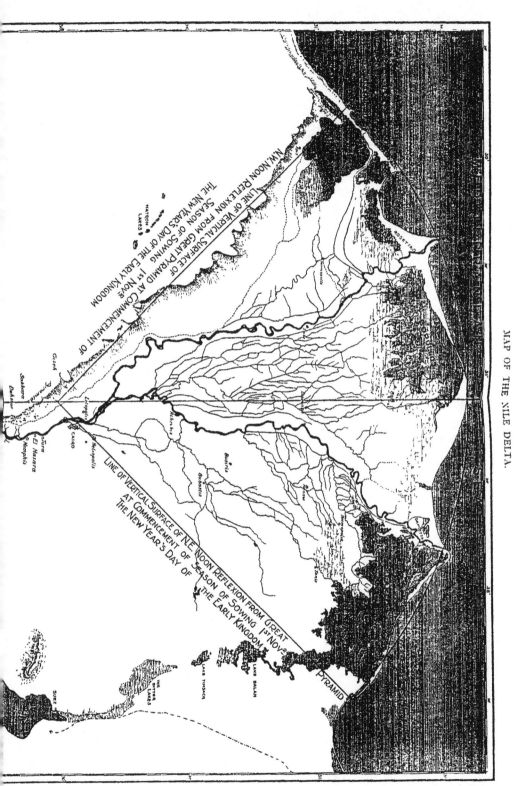

PLATE III.
MAP OF THE NILE DELTA.

both from the Pyramid's ancient name, "The Lights," and its structural evidences. Bearing in mind all the evidences pointing to special preparation and intention, it is clear that the site selected, and certain special details of construction referred to later, had some connection with this matter. It is in this connection that many of the Pyramid's structural features—and certain outstanding features of its environment—seem to suggest advanced problems for the physicist. These all tend to indicate that the Pyramid was designed and located upon the conception that the mid-day reflexions would be rendered visible. *Special features suggest advanced problems for the Physicist.* *Designed and Located on the conception that reflexions would be visible.*

That the atmospheric conditions within and bordering on the desert regions around Egypt furnish the essential conditions for the formulation of the conception noted is clear from the authentic observation quoted in ¶ 76b. (Section III of this Chapter.) In this case heliograph messages were read, not from the mirror disc—which was invisible to the accidental observer—but from the rise and fall of the actual beam of light reflected from the disc. The accidental observer was remotely placed with reference both to the point and line of projection. The atmospheric phenomenon can only be accounted for by the presence of myriads of minute particles in suspension in the air, such as are deemed to produce the phenomenal deep blue in the sky of dry desert atmospheres, and in atmospheres in proximity to such desert zones. (Refer ¶¶ 76, a and b, Sect. III.) *Authentic case of reflected beam visible in Egypt.* *Morse coded message read from beam projected from Heliograph when flash invisible.* *The Function of Atmospheric Dust in Dry Climates.* *Desert Atmospheres.*

The question of the Pyramid's reflected rays becoming visible is, then, a question, primarily, of atmospheric conditions around the Pyramid. Here the reader must remember that the Pyramid Designer was contemplating the "mass production" of reflexions on a scale beyond anything within ordinary human experience. Devices were accordingly perfected to prevent diffusion of the reflected light and to stabilise the reflected rays under the influence of variable surface refractions due to heat radiations. (Refer ¶¶ 18 and 19.) *Question primarily concerning Atmospheric Conditions.* *"Mass Production" of Reflexions.* *Accessory Details of Construction.*

It is important, however, that the reader should bear in mind the alternative questions as to whether the reflexions were transformed into visible effect or were themselves rendered clearly visible around noon-day. At the same time it simplifies matters for the general reader to adopt the view that the reflexions were visible. Description of the various phases of the Pyramid's phenomena will be made on this understanding. *Alternatives: (a) Reflexions transformed into visible effect, or (b) Reflexions visible at noon-day.* *Latter alternative adopted for description of phenomena.*

¶ 12. THE GREAT PYRAMID'S NOON REFLEXIONS. Plates V, VI, VII, VIII, and X.[1]

Exactly as a modern chronometer gives the hours, say of midnight, 6 a.m., noon, and 6 p.m., so the reflexions from the Great Pyramid gave accurately the days upon which the Winter Solstice, the Spring Equinox, the Summer Solstice, and the Autumnal Equinox occurred. This precisely defined the Solar Astronomical Year. *Great Pyramid's Noon reflexions fix the principal points of the Solar Astronomical and Solar Vegetation Years.*

[1]Technical details as Tabulated in Tables VI and VII at end of Section I.

The principal points of the Solar Vegetation Year, however, were equally well defined.   It is this definition of the Vegetation Year that forms one of the most striking series of phenomena connected with the Pyramid's exterior. For whilst the *noon* reflexion of the Pyramid's South face always pointed due South at the instant of noon—during Winter, Spring, Summer, and Autumn— it displayed the striking property of being elevated above the horizontal each day of Autumn, Winter, and Spring, and depressed below the horizontal during the entire extent of Summer.

South Noon
Reflexion
above the
horizontal
during
Autumn,
Winter, and
Spring,
below the
horizontal
during
Summer

¶ 13. THE PYRAMID'S PRECISE DEFINITION OF SUMMER LIMITS.

This is as shown on Plate V, Figs. B and b.   Fig. B represents the Pyramid and its noon reflexions as shown in plan.   Fig. b represents the elevation of the Pyramid and its reflexions as seen from the East.   The noon reflexions shown are for the day beginning Summer, and for the day ending Summer, respectively 6th May and 8th August—of modern Calendar—as stated in Table I.

South Noon
Reflexion
horizontal at
beginning and
ending of
Summer.

The diagrams show that exactly mid-way between the Vernal Equinox and the Summer Solstice, and, again, exactly mid-way between the Summer Solstice and the Autumnal Equinox, the beam reflected at noon from the Pyramid's South face, was truly horizontal.   This horizontal reflection defined the first noon of Summer and the last noon of Summer.   Between these two dates, 6th May and 8th August, the noon reflexion from the Pyramid's South face cast a triangular reflexion on the ground, and at no other period of the year.   The triangular south noon reflexions, therefore, define the days of Summer.   These south reflected images obviously shorten approaching the Summer Solstice, the shortest length of triangular image being attained at noon of the Summer Solstice, after which, again, the images lengthen until noon of the last day of Summer, when the noon reflexion becomes horizontal again.

Ten days after the commencement of Summer and ten days before the termination of Summer, at noon, the line RBCQ, formed by the East and West noon reflexions (Plate V, Fig. b), became a straight line running directly from East to West.

South, East,
and West Noon
Reflexions
Shortest and
North Noon
Reflexion
longest at
Mid-Summer

Plate VI shows the Pyramid reflexions for noon of the Summer Solstice. These are respectively the shortest noon reflexions of the year from the South, East, and West faces of the Pyramid, and the longest noon reflexion of the year from the North face of the Pyramid.

No Noon
Shadow during
Summer.

During the Summer half of the year no shadow was thrown by the Pyramid at the instant of noon, nor for an appreciable interval before and after noon.

PLATE IV.

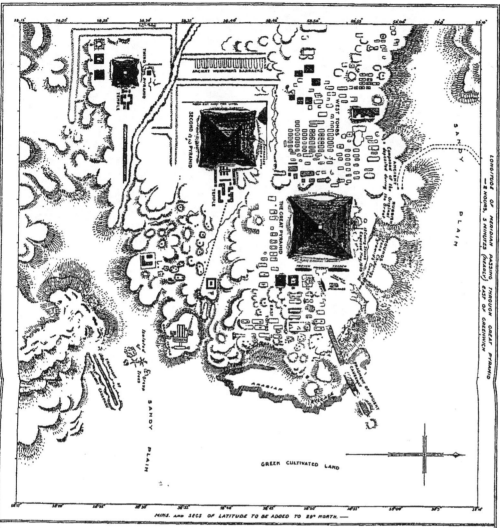

MAP OF THE PYRAMIDS AND TOMBS
ON THE PLATEAU OF GIZEH.

MERIDIAN SECTION THROUGH THE GREAT PYRAMID
(LOOKING WEST)

PLATE V.

PYRAMID NOON REFLEXIONS & SHADOWS

NOON REFLEXIONS OF
THE SUMMER HALF OF THE YEAR.

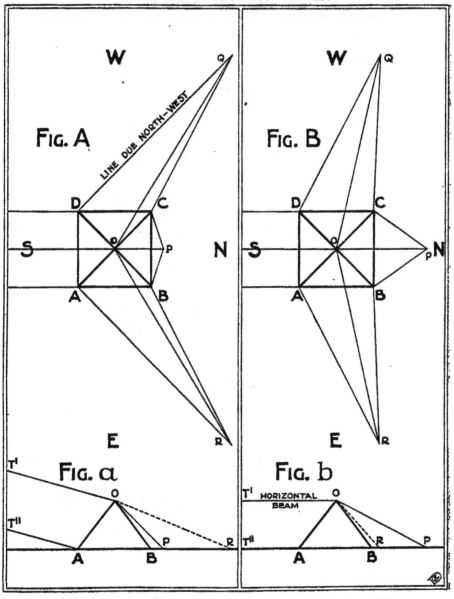

Autumnal Equinox or Vernal Equinox
REFLEXIONS.

Midway between Vernal Equinox,
and Summer Solstice,
Midway between Summer Solstice
and Autumnal Equinox
REFLEXIONS.

PLATE VI.

Pyramid Noon Reflexions & Shadows

NOON REFLEXIONS
AT SUMMER SOLSTICE.

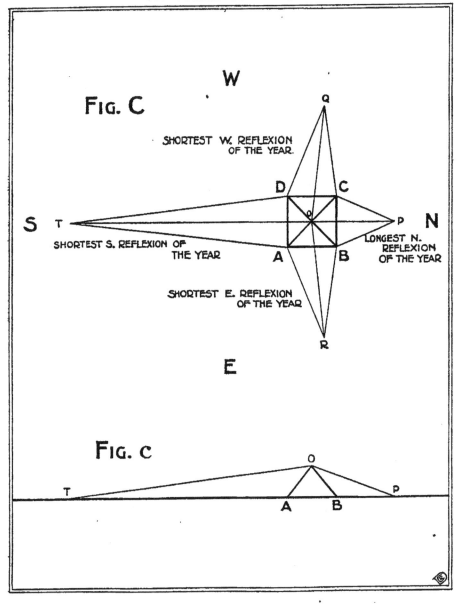

W

Fig. C

SHORTEST W. REFLEXION
OF THE YEAR.

SHORTEST S. REFLEXION OF
THE YEAR

SHORTEST E. REFLEXION
OF THE YEAR

LONGEST N.
REFLEXION
OF THE YEAR

E

Fig. C

PLATE VII.

Pyramid Noon Reflexions & Shadows

NOON REFLEXIONS & SHADOWS.
14-15 OCT. NOON SHADOWS 1ˢᵀ APPEARING.
27-28 FEB. NOON SHADOWS 1ˢᵀ DISAPPEARING.

NOON REFLEXIONS & SHADOWS.
OF THE WINTER HALF
OF THE YEAR.

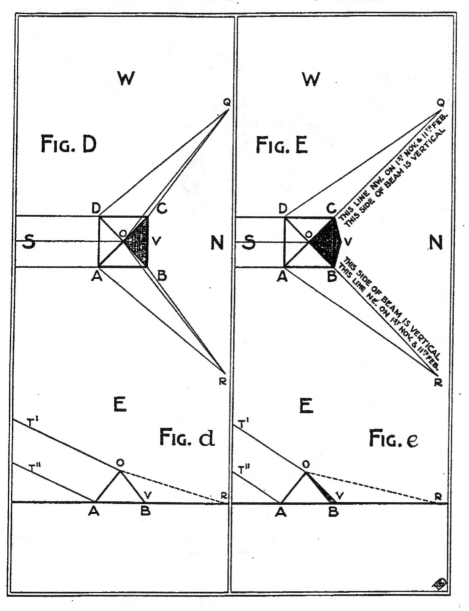

PLATE VIII.

Pyramid Noon Reflexions & Shadows

NOON REFLEXIONS AND SHADOW.
2 – 3 DEC. AND 11–12 JAN.

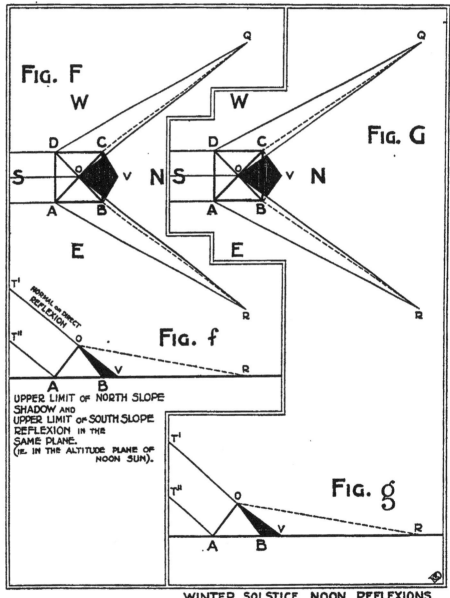

FIG. F

FIG. G

FIG. f

UPPER LIMIT OF NORTH SLOPE
SHADOW AND
UPPER LIMIT OF SOUTH SLOPE
REFLEXION IN THE
SAME PLANE.
(IE. IN THE ALTITUDE PLANE OF
NOON SUN).

NORMAL OR DIRECT REFLEXION

FIG. g

WINTER SOLSTICE NOON REFLEXIONS
AND SHADOW

¶ 14. THE PYRAMID'S EQUINOCTIAL NOON REFLEXIONS.

The noon reflexions from the East and West faces of the Pyramid projected *The East and West Noon* triangular images (Plates V to VIII) on the ground on each day of the year. *Reflexions* Almost East and West respectively at the Summer Solstice (Plate VI), the *define North-East and* Apex of each triangular image was North-East and North-West respectively *North-West Directions at* from the East and West corners of the South Base side of the Pyramid at the *the Equinoxes* instant of Vernal Equinoctial and Autumnal Equinoctial noon (Plate V, Fig. A).

This may be otherwise stated as follows :—(Plate V, Fig. A).

The East noon reflexion from the Pyramid projected a triangular image ARB, on the ground. This triangle consisted of a base, AB, lying on the Pyramid's East Base Side, AB, and of two other sides, which we may define, in terms of the plan, the South side, AR, and the North side, BR, of the triangular image. Thus defined, the line of the South side, AR, of the triangular image, pointed due North-East at Vernal Equinoctial and Autumnal Equinoctial noon. This was precisely the case during the period in history when the Pyramid was thus operating as a Sundial of the Seasons. In modern times the phenomenon noted would occur a day or so before the Vernal Equinox, and a day or so after the Autumnal Equinox.

Similarly defined (and with reference to Plate V, Fig. A), the line of the South side, DQ, of the triangular image, DQC, projected from the West face slope of the Pyramid, pointed due North-West at Vernal Equinoctial and Autumnal Equinoctial noon.

¶ 15. THE PYRAMID'S DEFINITION OF WINTER.

The solid beams of reflected light proceeding from the East and West face slopes of the Pyramid at noon had a further remarkable property defining Winter as distinct from Spring, Summer, and Autumn. Reference to Plates V to VIII shows that in all cases the East and West Solid noon reflexions had a sharply defined ridge line running from the Pyramid apex to the apex of each of the images projected on the ground.

The East and West noon reflected beams had, therefore, each a surface *Surface of* seen from the North side of the Pyramid, and a surface seen from the South *East or West Noon* side of the Pyramid. The side of the East or West noon reflected beam, as *Reflexion seen from* viewed from the South, always, throughout the year, appeared inclining away *North inclined overhanging* from the observer. The side of the East or West noon reflected beam, how- *towards observer in* ever, as viewed from the North side of the Pyramid, appeared inclining away *Winter and inclined* from the observer during Spring, Summer, and Autumn, but appeared over- *away from observer in* hanging towards the observer during Winter, as shown on Plate VIII, Figs. *Spring, Summer, and* F and G. *Autumn.*

At Beginning
and Ending
of Winter
this surface
truly vertical
and pointing
North-East
for East
reflexion
and
North-West
for West
Reflexion.

1st November
and
11th February
thus defined.
At the beginning and ending of Winter this surface of either reflected beam as seen from the North was a truly vertical surface lying, in the case of the East reflection, truly North-East, and in the case of the West reflection, truly North-West, in continuation of the Pyramid's base diagonals. This is as shown on Plate VII, Fig. E. In terms of the modern Calendar, the dates are respectively November 1st and Fébruary 11th. Referring to Table I, the reader will observe that the former date anticipates the beginning of winter by seven days, and that the latter date succeeds the termination of Winter by the like interval of seven days.

It is obvious that the difference was not due to any error in fixing the precise beginning and ending of Winter. Had this been the case, there would have been a similar error in fixing the beginning and ending of Summer. But the phenomenon of the horizontal South noon reflexion fixes the beginning and ending of Summer with definitive precision. The difference of seven days, then, in anticipating the beginning of Winter can only have been an intentional anticipation, as the reader will see.

¶ 16. THE PYRAMID'S WINTER SHADOWS (Plates VII and VIII).

Pyramid Noon
Shadows
during
Winter only.

October 14th
to
February 28.
A noon shadow was projected by the Pyramid during Winter and for sixteen or seventeen days before and after Winter. Between February 27-28 and October 14-15, no noon shadow appeared. During this period of the year a noon reflexion was projected by the North face slope of the Pyramid. On October 14-15, however, the noon reflexion disappeared and the first noon shadow made its appearance. (Plate VII, Figs. D and d.) Successive noons toward the Winter Solstice (Plate VII, Figs. E and e, Plate VIII, Figs. F and f), found the length of the noon shadow, projected on to the pavement base of the Pyramid, gradually lengthening towards the North, until at noon of the Winter Solstice it attained its greatest length due North (Plate VIII, Figs. G and g).

After the Winter Solstice the length of the noon shadow, projected on the pavement base, gradually shortened (Plate VII, Figs. E and e, Plate VIII, Figs. F and f), until at February 27-28 (Plate VII, Figs. D and d) it was " swallowed " by the Pyramid masonry, and the North noon reflexion made its first appearance, heralding the approach of the Vernal Equinox and the Summer *half* of the year.

Sowing
and Harvest
defined.
The initial and terminal datings of the noon shadow phenomenon defined respectively the beginning of early sowing, and the beginning of the barley and flax harvests in the ancient Delta. (The reader is referred to Plates III, IV, V, VI, VII, VIII, X, and XII, and to Section III, ¶¶ 67-72, 74 and 76, for the detailed descriptions of the various phenomena discussed.)

¶ 17. THE TEMPLE OF RAMESSU II AT ABU SIMBEL.

The influence of these initial and terminal datings of the Pyramid's noon shadow phenomenon in formulating later devices for automatically heralding the seasons is evidenced by the Temple of Ramessu II at Abu-Simbel. This temple was built with its central axis aligned towards the point of Sunrise of the day upon which the Pyramid's noon shadow first appeared, and of the day upon which it disappeared.

Now the sun's noon altitude for a certain point of the year when compared with the azimuth of its rising at the same point of the year over a long interval of years does not bear the precisely fixed relationship the Abu-Simbel alignment would lead one to suppose. For this reason, sunrise on the Abu-Simbel alignment cannot always occur on the same day as the Pyramid's noon shadow first appears or first disappears, respectively. Nevertheless the difference at the present time is not more than two days. The Sun rises on the Abu-Simbel alignment, at the present time, on October 16 and February 26,[1] whereas the Great Pyramid's limiting dates, for the present time, are October 14 and February 28 generally.

¶ 18. THE PYRAMID'S STRUCTURAL CORRECTION FOR REFLEXIONS.

To define more clearly the ridges and edges of the reflexions and to counteract the local dispersing effect of the variable surface refractions due to heat radiations from the Pyramid's surfaces, these surfaces were very slightly hollowed inwards towards the centre line of each face slope of the Pyramid. This slight hollowing, while tending towards stabilising and more clearly defining the reflected beams, was not sufficient to focus the reflected rays forming a beam of reflexion. The hollowing was not in the form of a concavely curved surface, but in *the general form* of two plane surfaces meeting along the centre line of each face slope. This feature, however, will be dealt with later.

That the hollowing feature noted was not merely the result of an afterthought is evidenced by the core masonry of the Pyramid. The stepped surface of each face slope of the core masonry was likewise hollowed in to the same extent,[2] preparatory to the external casing stones being added to form the smooth reflecting surfaces. This hollowing is so small in proportion to the Pyramid's mass, and extent of external surface, that it is not visible to the eye *unaided*. It can be observed, however, and its extent measured by careful sightings across and obliquely up each face escarpment. The reader must not confuse the evidence of hollowing in with the separate question of dilapidation. The two can be quite separately surveyed.

[1]Hon. E. M. Plunket. P.S.B.A., March, 1893.
[2]Petrie, " Pyramids and Temples of Gizeh," pp. 43 and 44.

¶ 19. THE EXTENT OF THE STRUCTURAL CORRECTION.

The structural effect of the hollowing inwards of each face slope of the Great Pyramid was that the Pyramid base sides were hollowed inwards between the corners of the Pyramid base. These corners were the four corners of a square of about 760 feet length of side. The central hollowing in of each base side is almost exactly three feet, as determined from Petrie's survey.[1] The ratio of hollowing in of base to length of base side is therefore about 1 in 250.

Centre of each Pyramid Base Side about one yard internal to Pyramid Base Square.

This receding camber was sufficient to make correction for the well-known optical illusion whereby a large plane escarpment appears to bulge outwards. Correction for this optical illusion was made by the ancient Egyptians in the case of their monolithic beams and lintels, and by the ancient Greeks in the case of their columns. A truly level beam appears to sag in the middle; a slight camber upwards eliminates the illusion. A large vertical column appears to overhang towards the observer on the ground; a slight tilt away from the observer removes the illusion.

Hollowing Inwards made correction for optical illusion.

¶ 20. NOON SHADOW AND STRUCTURAL CORRECTION.

In the centuries following the Pyramid's construction, the limit of the 14th October and 28th February noon shadow, once in about every hundred years would lie precisely on the line forming the North side of the Pyramid base square (although the coincidence nearly occurred once in each modern leap year period). Let us, for the purpose of illustration, suppose the period exactly one hundred years and that the shadow limit lay on the North side of the base square exactly at the middle date of the period. Then fifty years before, or fifty years after the middle date, the shadow limit lay 31½ inches within the North side of the Pyramid base square, or 31½ inches without the square respectively. These dimensioned limits are true whether the period is greater than or less than the hundred years assumed. For other years within the period, the limit of the noon shadow lay somewhere between the two limits, 31½ inches internal to or external to the North side of the Pyramid base square.

The Hollowing-in feature permitted 14 October or 28 February Noon Shadow Limit to be observed in relation to Side of Pyramid Base Square.

The noon shadow limits for 14th October and 28th February, when internal to the North side of the Pyramid base square, were, owing to the hollowing-in feature, always defined and measurable. The extent of hollowing at the centre of the base side gave a margin of about 4½ inches between the casing edge and the maximum internal limit of the noon shadow under consideration. This marginal space was just sufficient to permit of the noon shadow being clearly defined at its maximum internal limit. The marginal amount, therefore, confirms the hollowing effect as intentionally of the extent observed by Petrie's sightings.

[1] "Pyramids and Temples of Gizeh," pp. 43 and 44.

The reader will see for himself that owing to the hollowing-in feature, the particular year of the modern Leap-year cycle—generally four years—was defined by the extent of the North face slope that was covered by shadow down the centre at noon on 14th October or 28th February. In other words, the variations of the noon shadow limit automatically affected the intercalation of the Solar year.

The Shadow Limit automatically Intercalated the Solar Year.

¶ 21. THE GREAT PYRAMID'S ANNUAL MESSAGE TO THE DELTA.

Within two periods, then, of sixteen or seventeen days, we find that the Great Pyramid provided two outstanding phenomena defining fixed points of the Solar year. These were the North-East and North-West directed vertical surfaces of reflection at noon of 1st November and 11th February, and the North noon shadow limits on 14-15 October and 27-28 February. Both sets of phenomena were devised to be seen from the North.

Great Pyramid sited to enable its 14th October and 1st November and 11th February and 28th February Phenomena to be seen from the North.

Reference to Plate III—studied in relation to Plate VII—will show that the Pyramid site was selected with all this as part of the design.

The Great Pyramid is so situated that it is the centre of the quadrant of a circle that defines and includes the Delta (Plate III). The two Limiting Radii of the Quadrant lie North-East and North-West respectively, forming the angle of 90° subtending the quarter circle arc of the Delta coastline, from near the modern site of Port Said to near the modern site of Alexandria.

The Pyramid's situation and its accompanying coincidence with the centre of the Delta Quadrant might be deemed to be accidental were it not for the fact that the directions of the limiting radii of the quadrant were annually defined by the Vertical Surfaces of the Pyramid's East and West noon reflexions on 1st November.

Pyramid's North-East and North-West Vertical Surfaces of Noon Reflexions on 1st November define the Delta Quadrant.

¶ 22. THE GREAT PYRAMID'S PART IN ORGANISING CULTIVATION IN THE DELTA.

The significance of the Pyramid's phenomena and their datings is seen at once when we remember that the early sowing period in the Delta occurred between the 14th October and the beginning of the general sowing season on 1st November ; that the early harvesting period occurred between 11th February and the beginning of the general harvest season at 27-28 February, when barley was reaped and flax plucked.[1]

The Pyramid's Noon Phenomena define early Sowing Period 14th October 1st November and Early Harvest Period 11th February —28th February.

The appearance of noon shadow on the North Face of the Pyramid—seen only from the Delta—heralded early sowing on 14-15 October. The verticality of the surfaces of the East and West noon reflexions—seen only from the North—, and running truly North-East and North-West respectively, heralded the general beginning of the sowing season on 1st November.

Heralding of Agricultural Seasons intended for the Delta.

[1] For Wilkinson's Agricultural Datings refer Plate IX, cols. 7, 8, and 9.

The recurrence of the latter phenomenon again, at noon of 11th February gave warning to the Delta of the earliest date for an early harvest; and the disappearance of noon shadow from the North Face of the Pyramid on 27-28 February heralded to the Delta the beginning of the barley and flax harvests.

These facts immediately raise the question as to whether the ancient Egyptians at the time of the Pyramid Dynasties had not a fixed Calendar year, adjusted by intercalation to conform with the Solar year.

¶ 23. THE ANCIENT EGYPTIAN CALENDAR.

The Calendar Years, 360 and 365 days.

The Ancient Egyptians, we know, had two forms of Calendar Year. They had a Calendar Year of 360 days and a Calendar year of 365 days. The last five days of the latter Calendar Year were known from the earliest times as the " five days over the year." This expression clearly indicates that the earliest calendar year was that of 360 days.

Each Calendar Season 4 months of 30 days.

Both forms of Calendar year consisted of the same seasonal divisions (Plate IX, col. 2). There were three Calendar seasons, each of four months, and each month consisting of 30 days. The seasonal divisions were respectively :—

(1) SHAT, the Calendar Season of Sowing.

(2) PERT, the Calendar Season of " coming forth," *i.e.*, growing and harvest.

(3) SHEMUT, the Calendar Season of Inundation.

Calendar instituted when a November Agricultural Year was observed.

The Calendar year began with the Calendar Season of Sowing. This fact clearly indicates that the Egyptian Calendar was instituted when a November agricultural year was observed.

¶ 24. THE FIXED CALENDAR YEAR OF EARLY EGYPT.
Plates IX, X, and XI.

Earliest Calendar Year 360 days.

The latter fact seems to be very obvious. But that is not all. The earliest form of Egyptian Calendar was the Calendar year of 360 days. This began

Began with Calendar Season of Sowing.

with the Calendar season of Sowing. Such a definite designation implies a definite synchronism with the actual season of sowing at the time the designation was first given.

Designation made when a Fixed November Year observed.

It is obvious, therefore, that the earliest Calendar year of 360 days was a fixed Calendar year identified with the November Agricultural year.

Implies Intercalary Month added every 5 or 6 years.

A Calendar year of 360 days could only be a fixed Calendar year by intercalations of an additional month of 30 days at variable intervals of five or six years. That this was the form of Calendar employed—coincident with an intercalated

Fixed Year during period of Dynasties I to XVI.

Calendar year of 365 days—during the period of Dynasties I to XVI inclusive, is confirmed by the evidence discussed in Section II of this Chapter, and descriptions of Plates IX, X, and XI.

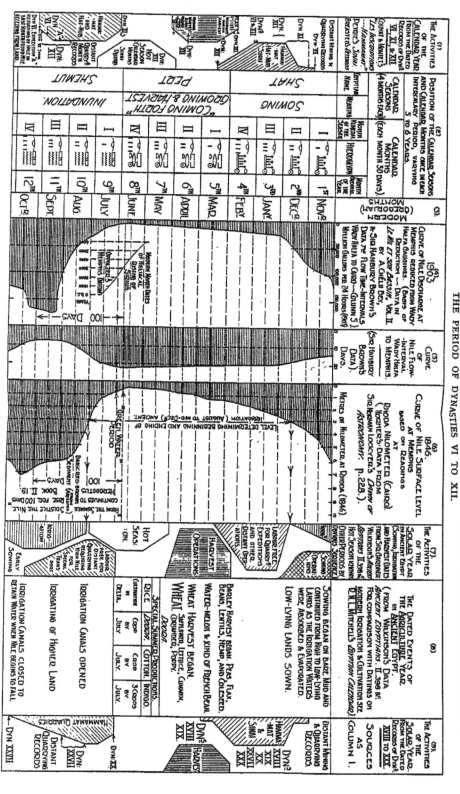

PLATE IX.

CHART SHOWING THE SEASONAL PHENOMENA AND ACTIVITIES OF THE *SOLAR YEAR* IN ANCIENT EGYPT COMPARED WITH THE SEASONAL PHENOMENA AND ACTIVITIES OF THE EARLY EGYPTIAN *CALENDAR YEAR* COMPILED FROM THE DATED RECORDS OF THE PERIOD OF DYNASTIES VI TO XII.

The data given graphically on this chart settle a vexed question of Egyptian Chronology. The two leading schools of Egyptological chronology disagree as to the extent of 1,460 (or 1,580) years in dating Dynasty XII. Both schools agree that the Egyptian Calendar year at the time in question slipped backwards 1 day in every four years, or a complete year in about every 1,500 years, and their rival systems of chronology are based on this theory. The data of the above chart, however, show clearly that the Egyptian Calendar year was a fixed year.

[To face p. 20.

CHART OF LIMITS OF EARLY EGYPTIAN INTERCALATED CALENDAR YEAR, EGYPTIAN SEASONS, AND GREAT PYRAMID NOON REFLEXION AND SHADOW PHENOMENA STATED WITH REFERENCE TO THE MODERN (GREGORIAN) MONTHS.

MODERN YEAR	JANY	FEBY	MAR.	APRIL	MAY	JUNE	JULY	AUGT	SEPT	OCTR	NOVR	DECR	MODERN YEAR
EARLY EGYPTIAN CALENDAR SEASONS OF INTERCALATED CALENDAR YEAR.	LATEST BEGINNING 180 DAYS AFTER AUTUMNAL EQUINOX		CALENDAR GROWING (HARVEST)				CALENDAR INUNDATION.			LATEST ENDING OF CALENDAR			EARLY EGYPTIAN CALENDAR SEASONS OF INTERCALATED CALENDAR YEAR.
	I	II	III	IV	I	II	III	IV					
	EARLIEST 150 DAYS AFTER AUT EQ.	CALENDAR GROWING (HARVEST)				CALENDAR INUNDATION			EARLIEST ENDING OF CALENDAR				
	I	II	III	IV	I	II	III	IV					
PYRD NORTH FACE AT NOON			LONGEST NOON REFLEXION AT SUMMER SOLSTICE										PYRD NORTH FACE AT NOON.
ACTUAL SEASONS.	EARLY HARVEST	SEE PLATE VII.			SEE PLATE VII			EARLY SOWING	SOWING.				ACTUAL SEASONS.
		ACTUAL GROWING (HARVEST)			ACTUAL INUNDATION.				THE 5 DAYS OVER THE CALENDAR YEAR.				

PLATE XI.

RECORDS OF THE PERIOD OF DYNASTIES VI TO XII OF DISTANT QUARRYING EXPEDITIONS TO THE QUARRIES AT WADY HAMMAMAT AND HAT NUB, AND TO THE MINES AND QUARRIES AT SINAI.

CALENDAR DATES OF HARVEST RECORDS	HAMMAMAT				HAT–NUB				SINAI				EARLY EGYPTIAN CALENDAR YEAR	
	DAY OF MONTH	YEAR OF REIGN	DYN	KING	DAY OF MONTH	YEAR OF REIGN	DYN	KING	DAY OF MONTH	YEAR OF REIGN	DYN	KING	CALENDAR MONTH	SEASON
					–	25th	VI	PEPY I					I	CALENDAR SEASON OF SOWING
	–3–	2nd	XI	MENTUHOTEP II									II	
	–15–	2nd	XI	MENTUHOTEP II										
	23/28	2nd	XI	MENTUHOTEP II										
	–1–	2nd/16th	XII	AMENEMHAT III / SENUSERT I									III	
	–13–	3rd/20th	XII	AMENEMHAT III / AMENEMHAT III					–12–	–	XII	AMENEMHAT III		
DYN. XII FLAX HARVEST (EL BERSHEH) 23rd–27th DAYS OF MONTH	–2–/–4–	1st/38th/11th/14th	VI/XII/XII/XII	ATY / SENUSERT I / SENUSERT II / SENUSERT III									IV	
SENUSERT I (DYN XII) YEAR 18 THROWS NUBIAN GRAIN INTO NILE IN THIS MONTH ON 8th DAY OF MONTH.	–15–	19th	XII	AMENEMHAT III									I	CALENDAR SEASON OF GROWING AND HARVEST
													II	
SENUSERT III (DYN XII) YEAR 16. PRIOR TO RECORD OF THIS MONTH SENUSERT III REAPED GRAIN & BURNT SAME IN NUBIA.												HOR–UR–RA'S XIIth DYNASTY RECORD AT SINAI OF HOT WEATHER MONTHS	III	
												BREASTED (RECORDS I p.322) PETRIE (SINAI p.169)	IV	
	–3–	8th	XI	SANKH KARA									I	CALENDAR SEASON OF INUNDATION
													II	
	– / –27–	– / 18th	XII / VI	AMENEMHAT I / PEPY·I	QUARRY-ING X+17 DAYS	–	VI	MERENRA					III	
	–3–	–.–	XII	AMENEMHAT I	BLOCK X+17 NILE TRANS-PORT	–	VI	MERENRA	–6–	18th	VI	PEPY I	IV	

Apart altogether from this evidence, however, we know that the noon phenomena of the Great Pyramid automatically fixed the November Agricultural year. Now the Calendar years of 360 and 365 days were in use in Pyramid times, and the November year, beginning the sowing season, had previously been fixed—the fixing being monumentalised in the names of the Calendar seasons. It is clear then that the Pyramid's noon phenomena gave a high degree of accuracy to an adjustment of the Calendar year in relation to the Solar year that had already been long previously effected. *Great Pyramid's Fixing of November year gave accuracy to Adjustment Already effected.*

The fixed November year, again, is confirmed by the dated *Calendar* records of the activities of the agricultural (or Solar) year during the period of Dynasties VI, XI, and XII. These are as graphically represented in Plate IX, Column 1, stated with reference to the Time Basis of Column 2, and as compared with actual conditions of Columns 7, 8 and 9, stated with reference to the Time Basis of Column 3.[1] *Dated Calendar Records Dynasties VI, XI, XII, confirm fixed November Year.*

¶ 25. THE FESTIVAL OF THE DEAD.

Attention has been directed (in ¶ 15) to the fact that the 1st November dating was intentionally observed instead of the beginning of Winter, seven days later. The 1st November Pyramid phenomena defined the first day of the fixed agricultural year of the Ancient Egyptians. It is with respect to this fixed 1st November year that the early Egyptian Calendar year was intercalated at the end of every five or six years. Hence the festival of the true beginning of the New Year was observed in Egypt at intervals of this duration as early as the time of Dynasties I and II.[2] *Period Egyptian Dynasties I and II, Calendar Year adjusted every 5 or 6 years to the Fixed 1st November Agricultural Year Beginning.*

At the time of Dynasty XII, the celebration of the New Year festival took the form of lighting lamps for the dead on the last day of the old year and the first day of the New Year.[3] As Dr. Frazer has pointed out, this proves that the New Year's Festival at this time was the ancient Festival of the Dead—the modern All Souls', or All Saints' (1st-2nd November).[4] *Period Dynasty XII, lamps lit for dead on 1st November—the date of the Festival of the Dead—All Saints—All Souls.*

"The custom," he remarks,[5] "was observed throughout the whole of Egypt," and is referred to by Herodotus (II, 62), as prevailing in the 5th Century B.C.

"On All Saints' Day, the 1st of November," Frazer continues, "the shops and streets in the Abruzzi are filled with candles, which people buy in order to kindle them in the evening on the graves of their relations: For all the dead come to visit their homes on that night, the Eve of All Souls', and they need lights to show them the way." *Ancient Custom still prevails in parts of Modern Europe on 1st to 2nd November.*

Similarly, he states, "The Miztecs of Mexico believed that the souls of the dead came back in the twelfth month of every year, which corresponded with our November. On this day of All Souls the houses were decked out to welcome the Spirits."[6] *Ancient Mexican Celebrations in November.*

[1] Detailed explanations are given in descriptions of Plates IX, X, and XI.
[2] For the data concerning this refer Section II, ¶ 56.
[3] Breasted, "Ancient Records," I, pp. 260-271. Frazer, "Adonis, Osiris, Attis," pp. 241-242.
[4] "Adonis, Osiris, Attis," pp. 241-2.
[5] Ibid., pp. 241-2.
[6] Ibid., pp. 244-3.

Frazer suggests that "The nominally Christian feast of All Souls' on November 2nd, appears to be an old Celtic festival of the Dead, adopted by the Church in 998 A.D.

"The Celts and the Teutons appear to have dated the beginning of their year from the beginning of Winter, the Celts reckoning it from the 1st of November and the Teutons from the 1st of October.

"The feast of All Saints' on November 1st, seems also to have displaced a heathen festival of the dead."[1]

¶ 26. OSIRIS AND THE FESTIVAL OF THE DEAD: ISIS AND THE GREAT PYRAMID.

In the dual aspect of Osiris as corn or vegetation-god and god of the dead,

the rites of Osiris embodied in one celebration, at the commencement of the November Vegetation Year, the rites of the agricultural deity and the rites of primitive ancestor-worship. In the sowing of the grain in November was seen the symbolic burial of the god; in its growth, his renewal of life; his resurrection; and, in harvest, the death and sacrifice of the god.[2] Thus Dr. Frazer states:—[3]

"Under the names of Osiris, Tammuz, Adonis, and Attis, the peoples of Egypt and Western Asia represented the yearly decay and revival of life, especially of vegetable life, which they personified as a god who annually died and rose again from the dead."

The rites of Osiris in ancient Egypt were annually celebrated on the day of the Festival of the Dead, November 1st. Owing to the fact that the

noon reflections of the Great Pyramid defined the day of the celebrations, Osiris, in later Egyptian times, was associated with the Pyramid. Hence the fact that Isis, the female counterpart of Osiris, was designated in later times, "the queen of the Pyramid," and the "mistress of the commencement of the year." When the November year was discarded for the Sothic or Sirius Year, Isis followed the alteration of the year's beginning, and was identified with the star Sothis or Sirius. The original November year beginning aspect of the goddess was Hathor, later absorbed by Isis.

¶ 27. THE GREAT PYRAMID NOT AN INSTITUTION OF EGYPTIAN RELIGION.

The accounts of Herodotus that Cheops (or Khuphu), the builder of the Great Pyramid, closed the Egyptian temples of the gods, and forbade sacrifice to the gods, and of the Egyptian priest, Manetho, that the same king "was arrogant towards the gods," have been confirmed by Professor Petrie's excavations at Abydos.[4] Furthermore, the simplicity of the Great Pyramid, and of other works belonging to the same reign, the utter lack of internal or external

[1] Ibid., pp. 254-5.
[2] A. Moret, "Kings and Gods of Egypt," pp. 69-108, 148-198.
[3] "Adonis, Osiris, Attis," p. 5.
    Both are standard works on this subject.
[4] Abydos II, pp. 10, 30, 48.

ornament and inscription, removes the Pyramid entirely from the particular kind of religious atmosphere associated generally with every form of Egyptian architecture.

It seems clearly obvious, then, that the First of November phenomena of the Great Pyramid had *not* been devised to ensure the celebration of the rites of ancestor-worship, or the rites of Osiris, on this particular day. The traditions concerning the festival, however, indicate that it was considered to be the anniversary of an historical event, rather than of an event belonging to the astronomical or vegetational phenomena of the year. This again, is confirmed by the Pyramid indicating this date rather than the true beginning of winter.

[margin: Cheops opposed to Egyptian forms of worship.]

[margin: Simplicity of Pyramid and contemporary work confirms this.]

[margin: The Pyramid's 1st November phenomena for different purpose than fixing Celebration of Osirian Rites.]

¶ 28. THE TRADITIONAL ORIGIN OF THE FESTIVAL OF THE DEAD.

As to the origin of the traditions concerning the festival of the dead, Haliburton[1] states as follows :—

In Mexico " the festival of the dead was held on the 17th of November, and was regulated by the Pleiades........They had a tradition that, at that time, *the world had been previously destroyed*, and they dreaded that a similar catastrophe at the end of a cycle would annihilate the race."

[margin: Mexican Festival of the Dead commemorated " Former Destruction of the World " in November.]

The 17th of November[2] occurs also as an alternative dating of certain cults in Egypt during Dynasties XII and XIX, in Ptolemaic Egypt, and at the time of Plutarch. It occurs in Ancient Rome as an alternative date to 1st November.

[margin: The alternative 1st November and 17th November datings for the Festival.]

According to Plutarch, the alternative dating, on the fixed Alexandrian (Julian) Calendar of his time, fell on the 17th day of the Egyptian month Athyr (Hathor).[3] In the XIIth Dynasty, the same alternative dating would be the 17th day of Month I, Season of Sowing,—the 1st month of the fixed 1st November year.

Reference to the Egyptian form of the traditional destruction of the world appears in the early Xth Dynasty Papyrus, Petersburg 1116A,[4] as " The Destruction of Mankind." The Xth Dynasty Papyrus states :—

[margin: Dynasty X and Dynasty XIX narratives of the Destruction of Mankind in November give the form of the Hebrew narrative of the Deluge on Day 17 Month II of Calendar of Genesis.]

" ......God......made heaven and earth (refer Gen. I, 1) at their desire. He checked the greed of the waters (refer Gen. I, 6-10) and made the air to give life to their nostrils (*i.e.*, by the removal of super-saturation from the atmosphere effected by process of Gen. I, 6 and 7. For previous conditions refer Gen. II, 5 and 6). They are His own images (refer Gen. I, 26, 27) proceeding from His flesh........He slew His enemies and destroyed His own children because of their plots in making rebellion." (Refer Gen. VI, 5-7, 11-13, for causes.)

The later form of the narrative, appearing in the tomb of Seti I of Dynasty XIX,[5] associates Hathor with the " Destruction of Mankind," which would account for the 17th day of the Egyptian month Hathor (the Athyr of Plutarch's account) being identified, in later times, with the Festival of the Dead.

[1] In Prof. C. P. Smyth's " Life and Work at the Great Pyramid," Vol. II, p. 390.
[2] Refer Section II, ¶ 55.
[3] Plutarch, *De Iside et Osiride*, Vol. II, p. 336.
[4] Translation by Dr. Alen H. Gardiner, " Journal of Egyptian Archæology," Vol. I, p. 34.
[5] Translation by Dr. Ed. Naville, " Records of the Past," 1st series, Vol. VI, pp. 105-112

¶ 29.   HATHOR AND "THE DESTRUCTION OF MANKIND."

The Constellation associated with the Festival of the Dead is the Ancient November Constellation of Pleiades.

Outstanding features of the XIXth Dynasty story of the " Destruction of Mankind " fix that narrative as the Egyptian rendering of the narrative of the Noachian flood in Genesis, and of the ancient Mexican tradition of the destruction of the world, referred to by Haliburton.   Commemoration of the latter, as quoted, " was regulated by the Pleiades."

The Pleiades associated with " Rain Giving."

Confirming the connection between the various forms of the narrative, Haliburton observes that the celebration of the festival of the dead by the Australian aborigines was held in November, when the constellation of the Pleiades is most distinct, and was specifically worshipped as " the giver of rain."[1]   He says again that " The month of November was formerly called in Persia ' The Month of the angel of death.' "[2]

Hathor the November Angel of Death, but originally " The Flood-gates of Heaven."

In the Egyptian XIXth Dynasty form of the tradition this " angel of death " appears as Hathor.   Hat-hor, as Sir Ernest Budge shows,[3] was originally ' Het-Heru,' " The House of Horus," " one special part of the great watery mass of heaven," and was therefore a special part of " the waters above the firmament," of Genesis I, 9, and probably, therefore, the Deluge " floodgates of heaven " of Genesis VII, 11.   The latter should more clearly be rendered " a finely spread restraining influence or natural law (*attenuated lattice-work* is the restricted application) upholding *the waters above the firmament*."   This suffi-

The 17th of the Month Hathor and the 17th of the Deluge Month.

ciently accounts for the 17th of the month Athyr (Hathor) being celebrated as the day of the festival of the dead in the Alexandrian Calendar period.   For in the narrative of Genesis the Noachian deluge is given as beginning on the 17th day of the second month of the Calendar year of Genesis.

The Seven Hathors and the Pleiades.

As to the association between Hathor and the ancient November constellation of Pleiades, the modern popular name—" the seven sisters "—of the latter constellation had its counterpart in Ancient Egypt as " the Seven Hathors."

Hathor associated with the Egyptian Flood.

The XIXth Dynasty narrative of the Destruction of Mankind states that " Ra ordered in the midst of the night[4] to pour out the water of the vessels, and the fields were entirely covered with water........and there came the goddess (Hathor) at the morning, and she found the fields covered with water, and she was pleased with it and she drank to her satisfaction, and she went away satisfied, and she saw no men........ "

This com-memorated by Festival of Hathor originally on New Year's Day,—1st November.

Then Ra ordered " that libations be made to her at every festival of the New Year."   The narrative defines this as the " festival of Hathor."   Obviously. it was originally New Year's Day, which in early Egypt fell on 1st November.

[1]Haliburton in Smyth's " Life and Work at the Great Pyramid," Vol. II, pp. 384-386.
[2]Ibid., p. 390.
[3]" Gods of the Egyptians," Vol. I, pp. 428-429.
[4]All Hallow's Eve or Hallowe'en ?

TABLE II.

ANCIENT INTERCALARY CYCLE AND ITS INTERCALARY PERIODS.

Cyclic years' duration.	Intercalated 360 days' Calendar Year. Duration on Cycle in Months.		Intercalated 365 days' Calendar Year. Duration on Cycle in Months.		Number of days in mean years of Cycle. Days.
6	73 =	2190	73 =	2190	2191.45632
11	134 =	4020	134 =	4020	4017.66992
17	207 =	6210	207 =	6210	6209.12624
23	280 =	8400	280 =	8400	8400.58256
28	341 =	10230	341 =	10230	10226.79616
34	414 =	12420	414 =	12420	12418.25248
40	487 =	14610	487 =	14610	14609.70880
46	560 =	16800	560 =	16800	16801.16512
51	621 =	18630	621 =	18630	18627.37872
57	694 =	20820	694 =	20820	20818.83504
63	767 =	23010	767 =	23010	23010.29136
68	828 =	24840	828 =	24840	24836.50496
74	901 =	27030	901 =	27030	27027.96128
80	974 =	29220	974 =	29220	29219.41760
86	1047 =	31410	1047 =	31410	31410.87392
91	1108 =	33240	1108 =	33240	33237.08752
97	1181 =	35430	1181 =	35430	35428.54384
103	1254 =	37620	1254 =	37620	37620.00000

TABLE III.

THE CONSTRUCTION OF THE INTERCALARY CYCLE OF 103 YEARS.

Cyclic Years' Duration	Cumulative Days for Duration in Mean Years of Cycle	360 Days' Calendar Year. Duration on Cycle: In Months	360 Days' Calendar Year. Duration on Cycle: In Days	360 Days' Calendar Year. Day I Month I Commencing Before (—) or After (+) Beginning of Mean Year of Cycle	365 Days' Calendar Year. Duration on Cycle: In Months	365 Days' Calendar Year. Duration on Cycle: In Days	365 Days' Calendar Year. Day I Month I Commencing Before (—) or After (+) Beginning of Mean Year of Cycle
0	0.	0	0	0.00	0	0	0.00
1	365.24272	12	360	— 5.24	12⅙	365	— 0.24
2	730.48544	24	720	— 10.49	24⅓	730	— 0.49
3	1095.72816	36	1080	— 15.73	36½	1095	— 0.73
4	1460.97088	48	1440	— 20.97	48⅔	1460	— 0.97
5	1826.21360	60	1800	— 26.21	60⅚	1825	— 1.21
6	2191.45632	73	2190	— 1.46	73	2190	— 1.46
7	2556.69904	85	2550	— 6.70	85⅙	2555	— 1.69
8	2921.94176	97	2910	— 11.94	97⅓	2920	— 1.94
9	3287.18448	109	3270	— 17.18	109½	3285	— 2.18
10	3652.42720	121	3630	— 22.43	121⅔	3650	— 2.43
11	4017.66992	134	4020	+ 2.33	134	4020	+ 2.33
12	4382.91264	146	4380	— 2.19	146⅙	4385	+ 2.09
13	4748.15536	158	4740	— 8.16	158⅓	4750	+ 1.84
14	5113.39808	170	5100	— 13.40	170½	5115	+ 1.60
15	5478.64080	182	5460	— 18.64	182⅔	5480	+ 1.36
16	5843.88352	194	5820	— 23.88	194⅚	5845	+ 1.12
17	6209.12624	207	6210	+ 0.87	207	6210	+ 0.87
18	6574.36896	219	6570	— 4.37	219⅙	6575	+ 0.63
19	6939.61168	231	6930	— 9.61	231⅓	6940	+ 0.39
20	7304.85440	243	7290	— 14.85	243½	7305	+ 0.14
21	7670.09712	255	7650	— 20.10	255⅔	7670	— 0.10
22	8035.33984	267	8010	— 25.34	267⅚	8035	— 0.34
23	8400.58256	280	8400	— 0.58	280	8400	— 0.58
24	8765.82528	292	8760	— 5.83	292⅙	8765	— 0.83
25	9131.06800	304	9120	— 11.07	304⅓	9130	— 1.07
26	9496.31072	316	9480	— 16.31	316½	9495	— 1.31
27	9861.55344	328	9840	— 21.55	328⅔	9860	— 1.55
28	10226.79616	341	10230	+ 3.20	341	10230	+ 3.20
29	10592.03888	353	10590	— 2.04	353⅙	10595	+ 2.96
30	10957.28160	365	10950	— 7.28	365⅓	10960	+ 2.72
31	11322.52432	377	11310	— 12.52	377½	11325	+ 2.48
32	11687.76704	389	11670	— 17.77	389⅔	11690	+ 2.23
33	12053.00976	401	12030	— 23.01	401⅚	12055	+ 1.99
34	12418.25248	414	12420	+ 1.75	414	12420	+ 1.75
35	12783.49520	426	12780	— 3.50	426⅙	12785	+ 1.50
36	13148.73792	438	13140	— 8.74	438⅓	13150	+ 1.26
37	13513.98064	450	13500	— 13.98	450½	13515	+ 1.02
38	13879.22336	462	13860	— 19.22	462⅔	13880	+ 0.78
39	14244.46608	474	14220	— 24.47	474⅚	14245	+ 0.53
40	14609.70880	487	14610	+ 0.29	487	14610	+ 0.29
41	14974.95152	499	14970	— 4.95	499⅙	14975	+ 0.05
42	15340.19424	511	15330	— 10.19	511⅓	15340	— 0.19
43	15705.43696	523	15690	— 15.44	523½	15705	— 0.44
44	16070.67968	535	16050	— 20.68	535⅔	16070	— 0.68
45	16435.92240	547	16410	— 25.92	547⅚	16435	— 0.92
46	16801.16512	560	16800	— 1.17	560	16800	— 1.17
47	17166.40784	572	17160	— 6.41	572⅙	17165	— 1.41
48	17531.65056	584	17520	— 11.65	584⅓	17530	— 1.65
49	17896.89328	596	17880	— 16.89	596½	17895	— 1.89
50	18262.13600	608	18240	— 22.14	608⅔	18260	— 2.14
51	18627.37872	621	18630	+ 2.62	621	18630	+ 2.62

THE CONSTRUCTION OF THE INTERCALARY CYCLE OF 103 YEARS.—(*Continued*).

Cyclic Years' Duration	Cumulative Days for Duration in Mean Years of Cycle	360 Days' Calendar Year.			365 Days' Calendar Year.		
		Duration on Cycle		Day I Month I Commencing Before (—) or After (+ Beginning of Mean Year of Cycle	Duration on Cycle		Day I Month I Commencing Before (—) or After (+) Beginning of Mean Year of Cycle
		In Months	In Days		In Months	In Days	
52	18992.62144	633	18990	— 2.62	633⅙	18995	+ 2.38
53	19357.86416	645	19350	— 7.86	645⅓	19360	+ 2.14
54	19723.10688	657	19710	— 13.11	657½	19725	+ 1.89
55	20088.34960	669	20070	— 18.35	669⅔	20090	+ 1.65
56	20453.59232	681	20430	— 23.59	681⅚	20455	+ 1.41
57	20818.83504	694	20820	+ 1.16	694	20820	+ 1.16
58	21184.07776	706	21180	— 4.08	706⅙	21185	+ 0.92
59	21549.32048	718	21540	— 9.32	718⅓	21550	+ 0.68
60	21914.56320	730	21900	— 14.56	730½	21915	+ 0.44
61	22279.80592	742	22260	— 19.81	742⅔	22280	+ 0.19
62	22645.04864	754	22620	— 25.05	754⅚	22645	— 0.05
63	23010.29136	767	23010	— 0.29	767	23010	— 0.29
64	23375.53408	779	23370	— 5.53	779⅙	23375	— 0.53
65	23740.77680	791	23730	— 10.78	791⅓	23740	— 0.78
66	24106.01952	803	24090	— 16.02	803½	24105	— 1.02
67	24471.26224	815	24450	— 21.26	815⅔	24470	— 1.26
68	24836.50496	828	24840	+ 3.49	828	24840	+ 3.49
69	25201.74768	840	25200	— 1.75	840⅙	25205	+ 3.25
70	25566.99040	852	25560	— 6.99	852⅓	25570	+ 3.01
71	25932.23312	864	25920	— 12.23	864½	25935	+ 2.77
72	26297.47584	876	26280	— 17.48	876⅔	26300	+ 2.52
73	26662.71856	888	26640	— 22.72	888⅚	26665	+ 2.28
74	27027.96128	901	27030	+ 2.04	901	27030	+ 2.04
75	27393.20400	913	27390	— 3.20	913⅙	27395	+ 1.80
76	27758.44672	925	27750	— 8.45	925⅓	27760	+ 1.55
77	28123.68944	937	28110	— 13.69	937½	28125	+ 1.31
78	28488.93216	949	28470	— 18.93	949⅔	28490	+ 1.07
79	28854.17488	961	28830	— 24.17	961⅚	28855	+ 0.83
80	29219.41760	974	29220	+ 0.58	974	29220	+ 0.58
81	29584.66032	986	29580	— 4.66	986⅙	29585	+ 0.34
82	29949.90304	998	29940	— 9.90	998⅓	29950	+ 0.10
83	30315.14576	1010	30300	— 15.15	1010½	30315	— 0.15
84	30680.38848	1022	30660	— 20.39	1022⅔	30680	— 0.39
85	31045.63120	1034	31020	— 25.63	1034⅚	31045	— 0.63
86	31410.87392	1047	31410	— 0.87	1047	31410	— 0.87
87	31776.11664	1059	31770	— 6.12	1059⅙	31775	— 1.12
88	32141.35936	1071	32130	— 11.36	1071⅓	32140	— 1.36
89	32506.60208	1083	32490	— 16.60	1083½	32505	— 1.60
90	32871.84480	1095	32850	— 21.84	1095⅔	32870	— 1.84
91	33237.08752	1108	33240	+ 2.91	1108	33240	+ 2.91
92	33602.33024	1120	33600	— 2.33	1120⅙	33605	+ 2.67
93	33967.57296	1132	33960	— 7.57	1132⅓	33970	+ 2.43
94	34332.81568	1144	34320	— 12.82	1144½	34335	+ 2.18
95	34698.05840	1156	34680	— 18.06	1156⅔	34700	+ 1.94
96	35063.30112	1168	35040	— 23.30	1168⅚	35065	+ 1.70
97	35428.54384	1181	35430	+ 1.46	1181	35430	+ 1.46
98	35793.78656	1193	35790	— 3.79	1193⅙	35795	+ 1.21
99	36159.02928	1205	36150	— 9.03	1205⅓	36160	+ 0.97
100	36524.27200	1217	36510	— 14.27	1217½	36525	+ 0.73
101	36889.51472	1229	36870	— 19.51	1229⅔	36890	+ 0.49
102	37254.75744	1241	37230	— 24.76	1241⅚	37255	+ 0.24
103	37620.00016	1254	37620	0.00	1254	37620	0.00

TABLE IV.

THE SERIES COMPRISING THE PERIOD OF THE CYCLE OF 721 YEARS.

No. of Series.	Interval in years.	Cumulative Years.	Intercalary year of Table II. equivalent to Year of Series.	Subtraction of periods of 103 years' cycles from cumulative years of series to obtain year in preceding column.
(1)	120	120	17	120 cumulative years of series. Deduct 103 =1 primary solar cycle. 17 Year of Tables II. and III.
(2)	120	240	34	240 cumulative years of series. Deduct 206 =2 primary solar cycles. 34 Year of Tables II. and III.
(3)	120	360	51	360 cumulative years of series. Deduct 309 =3 primary solar cycles. 51 Year of Tables II. and III.
(4)	120	480	68	480 cumulative years of series. Deduct 412 =4 primary solar cycles. 68 Year of Tables II. and III.
(5)	121	601	86	601 cumulative years of series. Deduct 515 =5 primary solar cycles. 86 Year of Tables II. and III.
(6)	120	721	103	721 cumulative years of series. Deduct 618 =6 primary solar cycles. 103 Year of Tables II. and III.

¶ 30. THE EARLIEST KNOWN EXAMPLE OF THE ALMANAC TRADITION.

Now we saw that in the celebration of the festival of the dead, the 17th day of the Egyptian fixed Agricultural (November) year appeared as an alternative dating to the 1st day of the fixed agricultural year which began on 1st November. From this it would appear that, originally, the 17th day of the second month of the Calendar year of Genesis was commemorated as the 1st day of the first month of the early Egyptian Calendar year, and that, at a later date, the persistence of the tradition, connecting the festival with the 17th day of the month, led to the adoption of the alternative Egyptian dating.

Hypothesis that the 17th day of Genesis Calendar Month II was originally adopted in Egypt as Day I Month I of the Agricultural Year.

This would identify early Egyptian Day I Month I on November 1st, with Day 17 Month II of the Calendar year of Genesis.[1] Day I Month II of the then current Calendar year of Genesis would therefore fall on October 16th (Gregorian), and, in consequence, Day I Month I of Genesis on September 16th (Gregorian). This would mean that the Calendar year of Genesis was an intercalated year of 360 days intercalated with respect to the Autumnal Equinox, which agrees with the data concerning the basis of the Biblical year prior to the Vernal Equinoctial basis of the luni-solar year adopted at the Exodus of Israel from Egypt.

Adoption implies that Genesis Calendar Year was an intercalated Year of 360 days based on Autumnal Equinox.

If this hypothesis is correct—and it is little more than a hypothesis until it is confirmed by reliable data—then the Great Pyramid's 1st November phenomena form the earliest known example of what is understood in modern times as " The Almanac Tradition."

The Pyramid's 1st November phenomena the earliest known example of " The Almanac Tradition."

¶ 31. THE CYCLES OF THE INTERCALATED CALENDAR YEAR.

In Section II of this Chapter—¶ 56—it is shown that both the Calendar year of 360 days and the Calendar year of 365 days in early Egyptian times received intercalations at the end of every five or six years. A series of such intercalary periods naturally fall into a cycle of 103 years of 365.24272 days, giving the mean value of the solar year over the entire period of astronomical time covered by historical records. (Section II, ¶ 56). Table II shows the construction of the cycle. The progressive durations of the years tabulated are for progressive intercalary years of cycle only. The Calendar of 360 days began on the same day as the Calendar of 365 days at the end of each intercalary period of Table II. The intercalary periods of Table II, as will be seen, are all in exact numbers of months of 30 days. Table III gives the comparative details for each year of the Cycle of 103 years. It will be shown later that this cycle and its intercalary periods were observed by the early Egyptians, had been derived from an earlier civilisation, and were still referred to in the early centuries of our Era.

The intercalated Calendar Years of 360 and 365 days coincided every five or six years.

A series of such intercalary periods automatically supplied a cycle of 103 Solar Years.

Tables II and III.

The Cycle used in earliest times; referred to in latest times in Egypt.

---

[1] This hypothesis, it will be found, requires a slight revision later.

¶ 32. THE CYCLIC SERIES OF THE 721 YEARS' PERIOD.

The Auxiliary Series,
(1) 120 Years
(2) 120 „
(3) 120 „
(4) 120 „
(5) 121 „
(6) 120 „

721 years.

An important auxiliary series of cycles dependent upon the intercalary periods of Table II, was a series of six cycles terminally coinciding with seven cycles of Table II, after the duration of 721 years. The auxiliary series consisted of four initial periods of 120 years each terminating at an intercalation of Table II, followed by a period of 121 years ending at an intercalation of Table II,—the 120 years not fulfilling this requirement—the terminal period, making

7 Cycles of 103 Years.

up the six repetitions of the auxiliary cycle, ending at the last intercalation of Table II. Table IV indicates how the auxiliary series was automatically

Series follows intercalations.

obtained.

The included periods of 30 years.

In following the years' duration of the 360 *days' Calendar* in Table III, and its successive repetitions, each period of 120 years included four periods of 30 years of the following total duration :—

30 years = 365 months of 30 days.
60   „   = 730   „   „
90   „   =1095   „   „
120   „   =1461   „   „

The necessary exception was the last 31 years' period of the 121 years of No. (5) of series in Table IV, which automatically followed the rule requiring the interval of the series to end at an intercalation.

Egyptian time measures translated numerically into linear measures.

The identities employed by the Egyptians in translating the numerical values of time measures into linear measures will shortly be seen. When this fact of the mythological basis of Egyptian civil and religious life is appreciated

The Cyclic Dimensions of certain underworld domains.

it will be understood why certain domains of the Egyptian Underworld are expressed as 309 *àtru* in length, and 120 *àtru* in breadth,[1]—numerically three

3 Cycles of 103 × 1 Cycle of 120.

cycles of 103 years and one cycle of 120 years respectively, indicating the connection understood as holding between the two cycles.

¶ 33. OTHER AUXILIARY CYCLES.

Other important cycles, dependent upon the 103 years' cycle of Tables II and III are :—

I. Commencing from zero year of Table III and following its successive repetitions :

The Cycle of 658 years. (360 and 365 days' Calendar.)

(a) An important cycle of 658 years of 365.2431611 days on the 360 days' Calendar basis and on the 365 days' Calendar basis.

The Cycle of 329 years. (365 days' Calendar).

(b) An important cycle of 329 years (half of above cycle) of 365.2431611 days on the 365 days' Calendar basis.

These two are the most important cycles in Egyptian chronology, and will be found frequently referred to in the Egyptian records.

[1]Budge, " Gods of the Egyptians," vol. I, p. 208.

II. Commencing from year 5 of the initial 103 years cycle (on 360 days' Calendar basis) :—

(a) A series of 200 Julian years.

(b) A series of 120 Julian years.

These agree and terminate exactly at the completion of 35 cycles of 103 years.

Cycles of 200, 120, 97, and 2920 years, commencing after 5 years' duration of initial 103 Cycle.

(c) A series of 97 years of 365.2577 days each closely approximating to the mean siderial year of 365.25637 (modern value).

(d) A cycle of 2920 Julian years, equal to two cycles of 1460 years, beginning at year 5 of the initial cycle of 103 years, and terminating at a year 2925 of the 103 years' cycle in continued repetition.

The most important cycle of these is that of 97 years as it is the one of the above four most often met with in Egyptian cyclic chronology.

The importance of the 97 years' cycle.

¶ 34. THE SED FESTIVAL AND THE SEP TEP SED FESTIVAL.

The series of ¶ 32 confirms Petrie's identification that the Egyptian period of the *Sep tep sed* Festival was an astronomical period of 120 years, and that the period of the *Sed* Festival was an astronomical period of 30 years. Four repetitions of the *Sed* Festival period were celebrated by the *Sep tep sed* Festival. *Sed* means *the tail* or *end*, and therefore refers to a Festival celebrated in the last or tail year of the period of 30 years. *Sep tep* means *the chief repetition* or *occurrence*. The *Sep tep sed* Festival was therefore, the *chief occurrence of the tail* or *end* Festival, in the last or tail year of the 120 years' period,[1] or, as ¶ 32 shows, of the 121 years' period once in every seven repetitions of the 103 years' cycle.

The Chief Festival of 120 years. The Festival of 30 years. The Tail or End Festival

In early times it was the custom, as will be seen, for the king, at the *Sed* Festival, to appoint his co-regent. The co-regent, then, began the reckoning of his reign from his first year of co-regency, thus dating from the *Sed* Festival. Successive kings, thus appointed in unbroken succession, would always celebrate their second *Sed* Festival in their 30th year of rule from co-regency. So far—for very early times—Breasted's opinion[2] is applicable that a king's *Sed* Festival was celebrated 30 years from his appointment as co-regent. But when Breasted infers from this that the *Sed* period was not an astronomical period and, further, that the *Sed* Festival was always celebrated 30 years from appointment as co-regent, his opinion fails to accord with the facts.

Ancient custom of Kings appointing their co-regent at the Tail Festival.
Breasted's opinion that the custom continued, and that period not astronomical.

Petrie has shown repeatedly that the co-regency theory does not hold during the greater period of Egyptian history. He has repeatedly claimed that the Egyptian evidence fixes the periods of 30 and 120 years as astronomical periods. The data of ¶ 32 now confirm this, in that Petrie's *astronomical* period is now seen to be an important period of a highly scientific series of *Calendar* cycles, based on an accurate determination of the value of the solar year for ancient times.

Petrie's opinion that custom not continued, and that period was astronomical.
This opinion confirmed by new knowledge of cycles.

[1]Petrie, " Researches in Sinai," p. 180.
[2]" History of Egypt " (1919), p. 39.

¶35. THE RITES OF THE SED FESTIVAL.

Egyptian Rites of "Sed" Festival derived from a previous Civilisation.

The *Sed* Festival and its rites were institutions that the early Dynastic Egyptians derived from an earlier civilization. The significance of the *Sed* period we know to be primarily calendric. But as to what was the original nature of the *Sed* Festival rites is a matter that can only be surmised from what we know concerning the ceremonies followed at the Festival during the times of the earliest Dynasties in Egypt.

Early Egyptians believed that the King at "Sed" Festival renewed his Spiritual and Physical Strength from the presence-form of the Dynastic God.

The purpose of the ceremonies at the time of the first two Egyptian Dynasties centred chiefly round the idea of ensuring the continuity of the Dynasty in both a spiritual sense and a physical sense. The king was the representative on earth of the god of his Dynasty. He was supposed to partake of the spiritual strength of his god, and to derive his physical strength from the god. What was believed to be the process of effecting this accession of Divine Power took place at the *Sed* Festival, when the king and his selected co-regent presented themselves before the Shrine of the " presence-form " of the Dynastic god.

¶ 36. THE RENEWAL OF THE KING.

Festival therefore alternatively designated the Festival of Renewal.

The reigning king was believed to *renew* his strength in the presence of the god. Hence the *Sed* Festival was also known as the Festival of *Renewal.*

The Reigning King renews and the Elected Co-Regent receives the power of the god.

The selected co-regent, as was believed, received, jointly with the reigning monarch, the power from the god's presence. If the reigning king died before the following *Sed* Festival or Festival of Renewal the power of the god continued in his successor. Such seems to have been the idea that formulated this early stage of the kingly doctrine of Divine Right, and of the constitutional formulæ[1]

" The King never dies."

persisting in our own times and kingdom, " The king is dead, long live the king,"

" The King is dead, Long Live the King."

and " The king never dies, he only demises the throne."

" Sed " Dancing and Running before the Shrine.

The divine right was supposed to pass from one Dynasty to another when the god failed to renew the king, or to accept or provide a successor belonging to the family. The king and his co-regent signified their renewal and accession of power by running or dancing before the shrine of the " presence-form " of the god. Similarly David, in the year in which he received the promise of his Everlasting Kingdom, danced before the Ark of the Covenant, in the presence of the Shekinah, when the Ark returned from the Philistines. St. Paul (Acts

David dances before the Ark.

15 " Sed " Periods from New Epoch of Israel.

XIII, 17-23) refers to this Establishing of the Kingdom in connection with the termination of a period of 450 years[2]—obviously a period dating from an Epoch in Israel's history. The period is an interval of fifteen *Sed* periods of 30 years. Can it be that the Biblical evidence here points to the continuance of certain ancient sacred rites and customs as these were understood amongst the Hebrews,

[1] Refer Ferrar Fenton's long note at the end of his translation of the 1st Book of Genesis, " Bible in Modern English " We do not agree entirely with Fenton's theory, but what he says has an important bearing upon this subject of the *Sed* Festival, as well as upon the question of the Antediluvian genealogies with which Fenton's theory deals.

[2] Refer Founding of Solomon's Temple, 480th year from Exodus. Another *Sed* Festival (I Kings, VI, 1). This throws light on the 450 years of Acts XIII, 17-23.

precisely as the Egyptians followed the rites and customs handed on to them by a former civilisation, that had reduced the central idea to the form presented by the rites of the *Sed* Festival in early Egypt ? That this is not improbable is evidenced by the common origin of the Deluge narrative of Genesis and the Egyptian narrative of the Destruction of Mankind, and all the associated Calendar data connecting the month date of the Festival of the Dead with the month date of the Noachian Deluge. Egyptian Religious Customs developed apart but had a source of origin in common with the Religious Customs of the Hebrews.

¶ 37. THE EPOCHS AND CYCLES OF GENESIS.

The truth concerning the connection inferred between the ancient Egyptian cycles and the customs and institutions belonging to the period of the early chapters of Genesis is seen at once by tabulating the chronology of the gene- alogies of Genesis, Chapter V. This is as stated in Table V,—"The Ante- diluvian Dynasties of Genesis V." The Chronology of the Genealogies of Genesis confirms above.

It is significant that whereas the initial dates (in Column 2, Table V), of the ten genealogical items, Adam to birth of Noah, do not bear any relation to the Calendar Cycles, the ten terminal dates, in Column 3, all fall at the beginning or ending of the last year of one or other of the Calendar Cycles dependent upon the cycle of 103 years. For this reason the years of the chronology are stated in Table V as A.K. or *Anno Kalendarii*.[1] The Terminal Dates of the Dynasties of Genesis are dates of the Festival of the End, dated with Epoch of Adam as origin

Two of the terminal dates end at the date of the Deluge ending. Of the remaining eight terminal dates, six coincide with the beginning or ending of the last year of a *Sed* period. Five of these belong to a *Sed* series beginning from o A.K., and one to a *Sed* series beginning from 622 A.K., the date of the birth of Enoch or Hanok. That this latter date was reckoned as a separate Epoch is proved by the 365 years of Enoch being dated from 622 A.K., and by the 365 years' period ending at 987 A.K., the termination of three cycles of 329 years from o A.K. The latter identity accounts for one of the remaining two terminal datings of column 3. The one terminal dating remaining coincides with the commencement of the last year of the twelfth cycle of 103 years from o A.K. One Exception a Cycle of 329 years. Another Exception a Cycle of 103 years.

We saw that the *Sed* Festival in Egypt was celebrated in the last year of each period. The chronology of the terminal dates of the dynasties of Genesis confirms that the terminal festivals were celebrated in any convenient month of the last year of a cyclic period.

¶ 38. THE CYCLE OF THE HOUSE OF ENOCH.

From Genesis V, 24, in conjunction with the dates in Table V, we discover that the translation of Hanok (Enoch) is dated at the termination of a cycle of 329 years. Later evidence from Egyptian sources will show this cycle to be the hitherto lost Phœnix cycle of Egyptian, Greek, and Roman tradition. Translation of Enoch at 3 Cycles of 329 years from Epoch of Adam. The 329 Years Period the Lost "Phœnix Cycle."

[1] The initial " K " for " C " is intentional, to avoid using A.C.

THE ANTEDILUVIAN DYNASTIES OF GENESIS V.

The House of	Duration of Dynasty from	to	The cyclic significance of the terminal dating.
ADAM	0 A.K.	930 A.K...	Commencement of last year of 31st Sed Festival from 0 A.K. Since 721+210=931 years.
SHETH	130 A.K.	1042 A.K...	14 Sed Festivals (420 years) from Epoch of Enoch at 622 A.K.
ENOSH	235 A.K.	1140 A.K...	Commencement of last year of 38th Sed Festival from 0 A.K. Since 721+420=1141 years.
KENAN	325 A.K.	1235 A.K...	Commencement of last year of XIIth Cycle of 103 years.
MAHALALEEL ..	395 A.K.	1290 A.K...	Commencement of last year of 43rd Sed Festival from 0 A.K. Since 721+570=1291 years.
JARED	460 A.K.	1322 A.K...	Termination of last year of 44th Sed Festival from 0 A.K. Since 721+601=1322 years.
HANOK (Enoch) ..	622 A.K.	987 A.K...	Termination of 3rd Phoenix Cycle of 329 years from 0 A.K. Since 3×329=987 years.
METHUSELAH ..	687 A.K.	1656 A.K...	Termination of 20 Sed periods from Epoch of Noah, 1056 A.K. Termination of Deluge and beginning of new era for Egyptian Sed periods.
LAMEK	874 A.K.	1651 A.K...	Commencement of last year of 55th Sed Festival from 0 A.K. The last Sed Festival of the Antediluvian reckoning from 0 A.K. Since 721+721+210 =1652 years.
NOAH	1056 A.K.	1656 A.K...	The last Sed period (20 periods) from Epoch of Noah, 1056 A.K. Termination of the Deluge, and beginning of New Era for Egyptian Sed Festivals.
NOAH (New Era) ..	1656 A.K.	2006 A.K...	A period of 350 years, the duration of Manetho's last Dynasty of Demi-gods; as the interval from the commencement of Dynasty of Adam to the commencement of the Dynasty of Noah, 1056 years, is the duration of Manetho's last Dynasty of gods.

Now the legend of the Phœnix is the story of its translation at the end of the Phœnix period or cycle. The legend of the Phœnix is thus the Egyptian or Greek mythological form of the translation of Hanok (Enoch). In Egyptian, *Pa* as a prefix to a proper name signified " the house of," or the " father of the house of " the individual designated by the proper name. Hence the Egyptian name Grecianised as " Phœnix " was apparently derived down from " Pa-Hanok " or " Pa-Enoch," the name of the father of the House of Enoch. The Phœnix cycle, therefore, is the cycle of Pa-Hanok, the Cycle of the House of Enoch.

The date for the translation of Enoch, 987 A.K.,—the termination of three Phœnix cycles—is 360,495 days from the cyclic beginning at 0 A.K. Now the summation of 900 years of 360 days and 100 years of 365 days—numerically 1000 " years "—is 360,500 days. From this almost exact coincidence (within five days), obviously originated the tradition identifying the Phœnix Cycle with a period of 1000 years (as Martial, Claudian, Lactantius, and Nonno). Beginning with Herodotus, however, the majority of the Greek and Latin writers reckoned the period at half this duration, or 500 " years." Apparently, then, both traditions originated from the fact that the translation of Enoch is dated in Genesis at 987 A.K., the completion of [900 years of 360 days]+[100 years of 365 days] numerically totalling 1000 " years."

¶ 39. THE EPOCH OF ENOCH AND THE EPOCH OF ABRAM.

Tacitus, and other writers, however, mention an alternative duration of 1460 or 1461 " years " for the Phœnix cycle. This obviously originated from the 365 years of the *life* of Enoch. $4 \times 365 = 1460$, and $4 \times 365\frac{1}{4} = 1461$ years. The initial 365 (or 365¼) years spanning the life of Enoch, begin from 622 A.K. as in Table V. Observe the significance, then, of the following summation.

Birth of Enoch .. .. = 622 A.K.

Interval of .. .. 1461 years

Hebrew date for Call of Abram .. .. .. = 2083 A.K.

The initial period again—the *life* of Enoch (Pa-Hanok)—is a " great year " or a year of years, 365 or 365¼ years. The Greeks gave the name " Phœnix " to the palm-tree branch, which as a hieroglyphic in Egyptian, denoted the " year "—365 or 365¼ days. Thus Horapollo (I, iii) refers to the " Phœnix, the palm branch " as signifying the " year " in Egyptian; (I, xxxiv) to " the phœnix, the bird " as signifying in Egyptian, " a soul continuing a long time here "; or (I, xxxv) " a man returning home after a long time from a foreign land."

¶ 40. THE CALENDAR YEAR OF GENESIS.

The Calendar Cycles, then, of the ancient Egyptians and of the early civilisation briefly pictured in the first eleven chapters of Genesis were identical. This confirms the hypothesis of ¶ 30 as to the intercalated Calendar year of

1st Calendar
Year of Genesis
began at
Autumnal
Equinox.
Genesis being based on the Autumnal Equinox. Day I, Month I of Genesis therefore began at the Autumnal Equinox in the zero year, o A.K., of Genesis. For several thousand years prior to 2000 B.C., the Autumnal Equinox could fall upon one or other of the days 21st, 22nd, or 23rd September (Gregorian)[1]

1655 years to
month dating
of Deluge
beginning.
From Genesis VII, 11, Day 17, Month II, fell in the 600th year from the Epoch of Noah. Being early in the then current year, as indicated by the month numeral, 599 years from the Epoch of Noah terminated at the beginning of Day 1, Month I of the 600th year. The Epoch of Noah is 1056 A.K. (Table V. from genealogies of Genesis Chapter V.) Hence Genesis VII, 11, refers to Day 17, Month II of 1655 A.K.

Autumnal
Equinox of
Zero Year
of Cycles of
Genesis fell
within 21-23
Sept.
(Gregorian).
Now the Calendar year of Genesis is the Intercalated Calendar Year of 360 days, and the cycles of Genesis V are the cycles dependent upon the statement of Table III. The rules of Table III, therefore, apply as commencing Day 1 Month I on one or other of the days 21, 22, 23 September (Gregorian) o A.K. If we knew the year B.C. in which o A.K. began we could reduce the range to one particular day of the three. The range of three days is, however, sufficient for purposes of identification

Calendar
Cycles
and Rules
give month
dating of
Deluge within
30th Oct. to
1st Nov.
(Gregorian).

Confirms
Purpose of
Pyramid's
1st November
Phenomena
and confirms
traditional
survival in
Modern
" All Hallow's
Eve."
Following the rules suggested, we find that Day 17, Month II in 1655 A.K. fell on one or other of the days 30th or 31st October or 1st November (Gregorian). As the narrative of Genesis places the Noachian Deluge as beginning on Day 17 Month II, 1655 A.K., it therefore gives the commencement of the Deluge on 30th or 31st October or 1st November (Gregorian). This explains the intention of the Pyramid's 1st November Phenomena, and why the Festival of the Dead is universally associated with a date generally ranging from 31st October (All Hallow's Eve or Hallowe'en) to 2nd November, the modern *All Souls.*

[1]In all *precise* Gregorian datings for ancient times, in this work, the datings have been calculated and are not, therefore, merely approximate datings. For such precise datings, the modern (Gregorian) rule of intercalation has been carried back into ancient times, together with the modern months. This was done for purpose of comparison with the solar year. When comparison with the siderial year or with the Sothic (or Sirius) year is required, the same process is adopted by carrying back the Julian year from 1582 A.D.—when it was discarded for the modern Gregorian year. The latter process is that adopted generally in astronomical calculations for ancient times. The single difference in the month datings, of Julian as compared with Gregorian, is that prior to 1582 A.D. the Julian Leap Year occurs every four years without exception, whereas the Gregorian rule omits three Leap years in every 400 years, otherwise following the Julian rule. This reduces to the following for A.D. years :—

Julian Rule :—All years A.D. divisible by 4 are Leap Years.

Gregorian Rule :—All years A.D.—except zero years of centuries—divisible by 4 are Leap Years. All zero years of centuries divisible by 400 are Leap Years. Thus, 1,600 A.D. was a Leap Year, but 1700, 1800 and 1900 A.D. were not Leap Years.

By following the astronomical reckoning of B.C. years whereby

Astronomical A.D. 1 =	Historical A.D. 1.		
,,	B.C. o =	,,	B.C. 1
,,	B.C. 1 =	,,	B.C. 2

and so on,

the same rules can be applied to B.C. reckoning. Unless, however, in the present work, a B.C. year is specifically defined as B.C. year of astronomical reckoning, it refers to B.C. year of historical reckoning.

SECTION I.   SUMMARY AND CONCLUSIONS.

¶ 41. CONCLUSIONS CONCERNING ORIGINS.

In what is generally and vaguely referred to as prehistoric times, there existed a highly developed state of civilisation. Much is to be *inferred* con- A Former Civilisation. cerning the various phases and branches of life and knowledge of this former civilisation. One thing, however, appears to be certain. It came to an end in Its Landmarks Vanished. such a manner that none of its works—except in the form of tradition—remained as a heritage to the civilisation that followed.[1]

The men who founded the origins of modern civilisation built on the oral traditions brought over from the former civilisation. In conception, co- Oral Tradition spanned the relation of ideas, and what we may term mental idiom, we find these origins to gap, and carried into be already highly developed. In forms of literary and artistic presentation the new period of civilisation they are, at first, archaic or amateurish in execution. Development, however, the conceptions, was rapid. Thus, of the first three Egyptian Dynasties, Professor Petrie co-relation of ideas, and the remarks " The rapid rise of art is the most surprising activity of this age...... mental idiom of the lost arts So soon as the dynastic race come in, there begins the enormous step in art, and sciences. rapidly developing to perfection within its natural limits."[2]

¶ 42. CONCLUSIONS CONCERNING THE TRADITIONAL CATASTROPHE AND ITS ANNIVERSARY.

According to the traditions from various sources, the former civilisation met with a catastrophic ending. In ancient Egypt, the tradition exists as " The Destruction of Mankind," in ancient Mexico and Peru as " The Destruc- The Traditional tion of the World," and in ancient Babylonia and Assyria, and in China, as Accounts of the former " The Deluge." These traditional accounts, when compared, indicate they are Civilisation's Catastrophic various versions of the Noachian Deluge narrative in the Hebrew Book of Ending. Genesis.

The day *generally* celebrated throughout the world, in ancient and modern times, as the Anniversary of the Catastrophe, is 1st November, with variation The Anniversary of the *generally* from 31st October to 2nd November. These represent in modern Catastrophe 1st November times, All Hallows' Eve, All Saints' Day and All Souls' Day. (Gregorian).

The Autumnal Equinoctial year beginning of Genesis, the 103 years' Calendar Cycle of Genesis, the Genesis Deluge year and month date combine to give the Genesis date for the Deluge as one or other of the three days, 30th October, 31st October, or 1st November (Gregorian).

---

[1]The statues of Easter Island, and some of the titanic rock temples of Asia have been referred to this period. But they tell us nothing, nor is their identification with the period certain.

[2]It must always be remembered, however, that in all stages and periods of civilisation the highest forms exist alongside the primitive and barbarous. Even the best authorities frequently permit themselves to forget this.

¶ 43. CONCLUSIONS CONCERNING THE FIXED CALENDAR YEAR OF EARLY DYNASTIC EGYPT.

Egyptian Calendar and Agricultural Year began 1st November (Anniversary Date).

Great Pyramid's 1st November Phenomena ensured against error.

Calendar Year a Fixed Year during Egyptian Dynasties I to XVI.

At the commencement of Egyptian Dynastic history, the Egyptian calendar year was instituted to begin from the anniversary of what the Egyptians designated the " Destruction of Mankind "—1st November. This coincided with the beginning of the agricultural year. The agricultural year commenced with the sowing season at the beginning of November. In consequence, the first Egyptian Calendar Season was the Calendar Season of Sowing. The outstanding phenomena of the noon reflexions of the Great Pyramid of Gizeh (Dynasty IV) defined the beginning of the agricultural year and the sowing season to all the inhabitants of the Nile Delta, annually on 1st November. The same phenomena on this date defined the Nile Delta as a truly Oriented Quadrant of a circle centred on the Great Pyramid. The Egyptian Calendar year, thus fixed, remained fixed from Dynasty I to Dynasty XVI.

¶ 44. CONCLUSIONS CONCERNING THE CALENDAR CYCLES AND THEIR ORIGIN.

The Intercalary Periods.

Their Natural Cycle of 103 Solar Years.

Connected " Sed " Festival Periods.

Connected Phœnix Cycle of 329 Years.

The Egyptian Calendar year of 360 days, at this time, received, every five or six years, the addition of a month of 30 days. A series of such intercalary periods automatically formed a Calendar Cycle of 103 solar years. This cycle was also the basis of the Egyptian *Sed* Festival period of 30 years, and of the *Sep tep sed* Festival period of 120 years. It was also the basis of the ancient Phœnix Cycle of 329 years. These and other connected cycles were derived by the Egyptians from the previous civilisation, from which they also derived the original form of their *Sed* festival ceremonies.

Originally Dynasties officially ended only at " Sed " Festivals.

The Origin of this in Genesis V.

Enoch translated at Phœnix Cycle ending.

Translation of Enoch originated Translation of Phœnix.

Pa-Hanok— Phœnix— House of Enoch.

In effect, the original conception followed made it impossible for a Dynasty to be declared *officially* ended other than at a *Sed* festival. That this was the conception held by the former civilisation is evident from the chronology of the genealogies of Genesis V. In every case the genealogical item ends in the last year of a *Sed* festival period, or in one exception at the end of a cycle of 103 years, and in another, at the end of a Phœnix cycle of 329 years.

From the last identity, the Phœnix cycle was seen to be the cycle of Pa-Hanok. the cycle of the House of Enoch ; and the translation of the Phœnix to be the mythological aspect of the Biblical translation of Enoch.

¶ 45. PYRAMID REFLEXIONS AND SHADOWS ; TEMPLE ALIGNMENTS ; AND ALIGNMENTS OF MEGALITHIC MONUMENTS.

Pyramid automatically defines points of Solar Year.

Idea borrowed for Temple Alignments.

The noon reflexions and shadows of the Great Pyramid automatically and accurately defined the principal points of the solar astronomical and the solar vegetation year. This idea of defining a required point of the solar year was borrowed by the Egyptian, Babylonian and Greek temple builders, as Lockyer and Penrose have shown. Instead of reflexions and shadows, they adopted temple alignments directed to the point of sunrise of the required day of the year. The same idea was borrowed by the Oriental maritime traders and mining specialists who established mining and other industrial colonies in Spain, Portugal, and Britain. Not having time nor the opportunity to adopt the elaborate temple architecture of the contemporary East, and—as the Belgian archæologist, Siret, has shown,[1]—not permitting the aboriginal inhabitants to understand the use of metals and metal tools, they devised the simple yet accurate constructions of the rough stone circle and of the rough stone alignment. As Lockyer has shown, the stone circle was an advance on the stone alignment, as the latter was an advance—by reason of its greater length generally—on the Oriental Temple Axis alignment.

Idea of Temple Alignments borrowed for Megalithic Monuments.

Oriental Colonists in Spain, Portugal, and Britain adopt "Rough" stone constructions intentionally

¶ 46. IS THE PYRAMID A GRAPHICAL EXPRESSION OF NATURAL LAW?

In light of the foregoing conclusions—and having regard to the extreme accuracy of workmanship in the Great Pyramid and the extreme accuracy of its definition of the points of the solar year—it would seem that the Great Pyramid was not built for the latter purpose only. All our conclusions take us back to the origins in the former civilisation. Can it be that the Great Pyramid has something to tell us concerning these origins, and concerning the basis of the lost sciences and arts of the past?

Other possible purposes of the Great Pyramid?

Lost Sciences and Arts of the Past?

The mathematical or astronomical reader may possibly have seen the clues that have suggested these questions. In the Great Pyramid we have four sloping surfaces at the same angle of slope, accurately oriented, and built at a selected latitude. These comprise four constants.

The Mathematical Clue of the Four Pyramid Constants.

We could understand the two structural constants having been purposely brought to a selected latitude and there oriented to enable the noon phenomena to define the 1st of November. But the chances against the same four constants defining the beginning and ending of Summer by a horizontal South reflexion, and the Equinoxes by North-East and North-West directions, are so overwhelming as to be deemed impossible. Yet the Equinoctial phenomenon and the phenomenon of the beginning and ending of summer, both resulting from the same simple combination of constants, prove the phenomena to have been intentional. Three precise series of independent coincidences of such a nature cannot happen by chance.

Mathematical Authority against the Identities, viewed as resulting from ordinary combination of factors.

Precision of Identities declares against chance and ordinary combination.

Now there is only one class of phenomena that can supply several such striking coincidences and identities from a simple combination, and that is the class of phenomena governed by Natural Law. Of a like simplicity to the case considered are the phenomena whose laws are expressed by the simple natural laws of Newton, Kepler, and Einstein.[2]

Within the Category of Natural Law Phenomena.

Analogy: Laws of Newton, Kepler, Einstein.

[1] D. A. Mackenzie, " Early Man in Britain," pp. 97 and 98.
[2] The statement of Einstein's *Law of Relativity* is simple. What is difficult is the *explanation* of its application in the various branches of science. The same difficulty will be experienced in regard to the Pyramid's application. The simplicity is obvious. Why it should be so is not obvious.

¶ 47. THE PYRAMID DESIGNER'S KNOWLEDGE OF ORBITAL MOTIONS.

Great Pyramid's Noon Phenomena are remotely derived functions of the Primary Functions of the Elements of the Earth's Orbit and its Motions.

Tentatively, therefore, we may accept as possible that the Great Pyramid is the solid geometrical expression of a natural law, or of certain natural laws known to a former civilisation, and that this expression refers to solar astronomical time, and hence, possibly, to orbital motions and elements. The possibility more nearly approaches certainty when the mathematician realises, as he must, that the outstanding noon phenomena of the Pyramid cannot be other than functions that are remote derivatives of other functions. These other functions can only be primary functions of the elements of the Earth's orbit and its motions.

The Relation between the Primary and Derived Functions necessarily known before Pyramid's Simple Expression of the Derived Functions could be evolved.

Obviously it was known, before the Pyramid design was put into being, that certain properties of the solar year could be reduced to the simple Pyramid expression of them. The knowledge of the simplicity of expression necessarily presupposes knowledge of the properties thus simply expressed. The possession of such knowledge by the Pyramid designer implies the possession of a knowledge of astronomy at least equal to that of modern times.

Such Knowledge at least equal to astronomical knowledge of Modern Times.

It may seem rash to suggest such an hypothesis thus early in our argument, but we are content to let the Pyramid's own evidence, and the evidence from archæological and literary sources, speak for themselves. The evidence from these sources has not hitherto been co-ordinated in this connection, but this will be accomplished in subsequent chapters, and the results of this co-ordination fully discussed.

The Direction of further Inquiry.

PYRAMID NOON REFLEXIONS DURING THE SUMMER HALF OF THE YEAR.

Astronomical points in the Solar Year.	Modern Calendar Dates.	Diagram Reference (Plates Nos. 5-8 inclusive).	SOUTH FACE REFLEXIONS.		NORTH FACE REFLEXIONS.		REFLEXIONS FROM EAST AND WEST FACES.			Sun's observed altitude at Pyramid.
			Inclination with Horizontal.	General characteristics and variations between dates.	Inclination with Horizontal.	General characteristics and variations between dates.	Constant inclination of Projection of E. and W. Reflexions on E. and W. Vertical Plane.	Azimuth of Apex Ridge of Reflexion E. and W. of N.	General characteristics and variations between dates.	
Vernal Equinox	20-21 Mar.	Fig. A	16°-17½' upwards	Reflexion gradually lowering	43°-43½' downwards		13°-43½' downwards	59°-16'-42"	Southern Limit of E. and W. reflexions point due N.E. and N.W. respectively	60°
Beginning of Summer, ¼-way Vernal Equinox and Summer Solstice.	6 May	Fig. B	0°-0' Horizontal	Unbroken Horizontal Reflexion. Length of reflected beam gradually lowering 7th May to 7th Aug. inclusively Beam broken by striking ground.	27°-25' downwards	Reflexion gradually lengthening	13°-43½' downwards	75°-57'	10 days after beginning of Summer Northern Limit of E. and W. reflexions lies E. and W. along North Base Side of Pyramid. Reflexions gradually shortening.	76°-17½'
Summer Solstice	19-20 June	Fig. C	Ancient 7°-4½' downwards Modern 7°-6' downwards	15 days before and 15 days after the Summer Solstice the South Reflexion makes an Angle of 90° with Sun's Altitude. 7th May to 7th Aug. inclusively Beam broken by striking ground.	Ancient 19°-42½' downwards Modern 20°-19' downwards		13°-43½' downwards	Ancient 83°-51½' Modern 83°-15'	Reflexions slightly N. of E. and W. respectively	84° for Ancient Egyptian Time 83°-23½' for Modern Times
End of Summer ¼-way Summer Solstice and Autumnal Equinox	8 Aug.	Fig. B	0°-0' Horizontal	Reflexion gradually rising Length of reflected beam gradually lengthening Unbroken Horizontal Reflexion.	27°-25' downwards	Reflexion gradually shortening	13°-43½' downwards	75°-57'	Reflexions gradually lengthening 10 days before end of Summer Northern Limit of E. and W. reflexions lies E. and W. of North Base Side of Pyramid.	76°-17½'
Autumnal Equinox	22-23 Sept.	Fig. A	16°-17½' upwards	Reflexion gradually rising	43°-43½' downwards		13°-43½' downwards	59°-16'-42"	Southern Limit of E. and W. reflexions point due N.E. and N.W. respectively	60°

GENERAL NOTE :—

No Shadow on or from the Pyramid at Noon during the Summer Half of the Year.

Between Vernal Equinox and beginning of Summer and again between end of Summer and Autumnal Equinox the E. and W. Reflexions in rotating towards the South and the North Reflexion in lengthening towards the North pass with their respective Ridge Lines through the same plane.

[To face p. 42.

TABLE VII.

PYRAMID NOON REFLEXIONS DURING THE WINTER HALF OF THE YEAR.

Astronomical points in the Solar Year.	Modern Calendar Dates.	Diagram Reference (Plates Nos. 5–8 inclusive).	South Face Reflexions. Inclination with Horizontal.	South Face Reflexions. General characteristics and variations between dates.	North Face Reflexions. Inclination with Horizontal.	North Face Reflexions. General characteristics and variations between dates.	Reflexions from East and West Faces. Constant Inclination of Projection of E. and W. Reflexions on E. and W. Vertical Plane.	Reflexions from East and West Faces. Azimuth of Apex Ridge of Reflexion E. of N. and W. of N.	Reflexions from East and West Faces. General characteristics and variations between dates.	Sun's observed altitude at Pyramid.
Autumnal Equinox	22–23 Sept.	Fig. A	16°–17½′ upwards	7 days later than Equinox, ridge of South reflexion lies in some plane as ridges of E. and W. reflexions.	43°–42½′ downwards	Reflexion gradually shortening.	13°–42½′ downwards	59°–16′–42″	Southern Limit of E. and W. reflexions point due N.E. and N. W. respectively.	60°
	14–15 Oct.	Fig. D	24°–26′ upwards		51°–51′ Last Reflexion First Shadow 51°–51′		13°–42½′ downwards	51°–2½′		51°–51′
	1 Nov.	Fig. E	30°–27½′ upwards	Reflexion gradually rising, but lower than Sun's altitude	45°–50′		13°–42½′ downwards	45°–0′	Northern Limit of E. and W. reflexions point due N. E. and N. W. respectively. This Limit is a Vertical Plane of Reflected Light.	45°–50′
Beginning of Winter ½-way Autumnal Equinox to Summer Solstice	8 Nov.		32°–35′ upwards		43°–42½′	Shadow gradually lengthening	13°–42½′ downwards	42°–53½′		43°–42½′
	2–3 Dec.	Fig. F	38°–9′ upwards	Direct or Normal Reflexion from face	38°–9′	With Shadow Ridge Line and South Reflexion Ridge Line in same straight line N. to S. (Sun's Altitude Line)	13°–42½′ downwards	37°–21′		38°–9′
				Reflexions gradually rising but higher than Sun's altitude						
Winter Solstice	21–23 Dec.	Fig. G	40°–17½′ Ancient 40°–41′ Modern	Highest Noon Reflexion of the Year	36° Ancient 36°–36½′ Modern	Longest Noon Shadow of the Year	13°–42½′ downwards	35°–13′ Ancient 35°–49½′ Modern		36° Ancient Egyptian Times 36°–36½′ Modern Times
				Reflexions gradually falling but higher than Sun's altitude						
	11–12 Jan.	Fig. F	38°–9′	Direct or Normal Reflexion from Face	38°–9′	(As for 2–3 Dec.)	13°–42½′	37°–21′		38°–9′
End of Winter	4 Feb.		32°–35′		43°–42½′		13°–42½′	42°–53½′		43°–42½′
	11 Feb.	Fig. E	30°–27½′	Reflexions gradually falling but lower than Sun's altitude	45°–50′	Shadow gradually shortening	13°–42½′	45°–0′	(As for 1st Nov.)	45°–50′
	28 Feb.	Fig. D	24°–26′		51°–51′ Last Shadow First Reflexion 51°–51′		13°–42½′	51°–2½′		51°–51′
						Reflexion gradually lengthening				
Vernal Equinox	20–21 Mar.	Fig. A	16°–17½′ upwards	7 days before Equinox, ridge of South reflexion lies in same plane as ridges of E. and W. reflexions.	43°–42½′ downwards		13°–42½′ downwards	59°–16′–42″	Southern Limit of E. and W. reflexions point due N. E. and N. W. respectively.	60°

[*To face p. 42.*

SECTION II.—ACCESSORY.

¶ 48. THE XVIIITH DYNASTY VAGUE CALENDAR YEAR.

It is an undisputed fact that during the entire duration of the XVIIIth Dynasty of Egypt, the Egyptian Calendar year consisted of 365 days without any intercalation. In other words, the Egyptians of this period had no equiva- lent for our Leap Year. This form of year is known as the Egyptian Vague (or Wandering) Year. It is so called, obviously, from the fact that it slips back round the Julian year of 365¼ days, at the rate of one day in four Julian years. The slip back amounts to one complete Calendar year of 365 days in 1460 Julian years. At this time the vague Calendar year began with Day 1, Month I, of the now *mis-named* Calendar Season of Sowing.

The Vague or Wandering Year in use during Dynasty XVIII without revision.

¶ 49. THE VAGUE CALENDAR YEAR FROM 6TH CENTURY B.C. TO 3RD CENTURY A.D.

It is also a fact beyond dispute that the vague *Calendar* year of 365 days was in use by the Egyptians from the 6th century B.C. to the 3rd century A.D. It continued in use even after 25 B.C., when the fixed Alexandrian (Julian) year was adopted for Egypt. The evidence concerning all this is too reliable and too surely established to require repeating. At this time, also, the vague Calendar year began with Day 1, Month I, of the now *mis-named* Calendar Season of Sowing.

The Vague or Wandering Year in use 6th Century B.C. to 3rd Century A.D. without revision

¶ 50. BETWEEN DYNASTY XVIII AND THE 6TH CENTURY B.C.

The evidence is also very complete that, between the period of Dynasty XVIII and the 6th Century B.C., a vague year was in use, with Month I of the so-called Calendar Season of Sowing as the first month of the Calendar year. But as to whether or not the vague year during this interval continued its tranquil *wandering* unaffected by legislation or other means of revision is a question that has failed to receive the critical treatment warranted by the evidence.

Vague Year in Use in Period Dynasty XVIII to 6th Century B.C.

But question as to whether subjected to revision.

¶ 51. EVIDENCE POINTING TO TWO REVISIONS.

The evidence indicates that the vague year was twice subjected to revision during the interval defined. It points to a first revision during the reign of Ramessu II (Dyn. XIX), and to a second revision during the reign of Uasarkon II (Dyn. XXII). The indications are that the first revision belongs to the 27th year of Ramessu II, and the second to the 22nd year of Uasarkon II.

Reference to Revision by Ramessu II and Revision by Uasarkon II

¶ 52. THE EFFECT OF THE REVISIONS.

The Two
Revisions
of the
Vague Year
considerably
complicate
Egyptian
Chronology
from
Dynasty XVIII
to 9th
Century B.C.

Neither of these revisions effected any considerable displacement of the Calendar year. But they so completely broke the uniform rate of the **vague year's** wandering that the solution of the astronomical chronology of the Dynasties is a considerably more complicated matter than has hitherto been supposed.

The data concerning the two revisions are deep rooted in the Egyptians' own presentation of their history. For this reason, consideration of the evidences will be given only as the various items of the data arise, and for the same reason, cannot be completed within the present volume.

The two regnal years are now, however, stated as an introductory basis of reference for the various items of the data as they emerge.

Vague Year
Unaltered
from Late
in the 9th
Century B.C.
to the
Middle of 3rd
Century A.D.

The date of the revision of Uasarkon II determines that the vague year continued its unbroken uniform rate of slip backwards round the Julian year —in spite of other two attempts at revision[1]—from late in the 9th century B.C. to the middle of the 3rd century A.D.

¶ 53. THE ASSUMPTIONS COMMONLY MADE.

The following assumptions have hitherto been made with the utmost assurance :

Common
Egyptological
Assumption :—
Vague Year
not subjected
to Revision
from 5700 B.C.
or alternatively
from 4240 B.C.
to 238 A.D.

(1) That the XVIIIth Dynasty vague year continued without revision— *i.e.*, uniformly slipping back without interruption, one day from the Julian year in every four Julian years—during the period intervening to the 6th century B.C. ; and

(2) That the same uniform rate of wandering had continued without revision or alteration, during the whole period of Dynastic history,— and earlier, from 5700 B.C. or alternatively from 4240 B.C. to 238 A.D. when Censorinus wrote concerning the Vague Year in his *De Die Natalis*.

¶ 54. THE FIXED YEAR OF PERIOD DYNASTIES VI TO XII.

Common
Assumption
of Unbroken
Sequence of
Unintercalated
Years of
365 Days.

Recorded
facts prove
otherwise.

Calendar Year
Intercalated
during period
of Egyptian
Dynasties
VI to XII.

Reference to
Egyptian Data
proving a Fixed
November
Agricultural
Year.

The basis of the common assumption is that the Egyptian Calendar— during the period of Dynastic history—always consisted of an unintercalated Calendar year of 365 days. Much might be said concerning the flaws in this assumption. The comparative charts, diagrams and data of Plates IX, X, and XI, however, render any such discussion superfluous.[2] Here we have the facts concerning the events of the seasons of the solar year compared with all the dated events of the defined seasons of the Calendar year in Egyptian records belonging to the period of Dynasties VI to XII inclusive. This comparison shows that during this period the calendar seasons coincided exactly with the actual seasons from which they derived their names. In other words, during Dynasties VI to XII, the Egyptians had a fixed (intercalated) year beginning at the commencement of the November Agricultural Year.

[1]Decree of Canopus, 238 B.C., and the Institution of the fixed Alexandrian (Julian) year 25 B.C.
[2]Refer detailed description of these, ¶¶ 73 to 75d.

¶ 55. THE XIITH DYNASTY RECORD OF THE HELIACAL RISING OF SIRIUS.

The first appearance of the Hittites during the reign of Senusert III of Egyptian Dynasty XII, during the reign of Khammurabi, the Babylonian *Hittites' First* contemporary of Abraham, and during the life of Abraham in Canaan, fixes the *Appearance* date of the beginning of the reign of Senusert III not earlier than 2100–1900 *Dynasty XII* B.C. This fixing of the date is apart from any real or imaginary astronomical *in Egypt.* fixing.

For many centuries around this period—*vide* Oppolzer's calculations— —Sirius rose heliacally at Memphis on 18th July (Julian) in three out of every consecutive four years, and on 19th July (Julian) in one out of every *The Heliacal* consecutive four years. From 2100 to 1900 B.C. (astronomical) these dates *Rising of Sirius* coincided with 1st July (Gregorian) and 2nd July (Gregorian) respectively. *Dynasty XII.* Hence from 2100 to 1900 B.C. (astronomical) Sirius rose heliacally on 1st July (Gregorian) in three out of every consecutive four years, and on the 2nd July (Gregorian) in one out of every consecutive four years.

Amongst a number of Papyri discovered at Kahun, and belonging to the period of Dynasty XII, were two mentioning the heliacal rising of Sirius in the 7th year of Senusert III. The account containing this notice narrates that on Day 25, Month III, Season Pert (Growing and Harvest), the superintendent *The XIIth* of the temple advised the governor that arrangements were being made for the *Dynasty* festival of the heliacal rising of Sirius which would take place on Day 16 of the *Heliacal Rising* following month. The narrative, continuing in diary form, gives, under Day *Day 17 of 8th* 17, Month IV, Season Pert, an inventory of the " festival offerings for the rise *Month.* of the star Sirius " on that date.

The heliacal rising therefore took place on 1st or 2nd July (Gregorian), 226 days after the commencement of the Calendar year. The current Calendar *Current* year, therefore began on the 17th or 18th November (Gregorian)—16 or 17 days *began on* after the fixed position of the true beginning of the year. *17–18th November (Gregorian).*

This interval, obviously, indicates why special attention was directed to *On 17th Day of* the Sirius rising in this particular year. In this year Sirius rose heliacally on *1st Calendar* Day 17 of the 8th Calendar Month, and the first day of the current Calendar *Fixed Pyramid* year began on Day 17 of the 1st month of the fixed Calendar year, as defined *1st November* by the Pyramid's 1st November phenomena. Here we find indicated the *Year.* connection between the two alternative month datings celebrated as the day of the Festival of the Dead. (Refer Sect. I, ¶¶ 28 and 29.)

¶ 56. THE FIXED NOVEMBER YEAR OF DYNASTIES I AND II.

Tables II and III have shown that the intercalations of the 360 days' *Annals of* year occurred at intervals of five or six years. The Annals of the early Dynasties, *Dynasties I and* of which the Palermo stone is a considerable fragment, indicate that the Festival *II give Feast of* of Sokar,[1] (Osiris) occurred after precisely this interval. *occurring every 5 or 6 Years.*

[1]Breasted, " Ancient Records," I, pp. 58-63.

Proves
Intercalations
Adjusting
Calendar Year
to Fixed 1st
November
Year.
Now Dr. Frazer ("Adonis, Osiris, Attis") has shown that the Festival of Sokar (Osiris) is identical with the Festival of the Dead. (Refer Sect. I, ¶ 26.) It therefore fell on the 1st November (Gregorian), (refer Sect. I, ¶ 25) which accounts for its celebration once only in every five or six years during the period of Dynasties I and II. The Palermo Stone, therefore, proves that an intercalary cycle kept the Calendar year adjusted to the 1st November year at the time of Dynasties I and II.

Both Calendar
Years..360 and
365 Days..thus
Adjusted.

The 103 Years'
Cycle.
Maspero and Budge, again, have shown repeatedly that the Epagomenal days—"the five days over the year"[1]—were known as early as the beginning of Egyptian Dynastic History. This necessarily implied that the year of 365 days was in use at the same time as the year of 360 days. As the latter was intercalated with respect to 1st November, the former must have been intercalated with respect to 1st November. It follows, then, that the two Calendar years followed the same Calendar Cycle. This is the case with the Calendar cycle of 103 years.

(Refer Tables II and III, Sect. I., ¶ 31.)

¶ 57. THE MONTH NAME REVISIONS FROM DYNASTY XII TO 6TH CENTURY B.C.

XXth Dynasty
Fixed Celestial
Sothic
Calendar.
The XXth Dynasty Calendar on the walls of the Temple of Amen at Medinet Habu give the months of the Celestial or Sothic (fixed) year and the month datings of the annual festivals. This has no relation to the contemporary *vague* or *wandering* year. Day 1 Month I begins with the Heliacal rising "Hathor"
Name of its 4th
Month. of Sirius, and Day 1, Month IV of the Calendar is the Day of the Feast of Hathor. The latter proves that *Hathor* was the name of the 4th month of the Calendar (and that *Mesore* was the name of the 1st month) at the time of Dynasty XX.

Period Dynasty
XII "Hathor"
4th Calendar
Month.

Period
Dynasty XVIII
"Hathor" 3rd
Calendar
Month.

9th Century
B.C. to 3rd
Century A.D.
"Hathor" 3rd
Calendar
Month.
This identification of the names for the Calendar months agrees with the identification for the period of Dynasty XII.[2] It does not, however, agree with the identification of month names for Dynasty XVIII. Hathor was the name of Month III, and Thoth the name of Month I of the Calendar at the time of Dynasty XVIII.[3] This, again, was the identification holding from the end of the 9th century B.C. to the middle of the 3rd century A.D.

3 Calendar
Revisions
between
Dynasty XII
and 9th
Century B.C.

High Nile
dating 3rd Year
Uasarkon II.
It is obvious then, that the Calendar was revised between Dynasty XII and Dynasty XVIII; again, between Dynasty XVIII and Dynasty XX; and again, between Dynasty XX and the end of the 9th century B.C. The latter revision certainly took place after the 3rd year of Uasarkon II, as is proved by the high Nile dating recorded for that year at Thebes. (Refer ¶¶ 48-53). Discussion of this subject will be resumed later.

[1] See also Petrie, "Historical Studies," p. 8.
[2] Petrie, "Historical Studies," II, pp. 8 and 22, and *Ancient Egypt*, 1917, p. 45; revision of "Historical Studies."
[3] Month name identifications on a clepsydra of Amenhotep III, Karnak. *Ancient Egypt*, 1917, pp. 42-45.

¶ 58. THE XXth DYNASTY CELESTIAL OR SOTHIC CALENDAR.

The XXth Dynasty fixed Sothic Calendar and its datings (¶ 57) are stated in Table VIII. The Gregorian month datings follow from the facts :— *XXth Dynasty Celestial Calendar Dating.*

(1) That Dynasty XX certainly began around 1200 B.C.

(2) That around, and for several centuries after 1200 B.C., Sirius rose heliacally three years in every consecutive four years on July 19th (Julian), and one year in every consecutive four years on July 18th (Julian).

(3) That July 18-19 (Julian) coincided with July 7-8 (Gregorian) from 1301 to 1100 B.C. inclusive.

Table VIII shows that the Feast of Sokar (Osiris) was celebrated on 31st *Festival Osiris Sokar.* October or 1st November (Gregorian). In spite, then, of the contemporaneous vague year Calendar, the XXth Dynasty Egyptians celebrated the Festival of *31st October— 1st November* Sokar—the Festival of the Dead—on the same day of the solar year as had been *(Gregorian) as Dynasties I* observed during the period of Dynasties I to XII. *to XII.*

¶ 59. THE PTOLEMAIC CELESTIAL OR SOTHIC CALENDAR.

This fixed Sothic Calendar and its festival datings, together with the *Ptolemaic Celestial* description of the festival rites of Osiris, as observed in Ptolemaic times, are *Calendar Dating.* contained in a long inscription in the Temple of Osiris at Denderah. The *Festival Osiris* essential festivals and their month datings are stated in Table IX. The *Khent-Amenti.* Gregorian month datings follow from the facts :— *28th-29th October (Gregorian).*

(1) That the inscription belongs to a period between 301 B.C. and 102 B.C. when the heliacal rising of Sirius occurred on one or other of the days July 19-20 (Julian).

(2) That from 301 B.C. to 102 B.C. July 19-20 (Julian) coincided with July 15-16 (Gregorian).

Table IX shows that the Ptolemaic Festival of Osiris Khent-Amenti takes the place of the XXth Dynasty Festival of Osiris Sokar. The Ptolemaic Festival lasted for 18 days—from Day 12, Month IV (October 24-25) to Day 30, Month IV (November 12-13)—"and set forth the nature of Osiris in his triple aspect as dead, dismembered, and finally reconstituted by the union of his scattered limbs. In the first of these aspects he was called Khent-Amenti, in the second Osiris-Sop, and in the third Sokar." The Festival of Osiris Khent-Amenti—the festival of the *dead* Osiris—fell on October 28-29 (Gregorian), a slip of three days being indicated from the original placing still retained in the time of the XXth Dynasty. The slip is accounted for, as will *The Nominal Sothic Year of* be shown later, by the fact that whereas the later Egyptian astronomer priests *365.25 Days* (Dynasty XX to Ptolemaic times) reckoned the Sothic year as 365.25 days, *The Nominal Solar Year of* they also reckoned the Solar year as 365.24 days, to obtain Precession of the *365.24 Days.* Solar year round the Sothic year once in 36,525 years. The difference between *Give Precessional* the true solar and the nominal solar year amounted to 2½ to 3 days between *Cycle of 36,525 Years* 1200 B.C. and 100 B.C.

TABLE VIII.

XXᴛʜ DYNASTY DATINGS OF ANNUAL FESTIVALS.

Brugsch, " Egypt under the Pharaohs " Vol. II, p. 156.		Gregorian Month Datings, for period 1301-1100 B.C.
New Year's Day, Rising of Sirius ..	.. Day 1, Month I	= 8th–9th July.
Feast of Hathor	.. Day 1, Month IV	= 6th–7th October.
Feast of Sacrifice	.. Day 20, Month IV	= 25th–26th October
Opening of the Tomb of Osiris ..	.. Day 21, Month IV	= 26th–27th October.
Feast of the Hoeing of the earth ..	.. Day 22, Month IV	= 27th–28th October
Preparation of the Sacrificial Altar in the Tomb of Osiris	.. Day 23, Month IV	= 28th–29th October.
Exhibition of the Corpse of Sokar (Osiris) in the Midst of the Sacrifice ..	.. Day 24, Month IV	= 29th–30th October.
Feast of the Mourning Goddesses ..	.. Day 25, Month IV	= 30th–31st October
Feast of Sokar (Osiris)	.. Day 26, Month IV	= 31st October–1st November.
Feast of Palms	.. Day 27, Month IV	= 1st–2nd November.
Feast of the Precession of the Obelisk ..	.. Day 28, Month IV	= 2nd–3rd November.
Feast of the Exhibition of the Image of Did (the symbol of Osiris)	.. Day 30, Month IV	= 4th–5th November.
Feast of the Coronation of Horus ..	.. Day 1, Month V	= 5th–6th November.

TABLE IX.

PTOLEMAIC DATINGS FOR THE OSIRIAN FESTIVAL RITES.

Budge, " Gods of the Egyptians," Vol. II, pp. 128-129. (for Osirian Festival Month Datings).	" Celestial " Calendar Month Datings.	Equivalent Gregorian Month Datings.
" Celestial " New Year's Day, Heliacal Rising of Sirius	.. Day 1, Month I	= 15th–16th July.
	Day 1, Month IV	= 13th–14th October.
Feast of the Hoeing of the earth ..	.. Day 12, Month IV	= 24th–25th October
Festival of *Pert* (" Coming forth " or " growing ")	.. Day 14, Month IV	= 26th–27th October.
Festival of Osiris Khent-Amenti ..	.. Day 16, Month IV	= 28th–29th October.
" Model of the god of the preceding year " taken out from its place and buried " suitably, and the new Osiris was " embalmed in the Sanctuary "	.. Day 24, Month IV	= 6th–7th November.
Feast of the Exhibition of the Image of Did, the symbol of Osiris	.. Day 30, Month IV	= 12th–13th November.

In the same period, the nominal solar year had receded from the Sothic year to the extent of ten days. This accounts for the ten days difference between the XXth Dynasty and the Ptolemaic seasonal datings.

Comparison of the two Calendars (Tables VIII and IX) again, shows that in both XXth Dynasty and Ptolemaic times, the Feast of the Exhibition of the Image of Did was attached to Day 30, Month IV. This indicates that certain festivals were not seasonal and that such festivals remained attached to the day of the month at which tradition of a certain period placed them. *Non-seasonal Datings of Two Calendars (Dynasty XX and Ptolemaic) Fixed.*

¶ 60. THE NUMERICAL DETAILS OF THE PTOLEMAIC FESTIVAL.

In the Ptolemaic celebration of the Festival, 34 Papyrus boats conveyed 34 images. These obviously were derived from, and symbolise, the 34 intercalary periods of the 103 years' cycle (Tables II and III). From Tables II and III, we observe as follows :—

34 intercalated years of the 360 days' calendar
    = 34 intercalated years of 365 days' calendar,
    = $34\frac{1}{2}$ years of 360 days (not intercalated),
    = 12,420 days = 414 months of 30 days each.

The numerical significance of the enumeration here becomes apparent, For, since

$$4 \times 414 \text{ months} = 1656 \text{ months},$$

and since the Osirian texts state that " one day counts for a month," so, presumably, one month counts for a year, and therefore, 1656 months symbolise 1656 years. This gives symbolically the date of the Noachian Deluge Ending 1656 A.K., as in Table V. *Numbers Associated with Ptolemaic Ceremonies Give Deluge Date 1656 A.K.*

A similar numerical identity—giving the Deluge Date 1656 A.K.—was found by Oppert,[1] in the case of the mythical chronology of the Babylonians. *Similar Babylonian Identity.*

¶ 61. THE HYKSOS CALENDAR RECORD OF AN INTERCALARY CYCLE.

From the earliest dynastic times, the Egyptians referred to the epagomenal days—the five days over the year—as the birthdays of certain gods and goddesses. These were, respectively, in the order of the days, Osiris, Horus, Set (Typhon), Isis and Nephthys. Now the civil calendar of 360 days was in use from Dynasty I to Dynasty XII at least, in conjunction with the Calendar year of 365 days. At this early period, then, the epagomenal days—the birthdays of the five gods or goddesses—coincided, between intercalary years, with certain five days of Month I, Season of Sowing. Immediately after an intercalation, Day 1, Month I of the 360 days' Calendar would follow the fifth of the Epagomenal days of the 365 days' Calendar. In the second year after an intercalation, Days 1 to 5, Month I, of the 360 days Calendar would coincide with the five Epagomenal days of the 365 days Calendar. *"The Five Days Over the Year." The Birthdays of 1. Osiris, 2. Horus, 3. Set, 4. Isis, 5. Nephthys. These Birthdays in Relation to Intercalated Calendar Year of 360 Days.*

[1] Gött, Gel. Nachrichten. 1877, p. 205.

Now there is precisely such a record as this on the back of the Rhind Mathematical Papyrus.[1] This Papyrus was compiled during the reign of a Hyksos king (Dynasty XV or XVI), and Egyptologists generally believe it to be of an earlier date than Asseth, the last Hyksos king.

The record states as follows :—

" Year II, Month I, Day 3, birth of Set ; the majesty of this god caused his voice (to be heard)."

" Birth of Isis, the heaven rained."

The record states that the birthday of Set (the third of the Epagomenal days) fell on Day 3, Month I, and that the birthday of Isis (the fourth of the Epagomenal days) followed, obviously on Day 4, Month I. As the coincidence noted always occurred in the second year after an intercalation, it is obvious that the Hyksos record indicates two facts. These are :—

(1) That in Hyksos times (Dynasties XV and XVI) the intercalated Calendar years of 360 and 365 days—in use from Dynasty I to XII— were still in use at the time of Dynasty XV or XVI.

(2) That such intercalations occurred at the intervals of five or six years found established at the time of Dynasties I and II.

The Hyksos Calendar record on the Rhind Mathematical Papyrus therefore proves, in conjunction with the preceding data, that the fixed November year and the conforming intercalated Calendar years of 360 and 365 days were in continuous use from Dynasty I to Dynasty XV or XVI.

¶ 62. EARLY EGYPTIAN EXAMPLES OF " THE ALMANAC TRADITION."

One point, however, requires to be cleared up. The Hyksos' Calendar record, under " birth of Set," on Day 3, Month I, states that " the majesty of the god caused his voice (to be heard)." This does not mean that thunder was heard on this day in the particular year recorded. Any ancient or modern almanac— by the kind of reference given—will show what is meant. The record is an early example of what we now term " The Almanac Tradition." Almost every Almanac, in any year, gives the anniversary of the Battle of Waterloo. In this case of the Hyksos' record, the day is the anniversary of the day upon which Set, at his birth, first rended the sky (the goddess Nuît) with his thunderbolts. Thus the *Egyptian Book of the Dead*[2] refers to Set as the god who " letteth loose the storm clouds and the thunder in the horizon of heaven." According to Plutarch, Set tore his mother's bowels at birth. Set's mother, Nuît, being the sky goddess.

Similarly, Isis was not only the primitive goddess of grain, but as such, was also the goddess of verdure, moisture and rain, and is referred to as " the wife of the lord of the Inundation, the creatrix of the Nile flood."[3] Her tears for

[1] Petrie, " Historical Studies," II.
[2] Budge, " Gods of the Egyptians," Vol. II, pp. 246-7.
[3] Budge, " Gods of the Egyptians," Vol. II, p. 214.
Moret, " Kings and Gods of Egypt," p. 106.

the dead Osiris were supposed to produce the Inundation. Hence the Hyksos record refers to Day 4, Month I of the current Calendar year as falling upon the anniversary of the " birth of Isis," when " the heaven rained." In this case also, as in the case of Set, we have an early example of the " Almanac Tradition." It is unnecessary, therefore, to point out that the record does not refer to rain falling upon this day in the particular year of the record.

Tradition Annually Recorded.

Hyksos' Calendar Record Not a Dated Record of Thunder and Rain.

This explanation has been rendered necessary owing to the fact that the dates of the Hyksos' Dynasties have been " fixed " from the supposed occurrence of rain on the day and month stated.

Fixing Hyksos' Date on Such Supposition.

¶ 63. THE ESTABLISHING OF THE VAGUE YEAR.

The Egyptian " Book of the Sothis," preserved by Syncellus, states that the vague or wandering year of 365 days was first instituted by the last Hyksos king, Asseth. The statement is :—" This king (Asseth) added the five Epagomenae and in his time they say the Egyptian year was reckoned as 365 days, having before this time counted only 360." Obviously, the statement means that prior to Asseth, the last Hyksos king, the civil Calendar of 360 days was the intercalated year, and that Asseth, who reigned not long prior to Dynasty XVIII, instituted, as the civil year, the unintercalated or vague year of 365 days.

The Last Hyksos King, Asseth, Introduces the " Vague " Year of 365 Days, as the Civil Calendar Year.

Two facts confirm this. These are :—

(1) That from Dynasties I to XV or XVI, according to the evidences discussed, the Civil Calendar year was an intercalated Calendar year, adjusted at intervals of five or six years, to the fixed 1st November Agricultural year.

Confirmed by Proofs of Fixed Year Dynasties I to XVI.

(2) That the month datings for the recorded heliacal risings of Sirius during Dynasty XVIII determine that the vague year was then in use, but had not long prior to Dynasty XVIII, been in its true 1st November-beginning position—with the Calendar Season of Sowing coincident with the actual Season of Sowing.

Confirmed by Vague Year Month Datings of Heliacal Risings of Sirius during Dynasty XVIII.

All the evidences, then, from the period of Dynasties I to XVIII, combine to prove :—

(1) That the year was a fixed November-beginning Agricultural year from Dynasty I to XVI.

Fixed Year Dynasties I to XVI.

(2) That the last king of Dynasty XVI first established the vague or wandering year ; and

(3) That the first Egyptian records. employing the vague year for month datings, are the records of Dynasty XVIII.

Vague Year Dynasty XVII Onwards

SECTION III.—DETAILED TECHNICAL DESCRIPTION OF PLATES.

Pyramids of Khufu and Khafra.

¶ 64. FRONTISPIECE.   UPPER PERSPECTIVE VIEW.   RESTORATION OF THE PYRAMIDS AND TEMPLES OF GIZEH PLATEAU.

Sphinx.

Khafra's Granite Temple.

The 1st (Great) Pyramid of Khufu (Dynasty IV) is shown on the right, and the 2nd Pyramid of Khafra (Dynasty IV) on the left.   In the right foreground appear the Sphinx and part of the Granite Temple of Khafra.   Leading from the latter is shown the causeway to the 2nd Pyramid.   The similar causeway to the Great Pyramid is shown in the right hand middle distance.

Pyramid Causeways.

Arrangement of Pyramids and Temples to avoid intercepting shadows and reflexions.

Attention is directed to the fact that none of the larger pyramids are in the line of the Great Pyramid's noon shadows or reflexions, and that the smaller pyramids and temples do not interfere with the projection of these.

¶ 65. PLATE I.   PLAN OF STONEHENGE.   STONE CIRCLE AND OUTER EARTH CIRCLE.

Reconstructed from Sir William Flinders Petrie's Survey, " Stonehenge," and from data in Mr. Edgar Barclay's " Stonehenge."

Stonehenge Alignment and Date.

" Slaughter Stone."

The axis line XY is shown as determined by Sir Norman Lockyer from the existing alignment.   As calculated by Lockyer, this alignment is directed to the point of Sunrise at the Summer Solstice, 1680 B.C. ± 200 years.   The fallen position of the so-called " Slaughter Stone " has nothing whatever to do with the sunrise alignment.

Outer Earth Circle and Lockyer's Theory.

The Earth Circle's Agricultural Year.

November 8.

February 4.

Lockyer considers that the construction of the outer Earth Circle was long prior to the erection of the Stone Circle.   He dates the Earth Circle about 2000 B.C., and considers from the existing evidence that the agricultural year was in use at that time.   Thus, standing at M on the Earth Circle, on left of Plate I, and looking over the upright stone A, in bottom left of Plate I, towards the corresponding upright stone B, on the middle right, gives the alignment pointing to Sunrise at commencement of Winter, November 8th, and end of Winter, February 4th.   The alignment AOB passes through O, the common centre of the Earth and Stone Circles.

May 6.

August 8.

Looking in the opposite direction over the upright stones, i.e., from N on the opposite side of the Earth Circle, gives the alignment BOA pointing to Sunset at the commencement of Summer, May 6th, and end of Summer, August 8th.

Earth Circle's Solstitial Alignment.

Standing at P on the Earth Mound, in the middle left of Plate I, and looking over the upright stone A in the lower left, gives the alignment PA pointing to Sunset of Winter Solstice.   Looking from Q on the Mound, in lower right of Plate, across the upright stone B, in middle right of Plate, gives the alignment QB pointing to Sunrise of Summer Solstice.   The Earth Circle, therefore, was designed to give both the points of the astronomical solar year, as well as the points of the agricultural solar year.

¶ 66. PLATE II. PERSPECTIVE VIEW OF STONEHENGE AT TIME OF
SUNRISE OF SUMMER SOLSTICE, 1680 B.C.

The direction of sunrise is indicated by the direction of the shadows thrown by the *Summer Solstice Sunrise View of Stonehenge.* upright stones of the Stone Circle.

The so-called "Slaughter Stone" is shown in its present fallen position at the Avenue *Uncertainty Concerning "Slaughter Stone."* opening of the Earth Circle. Not enough is known of its object to justify attempt at restoration. It may have been a portion of an Entrance Trilithon, similar to the five large Trilithons shown within the Stone Circle. But conjecture is futile.

Attention is directed to the short upright stone of the Stone Circle shown in right foreground. *Peculiarity concerning one short upright of Stone Circle and original Gap in Lintel Circle.* As Mr. Edgar Barclay has shown, the present condition of this stone is as it was quarried and erected. The gap in the Lintel Circle is therefore as originally constructed. The gap may have been left intentionally to permit of the entrance of the two high poles of banners, festoons or other decorations paraded at the celebrations of the rituals of the temple.

¶ 67. PLATE III. MAP OF THE NILE DELTA.

The central axis of the Nile Delta runs due North and South, and is the Meridian line *Great Pyramid Meridian Central Axis of Nile Delta.* passing through the Great Pyramid of Gizeh. This might be a coincidence were it not for the *Accident or Design.* fact that all the intentional phenomena of the noon reflexions and shadows of the Great Pyramid were symmetrical to the Delta with respect to this Meridian line.

Thus on 1st November, the Pyramid's East and West noon reflexions each presented a *Pyramid's 1st November Phenomena Define Nile Delta.* vertical surface of reflexion to the observer North of the Pyramid. These vertical surfaces defined the North-East and North-West directions respectively from the Pyramid's East and West sides. The line of each vertical surface was the continuation of the respective diagonal of the Pyramid's base, and therefore, made an angle of 45° with the central Meridian *Pyramid at Centre of Oriented Quadrant of Nile Delta.* line. This indicates one of the reasons for the selection of the Pyramid's site. The intention obviously was that the Great Pyramid should appear as the centre of the Quadrant of the Circle that defines the Nile Delta.

Again, as seen along the central Meridian line at each noon of Autumn, Winter, and *Pyramid's South Noon Reflexion above the Horizontal during Autumn, Winter, and Spring, but below the Horizontal during Summer.* Spring, the South reflexion from the Pyramid was thrown high into the air. Rising first above the horizontal at the commencement of Autumn, the elevation of this noon reflexion increased during Autumn, reached its maximum at Mid-Winter, and decreased towards and during Spring, finally falling below the horizontal at the termination of Spring. On the first day of Summer, this South noon reflexion became horizontal.

At Mid-Summer noon the reflexion reached its lowest depression, thereafter becoming less depressed, until it again became horizontal at noon of the last day of Summer.

¶ 68. PLATE IV. MAP OF THE PYRAMIDS, TOMBS AND TEMPLES ON THE
PLATEAU OF GIZEH; AND MERIDIAN SECTION THROUGH THE
GREAT PYRAMID.

Compiled from Col. Howard Vyse's "Pyramids of Gizeh," Prof. C. P. Piazzi Smyth's
"Life and Work at the Great Pyramid," Prof. W. M. Flinders Petrie's "Pyramids and
Temples of Gizeh," and Edgar's "Great Pyramid Passages," Vol. I.

The Meridian Section lies along the central axis of the Nile Delta figured on Plate III,
and defined as the Pyramid Meridian Line.

In the North-West corner of the Map Plan is figured part of a spur from the Gizeh
Plateau. The height of this spur is shown on the Meridian Section. From the data thus
given it is seen that the limiting point of the West noon reflexion from the Great Pyramid on

1st November lay on the spur referred to, and in the same level horizontal plane (practically) as the Pyramid pavement base. From this indication one might expect to find on the spur mentioned some boundary mark or other indication marking the limit of the first November noon reflexion, or some other evidence of this spur having been dressed down, or levelled up, to receive the projection at the level of the Pyramid base. No search, however, for such a boundary mark, or signs of dressing down has yet been made, for hitherto the reasons for its probable existence have not been disclosed.

In any case it is evident that the 1st November West noon reflexion did not extend beyond the spur shown.

In the case of the East noon reflexion on 1st November it is a different matter. This reflexion was projected on to the lower plane of the cultivated land, and therefore, continued considerably further than is figured on Plate VII. The same remark applies in the case of Plate VIII. The extent of the projection could not, however, alter the surface planes of the reflexions. Hence the *vertical* surface of the East noon reflexion on 1st November continued further in its direction due North-East.

¶ 69. PLATE V. THE NOON REFLEXIONS OF THE SUMMER HALF OF THE YEAR, *i.e.* during the period between the Vernal Equinox and the following Autumnal Equinox.

Fig. A gives plan of the noon reflexions at the Equinoxes, projected on to the plane of the Pyramid's base level. N. S. E. and W. refer to the North, South, East and West. The outstanding feature is supplied by the East and West noon reflexions. One base line of each of these reflexions, DQ for the West reflexion, and AR for East reflexion, runs due North-West and due North-East respectively, from the West and East corners of the Pyramid's South base side, DA.

Fig. a is the elevation of *Fig. A*. In this the South reflexion T¹OT¹¹A, is elevated as it is, in varying degrees of elevation during Autumn, Winter and Spring.

Fig. B gives plan of the noon reflexions at the beginning and ending of Summer. Ten days after the beginning of Summer, and ten days before the end of Summer RBCQ is a straight line—the North base side of the Pyramid produced—running due East and West.

Fig. b is the elevation of *Fig. B*. In this the South noon reflexion T¹OT¹¹A, is horizontal at the beginning and ending of Summer. (Refer last para. of note to Plate III.)

All these diagrams of Plate V show the North surfaces ORB and OQC of the East and West noon reflexions inclined southwards from the observer in the North. This general feature, with varying degrees of inclination southwards, held between 11th February and 1st November of each year.

¶ 70. PLATE VI. NOON REFLEXIONS AT THE SUMMER SOLSTICE.

Fig. C. Plan of Noon reflexions.

BPC is the longest North noon reflexion of the year.
DQC is the shortest West noon reflexion of the year.
ARB is the shortest East noon reflexion of the year.
ATD is the shortest South noon reflexion of the year.
Q and R reach their Southernmost limits.
Fig. c is the elevation of *Fig. C.*

¶ 71. PLATE VII. PYRAMID NOON REFLEXIONS AND SHADOWS.

Figs. D and E indicate on plan how the surfaces ORB and OQC of the East and West noon reflexions as seen from the North, gradually lost their inclination towards the South as 1st November approached, when they became vertical and pointed due North-East and North-West respectively, along the Pyramid base diagonals DOB and AOC respectively, produced to R and Q (*Fig. E*).

The reverse process happened on 11th February, when the surfaces ORB and OAC of the East and West reflexions again became vertical and pointed North-East and North-West respectively. Prior to this date, and since 1st November, these surfaces inclined, with varying degrees of inclination overhanging towards the observer in the North. After the 11th February they again assumed the inclination towards the South.

Fig. D shows the Pyramid's North face first appearing in noon shadow at 14th October, but throwing no shadow on the pavement base. On successive noons after 14th October, the shadow, thrown on to the pavement base, gradually extended, reached its Northernmost limit at the Winter Solstice, commenced to creep back after the Winter Solstice, and reached its final stage of coincidence with the North base line on 28th February (as on 14th October), after which it disappeared until the following 14th October.

Fig. E shows the extent of pavement shadow on 1st November.

Figs. d and e are the elevations of *Figs. D and E* respectively.

Side notes: Variations of East and West Reflexions. Their Vertical Surfaces on 1st November and 11th February are Directed North-East and North-West. Appearance and Disappearance, and Variations of North Noon Shadow.

¶ 72. PLATE VIII. PYRAMID NOON REFLEXIONS AND SHADOWS.

The diagrams here are typical of the Winter noon phenomena between 1st November and 11th February. *Figs. F and G* show in plan the surfaces ORB and OAC of the East and West noon reflexions, as seen by the observer in the North, overhanging towards the observer. In both figures the dotted lines on plan, BR and CQ, which lie on the Pyramid pavement base level, are covered or overhung by the sloping surfaces of reflexion ORA and OQD. The figures also show that the same sloping surfaces of reflexion overhang the noon shadow area of the Pyramid's North face slope, BOC.

Figs. f and g are the elevations of *Figs. F and G*.

Figs. F and f give the noon reflexion and shadow phenomena for 2nd December and 12th January. *Fig. f* shows that on these days the noon reflexion of the Pyramid's South face slope is normal to that surface, *i.e.*, the sun's noon rays are reflected directly back in the direction from which they came. In other words, the angle of incidence = angle of reflexion = 0°.

Figs. G and g give the noon reflexion and shadow phenomena for the Winter Solstice. R and Q are the furthest Northern limits of the year for the East and West noon reflexions respectively.

V is the furthest Northern limit of the year for the North noon shadow.

T¹OAT¹¹ (*fig. g*), is the highest elevation of the year for the South noon reflexion.

Side notes: The Peculiarity of the East and West Noon Reflexions during Winter. The Normal Noon Reflexion from South Face Slope 2nd December and 12th January. Winter Solstice Noon Phenomena.

¶ 73. PLATE IX. CHART SHOWING THE SEASONAL PHENOMENA AND ACTIVITIES OF THE *SOLAR YEAR* IN ANCIENT EGYPT COMPARED WITH THE SEASONAL PHENOMENA AND ACTIVITIES OF THE EARLY EGYPTIAN *CALENDAR YEAR* COMPILED FROM THE DATED RECORDS OF THE PERIOD OF DYNASTIES VI TO XII.

General remarks :—

So far as we are aware, this chart is the first comprehensive and comparative abstract of all the known data concerning the relation between the Calendar Year and the Solar Year in the period preceding the XVIIIth Egyptian Dynasty. A careful study of the data of this series of diagrams will well repay both the general reader and the Egyptological

Side notes: A New Comprehensive and Comparative Abstract of Fundamental Egyptological Data.

<table>
<tr><td>The Bearing of the Abstract upon the question of Egyptian Chronology.</td><td>student or expert. For within the bounds of one presentation are given all the scientific data upon which the accepted theory of modern Egyptological chronology stands or falls. The Chart shows that the Calendar Seasons synchronised with the actual Seasons during the period of Dynasties VI to XII, and not only so, but that the commencement of the Calendar Year at that time synchronised with the commencement of the actual Egyptian Agricultural Year.</td></tr>
</table>

As the accepted theory of Egyptological chronology is based on a *wandering* Calendar year at that time, the importance of the synchronisms of Plate IX must be evident to everyone giving the matter consideration. So certain is the Chart to tell its own story that we content ourselves with the single assertion, that the data are correctly plotted from all the known facts.

Explanation of Arrangement :—

¶ 73a. NILE FLOW AND HELIACAL RISING OF SIRIUS.

The Solar Year Time Basis of the Abstract.   *Column* (3) of Plate IX contains the time basis with respect to which all the various data in the remaining columns are arranged. In this column appear plotted to scale of duration in days, the months of the modern (Gregorian) year commencing with November.

Annual Curve of Nile Discharge.   *Column* (4), as explained on Chart, gives the typical annual curve of Nile Discharge at Memphis.

Heliacal Rising of Sirius. (Gregorian Month Datings).   Inset is the curve of Heliacal Risings of the Star Sirius at Latitude 30° N. The risings are stated with reference to the Modern (Gregorian) month dates reduced from Oppolzer's calculations giving the Julian month dates over the period indicated. (Oppolzer, " Ueber die Länge des Sirius-jahrs und der Sothis periode," Vol. 90, Sitzungsberichte, Vienna **Oppolzer's and Knobel's Calculations.** Academy). Oppolzer's calculations are extended back to 7171 B.C. by Dr. E. B. Knobel, Historical Studies. (Brit., Sch., Arch., Egypt., 1911, pp. 6 and 7.)

Oppolzer took the depression of the Sun at the time of the heliacal rising of Sirius as 10° 48′.

Heliacal Rising Defined.   The heliacal rising of a star is its first observed rising after it has been invisible for some time in close proximity to the sun.

XIIth Dynasty Sirius Rising.   Refer description Plate X for XIIth dynasty record of heliacal rising of Sirius.

Annual Curve of Nile Level.   *Column* (6) gives practically the same Nile flow data as *column* (4), but for gaugings taken 57 years earlier, and stated in terms of Nile level instead of discharge.

Comparison of Nile Data with Data of Herodotus.   These two columns give practically the fluctuations of Nile flow and its range of date variation. These agree with the statement of Herodotus for Memphis in the 5th century B.C. This statement is reduced to graphical comparison in *columns* (4) *and* (6).

Column (5) gives merely an intermediate stage of data in the derivation of *column* (4) data.

¶ 73b. THE ACTIVITIES OF THE YEAR.

Wilkinson's Activities of the Solar Year in Ancient Egypt   *Column* (7) gives the activities and seasonal phenomena of the *Solar* year in ancient Egypt, at the dates stated by Sir Gardner Wilkinson. These are accepted by all Egyptologists of repute as the reliable basis of this branch of study.

Graphs of Same.   In *Column* (7) the information is reduced to graphical form, diminishing of activity being indicated by the tapering off of areas.

Irrigation, Sowing, Harvest Graphs.   Wilkinson supplies the dates and data for the graphical areas of activity in Irrigation, Sowing and Harvest.

The hot season is known, the tapering off in graphical area representing diminution of Hot Season Graphs. heat.

The periods of activity for distant quarrying expeditions depended upon three factors. These are :—

(1) The need for the available labour in sowing and harvest, and to a less extent for irrigation purposes.

(2) The impossibility of efficient quarrying in the hot season. Distant Quarrying Factors.

(3) The need in certain cases of utilising the rise of the Nile to float large quarried masses on barges.

These three factors determined the two distant quarrying periods of the year shown in *Column* (7).

¶ 73c. THE DISTANT QUARRYING PERIODS.

The 1st distant quarrying period, then, fell within the months II, III, and IV of the first 1st Distant Quarrying Period. season of the Agricultural year, *i.e.*, December to February inclusive. It began as sowing operations were finishing. It ended as harvesting became active. This is the principal December to February inclusive. distant quarrying period, for Sinai, Hat Nub and Hammamat, when High Nile Flood was not required for river transport.

The 2nd distant quarrying period began towards the end of the hot season, as the Nile 2nd Distant Quarrying Period began to rise, beginning thus early in order to have the quarried masses ready for the high Nile in September or Early October, and to enable the workmen to return for the middle of Early July to Mid-October the irrigation period at latest, and in time for the early sowing.

¶ 73d. IRRIGATION, SOWING, HARVEST, ETC.

Column (8) gives the details of Wilkinson's dated information concerning Irrigation, Wilkinson's Dates and Data concerning Sowing, and Harvest. Each item of information is given opposite its place in the modern Irrigation, Sowing, Harvest. months as stated by Wilkinson.

Column (9) gives the same information with respect to the Solar year as column (7). But Graphs of Activities of whereas Column (7) is based on Wilkinson's researches on ancient crops and agricultural Solar Year activities, independently of the dated records, the areas of activity in Column (9) are plotted from Records of Period entirely from the dated records of the period from Dynasty XVIII to XXX inclusive. During Dynasties XVIII-XXX this period the *wandering* calendar year was in use, and it is from the known, or in some early The Vague cases the approximately known, position of this wandering calendar year in the solar year at or Wandering Year Datings various stages in the period that the modern month datings of the records are found. of the Graphs for Dynasties XVIII-XXX.

¶ 73e. GRAPHS OF YEAR'S ACTIVITIES.

The agreement between the areas of Column (7) and the areas of Column (9) confirms Agreement of Graphs from what it was scarcely necessary to confirm, the accuracy of the data based on Wilkinson's Wilkinson's Data and Activities of the Agricultural Year. Graphs from Data of

With Columns (1) and (2) we come to the important feature of the charting. Dynasties XVIII-XXX.

Whereas Columns (7) and (9) give the activities of the *Solar* year in relation to the Emphasis *modern months* of Column (3), Column (1) gives the activities of the *Calendar* year in relation concerning Graphs from to the *Calendar months* of Column (2). " Solar "

It will assist the reader to follow the matter more clearly if he can suppose, in the first Year Datings, and Graphs from Early instance, that Columns (1) and (2) bear no relation to Column (3). " Calendar " Year Datings.

¶ 73f. THE INDEPENDENT GRAPHS.

Necessity for
considering
the two sets of
Graphs, in
first instance,
as matters
apart, and
resting solely
on their own
respective
bases.
Let the reader understand that Columns (1) and (2) are drawn up, independent of Columns (3) to (9), from the early Calendar year datings of the period of Dynasties VI to XII, the areas of activity of the *Calendar* year being stated with reference to Column (2); that Columns (1) and (2), thus attached to each other, were moved into position until the areas of Column (1) were opposite the corresponding areas of Columns (7) and (9); and that when this

The Agreement
of the two
Sets of Graphs
when
considered
in relation.
had been effected it was found that the *Calendar* year and its *Calendar* seasons of the period in question agreed with the actual Agricultural year and its seasons.

Agreement
proves a Fixed
Calendar
Year for period
Dynasties
VI-XII.
Columns (1) and (2), when synchronised with all the data of Columns (3) to (9) prove that the Calendar year at the time of Dynasties VI to XII was a *fixed* Calendar year. In other words, during Dynasties VI to XII, the vague or wandering year was not in use.

¶ 73g. COLUMN (1), XIIth DYNASTY FLAX HARVEST CALENDAR DATING.

XIIth Dynasty
Flax Harvest
" Calendar "
Dating agrees
with actual
dating of Flax
Harvest.
One important item beginning in Column (1) is the Flax Harvest dating given on a XIIth Dynasty record. (*El Bersheh*, II, Pls. 8 and 9.) The flax harvest is recorded as taking place between Day 23 and Day 27, Calendar Month IV, Calendar Season of Sowing, *i.e.*, 112 to 116 days after the beginning of the Calendar Year. Wilkinson, for ancient times, gives Flax as plucked in Lower and Middle Egypt, late February or early March, *i.e.*, late in the actual Month IV of the actual Season of Sowing, or early in Month I of the actual Season of Harvest.

The Calendar Dating and the actual Dating therefore agree, and the Calendar year began in November.

¶ 73h. COLUMN (1), XIIth DYNASTY HOT SEASON RECORD IN SINAI.

XIIth Dynasty
complaint
concerning
Hot Season
Expedition
to Sinai.
This is a fine example of an exception proving the rule.

Hor-ur-ra states on record at Serabit, Sinai (reign Senusert III or Amenemhat III):—

Calendar
Months
of Hot Season
agree with
actual Months
of Hot Season.
" I arrived in this land in Calendar Month III, Calendar Season of Growing (and Harvest), although it was not the season for going to this Mine-land."

" ....The highlands are hot in Summer, and the mountains brand the skin....... It is—[*uncertain*]—for it in this evil Summer season."

" ....I succeeded in mining the good sort, and I finished in the Calendar Month I, Calendar Season of Inundation. I brought genuine costly stone for the luxuries more than anyone who came (hither)........It was better that the accustomed seasons thereof......" (Breasted, *Records* I, 322, 323).

The hot months here are the 7th, 8th, and 9th months of the Calendar year.

The actual hot months are May, June, and July, respectively the 7th, 8th, and 9th months from November inclusive. This again confirms that the XIIth Dynasty Calendar Year was a fixed November Year.

Plate XI gives a list of all the known VIth to XIIth Dynasty seasonal records used for plotting areas in Column (1), Plate IX.

¶ 74. PLATE X. CHART OF LIMITS OF EARLY EGYPTIAN INTERCALATED CALENDAR YEAR, EGYPTIAN SEASONS, AND GREAT PYRAMID NOON REFLEXION AND SHADOW PHENOMENA STATED WITH REFERENCE TO THE MODERN (GREGORIAN) MONTHS.

The top item of chart—below Scale of Modern Months—represents the maximum and minimum limits of two of the three Early Egyptian Calendar Seasons. The basis of the rule governing intercalation was that the 1st month of the Calendar year (Month I, Calendar Season of Sowing), never began later than 60 days after the Autumnal Equinox. The evidence determining this rule will be given in the various details of same as they are met with in the projected series of volumes. Meantime it is deemed that the practical and simple nature of the rule will appeal to the general reader. The Intercalated Limits of the Early Egyptian "Calendar" Seasons.
The Rule fixing the Limits.

The other items of the chart, in light of the explanation of the preceding plates explain themselves. It will, however, be noted that the East and West co-ordinates of the East and West Pyramid noon reflexions are equal and always of constant value.

¶ 75. PLATE XI. RECORDS OF THE PERIOD OF DYNASTIES VI TO XII OF DISTANT QUARRYING EXPEDITIONS TO THE QUARRIES AT WADY HAMMAMAT AND HAT NUB, AND TO THE MINES AND QUARRIES OF SINAI.

The reader will observe that the days of the months are both stated and plotted to the scale of days and months of the Calendar year. From this feature of the charting, it will be seen, for the First Distant Quarrying Period, that only one dating occurs in Month I of the Calendar Season of Growing (Harvest), and only one in Month I of the Calendar Season of Sowing. The others are all concentrated in the period from Day 3, Month II to Day 4, Month IV, Calendar Season of Sowing. This shows clearly enough that the active period began in early December, as irrigation and sowing activities diminished (only one dating occurs before the 15th day of Month II, Calendar Season of Sowing), and ended early February when return for the Harvesting Season was due. First Distant Quarrying Period.
Maximum Activity Mid-December to Early February.

The Second Distant Quarrying Period was governed by the requirements as to Nile transport. In some cases it saved time and labour in the handling of large blocks, to utilise the inundation waters for floating off the large quarried masses on shallow barges, then sailing these down the Nile, to navigate the barges over the inundated country, and close up to the building site, before the inundation began to recede from the land. Second Distant Quarrying Period.
Maximum Activity Mid-September to Mid-October.

In such cases, in later times, quarrying began as early as the beginning of July, in the end of the Hot season, for the purpose of having the work ready for floating off over the inundated land to the building site during the extreme height of the Inundation. In discussing such cases, Professor Petrie (*Ancient Egypt*, 1914, p. 91) states, " The hot season work was more usual in later times." Practise in Later Times.

For early times, at Hammamat only, there is the single record of Sankh-kara (Dynasty XI), on Day 3, Month I, Calendar Season of Inundation. The other records of the period of Dynasties VI to XII are all concentrated in the second half of Month III, and the first half of month IV of the Calendar Season of Inundation. (Refer Plate IX, comparing these limits, Column (2), with maximum Nile flood, Columns (3) and (4).) Seasonal Period of Greatest Activity (2nd Quarrying) in Early Times.

¶ 75a. THE NILE TRANSPORTATION RECORD OF UNA.

The Hat Nub record of Una's expedition during the reign of Merenra (Dynasty VI), mentions the quarrying, and then, during 17 days of Month III, Calendar Season of Inundation, the building of the barge, followed by transportation during a second period of 17 days. Una concludes " Although there was no water on the [*thesu*] I landed in safety at the pyramid (called): 'Merenra-shines-and-is-Beautiful'." (Breasted, *Records*, I, p. 149.) Una's statement concerning Nile Navigation conditions.

The uncertain word *thesu* is generally translated " flats " but as Breasted states, this is " a pure guess."   Whatever the word does mean, it cannot apply to any shallows or sand-banks on the normal course of the river itself, but to lowlying grounds off the normal course of the river, and flooded only at high level of inundation.   For the same word occurs in a connection that decides against *thesu* applying to shallows on the normal course of the river. This is in an inscription of the reign of Senusert III (Dynasty XII), (Breasted, *Records*, I, p. 300), referring to the celebration of the rites of the Osirian Festival.   The inscription states " I championed Uenefer at ' That Day of Great Conflict.'   I slew all the enemies upon the ' flats ' (*thesu*) of Nedyt.   I conveyed him (the god) into the Barque (called) ' The Great'."

The Reference is to Low-Lying Grounds covered at Inundation.
A statement bearing upon the problem.

¶ 75b. THE SEASON OF UNA'S ARRIVAL AT MEMPHIS.

Una's arrival when Nile was already receding from Inundated Land.

It is clear then, that the expedition of Una during the reign of Merenra (Dynasty VI), arrived at Memphis when the Nile was already receding from the ' flats ' (*thesu*) there.   He had obviously endeavoured to time his arrival at Memphis at highest Nile, but had been delayed by the construction of his barge in 17 days, or else had been unfortunate in having a slightly earlier high Nile than he had anticipated.

Petrie's Original Opinion.

All the other records of the period of Dynasties VI to XII confirm that these are the facts of the case, thus justifying Sir William Flinders Petrie's original opinion in the earlier editions of his " History of Egypt," Vol. 1, p. 95.

Budge's Opinion.

Sir Ernest Budge states, " Petrie argues from this statement that when Una arrived off Memphis in the month Epiphi (Month III, Calendar Season of Inundation), the waters of the Nile had subsided so greatly that he was unable to float the boat or barge with its heavy load over the land which had been recently inundated, for the depth of the water on the land did not permit him to do so.   So far all is clear, and this is undoubtedly what the words in the hieroglyphics indicate—but the possibility of deducing any date for the reigning king from this circumstance is too remote to be seriously entertained for a moment." (Hist. Egypt, Vol. 1, 152–3.)

¶ 75c. DEVIATIONS FROM UNA'S NARRATIVE.

The Calendar Month of Una's arrival at Memphis.

One remark in the above calls for comment.   The record does not state that Una arrived in Month III of the Calendar Season of Inundation.   The month of arrival with his load at Memphis, is not stated.   Una merely records that he quarried his stone, and then, in 17 days of the month stated, constructed his barge.   In the following 17 days, probably in Month IV of the Calendar Season of Inundation, he came to Memphis, when the Inundation had already commenced to fall, and therefore, at the end of September at the earliest, or mid-October at latest.

How theories can govern the Translating of Records.
The Effect of the discovery of the XIIth Dynasty Sirius Dating.
A revision of Chronology and a revision of the rendering of Una's Record

This long explanation has been rendered necessary by certain revisions of Egyptological opinion following the discovery of the XIIth Dynasty record of the heliacal rising of Sirius. The revisions are not due to any new light upon the inscription of Una, but due to the revision of the Sothic year theory of chronology, based on the theory of an uninterrupted vague Calendar year from the earliest times.   The theory of one school—that of the long chronology—makes the date of Merenra as 4190 B.C.   The theory of the short chronology gives the date of Merenra as 2570 B.C.   The former requires the arrival of the expedition of Una at Memphis to have been at the end of April, whereas the latter requires the end of March.   Both cases are in the height of the Harvest Season.

¶ 75d. LOCAL AND DISTANT QUARRYING.

The Local Quarrying Calendar Datings of Dynasty III.

We adhere to Petrie's original identification of the seasons for long distance quarrying expeditions, as that identification is free from the subsequent bias of the Sothic year chronological theory.   In this connection the reader must understand that *local* quarrying dates are not included.   Local quarrying, *i.e.*, quarrying adjacent to building sites, could

PLATE XII.

THE GEOMETRY OF THE GREAT PYRAMID'S NOON REFLEXIONS AND SHADOWS.

FIG. A1.

WEST FACE

EAST TO WEST SECTION OF PYRAMID THROUGH Z-Z BELOW & FIG A3

Sun's Ray at Noon

Horizontal

Constant
$\hat{\theta}$

Constant Plane of Reflected Ray to FIG. 3

Constant $\hat{\psi} = 13^\circ - 42' - 28\cdot 6$

FIG. A2.

PLAN.

SOUTH

Z

Z

Constant

Reflected Ray on Plan.

$\hat{D}$ varies with Sun's Altitude.

$\hat{\beta}$

FIG. A4.

HORIZONTAL PLANE ODQN

H_1

H

O

F_1

F

G

$\hat{D}$
$\hat{C}$

$90°$

ψ

90°

FROM DIAGRAMS
$Tan \hat{D} = Tan \hat{C} \cdot cos \psi$
$\theta = 5°3'14"3$ $\psi = 2\theta - 90° = \cdot 54226·5$

F_1 G   90°   O $\hat{\theta}$ F
F_1 G   90°   O $\hat{C}$ F
ψ 90°

[To face p. 61.]

For Correction of Sun's Altitudes in Ancient Times:—
Newcomb's Expression for Obliquity (ϵ) of Ecliptic
Epoch 1850 A.D. $\epsilon = -257'1·346 - 46·837"·0·0013" + 0·0007"$
T in units of Centuries from 1850
(−) Before 1850
(+) After 1850
Sun's Altitude = $\hat{C}$

VERTICAL PLANE OF MERIDIAN

HORIZONTAL PLANE.

SLOPE OF PYRAMID

PLANE OF WEST FACE

Sun's Ray at Noon

X

T

S

A

B

E

C

D

O

P

Q

N

M

H

H_1

ψ

$\hat{C}$

R

Z

Z

K

CONSTANT PLANE OF REFLECTED RAY

PLANE NORMAL TO PYRAMID FACE

L

G

F

REFLECTED RAY AT NOON

Y

FIG. A3.

FIG. C.

NORTH FACE NOON SHADOW.

NORTH TO SOUTH PYRAMID SECTION LOOKING WEST.

PLANE CONTAINING SHADOW

Sun's Noon Ray

$\hat{C_1}$

$\hat{C_1}$

θ_1

θ

Z

FIG. B.

NORTH FACE NOON REFLEXION.

NORTH TO SOUTH PYD. SECTION LOOKING WEST OF

SOUTH FACE NOON REFLEXION.

Sun's Noon Ray

NORMAL

Noon Reflected Ray

$\hat{C}$

γ

90°

be carried on by small parties at any season of the year. Thus the dated stones of Seneferu's *Local* Meydum Pyramid (year 17), range from Day 22, Month II, Calendar Season of Growing *Quarrying* and Harvest, to Day 8, Month III, Calendar Season of Inundation. With the fixed November *during* year, this gives a local quarrying period beginning in the end of April, when harvest *Harvest, but* activities diminished, to the beginning of September, when irrigation operations became *during Hot* active, and, following which, early sowing commenced. (Petrie, Historical Studies, pp. 10–11.)

This shows that *local* quarrying was carried on in the hot weather—the workmen *Proves a* probably slackening off during the heat of the day—but not during Sowing or Harvest. *Calendar*

Seneferu's local quarrying dates, therefore, confirm the fixed November Calendar for *period* the time of the IIIrd Dynasty. *Dynasties III to XII.*

In the case of long distance quarrying, large working and carrying parties, accompanied by a military escort, were supplied. The numbers necessary were not available during *Labour and* Sowing and Harvest, and such long distance expeditions were not undertaken during the *Escorts for* hot weather. An exception to the latter case is the expedition of Hor-ur-ra, whose record *long distance* refers to the exceptional circumstances, and the hardships incidental thereto. (Refer *expeditions.* ¶ 73h.)

¶ 76. PLATE XII. THE GEOMETRY OF THE GREAT PYRAMID'S NOON REFLEXIONS AND SHADOWS.

The East and West Noon Reflexions.

Figs. A_1, A_2, A_3, and A_4 are those needing most explanation, as the basal geometry of the East and West Noon reflexions is not an easily comprehended matter.

Fig. A_1 gives the simplest aspect of the West Noon Reflexion. Supposing the Sun *East and West* could be directly over the Pyramid at noon, Fig. A_1 would represent the precise approach *Reflexions for* of the sun's ray and the reflexion of the ray from the Pyramid's West Face. This would *"Supposed"* be for an altitude of the Sun of 90°, which the sun never has at the Great Pyramid's latitude. *of Sun at* In such case the reflected ray seen in plan would be directed due West. (Fig. A_2.) *Zenith.*

For lower altitudes, however, Fig. A_1 gives precisely the noon conditions as they would *How East and* be seen by an observer—*i.e.*, the reader looking at the view given—standing in the North *West reflected* and looking towards the Pyramid in the vertical plane of approach of the Sun's ray shown. *Noon Rays* However low the Sun at noon, the ray would always appear vertical, and the reflected ray *would be seen* would always appear at the same angle from the West face. As seen in plan, however, *North by an* the lower the noon sun, the more would the reflected ray be swung round from West towards *Pyramid* the North. (Fig. A_2.) *Meridian.*

We can sum up in the following statement:—

For a particular point on the West Face Slope of the Pyramid, the successive lines, *The constant* traced out by the Sun's noon ray to that point on successive noons of the Solar year, lie *Plane of the* in a vertical plane running due North and South, and the successive lines traced out by the *East and West* noon reflected rays from the same point on successive noons of the year lie in a plane inclined *Reflexions.* 13°.42′ 28″.6 below the horizontal. (Fig. A_1.)

Fig. A_3. XA is a typical Sun's noon ray to the point O on the West face slope of the Pyramid. The vertical plane of all such successive noon rays is the plane XAOBS.

OGFH is the constant plane of reflexion defined above, and shown in elevation in Fig. A_1, depressed at the constant angle of 13°.42′ 28″.6 below the horizontal. The horizontal plane in Fig. A_3 is OBPN. The Constant angle ψ between the two planes is represented by NOM.

Whilst the
Plane of
Reflexion
(for East and
West Noon
Reflexions)
is constant, and
the East or
West
Co-ordinate
respectively is
constant, the
Lower the
Sun's altitude
becomes at
Noon, the more
the East or
West Noon
Reflexion
veers round
towards the
North

XAO is the path of the Sun's noon ray for a particular day. The plane normal to the Pyramid's West Face Slope containing the Sun's noon ray XAO is the plane AOE. The angle of incidence with reference to the West Face Slope is, therefore, the angle AOE. The angle of reflexion must lie in the same plane continued. Hence AOE and OFL lie in the same plane, normal to the West Face Slope, and hence FOL is the angle of reflexion for the noon considered.

It is obvious, also, that DOC and KOH lie in the same plane, *i.e.*, the East and West vertical plane through the point O; that DC=HK and OD=OK; and OC=OH; and that OB=OG=DE=LK.

Fig. A$_4$ is a detail extracted from figure A$_3$, with the horizontal plane OBPN continued over the Constant Plane of Reflexion OHGF. A few minutes consideration will now enable the mathematical reader to connect the data of the four figures, A$_1$, A$_2$, A$_3$ and A$_4$, and to derive the relationship $\text{Tan } \hat{D} = \text{Tan } \hat{C}.\text{Cos } \psi$, from which the various dated phenomena have been derived for the East and West Faces.

The data for the East Face are, of course, identical with the data for the West Face.

Fig. B. This figure for the North and South Faces, is deemed to explain itself to the mathematical reader. It depends entirely upon the relationship :—

Angle of Reflexion=Angle of Incidence.

Fig. C. As above in case of South Face, but for the case of North Face noon shadows, the data depend upon the relationship :—

Sun's noon Altitude=Altitude of plane containing shadow from North Face of Pyramid.

¶ 76a. THE FUNCTIONS OF ATMOSPHERIC DUST.

Dry
Atmosphere
and large
numbers of
particles of
atmospheric
dust render
reflected
beams of
light visible.

The investigations of Mr. John Aitken (Quart. Jour. Roy. Met. Soc., July, 1896; Enc. Brit., 11th Ed., Vol. viii, pp. 713-715, Vol. xviii, pp. 278-279) into the phenomena and climatic effects of atmospheric dust have an important bearing upon the question of the Pyramid's noon reflexions being rendered visible. Aitken's observations have shown that for a dry atmosphere the transparency, brightness, and blueness of the sky—and in consequence, the tendency towards a beam of reflected light becoming visible—increase with the number of particles of atmospheric dust per unit volume of the atmosphere. In the case of a humid atmosphere he shows that for a given number of dust particles per unit volume of atmosphere, the density of the haze in the atmosphere increases as the degree of humidity increases. This is effected by the humidity *condensing* upon the dust, and increasing the size of the particles.

But humid
atmosphere
produces haze
in density
increasing with
number of
dust particles.

Minute size of
many of the
dust particles.
Too small to
settle through
the
atmosphere.
Surcharged
Accumulation
of these
prevented by
wind and rain.
Purifying
processes and
areas.
Sand Dust
driven from
African Deserts
into Europe.

Many of the dust particles are too small to be precipitated through the atmosphere in dry regions. For this reason, the atmosphere in dry regions would tend to become surcharged with the accumulation of the finer dust particles, were it not for the purifying processes of wind and rain. Driven from the dry accumulating regions into regions of humidity, the dust particles are weighted by the condensation of the atmospheric vapour, and are thus ultimately precipitated through the atmosphere in the form of rain. Aitken defines such regions of discharge as purifying areas for excess atmospheric dust. He states that " there is good reason for supposing that large quantities of sand are carried from the deserts by the wind and transported great distances, the sand, for instance, from the desert of Africa being carried to Europe." Thus he shows that the number of particles for inhabited areas and for the Sahara are high compared with the number of particles in mountain and sea zones, unless when these are being traversed by dust laden currents of air hurrying to a humid zone for discharge.

¶ 76b. CONDITIONS GOVERNING REFLECTED BEAMS BECOMING VISIBILE.

From these observations it is evident that the dry atmosphere of Egypt, closely adjacent as it is to the deserts on the East and West, must have a greater number of particles of atmospheric dust even than most dry climates. There should, therefore, be a greater tendency towards reflected beams of light being rendered visible in Egypt than in more humid climates, or in dry climates where the density of atmospheric dust is lower. That such is the case is clear from the following authentic observation. The description is extracted from a letter to us by Capt. F. A. Whitaker, R.E.—late Chief Instructor, 5th (and later 4th) Army Signals, B.E.F.

"At the time of which I write I was Brigade Signal Officer to the 92nd Infantry Brigade and our Headquarters were established in a hollow between sandhills about five miles East of Ballah on the Suez Canal.

This place, at the time, was the Railhead, and named Ballybunion after the Birthplace of the Engineer who constructed the Railway.

Our front line was situated about a mile further East and was held by the 11th and 13th East Yorks on the Left and Right Sectors respectively. In maintaining communications with the forward Infantry and our base on the Canal, considerable difficulty was experienced with all systems of Telegraphy and Telephony on account of corrosive effect of the sand on the insulation of the cables.

The uncertainty of telegraphy made us fall back on visual signalling, both by Day and Night. In some cases the distances between visual Stations were great so the Heliograph was chiefly used during the daylight. In order to receive Heliographic messages from our advanced post, I had to establish a visual Station on a sandhill a short distance South of our camp, and named the position Helio Hill.

One particularly bright and clear day—the 22nd of February, 1916—I was endeavouring to establish visual communication with the 34th Infantry Brigade on our right, who were supposed to be situated among the sandhills some five miles East of El Ferdan. As we only had a vague idea of their position it was necessary to sweep the horizon with the reflected light from the Helio mirror.

It was while occupied in this sweeping process that the incident to which I have referred, occurred.

Unintentionally I traversed the light a little too much towards the East—the direction in which we expected the enemy to be—when almost immediately, one of the Signallers drew my attention to a peculiar ray of light which seemed to come from a point due South-East of our position (Helio Hill). I noticed that this ray was vibrating in a vertical manner—that is, the beam appeared to rise and fall.

Although this ray was concentrated on some place to the South of our position it was possible to realize that the periodicity of the vibrations resembled the Morse Code.

In fact for quite a time we were able to recognize the letters R and U. These two letters sent together mean ' Who are you ? ' in Army code.

The first thought that flashed through my mind was that we had made a ' Faux pas,' and had given our position away to the Turks. However, after waiting awhile, the signals changed to W. H. D., which represented the ' call sign ' of the Worcester Yeomanry.

It then occurred to me that possibly the ray we were reading was from a heliograph belonging to a cavalry patrol of this regiment. Consequently I aligned the Helio on the point on the horizon from which the ray seemed to emanate and gave one answering flash.

This was instantly answered by the ray being traversed on to our position, so that we received the full flash of the light.

To cut a long story short, it turned out that the signals were transmitted by the Worcester Yeomanry, and that they were patrolling in a North-easterly direction some 10 miles East of our position when they observed our unintentional flash, which they took to be a ' call up.'

By the time the column had halted and their signallers had set up the Helio, our position was not quite clear to them, so they guessed the direction, called R. U., and waited our reply.   This accounted for the light being considerably to our right.

It appeared remarkable to me, at the time, that we should have been able to read Morse Code from a Heliograph ray, when the mirror disc was invisible.

The only way I can account for this phenomenon is that the light from the sun was very intense and the mirror of the Heliograph concentrated the reflected light into a narrow beam, thus making the ray so strong that it could be seen by an observer who was not in line with the beam."

The almost certain conclusion that the Pyramid's noon reflexions were visible. If such a tiny ray of light as that reflected from the heliograph could be visible from a distance under the conditions observed, obviously the huge volume of the reflected beams projected from the Pyramid would be more clearly visible under the same conditions, or visible at least to the same extent under conditions considerably less favourable.

CHAPTER II.

THE EVIDENCES OF SCIENTIFIC ORIGINS IN ANCIENT EGYPT.

SECTION I.—GEOMETRICAL METROLOGY[1] AND DYNASTOLOGY.

¶ 77.   THE SYSTEM OF MEASURES OF THE MEGALITHIC BUILDERS.

The evidence of archæology, folklore, and tradition—together with the astronomical alignments and datings—has established the Eastern origin of the builders of Stonehenge. This evidence has shown that the astronomical ideas of the British megalithic builders had been formulated in ancient Egypt. This formulation reached its highest phase of constructional expression in the work of the Great Pyramid builders. *Work of Great Pyramid Builders the best expression of the science passed on to the British megalithic builders.*

The connection thus established as holding between early Britain and ancient Egypt leads at once to a further discovery. The megalithic builders who monumentalised in Britain the science of the ancient Egyptians employed in their constructions a system of measures in use in ancient Egypt.   The route of the megalithic builders is the route of the ancient system of measures from the East into Britain. *British megalithic builders employed a system of measures in use in ancient Egypt.*

The data confirming this have been supplied by the painstaking researches and comprehensive metrological classifications of Professor Petrie.

¶ 78. THE AREA OF STONEHENGE CIRCLE.

From Petrie's data we find that the Stonehenge Circle is a constructional expression of the geometrical relations holding between the ancient Egyptian square and linear systems of measures.   Its constructional diameter—shown on Plate I—is an important Egyptian unit of linear measures.   The area defined by this diameter—*i.e.*, the circular area precisely internal to the outer ring of stones, is the exact area of an important Egyptian unit of square measure. *Stonehenge an expression of relationship of ancient Egyptian square and linear systems of measures. Stonehenge stone circle diameter and area are Egyptian units of measure.*

[1] In this section, where metrological references are not stated, the researches and classifications of Prof. W. M. Flinders Petrie are to be understood. " Inductive Metrology :" " Weights and Measures " in Enc. Brit. (11th Ed.), vol. xxviii, pp. 482-484 : and " Stonehenge."

The Egyptian Aroura and the ¼-Aroura.

Aroura Square side 100 common cubits long.

Common cubit 20.63 British inches.

¼-Aroura Circle diameter the diameter of Stonehenge stone circle.

The great unit of surface measure in ancient Egypt was the *aroura*. This was a square of length of side of an hundred common Egyptian cubits of 20.63 British inches each. This square was divided into four quarter squares ; the quarter *aroura* being thus employed as a separate unit of square measure. The diameter of the circle of equal area to the area of the quarter *aroura* is 1163 British inches. A circle of this diameter falls precisely internal to the outer ring of stones forming the circle of Stonehenge. The diameter indicated by the present remaining stones of the circle, as determined by Petrie's survey, is 1168 British inches. Petrie argues that the measure of this diameter is derived from Egypt, where it occurs generally as 1162 or 1164 British inches.

¶ 79. THE SOLAR YEAR AND THE AROURA.

The Solar year relations of the Stonehenge ¼-Aroura.

The Solar year relations of the Egyptian ¼-Aroura.

Horapollo on the ¼-Aroura and the Egyptian year.

The Egyptian square year and circle year.

Herodotus on the Aroura square.

The Samian Cubit 20.62 British Inches. The Egyptian Cubit 20.63 British Inches.

Thus at Stonehenge we find the Egyptian quarter *aroura* set out in circular structural form to define, by its alignments, the points and circuit of the solar year. A similar association held between the quarter *aroura* and the year in ancient Egypt. For as Horapollo states :—[1]

" To represent the *current year*, they (the Egyptians) depict the fourth part of an *aroura :* now the *aroura* is a measure of land of an hundred cubits. And when they would express a year they say *a quarter*."

Hence in the Egyptian inscriptions there are two hieroglyphic representations of the year—one indicated by *a square*, and the other by *a circle*.

Herodotus,[2] again, states that " the *aroura* is a square of a hundred cubits, the Egyptian cubit being the same as the Samian."

The cubit of Samos, as determined by Petrie, is 20.62 British inches, whereas the best average (Petrie's) for Egypt is 20.63 British inches.

¶ 80. THE ORIGIN OF THE AROURA.

The Solar Year 365.242 days.

The circumference of Circular ¼-Aroura 3652.42 units ; its diameter 1162.6 units.

Rectangle :— Circumference × Diameter.

= Aroura.

= 3652.42 × 1162.6.

Equal Square :— 2060.66 × 2060.66 = Aroura.

The statement of Horapollo—confirmed by the relations of the Stonehenge Circle—indicates that the *aroura* was derived from a representation of the year in measures. The original representation was in the form of a circle. The circumference of this circle measured 3652.42 selected units of length. This represented the circle of the solar year to a scale of 10 selected units of length to a day. The diameter then measured 1162.6 selected units of length.

To reduce the circular area thus defined to a form suitable for land measuring, a rectangle was formed of length 3652.42 equal to the circumference of the circle, and of breadth 1162.6 equal to the diameter of the circle. The area of this rectangle was therefore equal to four times the area of the circle.[3] The rectangle thus produced was the intermediate stage of the *aroura*. Transformed into the form of a square of equal area, the *aroura* became a square of length of side 2060.66 selected units.

The sequence of derivation is shown on Plate XIII (refer Sect. III, Description of Plates, ¶ 135).

[1] Hieroglyphics, Bk. I, v.
[2] II, 168.
[3] Since area of circle $= \frac{\pi d^2}{4}$ and area of rectangle = circumference × diameter, $= \pi d \times d, = \pi d^2$.

PLATE XIII.

EQUAL AREAS

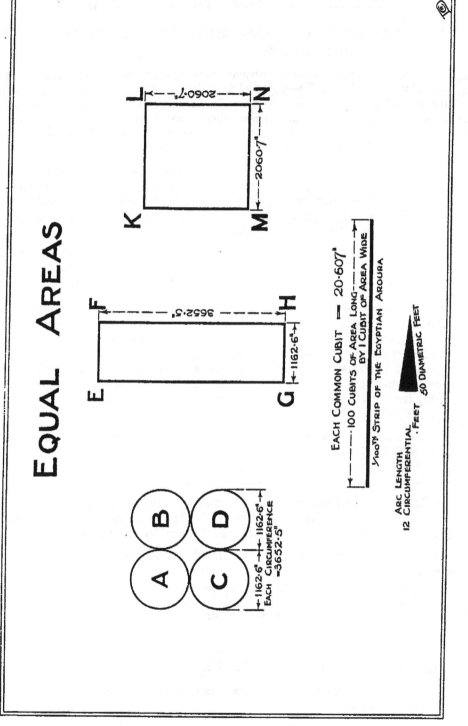

¶ 81. THE ORIGINAL LINEAR UNIT AND THE ORIGIN OF THE COMMON CUBIT.

Side of Square Aroura =2060.66 units =100 common Egyptian Cubits of 20.6066 units (Actually 20.63 British Inches)

1 primitive unit=1.0011 British inches

The division of the *aroura* square side into 100 parts—as observed by Herodotus and Horapollo—supplied the common Egyptian cubit of 20.6066 units=20.63 British inches. The most general value of the common Egyptian cubit observed by Petrie in the best work of the Pyramid builders is 20.629 British inches, from which the original selected unit=1.0011 British inches, as stated to 4th decimal place, or $\frac{11}{10000}$ths of an inch longer than the British inch.

The latter values agree closely with the mean Gregorian year value of 365.2425 days as basis, giving a basal circumference of 3652.425 selected units of length. These units we may now define as " Primitive inches," and hereafter refer to simply as P inches, or P″, avoiding confusion with British inches by stating the latter as B inches, or B″.

¶ 82. THE ANCIENT EGYPTIAN SYSTEM OF MEASURES.

Ancient Egyptian measures devised to avoid π relationship in calculations

Simple relations established between circles and segments of circles on one hand and straight line figures on the other hand.

With the preceding data as basis, it is found that the ancient Egyptians formulated a system of measures that, in the case of circular areas, and sectors of circles, avoided the repeatedly recurring trouble of the π relationship. By employing in their everyday work separate units and scales for circumferences, diameters, and areas, they avoided calculations that embodied the troublesome ratio of diameter to circumference. Simple formulæ were drawn up from which the circumferences and areas of circles, or sectors of circles, were immediately obtained from the diameter, or *vice versa*.

Sectors were correctly treated by analogy as triangles, by the following true relationship :—

Area of Sector .. .. = " Base " of Sector × " height " of Sector.
= Arc of Sector × radius.

The geometrical analogy leading to this relationship is explained for the particular case of quadrants in Plate XIV. The same treatment holds for similar sectors, *i.e.*, sectors whose arcs are subtended by the same angle.

Different Units of Measure :— Linear Digits, Feet and Cubits —for Diameters, Circumferences, and Straight Line Figures

The principal units of measure formulated to effect the various translations were the following :—

The Linear Digit, Foot and Cubit of Diameter.
The Linear Digit, Foot and Cubit of Circumference.
The Linear Digit, Foot and Cubit of Square Measure.

¶ 83. THE SYSTEM OF LINEAR UNITS.

(The algebraic relationship of units is as stated in Section III. Description of Plates, ¶ 137a).

PLATE XIV.

GEOMETRICAL ANALOGY

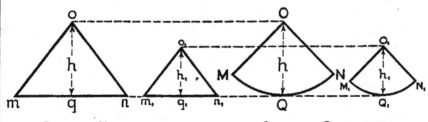

SIMILAR TRIANGLES   SIMILAR QUADRANTS

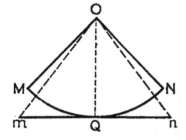

QUADRANT ARC DEVELOPED
ON MID-TANGENT GIVES
TRIANGLE OF EQUAL AREA

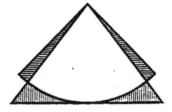

VERTICAL SHADED AREAS
EQUAL
HORIZONTAL SHADED AREAS

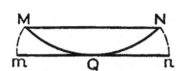

EGYPTIAN CONCEPTION OF
QUADRANT ARC DEVELOPMENT
MQN TO mQn

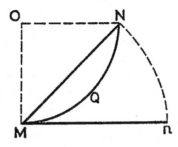

ORDINARY CONCEPTION OF
QUADRANT ARC DEVELOPMENT
MQN TO Mn

To obtain the Units of Diameter, the standard diameter of 1162.6 P″ (=1163.88 B″) was divided into :—

(a)   64 diametric cubits of 18.1656 P″ each (18.1856 B″).
(b)   100   „   feet of   11.626 P″ „ (11.6388 B″).
(c) 1600   „   digits of 0.7266 P″ „ (0.7274 B″).

The Units of Circumference ,were obtained by dividing the standard circumference of 3652.425 P″ (=3656.44 B″) into :—

(a)   200 circumferential cubits of 18.2621 P″ (18.2822 B″).
(b)   300   „   feet of   12.1748 P″ (12.1881 B″).
(c) 5000   „   digits of 0.7305 P″ (0.7313 B″).

The Linear Units of Square measure were derived by dividing the side of the square of area equal to the area of the standard circle into :—

(a)   50 common cubits of 20.6066 P″ (20.629 B″).
(b) 1600 linear digits of   0.6440 P″ (0.6447 B″).

An illustration of the various units in operation is figured on Plate XIII. Here the 1/100th strip of *aroura, i.e.,* a strip of 100 common cubits long by 1 common cubit wide,=area of sector, of arc length 12 circumferential feet, and diameter 50 diametric feet. Worked examples are given in Section III, ¶ ¶ 137, b and c.

¶ 84. THE SACRED HEBREW CUBIT.

Comparative scales of the various units are figured on Plate XV. Reference to this shows that there are 25 Diametric Digits in the Diametric Cubit, and 25 Circumferential Digits in the Circumferential Cubit. These suggest that the Basal Cubit of the original Primitive inch system consisted of 25 P.

inches. This gives the value of the Sacred Hebrew Cubit as derived by Sir Isaac Newton, and since confirmed by the metrological researches of Oppert, Petrie, and others. This again confirms the sequence as to Euphratean origins obtained in Chapter I.

The Sacred
Hebrew Cubit
in Egypt
during period
of Semitic
Domination in
Dynasty XVIII.

Completing this connection, Petrie finds the 25 inches' cubit in use in Egypt during the period of Dynasty XVIII. At this time the Egyptian language and the political and religious institutions of Egypt were strongly influenced by a powerful Semitic faction in Egypt.[1] Around the same time

Stonehenge and similar monuments were being built in Britain by a race whose astronomical and metrological cults evidence Egyptian influence, yet whose folklore and traditions indicate Semitic origins.

Hebrew Sacred
Cubit not
Egyptian, but
Egyptian Units
of measures
derived from it.

The Sacred Cubit of 25 P. inches (Plate XV) never occurs in Egypt unless during periods of Semitic dominance. The other systems of Plate XV belong to the whole period of Egyptian history. The fact that these systems were derived from the scale of the Sacred Cubit of 25 P. inches again confirms that the

Egyptian units of measure were not formulated in Egypt. The sacred system and its derived Egyptian Units all clearly belong to the period of the former civilization pictured in ¶ ¶ 41-47.

[1] Petrie, " Hist. Egypt," Vol. II, pp. 146-152.

PLATE XV.

COMPARISON OF ANCIENT SCALES OF MEASUREMENT (REDUCED)

SACRED SCALE

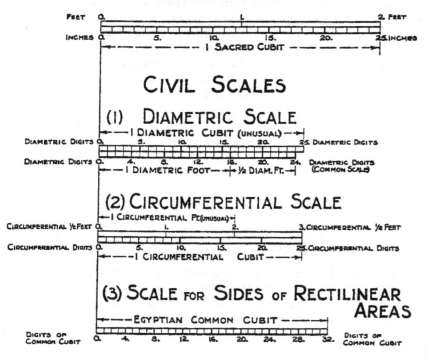

FEET 0. 1. 2. FEET
INCHES 0. 5. 10. 15. 20. 25. INCHES
← 1 SACRED CUBIT →

CIVIL SCALES

(1) DIAMETRIC SCALE

← 1 DIAMETRIC CUBIT (UNUSUAL) →
DIAMETRIC DIGITS 0. 5. 10. 15. 20. 25. DIAMETRIC DIGITS
DIAMETRIC DIGITS 0. 4. 8. 12. 16. 20. 24. DIAMETRIC DIGITS (COMMON SCALE)
← 1 DIAMETRIC FOOT → ½ DIAM. FT.

(2) CIRCUMFERENTIAL SCALE

← 1 CIRCUMFERENTIAL FT (UNUSUAL) →
CIRCUMFERENTIAL ½ FEET 0. 1. 2. 3. CIRCUMFERENTIAL ½ FEET
CIRCUMFERENTIAL DIGITS 0. 5. 10. 15. 20. 25. CIRCUMFERENTIAL DIGITS
← 1 CIRCUMFERENTIAL CUBIT →

(3) SCALE FOR SIDES OF RECTILINEAR AREAS

← EGYPTIAN COMMON CUBIT →
DIGITS OF COMMON CUBIT 0. 4. 8. 12. 16. 20. 24. 28. 32. DIGITS OF COMMON CUBIT

ANCIENT EGYPTIAN π RECORD

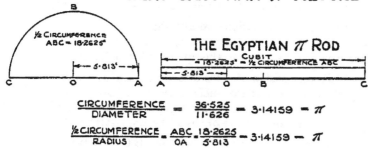

B
½ CIRCUMFERENCE ABC = 18·2625″
← 5·813″ →
C O A

THE EGYPTIAN π ROD
CUBIT
← 18·2625″ = ½ CIRCUMFERENCE ABC →
← 5·813″ →
A O B C

$$\frac{\text{CIRCUMFERENCE}}{\text{DIAMETER}} = \frac{36·525}{11·626} = 3·14159 = \pi$$

$$\frac{½ \text{ CIRCUMFERENCE}}{\text{RADIUS}} = \frac{\text{ABC}}{\text{OA}} \frac{18·2625}{5·813} = 3·14159 = \pi$$

¶ 85. THE FOOT OR SACRED HALF-CUBIT OF 12½ INCHES.

The Sacred Half-cubit. (12½ inches).
According to Petrie, the half-cubit (12½ inches) appears in Babylonia as the foot of the Babylonian system of measures. It appears also in ancient Greece *Its Track :— Babylonia, Greece,* (12.44 to 12.62 B″), in Etruria (12.45 B″ average), in what Petrie deems to be *Etruria,* *Roman* Britain, and in medieval England (12.47 B″ average). The migratory *Roman Britain,* sequence indicated clearly confirms the Euphratean connections established in *Medieval England.* Chapter I.

Ancient Cornwall Acre, 40 perches × 4 perches, with perch = 16 feet.
A statute of Richard I, belonging to the year 1199, defines an acre in Cornwall as " 40 perches in length and 4 in breadth and every perch of 16 feet in length."[1] Cornwall was the principal British centre of the Oriental colonists from 2000 B.C. onwards. Their influence still predominates in the folklore, *The Coming to Cornwall of the Sacred Half-Cubit.* traditions, and customs of Cornwall. It is obviously from this race, with its Mediterranean and Atlantic ports of call, that ancient Greece, Etruria and Britain derived the Sacred half-cubit of 12½ P. inches.

Ancient Perch : 16 feet of 12½ inches = 200 inches.
Now 16 feet of 12½ P. inches give the ancient perch in Cornwall as consisting of 200 P. inches. The modern perch or rod consists of 16½ feet of 12 inches, or 198 inches. The numerical interchange and the reason for it are *Modern Perch : 16½ feet of 12 inches = 198 inches.* obvious. The inch remained the basal unit, unchanged, except for small local variations. The perch also remained practically unchanged—losing but 1% of its original value.

¶ 86. THE RELATION BETWEEN ANCIENT AND MODERN
BRITISH MEASURES.

The manner of effecting the change from the ancient to the modern value of the perch or rod suggests that the numerical relations between the perch and *Ancient Furlong : = 40 perches* the higher units were maintained. Now there are 40 perches or rods in the *= 40 × 200 ins. = 8,000 inches.* furlong, and 8 furlongs in the mile. With the ancient perch as 200 inches, this *Ancient Mile : = 8 furlongs* gives the primitive basal furlong as consisting of 8,000 inches, and the primitive *= 64,000 inches.* basal mile of 64,000 inches.

Ancient Unit of 10 acres.
An acre in Cornwall (in 1199 A.D. and earlier) was measured as 40 perches by 4 perches. This is the $\frac{1}{10}$th strip of a square of 10 acres area. The side of *As a square its circuit = Half-a-mile, or 32,000 inches* the square of 10 acres therefore measured 1 furlong, or 8,000 inches, and the circuit of the 10 acres square, 4 furlongs or the half-mile,—32,000 inches.

Ancient and Modern Relation :— 640 acres = 1 sq. mile
Following from these relations we find that
$$640 \text{ primitive acres} = 1 \text{ sq. mile (primitive.)}$$
This relation between the acre and the square mile still holds.

The decimal subdivision of areas into $\frac{1}{10}$th and $\frac{1}{100}$th strips of squares— indicated by the definition of the ancient acre in Cornwall—is both Egyptian and Semitic. It occurs in the case of the Egyptian *aroura*. The 10 acre square was a large unit of square measure of the Hebrews. (Isaiah v. 10.)

[1] 10th Richard I, statute " Inter Fines " states " Acra in Cornwal continent 40 perticata in longitudine et 4 in latitudine et qua libet perticata de 16 pedibus in longitudine."

¶ 87. THE MEDIEVAL ENGLISH PROCESS OF COMPROMISE.

A decimal subdivision of the ancient Perch of 200 inches gave the ancient Ell or yard of 40 inches. Petrie gives the latter as averaging 39.66 B". The foot of this system—the Belgic Foot—is ⅓ of the ell or yard=13⅓" (13.22 B" Petrie). With this system Petrie finds a longer mile of 10 furlongs in use from as far back as the 13th century. This system is as follows :— *Ancient Yard : =40 inches =3 Belgic feet of 13⅓ inches. The Ancient Long Mile of 10 furlongs.*

Belgic Foot.	3= Yard.	2= Fathom.	10= Chain.	10= Furlong.	10= Mile.
13⅓".	40".	80".	800".	8,000".	80,000".

Its Decimal System.

Petrie's values extended from his average of the Belgic foot in England (13.22") are :—

Foot.	Yard.	Fathom.	Chain.	Furlong.	Mile.
13.22.	39.66.	79.32.	793.	7,932.	79,320 B".

It will be observed that the furlong (8,000") is of the same value as was obtained in ¶ 86.

The reason for the difference evidenced by Petrie's examples is that these are all from buildings belonging to the 10th to 15th centuries, when the Belgic foot and the foot of 12½ inches still competed with the legal foot of 12 inches instituted in the 10th century. The legal foot altered the perch or rod to 198" in place of the former 200", which contained 15 Belgic feet of 13⅓ P inches. To effect a compromise between the two competing systems, the perch or rod of 198" was reckoned as containing 15 Belgic feet. This gave an adjusted foot of 13.2 P" (13.22 B", as Petrie above). *Petrie's Examples of Belgic Foot derived from buildings of 10th-15th centuries. Legal foot of 12 inches instituted in 10th century. Compromise effected between two systems :— Relation retained that 15 Belgic feet =1 perch.*

Petrie, however, observes that the latter foot originated around Asia Minor, averaging there 13.35 B", and passed to Greece as 13.36 B". Now 13⅓ Primitive inches of value 1.0011 British inches (¶ 81) equal 13.348 B. inches, or to 2nd place, 13.35 B. inches, as in Asia Minor. *1% reduction in perch made 1% reduction in Belgic foot.*

¶ 88. THE EGYPTIAN METROLOGICAL EVIDENCE.

Returning to consideration of the Egyptian system of diametric and circumferential measures and their linear standards for areas, we find that all the values of ¶ 83 are found indicated in the structural measurements of the ancient Egyptians. A half diametric foot and the circumferential cubit were actually, in one case noted by Petrie, found on the same cubit rod. This is a graphical representation of the π relationship, as the half diametric foot (5.813 P") was the radius of a circle of 36.525 P" circumference, of which the circumferential cubit (18.2625 P") was the half circumference. (Refer Plate XV, lower portion.) *Structural Measurements in Egypt give ancient diametric and circumferential units and linear units for areas. An Egyptian π Rod.*

Metrologists, having failed to observe the origin of the system of measures, have universally supposed the diametric digit (0.7274 B"), and the circumferential digit (0.7313 B"), and also the diametric cubit (18.1856 B"), and the *Metrologists confuse diametric digit and circumferential digit, and the respective cubits.*

circumferential cubit (18.2822 B″), to be variable values of the same digit and the same cubit respectively. They therefore average the two values, in each case, obtaining the mean values as follows :—

The mistake in averaging two separate systems.

Diametric Cubit	.. = 18.1856 B″.
Circumferential Cubit .. ./	.. = 18.2822 B″.
Mean Cubit of Metrologists	.. = 18.2339 B″.

This is stated by Petrie as 18.23 B″. Again,

Diametric Digit	.. = 0.7274 B″.
Circumferential Digit	.. = 0.7313 B″.
Mean Digit of Metrologists	.. = 0.72935 B″.

This is stated by Petrie as averaging 0.729 B″. From Greek remains Petrie obtained 0.7296 B″.

Possibility that Egyptians themselves, at an early date, merged the two systems into one for ordinary use. It is quite possible, however, that for ordinary everyday commercial use, the two separate systems were merged into a single "rule-of-thumb" system at a comparatively early date in the dynastic history of Egypt. After all, as we have seen, Egypt is only a stage in the tracing of origins to their source in a former civilisation. The Egyptians, at an early date, lost the meaning and application of much that they have handed on to later days for elucidation.

¶ 89. THE GREEK SYSTEM OF MEASURES DERIVED FROM EGYPT.

Petrie's values for the Greek Decimal System of Linear Measures. With the average values of ¶ 88 as basis, Petrie has grouped the known data from buildings in Greece as follows :—

Old Digit	$\begin{cases} 25 = \text{Cubit}: 4 = \\ 100 \quad .. \quad .. \quad .. = \end{cases}$	Orguia.	10 = Amma.	10 = Stadion.
B″ 0.729.	18.2.	72.9.	729.	7296.

But with the stadion = 7,296 B″, as stated by Petrie above, the values are accurately :—

The Mean Values of Egyptian Diametric and Circumferential Measures.

Old Digit.	Cubit.	Orguia.	Amma.	Stadion.
B″ 0.7296.	18.24.	72.96.	729.6.	7296.

Thus indicating that the system tabulated is the mean of the two early Egyptian systems—diametric and circumferential.

Petrie further shows that the cubit of 18.24 B″, was also divided by the Greeks into 24 digits, obtaining the new Greek digit as 0.76 B″.

He shows again that the Greek foot was taken as $\frac{2}{3}$ of the mean cubit of 18.24 B″, and therefore as 12.16 B″. This is closely approximate to the Egyptian diametric foot of 12.1748 P″=12.188 B″. (¶ 83.)

The resulting Greek system, as stated by Petrie, is as follows :—

	Foot.	10=Acaena.	10=Plethron.
B″.	12.16.	121.6.	1216.

The early Greeks also used the diametric foot of 11.626 inches.   (¶ 83.)

¶ 90. THE ROMAN SYSTEM OF MEASURES.

The Roman system of measures was derived—through the Greeks—from the Egyptian diametric system. Its basis was the diametric digit of 0.7266 inches, and the diametric foot of 11.626 inches (¶ 83). As an average from existing Roman remains, Petrie gives the system as follows :—

Digitus.	4=Palmus.	4=Pes.	5=Passus.	125=Stadium.	8=Milliare.
B″ 0.726.	2.90.	11.62.	58.1.	7,262.	58,100.

The above system was used by the Romans in Britain and Africa.

The Roman foot appears in Medieval England as 11.6 B″.

¶ 91. ANCIENT RECORDS OF AN EGYPTIAN PYRAMID OF MEASURES.

The data from ancient Egyptian documentary sources show that the various metrological dimensions and standards of linear and square measure were preserved in the form of an existing Pyramid. The primary unit of measurement, the various outstanding dimensions and structural peculiarities, and the angles of the face slope and the Apex angle of this existing Pyramid are all precisely defined by the Egyptian literary data.

The data define as follows :—

(1) *GENERAL BASIS OF PYRAMID'S DESIGN.*

(a) That the unit of dimensions   ..   .. = 1 P. inch.
  = 1.0011 Brit. inch.
(b) That the angle of face slope with horizontal = 51°–51′–14″.3.
(c) That the apex angle ..   .. = 76°–17′–31″.4.
(d) That the base square circuit   ..   .. = 36,524 or 5 P. inches.
  and (defined independently) ..   .. = 1,772 common Egyptian cubits (of 20.63 B. inches).
(e) That the height from base to apex..   .. = 5,813 P. inches.

The data define (b) and (c) independently of (d) and (e).

(ii) *DETAILS OF DESIGN.*

A Square Circuit 25,827 at level 1,702½.

A Square Circuit 29,220 at Level 1,162.6

The latter defining " Aroura " Rectangle 3652.5 × 1162.6

Pyramid Vertical Section Area = Square of Side 5151.6.

(a) That the Pyramid indicated a square circuit of 25,826 or 7 P. inches (the sum of the diagonals of the base square) at a height of 1702½ P. inches above the base, both dimensions being given independently of the other.

(b) That the Pyramid indicated a square circuit of 29,220 P. inches at a height of 1162.6 P. inches above the base.

(c) That the latter defined, in elevation, the *aroura* rectangle of 3652.5 P. inches × 1162.6 P. inches, and a series of such rectangles (eight in all) encircling the Pyramid as seen in its four elevations of circuit.

(d) That the Pyramid vertical section was equal in area to a square of length of side = 5151.6 P. inches ; this being defined independently of the other relations.

The quarter-*aroura* goes into the latter square, or the area of the Pyramid section, 25 times.

¶ 92. THE FICTITIOUS PYRAMID DYNASTOLOGY OF THE EGYPTIANS.

Conception of Ancient Egyptians that the Standard Pyramid Measures denoted duration of Astronomical Periods.

On this conception Egyptians framed their Mythical Systems of Dynastic Chronology.

The Pyramid measures thus standardised were all associated with the geometry of the year. For this reason, and for other reasons to be explained later, the Egyptians of various periods, subsequent to the erection of the monument, deemed that all its measurements denoted the duration in years of astronomical periods. In accordance with this conception, they formulated various systems of fictitious or mythological chronology. Each cult had its particular system, always, however, based numerically on the Pyramid year cycle geometry. Each system claimed to be a presentation of the chronology of the Egyptian Dynasties—Divine and human. The systems all differed considerably, so that it is impossible to synchronize the various intervals given for the same Dynastic periods.

Various Versions of such Dynastic Systems edited by Egyptian Priest Manetho in 3rd Century B.C.

Manetho's King Lists preserved by Julius Africanus and Eusebius in 3rd Century A.D

All the systems in existence in the third century B.C., were edited by the Egyptian priest, Manetho, and entered in his work on Egyptian History, " Ægyptiaci," written in Greek. Several versions of the systems of fictitious chronology, known as the Egyptian " King Lists," were extracted from Manetho's work by Julius Africanus in the third century A.D. The composite nature of the King Lists as given by Africanus is seen by analysis of the various alternative details of summations of years.

Another version was preserved by Eusebius—also in the third century A.D.—together with the version known as the Armenian Version of Eusebius. The versions of Africanus and Eusebius were, in turn, preserved by George Syncellus about 800 A.D. With the exception of certain important extracts from Manetho's history, preserved by Josephus in his *Contra Apion.*, this is all that now remains of Manetho's notable work.

Version of Eusebius as old as 5th Century B.C.

To account for the difference between the chief version of Africanus and the version of Eusebius, Syncellus accused Eusebius of tampering with the figures as given by Manetho. The analysis given in this chapter, however, shows that the version preserved by Eusebius, as stated to the reign of Amasis II, was in existence in the fifth century B.C.—700 years before Africanus was born, and 200 years before Manetho.

CHART SHOWING THE GEOMETRICAL, ASTRONOMICAL, AND NUMERICAL BASES OF THE FICTITIOUS CHRONOLOGIES OF THE ANCIENT EGYPTIAN KING LISTS.

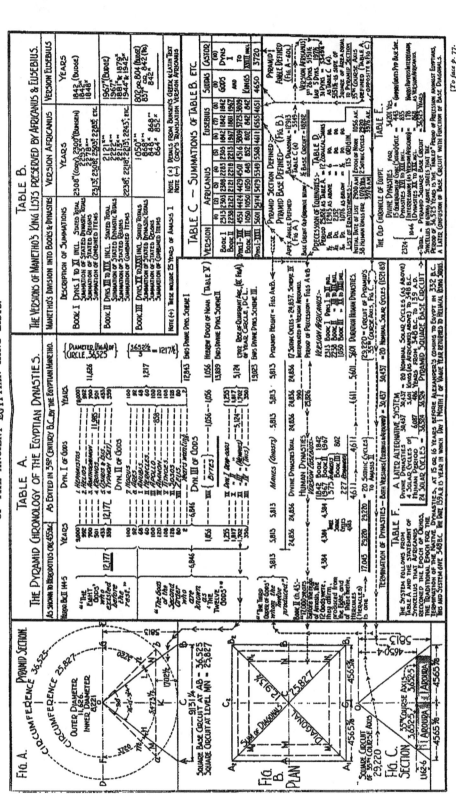

[To face p. 77.

The data here given deal with another question of Egyptian chronology, related to the question already noted by the data of Plate IX. One of the important schools of Egyptological chronology, as noted in the notes to Plate IX, claims that the Egyptian King Lists of Manetho confirm its system of so-called astronomical chronology. The data shown above, however, disprove the claim, since they prove not only that the King Lists as shown above were fabricated without any governing geometrical method from the dimensions of the Great Pyramid, but also that such Sothic Cycles as were involved in this fictitious arrangement do not synchronise with the Sothic cycles that form the basis of the modern system of Egyptological chronology mentioned. It is fair, however, to add as stated by Professor Breasted that the view of this school "is inherited from an older generation of Egyptologists . . . and . . . is now maintained only by a small and constantly decreasing number of modern scholars." These generally refer to dates, fixed from the data given above, as the dates of "the Egyptians' own chronology."

Other associated numerical details are found in records of the period of Dynasties XVIII and XIX.

A typical tabulation and analysis of the King Lists of Manetho—and the different versions of these and other lists—are shown on Plate XVI. Had this matter been dealt with otherwise than by the comprehensive tabulation and analysis given, the subject-matter would have extended to many tedious pages of text, without giving a fraction of the elucidation resulting from the graphical presentation of Plate XVI. For the statement of Manetho's, and other King Lists, and for the historical evolution of the various dynastic schemes of Plate XVI, the reader is referred to the Appendix.

[margin: Graphical Presentation of the Associated Data. Plate XVI Its Elucidating Features.]

¶ 93. EGYPTIAN KING LISTS DEFINE THE STANDARD PYRAMID.

Reference to Plate XVI shows that the numerical details of the King Lists define the standard Pyramid as follows :—

[margin: Dynastological Dimensions of Standard Pyramid.]

(a) THE HEIGHT OF THE STANDARD PYRAMID.

Table A.   Dynasty of Manes = 5,813.
         = Radius of Circle, 36,524 or 5.
Hephaistos to Osiris *and* Isis = 2 × 5,813 = 11,626.
         = Diameter of Circle, 36,524 or 5.

[margin: Height :— Dynasty of Manes = 5,813 years.]

(b) THE BASE CIRCUIT OF THE STANDARD PYRAMID.

Table E.   Old Chronicle. Gods and Kings = 36,525.
Table F.   Gods and Kings to 139 A.D. .. = 36,524.

[margin: Base Circuit : Total gods and kings = 36,525 years.]

(c) THE BASE SQUARE OF THE STANDARD PYRAMID.

The diagonal is defined by the two sides, each 9,131¼, and totalling 18,262½. The resulting diagonal is 12,913¼. This relationship is given as follows :—
(Fig. B).   Base Diagonal   ..   ..   .. = 12,913¼ (obviously period Gods).
Version Africanus.   Table C (4)   ..   .. = 5,349 Human Kings.

2 Sides defining Diagonal   ..   ..   .. = 18,262½ Gods and Kings.

[margin: Base Sides and Diagonals. 2 Sides 18,262 Diagonal 12,913 Difference 5,349 Years of Kings.]

The half-side of the base square is defined by Table C (7), Version Eusebius, Kings = 4,565. (Fig. B.)

[margin: ½-Base :— Kings = 4565 years.]

(d) THE ANGLE OF SLOPE OF THE STANDARD PYRAMID.

The Pyramid half base side and the Pyramid height define the Pyramid angle of slope as 51°-51′-14″.3. This however, is independently defined by Table C (10), Version Castor, Kings = 3,720 (Fig. A), the arc of the circle of 25,826 or 7 corresponding to the angle 51°-51′-14″.3.

[margin: Face Slope 51°-51′-14″.3. Equivalent Arc of 25,827 Circle = 3,720. Years of Kings.]

Again, the apex angle is defined as the corresponding arc of the circle of 25,827, thus Table C (2), Kings = 5,474 for 5,473½ exact. (Fig. A.)

[margin: Apex Angle :— Arc of Circle = 5,473½ Years of Kings.]

These relations prove that relations (a) to (c) apply to the Standard Pyramid, and not alone to the year circle of 36,524 or 5 circumference.

[margin: Definition of Angles proves Pyramid Intention.]

(e) *THE SQUARE CIRCUIT OF* 25,826 *or* 7.

Divine
Dynasties=
25,826 years.

This is equal to the summation of the Base Diagonals (Fig. B). The circuit occurs at level MN of Fig. A., where height of MN above base = KC = 1,702½. This is defined in Table A as Dynasty III of Demi-gods (Memphis) = 1,702.

Sum of Base
Diagonals and
Square Circuit
at level 1702½
Dynasty III
Demi-gods.

$MN = \dfrac{25,826 \text{ or } 7}{4}$. So that square circuit round Pyramid at MN = 25,826 or 7 = Divine Dynasties (Table A).

(f) *SQUARE OF AREA EQUAL TO STANDARD PYRAMID SECTION.*

The side of this square is 5,151½. This is defined as follows :—

Side of Square
of equal area
5151½.

Years of Kings
1st 26
Dynasties.

Version Africanus, 1st 26 Dynasties =	5,151½
Last 5 Dynasties =	197⅔
Table C (4). 31 Human Dynasties =	5,349⅙

This connects with item (c) above, 5,349 being common to both, and identifying 5,151½ with the same geometry as includes the half base circuit, 18,262½ and the base diagonal, 12,913¼.

¶ 94. EGYPTIAN KING LISTS DEFINE THE STANDARD UNIT.

1st 15 Kings
Old Chronicle
443 years.

The Old Chronicle of Egypt (Plate XVI, Table E) gives, for the first 15 generations of the Cynic (Sothic) Cycle, the duration of 443 years. This is the initial item of the human dynasties in this List.

Base Side
9,131¼ inches
=443 Common
Cubits

Now the base side AB (Plate XVI, Figs. A and B) of the Standard Pyramid consists of 9,131¼ units, and a measure of 9,131¼ Primitive inches (each 1.0011 B. inches) consists of 443.1 Common Egyptian Cubits of 20.6066 P. inches (20.63 British inches). The occurrence of the number 443 in the Old Chronicle therefore proves that the base side of the Standard Pyramid consisted of 443

This defines
Unit of
Standard
Pyramid as
1 inch=1.0011
British Inch.

common cubits, and that this measure equalled $\dfrac{36,524 \text{ or } 5}{4}$ standard units. As the common cubit is known (20.63 B″), the identity gives the standard unit as the Primitive inch of the value of 1.0011 British inch.

It should, perhaps, be explained that 443, whilst defining the standard Pyramid base in common cubits, is also half the numerical value of the length of side of a square of area equal to a quadrant of radius 1,000 units of any value. Hence its importance as an independent number, accurately calculated as 443.1134627, regardless of the value of unit. It is the latter value that defines the Primitive inch as 1.0011 B. inches, from the identity 36.524 P. inches = 4 × 443.1134627 cubits of 20.63 British inches.

1st 15 Kings of
Eratosthenes
443 years, to
end of reign of
Builder of
Great
Pyramid.

That the number 443 was known to be connected with the Standard Pyramid, and that the latter was identified with the Great Pyramid is proved by the following :—

(a) That the King List of Eratosthenes gives the duration of the first 15 Dynastic kings of Egypt as 443 years—this proving that the 15 generations of the Old Chronicle for 443 years are the first 15 Dynastic Kings.

This associates
the Standard
Pyramid of
lists with the
Great
Pyramid.

(b) That the 15th Dynastic king of the list of Eratosthenes is Saophis I, with whose reign inclusive the 443 years end.

(c) That the Saophis I of Eratosthenes is the Suphis I of Manetho, the IVth Dynasty king Khufu—the Cheops of Herodotus—who built the Great Pyramid.

¶ 95. THE ORIGINAL OLD CHRONICLE OF EGYPT.

The occurrence of 443 as the number of years for the first 15 dynastic kings of Egypt, and the fact that 443 is the number of common cubits in the Standard Pyramid's base side suggest a further identification. This is that the Divine Dynasties and the first 15 human kings were given the duration of 4×443 years, this being derived from the Standard Pyramid's base circuit of 1,772 common cubits=36,524 or 5 primitive inches. The latter identity thus obviously suggested the later extension to the duration of Gods and Kings for 36,525 years, as given in the Old Chronicle.

Square Circuit of 36,525 P. Inches = 1772 Common Cubits.

If the suggestion above is correct the detailed statement of the system suggested should confirm itself. Thus, as suggested,

Original Old Chronicle

Originally, Gods and Demi-gods .. .. = 3 × 443 = 1,329	Gods	1772
First 15 human kings .. .. = 443	Kings	1881
		3653

$$1,772$$

Remaining human kings, as Old Chronicle .. .. .. = 1,881

Defines "Aroura" Rectangle 3652½ × 1162.6.

Definition of Length of *Aroura* Rectangle 3,652½ (Plate XVI, Fig. C) 3,653

Now the height of the *aroura* rectangle is 1162.6 and the Standard Pyramid section as represented in Plate XVI, Fig. C, contains two *aroura* rectangles. Confirming the relationship inferred,

Old Chronicle Human Kings 2 × 1162 years.

The Old Chronicle, 1st 15 human kings .. .. = 443	
remaining do. .. .. = 1,881	

Defines Two "Aroura" Rectangles.

$$2 \times 1,162 = 2,324$$

defining the height of the two *aroura* rectangles—deleting the decimal of an inch.

¶ 96. THE MYSTERY OF MANETHO'S 113 GENERATIONS.

Now the generations of Gods and kings in the Old Chronicle are totalled as follows :—

(a) { 15 Gods
     8 Demi-gods }

(b) { 15 generations of Cynic Cycle
     8 kings of Dynasty XVI }

(a) and (b) obviously a duplication.

Old Chronicle added 113 descents for Gods and Kings stated as for 30 Dynasties only.

(c)   67 kings, Dynasties XVII to XXX inclusive.

Total 113 gods and kings.

Syncellus. in introducing the List, however, states that the 30 dynasties contained 113 descents.

This, again, is explained by another statement from Syncellus concerning Manetho's Dynasties. This is as follows :—

Manetho's Human Kings of 30 Dynasties stated as 113 generations for 3555 years.

" The period of the 113 generations described by Manetho in his three volumes, comprises a sum total of 3,555 years."

Connection
with Original
Old Chronicle
Period of
3652 years.
The latter total is one cycle of 97 years (¶ 33, ii (c),) short of 3,652 years, the basal total of the original Old Chronicle. It is also derived as follows:—

Circuit of square equal in area to circle of 29,220 circumference
(Plate XVI, Table A, and Fig. C)   ..   ..= 32,970
Manetho's 113 generations ..   ..= 3,555

The 3555 of
Syncellus
connects 29,220
of Manetho and
36,525 of later
Old Chronicle.
Total of later Old Chronicle   ´   ..   ..= 36,525

These details and identities all assist in confirming that the later systems of the Lists were expanded from an original form—similar to that inferred for the original Old Chronicle—in which the basal total was 3,652 or 3 years.

Evidence of
expansion of
later systems.

Hence human period of Old Chronicle ..   ..   ..= 2,324 years.
add 2 Nominal Solar Cycles   ..   ..= 3,044 years.

Version Africanus, Plate XVI, Table C (5)   ..   ..= 5,368 Years.
                                                          Kings.

¶ 97. THE VERSION OF CASTOR.

In one version of Castor we have the following :—
Gods and demi-gods to Anubis, inclusive   ..= 1,333 years.
Remaining demi-gods..   ..   ..= 217
Human kings ..   ..= 2,100

Total = 3,652½ vague years = 3,650 Sothic years.

Version of
Castor
confirms
original
system of
Old Chronicle
of Egypt.
The statement confirms the general arrangement of the inferred original Old Chronicle. In detail it is confirmed by the 217 years of Castor appearing as the duration of the eight demi-gods in the Old Chronicle, and by the initial period of Castor—1,333 years—agreeing within four years with the inferred initial 1,329 years of the original Old Chronicle.

The original Old Chronicle, therefore, defined the inscribed *aroura* rectangle, 3652.5 × 1162.6 (Plate XVI, Fig. C), and the square base circuit (1,772 common cubits) of the Standard Pyramid.

¶ 98. THE SQUARE CIRCUIT OF 29,220.

Gods and Kings
to Amasis II
29,220 years,
circuit of
standard
Pyramid at
1162.6 level
defining
"Aroura"
rectangles.
At the upper level of the *aroura* rectangles in the Standard Pyramid section (Plate XVI, Fig. C)—i.e., at level 1162.6—the square circuit is 29,220. This is the total number of years for gods and kings to the first year of Amasis II (Plate XVI, Table A). Comparison of the data narrated to Herodotus by the Egyptian priests in the 5th century B.C., with the statement of the Lists according to the version of Eusebius establishes this identity. It also establishes two important conclusions. These are,

Version of
Eusebius in
use in 5th
Century B.C.
(a) That the version preserved by Eusebius was the version in use in the 5th Century B.C.

Theory of
Sothic Cycle
ending in
570 B.C.
(b) That a Sothic cycle was supposed to have ended in the 1st year of Amasis II (570 B.C.).

Now this clashes with the later theory that a Sothic cycle of 1,460 Sothic years ended in 139 A.D., which theory is the fundamental basis of the various modern Egyptological chronologies. Why the Egyptians of the 5th century B.C. adopted a theory equally erroneous is a matter that will be dealt with later. The fact of immediate importance is that they knew nothing concerning a Sothic cycle that was due to end in 139 A.D.

¶ 99. THE 35th COURSE OF THE GREAT PYRAMID.

The level of the Standard Pyramid circuit 29,220 (Plate XVI, Fig. C) is again defined as follows :—

   Version Africanus, Human Kings = 4,651. Table B (8), Plate XVI.
   Version Suidas, Gods and Kings = 4,650. Table B (9), Plate XVI.

The level of the circuit 29,220—1162.6 above the base—being 4650.4 below the Apex of the Standard Pyramid.

Now 1162.6 Primitive inches is the precise level of the axis of the 35th course of masonry in the Great Pyramid. This course is 50 P. inches deep, 25 inches (the Sacred Cubit) above and below the axis of the course at 1162.6 P″. As seen from a distance this 35th course is the most outstanding course in the Pyramid. It occurs after a series of courses generally 26 inches deep. With the exception of the two lowest courses, it is the deepest course in the Pyramid. This sudden increase in depth can only have been for the intention of pointing to the fact that the 35th course axis defines the *aroura*, and the height of 1162.6 P. inches. This intention is confirmed when we study the accurate Great Pyramid survey data of Professor Petrie in relation to the fact concerning the hollowing-in feature observed by him and discussed in our ¶¶ 18–20. The angle of slope of the Standard Pyramid derived in ¶ 93 (d) is also the angle of slope of the Great Pyramid, 51°–51′–14″.3.

¶ 100. THE DYNASTOLOGICAL STANDARD PYRAMID
THE GREAT PYRAMID.

The square circuit of the Standard Pyramid base, by data of ¶ 94, is 36,524 P. inches. With 1 P. inch=1.0011 British inch, as derived in ¶ 81, and independently in ¶ 94, this circuit equals 36,564 British inches. The side of the square base of the Standard Pyramid was, therefore, 9,141 British inches. With the same hollowing-in feature as the Great Pyramid—which is hollowed in to a maximum extent of about 36 inches at the centre of each face slope—the dimension of 9,141 British inches between the centre of one base side and the centre of the opposite base side of the Standard Pyramid would be reduced by 2 ×36 inches, or 72 inches. The distance between centres of face slopes at the base of the Standard Pyramid would be 9,069 British inches (9,059 P. inches).

Four values obtained by Petrie for the corresponding dimension in the Great Pyramid are as follows:—

9069.4 B. inches ⎫
9067.7 „   „   ⎬ Petrie's stated range of possible error
9069.5 „   „   ⎬ being ± 0.6 B. inch for each side.
9068.6 „   „   ⎭

Average value = 9068.8 B. inches ± 0.6 B. inches.

The value for the Great Pyramid, then, is identical with the value for the Standard Pyramid of the Dynastological Lists. Now the angle of slope of the Great Pyramid is 51°-51'-14".3, as defined by the existing casing slope.

This is identical with the angle of slope derived in ¶ 93 for the Standard Pyramid. The Standard Pyramid of the Dynastological Lists is, therefore, the Great Pyramid of Gizeh.

¶ 101. THE DIMENSIONS OF THE GREAT PYRAMID.

The base circuit of the Great Pyramid then, is 36,524 primitive (or Pyramid) inches. Its base diagonals add 25826.5 Pyr. inches. Its height is 5,813 Pyr. inches, the radius of the circle of 36,524 Pyr. inches circumference. The axis of its 35th course defines the rectangular *aroura*, and its circuit the measure of 29219.4 Pyramid inches, expressed as 29,220 in the Dynastological Lists.

The reader will find this matter all clearly explained and diagrammatically illustrated on Plate XVII, where Petrie's surveyed measurements have been reduced to Pyramid inches.

The general appearance of the 35th course is diagrammatically represented by the suddenly thicker course shown on Figs. a, b, and c of Plate XVII.

The hollowing in of the core masonry escarpments, prior to the placing of the casing stones, is illustrated in diagrammatic perspective on Plate XVIII.

The reader will find a more detailed and precise discussion in Chapter III. In this it will be shown that the extent of hollowing-in is geometrically connected with the displacement of the plane of the Great Pyramid's Passage System, and that the amount of this displacement (286.1 P") is a well defined geometrical dimension of the Great Pyramid.

As stated on Plate XVII, the resulting value of the Pyramid inch (accurately derived from ¶¶ 81 and 94) divides precisely 500,000,000 times into the Polar Diameter of the Earth, according to the latest determination of the latter by the U.S.A. surveys of 1906 and 1909.

It is a matter for further discussion to show whether the coincidence is due to accident or design. This will be considered further in Chapter III.

DIAGRAMMATIC REPRESENTATION OF PROFESSOR PETRIES RECONSTRUCTION, AND OF THE NEW RECONSTRUCTION
OF THE GREAT PYRAMID FROM PETRIE'S SURVEY.

[To face p. 84.

PLATE XVIII.

DIAGRAMMATIC PERSPECTIVE VIEW ILLUSTRATING FEATURES
OF GREAT PYRAMID'S CORE MASONRY.

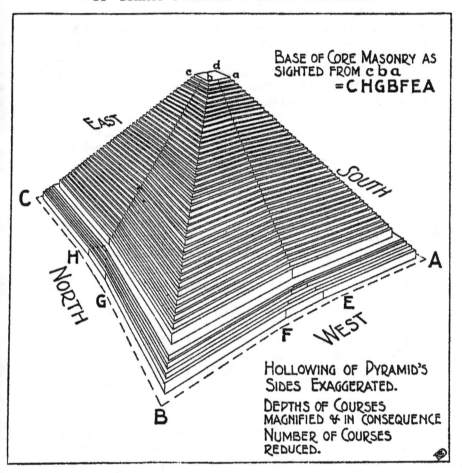

BASE OF CORE MASONRY AS
SIGHTED FROM c b a
= C H G B F E A

EAST

SOUTH

C

A

H

G

E

NORTH

F   WEST

B

HOLLOWING OF PYRAMID'S
SIDES EXAGGERATED.

DEPTHS OF COURSES
MAGNIFIED & IN CONSEQUENCE
NUMBER OF COURSES
REDUCED.

¶ 102. A PRECESSIONAL CONSTANT?

Connected with this question of intention is an important question relating to the significance the ancient Egyptians attached to the measurement of 25,826 or 7 Pyramid inches. (Plate XVI, Figs. A and B.) Up to the time of the Persian Conquest, they recognised 25,826 or 7 years to be the duration of the great astronomical cycle known as the period of the Precession of the Equinoxes. As a statement of the period of Precession it is as accurate as any modern determination. Whether, however, it is the precise interval or not does not immediately concern us. The matter of importance is that it

Great Pyramid
Measure of
25,826·7 P"
reckoned in
Dynastological
lists as
indicating
period of
Precession of
Equinoxes.

Its accurate
estimate of
precession

It is a simple function of the year value.

The period suitable as a constant of precession.

Was it used as such ?

is a simple mathematical function of the numerical value of the Solar Year. As such it is a useful constant to which to refer variations in the annual rate of Precession, or variations in the mean rate of Precession over a number of years. Whether it was formerly employed in this manner, and for the purpose stated, will be settled by the evidence discussed later.

78½ Phœnix cycles equal Pyramid's Precessional Constant.

  The period in years=50$\sqrt{2}$ times the Solar year in days=25826.54. Now 78½ Phœnix cycles of 329 years (¶¶ 33, 37, and 38)=25,826½ years of the Phœnix cycle or 25,826.54 mean solar years. In this identity the half year of the Phœnix cycle must terminate, in accordance with the Calendar rulings, at Day 1, Month VII of the Calendar Cycle of 103 years. This fixes that the period of 25,826½ years was recognised as a cycle.

Duodecimal division of 25,826 period in Dynastological List proves intentional association with Precession of Equinoxes.

  As shown on Plate XVI, Table D, the division of the Period into 24— the Babylonian divisions of the ecliptic—indicates that the cycle was identified with the twelve divisions or signs of the Zodiac. The 1,076 years of Eratosthenes would, therefore, represent precession through a half Zodiacal Sign, at the rate of 25,826 years for the 12 signs. One summation of the totals of the Version of Africanus—a summation not shown on Plate XVI—gives 4,305 or 6 years to the beginning of Dynasty XIX. This represents precession through two Zodiacal signs. It seems clear enough from these identifications that the earlier Egyptians, at least, recognised the period of 25,826½ years to be the Period of the Precession of the Equinoxes round the Zodiacal signs.

¶ 103. THE EARLY KNOWLEDGE CONCERNING PRECESSION.

48th century to 4th Century B.C., actual precession through 60° (2 Zodiacal signs) occupied 4380 years.

  Now, although the interval of 25,826½ years is the period—or almost exactly the period—of the Precession of the Equinoxes, the annual rate varies considerably. For this reason, the mean rate between the 48th century and the 4th century B.C., moved the Equinox round 60° of the ecliptic or through two Zodiacal signs in 4,380 years. Now 4,380 Sothic years equal 4,383 vague years.

Hence 4383 years of Human Kings to Amasis II.

The latter is the stated interval at the time of the 5th to 3rd centuries B.C. for the duration of human kings to the 1st year of Amasis II, 570 B.C. (Plate XVI, Table A, and ¶ 98.)

Identity presupposes knowledge, or tradition based on previous knowledge concerning actual rate of precession.

It seems clear enough that a coincidence of this nature could only have originated from a knowledge of the obvious basis of the identity, or from a tradition concerning such knowledge. The knowledge concerning, and the reason for effecting the identity appear to have governed the framing of the List around the year 570 B.C. It is equally certain that

Knowledge lost before 3rd century B.C.

this knowledge was lost before the 3rd century B.C., although the identity remained. At least the knowledge was never imparted to the Greeks.

¶ 104. SYNCELLUS AND THE OLD CHRONICLE ON THE PRECESSION OF THE EQUINOXES.

Later systems of Dynastological lists substitute 36,525 years for 25,826 years as period of precession.

  The latter facts are clear from the nature of the list of Africanus, as developed in Plate XVI, Tables A and F. and from the later form of the Old Chronicle of Egypt (Plate XVI, Table E). These both indicate that the cycle of 25,826 years had been confused with a supposed precessional cycle of 36,525 years. This, indeed, is stated by Syncellus, in relating concerning the 36,525 years' summation of the Old Chronicle. Syncellus states that the period of 36,525 years " relates to the fabled periodical revolution of the Zodiac among the Egyptians and Greeks, that is, its revolution from a particular point to the same again, which point is the first minute of the first degree of that equinoctial sign which they call the Ram, as it is explained in the Genesis of Hermes and in the Cyrannian books." The Statement of Syncellus concerning the late traditional cycle of precession, 36,525 years.

The sign here taken as datum belongs to later Egyptian times, when the Equinox fell in the Ram (Aries). In earlier times, the sign was Taurus, in which actual sign the Equinox fell from 4,700 B.C. to 1,800 B.C.—since the extent of the sign, as defined by its stars is about 40°. The actual extent of Aries (the Ram) is about 20°—as defined by its stars. The Equinox therefore fell in the Ram between 1,800 B.C. and 320 B.C.[1] About 320 B.C., the 1st point of Aries, defined by Syncellus above, therefore marked the diurnal commencement of the Vernal Equinoctial Year. This gives the epoch of the death of Alexander the Great (323 B.C.), and accounts for the origin of the theory that ended the alleged precessional period of 36,525 years about this time. Why this alleged precessional period was represented as ending at the Zodiacal 1st point of Aries around the date of Alexander's conquest of Egypt.

¶ 105. HOW THE DURATION OF 36,525 YEARS WAS IDENTIFIED AS PERIOD OF PRECESSION.

It is clear that the confusion arose first from the period of 4,380 years. Originally this was identified correctly as the number of years taken by the Equinox, between 4,700 B.C. and 320 B.C. to travel backwards through 60° of the ecliptic, from 1st point of Gemini, through Taurus and Aries, to 1st point of Aries. The termination of this period was then prematurely attached to 570 B.C., the 1st year of Amasis II, and identified as three Sothic cycles of 1,461 vague years, = 4,383 vague years, = 4,380 Sothic years. 25 of these Sothic cycles = 36,525 vague years; whereas the Sothic cycle fails to divide into the Precessional period of 25,826½ years. The latter, however, contains 78½ Phœnix cycles of 329 years. The Phœnix cycle in the Hebrew Chronology is associated with a period of 1,461 solar years (¶ 39), and from this originated the erroneous identification—noted by Tacitus (¶ 39)—that the Phœnix cycle was a period of 1,461 years. This sequence of error was obviously the origin of the late conception that the period of Precession was 36,525 years. Precession from 1st point of Gemini at 4,700 B.C. to 1st point of Aries at 320 B.C. = 4,380 years.
4,380 Sothic Years = 3 Sothic cylces.
25 Sothic cycles = 36,525 vague years.
Phœnix cycles make up true period of Precession, 25,826½ years.
Phœnix cycle erroneously identified with Sothic cycle.
Hence false Phœnix cycles lead to period 36,525 years, being conceived as Precessional period.

¶ 106. PERIOD OF PRECESSION ALWAYS NUMERICALLY ASSOCIATED WITH BASE OF GREAT PYRAMID.

Apart, however, from the sequence noted, tradition obviously held that the true period of Precession was given by the Pyramid base, tradition failed to preserve the knowledge that the numerical value of the period was contained in the sum of the diagonals of the base square. The later Egyptians, therefore, Tradition that Great Pyramid base gave true Precessional Period.
Identification with base diagonals lost.

---

[1] The basis of the calculations giving these dates, together with the whole question of the astronomical divisions of the Zodiac will be dealt with later.

Identification
with base
circuit
adopted.
How
Hipparchus
obtained his
rate of
precession.
adopted the circuit of the base square as giving the period of Precession.   They passed this period of 36,525 years on to the Greeks.   The period is equal to an annual rate of Precession of 35.5 secs. of angle.   Hence Hipparchus (circ. 150 B.C.) " determined " the rate of Precession as 36 secs. of angle.

The Nominal
Solar Year,
365.24 days,
recedes
through
the nominal
Sothic Year,
365.25 days,
in 36,525 years,
giving a true
application
of Precession,
but not an
astronomical
application.
The period was also reckoned as containing not only 25 Sothic Cycles, but 24 nominal Solar cycles of 1521.875 vague years.   (Refer ¶ 59.)   The nominal Solar year of 365.24 days was reckoned to travel completely backwards round the nominal Sothic year of 365.25 days in 36,525 years.   The vague year also travelled backwards completely round the nominal solar year in 1521.875 vague years.   This gives the complete explanation of the late conceptions concerning Precession.

Hence the system of Africanus (Plate XVI, Table A) gave the Divine and Human Dynasties as of the duration of 20 nominal solar cycles of 1521.8 years, or 30,437 years.

¶ 107. " PYRAMID " THE GRECIANISED FORM OF HEBREW " URIM-MIDDIN "—" LIGHTS-MEASURES."

Greek Science
derived from
Egypt and
Chaldæa.
In section II of this chapter a synopsis of the evidences concerning the origins of Greek Science and Philosophy is given.   The facts, and the sequence of facts, of this synopsis, clearly show that the Greek philosophers derived what was new and original in their science and philosophy from the oral traditions of the priesthood of Egypt and Chaldæa—but chiefly from Egypt. The same sequence of facts was seen in the case of the knowledge of the megalithic builders of the Mediterranean and Atlantic seaboards.

Zonares on
Greek
Arithmetic and
Astronomy
derived from
Egypt and
Chaldæa.
It was obviously of no recent derivation or migration of science that Zonares[1] wrote, in treating of arithmetic and astronomy, when he stated—

" It is said that these came from the Chaldees to the Egyptians, and thence to the Greeks."

Name
" Pyramid "
of Chaldæan
origin.
Great Pyramid
name in Egypt
" Khuti "=
" The Lights."
In Hebrew
" Lights "=
" Urim."
Chaldee " Ur "
becomes
Phrygian
" Pur," Greek
" Pyra " (pL)=
" Beacon
Fires."
The truth in this remark is monumentally confirmed by the lasting name of the monument perpetuating the early knowledge to which Zonares refers. For the name " Pyramid "—like all the constructional conceptions embodied in the Great Pyramid—is primarily of Euphratean derivation.   The Egyptian name for the Great Pyramid is " Khuti "—" the Lights."   In the Semitic languages the equivalent name is " Urim "—" the Lights."   In Phrygian and Greek, the root " Ur " (light) became successively " Pur " and " Pyr " (fire), and " Pyra " (a plural) " beacon fires."

Thus Plato, in his " Cratylus " (Taylor's translation), says, " Do you know on what account ' Pur ' (Pyr) was so called ?   Consider whether this is not of barbaric origin—for it is by no means easy to adopt this to the Greek tongue ; and it is manifest that the Phrygians thus denominate ' fire ' with a trifling deviation."   Thus ' Pur ' (Pyr) is a form of the Hebrew ' Ur '—' light.'   The

[1] Lib. I, vi.

addition of the labial ' p '—as also ' b ' and ' f,' hence ' burn ' and ' furnace '—
is a frequent change observed in roots passing from one language to another.
Hence ' Uri '=' fiery.' Here both words contain the same original root.

Again in Hebrew, 'middin '='measures,' 'madadu'='to measure'; in
Sanscrit, 'ma,' 'mad,'='to measure'; in Zend, 'meêtê,' 'matê'; Latin, 'modus,'
' a measure '; Greek, 'metron '; Anglo-Saxon, 'metan,' 'to measure.' *(Hebrew "Middin "=" Measures.")*

Examples—' Aga-medes,' *Semitic*, ' The Great Measurer,' or *Greek*, ' the
very wise ' *Phoenician*, ' Baal-middoh,' ' the Lord of the measures.' *(Phœnician "Baal-Middoh "=" The Lord of the Measures.")*

In Chaldee and Hebrew, ' Urim '=' Lights,' with the labial ' p,' as in
Phrygian, ' Urim '=' Purim '=' Lights.' Greek ' Pyra '=' beacon fires '
(lights).

In Chaldee and Hebrew, 'middin '=' measures." Hence the Chaldee-
Hebrew name for the Great Pyramid—in Egyptian, ' Khuti,' ' the Lights '—
is ' Urim-middin ' (Purim-middin)=' Lights–Measures.' *(Purpose of Great Pyramid defined in Hebrew by name 'Urim-middin '= 'Lights-Measures.')*

In Greek this becomes ' Pyra-midos,' ' Pyra-mid.'

The name ' Pyramid,' therefore, monumentalises the external purpose
of the Great Pyramid. It is a "beacon of reflexions," and a "monument of
measures." *(Grecianised form of name = 'Pyra-middin,' 'Pyra-Midos,' 'Pyramid.')*

It is of importance to observe that the Greek name is not derived from
two Greek roots, but is the Grecianised form (Pyramidos) of the Semitic name
' Urim-middin,' or possibly of a composite Phrygian and Phœnician form of
the name—' Purim-middoh.'

¶ 108. THE PYRAMID OF THE DYNASTOLOGICAL LISTS AND OF THE BOOK OF THE DEAD.

In the compilation of the ancient Egyptian King Lists, Egyptologists
recognise three main periods when such compilations were made. These are,
in order, *(Egyptian Dynastological Lists :—)*

Three periods of compilation.

(1) The early period of Dynasties V–VI—e.g., the King Lists of the Stele of Palermo,
and of the Cairo fragments. The kings of these dynasties built Pyramids at
Abusir and Sakkarah. *(1) Dyns. V & VI*

(2) The period of Dynasties XVIII and XIX—e.g., the Karnak List and the Turin
Papyrus List (Dyn. XVIII), and the Lists of Abydos and Sakkarah (Dyn. XIX). *(2) Dyns. XVIII & XIX*

(3) The Saïte Restoration Period—Dyn. XXVI—from the compilations of which
period as we have seen, the Lists of Manetho were derived in part. *(3) Dyn. XXVI*

In the evolution of the Egyptian Sacred writings, Egyptologists recognise
three similar periods as follows :— *(Egyptian Sacred writings :—)*

Three periods of compilation.

(1) The period of Dynasties V and VI, when the funerary texts, commonly known as
the Pyramid texts, were carved. These deal with the life of the king in the
future life. From them originated the later so-called *Book of the Dead*, chapters
of which were in existence as early as the XIIth Dynasty. *(1) Dyns. V-VI*

(2) The period of the XVIIIth to XXth Dynasties when the collection known as the
Theban Recension of the *Book of the Dead* was prepared. *(2) Dyns. XVIII-XIX*

(3) The period of the XXVIth (Saïte) Dynasty, when the Saïte Recension of the *Book
of the Dead* was compiled *(3) Dyn. XXVI*

The Egyptian "Book of the Dead" employs Great Pyramid features as an allegory of the future life.

To the latter recension belongs the version entitled " The Book of the Master of the Hidden House," in which, as Mr. Marsham Adams[1] has shown, the soul of the departed is pictured as following the passages and chambers of the Great Pyramid. In this version the Pyramid itself is pictured as an allegory in stone of the ways and trials of the future life.

¶ 109. THE SECRET HOUSE OF THE SAÏTE RECENSION

Maspero's opinion :—

Purpose of Pyramids and Book of the Dead related.

As a result of Mr. Adams' researches, Sir Gaston Maspero concluded that " The Pyramids and the ' Book of the Dead ' reproduce the same original, the one in words, the other in stone."[2] In quoting the preceding, Mr. Adams refers to " the prevalence of a tradition among the priests of Memphis," a fact which he says he " learned later from the same authority," supporting his " contention that the Secret House was the scene where the neophyte was initiated into the mysteries of Egypt."

Egyptian efforts to refer back sacred writings to Pyramid period.

Accordingly every possible attempt was made by the compilers of the various chapters of the Book of the Dead to refer back the origin of the ritual and symbolism to the Pyramid Kings of Memphis—the builders of the Pyramids of Gizeh. Thus a passage in the cxxxviith chapter of the Book of the Dead states that that chapter was found by Heru-tat-ef, son of Khufu, the builder of the Great Pyramid.

Significance of attempt of XXVIth Dynasty to ape the customs and institutions of Pyramid period.

Now it was during the XXVIth (Saïte) Dynasty that the order of chapters of the Book of the Dead was drawn up, and when, as Breasted states,[3] " the worship of the (Pyramid) kings, who had ruled at Memphis in these remote days, was revived.......Their Pyramids were even extensively restored and repaired. The archaic titles.........in the government of the Pyramid builders were again brought into requisition, and in the externals of government everything possible was done to clothe it with the appearance of remote antiquity."

Dynastological Date for Origin of Dynasty XXVI is numerically the arc of 36,525 circle giving Pyramid Angle of Slope.

Hence in the Saïte system of Dynastology, preserved in the version of Africanus, the duration of years stated to Psammetichos, the first actual king of Dynasty XXVI (Saïte), is given as 5,271, the length of the arc of the 36,525 circumference, measuring the angle of slope of the Standard Pyramid. Reduced to modern angular measure this angle of slope is 51°–51′–14″.3, the angle of slope of the Great Pyramid of Gizeh.

It was during the reign of Psammetichos (Psamtek I)—as Herodotus states—that Greek colonists first settled in Egypt.[4] For the significance of this settlement, and its date in relation to the history of Greek Geometry and Astronomy, the reader is referred to Section II of this chapter, and Table X.

---

[1]" The Book of the Master," by Marsham Adams.
[2]Quoted from a letter to Mr. Marsham Adams, " The Book of the Master," p. iv.
[3]A History of Egypt, p. 370.
[4]Refer Annals of Assurbanipal re Gyges and Lydians. This gives the date as 661 B C. when the Carian colonists of Herodotus apparently accompanied the Lydians as mercenaries

¶ 110. COPTIC CHRISTIANITY AND "THE BOOK OF THE DEAD."

Thus it is that from the remotest periods of authentic history, an *The Ancient Mystery of the Pyramids.* atmosphere of mystery has enshrouded all expression of thought and opinion concerning the Pyramids of Gizeh. Essentially geometrical in form, the *Survival in Book of the Dead.* Pyramids, by influencing the expression of theological conceptions, supplied religious allegory with an unfailing source of geometrical symbolism. It is this pyramid allegory of which a corrupt survival exists in the Egyptian *Book of the Dead.*

It is from the *Book of the Dead* that the Coptic descendants of the ancient *"The Book of the Dead" influences Coptic Christianity and Early Christian Gnosticism* Egyptians derived the mystical and allegorical element which was introduced into early Christian gnosticism. The literature of early Christian gnosticism abounds in mystical pyramid figures and associated astronomical conceptions and constellations.

To the Copts is due the survival, to the present day, of the ancient Egyptian *The Importance of Coptic in assisting to solve the problem of the Ancient Egyptian Language.* Calendar and month names. To them we owe the retention of a dialect of the ancient Egyptian language, and with it, much that has tended to facilitate and elucidate the translation of ancient hieroglyphic texts. Hence the importance and value attaching to any traditions concerning the Great Pyramid that can be reliably identified as of Coptic origin.

¶ 111. COPTIC TRADITION AND THE GREAT PYRAMID.

Regarding the Coptic traditions, Dr. Sprenger, in Appendix to Vyse's "Pyramids of Gizeh," vol. II, observes that "the traditions of the ancient Egyptians were preserved by their descendants, the Copts, who were held in *Coptic Traditions concerning the Pyramids and their purpose.* great esteem by the Arabs........It may be remarked that the Arabian authors have given the same accounts of the Pyramids, with little or no variation, for above a thousand years ; and that they appear to have repeated the traditions of the ancient Egyptians, mixed up with fabulous stories and incidents, certainly not of Mahometan invention."

The account of Masoudi (died 345 A.H.=957 A.D.), in the Arabic MS. of the Akbar-Ezzeman, at Oxford, relates that "Surid ......one of the kings *Arabic MSS. Translations of Early Coptic MSS. concerning the Pyramids* of Egypt before the flood, built the two great Pyramids." In this narration the Great Pyramid is referred to as "the Eastern Pyramid." Dr. Sprenger states that "Masoudi affirms, in the Akbar-Ezzeman that he wrote his account of Surid from a Coptic modern history."

The narration of Masoudi is as follows :—

".......He (Surid) also ordered the priests to deposit within them *The Great Pyramid :— Contained Records of Arithmetic and Geometry.* (the Pyramids), written accounts of their wisdom and acquirements in the different arts and sciences.......with the writings of the priests containing all manner of wisdom, the names and properties of medical plants, and the sciences of arithmetic and geometry, that they might remain as records, for the benefit of those who could afterwards comprehend them."

Astronomical
and Historical
Cycles affecting
past and
future time.

" ....In the Eastern Pyramid (the Great Pyramid) were inscribed the heavenly spheres, and figures representing the stars and planets...."

" The king, also, deposited.......the positions of the stars and their cycles ; together with the history and chronicle of time past, of that which is to come, and every future event' which would take place in Egypt."

Great Pyramid
Dedicated to
History and
Astronomy.

Similarly the MS. of Makrizi states that " the first (the Great) Pyramid was especially dedicated to history and astronomy ; the second (Pyramid) to medical knowledge."

Tohfat Alagaib states that the Great Pyramid contained " plans of the stars, and historical and prophetic records."

¶ 112. THE SOURCE OF COPTIC TRADITIONS.

According to the accounts of Masoudi and Al Kodhai, a papyrus, found in the monastery of Abou Hormeis, and said to have been inscribed with ancient " Coptic " characters, gave the following account of the Pyramids :—

" Upon the walls were written the mysteries of science, astronomy, geometry, physics, and much useful knowledge, which any person, who understands our writing, can read."

Coptic
Traditions
erroneously
identified the
pictured
Pyramid
Passages of
" The Book of
the Dead " with
the Passages of
the Great
Pyramid.

The Pyramids of Gizeh, we know, contain no such hieroglyphic inscriptions as the traditions imply. It is only such texts as that of the *Book of the Dead*, which picture the passages and chambers of the Standard Pyramid of the Dynastological Lists, or Secret House of the *Book of the Dead* as lined with instructions and formulæ, and with mythical figures and stars. It is to these that the traditions refer, and from such texts as these that the traditions obtained authority for identifying the Standard Pyramid of the Dynastological Texts with the Great Pyramid of Gizeh.

Importance
of Coptic
Traditions :—
Association of
Sacred House
of the " Book of
the Dead," and
the Standard
Pyramid of the
Dynastological
Lists, with the
Great Pyramid

The fact therefore remains that Coptic tradition associates the Great Pyramid with the symbolising of astronomical and geometrical figures, just as the Egyptian Ancestors of the Copts associated the Great Pyramid with their ideal secret house in the *Book of the Dead*, and with their geometrical Dynastology, cosmical year circle, and Sothic cycle mythology.

SECTION I—SUMMARY AND CONCLUSIONS.

Thesis that a
" Prehistoric "
Civilization
reached same
advanced stage
of astronomical
knowledge as
Modern
Science of
Gravitational
Astronomy.

Not necessarily
on same lines
or research.

¶ 113. PREVIOUS CONCLUSIONS AND NEW DATA.

In the Summary and Conclusions of Chapter I (Section I, ¶¶ 40–46), it was seen that a high state of civilisation flourished in times classified as " prehistoric." The culture of this civilisation was seen to have reached an advanced stage of scientific knowledge. It was not suggested that scientific development had proceeded along the same lines as modern scientific research.

It was, however, suggested, *by the evidence*, that results had been attained in the science of astronomy in no way inferior to the results of modern gravitational astronomy.

In one particular line of inquiry, the indications pointed clearly to an advanced knowledge concerning the elements of the planetary orbits. These indications suggested that this knowledge had been recognised to be capable of simple expression as a system of Natural Law; the system being capable of complete definition in solid geometrical form. This was indicated as of Pyramidal form.

"Prehistoric" Knowledge concerning Elements of Planetary Orbits.

Embodied in a system of Natural Law defined in solid geometrical form.

The evidence discussed afforded reliable grounds for tentatively accepting the hypothesis that the Great Pyramid of Gizeh was the structural expression of this system of Natural Law. It suggested that the Pyramid was constructed to perpetuate this knowledge at a time when the remote founders of the Euphratean, Egyptian, and Mediterranean civilisations were reconstructing their systems of national life upon the fragments of oral tradition remaining from the former civilisation.

Great Pyramid a structural expression of this.

Its construction a link between the "Prehistoric" civilisation and the beginning of Historical civilisation

The discussion of the new evidence adduced in the present chapter indicates that the hypothesis suggested by the preliminary data is confirmed by the oral traditions concerning the Great Pyramid, by its association with the original scientific system of primitive measures, and by its external measures and principal features.

New Data concerning Systems of Measures, Oral Tradition, and External Measures of Great Pyramid confirm thesis.

¶ 114. A POLAR DIAMETER INCH.—ACCIDENT OR INTENTION.

The evidence upon which the preceding conclusion is based leads to the further inference that the *external features* of the Great Pyramid are primarily concerned with a geometrical representation of the dimensions and motions of the Earth and its orbit. The unit for the geometrical representation of dimensions must necessarily be a simple function of (a) the Earth's Polar diameter, (b) the Sun's diameter, or (c) the Earth's mean distance from the Sun. Otherwise the representation can have no meaning or application. It seems to be clearly evident that of the three possible units that derived from the Earth's Polar Diameter is the most suitable for representing the other two dimensions in terms tangible to the Earth's scientific inhabitants.

Necessary Basis of Ancient Science a Knowledge of Length of Earth's Polar Diameter.

Intentionally, or by accident, the Great Pyramid unit of measurement—the Primitive inch—is the simplest possible function of the Earth's Polar Diameter. The Earth's Polar Diameter measures exactly 500 million Primitive inches. The value giving this result was derived from three independent sources :—

Primitive Inch, Great Pyramid Inch, and Inch defined by Egyptian King Lists are all equal.

500 Million of such inches = Earth's Polar Diameter.

(a) The common sources of Egyptian metrological data (¶ 81).

(b) The ancient Egyptian Dynastological Lists (¶ 94).

(c) The external measurements of the Great Pyramid (¶ 101).

The three independent sources agree in associating the Primitive inch value with the representation of cyclic functions of the Earth's motion in its orbit. This tends to confirm that the simple relationship between the Earth's Polar Diameter and the Primitive inch can scarcely have been an accidental

Associated Data indicate Relationship as possibly intentional.

Requisite
Additional
Data to
establish
intention :—
Association
with simple
relationships,
Sun's
Diameter,
Mean Sun
Distance, Orbit
Eccentricity,
and variations.
Independent
Angular Check
Measurements

relationship. It cannot, however, be established that the relationship was intentional until the Pyramid's geometrical system is shown to extend the relationship to the Sun's diameter, the mean Sun distance, and the variations in the eccentricity of the Earth's orbit. These values should be confirmed, as to intention, by the representation of *independent* heliocentric or geocentric angular measurements where possible. At least, this is what one would expect to find in a geometrical system of the nature inferred, and in which the Designer's express purpose was to establish the certainty of his intentions.

¶ 115. THE PRIMARY METROLOGICAL SYSTEM.

The Sacred
Hebrew Cubit,
of 25 P. inches,
preserved by
Pyramid and
Hebrews.
Never used in
Egypt except
by Semites.

The Primitive inch—the inferred Polar diameter inch—is the basal unit of the Primary Metrological system of the former civilisation. An important unit of this system was the Sacred Cubit of 25 P. inches. The latter has been preserved by the measurements of the Great Pyramid, and by the Hebrews. It never occurs in Egypt except during periods of Semitic domination.

The Sacred
½-Cubit
originates the
Modern Foot.

Apparently from the half cubit (12½″) of this system originated the 12⅓″ foot of ancient Roman remains, and of ancient British and Medieval English remains. Of the same origin is the old Rhineland foot, and the foot in Switzerland and Austria.

The Primitive
Inch originates
the Modern
Inch, Zoll,
Tum, and
Pouce.

The Primitive inch (1.0011 B″) is also the original of the British Inch, of the old German, Austrian and Swiss *Zoll*, of the Danish *tomme*, and Scandinavian *tum*, and of the old French *pouce*. This origin, at least for the British Inch, is confirmed by the connection between the sacred half-cubit and the decimal division of the Hebrew unit of 10 acres in ancient Cornwall, where the side of the 10 acres square occurred as a furlong of 8,000 inches. (¶¶ 85 and 86.)

¶ 116. THE SECONDARY METROLOGICAL SYSTEM.

Secondary
Metrological
System
devised to
Avoide use
of π.
Its basis the
Year Circle.
Diametric and
Circumferen-
tial Units, and
Linear Units
for Areas.

The Secondary Metrological System of the former civilisation is very clearly defined. It appears to have been formulated to avoid in calculations the use of the ratio, $\frac{circumference}{diameter}=3.14159$. A Standard Year Circle of 3652.42 Primitive inches was adopted. The Standard Diameter of this circle was divided into Diametric Digits, Diametric Feet, and Diametric Cubits. The Standard Circumference was divided into Circumferential Digits, Circumferential Feet, and Circumferential Cubits. These linear units have all been preserved by the Egyptians.

The Origin of
the Unit of
Square
Measure
The "Aroura."
The
"¼-Aroura"
Year Circle.

A standard of Square Measure was formulated as follows :—A Rectangle of length equal to the circumference of the Standard Circle, and of breadth equal to the diameter of the Standard Circle was the standard unit of square measure. It was equal in area to the area of four standard Circles. The Standard Rectangle was transformed into a square of equal area. The side of this square was divided into a hundred parts. The linear unit thus obtained was adopted as the cubit for measuring sides of rectangular figures. This cubit has been preserved by the Egyptians as their common cubit of 20.63 British inches. The "Aroura" Rectangle and "Aroura" Square. The Common Egyptian Cubit.

Simple rule-of-thumb relations connected the diametric and circumferential units with the linear units of rectangular figures. The Secondary system was obviously formulated at a time when the uncultured many were organised to carry out highly skilled work under the intermittent direction of a cultured few. The system appears in use in ancient Egypt in the earliest Dynastic times—and possibly in pre-dynastic times—before the Pyramids were built. System for use of the Uncultured Many under Intermittent Direction of a Cultured Few. System in use before the Pyramids.

¶ 117. THE GREAT PYRAMID'S EXTERIOR.

In Chapters III and IV it will be seen that the Great Pyramid contains a single comprehensive system of geometry representing the complete derivation of the Secondary System of Measures in terms of the Solar year to the scale of 1P. inch to a day. From this, and the data in the present chapter, it follows that the Great Pyramid represents the geometry of the year circle to three decimal scales, The Great Pyramid's three scales 1 10 100.

(a) 1 P. inch to a day. (Plates XXXV and XLIII.)
(b) 10 P. inches to a day. (¶¶ 95 and 99.)
(c) 100 P. inches to a day. (¶¶ 100 and 101.)

Its 35th course defines the Sacred Cubit of 25 P. inches, and the *aroura* rectangle of 3652.4 P. inches by 1162.6 P. inches. The Square circuit of *any* horizontal plane of the Pyramid is equal to the circumference of a circle of radius equal to the Pyramid height above the horizontal plane considered; and the area of the right vertical section of the Pyramid above this horizontal plane is equal to the area of the quadrant of the circle defined. Its 35th Course defines the Rectangular "Aroura." Pyramid's Horizontal Circuit= Circumference of Circle whose Radius equals Pyramid height above Circuit considered.

The datum of this representation is the Pyramid's base circuit of 36524.2+P. inches, representing the value of the solar year on the scale of 100 P. inches to a day. Pyramid's Base Circuit = 36,524 Primitive inches.

¶ 118. THE EGYPTIAN KING LISTS DEFINE THE GREAT PYRAMID.

It was at a comparatively late period of Egyptian history that the Egyptians constructed their various systems of fictitious chronology. This they did by substituting years of alleged Egyptian history for Pyramid inches in important measurements of the Great Pyramid. The principle upon which they proceeded in such cases was outlined by Dr. Sprenger about a century ago. Sprenger stated, regarding the Egyptians, that, with them, "an idea, a period of time, or any remarkable occurrence, were frequently connected with ideal persons in mythology, and when any similarity existed, received the same appellation."[1] Fictitious Chronology of Egyptian King Lists compiled from Great Pyramid's Measurements. Sprenger defines factors governing such fictitious compilations of Egyptians.

[1] Vyse's "Pyramids of Gizeh," Vol. II, Appendix.

The factors in the case of the Mythical Chronology of the King Lists.

"The idea" in the particular case under consideration was that oral tradition associated the Pyramid's measures with astronomical cycles and orbital motions. This supplied the data for their various "periods of time." and for identification with "remarkable occurrences" in history and astronomy.

Supposing that Great Pyramid had been demolished, its principal Features, Dimensions, and its Units could be reconstructed from the Egyptian King Lists.

So extensively did the Egyptians adopt the outstanding measurements of the Great Pyramid in their fictitious systems of chronology that the Great Pyramid's external *features, dimensions,* and *units* can be derived without any prior reference to the Great Pyramid. Were the Great Pyramid not now in existence its external form, dimensions, and units, together with its principal external features, could be reconstructed entirely from the Dynastological Lists of the Egyptians.

¶ 119. THE KNOWLEDGE IN THE KING LISTS AND THE LACK OF UNDERSTANDING.

Analysis of Pyramid Data of King Lists indicates that the Later Egyptians knew the general purpose of the Pyramid, but were unable to give expression to this purpose in detail.

The unsystematic manner in which the Egyptians adopted Pyramid measurements as the basis of astronomical periods in their King Lists clearly indicates that they had nothing but a general vague tradition to guide them. They proceeded to extract measurements without regard to sequence or principle. Scientific principle demands that a graphical representation of a period of time cannot be made along an axis defining radii and diameters, and at the same time be made round a circuit defining a circumference. The latter method of representation is possible, the former unlikely, but both together are impossible in a scientific representation.

They knew Base defined Precessional Period, but identified same with Base Circuit instead of Base Diagonals

The compilers of the King Lists, however, added the measurements of radii to the measurements of arcs, horizontal distances to vertical distances, and totalled measurements in cubits together with measurements in inches. The single idea they did adhere to was that the Pyramid base circuit contained a representation of the Period of Precession. One school adopted the sum of the base diagonals as giving the period in inches for years. Another school adopted the base circuit in inches for years, as defining the Period. The difference between the two conceptions amounted to 10,698 years, or twice the duration of the human kings given in one summation of the Lists preserved by Africanus. (Plate XVI, Table C (4).)

Other items of knowledge preserved intact but without intelligent understanding.

Nevertheless, in their oral tradition, possibly without much understanding of the facts, the Egyptian priests retained many valuable items of astronomical knowledge. This is indicated by the manner and sequence in which the Greeks derived their knowledge of science from the Egyptians. (Refer Section II of this Chapter—and Table X.)

¶ 120. THE SUGGESTED LINES OF FURTHER INQUIRY.

The traditional association of the Pyramid's base with the idea of Precession leads to a further possible inference.   The difference between the solar year and the siderial year is the annual amount of precession measured in time.   This and the Pyramid base connection suggest that while the base square circuit gives the value of the Tropical year, the perimeter of the hollowed-in base may have been intended to give the value of the Siderial year.

New Data suggest that Pyramid Base and its features should define not only the Tropical (Solar) Year but the Siderial Year.

By following up this suggestion, the reader will find the intention of the Pyramid rapidly developing in Chapter III.   From this suggestion, the external features, dimensions, and units of the Great Pyramid, when *studied in plan,* will be found to give, precisely and accurately, every essential value of the Earth's orbit, and its motions.   These will be found to include the values of the Anomalistic, Siderial and Solar years, the mean Sun distance, the Sun's diameter (independent linear and angular representations), and the maximum and minimum values of the eccentricity of the Earth's orbit.

Development of Inquiry suggested supplies more confirming Data than suggestion indicated.

From these representations the reader will be able to appreciate how and why Pythagoras—having studied the science of the Egyptians—was enabled to enunciate, over 2,000 years before the truth was generally realised, that the planets revolve round the Sun.   (Refer Section II, ¶¶ 126 and 129 to 133, and Table X.)

The Further Data throw light upon the origin of the Pythagorean system of Astronomy.

SECTION II.—THE ORIGINS OF GREEK GEOMETRY AND ASTRONOMY.

¶ 121. THE ANCIENT MYSTERIES OF ORIENTAL CULTS.

Ancient Knowledge preserved by oral instruction.
Oral instruction was the means of perpetuating the knowledge preserved by the cults of the ancient East. Hence we find, in both Egypt and Chaldæa, much monumental and other structural evidence of a higher knowledge, but
Hence paucity of direct literary reference.
no literature with regard to its principles and essential details. Literature there is, of a kind, as we have seen in the cases of the Egyptian Dynastological Lists, and the Book of the Dead. In general—as in the cases cited—it is the
Ancient Literature purposely distorted the facts of knowledge in form of a Priestly Code of Reference
literature dispensed by the priesthood for the mystification of the laity, or at best, the coded literature beloved of the mythologist and kabbalist, to understand which required oral instruction by admission into the several orders of the cult, and, for a complete unveiling, admission into the ultimate Inner Priesthood.

Analysis of such records indicates that Codes preserved the Central Facts of Ancient Knowledge without preserving understanding of the derivation and application of the facts.
The explanation of phenomena and ideals furnished by the popular literature were generally distorted and untrue. Furnished by the coded literature, the explanations were so hedged about by intentional obliquities, so obscured by fables and spurious mysteries, and so entangled in its code, as to be beyond the comprehension of those without the cult. The evidence discussed has shown that such explanations, when made, did not give an understanding of the ancient science. They merely revealed the traditional knowledge concerning the facts that had been derived from a former understanding of the causal relation between the facts and the scientific phenomena expressed by them.

¶ 122. KNOWLEDGE PRESERVED AS A MYSTERY: UNDERSTANDING LOST.

Distortion of Facts extended to Art.
With such an artificial basis for the national ideals, art itself became distorted in its representation of such phenomena as the heavenly bodies and their motions—apparent or real. This distortion was maintained even in the
Utilisation of Facts of Knowledge controlled by Priesthood.
coded literature that formed what we may term the index of reference for the priests of the Inner Mysteries. Hence we find that in Chaldæa, and still more particularly in Egypt, the scientific knowledge retailed by the priesthood, for
Empirical Rules " Rationed " out to Populace.
use and application in the national life, had been filtered down to " rule-of-thumb " dogmas, and rough empirical axioms, postulates and formulæ.

The mistake of supposing that the Empirical Rules indicate extent of knowledge possessed by the Ancients.
In reiteration of such dogmas and empirical formulæ the monuments, papyri and traditional literature are clamourously persistent. The approximate nature of these rules is so evident that it has become the custom to pass unchallenged the assertion that the ancient Egyptians and Chaldæans performed their vast and accurate engineering and other scientific works upon a purely empirical and " rule-of-thumb " basis.

The hypothesis underlying this assertion is not only illogical; it is not in accordance with what we know regarding the relations between State and Priesthood.

¶ 123. THE SUPPRESSION OF LEARNING.

The Priesthood saw in the State the means whereby it could obtain power, *Priesthood organised its knowledge and resources to control machinery of State.* possessions and obedience. Accordingly, the priesthood centred its efforts and organised its resources and knowledge towards obtaining control of the machinery of State. Its object was so to formulate the constitution that the State should be dependent upon the Priesthood.

The Priesthood possessed the knowledge necessary for almanac organisa- *Priesthood possessed the Exclusive knowledge of fundamental principles of Almanac Organisation, and of constructional and other scientific works.* tion and the scientific knowledge embodied in the vast engineering and other scientific works carried out by the State. That knowledge was given no clear literary expression, lest the State, by possession of this, should become inde- pendent of the Priesthood. Hence it is obvious that the few empirical rules, of which the monuments and papyri give us evidence, were vastly less than the unwritten knowledge of the silent Inner Priesthood.

Schooled to dependence upon the Priesthood, the ancient Egyptians, and to *Conditions devised and enforced to ensure that the nation must rely upon the informed guidance and judgment of the Priesthood.* a less extent, the ancient Chaldæans, made little or no independent attempt to seek the first principles underlying the empirical rules retailed by the Priesthood. The extent of this dependence—or rather, the extent to which this dependence was enforced—is illustrated by the enforced legalisation in Egypt of the vague or shifting year.

In Chaldæa a similar process was effected by means of the authority of the astrological texts, defining the supposed causal relations between the acts of kings, princes, and populace, and the produce and other phenomena of the seasons.

¶ 124. STATE-CONTROL IN ANCIENT EGYPT.

With the institution of the vague year in Egypt, the Priesthood brought *The Vague Year and the Calendar Seasons.* into being a new process of State control. The vague year thereafter carried the calendar seasons backwards round the Solar year. The Calendar Seasons *State Control of the Year and Agriculture.* came to have no meaning. The knowledge of the accurate recurrence of times and seasons was confined to the rulers and priests of the Solar deities. Only by giving abundance of gifts to the solar gods could the husbandman be assured of a plentiful harvest. A system of State-control was thus established whereby *The Gods Responsible* wealth accrued to state and priest craft, and ultimate responsibility was referred *The people responsible to the Gods.* to the gods. A goodly harvest implied that the gods were pleased ; a poor harvest that the gods were dissatisfied with the offerings of the people. State *State and Priesthood absolved.* and priesthood might receive reflected glory ; never blame.

¶ 125. THE DISTORTION OF KNOWLEDGE LEGALISED.

All common rules of life and things material were ultimately depicted as *The Solar Deity as formal cause.* having conception and source in the life-giving rays of the sun. The sun, from the XVIIIth Dynasty onwards, whatever the deity with which it was identified, was the great Formal Cause, which by means of its seasonal phenomena of the year, and the dependent phenomena of Nile inundation, made Egypt " the gift of the Nile."

The Cyclical
Basis of the
Solar Cult.
The theogony and cosmogony of the ancient Egyptians were, in consequence, formulated on a cyclic basis having its origin in the value of the year. This was already expressed in the Pyramid's geometry of the year circle. The numerical functions of this geometrical scheme were diverted by the priesthood into the channels of State-control, and were applied to the measurement of all effects attributed, by the Priests, to the influence of the Solar deity, Amen-Ra.

Fabulous
Chronology
and Pyramid
Year Circle
Geometry.
As a crowning monumentalisation of the omniscience of Amen-Ra the whole history of the Divine and Human Dynasties of Egypt was built around a fabulous chronology composed of nominal solar and Sothic cycles, and numbers of years that were in reality but geometrical functions of the Pyramid, and its year circle and astronomical cycles.

The absorbed
cults
responsible
for differing
versions of the
Dynastological
Lists.
Many of the old cults absorbed by the dominant cult of Amen-Ra still partly retained their individuality by worshipping their original gods under the aspect of the leading attributes of Amen-Ra. This was the effect intended, but owing to this fact, the Egyptian Lists contain differing versions of the mythological chronology of the year circle and its Pyramid functions applied to the Divine and Human Dynasties.

¶ 126. THE PARTIAL UNVEILING OF THE MYSTERIES OF EGYPT.

Independent
thinkers of
Greece glean
scientific
information
from priests
of Egypt.
It was only after the seed of freedom, sown by the rising Greek nations, had produced independent philosophers, and when these philosophers had commenced to visit the Egyptians and Chaldæans, that the meagre information gleaned from the priests and independently derived from the empirical rules, was reduced to its crude Greek first principles. Thus, Professor G. Forbes
Egyptian
Priests
reluctant
to impart
information.
states that " the Egyptian priests tried to keep such astronomical knowledge as they possessed to themselves "; and, as indicating the reluctance with which they parted with information, Sir G. Wilkinson states that " Iamblichus says
Pythagoras
derives
data for his
Philosophical
System and for
his scientific
systems of
astronomy,
numbers,
geometry, and
music from
Egyptian
Priests.
Pythagoras derived his information upon different sciences from Egypt; he learnt philosophy from the priests; and his theories of comets, numbers, and music were doubtless from the same source; but the great repugnance evinced by the Egyptian Priests to receive Pythagoras, will account for their withholding from him much that they knew, though his great patience, and his readiness to comply with their regulations, even to the rite of circumcision (Clem. Strom. i, p. 302) obtained for him more information than was imparted to any other Greek (Plut. de Is. s. 10)."

In light of the facts we now possess from the monuments, the ancient accounts of the sojourn of Pythagoras in Egypt picture him as a skilful cross-examiner eliciting information from a reluctant Priesthood. We can picture the Egyptian Priests striving to impress Pythagoras with the vast extent of their own learning and at the same time seeking to obscure the real facts—and their ignorance of the derivation of the facts—by dogmatic and mystifying assertions. Nevertheless, their long association with a credulous and easily satisfied laity ill fitted them for dealing in debate with an intellect so original, independent, and penetrating as that of Pythagoras.

Pythagoras a skilful cross-examiner pandering to the vanities of the Egyptian Priests, and conforming to their rituals, painstakingly extracts from their veiled admissions scientific facts of priceless value.

¶ 127. THE HELLENIZING OF EGYPT. 7TH CENTURY B.C. TO 7TH CENTURY A.D.

Coincident with the political and commercial rise of the Greek States, and the development of Hellenic science and arts, we can trace the decline, politically and commercially, of Egypt, and the accelerated decadence of Egyptian science and art. Greek philosophers hastened to absorb the virtues of the dying race—and many of its vices. Greek mercenaries, from the middle of the 7th century B.C. onwards, found military employment in Egypt. Pandering to the cults, the Greeks gradually undermined, throughout a succession of generations, the basis of the Egyptian national constitution. Slowly they Hellenized a nation for whom Hellenism meant disintegration.

Rise of Greek States coincident with decline of Egypt.

Period of close intercourse between Greeks and Egyptians.

The peaceful penetration of Egypt by the Greeks.

After the conquest of Egypt by Alexander the Great, the Greeks monumentalised their indebtedness to the Egyptians in the sciences and arts, by founding, during the reign of Ptolemy I, the famous library of Alexandria. From this age onwards, a long succession of Greek geometers, astronomers and philosophers, in the various schools of Alexandria, maintained the connection that previously had been more remotely held. Here all the learning that was gleaned and developed from the priests of the dying cults was reduced to literary form and method. Ultimately, however, in the age of Theon, and his daughter Hypatia, the schools themselves declined by falling completely under the pernicious spell of Egyptian dogma. In 642 A.D., the famous library was burnt by the orders of the Caliph Omar.

Alexander conquers Egypt. Founds Alexandria.

Alexandrian Greeks found Astronomical, Geometrical and Philosophical Schools and the great Library of Alexandria. Knowledge gleaned from oral tradition of Egyptian Priests reduced to system in writing.

"A cloud of witnesses" says Mr. R. Brown, Junr—in his "Primitive Constellations"—"testify to the connection between the wisdom of the East and the earlier sages of Hellas. The treasures of the library of Alexandria, the lore of such Chaldæan sages as Kidén, Naburianos, and Soudinos (*vide Strabo*, XVI, i, 6) were at the service of Hipparchus"; and again, quoting from the Scholiast on Aratos (*Diosèmeia.* 21) "the Hellenes received them from the Egyptians and Chaldæans."

Alexandria the Treasure City of the Wisdom of Egypt and Chaldæa.

¶ 128. THE SIGNIFICANT CONTRAST IN GREEK PRESENTATION OF SCIENCE.

Greek Scientific inquiry began in Egypt with XXVIth Egyptian Dynasty, which attempted restoration of cults and constitution of Pyramid Times.

The almost spontaneous rise and rapid development of Greek science date from the period during which Greek philosophers first visited Egypt. This dates back to the middle of the 7th century B.C., when the XXVIth Egyptian Dynasty began, and asserted its supremacy after the withdrawal of the Assyrians. At this time we saw that the Egyptians attempted a tawdry restoration of the manners, customs, arts, and sciences of the Pyramid age (¶ 109).

Sharp Contrast in presentation of Egyptian Science as given by the Greeks :—
Advanced Scientific facts enunciated.
True first principles of these necessary for their discovery.
Greeks explain the facts as derived from puerile first principles— clearly invented to meet contemporary criticism.

The " discoveries " of the Greek philosophers dating from this age can be definitely divided into two classes. These are divided by the clearly marked sharpness of contrast in passing from one class to the other. On the one hand there are enunciations that are certainly the result of mature thought and experienced observation during a long succession of trained philosophers. On the other hand, enunciations, clearly the result of less mature thought, and of less experienced observation—more pertaining to the environment one would associate with a nation's first crude gropings amongst hypotheses of science— were claimed as equally great discoveries of the same philosopher.

Thales describes Lunar eclipses correctly.
Yet indicates his ignorance of the essential First Principles by stating that the Earth floats on water.

Thus Thales of Miletus—the first of the Greek philosophers to visit Egypt for scientific instruction—while stating that the eclipses of the moon were caused by the earth cutting off the sun's light from the moon, indicated his own ignorance of the necessary advanced conceptions for arriving at this conclusion, by stating that the earth floated upon water. As to the extent of his experience, prior to his visit to Egypt, that is given by Hieronymus of Rhodes in his statement that Thales " never had any teacher except during the time he went to Egypt and associated with the Priests." (*ap. Diog. Laer.* I, 27).

¶ 129. THE LEARNED EVASIONS OF PYTHAGORAS.

The Advanced Planetary system of Pythagoras.
Its Modern Counter-part.
Absurdity of " First Principles " alleged by Pythagoras as basal premises of his system.
Their similarity to the mystifying dogmas of Egyptian Priests.
The advanced Planetary System calls for advanced first principles.

Pythagoras of Samos, who next of the Greek philosophers visited Egypt, stated that all the planets revolved around a common centre. This was not accepted by scientific circles in Europe until 2,000 years later. Pythagoras, however, indicated the vast unlikelihood of his having originated this conception by claiming to have deduced his system from " fantastic first principles, of which the following are examples : ' The circular motion is the most perfect motion,' ' Fire is more worthy than Earth,' ' Ten is the perfect number.' "[1] These so-called " first principles " bear a striking resemblance to the mystifying dogmas retailed by the Egyptian Priests—or to the catchword oratory of a modern type of aspirant to state-control—chanted to satisfy inquiring reason by voluminous reiteration rather than by wealth of argument. It is clear that the true first principles were as much the product of the same advanced state

[1] Professor G. Forbes, " History of Astronomy," p. 14.

of knowledge as the advanced planetary hypothesis immediately deduced from *That the latter were unknown* them, and that these advanced first principles were quite unknown to Pytha- *to Pythagoras indicates* goras, and possibly unknown to his Egyptian instructors. *system was not deduced by him.*

However this may be, it seems clear enough that Pythagoras derived his *His system derived from* system from the Egyptian Priests. It is certain that the latter were, for many *Egypt.* centuries, the custodians of much valuable scientific knowledge. This they ex- *Had been preserved by* plained on premises palpably absurd, but admirably adapted to suit the end *Egyptians but not deduced* they had in view. *by them.*

¶ 130. THE LOST ART OF NUMERICAL AND GEOMETRICAL EVALUATION.

The religious and philosophical conceptions preserved by the Egyptian *Association of Philosophical* Priests were similarly expressed by them in geometrical and numerical forms *Conceptions in Egypt with* that appear in no wise to suggest the symbolic use to which they were put, but *Geometrical and Numerical* appear rather to suggest the traditional survival of a symbolism of which the *Ideas indicates the survival of* art was lost. *an Ancient Symbolism.*

Now it is a fact that *there is* a geometrical or numerical basis attaching *The Geometrical* itself to most natural phenomena. We have merely to cite Kepler's Laws of the *and Numerical Bases of* planets, Newton's Gravitational Laws, or Einstein's Laws of Relativity (includ- *Natural Law.* ing Newton's Laws in the same mathematical category as the Laws of other *Physics,* branches of Physics). There are also the complicated mathematical series *Chemistry, Gravitational* associated with the formation of flower petals, and certain microscopical *Astronomy, Botany,* growths, and the marvellous geometrical forms of snowflakes and crystals. *Biology, and Crystallography.*

We are carried further in this subject by investigation of the Periodic Law *The Periodic* of the Chemical Elements (and the connected periodicities of Isotopy), Radio- *Law of the Chemical* activity, the Electronic Theory of Matter, Harmonics, etc. *Elements*

Isotopy

Radio-activity.

¶ 131. BODE'S LAW.

A close approximation to numerical harmony occurs in the case of the planetary distances from the sun. This relationship is expressed by the series *Bode's Law of* of Bode's Law—0, 3, 6, 12, 24, 48, 96, 192, 384, where 0 is the origin at Mercury. *Planetary Distances.* On this scale of relative distances, Mercury is distance 4 from the Sun. Adding this to the series given, the relative distances from the Sun are, according to Bode's Law :— 4, 7, 10, 16, 28, 52, 100, 196, & 388, *The Basis of the Series* the real distances being *that Earth's Distance=10.*

3.9, 7.2, 10, 15.2, ——, 52, 95.4, 191.8, & 300.6.

In this series the distance of the Earth from the Sun is 10, and the outstanding exception is the case of Neptune.

The distance 28 in Bode's series indicates the mean semi-major axis of the belt of orbits of the 91 minor planets that lie between Mars (15.2) and Jupiter (52).

Pythagoras on 10 in relation to his Planetary System.

Was Bode's Law known to originators of the system?

Now when we remember that the advanced Planetary System of Pythagoras was claimed by him as derived from such " first principles " as " Ten is the perfect number," and that " all things are numbers," we see a possible hint that the relations of Bode's Law were not unknown to the originators of the system. Thus Dr. A. S. Pringle-Pattison states that in the Solar System of Pythagoras " The distance of the revolving orbs from the central fire was determined according to simple numerical relations, and the Pythagoreans combined their astronomical and musical discoveries in the famous doctrine of ' the harmony of the spheres.' "[1]

¶ 132. THE SOURCE OF THE PYTHAGOREAN THEORY THAT "ALL THINGS ARE NUMBERS."

Evidence of a former science of Geometrical and Numerical Classification and Co-relation of Data and Phenomena.

Egyptian attempts at its revival haphazard and foolish.

There is evidence that in early Egyptian times there was a definite conception—derived undoubtedly from the former civilisation—associated with the symbolising of phenomena and ideas on geometrical or numerical bases. In the works of the later Egyptians, however, where such symbolical intention can be traced, everything indicates that the geometrical and numerical symbolism was no longer associated with a rational basis. The symbolic art had been lost. Nothing remained but a blind faith in its existence, and haphazard and foolish attempts at its realisation in the case of the Egyptian King Lists.

The Tradition passing to Pythagoras led him to the Independent Discovery of many valuable Numerical and Geometrical Identities in Natural Law.

The Conclusion to be derived from analysis of historical progress of Greek Science.

This blind faith in a geometrical or numerical ordering of things and phenomena—though applied haphazard—ruled the geometrical, astronomical, and musical systems of Pythagoras. The boundless enthusiasm and tireless energy inseparable from faith of this nature, undoubtedly led Pythagoras to the discovery of more geometrical and numerical problems and principles than he ever received from his Egyptian tutors. It is, however, clearly certain that the bulk of his epoch-making " discoveries " and enunciations were derived from the Egyptians, and that similar advances in geometrical and astronomical thought associated with his successors were likewise derived from Egypt and Chaldæa. No other conclusion is possible when one studies an analytic tabulation of the historical progress of Greek science. An analytic statement of this character is given in Table X.

[1]Enc. Brit. (11th Edit.), Vol. XXII, p. 700a.

TABLE X.

SYNOPTICAL HISTORY OF GREEK GEOMETRY AND ASTRONOMY.

Thales (640-546 B.C.), of Miletus.

GEOMETRY :—

ASTRONOMY :—

About 600 B.C., visited Egypt, and studied science there.

Hieronymus of Rhodes (*ap. Diog. Laer I, 27*) says, " He never had any teacher except during the time when he went to Egypt and associated with the priests."   On his return from Egypt he founded the Ionian School of Astronomy and Philosophy.

Originated the equation and proportion, and was thus in a sense the originator of Algebra. Is recognised to have been the founder not only of Greek geometry, but also of Greek astronomy and philosophy. He also " founded," on a scientific basis, the geometry of the circle and of points and lines. (Proclus, *In primum Euclidis Elementorum Librum Commentarii ;* Prof. G. J. Allman, " Greek Geometry from Thales to Euclid " ; Enc. Brit., Vol. 26, pp. 720-721.)

He taught " that the sun, moon, and stars are not mere spots on the heavenly vault, but solids ;   that the moon derives her light from the sun, and that this fact explains her phases ; that an eclipse of the moon happens when the earth cuts off the sun's light from her." (Prof. G. Forbes' "Hist. Astron." p. 13). He also taught the sphericity of the earth, and the obliquity of the ecliptic. (Dr. F. R. Moulton's " Celestial Mechanics," p. 30 ; Miss A. Clerke in " Enc. Brit " Vol. 2, p. 809.)

Pythagoras (569-470 B.C.), of Samos.

Travelled widely in the East, visiting Chaldæa, and penetrating as far as the Ganges.

About 500 B.C. he visited Egypt, and studied science there.   Returning from his travels, he founded a School of Astronomy and Philosophy in Sicily.

The Pythagorean doctrine of the immortality of the soul is clearly of Egyptian origin, whereas the connected Pythagorean doctrine of transmigration of the soul is certainly of a more easterly origin.

The Pythagorean idea of placing natural phenomena on a numerical basis, of associating numbers with conceptions and entities, is also clearly Egyptian in its origin.   Thus of the ancient Egyptians Dr. Sprenger states "An idea, a period of time, or any remarkable occurrence, were frequently connected with ideal persons in mythology, and when any similarity existed, received the same appellation." (Vyse's " Pyds. and Temp. of Gizeh," Vol. II, Append.). Hence the importance of the following from Dr. A. S. Pringle-Pattison : " Impressed by the presence of numerical relations in every department of phenomena, Pythagoras and his early followers enunciated the doctrine that 'all things are numbers.' Numbers seemed to

Originated that branch of geometry associated with his name, and dealing chiefly with areas and solids. He is credited with a knowledge of certain properties of Conic Sections, and the discovery of the law of the three squares (Euclid I, 47) is attributed to him. Diogenes Laertius states that " it was Pythagoras who carried geometry to perfection, after Moeris (Amenemhat III of the XIIth Egyptian Dynasty) had first found out the principles of the elements of that science.. ...... ; and the part of the science to which Pythagoras applied himself above all others was arithmetic." Prof. Allman states "According to Aristoxenus, the musician, Pythagoras seems to have esteemed arithmetic above everything, and to have advanced it by diverting it from the service of commerce and by likening all things to numbers. Diogenes Laertius (viii, 13) reports on the same authority that Pythagoras was the first person who introduced measures and weights among the Greeks." In the system of Pythagoras " Ten " was a sacred number and the most perfect number. He was acquainted with arithmetical, geometrical, and harmonical proportion, and concerned himself with finding

" He taught that the earth both rotates and revolves, and that the comets as well as the planets move in orbits around the sun. He is credited with being the first to maintain that the same planet, Venus, is both evening and morning star at different times." (Moulton, p. 31.)

Pythagoras " learned on his travels......to recognise the obliquity of the ecliptic, and to regard the earth as a sphere freely poised in space. The tenet of its axial movement was held by many of his followers." (Miss A. M. Clerke, Enc. Brit., Vol. 2, p. 809.)

" Copernicus in the sixteenth century claimed Pythagoras as the founder of the (heliocentric) system which he, Copernicus, revived." (Forbes, p. 14.)

Authorities, however, differ as to whether the system of Pythagoras was truly heliocentric. Thus Dr. A. S. Pringle-Pattison (Enc. Brit., Vol. 22, pp. 699-700) states that the Pythagoreans conceived " the earth as a globe self-supported in empty space, revolving with other planets round a central luminary.... The Pythagoreans did not, however, put the sun in the centre of the system. That place was filled by the central fire."

TABLE X—*(continued).*

GEOMETRY :—	ASTRONOMY :—

them, as Aristotle put it, to be the first things in the whole of nature, and they supposed the elements of numbers to be the elements of all things, and the whole heaven to be a musical scale and number. (*Meta.* A. 986a.).   Numbers, in other words, were conceived at that early stage of thought not as relations or qualities predicable of things, but as themselves constituting the substance or essence of the phenomena—the rational reality to which the appearances of sense are reducible." (Enc. Brit., Vol. 22, p. 699.) Pythagoras discovered

geometrical representations of numbers. He also elaborated the conceptions of the equation and proportion as " originated " by Thales.
(Authorities as above, and Enc. Brit., Vol. 22, pp. 700-703.)

The intermediate interpretation of Prof. G. Forbes seems the most likely interpretation. This is that Pythagoras " is supposed to have said that the earth, moon, five planets, and fixed stars all revolve round the sun, which itself revolves round an imaginary central fire called the Antichthon." This conception is quite modern.

—or more probably derived from the Egyptians —the mathematical proportions of the intervals of the diatonic scale.

Democritus (circ. 570-460 *B.C.*).
He studied astronomy for 5 years (or 7 years ?) in Egypt (Diodor., i, 98), and claimed to have been a disciple of the Egyptian priests and the Magi, having visited also Persia and Babylon (Clem. Str., i, p. 304). He knew of the obliquity of the ecliptic.

Anaxagoras (born 499 *B.C*) studied astronomy in Egypt. " He held that in a solar eclipse the moon hides the sun, and in a lunar eclipse the moon enters the earth's shadow." (Forbes, p. 14).

Eudoxus (408-355 *B.C.*) *of Cnidus.*
Visited Egypt with Plato.

His geometrical work comprised the establishing of expressions for the volumes of the pyramid, prism, cone, and cylinder.

In astronomy, he first suggested arbitrarily representing the apparent motions of the sun, moon, and planets as taking place upon revolving spheres ; the motion of each planet being resolved into its components, each component being given a separate revolving sphere.   The hypothesis was not stated as an actual belief, but rather as a mathematical conception—failing any then more satisfactory conception—to permit of the formulating of rules and methods for making astronomical calculations.   This system— the Eudoxian or " homocentric "—was elaborated by Callipus and Aristotle in the middle of the 4th century B.C. (about 350-330 B.C.)

Plato (429-350 *B.C.*), *the Athenian philosopher.*
Visited Egypt and Cyrene. In Egypt he conversed with the Egyptian priests. He was the pupil of Socrates, and was a follower of Pythagoras.

Plato touched upon astronomical and geometrical questions, only when these came within the scope of his system of philosophy.   In no strict sense can he be termed a mathematician nor yet an astronomer.   He, however, " proposed to astronomers *the problem of representing the courses of the planets by circular and uniform motions."* (Forbes, p. 17.)

TABLE X—(continued).

	GEOMETRY :—	ASTRONOMY :—
Euclid lived during the reign of Ptolemy I, king of Egypt (323-285 B.C.) He is said to have founded the school of mathematics at Alexandria.	Euclid's great geometrical work is "The Elements," contained in thirteen books, in which is laid down the fundamental basis of that branch of modern mathematics known as Euclidian geometry.	One work, Euclid's *Phaenomena*, is of an astronomical nature and deals with problems concerning the apparent motion of the celestial sphere.
	It is generally admitted that few of the propositions, theorems, etc., in Euclid's *Elements* are original. Euclid merely compiled and arranged the hitherto unsystematized geometrical work of his predecessors. He placed	the geometry of the line and the circle on a soundly logical basis and in a sequence that has had more influence upon modern method than authorities have taken the pains to note or admit.
Aristyllus and Timocharis (circ. 320-260 B.C.) of the school of Alexandria.		They observed at Alexandria, and constructed the first star-catalogue.
Aristarchus (320-250 B.C.) of Samos. Studied astronomy at Alexandria.		He wrote a work on "Magnitudes and Distances" describing a *theoretically* sound method of determining the relative distances of the sun and moon. He correctly determined the sun's diameter at half a degree, and according to Archimedes had formulated a heliocentric planetary system in advance of the more complicated heliocentric system of the Pythagoreans.
Archimedes (circ. 287-212 B.C.) of Syracuse in Sicily. Studied mathematics at Alexandria.	His geometrical works comprise treatises on the sphere and cylinder, on the measurement of the circle (showing that the value of π is between $3\frac{1}{7}$ and $3\frac{10}{71}$), on conoids and spheroids, on spirals, etc.	A work of an astronomical nature was his now lost work *On Sphere-making.* Professor F. R. Moulton under the heading of "Dynamical Astronomy," states that "Archimedes is the author of the first sound ideas regarding mechanical laws. He stated correctly the principles of the lever and the meaning of the centre of gravity of a body.................It is a remarkable fact that no single important advance was made in the discovery of mechanical laws for nearly 2000 years after Archimedes, or until the time of Stevinus (1548-1620), who was the first, in 1586, to investigate the mechanics of the inclined plane, and of Galileo (1564-1642), who made the first important advance in Kinetics."
Eratosthenes (276-196 B.C.) A Greek astronomer in charge of the library at Alexandria in the reign of Ptolemy III, Euergetes.	He determined (approximately correct) the value of the obliquity of the Ecliptic, and the circumference of the earth. His version of the Egyptian Dynastic Chronology contains periods derived from Genesis, from the true period of the Precession of the Equinoxes, and from the Pyramid base measure in common Egyptian cubits. (Refer Plate XVI and ¶¶ 94 and 102.)	

TABLE X—*(continued)*.

	GEOMETRY :—	ASTRONOMY :—
Apollonius of Perga Lived during the reigns of Ptolemy III Euergetes, and Ptolemy IV Philopater (B.C. 247-205). He studied mathematics at Alexandria.	Apollonius wrote the famous treatise on conic sections that earned for him the title, " the great geometer."	In astronomy Apollonius originated the working hypothesis of epicycles, which hypothesis formed the basis for all astronomical conceptions and observations from Ptolemy to Copernicus. The hypothesis of epicycles originated from the " homocentric " system of Eudoxus, but was a considerable advance on the latter, from point of view of application to practical problems.
Hipparchus (190-120 *B.C.*) Born at Nicæa in Bithynia. He settled at Rhodes and possibly later at Alexandria.	He founded the science of trigonometry, plane and spherical, and compiled the first table of chords.	He is said to have founded the science of observational astronomy. More accurately, we may say that he was the first of a long series of practical astronomers whose observations were placed on record.

He is similarly stated to have invented the planisphere, which, however, he borrowed from the Chaldæans. Astronomical historians are now generally agreed that Hipparchus owed much of his observational data to the long series of observations that had been carried out by the Chaldæans for many centuries, if not for close on 2000 years, before his time. Thus Prof. Forbes states (p. 18) that " making use of Chaldæan eclipses, he was able to get an accurate value of the moon's mean motion." This is in fact stated by Ptolemy in his *Almagest*. (Refer Prof. Simon Newcomb's use of the data of Hipparchus and Ptolemy, in his " Researches on the motion of the Moon," published by U.S.A. Govt. Printing Office, 1878.)

Probably much of the Chaldæan data of Hipparchus was derived from the works of the Chaldæan priest of Bel, Berosus or Berossus (the Greek form of his name), who " appears to have compiled his works in the reign of Antiochos II, B.C. 261-46." (Brown's " Prim. Constell." Vol. II, p. 331.) As Mr. Brown states, " he (Berosus) also compiled various astronomical treatises, which have unfortunately been lost ; they furnished material for Greek writers such as Diodorós, and the most important of them was a translation of what Prof. Sayce calls ' the standard astrological work of the Babylonians and Assyrians.' ......Opinions of Bêrósos respecting the moon have been preserved by Plutarch, Stobaios, and Vitruvius, and the latter (*De Architect*, IX, iv, 7) states that he treated of the properties of the signs of the Zodiac, of the planets, and of the sun and moon ; and that he established a school of learning in the island of Kôs." Kos or Cos, the modern Turkish Island of Stanko,

is at the mouth of the Gulf of Halicarnassus (Asia Minor), and about 50 miles North-West of the Island of Rhodes where Hipparchus had settled.

Centuries before Hipparchus, the Chaldæans, Egyptians, and Chinese knew of the " Precession of the Equinoxes." It is, however, claimed for Hipparchus that he discovered the " Precession " quite independently of the ancients from a comparison of his own observations and those of Timocharis at Alexandria. Syncellus in his " Chronographia " states that the " fabled period " of the Precession, amongst the Egyptians and Greeks, was a period of 25 Sothic Cycles of 1461 " years," or altogether 36,525 years. This gives a rate of 35¼" of angle per year, and the rate determined by Hipparchus was estimated by him as not less than 36". As to whether the rate of Hipparchus was influenced by the rate of the " fabled period " noted by Syncellus, or that of Syncellus derived from Hipparchus it is for our further discussion to show.

Hipparchus was the first to observe and appreciate the elements of the orbit of the earth, (or rather the apparent orbit of the sun), and the orbit of the moon, and by many bold conceptions based on his own vast experience of celestial observation—conceptions that were vastly in advance of his times—he anticipated in many features the basal requirements of the modern astronomical Ephemeris. He compiled the first solar tables, and also compiled a catalogue of 1080 stars on a constellational basis borrowed from the Chaldæans. His realization of the eccentricities of the orbits was a further great advance in geometrical astronomy. He, however, believed that all bodies revolved round the earth as centre.

TABLE X—*(continued)*.

Menelaus of Alexandria flourished towards the end of the 1st century B.C. His mathematical work considerably advanced the science of Spherical Trigonometry and Astronomy.

Ptolemy (*fl. circ.* 120-160 A.D.) was a native Egyptian, famous not only for his classical treatment of mathematical, astronomical, and geographical problems, but also for his having preserved in his great astronomical work, the *Almagest*, astronomical and chronological data—containing observations and records of Hipparchus and the Chaldæans—that has enabled history to be placed on a scientifically accurate basis.

Ptolemy may be said to have done for the spherical geometry and trigonometry of Hipparchus and Menelaus what Euclid did for the work of the earlier geometers. He also combined and systematized the "eccentric" hypothesis of Hipparchus, and the "epicyclic" hypothesis of Apollonius of Perga.

¶ 133. THE QUANTITATIVE AND QUALITATIVE RELATIONS OF EGYPTIAN AND GREEK KNOWLEDGE.

One obvious conclusion is to be derived from the analytic statement of Table X. This is, that if what Pythagoras learnt in Egypt enabled him to construct a system of geometry and astronomy excelling that of his teachers, there was clearly no necessity for his successors to visit Egypt for further knowledge of geometry and astronomy.

Successive Greek Philosophers visited Egypt for reason that their predecessors had merely touched the fringes of Egyptian Knowledge.

It is also obvious that the Egyptian priests would scarcely permit the Greeks to learn as much geometry and astronomy as they themselves knew, and that the Greeks—quick to discern scientific knowledge in the meagre information meted out to them—would have been equally quick to discern when no further knowledge was available. From this it would seem to follow that most, if not all, of the knowledge independently discovered by the Greeks was previously known to the Egyptians. For although the Greeks made great advances in geometry and astronomy, the fact remains that they still continued to seek improvement in Egypt. This is the fact that gives some measure of the amount of geometrical and astronomical knowledge that the Egyptian Priests possessed —knowledge of these subjects as distinct from understanding concerning their origination and the derivation of their first principles.

From first to last, the Greeks obtained but an insignificant fraction of the knowledge the Egyptian Priests possessed.

¶ 134. GREEK MEASURES AND SCIENCE CONTEMPORANEOUSLY FROM EGYPT.

Of this knowledge we have already had evidence in our consideration of the origin of the Egyptian systems of measures. The connection between geometry and measures naturally suggests that the Greeks derived both from Egypt about the same time. Thus, as noted by Herodotus in the 5th century B.C.,

Greek Geometry and Greek Measures from Egypt suggest contemporaneous derivation.

Cubit of Samos
and its
Geometrical
relations
suggest
grounds for
inquiry as to
application of
cubit. the inhabitants of Samos were already using the Egyptian common cubit of 20.63 B". It is the existence of this cubit, and the obvious manner of its derivation, that led to the discovery of the relatively high geometrical and mathematical skill attained by the former civilisation from which the oral traditions of the ancient Egyptians had descended.

That
Pythagoras
came from
Samos suggests
origin of his
interest in
Geometry. The use of this cubit in Samos would naturally lead to the Samians making further inquiry concerning its application to the measurement of areas. Not improbably it was this desire that led Pythagoras—whose earlier years are identified with Samos—to interest himself in the measurement of areas. Now

Credited with
Introduction
of Weights and
Measures
amongst
Hellenes after
his visit to
Egypt. it is stated by Aristoxenos, the musician, that Pythagoras "was the first person who introduced weights and measures amongst the Hellenes" (Diog. Laert. *Pythagoras*, xiii), and Professor G. J. Allman[1] states that "on examining the purely geometrical work of Pythagoras and his disciples......we observe that it is much concerned with the geometry of areas, and we are indeed struck with its Egyptian character."

The Pytha-
gorean
Systems of
Astronomy,
Measures and
Numbers
derived from
an Original
System
in use by the
Lost
Civilisation of
"Prehistoric"
Times. It is certain, therefore, that the basal geometry of the Pythagorean system was that of the Egyptians. This Egyptian system was based upon the conception of the year circle and its square of equal area—from which the Samian or common Egyptian cubit was derived—and was derived originally from the scientific system of the civilisation that had preceded the period of the early Egyptian, Babylonian, and Mediterranean civilisations. It is to this former lost civilisation that we must refer the origination of the heliocentric planetary system of Pythagoras.

[1]Enc. Brit. (11th Edit.), Vol. XXII, p. 701c.

SECTION III.—DESCRIPTION OF PLATES.

¶ 135. PLATE XIII.   EQUAL AREAS.

A rectangle constructed of length equal to the circumference of any given circle and of breadth equal to the diameter of the given circle is in area equal to four times the area of the given circle. *Area of any 4 equal circles= diameter (D) × circumference (C.).*

Thus, let C = Circumference of Given Circle.

and   D = Diameter of Given Circle. *Defines a rectangle of area equal to area of 4 circles.*

$$\pi = \frac{C}{D} = 3.14159+.$$

Then C = πD, Therefore D = $\dfrac{C}{\pi}$ *Side of square of area equal to area of 4 circles = √D × C*

Area of Circle = $\dfrac{\pi D^2}{4}$

4 times Area of Circle = $\pi D^2 = \pi D \times D = \pi D \times \dfrac{C}{\pi} = D \times C.$

Area of Rectangle of area 4 times area of circle = D × C.

Also, square of area 4 times area of circle = D × C.

Side of Square = $\sqrt{D \times C}$.

The ancients formulated their metrological systems upon the above relations and the year circle of 3652.42 Primitive inches in circumference—a representation of the solar year to the scale of 10 P inches to the day. This gave a circle of 1162.6 diameter. Four of such circles are represented as A, B, C, and D on Plate XIII. EFGH is the corresponding rectangle of equal area. Its length FH = EG = 3652.42 P″., and its breadth EF = GH = 1162.6 P.″. KLMN is the corresponding square of equal area. Area KLMN = (3652.42 × 1162.6) square P. inches. Side of square = KL = LN = $\sqrt{3652.42 \times 1162.6}$ = 2060.66 P.″. The three equal areas—4 circles, rectangle, and square—were defined as the *aroura*, the great unit of square measure. *Basis of Primitive Scientific Metrological System :— 3652.4 P. inches × 1162.6 P. inches defines rectangle of equal area. The "Aroura."*

Each of the circles A, B, C, and D falls precisely internal to the outer circle of stones at Stonehenge. *Stonehenge Circle=¼ "Aroura" Circle*

The circumference of 3652.42 P″ was divided into 200 circumferential cubits of 18.2621 P″. The diameter of 1162.6 P″ was divided into 100 diametric feet of 11.626 P″. The side of the square of equal area (the *aroura*) was divided into 100 common cubits of 20.6066 P″. This supplied three systems of linear units—a system of circumferential units, a system of diametric units, and a system for the linear measurement of straight line plane figures. Each system has its own cubits, feet, and digits. *Derivation of three systems for common use. Separate Cubits, Feet, and Digits for circumferences, diameters, and linear measurement of straight line plane figures*

The three systems were therefore derived from a system of Primitive Inches. The Primitive inch was of the value of 1.0011 British inches. Accidentally or intentionally, this is a 500 millionth part of the Earth's Polar Diameter. *The original or Basal system, a system of Earth's Polar diameter inches.*

The derived systems were originally invented for *common use* for the purpose of avoiding calculations involving π. Simple formulæ connected the three systems. The result of one such simple calculation is shown in the lower portion of Plate XIII. Here the $\frac{1}{100}$th strip of the *aroura* square is equal to the area of the segment of the circle of radius 50 diametric feet and of arc length 12 circumferential feet. Typical formulæ for the calculations are given in ¶ 137C. *Simple formulæ avoiding π.*

The original or basal system and the three derived systems are illustrated to comparative scale on Plate XV (refer ¶¶ 137, 137a, b and c for description, formulæ, and worked examples). *Typical example of calculated equal areas.*

¶ 136. PLATE XIV. GEOMETRICAL ANALOGY.

Simple relationship between Quadrants and their Isosceles Triangles of equal area and equal definitive linear measures

As a corollary of the relationship of ¶ 135, the area of a quadrant of a given circle= Length of Quadrant arc × ½ radius. This defines the area of a triangle of area equal to the quadrant area. The perpendicular height of the triangle= the quadrant radius and the base of the triangle= the length of the quadrant arc.

Plate XIV shows the relationship for the case of two similar isosceles triangles mOn and $m_1O_1n_1$, and two quadrants MON and $M_1O_1N_1$.

Larger Figures.	Smaller Figures.
Triangle height h=Quadrant radius h.	Triangle height h_1=Quadrant radius h_1
Triangle base mn=Quadrant arc MN.	Triangle base m_1n_1=Quadrant arc M_1N_1.
Triangle area mOn=Quadrant area ONQMO	Triangle area $m_1O_1n_1$=Quadrant area $O_1N_1Q_1M_1O_1$

The base angle of both triangles is the base angle of the Great Pyramid's right vertical section, 51°-51'-14".3.

The underlying conception of circular arc developments.

The importance of the Mid-tangent in the conception.

The conception underlying this representation in the Pyramid is that the Isosceles triangle of area equal to the quadrant area is constructed from the development of the quadrant arc on its mid-tangent. Thus on left hand side of middle Plate XIV, Q is the middlepoint of the quadrant arc MQN and mQn is the tangent at mid-point Q. The quadrant arc MQN is developed on to the tangent mQn, so that when QM is straightened out along Qm, M gives the point m, and when QN is straightened out along Qn, N gives the point n. The process is illustrated on the bottom left hand figure. Hence QM= Qm, QN= Qn, and MQN= mQn. Joining Om and On, we find that although the area has been distorted and the definitive linear dimensions retained,—OQ common to both, and MQN= mQn—the area of the isosceles triangle mOn is nevertheless equal to the area of the quadrant OMQNO. When one comes to think of it, this is a very remarkable and simple property. It is, however, a property that is seldom conceived in tangible form by the mathematician.

Similar sectors developed give similar triangles.

Areas in comparative series equal.

The same conception and simple relationship extend to sectors and triangles. Similar sectors, when developed, give similar triangles, each of area equal to the area of its sector, and of definitive dimensions equal to the definitive dimensions of its sector.

¶ 137. PLATE XV. COMPARISON OF ANCIENT SCALES OF MEASUREMENT.

Derivation from Year Circle Geometry and Primitive Inch.

The systems of measures briefly described in ¶ 135 are illustrated to comparative (reduced) scale on Plate XV. ¶ 135 described how the circumferential cubit, the diametric foot, and the common cubit were derived from the original linear unit, the Primitive Inch. Direct diagrammatic illustration is given in the lower portion of Plate XV. This gives a representation (right hand figure) of an Egyptian cubit rod noted by Professor Petrie.[1] Its length is the circumferential cubit, and on it is marked off the length of the diametric half-foot. The right hand figure illustrates the manner of direct derivation from the year circle geometry and the original Primitive inch.

THE DIAMETRIC SCALE :—

The Diametric Scale.

With the derived diametric foot (11.626 P″) as basis, this was divided off into 16 digits— each of value 0.7266 P″. The number of digits is from Petrie.[1]

Its primary unit the diametric foot of 11.626 primitive inches.

Whereas one and a half diametric feet contained 24 diametric digits, the diametric cubit was reckoned to contain 25 diametric digits. This is the real origin of " the well-known ratio of 25 : 24," noted by Petrie.[1] (Refer ¶¶ 88-90.)

[1]Enc. Brit. (11th Edit.), Vol. xxviii, p. 483 c.

THE CIRCUMFERENTIAL SCALE :—

With the derived circumferential cubit (18.2621 P″) as basis, this was divided off, like the diametric cubit, into 25 digits—each of value 0.7305 P″. The number of digits is from Petrie.[1] The circumferential cubit also contained one and a half circumferential feet.[1] Petrie here remarks that this foot "although very well known in literature, is but rarely found........The Greek system, however, adopted this foot as a basis for decimal multiplication." (Refer ¶¶ 88 and 89).

The Circumferential Scale. Its primary unit the circumferential cubit of 18.2621 primitive inches.

THE LINEAR SCALE FOR SIDES OF RECTILINEAR AREAS :—

With the derived cubit (20.6066 P″) as basis, this was divided off into 32 digits—each of value 0.644 P″. The number of digits in the early Babylonian and Egyptian examples of this cubit is from Petrie.[2] Petrie explains that the later division into 28 digits was due to a confusion of this system with the systems herein defined as diametric and circumferential. Thus, 28 circumferential digits = 20.454 P″, closely approximating to the true value of 20.6066 P″ for the common cubit.

Linear Scale for Square Measures. Its primary unit the common cubit of 20.6066 primitive inches.

¶ 137a. THE ALGEBRAIC RELATIONSHIP OF UNITS. (PLATE XV.)

For any given circle,

Let Diameter = D diametric cubits = d diametric feet = δ diametric digits.
Circumference = B circumferential cubits
       = b circumferential feet
       = β circumferential digits.

Algebraic Symbols.

Side of Square of equal area
       = L common cubits
       = λ digits of common cubit.

Area of Circle = $\begin{cases} \text{L}^2 \text{ square cubits (common)} \\ \text{or H square cubits (common)} \end{cases}$

$= \begin{cases} \lambda^2 \text{ sq. digits} \\ \text{or h sq. digits} \end{cases}$ = A *arourae.*

Then δ = 16d = 25D   ..   .. (1)

$\beta = \dfrac{50b}{3} = 25B$ ..   .. (2)

λ = 32L   ..   .. (3)

Formulæ of relationship between units of same scale.

And b = 3d }
     B = 2d }   ..   .. (I)

$L = \dfrac{d}{2}$ }
λ = 16d }   ..   .. (II)

$H = \dfrac{d^2}{4}$ }
h = (16d)² }   ..   .. (III)

Formulæ of relationship between units of different scales.

$A = \dfrac{d^2}{40,000}$ }   ..   .. (IV)

If any one value—A B b, d, H, h, L, or λ—be given, all the other values can be found directly from the formulæ I to IV.

Method of using formulæ.

If any one of the values D, δ, or β is then required, it can be derived from formulæ (1) and (2).

[1] Enc. Brit. (11th Edit.), Vol. xxviii, p. 483 b.
[2] Ibid. p. 482 d.

If any one of the values D, δ, or β is given, its value in terms of d—for D and δ—and in terms of b or B for β, can be found from formulæ (1) and (2), and thereafter substituted in formulæ I to IV, as

$$d = \frac{25D}{16} \; ; \quad d = \frac{\delta}{16} \; ; \quad \text{or } b = \frac{3\beta}{50} \; ; \quad B = \frac{\beta}{25} \; .$$

¶ 137b. EXAMPLES OF SIMPLE RELATIONS. (PLATE XV).

An important simple relation between diameter and side of square of equal area.

One important relation is obtained from the formulæ as follows :—

A given diameter = δ diametric digits.

From Formula (II) :—

Length of side of square of equal area, in digits of common cubit = λ = 16d.

From (1) :— δ = 16d.
Hence λ = δ.

Otherwise expressed, the length of side of the square of area equal to the area of a given circle contains the same number of digits of the common cubit as the diameter of the given circle contains diametric digits.

Example for a given diameter :—

A worked example of the above is given for a circle of diameter measuring 2,000 diametric digits.

FOR DIAMETER :—

Various statements for diameter in different units.

From (1) :— δ = 2,000 diametric digits.

$$d = \frac{\delta}{16} \text{ diametric feet} = \frac{2,000}{16}$$

= 125 diametric feet.

$$D = \frac{\delta}{25} \text{ diametric cubits} = \frac{2,000}{25}$$

= 80 diametric cubits.

FOR CIRCUMFERENCE :—

From (1), (2) and (I) :—

Various statements for circumference in different units.

$$\beta = \frac{25\delta}{8} \text{circumferential digits} = \frac{25 \times 2,000}{8}$$

= 6,250 circumferential digits.

$$b = \frac{3\delta}{16} \text{ circumferential feet} = \frac{3 \times 2,000}{16}$$

= 375 circumferential feet.

$$B = \frac{\delta}{8} \text{circumferential cubits} = \frac{2,000}{8}$$

= 250 circumferential cubits.

FOR SIDE OF SQUARE OF EQUAL AREA :—

Various statements (linear and square) for square of equal area in different units.

λ = δ = 2,000 digits of common cubit.

$$L = \frac{\lambda}{32} = 62\tfrac{1}{2} \text{ common cubits.}$$

AREA OF SQUARE OF EQUAL AREA :—

λ^2 = 2,000 × 2,000 = 4 million sq. digits of common cubit.

$$L^2 = \left(\frac{\lambda}{32}\right) = 3906.25 \text{ sq. (common) cubits.}$$

$$A = \frac{d^2}{40,000} = \frac{125 \times 125}{40,000} = 0.390625 \; aroura.$$

¶ 137c. THE SIMPLE CALCULATIONS FOR AREAS OF SECTORS AND SEGMENTS OF CIRCLES.

Let m = No. of Circumferential Cubits in a given Sector arc, of diameter d diametric feet, for circle of B circumferential cubits.

Area of whole circle $= \dfrac{d^2}{4}$ common square cubits. (From ¶ 137a, Formula III).

Number of the given sectors in circle $= \dfrac{B}{m} = \dfrac{2d}{m}$ (¶ 137a, Formula I).

Therefore, Area of given Sector $= \dfrac{d^2}{4} \times \dfrac{m}{2d} = \dfrac{md}{8}$ common square cubits.

Area of sector in common square cubits= ¼-sector are in circumferential cubits × Radius in diametric feet.

Otherwise expressed, the area of a given sector in common square cubits is equal to one-eighth the product of the number of circumferential cubits in the sector arc and the number of diametric feet in the diameter of the circle ; or, is equal to a quarter of the product of the number of circumferential cubits in the sector arc and the number of diametric feet in the radius of the circle.

To obtain the area of the segment in the given sector, in common square cubits, deduct the area of the isosceles triangle of the given sector from the area of the sector as above obtained in common square cubits.

The area of segment=area of sector—area of sector triangle.

¶ 138. PLATE XVI. CHART SHOWING THE GEOMETRICAL, ASTRONOMICAL, AND NUMERICAL BASES OF THE FICTITIOUS CHRONOLOGIES OF THE ANCIENT EGYPTIAN KING LISTS.

General remarks :—

The chart is a record of facts that have been long in existence—in some cases for several thousand years. The elements that are distinctly new are the co-ordination of these facts and the self-evident origin and significance of the facts revealed by this co-ordination.

Facts Long Known.
Co-ordination New.

The outstanding new facts derived from the statement of the chart are the following :—

New facts from Co-ordination.

(1) That the Egyptian King Lists of the Egyptian Priest, Manetho, do not contain a true statement of ancient Egyptian Chronology. (¶¶ 92, 118 and 119.)

Chronology of Egyptian King Lists fictitious.

(2) That prior to the 3rd century B.C., the Egyptians knew nothing concerning the hypothesis now adopted as the basis of modern Egyptological chronology. (¶ 98 and Appendix.)

Modern Egyptological theory of chronology unknown.

(3) That the King Lists contain a written record of the numerical values of all the external linear and angular measurements of a Standard Pyramid (¶¶ 93, 95–99, 118 and 119), in terms of units specified in the Lists as of values equal to 1.0011 British inches and 20.63 British inches respectively. (¶ 94.)

A written record of the measurements and units of a Standard Pyramid.

(4) That the Standard Pyramid of the Egyptian King Lists is the Great Pyramid of Gizeh. (¶¶ 94, 99–101 and 118.)

The Standard Pyramid is the Great Pyramid.

The complete statement of Manetho's Divine Dynasties is as given in Table A of chart. This is precisely as stated by Sir Ernest Budge, "Book of Kings," Vol. I, pp. lx and lxi.

The detailed statement of Manetho's Human Dynasties is as given in the Appendix. This is precisely as stated in Baron Bunsen's Greek and Latin Text ("Egypt's Place," Vol. I, Appendix), for the versions of Africanus and Eusebius, and in Cory's "Fragments" (Hodge's Edition, 1876). The other lists are preserved in the same works. Statements of Manetho's Lists also appear in Budge's "Book of Kings," Vol.I, his "History of Egypt," Vol. I, in Sayce's "Ancient Empires of the East" (Appendix), and in the various volumes of Petrie's "History of Egypt." These, however, generally omit some important details and statements peculiar to the Version of Africanus. Budge's statement ("Book of Kings," Vol. I) of the basal totals of years for the Version of Eusebius for Manetho's Book I, II and III has been adopted in the chart (Table B). The stated totals for the same books, according to the Version of Africanus, have been adopted from Cory in the chart (Table B).

Authorities for statement of Egyptian King Lists.

¶ 138a. SOME DETAILS CONCERNING THE VERSION OF AFRICANUS.

Four features affecting the statement of the Version of Africanus in Tables B and C call for special remark.

Pepy II Died 100 Years Old after Reigning 95 Years.

Stated duration Dynasty VI (Africanus) 203 years.

Added Duration 198 Years.

(1) Under Dynasty VI, it is stated that the fourth king, "Phiŏps, who began to reign at six years of age, reigned till he had completed his 100 year." The stated total for the duration of the dynasty—given as 203 years—includes reign of Phiŏps (Pepy II) as of duration of 100 years. Accordingly " 203 years " appears in the summations giving one series of fictitious totals for Book I. But the reign of Pepy II was 94 or 95 years, and the total of the Dynasty therefore 197 or 198. Petrie (Hist. Egypt, Vol. I, Dyn. VI) adopts 95 and 198 years respectively. This agrees with the summations giving another series of fictitious totals for Book I, whereas 94 and 197 years fail to give summations agreeing with any fictitious system.

Dynasty XVIII.

Amosis I.

Statement of duration of reign, 25 years, omitted, but included in added summations of some systems.

(2) Under Dynasty XVIII the name of the first king appears as Amosis (Amosis I), with duration of reign omitted. Other versions give this reign as 25 years. Accordingly one series of fictitious totals for Book I, Version Africanus, omits the reign of 25 years, and another series includes the reign as 25 years ; both series supplying the numerical bases of their respective systems of fictitious construction.

The 1050 Years of Africanus, Book III.

Interregnum between Dynasties XIX and XX.

Harris Papyrus.

Duration, 182 Years (Africanus).

178 Years (Old Chronicle)

(3) In Book III the stated total duration of time after Dynasty XIX and up to end of Dynasty XXXI is given as 1,050 years, whereas the added stated totals for Dynasties XX to XXXI inclusive amount to 868 years. This indicated the theory of an interregnum of 182 years between Dynasty XIX and Dynasty XX. Such an interregnum is mentioned in the Harris Papyrus. This was written in the early period of Dynasty XX, under king Ramessu III, who was closely associated with the events that terminated the Interregnum. It would seem that there are good grounds for adopting this theory of the Version of Africanus.

Again, the Old Chronicle gives the statement of 2,324 years for the duration of all human Dynasties. Its stated totals for duration of Dynasties, however, amount to 1,881 years. This gives an unplaced interregnum of 178 years— 4 years short of the total of Africanus for the Interregnum between Dynasty XIX and Dynasty XX. As the Old Chronicle totals for Dynasties XX to XXX inclusive amount to 868 years—as in Dynasties of Book III, Africanus—it would appear that the two periods are identical.

The 990 years interpolated in Version Africanus.

(4) At the end of Dynasty XXIV in the Version of Africanus, there occurs the statement " Total 990 years."

The query concerning 31 years.

Custom of entering such queries in MSS.

Now in the statement of the previous dynasty there occurs a note that throws some light upon this. The note is $Z\dot{\eta}\tau$ $\check{\epsilon}\tau\eta$ $\lambda\acute{a}$, read as " Zet 31 years." For long Zet was supposed to be an unknown king's name. It appears in no other version of any List. Professor Petrie and Mr. F. W. Read have shown, however, that $\zeta\eta\tau$ was commonly entered in such MSS. as Manetho's by editors, critics and scholiasts to indicate a query.[1] Petrie explains that Manetho here added a query concerning 31 years that belonged to a system of summation, but could not be accounted for by the summation of details. The added totals of Africanus, including the 31 years noted, by agreeing with the system framing the summations, confirm Petrie's explanation.

The Entry of 990 Years. A query concerning this as referring to a period to complete a requisite total.

The summation of Plate XVI, Table A indicates that the statement of Africanus concerning the 990 years is to be similarly explained. 990 years added to 24,837 years, the duration of the Divine Dynasties, give 25,827 years, the sum of the Pyramid's base diagonals. 990 years added to the 4,611 years of Eusebius for the human kings, give the 5,601 years of Africanus for the human kings.

[1] *Ancient Egypt*, 1914, p. 32. 1916, p. 150.

¶ 139. PLATE XVII. DIAGRAMMATIC REPRESENTATION OF PROFESSOR PETRIE'S RECONSTRUCTION, AND OF THE NEW RECONSTRUCTION OF THE GREAT PYRAMID FROM PETRIE'S SURVEY.

This Plate fully explains itself. One item, however, may require amplification; the relation between the dimensions on diagrams of Plate XVII, stated in Primitive or Pyramid inches, and the dimensions according to Petrie's survey in British inches.

Petrie's survey for the mean square side defining the corners of the existing core surface base gave a length of 9001.5 B″ ± 1.0 B″. Reduced to Pyramid inches (on basis of ¶¶ 81, 94 and 101), this is 8991.6 P″, ± 1.0 P″ or, as stated in round numbers of inches as on Plate XVII, Figs. A, B and C, 8,991 P″. *Size of side of base square of core masonry plane surfaces, 8,991 P″.*

Petrie's mean distance between the centres of two opposite sides of the core masonry base—*i.e.*, as along line of AB, Figs. A, B and C; or on Section AB, Figs. a, b and c—gave 8,929 B″, or in round numbers of P. inches, as on all figs. of Plate XVII, 8,919 P″. *Distance between opposite centres of core masonry base sides, 8,919 P″.*

The other relations defining the casing base square, and its central hollowing in, are as given in ¶¶ 99–101.

As to what Petrie means by a core plane face, the reader is referred to Plate XVIII and ¶ 140.

It is unfortunate that Professor Petrie, in observing the core masonry hollowing, did not extend the same feature to the restoration of the casing. By reason of this unfortunate omission, scientists for 42 years have been led to believe that the theory of the late Astronomer Royal for Scotland—Professor Piazzi Smyth—requiring a Great Pyramid base circuit of 36,524 Pyramid inches, was nothing more than a delusion. It is equally unfortunate that Professor Smyth saddled his theory with corollaries and side issues rightly deemed by his scientific contemporaries to be fallacious. *The unfortunate effect of an incorrect restoration of the Great Pyramid.*

¶ 140. PLATE XVIII. DIAGRAMMATIC PERSPECTIVE VIEW, ILLUSTRATING FEATURES OF GREAT PYRAMID'S CORE MASONRY.

As explained on the Plate, the hollowing-in of the core face escarpments, and the depths of courses are considerably exaggerated. In consequence of the latter, the number of courses is reduced. The thicker 5th course, however, gives a general idea of the appearance of the 35th course. The view illustrates the Pyramid's appearance prior to the addition of the casing.

What Petrie means by a core plane face is defined by the plane geometrical surfaces cCBb and bBAa. Petrie's core plane base is the actual square defined by the corner points C, B, A and D (the last unseen). This base square was obtained by sighting down from c, b, a and d, along the line of the stepped (arris) edges, cC, bB, aA and dD (the last unseen). The core base square is defined by the straight lines CB, BA, AD (unseen) and DC (unseen). *Petrie's Core Plane Faces. And Core Plane Base.*

The hollowed-in effect is defined on the base by the lines CHGB and BFEA. HG and FE are each about 36 inches horizontally internal to the square base sides CB and BA. HG and FE were obtained by sighting down the stepped core courses from c to H and b to G; and from b to F and a to E. *Definition of Pyramid's Hollowed-in effect.*

Petrie states, " The form of the present rough core masonry of the Pyramid is capable of being very closely estimated. By looking across a face of the Pyramid, either up an edge, across the middle of the face, or even along near the base, the mean optical plane, which could touch the most prominent points of all the stones, may be found with an average *How Petrie determined the Core Plane Base.*

variation at different times of only 1.0 inch.   I therefore carefully fixed, by nine observations at each corner of each face, where the mean plane of each face would fall on the socket floors ; using a straight rod as a guide to the eye in estimating.   On reducing these observations to give the mean form of the core planes at the pavement level, it came out thus :—

Core Plane Sides.

B″.

N.	..	..	..	..	..	9002.3
E.	..	..	..	..	..	8999.4
S.	..	..	..	..	..	9001.7
W.	..	..	..	..	..	9002.5

Mean	..	..	..	..	..	9001.5
Mean difference..		..	..	..	1.0."[1] (Refer ¶ 139.)

On pp. 43–44, Petrie then states as to "the faces of the core masonry being very distinctly hollowed."   "This hollowing," he continues, "is a striking feature ; and beside the general curve of the face, each side has a sort of groove specially down the middle of the face........ The whole of the hollowing was estimated at 37 B″ on the N face.........."

[1]Pyds. and Temples of Gizeh, pp. 37, 38.

CHAPTER III.

THE ELEMENTS OF
ANCIENT GRAVITATIONAL ASTRONOMY.

SECTION I.—THE PYRAMID'S EXTERNAL DEFINITION OF THE EARTH
AND ITS ORBIT.

¶ 141. THE ANALYTICAL APPLICATION OF PETRIE'S PYRAMID
SURVEY DATA.

Professor Petrie's admirable survey data for the Great Pyramid are so *Accuracy of Petrie's survey data.* comprehensive and accurate as to enable us to settle three momentous questions. These questions, which are closely inter-related, may be expressed as follows :—

(1) How far the existing measurements give evidence concerning the *Basis for determining designer's intentions,* designer's intentions,

(2) How far they indicate the extent of workmen's errors, and *Workmen's errors,*

(3) How far they indicate the extent of internal and external movements *Movements due to subsidence and earthquake.* due to subsidence and earthquake shock.

To form the necessary basis for the analytical investigation for the *Conversion of data to Pyramid azimuth for analytical purposes.* above, Petrie's system of Survey Co-ordinates has had to be converted into an equivalent system of co-ordinates oriented with respect to the mean azimuth[1] of the Great Pyramid. All the necessary data—Petrie's original co-ordinates and the new equivalent Pyramid azimuth co-ordinates—are *Tabulation of conversion.* given in relation on Plate XIX, to enable the mathematical reader to check the conversion for himself.

Subtraction of related co-ordinate units of Plate XIX—*i.e.* for co- *The special feature of Petrie's Pyramid base and socket corner distances.* ordinates from the same base and on the same straight line—and conversion of the units into British inches give all the Pyramid's true azimuth base distances shown on Plate XX. Plate XX also shows Petrie's oblique distances between base points and diagonal corners of sockets. The latter

[1]For Plate XX, the azimuth of a line running true North—or of the perpendicular to a line running true East and West—is defined as 0°. The azimuth of a line West of true North is defined as (—) angle from true North line. The azimuth of a line East of true North is defined as (+) angle from true North line.

The azimuth of the Pyramid's base diagonals as defined by the corners of the rock-cut sockets is —0° 3′ 43″.

distances are not stated with reference to any common azimuth. They are nothing more, in each case, than the direct distance in a straight line between two stated points. In this form, Petrie's distances are not a suitable basis for the analytical investigation of all the related data.

¶ 142. THE   SIGNIFICANCE   OF   PETRIE'S   PYRAMID   BASE
        DISTANCES.

In one application, however, Petrie's base distances are of direct value for analysis. They determine the existing form of the square defining the central extent of base hollowing-in. This is the square RQPS on Plate XX.

The North side, QP, of this square = 9069.4 B", and defines the line of
    CD where casing was found and surveyed.
The East side, PS, of this square = 9067.7 B", and defines the line of EF
    where casing was found and surveyed.
The South side, RS, of this square = 9069.5 B", and defines the line of
    GH where casing was found and surveyed.
The West side, RQ, of this square = 9068.6 B", and defines the line of BA
    where casing was found and surveyed.

The close agreement of the North and South measurements, 9069.4 and 9069.5 B" respectively, and the variation of 0.9 B" between the East side (9067.7 B") and the West side (9068.6 B") suggest—

(1) That the North and South measures define the intended or original
    value as 9069.5 B"; and

(2) That the shorter measurements of the East and West sides, 1.8 B"
    and 0.9 B" respectively, less than 9069.5 B" indicate workmen's
    errors in building; or

(3) That reduction of the original central base distance between the
    North and South base edges—i.e. between CD on North face and
    GH on South face—is due to the drawing-in effect of a large
    cavern subsidence in the natural rock below the Pyramid, and to
    the major axis of this subsidence running in a direction approxi-
    mately South and North.

The minute accuracy of detail in the finishing of beds, joints, and external surfaces of the Pyramid, and the remarkable precision of workmanship evidenced by the tightly fitting blocks, seem to indicate that the same minute accuracy and precision of workmanship extended to the external form of the Pyramid as a whole. In such event, the existing variation in the base distances is due to distortion by subsidence.

¶ 143. THE   GENERAL   EVIDENCE   CONCERNING   PYRAMID
        SUBSIDENCE.

Now if the slightly shorter distance between the North and South base sides, as compared with the distance between the East and West base sides, is

PLATE XIX.

THE REDUCED CO-ORDINATES OF PROFESSOR PETRIE'S SURVEY DATA.

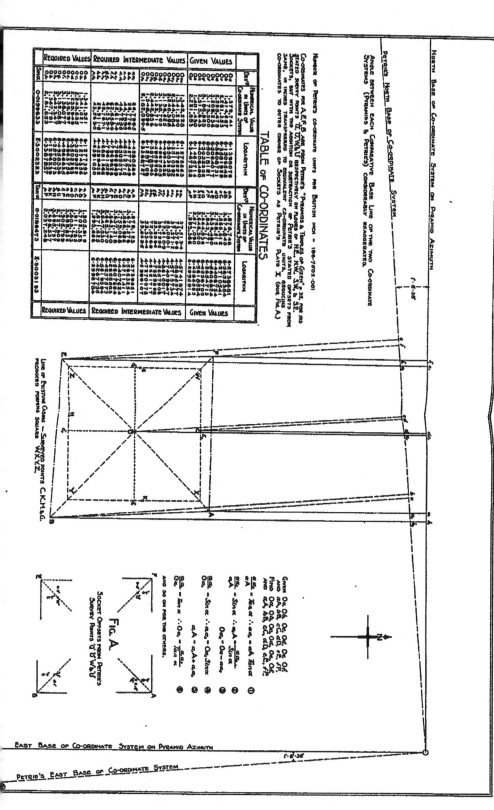

due to the subsidence effect inferred, the Great Pyramid should contain the following indications of such subsidence :— How subsidence movement would affect Pyramid :—

(1) The courses of the Pyramid masonry should indicate a slight dip inwards, towards the centre. Inward dip of courses,

(2) The existing top platform of the Pyramid masonry should not be truly central to the Pyramid's base square, unless in the remarkably accidental case of the axes of subsidence crossing below the Pyramid's base centre, and possessing the same orientation as the Pyramid base. Top platform square not central.

(3) The angle of the Entrance Passage with the horizontal in a Northerly direction should be greater than the angle of the Ascending Passage with the horizontal in a Southerly direction—presuming both to have been of the same inclination originally. Descending Passage steeper; Ascending Passage flatter,

(4) The angle of the Entrance Passage, continued as the Descending Passage, should increasingly accelerate its angle of dip after it leaves the masonry courses, and as it descends further into the natural rock. Descending Passage increasingly steeper in natural rock,

(5) The Chambers within the Pyramid masonry should be buckled and crushed in such direction of distortion as agrees with the approximate North and South direction of the major axis of subsidence indicated by the Pyramid's external variations. (¶ 142 (3).) Distortion and fractures in chambers.

Every one of the five indications outlined are defined by the existing state of the Great Pyramid's masonry as surveyed and measured by Professor Petrie. The external and internal evidences of subsidence are discussed in detail in Sections II and III of this Chapter. All above effects exist in Pyramid, observed and measured by Petrie.

¶ 144. THE PURPOSE OF THE PYRAMID'S SOCKETS.

Petrie has shown that the four corner sockets of the Great Pyramid were primarily cut to fix the alignments of the two diagonals of the Pyramid base. In three cases the alignments of the diagonals are fixed by the outer corner of each of three sockets, L, K, and M, for the N.W., N.E., and S.E. sockets respectively, as figured on Plate XX. In the case of the S.W. socket, the socket surface was carried to UX, $17\frac{1}{2}$ inches to the West of the point Z on the diagonal ZK. The point Z, defining the diagonal alignment is, however, indicated by a chiselled line WZ cut by the original workers for this purpose. Sockets cut to define base diagonal alignments prior to construction. The chiselled line on the S.W. socket.

As shown on Plate XX, the true East to West distance from East side of S.E. socket to West side of S.W. socket—i.e. between M and the line UX produced—is 9140.63 B″. Petrie gives the oblique distance XM as 9141.4 B″. Now the true geometrical Pyramid base side $\frac{36,524.24}{4}$P″ =9131.06 P″ =9141.1 B″. From this it is obvious that this distance over the two sockets was the original setting-out dimension for the corner to corner distance of the Pyramid's base side. Distance between East side of S.E. socket and West side of S.W. socket set out prior to construction to define width of Pyramid base square of 36,524 P′ circuit.

The existing distance is 0.47 B" shorter than the true distance. In the same way the sum of the true azimuth co-ordinates betweem AB and EF (Plate XX), at the centre of the base, is 9068.83 B" or 0.62 B" shorter than the mean of the measurements indicated as original by the distorted oblique distances QP and RS, 9069.4 and 9069.5 B" respectively. (¶ 142.) The shortening effect on base measurements due to subsidence would naturally be greatest across the centre between two opposite base sides. In consequence, we may take the shortening of North base as not greater than the mean of the other two variations noted, $\dfrac{0.47+0.62}{2} = 0.54$ B".

¶ 145. THE ORIGINAL SETTING-OUT LINES OF THE PYRAMID BASE.

As stated by Petrie, the existing definition of the base diagonals—owing to subsidence distortion—does not give precisely rectangular diagonals. The amount of error from true rectangular diagonals is shown by the azimuth co-ordinates of the half diagonals on Plate XX. The intentional or original setting out can be very closely approximated by taking the existing North base socket distance LK (+its correction of ¶ 144, *i.e.* 0.54 B") and the existing South base socket distance ZM (+its correction of ¶ 144, *i.e.* 0.47 B"), and by taking O the centre of the base as fixed ; then with these as data we can correct the angles LOK and ZOM each to a right angle, to give the closely approximate true original socket corners L, K, M, and Z.

The result is that the half diagonals OL, OK, OM, and OZ to the socket corners L, K, M, and Z respectively, are defined by four true squares respectively of length of side 4567.41 B", 4562.10 B", 4570.55 B", and 4553.05 B". The result is confirmed, not only as to its supplying the original intention, but as to its definition of the original construction, by the S.E. socket corner M becoming the precise corner of the Pyramid square base of 36524.25 P" circuit. The azimuth distance between UX produced and the S.E. socket corner M is also the length of the base side for the Pyramid circuit 36524.25 P".

The Pyramid was therefore set out in preliminary lines as follows :—

(1) The socket corners defined the lines of the base diagonals.
(2) One socket corner (the S.E.) defined the S.E. corner of the Pyramid.
(3) The distance between the East side of the S.E. socket and the West side, UX produced, of the S.W. socket defined the South base side of the Pyramid.

¶ 146. THE TWO VERSIONS OF PYRAMID RECONSTRUCTION.

Remembering that Professor Petrie's reconstruction defines the hollowing-in of the core without applying the same feature to the casing, and that the new reconstruction, adopted in the present work, applies the hollowing-in to

THE MEASUREMENTS AND LEVELS OF THE EXISTING DETAILS OF THE GREAT PYRAMID'S EXTERIOR.

[To face p. 120.

the casing, the reader will find instructive matter in the details of Plates XXI and XXII. These show the appearance of the South-East corner casing stone according to the two different reconstructions.

It should be understood that Petrie carries down the masonry of the corner casing stones to the socket floors in all cases. The discovery of the Lisht Pyramid sockets and their foundation deposits (refer Section III, ¶ 197a) may have caused Professor Petrie to modify his reconstruction in this detail. But even this modification could scarcely redeem the evident weakness of his reconstruction as applied to the South-East socket corner casing stone. A reconstruction stands or falls under its critical application to detail. Apart, then, from the identities established concerning the intentional circuit of the Pyramid's base, we are assured that a critical technical examination of the two reconstructions, as applied to the detail of Plates XXI and XXII, will settle the matter conclusively, to the satisfaction of the thesis advanced in the present work.

(margin note: Sockets and foundation deposits. Lisht Pyramid sockets.)

(margin note: The importance of the comparison of the two reconstructions.)

¶ 147. THE EFFECT OF SUBSIDENCE ON FORM OF PYRAMID'S BASE.

The nett effect of the correction of the right angles of the base diagonals in ¶ 145 is as follows :—

(margin note: Rectangular correction of diagonals shows that central subsidence has reduced Pyramid's central base width by 0.67 B″ across East to West and 2.10 B″ across North to South.)

(1) That subsidence effect has reduced the true azimuth distance *between the centres of* the East and West casing base sides by the total amount of 0.67 inch.

(2) That the same effect has reduced the true azimuth distance *between the centres of* the North and South casing base sides by the total amount of 2.10 inches.[1]

These corrections applied to the distances *between* the hollowed-in base sides give a constant distance of 9069.5 B″, East and West, or North and South, between centres of base sides. The East to West distance given by the existing slightly distorted features of the North and South base sides, as surveyed by Professor Petrie, still gives this value (¶ 142). This indicates that the Pyramid masonry, in centrally sliding slightly inwards, could not very appreciably reduce its external base length owing to the tightly fitting blocks. Externally it compromised by slightly skewing the external form of its base to retain its external base length practically unaltered, and at the same time produce the necessary diminution of azimuth co-ordinates to satisfy the subsidence conditions. This distortion of the external form of the Pyramid base bears relation to the distortion of the socket base only as effect to cause.

(margin note: This gives constant original central width across Pyramid base—between any two faces—as 9069.5 B″.)

(margin note: Construction of Pyramid ensured that subsidence reduction across centre—between opposite faces—should be a maximum; but between corners of each base side a minimum—almost inappreciable.)

All the data, then, at our disposal combine to show that the external corner to corner measures of the Pyramid remained practically unaltered, although very slightly skewed in direction. At the same time, the effect of

---

[1] This movement, due to subsidence, is discussed further in Section II (¶¶ 180–182), in light of data emerging from inductions subsequent to the stage here discussed.

PLATE XXI.

RECONSTRUCTION OF THE SOUTH-EAST CORNER CASING STONE.

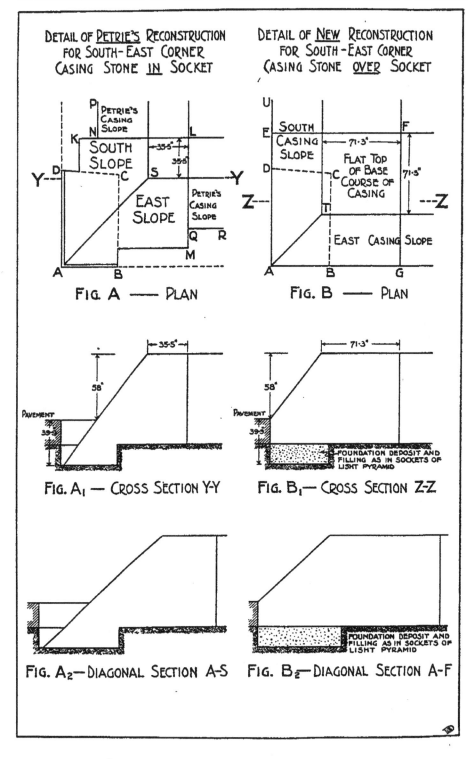

DETAIL OF PETRIE'S RECONSTRUCTION FOR SOUTH-EAST CORNER CASING STONE IN SOCKET

DETAIL OF NEW RECONSTRUCTION FOR SOUTH-EAST CORNER CASING STONE OVER SOCKET

FIG. A —— PLAN

FIG. B —— PLAN

FIG. A₁ — CROSS SECTION Y-Y

FIG. B₁ — CROSS SECTION Z-Z

FIG. A₂ — DIAGONAL SECTION A-S

FIG. B₂ — DIAGONAL SECTION A-F

PLATE XXII.

ISOMETRIC AND OBLIQUE PROJECTIONS OF SOUTH-EAST
CASING STONE RECONSTRUCTIONS.

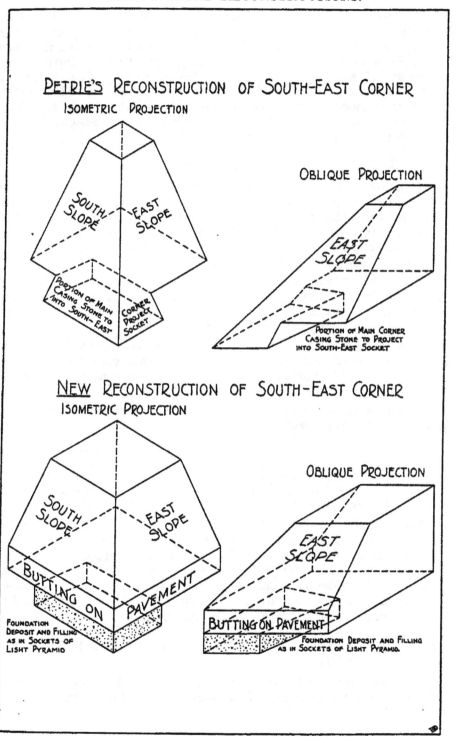

Explains why
core masonry
hollowing is
37″ at centre
of North face.
the subsidence brought the hollowed-in central portion of the North base and of the South base in each case 1 inch nearer the centre of the Pyramid (¶ 147, Case 2) ; and in the case of the East and West sides ½ inch nearer the centre of the Pyramid (¶ 147, Case 1). In consequence, the hollowing-in extent of about 36″ would be increased by subsidence to 37″ on North and South base sides, and to 36½″ on East and West base sides. 37″ is the value obtained by Professor Petrie from his sightings down the North face slope of the core masonry. This agrees with the value deduced for the North face including subsidence effect.

¶ 148. THE PYRAMID'S DISPLACEMENT FACTOR.

Analysis of
subsidence
movements
shows that
Pyramid base
was defined
by a square
of 36,524 P″
circuit—
corner to
corner—and
by an inner
square margin-
ally 35.76 P″
internal to
the other, and
of circuit
286.1 P″ less
than the
circuit of the
outer square.
286.1 P″ a
geometrical
measure of
the Pyramid.
Also the dis-
placement of
the Passage
System.

Criticism, therefore, has shown that the Pyramid was set out to a base line of 9141.1 B″, that its distance between centres of opposite base sides was 9069.5 B″, and, independently, that its base sides were centrally hollowed to the extent of about 36″. The difference between the first two values, 9141.1 and 9069.5 B″, gives twice the extent of hollowing-in as 71.6 B″, and therefore the hollowing-in as 35.8 B″ =35.76 P″.

The actual Pyramid base circuit is therefore defined by two squares, one marginally 35.76 P″ internal to the other. The outer square, defining the base corners, is 36,524.24 P″ circuit, and the inner square is 8 × 35.76 P″ (or 286.1 P″) less in circuit than the outer square.

Now 286.1 P″ (286.4 B″) is an important geometrical value of the Pyramid. It is also the measurement of the displacement of the North to South Vertical Axial Plane of the Pyramid's Passage System Eastwards from the North to South Central Vertical Plane of the Pyramid.

The existing displacement of the Passage System, as defined, was measured by Professor Petrie as follows :—

	Petrie's stated possible range of error.
Entrance Door on North Face	=287.0 B″±0.8 B″.
Entrance Passage End in Natural Rock	=286.4 B″±1.0 B″.
Beginning of Ascending Passage	=286.6 B″±0.8 B″.
End of Ascending Passage	=287.0 B″±1.5 B″.

The
geometrical
definition
of external
hollowing
displacement,
Passage
displacement,
and 35th
course axis.

Plates XXIII, XXIV, and XXV (Figs. A, A₁, and A₂) show how the hollowed-in base feature, the 35th course axis, and the displacement of the Passage System are all geometrical functions of a composite system of geometry featuring the solar year to the scale of 10 P″ to a day, and to the scale of 100 P″ to a day. To convey the full significance of this to the reader it is necessary first to define the precise value of the solar year intentionally identified with the Pyramid's base square circuit.

¶ 149. THE INTENTIONAL VALUE OF PYRAMID'S BASE CIRCUIT.

In ¶¶ 102–104 it was shown that the period of 25,826½ years was identified with the period of the Precession of the Equinoxes. In ¶ 102 it was explained that 78½ Phœnix cycles gave the identity 25,826½ Phœnix years (or inter-calated Calendar years) =25,826.54+Solar years. Accurately, the identity defines the precise numerical values of the Pyramid's base diagonals and of the base square circuit as follows :—

(1) *INITIAL HALF PHŒNIX CYCLE.*

From Table III.	103 years' cycle	=37,620 days
Do. (365 days' column)	61 years of next cycle	=22,280 ,,
	½ Calendar year	= 180 ,,
	164½ years on cycle	=60,080 days.

(2) *NO. OF DAYS IN THE PHŒNIX CYCLE.*

From Table III.	3 cycles of 103 years	=309 years	=112,860 days
Do. (365 days' column)	20 years	= 20 ,, =	7,305 ,,
	Phœnix cycle	=329 years	=120,165 days.

(3) *TOTAL PRECESSIONAL PERIOD.*

78 Phœnix cycles	=25,662	years	=9,372,870 days
From (1) above	164½	,, =	60,080 ,,
Precessional period	=25,826½ years		=9,432,950 days.

The years are intercalated Calendar years.

(4) *PYRAMID BASE CIRCUIT AND DIAGONALS.*

Let N =No. of days in solar year, and
P =Precessional period in years.

Then from above

$$P = \frac{9,432,950}{N} \quad .. \quad .. \quad .. \quad .. \quad .. \quad (I)$$

and from Pyramid base relationship

$$P = \frac{100\ N}{\sqrt{2}} \quad .. \quad .. \quad .. \quad .. \quad .. \quad (II)$$

Solving the simultaneous equations I and II, we get

$$N = 365.2424650 \text{ days.}$$

Then, Pyramid base circuit =36,524.2465 P″,
and Sum of Base Diagonals =25,826.542378 P″.

These are the values adopted for the geometrical representation developed in Plates XXIII, XXIV, and XXV.

¶ 150. THE PROBLEM AND ITS PLANE.

It has been suggested by the evidence discussed in the two preceding chapters that the external features of the Great Pyramid were intended to

The Phœnix cycle chron-ology and Calendar rules define the numerical value of Pyramid base square circuit as 36,524.2465 and the numerical values of the sum of the base diagonals (and constant of Precession) as 25,826.542378.

PLATE XXIII.

THE GREAT PYRAMID'S EQUAL AREA GEOMETRY DEFINES DISPLACEMENT OF PASSAGE SYSTEM.

Fig. A.

EAST TO WEST VERTICAL SECTION

SQUARE CIRCUIT OF PLANE B_2 A_1 B_1
= SUM OF DIAGONALS OF SQUARE
OF PLANE D_2 J_1 D_1

ARC A_2 A_1 A_3
— LINE B_2 A_1 B_1

ARC J_2 J_1 J_3
LINE D_2 J_1 D_1

NOTE :—
POINTS E_1 & E_2 DO NOT
LIE ON ARC A_2 A_1 A_3

SQUARE OF AREA
EQUAL TO
QUADRANT AREA
O A_2 A_1 A_3

Fig. B.
PLAN

CASE I (FIG. A):—
FOR CASE OF D_2 J_1 D_1 (FIG. A) — M_2 M_1 (FIG. B),
D_2 D_1 CIRCUIT = 36,524·2465
k_3 F_1 — F_1 k_1 = 2,861·022156 (FIG. A ONLY)

CASE II (FIG. A)
FOR CASE OF D_2 J_1 D_1 (FIG. A) — N_2 N_1 (FIG. B),
D_2 D_1 CIRCUIT = 3652·42465
k_3 F_1 — F_1 k_1 = 286·1022156 (IN FIGS. A & B)

PLATE XXIV.

THE GEOMETRY OF THE PASSAGE SYSTEM DISPLACEMENT.

SECONDARY SYSTEM

CIRCUIT AT $D_1 D_2$ = 3652·42465
$D_1 D_2$ = 913·1061625; $O_1 J_1$ = 581·3014373
$O A_1 - O A_2 - O A_3$ = 411·04218823
$B_1 B_2$ = 645·66355945; $O_1 - E_1 E_2$ = 364·2766547
CIRCUIT AT $B_1 B_2$ = 4 × ARC $A_3 A_1 A_2$
$k_1 k_3$ = 572·20443I2

HENCE $F k_1 - F k_3 - K_1 P - K_3 P$
= $X p$ - 286·1022156

SECONDARY SYSTEM:-
$\frac{1}{10}$ᵗʰ LINEAR SCALE
OF PRIMARY SYSTEM

Line of Central Vertical (North & South) Plane of Passage System

PRIMARY SYSTEM
CIRCUIT AT $R_1 R_2$ = 36524·2465
$R_1 R_2$ = 9131·061625
O P = 5813·0143730

R_2

R_1

$K_3 \; P \; K_1$

X

E_3
$E_1 E_2 E_4$

form a geometrical representation of the dimensions and motions of the Earth and its orbit (¶ 114). Any such representation must, of necessity, be made with reference to a plane representing the plane of the Earth's orbit. The plane of the Great Pyramid pavement is defined as this natural plane, as it is the plane of the Pyramid's base square, defining the circuit of the solar year. For the necessary geometrical representation the Great Pyramid's base plane, therefore, represents the plane of the Earth's orbit. This, then, is the natural plane for the geometrical and comparative representation of all values defining the dimensions and motions of the Earth and its orbit. These values, in consequence, need only be looked for in relation to the Pyramid's external features as defined in plan.

¶ 151. THE THREE YEAR VALUES.

Consideration of the Earth's motion in its orbit is complicated by several factors. These complications, however, make it a considerably easier matter to specify the intention of any geometrical representation of the elements of the Earth and its orbit. One of the complications referred to is that there are three different year values defining the revolution of the Earth round its orbit. These are the Solar (or Tropical) year, the Sidereal (or Stellar) year, and the Anomalistic (or Orbital year).

The interval between successive autumnal or vernal equinoxes—or between successive summer or winter solstices—defines the Solar year. The interval between the Earth's position, at any time in the year, in relation to the fixed stars, and its next return to that position defines the Sidereal year. The interval between successive annual returns of the Earth to the point—defined as Perihelion—in its orbit nearest the Sun defines the Anomalistic year.

The Solar year is slightly *less than* 365¼ days, the Sidereal year is slightly *more than* 365¼ days, and the Anomalistic year is slightly longer than the Sidereal year. Were the Earth's axis rigidly constant in its inclination, and in the direction of its inclination, the Solar year would be of the same length as the Sidereal year. Were the plane and axes of the Earth's orbit rigidly fixed in relation to the fixed stars, the Anomalistic year would also be of the same length as the Sidereal year. The Solar and Anomalistic years are therefore departures from the Sidereal year, due to circumstances other than the primary functions governing the Earth's rotation and revolution.

¶ 152. THE SIDEREAL YEAR DATUM.

The Sidereal year is therefore the basal period for the other forms of the year. As such—presuming our premises concerning the Pyramid's purpose to be correct—it should be the year value defined by the true circuit of the Great Pyramid's base. Now the square circuit of the Great Pyramid's base defines the Solar year. This square circuit touches the true Pyramid base at four points only—the four corners. The true circuit of the Pyramid's base is the circuit of the hollowed-in perimeter of the casing base edges. This circuit is longer than the square (corner to corner) circuit defining the Solar year, and the Sidereal year is longer than the Solar year. In other words, the hollowed-in base circuit is the true constructional base circuit, as the Sidereal year is the true constructional year circuit of the basal dynamics of the Earth's orbit. The question, then, to be settled is whether the hollowed base circuit gives the value of the Sidereal year to the scale of 100 P″ to a day.

¶ 153. THE COMPLETED GEOMETRY OF THE GREAT PYRAMID'S EXTERIOR.

Plate XXV illustrates how the representation in plan should indicate the three values of the year. This is derived from the geometrical sequence of Plates XXIII and XXIV in relation to the geometry of the 35th course axis and the *aroura*. The derivation of the 35th course axis connection is illustrated on Figs. A and A_1 (Plate XXV). In Fig. A_1 (Plate XXV), the apex Pyramid circuit at level acb =3652.42465 P″, and this is equal to the apex Pyramid circuit $D_2J_1D_1$ (Plate XXIV). The connected geometry of the latter defines the displacement of the axis of the Passage System and the displacement of the central hollowing-in of the Pyramid's base sides. The circuit of the apex Pyramid at acb (Plate XXV, Fig. A_1) is therefore equal to the 35th axis length EG =FH (Plate XXV, Fig. A). The rectangular *aroura* defined by the latter are EGRC and EFQC, and these are respectively equal in area to the *aroura parallelograms* EGBH and EFAD (the two horizontally shaded areas of Plate XXV, Fig. A). The two latter define the centrally hollowed-in area as DEH, in elevation on Fig. A, and as $D_1E_1H_1$ in plan, Fig. B, Plate XXV.[1] The maximum extent of hollowing-in (35.762777 P″ horizontally from the geometrical plane face of the Pyramid's slope) applies to the whole area DEH (Fig. A), and along the line EO (Fig. A) to the base of the apex Pyramid at c (Fig. A_1). The broadly fluted (or scooped-leaf) effect necessary to taper off the hollowing towards the apex is illustrated on Figs. A_1 and A_2 (Plate XXV).

¶ 154. THE THREE ASTRONOMICAL YEAR-CIRCUITS OF THE PYRAMID BASE.

The restoration of ¶ 153 is the one restoration that satisfies all the structural and geometrical features of the Great Pyramid. The real test of its having been the intentional geometrical arrangement is the extent to which it satisfies the conditions postulated in ¶¶ 150–152.

These conditions were—

(1) That the actual (hollowed-in) structural circuit (AD₁H₁B, etc., in Fig. B, Plate XXV) of the Pyramid's base should give the value of the Sidereal year to a scale of 100 P″ to a day ; and

---

[1]For the relation between point G on Plate XX, as there defined, and point D on Plate XXV, as there defined, the reader is referred to the further discussion on subsidence effects in Section II, ¶¶ 180–182.

PLATE XXV.

THE PYRAMID BASE DEFINES THE EARTH AND ITS ORBIT, IN DIMENSIONS AND MOTION.

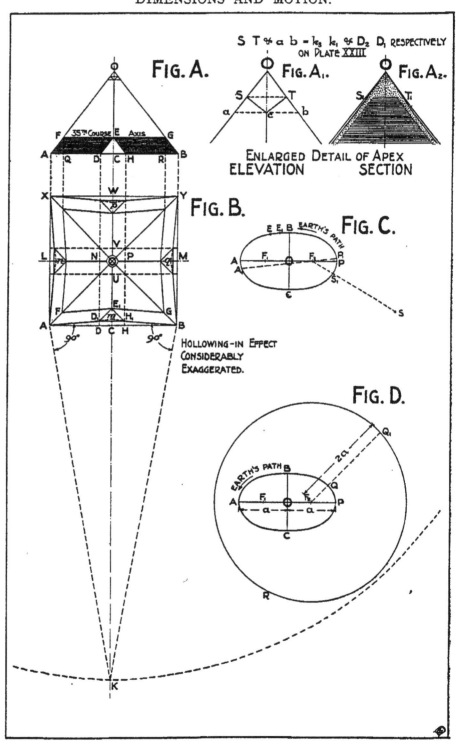

(2) That the geometrical circuit (AmBqYpXnA in Fig. B, Plate XXV), internal to the structural circuit, and defined by it, should give the value of the Anomalistic year to the scale of 100 P″ to a day, precisely as the external geometrical circuit (ADCHB, etc., Fig. B, Plate XXV) gives the value of the Solar year to this scale.

Now the external geometrical base circuit, as defined, is 36,524.2465 P″, representing, to the scale defined, a good average value for the Solar year for a long period of history from ancient to modern times. *Solar year base circuit 36,524.2465 P″.*

The actual structural base circuit, as defined, and resulting from the geometry described, is 36525.6471536 P″, representing, to the scale defined, a good average value for the Sidereal year. The resulting value of 365.256471536 days for the Sidereal year is only 8.6 seconds of time longer than the value for the present time,[1] 365.25637 days. *Sidereal year base circuit. 36,525.647 P″.*

The internal geometrical base circuit, as defined, and resulting from the geometry described, is 36525.997317 P″, representing, to the scale defined, a good average value for the Anomalistic year. The resulting value of 365.25997317 days for the Anomalistic year is only 33½ seconds of time longer than the value for the present time,[1] 365.2595844 days. *Anomalistic year base circuit. 36,525.997 P″.*

In a representation intentionally giving the values stated, one would expect the intention to be emphatically declared by the associated representation of other related values. So far, the Pyramid's base geometry defines the Earth's annual orbit, in terms of its three forms of year. The intention would be completely defined by the connected representation of the related astronomical knowledge concerning the dimensions and form of the Earth's orbit. (Refer ¶¶ 114 and 120.) *Suggests that intention of above representation would be completely expressed by other connected dimensional values of Earth's orbit.*

¶ 155. ASTRONOMICAL RELATIONSHIP OF THE THREE FORMS OF THE YEAR. (Plate XXV, Fig. C.)

The path or orbit of the Earth round the Sun is an ellipse, ACPB, of which F_1 and F_2 are the two foci. The Sun's centre is at the focus F_2. O is the centre of the orbit. AOP is the major axis, and BOC the minor axis of the elliptic orbit. *Earth's elliptical orbit. The Sun in one focus. Major Axis. Minor Axis.*

The ellipse figured is considerably exaggerated as a representation of the Earth's elliptical orbit. The latter, to any ordinary scale of representation, cannot be distinguished from a circle. *Earth's elliptic orbit nearly a circle.*

When the Earth is nearest the Sun it is at P—on the major axis—whence P is called Perihelion. *Perihelion.*

When the Earth is farthest from the Sun it is at A—also on the major axis—whence A is called Aphelion. *Aphelion.*

[1]For further explanation and additional data concerning the astronomical relationship of the three forms of year—and for data concerning their variations—the reader is referred to Chapter IV, Section II, and Plates XLIV–LVI inclusive.

The Earth travels round its orbit in the direction of the arrow, *i.e.* direction BACPB.

Now let S be a fixed point in the heavens, and E the equinox for a particular year. Owing to a slow movement of the Earth's axis,[1] the equinox of the following year does not occur at E, but at a point E_1, about 50″ of angle (or 20 minutes of time) short of E.

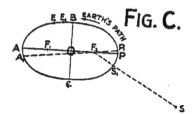

The Solar year is therefore the interval in days taken by the Earth to travel round the distance $EACPBE_1$, whereas the Sidereal (or Stellar) year—fixed from the immovable point S, and its immovable radius F_2S_1S—is the interval in days taken by the Earth to travel round the distance S_1PBACS_1.

The Solar year is therefore shorter than the Sidereal year by the interval E_1E—about 50″ of angle, or about 20 minutes of time.

The Equinox is not, however, the only point that moves. In the course of the Earth's revolution round its orbit, the orbit itself is not stationary, but moves round in the direction of the Earth's revolution. In the course of one revolution of the Earth round its orbit, the major axis AF_2P moves round to the position $A_1F_2P_1$. Hence, commencing, say, from perihelion at P, the Earth travels round PBACPP₁ to return to perihelion. This revolution defines the Anomalistic or Orbital year. It is longer than the Sidereal year by the time it takes the Earth to travel from P to P_1. PP_1 is about 11.5″ of angle, or about 4.6 minutes of time. (Refer also Plates LV and LVI.)

¶ 156. THE MEAN SUN DISTANCE AND THE EARTH'S ORBITAL MOTION. (Plate XXV, Fig. C).

F_2P =the shortest distance between the Earth and Sun.
F_2A =the longest   „   „   „   „

The mean of these is OP=OA, and this distance, in astronomical nomenclature, is defined as the *mean sun distance*.

The eccentricity of the elliptic orbit is

$$e = \frac{OF_2}{OP} = \frac{OF_1}{OA} = \frac{F_1F_2}{AP}.$$

The value of this eccentricity (e) is variable. Its value for 1900 A.D. is 0.016751. Its greatest value during the past 60,000 years occurred about 11,600 B.C. It was then something over 0.019. Since that time it has been slowly but constantly diminishing, and will continue to diminish until about 26,000 A.D. The value of e will then be about 0.004, when the Earth's orbit will be as nearly a circle as it is ever likely to be.

[1]For explanation of this movement refer Chapter IV, Section II, and Plates Nos. XLIV–LVI inclusive.

To determine accurately the functions of the year, at any period, know-ledge of these and other values, as well as of the laws governing motion in elliptic orbits, is a matter of fundamental necessity. Without going extensively into the subject of the Laws of Planetary Motion, attention is directed to an important corollary of these laws which has an important bearing upon the question of the Sun's mean distance.

Knowledge concerning these and other values, and their variations, and the laws governing same, of fundamental necessity.

¶ 157. THE MAJOR AXIS OF THE ORBIT A DYNAMICAL CONSTANT. (Plate XXV, Fig. D.)

In Fig. D, ABPC is the elliptic orbit of Fig. C, with the Sun in focus F_2.

In Fig. D let $OA = OP = a$.

Then $AP = 2a = $Major axis.

With centre F_2 at the Sun, and radius $F_2Q_1 = AP = 2a$, describe the circle Q_1R.

Definition of the " Earth's Speed Circle."

The corollary to which attention is directed is as follows :—

The speed of the Earth round its elliptic orbit is at every point, such as Q, equal to the speed which the Earth would acquire in falling to the ellipse at Q, from Q_1 on the circumference of a circle (Q_1R) with centre at the Sun (F_2), and radius (F_2Q_1) equal to the major axis (AP) of the elliptic orbit.

FIG. D.

The period of the Earth's revolution round its orbit " independent of every element except the major axis."

Thus the speed of the Earth at Q in the elliptic orbit is equal to the speed the Earth would acquire at Q in falling towards the Sun from Q_1 to Q.

From this it follows that " *the period* " of the Earth's revolution round its orbit is " *independent of every element except the major axis.*"[1]

For purpose of brevity, rather than accuracy of definition, we will term the circle Q_1R the " Earth's Speed Circle."

¶ 158. THE GEOMETRICAL REPRESENTATION OF THE RANGE OF VARIATIONS IN RELATION TO THE BASAL CONSTANT.

The single constant geometrical feature of the Earth's orbit is therefore the Earth's " Speed Circle," with its centre occupied by the Sun. Referring again to Fig. D of Plate XXV, we see that the Earth's orbit ABPC revolves in an anti-clockwise direction about the fixed point F_2, defined as the centre of the Sun, and the centre of the Earth's Speed Circle RQ_1. Thus the point O

The Earth's " Speed Circle " the only constant feature of orbit. All points of orbit slowly revolve round heliocentric focus of orbit.

[1] Refer Moulton's " Celestial Mechanics," pp. 150-151.

Heliocentric
focus the
fixed centre
of the Earth's
" Speed
Circle."
The history
of an orbit's
motions and
dimensions
cannot be de-
picted by an
ellipse.
describes a circle around F_2. Points P, F_1, and A on the major axis, and points B and C on the minor axis, also each describe their independent circles around F_2 as centre. None of these points, then—other than the fixed centre of the Sun, F_2—can be deemed as suitable for the origin of co-ordinates for any graphical representation of the Earth's orbit defining the limits of its movements and variations. Nor, indeed, can the orbit for any particular date be graphically represented as defining in general geometrical terms the limiting values of orbital cycles.

Two circles,
both concen-
tric with, and
internal to,
the Earth's
" Speed
Circle,"
define the
annular zone
of variation of
the centre of
the Earth's
orbit.
Now, since the distance F_2O is a variable distance, and since O rotates around F_2 as a fixed centre, it is clear that a circle of radius F_2O, minimum value, and an outer circle of radius F_2O, maximum value, completely define the limits of variation of the centre of the orbit from the Sun. During the long period of the rotation of the orbit round the Sun (over 108,000 years) the curve traced by the centre point O of the orbit lies within the ring defined by the maximum and minimum circles.

The three
heliocentric
circles com-
pletely define
in geometrical
terms the
historical
range of the
orbit's motions
and dimen-
sions.
These two circles, together with the Earth's " Speed Circle "—all concentric with the Sun—completely define, in general geometrical terms, the fixed element of the Earth's orbit—i.e. its major axis—and the range of variation of the variable elements. A representation of this nature is the necessary geometrical basis for any further representation defining the variable elements in relation to any standard system of astronomical chronology.

¶ 159. GREAT PYRAMID'S EXTERNAL GEOMETRY DEFINES
THE EARTH'S ORBIT AND ITS VARIATIONS.

Geometrical
definition
of limiting
values of
eccentricity(e).
With e=eccentricity of Earth's orbit, then (Fig. D of Plate XXV) :—

$$\text{Maximum value of } e = \frac{\text{Diameter of max. circle of radius } F_2O}{\text{Radius } (F_2Q_1) \text{ of Earth's Speed Circle}},$$

and

$$\text{Minimum value of } e = \frac{\text{Diameter of min. circle of radius } F_2O}{\text{Radius } (F_2Q_1) \text{ of Earth's Speed Circle}},$$

F_2O being variable within its defined limits, and F_2Q_1 being a constant = the major axis of the Earth's orbit =AOP.

The geometry
of the
Pyramid's
base plan
gives the
above com-
plete defini-
tion.
Now the two limiting values of e are known, and are precisely defined by the proportions of the Pyramid base geometry shown in Fig. B, Plate XXV. In this representation (Fig. B), the base centre, O, represents the Sun's centre. NOP and UOV represent the rectangular diameters of the minimum circle passing through NVPU. These diameters are defined by the central hollowing-in widths of the Pyramid base sides. The maximum circle is defined by the circle, CLWM, inscribed within the Pyramid's geometrical base square. Its diameter is the Pyramid base side length, LOM or WOC.

The radius of the Earth's " Speed Circle " is defined by the distance, OK, K being the intersection of the perpendiculars, AK and BK, from the converging base side lengths, AD_1 and BH_1 respectively. Other points such as K are defined by all four sides of the Pyramid's base, this definition completing the circuit of the Earth's " Speed Circle." The radius OK of this circle, by geometrical construction, is 470860.606 P". The diameter VOU of the minimum circle, by geometrical construction, is 1826.212325 P", and the diameter of the maximum circle is 9131.061625 P".

From these values—

$$\text{Minimum value of } e = \frac{\text{VOU}}{\text{OK}} = \frac{1826.212325}{470860.606}$$
$$= 0.003878414$$

and

$$\text{Maximum value of } e = \frac{\text{WOC}}{\text{OK}} = \frac{9131.061625}{470860.606}$$
$$= 0.01939207.$$

These values are respectively the least and the greatest possible values of e—the eccentricity of the Earth's orbit—as accurately as modern astronomy can determine these values.

Again,

$$\text{radius OK} = 470,860.606 \text{ P"}$$
$$= 471,378.552 \text{ B"}$$
$$= 7.43968674 \text{ miles.}$$

This distance, multiplied by 25,000,000

$$= 185,992,169 \text{ miles,}$$
$$= \text{Major axis of Earth's orbit,}$$
$$= \text{Twice Mean Sun Distance.}$$

Whence Mean Sun Distance = 92,996,085 miles.

Professor Simon Newcomb[1] gives for the latter a mean value of 92,998,000 miles.

Thus we have found (¶¶ 101 and 114) that

$$\text{1 Pyr. inch} = \frac{1}{250,000,000} \text{ Polar radius of Earth,}$$

and that Pyramid's " Speed Circle " radius OK

$$= \frac{1}{25,000,000} \text{ Radius of Earth's " Speed Circle."}$$

The scales are therefore decimally related, as we had inferred they would be in a representation of this nature (¶ 114).

For modern variations in the determination of the value of the Sun's Mean Distance, the reader is referred to Section III, ¶ 201.

[1] Enc. Brit. (11th Edit.), Vol. XXI, p. 717, Table I.

Marginal notes:

Pyramid's definition of Earth's " Speed Circle " and related maximum and minimum values of eccentricity.

Pyramid's Minimum e and Maximum e.

Pyramid's " Speed Circle " radius $\frac{1}{25,000,000}$th of Earth's " Speed Circle " radius.

Pyramid's relative scales of definition of Earth's polar radius and " Speed Circle " radius, $\frac{1}{250,000,000}$ and $\frac{1}{25,000,000}$.

Pyramid value for Sun's Mean Distance, 92,996,085 miles

SECTION I.—SUMMARY AND CONCLUSIONS.

¶ 160. THE GEOMETRICAL EXPRESSION OF NATURAL LAW.

Pyramid's Polar diameter inch intentional.

The Great Pyramid has now clearly established its intention in regard to its inch-unit. It defines that this unit is a Polar diameter inch-unit of the value of one 500-millionth part of the Earth's Polar diameter.

Its use defines all Earth and orbital distances and motions as simple functions of the Earth's Polar diameter and the year.

In conjunction with a simple, yet extensive system of solid geometry, the Pyramid inch-unit, as applied to the dimensions and form of the Pyramid's exterior, defines a further intentional representation. This is to the effect that all dimensions (angular and linear), and all motions—as well as variations in these dimensions and motions—of the Earth and its orbit, are simple functions of the Earth's Polar diameter and of the period of the Sidereal Year in solar days.

This definition is the Natural Law relationship inferred from the reflexion phenomena.

In other words, the Great Pyramid's external system of geometry is the graphical expression of the Natural Law relationship inferred from the mathematical clue of the four Pyramid constants that defined, by the noon reflexion phenomena, the principal points of the year (¶¶ 46 and 47).

Intentional presentation in terms of Gravitational Laws.

The manner in which the Pyramid's base plan simply defines the dimensions and limiting areas of dimensional variations of the Earth's orbit shows clearly that the intention was to present these as governed by the Laws—or, as the Pyramid seems to define, an all-including Law—of Gravitation (¶¶ 157, 158).

Numerical value of Pyramid base circuit measurement independent of surveyed measurements, yet agrees with latter.

This comprehensive graphical representation is independent entirely of any question as to the accuracy of any survey or measurement of the Pyramid's base, yet this independent representation agrees precisely with the accurate modern survey measurements. The intentional numerical value of the circuit of the Pyramid base square is

Defined in terms of known duration of Phœnix Cycle.

defined in terms of the known duration of the Phœnix Cycle, or the Cycle of the House of Enoch (¶ 149). In this connection the relations established in ¶¶ 38 and 39 possess a remarkable numerical significance.

Fragments of the ancient scientific system in use in Egypt before arrival of Pyramid builders.

A fact requiring emphasis, in connection with the use of the Polar diameter inch in the Pyramid, is that this unit and the year circle form the necessary basis for the derivation of the Egyptian common cubit and the Egyptian *aroura*. Nevertheless, the common cubit was in use in Egypt—but without the inch as a contemporary unit—before the Pyramid builders had arrived. This confirms what we have previously seen, that the early Egyptians had derived from the former civilisation a fragment of the science that the designer of the Great Pyramid knew in its entirety.

¶ 161. THE SYMBOLICAL DEFINITIONS OF THE PYRAMID'S BASE CIRCUIT.

Form of Pyramid's constructional base perimeter defines relations of the Earth and its orbit.

Whilst the solid geometrical relations of the Pyramid define the form of the Pyramid's base perimeter, it is the constructional form of the latter that defines, in the plane of the base, all the principal relations of the Earth and its orbit. The Pyramid's base perimeter is defined as a symmetrical figure formed of twelve lines. Its corners define an external square, and the lines of its perimeter from its corners, when produced to meet inside the centre of each base side, define a symmetrical figure formed of eight lines. (Plate XXV, Fig. B.)

The twelve-line figure is the actual constructional base circuit of the Pyramid, and defines the Sidereal year to the scale of 100 Polar diameter inches to a day.

The external square circuit of the Pyramid's actual base corners, defines the Solar (or Tropical) year to the scale of 100 Polar diameter inches to a day.

The eight-line figure defines the Anomalistic (or Orbital) year to the scale of 100 Polar diameter inches to a day (¶ 154).

This is a graphical representation indicating that the Sidereal year is the actual constructional year value of orbital motion, that the Solar year is the *apparent* basal year value, and that the Anomalistic year is the most obscure value of the three. This is an exact representation of an astronomical truth.

Constructional base perimeter of twelve lines defines circuit of Sidereal year.

This perimeter defined by and internal to a square defining circuit of Solar year.

The same perimeter defines an internal circuit of eight lines defining circuit of Anomalistic year.

The symbolical definition of the three relations.

¶ 162. THE GEOMETRICAL REPRESENTATION OF THE ORBIT'S HISTORY.

The geometry of the Pyramid's base is an exact representation of an astronomical truth, *i.e.* that the speed of the Earth at any point in its orbit can be determined from the following data :—

The Pyramid's base plan defines the framework for the geometrical representation of the history of the Earth's orbit.

(a) A circle with its centre at the focus of the Earth's orbit occupied by the Sun, and of radius equal to the length of the major axis of the Earth's orbit, *i.e.* twice the mean Sun distance ; and

(b) The direction and distance of the free focus of the Earth's orbit in relation to the focus occupied by the Sun.

Definition of Constants :— Length of major axis of orbit ; heliocentric focus.

The Pyramid's base geometry represents the radius and circle of (a) accurately to a scale of $\dfrac{1}{25{,}000{,}000}$ and defines the annular field of (b) to the same scale. The latter representation (*i.e.* of (b)) may be described as the definition of the orbital field of the free focus. The orbit of the free focus is completed in each cycle of about 21,000 years. The orbits of a series of such successive cycles, owing to the variation in the distance of the free focus from the heliocentric focus, completely traverse the annular zone between its circle of minimum radius and its circle of maximum radius.

Definition of annular zone containing all possible positions of the free focus thus defining limits of variation of orbit's eccentricity.

The radius of the constant circle of (a) above precisely represents the value of the constant length of the major axis of the Earth's orbit. Consequently, it represents the Sun's mean distance as half this value. The Sun's mean distance is, therefore, represented as a radius, to the scale of

Scalar relation between representations of Earth's Polar radius and Sun's mean distance.

$\dfrac{1}{25{,}000{,}000}$, and, as previously shown (¶¶ 101, 114, 159), the Earth's Polar

radius is represented by the Pyramid inch to the scale of $\dfrac{1}{250{,}000{,}000}$.

¶ 163. THE QUESTION OF UTILITARIAN MOTIVE.

Nothing so far learned of particular value from utilitarian standpoint.

All these and other identities have been established as related identities in this chapter, and in preceding chapters. That they are intentional identities can scarcely now be doubted. But what new item of knowledge have we learned that is of any practical value, from the standpoint of the utilitarian, apart from its interest as pertaining to matters of scientific and archæological curiosity? Very little, indeed, when viewed from the stand-point of any utilitarian basis.

Scientific facts given by Pyramid already known as facts of modern science.

We have certainly learned that the dimensions and motions of the Earth and its orbit are all related functions of the simplest units of these dimensions and motions. This, however, we have known in a slightly different form from the Laws of Newton and Kepler. The rational development of Einstein's Theory of Relativity now gives us reason to hope that these and the laws of other branches of science may be shown to be but varying phases of one Universal Law of Nature.

What other motive, if any, lies behind the design and construction of the Great Pyramid?

The most we have learned, then, from the Pyramid's geometry so far—taken as a whole—has not very materially advanced our knowledge of science beyond what we have already known *in general terms.* What we have learned may have caused us to alter our conceptions concerning the origin and development of ancient civilisations. But was this the sole reason that prompted the design and construction of a monument of the nature of the Great Pyramid? Surely there was some utilitarian motive behind a project of this nature.[1]

¶ 164. OMISSIONS THAT SUGGEST POSSIBLE MOTIVES.

Pyramid gives us an ancient geometrical system of Natural Law in relation to the motions of the Earth and its orbit.

Let us consider, then, what are the outstanding features of the facts, from this standpoint of possible motive. The facts have proved to us that a certain stage of world civilisation, at an unknown—or hitherto supposedly undefined—period in the past had evolved a geometrical system of Natural Law, in relation to the motions of the Earth and its orbit, equal to, superior to, or more comprehensive than the modern system of expressing this Natural Law.

So far it has failed to indicate the date of the civilisation using this system; or as to how the scientific facts were derived.

The facts of importance in this statement of the case are that we have not yet learned anything concerning the precise, or even the approximate date of the stage of civilisation thus made known; and that we have not yet derived a single *tangible* indication as to how the savants of that period discovered their facts of science—*whether by methods of modern times, by methods unknown to modern times, or by the development of faculties now atrophied by long disuse.*

The Pyramid's design postulates that knowledge of the facts of science defined by the Pyramid must precede the discovery of the Pyramid's definition of these facts.

Another feature that must have become increasingly evident to the careful reader is of equal importance. This is that, in order to discover the scientific facts embodied in the Great Pyramid, it is essential that the investigator should have previous knowledge of these very facts. Was the object of the designer, then, merely to show a later civilisation that the precise science of gravitational astronomy had been known long previously? Was this the

[1]For the evidence against the Tombic Theory refer Section III, ¶ 208 and context.

sole object of a work so vast, and so painstakingly executed in the minutest detail ? The fact that the riddle of the Great Pyramid can only be read by one already in possession of the knowledge embodied in its design surely supplies a clear indication of a more utilitarian motive than we have so far seen.

This a clear indication of motive.

¶ 165. THE PYRAMID DESIGNER'S FORETHOUGHT.

. To answer the preceding questions we must reach our objective in stages. One thing we have seen to be clear. This is that the designer of the Pyramid deemed he was projecting his knowledge into a future stage of civilisation that could interpret his intention. He foresaw that the contemporary language in which the facts could be conveyed would lose its meaning and idiomatic significance. It might be lost entirely, or at least be capable of mistranslation or misinterpretation. This foresight has certainly been justified.

Pyramid's science intended to be read by a future race to whom the science was already known.

The designer's foresight in not committing his knowledge to writing in any contemporary language.

The design was therefore formulated, without the aid of written expression, to embody in its external features a geometrical symbolism in Earth standard measurements. This symbolism was to be interpreted in an age already in possession of the knowledge embodied in the symbolism projected. The modern elucidation of this symbolism clearly justifies the remarkable forethought that both conceived the future conditions and created the design to meet them. Forethought of this nature was never expended merely to teach a future race of mankind facts of science it already knew.

Geometrical symbolism a universal means of scientific communication.

Earth's Polar diameter a universal scale of measurement.

Forethought justified by the interpretation of the ancient science as defined in these terms.

We are compelled, then, to come to the conclusion that the Pyramid's external features were designed to attract and direct attention to a further message of greater importance. Granting the forethought displayed, of what nature could this further message be ? Clearly to tell the future race of mankind what it could not possibly know, or to confirm what could have no other possible physical means of being confirmed. A definitive limiting of future possible knowledge in this way can only relate to a break in the continuity of something essential to a race of mankind possessing the scientific knowledge defined ; a break that had taken place before the Pyramid was built, and that could not be restored otherwise than by being passed on from the former civilisation to the then remotely future civilisation.

Such forethought expended in vain unless expended for the purpose of teaching the future race something it could not possibly know.

A vital break in a continuity essential to mankind.

¶ 166. THE INDICATIONS OF A CHRONOLOGICAL CONNECTION.

The inferred break in continuity can only be conceived as relating to some factor affecting the history of the previous civilisation, and related— or that should be related—to the history of the present stage of civilisation. However we look at this aspect of the problem, we are compelled to see that the *primary essential* for restoring the inferred relation must be of a chronological nature. This, indeed, is the one obvious connection suggested by the Great Pyramid's exterior. Here everything is connected with astronomical

The motive suggested inferred as relating to a factor that should be a common factor in the two systems of civilisation.

This inference suggests that the first step in deriving the factor noted is essentially of a chronological nature.

This is confirmed by Pyramid's external indications.

A standard chronology necessarily defined by astronomical cycles.
The various cycles that could be employed to define such a system :—
The Precessional cycle,
The cycle of motion of Equinox from Perihelion,
The cycle defining variation in eccentricity,
The cycle of the revolution of the instantaneous axis of rotation of the Ecliptic.

cycles, and astronomical cycles are the only possible means of affording a reliable datum for the chronological relations of two isolated periods of mankind's history.

Now there are two outstanding astronomical cycles associated with the Pyramid's exterior. There is the cycle of the Precession of the Equinoxes, associated in the Pyramid geometry with a standard period of reference of 25,826.54 Solar years. And there is the cycle of the revolution of the Autumnal Equinox from Perihelion to Perihelion.

There is also the cycle defining the variations in the eccentricity of the Earth's orbit. In addition to these, there is a cycle not hitherto mentioned. This is a cycle defining an important feature of a very slight variation in the Ecliptic due to planetary attractions. The important feature mentioned is what is known as the instantaneous axis of rotation of the Ecliptic. This axis is analogous to the major axis of the Earth's orbit, and, like the latter, has a slow revolution round the orbit. This movement—if its rate during the past 6000 years be taken as basis—completes a revolution of the Ecliptic in about 49,000 years.

¶ 167. DEFINITION OF A SINGLE CYCLE INSUFFICIENT.

The representation of the variable annual values for one cycle not sufficient to define representation as intentional.

A complete and accurate definition of the variable annual rates of any one of the cycles mentioned for every year over a long period of time covering the current years of the present chronological era and the years of a chronological era of past history would be sufficient to effect a chronological connection. It would not, however, suffice to define the representation of the values as intentional. A single representation would always be open to doubt on the grounds of accidental coincidence.

There are also two other reasons why a single representation could not be accepted as certain evidence in the relation mentioned. These are—

Reasons :—
(1) Modern values for ancient times not sufficiently reliable for identity.

(2) An ancient representation of accurate modern values requires an independent means of defining the representation as intentional.

(1) That, whilst modern astronomy is very accurate in its definition of the variable annual rates over a period of 600 years of modern time, its values covering a period of 6000 years back from the present are not so reliable ; and

(2) That, presuming certain remotely ancient astronomers knew the accurate values for their own times, and also knew the accurate values for years of modern times, it would be necessary for them to define both facts in such certain terms as could not fail to be accepted by modern astronomers.

Any chronological definition of present in relation to past history on the Great Pyramid's geometrical system would require to satisfy these conditions.

¶ 168. THE POSSIBLE MAXIMUM DEFINITION.

Scientific zero datum of chronology.

The most scientifically appropriate zero date of any system of astronomical chronology is the date at which longitude of Perihelion is 0°. With this as basis, definition of intention, and definition of accurate knowledge of Longitude of the astronomical values of rates and angles for both ancient and modern Perihelion. 0°. times would be completely established as follows :—

(1) By the representation of a year of past time, which we term Date A, For Dates defined in relation to the date at which longitude of Perihelion A and B :— Longitude of was 0°, and of a year of present time, which we term Date B, for Perihelion. which the longitude of Perihelion, defining the modern Date B, is given by the representation.

(2) By the representation of the total angle of Precession between Total Date A and Date B. Precession.

(3) By the representation of the angle between the instantaneous axis Longitude of rotation of the Ecliptic at Date A, and the same axis at Date B— Ecliptic instantaneous or by the definition of the longitudes of the axis at both dates, axis of that for Date B agreeing with the modern value. rotation.

(4) By the representation of the annual rate of motion of the Equinox Annual rates, separation of in relation to Perihelion for every year from Date A to Date B, Equinox and the rate for Date B agreeing with the modern accepted rate for Perihelion. Date B.

(5) By the representation of the annual rate of Precession for every year Annual rates, from Date A to Date B, the rate for Date B agreeing with the Precession. modern accepted rate for Date B.

(6) By the representation of the annual values for the motion of the Annual rates, Revolution of instantaneous axis of the Ecliptic for every year from Date A to Ecliptic instantaneous Date B, the rate for Date B agreeing with the modern accepted axis of rate for Date B. rotation.

(7) By the representation of the annual values for the eccentricity of the Eccentricity Earth's orbit from Date A to Date B, the rate for Date B agreeing Earth's orbit. with the modern accepted rate for Date B.

(8) By the conversion and integration of the values in (4), (5), and (6), Integration of rates give giving accurately the angles defined by (1), (2), and (3). same total angles.

(9) By the values in (4), (5), and (6) not being measured values dependent All values upon any Pyramid measurer or surveyor, but by their being values primarily geometrical that are primarily functions of the Pyramid's external geometry, Pyramid values, and that, secondarily, agree with the accurate measurements of a agreeing with accurately reliable Pyramid measurer and surveyor such as Professor Flinders measured Petrie (for linear measurements), or Professor Piazzi Smyth (for Pyramid values. angular measurements). (Refer Section II, ¶¶ 170-175, regarding the relative value of Petrie's and Smyth's independent measurements.)

¶ 169. THE DEFINITION ESTABLISHING INTENTION.

If items (1) to (5) and (8) and (9) are established, the conditions are satisfied as fully as any astronomer could desire.

If item (9) is established, it will be proved that the Great Pyramid's system of geometry is a graphical representation of Natural Law, defining

**What would be
implied by a
definition such
as that out-
lined :—
Restoration of
chronological
relations with
previous
civilisation.**

**Intention of
definition
established.**

**Established
that former
civilisation
more highly
skilled than
modern in the
mathematical
basis of the
practice of
living.** the linear and angular measurements of the Earth and its orbit ; defining the annual rates and periods of the cyclical motions of the Earth and its orbit ; and defining a system of astronomical chronology that can be the basis of related reference for every period of highly developed stage of civilisation in the world's history.

With these items established as identities, the identities become intentional identities. With the latter established, there will be proved that a former civilisation was more highly skilled in the science of gravitational astronomy—and therefore in the mathematical basis of the mechanical arts and sciences—than modern civilisation. And what will this mean ? It will mean that it has taken man thousands of years to discover by experiment what he had originally more precisely by another surer and simpler method. It will mean, in effect, that the whole empirical basis of modern civilisation is a makeshift collection of hypotheses compared with the Natural Law basis of the civilisation of the past.

PLATE XXVI.

VIEW OF EXISTING NORTH BASE CASING STONES, LOOKING WESTWARDS.
FISSURE IN NATURAL ROCK, WHERE PAVING REMOVED, SHOWN IN RIGHT
FOREGROUND.

A.C. DE JONG.

PLATE XXVII.

VIEW OF EXISTING NORTH BASE CASING STONES AND PAVEMENT SLABS.
AL MAMOUN'S FORCED ENTRANCE SHOWN ON 7TH COURSE OF MASONRY.

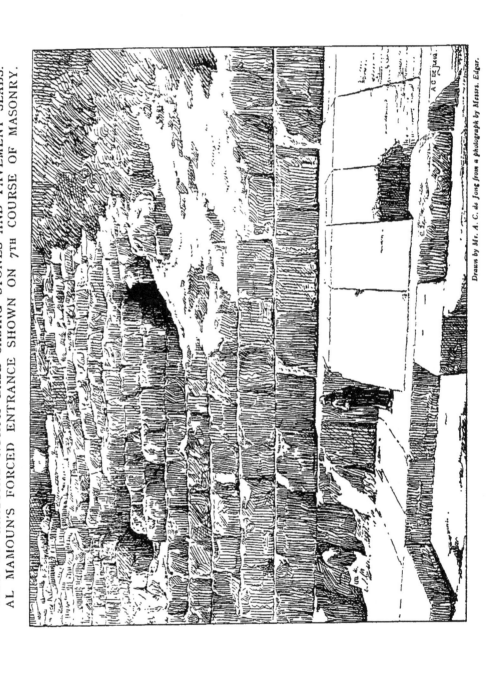

Drawn by Mr. A. C. de Jong from a photograph by Messrs. Edgar.

PLATE XXVIII.

NEAR VIEW OF EXISTING NORTH BASE CASING STONES AND PAVEMENT
SLABS, SHOWING FISSURE IN NATURAL ROCK, WHERE PAVING REMOVED,
IN LEFT FOREGROUND.

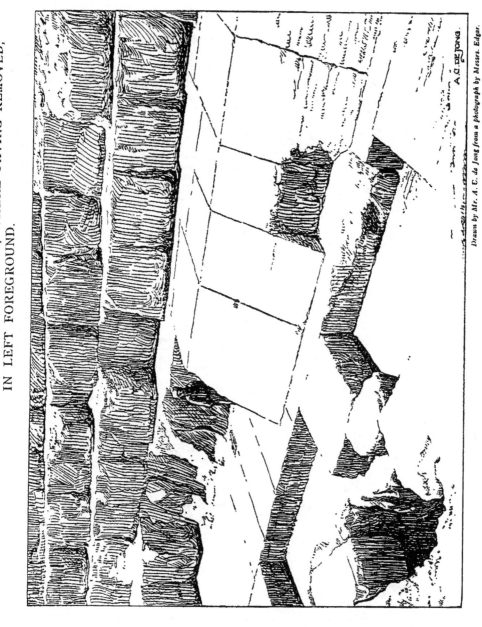

A. C. DE JONG.

Drawn by Mr. A. E. de Jong from a photograph by Messrs. Edgar.

PLATE XXIX.

VIEW OF EXISTING STATE OF NORTH ESCARPMENT SHOWING EXISTING BASE CASING STONES, AL MAMOUN'S FORCED ENTRANCE—INDICATED BY FIGURE—AND EXISTING STATE OF ENTRANCE TO THE DESCENDING (OR ENTRANCE) PASSAGE.

Drawn by Mr. A. C. de Jong from a photograph by Messrs. Edgar.

SECTION II.—PYRAMID MEASURES AND DETAILS, AND SUBSIDENCE
DISTORTION.

¶ 170. BASIS FOR COMPARISON OF GEOMETRICAL AND MEASURED DISTANCES.

It is futile to discuss any geometrical theory of the Great Pyramid's *Geometrical distances* measurements—internal and external—unless the geometrical distances *must agree with measured* required by theory agree with the corresponding measured distances. *distances.* In other words, fact must not be altered to conform to geometrical requirements.

The actual measurements to be taken as a basis must be those taken by *Measured distances must* responsible scientific measurers. The taking of linear, as well as angular, *be those taken by responsible* measurements is not the simple matter it may appear to those inexperienced *scientific measurers.* in the precise determination of dimensions.

The two best sets of angular and linear measurements of the Great *Professor Smyth's* Pyramid are those of Professor C. Piazzi Smyth, late Astronomer Royal for *angular measurements,* Scotland, and Professor W. M. Flinders Petrie. The former, with his long *and Professor Petrie's linear* and varied experience in observational astronomy, possessed the necessary *and survey measurements* qualifications and apparatus for the taking of reliable angular measurements *the best data for an accurate* of a high degree of precision. Professor Petrie, whose archæological survey *basis of study.* methods first laid the basis for modern scientific archæological exploration, and whose experience in previous geodetic and other survey work eminently fitted him for the task of surveying the Great Pyramid, has undoubtedly produced the best set of linear measurements to date.

¶ 171. RELATIVE VALUE OF THE TWO SERIES OF MEASUREMENTS AVAILABLE.

Adopting Smyth's angular measurements for the interior details—upon *Petrie adopts Smyth's pre-* which measurements Petrie could not improve—Petrie took special pre- *cise angular measurements,* liminary precautions in designing and preparing the most reliable measuring *and improves on Smyth's* appliances obtainable for linear measurements.[1] *appliances and methods*

Compared with Petrie's steel tape and special chain, 1200 and 1000 *for linear measurements.* inches respectively, and his self-compensating accessory appliances, Smyth's comparatively short measuring rods and accessories were primitive indeed. There are, in consequence, cumulative differences between the two independent sets of linear measurements. Thus Smyth makes the Entrance

[1]These are as described in Petrie's " Pyramids and Temples of Gizeh," pp. 10-15.

(Descending) Passage about 3 inches shorter than Petrie's measurement for this.   Petrie accounts for the differences as follows :—

" (1) By his (Smyth's) being all piecemeal measures added together ;
" (2) By the rude method of making scratches with a screw-driver to mark the lengths of the rod on the stone (' Life and Work,' II, 46) ; and
" (3) By there being ' always a certain amount of risk as to the measuring rod slipping on the inclined floor ' (' Life and Work,' II, 35).
" All these errors would make the reading of the length shorter than it should be."

It must be understood, of course, that these remarks concerning the relative value of the two series of linear measurements apply to the interior of the Pyramid only.   Professor Smyth never surveyed the Pyramid's exterior.   In fact, he never knew the precise or approximate measured relations of the Pyramid's base—unless in theory—until Professor Petrie's survey had been published, almost 20 years after Smyth's work at the Pyramid.

Why the interior measurements of the Pyramid are mentioned at this stage is for the reason that it is from the existing condition of the interior we have the clearest evidence concerning the cause and direction of the movements that affected the exterior of the Pyramid (¶¶ 141–147).

¶ 172.   THE CRITICAL VALUE OF PETRIE'S MEASUREMENTS.

The fact of moment is that Petrie's appliances were prepared and his linear measurements taken with a critical knowledge of the defects in Smyth's appliances for linear measurements, and of the inaccuracies liable to occur in the application of Smyth's method of measurement.   This is not to say that had Petrie been in Smyth's place as original reliable measurer, Petrie's apparatus and methods would have been any better than those Smyth adopted.

The truly scientific worker always endeavours to improve upon the apparatus and methods of his predecessors, and to benefit by their experience. Smyth published an account of the defects in his appliances and method of measurement.   Petrie, accordingly, designed his appliances and formulated his system of measurement to eliminate the defects revealed by Smyth's experience.

Apart, then, from any question of preference a possibly biassed judgment might accord to actual measurements most nearly agreeing with geometrical measurements, Petrie's statement of his linear measurements must receive preference as the most reliable statement of the Pyramid's measures as they now exist.   Against this we must place the fact that Petrie's measurements clearly were taken to disprove Smyth's theories.   Were this not a fact, Petrie could scarcely have failed to see that his own survey and set of

measurements, and his comprehensive classification of ancient metrology, contained more distances of geometrical significance than Smyth, or any of his innumerable contemporaries and followers, ever claimed or showed in measurement.   This is true both in regard to the Pyramid's external measures and internal measures.

¶ 173. HOSTILE DATA CONFIRMING INDUCTION.

The possibly small bias evidenced in Petrie's measurements is more than balanced by another fact to be admitted, viz. that Smyth's measurements were taken with the hope of finding confirmation of his own and John Taylor's theories. The influencing bias—unwitting, but psychologically unavoidable —is evidenced in several outstanding cases in the statements of both measurers, Smyth and Petrie ; more by unwittingly biassed judgment authorising the selection of averages, than in judgment controlling the taking of any particular measurement.

The exponent of a theory, or the holder of a preconceived belief, must always be considered, from any critical point of view—whether friendly or hostile—as potentially and psychologically, though possibly unwittingly, biassed in favour of evidence that accords with his theory or preconceived belief. This, it must be granted, is a fair statement of the mentality that should be adopted to consider logically any statement concerning the results of inductive analysis. It is not a statement, however, that can be applied in the particular instance of Petrie's data—hostile to Smyth's theories— confirming the latter in a manner never imagined by Smyth or any of his followers.

Of such cases, Sir John Herschel [1] stated :—

" The surest and best characteristic of a well-founded and extensive induction is, when verifications of it spring up, as it were, spontaneously into notice from quarters where they might be least expected, or from among instances of that very kind which were at first considered hostile. Evidence of this kind is irresistible, and compels assent with a weight that scarcely any other possesses."

¶ 174. BIASSED OPINION DELAYING PROGRESS OF DISCOVERY.

One good instance of the truth of Herschel's statement is seen in the case of the origin of the Common Egyptian Cubit from the Primitive Polar Diameter Inch and the Year Circle geometry. Petrie was hostile to the latter, and Smyth hostile to the former. Yet the admirable classifications of Petrie's inductive metrology have shown us that the Common Egyptian Cubit is a simple function of Smyth's Pyramid Inch, and that the latter is truly a Polar Diameter Inch.

Again, with no precise measurement of the Pyramid's base to guide him, Smyth, from a few remotely secondary external and internal details of the Pyramid's construction, inferred that the circuit of the Pyramid base consisted of 36,524.2 Polar Diameter inches, and that the Pyramid's height was the radius of a circle of the latter circumference. Smyth even supposed originally that the pavement upon which the Pyramid was built formed part of the casing, and that the Pyramid base level was at the bottom of the pavement blocks.

[1] " On the Study of Natural Philosophy " (1830), p. 170.

Side notes:
- The influence of biassed opinion in the two series of data.
- Bias psychologically inseparable from preconceived belief.
- But does not detract from the value of data collected under bias, and hostile to a theory, verifying that theory.
- Sir John Herschel's statement concerning such cases.
- Examples of above:—Egyptian Common Cubit cited by Petrie as opposed to Smyth's Pyramid Inch.
- Smyth ridicules value of Egyptian Common Cubit.
- Yet Egyptian Common Cubit of Petrie's value verifies Pyramid Inch of Smyth's value.
- Smyth's original theory—without precise data—correct on general lines, but wrong in application to detail.

It was not until Petrie—nearly 20 years after Smyth's work at the Pyramid—published his results that Smyth indicated, in his later editions, the casing blocks sitting on the pavement. Petrie, on the other hand, whilst observing the hollowing-in of the core, failed to see that the purpose of this was to provide the backing surface for a similar hollowing-in of the casing. This oversight delayed the presentation of the Pyramid's message for a further period of 20 years. For Petrie declared that his survey failed to confirm Smyth's theory in any single detail, except the casing angle of slope. This declaration was given additional weight by Smyth readjusting his theory to suit what he supposed Petrie's survey to indicate. Smyth's readjustment required the circuit of 36,524.2 to be at a level where it could neither be indicated nor measured, *i.e.* in the natural rock at the level defined by him as the mean socket floor level.

¶ 175. SMYTH'S THEORY CONCERNING PYRAMID'S PURPOSE CORRECT.

Investigation showed the absurdity of this readjustment. For, apart entirely from the obviously untenable nature of the readjusted theory, neither the mean socket floor level, nor yet the lowest socket floor level, gave the true level for the Pyramid base circuit, unless by altering the angle of slope of the Pyramid. As this further readjustment destroyed all the other essentials of the theory, it was reasonably assumed in sequence by accredited authorities—

(1) That Petrie's survey was correct ; and hence
(2) That Smyth's theory was wrong.

They gave not a moment's consideration to the other possible and reasonable sequence—

(1) That Petrie's survey, being correct, might show
(2) That Smyth's theory was correct on premises other than Smyth's, and on premises other than Petrie inferred from his reliable survey data.

We now realise that the sequence is as follows :—

(1) That Petrie's survey is correct ; and
(2) That, in consequence, Smyth's theory concerning the purpose of the Pyramid is correct.

This is precisely the kind of verification that Sir John Herschel defined as being " the surest and best characteristic of a well-founded and extensive induction."

¶ 176. EFFECT OF SUBSIDENCE ON PYRAMID PASSAGES.

One other feature essential in any analytical investigation of the Great Pyramid's measures, but that has never been properly discussed in this connection, is the question of subsidence. It is true that Professor Petrie specially discusses the effects of subsidence in the King's Chamber ; but he has passed over in silence the necessarily related effect of the same movement Rate of upon the angle of inclination of the Passages. He states that the angle of steepening and flattening inclination for the Ascending Passage is slightly flatter than, and for the of slopes of Passages follow Descending Passage slightly steeper than, Smyth's theoretical angle for these known law of subsidence. Passages. This, however, is precisely the condition in these Passages that would follow from subsidence movement.

Smyth's theoretical angle for both passages is 26° 18' 9".63 with the Proves that horizontal. Subsidence below the centre of the Pyramid's mass would Smyth's theoretical increase the angle of the Descending Passage and decrease the angle of the Passage angle of slope was Ascending Passage. Accordingly we find that the mean angle of the built angle of Descending and portion of the Descending Passage is 26° 26' 43" (Smyth and Petrie), of the Ascending Passages. first Ascending Passage, 26° 2' 30" (Petrie), and of the Grand Gallery, 26° 17' 37" (Smyth and Petrie).

The distortion of the King's Chamber proves that subsidence has taken place. The fact that subsidence has taken place below the Pyramid proves that the angle of the Descending Passage has steepened, and that the angle of the Ascending Passage has flattened. The massive and rigid construction of the Grand Gallery has been able largely to resist relative movement between its various parts. It has subsided almost bodily, thus almost exactly retaining its original angle of slope, being now only 33 seconds of angle flatter than the theoretical angle of 26° 18' 10".

That 26° 18' 10" was the original angle of slope is clearly shown by Original angle Petrie's detailed measurements. of slope, 26° 18' 10".

¶ 177. SMYTH'S THEORETICAL ANGLE CONFIRMED.

At Petrie's floor distance of 990 B" down the Descending Passage from Descending the original Entrance Doorway, the Passage suddenly commences to increase Passage length 515 its dip. Between the latter point and Petrie's floor distance 1505 B", near inches back from base, which—within an inch or two—the Descending Passage intersects the subsided angle of slope, Pyramid base level, the angle of slope of the Passage floor line is 26° 34' 0". 26° This is obtained from Petrie's offsets from his theodolite altitude of 26° 31' 23", stated as the mean angle for the whole Descending Passage length to its termination deep in the natural rock.[1]

The effect of subsidence movement below the Pyramid's base level on 1st Ascending the Descending Passage immediately above the base level is therefore Passage mean subsided angle 26° 34' 0", less the original angle of slope. Presuming the latter to be of slope, 26° 2' 30". 26° 18' 10", Smyth's theoretical angle—we obtain 15' 50" as the amount by which the Descending Passage, immediately above the base level, has been Restoration steepened by subsidence in the natural rock below the base level. Now this to a common angle for both amount is also the amount by which the portion of the Ascending Passage gives 26° 18' 15". nearest the natural rock has been flattened. This portion of the Ascending Passage should therefore be 26° 18' 10", less 15' 50"=26° 2' 20", whereas Theoretical the mean angle of slope of the 1st Ascending Passage is 26° 2' 30".[2] 26° 18' 10".

[1] " Pyramids and Temples of Gizeh," p. 58.   [2] Ibid., p. 61.

¶ 178. SIGNIFICANCE OF EXISTING CENTRIC POSITION OF STEP AND QUEEN'S CHAMBER.

Another detail, however, confirms the latter conclusion. Petrie's interior linear and angular measurements show that the existing centre of the Queen's Chamber and the existing termination of the Grand Gallery floor at the Great Step both lie in the central vertical East to West plane passing through the centre of the Pyramid's square base area. This coincidence is obviously intentional. Petrie accepts it as such, and therefore
as a feature of the original design and construction.

The significance attaching to this feature still existing, is that it supplies an important indication as to the approximate location of the centre of subsidence. It indicates that this centre was not so sufficiently remote from the Pyramid's base centre as to produce appreciable horizontal North to South displacement of the Great Step and of the centre of the Queen's Chamber. As a result, near these points, the tangents to the curve of the
subsided core courses of the Pyramid would not be far from the horizontal, unless where locally buckled by thrusting. As a corollary of this, the subsided Grand Gallery floor near the Great Step should still retain its original angle of slope of 26° 18' 9".63. Professor Petrie's offsets to the Grand Gallery floor from his altitude line in the last 213½ inches towards the Great Step prove this to be the case.[1] The existing vertical distance between the foot of the Great Step at the South end of the Grand Gallery and the floor level at the North end of the Grand Gallery is 0.54 B" less than for the original angle of 26° 18' 9".63.

¶ 179. SIGNIFICANT EFFECT OF RESTORATION OF ORIGINAL PASSAGE ANGLE.

The still existing centrally located position of the Great Step and Queen's Chamber, however, supplies us with a more certain basis for testing Smyth's theoretical angle for the Passages than any of the above lines of inquiry.
This is, that if the location defined is the original location—and there is no disagreement on this question—and if the angle of slope of the Passages was originally 26° 18' 9".63, then with Petrie's existing Passage lengths from the existing Entrance Doorway on the North face to the junction of the Passages, and from the junction to the Great Step, both applied along the inferred original angle of 26° 18' 9".63, the Great Step and the centre of the Queen's Chamber should still be in the same central location. Calculation along the lines defined agrees precisely with the conditions inferred.

Thus Petrie states that his survey data, Passage measurements and angles define—

(1) Existing face of Great Step as 0.4 B" South of existing centre of Pyramid, with probable error of ±0.9 B"; and

[1] "Pyramids and Temples of Gizeh," p. 71.

(2) Existing centre of Queen's Chamber as 0.3 B″ North of existing centre of Pyramid, with probable error of ±0.8 B″.

Petrie accepts from these that the central location was intentional.

Adopting the centric position of the Great Step, Petrie's Passage floor distances, the constant angle of Passage slope of 28° 18′ 9″.63, and Petrie's Entrance Doorway on Pyramid face at 668.28 B″±0.1 above pavement base, we obtain as follows :— *Petrie's Passage distances on original angle of slope give the same centric position.*

Horizontal Distance, Great Step to North End, Grand Gallery	=1627.5331 B″.
Horizontal Distance, North End, Grand Gallery to Junction of Passages	=1386.6529 B″.
Horizontal Distance, Junction of Passages to Petrie's Entrance Doorway	= 995.6504 B″.
	4009.8364 B″.
Horizontal Distance, Petrie's Entrance Doorway to Petrie's existing North Casing Base	= 524.1 ±0.3 B″.
Centre of Pyramid to existing North Casing Base ..	=4533.9364±0.3 B″.
The same distance on Plate XX =distance O to CD ..	=4533.7100
The difference lies within Petrie's range of possible error	0.2264±0.3 B″.

¶ 180. PASSAGE DISTANCES PROVE HORIZONTAL INWARD MOVEMENT OF BASE CENTRES.

In the above series of additions the existing North casing base point at 524.1±0.3 B″ horizontally from Petrie's Entrance Doorway, was taken without any reference to the question of the angle of the Pyramid's face slope. This has been shown to have been originally exactly 51° 51′ 14″.3.

Petrie has proved conclusively that the floor of the Entrance Doorway certainly commenced at 668.28 ±0.1 B″ above the Pyramid's Pavement Base. The level and depth of the 19th course of masonry determine that the Entrance Doorway emerged with its roof line at the top of the course and its floor line at the bottom of the course. Near the Entrance, the existing bottom level of this course is 668.28±0.1 B″, as Petrie has shown. Nothing can be more certain than that this gives the original floor level of the Passage at the Entrance on the face slope. *Original Entrance Doorway emerged on Pyramid face in depth of the 19th masonry course.*

We therefore have two certain facts to guide us. The Entrance floor on face slope was 668.28±0.1 B″ above the Pavement, and the angle of slope was 51° 51′ 14″.3. From these we find that the original horizontal distance from casing base to Entrance floor was 524.91 B″±0.1, or 0.8 B″ *Entrance floor originally 524.8 B″ horizontally from central edge of North casing base.*

longer than the existing indications tend to show. Adding the latter in the series of horizontal passage distances of ¶ 179 we obtain—

	PLATE XXX Original.	PLATE XXX Petrie's existing.
Horizontal distance, Great Step to Entrance Floor	=4009.84 B″	4010.91 B″±0.6
Horizontal distance, Entrance Floor to original North Casing Base.. ..	= 524.91 B″±0.1	524.10 B″±0.3
Horizontal distance, Great Step to North Casing Base	=4534.75 B″±0.1	4535.01 B″±0.9
Deduct, Plate XX, existing distance O to DC	=4533.71	

Original horizontal length from Entrance to Step proves existing North Base has moved 1 inch inwards,

and

Extent to which centre of North Casing Base has been drawn in by subsidence towards centre of Pyramid. } 1.04 B″±0.1.

That there was a separate Northwards relative horizontal movement between core masonry courses, increasing in extent from nothing at the base course to a maximum at the top course.

In ¶ 147 this was independently obtained as 1.0 inch average for each casing face, or a total drawing together of the centre of the North casing base and the centre of the South casing base of 2.1 inches. (Refer also ¶¶ 142-145.) The existing details and measurements discussed above show further that, in addition to this general movement, there was a relative horizontal movement between the masonry courses of the Pyramid core; that this movement became in extent cumulatively greater for higher courses; and that the general direction of the movement of successive courses was towards the North side, steepening the Pyramid's face slope from its original 51° 51′ 14″.3 to 51° 53′ 20″ between the existing base and the existing 19th masonry course. The nature of the relative movement indicates that the angle of North face slope should become steeper for higher courses.

¶ 181. INDICATIONS OF FURTHER MOVEMENT INWARDS OF SOUTH BASE CENTRE.

Petrie's surveyed point on South casing base edge.

Lies 113.6 B″ external to maximum hollowed-in base strip.

Indicates a further movement inwards of central area of Pyramid South base to extent of 1.11 B″.

Total inward movement of centre of South base now 2.17 B″.

One feature not entirely dealt with concerns the South base point G on Plate XX. G is the point located and surveyed in by Petrie. In ¶ 147— and prior to the geometrical definition of the central width of maximum hollowing-in—this point was considered as lying on the base edge of this central area, i.e. on the line D_1H_1 of Fig. B, Plate XXV. Actually, by comparing Plate XX, for point G at 1028.7 B″ from centre of base, with Plate XXV, for Point D_1 on Fig. B at 914.1 B″ from centre of base, we find that Petrie's South base survey point (G on Plate XX) lies on the line D_1A of Plate XXV, Fig. B, and 113.6 B″ from D_1 towards A. In this position on the geometrical Pyramid base, point G (Plate XX) should be 1.11 P″ further South than the maximum hollowed-in base line D_1H_1 (Plate XXV). Its distance South from the base centre should therefore be 4535.85 B″, whereas the corresponding existing distance is 4533.69 B″, or 2.17 B″ less than the existing distance.

Now we have already seen that the centre of the South base has moved inwards, owing to subsidence movement, at least 1 inch. The Passage data of ¶ 180 have confirmed the data of ¶ 147 by indicating that the North base has moved inwards 1.04 B″ ±0.1. The total movement of North base centre and South base centre inwards was estimated in ¶ 147 as 2.1 B″. To this we must now add an additional 1.11 inches for South base movement extra to that estimated. This gives the total movement inwards between the centres of opposite base sides as 3.21 inches—2.17 inches inwards on South side, and 1.04 inches inwards on North side. The movement, as defined, is confirmed by two features of the Pyramid's exterior.

[margin note: Movement confirmed by two other external features of the Pyramid.]

¶ 182. THE MOVEMENT OF THE SOCKETS, AND THE DISTORTION OF THE CORE ESCARPMENTS.

One of the features referred to has already been considered in ¶¶ 145 and 180, and the other at the end of ¶ 180. The former showed that the side of the *true* square defining the half-diagonal OM (Plate XX) required to be 4570.55 B″, whereas the existing East side of this square is 4567.02 B″, or 3.53 B″ less than the true square defining the half-diagonal. This indicates a movement of the South-East socket 3.53 B″ towards the North. Professor Petrie's data on his Plate X presuppose correction for this movement without drawing attention to the actuality of the movement, since his survey data on pages 38, 39, and 206 do not agree with his data on his Plate X.

[margin note: Distortion of existing socket distances defining base diagonals indicates necessary extent of natural rock movement to effect the above Pyramid base movement.]

A ground movement is necessarily greater than a compactly massive building movement effected by it. Hence the Pyramid masonry base movement is less than the South-East socket movement.

The second feature referred to is the distortion of the Pyramid's core escarpments. The North core escarpment up the centre of the North face is steeper than the South core escarpment up the centre of the South face (confirming ¶ 181). The former, from the base to the existing top, is 51° 54′ 24″, whereas the latter is 51° 51′ 13″, or within 1″ of the true angle of slope of the casing. This difference of angle would be the exact effect of the return ground wave, or "echo" wave of the earth tremor of a subsidence that had produced a steeper dip in the Pyramid's courses inwards from the South side than inwards from the North side.

[margin note: Direction of distortion of core masonry confirms nature of Pyramid base movement. Indicates nature of base subsidence and Earth tremor effect producing the distortions and movements.]

¶ 183. RELATION BETWEEN PASSAGE SUBSIDENCE AND SUBSIDENCE OF COURSES.

The general form of the subsidence effects on the Great Pyramid can be obtained from a study of the subsidence effects in the Passages and Chambers. We have seen that the original angle of slope of the Descending and Ascending Passages was 26° 18′ 9″.63. Correcting all Passage points to their original positions at this angle of inclination, commencing from the Entrance inwards, will give us the extent of subsidence at all such Passage points.

[margin note: Comparison of points of the Passages at original angle, and the corresponding points of the existing Passages gives subsidence a all such points.]

Thus we find that the levels of the original and existing principal floor points of the Passages—and their extent of subsidence—are as follows :—

	Original.	Existing.	Extent of Subsidence.
	B″.	B″.	B″.
Floor junction of Descending and Ascending Passages	176.1	172.9 ±.2	3.2
Floor joint, North End, Grand Gallery	861.5	852.6 ±.3	8.9
Foot of Great Step, Grand Gallery	1666.0	1656.5 ±.5	9.5
Top of Great Step,[1] Grand Gallery (35.87 B″)	1701.87	1692.36±.5	9.5

Plate XXX gives a graphically illustrated comparative statement of all the existing and original dimensions of the Passages, together with a statement of the cumulative subsidence in the Passages.

The above tabulation shows, in accordance with the laws of central mass subsidence, that the subsidence effects follow, progressively increasing, from the North base inwards towards the centre. This progressive increase continues beyond the centre into the King's Chamber, where the lowest floor point is 2.4 B″ lower than the top of the Great Step. The total extent of subsidence, therefore, at the level of the King's Chamber and at the South-East corner of the King's Chamber is 9.5 B″ +2.4 B″ =11.9 B″. The subsidence at the Pyramid's base vertically below this is necessarily greater than this amount, owing to the cumulative loss of subsidence in ascending order of courses, for points of courses on the same vertical. This cumulative loss of subsidence holds for every vertical line passing through the courses, and is due to the well-known structural effect of " flat-arching."

¶ 184. BASIS OF SUBSIDENCE DIAGRAMS.

Proceeding, then, in the same way for the Descending Passage, we find that its lower sloping end in the natural rock—about 303 B″ horizontally North from the Pyramid's base centre—has subsided 20 B″, and at its entrance into the natural rock has subsided 4 B″. Proceeding thus for all intermediate points in this Passage we obtain the cumulative extent of subsidence from the North face inwards towards the centre. This gives, in the natural rock, the extent of settlement of the base courses at points vertically above the

[1]It is as well to state here that Professor Petrie has an unfortunate error in his calculations for the level of the Step, and, in consequence, for every point beyond that. All his other existing levels for the Passages have been correctly reduced from his data. In this case, however, he has stated the End of the Gallery as 2.39 B″ higher than his own data prove it to be. This can be shown from a simple statement of the facts. His horizontal distance for the Grand Gallery agrees with his sloping distance and angle of slope for the Gallery, but does not agree with his vertical rise for the Gallery floor. The latter gives a steeper angle of slope than the original angle of 26° 18′ 9″.63, whereas Petrie's stated existing angle is less than this.

His offsets from his theodolite altitude line determine that the foot of the Great Step is 0.54 B″ vertically lower than the same for an altitude of 26° 18′ 9″.63. As the rise from the commencement of the Gallery to the foot of Step with the latter angle is 804.47 B″, the existing rise is 803.93 B″, whereas Petrie's rise is 2.39 B″ higher. Refer also Notes on Plate XXX.

TABLE A. ENTRANCE & ASCENDING PASSAGES & ANTECHAMBER & KING'S CHAMBER.

1	2 SLOPING FLOOR DISTANCES OF PASSAGES	3 HORIZONTAL DISTANCES OF PASSAGE FLOORS			4 VERTICAL DISTANCES OF PASSAGE FLOOR POINTS ABOVE BASE		
		A ORIGINAL	B EXISTING	C DIFF.	A ORIGINAL	B EXISTING	C SUBSIDENCE
KINGS CHAMBER 5th	8"	536.88	536.92	+ 0.04	1701.87	VARIABLE	PLUS EXTRA
2nd PASSAGE ENDS		330.59	330.49	− 0.10	1701.87		
			259.73		1701.87		
2nd PASSAGE BEGINS		229.43	229.42	− 0.01			
			195.49				
			180.58				
			174.60				
			173.47		1701.87		
			153.11				
			136.58				
GRANITE FLOOR BEGINS 1st PASSAGE ENDS		126.28	126.22	− 0.06	1701.87		
		113.04	113.34	+ 0.30			
1st PASSAGE BEGINS		61.02	61.33	+ 0.31	1701.87		11.06
TOP OF STEP	0	0.00	0.00	0.00	1701.87		
FOOT OF STEPS		0.00	0.00	0.00	166.02	165.53	9.49
		21.55	193.18	193.18	157053	156103	9.50
GRAND		51.55	462.12	461.62	−0.50	1437.60	1427.21	10.39
		81.55	731.06	730.57	−0.49	1304.66	1294.29	10.37
GALLERY		111.55	100.000	99.947	−0.53	1171.73	1161.38	10.35
		141.55	1268.94	1268.72	−0.22	1036.80	1028.96	9.84
		155.14	1390.77	1390.67	−0.10	978.58	968.99	9.59
FLOOR JOINT (GRAND GALLERY)		1615.5	162.7.78	1627.78	+ 0.25	861.55	852.57	8.98
		1997.3	1790.51	1790.98	+ 0.47	780.99	772.46	8.53
		2142.3	1920.50	1921.16	+ 0.66	716.74	708.65	8.09
1st		2317.3	2077.38	2078.59	+ 1.21	639.19	632.17	7.02
ASCENDING		2522.3	2261.16	2262.98	+ 1.82	548.36	542.57	5.79
PASSAGE		2712.3	2431.49	2434.14	+ 2.65	464.16	459.95	4.21
		2842.3	2548.03	2550.39	+ 2.36	406.56	401.88	4.68
		3102.3	2781.10	2784.94	+ 3.84	291.35	287.63	3.72
		3293.3	2952.33	2955.30	+ 2.97	206.72	203.33	3.39
FLOOR JUNCTION		3362.3	3014.19	301721	+ 3.02	176.14	172.98	3.16
		3482.94	3122.34	3125.19	+ 2.85	229.60	227.00	2.60
ENTRANCE		3762.94	3373.35	3376.02	+ 2.67	353.67	351.54	2.13
PASSAGE		4012.94	3597.47	3599.81	+ 2.34	464.45	462.98	1.47
ENTRANCE FLOOR		4472.94	4009.84	4010.91	+ 1.07	668.28	668.28	0.00
Hth BASE CASING		4534.75	4535.01	+ 0.26				

TABLE B. DESCENDING PASSAGE.

1	2 SLOPING FLOOR DISTANCES OF PASSAGE FROM ENTRANCE DOOR		3 HORIZONTAL DISTANCES OF PASSAGE FLOORS FROM STEP VERTICAL			4 VERTICAL DISTANCES OF PASSAGE FLOORS ABOVE + OR BELOW − BASE		
	A ORIGINAL	B EXISTING	A ORIGINAL	B EXISTING	C DIFF.	A ORIGINAL	B EXISTING	C SUBSIDENCE
ENTRANCE DOOR SILL	0.00	0.00	4009.84	4010.91	+ 1.07	+ 668.28	+ 668.28	0.00
	460.00	460.00	3597.47	359.981	+ 2.34	+ 464.45	+ 462.98	1.47
	710.00	710.00	3373.35	337602	+ 2.67	+ 353.67	+ 351.54	2.13
	990.00	990.00	3122.34	3125.19	+ 2.85	+ 229.60	+ 227.00	2.60
FLOOR JUNCTION ASCENDING PASSAGE	1110.64	1110.64	3014.19	3017.21	+ 3.02	+ 176.14	+ 172.98	3.16
ROCK W. WALL TOP		1318.50						
ROCK E. WALL TOP		1347.50						
EAST WALL BEGINS	1500.61	1505.00	266459	266459	± 0.00	+ 3.38	+ 3.37	6.75
BUILT-IN STONES JOINT		1569.00						
IN FISSURE ENDS		1595.00						
		1629.00						
	1735.94	1741.00	2453.63	245353	− 0.10	− 100.90	− 109.23	8.33
	2062.97	2069.00	2160.45	216020	− 0.25	− 245.61	− 255.63	9.82
	2473.97	2481.00	1792.01	1791.56	− 0.45	− 427.93	− 439.62	11.69
EAST WALL FISSURE IN ROCK		3086.00						
		3116.00						
	3700.95	3711.00	692.06	691.06	− 1.00	− 971.62	− 988.98	17.36
		4113.00						
END OF EAST SIDE FLOOR SLOPE WEST SIDE	4134.60	4146.14	303.10	301.89	− 1.21	− 1163.90	− 1183.59	19.69
		4148.34		299.90			− 1184.58	
SLOPE PRODUCED TO STEP VERTICAL	4472.94	4483.64	0.00	0.00		− 1313.70	− 1334.29	20.59

TABLE C. QUEEN'S CHAMBER & PASSAGE.

1	2 HORIZONTAL DISTANCES FROM STEP VERTICAL		3 CEILING OF PASSAGE & 1st COURSE OF CHAMBER LEVEL ABOVE BASE		
	ORIGINAL	EXISTING	ORIGINAL	EXISTING	SUBSIDENCE
LEVEL OF TOP DOORWAY GRAND GALLERY	1627.53	1627.78	914.25	905.27	8.98
			131.578	903.8	10.45
			1004.78	914.25	902.3	11.95
			627.78	914.25	902.4	11.85
			320.78	914.25	901.0	13.25
Hth WALL QUEEN'S CHAMBER	103.15	103.88	914.25		
BELOW ROOF APEX QUEEN	± 0.00	1.28	914.25	901.3	12.95
Sth WALL CHAMBER	−103.15	−101.72	914.25		

1st ASCENDING & ENTRANCE PASSAGES −
PETRIE'S MEAN PERP. HEIGHT = 47.36 B" = 47.31 P"
GIVING VERT. HEIGHT = 57.64 B" = 57.78 P"
GRAND GALLERY VERTICAL HEIGHT
= 1st ASCENDING PASSAGE VERT. HEIGHT + PASSAGE DISPLACEMENT
= 57.78 B" + 286.1 P" = 338.88 P" = 339.25 B"
SMYTH'S MEASURED MEAN = 339.20 B"

NOTE :—

TABLE A.—Column 2. Existing Distances are equal to Original Distances within limits of Accurate Measurement.
Column 3c (1) Variations in Wall Measurement.
(2) Variations in Floor Measurement; the Floor Blocks in Antechamber, King's Chamber, Great Step and connecting Passages being fitted between Walls.
Sudden variations in Horizontal Floor Differences and Subsidences (columns 3c and 4c) are due to Buckling of Passage Floor Blocks.

TABLE B.—Column 2b (3) By Edgar's steel tape Minimum Measurement of Floor (East Side). Perpendicular from end of Roof Slope on West Side (by Edgar's steel tape) gives same measurement.
This measurement shows that Max. Horizontal Movement due to Vertical Subsidence is only 1.21 B" South of original. This is confirmed by Azimuth of Passage being not more than ± 1.0 B" (as Petrie) off true Original Azimuth.
(4) By Edgar's steel tape Maximum Measurement of Floor West Side.

Sloping Floor Distances of built Passages are Prof. Petrie's measured Distances. Petrie has an error, however, in reducing the Vertical and Horizontal Distances of his Grand Gallery Floor length. Correction for this affects the statement of all levels above Foot of Great Step and gives Face of Step as 0.58 B" horizontally South of Petrie's erroneously stated position, and Foot as 2.39 B" higher than Petrie's erroneously stated level. All Horizontal Distances of Ascending and Descending Passages from Face of Step are therefore 0.58 B", as Table A, more than Petrie's erroneously reduced distances, and all levels above foot of Step are 2.39 B" higher than the corresponding levels given by Petrie.

[To face p. 156.

Passage points taken. The general rate of increase of subsidence again indicates that the maximum extent of subsidence is nearer the South base side than the North base side, thus confirming the indication of the King's Chamber in ¶ 183, and confirming the inference derived in ¶¶ 181 and 182, as to the additional movement of the South base side inwards at its centre towards the centre of the Pyramid's base area.

[margin: Indicates maximum subsidence nearer South than North base side.]

The extent of subsidence thus obtained at all observed points in the Descending and Ascending Passages, and in the Antechamber and King's Chamber, enables us to plot a diagram of subsidence. To make this diagram of use in studying the related movements, it is necessary to magnify the subsidence movement. We can produce a true-to-scale representation of subsidence by drawing the Pyramid and its Passages to a certain scale, and then drawing all existing variations horizontally and vertically from their original positions as ten times their true extent. All that this amounts to is that we are imagining the subsidence effects to be ten times greater than they actually are.

[margin: Measured variations in subsidence in all Passages form basis for diagrams of general Pyramid subsidence. Subsidence in diagrams shown as ten times actual subsidence.]

Drawn in this manner, Plate XXXI represents the subsidence of all the Pyramid's courses and Passages, as indicated by the existing variations of the floor or axis levels of the Passages. Similarly Plate XXXV gives the subsidence effects in the King's Chamber and Antechamber, and in their connecting Passages.

[margin: General diagrams of Pyramid subsidence. Diagram of King's Chamber and Antechamber subsidence.]

¶ 185. PYRAMID COURSES AND HORIZONTAL COURSES OF CHAMBERS.

Study of the precisely determined relative amounts of subsidence in the Passages and Chambers in relation to the two subsidence diagrams—Plates XXXI and XXXVa—establishes the following identities between horizontal passage and chamber masonry courses on the one hand, and the horizontal courses of the Pyramid core masonry on the other hand:—

	Existing Lowest Level.	Sub-sidence.	Origin-ally.	Existing Levels of Courses on Pyramid Core Face.		Top of Course Nod. Plate XX.
				S.W.	N.E.	
	B″.	B″.	B″.	B″.	B″.	
Ceiling level of King's Chamber	1920.7	11.8	1932.5	1931.7	1931.7	59th
Ceiling level of Antechamber ..	1840.3	11.2	1851.5	1851.5	1851.9	56th
Base of walls of { King's Chamber	1685.4	11.8	1697.2	1697.7	1697.6	50th
{ Antechamber	1686.0	11.2				
Top of North and South walls, and course of East and West walls, Queen's Chamber	1018.9	12.6	1031.5	1030.9	1031.0	30th

[margin beside table: King's Chamber ceiling top of 59th course. Antechamber ceiling top of 56th course. King's Chamber and Antechamber wall base top of 50th course. Top of North and South walls and course level of East and West walls in Queen's Chamber top of 30th course.]

As to the variations in depths of existing masonry courses, Petrie, in his Plate VIII, gives these as follows:—

For 59th course, 1 inch variation ; 56th course, 0.4 inch ;
50th course, 0.2 inch ; 30th course, 1.5 inch.

Latter level at height giving length of side of ¼-Aroura square = 1030.33 P″, and ceiling of horizontal Passage to Queen's Chamber at level of ceiling of 1st Ascending Passage entrance to Grand Gallery.

The above statement of levels shows that the level of the original top of the North and South walls of the Queen's Chamber was 1030.33 P″=1031.46 B″, the length of side of the quarter-*aroura* square. Since the height of the North and South walls is 184.4 B″=184.2 P″, the original level of the Chamber floor was 846.130 P″=847.06 B″. The existing level being 834.4 B″, the extent of subsidence in the Queen's Chamber is 12.66 B″. This amount of subsidence here agrees with the cumulative rate of increase of subsidence effect on the courses from the Great Step vertically downwards to the centre of the base area. The same restoration gives the original level of the ceiling of the horizontal Passage to the Queen's Chamber coincident with the original level of the ceiling of the 1st Ascending Passage at the Entrance to the Grand Gallery, *i.e.* at 914.4 B″.

¶ 186. PYRAMID'S CONSTRUCTIONAL DETAILS DESIGNED TO MEET SUBSIDENCE EFFECTS.

Rock fissures indicate cause and nature of subsidence.
Existed prior to construction.

Plate XXXI shows clearly the cause and nature of the subsidence. The cause is seen in the several fissures in the natural rock portion of the Descending Passage. These had existed when the Passage was cut in the natural rock. Two of them have been built up with blocks by the original builders.

Fissures due to collapse of a subterranean cavern deep in limestone forming the Nile Valley.
Designer of Pyramid's constructional details aware of this, and took constructional measures to meet contingencies likely to arise from conditions noted.

These fissures are the evidence of the collapse of a subterranean cavern deep in the limestone forming the Nile Valley, which contains many examples of this cause of subsidence. This subsidence, as we saw, occurred prior to the building of the Pyramid. Indeed, many special details of the Pyramid's construction indicate that the designer of the constructional details was aware of the subsidence, and took special constructional measures to meet its effects. This is evident particularly in the construction of the masonry chambers and in the construction of the Grand Gallery. In fact, the Great Pyramid is as perfectly designed to meet, and adjust itself to, the conditions of subsidence as it well could be ; more perfectly designed for its substrata conditions than St. Paul's Cathedral, for example, was designed to meet the conditions of its substrata.

The precarious stability of fissured foundation strata.
Effect of central mass of Pyramid on same.

Where limestone fissures occur there is instability, particularly under added burden to the strata in which they occur. The designer of the Pyramid's constructional details foresaw the possibility of the existing precarious stability of the fissured strata being disturbed by the superimposed central mass of the Pyramid's masonry. That his details, devised to meet the expected vertical movement, were effective is proved by the fact (shown by ¶ 180) that the Passage lengths, in spite of subsidence, have remained unaltered.

¶ 187. THE CONSTRUCTIONAL PURPOSE OF THE TERRACED
        ROCK CORE.

The designer of the Pyramid's constructional details foresaw that the slightest tremor due to adjacent cavern collapses—which collapses in such strata are the minor causes of earthquakes—would disturb the precarious stability of the strata below the Pyramid. He foresaw that the central mass of the Pyramid's masonry, in such case, would bring its maximum intensity of pressure to bear upon a square considerably internal to the Pyramid's base square ; and that such local concentration of pressure would, by dynamic impulse of momentary subsidence due to Earth tremor, punch the central area, along its fissure surfaces, below the level of the natural rock base.

To meet this eventuality, the natural rock was left terraced upwards towards the Pyramid's centre. The constructional object of this was obviously to form the nucleus of an arch, so that when the terraced centre was affected by local Earth tremor, the momentary impulse of the central mass of masonry should, by the accentuation of " flat-arching," be largely diverted as arch thrust effect clear of the central area. The design, in effect, provided a shock-absorber ; but a shock-absorber designed to " throttle " two separate shocks, or series of shocks.

Terraced rock core for purpose of inducing arching effect in courses under subsidence, and as a " shock-absorber " to " throttle " dynamic movements due to Earth tremors accompanying or causing subsidence.

The first shock was that instantaneously reacting to the Earth tremor, producing vertical movement. Vertical movement of the fissured area—like the effect of central failure, due to shearing, on the fixed ends of a beam—produced the second series of shocks : (1) an upward and outward kick of the freed external strata ; and, on its completion, (2) a reaction wave outwards from its centre. Both these secondary effects were " damped " or " throttled " by the incidental thrust of the arching effect noted.

The " echoing " return of the latter ground wave—always accompanying such earthquake effects—would produce, as it does in such earthquake movements, an undulatory movement inwards towards the centre. This would be largely resisted by the terraced natural rock core. Nevertheless, and for the reasons noted in ¶ 182, the centre of the South base was jolted inwards 2.17 B″, and the centre of the North base 1.04 B″.

The undulatory movement that jolted the South base centre further inwards than the North base centre was moved inwards.

¶ 188. THE SOUTH AND NORTH MOVEMENT OF MASONRY
        COURSES.

Plate XXXI indicates the central " punched-in " area of maximum subsidence. This effect would have been considerably increased had the central terracing of the natural rock core been omitted. This " shock-absorber " detail has made it possible at this date to derive from the existing measurements and structural indications, the precise purpose of the Pyramid's design and construction. We may, therefore, take it as certain that the design of the constructional details has effected its purpose. The designer of these details has therefore been justified in his conclusions concerning subsidence,

That the " shock-absorber " detail of construction has served its purpose justifies the principles of design and the forethought displayed in regard to subsidence.

and in his design to meet the effects of such subsidence as he inferred might take place, and that has taken place.

The indications supplied by the variations in level of the Passages have determined the subsidence of the masonry courses. These, as shown on Plate XXXI, indicate that the " punched-in " area of fissured rock is more deeply " punched-in " near the South base side than near the North base side. This shows that the dip of the courses inwards on the South side is steeper than on the North side ; and that, in consequence, the surrounding undulatory movement due to the " echoing " Earth wave, mentioned in ¶¶ 182 and 187, would have the effect of jolting the whole of the southern portion of the masonry bodily inwards, producing a relative horizontal movement along successive courses from base to apex. This relative movement of courses would increase the horizontal slip between courses in proportion to the height of a course above the base, this increase being due to the decrease of super-imposed mass, and to the consequent increased opening of vertical East to West joints towards the North face.

¶ 189. THE JOLTING OPEN OF JOINTS IN THE NORTHERN SIDE OF THE CORE MASONRY.

The reader can experimentally obtain the conditions of the last effect for himself. Place a long line of blocks in end-to-end contact on a table and build on this successive similar and equal courses of end-to-end blocks, in such manner that all the initial ends butt firmly against a rigid vertical board. Strike the rigid vertical board with a hammer and examine the end-to-end joints between blocks in each successive course. The end-to-end joints near the vertical board will generally remain tightly closed, and will only be found to have opened out towards the further end of the courses, and to an increasing extent for the higher courses. Owing to the latter effect, the originally vertical surface formed by the ends of the courses away from the source of shock will be found to be inclining over.

If the effect described took place in the Pyramid from the South side, as all the structural and subsidence evidences have indicated, then the existing top platform of the Pyramid should show a greater distance from the Pyramid's centre to the North face of the core escarpment than from the Pyramid's centre to the South, East, and West core escarpments. Petrie gives the distances obtained by him at the mean level of 5408.5 B″ above the base as follows :—

	Mean.
Centre of Pyramid base horizontally to the core masonry faces on the	N. side 224.5 ±0.7
	E. side 214.1 ±0.3
	S. side 215.0 ±0.4
	W. side 217.6 ±1.0

thus confirming the movement as described.

Thus it will be seen that, although the distance to the South core face is only 0.85 B″ less than the mean of the distances to the East and West core

N — S (compass)

HORIZONTAL AND VERTICAL MOVEMENTS
DUE TO SUBSIDENCE SHOWN 10 TIMES
GREATER THAN ACTUAL MOVEMENTS

CONFIRMING GENERAL DIP OF COURSES.
PETRIE STATES "I CONTINUALLY
OBSERVED THAT THE COURSES
OF THE CORE HAD DIPS OF AS
MUCH AS ½ TO 1." "PYRAMIDS & TEMPLES
OF GIZEH" p.42.

ANCIENT FORCED ENTRY VIA GROTTO INTENTIONALLY
LOCATED TO PASS THROUGH NEW FISSURES TO
INSPECT SAME.
ANCIENT FORCED ENTRY MADE SOUTH TOP END
OF GRAND GALLERY FOR INSPECTION OF
CRACKS ETC IN CHAMBERS OF
CONSTRUCTION.

ALL KNOWN FISSURES
LETTERED AS G–H
CONSECUTIVELY TO V–W.

CHAMBERS OF CONSTRUCTION

KING'S CHAMBER

GRAND GALLERY

QUEEN CHAMBER

HORIZONTAL PASSAGE

FIRST ASCENDING PASSAGE

DESCENDING PASSAGE

GROTTO

WELL SHAFT

NATURAL ROCK

NATURAL ROCK

ANCIENT FORCED ENTER

FORCED PASSAGE SUNDRY KINGS

APPROXIMATE LIMITS
OF PLANE OF FISSURE
DEFINING MAXIMUM
SUBSIDENCE

CENTRAL AREA OF SUBSIDENCE

[To face p. 160.]

faces, the distance to the North core face is 8.65 B″ greater than the latter. *Central slope of South, East, and West core escarpments. 51° 51′ 14″, but for North core escarpment. 51° 54′ 24″.* It is this extra distance that has made the existing angle of slope 51° 54′ 24″ from the centre of the North core base to the top core platform,[1] whereas the existing angles of slope of the centres of the South, East, and West core escarpments are not appreciably different from the original angle of 51° 51′ 14″.3.

¶ 190. THE GEOLOGICAL DATA.

When it is remembered that the stratification of the Gizeh Plateau, upon *Strata of Gizeh Plateau and Nile Valley limestone.* which the Great Pyramid stands, and of the whole of the adjacent Nile Valley consists of limestone, the geological reasons for the subsidence effects are *Nile bed a limestone fault.* clearly to hand.[2] The Nile bed itself is formed in a great limestone fault, " eroded into a gorge, fed by water-tunnelled caverns in the cliffs," and now *Water-tunnelled caverns.* " filled with debris, forming the present Nile bed." Here are evidences of the cause of subsidence, in the examples of collapses of underground caverns *Collapses of these.* and grottos. As Petrie states,[3] " large caverns have collapsed at some hundreds of feet below the present Nile (Fig. 4)."

One such smaller cavern or grotto, but not collapsed, is already known *Grotto in Pyramid's terraced rock core.* under the Pyramid masonry (Plate XXXI), and within the natural rock core, terraced to receive and to bind into the masonry courses of the *A deeper cavern indicated by fissures.* Pyramid. Not this grotto, however, but a larger unexplored cavern, by collapsing prior to the Pyramid's construction, has been the cause of the rock fissuring and instability of strata discussed in ¶¶ 186–188.

¶ 191. THE EARLIEST FORCED ENTRY TO UPPER CHAMBERS.

The Pyramid's structural indications are fairly conclusive that sub- *External effects of Pyramid subsidence shown not many genera- tions after construction, when data concerning construction still known.* sidence effects were observed on the external surface of the Pyramid not long after it was built, possibly within a few generations from the time of its construction, and certainly before precise details and measurements of its internal construction were lost or forgotten. The latter conclusion is certain from the entry for examination of the effects of the subsidence upon the Chambers.

When the Pyramid was built, all access to its upper chambers was closed *All access to Ascending Passage originally closed.* by the granite plug or plugs at the lower end of the 1st Ascending Passage (Plate XXXI). To hide the fact that a Passage began here, a limestone *Access to Descending Passage and Subterranean Chamber only.* block was inserted to make the roof of the Entrance or Descending Passage

[1]It will be observed that this general angle for the entire centre line of the North core escarpment from base to existing top platform agrees with the existing indications of casing slope for North face, from existing casing base to Entrance sill indicated by existing line of Entrance Passage, and its intersection with the existing base level of the 19th masonry course, near the existing Entrance. The latter definition, as obtained by Petrie, gives existing angle of North face casing, in its first 700 inches of height, as 51° 53′ 20″±1′. (Refer ¶ 180.)

[2]Refer Petrie's " Hist. Egypt," Vol. I (1894 Edit.), pp. 1–6.

[3]Ibid., pp. 3 and 4, illustr. Fig. 4. For such collapses originating earthquakes, refer Sir Archibald Geikie's " Text-book of Geology," pp. 369, 477–479.

PLATE XXXII.

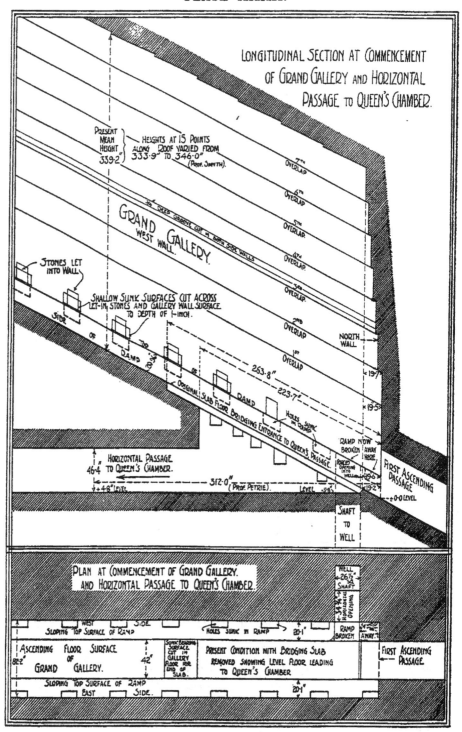

LONGITUDINAL SECTION AT COMMENCEMENT OF GRAND GALLERY AND HORIZONTAL PASSAGE TO QUEEN'S CHAMBER.

PLATE XXXIII.

WEST WALL OF GRAND GALLERY.

NORTH WALL OF GRAND GALLERY

RAMP.

WEST WALL of HORIZONTAL PASSAGE TO QUEENS CHAMBER

FLOOR OF HORIZONTAL PASSAGE TO QUEENS CHAMBER

EAST RAMP OMITTED

ISOMETRIC PROJECTION SHOWING FORCED OPENING INTO WELL-SHAFT ·

A.C. DE JONG

continuous past the 1st Ascending Passage. Entry to the upper chambers was thus effectively closed. It was possible only to use the Descending Passage to gain entry to the Subterranean Chamber.

When it was observed, however, that an internal movement had taken place, steps were taken by the keepers of the Pyramid to force an entry. The manner in which this entry was effected forces us to two conclusions :

The early forced entry to upper Passages, etc.

Manner in which effected confirms Arab accounts of limestone plugs, and that data of construction still known when early entry was made.

(1) That the Arab accounts of Al Mamoun's later forced entry in the 9th century A.D. are correct in stating that the 1st Ascending Passage above the plugs was filled with limestone blocks, which had to be broken up one by one, by the Arabs (refer also ¶¶ 208 and 208a) ; and

(2) That the plans of the Pyramid, or the data of its construction and ground conditions, were still in existence when the first entry was effected for inspection.

PLATE XXXIV.

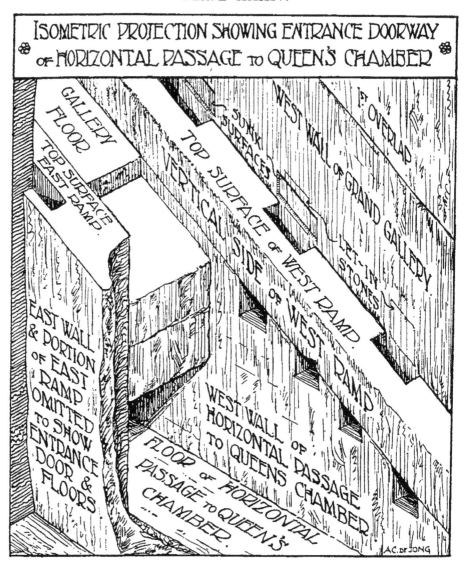

ISOMETRIC PROJECTION SHOWING ENTRANCE DOORWAY of HORIZONTAL PASSAGE TO QUEEN'S CHAMBER

¶ 192. THE TUNNELLING OF THE WELL-SHAFT.

Entry by tunnelling up through natural rock to grotto.

Instead of seeking to tunnel through the masonry as the Arabs did later, the early keepers of the Pyramid commenced their tunnelling in a gradually sloping direction from the Descending Passage, up through the natural rock terracing to the grotto (Plate XXXI). Here they organised their depot for tools and rest, and for the bye-passing of workers and materials. Their reason for commencing their tunnel so deep in the natural rock was *Grotto selected and organised as depot and bye-pass.* obviously to intersect, for purpose of inspection, the two fissures, PQ and MN, shown on Plate XXXI. This seems to indicate that the fissures not built up in the Descending Passage had developed as newly visible in the Passage at the time of the subsidence that had occasioned the visit of inspection considered.

From the grotto they then continued with a rough shaft approaching *Accurate setting out of forced tunnel to enter West lower end of Grand Gallery ramp.* towards the commencement of the Grand Gallery. When they had proceeded sufficiently far with this, by their rough initial methods of aligning, they made an accurate survey from a fixed point of the Pyramid's construction to determine the exact location of their tunnel end in azimuth, altitude, and distance from this fixed point. Referring to the then known data concerning the Pyramid's interior, the keepers thus obtained the location of their tunnel end in relation to the end of the Grand Gallery. They next continued their rough tunnel to a point vertically behind the first (lowest) ramp stone on the West side of the Grand Gallery. This effected, a perfectly vertical shaft— the so-called Well-shaft—was driven upwards to the predetermined point at which the keepers intended to force an entry into the Gallery. Reaching this point behind the first ramp stone, as shown on the Frontispiece (right- *Ramp stone forced out from vertical tunnel shaft into Grand Gallery.* hand view) and Plate XXXII (plan), they forced the ramp stone upwards and outwards. That this is the manner in which the ramp stone was forced is shown by the fractured appearance of the ramp around the Well-shaft. This is accurately illustrated on the Isometric Projection shown on Plate XXXIII.

¶ 193. THE EARLIEST INSPECTION OF THE SEALED CHAMBERS.

Having gained an entry, the keepers proceeded to an inspection of the *The opening of the Grand Gallery floor slab covering Entrance to Queen's Chamber.* Chambers. To inspect the Queen's Chamber, they had, perforce, to break or remove the Grand Gallery floor slab that originally bridged the Entrance Passage to the Queen's Chamber, as indicated by the existing details. These are as shown on Frontispiece (right-hand view), and Plates XXXII, XXXIII, and XXXIV. This done, they found little or no serious indications of failure in the Queen's Chamber.

Proceeding to the Antechamber and King's Chamber, they found here *Inspection of Antechamber and King's Chamber.* indications of possible instability due to the movement that had caused inspection to be made. In the King's Chamber they found the ceiling beams cracked along their South ends inside the Chamber. The cause of this *Visible cracks and openings cemented over or plastered to give indications of further movement.* fracture is clearly indicated by the general form of subsidence shown on Plates XXXI and XXXV. To enable any further movement or fracture to be indicated, the keepers evidently smeared the cracks and open joints with cement or plaster. Thus Petrie states, regarding these ceiling-beams, that " Round the S.E. corner, for about 5 feet on each side, the joint is daubed up with cement, laid on by fingers. The crack across the Eastern Roof-beam has been also daubed with cement, looking, *therefore*, as

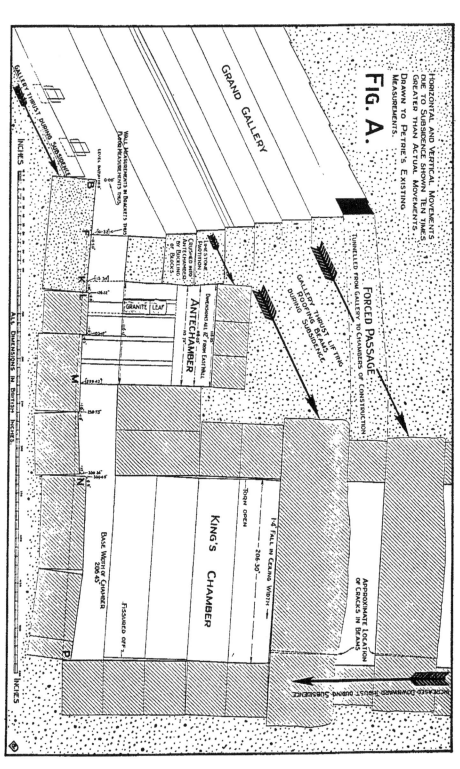

SUBSIDENCE DISTORTION DIAGRAM OF EXISTING KING'S CHAMBER, ANTECHAMBER, ETC.

In Section—Limestone Stippled : Granite Hatched in Parallel Lines.

PLATE XXXVb.

PLAN OF KING'S CHAMBER, ANTECHAMBER, AND QUEEN'S CHAMBER—ORIGINAL MEASUREMENTS.

In Section—Limestone Stippled; Granite Hatched in Parallel Lines.
For Enlargement of Table, see Addendum to Plate XXXV.

FIG. B.

ORIGINAL DISTANCES FROM FACE OF GREAT STEP TO SOUTH WALL OF KING'S CHAMBER

PLATE XXXV REF.	PLATE XXXVI REF.	ORIGINAL DIMENSIONS PYRAMID INCHES	BRITISH INCHES	GEOMETRICAL DIMENSIONING IN PYRAMID INCHES
B	1	0·000000	0·000	
R K	— 4	103·032997 112·916514	103·146 113·041	
L	5	126·143804	126·283	
—	10	149·440760	149·605	
=	11	171·046657	171·235	
=	12	177·660302	177·866	
M	13	229·176801	229·429	
N	14	330·223128	330·586	
P		536·289122	536·879	

if it had cracked *before* the chamber was finished. At the S.W. corner, plaster is freely spread over the granite, covering about a square foot altogether." (The first *italics* are ours, the second Professor Petrie's own.)

¶ 194. THE INSPECTION TUNNEL TO CHAMBERS OF CONSTRUCTION.

To gain access to the important Chambers of Construction over the King's Chamber, the keepers next drove an opening into the East wall of the Grand Gallery at its upper or South end. This is as shown on the Frontispiece and Plate XXXVI.

Tunnelling clear of the wall blocks of the Gallery, the workers turned their tunnel towards the South, as shown on Plate XXXVI, to enter the Chambers of Construction at the upper level of the ceiling blocks of the King's Chamber. Here they found that the indications of instability were not so serious as they had feared, for they did not proceed higher than the 1st Chamber with their inspection.[1] Modern tunnelling upwards into the four higher Chambers has shown that the use of limestone (in lieu of granite) supporting blocks, bearing the ends of the higher granite roofing beams, has caused the shock of subsidence to be partly broken by crushing and " plastic " flow of the limestone. In other words, the higher Chambers of Construction were purposely built weaker than the lowest Chamber and ceiling beams of the King's Chamber, to act as a succession of " buffers " between the superimposed mass of the Pyramid and the King's Chamber, during the expected subsidence movement.

Inspection tunnel driven from top of Grand Gallery to upper surface of King's Chamber ceiling beams.

Higher Chambers of Construction built weaker to give way slightly under subsiding superimposed load.

To permit of this " buffer " effect being fully developed, the beams or slabs of the Chambers of Construction were not built into the East and West walls, from which, as shown by the adhering plaster, the upper Chamber has subsided as much as 3 inches. Hence, instead of indicating bad workmanship —as has been supposed by some authorities not conversant with the design of constructional devices for counteracting the effects of subsidence movement that cannot be prevented — the workmanship in these Chambers is the necessary effect of good design. An entirely rigid system of construction, with uniform workmanship from the lowest to the highest Chamber, would

Object being to break the shock of direct communication to the more rigid construction of lowest Chamber of Construction and King's Chamber.

[1] The question of an early forced entry into the Pyramid for inspection has been discussed at greater length than many readers may deem to be warranted by the relative importance of the facts. The reason is that many theories of intention have been attached to the so-called " Well-shaft "—by which we deem this earliest entry was made—and to the access tunnel to the Chambers of Construction.

We have tried to shorten the presentation of what seemed to us to be the true explanation, by adopting the narrative form rather than the inductive form of presenting the data. The reader, therefore, should understand that where the narrative form may seem to savour of assertion, in the presentation of what actually has been evolved by inductive analysis, this is entirely due to the abbreviated form adopted. Where assertion may seem to exist, the reader, it is hoped, will find the confirming data in the context.

Two facts of importance in this connection are (1) that the ramp stone in the Grand Gallery clearly was forced into the Grand Gallery from the so-called Well-shaft; and (2) that the forced inlets were evidently all carefully selected to be at such points as would not destroy or interfere with the purpose of any essential feature of the Pyramid's Passage construction.

PLATE XXXVI.

Limestone in Section shown in Stippled Effect; Granite in Section shown Hatched in Parallel Lines.

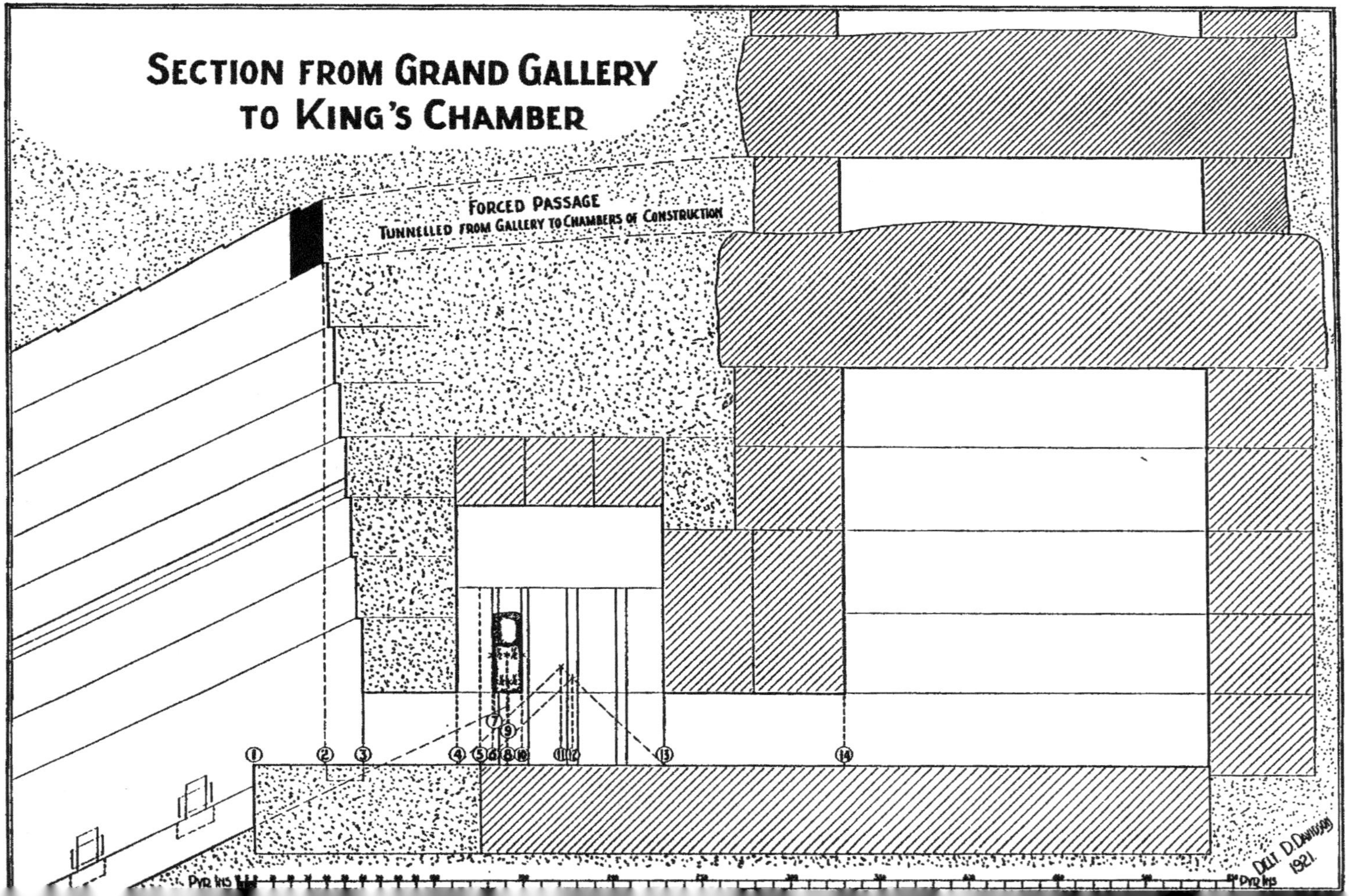

SECTION FROM GRAND GALLERY
TO KING'S CHAMBER

FORCED PASSAGE
TUNNELLED FROM GALLERY TO CHAMBERS OF CONSTRUCTION

have been disastrous. A voussoir arch construction would have been more disastrous still, as the final stage of settlement has produced an opening out of the King's Chamber walls. This opening out, in conjunction with the tilting thrust from the Grand Gallery, illustrated on Plate XXXV, Fig. A, would have produced a rocking motion and a kicking-up effect on the North haunching of a voussoir arch construction, as well as an opening out of the span of the arch. The complicated combination of stress movements between the voussoirs would have produced failure.

SECTION III.—DETAILS CONCERNING PLATES.

¶ 195. PLATE XIX. THE REDUCED CO-ORDINATES OF PROFESSOR PETRIE'S SURVEY DATA.

Plate XIX for technical reader only.

The data given on Plate XIX are self-explanatory to the technical reader. The purpose of the Plate is to enable the technical reader to check the calculations giving the co-ordinates of Plate XX.

Supplies data for co-ordinates of Plate XX.

Close agreement with Petrie's data.

It should be sufficient for the general reader to observe how closely the newly calculated co-ordinates of Plate XX agree with Professor Petrie's calculated distances, as given on Plate XX.

¶ 196. PLATE XX. THE MEASUREMENTS AND LEVELS OF THE EXISTING DETAILS OF THE GREAT PYRAMID'S EXTERIOR.

Sources of data.

The data given on Plate XX are self-explanatory. The direct measurements of the base square are Professor Petrie's. The true Pyramid azimuth co-ordinate measurements are from Petrie's survey data given on Plate XIX. The plan of the base sockets—shown to a magnified scale as compared with the scale of base co-ordinates—is from Professor Smyth's " Life and Work," Vol. I, p. 138, etc.

Related movements due to ground subsidence and consequent reactions on Pyramid masonry courses.

The adopted azimuth system.

As explained in Sections I and II of this Chapter, ground subsidence has shifted the sockets, both in relation to their original azimuth and in relation to each other, and at the same time, by consequent minor earthquake effects has shifted the base courses of the Pyramid in relation to the shifted positions of the sockets. The sum of all apparent movements, as examined in detail, varies from ⅛ of an inch to 3½ inches. (¶¶ 141–145, 180–182.) What we have termed the Pyramid's " true azimuth co-ordinate system " is the azimuth system as defined by the existing socket corners—outmost from the Pyramid's base centre. This azimuth system was adopted as the system of reference for the various related—primary and secondary—movements.

The point of origin for setting out the base square and the oriented definition of the distance between the Pyramid's East and West sides.

Preliminary or final ?

The existing evidences of the various related movements have shown (¶¶ 145, 180, and 181) that the point M of the S.E. socket was adopted as the point of origin for setting out the Pyramid's base square and diagonals, and that the distance between the East side of the latter socket and the West side UX of the S.W. socket defined the length of the Pyramid's base side. Even in the event of the technical reader failing to agree with all our conclusions concerning the related base movements, it will nevertheless have to be conceded that the point M formed the point of origin for preliminary setting out, and that the distance between the East side of the S.E. socket and the West side of the S.W. socket formed the preliminary definition of the Pyramid's base width from East to West. (¶¶ 145, 180, and 181.)

The Pyramid courses.

The geometrically defined special apex Pyramid in relation to the existing topmost course.

The levels of the Pyramid courses are as obtained by Petrie. The reader should note that the geometrical considerations of Plates XXIII, XXIV, and XXV (Fig. A₂) require that the special apex Pyramid should be 364.27665 P″ =364.68 B″ high. The Pyramid's geometrical height being 5813.01 P″ =5819.40 B″ gives base of original apex Pyramid, or top surface of the highest course of masonry at 5454.72 B″ above the base. This agrees with the highest existing course, the 203rd course, at 5451.8 B″, thus leaving 2.9 B″ for subsidence of the highest course. Owing to the cumulative effect of the flat-arching of the courses, from the centre of the base to the topmost course, as explained in ¶¶ 183 and 184, the subsidence at the apex would not be more than this. The special apex Pyramid would not be a single apex stone, but an apex Pyramid of finer (casing) limestone. The reader must not confuse the apex Pyramid with the apex stone.

¶ 196a. THE CEREMONY OF ORIENTING THE FOUNDATION.

The ceremony of setting out—or orienting—the foundations of a building is extremely ancient. The ceremony was known as "the stretching of the cord." It is referred to, without explanation, in an Egyptian inscription of Amenemhat I, the first king of Dynasty XII. At that time the ceremony was already ancient. *Egyptian evidence as to the antiquity of the ceremony of setting out the foundation.*

The "measuring cord" is allegorically taken as defining the function of Israel in relation to the world in Deut. xxxii, 8 and 9, and context. In verse 9 the true rendering of the Hebrew reads "Jacob is the measuring cord of His inheritance." Again in Job xxxviii, 4, 5, and 6, the "stretching of the cord" and the cutting of the sockets for defining the laying out of the foundations are referred to as follows :— *References to the ceremony in the Old Testament. The stretching of the cord, the sockets, and the corner stone referred to in Job.*

> "Where wast thou when I laid the foundations of the earth? . . .
> "Who hath laid the measures thereof? . . .
> "Who hath stretched the line (or cord) upon it?
> "Whereupon are the sockets made to sink? or who laid the corner stone thereof?"

The Egyptian inscriptions generally indicate the process of orientation being effected by "stretching the cord" on an alignment towards a particular star. All the astronomical and Egyptological data in relation to this are fully discussed in Sir Norman Lockyer's "Dawn of Astronomy."[1] *Star alignments.*

¶ 196b. THE GODDESS OF THE FOUNDATION.

In the Egyptian sculptures and texts the goddess Sefkhet-Ååbut[2] — "the goddess of the laying of the foundation," and the goddess associated with the chronological repetitions of "seven"—is pictured as assisting the king in the ceremony of "stretching the cord." This goddess is represented as the guardian of the cycles of 30 and 120 years, and is pictured accompanied by the symbols of these. In consequence, the principal foundation ceremonies were held at the festivals of the termination of these cycles. Obviously the chronological aspect of her connection with "seven" relates to the seven primary cycles of 103 years, which were equal to six groups of *Sep tep sed* periods (¶ 34). *The goddess Sefkhet-Ååbut and the foundation ceremony. "Stretching the cord." The guardian of chronological repetitions of "seven." The "Sed Hebs" and the series of seven cycles of 103 years.*

The head-dress of the goddess consists of an arch, or pair of horns inverted, over a seven-rayed star, or seven-petalled flower. Here we have, apparently, a hieroglyphic representation of the rainbow, which in the Babylonian goddess Ishtar is signified by "the jewelled collar of Ishtar."[3] The Rev. C. J. Ball shows that the latter symbol was derived from the Chinese. Accordingly we find that the Chinese equivalent of Noah, the patriarch Fu-hi, was "born of a rainbow," "was manifested on the mountains of Chin, immediately after that great division of time which was produced by the deluge," and that "he carefully bred *seven* different kinds of animals which he used to sacrifice to the Great Spirit of heaven and earth."[4] *The emblem of the Noachian rainbow covenant. The jewelled collar of Ishtar. Chinese connection. The rainbow covenant in Chinese tradition.*

[1] The only criticism one feels inclined to offer in connection with this work is that Lockyer seems to have had too few definitive statements of alignment and too many stars upon which to align. He was, therefore, able to fix many of his datings in accordance with systems of Egyptological chronology that are not now accepted. Criticism, however, does not apply to his solar alignments. Refer ¶¶ 1–4 and footnotes.

[2] Budge, " Gods of the Egyptians," Vol. I, pp. 424–426 and 430.

[3] Rev. C. J. Ball, " Light from the East," pp. 40 and 201.

[4] Faber's " Pagan Idolatry," Vol. II, pp. 343–344.

¶ 196c. THE DELUGE ELEMENT AND EPOCH.

Confirming the connection suggested, Ball points out that Iris, the goddess of the rainbow, " is associated with Aphrodite (Ishtar) in Homer (II, 5, 353, *seq.*) " ; and Budge, that Aphrodite was identified with the Egyptian Hathor,[1] and that the goddess Sefkhet-Áábut, in one Egyptian representation, is represented as Hathor. The latter, again, was originally, according to Budge, " only one special part of the great watery mass of heaven."[2] The clear meaning of the latter statement becomes apparent when we remember that Hathor was instrumental in effecting the " Destruction of Men " in the Egyptian equivalent of the Deluge narrative (¶ 28). Hence the association with " seven " obviously originated the " seven Hathors " —the seven fairy goddesses of the Egyptians. Obviously, again, these were identi- fied with the " seven *Pleiades* "—associated traditionally with the Deluge (¶ 29) —since, in early Euphratean astronomy, the " seven *Pleiades* " (or particularly, the star *Alcyoné*) were known as " The Foundation."[3]

This completes the identifications associating the goddess Sefkhet-Áábut, the goddess of the foundation ceremony, with the Deluge rainbow covenant of Gen. ix, 13. The identifications further suggest that the cycles of 30 and 120 years, represented as controlled by the goddess, began from an epoch that was the ancient Egyptian equivalent date for the Hebrew Deluge ending. This is confirmed by the facts concerning the Deluge Calendar of Genesis, and the facts concerning the early Egyptian November year-beginning discussed in Chapter I, Sections I and II.

¶ 196d. THE RAINBOW ANGEL OF REVELATION.

The identifications outlined show that the goddess Sefkhet-Áábut was the Egyptian (female) version of the " Rainbow Angel " of Revelation, Chapters x and xi. It is this angel who defines " the times," as *Palmoni*—" the wonderful numberer "[4] or " numberer of secrets "—in Daniel viii defines " the times." The " Rainbow Angel " " was clothed with a cloud, and a rainbow was upon his head." He was " the Seventh Angel," and at his cry " seven thunders uttered their voices." His final declaration was that " there should be time no longer."[4] Comparing the latter with Daniel viii, 13–19, we see that the functions of *Palmoni* and the Rainbow Angel are identical, and that the Egyptian goddess Sefkhet-Áábut was represented as exercising the same functions.

¶ 197. PLATE XXI. THE SOUTH-EAST CORNER CASING STONE.

The reconstruction defined as Professor Petrie's in Figs. A, A₁, and A₂, results entirely from his data in the text of his work and from his Plate X. The new reconstruction shown on Figs. B, B₁, and B₂ follows from the data discussed in Sections I and II of this Chapter—particularly in ¶¶ 144, 145, 146, and 196. A model of Petrie's reconstruction for the S.E. corner casing stone will convince any experienced constructional engineer, architect, or building craftsman, that a corner stone of its shape and proportion could not be safely handled into position, and that the stone, in position, would not be reliable. This has been the conclusion, without exception, of many experienced engineers, architects, and contractors, to whom we have shown such a model during the past thirteen years.

It is unfortunate that Professor Petrie, in selecting one of the four corner stones to define a typical case of his theory of reconstruction for all four, did not select the S.E. corner stone. Had he done so, we feel confident he would have

---

[1] " Gods of the Egyptians," Vol. I, p. 435.
[2] Ibid., pp. 428–429.
[3] Brown, " Primitive Constellations," Vol. I, p. 57.
[4] In this connection the reader is referred to ¶ 36 and footnote.

revised his theory of reconstruction. Had he been led to a revision of his theory of the sockets and the corner casing stones, it is highly probable that the revision of the latter would have led him to discover the true hollowed-in base plan.

The reader should understand that the new reconstruction shown on Figs. B, B₁, and B₂ may not be absolutely correct in every detail. It is more than probable that the pavement was carried over the socket, and that the casing stone rested on the pavement—in all other respects, precisely as shown on Figs. B₁ and B₂. *For new reconstruction, pavement probably supported the corner casing stones.*

¶ 197a. SOCKET DEPOSITS.

What makes the latter alternative probable is the more recently derived evidence from the Lisht Pyramid of Senusert I (Dynasty XII). This is given by Dr. Albert Lithgoe as follows :—[1] *Foundation deposits of Lisht Pyramid sockets.*

> " Under the platform (of the Pyramid) there was found at each of the four corners of the Pyramid a ' foundation-deposit.' These were practically identical in character, and in each instance had been placed in a square pocket about 80 cm. in diameter, and 1 metre in depth, excavated in the bed-rock upon which the platform rested. The bottom of the pocket had been covered in each case with about 5 cm. of clean gravel upon which were some 25 to 30 small pottery model dishes and vases, while scattered among them were a number of lozenge-shaped blue glass beads. On these objects were laid the skull and some of the bones of an ox which had been sacrificed as a part of the ceremonial. The pocket had then been completely filled with gravel, on which, at about half its depth, was laid a small model brick of sun-dried Nile mud. Finally the pockets were covered by massive limestone blocks, which in each case formed the corner blocks of the Pyramid platform."

The engineer or architect will probably agree, for the particular case of a corner stone partly resting on the natural rock and partly on socket filling of the nature described for the Lisht Pyramid, that such construction as is shown on Figs. B, B₁, and B₂ would not be altogether good design or construction. In such event, it is likely that the pavement spanned the socket and carried the corner casing stone. Of course, it was the usual Egyptian practice to cover the foundation area of their Pyramids and other heavy constructions with a layer of sand upon which to bed their base blocks. This is good practice so long as the sand is not free to move after bedding. What is not good practice is to have a block such as AGFE on Plan (Fig. B) with its corner A resting on sand or gravel filling and its corner F on bed-rock. *If Great Pyramid sockets filled in as for case described, this would confirm that corner casing stones rested on pavement slabs spanning sockets.*

On the other hand, the foundation deposits of the Great Pyramid's sockets may have been filled round with run-in lead,[2] or with other hard filling, in which case the whole foundation area of the Pyramid base—as normal in such work—may have been covered with fine sand internal to the surrounding pavement, the core base blocks, and possibly also the corner casing stones being thereafter laid, as shown on Figs. B₁ and B₂. All known casing blocks near the centre of the four base sides, however, rest upon the pavement, as shown on Plates XXVI–XXIX. *If Great Pyramid sockets filled in with hard filling, corner casing blocks may have rested directly on same, as shown on Plates.*

¶ 198. PLATE XXII. ISOMETRIC AND OBLIQUE PROJECTIONS OF SOUTH-EAST CASING STONE.

The isometric and oblique projections of Professor Petrie's reconstruction refer to the defects mentioned in ¶ 197. These two views clearly illustrate the difficulty of handling without injury a stone altogether 8 feet high, according to Petrie's reconstruction, from extreme base to top surface, only 3 feet square on top, and with a base diagonal—AL on Fig. A, Plate XXI—of over 13 feet, ending in the weak projecting footing provided to fit into the socket. *Petrie's S.E. corner casing stone:— Top, 3 feet square; height, 8 feet; base diagonal over 13 feet long, ending in weak projecting footing.*

[1] Journal " Ancient Egypt," 1915, Part IV, p. 145.
[2] The Coptic tradition of the Masoudi Arabic MS. mentions run-in lead in connection with the Great Pyramid pavement.
Vyse's " Pyramids of Gizeh," Vol. II, Sprenger's Appendix, p. 325.

The isometric and oblique projections of the corner stone, according to the new reconstruction, give a stone 6 feet square on top, 5 feet high, if resting on the pavement—or 6 feet 6 inches high, if resting on the rock surface—and 9 feet 9 inches square on its base surface. All the known casing stones *in situ* are of this or greater proportion. Many of them are of a much greater top thickness than 6 feet, running into and beyond the mean core surface. This shows that the base casing stone course was thicker than the casing stone courses above it, and hence, in all probability, that the corner base casing stones were larger in plan than is indicated by Plate XXI, Fig. B.[1] Otherwise the casing of the Pyramid is more or less uniform, about 6 feet thick on the top surface of courses.

Petrie's reconstruction requires the 6 feet thickness down the centre of each face slope, and a 3 feet thickness at the corners or approaching the arris edges. This is the reverse of sound construction in any form of building. Additional thickness is more necessary at returns of courses than in straight lengths of courses.

¶ 199. PLATE XXIII. GEOMETRICAL DEFINITION OF PASSAGE DIS-
    PLACEMENT.

In Fig. A, Case I, D_2OD_1 represents the East to West vertical section of the Pyramid.

For Fig. A, Case II, D_2OD_1 represents an apex vertical section whose linear dimensions are $\frac{1}{10}$th the linear dimensions for Case I. This apex section forms the basis for the geometrical definition (1) of the Apex Pyramid; (2) of the hollowing-in features of the Pyramid's casing slopes; and (3) of the displacement of the Pyramid's Passage System. Explanation of Case II, as defining the features noted, will also form the explanation for Case I, if 10 times the dimensions of Case II be substituted.

Fig. A, Case II :—

With centre O, and radius $OJ_1 = 581.3014373$ P″, describe the quadrant arc $J_2J_1J_3$, $= \frac{3652.42465}{4}$ P″. Complete the quadrant $J_3J_1J_2O$.

With O as apex, and the central radius OJ_1 of the quadrant as perpendicular height, form the triangle D_2OD_1, with base $D_2J_1D_1 =$ length of quadrant arc $J_2J_1J_3$. Then area of triangle $D_2OD_1 =$ area of quadrant $J_3J_1J_2O$.

Draw the chord $J_2A_1J_3$ to cut the perpendicular OJ_1 at A_1, and to cut OD_2 at B_2, and OD_1 at B_1. Then $B_2A_1B_1 = \frac{2582.654}{4}$ P″, 2582.654 P″ being $\frac{1}{10}$th the Precessional circuit. (Hence for Case I, $B_2A_1B_1$ represents the level of the Precessional circuit.)

Now, with centre O, and radius OA_1, describe the quadrant arc $A_2A_1A_3$, which is of equal length to $B_2A_1B_1$. (Hence for Case I, quadrant $A_3A_1A_2O$ is the quadrant of the Precessional Circle.)

Draw E_3OE_4 through O and parallel to J_2J_3 and D_2D_1. On E_3OE_4 construct the square $E_1E_2E_3E_4$ of area equal to the quadrant area $A_3A_1A_2O$, and equal to the Pyramid sectional area B_1OB_2, and such that $E_3O = E_4O = E_2F_1 = E_1F_1$. Then $OF_1 = E_3E_4 = E_1E_2 = 364.2766547$ P″.

Now produce $E_2F_1E_1$ to cut the Pyramid face line OD_2 at k_3 and OD_1 at k_1. Then $F_1k_3 = F_1k_1 = 286.1022156$ P″. The line $k_3F_1k_1$ represents the level of a square circuit at the Pyramid's apex, of length of side $k_3F_1k_1 = 2F_1k_1 = 2F_1k_3 = 2 \times 286.1022156$ P″.

[1] Similar thickening applied to Petrie's reconstruction would necessarily make his detail still weaker for handling and bedding in position.

The plan of this square in relation to the plan of the Pyramid's base square $M_1M_2M_3M_4$ is shown on Fig. B as $N_1N_2N_3N_4$, in which $k_3F_1k_1$ represents the line $k_3F_1k_1$ in Fig. A. Producing N_2N_3 in Fig. B to intersect, in plan, the Pyramid's North base side M_1M_2 at Y, and its South base side at W, gives the line $WN_3k_3N_2Y$ defining the plan of the central vertical axial plane of the Pyramid's Passage System, uniformly removed the distance $YZ=k_3F_1=WU=286.1022156$ P" eastwards from the Pyramid's North to South central vertical plane, represented in plan by the line UF_1Z.

Point T in Fig. B represents the centre of the Entrance Doorway on the North face slope of the Pyramid.

¶ 200. PLATE XXIV. THE COMPLETE GEOMETRY OF THE DISPLACEMENT.

Plate XXIV represents the East to West vertical section R_2OR_1 of the Pyramid, shown in plan as the line R_2R_1 in Fig. B, Plate XXIII. The apex geometrical construction is identical in line and letter references with Case II, Fig. A, Plate XXIII. Plate XXIV diagram is, therefore, a composite representation of the geometrical constructions of Plate XXIII, Figs. A and B. *The composite geometry of Figs. A and B of Plate XXIII.*

The vertical line K_3B_2 represents the elevation, as seen from the North, of the central vertical axial plane of the Passage System, with the point X at height K_3X representing the *level* of the centre of the Entrance Doorway on the North face slope.

With these key explanations the general reader should be able to follow the sequence of geometrical construction in Plates XXIII and XXIV without further elaboration. The sequence of geometrical construction bears an important relation to the geometrical constructions of Plate XXV.

¶ 201. PLATE XXV. THE PYRAMID BASE AND THE EARTH'S ORBIT.

Plate XXV has been sufficiently explained in ¶¶ 153 to 159. One item, however, requires amplifying. This concerns the Pyramid's value for the mean sun distance as compared with the various modern values by different methods. The four principal methods of determination giving reliable results are the following :— *The four principal modern methods of obtaining the sun distance.*

(1) By measurement of planetary parallaxes ;
(2) By the velocity of light ;
(3) By means of the determination of the relative masses of the Earth and the Sun ; and
(4) By means of the parallactic inequality of the Moon's motion.

Results by the four different methods do not precisely agree. The total range of difference is about 500,000 miles. Until they do agree by all four methods— within a minute range of variation—the mean sun distance cannot be stated as known precisely. It is not sufficient for a series of independent observations or calculations by one method alone to agree within a minute range of variation. In such case— until observations or calculations by the other methods agree within the same range of variation—it must be assumed that that agreement has been rendered possible by errors common to the method or apparatus employed. *Range of variation in comparison of values by the four independent methods, 500,000 miles.*

At present the range of variation in the determination of the sun's parallax by the various methods ranges from 8".762 to 8".806. These limits give a value for the sun distance ranging from 93,300,000 miles to 92,830,000 miles respectively. The Pyramid's value for the sun distance—92,996,085 miles, as in ¶ 159—represents a parallax of 8".791, which agrees closely with the added mean of methods (1), (2), and (4), 8".806, 8".781, and 8".773 respectively. Professor Newcomb's experiments in connection with method (2) derived a parallax of 8".79. *Expression of results by all four methods. Sun distance =93,050,000 ±250,000 miles.*

Present
opinion :—
Sun distance,
92,900,000±
100,000 miles.
The general *opinion* at the present time is that the sun distance lies between 92,800,000 miles and 93,000,000 miles. Observational astronomers declare in favour of the lower value. The best modern statement, however, is 92,900,000 ±100,000 miles.

¶ 202.   PLATE XXVI.   VIEW OF NORTH BASE CASING STONES, LOOK-
ING WESTWARDS.

View in
relation to
centre of
North base
side.

Nineteen stones
"in situ."

Fourteen stones
in good con-
dition, giving
base line of
63 feet 4 inches

One of these
limits can be
located on the
South base
side, but is
covered with
debris.

Plate XXVI gives a general view of the extent of casing stones existing on the North base side. The figure standing at the first casing stone is not many feet removed from the centre of the North base side. The complete extent of pavement shown in the foreground, and extending beyond the casing stones, was uncovered by Mr. L. Dow Covington during 1909 to 1910. The total number of casing stones uncovered is nineteen, of which the first fourteen, in the view shown, give an unbroken base line of 63 feet 4 inches. This is not sufficient to locate the point H of Fig. A, Plate XXV, the western limit of the hollowed-in central surface at the base. To locate this limit, the only known certain point where casing exists at the necessary distance from the centre of a base side is at G on the South base. This has not been cleared. Petrie sunk a shaft through debris at the point noted, and surveyed the points obtained by means of a plumb line. A complete clearance near this point would be necessary to define the change of direction in the South base line.

Attention is directed to the fact that the casing stones sit on the pavement. In his earlier editions, prior to Petrie's survey, Smyth showed the pavement erroneously as the lowest casing course.

¶ 203.   PLATE XXVII.   VIEW OF NORTH BASE CASING STONES AND
AL MAMOUN'S FORCED ENTRANCE.

The figure shown is in the same position as in the view of Plate XXVI. The joints between the casing stones are shown as visible for purpose of illustration. Actually they are only perceptible under the closest inspection.

Account of
Al Mamoun's
forced entry
about 800 A.D.

The curious
circumstance
that led to
access being
gained when
operations
were about to
be stopped.

The discovery
of the 1st
Ascending
Passage.

Al Mamoun's forced entrance is shown on the 7th course, and, as pictured, vertically above the first existing casing stone. This entry was made about 800 A.D. in the hopes of obtaining access to the treasures that, according to tradition, were hidden in the Pyramid. A curious circumstance is related in connection with this undertaking. This is to the effect that the excavation—having proceeded a con-siderable distance into the core masonry—was upon the point of being given up, when the workmen heard what appeared to be the sound of a stone falling, slightly eastwards of their tunnel end. Altering the direction of their tunnel eastwards towards the point indicated by the sound referred to, the workers soon reached the Descending Passage at a point below the junction. Here they found the stone whose fall had redirected their operations. The shape of the stone showed that it had been the roofing stone of the Entrance Passage that had hidden the beginning of the 1st Ascending Passage.

Arab accounts
of innumerable
limestone
blocks broken
up, and ex-
tracted from
1st Ascending
Passage.

Finding that the Descending Passage did not lead to the hoped-for treasure, the workers redirected their attentions to finding an entrance to the 1st Ascending Passage. The Arab accounts relate that many limestone plugs had to be extracted from the Passage above the granite plugs before entrance was effected. (Refer ¶ 191.)

¶ 204.   PLATE XXVIII.   NEAR VIEW OF NORTH BASE CASING STONES.

Near view of
North base
showing rock
fissure.

The standing figure is again in the same position as in Plates XXVI and XXVII. The fissure below the pavement shown in the left foreground is also shown partly, in the right foreground of Plate XXVI and in section on Plate XXXI, as fissure GH.

¶ 205. PLATE XXIX. GENERAL VIEW OF NORTH BASE SHOWING CASING STONES, AL MAMOUN'S ENTRY, AND EXISTING ENTRANCE TO ENTRANCE PASSAGE.

The figure seated on the 5th course of core masonry is shown pointing to Al Mamoun's forced entry on the 7th course. Above, to the left, is shown the system of relieving slabs or blocks over the beginning of the Entrance Passage, designed to prevent subsidence pressure jamming the vertically rotating pivoted block that originally closed the Entrance Doorway. These relieving blocks are also shown in section over the Entrance in Plate XXXI. *Constructional feature to prevent subsidence jamming pivoted block of Entrance Doorway.*

The pivoted doorway was not known to Al Mamoun's workers until after access had been gained by tunnelling; the casing being complete until Arab demolition around 800 A.D. It would appear, however, that subsidence had distorted the casing and buckled it loose on the core masonry, making it a simple matter, once the casing had been undermined near the base, for demolition to continue. Many of the greater buildings of Cairo about 1000 A.D. were built of the casing blocks. *Subsidence effects on casing assisted Arab demolition.*

¶ 206. PLATE XXX. EXISTING AND ORIGINAL MEASUREMENTS OF THE GREAT PYRAMID'S PASSAGES.

The bases of the comparative statements of Plate XXX are—

(1) That the original angle of slope of the Passages is known. (¶¶ 176 and 177.)
(2) That the existing sloping lengths of the built portions of the Passages are known, and that critical examination shows that these have not appreciably altered since construction. (¶¶ 180 and 186.)
(3) That, in consequence of (2), subsidence has altered the horizontal and vertical positions of all points along ABCD without appreciably altering their passage floor distances in relation to the points A, B, C, and D. (¶¶ 179, 180, 183, and 185.)
(4) That the floor from the Great Step to the King's Chamber originally lay in one horizontal plane.
(5) That the roof of the horizontal passage to the Queen's Chamber originally lay in one horizontal plane at the level of the termination of the roof of the 1st Ascending Passage. *The bases of the comparative statements of existing and original Passage lengths and their horizontal and vertical co-ordinates.*
(6) That subsidence in the natural rock below the Pyramid's base—unlike its effect on the built mass of blocks above—vertically lowered all points in the rock-cut portion of the Descending Passage between C and E, without sensibly moving the points horizontally. (Plate XXX, Table B, Cols. 3 A and B, and note 3 to Table B.)
(7) That, in consequence of (6), floor distances from C towards E were all cumulatively stretched during subsidence, with the maximum amount of extension for the total sloping floor distance CE. (Plate XXX, Table B, Cols. 2 A and B.)
(8) That reconstruction on the bases of (6) and (7) shows that E was originally 1162.6 P" below the base (Plate XXX, Table B, Col. 4 A), this being also the measurement of the height of the 35th course axis above the base. *A geometrical datum connecting with the geometrical construction of the 35th course.*

The existing measurements are all from Professor Petrie, except in the case of CE, which Petrie could not measure accurately owing to accumulations of debris. The Edgars,[1] as a result of Dow Covington's clearances in the Descending Passage, were able to measure the length CE as given on Plate XXX. *Sources of existing measurements.*

The horizontal and vertical distances of points in the sloping passages are reduced from Petrie's passage distances, angles, and offsets. The notes to Plate XXX and footnote to ¶ 183 direct attention to an error in Petrie's reduction of his measured *Petrie's error in stating the horizontal and vertical position of the Great Step.*

[1] "Great Pyramid Passages," Vol. II, p. 8.

data to the statement of the horizontal and vertical position of the point A, and all points higher and beyond point A in Plate XXX.

For the original horizontal distances from the Great Step into the King's Chamber (Plate XXX, Table A, Col. 3 A) refer Plates XXXV (Table) and XLIII, and ¶¶ 211 c and d.

¶ 207. PLATE XXXI. SUBSIDENCE DISTORTION OF THE GREAT PYRAMID.

Plate XXXI has been prepared from the data given on Plate XXX. Explanation of the relation between Plates XXX and XXXI has been given in ¶¶ 176 to 194.

The result of the "jolting" effect described in ¶¶ 187 to 189 is shown clearly by the eccentric position of the top platform, as shown on Plate XXXI. The angle of the South stepped core slope with the horizontal, according to Petrie's survey data, is not sensibly different from the original casing slope—51° 51′ 13″ as against the original 51° 51′ 14″. Owing to the cumulative jolting open of the joints of the courses towards the North face, the angle of the North stepped core slope with the horizontal is now 51° 54′ 24″. This is as described in ¶ 182.

Certain minor features of Plate XXXI may be open to discussion and revision. We are confident, however, that, in the main, the data and conclusions upon which the features of Plate XXXI are based, and the general presentation of these features, give a true representation of the facts.

¶ 208. PLATE XXXII. PLAN AND SECTION OF NORTH END OF GRAND GALLERY.

The features illustrated in this Plate are shown in perspective on the right-hand side of the Frontispiece. Both plates show the holes for the beams that originally carried the slab closing the entrance to the horizontal passage leading to the Queen's Chamber. The shallow depth of the slab, and the closeness of the beams for such a shallow slab, show that the slab was merely a temporary bridging contrivance used in course of construction. (Refer also Plates XXXIII and XXXIV.)

Now the depth and width of the granite plugs closing the lower end of the 1st Ascending Passage clearly show that the plugs were built into the passage when the Pyramid masonry had reached the height of the plugs. This is certain from the fact that half an inch of clearance at the sides and top in the 1st Ascending Passage would not be sufficient to ensure the granite plugs being lowered from the Grand Gallery without risk of jamming in the descent of the 1st Ascending Passage. As existing, the depth of the plugs is greater than the depth of the upper end of the 1st Ascending Passage, and equal to the geometrical (original) depth of the Passage. It is clear, then, that the granite plugs were in position before the Pyramid courses had reached the height of the lower end of the Grand Gallery. The purpose of the bridging slab was not, therefore, for temporary bridging access *via* the 1st Ascending Passage.

It is obvious, also, that the plugging of the 1st Ascending Passage when the Pyramid courses had reached the height of the plugs precludes the idea that the Great Pyramid was intended as a tomb, unless the king conveniently died when the work had not long been commenced. (Refer Plates XXXV and XXXIX.)

¶ 208a. THE CONSTRUCTIONAL GAUGE RUNGS OF THE GRAND GALLERY.

A clue to the purpose of the bridging slab is seen in the holes sunk in the ramp stones, exactly opposite each other on both ramps, and in the let-in stones—over each ramp hole except the first two—opposite each other in the walls of the Grand

Gallery. This is illustrated on the Frontispiece and Plate XXXII. Obviously, we Gauge stone rungs originally extended across Gallery to retain ramps and wall blocks in position during construction. have here evidence that the ramps and lower wall course of the Gallery were constructed with gauge stones built across from ramp hole to opposite ramp hole like the rungs of a ladder, to retain the ramp stones, and the lower wall course on each side, the required distance apart during construction of the higher courses, and whilst the masonry external to the Gallery was progressing. This would necessitate vertically pendant projections from either end of the stone rungs or gauges fitting into the ramp holes; and, in all cases except the first two rungs, projecting shoulders The necessary shoulders and pendant projections account constructionally for features hitherto inexplicable. to retain the side walls their required distance apart above the ramps. The pendant projections would account for the ramp holes, and the bearing resistance of the projecting shoulders would account for the shallow sunk surfaces shown across the let-in stones and Gallery wall surfaces on both sides.

Further, to retain the ramps apart, we can see the constructional advantage to Limestone blocks held between gauge rungs, and of width (with wedges) to prevent base movement of ramps. be gained by placing blocks of limestone on the Gallery floor between the ramps, and between successive gauges or rungs. This would account for the temporary bridging slab over the entrance to the horizontal passage to the Queen's Chamber. On completion of the Gallery construction and the King's Chamber, and prior to Cutting out of successive rungs after construction released blocks for descent into 1st Ascending Passage. roofing these in, finally to close all access, the rungs or gauges would be cut out. Commencing from the lower end, successive rungs would be removed, thus releasing successive limestone blocks for descent into the 1st Ascending Passage. The number of rungs—extending the whole length of the Grand Gallery—and their clear distance apart are just sufficient to accommodate the number and size of blocks necessary to fill the 1st Ascending Passage from the upper end of the granite plugs to the beginning of the Grand Gallery. This agrees with the Arab accounts, noted This explains Arab accounts concerning such blocks in 1st Ascending Passage. in ¶¶ 191 and 203, as to the large numbers of limestone blocks said to have been broken up and extracted, one by one, from the 1st Ascending Passage. The cutting or sawing out of the rungs or gauges left the let-in stones as now existing on both sides of the Gallery. The first two rungs did not require extensions projecting into the Gallery walls, as these were retained apart by the adjacent masonry roofing-in the end of the 1st Ascending Passage.

The limestone plugs filling the 1st Ascending Passage would account for the The relation of this feature to route of earliest forced entry for inspection of subsidence effects. forced entry for the purpose of inspecting the effects of subsidence being directed towards the beginning of the Grand Gallery, rather than by the considerably shorter route directly from the Descending Passage below the junction to the 1st Ascending Passage above the granite plugs still in position. (Refer ¶¶ 191 and 192, and Plates XXXV and XXXIX.)

¶ 209. PLATE XXXIII. ISOMETRIC PROJECTION AT BEGINNING OF GRAND GALLERY.

Here the East wall and East ramp of the Grand Gallery are supposed to be The missing ramp stone. removed for purpose of illustration. The view clearly shows how the first Commencement of Gallery. ramp stone of the West ramp was forced out from below, as described in ¶ 192. It also shows how the roofing block ending the 1st Ascending Passage acted as a gauge Gauge blocks. retaining the East and West walls of the Gallery in position during construction, and without necessitating the two lower gauge rungs (discussed in ¶¶ 208 and 208a) being provided with projections into the walls, or with retaining shoulders.

¶ 210. PLATE XXXIV. ISOMETRIC PROJECTION SHOWING ENTRANCE DOORWAY OF PASSAGE TO QUEEN'S CHAMBER.

The view shows how the bridging slab was carried by the sunk area of the Grand The beam holes and bearing for the temporary bridging slab. Gallery floor and by the beams—the wall holes for the latter being shown below the West ramp stone.

Necessity for
gauge rungs
and wedged
plug blocks
in constructing
ramps.
Evidences of
gauge rungs
and their
retaining
shoulders.
Attention is directed to the fact shown that the ramp rests on the surface plane of the Grand Gallery floor, thus necessitating the use of the gauge rungs and wedged plug blocks on the floor (discussed in ¶¶ 208 and 208a) to retain the ramps in position during construction. The cut-off ends of the gauge rungs are shown as the " let-in stones " in the Gallery wall. The positions of the retaining shoulders of the gauge rungs—to keep the wall blocks in position during construction—are indicated by the sunk surfaces crossing the let-in stones, and continuing on the wall block for approximately the width of the ramp holes.

¶ 211. PLATE XXXV. ANTECHAMBER, KING'S CHAMBER, AND CON-
NECTING PASSAGES.

Distortion in
Chambers and
Passages due
to subsidence.
Source of data.
Plate XXXV, Fig. A.—This illustrates the effects of subsidence movement on the masonry of these Chambers and Passages. The distortion data are compiled from Petrie's distortion diagram of the King's Chamber, his continuous floor measurements, his series of measurements in the Antechamber, and his measurements of the over-hang of the Grand Gallery. These data would have been more definitively complete had Petrie measured the variations from the vertical in the Antechamber walls. The data, however, are fairly certain, from the co-ordination of the King's Chamber distortion data and the series of measurements noted.

Grand Gallery
thrust upheld
North end of
Chambers, etc.
Shearing-in of
partition wall
between
Gallery and
Antechamber.
Nature of
combined
movements
causing cracks
in King's
Chamber roof-
ing beams.
Distortion and
fractures due
to a vertically
rotating move-
ment.
Plates XXXI and XXXV (Fig. A), studied in relation, show that during the subsidence movement the axial thrust and rigidity of the Grand Gallery construction upheld the North end of the constructional mass of these chambers. The same tilting thrust, communicated from the Grand Gallery walls and ratchet roofing slabs, obviously pushed and lifted the mass of masonry above the Antechamber slightly upwards and towards the King's Chamber. As Petrie has observed, these chambers are not bonded into the surrounding Pyramid masonry courses, and were, therefore, free to move. The reaction and mass of the Pyramid's masonry courses over and South of the King's Chamber, however, resisted the proportionate deformation of the superimposed mass of the Chambers of Construction by inducing it to act as a vertical cantilever. The resulting bending in the vertical is shown on Plate XXXI, and the effect of this, the cracking of the roofing beams of the King's Chamber near its South wall, is shown on Plate XXXV, Fig. A. In effect, the King's Chamber, in subsiding, was lifted up on its North side by the tilting thrust from the Grand Gallery. The same movement, as shown on Fig. A, Plate XXXV, has sheared the South-end masonry of the Grand Gallery into the Antechamber.

The effect of the thrust upon the floor blocks, from the Great Step into the King's Chamber, is very clearly shown on the latter diagram. It is important to remember that these flooring blocks are built between and independent of the side walls of the Chambers and Passages. The movement of the latter bears no relation to the accompanying compression of the former. This explains the significance of notes (1) and (2) to the measurements of Plate XXX, Table A, Column 3 C.

¶ 211a. " THE FLOW OF SOLIDS " UNDER GREAT CONTAINING
PRESSURES.

Movement of
walls appreci-
able ; relative
movement be-
tween integral
parts of floors
slight.
Walls built
more free to
move than
floors.
When we come to examine closely into this question of the difference between the wall movements and the floor movements—in the horizontal—we find that, whereas walls have been moved in relation to the floors and in relation wall to wall, the floor lengths have nowhere been *very* appreciably altered. This is accounted for by the fact—evidenced by the constructional details and by nature of movement and distortion effects (Plate XXXV, Fig. A)—that the walls were more liable to distort in the direction of movement than the floors. The floors, as noted in ¶ 211, are built between the walls, and are formed of closely fitting blocks. These, although

liable to buckle and subside unequally, were not free to diminish in length, unless Floors laid by crushing, or by means of a recognised internal movement in the material, known between walls. as " solid flow," towards an exposed surface.

For the molecular flow of all apparently rigid and brittle materials under Molecular extreme containing pressure, the technical reader is referred to the classical experi- flow of rigid ments of three eminent independent investigators, MM. Tresca, Considère, and materials. Mesnager. As expressed by Professor W. H. Burr,[1] the law of the " Flow of Solids " is as follows :—

" If a mass of material be enclosed on all its faces, or outer surfaces, but The law of one or a portion of one, and if external pressure be brought to bear on those Solids." faces, the material will be forced to move to and through the free surface ; *in other words, the flow of the material will take place in the direction of least resistance.*"

The movement is analogous, and similar to the phenomenon of " creep " in Analogy— coal mines. This analogy with " creep " explains much in connection with distor- coal mines. tion in mass and distortion in detail within the Great Pyramid.

¶ 211b. THE TILTING AND DISTORTION OF THE STEP BLOCK.

Apart from the partial movement of walls in relation to floors, the diagram of The pushing Plate XXXV, Fig. A, shows that the face of the Step has been pushed upwards and movement on tilted away from the South (or upper) end of the ramps, and from the South end of Great Step the sloping floor in the Gallery. It is essential to remember that Petrie, in noting block. this, states :—

" The ends of the ramps are parted away from the face of the Step by Petrie on same. 0.30 inch on East, and 0.44 inch on West, an amount which has been duly subtracted from my length measures of the Gallery."

Petrie, therefore, admits that this amount of separation has occurred since Horizontal construction. His statement also shows that movement along the West wall was extent of greater than movement along the East wall. This is confirmed by all his measures movement. in the Chambers here.

¶ 211c. MOVEMENT OF WALLS IN RELATION TO FLOOR.

Referring to Petrie's measurements on the horizontal surface of the Great Step, Movement and stating in terms of Fig. B, Plate XXXV, we find as follows :— wall exceeded that along East wall.

At East wall	..	..	..	..	..	AE =61.00 B".
On Petrie's line of continuous measurements through the Passages and Chambers	.. }	BF =61.32 B".
At West wall	..	..	..	..	..	DH =61.50 B".

We may presume that AE, BF, and DH were all intended to be of equal distance. Structural The fact, then, that movement along the West wall exceeded movement along the original Step East wall indicates that the East wall distance, AE =61.00 B", most nearly approxi- length. mates to the original dimension. Taking, then, the length of the Step as 61.00 B" Approxima tely originally, the existing distance BF =61.32 B" would show that the wall-point F Movement on has moved, in relation to the floor, a distance of 0.32 B" towards the South. This Petrie's line would mean that the whole wall distance FK (on Plan in Fig. B, Plate XXXV, or 0.32 B". in Elevation in Fig. A, Plate XXXV) has been pushed bodily by buckling, crushing, and shearing, into the Antechamber. That such movement has taken place is clearly shown by the existing state of the partition wall between the Grand Gallery and the Antechamber. (Fig. A, Plate XXXV.)

[1]" The Elasticity and Resistance of Engineering Materials," pp. 857, 858.

¶ 211d. MOVEMENT OF WALLS CONFIRMED IN EXTENT.

Identical extent by which partition wall between Gallery and Antechamber has been sheared into the latter along Petrie's line of measures.

Now the existing length between the North *wall*-point K and the South *wall*-point M (Plate XXXV) in the Antechamber—measured along the floor surface, but not between two *structurally* defined *floor*-points—is 116.08 B″. The geometrical length for this is 116.26 P″, the diameter of the year circle of 365.242 P″ circumference. This geometrical length 116.26 P″ is equal to 116.39 B″. Comparison, then, shows as follows :—

Geometrical length of Antechamber for KM   ..   ..   =116.39 B″.
Existing wall length at floor level for KM   ..   ..   =116.08 B″.

Difference due to shearing-in of partition wall ..   ..   = 0.31 B″.
Whereas, as shown in ¶ 211c, the related movement of
the connected wall-point F, in relation to the floor
distance BF   ..   ..   = 0.32 B″.

The restorations of Step length and Antechamber length mutually confirming each other.

Step length, 61.0 B″.

Antechamber length, 116.26 P″, the diameter of the year circle.

If, therefore, we push the wall partition FK back towards the Step to this extent of 0.31 B″, we obtain BF =61.01 B″, practically the same as existing AE =61.00 B″. (Plate XXXV, Fig. B.) This confirms that the original Antechamber length is equal to the geometrical length of 116.26 P″. The complete geometry of the Antechamber and King's Chamber, as derived from Professor Petrie's measurements, is given in the Table and diagram of Plate XXXV, Fig. B, and in geometrical construction on Plate XLIII. Comparison of the measured existing distances in British inches and the geometrical distances in British inches (Plate XXX, Table A) shows that the difference in each case is inappreciable, except in the case above considered, and identified by note 2 to Table A, Plate XXX. Such slight differences as do exist are clearly due to the causes mentioned in ¶ 211a.

¶ 211e. PLATE XXXVI. ANTECHAMBER AND KING'S CHAMBER AS
           ORIGINALLY BUILT.

Plate XXXVI is a longitudinal section through the Antechamber and King's Chamber, showing the Chambers and Passages as these were originally built.

Plate XXXVI gives reference numbers for the Table in Plate XXXV, Fig. B.

The points numbered as shown, 1 to 14, form the reference numbers for Column (2) of the Table on Plate XXXV, Fig. B. The complete continuous series of measurements corresponding to these points will be given later, when the geometrical basis is extended. It was not the intention to deal, in detail, with the Antechamber and King's Chamber at this stage.

Forced passage to Chambers of Construction.

The forced passage shown in Plate XXXVI from the North end of the Grand Gallery to the lower or first Chamber of Construction above the King's Chamber is that referred to in ¶ 194, and shown in perspective (entry only) on the Frontispiece (left-hand view).

CHAPTER IV.

THE ANCIENT SCIENCE OF CHRONOLOGY: ITS ORIGIN AND PURPOSE.

Section I.—The Astronomical Ephemeris Intact, and the Literary
Fragments of its Application.

¶ 212. THE FIRST INDICATION OF A CHRONOLOGICAL
SCIENCE.

The Summary and Conclusions of Chapter III have led us to the inference *The essential datum of a scientific chronological scheme:—* that the Great Pyramid Passages contain a geometrical representation of a *Date at which longitude of* system of astronomical chronology. We saw that this should be defined in *Perihelion 0°.* terms of the general geometrical scheme of the Pyramid's exterior. The basis of representation that would completely establish the definitive intention of the representation was stated in ¶¶ 168 and 169. In this statement it was shown that the essential datum for any such representation, as well as the most scientifically appropriate date of any system of astronomical chronology, is the date at which the longitude of Perihelion is 0°—*i.e.* the Earth[1] at its Autumnal Equinox and Perihelion coincident. (Refer Section II, Plate LV.)

Presuming that we have followed the Pyramid's external indication, as *Sum of base angles of Pyramid section = 103° 42′ 28″.6 =longitude of Perihelion at 2045 A.D.* the design intended we should, we may expect the exterior of the Pyramid to supply an indication of the specified angle of the inferred intentional definition of the longitude of Perihelion (¶ 168 (1)). Now the Pyramid's right vertical section defines the Pyramid's external angular relations. The angular relations are completely expressed by the two equal base angles, each 51° 51′ 14″.3. The sum of these is 103° 42′ 28″.6. This is the longitude of Perihelion in the year 2045 A.D.

As will be shown later, when we deal with the mathematical relations *Longitude of Perihelion 0° at 4043–44 B.C.* of the data, Perihelion and the Earth at its Autumnal Equinox coincided at *Interval between two dates, 6087 to 6088 years.* 4043–44 B.C. (4042–43 B.C. astronomical).[2] It will be sufficient, meanwhile, for the general reader to know that Dr. A. C. D. Crommelin (of Greenwich

---

[1] The reader acquainted with the nomenclature of modern astronomy should carefully observe the point of view here presented and adopted.

[2] For astronomical and historical B.C. refer note, p. 38. From mid. 4042 B.C. (astronomical) to mid. 2045 A.D. is a period of exactly 6087 years=mid. 4043 B.C. (historical) to 2045 A.D.

Observatory) gives the date for this coincidence as 4040 B.C. (astronomical), stated to the nearest decade.

¼th base circuit of Pyramid = 6087.3744 P. inches.

Period of Egyptian King Lists, 6087 years, ending in 139 A.D.— the Sothic Cycle datum of Censorinus.

The interval, then, between the longitude of Perihelion 0°, at 4043–44 B.C. (historical), and the longitude of Perihelion 103° 42′ 28″.6, at 2045 A.D., is a period of 6087 to 6088 years. The latter period is numerically ⅙th of the Pyramid base circuit of 36,524. From this it seems clear that the period of 6087 to 6088 years, if here indicated intentionally, defines something more than merely the longitude of Perihelion at 2045 A.D. and at 4043–44 B.C. As to this interval of 6087 to 6088 years forming a period of the mythical chronology of the Egyptian King Lists—to complete the total of 36,524 years to 139 A.D.—the reader is referred to Plate XVI, Table F.

This dual identity justifies further investigation. The general indication seems to be that what the Pyramid's exterior supplies as an index, the Pyramid's interior should reveal in detail.

¶ 213. THE DATUM OF THE EARLIEST ZODIAC.

An original division of the Zodiac into 6 Zodiacal signs of 60° each.

The period of 6087 to 6088 years—apart from the particular identity (¶ 212) associating it with the sum of the base angles of the Pyramid's vertical section—clearly indicates the division of the year circle into 6 equal parts of 60° each. This confirms Professor Jensen's and Sir Norman Lockyer's independent conclusions that an original division of the Zodiac contained only 6 Zodiacal signs.[1] This is the number of divisions in the Zodiac evidenced by the earliest Babylonian records. Then we find that early Chinese astronomy divided the circle into 36,524 parts, and decimal subdivisions of this.[2] With the original early Zodiacal scheme of 6 signs, this gives 6087⅓ parts per sign of 60°. Half of this division, again, as explained in Section II, ¶ 303, appears as a period of 3043 to 3044 years, in connection with the mythical chronology of the Hindoo Kali-Yug. An interesting identity confirming this is suggested by the association of the " Kali-Yug "—*literally* " the *black* way "—with the Hindoo Lunar Zodiac, which is a system of *nocturnal* signs.

Chinese 36,524 divisions in circle of ecliptic, giving 6087⅓ divisions per early Zodiacal sign.

Hindoo nocturnal Zodiac of 3043 to 3044 for each of 12 signs.

This Zodiac dated with reference to a zero at 4699 B.C., representing Equinox at toe of Castor in Gemini— the last point of Taurus.

Mr. R. Brown, jun., gives the origin of the earlier representation of the Zodiac at the extreme limit of Taurus, or the commencement of the later Gemini—at the toe of Castor. (Refer Plates XLVIII and L.) His date for the Equinox at the latter point is 4698 B.C. (astronomical)=4699 B.C. (historical).[3] Brown's date is not quoted as having been accurately calculated, but to give the general reader independent evidence. In this case, Brown's date agrees with the precise calculations. Whether it was precisely calculated, or derived by the ordinary approximate method of rotating the precessional globe, therefore, does not matter.

60° of Precession—back through original Taurus— ended 317 B.C. after interval of 4381 Solar years.

From 4699 B.C. " precession " through 60° of the Zodiac brought the Equinox back from the true termination of the Zodiacal Taurus to the true

---

[1]For explanation and discussion of this, the reader is referred to Section II of this Chapter, and Plates XLVIII–LIV.
[2]" Enc. Brit.," Vol. VI, p. 317b (11th Edit.).
[3]" Primitive Constellations," Vol. I, p. 56.

first point of the Zodiacal Aries. This 60° of precession was completed in the year 317 B.C. (historical). The interval was almost precisely 4381 Solar years (accurately 4381.7 years, as shown later). This was dealt with in ¶¶ 103–104, where the dates were given to the nearest decade, as 4700 B.C. (historical) and 320 B.C. (historical).

Now, as was pointed out in ¶¶ 103–104, 4380 Sothic years =4383 vague years =3 Sothic cycles. The precise relation now indicated is that 4380 *Solar* years =4383 vague years, less ⅕th of a year. That this relation was inferred from a Pyramid relation seems to be indicated by the use made of it in the compilation of the Egyptian King Lists (Plate XVI, Table A, and ¶¶ 98, 103, and 104). The King Lists give a period of 4384 vague years, =4381 Solar years. The period as a Pyramid period is therefore associated with the early division of the Zodiac into 6 signs with reference to a pre-cessional origin at 4699 B.C. (historical).

Originates theory of 3 Sothic cycles of Egyptian King Lists. 4380 Sothic years =4383 vague years.

¶ 214. THE DATUM OF A CONTEMPORARY INDEPENDENT ZODIAC.

There was, however, an early independent division of the Zodiac into 12 signs, with reference to an origin for precession at 4000 B.C. (historical). This is clearly shown by Plates XLVIII and L to LIV, and Section II of this Chapter. The two Zodiacal systems—the system of 6 signs from 4699 B.C. (historical), and the system of 12 signs from 4000 B.C. (historical)—originated in the period of the former civilisation. When the purpose of the two independent systems was forgotten, the constellations of both systems were reduced to a composite system. Hence the unequal divisions of the 12 Zodiacal signs as they have come down to us. The relative extents of the existing signs, Taurus and Aries, as figured on Plate XLVIII—respectively about 40° and 20°—indicate that the compromise between the two systems was effected when the Equinox had receded 40° back through the 60° Taurus, about 1770 to 1800 B.C. The hindquarters of an original 60° complete bull Taurus were omitted to make way for an original 30° sign Aries, now compressed into 20°. It is to be observed that all the early representations of Taurus picture a complete bull.

An independent Zodiac of 12 signs dated with reference to a zero at 4000 B.C.

Existing extents of Zodiacal signs the result of a composite system effected about 1770 to 1800 B.C.

Now it is the chronological epoch of the system of 12 signs that forms the epoch for the chronological system of the Old Chronicle of Egypt. This, according to Plate XVI, Tables E and F jointly with ¶ 95, gave an original system of 3652, 3652½, or 3653 years, ending "15 or 16 years" (as given by Syncellus) before Alexander's coming to Egypt in 332 B.C. The two alternatives are as follow :—

The epoch of the 12 Zodiacal signs the chronological epoch of the Old Egyptian Chronicle. Its 3652-53 years from 4000 B.C. end at 348 to 347 B.C., the epoch of Okhos, according to Syncellus.

	(a)			(b)	
Alexander in Egypt ..	332 B.C.	..	..	332 B.C.	⎫ Plate XVI,
15 years before ..	15	16 years	16	⎬ Table F.
Epoch of Okhos ..	347 B.C.	..	..	348 B.C.	⎭
Old Chronicle	3653 years	..	..	3652 years as ¶ 95.
	4000 B.C.			4000 B.C. (hist.).

This is the epoch of precession for the original 12 signs of the Zodiac, as 4699 B.C. (historical) is the epoch of precession for the original independent 6 signs of the Zodiac. The epoch of Okhos is not, therefore, the date of the commencement of the reign of Okhos, but the date—in the reign of Okhos—of the termination of $3652\frac{1}{2}$ years from the secondary Zodiacal epoch at 4000 B.C.

¶ 215. THE NUMERICAL INDICATIONS OF A SCIENTIFIC CHRONOLOGY BASIS.

Indications agree with accounts of Coptic MSS. identifying the Pyramid with astronomical cycles, and in associating same with the Passage system.

Now the Egyptian King Lists first supplied us with the dimensions—angular and linear—and with the units and purpose of the Great Pyramid's exterior. They now supply us with indications pointing to a knowledge concerning precisely defined astronomical variations certainly not represented *in detail* by the geometry of the Pyramid's exterior. The obvious conclusion—already suggested by ¶¶ 164–166—is that we must extend our investigations for such data to the interior of the Pyramid. That such data were supposed by the Egyptians and Copts to be contained within the Pyramid is directly stated in the MSS. of the Akbar-Ezzeman and of Makrizi (¶¶ 111 and 112).

The latter should define the astronomical variations and longitudes with reference to the interval of 6087 years, should define in astronomical terms the initial and terminal dates of this period, and should define the zero dates of the two Zodiacal systems.

Proceeding, then, with the indications from the King Lists, as we did in the case of the Pyramid's exterior, let us examine precisely what we have obtained as indicative of the geometrical representation of the Pyramid's interior. The following indications have been suggested :—

(1) That the Pyramid should define—

   (a) Longitude of Perihelion 0° at 4043–44 B.C. (historical) ; and
   (b) Longitude of Perihelion 103° 42′ 28″.6 at 2045 A.D., in terms of the interval of 6087 to 6088 years, and in terms of the annual variations during this interval.

(2) That the Pyramid should define—

   (a) A Zodiacal epoch at 4699 B.C. (historical) ; and
   (b) A Zodiacal epoch at 4000 B.C. (historical), in terms of a defined interval in years for a defined angle of total precession, and in terms of the annual variations during this interval.

¶ 216. INDICATIONS OF CHRONOLOGICAL SCALE AND ZERO.

Autumnal Equinox 1000 B.C. the central date of two periods— A period of 6087 years, and a period of 6000 years.

From 1 (a) and (b) above, we observe that the Autumnal Equinox of 1000 B.C. is the exact centre of the period of 6087 years, beginning in Spring 4043 B.C. (historical) and ending in Spring 2045 A.D. This brings the system of 1 (a) and (b) into the scale of system 2 (b) above, and indicates that the latter, with Autumnal Equinox 4000 B.C. as zero, gives a scale of years as follows :—

	Year	0 begins Autumnal Equinox			4000 B.C.
	Year 1000	,,	,,	,,	3000 ,,
	Year 2000	,,	,,	,,	2000 ,,
Centre of Systems.	Year 3000	,,	,,	,,	1000 ,,
	Year 4000	,,	,,	,,	1 A.D.
	Year 5000	,,	,,	,,	1001 ,,
	Year 6000	,,	,,	,,	2001 ,,

Now from Autumnal Equinox 2001 A.D. to Spring 2045 A.D.—when the period of 6087 years terminates—is an interval of 43½ years. And from Autumnal Equinox 4000 B.C. (historical) back to Spring 4043 B.C. (historical)—when the period of 6087 years began—is also an interval of 43½ years.

The Autumnal Equinox of 1000 B.C. (historical) is therefore the central date of the two systems :—

(1) The system of 6087 years, defining the motion of the Equinox in relation to Perihelion ; and
(2) The scalar system of 6000 years.

The latter system, with its indicated division into periods of 1000 years, we would expect to find as the basal system for numerical reference of the other systems. In other words, the Autumnal Equinox of 4000 B.C. should be the commencement of year 0 of the chronological system of reference for all astronomical systems geometrically represented in the Pyramid's interior geometry.

¶ 217. FRAMEWORK FOR THE GEOMETRICAL DEFINITION OF ASTRONOMICAL EQUATIONS.

The chronological framework outlined by the two systems of ¶ 216 possesses a very significant property. Its general arrangement is the one arrangement that can possibly form the basis of any true geometrical representation of variations in astronomical values. The plotted values of these variations in the form of a curve can convey no *precise* geometrical significance unless they are accompanied by a geometrical expression of the equation to the curve, and of the basal constants of that equation.

The equation to a curve of regularly varying astronomical values can be geometrically expressed in one way only. This geometrical expression can be effected only *with reference to the point representing the central date* of the definite period of time selected for the consideration of the astronomical values. The Autumnal Equinoctial date of 1000 B.C. indicated by the framework of the systems of ¶¶ 215 and 216 is just such a central date to the respective periods of 6087 and 6000 years.

¶ 218. ALGEBRAIC INTERPOLATION.

All astronomical variations with respect to time are ultimately reducible to—and for practical application have to be reduced to—the general algebraic form

$$P = A + B.t + C.t^2 + D.t^3 + E.t^4 + \text{etc.},$$

where A, B, C, D, E, etc., are constants, each ($\pm$), for each particular astronomical series of values.

t is the ($\pm$) number of years from a definitely specified date, termed the Epoch, and

P is the required astronomical value at t years before ($-$), or after ($+$), the Epochal year.

In general, the terms beyond $C.t^2$ are negligible. This is particularly the case in regard to the annual value of the rate of precession, and the annual value defining the rate of separation of the Equinox and Perihelion. These are completely defined, over the longest periods of time that can apply to any extent of history, by the general formula

$$P = A + B.t + C.t^2.$$

¶ 219. GEOMETRICAL INTERPOLATION.

The ordinary algebraic or arithmetical method of interpolation for values expressed by the above formula requires values of P to be determined for five dates at equal intervals apart. For values expressed by the same formula, the geometrical method of interpolation, shown on Plate XXXVIIa (left hand), requires values of P for three dates only, at equal distances apart. As explained on Plate XXXVIIa (left hand), the equation is completely defined—

(1) By the total interval T in years ;
(2) By the value of P, $= P_3$, for the mid-date of this interval ;
(3) By a first term constant p_3 for the mid-date ;
(4) By a second term constant Q.

The geometrical construction gives the relations

$$B = \frac{2p_3}{T} \quad \text{and} \quad \frac{2Q}{T^2} = C$$

as defining the formula for the Epoch of reference at the mid-date of the interval T.

$$P = A + B.t + C.t^2$$

when

$$Q = 0 \text{ (} i.e. \text{ in Fig. A, Plate XXXVII, } p_3 = p_0 = p_6\text{)}$$
$$P = A + B.t,$$

which is the equation to a straight line.

In Plate XXXVII time is represented as proceeding from right to left, *i.e.* from point 0 towards point 6. The point 0 is therefore $\frac{T}{2}$ years before the mid-point 3, and the point 6 is $\frac{T}{2}$ years after the mid-point 3. Since the Epoch of reference for the general formula, as given, is at the date represented by the mid-point 3, time (t) measured forward from mid-point 3—*i.e.* to the left—is positive (+), and backwards from mid-point 3—*i.e.* to the right—is negative (−).

General formula, P = A+B.t+C.t². is for t positive (+), forward from mid-date of defining period T.

The special case defining the formula

$$P = A - B.t + C.t^2$$

is illustrated on Plate XXXVIIb (right hand).

All special cases of the general formula are dealt with in Section III, ¶¶ 304 to 304h, together with amplification of the data here supplied.

Special cases and fuller data.

¶ 220. THE FORMULA DEFINED FOR A CHANGE OF EPOCH.

The formulæ of ¶ 219—*in the form stated*—are applicable only for time (t) measured in relation to the mid-date as Epoch of reference. The data of the graphical representation are applicable, however, to any other Epoch, and, from the general formula already given, can be readily translated into a general formula with reference to time (t_1) measured in relation to the new Epoch.

Let the new Epoch be T_1 years ahead of the mid-date Epoch ; let t_1 represent years measured from the new Epoch ; and let the value of P for the new Epoch be P_x. (Plate XXXVIIa, left hand.)

Then, with reference to the new Epoch, we have the general formula

For Epoch X, P = Pₓ+$\frac{2m}{T}$.t₁ +$\frac{2Q}{T²}$.t₁² where m = p₃ + $\frac{2Q.T_1}{T}$.

$$P = P_x + \frac{2m}{T}.t_1 + \frac{2Q}{T^2}.t_1^2,$$

T above being the value of T in Plate XXXVII, and m being a constant to be determined from the relations of the general formula for the mid-date Epoch, as effected by the change of Epoch.

In Section III of this Chapter, ¶ 304d, it is shown that

$$m = p_3 + \frac{2Q.T_1}{T}.$$

(Refer also Plate XXXVIIa, left hand for fuller data concerning m.)

The special case defining the formula $P = P_x - \frac{2m}{T}.t_1 + \frac{2Q}{T^2}.t_1^2$, is illustrated on Plate XXXVIIb (right hand).

The special cases for the change of Epoch are fully dealt with in Section III, ¶¶ 304d–304h, together with special cases for the value of m.

Special cases for change of Epoch, and special cases for m.

GEOMETRICAL INTERPOLATION FOR CASE ALGEBRAICALLY DEFINED $P=A+Bt+Ct^2$

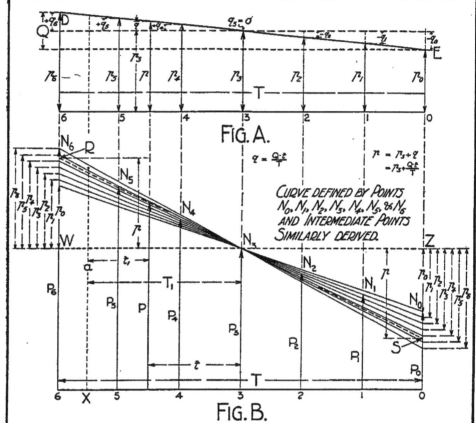

FIG. A.

$q = \dfrac{Q \cdot t}{T}$

$p = p_3 + q$
$= p_3 + \dfrac{Q t}{T}$

CURVE DEFINED BY POINTS $N_0, N_1, N_2, N_3, N_4, N_5$ & N_6 AND INTERMEDIATE POINTS SIMILARLY DERIVED.

FIG. B.

FOR EPOCH OF REFERENCE AT MID-DATE 3 :—

$P = P_3 + \dfrac{2p_3 t}{T}$ FROM FIG. A. $p = p_3 + \dfrac{Q t}{T}$

HENCE $P = P_3 + \dfrac{2p_3}{T}\cdot t + \dfrac{2Q}{T^2}\cdot t^2$ GENERAL FORMULA.

SINCE P_3, p_3 & T ARE CONSTANTS

LET $P_3 = A$, $\dfrac{2p_3}{T} = B$, & $\dfrac{2Q}{T^2} = C$

THEN $P = A + Bt + C\cdot t^2$

THE ONLY VALUES NECESSARY TO DEFINE EQUATION GEOMETRICALLY ARE,
(1.) THE INTERVAL T IN YEARS, WITH MID-DATE 3 OF INTERVAL.
(2) VALUE OF p_3 AT MID-DATE 3.
(3) VALUE OF Q FOR INTERVAL.
(4) VALUE OF P_3 AT MID-DATE 3.

THE STRAIGHT LINE R N_3 S IS FOR ANY GIVEN VALUE OF p, DEFINING THE CORRESPONDING VALUE OF P, FROM WHICH FOLLOWS THE STRAIGHT LINE EQUATION $P = P_3 + \dfrac{2p_3 \cdot t}{T}$

FOR EPOCH OF REFERENCE AT ANY DATE X AHEAD OF THE MID-DATE EPOCH :—
LET NEW EPOCH X BE T YEARS AHEAD OF MID-DATE EPOCH
$t_1 =$ YEARS FROM NEW EPOCH X.
(+ FORWARD ; − BACKWARD)
AND LET $a =$ VALUE OF P AT DATE OF NEW EPOCH X
THEN $P = a + bt_1 + c\cdot t_1^2$
$b = \dfrac{2m}{T}$
$c = \dfrac{2Q}{T}$

THE VALUE OF $m = p_3 + \dfrac{2Q\cdot T_1}{T}$

WHEN T_1 PRECEDES THE MID-DATE EPOCH :—
$m = p_3 - \dfrac{2Q\cdot T_1}{T}$

THE EQUATION MAY BE DEFINED GEOMETRICALLY AS FOLLOWS :—
(1) INTERVAL T IN YEARS WITH THE INTERVAL T_1 YEARS AHEAD
(2) VALUE OF m.   OF MID-DATE.
(3) VALUE OF Q FOR INTERVAL.
(4) VALUE OF a FOR NEW EPOCH X.

GEOMETRICAL INTERPOLATION FOR
CASE ALGEBRAICALLY DEFINED $P=A-Bt+Ct^2$

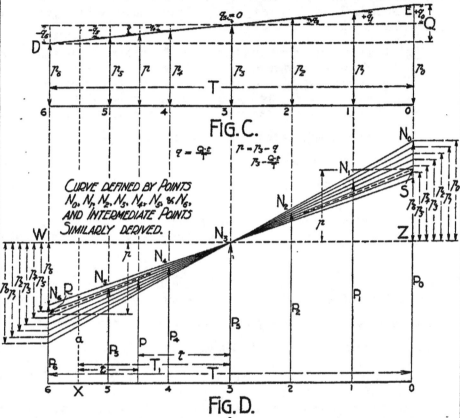

FIG. C.

CURVE DEFINED BY POINTS
$N_0, N_1, N_2, N_3, N_4, N_5$ & N_6.
AND INTERMEDIATE POINTS
SIMILARLY DERIVED.

FIG. D.

FOR EPOCH OF REFERENCE AT MID-DATE 3:-
$P = P_3 - \frac{2\pi \cdot t}{T}$ FROM FIG.C. $\pi = \pi_3 - \frac{Q \cdot t}{T}$
HENCE $P = P_3 - \frac{2\pi_3}{T} \cdot t + \frac{2Q}{T} \cdot t^2$ GENERAL FORMULA.
SINCE P_3, π_3 & T ARE CONSTANTS
LET $P_3 = A$, $\frac{2\pi_3}{T} = B$, & $\frac{2Q}{T} = C$
THEN $P = A - Bt + C \cdot t^2$.

THE ONLY VALUES NECESSARY TO DEFINE EQUATION
GEOMETRICALLY ARE,
(1.) THE INTERVAL T IN YEARS, WITH MID-DATE 3 OF INTERVAL.
(2) VALUE OF π_3 AT MID-DATE 3.
(3.) VALUE OF Q FOR INTERVAL.
(4.) VALUE OF P_3 AT MID-DATE 3.

THE STRAIGHT LINE $R N_3 S$ IS FOR ANY GIVEN
VALUE OF π, DEFINING THE CORRESPONDING VALUE
OF P, FROM WHICH FOLLOWS THE STRAIGHT
LINE EQUATION $P = P_3 - \frac{2\pi \cdot t}{T}$

FOR EPOCH OF REFERENCE AT ANY DATE X AHEAD
OF THE MID-DATE EPOCH:—
LET NEW EPOCH X BE T_1 YEARS AHEAD OF MID-DATE EPOCH.
t_1 YEARS FROM NEW EPOCH X
(+FORWARD; −BACKWARD)
AND LET a = VALUE OF P AT DATE OF NEW EPOCH X
THEN $P = a - b t_1 + c t_1^2$
$b = \frac{2m}{T}$
$c = \frac{2Q}{T}$
THE VALUE OF $m = \pi_3 - \frac{2Q \cdot T_1}{T}$
WHEN T_1 PRECEDES THE MID-DATE EPOCH:—
$m = \pi_3 + \frac{2Q \cdot T_1}{T}$

THE EQUATION MAY BE DEFINED GEOMETRICALLY AS FOLLOWS:—
(1.) INTERVAL T IN YEARS WITH THE INTERVAL T_1 YEARS AHEAD
(2) VALUE OF m. OF MID-DATE.
(3.) VALUE OF Q FOR INTERVAL.
(4.) VALUE OF a FOR NEW EPOCH X.

¶ 221. GEOMETRICAL DEFINITION OF FORMULA FOR THE NEW EPOCH.

For a geometrical representation such as Plate XXXVII, but represented with reference to an Epoch that is not the mid-date of the representation, the general formula, $P = a + b.t_1 + c.t_1^2$, is completely defined with respect to its Epoch X if the following data are given :—

(1) The geometrical representation of the Epoch X as T_1 years from the mid-date of the defined interval T years.

(2) The geometrical representation of the value of P_x in connection with the point defining the Epoch X, this giving the value of $a = P_x$.

(3) The geometrical representation of the value of m in connection with the point defining the Epoch X, this giving $b = \dfrac{2m}{T}$.

(4) The geometrical representation of the value of Q in connection with the point defining the Epoch X, this giving $c = \dfrac{2Q}{T^2}$.

It is important to observe that the geometrical representation of these values should give P_x, m, and Q as co-ordinates at the point geometrically defining the Epoch.

For the representation to prove its intention, and to supply data easily capable of being converted into algebraic form, its scalar system should be given in terms of round hundreds or thousands of years. In other words, the interval T years—as also $\dfrac{T}{2}$ years—should be in round thousands of years, to cover a sufficiently long period defining variations in annual astronomical values. The inferred Pyramid scalar system of chronology—in which the interval T is 6000 years, and in which, as the evidence indicates, the mid-date is clearly defined (¶¶ 215 and 216)—is just such a framework as is necessary to define the associated astronomical relations of ¶¶ 212–216 in terms of the system of geometrical interpolation of Plate XXXVII.

¶ 222. THE VARIATIONS OF THE PRECESSIONAL RATE.

Now it so happens that the diagrams of Plate XXXVIIa (left hand), as defined, graphically represent—

(a) precisely the conditions of Precession, for

P = the annual value of the rate of Precession expressed in seconds of angle ;

and Plate XXXVIIb (right hand)—

(b) the exact conditions of Precession, for

P = the annual value of the rate of Precession expressed as years per 360°.

This is obvious from the following :—

$$\text{Rate in P years per } 360° = \frac{360°}{\text{Annual rate of Precession in angle}}.$$

Annual rate of Precession expressed as years per revolution of ecliptic = $a - b.t_1 + c.t_1{}^2$.

As the annual angular rate increases the annual rate in years per 360° diminishes. Hence for (a)

$$\text{Annual angular rate of Precession} = a + b.t_1 + c.t_1{}^2 ;$$

but for (b)

$$\text{Annual rate of Precession in P years per } 360° = a - b.t_1 + c.t_1{}^2.$$

It will assist the reader to follow the Pyramid's elucidation of this matter if we give some explanation of the basal data and formula universally adopted by modern astronomers in dealing with Precessional values.

¶ 223. NEWCOMB'S DATA FOR PRECESSION.

In the middle of the 19th century the Precessional value adopted by astronomers was Bessel's value—50″.2346 +0″.000244t forward from 1850 A.D. Leverrier gave the value for 1850 as 50″.2357 for the Julian year, and Oppolzer as 50″.2346 for the tropical year.

The older data of Bessel, Leverrier, and Oppolzer.

During the second half of the 19th century the Struve-Peters' value— 50″.2522 +0″.000227t forward from 1850 A.D.—gradually superseded the earlier accepted values. In 1897, however, Professor Simon Newcomb published the results of his researches in "Astronomical Papers of the American Ephemeris" (Vol. VIII). Since that date his value and formula have been universally adopted by astronomers.

The late 19th century Struve-Peters' data. Superseded by Newcomb's data.

Newcomb's calculations cover the period from 1600 A.D. to 2100 A.D. His values for years at intervals ten years apart, from 1600 A.D. to 2100 A.D., tabulated in Bauschinger's "Tafeln zur Theoretischen Astronomie," Taf. XXX, give the formula 50″.2453 +0″.0002222t from 1850 A.D., the central date of his calculations.

Outline of Newcomb's data. Period covered by calculations 500 years from 1600 A.D. to 2100 A.D.

This formula is derived from the following :—

Date A.D.	Value, Secs. of Angle.	Difference in 250 years.	
1600	50.1897		
		+0.0556	Average difference in 250 years =0.05555 or 0.0002222 per year.
1850	50.2453		
		+0.0555	
2100	50.3008		

Examination of the complete table in Bauschinger's work shows that the slight inequality in the two differences is due to the values being stated only to the 4th decimal place. For the same reason, the value in "The Nautical Almanac"—50″.2453 +0″.0002225t from 1850 A.D.—has been interpolated from Newcomb's values from 1750 to 1950 A.D.

Bauschinger, again, in his " Bahnbestimmung der Himmelskörper," p. 79, gives the formula $50''.2453 + 0''.0002218t$, which cannot be precisely obtained from the data in his " Tafeln," within any selected limits.

¶ 224. NEWCOMB'S FORMULA FOR PRECESSION.

Newcomb's formula in angular rate per year.
In annual rate expressed as period of revolution.
A = 25,793.46.
B = −0.114.
And, within range of calculations (500 years), C negligible.

In the present work we have adopted Newcomb's formula as derived from the complete range of his data, and to apply equally to his data both before and after 1850 A.D.

This gives

Annual rate of Precession $= 50''.2453 + 0''.0002222t$.

Converting this into the rate expressed as the number of years to complete a revolution (360°), we obtain

$P = 25,793.46 - 0.114t$ with t positive (+) forward from 1850 A.D.

Extreme accuracy of Newcomb's formula.

The formula strictly applies only to the period 1600 A.D. to 2100 A.D. covering the range of Newcomb's calculations. It gives, however, extremely accurate results for many thousands of years before and after this period, as the reader will see. This indicates that the constant C in the formula $P = A + B.t + C.t^2$—negligible within the range of Newcomb's calculations—must be an extremely small quantity.

In Newcomb's formula (Epoch 1850 A.D.)

$A = 25,793.46$; $B = −0.114$; and $C = 0$.

¶ 225. PYRAMID'S GEOMETRICAL CONNECTION BETWEEN EXTERIOR AND INTERIOR.

Pyramid's period of reference for 90° of Precession
$= \dfrac{25,826.54}{4}$
years.

Now the measure of 25,826.54 P″—supplied by the sum of the Pyramid's base diagonals and by the precessional circuit—is indicated as the measure of the Pyramid's standard period of reference for variations in the rate of Precession (¶ 166). One quarter of this period (or 6456.635 years) is, therefore, the Pyramid's standard period of reference for 90° of Precession.

The importance of the Pyramid's external relations.
2861.022 P″ and 286.1022 P″.

In Case I, Fig. A, Plate XXIII, the value of 2861.02215624 P″ was obtained as an important relation in the geometrical scheme of the Pyramid's right vertical section. We now see that this value, and its $\frac{1}{10}$th subdivision (Fig. B, Plate XXVII), form the key to the relationship between the Pyramid's external and internal geometrical systems. For

Sine of Passage angle
$= \dfrac{4 \times 2861.022}{25,826.54}$.

(a) A triangle of vertical 2861.02215624 P″ and hypotenuse 6456.6355945 P″ (Plate XXXVIII, Fig. A) defines the angle of slope of the Pyramid's Passages with the horizontal as 26° 18′ 9″.63. (¶¶ 176–179.)

286.1022 P″ = Displacement of Passage System.

(b) A horizontal distance of 286.1022156 P″ Eastwards from the North to South central vertical Plane of the Pyramid defines the North to South central vertical plane of the Passage system. (¶ 148 and Plate XXIV.)

(c) A vertical distance of 286.1022156 P″ above the roof line (and that line produced) of the 1st Ascending Passage defines the roof line (and that line produced) of the Grand Gallery. Since the known vertical height of the 1st Ascending Passage is 52.78 P″ (Plate XXX, confirmed later by geometrical considerations), the vertical height of the Grand Gallery is 338.88 P″ =339.25 B″; Professor Smyth's average of 15 measured heights being 339.2 B″.

The external measures of 25,826.54, 2861.022, and 286.1022 P″, therefore, form the connecting data between the external and internal geometrical systems, and define the angle of slope of the Passages with the horizontal.

¶ 226. THE CONNECTION CONFIRMED BY INDEPENDENT DATA.

The connection between the Pyramid's external geometry and its internal geometry and the definition of the angle of slope of the Passages are independently defined by the following :—

(1) With the Pyramid's height (5813.014373 P″) as hypotenuse and half the side of the square of area equal to the Pyramid's vertical section (½ of 5151.6498562 P″ =2575.8249281 P″) as vertical, the resulting angle of slope is 26° 18′ 9″.63—the Passage angle of slope with the horizontal. (Plate XXXVIII, Fig. B.)

(2) In ¶¶ 94–97, it was shown that the Pyramid's base side=443.1134627 common Egyptian cubits=365.242465 Sacred Cubits of 25 P″. With 443.1134627 P″ as vertical and 1000 P″ as hypotenuse, the resulting angle of slope is 26° 18′ 9″.63—the Passage angle of slope with the horizontal. (Plate XXXVIII, Fig. C.)

Now relation (a) of ¶ 225 clearly indicates that precession is represented to the scale of 1 P″=1 solar year, along the angle of slope of the Passages. Relation (2) above now indicates further that the chronological scale is geometrically defined as divided into scalar units of 1000 P″ representing 1000 solar years.

The vertical intervals of this scale are 443.1134627 P″, 443 being the basal number of the Old Egyptian Chronicle chronology.

¶ 227. THE CONNECTION DEFINED IN THE OLD CHRONICLE OF EGYPT.

The zero date of the Old Chronicle system of chronology is given as 4000 B.C. (¶¶ 214–216 and Plate XVI—comparison of data of Tables F and E with data of ¶¶ 94–97). From this as zero date, 3×443 years, or 1329 years, are given as preceding the beginning of the Dynasties of Egypt (¶ 95). With the above significance attaching to 443.1134627 P″ as a vertical distance, we see the origin of the 1329 initial " years " of the Old Chronicle system.

PLATE XXXVIII.

GEOMETRY OF PASSAGE SLOPES.

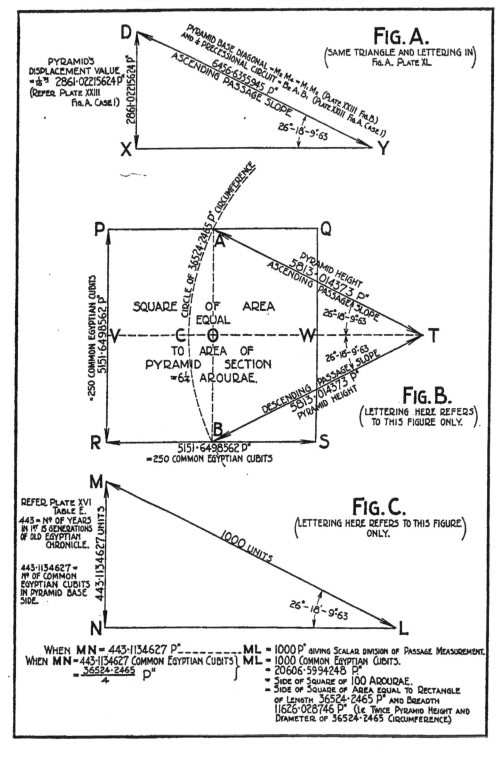

FIG. A.
(SAME TRIANGLE AND LETTERING IN Fig. A. PLATE XL)

PYRAMID'S DISPLACEMENT VALUE = $\frac{1}{18}$th 2861·02215624 P" (REFER PLATE XXIII Fig. A. CASE I)

PYRAMID BASE DIAGONAL = M₂ M₄ = M₁ M₆ (PLATE XXIII Fig. B) AND ¼ PRECESSIONAL CIRCUIT = B₂ A₁ B₁ (PLATE XXIII Fig. A. CASE I) 6456·6355945 D"

ASCENDING PASSAGE SLOPE

2861·02215624 P"

26°–18'–9"·63

FIG. B.
(LETTERING HERE REFERS TO THIS FIGURE ONLY.)

CIRCLE OF 36524·2465 D" CIRCUMFERENCE

=250 COMMON EGYPTIAN CUBITS 5151·6498562 P"

SQUARE OF AREA EQUAL TO AREA OF PYRAMID SECTION =6¼ AROURAE.

PYRAMID HEIGHT 5813·014373 P"
ASCENDING PASSAGE SLOPE
26°–18'–9"·63

26°–18'–9"·63
DESCENDING PASSAGE SLOPE 5813·014373 P" PYRAMID HEIGHT

5151·6498562 D" =250 COMMON EGYPTIAN CUBITS

FIG. C.
(LETTERING HERE REFERS TO THIS FIGURE ONLY.)

REFER PLATE XVI TABLE E.
443 = N° OF YEARS IN 1ˢᵗ 15 GENERATIONS OF OLD EGYPTIAN CHRONICLE.

443·1134627 = N° OF COMMON EGYPTIAN CUBITS IN PYRAMID BASE SIDE.

443·1134627 UNITS

1000 UNITS

26°–18'–9"·63

WHEN MN = 443·1134627 P" ————— ML = 1000 P" GIVING SCALAR DIVISION OF PASSAGE MEASUREMENT.
WHEN MN = 443·1134627 COMMON EGYPTIAN CUBITS) ML = 1000 COMMON EGYPTIAN CUBITS.
= $\frac{36524·2465}{4}$ P"
= 20606·5994248 P"
= SIDE OF SQUARE OF 100 AROURAE.
= SIDE OF SQUARE OF AREA EQUAL TO RECTANGLE OF LENGTH 36524·2465 P" AND BREADTH 11626·028746 P" (i.e. TWICE PYRAMID HEIGHT AND DIAMETER OF 36524·2465 CIRCUMFERENCE)

SECTION OF THE PASSAGES OF THE GREAT PYRAMID.

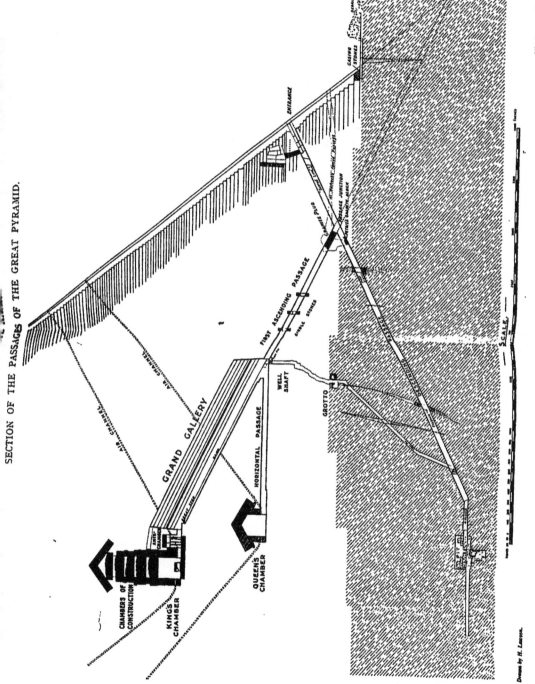

Drawn by H. Lange.

[To face p. 198.]

The alleged period was clearly derived from a vertical Pyramid distance of 1329.3403881 P″ defining a Passage sloping distance of 3000 P″ that represents an initial period of 3000 solar years from 4000 B.C.

The initial period, thus defined and dated, gives us the half interval of T in our astronomical formula (Plate XXXVII) and supplies us with the mid-date—a pivoting date for the tilting line of Plate XXXVII—1000 B.C., necessary for the geometrical representation of the essential data defining the formula. *This all shows that the Pyramid's interior system of geometry gives the mid-date of its scalar period of* 6000 *years as fixed by a well-defined structural bisection.*

¶ 228. THE SCALAR AXIS OF THE PASSAGE SYSTEM.

The Pyramid's chronology line is therefore identified as a line at the angle of slope of the Passages.   Relation (a) of ¶ 225 shows that this line is defined by the floor line or roof line of the 1st Ascending Passage, and those lines produced, or with a line parallel to and between those lines.   The floor and roof lines thus produced meet the line of the North face slope of the Pyramid produced, as shown on Plate XXXIX.   This, obviously, is an essential geometrical construction.

Relation (a) of ¶ 225, however, also shows that an essential geometrical definition of a chronological datum is associated with the Precessional circuit level, and with the central point of that level, point D in Fig. A, Plate XL. The latter point is necessarily the point of origin for the geometrical construction of the relation (a) of ¶ 225, illustrated in Fig. A, Plate XXXVIII, since it is then the point common to the two geometrical definitions of the ¼-period of reference for the cycle of Precession.

Fig. A, Plate XL, illustrates the geometrical construction resulting from the latter identification.   The line DY at the Ascending Passage angle of slope, and with D on the central vertical axis of the Pyramid and at the level (DE) of the Precessional circuit, intersects the line EBF of the North geometrical casing slope produced at the point F.   The line DF thus defined is of the length of 5886.3105287 P″, as determined from the geometrical relations of its construction.   This line DF, for the lack of a better term, we may define as " the Scalar Axis of the Passage System."   This " Scalar Axis," as will be shown, constitutes the principal axis of construction for the geometry of the Passage System and for defining its scalar and astronomical systems of chronology.

¶ 229. THE RESULTING GEOMETRICAL SYSTEM OF ASTRONOMICAL CHRONOLOGY.

The various progressive geometrical constructions, following in sequence from the data considered above, are as shown on Plates XL, XLI, XLII, and

Geometrical
construction
of Great
Pyramid's
Passage
System defines
(1) Scalar
chronology
system of
6000 years
and its mid-
date, and
astronomical
period of the
King Lists,
6087 to 6088
years, and its
mid-date
coincident
with mid-date
of scalar
system; and

XLIII.[1] From these it will be seen that two outstanding results accrue, as follow :—

(1) That the geometry of the Pyramid's Passage System defines—

(a) A scalar system of 6000 P″ with its initial, central, and terminal points all intentionally defined by outstanding structural features of the Pyramid; this scalar system being obviously the representation from which was derived the scalar system of the astronomical chronology of the Egyptian King Lists (¶¶ 212, 215–217, and 227).

(b) A system of 6087.94 P″ with its principal points similarly defined, and with its centre at the centre of the scalar system; this obviously being the representation of an astronomical system of 6087.94 Solar years, adopted as the astronomical basis of the chronology of the Egyptian King Lists (¶¶ 214–217).

(2) Passage
Entrance
level, Passage
height, and
sloping
Passage
lengths
identical with
Petrie's.

(2) That the resulting level of the existing Doorway, the perpendicular heights of the sloping Passages, and the floor lengths of the Entrance and Ascending Passages as given by the geometrical system are all exactly of the respective values measured by Professor Petrie (Plate XLI, Figs. G, H, K, and L).

Extent of
agreement
reached, and
extent remain-
ng to be
proved.
Pyramid's
chronology
must define
its own
connection
with modern
astronomical
time.

The former of these two groups of results confirms the induction of ¶ 166 concerning the chronological purpose of the Pyramid. The latter group of results satisfies the metrological and geometrical conditions postulated in ¶ 170. What we have now to consider is the extent to which the Pyramid's chronology satisfies the astronomical conditions of ¶¶ 167–169. In other words, we have yet to show that the Pyramid's chronology defines its years in definite astronomical terms in relation to current time. It is essential that the Pyramid should do so *independently of evidence from any external source other than the science of gravitational astronomy.*

¶ 230. THE PYRAMID'S GEOMETRICAL FRAMEWORK FOR ASTRONOMICAL FORMULÆ.

To effect the latter requirements it is necessary to examine the geometrical data of the Passage chronology system in the light of the astronomical relations of Plate XXXVII, and of ¶¶ 217–224. In doing so we shall find that the purpose of the Passage chronology proclaims itself.

The sloping
Passage lines,
and lines
produced,
define the
geometrical
framework.

The geometrical framework for the astronomical equations of Plate XXXVII and ¶¶ 213–222 is very clearly defined, both by the Descending Passage, and that Passage produced, and by the Ascending Passages, and

[1]These Plates will be found, when studied in related sequence, to supply in themselves their own explanation of the various geometrical processes, and of the relation of each successive Plate to that preceding. For this reason, the constructions are not described in detail in the text at this stage. If, however, the reader meets with any difficulty in following the geometrical sequence of the Plates, reference should be made to Section III of this Chapter, ¶¶ 307–310a.

those Passages produced. A vertical line drawn from the former to the latter gives a point in both Passages, or in their produced alignments, representing the same date. This is the universal method of co-ordinate construction and symbolism.

Adopting the term *Anno Pyr.* (A.P.) as signifying years of the Pyramid chronology system, the geometrical framework for the astronomical formula of interpolation is defined by the following description (Plate XL, Figs. C and F) :— Term adopted
for years of
Pyramid
chronology.
A.P.

0 A.P. (Plate XL, Fig. C).—Point H on the floor line produced of the Ascending Passage, MHU. This point H is defined by the intersection of the floor line produced, MHU, with the perpendicular, KH. This perpendicular, KH, falls from the point of intersection of the line produced of the North geometrical face slope of the Pyramid (line EBU), and the line produced of the roof of the 1st Ascending Passage (line W_1K). 0 A.P. defined
by intersection
of Pyramid
face line
and line of
Ascending
Passage.

This point, H, we may term "lower 0 A.P.," to distinguish it from the "upper 0 A.P." on the floor line produced of the Entrance Passage. The latter point is defined by the vertical from the lower 0 A.P. (Fig. F).

0 A.P. is the zero date of the geometrical framework for the astronomical formula.

3000 A.P.—Defined by the point of intersection of the roof line of the Descending Passage and the Pyramid's base. The vertical line passing through this point of intersection gives 3000 A.P. on the floor lines of the Descending and Ascending Passages (Plate XL, Fig. F). 3000 A.P.
defined by
intersection
of Pyramid
base and roof
line of
Descending
Passage.

3000 A.P. is the mid-date of the geometrical framework for the astronomical formula.

6000 A.P.—The point defining this date is horizontally 141.3369423 P″ South of the Pyramid's central vertical axis (Plate XL, Fig. F). This distance marks the precise central point of the Granite Leaf in the Antechamber.[1] The point defining 6000 A.P. is therefore the point V, in Plate LXVa, on the line AV, representing the floor line of the Grand Gallery continued beyond the Great Step. 6000 A.P.
defined by
intersection of
Grand Gallery
floor line
and vertical
from centre
of Granite
Leaf.

Other scalar points—2000, 2500, 5000 A.P.—are equally well defined. (Refer Plate XL, Fig. F.)   The above statement, however, is given as the essential basis for the astronomical formula.

¶ 231. THE PYRAMID'S EPOCH OF REFERENCE FOR ASTRONOMICAL VALUES.

The Pyramid's Epoch of reference (¶ 219) for the geometrical representation of astronomical values is clearly defined by the intersection of the three principal axes of geometrical construction for the Passage System and its graphical chronology.   These three principal axes are— The meeting-
place of three
principal
geometrical
axes defines
the Pyramid
Epoch of
reference.

(1) The central vertical axes of the Pyramid ;
(2) The horizontal line of the Precessional circuit (¶ 225) ; and
(3) The " Scalar Axis " of the Passage System (¶ 228).

The geometrically indicated Pyramid date for this meeting-place of the axes is 5842.3397932 A.P. (Plate XL, Figs. C and F). This is the Pyramid dating—indicated by the floor-line distance from 0 A.P.—of the Great Step, The Pyramid
dating for the
Great Step.

---

[1]For the structural relations between the Granite Leaf and the Granite Wainscots of the Antechamber, the reader is referred to Plates LVII and LVIII.

THE GEOMETRY OF THE GREAT PYRAMID'S PASSAGE SYSTEM.

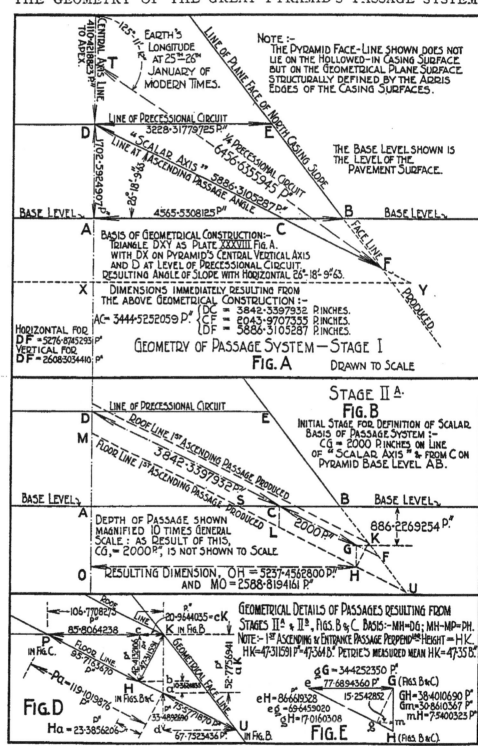

THE GEOMETRY OF THE GREAT PYRAMID'S PASSAGE SYSTEM.

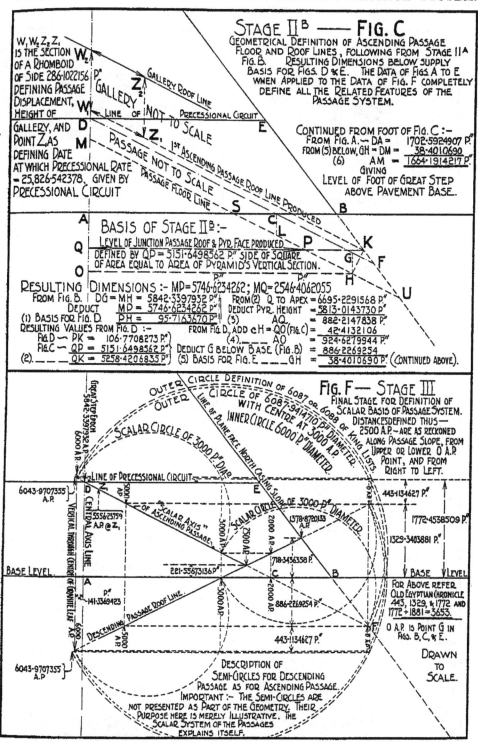

NOTE.—A.P. denotes *Anno Pyr.* in Fig. F and in following plates; o A.P. being the zero date of the Pyramid's scalar system of astronomical chronology. Hence the clear definition of o A.P., 2000 A.P., 3000 A.P., 5000 A.P., and 6000 A.P.

GEOMETRICAL DETAILS OF THE GREAT PYRAMID'S PASSAGE SYSTEM.

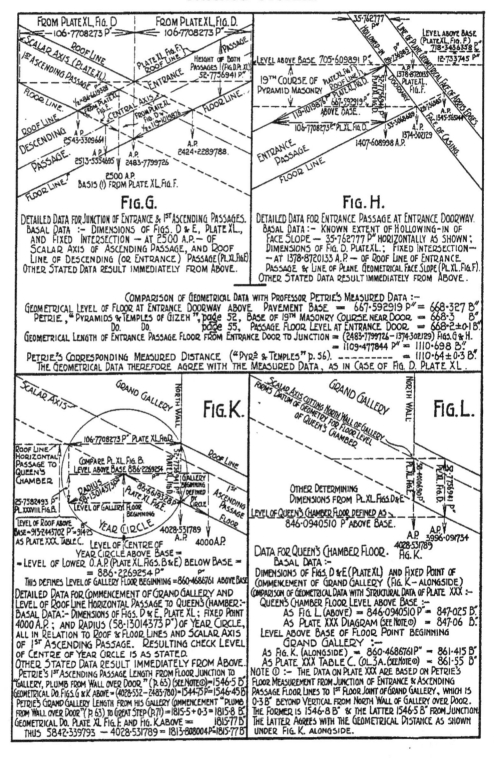

GEOMETRICAL DETAILS OF THE GREAT PYRAMID'S PASSAGE SYSTEM.

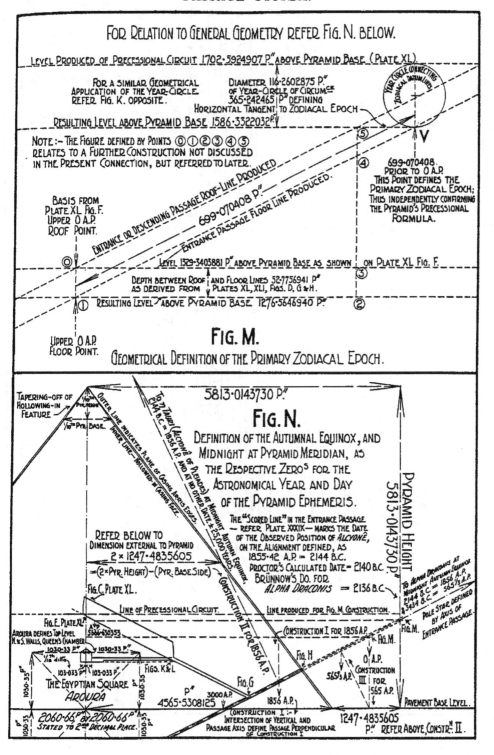

FOR RELATION TO GENERAL GEOMETRY REFER FIG. N. BELOW.

LEVEL PRODUCED OF PRECESSIONAL CIRCUIT 1702·5924907 P." ABOVE PYRAMID BASE. (PLATE XL)

FOR A SIMILAR GEOMETRICAL APPLICATION OF THE YEAR-CIRCLE REFER FIG. K. OPPOSITE.

DIAMETER 116·2602875 P." OF YEAR-CIRCLE OF CIRCUM.ce 365·242465 P." DEFINING HORIZONTAL TANGENT TO ZODIACAL EPOCH

RESULTING LEVEL ABOVE PYRAMID BASE 1586·3322032 P."

NOTE:— THE FIGURE DEFINED BY POINTS ⓪①②③④⑤ RELATES TO A FURTHER CONSTRUCTION NOT DISCUSSED IN THE PRESENT CONNECTION, BUT REFERRED TO LATER.

699·070408 PRIOR TO O A.P. THIS POINT DEFINES THE PRIMARY ZODIACAL EPOCH; THUS INDEPENDENTLY CONFIRMING THE PYRAMID'S PRECESSIONAL FORMULA.

BASIS FROM PLATE XL FIG. F. UPPER O A.P. ROOF POINT.

ENTRANCE OR DESCENDING PASSAGE ROOF-LINE PRODUCED

699·070408 P."

ENTRANCE PASSAGE FLOOR LINE PRODUCED

LEVEL 1329·3403881 P." ABOVE PYRAMID BASE AS SHOWN ON PLATE XL FIG. F.

DEPTH BETWEEN ROOF AND FLOOR LINES 52·7756941 P." AS DERIVED FROM PLATES XL, XLI, FIGS. D, G & H.

RESULTING LEVEL ABOVE PYRAMID BASE 1276·5646940 P."

UPPER O A.P. FLOOR POINT.

FIG. M.

GEOMETRICAL DEFINITION OF THE PRIMARY ZODIACAL EPOCH.

TAPERING-OFF OF HOLLOWING-IN FEATURE

OUTER LINE INDICATES PLANE OF CASING ARRIS EDGES

INNER LINE— HOLLOWING-IN CASING FACE

TO η TAURI (ALCYONÉ OF PLEIADES) AT MIDNIGHT AUTUMN EQUINOX 2144 B.C. = 1856 A.P. AND AT NO OTHER DATE ± 25,000 YEARS.

5813·0143730 P."

FIG. N.

DEFINITION OF THE AUTUMNAL EQUINOX, AND MIDNIGHT AT PYRAMID MERIDIAN, AS THE RESPECTIVE ZEROS FOR THE ASTRONOMICAL YEAR AND DAY OF THE PYRAMID EPHEMERIS.

REFER BELOW TO DIMENSION EXTERNAL TO PYRAMID 2 × 1247·4835605
=(2×PYR. HEIGHT)−(PYR. BASE-SIDE)

FIG. C. PLATE XL.

THE "SCORED LINE" IN THE ENTRANCE PASSAGE — REFER PLATE XXXIX — MARKS THE DATE OF THE OBSERVED POSITION OF ALCYONÉ, ON THE ALIGNMENT DEFINED, AS 1855·42 A.P. = 2144 B.C. PROCTOR'S CALCULATED DATE= 2140 B.C. BRÜNNOW'S DO. FOR ALPHA DRACONIS = 2136 B.C.

PYRAMID HEIGHT 5813·0143730 P."

TO ALPHA DRACONIS AT MIDNIGHT AUTUMN EQUINOX A.P. 2144 B.C. = 1856 A.P. 3434 B.C. = 565⅓ A.P.

POLE STAR DEFINED BY AXIS OF ENTRANCE PASSAGE

LINE OF PRECESSIONAL CIRCUIT.

LINE PRODUCED FOR FIG. M. CONSTRUCTION.

FIG. E. PLATE XL.
AROURA DEFINES TOP LEVEL N. & S. WALLS, QUEEN'S CHAMBER.

5066·650353

1030·33 P."

1030·33 P."

103·033 P."

103·033 P."

CONSTRUCTION I FOR 1856 A.P.

CONSTRUCTION II FOR 1856 A.P.

CONSTRUCTION I FOR 1856 A.P.

FIG. M.

FIG. H

FIGS. K & L

FIG. G

O A.P. CONSTRUCTION III FOR 565 A.P.

565⅓ A.P.

THE EGYPTIAN SQUARE OR AROURA

P." 4565·5308125

3000 A.P.

1856 A.P.

PAVEMENT BASE LEVEL.

2060·66 P." BY 2060·66 P." STATED TO 2ND DECIMAL PLACE.

CONSTRUCTION I :— INTERSECTION OF VERTICAL AND PASSAGE AXIS DEFINE PASSAGE PERPENDICULAR OF CONSTRUCTION I

1247·4835605 P." REFER ABOVE, CONSTRN. II.

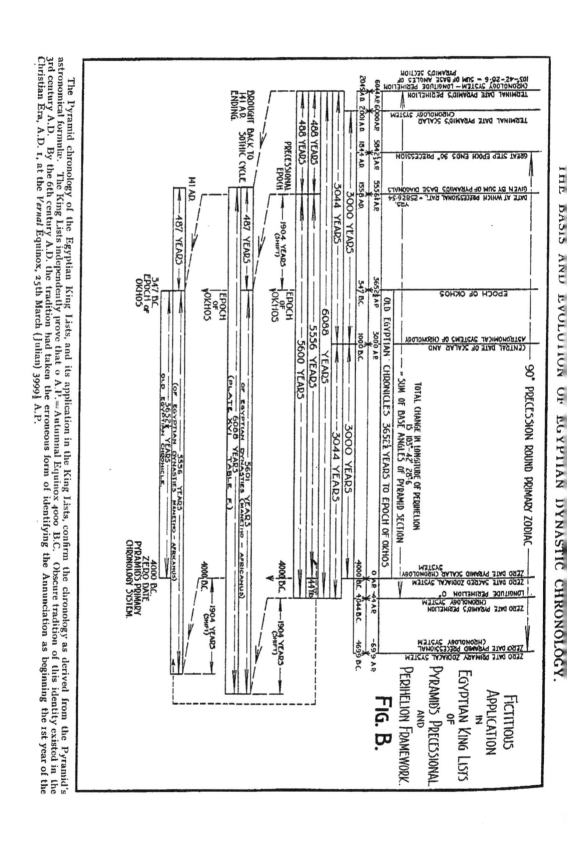

FICTITIOUS APPLICATION IN EGYPTIAN KING LISTS OF PYRAMID'S PRECESSIONAL AND PERIHELION FRAMEWORK.

FIG. B.

The Pyramid chronology of the Egyptian King Lists, and its application in the King Lists, confirm the chronology as derived from the Pyramid's astronomical formulæ. The King Lists independently prove that o A.P.=Autumnal Equinox 4000 B.C. Obscure tradition of this identity existed in the 3rd century A.D. By the 6th century A.D. the tradition had taken the erroneous form of identifying the Annunciation as beginning the 1st year of the Christian Era, A.D. 1, at the *Vernal* Equinox, 25th March (Julian) 3999½ A.P.

THE GREAT PYRAMID'S ASTRONOMICAL CHRONOGRAPH AND GEOMETRICAL EPHEMERIS.

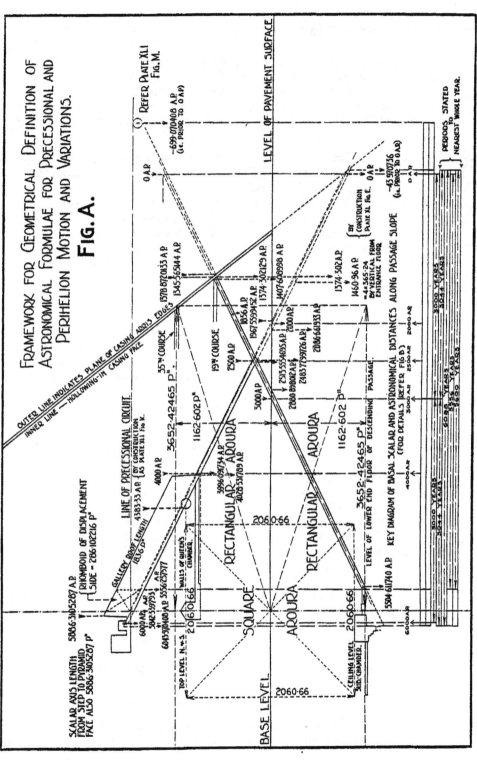

FRAMEWORK FOR GEOMETRICAL DEFINITION OF ASTRONOMICAL FORMULAE FOR PRECESSIONAL AND PERIHELION MOTION AND VARIATIONS.

FIG. A.

As defined and confirmed by the Pyramid's various and independent astronomical formulæ and their integrated angular values : (1) o A.P. = Autumnal Equinox 4000 B.C. ; (2) 3000 A.P. = Autumnal Equinox 1000 B.C. ; and (3) 6000 A.P. = Autumnal Equinox 2001 A.D.

NOTE.—A.P. denotes *Anno Pyr.*

Primarily
associated
with
Precession.
Symbolism
indicates
Great Step
dating.

which terminates the actual structural definition of the sloping floor of the 1st Ascending Passage and Grand Gallery. The Great Step is therefore indicated as marking the Pyramid's date for its Epoch of reference. The close geometrical association with the Precessional circuit of reference and with the $\frac{1}{4}$-period of the cycle of reference—25826.54 years—indicated by this circuit clearly points—

(a) As com-
pletion of 90°
Precession from
a Zodiacal
Epoch.

(a) To the Great Step dating marking the specific termination of a period of years defining $\frac{1}{4}$-Precession (i.e. 90° of Precession) from an ancient Zodiacal Epoch ;

(b) As Epoch
of reference
for Precession
and annual
rates of
Precession.

(b) To the Great Step dating being an Epoch of reference primarily for the cycle of Precession and for the representation of the variable annual rate of Precession with reference to this dating and with reference to the Pyramid value of 25826.54 ; and

(c) As asso-
ciated with
year in which
annual Preces-
sional rate =
25,826.54.

(c) To the Great Step dating being associated, in a manner to be defined by its geometrical connections, with the year in which the annual rate of Precession equalled the Pyramid value of 25,826.54.

¶ 232. THE FORMULA FOR THE GREAT STEP EPOCH.

Above
indications
should be
given at
Great Step.
Each indica-
tion should
confirm the
other inde-
pendently.
Great Step
dating to be
defined.
Precessional
formula to
be defined for
Great Step
Epoch.
Chronological
base line
on line of
Passage slope.
Co-ordinates
defining
formula should
be given as
verticals at
Great Step.

The geometrical connections of the Great Step should therefore supply the data for the indications, a, b, and c, of ¶ 231. These should be given in such manner that the data for each indication are independent of and yet precisely confirmatory of the other indications. These conditions, we shall find, are entirely and accurately fulfilled.

The Great Step dating, so far, has not been defined in terms of modern astronomical chronology by the Pyramid geometry. The first essential for this is to find the geometrical definition of the constants for the formula supplying the annual variation in the Precessional rate with reference to the Epoch of the Great Step dating. As the chronological base line for this definition of the constants lies along the Passage slope, the co-ordinates for the constants may be indicated either as perpendiculars to this slope or as verticals from the slope. The verticality of the Great Step is clearly indicative of the latter. We have, therefore, to consider the various vertical co-ordinates at the Great Step. This procedure is directed by the principles derived for the formula for an Epoch other than the mid-date Epoch of the geometrical framework (¶¶ 220 and 221).

¶ 233. THE CO-ORDINATES FOR THE GREAT STEP.

The three
principal
structural
co-ordinates
at Great Step—
(1) Step
height ;
(2) Vertical
height of
Grand Gallery ;

The principal structural co-ordinates indicated at the Great Step are—

(1) The Step height ; and

(2) The vertical height of the Grand Gallery from the foot of the step.

To these we must add a third small vertical co-ordinate. This is the difference between the top of the Step and the level of the Pyramid's Preces-

PLATE XLIII.

THE GEOMETRY OF THE ANTECHAMBER AND KING'S CHAMBER.

EAST WALL OF KING'S CHAMBER

GRANITE FLOOR

365·242

FORCED PASSAGE
TUNNELLED FROM GALLERY TO CHAMBERS OF CONSTRUCTION

58·13   CEILING   58·13

(QUADRANT ARC DEVELOPMENT)

91·31

58·15

EAST WALL OF ANTECHAMBER

36·524

58·15   GRANITE WAINSCOT   58·15

TOP OF 103·033

58·15

91·31

105·033

(QUADRANT ARC DEVELOPMENT)

58·15·033

103·033

SQUARE CIRCUIT EQUAL TO CIRCUMFERENCE OF CIRCLE 565·242

91·31

INDEX SQUARE
Square Side ⅟₁₀₀₀ Pyr. Base Side

SQUARE
AREA
Area ⅟₁₀₀₀₀₀₀
PYRAMID BASE AREA

91·31

INDEX
PYRAMID
⅟₁₀₀ᵗʰ Scale

FACE OF STEP

LIMESTONE FLOOR

To face p. 208.

In Section—Limestone Stippled : Granite Hatched in Parallel Lines.

sional circuit. On Plate XXX, and in ¶ 183, it was shown that Petrie's structural measurements at the geometrical slope of the Passages give the top of the Great Step and the level of the horizontal floor into the King's Chamber as 1701.87 B". Now this level is 2.59 P" lower than the Precessional circuit level at 1702.5924907 P"=1704.46 B".

The latter difference of 2.59 P", again, is confirmed by the geometrical relations of Plates XL to XLIII. The level of the foot of the Step is defined as 1664.1914215 P"=1666.02 B", above the base (Plate XL, Fig. C, Item 6) ; whereas, on structural evidence, Plate XXX obtained this as 1666.0 B" (¶ 183). The geometrical relations therefore define the foot of the Great Step (at 1664.1914215 P") as 38.4010692 P" lower than the Precessional circuit level at 1702.5924907 P". The difference in level is clearly at least 2.59 P" greater than the height of the Great Step, which both Smyth and Petrie average as 35.87 B". The geometrical relations of the Great Step should settle the question as to the precise value of the difference.

¶ 234. THE VERTICAL DISPLACEMENT OF THE GREAT STEP.

Two possibilities present themselves. The first appears to be defined by the sloping distance of the Grand Gallery floor line produced to intersect the horizontal floor line from the Step to King's Chamber. A step height of 35.826577 P" (=35.866 B") gives the latter sloping distance as 80.8520116 P". On the Pyramid's chronology system this represents a period of 80.8520116 solar years=29530.588 days=1000 lunar months. The round number of 1000 months here is convincing, since it follows the principle of the scalar chronology system. This relation, then, gives the difference as follows :—

Foot of Step to Precessional Circuit	..	=38.401069 P".
Step height, as derived above	.. ..	=35.826577 P".

$$\left.\begin{array}{l}\text{Step Level surface, and King's Chamber floor}\\ \text{below Precessional Circuit} \quad .. \quad ..\end{array}\right\} = 2.574492 \text{ P"}.$$

Now Newcomb's data and formula for Precession (¶¶ 223 and 224) indicate that within the range of 500 years covered by his calculations the value of C in the precessional formula is zero, when A is stated to 2 decimal places in years, and B to 3 decimal places ; the latter as −0.114 for Epoch 1850 A.D. In algebraical effect, this means that the value of Q in the formula of ¶ 221 must be less than 10 in the relation $C = \dfrac{2Q}{T^2} = \dfrac{2Q}{(6000)^2}$.

Now if we adopt the vertical displacement of the Step as 2.574492 P", and this value as indicating the value of Q, we obtain

$$C = \frac{2Q}{(6000)^2} = \frac{2 \times 2.574492}{(6000)^2}$$
$$= 0.0000001430273$$
$$= \frac{286.0546}{2 \times 10^9}.$$

Value of C
from this
suggests that
C =
$\frac{286.1022156}{2 \times 10^9}$
and that
Q = 2.57492,
a function of
the Passage
displacement.

The latter value suggests the second alternative for the vertical displacement of the Step, as a function of the horizontal displacement 286.1022156 P″.

Thus—

$$C = \frac{286.1022156}{2 \times 10^9}$$
$$= 0.0000001430511078$$
$$= \frac{2 \times 2.57492}{(6000)^2}$$

giving

$$Q = 2.57492.$$

We may provisionally adopt the latter value for the trial formula, since the difference between the two alternatives will be quite inappreciable.

¶ 235. THE TRIAL VALUES OF THE STEP CO-ORDINATES.

Newcomb's
data indicate
that Grand
Gallery height
is co-ordinate
for b in
formula.

Newcomb's formula, again, suggests the value of the co-ordinate for the value of B in his formula (¶ 224). Here B = 0.114. Newcomb's Epoch, however,—not being the mid-date Epoch for the Pyramid formula—for comparison with the latter, requires to be expressed in terms of the formulæ of ¶¶ 221 and 222.

This is

$$P = a - b.t_1 + c.t_1^2$$

where

$$b = 0.114 = \frac{2m}{6000}.$$

Hence value of

$$m = 342.$$

Now since m is the vertical co-ordinate for Newcomb's Epoch, the relation obtained clearly suggests that the Great Step co-ordinate for m—for the Great Step Epoch—is supplied by the vertical height of the Gallery. This we saw in ¶ 225 to be given by the addition of the Passage displacement distance to the vertical height of the 1st Ascending Passage. The latter is now accurately known as defined by its geometrical relations $W_1W_2Z_2Z_1$ in Plate XL, Fig. C.

Thus—

Vertical height of 1st Ascending Passage	= 52.7756941 P″.
Passage Displacement	= 286.1022156 P″.
Vertical height of Gallery	= 338.8779097 P″.

This gives

$$m = 338.8779097$$

and

$$b = 0.1129593032.$$

Our trial formula for the Great Step Epoch may therefore be stated as follows :—

$$P = a - b.t_1 + c.t_1^2$$

where

a = the still unknown rate of P for the year of the unknown Epoch
b = 0.1129593
c = 0.00000014305.

The trial formula thus obtained :—
P =
a − b.t₁ + c.t₁' ;
a to determine ;
b = 0.1129593 ;
c =
286.1022156 / 2 × 10⁹ .

¶ 236. THE DATE OF THE GREAT STEP EPOCH.

Now we saw that the Great Step is geometrically associated with the Precessional circuit 25826.54 (¶ 231 and Plate XL, Fig. C). This naturally suggests that the Great Step defined the date at which the annual rate of Precession was 25,826.54. In this relation, however, we must consider the displacement of the Passage system. The central vertical axis of the Great Step is 286.1022 P″, East of the central vertical axis of the Pyramid, which is defined by the centre of the Precessional square of 25826.54 P″ circuit, and by the intersection of the base diagonals, which total 25826.54 P″.

The relation indicated between Great Step Epoch and date at which Precessional rate is 25,826.54.

Entering the Pyramid on the North Face, we pass along the sloping Passages in the direction of advancing time, according to the Pyramid's chronology. From this standpoint of advancing with the chronology, the whole Passage system is displaced 286.1022 P″ to the left of the Pyramid's North to South vertical plane. As the left is subordinate to the right, in both ancient and modern symbolism, the displacement is in the negative direction rather than in the positive direction. The displacement then represents a negative quantity of 286.1022, and therefore a deduction of this amount.

The Passage displacement of 286.1 indicated as a negative quantity in relation to Great Step.

Now, what do we require that this deduction can give us ? We saw that the primary necessity is the indicating of the date of the Great Step Epoch in terms of current chronology. This would be defined if we knew the interval in (±) years separating the date of the Epoch and the date at which P = 25,826.54. Taking the rhomboid of displacement, shown at $W_1 W_2 Z_2 Z_1$ in Plate XL, Fig. C, as defining this—

The significance of the rhomboid of displacement of side 286.1 P″.
Basis of Pyramid's Precessional formula :—
Precessional rate, 25826.54 at date 286.1 years prior to Great Step Epoch.

$$a - b.t_1 + c.t_1^2 = 25,826.542378$$

with

$$t_1 = -286.1022 \text{ years}$$
$$b = 0.1129593$$

and

$$c = 0.00000014305.$$

Solving the equation

$$a = 25,794.212764.$$

Now a is the value of P for the year of the Epoch. The Great Step dating is therefore the year in which the Precessional rate was 25,794.212764. This is the rate for 1844 A.D., and for no other year within a range of considerably over 30,000 [1] years before or after 1844 A.D.

Defines the Great Step Epoch as 1844 A.D.

[1] Outside a range of ±20,000 years from 1844 A.D. a fourth term (d.t³), and possibly a fifth term (e.t⁴), should come appreciably into effect in the formula for P.

Newcomb's formula gives the rate for 1st January 1844 A.D. as 25,794.14 years.

¶ 237. THE METHOD OF CHECKING.

Formula defines initial date 0 A.P. = Autumnal Equinox 4000 B.C. Great Step dating 25th January 1844 A.D.

Again, since the Pyramid chronology system defines the Great Step dating as 5842.3397932 A.P., our trial formula, by giving this as falling in 1844 A.D., defines 0 A.P. as commencing at the Autumnal Equinox 4000 B.C. and the Great Step dating as 25th January (Gregorian) 1844 A.D.[1] The rigid conditions laid down in ¶¶ 231 and 232, however, require that this definition should be independently confirmed.

Two independent series of data should give 25th January 1844 A.D. as date of completion of 90° of Precession from a definitely indicated ancient Zodiacal Epoch. Newcomb's formula gives Epoch as 4699 B.C.

Indication (a) of ¶ 231 requires that the Step dating should be defined as marking the specific completion of 90° of Precession from an ancient Zodiacal Epoch. Our conditions demand that our formula, to be proved correct, should give the date of this Epoch and that the date thus obtained should agree precisely with a date independently supplied by the Pyramid's geometrical system.

With Newcomb's formula, again, to guide us, we find that this gives us a period of 6541.75 years for 90° back from 1st January 1844. Newcomb's formula, therefore, fixes the Zodiacal Epoch at 4699 B.C. We shall see how close this is to the result of the Pyramid formula.

¶ 238. THE PYRAMID'S INTEGRATION OF PRECESSIONAL VALUES.

Method of calculation by Pyramid formula.

To employ our Precessional formula in the manner indicated, the application depends upon the relationship that *for 90° of Precession* reckoned back from the Epoch—

The Exact Average value of P for $(-t_1)$ years $= 4.t_1$.

The procedure is as follows :—

$$P = a - b.t_1 + c.t_1{}^2.$$

By the process of integration we obtain

Average value of P for Interval $(-t_1)$ years $= \dfrac{a.t_1 - \dfrac{b}{2}t_1{}^2 + \dfrac{c}{3}t_1{}^3}{t_1}$

$$= a - \frac{b}{2}t_1 + \frac{c}{3}t_1{}^2$$

where

$$a = 25,794.212764$$
$$b = 0.1129593$$

and

$$c = 0.00000014305.$$

[1] This dating is obtained by taking 5842.00 A.P. = Autumnal Equinox 1843 A.D.

With the above formula and constants, the relation

$$\text{Average } P = 4.t_1 \text{ (for 90°) holds for}$$
$$t_1 = 6541.42 \text{ years,}$$

as against Newcomb's 6541.75 years (¶ 237).

Newcomb's formula and the Pyramid formula therefore agree in giving the date 4699 B.C. as representing the date for 90° Precession back from 1844 A.D.

Now the interval of precisely 6541.4102013 years back from the Great Step Epoch is independently given by the Pyramid's geometry. A distance of 6541.4102013 P″ from the Great Step vertical, measured along the chronological floor line produced of the Descending Passage, reaches a point (V on Plate XLI, Fig. M) 699.070408 P″ beyond (*i.e.* chronologically prior to) the point indicating Upper o A.P., and 116.2602875 P″ vertically below the level of the Precessional circuit. Now the latter vertical distance is the diameter of a circle of circumference 365.242465 P″—defining the value of the Pyramid's mean solar year. The geometrical symbolism of the solar year therefore connects the levels of the two points defining the initial and terminal dates for 90° of Precession round the Zodiac.

Date of
Zodiacal
Epoch, in
relation to
Great Step
Epoch, given
as 4699 B.C.
by independent
geometrical
indications
of Passage
System.

Similar applications of the year circle are shown on Plate XLI, Fig. K, and Plate XLIII. In the first of these, the geometry of the year circle defines the commencement of the Grand Gallery—and by connection with Fig. L, the level of the Queen's Chamber floor—in relation to 4000 A.P. of the Scalar system of chronology. In the second case, the Great Step, Antechamber, and King's Chamber all appear as a single exposition of the Geometry of the year circle.

The chrono-
logical signi-
ficance of the
geometry of
the year
circle.

¶ 239. THE PYRAMID'S ASTRONOMICAL ALIGNMENTS.

Referring now to Plate XLI, Fig. N, it will be seen that the Pyramid's geometrical system gives two independent constructions defining the date 1856 A.P. = 2144 B.C., and another similar construction defining the date 565⅓ A.P. = 3434 B.C. The interest attaching to these constructions and their datings is that at the time of both dates—but not at any date preceding the latter, succeeding the former, or intervening between the two dates—the pole star of ancient times, *a Draconis*, would be seen by an observer at the bottom of the Pyramid's Descending Passage precisely at midnight of the Autumnal Equinox.[1] Strictly speaking, the condition would hold approximately for several years before and after both dates.

Pyramid's
geometrical
constructions
define two
dates, 2144
B.C. and 3434
B.C.

Entrance
Passage angle
and the pole
star at 2144
B.C. and
3434 B.C.
Autumnal
Equinoctial
midnight.

Attention to the fact noted was first directed by the calculation of Sir John Herschel in 1836 A.D. Herschel gave the date for *a Draconis* on the Entrance Passage alignment at Autumnal Equinoctial midnight as approximately 2160 B.C.[2] Professor Piazzi Smyth's later calculation gave the date

Dates
calculated by
Sir John
Herschel,
Professor
Smyth, Dr.
Brünnow, and
Richard
Proctor.

[1] The accurate conditions of observation for the precise alignment require the observer to sight the star through two apertured diaphragms or partitions fixed into the Passage at a considerable interval apart.

[2] Col. Howard Vyse's " Pyramids of Gizeh," Vol. II, Appendix, pp. 107–109.

as 2170 B.C.[1] The latter authority also pointed out that the perpendicular from the Entrance Passage slope at the same date, 2170 B.C., and at Autumnal Equinoctial midnight was directed to the star *Alcyonê* of *Pleiades* (*η Tauri*).[1] This is as illustrated on Plate XLI, Fig. N. Dr. Brünnow, Astronomer-Royal for Ireland, by superior methods, next calculated the *a Draconis* alignment as occurring in 2136 B.C.[1] As Richard Proctor's later determination of the *Alcyonê* alignment gave the date 2140 B.C.,[2] the two alignments were again brought into close agreement as to date, but 30 years later than Smyth's dating, and 20 years later than Herschel's dating. Dr. Brünnow's calculations also gave the date 3443 B.C. for the earlier *a Draconis* alignment.

¶ 240. THE PYRAMID'S "SCORE" DATING CONFIRMED.

The best determinations, then, give—

(1) The first *a Draconis* alignment at 3443 B.C., as against the Pyramid's geometrically defined 3434 B.C. ; and

(2) The second *a Draconis* alignment, and the independent *Alcyonê* alignment at 2136–2140 B.C., as against the Pyramid's geometrically defined 2144 B.C.

Now it is obvious that *a Draconis* or *Alcyonê* might be slightly on one side of the Meridian at Autumnal Equinoctial midnight of, say, 2145 B.C., and slightly on the other side of the Meridian at Autumnal Equinoctial midnight of the following year 2144 B.C. The amount on one side more than the other would determine the fraction of the year at which the true passage of the star took place. Hence we find that a "scored line" on both walls of the Entrance Passage defines the date as 1855.42 A.P. (*i.e.* the early spring of 2144 B.C.). The date defined by the "scored line" is obviously given as an actually observed check result confirming the geometrical indication.

Sir John Herschel naturally and logically concluded that the Entrance Passage slope defined the date of the Pyramid's construction as around 2160 B.C. His reasons for this conclusion are identical with Sir Norman Lockyer's reasons for dating the construction of ancient Temples by their astronomical alignments. Herschel's dating, however, was overruled by the Egyptologists of his time, who based their chronology upon the Egyptian King Lists. We now see that the latter basis is entirely fictitious, being, in fact, a misrepresentation of Pyramid chronology.

¶ 241. THE FOUNDATION-STAR.

Professor Piazzi Smyth maintained, however, that Herschel's datum was confirmed by the "score" and its indication of the synchronous *Alcyonê* dating, and concluded, in face of the solid opinion of his Egyptological

[1] Professor C. P. Smyth, "Our Inheritance," 3rd Edit., p. 348.
[2] Ibid., added in 5th Edit.

contemporaries to the contrary, that their King Lists and its chronology were in the main spurious. The new data entirely confirm Smyth in this general statement of his contention. It does not, however, follow of necessity, that the " scored line " defines the date of the Pyramid's construction as around 2144 B.C. In the event of an entire lack of evidence to the contrary, the " scored line " might be deemed to indicate the probability of 2144 B.C. defining the Epoch of the Pyramid's foundation. Until, however, it can be proved from Egyptological or other archæological data that the reign of the Great Pyramid king, Khufu, included the year 2144 B.C., the matter must remain in abeyance.

It is, nevertheless, a remarkable fact that Euphratean tradition seems to identify *Alcyonê* with the ceremony of foundation-laying. The significance of this identification lies in the fact that the Pyramid builders have been traced to an Euphratean origin (¶¶ 5, 6, 7, 8, 45, 77–85, and 107). Now, Brown, in his " Primitive Constellations,"[1] states as follows :— *(margin: Euphratean origin of Pyramid builders.)*

> " Alaparos (the second of the ten antediluvian kings of Euphratean legend) is equated with *Alcyonê* (η *Tauri*). The Euphratean astronomical abbreviation of the Sign is *Te* or *Te-te*, the highly abraded form of the Akkadian dimmena (' foundation-stone ') =Assyrian, *timmena—timmen—timme—tim—tim—tem—te* (' foundation '). The ' Foundation '-star (*Temennu*) is the Pleiad, or particularly *Alcyonê*." *(margin: Euphratean Astronomy defines Alcyonê as the " Foundation-star.")*

¶ 242. ASTRONOMICAL DAY BEGINNING AT MIDNIGHT.

Apart, then, from the question of the date of the Pyramid's foundation, the geometrical chronology of the Pyramid defines the *Alcyonê* and *a Draconis* alignments—indicated by the direction of the " scored line " and the inclination of the Entrance Passage—as occurring in the year 2144 B.C. The " scored line " again defines the same date in terms of the same system of chronology. *(margin: "Scored line" emphatically confirms the other data fixing 2144 B.C. dating.)*

Now the *Alcyonê* alignment is defined by two separate geometrical constructions (Plate XLI, Fig. N) associating the *Alcyonê* date with the zero date, o A.P., of the scalar chronology, and with the principal features of the Pyramid's external geometry. *Alcyonê* is, therefore, appropriately identified with the " Foundation " or basis of the scalar system of chronology. *(margin: Alcyonê geometrically defined as related to the " Foundation " of the Pyramid's scalar system of chronology.)*

The " scored line " then emphasises the importance of the identification by defining its relation to the chronology system as determined from actual observation on *Alcyonê* at midnight of two successive Autumnal Equinoxes, that of 2145 B.C. and that of 2144 B.C. The chief features of this emphatic definition are that it fixes the Pyramid meridian and the astronomical day of Pyramid time, as associated with midnight, as the zero for reckoning for days, and that it fixes the commencement of the Pyramid's solar year at the Autumnal Equinox. *(margin: Pyramid's astronomical day defined as beginning at midnight at the Pyramid, and its solar year as beginning at the Autumnal Equinox.)*

These indications were not addressed to the Pyramid builders' contemporaries to whom the facts were known. They were obviously directed *(margin: These indications addressed to the future.)*

[1] Vol. I, p. 57.

Purpose to
define zero
relations
for complete
definition of
Great Step
Epoch as
midnight
ending the
25th January
1844 A.D.

to the future civilisation, together with the indication of the Epoch of reference for the Pyramid's message. This Epoch of reference is defined as 5842.3397932 A.P. =25th to 26th January 1844 A.D. If the decimals beyond the year denote the fraction of the year from the Autumnal Equinox, then the hour is defined as late in the 25th or early in the 26th January 1844 A.D. Similarly, the definition of the Earth's longitude at the Epoch (Plate XL, Fig. A) is given as 125° 11′ 12″.[1] This fixes the hour as late in the evening of 25th January 1844 A.D.

Clearly, then, the " score " definition of the Pyramid's day as beginning at midnight, was intended to relate to the Epoch of reference for the Pyramid's message. This defines the Great Step Epoch as midnight ending the 25th of January 1844 A.D.

¶ 243. THE PYRAMID'S PRECESSIONAL CHRONOLOGY.

The three
independent
proofs.

Now we saw that three independent series of geometrically defined values define the Pyramid's chronological system in terms of the variation in the rate of the Precession of the Equinoxes. The three independent definitions are as follow :—

Great Step
Epoch, 25th
January 1844
A.D.

(1) The Precessional rate for the Great Step Epoch is the known Precessional rate for 1844 A.D., and for no other year within a range of over ±30,000 years from 1844 A.D. (¶ 236.)

Ancient
Zodiacal
Epoch, 6541.41
years earlier
at 4699 B.C.

(2) The Precessional formula—whether the formula be Newcomb's or the Pyramid's—gives 90° of Precession prior to 1844 A.D. as commencing at the Zodiacal Epoch 4699 B.C. (¶¶ 237 and 238.)

Additional
independent
proof by
" score "
relations.

(3) The Pyramid's chronological geometry defines an interval of 6541.41 years (independently given by (2) above) between its two Zodiacal Epochs—the Great Step Epoch (1844 A.D.) and the ancient Zodiacal Epoch (4699 B.C.). (¶ 238.)

All these, again, are confirmed by the " score " relations and dating of ¶¶ 239–242.

Trial formula
proved
intentional
and accurate.

Our trial formula and trial constants (¶¶ 235 and 236) may, therefore, be adopted as intentional and as correctly supplied by the Pyramid's geometrical data, since they satisfy the conditions of ¶ 168, Cases 2, 3, 8, and 9. For further consideration of the formula and its special cases and applications,

---

[1]The geometrical construction (Plate XL, Fig. A) defining this was suggested as follows :— The " Scalar Axis " construction is defined entirely by the geometry of the ¼-Precessional Period of Reference, i.e. Pyramid total width at level DE =6456.6355945 P″ ; " Scalar Axis " is defined from centre point D of same, and as distance DY =6456.6355945 P″ ; DY cuts the Pyramid face line produced at F.

The point D defines the chronological termination of ¼-Precession. ¼-Precession is geometrically symbolised by 6456.6355945 P″ in the Pyramid. All this suggested

F as centre, and FT=6456.6355945 P″, as radius.

FT was then found to make an angle of 125° 11′ 12″ with the vertical axis from Step to Apex. This angle defines Longitude of Earth for 25th to 26th January in modern times, thus agreeing with the A.P. date for the point D—i.e. at the Great Step and vertical axis to Apex.

and for comparison of its data for modern times with Newcomb's data, the
reader is referred to Section III of this Chapter, ¶¶ 304 to 304h.

The precise result of the definitive fixing of the Pyramid's Precessional Defines Scalar chronology datum ; 0 A.P. =Autumnal Equinox 4000 B.C.
chronology is that it also defines the Pyramid's Scalar chronology. On the
latter system the Great Step Epoch is 5842.3397932 A.P. This defines o A.P.
as commencing at the Autumnal Equinox, 4000 B.C., and the Great Step
Epoch as midnight ending 25th January 1844 A.D.

The reader will observe that the three independent proofs above apply
as much to the Scalar chronology as to the Precessional chronology.

It should also be explained that the completion of 60° of Precession from 1st Point of Zodiacal Aries reached at 317 B.C.
the Zodiacal Epoch 4699 B.C.—as obtained by the Pyramid's Precessional
formula—occurred after a period of 4381.7 solar years, ending in 317 B.C.
(refer ¶ 213).

¶ 244. THE PYRAMID'S ORBITAL OR PERIHELION CHRONOLOGY.

In addition to this definition of Precessional chronology, we find also The Pyramid defines the Earth's Orbital chronology as well as its Precessional chronology.
a definition of the Earth's Orbital chronology (¶ 168, Cases 1, 4, 8, and 9).
The latter we may define as the chronology of the Longitude of Perihelion,
and of the rate of change of the Longitude of Perihelion. The angular
measurement of the Longitude of Perihelion is the angular distance separating Relation between Precessional rate and rate of change of Longitude of Perihelion.
the place of the Autumnal Equinox from Perihelion. The rate of change of
this angle is, therefore, largely due to Precession (refer Plates LV and LVI).
As a matter of fact, about the ⅞th part of the rate is due to Precession and ⅞th due to Precession, ⅛th due to movement of orbit.
the remaining ⅛th due to the movement of Perihelion in the opposite direction.
Viewed in relation to the algebraic effect of the composite movement, the
algebraic effect of the movement of Perihelion will be small as compared with
the algebraic effect of the Precessional movement. In other words, we may
expect the factors for our Pyramid formula expressing the composite movement to indicate the dominant influence of the constants of our Pyramid
Precessional formula.

We find, accordingly, that the Orbital chronology is defined in relation Length of Pyramid's "Scalar Axis" defines Longitude of Perihelion 0° at 4044 B.C., 5886 years prior to Great Step Epoch, 1844 A.D.
to what we have termed the " Scalar Axis " of the Passage System (¶ 228).
As shown on Plate XL, Fig. A, this axis line (DCF) cuts the Pyramid face
line at a point (F) 5886.3105287 P″ back along the Ascending Passage slope
from the intersection (D) of the vertical Step axis and the horizontal precessional circuit. Chronologically, this defines 5886.3105287 solar years
prior to the Great Step Epoch at 5842.3397932 A.P. (=25th January 1844) ;
or 43.9707355 solar years prior to o A.P. (=Autumnal Equinox, 4000 B.C.). 4044 B.C. defined as " Initial Perihelion Epoch."
The date thus defined falls in 4044 B.C., and clearly indicates the date at
which the Longitude of Perihelion was 0° (refer ¶ 212). We may term the
latter date the Initial Perihelion Epoch.

What remains to be shown is that the date thus defined is independently
fixed by the Pyramid's data for the Longitude of Perihelion, and for the rate
of change of the latter.

¶ 245. " THE CHAMBER OF THE ORBIT " AND ITS ORBITAL CONSTANTS.

Imagery of Egyptian religious texts identifies the Pyramid's Grand Gallery as the " Chamber of the Orbit."

From consideration of the imagery of the Egyptian religious texts in relation to the Passages and Chambers of the Great Pyramid, Mr. Marsham Adams makes a remarkable identification in regard to the Grand Gallery and the groove cut parallel to the floor in each of its side walls.[1] The latter groove is figured on Plate XXXII, above the 3rd overlap. Adams defines the Gallery as " The Chamber of the Orbit," and associates the Wall Groove with the symbolism of the Orbit.

The Grand Gallery Wall Groove and symbolism of the Orbit.

Wall Groove defines constant b of Pyramid's formula for Orbital chronology.

The remarkable feature of this identification is that it is this particular groove and its vertical relationship to the Scalar Axis of the Passage system at the point (D in Fig. A, Plate XL) defining the Great Step Epoch that defines the constant b in the Pyramid's formula for Orbital chronology. Professor Petrie has shown [2] that the lower edge of the wall groove is at half the height of the Gallery. The geometrical definition of the vertical height of the Gallery gave 338.8779097 P″ (¶¶ 235 and 236). The half-height is, therefore, 169.43895485 P″.

Co-ordinate for constant b represented from " Scalar Axis " at Great Step Epoch, 1844 A.D.

$m = 131.0378857$

$b = \dfrac{2m}{6000}$

$b = 0.043679295.$

The latter value for the Great Step Epoch gives a co-ordinate from the foot of the Great Step. The indications discussed in ¶ 244, however, show that the co-ordinate for the Perihelion relations must be measured from the " Scalar Axis " of the Passage system, at the Great Step vertical axis. The co-ordinate must, therefore, be measured from the point D (Fig. A, Plate XL), which, as shown in ¶ 234, is 38.4010692 P″ above the foot of the Step. The co-ordinate value is therefore $(169.43895485 - 38.4010692) = 131.0378857$.

This gives the value for m in the relation $b = \dfrac{2m}{T}$; T, as before, being 6000 years. From this $b = 0.04367929523$.

C is same value as for Precessional formula.

As will be shown, by the application of the formula, the value of C remains as before, and is defined by the co-ordinate from point D (Fig. A, Plate XL) to the top of the Great Step (¶ 234). The value of C $= 0.0000001430511$.

There remains to be found the value of a.

¶ 246. THE INDEPENDENT USE OF GEOMETRICAL AND SCALAR VALUES.

Period of reference for Precessional rate was defined geometrically since geometrical value was related to 1844 A.D. date.

In the case of the Precessional formula, the value of a was obtained from the defined value of P for a year geometrically related to the Great Step Epoch. A similar method of definition holds for the Orbital formula.

In the Precessional formula the period of reference for P was the geometrical period $25,826.54$ defined by the sum of the diagonals and by the Precessional circuit. The latter value was seen to be the basal value of

---

[1] " The Book of the Master," pp. 181, 182. This remarkable work was referred to in ¶¶ 108 and 109.
[2] " Pyramids and Temples of Gizeh," pp. 73, 74.

reference adopted in the geometrical system as giving the Precessional rate for a year within easy range of the basal Epoch at the Great Step. In the case of the Orbital formula, no such *geometrical* period of reference occurs within easy range of the Great Step Epoch (1844 A.D.). The latter date, and its relations in the Pyramid scheme, show that the data were presented for modern times, and for values within the accurate range of calculations for modern times. The Orbital period of reference for modern times is the handy period of 21,000 years, *i.e.* modern authorities, in referring to the change of Longitude of Perihelion, and when stating its rate, express it as a cycle of 21,000 years, this representing the nearest round number of thousand years defining the annual rate in modern times.

Geometrical period of reference for Orbital rate not suitable for 1844 A.D. Nearest value is the numerical value, 21,000 for modern times.

Now the data of Plates XL to XLIII show that the Pyramid's Passage geometry defines, not only a system of astronomical chronology, but also a related system of scalar chronology. The basis of the latter, although geometrically derived, is entirely numerical and is expressed in intervals of thousands of years from 0 A.P. to 6000 A.P. (*i.e.* from 4000 B.C. to 2001 A.D.). For the Ascending Passages this numerical or scalar system is defined by the " Scalar Axis " of the Passage system. The latter, again, is the base line for the constants of the Orbital formula (¶ 245). This clearly suggests that the numerical or scalar definition extends to the expression of the Orbital formula. It suggests that the numerical rate of 21,000 years was adopted as the period of reference. The scalar chronology should, therefore, have been framed to give the representation of this value for a scalar year within range of modern times. The only suitable scalar year is the year 6000 A.P. $=2001\frac{3}{4}$ A.D.

The Scalar Axis is geometrically defined measured off into divisions representing intervals of 1000 years.

This Scalar Axis is axis of reference for Orbital formula's constants.

Suggests Scalar rate 21,000 at Scalar date 6000 A.P.

¶ 247. THE ORBITAL OR PERIHELION FORMULA.

From our trial data we have obtained the Orbital formula as follows :—
For Epoch 5842.3397932 A.P. (25th January 1844 A.D.)—

$$P = a - b.t_1 + c.t_1{}^2$$

where

$$b = 0.04367929523 \ (¶ \ 245)$$
$$c = 0.00000014305\text{II} \ (¶ \ 245)$$

and

a   unknown.

For 6000 A.P. (2001¾ A.D.)—

$$P = 21,000 \ (¶ \ 246)$$
$$t_1 = 6000 - 5842.3397932$$
$$= 157.6602068.$$

Trial Orbital (or Perihelion) formula :— Epoch, 1844 A.D.—
$P =$
$a - b.t_1 + c.t_1{}^2,$
$a =$
21,006.883208,
$b =$
0.043679295,
$c =$
$\dfrac{286.1022156}{2 \times 10^8}$.

Substituting these in the formula above gives

$$a = 21,006.883208,$$

which is the value of P for the Great Step Epoch. Converting the formula (by the conversion rules and data of ¶¶ 220 and 221) to the Epoch 4044 B.C.

Epoch
4044 B.C.
Longitude of
Perihelion, 0°,

a =
21,269.051404,

b =
0.04536338,

c as before.

—the Initial Perihelion Epoch (¶ 244) when the Longitude of Perihelion was 0°—we obtain

$$P = a - b.t_1 + c.t_1{}^2$$

where

$$a = 21,269.051404$$
$$b = 0.0453633817$$
$$c = 0.0000001430511.$$

Longitude of
Perihelion =
Sum of base
angles of
Pyramid
section at
2045¼ A.D.

Solving for the date at which Longitude of Perihelion = 103° 42′ 28″.6 = Sum of base angles of Pyramid's right vertical section [1] (refer ¶ 212), we obtain

$$t_1 = 6087.941471 \text{ years from Initial Perihelion Epoch, and ending at } 6043.9707355$$
A.P. (2045¾ A.D.).

Interval of
6087.94 years
confirms
formula.

This relation, by establishing the inductions of ¶¶ 212 to 217, confirms the formula and establishes the intention and accuracy of the Pyramid's values from which the formula is derived.

Longitude of
Perihelion 90°
in 1246 A.D.

Application of the formula to the determination of the date at which the Longitude of Perihelion was 90° gives the latter at 5287.61 years from the Initial Perihelion date. The date for Longitude of Perihelion 90° is therefore 5244.64 A.P., this falling in 1246 A.D. (refer Plate LVI).

For further consideration of the formula and its special cases and applications, and for comparison of its data with the accepted data for modern times, the reader is referred to Section III of this Chapter, ¶¶ 304i and j.

¶ 248.   SIX INDEPENDENT PROOFS OF PYRAMID CHRONOLOGY.

Orbital
chronology
fixed by three
independent
definitions.

The reader should note that the Orbital (or Perihelion) chronology is fixed by three independent definitions of a nature similar to the three independent definitions of the Precessional chronology in ¶ 243. This means

Six independ-
ent definitions
of Passage
chronology
with Great
Step Epoch,
25th January
1844 A.D.

that the geometry of the Passage system of the Great Pyramid gives six independent definitions of a system of astronomical chronology, in all of which definitions the Great Step figures as defining an Epoch of reference at midnight ending the 25th January 1844 A.D.

Postulated
conditions
satisfied as
to definition
of intention.

The conditions of ¶¶ 168 and 169, as to the extent of definition establishing intention in the relation considered, are therefore completely fulfilled. The six independent proofs, however, define considerably more than the

Data further
define the
period for
which the
Pyramid's
Message was
designed.

conditions postulated require. They define specifically that all the astronomical values forming the key or keys to the elucidation of the Pyramid's purpose and intention fall within a period of 487 years, embracing the period of modern times.

¶ 249.   THE ERA OF THE PYRAMID'S MESSAGE DEFINED.

Era defined—
(1) Initially
by base
diagonals ;
(2) Terminally
by base angles.

The initial date of the latter period is defined as the year in which the Precessional rate is given by the *Sum* of the Pyramid's *base diagonals* ; the

[1] Analogously the basal period of reference for the Precessional formula is given by the sum of the diagonals of the Pyramid's base square.

terminal date as the year in which the Longitude of Perihelion will be equal to the *Sum* of the *base angles* of the Pyramid's right vertical section. The analogous summation of base details in both cases is clearly not unintentional. The initial date is 286.1022 years prior to the Step Epoch at 5842.33979 A.P., and is, therefore, at 5556.23759 A.P.—less than a month prior to the commencement of 1558 A.D. (Plate XL, Figs. C and F). The terminal date is 6043.9707 A.P., or 2045¾ A.D. Step Epoch by Passage displacement Era of Message 1558 A.D. to 2045 A.D.

It is a remarkable fact that the Initial Date—ushering in the reign of Elizabeth in England—should be identified by Whewell, in his "History of the Inductive Sciences," with what he defines as the "Inductive Epoch of Copernicus"—the Epoch beginning "The History of Formal Astronomy after the Stationary Period." It is further remarkable that prior to the Great Step Epoch gravitational astronomy was not sufficiently advanced *in accuracy* to check the translation of the Pyramid's co-ordinates with the degree of precision now possible. Since the date of the Step Epoch onwards, the attention of astronomers has been repeatedly directed to the solution of the Pyramid's astronomical purpose. The era of Inductive Science following the "Stationary Period." Historical coincidence and the Great Step Epoch.

That these relations to the facts are something beyond mere accidental coincidence is at once apparent when we examine the use to which the ancient Egyptians put the data we have been considering. Significant use of Pyramid data in Egyptian King Lists.

¶ 250. THE NEW ERA ANTICIPATED BY THE KING LISTS.

The complete period of the Pyramid's orbital chronology is 6087.94 solar years, extending from Longitude of Perihelion 0° in 4044 B.C. to Longitude of Perihelion twice the Pyramid base angle, at 2045 A.D. The period was borrowed by the Egyptian compilers of the Egyptian King Lists. It was fictitiously applied to build up a scheme of false chronology. Hence we find that a period of 6087 or 6088 years (¶¶ 212–215, and Plate XVI, Table F) was deemed to terminate in one or other of the four years 137, 138, 139, and 140 A.D., in which, as Oppolzer's astronomical calculations have shown,[1] Day 1, Month I of the shifting Egyptian calendar coincided with the day upon which Sirius rose heliacally (refer ¶¶ 49, 53, and 73a). Pyramid's orbital period of 6087.94 years borrowed by Egyptian King Lists. Alleged termination, 137-140 A.D. Identified with Sothic Cycle ending.

Writing in the year 238 A.D., Censorinus [2] gives the year for shifting Day 1, Month I coincident with the heliacal rising of Sirius as 139 A.D. Now the coincidence noted occurred on 20th July (Julian) in 137 to 139 A.D. inclusive, and on 19th July (Julian) in 140 A.D. The latter is the dating of Palladius (vii. 9). An Alexandrian coin, dated in the 6th year of Antoninus Alexandrian coin dates epoch as 143 A.D.

---

[1] "Ueber die Länge des Sirius Jahrs und der Sothis Periode," 90th vol., *Sitzungsberichte*, of the Vienna Academy.
Petrie and Knobel in "Historical Studies," pp. 6 and 7.
[2] *De Die Natali*, Chapters XVIII and XXI. Censorinus makes a mistake in giving the day as 21st July (Julian) instead of 20th July (Julian) for 139 A.D., as Oppolzer has shown. The ancient latitude datum for the heliacal rising of Sirius was Memphis. This, during the 2nd century A.D., gave the heliacal rising as occurring generally on 20th July (Julian), or, dependent upon leap year, on 19th July (Julian). In 238 A.D., however, and at the more northerly latitude of Alexandria, Sirius would be seen to rise heliacally on 21st July (Julian), Censorinus thus giving the latter date as the "time the Dog-star is wont to rise in Egypt."

Pius,[1] ascribes the ending of the cycle to the year of the dating, and therefore to 143 A.D.

We find, therefore, that the alleged termination of the period of 6087 or 6088 years was variously identified with one or other of the years 139 to 143 A.D. For the month datings of the heliacal rising of Sirius, these years cover the period of four years from 4137¾ to 4141¼ A.P., in the Pyramid scheme of scalar chronology. These were given by the Egyptians as alternative terminal dates for the Pyramid's astronomical period of 6087.97 years. The 487.7 years' period—the period to which the Pyramid's message is defined as applying—would therefore be explained by the Egyptians as ending in 4137¾–4141¼ A.P., and as beginning at one or other of the years 3650 to 3654 A.P. (350 to 346 B.C.). The latter range of dates includes the date of the Epoch of Okhos (¶ 214)—given by Syncellus as 347 or 348 B.C. The version of Castor (¶ 97) gives the dynasties of the Egyptian kings as ending at 3650; the Old Chronicle, as ending at 3652, 3652½, or 3653 (¶¶ 95 and 214).

¶ 251. THE FORGERIES OF THE EGYPTIAN KING LISTS.

The Egyptian priests, then, re-edited the dynastic records of their kings in such manner as to expand the period of Egyptian history to cover the period of the Pyramid's orbital chronology. To effect this purpose, dynasties that had existed contemporaneously were represented as having reigned in succession. Obscure dynasties—whose existence is scarcely noted in the records of the greater contemporary dynasties—were given the longest durations of continuous rule possible; the reason being that where no records were known to exist, fictitious duration could be given with less chance of the fiction being discovered. Such fictitious expansion had already become the fashion in the later years of the XVIIIth Dynasty. The fashion was then set to identify the chronology of the kings with the Pyramid's precessional and orbital systems of chronology. Such a system exists in the Turin Papyrus. The fashion thus set continued after native kings had ceased to rule in Egypt. The last expansion effected the final identification with the complete orbital chronology of the Great Pyramid.

Now the Pyramid's orbital chronology continues for 1904 years beyond the close of the native history of Egypt. Expansion of the native dynasties could not well be projected into the future. The expansion was therefore projected into the past. To effect the necessary identification with the Pyramid's orbital chronology, the latter was presented moved backwards in time to the extent of the 1904 years it projected into the future beyond the close of the native Egyptian history. The date of the Longitude of Perihelion 0°—defined by the Pyramid as 4044 B.C., 3697 years prior to the Epoch of Okhos at 347 B.C., when the dynasties were identified as ending—was therefore pushed backwards 1904 years prior to 4044 B.C., to 5948 B.C. At this

[1]Torr, "Memphis and Mycenæ," p. 54.

remote date, it was claimed, the 1st dynastic king of Egypt, the traditional Menes, began his reign. The date is remotely beyond the range of any item of the Pyramid's astronomical chronology. It is 1205 years prior to the Pyramid's earliest Zodiacal Epoch at 4699 B.C. It is, therefore, beyond the range of the ancient civilisation that had long preceded the dawn of Egypt's history.

¶ 252. THE ORBITAL CHRONOLOGY OF THE KING LISTS.

The following is a comparative statement of the true terminal datings of the fictitious chronology of the King Lists :—

Comparative statement of true terminal datings of the fictitiously applied orbital chronology of the Egyptian King Lists.

True Pyramid Date.

Termination of alleged 5601 years of Egyptian Dynastic History, Version Africanus, Plate XVI, Table A. Epoch of Okhos and termination of Old Chronicle 3652½ years of Dynastic History.
Alleged year for Precessional rate 25,826.54 (Plate XVI). } 3652.42 A.P. = 347 B.C.

Pyramid's terminal period of 487.77, represented by the King Lists as beginning with the New Era of European Civilisation identified with Alexander's conquests. } 487.77 years' Interval.

Year in which the heliacal rising of Sirius fell on shifting Day 1, Month I. Alleged year of termination of Pyramid's Orbital Period of 6087 or 6088 years from fictitious date of commencement of Egyptian Dynastic History. } 4140.19 A.P. = 141 A.D.

Now the actually defined interval of the Pyramid's period, between the date of Longitude of Perihelion 0° and the date of the Precessional rate 25,826.54 years, is a period of 5600.2 solar years—from a date 43.97 years prior to 0 A.P. to the date 5556.2 A.P. In the King Lists (Version Africanus, Plate XVI, Table A) this period appears as 5601 years for the duration of the human kings, as tabulated above. As shown in the tabulation, this fictitious scheme was devised to terminate the period at the Epoch of Okhos—defined as 347 B.C. A terminal period of 486 or 487 years (Plate XVI, Table F) was reckoned as completing the period of 6087 or 6088 years to 139 A.D. or 140 A.D., at which latter date it was calculated Sirius would rise heliacally on shifting Day 1, Month I.

The origin of the 5601 years of the King Lists. A true astronomical period. Defined by Pyramid as ending 1558 A.D. By King Lists as ending 347 B.C.

This scheme of the King Lists is, therefore, as follows :—

The use of the 487 years' interval in King Lists to complete astronomical period of 6087 or 6088 years.

Human Kings 5600.2 years stated as ..	5601	5601
Terminal Period 487.77 ,, ,, ..	486	487
Astronomical Period 6087.97 ,, ,, ..	6087 or	6088
As in Plate XVI, Table F, add 20 nominal Solar Cycles	30437	30437
Pyramid's Base Circuit	36524 or	36525

¶ 253. ALTERNATIVE ORBITAL CHRONOLOGY IN THE KING LISTS.

Pyramid's Precessional date, 1558 A.D., represented as date of Epoch of Okhos, 347 B.C.; Perihelion date, 2045 A.D., as Sothic Cycle ending 141 A.D.

In effect, the latter scheme of the Version of Africanus indicates that the alleged period of 5601 years of the Egyptian kings was presented as ending at the defined Pyramid date 5556 A.P. (¶ 249), and the additional period of 487 years as ending at 6043 A.P. (¶ 249). The periods were actually presented as ending at 348 or 347 B.C., and 140 or 141 A.D. respectively, thus anticipating the actually defined dates by 1904 or 1905 years.

The version of the King Lists given in terms of Pyramid's scalar chronology.

Confirming this statement of the system of the Lists in years of A.P. or scalar reckoning, 5556 A.P. and 6043 A.P. respectively, we find that one alternative version of Africanus is obtained as follows :—

Manetho's Dyns. of Human Kings.	Years.	
Book I	2293	Plate XVI, Table B.
Book II	2213	,,
Book III	1050	,,
Total	5556 to 348–7 B.C.	=3652–3 A.P., Old Chronicle.
Terminal period	487 B.C. to 140–1 A.D.	=4139–40 A.P., Old Chronicle.
	6043	

" 6043 years " being derived from the true A.P. dating for Longitude of Perihelion = the sum of the base angles of the Pyramid's vertical section, i.e. datum for 2045 A.D. (Plate XLI, Fig. F.)

But zero date at 4000 B.C. represented as at 5903 B.C. or 5904 B.C. Comparison with Old Chronicle independently fixes Pyramid's astronomical dates.

Now we have seen that the Old Chronicle chronology is identical with the Pyramid's chronology (¶¶ 214 and 237). Here we see that the version of the King Lists considered gives 1904 years more than the Old Chronicle for the date 3652 A.K. = 347 B.C. As the Old Chronicle dating is correct, the application of the King Lists is wrong. The period belongs, however, to the same system of chronology as the Old Chronicle. The difference of 1904 years added to 347 B.C. gives the date 1558 A.D. for 5556 A.P. of the King Lists. The terminal period of 487 years, therefore, ends in 2045 A.D.

¶ 254. RELATION BETWEEN PYRAMID'S CHRONOLOGY AND ITS MESSAGE.

The Egyptian King Lists add an additional series of proofs to the several series supplied by the Pyramid's astronomical data.

Comparison of the King Lists and the Old Chronicle, therefore, independently proves—

(1) The period of 6087–8 years for the Orbital Chronology ;
(2) The date 4044 B.C. for the Longitude of Perihelion 0°, and the date 2045 A.D. for the Longitude of Perihelion 103° 42′ 28″.6 ;
(3) The date 1558 A.D. for the Precessional rate 25,826.54 ; and
(4) The 487 years' period for the application of the Pyramid's message as being from 1558 A.D. to 2045 A.D.

The outstanding feature of the identification noted is that the Egyptian priests represented the period of 487 years as belonging to a new era of civilisation. The Pyramid period of 5600 years is given by the King Lists as the period of Native Egyptian Dynastic history prior to the Epoch of the Persian Okhos—15 or 16 years prior to Alexander's coming to Egypt. The Pyramid's terminal period of 487 years is not, therefore, identified with Egyptian native history. It is placed as ushering in the new era of *European* civilisation beginning with Alexander the Great. *(Outstanding feature of Lists that the terminal period of 487 years is associated with a new era of European civilisation.)*

This feature of the Lists points clearly to the existence of an ancient tradition or record ascribing to the Pyramid symbolism, the definitely expressed intention of its message being associated with the conception of a future stage of *European* civilisation. Now the initial date for this period is defined by the Pyramid's astronomical data as 1558 A.D. The period itself is defined as ending in 2045 A.D. The period thus defined is actually the era of modern civilisation. Our further task will be to investigate whether these evidences of design and intention are purely accidental or whether they are the result of a knowledge of some Natural Law, knowledge that was possessed by the designer of the Pyramid, but which perished with him, or with the race and civilisation to which he belonged. We must consider whether this Natural Law is a law that is not now admitted to exist, but which, nevertheless, is a law, the knowledge and understanding of which are necessary to the full fruition of all human endeavour. *(Era defined by Pyramid as commencing 1558 A.D. The era identical with the era of modern civilisation. A question of moment.)*

Section I.—Summary and Conclusions.

¶ 255. THE QUEST.

In the Summary and Conclusions of Chapter III (Section I, ¶¶ 160 to 169) we saw that the arrangement and dimensions of the Pyramid's base plan completely defined the Earth's orbit and its variations in relation to astronomical time and space. The manner in which this was defined supplied us with certain simple geometrical relations and values that were seen to be expressive of an all-including Law of Gravitation. The whole geometrical expression of this Universal Law of astronomical time, space, and causality was seen to define the basal principles of an exact science of astronomical chronology. *(Exterior of Pyramid defines causal relations of the Earth and its orbital functions in time and space. The Universal Law relating to time, space, and causality. Principles of science of astronomical chronology.)*

The question of utilitarian motive concerning the design and construction of the Great Pyramid was seen to resolve itself into the obvious intention of conveying a message to a future stage of world civilisation. This message was indicated as being concerned with the handing on of a higher scientific knowledge than the future stage of civilisation could possibly attain. It appeared that this implied impossibility of attainment was due to the atrophy of faculties whose former normal employment had been in a particular realm of knowledge, unattainable without the aid of those faculties, and that the designer of the Pyramid knew that this atrophy would occur. The logical *(The Pyramid's message to a future race. The designer's certainty of the need for the message. The question of atrophied faculties and their revival or restoration.)*

inference was that it was deemed by the designer that the employment of these faculties would be a question of vital necessity to the stage of civilisation that could interpret the Pyramid's astronomical indications.

¶ 256. NATURAL LAW AND ANALOGY OF LAW OF CONTRACT.

Significance of attention being directed to the facts of the former knowledge as applied by its former exponents. The question of utilitarian motive and the indications converging thereon, combined to suggest that the Great Pyramid's message was concerned with the means whereby the atrophied faculties could and would be restored. It was indicated that the consideration of the facts of the former knowledge as applied by its past exponents would lead to the restoration of these faculties. This necessarily required a chronological connection between the period of the application of these facts and the period of the future civilisation.

Analogy between the Natural Law symbolism and the Law of Contract. In fact, as the matter is now presenting itself, it would seem as if the human race were, figuratively speaking, hereditarily party to a contract in terms of Universal Natural Law. That these terms required the fulfilling of certain obligations by all the parties to the contract ; that certain rights and privileges accrued in consequence ; and that these rights and privileges automatically lapsed as the obligations failed to be fulfilled. To continue the allegory as it seems to be presented, it would appear, not only that certain rights and privileges of the human race have lapsed—as a result of the failure of the human race to meet the obligations imposed upon it—but that failure, continuing to a time appointed in the contract, must be met by a suitable penalty provided for in the contract in accordance with the terms of its Natural Law. In the case of such penalty being applied, its purpose would necessarily be the enforcing of the conditions of the contract. Such enforcement—particularly in the case of ignorance of hereditary obligations—would be preceded by the reiteration of the conditions as the time appointed approached. Thus, in Law, " Time is the essence of the Contract." Hence **Significance of Pyramid's definition of chronology.** the significance of the Pyramid's definition of a scientifically accurate system of astronomical chronology.

¶ 257. THE TIME AND OTHER ESSENTIALS OF THE LAW.

Pyramid's external relations supplied a scientific framework for astronomical chronology. The first stage, therefore, of the developing of the Pyramid's message was seen to be concerned with the chronological connection. The Pyramid's external indications directed us to the elements of the framework supplying this connection. The framework supplied was seen to define the outlines of an exact scientific system of astronomical chronology.

The scientific system found defined in detail by the Pyramid's Passage system. The Pyramid's internal system of Passages and Chambers was then found to define the exact scientific system of astronomical chronology to which the external relations directed us. The co-ordinates of this graphical **Co-ordinates of system connect with exterior.** system were indicated as connected with the Pyramid's external geometry of the year circle, and with such simple geometrical functions of that as define the hollowing-in of the base square. The latter definition, again, was seen to portray the properties and values of the Earth and its relations to its orbit.

The chronology indicated was thus seen to be expressed as derived from the same simple geometrical relations as comprise the principles of the Pyramid's Universal Law of Gravitation.

An extension of the same Universal Law of Gravitation.

¶ 258. THE TEST CONDITIONS OF THE TIME-ESSENTIAL.

Certain conditions were laid down as to the manner in which the Pyramid's chronology should be defined in precise astronomical terms (¶¶ 167–169). These conditions were purposely formulated to be the severest test that modern astronomy could apply. They were formulated to require that the Pyramid should define its chronology in relation to modern times as definitely as " The Nautical Almanac and Astronomical Ephemeris " defines the current year.

The rigorous test conditions for the Pyramid's astronomical data.

The chief features of the conditions were—

Chief features of the test conditions.

(1) That the Pyramid Ephemeris should define years of modern time by the indication of precise astronomical values for these years ;

(2) That it should give, in each case, independent check values—all precisely agreeing as to the definition of the year, and as to the intention of such definition in each particular case ; and

(3) That in each case the year so precisely defined should be the one particular year that could be so defined within the entire possible range of human history.

Another rigorous element of the conditions was that years of remotely ancient time should be similarly defined, in order to show that they were intended to confirm the deductions drawn, and to assist in establishing the intention of the whole system. It was necessary that the ancient years thus defined should be so harmoniously related to the modern connections that no investigator, regarding the system as a whole, could fail to observe its definite intention. The conditions for the latter requirement were such that their fulfilment would establish emphatically the impossibility of every indicated value, for ancient and modern times, being other than the precisely exact value in each case ; and other than the natural consequence of the accurate representation of the operation of an Universal Law of Gravitation.

The range of application of the test conditions. Conditions required Pyramid's astronomical data to be specifically defined as Natural Law data.

¶ 259. THE TEST CONDITIONS FULFILLED.

All these conditions have been applied to the Pyramid's Passage system of astronomical chronology discussed in the present chapter. The conditions, in every case, have been completely fulfilled. In addition, new evidence has arisen during the course of our investigation. This has clearly and fully established the system as intentional and exact, and has indicated other methods of interpreting the message of the Pyramid.

Conditions fulfilled. Additional evidence. Further elucidation of the Pyramid's message.

The key to the Pyramid's Passage system of astronomical chronology is now seen to lie in the geometrical quantity defining the central displacement of the Pyramid's base sides. This same quantity defines the displacement of the central vertical plane of the Passage system, and defines the purpose

The base displacement value = Passage displacement value = key to chronology system.

of this displacement (¶¶ 225, 234, 235, 236, 245, 249, and 254; Plate XL, Fig. C).

Displacement
value in base
defines Earth
and its orbit,
and variations
in time and
space.
Also defines
variations in
Precessional
and Orbital
rates of
motion, and
by these fixes
all dates in
Pyramid's
chronology
system.
Independent
algebraic and
geometrical
check data.

This quantity—in Chapter III, ¶¶ 148-159—was seen to define, by its application to the Pyramid's base circuit, all the relations in time and orbital space between the Earth and its orbital values and variations. The same displacement value, by its application to the geometrical elements of the base circuit, and the Pyramid's vertical section, is now seen to define all the variations in the rates of Precessional and Perihelion motion (Plate XL, Fig. C). By this definition it fixes the Pyramid's chronology system in relation to the modern system of astronomy (¶ 236). It gives, what one might have deemed to be impossible, the geometrical definition of the algebraic formulæ for these rates of motion (¶¶ 234-238, 243-249). The integration of the respective formulæ supply the total angle of Precession (¶ 238), and the change in the Longitude of Perihelion (¶ 247)—in each case between two independently specified dates. In each case, again, the interval in years is also supplied by the Pyramid in the form of geometrical indications independent entirely of the formula. In each case the initial date is a remotely ancient date, and the terminal date a year within the range of modern times.

¶ 260. PRECESSIONAL AND ORBITAL CHRONOLOGICAL SYSTEMS DEFINED.

Pyramid's
Precessional
values define
1844 A.D. and
4699 B.C.
Interval of 90°
Precession
from toe of
Castor.

In the case of the Precessional values, the terminal date is defined as midnight ending the 25th January 1844 A.D. (¶¶ 239-242 and Plate XL, Fig. A). This is geometrically indicated as the completion of 90° of Precession from an ancient Zodiacal Epoch (¶ 238, and Plate XLI, Fig. M). The latter is algebraically and, by independent indications, geometrically defined as 4699 B.C. The latter identification fixes the date at which the Autumnal Equinox coincided with the last point of the Zodiacal sign, Taurus, or the first point of Gemini. The latter is defined by the toe of Castor (Plates XLIV, XLVIII, and L).

Pyramid's
values for
orbital motion
define Longi-
tude of
Perihelion 0°
at 4044 B.C.
and Longitude
103° 42' 28".6
at 2045 A.D.
The meaning
of the Passage
displacement.

In the case of the Perihelion values the initial date is defined as 4044 B.C. (¶¶ 244 and 247). This is defined as the date at which the Longitude of Perihelion was 0° (Plate LV). The terminal date is indicated as 2045 A.D., this being defined as the date at which the Longitude of Perihelion will be 103° 42' 28".6—the sum of the base angles of the Pyramid's vertical section (¶ 247). This indication of the summation of two equal values associated with the base is confirmed by a similar indication. The date at which the Precessional rate equalled the sum of the Pyramid's base diagonals is defined as 286.1 years—the Passage displacement value and the base displacement value—prior to the 25th January 1844 A.D. (¶¶ 236 and 249).

¶ 261. THE SCALAR CHRONOLOGY DEFINED.

Six independ-
ent series of
astronomical
proofs of the
chronology
systems.

Altogether there are six independent series of astronomical values supplied fixing and confirming the system of chronology outlined (¶ 248).

The chronology thus established is confirmed to the second decimal place of a year over an interval of 6541.41 years in one case, and of 6087.94 years in another.

The former interval is defined as the period of Precessional chronology, and the latter as the period of Orbital (or Perihelion) chronology. The former is geometrically and algebraically defined as beginning at 4699 B.C., and the latter at 4044 B.C. (¶¶ 238, 247, and 250).

The arithmetic basis for the related definition of these two systems of astronomical chronology is geometrically defined as a scalar system of 6000 years (¶¶ 212–216, 230, 237, 243, 246, and Plate XL, Fig. F). The manner in which this is framed and indicated supplies the precise equivalent for the modern astronomical formula of interpolation (Plate XXXVII, and ¶ 230). This scalar system is central to the Orbital chronology, and is its algebraic datum (Plate XL, Fig. F, and ¶¶ 216, 227, 229, and 244). It is also the algebraic datum for the Precessional chronology (¶¶ 236–238 and 243).

The scalar system of chronology 6000 years. 4000 B.C. to 2001 A.D. Centre of scalar system specifically defined as centre of orbital system of chronology 1000 B.C.

The central point of the scalar system is geometrically and structurally defined as representing the Autumnal Equinox 1000 B.C. The initial and terminal points of the scalar system are similarly defined as representing the Autumnal Equinox at 4000 B.C. and 2001 A.D. respectively (Plate XL, Fig. F, and ¶¶ 216, 230, and 243).

¶ 262. THE CONFIRMING APPLICATION OF THE EGYPTIAN KING LISTS (¶¶ 212–216, and 250–254).

The chronological and astronomical periods and datings of Epochs thus established by the Great Pyramid's system of geometry are independently established by the chronological systems of the ancient Egyptians. The chronological basis and Epochs of the original Old Chronicle of Egypt are identical with the basis and Epochs of the Pyramid's scalar system of chronology. The chronological periods of the King Lists are identical with the astronomical periods of the Pyramid's Orbital (or Perihelion) and Precessional systems of chronology. Synchronistic comparison of these periods of the King Lists and their alleged Epochs with the chronology and true Epochs of the Old Egyptian Chronicle independently establishes the astronomical datings of the Pyramid's Orbital and Precessional systems of chronology, in relation to modern time. The comparison also proves that the King Lists fictitiously identified the chronological datings of the Pyramid's Orbital and Precessional chronologies as, in each case, 1903 to 1905 years prior to their actual astronomical definition.

Chronological datum of the Old Egyptian Chronicle identical with Pyramid's scalar chronology. Total periods of Egyptian King Lists identical with Pyramid's astronomical periods. Synchronising Old Chronicle and King Lists independently supplies Pyramid's astronomical datings in relation to modern time.

One striking feature, common to the presentation of the King Lists and the Pyramid's presentation of the astronomical data, concerns a terminal period of 487 years. This is defined by the Pyramid as the period—from 1558 A.D. to 2045 A.D.—to which the Pyramid's message was designed to apply. The period thus defined is, strangely enough, the period of a new active phase of European civilisation, following a long " stationary " period

Pyramid's terminal period defining era of modern European civilisation applied in King Lists to define era of European civilisation commencing with Alexander the Great.

of civilisation. In the Egyptian King Lists, the period is identified as beginning the active period of European civilisation ushered in by the conquests of Alexander the Great. The beginning of the terminal period is thus marked by the Lists as the definitive close of the " quiescent " period of native Egyptian history, and as defining the Epoch of the passing of the source of world dominion from the East to the West.

¶ 263. THE MATHEMATICAL ENIGMA OF THE PYRAMID.

The coincidence thus holding between the historical conditions of the anticipated Epoch and the historical conditions of the true Epoch of application, as astronomically defined in the Pyramid, directs our attention to an important feature of the mathematical relations of the Pyramid's geometrical, astronomical, and scalar data. This is a feature that must, of necessity, have become a matter of increasing perplexity to the mathematician. The problem presented is akin to that discussed (in ¶¶ 46 and 47) in relation to the Pyramid's noon reflexion phenomena and the four mathematical constants.

The new problem may be illustrated by considering the analogy between the various relations of the Earth and its orbit and the structural parts— and functions of those parts—in a modern work of construction. In designing the latter, the architect or engineer employs a scale of measurement. This may be the English system of feet and inches, or the continental metric system. Any other architect or engineer—not having seen the original plans, and not knowing what system of measurement was adopted in the construction—can find from the structural dimensions of the building what scale of measurement was adopted. This is generally a simple matter, owing to the fact that in the majority of dimensions, architects or engineers use simple multiples or subdivisions of the units of their scale of measurement.

When, however, the construction is a piece of complicated machinery in which all dimensions are intimately related to the mechanical functions, dynamical effects and structural relations holding between the various parts of the machine, the search for the scale of measurement becomes a very complicated matter indeed. Let us add to these conditions that the scale of measurement was purposely designed for this one piece of machinery only, and that the scale was designed to simplify the mathematical relations between the various complicated factors of the machine. In such case it is a mathematical impossibility for the scale of measurement to be known other than by its being disclosed by the designer himself.

¶ 264. THE DESIGN AND ITS RELATIONS.

The latter conditions apply to the case of the scalar system of the Pyramid's astronomical relations. All these relations are seen to be mathematical functions expressed in terms of the scalar system. The scalar system is not an interpolated haphazard application of a system of measurement; it bears throughout an intimate relationship to all the astronomical values. Without the scalar system, the astronomical values cannot be expressed in terms of the Universal Natural Law governing the system. The Pyramid's scalar system is, therefore, seen to be the scalar system of Universal Natural Law. The Great Pyramid makes known this scalar system. The necessary conclusion is that the scalar system was disclosed by its inventor to the Pyramid's designer, or that the Pyramid's designer was the inventor of the scalar system. The Inventor of the scalar system was, however, necessarily the Inventor of the Universal Natural Law. The Inventor of the latter is, necessarily, the Creator of the Universe. *The Pyramid makes this known, otherwise its derivation would be mathematically impossible. The scalar system is the numerical basis of the Natural Law dominating the system of astronomical cycles.*

We cannot safely come to any other conclusion than that the designer of the geometrical system of the Great Pyramid was also the Designer of the Universe. The design of the Pyramid was necessarily revealed to its builder—together with the purpose of the design—by the Great Architect of the Universe. *The scalar system necessarily revealed by the designer of the Natural Law. The Pyramid's system necessarily a matter of Divine revelation.*

¶ 265. MODERN EFFORT IN RELATION TO MODERN DIS-COVERY.

The mathematical reader, building his inferential premises upon the mathematical discoveries of Newton, Kepler, Laplace, Gausz, Euler, Leverrier, Adams, Kelvin, J. J. Thomson, and Einstein, may deem that the conclusion as stated may require modification. He may consider that the sequence of modern discovery falls into the same category as the "discovery" of the Pyramid method of presenting the facts of Universal Law. We may term the various categories of such modern discoveries, branches of the wider field of the Pyramid's system of application. The modern discovery most nearly approaching the extent of this field is that contained in Einstein's pronouncement of his hypothesis of the Universality of his Principle of Relativity. *The outstanding peculiarity common to epoch-making mathematical discoveries. Newton, Kepler, Laplace, Gausz, Euler, Leverrier, Adams, Einstein.*

The nature of Einstein's discovery, and also the nature of Newton's and Kepler's discoveries, place all such outstanding scientific discoveries in a single enigmatical category. All such discoveries came as instantaneous rays of light to their discoverers. Any research worker knows the process and its instantaneousness, and all students of the history of mathematics know how it has been such lightning flashes that have pointed the way from discovery to discovery. Effort indeed is, and always has been, necessary. Effort is the research worker's process of acquiring his equivalent of the language whereby facts may be revealed to him in terms of the field of effort relating to these facts. *The process of research. Enlightening flashes of knowledge exceeding the speed of thought. The relation of effort to the essential discovery.*

Newton could not prove his laws before he applied them, yet he knew them before their application was made. Indeed, it is a certain matter that Einstein cannot prove his theory absolutely by mathematical processes exclusive of the experimental field. Yet the theory preceded the application. It has been the same with all epoch-making mathematical discoveries. For *Discovery of the laws precedes their application. Application proves the laws.*

The "language" of effort and the tardy acceptance of new discoveries in Natural Law.

this reason, such discoveries take a long time to be accepted. Other workers have to acquire the " language " of the discoverer's field of effort. They are, for this reason, seldom the accredited authorities contemporary with the discoverer. One merely has to cite the known instance of Newton and his own University, Cambridge ; but since then Cambridge has made good in many fields of importance equal to Newton's field of research.

¶ 266. THE HIGHER INDUCTION AND ITS FIELD.

The creation of a new field of Inductive Thought defined.
The process of Higher Induction.
Intellectual effort in the new field attunes the mind to synchronise with the laws of influence within the field.
Synchronisation begets knowledge, and knowledge discovery of the law.

Now the astronomical chronology of the Great Pyramid defines the period from 1558 A.D. to 2045 A.D. as the period of the *creation* of a new Era of Inductive Thought. In thus defining, it gives to *Induction* its larger scientific meaning. It defines the process of the period as the Creation by Higher Induction of a *Field of Intellectual Influence* analogous to the creation, by induction, of the field of Physical influence. Minds attuned to this intellectual influence, by effort in its field, felt their efforts being directed along a definite path. Accommodating their effort to the influence felt in the new direction, their effort synchronised with the directing Law. This being perceived, led to the enunciation of the Law. The process in effect lies in synchronising one's will and effort with a stream of energy from the Godhead—whether realised as such or not. Such, in effect, is the process of Revelation. In the life of the Christian the process of synchronisation is faith.

Revelation, realised and unrealised.
Pyramid's enunciation of Natural Law compared with modern enunciations of Natural Law.

The discoveries of Newton, Kepler, and their great successors all fall, therefore, within a similar category to that of the scientific Revelation of the Great Pyramid. The latter, again, defines the chronological field of the former, which advances the Pyramid's science into a category of Revelation infinitely beyond that defining the process of modern scientific discovery.

¶ 267. THE VITAL QUESTION—FACT OR THEORY?

Sceptical criticism and the directing conclusions.
The factor possibly influencing premature pronouncement of certainty.
Conclusions adopted as framing a hypothesis of Revelation concerning the Pyramid and its message.

The sceptical critic may pronounce that the fullness of our conclusions is scarcely warranted by the data upon which the conclusions have been based. It may be that there would be some show of reason in this pronouncement. It is possible that what we know further concerning the Pyramid's indications and the message proclaimed by such indications, may have influenced our statement of the conclusions. But then, it is not easy for one acquainted with the facts to see matters from the point of view of those unacquainted with the facts. If, then, it should appear that the conclusions claim to be more far-reaching than the data warrant at this stage, we are content to let the matter stand as a hypothesis of Revelation that requires to be confirmed as completely as the Pyramid's scientific purpose has been established.

The pivot of judgment.

The whole matter hinges upon the question of the Pyramid's accidental or intentional definition of the modern era of European civilisation and

discovery, and upon the accidental or intentional application—by the
Egyptian King Lists—of the period thus defined to the era of European
civilisation ushered in by Alexander the Great. The latter application
seems to be confirmed as an intentional application by the various statements
of the Coptic traditions quoted in the Arabic MS. accounts of Masoudi,
Al Kodhai, and Makrizi (¶¶ 111 and 112). These all define the geometrical
and astronomical purpose of the Great Pyramid, and associate it with
astronomical cycles and with the prophetic elucidation of future history.

The question of accident or intention.
Coptic traditions concerning Pyramid's astronomy confirmed.
Coptic traditions concerning Pyramid prophecy.

¶ 268. THE HEBREW NAME OF THE PYRAMID.

In this connection we are driven to a reconsideration of the name of the
Great Pyramid. In Egyptian the name is "Khuti"—"The Lights." In
Chaldee and Hebrew the equivalent name is "Urim"—"The Lights."
In Hebrew, however, "Urim"—"The Lights"—is used almost exclusively
to denote "Revelation"; hence the Divine Oracle, "Urim and Thummin"
—the Hebrew means of communication with Jehovah in the Holy of Holies
of the Temple. It was associated with the Shekinah, the Ark of the Covenant,
and the High Priest's Breastplate.

The Pyramid name—"The Lights."
In Hebrew, "Revelation."
"Urim and Thummin."
The Divine Oracle.

Now we saw that the original of the name "Pyramid" was the Chaldee
"Urim-middin," literally "The Lights—The Measures." In its Hebrew
sense we now see that the name signifies literally "Revelation—Measures,"
this defining that the Great Pyramid is "The Metrological or Geometrical
Expression of Divine Revelation."

Hebrew name for the Great Pyramid signifies "the Geometrical Expression of Divine Revelation."

If this definition is correct, we have a complete explanation of the statement in Jeremiah xxxii, 18–20—

Jeremiah on a Divine Revelation set up in permanent form in Egypt.

"The Great, the Mighty God, the Lord of Hosts, is his name, Great
in counsel, and mighty in work........Which hast set signs and
wonders in the land of Egypt, even unto this day........"

This explanation would account for the use of a Pyramid symbolism in
the allegorical language of the Old and New Testaments. In such allegorical
references, the mystical body of Christ is likened to the Pyramid with Christ
Himself as the Apex-stone—the Headstone of the Chief Corner.[1]

The Bible's Pyramid allegory.
Jesus Christ the Apex.

[1] The Apex-stone="The Head of the Corner" (1 Pet. ii, 7)=Jesus Christ;
                ="The Stone which the builders rejected" (Ps. cxviii, 22; Matt. xxi, 42;
                        Acts iv, 11; 1 Pet. ii, 4 and 7).
Also 1 Cor. x, 4; Deut. xxxiii, 3, 4; Ps. xviii, 2; 1 Sam. ii, 2; Gen. xlix, 24; Dan. ii, 45.
The individual living stones or "lively stones" comprising the structure (1 Pet. ii, 5 and 9;
Eph. iv, 13-16).
Relation between the "Head" and the "Body"—The Structure=The mystical Body of
Christ (Eph. i, 17-20; ii, 19-22; iv, 13-16).
"The Measure of the Stature of the Fullness of Christ" (Eph. iv, 11-13; ii, 16).
Complete symbolism of Pyramid's immutable science (The Divine Universal Law)="In
whom (Christ) are hid all the treasures of wisdom and knowledge" (Col. ii, 3); and by whom
God "created all things" (Eph. iii, 9).
The Purpose outlined by the Bible's Pyramid allegory (Matt. xxi, 42; Dan. ii, 34, 35, 44,
and 45; Is. xxviii, 16-18; Rom. viii).
The Divine "Reconstruction" (Ezek. xxxvi, 32-37); "the restitution of all things"
(Acts iii, 21).

¶ 269. THE RELEASING OF CHAOS,

If, then, our conclusions herein are correct, if the Pyramid contains a message to the modern era it defines so thoroughly, we would expect the Pyramid's indications to declare emphatically, not only the historical relations of past time, but also the detailed events of significance related to current history. It has seemed to define intentionally as such the era of development of modern inductive science. The chief feature of such development in current times has been the misdirection of scientific knowledge. Man has applied his discoveries in science to the creation of machinery of destruction. Man has set in motion relentless energies that he cannot now control. He has made of his boasted world of civilisation a chaotic shambles. He is devising the means of protecting himself from the energies already released, and in thus devising, is releasing new and more terrible energies for his own destruction.

If ever a Divine message was prepared for the human race, it was prepared for the current time more certainly than for any previous period of human history. We would expect that a Divine message of this nature would define the conditions now current if it applied to those conditions. We would expect it to give the precise dates of such events as determined and shaped the period of waste and terror just past, and that, in spite of the best intentions, are even now determining and shaping a period of waste and terror of greater significance ahead. But the definition of such would be cold comfort to possess, unless indeed the definition contained a remedy, and the certain indications of the remedy being applied. In looking for the definition of the current conditions we are, therefore, seeking for the remedy, and for the definitive indication that the remedy will be applied. If we can establish this certainty we need not concern ourselves with the age-long problem concerning why God permits destruction. We shall content ourselves with the knowledge that God will prevent the extinction of the human race, and that He will restore it. Then we shall understand why the Hebrew prophet Isaiah proclaimed :—

> " In that day shall there be an altar to the Lord, in the midst of the land of Egypt, and a pillar at the border thereof to the Lord.
> " And it shall be for a sign and for a witness unto the Lord of Hosts in the land of Egypt ; for they shall cry unto the Lord because of the oppressors, and he shall send them a saviour, and a great one, and he shall deliver them."[1]

In understanding the significance attaching to this prophecy we shall see that the Pyramid teaches us more concerning the Bible than its destructive critical " exponents " have hitherto permitted us to know. For this reason we have avoided throughout any refutation of the opinions of the destructive critics. The Bible, being what it claims to be—and the Pyramid establishes this beyond cavil—stands as its own authority, and by its own clear exposi-

[1] Is. xix, 19, 20. The whole chapter should be read in this connection. For the geographical location of the " altar " and " pillar " referred to, " in the midst of " and at the same time " at the border thereof," refer Plate III.

tions, in the fullness of its own appointed time, shall confound the destructive critic and refute his opinions.

"Therefore, behold, I will proceed to do a marvellous thing among this people, even a marvellous work and a wonder: for the wisdom of their wise men shall perish, and the understanding of their prudent men shall be hid."[1]

Isaiah proclaims the Ephemeral nature of human wisdom.

¶ 270. TWO PERSPECTIVES—1911 AND 1923.

Professor F. Soddy, in his " Matter and Energy "—published in 1911— throws some light upon the feature of modern science dealt with in ¶ 265. This statement is remarkable as having been made before the war. He states (pp. 245–253) :—

The outlook of civilisation in 1911.

"Civilisation, as it is at present, even on the purely physical side, is not a continuous self-supporting movement. The conditions under which it originates determine its period and fix the date of its decline. It becomes possible only after an age-long accumulation of energy, by the supplementing of income out of capital........It reaps what it has not sown, and exhausts, so far, without replenishing."

Modern civilisation "reaps what it has not sown—exhausts without re-plenishing."

"........It is perfectly obvious that........a turning-point is being reached in the upward progress which has hitherto kept pace with the advancement of knowledge........So far, Science has been a fair-weather friend. It has been generally misunderstood as creating the wealth that has followed the application of knowledge. Modern science, however, and its synonym, modern civilisation, create nothing except knowledge. After a hand-to-mouth period of existence, it has come in for, and has learned how to *spend*, an inheritance it can never hope to restore........ "

" A turning-point is being reached." " Modern science and modern civilisation create nothing except knowledge."

"........The world is great enough and rich enough to supply human aspirations and ambitions beyond all present dreams. But the human intellect must keep pace in its development with the expanding vision of natural abundance."

The necessity that the " human intellect should keep pace with development."

Some three or four years after this was written the war had foreshortened the perspective of the picture here presented. In the light of the after-effects of war, the statement assumes a new and terrible significance, not to genera-tions yet unborn, but to the living generation of our " tragic Epoch." The war and its aftermath—the double harvest of modern civilisation—have clearly accelerated the operating of the factors relating to civilisation, " as it is at present," which factors, to quote Professor Soddy, " determine its period and fix the date of its decline."

The outlook of civilisation in 1923. " The tragic Epoch."

In thus dealing with the pessimistic side of the problem, we do so with the certain knowledge that the factors of destruction will be diverted through successive phases of chaos to their own undoing, and that the Pyramid's message is concerned with the means whereby this will be effected.

The nature of the Pyramid's message.

[1] Is. xxix, 14.

SECTION II.—PRECESSION, THE ZODIAC AND ORBITAL MOVEMENT.

¶ 271. THE EFFECT OF THE EARTH'S EQUATORIAL PRO-
TUBERANCE.

The Earth flattened at the Poles, bulged outwards along the Equator.

The figure of the Earth is in the form of an oblate spheroid. In consequence, the Earth's equatorial diameter is longer than its polar diameter. The equatorial diameter is roughly $\frac{1}{300}$th longer than the polar diameter. For a meridian section (*i.e.* a section of the Earth passing through both poles) Bessel determined the ellipticity of the section (or its polar flattening) as $\frac{1}{299.15}$. The U.S.A. Geodetic Survey results, 1906 and 1909, give the data as follows :—

	Equatorial Radius.	Reciprocal of Flattening.	Polar Radius.
	Metres.		Metres.
1906 U.S.A. Survey	6,378,283	297.8	6,356,868
1909 ,,	6,378,388	297.0 ± 0.5	6,356,909

The attraction of any body acting in a plane oblique to the plane of Earth's equatorial bulge tends to pull the latter into the plane of attraction. The Earth's mechanical factors counteract the tendency by producing a " wobbling " of the Earth's axis.

The Earth, therefore, has what is known as an equatorial bulge. There is consequently a maximum concentration of matter around the equator. The attraction of other bodies of the solar system—when exerted in planes oblique to the plane of the Earth's diurnal rotation—act upon the Earth's equatorial protuberance. The *tendency* of such action is to pull the equatorial plane into the plane of attraction of a particular body. The mechanical factors governing the Earth's diurnal rotation *resent* the action, and counteract the tendency of such action. This they do by absorbing the effect of the pull in a secondary rotation. Thus a spinning-top may be observed rotating tranquilly round its vertical axis. The slightest external force tending to deflect its plane of rotation will, however, be met immediately by a counteraction, in the form of secondary rotation, appearing as a " wobbling " motion to the observer. Both the action and the counteraction—in the case of the Earth—are due to the Law or Laws governing matter and the motion of matter.

¶ 272. FIXED SPINNING-TOP, SPINNING VERTICALLY.

Illustration :—Spinning-top.

Now let the spinning-top in the illustration given be supposed to have a fine pencil projecting upwards as a continuation of its spinning axis, and let this pencil be supposed to mark the movement of the axis on a horizontal Case I :— Fixed spinning, vertical rotation undisturbed. sheet of cardboard. In the first case, the top was described as spinning "tranquilly" on a vertical axis. In this case, no movement of the axis would be indicated on the cardboard. The pencil would mark a point only on the cardboard.

In the second case, the tranquil motion was disturbed by an external Case II :— Fixed spinning vertical rotation uniformly disturbed. force. In this case, let the point of the spinning-top be fixed in a tiny frictionless cup to prevent lateral movement of the point. Let the external force be represented by the constant pressure of a fine jet of water impinging obliquely downwards on the bulging portion of the top's surface. The pressure thus produced is equal to an attraction or pull in an exactly opposite " Precession " illustrated. direction. In this case the top will spin with the " wobbling motion " already referred to, the " wobble " or secondary rotation being indicated by the pencil tracing a circle on the cardboard, with the originally fixed point as centre Cycle of Precession for the case illustrated. of the circle. The path of this circle defines what is termed the " Precession " of the axis of the spinning-top. The top may perform 10, 20, 50, or any number of its primary rotations within the space of time it takes the pencil axis to trace out one revolution of the secondary motion. In this case, the number of primary rotations defines the cycle of Precession of the secondary motion.

In the latter case, the pencil axis describes a cone with its original vertical position as axis of that cone.

¶ 273. SPINNING-TOP, SPINNING OBLIQUELY, FIXED, OR FREE.

Let it be supposed that a fixed spinning-top is arranged to spin with its Illustration :— Spinning-top. axis stationary in a given inclined direction, so long as it is not subjected to the additional pressure or attraction described in the preceding ¶ 272, Case II. Case Ia :— Fixed spinning, inclined rotation undisturbed. The spinning-top can be fixed on a table, spinning at a given inclination to the table. The pencil axis in such case will mark a single point only on the sheet of cardboard, as in Case I of ¶ 272.

With the application of a uniform external force as in Case II of ¶ 272, Case IIa :— Fixed spinning, inclined rotation uniformly disturbed. the pencil axis will describe a cone with its original inclined position as axis of that cone, and its point will describe a circle on the cardboard about the original fixed point as centre of circle.

Let the top, designed to spin at a fixed inclination to the table, be also Case IIIa :— Case Ia spinning in a fixed circle. designed to move freely on the surface of the table. Let it be then constrained to move in a fixed circle at a uniform rate, with its spinning axis at a fixed inclination to the surface of the table, and pointing in a fixed direction. Thus, if the axis of the spinning-top is inclined at 66½° to the table surface and its direction of inclination towards, say, the South end of the table, the spinning-top will move round the circle, spinning at a constant rate of, say, 365 rotations per complete revolution of the circle, without altering the angle of inclination and the direction of inclination towards the South end of the

Illustration of
the Earth's
orbital motion
neglecting
precession.

table. This illustrates precisely the conditions of the Earth in its orbit if we suppose the Earth to be free from any external attractions affecting its equatorial protuberance.

¶ 274. THE EARTH AS A SPINNING-TOP.

**Illustration
of plane of
Earth's orbit
(and Ecliptic),
polar axis of
rotation, and
its inclination
to plane of
Ecliptic.**

In the case given, the plane of the table represents the plane of the Earth's orbit—or the plane of the Ecliptic—the axis of the top represents the Earth's polar axis, the pencil point represents the continued Northern projection of the Earth's polar axis, and the angle of 66½° with the table surface represents the inclination of the polar axis with the plane of the Ecliptic. The last feature, however, is otherwise defined. The manner in which this is effected is best understood by comparing Case I with Case Ia.

**If Earth were
spinning
vertically in
its orbit, the
polar axis of
rotation would
coincide with
the Ecliptic
axis.**

In Case I, as illustrating the case of the Earth spinning on a vertical axis, the Earth's polar axis would be said to coincide with the Ecliptic axis. The Ecliptic axis is therefore the line that the Earth's axis of rotation would possess were the Earth spinning vertically. In Case IIIa, then, the inclination of the Earth's polar axis with the plane of the Ecliptic—i.e. 66½°—is also explained in an inclination of 23½° with the Ecliptic axis.

**If Earth's
equatorial
protuberance
were
undisturbed
by external
attractions,
Earth's polar
axis would
point always
in the same
direction, i.e.
there would
be no pre-
cession of the
polar axis.**

Case IIIa shows that, *were the Earth free from any external attractions affecting its equatorial protuberance*, the polar axis of the Earth would point in a constant direction—i.e. towards the same region of the heavens—throughout each successive day, month, and year of the Earth's existence, unaffected by successive repetitions of its diurnal rotations and successive annual revolutions.

Plate XLV illustrates the direction the Earth's inclination occupies throughout the year in modern times, and which it would always occupy were the conditions as assumed above.

To the inclination of the Earth's polar axis with the Ecliptic plane are due the seasons and the vegetational phenomena of the seasons.

¶ 275. PRECESSION OF THE EQUINOXES.

**Case IVa :—
Case IIa
spinning in a
fixed circle.
Polar axis
inclined and
equatorial
protuberance
subjected to
external
disturbance.
Resulting
" wobble "
produces a
slow change
in the "direc-
tion" of the
inclined axis.
This change of
direction of
the polar axis
is " Preces-
sion."**

If now we add the special conditions of Case IIa to the conditions of Case IIIa, we have an exact illustration of the Earth's *principal* motions in its orbit. These motions can therefore be illustrated by a spinning-top—

(1) Performing 365 rotations in the course of its revolution round the circle defining the yearly orbit, during which its axis of inclination remains *sensibly* the same, and the direction of its inclination *sensibly* the same ; but

(2) In the course of about 26,000 revolutions of its orbit (*i.e.* in about 26,000 years) the axis of inclination describes the cone referred to in Case IIa, pointing, at the end of this period, in the same direction as it pointed at the beginning.

The latter movement is illustrated by the successive stages presented by Plates XLIV to XLVII. Each Plate shows four successive positions of the Earth in its orbit during a year. Positions on other days of the same year have the same direction of inclination. Thus Plate XLIV represents the direction of inclination of the Earth's axis during the year 4699 B.C. Plate XLV represents the direction of inclination of the Earth's axis during the year 1844 A.D.—the direction having altered 90° between 4699 B.C. and 1844 A.D. Plate XLVI represents the direction of inclination of the axis during the year 8203¼ A.D.—the direction having altered 180° between 4699 B.C. and 8203¼ A.D. Plate XLVII represents the direction of inclination of the axis during the year 14,390 A.D.—the direction having altered 270° between 4699 B.C. and 14,390 A.D. The direction then returns to the position represented on Plate XLIV, which now represents the direction of the axis for the year 20,415 A.D.—the direction having turned round 360° between 4699 B.C. and 20,415 A.D. Between these two dates, the cycle of Precession is a period of 25,112¾ years. For other earlier dates, the period is greater ; for later dates, the period is less. Thus for precession of 360° prior to 1844 A.D., the precessional cycle is a period of 27,376.1 years, beginning at 25,533 B.C. and ending at 1844 A.D. ; and for precession 360° forward in time from 1844 A.D., the precessional cycle is a period of 24,442.2 years, beginning at 1844 A.D. and ending at 26,286 A.D.

Marginal notes: Direction changes completely round 360° in about 26,000 years. Plates XLIV to XLVII illustrate directions of Earth's polar axis for successive directions 90° apart, and at the dates stated in each case. Precessional cycle, 4699 B.C. to 20,415 A.D. = 25,112¾ years. Precessional cycle :— 25,533 B.C. to 1844 A.D. = 27,376 years. 1844 A.D. to 26,286 A.D. = 24,442 years. 11,434 B.C. to 14,390 A.D. = 25,822.65 years, i.e. central to 1844 A.D.

For 180° prior to 1844 A.D., ½ period   ..   ..   =13,276.20 years.
And for 180° after 1844 A.D., ½ period   ..   ..   =12,546.45   ,,

Precessional period 11,434 B.C. to 14,390 A.D.
Cycle   ..   ..   =25,822.65 years.

These periods follow from the formula and method of ¶ 238.

¶ 276. THE SOLAR DAY AND THE SIDEREAL DAY.

Now, in ¶¶ 273 and 275, 365 rotations were taken as illustrating the case of the revolution of the Earth round its orbit. *Strictly speaking*, this is untrue —even as an approximation.

In the course of a solar year, the Sun *appears* to revolve round the Earth 365.2422 times, thus defining the number of days. If, however, the Sun were hidden for a year, we would observe that the stellar heavens *appear* to revolve round the Earth 366.2422 times in a solar year. The reason is that the Earth in revolving *externally* round the Sun, is performing its revolution internally to the stellar heavens. The stellar heavens, therefore, appear to revolve 366.2422 times to the Sun's apparent 365.2422 times. Hence the apparent diurnal revolution of the stellar heavens is termed a " sidereal day " and the diurnal revolution of the Sun is termed a " solar day." The latter is the day as commonly known. The former is an astronomical unit employed in the "Nautical Almanac" and astronomical ephemerides. Hence,

Marginal notes: The solar year = 365.2422 solar days (or "apparent" revolutions of the Sun) ; = 366.2422 sidereal days, (or "apparent" revolutions of the stellar heavens).

One *Solar* Year =365.2422 solar days,
    ,,   ,,   =366.2422 sidereal days.

PLATE XLIV.

PRECESSION OF THE EQUINOXES—THE SOLAR YEAR
IN 4699 B.C.

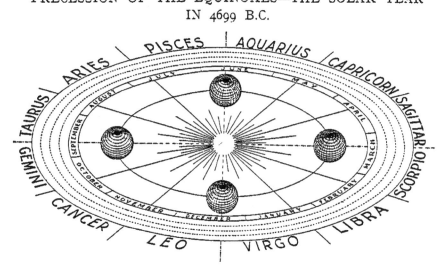

PLATE XLV.

PRECESSION OF THE EQUINOXES—THE SOLAR YEAR
IN 1844 A.D.

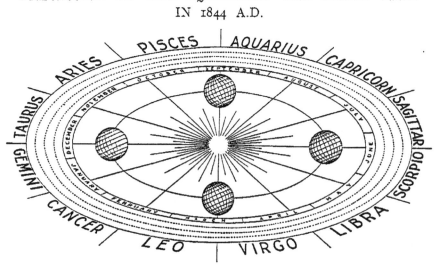

PLATE XLVI.

PRECESSION OF THE EQUINOXES—THE SOLAR YEAR
IN 8203¼ A.D.

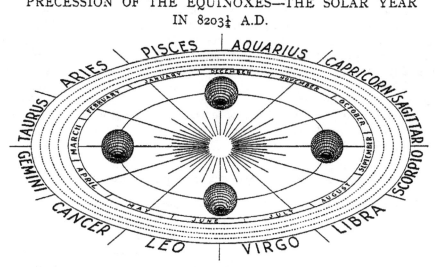

PLATE XLVII.

PRECESSION OF THE EQUINOXES—THE SOLAR YEAR
IN 14,390½ A.D.

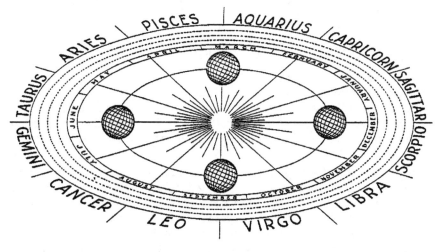

The solar year, defined as consisting of 366.2422 sidereal days, is termed the "Sidereal year" in some elementary works on astronomy, and in others that ought to know better. This designation, however, is a misnomer. The Sidereal year—as defined in ¶¶ 150 and 155—is the duration in solar days of the Earth's complete revolution of the stellar heavens. The amount by which the solar year falls short of the sidereal year is determined by the extent to which the direction of the Earth's polar axis is altered, by its precessional factors, in the course of a year. The resulting slip backwards of the solar year round the stellar heavens is illustrated in successive stages by the modern month indications of Plates XLIV–XLVII inclusive.

¶ 277.   THE VARIOUS ELEMENTS OF PRECESSION.

Now the plane of the Earth's orbit is necessarily the plane in which the Sun's attraction acts on the Earth. Owing to the inclination of the Earth's axis of rotation to the plane of the orbit, the plane of the Earth's equatorial protuberance is oblique to the plane of the Sun's attraction. In consequence, the latter attraction tends to pull the plane of the equatorial protuberance into the plane of the Earth's orbit. The Earth counteracts this tendency by means of the "wobbling" motion described in ¶¶ 271, 272, and 275. The resulting slow change of direction of the Earth's axis—measured by its annual extent of change—is termed "Solar Precession."

Again, the plane of the Moon's orbit round the Earth being oblique to the plane of the Earth's equatorial protuberance, a similar action and counter-action result. Precession resulting from this is termed "Lunar Precession."

As the orbits of all the other planets are oblique to the plane of the Earth's equator, a similar resultant action and counteraction are due to planetary attractions. Precession resulting from this is termed "Planetary Precession."

The algebraic sum of all three Precessional values is the total precession, and is termed "General Precession."

¶ 278.   APPARENT—AS DISTINCT FROM ACTUAL—MOVEMENTS.

To an observer on the Earth, the Earth appears to be stationary. The Sun appears to perform a complete revolution round the Earth in the course of a solar day, and the stellar heavens to perform a complete revolution round the Earth in the course of a sidereal day (¶ 276). Similarly, the moon and all the planets appear to revolve round the Earth each in a period of approximately a solar day.

The apparent paths of the Sun, Moon, and Planets in the stellar heavens always lie within a particular belt or girdle encircling the heavens. This belt is termed the Zodiacal belt, or, simply, the Zodiac. The central encircling line of the Zodiac is the Ecliptic, or apparent path of the Sun. The apparent path of the Sun is therefore traced in the stellar heavens, although, whilst the Sun is visible, the stars, defining the Sun's course, are themselves invisible.

The stellar heavens, therefore, appear as a vast globe encircling the Earth. To the ordinary observer, the Earth appears to be the centre of the stellar globe. With minor modifications—affecting geocentric and heliocentric points of reference—the point of view of the ordinary observer has been adopted as the basis of presentation for astronomy in ancient and modern times.

Stellar heavens appear as a celestial sphere, with the Earth in the centre.

¶ 279. THE CELESTIAL SPHERE.

The axis of apparent rotation of the stellar globe is the polar axis of the Earth produced. The Earth's polar axis produced into the northern hemisphere of the stellar globe defines the celestial North Pole. All the stars in the northern celestial hemisphere appear to revolve daily around the point thus defined ; and similarly in the southern celestial hemisphere, with reference to the celestial South Pole.

Earth's polar axis produced defines polar axis of celestial sphere. Celestial North Pole and Celestial South Pole thus defined.

Similarly, the plane of the Earth's equator produced in all directions defines the plane of the celestial equator. Its line of intersection with the apparent stellar globe defines the line of the celestial equator.

Plane of Earth's equator produced defines the celestial equator on the celestial sphere.

Now if the polar axis of the Earth had been perpendicular to the plane of the Earth's orbit, the plane of the Earth's equator would have coincided with the plane of the orbit. As the plane of the latter produced defines on the stellar globe the line of the Ecliptic, or the apparent annual path of the Sun, it is obvious that, with the condition assumed, the polar axis of the stellar globe would have coincided with the axis of the Ecliptic, and the celestial equator with the Ecliptic.

Plane of Earth's orbit produced defines the Ecliptic, or apparent annual path of Sun round the celestial sphere. Had Earth's polar axis been perpendicular to plane of its orbit, the celestial equator would have coincided with the Ecliptic, and the polar axis with the axis of the Ecliptic.

Owing, however, to the tilt of the Earth's axis being about 23½° from the position assumed above, the North Celestial Pole is about 23½° removed from the Pole of the Ecliptic. The latter is unaffected by the tilt. The result is that the *yearly* path of the Sun appears to be performed round the Ecliptic as the middle circumference of a sphere of which the axis of revolution is the Ecliptic axis, and that the daily apparent revolution of the stellar globe is effected about the celestial polar axis. One effect of the latter apparent revolution is that the imaginary point of the Ecliptic North Pole daily appears to revolve around the North Celestial Pole, and that the imaginary line of the Ecliptic traced by the apparent annual journey of the Sun round the stellar globe appears to revolve daily with the stellar globe.

Tilt of Earth's axis produces tilt of plane of celestial equator 23½° from the Ecliptic plane, and North Celestial Pole 23½° from North Ecliptic Pole. Ecliptic North Pole appears to revolve daily round North Celestial Pole, and the Ecliptic to revolve daily with the celestial sphere.

¶ 280. THE TWO AXES OF ASTRONOMICAL REFERENCE.

The polar axis of the stellar globe is therefore the axis of reference for the day and the year, since all motions within the year appear to be performed relative to that axis. Owing to Precession, however, the celestial polar axis changes direction with the Earth's polar axis. The stellar globe for one year, therefore, does not bear the same relation to the fixed stars as the stellar globe for another year. In 6500 years the stellar globe turns round 90° in relation to the fixed stars, whereas in the same interval the Ecliptic and

The polar axis of the celestial sphere is the axis of astronomical reference for the day and the year. Owing to Precession polar axis of one year does not occupy the same position as the polar axis of any other year.

Polar axis
turns round
90° in direc-
tion in 6500
years ; in the
same time
Ecliptic axis
shifts less than
1°.

Ecliptic axis
becomes axis
of reference
for Precession.

Ecliptic North
Pole the point
of reference for
North Celestial
Pole of differ-
ent dates.

North Celestial
Pole defined
as slowly
revolving
round Ecliptic
North Pole.

Precession
defined in
relation to
the celestial
sphere and the
signs of the
Zodiac.

the Ecliptic axis have shifted less than 1° in relation to the fixed stars, or to be more precise, in relation to their original positions at the beginning of the interval considered.

The Ecliptic North Pole is therefore taken as the point to which the positions of the North Celestial Pole for different dates are referred. The Ecliptic axis is thus the axis of reference for Precession, and the Ecliptic North Pole is the point of reference for Precession of the North Celestial Pole. The North Celestial Pole is, in consequence, defined as revolving slowly round the Ecliptic North Pole. As thus defined, the movement is illustrated on Plate XLIX, the various positions of the North Celestial Pole being shown for dates from 5000 B.C. to 2500 A.D. Complete illustration of the movement in relation to the celestial hemisphere north of the Ecliptic, and in relation to the fixed stars thereon, is shown on Plate XLVIII. This shows the relations between the North Celestial Pole and the Equinoctial and Solstitial Colures, and by these relations illustrates the meaning of " The Precession of the Equinoxes," round the Zodiac.

¶ 281. THE EARLIEST ZODIACAL DATE.

The star groups
and their
figures
defining the
Zodiacal Signs.

Twelve signs
recognised as
handed on to
modern times.

Earliest date
of origin :—
Midnight of
Autumnal
Equinox,
4699 B.C.,
indicated at
first point
of Gemini =
last point of
Taurus.

Earliest
historical
references in
no case refer
to a year
beginning in
Gemini.

All earliest
references are
to a year
beginning in
Taurus.

Earliest date
of Zodiacal
signs and of
earliest
historical
records is
therefore not
earlier than
4699 B.C.

At a remote date in history the constellations or star groups of the Zodiac were divided off into equal spaces in the Ecliptic. As these have come down to us, the star groups indicate a division into twelve Zodiacal Signs. The constellational figures associated with these signs and their designations are as shown on Plate XLVIII.

R. Brown, jun., in his " Primitive Constellations,"[1] places the date of origin for the figures shown as 4698 B.C. (astronomical) =4699 B.C. (historical). This date agrees with the various other lines of independent evidence discussed in Section I of this Chapter. Brown's date of origin depends upon the following :—

The toe of Castor, beginning the sign Gemini, also marks the termination of the sign Taurus. At the date 4699 B.C. (historical) a given meridian on the Earth passed through the point thus defined precisely at midnight of the Autumnal Equinox of that year ; or, alternatively, the Sun occupied the point thus defined at noon of the Vernal Equinox of that year. This can be independently confirmed from the present position of the toe of Castor, and from Newcomb's formula for Precession (¶ 224). The resulting relation between the modern months of the solar year and the Zodiacal signs for 4699 B.C. is as shown on Plate XLIV. The first month of the Equinoctial year therefore coincided with the Zodiacal sign Gemini in 4699 B.C. In successive later years, owing to Precession, the beginning of the year slipped backwards gradually through the sign Taurus. Now the earliest known historical records in no case refer to an Equinoctial year beginning in Gemini. They all refer to an Equinoctial year beginning in Taurus. Brown therefore placed the date of origin at the last point of Taurus, thus fixing the date at 4699 B.C. (historical).

[1] Vol. I, p. 56.

¶ 282. TAURUS PRE-EMINENT IN EARLIEST HISTORICAL TIMES.

This identification explains the predominance of the Bull, as a symbol of leadership, headship, and general pre-eminence, in ancient Euphratean and Egyptian imagery. This particular symbol appears in the earliest records of the two countries. These records are therefore not anterior to the date 4699 B.C., when the Equinoctial year first began in Taurus. The records clearly prove that they belong to a much later date, when the symbol of the Bull was already a symbol of long-established use. This conclusion is interesting as indicating that pre-dynastic civilisation in Egypt and Mesopotamia —when the rites of the Bull were already woven inextricably into the traditional rituals of the priests—belongs to a period considerably later than 4699 B.C. The epoch of Mena in Egypt and the epoch of Sargani of Akkad are therefore of a still later date or dates.

Long after Taurus had ceased to begin the Equinoctial year, Vergil wrote that " the white bull with the golden horns opens the year." Vergil's statement is clearly a survival of the tradition of a former fact of historical chronology. On the other hand, the existence of the dominant symbol of the Bull in the earliest records of oriental civilisation indicates the total lack of any similar survival of a tradition associating any other sign than Taurus with the beginning of the year. Taurus was already the Sign of tradition when the earliest existing records were inscribed. No existing human relic of an intelligent civilisation can be reliably connected to a date as remote as 4699 B.C. The single fact witnessing to the existence of an organised intelligence at this date is the fact enshrined in the star groups and figures of the Zodiac.

[Side notes: The Bull the symbol of pre-eminence in earliest Euphratean and Egyptian times. Symbolic application indicated long-established use. Proves that pre-dynastic civilisation in Egypt and Mesopotamia —when Bull symbol of pre-eminence was used—was long after 4699 B.C. Epoch of Mena in Egypt, and epoch of Sargani of Akkad still later. Tradition of Bull's pre-eminence long survived its astronomical identification with beginning of the year. Lack of such survival in earlier times, and in the case of the sign preceding Taurus—and now known as Gemini—confirms the inference derived above. Taurus already the Sign of tradition when earliest records were inscribed.]

¶ 283. THE LUNAR ZODIAC OF NOCTURNAL SIGNS.

The later conception of the Zodiac pictured the Zodiacal Signs as the various stations or houses of the Sun during the Solar year. In this conception, knowledge of the signs as Nocturnal (visible) Signs necessarily preceded their use as Diurnal (and invisible) Signs. The early Zodiac depicted the signs as nocturnal. This conception requires the astronomical assumption of an imaginary Anti-Sun in the Zodiac at midnight in place of the modern conception of the visible Sun in an invisible Zodiac at noon. Now the Anti-Sun would be indicated by the projection of the Earth's shadow on to the celestial sphere, if we can imagine the projection to be possible. The equivalent indication is given at a total lunar eclipse. The Moon, entering the Earth's shadow, indicates the place of the imaginary Anti-Sun in the Zodiac.

[Side notes: The late Zodiacal conception :— A visible Sun following its annual (Ecliptic) path through the invisible signs of the Zodiac. Early conception :— The Nocturnal Zodiac of visible signs, with full Moon, slightly above or below the Ecliptic, defining the position of the Anti-Sun.]

The Moon, therefore, becomes the ideal medium for defining the path of the Anti-Sun along the Ecliptic in the Zodiac. Successive total lunar eclipses define the Ecliptic. With the latter known, successive full moons, slightly above or slightly below the Ecliptic, determine the precise position of the

[Side notes: Successive total lunar eclipses defined the Ecliptic.]

Hence the
significance
of the early
lunar Zodiac.
Anti-Sun on the Ecliptic.[1]   The earliest Zodiac is, therefore, the Lunar Zodiac —a system of Nocturnal Signs.

Full Moon at
the horns of
Taurus at the
year's begin-
ning originated
horned head-
dress of various
ancient deities
of the year.
From the conception of the Lunar Zodiac originated the many anciently pictured forms of horned head-dress supporting a Moon—the latter often hieroglyphically represented in the shape of a crescent to avoid its being confused with the Sun—figured as crowning various deities of the year.   The Lunar Zodiac is the Zodiac of the ancient Euphrateans.

¶ 284. THE EARLIEST ALPHABET.

Taurus as first
sign preceded
earliest
formulation
of Semitic
languages.
The first sign of this ancient Zodiac was identified with *Taurus* before the existence of the Semitic languages, since in Chaldæan and Hebrew—and in the early forms of Semitic language—*Taurus* was signified by *Alap* or *Aleph*, the first letter of the Chaldæan and Hebrew alphabets.   As *alap* First letter of
latter derived
from "Taurus,"
Euphratean
name being
"Alap." signifies *a bull*, the name long preceded the alphabet and the written or inscribed language.   Hence, too, that the letter A is derived from > and >, The primitive
form of the
letter A
derived from
bull's horns. originally the symbol of the horns of the bull.   Petrie[2] shows that the latter symbol is met with in Egypt and along the Mediterranean during predynastic times in Egypt—*i.e.* long before the reign of Mena.   Its use is therefore Letter found
in primitive
Mediterranean
"signary,"
prior to 1st
Dynasty in
Egypt. remotely later than 4699 B.C., when Taurus = *Alap* began to be the first sign. Long-established identification as the First Sign of the year was necessary before it could give its contribution to the Mediterranean *signary*[3] that formed the primitive alphabet.

1st Dynasty of
Egypt there-
fore long after
4699 B.C.
Petrie shows that the letter A was in use in Egypt prior to Mena, the first Dynastic king, and makes the significant statement that—

"The history
of the alphabet
is as old as
civilisation"
(Petrie).
" The history of the *alpha*bet is as old as. civilisation."[3]   (The partial italics are ours.)

¶ 285. THE TWO ORIGINAL ZODIACAL SYSTEMS.

Existing ex-
tents of the
various star
groups and
their existing
traditional
figures as
recognised in
modern times
define that
existing
system is a
compromise
between two
ancient
systems.
Referring to Plate XLVIII, the reader will see that generally the signs are alternately long and short, and also, generally, that any two adjacent signs are equal in extent to any other two adjacent signs.   Generally speaking, the signs are alternately about 40° and 20°.

Thus the extent of Taurus from the toe of Castor to tail of Aries is 40° ; Aries = 20° ; total 60°.

Pisces + Aquarius ..	= 60°
Capricornus + Sagittarius	= 60°
Scorpio + Libra ..	= 60°.

Then the rule is disturbed at Virgo and Leo—

Virgo = 40° ; and	Leo = 30°
Cancer = 30° ;	Gemini = 20°.

---

[1] This point of view is adopted merely for purpose of illustration, as the Anti-Sun can be determined very simply by ordinary methods.
[2] " The Royal Tombs of the 1st Dynasty," I, pp. 31, 32.
[3] Ibid., I, p. 32.

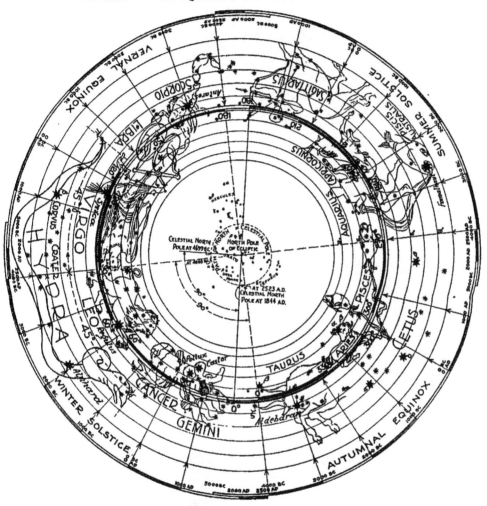

STELLAR DEFINITION OF THE SIGNS OF THE ZODIAC.

PLAN OF THE CELESTIAL HEMISPHERE NORTH OF THE ECLIPTIC, TOGETHER WITH DEVELOPED SURFACE OF PORTION OF THE CELESTIAL HEMISPHERE SOUTH OF THE ECLIPTIC.

The Ecliptic is the middle circumferential line of the three circumferential lines defining the Ecliptic Scale of the Zodiacal Signs.

The Outer Scale of years, when projected radially inwards, as indicated, on to the Ecliptic Scale, gives the dated precession of the Equinoxes and Solstices through the Zodiacal Signs.

[To face p. 246.

The Zodiacal figures of Plate XLVIII show clearly enough that the figures as we know them depict a compromise between two distinct systems defining two distinct epochs ; the figures also defining the date at which the compromise was effected. One system has date of origin clearly defined as 4699 B.C.

The primary system is a system of six signs of 60° each, with epoch at 4699 B.C. The secondary system is a system of twelve signs of 30° each, with epoch at 4000 B.C. The date at which the compromise system was effected was the date at which Precession had brought the Equinox 40° back through Taurus from the toe of Castor. This defines the date as around 1780 B.C. The other system has date of origin as clearly defined as 4000 B.C.

The two epochs are, respectively, the ancient epoch (4699 B.C.) of Precessional Chronology, and the ancient epoch (4000 B.C.) of Scalar Chronology, fixed by the Pyramid's astronomical indications and formulæ, and independently by the astronomical data of the Egyptian King Lists, discussed in Section I of this Chapter. The star groups and their traditional figures therefore confirm the evidences from the Pyramid and Egyptian King Lists establishing epochs at 4699 B.C. and 4000 B.C.

¶ 286. AUTUMNAL EQUINOCTIAL MIDNIGHT—VERNAL EQUINOCTIAL NOON.

Now, before considering what Jensen, Lockyer, and Brown have all independently written to the same effect, let us consider what the Zodiacal figures—and the extent of each round the Ecliptic—can tell us in this relation. In the first place, we have seen the primary necessity for the conception of nocturnal (visible) signs prior to the conception of the Sun's annual progress through the diurnal (invisible) signs. This agrees with the Pyramid's definition of the zero datum for the astronomical day at midnight instead of at noon, as in the modern astronomical day[1] (¶¶ 239–242). Early conception of a nocturnal Zodiac agrees with Pyramid's definition of a midnight beginning for the astronomical day.

In the earliest ancient system of time the zero datum for the year was the Autumnal Equinox. This also agrees with the defined datum of the Pyramid. Consequently, we find that the earliest Euphratean year in use began at the Autumnal Equinox. About the time of Khammurabi, of the Amorite Dynasty of Babylon (the Amraphel of Gen. xiv, 1), the contemporary of Abraham and of Senusert III of Dynasty XII in Egypt, we find two forms of Euphratean year in current use—one commencing from an Autumnal Equinoctial datum and the other commencing from a Vernal Equinoctial datum. The latter year-beginning gradually gained complete ascendancy over the earlier Autumnal Equinoctial year-beginning. The period of transition from one to the other lies within the period 2200 to 1400 B.C. By 1400 B.C. we find that the Vernal Equinoctial year-beginning was the system adopted for civil reckoning amongst all the nations of Semitic origin. Coincidently, the order of the signs for the year was retained. Taurus was still considered the sign identified with the first month of the Vernal Equinoctial year, as it had been the first sign of the Autumnal Equinoctial year. The Early Zodiacal year zero at Autumnal Equinox, as in Pyramid's chronology. Two Euphratean forms— Autumnal and Vernal Equinoctial— in use at time of Abraham. Vernal Equinoctial year-beginning gains ascendancy about 1800 B.C. Semitic civil year. Order of Zodiacal signs retained. Retention necessitated conception of diurnal signs or the latter necessitated the former.

[1]It should be observed, however, that future " Nautical Almanacs " have to be compiled with midnight as the zero datum of the astronomical day ; a reversion to ancient practice.

New conception of Sun in Taurus at Vernal Equinoctial noon in place of earlier conception of Anti-Sun in Taurus at Autumnal Equinoctial midnight.

identity, however, now depended upon the conception of the Sun at noon in Taurus, near the beginning of the Vernal Equinoctial year, in place of the earlier conception of the Anti-Sun in Taurus at midnight, near the beginning of the Autumnal Equinoctial year (¶¶ 281–284).

The change obviously resulted from one or other of two alternative conceptions. Either

Date of change of conception is date of formulation of twelve Zodiacal signs as now known.

(1) The change of year-beginning determined the change of conception from midnight to noon, and from visible (nocturnal) signs to invisible (diurnal) signs ; or

(2) The new conception of the Sun passing through the invisible signs determined the change from midnight to noon, and from the Autumnal to the Vernal Equinoctial year-beginning.

Circa 1780 B.C.

The precise sequence of change is unimportant. What is important is that the central date of the transition period is the date, 1780 B.C., at which the compromise system of twelve irregular signs was effected (¶ 285).

¶ 287. THE ORIGINAL TAURUS OF THE PRIMARY ZODIAC.

Figure of Taurus originally a full Bull extending to Pisces. Jensen's evidence from Babylonian mythology confirms the astronomical indications.

Reference to Plate XLVIII shows the date at which the compromise was effected, and at which the change of year-beginning was permanently established as related to the Zodiac. The relation between the figures of Taurus and Aries indicates clearly that the full figure of the Bull originally extended to Pisces. This has been independently shown by Jensen from consideration of the early Babylonian astronomical mythology. He shows that the Babylonian Taurus was originally a complete Bull extending to the Fish of Ea.[1]

Astronomical indications show that Aries was inserted about 1780 B.C. into remaining 20° of Taurus not already traversed by the Precessional motion of the Equinox.

The extent of the inserted figure of Aries (Plate XLVIII) indicates that Precession had already brought the Sun at Vernal Equinoctial noon—at the date of insertion—40° backwards into Taurus from the toe of Castor. This being so, Aries could not well be extended into the portion of Taurus through which Precession had already brought the Sun. On the other hand, the defined extent of Pisces limited extension of Aries in the other direction.

Taurus originally 60° in primary system with epoch at 4699 B.C.

The defined limits for the figuring of Aries marked the 20° of the original Taurus still to be covered by Precession. This shows that the figure Aries as shown was inserted around the date 1780 B.C., when the position of the Sun in Taurus at the Vernal Equinox determined the point at which the tail of Aries could be placed.

This all clearly shows that Taurus was originally—at least in the system with epoch at 4699 B.C.—a sign of 60°, representing the full-figure Bull of the Babylonian astronomical mythology.

¶ 288. THE ORIGINAL PISCES OF THE PRIMARY ZODIAC.

A similar compressed insertion of Aquarius into remaining extent of Pisces.

Again, in the case of Pisces and Aquarius (two water signs), Pisces is much the longer and Aquarius has been crushed into the same small compass

[1] " Kosmologie der Babylonier," p. 315; quoted by Lockyer, " Dawn of Astronomy," p. 397.

PLATE XLIX.

(Enlargement of Central Portion of Plate XLVIII.)

THE PRECESSIONAL MOVEMENT OF THE NORTH CELESTIAL POLE.

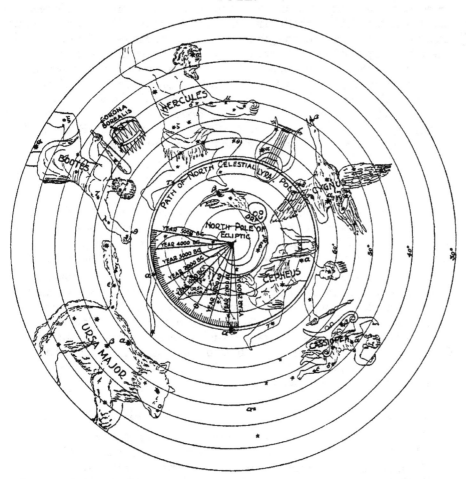

PLAN OF THE CONSTELLATIONS ROUND THE NORTH POLE OF THE ECLIPTIC.

The thick circumferential line defines the Path of the North Pole of the Heavens. The position of the North Pole of the Heavens for any date is given by the intersection of the radially dated line for that date with the latter circle.

as Aries. In fact, reference to Plate XLVIII will show that Aquarius had to overlap the tail of Capricornus—the fish-goat.

Jensen's
evidence
confirms
astronomical
indications.
Pisces origin-
ally 60° in
primary (4699
B.C.) system.

In this case, the original 60° sign of the primary Zodiac—of epoch 4699 B.C.—was the complete sign of the Fishes, including the portion of the inserted figure of Aquarius not overlapping into Capricornus. This seems to show that the sign originally figured Piscis Australis joined with the bound fishes that now form the star group of the modern Pisces. The band joining the two groups obviously intersected the Ecliptic at the point defining the 60° extent of the original Pisces. The same connection is to be inferred from the water stream passing from the Pitcher of Aquarius to *Formalhaut* in the mouth of the Southern Fish. Jensen has shown that the whole extent of Pisces, including Aquarius, formed one original sign of early Babylonian astronomy—the Fish-Man. Another Euphratean name for Pisces is " the Cord," thus naming the connecting band of the bound fishes.

¶ 289. THE ORIGINAL CAPRICORNUS OF THE PRIMARY ZODIAC.

A similar
compressed
insertion of
the torso of
Sagittarius
into the
remaining
extent of
Capricornus.
Jensen's
evidence
confirms.

The compressed insertion in this sign is indicated by the 20° extending from the bow to the right elbow of Sagittarius, as measured along the Ecliptic. The lower (horse) body of Sagittarius is all below the Ecliptic, and was therefore extended, as not defining the Precessional extent along the Ecliptic.

Obviously the sign Capricornus originally extended 60° from the left thigh of Aquarius to the bow of Sagittarius. Jensen has shown that the original Babylonian sign—the Goat-man or Goat-fish—included both Capricornus and Sagittarius. The Goat-man and Goat-fish identification—together with the figures as now known—suggest an original figure with a Centaur torso[1] holding the bow and arrow of Sagittarius, supported on the forequarters of a goat, and terminating with a fish-tail hindquarters just emerged from the watery sign of the Fishes.

¶ 290. THE ORIGINAL SCORPIO OF THE PRIMARY ZODIAC.

A similar
compressed
insertion of
Libra into the
remaining
extent of
Scorpio.
Jensen's
evidence
confirms.

In this case again the Balance (Libra) is compressed within the extent of 20°. The position of the Balance suggests that the pans were originally the " horns " of the Scorpion. Jensen confirms this by stating that " the Greeks have often called it (Libra) χηλαι, ' claws ' (of the Scorpion) ; and, according to what has been said above (p. 312), the sign for a constellation in the neighbourhood of our Libra reads in the Arsacid inscription ' claw(s) ' of the Scorpion. These facts are very simply explained on the supposition that the Scorpion originally extended into the region of the Balance, and that originally α and β Libræ represented the ' horns ' of the Scorpion."[2]

---

[1]Brown, " Prim. Constell.," Vol. II, pp. 44, 45. " *Sagittarius*, the *Archer*, is represented on the monuments (1) as a man with a bow ; (2) as a Centaur ; and, according to Lenormant, (3) by an Arrow, on the principle, familiar to symbolism, of a part for the whole." " In Lajard *M*, Pl. XIII, 8, he appears as a seated Bowman. In Pl. LIV, A 12, he is a Bowman kneeling on one knee near a star."
[2]Quoted by Lockyer, " Dawn of Astronomy," p. 401.

Reference to Plate XLVIII also seems to show that the tail of the Scorpion originally extended to the bow of Sagittarius. In fact, some modern representations do actually figure the tail as of the extent here inferred for ancient times. Thus defined, the original Scorpio extended from the bow of Sagittarius to the feet of Virgo—an extent of 60°.

¶ 291. THE ORIGINAL VIRGO OF THE PRIMARY ZODIAC.

The original Virgo—in accordance with the indications of the signs discussed—consisted of 60° from the foot of the Virgin as now figured to the middle of Leo as now figured. The present extent of Virgo is 40°, and therefore confirms the other indications discussed. *A similar curtailing of Virgo is indicated, but Leo, whilst inserted, was not compressed but retained as 30°.*

Now Jensen has shown that the original Virgo was the early Babylonian sign of the *Ear of Corn*. The latter is now identified with the star *Spica* (see Plate XLVIII). From *Spica* to the tail of Leo is 30°, and Leo, again, is 30°. Here we have the overlapping of the two early Zodiacal systems. The tail of Leo and the head of Virgo define the position of the Anti-Sun at the Winter Solstice 4000 B.C.—the epoch of the secondary Zodiacal system of twelve signs. The same point also defines the position of the Sun at the Summer Solstice 4000 B.C. *Leo occupies 20° of original Virgo and 10° of original Cancer. Reason for retention that Leo thus occupies its actual place in the system of twelve signs based on 4000 B.C.*

Obviously the definition of the Solstice for this epoch led to Leo being inserted from the secondary system of twelve signs, without alteration of its position and without compression. The 60° sign of the Ear of Corn in the primary system had, however, to be reduced to the 40° extent of the adopted figure of Virgo. *Dividing line of Virgo and Leo defines meridian at midnight Winter Solstice 4000 B.C.*

The resulting arrangement left Leo—adopted entire from the secondary system—extending 10° into the original 60° sign Cancer (the Crab).

¶ 292. THE ORIGINAL CANCER OF THE PRIMARY ZODIAC.

The insertion of Leo entire, as explained in ¶ 291, robbed the original Cancer of the primary Zodiacal system of 10° of its extent. This left 50° in which to adjust the new figure of Cancer and in which a compressed Gemini from the secondary system was to be inserted. As in the case of Aries, the torso of Sagittarius, and the Balance, Gemini was compressed into the extent of 20°, as shown on Plate XLVIII. This completed the circuit of the Zodiac and the readjustment of the star groups that effected a compromise between the primary system of six signs of 60° each, with epoch at 4699 B.C., and the secondary system of twelve signs of 30° each, with epoch at 4000 B.C. *Original 60° of Cancer robbed of 10° by Leo and 20° by compressed insertion of Gemini.*

¶ 293. LOCKYER'S DEFINITION OF THE ORIGINAL SIX SIGNS.

Not seeing the clear indication of the original secondary system of twelve signs, Sir Norman Lockyer concluded from Jensen's and his own researches *Lockyer's statement of the original six signs :—*

that there was a single original system of six signs. He therefore stated as follows :—

"The original Zodiac consisted only of six constellations : Taurus, Crab (or Tortoise), Virgin (or Ear of Corn), Scorpion, Capricornus, Pisces."[1]

Lockyer, however, had previously quoted Jensen as stating that, although the facts are as given in our ¶ 290, "we cannot doubt the (independent) existence of an eastern balance (Libra)." The facts are that "the Balance" belonged to an independent ancient system of twelve signs, distinct from the primary ancient system of six signs, and that it was based on an independent epoch.

The historical facts show that the change from Nocturnal to Diurnal conception of the signs, from Anti-Sun to Sun, and from Autumnal Equinoctial datum to Vernal Equinoctial datum, had already been effected in the case of the system of twelve signs. The facts established in Section I of this Chapter lead us now to the inference that this latter system was a sacred system associated with the sacred system of Scalar Chronology. In the same way we saw that the civil systems of measures were distinct from the sacred system of measures, and yet geometrically related. Similarly, the Precessional system of chronology associated with the primary Zodiacal system is related to the sacred Scalar system of chronology associated with our so-called secondary Zodiacal system.

¶ 294. BROWN ON NOCTURNAL AND DIURNAL SIGNS.

The sacred system of twelve signs had already conformed to the diurnal Vernal Equinoctial datum, and the system of six signs was still nocturnal and Autumnal Equinoctial at the date of the establishing of the composite system. This is proved by the fact that the sacred signs, inserted into the system of six signs, were, when inserted, already known as diurnal signs, whereas the six original signs were contemporaneously known as nocturnal signs. Thus Brown states as follows :—[2]

"The primary name of the Euphratean Moon-god appears to have been Nannar........In Euhemeristic legend he becomes a Persian satrap, Nannaros........He is styled 'the strong Bull, whose horn is powerful '........ ; and the connection in idea between the moon and the bull, ox, or cow, is so obvious as to be inevitable. In the Hittite characters the Bull's head is actually combined with the crescent........ The lunar Bull is reduplicated in the Zodiacal *Taurus*, hence called a ' nocturnal ' sign and connected with the second of the ten antediluvian kings, Alaparos (=Akkadian, *alap*, bull+*ur*, ' foundation '), ' the Bull of the Foundation,'........"

[1] " Dawn of Astronomy," p. 401.
[2] " Prim. Constell.," Vol. I, p. 56 ; Vol. II, pp. 230, 231.

" Originally the first of the Zodiacal Signs, the *Bull* is a lunar re- Nocturnal signs :—
Taurus,
Cancer, Virgo,
Scorpio,
Capricornus,
and Pisces.
duplication. In this case the configuration of the stars aptly coincides
with the lunar idea........ it will be found that *Aries, Gemini, Leo, Ara*
(now *Libra*), *Sagittarius*, and *Aquarius* are in nature diurnal Signs ; whilst
Taurus, Cancer, Virgo, Scorpio, Capricornus, and *Pisces* are in nature Diurnal signs :—
Aries, Gemini,
Leo, Libra,
Sagittarius,
and Aquarius.
nocturnal Signs. This fact........ has been faithfully preserved by
astrology down to the present time."

¶ 295. THE ESSENTIAL FACTS OF THE PROBLEM.

The central facts that we must remember in determining the origin and Both Zodiacal systems established by able astronomers.
purpose of the Zodiacal Signs are as follow :—

(1) That the original Zodiacal Signs—both systems—were established by The signs established as basis of reference for successive equinoctial years.
a highly civilised people, who knew as much about astronomy as
we do in modern times ;

(2) That the original signs were established as a fixed astronomical means
of reference—obviously to form the basis of reference for deter- The two Zodiacal systems were related.
mining the sidereal relations between successive equinoctial
years ; and

(3) That the original sacred system of twelve equal signs was related to Both originally nocturnal and Autumnal Equinoctial in basis and datum.
the original precessional system of six equal signs ; that both
systems were originally nocturnal and Autumnal Equinoctial in
basis and datum respectively ; and that both systems reveal a Relation of both systems to the Natural Law governing the connected systems of Chronology.
stellar framework defining the causal relation between Natural
Law on the one hand, and Astronomical and Sacred (Scalar)
Chronology on the other hand.

The central facts enumerated all necessarily follow from the certain conclusions derived in Section I of this Chapter. With these facts as basis, we
should be able to derive some further conclusions concerning the purpose of
the two original Zodiacal Systems.

¶ 296. ASTRONOMICAL PURPOSE OF THE TWO ZODIACAL SYSTEMS.

Now, in Chapter I, ¶¶ 30–40, we saw that the calendar year of the ancient Relation of ancient intercalated calendar year of 360 days to the Zodiacal systems and their connected systems of chronology.
times, identified with the period we are considering, was Autumnal Equinoctial
in its basis. Its calendar year was an intercalated calendar year of 360 days.
The basal cycle was a cycle of 103 mean solar years (Tables II, III, and IV).
Table III shows that any calendar month, within the period of the cycle, had
a range of 60 days for the movement of its calendar period of 30 days within
the fixed solar year. Thus Day 1, Month I could not begin later than 3.49
days after the mean Autumnal Equinox of the Cycle (Table III, Cyclic years'
duration, 68), nor earlier than 26.21 days prior to the mean Autumnal Equinox
of the Cycle (Table III, Cyclic years' duration, 5). Any day of the calendar
year had, therefore, a range of shift of 30 days in the fixed solar year, and any
month of 30 days covered a complete range of 60 days in the fixed solar year.

The primary Zodiacal Sign of 60° therefore formed a suitable basis of reference for the 60 days' range of a calendar month, while, at the same time, defining in *stellar* terms the Natural Law basis of the Precessional Chronology framed with 4699 B.C. as epoch.   The Scalar or Sacred Chronology system— with epoch of origin at 4000 B.C.—is, however, defined as the system adopted for historical reference.   The calendar cycle of 103 years was employed in this relation.   Hence, the Sacred system of twelve Zodiacal Signs—each of 30°— with epoch of origin at 4000 B.C., was naturally adopted as the basis of reference for the ideal fixed months of the *Equinoctial* year, with respect to which the calendar months were intercalated on the cycle of 103 years. Precession of the twelve ideal fixed months could therefore be measured in relation to the twelve Zodiacal Signs of the Sacred (or Scalar) system of chronology.

¶ 297. " THE LIGHTS " IN THE ZODIAC.

We have seen that the original Zodiacal system of nocturnal signs required the full moon to define the position of the Anti-Sun (¶ 283).   We have also seen that the system of twelve signs, with epoch of origin at 4000 B.C., was originally nocturnal and Autumnal Equinoctial.   Plate XLVIII shows how the figure of Taurus defines the latter epoch.   The line joining the tips of the horns of the Bull, the stars β *Tauri* and ζ *Tauri*, respectively above and below the Ecliptic, cuts the Ecliptic at the point occupied by the Autumnal Equinox at 4000 B.C.   This point defines the limit of the 30° sign Taurus in the Sacred system of twelve Zodiacal signs.   Brown[1] tells us that the Euphratean names for these stars are as follow :—

β *Tauri* = " The Northern-light of the Chariot."
ζ *Tauri* = " The Southern-light of the Chariot."

But the Euphratean name for Taurus is " the Directing Bull."   How then " the Lights " of the Chariot came to be associated with the tips of the Bull's horns is a question requiring to be cleared up.

Now in the same sign we have the Pleiades.   In this group, *Alcyonê* is defined as " the Star of the Foundation " (¶ 241).   The Pyramid's geometrical chronology connects *Alcyonê* directly with " the foundation " date of the Scalar chronology, *i.e.* with the Autumnal Equinox of 4000 B.C. (¶¶ 239–242, and Plate XLI, Fig. N).   The Pyramid itself was known as " the Lights," and the tips of the Bull's horns were known as " the Lights " of " the Chariot."   These define the position of the Autumnal Equinox at 4000 B.C. The Zodiacal system, being nocturnal, defines the position of the Anti-Sun at midnight of the latter date.   The Anti-Sun was defined by full moon, and the Autumnal Equinoctial full moon of 4000 B.C. occurred at the tips of the Bull's horns at midnight beginning 22nd September (Gregorian).[2]   This

[1] " Prim. Constell.," Vol. II, p. 209.
[2] The meridian taken as defining midnight of this date is the Pyramid meridian.   With this midnight datum and date, the total value for lunar acceleration and tidal retardation of Earth's rotation—amounting in total effect to less than 1 day in 6000 years back from the present date— agrees with Newcomb's modern value.

dating fixes the precise hour (midnight) of the zero epoch of the Pyramid's Sacred (Scalar) chronology. Similarly, the hour of the Great Step epoch (1844 A.D.) was defined as midnight in relation to the zero epoch (4000 B.C.) by means of the *Alcyonê* and *α Draconis* alignments (¶¶ 239–242). The reader is also referred to the first quotation in ¶ 294, referring to Taurus as " the Bull of the Foundation."

¶ 298. THE CHANGES IN THE CALENDAR YEAR.

The change of conception from Anti-Sun and full moon in the Zodiac at Autumnal Equinoctial midnight to the Sun in the Zodiac at Vernal Equinoctial noon required a change in the lunar conception from full moon to new moon. We find, therefore, that from around 1780 B.C. onward, the new moon regulates the beginning of the months of the luni-solar calendar of the Semitic peoples. The Autumnal Equinoctial year basis of the original luni-solar calendar is evidenced by the pre-Exode calendar of the Israelites. At the Exodus, this was altered to the Vernal Equinoctial beginning.

Change from nocturnal and Autumnal Equinoctial datum to diurnal and Vernal Equinoctial datum necessarily alters lunar datum from full moon to new moon.

The history of the calendar of the Old Testament is therefore, briefly, as follows :—

The stages leading up to the establishing of the Semitic luni-solar Vernal Equinoctial year with its new moon beginning.

Adamic	{ Autumnal Equinoctial year ; { Intercalated 360 days calendar.
Early Semitic	{ Autumnal Equinoctial year (luni-solar) ; { Intercalated 354 days year ; { Month beginning regulated by full moon.
Later Semitic (pre-Exode)	{ Autumnal Equinoctial year (luni-solar) ; { Intercalated 354 days year ; { Month beginning regulated by new moon ; { Conception derived from contemporary luni-solar Vernal Equinoctial year.
Israelitish (post-Exode)	{ Vernal Equinoctial Sacred year (luni-solar) ; { Intercalated 354 days year ; { Month beginning regulated by new moon.

¶ 299. OSIRIS AND THE MOON IN TAURUS.

Confirming the change of conception as it affected Egypt, Lockyer shows that, although later identified with the Sun, Osiris was in earlier times in Egypt identified with the Moon. As Moon-god, Osiris was represented with horned and lunar head-dress, symbolic of the full moon at the tips of the horns of Taurus. This aspect of Osiris necessarily belongs to the stage of evolution intermediate between the original form of Osiris as primitive Corn-god, and the later form of Osiris as the Sun-god. As Lockyer states—

*Evolution of Osiris :—
(1) Corn-god ;
(2) Moon-god ;
(3) Sun-god.*

The horned and lunar head-dress of Osiris.

The Moon in Taurus (nocturnal).

Lockyer on Osiris as a Moon-god.

" If in later times he represented both Sun and Moon, as he certainly did, it is not probable that he did so from the beginning. All the special symbolism refers to him as a Moon-god ; he is certainly a Moon-god in the myth of Isis and Osiris. . . . . . ."

" Now we can easily understand an evolution beginning with a

Moon-god and ending with a Sun-god. But the contrary is almost unthinkable; besides, we know that in Egypt it did not happen; the solar attributes got hardened as time went on."[1]

Sayce on the Moon-god.

Lockyer again quotes Professor Sayce (Hibbert Lectures), as follows:—

" According to the official religion of Chaldæa, the Sun-god was the offspring of the Moon-god........Such a belief could have arisen only where the Moon-god was the supreme object of worship........To the Semite the Moon-god was the lord and father of the gods."

And Lockyer here adds that " in modern German, even, the Moon is masculine and the Sun feminine."

¶ 300. THOTH AND THE FULL MOON AT AUTUMNAL EQUINOX.

Original Egyptian Moon-calendar of Thoth Autumnal Equinoctial in its indications.

From these and other evidences, Lockyer concludes that " it becomes a question whether the original moon-calendar of Thoth (here referring to the Egyptian god of that name and to the *primitive* Egyptian calendar) did not refer to a year beginning at the Autumnal Equinox. This is a suggestion resulting from later enquiries, and hence I have not referred to it in the chapters on the year."[2]

Thoth-lunus and Khons-lunus.

Full Moon between Bull's horns.

He has, however, previously figured, on page 29, Khons-lunus and Thoth-lunus as two early Egyptian Moon-gods, stating that " with the Moon we find two gods connected—Thoth-lunus and Khons-lunus—although the connection is not a very obvious one." In the representations of the gods shown, however, appears the well-known form of head-dress—the full Moon between the Bull's horns.

Eye of Thoth " the full Moon."

"The measurer and regulator of the seasons."

Thoth, again, in the Egyptian " Book of the Dead," is referred to as the Moon-god who acted as " the measurer and regulator of the seasons." In this connection, Budge states that the " Eye of Thoth " is " *the full moon*," as the " Eye of Ra " is the midday Sun. Here we have direct evidence of the change of conception from Anti-Sun to Sun, from midnight to midday, and from the nocturnal Zodiac to the diurnal Zodiac.

The significant full Moon record of Tahutmes III.

The continuance of the older conception of the full Moon, beginning the cycle of the lunation identified with a particular month, is indicated in an inscription of Tahutmes III. The latter refers to the Festival of the (apparent) New Moon as " *the same (moon) as* " the full Moon that had occurred 17 days previously on the anniversary of the Royal Coronation, although the calendar in use at the time was the vague year calendar of 365 days.

¶ 301. EQUINOXES AND ZODIAC AT 4699 B.C. AND 4000 B.C.

The celestial sphere at 4699 B.C. and 4000 B.C.

Plates L to LIV show how the Zodiacal figures appeared on the celestial sphere at the two ancient Zodiacal epochs, 4699 B.C. and 4000 B.C. respectively. The diagrams given represent the sky as it appeared above the southern horizon at latitude 45° North. Points lettered as W, S, and E

[1] " Dawn of Astronomy," pp. 389 and 390.   [2] Ibid., p. 393.

represent the West, South, and East points of the horizon respectively. Point Z is the zenith; ZS is the meridian. Other features are as defined on Plates.

At midnight, Autumnal Equinox, 4699 B.C., the position of the Anti-Sun was at the toe of Castor as defined by the line intersections of Plate L. The vertical position of Orion below same, and symmetrical about the meridian, should be noted as confirming the zodiacal arrangement designed with respect to 4699 B.C. *The position of Zodiacal signs on celestial sphere at midnight of Autumnal and Vernal Equinoxes, 4699 B.C.*

At the same instant the Sun lay on the point defined on Plate LI. Otherwise stated, Plate LI represents the midnight sky at the Vernal Equinox of 4699 B.C. The position of the Anti-Sun is defined by the northern tip of the bow of Sagittarius. The meridian passes vertically down the bow.

Plate LII represents the sky at midnight of Autumnal Equinox, 4000 B.C. The line joining the tips of the Bull's horns defines the position of the Anti-Sun. At the same instant the full moon appeared as if balanced on the tips of the horns, slightly above the Ecliptic. *The same for 4000 B.C.*

Plate LIII shows the meridian on the tip of the arrow of Sagittarius at midnight of the Vernal Equinox, 4000 B.C. The intersecting lines define the position of the Anti-Sun.

Plate LIV shows how the meridian defined the dividing line of Virgo and Leo at midnight of the Winter Solstice, 4000 B.C. The position of the Anti-Sun is defined by the intersection of the meridian and the Ecliptic. At the same time, Hydra—the symbol of the Leviathan of the Old Testament —extended 90° along the celestial equator, 45° on each side of the meridian. *Definition of Solstice at 4000 B.C.*

¶ 302. PERIHELION AND THE ZODIACAL SIGNS.

The motion of Perihelion and of the axes of the Earth's orbit has been dealt with in ¶¶ 150–159. Plates LV and LVI illustrate the motion in relation to the Zodiac. The Zodiacal Signs are figured as twelve signs of 30° each based on the arrangement with respect to 4699 B.C., although, strictly speaking, the latter arrangement is always associated with its own system of six signs. The same remark as to the twelve signs applies also to Plates XLIV–XLVII.

Plate LV shows the position of the Earth's orbit and of the Equinoxes and Solstices at 4044 B.C. The latter date is the epoch defined by the Pyramid for longitude of Perihelion 0°, i.e. the Autumnal Equinox coincided with Perihelion at point A, when the Anti-Sun lay in Taurus, and the Sun in Scorpio. The other points of the solar year are as shown. *Position of Perihelion (longitude 0°) at 4044 B.C. in relation to the Zodiacal signs and the solar year.*

Plate LVI shows the position of the Earth's orbit when the Autumnal Equinox had moved 90° from Perihelion, i.e. longitude of Perihelion = 90°. This occurred at 1246 A.D. The original position of Perihelion at 4044 B.C. is shown at a, and the position for 1246 A.D. is shown at A. Perihelion has moved forward round the orbit from a in Taurus to A in Gemini, and in the same interval the Autumnal Equinox has moved back round the orbit from a in Taurus to its position in Pisces shown for 1246 A.D. *Position of Perihelion (longitude 90°) at 1246 A.D. in relation to the Zodiacal signs and the solar year.*

PLATE L.

PRECESSION OF EQUINOXES.

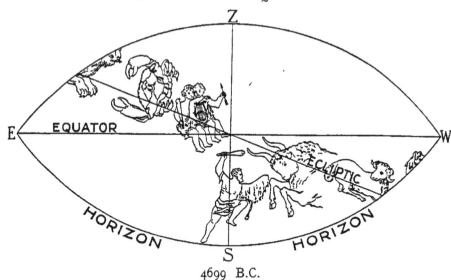

4699 B.C.

Sky above Southern Horizon at Latitude 45° North.
Visible at Midnight, Autumnal Equinox.
Invisible at Noon, Vernal Equinox.

PLATE LI.

PRECESSION OF EQUINOXES.

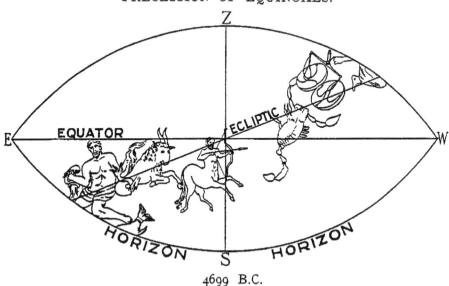

4699 B.C.

Sky above Southern Horizon at Latitude 45° North.
Visible at Midnight, Vernal Equinox.
Invisible at Noon, Autumnal Equinox.

PLATE LII.

PRECESSION OF EQUINOXES.

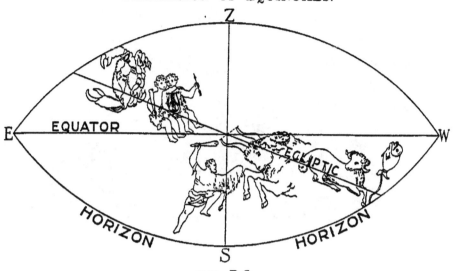

4000 B.C.

Sky above Southern Horizon at Latitude 45° North.
Visible at Midnight, Autumnal Equinox.
Invisible at Noon, Vernal Equinox.

PLATE LIII.

PRECESSION OF EQUINOXES.

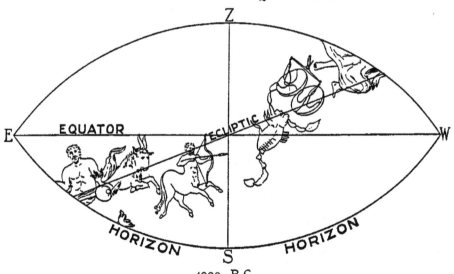

4000 B.C.

Sky above Southern Horizon at Latitude 45° North.
Visible at Midnight, Vernal Equinox.
Invisible at Noon, Autumnal Equinox.

PLATE LIV.

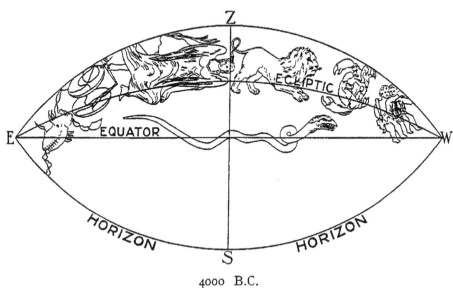

4000 B.C.

Sky above Southern Horizon at Latitude 45° North.
Visible at Midnight, Winter Solstice.
Invisible at Noon, Summer Solstice.

Note :—Hydra extended along the Celestial Equator 45° Eastward and 45° Westward from the Meridian.

PLATE LV.

THE MOTION OF THE EARTH'S ORBIT.

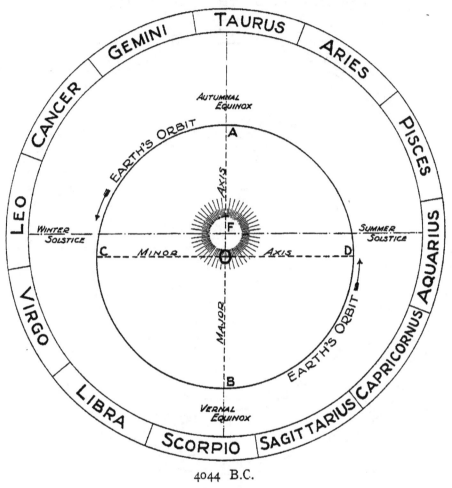

4044 B.C.

Position of the axes of the Earth's Orbit in relation to the Equinoxes and Solstices and in relation to the Zodiacal Signs.

Note :—Perihelion at A, Aphelion at B.

PLATE LVI.

THE MOTION OF THE EARTH'S ORBIT.

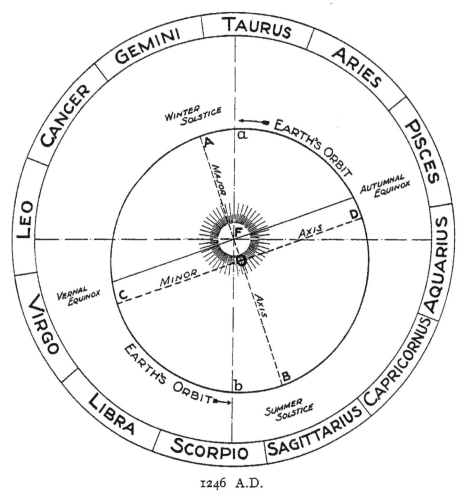

1246 A.D.

Positions of the axes of the Earth's Orbit in relation to the Equinoxes and Solstices and in relation to the Zodiacal Signs.

Note :—Perihelion for 1246 A.D. at A ; for 4044 B.C. at a.
Aphelion for 1246 A.D. at B ; for 4044 B.C. at b.

¶ 303. THE HINDOO LUNAR ZODIAC AND THE KALI-YUGA.

In ¶ 59 we saw that the Egyptian priests had a nominal solar year of 365.24 days. The vague year was reckoned to slip a complete revolution round the nominal solar year in 1522 vague years (accurately 1521.875, as in ¶ 106). The latter interval we termed the Nominal Solar Cycle (¶¶ 59 and 106). *In Egypt :— Nominal solar year and vague year produce cycle of 1522 vague years.*

It was also shown, in ¶ 106, that the nominal solar year of 365.24 days slipped backwards round the nominal Sothic year of 365.25 days in 36,525 years. For this reason, the later Egyptians erroneously identified the latter period as the period of the Precession of the Equinoxes (¶¶ 103–106). With the latter conception, the Zodiacal system of twelve signs gave Precession through one sign in 3043.75 =2 Nominal Solar Cycles, generally reckoned as 3044 years. In Section I of this Chapter we saw that this period is defined as the half period of the Pyramid's Perihelion chronology. (Refer also to Plates XLb, Fig. F, and XLII, Figs. A and B ; and Plate XVI, Table A, *re* 10 signs =30,437 years.) *Nominal solar year and nominal Sothic year produce "Precessional" cycle of 36,525 years. "Precession" through one sign as above =3044 years ; =half period of Pyramid's Perihelion chronology.*

In ¶¶ 283 and 294 we saw that the original Zodiacal signs were nocturnal signs. We have quoted Brown (in ¶ 294) to the effect that the original Lunar Zodiacal signs were nocturnal. Now the facts of importance are that the Hindoo Lunar Zodiacal signs are nocturnal, and in their traditions are associated with the mythical period of the Hindoo *Kali-Yuga*—the *Iron Age*, but literally, the *Black Way*. Now the Zodiac was the dark path or *black way* of the moon and the planets. In Egypt the period of 3043–4 years was associated with the idea of Precession through one sign of this " *Black Way*," and in India the period is associated with the Hindoo *Kali-Yuga*, or Black Way.[1] *Original Zodiac nocturnal. The " Kali-Yuga " or " Black Way " of the moon and planets. Hindoo lunar Zodiac nocturnal, and 3044 years associated with the " Kali-Yuga."*

[1] For the connection between the period of 3043–4 years and the *Kali-Yuga*, the reader is referred to Dr. J. F. Fleet's identifications in " Royal Asia. Soc. Jour." (April 1911) ; " Ency. Brit." (11th edition), Vol. XIII, " Hindoo Chronology," pp. 496, 497.

SECTION III.—DESCRIPTION OF PLATES.

¶ 304. GENERAL REMARKS CONCERNING PLATE XXXVII.

Pyramid's Graphical Calculus.

New special method of interpolation.

Geometrical definition of algebraic formula.

Plate XXXVII illustrates a special case of Graphical Calculus. So far as we are aware, this has not hitherto been known in the form here applied. It should be of interest to the mathematical reader to know that this special case and its application were derived from the geometrical framework of the Pyramid's passages and the connected system of co-ordinates. These were seen to indicate a geometrical method of interpolation. When this was clearly understood it was seen that the method thus given supplied all the essential data for the complete definition of the universal algebraic formula

$$P = A + B.t + C.t^2.$$

Method can be extended in application to greater number of algebraic terms.

The mathematical reader will see that there is no limit to the application of the method. He will see that, with Fig. A as basis, a succession of diagrams, such as Fig. B, each defining its succeeding figure, as Fig. A defines Fig. B in Plate XXXVII, can be employed to supply the algebraic relationship

$$P = A + B.t + C.t^2 + D.t^3 + \ldots \ldots N.t^{(n-1)}.$$

Of course, it must be realised that a graphical representation of the formula

$$P = A + B.t + C.t^2$$

The limited number of terms given by Pyramid as defining Precessional and Perihelion motions when annual rate is taken as No. of years per 360°.

would not supply the conditions for a series of values whose variations are given by the formula

$$P = A + B.t + C.t^2 + D.t^3.$$

What the Pyramid Passage Geometry establishes is that, *within its defined chronological limits*, the formula $P = A + B.t + C.t^2$ expresses the precise conditions of variation for Precessional and Perihelion motions *only when these are expressed in the form*

Annual Rate = No. of years per 360°.

¶ 304a. GENERAL EXPLANATION OF PLATE XXXVII.

Explanation of the function of the tilting line on the fixed pivot of the mid-date co-ordinate in Fig. B, Plate XXXVII.

The principle of application is best understood from Fig. B. Points 0, 1, 2, 3, 4, 5, and 6 are points equal distances apart along the base line of co-ordinates. The equal distances represent equal periods of time in years along the base line from point 0—*i.e.* from right to left. Point 3 represents the mid-date of the period 0 to 6. The period 0 to 6 is T years.

The vertical co-ordinates P_0, P_1, P_2, P_3, P_4, P_5, and P_6 represent the annual values of a certain astronomical rate of motion for the years represented by the points 0, 1, 2, 3, 4, 5, and 6 respectively. In this representation P_3 is the annual value for the mid-date at point 3. Then P_3 = vertical $3N_3$.

The basis of the geometrical definition of the algebraic formula is that N_3 is a fixed pivot for a tilting line RN_3S. Each year has a particular tilt for the line RN_3S. The vertical co-ordinate from the point representing a particular year intersects the tilting line for the particular year. The point of intersection gives the height of the co-ordinate defining the value of P for the particular year. All such points of intersection (*e.g.* N_0, N_1, N_2, N_3, N_4, N_5, and N_6) define the curve for the annual values of P (*e.g.* P_0, P_1, P_2, P_3, P_4, P_5, and P_6 respectively).

When the value of P is expressed by the algebraic formula $P = A + B.t + C.t^2$, the vertical increment of displacement for the tilting line is a constant for successive years. In other words, for the case defined, the vertical displacement of the tilting line is proportionate to the time in years. It is, therefore, expressed by a straight line equation. The straight line defining the algebraic relations is as shown on Fig. A. Relation of the values of Fig. A to the vertical displacement of the tilting line of Fig. B.

¶ 304b. PLATE XXXVII. THE GENERAL FORMULA FOR THE MID-DATE EPOCH.

In Fig. A the base line of co-ordinates is the time base of Fig. B. Points 0, 1, 2, 3, 4, 5, and 6 in Fig. A, therefore, represent the same dates as points 0, 1, 2, 3, 4, 5, and 6 in Fig. B. The co-ordinate at any point in Fig. A determines the amount of vertical end displacement of the tilting line in Fig. B for the corresponding point in Fig. B. Thus for point 2 in Fig. A, the value of p is p_2. This value, applied at the points W and Z of Fig. B—as shown on the diagram,—fixes the position of the tilting line for the date represented by the point 2 in Fig. B. The vertical line $2N_2$ from point 2 in Fig. B intersects the tilting line defined at point N_2. The co-ordinate $2N_2$ gives the value of P for the date represented by the point 2. Similarly for the other points. The geometrical relations of Figs. A and B, Plate XXXVII.

Now, let p be any required value in Fig. A, at a given time, t, forward from the mid-date represented by the point 3. From Fig. A, $p = p_3 + q$. Then, since $p_6 - p_0 = Q$, as shown on Fig. A, and since DE is a straight line, $\frac{q}{t} = \frac{Q}{T}$, or, by simple proportion, $q = \frac{Q.t}{T}$. But since $p = p_3 + q$, $p = p_3 + \frac{Q.t}{T}$. Otherwise stated, $q = \frac{Q.t}{T}$, is the amount by which the value of p at time, t, from the mid-date exceeds the value of p at the mid-date. The corresponding algebraic relations.

In Fig. B, P at time, t, from the mid-date is obtained from the value of p obtained in Fig. A. The position of the tilting line at time, t, from the mid-date is the dash line RN_3S. The tilt is such that RW = the value of p obtained from Fig. A. Then, considering the triangle RWN_3, Detailed explanation of the derivation of the general formula of interpolation for the mid-date epoch.

$$\frac{RW}{WN_3} = \frac{P - P_3}{t} \quad \text{or} \quad \frac{p}{\frac{1}{2}T} = \frac{P - P_3}{t}.$$

Therefore $$P - P_3 = \frac{2p.t}{T},$$

and since $$p = p_3 + \frac{Q.t}{T},$$

$$P - P_3 = \frac{2p_3.t}{T} + \frac{2Q.t^2}{T^2}.$$

$$\therefore \quad P = P_3 + \frac{2p_3.t}{T} + \frac{2Q.t^2}{T^2}$$

which is of the general form

$$P = A + B.t + C.t_2;$$

where A, B, and C are constants,

$$A = P_3,$$

$$B = \frac{2p_3}{T},$$

and

$$C = \frac{2.Q}{T^2}.$$

¶ 304c. SPECIAL CASES FOR THE MID-DATE EPOCH.

Case I.—
For p and P
both increasing
with time (t),
B and C are
both positive
(+).

Case I.—For the case illustrated on Plate XXXVII, Figs. A and B, the values of p and P both increase with the time.

In this case, B is positive (+) and C is positive (+), the formula being

$$P = A + B.t + C.t^2;$$
$$\left. A = P_3, \quad B = \frac{2p_3}{T}, \text{ and } C = \frac{2.Q}{T^2} \right\} \qquad \cdots \qquad \cdots \qquad \cdots \quad I$$

Case II.—
For p and P
both decreas-
ing with time
(t), B is
negative (—)
and C is
positive (+).

Case II.—For the case illustrated on Plate XXXVII, Figs. C and D, the values of p and P both decrease with the time.

In this case, B is negative (—) and C is positive (+).

The general reader will see why C is positive if he understands that Case II is the equivalent of Case I with the direction of time reversed, *i.e.* t negative (—) in Case I.

Then $\qquad\qquad\qquad P = A - B.t + C.t^2$

since $\qquad\qquad\qquad (-t)^2 = (-t) \times (-t) = +t^2.$ $\qquad \cdots \qquad \cdots \qquad \cdots \quad II$

As before $\qquad\qquad\qquad A = P_3, \quad B = \frac{2p_3}{T}, \text{ and } C = \frac{2.Q}{T^2}$

Case III.—
For P increas-
ing and p
decreasing
with time (t),
B is positive
(+) and C is
negative (—).

Case III.—For the value of P increasing with the time, and the value of p decreasing with the time (Plate XXXVII, Fig. C in conjunction with Fig. B), B is positive (+) and C is negative (—).

Then $\qquad\qquad\qquad P = A + B.t - C.t^2 \qquad \cdots \qquad \cdots \qquad \cdots \qquad \cdots \quad III$

with values of A, B, and C as before.

Case IV.—
For P decreas-
ing and p
increasing
with time (t),
B and C are
both negative
(—).

Case IV.—For the value of P decreasing with the time, and the value of p increasing with the time (Plate XXXVII, Fig. A in conjunction with Fig. D), B is negative (—) and C is negative (—), as may be proved independently by taking, in Case III, the direction of time reversed.

Then $\qquad\qquad\qquad P = A - B.t - C.t^2 \qquad \cdots \qquad \cdots \qquad \cdots \qquad \cdots \quad IV$

with values of A, B, and C as before.

¶ 304d. GENERAL FORMULA FOR CHANGE OF EPOCH.

Detailed
explanation of
the derivation
of the general
formula of
interpolation
for a change
of epoch.

To transfer to a formula for an epoch other than the mid-date epoch, proceed as follows:—

Let X in Fig. B, Plate XXXVII, represent the new epoch, T_1 years after the mid-date epoch.

Then, as shown on diagram, Fig. B, value of P at date X of epoch $= P_x = a$. From concluding formula of ¶ 304b,

$$P = P_3 + \frac{2p_3}{T}.t + \frac{2.Q}{T^2}.t^2 \quad \cdots \qquad \cdots \qquad \cdots \qquad \cdots \qquad \cdots \quad (1)$$

$$P_x = P_3 + \frac{2p_3}{T}.T_1 + \frac{2Q}{T^2}.T_1^2 \qquad \cdots \qquad \cdots \qquad \cdots \qquad \cdots \quad (2)$$

Subtracting, we obtain

$$P - P_x = \frac{2p_3}{T}(t - T_1) + \frac{2Q}{T^2}(t^2 - T_1^2);$$

$$P = P_x + \frac{2p_3}{T}(t - T_1) + \frac{2Q}{T^2}(t^2 - T_1^2) \qquad \cdots \qquad \cdots \qquad \cdots \quad (3)$$

Now, as on diagram, Fig. B, let t_1 be the number of years for values of P in relation to the new epoch X, but t_1 being taken as positive[1] ($+$), forward from date X.

Then
$$t_1 = t - T_1 \quad .. \quad .. \quad .. \quad .. \quad .. \quad (4)$$

In formula (3) above, the value of P for the new epoch X is stated as a function of the value of p for the mid-epoch.

By analogy with the mid-epoch formula (¶ 304b), let

$$P = P_x + \frac{2m}{T}.t_1 + \frac{2Q}{T^2}.t_1{}^2 \quad .. \quad .. \quad .. \quad .. \quad (5)$$

stated in terms applicable to the new epoch ; m being a constant for the new epoch, analogous to p_3 for the mid-epoch.

It is required to state m in terms of p_3, or *vice versa*. Expressing formula (5) in terms of formula (4) we obtain

$$P = P_x + \frac{2m}{T}(t - T_1) + \frac{2Q}{T^2}(t^2 - 2t.T_1 + T_1{}^2) \quad .. \quad .. \quad .. \quad (6)$$

Subtracting formula (3) from formula (6)

$$\left. \begin{array}{l} m = p_3 + \dfrac{2Q.T_1}{T} \\[2mm] p_3 = m - \dfrac{2Q.T_1}{T} \end{array} \right\} \quad .. \quad .. \quad .. \quad .. \quad (7)$$

and

The resulting general formula for a change of epoch is

$$P = a + b.t_1 + c.t_1{}^2,$$

where

$$a = P_x = P \text{ for new epoch X}$$

$$b = \frac{2m}{T}$$

$$c = \frac{2Q}{T^2}$$

$$m = p_3 + \frac{2Q.T_1}{T}$$

when T_1 is ahead of the mid-epoch.

¶ 304e. SPECIAL CASES FOR THE CHANGE OF EPOCH.

As before, we can express the preceding general formula in the following forms :—

Case I.—Values of p and P both increasing with the time. (Plate XXXVII, Figs. A and B.)

where

$$\left. \begin{array}{l} P = a + b.t_1 + c.t_1{}^2 \\[2mm] a = P_x = P \text{ for new epoch X} \\[1mm] b = \dfrac{2m}{T} \\[2mm] c = \dfrac{2Q}{T^2} \\[2mm] m = p_3 + \dfrac{2Q.T_1}{T} \left\{ \begin{array}{l} \text{when } T_1 \text{ follows} \\ \text{the mid-epoch} \end{array} \right. \\[3mm] = p_3 - \dfrac{2Q.T_1}{T} \left\{ \begin{array}{l} \text{when } T_1 \text{ precedes} \\ \text{the mid-epoch} \end{array} \right. \end{array} \right\} \quad .. \quad .. \quad \text{V}$$

or

---

[1] In diagram, Plate XXXVII, Fig. B, t_1 is shown as a negative ($-$) value of time.

Case II.—
Formula for
p and P both
decreasing
with time.

Case II.—Values of p and P both decreasing with the time. (Plate XXXVII, Figs. C and D.)

$$P = a - b.t_1 + c.t_1{}^2,$$

where a, b, and c are as above, and

$$m = p_3 - \frac{2Q.T_1}{T} \left\{ \begin{array}{l} \text{when } T_1 \text{ follows} \\ \quad \text{the mid-epoch} \end{array} \right.$$

or

$$= p_3 + \frac{2Q.T_1}{T} \left\{ \begin{array}{l} \text{when } T_1 \text{ precedes} \\ \quad \text{the mid-epoch} \end{array} \right.$$

$$\qquad \text{..} \qquad \text{..} \qquad \text{VI}$$

Case III.—
Formula for P
increasing and
p decreasing
with time.

Case III.—Value of P increasing, and value of p decreasing with time. (Plate XXXVII, Figs. C and B.)

$$P = a + b.t_1 - c.t_1{}^2,$$

where a, b, and c are as above, and

$$m = p_3 - \frac{2Q.T_1}{T} \left\{ \begin{array}{l} \text{when } T_1 \text{ follows} \\ \quad \text{the mid-epoch} \end{array} \right.$$

or

$$= p_3 + \frac{2Q.T_1}{T} \left\{ \begin{array}{l} \text{when } T_1 \text{ precedes} \\ \quad \text{the mid-epoch} \end{array} \right.$$

$$\qquad \text{..} \qquad \text{..} \qquad \text{VII}$$

Case IV.—
Formula for P
decreasing and
p increasing
with time.

Case IV.—Value of P decreasing, and value of p increasing with time. (Plate XXXVII, Figs. A and D.)

$$P = a - b.t_1 - c.t_1{}^2,$$

where a, b, and c are as above, and

$$m = p_3 + \frac{2Q.T_1}{T} \left\{ \begin{array}{l} \text{when } T_1 \text{ follows} \\ \quad \text{the mid-epoch} \end{array} \right.$$

or

$$= p_3 - \frac{2Q.T_1}{T} \left\{ \begin{array}{l} \text{when } T_1 \text{ precedes} \\ \quad \text{the mid-epoch} \end{array} \right.$$

$$\qquad \text{..} \qquad \text{..} \qquad \text{VIII}$$

¶ 304f. TOTAL MOTION FOR A GIVEN INTERVAL.

Integration
for derivation
of true mean
value of P
for interval t.

To obtain the true mean value of P for a given time, t, from the epoch in the formula

$$P = A + B.t + C.t^2$$

integrate thus—

$$\int P.(dt) = A.t + \frac{B}{2}.t^2 + \frac{C}{3}.t^3.$$

Rigorous
method of
obtaining
total angle
covered by
motion in
interval t
years.

Then the true mean value of P for time, t, from the epoch

$$= \frac{\int P.(dt)}{t} = \frac{A.t + \frac{B}{2}.t^2 + \frac{C}{3}.t_3}{t}$$

$$= A + \frac{B}{2}.t + \frac{C}{3}.t^2 \quad \text{..} \quad \text{..} \quad \text{..} \quad \text{..} \quad \text{IX}$$

where P is the annual motion expressed as the period of a cycle.

Then the true mean value of P for 90° of total movement is such that

$$4t = P.$$

$$\therefore \quad 4t = A + \frac{B}{2}.t + \frac{C}{3}.t^2,$$

and
$$\frac{C}{3}.t^2 + \left(\frac{B}{2}-4\right).t + A = 0$$

$$t = \frac{-\left(\frac{B}{2}-4\right) \pm \sqrt{\left(\frac{B}{2}-4\right)^2 - \frac{4C}{3}.A}}{\frac{2C}{3}}$$

$$t = \frac{12 - \frac{3B}{2} \pm 3\sqrt{\left(\frac{B}{2}-4\right)^2 - \frac{4A.C}{3}}}{2C} \quad .. \quad .. \quad .. \quad .. \quad X$$

Again,

for 360° $\quad t = P$ ⎫
,, 180° $\quad 2t = P$ ⎪ Corresponding alterations being
,, 60° $\quad 6t = P$ ⎬ made in formula X.
,, 30° $\quad 12t = P$ ⎭

Let $\theta =$ Total angle covered by motion in t years; then $\frac{360.t}{\theta} = P$

and
$$t = \frac{-\left(\frac{B}{2}-4\right) \pm \sqrt{\left(\frac{B}{2}-4\right)^2 - \frac{4C}{3}.A}}{\frac{240C}{\theta}} \quad .. \quad .. \quad .. \quad XI$$

Owing generally to formulæ X and XI resolving themselves into a quotient of two **Simple method** small quantities, and to other complicated factors of arithmetical reduction, it is **of successive approximation.** generally simpler and quicker to employ formula IX with trial and error value of t to give $4t = P$ for 90° of total movement, or $\frac{360.t}{\theta} = P$ for θ in degrees of total movement. Two or three brief calculations are generally sufficient, as the reader will find by trial.

¶ 304g. VALUES IN PRECESSIONAL FORMULA FOR DIFFERENT EPOCHS.

Basis :—¶ 236.

$$P = a - b.t_1 + c.t_1^2.$$

For epoch midnight ending
25th January 1844 A.D. ⎰ $a = 25,794.212764,$
⎱ $b = 0.1129593,$
⎩ $c = 0.0000001430511,$

Values in formula for epochs at 1844 A.D., and

and formulæ VI, ¶ 304e—

Epoch : Autumnal Equinox.	Values in years of			At 1000 years' intervals from 4000 B.C. to 2001 A.D.
	a.	b.	c.	
4000 B.C. = 0 A.P.	26,459.038617	0.1146308096		
3000 B.C. = 1000 A.P.	26,344.550859	0.1143447074		
2000 B.C. = 2000 A.P.	26,230.349202	0.1140586052	Constant for all	
1000 B.C. = 3000 A.P.	26,116.433648	0.1137725030	Epochs,	
1¾ A.D. = 4000 A.P.	26,002.804196	0.1134864008	0.0000001430511	
1001¾ A.D. = 5000 A.P.	25,889.460847	0.1132002986		
2001¾ A.D. = 6000 A.P.	25,776.403599	0.1129141964		

Influence of the Pyramid's displacement factor.

It will be noticed that b reduces its value by 0.0002861022 per 1000 years' change of epoch ; 286.1022 being the numerical value of the Pyramid's Passage Displacement, and of the displacement of the Pyramid's central extent of base side (¶¶ 225, 233–235).

¶ 304h. PRECESSIONAL FORMULA FOR ANNUAL ANGULAR RATE.

Epoch 1850 :— P in cyclic time.

P as annual angular rate.

The Pyramid's precessional formula for epoch 1st January 1850 A.D. is as follows :—

$$P = 25{,}793.542356 - 0.11295760522t + 0.00000014305t^2,$$

whereas Newcomb's for the same epoch is

$$P = 25{,}793.46 - 0.114t \quad .. \quad .. \quad .. \quad \text{(refer ¶ 224)}$$

(applicable from 1600 to 2100 A.D.).

Newcomb's corresponding formula.

The Pyramid's precessional value, when expressed as the rate in seconds of angle per year (for 1st January 1850 A.D. epoch)

$$= 50''.2451343097 + 0.0002200383835t + 0.0000000068447t^2 \,;$$

whereas Newcomb's formula for the same epoch is

$$50''.2453 + 0.0002222t \text{ (refer ¶ 224)} \,;$$

Bauschinger's corresponding formula.

Bauschinger's being

$$50''.2453 + 0.0002218t \text{ (refer ¶ 223)}.$$

Mathematical defect in interpolative statement of angular rates as derived from true interpolative statement of cyclic time rates.

The above data are for comparison only. The reason for emphasising this is that, if the formula for P (expressed as years of Cycle) *precisely* agrees with the formula $P = a - b.t_1 + c.t_1^2$, it is mathematically certain that when the data derived from the same are converted into the formula

Seconds of angle per year $= a + b.t_1 + c.t_1^2,$

the latter formula does not *precisely* define the motion *over the long periods* accurately covered by the cyclic form of the same.   The formula thus obtained, however, is very accurate indeed ; when integrated to obtain the total angle of precession over a long interval a very slight discrepancy occurs.   It is not very material, but serves to show that the angular functions cannot be as accurately expressed by the general interpolation formula $P = a + b.t_1 + c.t_1^2$, as in the case of the cyclic functions thus expressed.

¶ 304i. PERIHELION MOTION.

$$P = a - b.t_1 + c.t_1^2.$$

Values in formula for epochs 2001 A.D., 2045 A.D., and 4044 B.C.

Basal Data :—

P for 6000 A.P. (2001¾ A.D.) = 21,000 $\quad .. \quad .. \quad$ (¶ 246)

Epoch, midnight ending 25th January 1844 A.D. :—

$$\left. \begin{array}{l} a = 21{,}006.883208 \\ b = 0.04367929523 \\ c = 0.0000001430511 \end{array} \right\} \text{ refer ¶ 247.}$$

Other Epochs :—

Epoch 6043.9707355 A.P. = 2045¾ A.D. :—

$$\left. \begin{array}{l} a = 20{,}998.081926 \\ b = 0.04362160826 \\ c = 0.0000001430511 \end{array} \right\} \text{ refer ¶ 247.}$$

Epoch 43.9707355 prior to 0 A.P. =4044 B.C., when longitude of Perihelion
=0° :—

$$a = 21,269.051404$$
$$b = 0.0453633817 \quad \Big\} \text{ refer } \P \text{ 247.}$$
$$c = 0.0000001430511$$

The latter values, when employed with the method of ¶ 304f, give the longitude of Perihelion 90° at 1246¼ A.D., and longitude of Perihelion 103° 42′ 28″.6 (the sum of the base angles of the Pyramid's vertical section) at 6043.97 A.P. =2045¾ A.D. (refer ¶ 247).

Longitude of Perihelion 90° at 1246¼ A.D. and 103° 42′ 28″.6 (sum of base angles of Pyramid section) at 2045 A.D.

Epoch : Autumnal Equinox.	Values in Years of			
	a.	b.	c.	*Values in formula for epochs 1000 years apart from 4000 B.C. to 2001 A.D.*
4000 B.C. = 0 A.P.	21,267.054970	0.0453508015		
3000 B.C. =1000 A.P.	21,221.747219	0.0450646993		
2000 B.C. =2000 A.P.	21,176.825571	0.0447785971	Constants for all	
1000 B.C. =3000 A.P.	21,132.190025	0.0444924949	Epochs,	
1¼ A.D. =4000 A.P.	21,087.840581	0.0442063927	0.0000001430511	
1001¼ A.D. =5000 A.P.	21,043.777239	0.0439202905		
2001¾ A.D. =6000 A.P.	21,000.000000	0.0436341883		

¶ 304j. MODERN PERIHELION VALUES COMPARED WITH THE PYRAMID'S.

In Gausz's " Tafeln " (Edit. 1917)—
Longitude of Perihelion for 1st January 1910 A.D.
is given as   ..   ..   101° 23′ 3″.0
Pyramid's value for same is   ..   ..   ..   101° 22′ 54″.4

Difference ..   ..   0° 0′ 8″.6

Modern stated longitude of Perihelion for 1910 A.D. 8″.6 only in excess of Pyramid's value for same date.

Having regard to the circumstances of the two presentations, one contemporaneous with and the other remotely anterior to the longitude defined, anything smaller than the difference of 8″.6 obtained can scarcely be imagined. In fact, the difference falls within the modern limits of error in determining the longitude of Perihelion. *Difference within modern limits of error.*

Again, when the Pyramid's Perihelion cyclic value of P for 1st January 1910 A.D. (i.e. 21,004.001 years) is transformed into the equivalent annual value for the change of longitude of Perihelion, the value, stated to 2 decimal places, is .. 61″.70 whereas Gausz, " Tafeln " (Edit. 1917), gives for 1910 A.D. ..   ..   .. 61″.68

Difference ..   ..   .. 0″.02

Modern stated annual rate of change in longitude of Perihelion for 1910 A.D. 0″.02 only less than Pyramid's value for same date.

Again, the small difference of 0″.02 falls within the modern limits of error in determining the annual rate of change of the longitude of Perihelion. *Difference within modern limits of error.*

It should be noted by the reader that research on the motion of Perihelion has not been so extensive or complete as in the case of Precessional motion ; and that the

Research on
motion of
Perihelion
compared with
research on
Precessional
motion.
determination of the annual values related to Perihelion, for any particular year, is complicated by the intricate factors governing the elements of all the planetary orbits of the Solar System.

¶ 305.   PLATE XXXVIII, FIGS. A, B, AND C.   DEFINITION OF PASSAGE SLOPE.

Connected
relations of
Plate
XXXVIII.
Figs. A, B, and C of Plate XXXVIII, as figured and lettered, largely explain themselves.   Essential details of Fig. A are given in ¶ 225, and of Figs. B and C in ¶¶ 226 and 227.   The relation between the three figures of Plate XXXVIII and the various stages of Plate XL are given in ¶¶ 228 to 231.   An important relation between Plate XXXVIII, Fig. A and Plate XL, Fig. A is defined in footnote to ¶ 242.·

Scalar Axis
of Ascending
Passage
defined in
relation of
general
geometry of
Pyramid.
The general reader, with but a slight knowledge of geometrical methods, will see that the Scalar Axis construction of Plate XL, Fig. A—here derived from Plate XXXVIII, Fig. A—can be obtained directly as a geometrical construction from Plate XXIII, Fig. A, Case I.   The construction was omitted, as a possible over-elaboration.

The method, however, is as follows :—Referring to Plate XXIII, Fig. A, Case I, let the Section shown be a North to South Vertical Section—

$$F_1 k_1 = 2861.022156 \ P'',$$

and

$$B_2 A_1 B_1 = 6456.6355945 \ P''.$$

Method
explained as
relating to
Plates XXIII,
XXXVIII, and
XL.
From k_1 drop a vertical to cut $A_1 B_1$ at a point which we may term p.   Then $A_1 p = 2861.022156 \ P''$.   On and below $A_1 p$ construct a square of which $A_1 p$ is the upper horizontal side.   The lower horizontal side of this square is then 2861.022156 P'' below the precessional circuit level $A_1 B_1$.   Continue the lower horizontal side to pass through and beyond the geometrical North face slope of the Pyramid, produced below the base.   The line thus obtained is the line XY in Plate XL, Fig. A.   Now, with $B_2 A_1 B_1 = 6456.6355945 \ P''$, of Plate XXIII, Fig. A, Case I, as radius, and point A_1 as centre, describe a circle to intersect the lower horizontal line above defined. The intersection occurs at point Y of Plate XL, Fig. A.

¶ 306.   PLATE XXXIX.   GENERAL SCHEME OF PASSAGE SYSTEM.

Projection of
1st Ascending
Passage
indicates
geometrical
datum and
basis of
geometrical
construction.
Plate XXXIX illustrates how the structural indications, as seen in a sectional elevation taken along the plane of the axes of the Passages, suggest the geometrical framework of the Passage system.   The roof and floor lines of the 1st Ascending Passage are shown produced to intersect the line produced of the North face slope. This intersection naturally forms a geometrical zero datum for measurements along the Passage slope.   The indication thus supplied leads to the various geometrical constructions and astronomical identities of Plates XL, XLI, and XLII.

The Edgars'
error in
reconstruction
of the Pyramid
base and of the
Passage
system.
Error not in
data of text
but in drawn
data.
At first sight the drawing may seem to be an exact copy of the splendid Plate appearing in Messrs. Edgars' work.[1]   We willingly acknowledge our indebtedness to the Edgars for many new details furnished by them as a result of their and Dow Covington's investigations and measurements.   The Plate furnished by the Edgars, however, supplies a measurement horizontally from the Great Step to North base casing edge, 36 inches in excess of the true distance obtained by Petrie's survey. This shows that the Edgars theoretically reconstructed the measurement of the casing base by ignoring Petrie's survey ; precisely as Petrie theoretically reconstructed the casing corners and arris edges by ignoring the hollowing-in feature observed by him.

[1] " Great Pyramid Passages," Vol. I, Plate IX.

Petrie's total Passage floor distance from the hollowed-in casing face to the vertical face of the Great Step is precisely as shown on Plate XXXIX. In the Plate supplied by the Edgars, owing to the casing stones being shown in section, where our Plate shows the arris edge in elevation, the total distance (Edgars') from the Great Step to the casing face thus obtained is 28¾ inches longer than Petrie's, or any other measurement. This fact is not noted in the text of the work referred to. It is doubtful even if the Edgars knew of the discrepancy. The reader will find it, however, by scaling the plate referred to. Strangely enough, the error occurs, not in the Entrance Passage length, but in the Grand Gallery length. A corresponding error occurs in the horizontal length of the Passage to the Queen's Chamber. *[margin: Existing base casing stones shown displaced 36 inches. Owing to same Grand Gallery length scales 28¾ inches too long.]*

¶ 306a. A PUZZLE OF SIXTY YEARS' STANDING.

The reason for the error of 28¾ inches in excess for the Grand Gallery—as scaled from Messrs. Edgars' Plate—will appear when the reader refers to our Plate XLI, Fig. H. In thus drawing attention to Edgars' mistake in reconstructing, the intention is not merely to criticise. The same initial error occurred in the first published series of articles dealing with the preliminary discoveries of the present work.[1] The error in our case affected, not the Gallery length, but the Entrance Passage length. When we observed that our geometrical length for the latter was 28¾ inches in excess of Petrie's measured length for the Entrance Passage, the reason for the difference appeared at once. Prior to this we had unwittingly adopted the same view as the Edgars concerning the casing base. The observing of the error noted supplied the first indication of the hollowing-in feature. The hollowing-in feature was, in fact, suggested to us by the geometrical indications prior to any knowledge on our part that Petrie had observed the precise extent of hollowing-in on the core escarpments. *[margin: Error due to not realising hollowing-in feature. The same error occurred in initial form of present discoveries (1909-1910). This gave our original Entrance Passage length 28¾ inches too long. Discovery of this error led to discovery of hollowing-in independently of Petrie's statement.]*

The same error of 28¾ inches will be seen to have perplexed Professor Smyth. In his "Life and Work" Plates, and in the first three (or four) editions of his "Our Inheritance," the Great Step and the centre of the Queen's Chamber are both shown thrown to the South of the Pyramid's central vertical axis. In his 5th Edition of the latter work, however, Smyth adopted Petrie's Passages and his casing base at pavement level. At the same time Smyth adopted the untenable theory already dealt with in ¶¶ 174 and 175. *[margin: Smyth's original (1864) and revised (circa 1890) casing base of Pyramid in error for the same reason.]*

¶ 307. PLATE XL, FIGS. A, B, AND C. THE SCALAR AXIS AND SCALAR ZERO.

The preliminary geometrical bases of Plate XL appear on Plate XXIII, Fig. A, Case I, and Plates XXXVIII and XXXIX, for which refer ¶¶ 305 and 306. These bases define the constructions for the Scalar Axis, DCFY of Plate XL, Figs. A, B, and F. The geometrical indications that supplied the important angular relation of the line FT are supplied in the footnote to ¶ 242. *[margin: Sequence of geometrical construction:— Plates XXIII (Fig. A), XXXVIII, XXXIX, and XL.]*

It should be noted by the reader that the reference lettering in the diagrams of Plates XL and XLI is unchanged throughout. *[margin: Reference lettering of Plates XL and XLI constant throughout.]*

The dimensions throughout are accurately calculated in all cases from the various geometrical bases adopted. The reader should observe that the only basal *dimensional* feature adopted in Plate XL, Fig. B, extra to the dimensional features resulting from the geometrical construction of Fig. A, is the scalar distance of 2000 P". The verticals 886.2269254 P" and 2588.8194161 P", and the horizontal 5237.4561800 P" follow as calculated results from the adoption of CG =2000 P". In Plate XL, Fig. B, the dimensions of GH and HK are unknown. GH and HK are merely figured here *[margin: All dimensions are calculated from geometrical bases, i.e. without any basis derived from measured distances. Plate XL, Figs. A and B, sequence of essential data.]*

[1] These were written by D. Davidson in 1909, and published in 1910. The articles are now out of print.

as further geometrical indications supplied by the constructions of Plate XXXIX and Plate XL, Fig. B.

Fig. C :—
The geometrical function of the square of equal area.
Defines the scalar zero for Passage measurements. Plate XL, Fig. C, supplies the geometrical basis for the determination of the dimensions of GH and HK. K is the point of intersection of the 1st Ascending Passage roof line and the face of the Pyramid, both produced to effect the intersection. The horizontal QPK through the point of intersection, K, cuts the 1st Ascending Passage floor line at P, such that the horizontal distance QP from the Pyramid's central vertical axis is 5151.6498562 P″. The latter dimension is the length of the side of the square of area equal to the area of the Pyramid's right vertical section. This dimension defines the co-ordinates of the point of intersection K, and also the scalar zero for passage measurements.

¶ 307a. PLATE XL, FIGS. C, D, AND E. THE SEQUENCE OF
    CALCULATIONS.

Manner of definition of scalar zero. The manner in which the latter are defined is as follows :—

The sloping Passage distance DG = MH is known from Plate XL, Fig. B.

In Plate XL, Fig. C, QP being given supplies by calculation the sloping Passage distance MP.

Fig. D :—
1st Ascending and Entrance Passage height. Then MH−MP = PH, as shown in the text of Fig. C. This gives the basis for the calculations supplying all the co-ordinates related to the Passage height. These are as figured on Plate XL, Fig. D.

Fig. E :—
Vertical height from Passage floor to Scalar Axis. Similarly, as shown on Plate XL, Fig. C, the vertical height between the Passage floor and the Scalar Axis is derived from the combined data of Fig. C and Fig. D. The resulting calculated co-ordinates are as shown on Fig. E.

All the co-ordinates of K and G, in Figs. D and E, are bases, perpendiculars, and hypotenuses of right-angled triangles, with the hypotenuse in each case making an angle of 26° 18′ 9″.63 with the base. Angle KŪd (in Fig. D) = 51° 51′ 14″.3, the Pyramid base angle.

Complete dimensions of 1st Ascending Passage.
Vertical distance of Great Step above the pavement base. The relations of Figs. D and E, thus calculated, enable us to complete all the geometrical dimensions—vertical, horizontal, and sloping—of the 1st Ascending Passage produced between the Pyramid's central vertical axis and its geometrical North face slope produced. The important resulting vertical dimension, shown on Fig. C, is the vertical distance AM of the point M, the foot of the Great Step, above the pavement base level, AB.

The above is merely a skeleton outline of the geometrical sequence and of the sequence of calculations, to enable the general reader to piece together the various stages and calculations of Plate XL, Figs. A to E. The diagrams were prepared to be self-explanatory.

¶ 307b. PLATE XL, FIG. C. THE RHOMBOID OF DISPLACEMENT.

The rhomboid of displacement.
Each side 286.1 P″.
Structural definition of the planes of all sides except the North. An important geometrical detail shown on Plate XL, Fig. C, is the rhomboid[1] of displacement, of which $W_1W_2Z_2Z_1$ is the side elevation, or rhombus elevation. The twelve dimensional lines forming its edges are each 286.1 P″. The rhomboid thus defined is a solid figure bounded on its upper surface by the plane of the Grand Gallery roof, W_2Z_2 ; on its lower surface, by the plane of the 1st Ascending Passage roof produced, W_1Z_1 ; on its West side, by the North to South central vertical plane of the Pyramid ; on its East side, by the central vertical plane of the passage axis ; on its South side, by the East to West central vertical plane of the Pyramid ; and on

---

[1]The designation, although not precisely correct, will be better understood by the majority of readers. The correct term is " rhombohedron."

its North side, by the East to West vertical plane passing through the line Z_1Z_2. Implied
geometrical
definition of
the latter.
The latter plane is the only one of the six planes of the rhomboid that is not *structurally*
defined. Its purposely implied geometrical definition, however, is one of the most Completes the
geometrical
important items in the Pyramid's astronomical symbolism. In conjunction with the definition of
passage displacement and the base side displacement, it completes the geometrical the Preces-
definition of the Precessional and Perihelion relations of the Earth and its orbit. sional and
Perihelion
This is fully explained in Section I of this Chapter, together with the fact that the relations of
ultimate purpose of the astronomical symbolism is independently revealed in the the Earth and
its orbit.
literature of the ancient Egyptians.

The true Scalar relation of the rhomboid of displacement to the Grand Gallery True Scalar
relation shown
on Plate XLII.
is shown on Plate XLII, Fig. A.

¶ 307c. PLATE XL, FIG. F. THE ZERO DATE OR EPOCH, o A.P.

Fig. F of Plate XL shows the Scalar line of the Descending Passage added to the Fig. F :—
Scalar Axis of the Ascending Passage. The Descending Passage Scalar line is the Scalar line of
Descending
roof line of that Passage produced. The two axes intersect at a point 2500 P″ along Passage.
the Ascending Passage Scalar Axis from the zero scalar point G of Figs. B and C. Definition of
upper and
In Fig. F this is indicated as the lower o A.P. point. The vertical line from the latter lower 0 A.P.
to the roof line produced of the Descending Passage defines, on the latter line, the upper Solar years
o A.P. point as shown on Fig. F. A distance in Pyramid inches from o A.P., upper or represented by
Pyramid inches
lower, measured along the Descending Passage line or the Ascending Passage line measured along
Descending
respectively, represents the number of solar years (defined in the diagram as Anno or Ascending
Passage lines
Pyr. or A.P.) from the zero date or Epoch represented by the point o A.P. (upper or from 0 A.P.
lower). Thus any two points, one on the Descending Passage line and the other (upper or
lower) as
on the Ascending Passage line, joined by a vertical line, represent the same date A.P. Epoch.
With this explanation we think the diagram of Fig. F should explain itself to the
general reader. Intersection
of Descending

The astronomical significance of the diagram has been explained in ¶¶ 229 and Passage roof
230, and is further simply illustrated on Plate XLII, Figs. A and B. When the line and level
of pavement
reader observes, however, that the Descending Passage roof line intersects the level base at 3000
of the Pavement base at 3000 A.P., and that this is the centre point of the circle of A.P. is the
centre of
diameter 6087.94 P″, and also of the circle of 6000 P″, and observes how the two circles of
diameters are geometrically defined, he cannot fail to see that the diagram represents 6087.94 P″,
and of 6000 P″
the chronological framework of ¶¶ 229 and 230, for the definition of the general diameter, both
geometrically
formula geometrically expressed by Plate XXXVII, Figs. A and B. defined.

The central date for a similar geometrical framework for the algebraic expression Chronological
framework for
of astronomical variations other than those based on the framework of Fig. F is the definition
of the general
suggested by the point 2500 A.P. being represented as a central point of intersection. formula.
This, however, has not been developed in the present volume. Similar central
date, 2500 A.P.,
suggested by

The complete definition of the Passage System—with all its dimensions, longi- the construc-
tudinal, sloping, vertical, and perpendicular—is obtained by adding the details of tion but not
here developed.
Figs. C, D, and F of Plate XL to the framework of Fig. F. This is effected on Plates Complete
XLI and XLII. As shown on Figs. G, H, K, and L of Plate XLI, the dimensions definition of
Passage
thus obtained—entirely from geometrical data—are identical with Professor Petrie's System
obtained.
measured dimensions. All dimensions
identical with
Petrie's.

¶ 308. PLATE XLI, FIG. G. PASSAGE JUNCTION DATINGS.

Intersection
of Descending
In Plate XLI, Fig. G, the point 2500 A.P.—defined by the intersection of the Passage roof
Descending Passage roof line and the Ascending Passage Scalar Axis, as given by line and
Plate XL, Fig. F—is the given point for the construction. The vertical from the Ascending
Passage
latter point to the floor line of the Ascending Passage (Fig. G) is equal to GH in Scalar Axis
at 2500 A.P.,
Fig. E (Plate XL). The corresponding sloping floor distance of the Ascending the given
point of the
construction.

Intersection of
Descending
Passage roof
line and
Ascending
Passage floor
line at
2543.33 A.P.
The relations
giving all the
other datings
in Fig. G.
Passage in Fig. G (Plate XLI) equals He in Fig. E (Plate XL). Hence the distance along the Descending Passage roof line from 2500 A.P. to the Ascending Passage floor line, and the equal distance along the Ascending Passage floor line from 2500 A.P. vertical to the roof line of the Descending Passage, in Fig. G (Plate XLI), each equal ⅓He in Fig. E (Plate XL). This defines the intersection of the Descending Passage roof line and the Ascending Passage floor line as 2543.3309664 A.P., as shown on Fig. G (Plate XLI). Again, the Passage height at the Passage Junction in Fig. G (Plate XLI) is equal to the height Ka in Fig. D (Plate XL). Hence the distance from the roof junction of the Passages to the intersection of the Descending Passage roof and Ascending Passage floor in Fig. G (Plate XLI) are each equal to ½aP in Fig. D (Plate XL). From these relations follow all the other A.P. datings of Fig. G (Plate XLI).

All datings
agree with
Petrie's
measurements.
The resulting datings all agree with Petrie's measurements, as explained on Plate XLI, Figs. G and H.

¶ 308a.   PLATE XLI, FIG. H.   THE ENTRANCE PASSAGE DOORWAY DATINGS.

The point for
the construc-
tion 1378.87
A.P. at inter-
section of
the Entrance
Passage roof
line produced
and the plane
of the arris
edges of the
North face
slope.
Intersection
of Passage
roof line and
the hollowed-
in face of the
casing slope
at 1407.6 A.P.
In Fig. H, Plate XLI, the point 1378.8720133 A.P.—defined by the intersection of the Entrance Passage roof line produced and the plane of the arris edges of the Pyramid's North face slope, as given by Fig. F, Plate XL—is the given point for the construction. The horizontal extent of hollowing-in (refer ¶ 148) is 35.762777 P″. The corresponding Passage roof distance, as given on Fig. H, Plate XLI, is 28.736985 P″. This gives the dating for the intersection of the Passage roof line and the hollowed-in face of the casing slope of the Pyramid's North face as 1407.608998 A.P. The application of the dimensions of Fig. D, Plate XL, then gives the dimensions of the Entrance Passage Doorway as shown. These, in conjunction with the angle of Pyramid face slope, give the other datings as shown on Fig. H, Plate XLI.

Construction of
Plate XLII,
Fig. A, giving
dating at
1460.96 A.P.
(4 × 365.24),
confirms
Entrance
Doorway
datings as
intentional.
Application of
year-cycle
geometry.
The application of the Scalar Axis of the Ascending Passage to the Entrance Passage—but, of course, at the reverse angle—is not shown on Plates XL and XLI. When, however, the vertical from the sill of the Entrance Doorway is projected to intersect the Scalar Axis of the Ascending Passage produced below the Pyramid base, and the construction of Fig. E (Plate XL) is applied to the point and vertical thus defined, the resulting dating is 1460.96 A.P., or 4 × 365.24. This construction is shown on Plate XLII, Fig. A. The dating thus obtained clearly confirms the datings of the Entrance Doorway as intentional.

The dating thus defined is obviously intended to represent the development of successive applications of the year-circle geometry shown in Figs. K and M, Plate XLI, in Fig. A, Plate XLII (at 4383 A.P. = 12 × 365¼, in Grand Gallery), and in Plate XLIII (defining the year-circle geometry of the dimensions of the King's Chamber and Antechamber).

¶ 308b.   COMMENCEMENT OF GRAND GALLERY AND PASSAGE TO QUEEN'S CHAMBER.

Scalar point
4000 A.P. the
point for the
construction.
Gives point
4086.66 A.P.
as centre of
year circle
defining
commence-
ment of Grand
Gallery at
02 8.53 A.P.
In Fig. K, Plate XLI, the Scalar point 4000 A.P. is the given point for the construction. The application of Fig. E, Plate XL, to 4000 A.P. in Fig. K, Plate XLI, gives the point 4086.6619328 A.P. This is taken as the centre of the year circle of circumference 365.242465 P″ and radius 58.13014373 P″. The circle as described (Plate XLI, Fig. K) cuts the Ascending Passage floor at 4028.531789 A.P., thus defining the commencement of the Grand Gallery. This agrees with Petrie's measurements, as explained on the diagram.

With the floor point commencement of the Grand Gallery as the given point for *This the point for further construction defining roof termination of 1st Ascending Passage and level of roof line of Queen's Chamber Passage.* further construction in Fig. K, Plate XLI, the construction of Plate XL, Fig. D, is then applied. This defines the roof point terminating the 1st Ascending Passage. The horizontal line drawn from the point thus obtained gives the level of the roof line of the horizontal passage into the Queen's Chamber. The level thus geometrically obtained (Plate XLI, Fig. K) agrees with the level obtained in Plate XXX, Table C, from the structural and measured data.

The use of the year circle as above is dealt with in ¶ 308a (refer also Plates *Latter agrees with level obtained from structural and measured data.* XLI (Fig. M), XLII (Fig. A) and XLIII).

¶ 308c. QUEEN'S CHAMBER FLOOR LEVEL.

In Fig. L, Plate XLI, the floor commencement of the Grand Gallery is the given *Given point for construction 4028.53 A.P., commencement of Grand Gallery floor.* point of construction, 4028.531789 A.P. To this is applied the construction of Plate XL, Fig. E, obtaining the point 4115.193722 A.P. The application of Plate XL, Fig. D, to the latter point gives the point 3996.091734 A.P., on the floor line of the 1st Ascending Passage, as shown on Fig. L, Plate XLI. The horizontal line drawn *Defines level of Queen's Chamber floor as obtained from structural data.* from the latter point defines the level of the Queen's Chamber floor. The level thus obtained, and the level for the roof termination of the 1st Ascending Passage (obtained from data of Fig. K, Plate XLI) both agree with the levels obtained in Plate XXX, as explained in the text of Fig. L, Plate XLI.

¶ 308d. GEOMETRICAL DEFINITION OF THE PRIMARY ZODIACAL EPOCH.

In Plate XLI, Fig. M, the upper horizontal dash-line is the continuation of the *Application of year circle defines the primary Zodiacal epoch 699.07 years prior to 0 A.P.* line of Precessional circuit figured as DE in Fig. F, Plate XL. (refer also Fig. N, Plate XLI, for the relation of Fig. M to the general geometry of the Pyramid). The horizontal line thus produced is adopted as the upper horizontal tangent to the year circle shown on Fig. M, Plate XLI. The lower horizontal tangent to the year circle cuts the floor line of the Entrance Passage produced at the point V. The latter point is −699.070408 A.P. (*i.e.* is indicated as representing 699.070408 years prior to 0 A.P.). The significance of this definition is dealt with in ¶¶ 213, 243, 260, 281, 282, 285, and 301. For similar applications of the year circle refer ¶¶ 308a and 308b, and Plates XLII (Fig. A) and XLIII.

¶ 308e. THE *ALCYONÊ* AND *ALPHA DRACONIS* ALIGNMENTS FOR 2144 B.C.

The principal feature of Fig. N, Plate XLI, relates to the *Alcyonê* and *Alpha Draconis* alignments for 2144 B.C. (refer ¶¶ 239 and 240).

Construction I, defining the *Alcyonê* alignment, is as follows :—

From Upper 0 A.P. (Fig. N) on floor line of Entrance Passage produced (*i.e.* *Construction I, defining "Alcyonê" alignment at Autumnal Equinox 2144 B.C. (1856 A.P.).* point 1 in Fig. M) draw a horizontal line to intersect the Pyramid's geometrical face (*i.e.* the plane of the arris edges). From the point of intersection thus defined drop a vertical line to intersect the central axis line of the Entrance Passage. Through the point of intersection thus obtained draw a line perpendicular to the floor and roof of the Entrance Passage. The floor point obtained is defined as 1856 A.P. =2144 B.C. (¶ 239). This latter date is the date of the *Alcyonê* alignment. The perpendicular produced as shown points to *Alcyonê* at midnight of the Autumnal Equinox, 2144 B.C.

Construction II, defining the *Alcyonê* alignment, is as follows :—

With the Pyramid height as a given side, complete the square shown on *Alternative construction defining the "Alcyonê" alignment for same date.* Fig. N, Plate XLI. The base side of the square obtained extends, as shown,

Scored line
on walls of
Entrance
Passage at
1855.42 A.P.
marks date of
observed
position of
" Alcyonê " on
alignment
thus defined.
1247.4835605 P″ beyond the Pyramid base. Take twice this distance as a Pyramid half-width at the level shown. From the point of intersection of the horizontal line thus defined with the Pyramid's geometrical face (*i.e.* the plane of the arris edges) drop a perpendicular to the Entrance Passage. The line of the perpendicular thus obtained points to *Alcyonê* at midnight of the Autumnal Equinox of 1856 A.P. =2144 B.C. (¶¶ 239 and 240). The floor point of the Entrance Passage defined by the perpendicular is 1856 A.P. =2144 B.C.

" Alpha
Draconis "
alignment for
2144 B.C.
given by
inclination of
Entrance
Passage.
The actual perpendicular scored line on the walls of the Entrance Passage is at 1855.42 A.P., marking the date of the observed position of *Alcyonê* on the alignment geometrically defined.

The *Alpha Draconis* alignment for 1856 A.P. is given by the inclination of the Entrance Passage.

" Alpha
Draconis "
alignment for
3434 B.C.
Construction III, defining the alternative *Alpha Draconis* dating (at 3434 B.C.), is as follows :—

From Upper o A.P. floor point drop a vertical to the pavement base. From the point on the pavement base thus obtained draw a perpendicular[1] to intersect the floor line of the Entrance Passage produced. The point of intersection thus obtained is 565.6630020 A.P. =3434 B.C., at which date also the Entrance Passage pointed to *Alpha Draconis*.

¶ 308f. ASTRONOMICAL CALCULATION OF POSITIONS OF *ALCYONÊ* AND *ALPHA DRACONIS*.

Adoption of
Newcomb's
method for
independent
astronomical
calculations
for positions
of " Alcyonê "
and " Alpha
Draconis " at
above dates.
Calculation by
Pyramid's
Precessional
formula
necessitates
revision of
all Newcomb's
formulae.
Determination
of Pyramid's
formula for
longitude of
instantaneous
axis of
rotation of the
Ecliptic also
necessary for
extreme
accuracy.
To obtain an independent astronomical calculation for the position of *Alcyonê* at 2144 B.C., and of *Alpha Draconis* at 2144 B.C. and 3434 B.C., as shown on Plate XLI, Newcomb's rigorous method of reduction should be adopted. This is as given in Newcomb's " Compendium of Spherical Astronomy," pp. 260–268. To effect the calculation by means of the Pyramid's Precessional formula, all Newcomb's formulæ from p. 232 to p. 246 would require to be revised in accordance with the Pyramid's Precessional formula. Precise values for the proper motions of *Alcyonê* and *Alpha Draconis* for long periods are also necessary.

To carry the revision to its ultimate refinement it would be necessary to determine the Pyramid's formula for the longitude of the Nodes of the instantaneous axis of rotation of the Ecliptic, and for the angular rates related to this (¶¶ 166–168). Indications pointing to the framework of the Pyramid formula for these have been observed but not developed. Newcomb's formulæ for these are, however, very reliable, even when applied over the long periods of time dealt with in this volume.

It was intended to include in the present volume the revision of Newcomb's method in accordance with the Pyramid's Precessional formula. The work had, in fact, been completed—as we had supposed—when an error was discovered in our first reduction of the Pyramid formula. This error has been corrected in the present volume, so far as the Pyramid formula is concerned. Since, however, it entailed a large amount of work to eliminate the error from the revision of Newcomb's method, this portion of the work was not again gone into.

Method of
effecting the
revision.
For the benefit of any mathematical reader who may wish to attempt the revision referred to, we would suggest that the first step in Newcomb's process of successive approximation—where this process is met with in Newcomb's work—should be the adoption of Newcomb's final result ; further successive approximation being effected by the inclusion of the data from the Pyramid formula.

[1]The length of this perpendicular is 1144.3962540 P″ =4×286.0990635 P″. Here 286.0990635 P″ falls short of the Pyramid's displacement value, 286.1022156 P″, by the extent of 0·0031521 P″ only.

¶ 308g. ASTRONOMICAL WORKS—ELEMENTARY AND REFERENCE.

The mathematical reader, wishing to study the related mathematical astronomy from its first principles, is recommended to study, in the order given, the following works :— General elementary work :— Barlow and Bryan's.

Barlow and Bryan's "Mathematical Astronomy."
Chauvenet's "Spherical Astronomy."
Newcomb's "Compendium of Spherical Astronomy."
Moulton's "Celestial Mechanics."
Watson's "Theoretical Astronomy."
Bauschinger's "Bahnbestimmung des Himmelskörper" and "Tafeln."
Oppolzer's "Bahnbestimmung."

General data for astronomical calculations :— Chauvenet's and Newcomb's.
General data for modern Precessional calculations :— Newcomb's.

The last four works deal with the elements of planetary orbits, in addition to Precession. Professor Moulton's work forms a good introduction to Professor Watson's. The general elements of the subject are very ably expounded in Barlow and Bryan's work, and with a minimum of mathematics. For the purpose of precise calculation, however, the essential works are Newcomb's and Bauschinger's for Precession, and Watson's, Bauschinger's, and Oppolzer's for determination of the elements of the planetary orbits. Good geometrical explanations of Precession and orbital motion are given in Newton's *Principia*. Mathematical explanation of Precession and related formulæ :— Bauschinger's and Oppolzer's.
Ditto for orbital elements :— Watson's, Bauschinger's and Oppolzer's.
Elementary :— Moulton's.

¶ 309. PLATE XLII, FIGS. A AND B. THE PYRAMID'S ASTRONOMICAL FRAMEWORK AND THE EGYPTIAN KING LISTS.

Plate XLII—as illustrating the relations between the Pyramid's framework for the geometrical definition of the Precessional and Perihelion formulæ and the periods of the Egyptian Dynastic Lists—explains itself when studied in connection with ¶¶ 212–216, and 249–254, for the Egyptian Lists, and with ¶¶ 217–248 for the Pyramid's astronomical framework. Pyramid's astronomical framework and periods of Egyptian King Lists.

All the A.P. datings figured on Plate XLII, Fig. A, result directly from the details of Plates XL and XLI. The datings 1461 A.P. and 4383 A.P. are dealt with in ¶ 308a. Periods of 1461 and 4383 years defined from 0 A.P.

The reader should observe how the 35th course axis and the rectangular *aroura* define the floor termination of the Descending Passage. This agrees with the reconstruction of Plate XXX, for which refer ¶ 206. It will also be observed that the square *aroura* defines the ceiling of the Queen's Chamber and the ceiling of the Subterranean Chamber. The latter ceiling, as geometrically fixed, is really a few inches from the ceiling level, resulting from the reconstruction of Plate XXX and Professor Petrie's data for the Subterranean Chamber. Local variations in subsidence of the natural rock, as evidenced by the fissures of Plate XXXIX, would account for the difference. The related geometry of the square and rectangular *arouræ* seem certainly to define the geometrical intention. The geometry of the rectangular and square "aroura."
Defines ceiling levels of Queen's Chamber and Subterranean Chamber, and floor end of Descending Passage.

The dating for the South roof termination of the Grand Gallery is shown as 5886.3105287 A.P. This agrees with Petrie's measurement in relation to the Great Step and the data discussed in relation to subsidence distortion (¶¶ 143, 147, 180–189). The dating gives the same geometrical measure as Plate XL, Fig. A, gives for the Scalar Axis from Great Step to face of Pyramid produced. The resulting length for the Grand Gallery roof is 1836 P″, an important Pyramid dimension dealt with later. Upper roof termination of Grand Gallery.
Length of Grand Gallery roof 1836 P″.

¶ 310. PLATE XLIII (AND PLATES LVII AND LVIII). THE GEOMETRY OF THE CHAMBERS.

Plate XLIII clearly defines the geometrical constructions forming the basis of all the dimensions of the Antechamber, King's Chamber, and connecting Passages. The geometrical definition of dimensions of Chambers.

PLATE LVII.

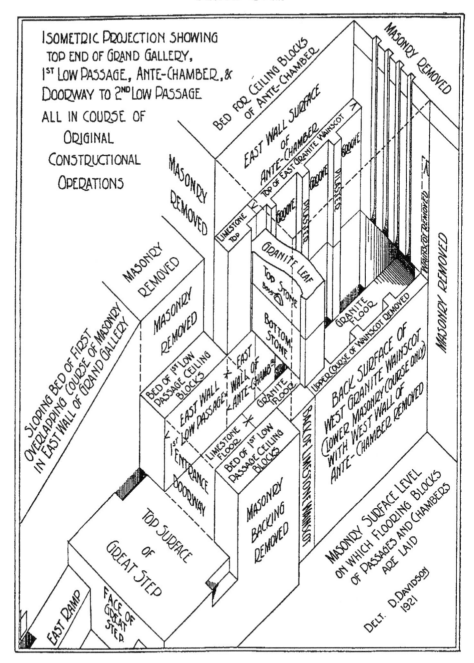

ISOMETRIC PROJECTION SHOWING TOP END OF GRAND GALLERY, 1ST LOW PASSAGE, ANTE-CHAMBER, & DOORWAY TO 2ND LOW PASSAGE ALL IN COURSE OF ORIGINAL CONSTRUCTIONAL OPERATIONS

DELT. D. DAVIDSON 1921

PERSPECTIVE VIEW OF SOUTH END OF GRAND GALLERY, GREAT STEP, ANTECHAMBER, AND CONNECTING LOW PASSAGES.

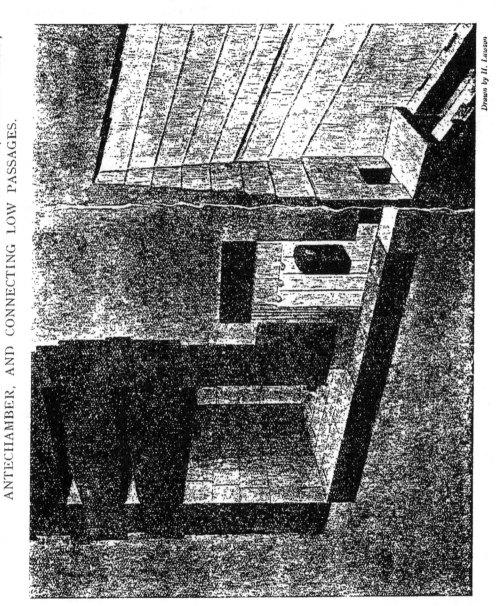

Drawn by H. Lawson

Plates XXXVb and XLIII. This should be studied in relation to Plate XXXVb, where the geometrical constructions are extended to the Queen's Chamber, shown in plan, as geometrically related to the Great Step, Antechamber, and King's Chamber.

The geometrical dimensions of the King's Chamber in plan are shown on Plate XXXVb. These are all multiples of the length of side of the square of area equal to the year circle, both of which are defined in the Antechamber (Plate XLIII). The same relationship is shown in the Queen's Chamber (Plate XXXVb).

The geometry of the linear and surface measures of the Antechamber.

The various Antechamber relations are as follows (Plate XLIII) :—

(1) Antechamber circle 365.242465 P″ in circumference ; its centre defining the mid-height of bottom stone of the Granite Leaf, and its developments of upper quadrant arcs defining the ceiling.

(2) Horizontal development of Antechamber circle, 365.242465 P″, defining distance from centre of Antechamber to South wall of King's Chamber.

(3) $\frac{1}{10}$th latter distance—i.e. 36.5242465 P″—defining distance from North End of Antechamber to South face of Granite Leaf.

(4) $\frac{1}{100}$th Pyramid square side and Pyramid height (i.e. defining circumference and radius of the year circle, 365.242465 P″) geometrically define the distance from face of the Step to South face of the Granite Leaf, and also height of the Antechamber from floor to ceiling $=58.1301437$ P″

$$+\frac{365.242465}{4} \text{ P″} =149.440760 \text{ P″}.$$

(5) The Antechamber granite square, of area equal to the area of the Antechamber year circle, defined by the height of East granite wainscot (103.032997 P″) and by the length of granite floor in Antechamber (103.032997 P″).

¶ 310a.   GEOMETRICAL RELATIONS BETWEEN THE THREE CHAMBERS.

Linear and surface relations in Antechamber, Queen's Chamber, and King's Chamber.

Height relations in King's Chamber and Antechamber.

The latter distance (103.032997 P″) is the unit for the dimensions of the King's Chamber and Queen's Chamber (refer Plate XXXVb). The length of the King's Chamber is 4×103.032997 P″ ; its breadth is 2×103.032997 P″ ; and its cubic diagonal from, say, its N.E. floor corner to its S.W. ceiling corner is 5×103.032997 P″. These cubic relations define the height of the King's Chamber as $5\sqrt{5}$ common Egyptian cubits. As defining the derivation of the common Egyptian cubit from the Pyramid inch and the Antechamber year circle, we find that the height of the West granite wainscot of the Antechamber is $50\sqrt{5}$ P″. Thus, King's Chamber height $=11.1803399$ common Egyptian cubits of 20.6065994 P″, and Antechamber West wainscot height $=111.803399$ P″. Expressed in P inches, the King's Chamber height is 230.3887855 P″.

Continuous measurements through Chambers, Plates XXX and XXXVb.

The continuous series of measurements from the Great Step to the South wall of the King's Chamber, as derived from the geometrical relations discussed, are tabulated on Plates XXX and XXXVb.

The structural features of the Chambers, Plates LVII and LVIII.

Plates LVII and LVIII have been included here to illustrate the structural features of the Chambers, since it is upon an understanding of these features that appreciation of the geometrical relations depends.

¶ 311.   PLATES XLIV–LVI.   THE ZODIACAL SIGNS.

These Plates are fully dealt with in Section II of this Chapter. One point, however, requires clearing up, as it is frequently the cause of misunderstanding. The Zodiacal Signs depicted in the Plates referred to are the fixed stellar signs. They mark the twelve fixed months of the Sidereal year. Strictly there should be no other application of the designation "Zodiacal Signs." Unfortunately, another application to the Solar year has been adopted. At the time this application was first made, the apparent position of the Sun at the Vernal Equinox coincided with the 1st point of the true Zodiacal Sign *Aries*. *Aries* was adopted as the first sign of the Solar year; the signs were reckoned to be 30° each; there were, therefore, three signs from an equinox to the succeeding solstice, and three signs from a solstice to the succeeding equinox. In other words, the twelve signs were reckoned to be the astronomical divisions of the twelve months of the *Solar* year.

The distinction to be drawn between the true fixed Zodiacal Signs of the Sidereal year and the misnamed Zodiacal Signs of the modern Solar year in astronomical ephemerides.

Since that time, owing to Precession, the Sun at the Vernal Equinox is seen to lie in the sign *Pisces*, remotely distant from the 1st point of the stellar sign *Aries*. Nevertheless, the Sun at the Vernal Equinox is still spoken of as entering the 1st point of Aries.

A point that is worthy of notice is that the ancient Chaldæan astrologers employed the *stellar* Zodiacal Signs in determining their astrological predictions, whereas modern astrologers employ the misplaced and misnamed solar signs. Whatever may have been, or may be, the predictive bases of the two schools of astrology, it seems clear that the two bases can have nothing *astronomically* in common. In making this statement, we neither profess to accept nor reject the principles of a subject concerning which we know little beyond the fact noted. A fact not generally known is that both Kepler and Newton contributed much to the modern development of astrology.

Ancient Chaldæan astrology and modern astrology.

[Plates LVII and LVIII explain themselves, but are referred to in ¶ 310a, in relation to Plates XXXV and XLIII.]

CHAPTER V.

THE CHRONOGRAPH OF HISTORY.

SECTION IA.—THE SYNCHRONOUS HISTORY OF EGYPT, BABYLON, ASSYRIA,
AND ISRAEL.

¶ 312. THE EVOLUTION OF THE FICTITIOUS CHRONOLOGY OF THE EGYPTIANS.

Each fictitious system of Egyptian chronology was evolved from the original Pyramid system.
The resulting restoration of Egyptian chronology is confirmed by many independent lines of astronomical data from ancient Egyptian sources.

The investigations and conclusions of the preceding Chapter have shown that all the systems of Egyptian chronology were derived from the Great Pyramid's scalar and astronomical systems of chronology. By tracing each system back along the historical lines of its evolution, each particular system is seen to be derived from the same original Pyramid system or systems. The essential results of the researches in this connection are given in tabulated form with explanatory annotations at the end of this Section (Ia). This will be fully dealt with in relation to Egyptian Dynastic history in the proposed second volume of our work. The tabulations and annotations given are, in the meantime, quite sufficient to show that we are not now dealing with a matter of theory, but with a matter of fact that is demonstrated with scientific precision. The reader will find that the ultimate statement of Dynastic history, given in chronological outline, and as resulting from the tracing of the several evolutionary processes, is confirmed by many independent lines of astronomical data. The latter are derived from various, and independent, ancient Egyptian sources.

¶ 313. A UNIVERSAL SYSTEM OF ANCIENT CHRONOLOGY.

Ancient Egyptian zero datum of chronology 4000 B.C.

The results of our investigations show that the zero datum of all the original statements of Egyptian chronology, as in the case of the Old Chronicle, is the Autumnal Equinox of 4000 B.C., and that the chronological references are to cycles of 103, 97, and 329 years from the zero datum (¶¶ 31–33 and Tables II–IV). The Calendar in use, however, is based on the November year in Egypt, a datum that will be explained shortly.

Egyptian use of cycles of the Book of Genesis indicates that zero epoch of Genesis is 4000 B.C.

Now the cycles noted were all seen to be employed in the statement of the Dynastic chronology of Genesis v (Table V and ¶¶ 34–40). This would seem to indicate that the 4000 B.C. zero datum of the Egyptian chronology is the zero datum of the Dynastic chronology of the Hebrew Book of Genesis. Confirming this, our tracing of the Egyptian systems shows that the various basal epochs of the original Egyptian systems are identical with the epochs of Genesis (Table V). These are respectively :—

The Chinese epoch of the beginning of the Dynasty of Noah at 2944 B.C. =1056 A.K. confirms 4000 B.C. as zero chronological epoch.

Other confirming data from Egyptian and Chinese sources.

B.C.	Egyptian Epochs.			Hebrew Designations (Table V).
4000	=	0 A.K.	..	.. Epoch of Adam.
3378	=	622 A.K.	..	.. Epoch of the birth of Enoch. ⎫
				Interval 365 years. ⎬
3013	=	987 A.K.	..	.. Epoch of the House of Enoch. ⎭
				Termination of 3 Phœnix cycles. Castor's alleged Egyptian Dyn. I–IV, incl.
2944[1]	=	1056 A.K.	..	.. Epoch of Noah. (Manetho's Dynasty of Bytes, Plate XVI, Table A.)
2355	=	1645 A.K.	..	.. 5 Phœnix cycles end.
2345	=	1655 A.K.	..	.. Hebrew Deluge begins.
2344	=	1656 A.K.	..	.. Hebrew Deluge ends. (1680 Calendar years, as in Egyptian Divine Dynasties of Suidas.)

The latter dating is given by the Egyptians and Babylonians, in terms of unintercalated Calendar years of 360 days, as 1680 years.

The Chinese *Shu-King* [1] also gives the Epoch of Fu-hi, the Chinese Noah,[2] as 2944 B.C. (hist.), and places the date of the Chinese Deluge within the reign of Yaou, which is given as 2356–2254 B.C.[3] (hist.), thus including the Hebrew Deluge date 2345–2344 B.C. The alleged first year of the reign of Yaou is the last year of the 5th Phœnix cycle from 0 A.K. = 4000 B.C. For the significance of this identity refer ¶¶ 34–40 and Table V.

¶ 314. THE PHŒNIX CHRONOLOGY OF ANCIENT EGYPT.

In ¶ 102 we saw that the Phœnix cycle was recognised as related to the Pyramid's period of reference for Precession. Thus, 78¼ Phœnix cycles =25,826.5 years. In ¶ 149 we saw that the Calendar statement necessitated the half period (or 164¼ years) beginning the chronological placing. This aspect of the Phœnix cycle was required by the change from Autumnal Equinoctial year-beginning to Vernal Equinoctial year-beginning (¶ 286). Accordingly we find the first use of this form in Egypt beginning at 2138½ A.K. = 6½ Phœnix cycles. The date is given by the Egyptian data (Table XI and Annotations) as 31½ years prior to the beginning of the XVIIIth Egyptian Dynasty.

The Great Pyramid, the Phœnix cycle, and the Precession of the Equinoxes.

78¼ Phœnix cycles = 25,826¼ years.

The initial half-cycle.

The Phœnix cycle of the Hyksos, 31½ years prior to Dynasty XVIII.

In the first year of the new Phœnix cycle, the last Hyksos (or Shepherd) king began Day 1, Month I of the 365 days Calendar year at the Semitic *Autumnal* Equinoctial *New* Moon (14th September (Greg.) 1861 B.C.). This

The luni-solar Equinoctial beginning of the newly instituted "vague" year.

---

[1]W. G. Old, " The *Shu-King*," Appendix, pp. 301, 302.
[2]Refer ¶ 196b.
[3]W. G. Old, " The *Shu-King*," pp. 301, 302. The " Enc. Brit." (11th Edit.), Vol. VI, p. 192, gives one year earlier.

The observed Egyptian Phœnix cycles.

is explained more fully in the annotations to Table XI.[1] In the course of the Egyptian war of independence, which began at this time, the intended intercalations were never made. *For the first time* in Egyptian history, the Calendar of 365 days became the unintercalated vague year Calendar (refer ¶¶ 43–63, and 73–75d). The series of Phœnix cycles are discussed and established in Table XI and Annotations.

The monumental and astronomical chronology of Egyptian Dynasties XVIII and XIX.

The years of the various reigns of Dynasties XVIII and XIX are known (Tables XII and XIII).[1] From the Hyksos date above noted, the chronology of Dynasties XVIII and XIX is as stated in Table XIV. Then, from the Hyksos Calendar datum, we can find the Calendar datings of new and full moons, and heliacal risings of Sirius, for any particular year of a king's reign. The vague Calendar datings for several new moons, one full moon, and two heliacal risings of Sirius are given for stated regnal years of Dynasty XVIII. In each case these agree exactly with the calculated datings. The chronology of the Egyptian Lists, the Phœnix chronology, the recorded regnal years and astronomical datings are thus all found to be in agreement.

The Harris Papyrus interregnum between Dynasties XIX and XX.

The chronology thus fixed proves that a long interregnum of anarchy and famine—as stated in the XXth Dynasty Harris Papyrus, and as independently shown by the King Lists of Manetho (Africanus' Version) and the Old Chronicle of Egypt (Plate XVI, Table E, and ¶ 138a (3))—occurred between Dynasties XIX and XX. This explains what has hitherto been one of the most perplexing problems of Egyptian chronology.

¶ 315. THE NEW EPOCH FOR EGYPTIAN *SED* FESTIVALS AND THE NOVEMBER YEAR-BEGINNING.

With fixed beginning of Calendar and Epoch the Calendar cycles give month datings of Deluge as beginning All Hallows' Eve, 2345 B.C., and ending 5th November 2344 B.C.

Again, as stated, the original systems of Egyptian chronology indicate the date of the Hebrew Deluge ending, 1656 A.K., as an Epoch of Egyptian chronology. Now with midnight beginning 22nd September (Greg.) o A.K. (4000 B.C.) as zero datum (¶ 297), and our cycle of 103 years (Table III, and ¶¶ 31 and 196b and c) as basis, the Hebrew Deluge datings can be stated in terms of modern Gregorian month datings. Thus the dating for the beginning of the Deluge, 1655 A.K., 17th day of Month II = 31st October (Greg.) (All Hallows' Eve), 2345 B.C. (hist.) ; and for the termination of the Deluge, 1656 A.K., 27th day of Month II = 5th November (Greg.), 2344 B.C. (hist.). (Refer ¶ 30 and footnote, also ¶ 196c.)

6th November 2344 B.C. began new calendar year datum and Epoch of Egyptian "Sed" festivals.

With the latter month dating and year as terminal bases, the Egyptians began a new series of *Sed* periods—without altering the succession of Calendar cycles of 103 years from o A.K.—beginning their intercalated calendar year of 360 days with Day 1, Month I at 6th November 1656 A.K. = 2344 B.C. (hist.). The result of the cycle of 103 years being retained based on o A.K. is that each repetition of the 103 years' cycle began with Egyptian Day 1, Month I at 17th, 18th, or 19th November (Greg.), as com-

[1]Tables XI, XII, XIII, and XIV, and all tables referred to in this Section Ia, are placed to follow Section Ia of this Chapter.

pared with Euphratean Day 1, Month I at 21st, 22nd, or 23rd September (Greg.) respectively. The precise day of the Gregorian months can be determined from Plate LIX.[1] For comparison of calendar datings thus obtained with the calendar datings of recorded heliacal risings of Sirius prior to the Hyksos Calendar revision, Sirius risings in terms of Julian month datings can be obtained from Plate LX. Comparison is effected by transferring the Julian month datings into their equivalent Gregorian month datings for the particular year considered.

¶ 316. THE ASTRONOMICAL BASES OF ANCIENT EGYPTIAN CHRONOLOGY.

In ¶¶ 56–60 and Tables VIII and IX, we saw that the true anniversary of the date of the Deluge ending was celebrated in spite of the Hyksos revision of the year, and in spite of the vague year calendar. This confirms that the Egyptian priests still secretly observed the ancient cycles in unbroken succession (¶¶ 123–125 and 315).

Accordingly we find that the *Sed* periods are recorded continuously in unbroken succession until the 27th year of Ramessu II (Table XI, Annotations). All such periods recorded for the regnal years. of Dynasties XII and XVIII agree absolutely with the chronological years obtained as stated in ¶¶ 312–315. The periods thus recorded are in all cases based on a datum at 1656 A.K. The chronology of Dynasty XII is given on Table XV.[2]

There are therefore five independent lines of evidence fixing the chronology of Dynasties XII to XX. These are—

(1) The chronological statement of the original Egyptian systems.
(2) The Phœnix chronology on the series of 329 years' cycles from 4000 B.C.
(3) The fixed calendar datings prior to 1861 B.C. and the vague calendar datings after 1861 B.C., for recorded heliacal risings of Sirius.
(4) The vague calendar datings for recorded new and full moons.
(5) The recorded *Sed* festivals on the series from 2344 B.C.

The data concerning the *Sed hebs* as they affect Dynasties XII, XVIII, and XIX are given on Tables XV and XVI.[2]

Similar identities—complicated, however, by two revisions of the year- beginning, one in 1532 B.C. and another in 874 B.C.—fix the Egyptian chronology from the time of Dynasty XX to the time of Alexander the Great, and later. The complications referred to have been cleared up owing to the fact that the revisions noted were made, in each case, at the beginning of a Phœnix cycle, and owing to other check astronomical data confirming (refer Table XI, Annotations, and Table XXIV, and Annotations).

[1]This Plate, in conjunction with Table III, gives the Deluge month datings above stated and for the years stated.
[2]Tables XV and XVI follow at the end of Section Ia of this Chapter.

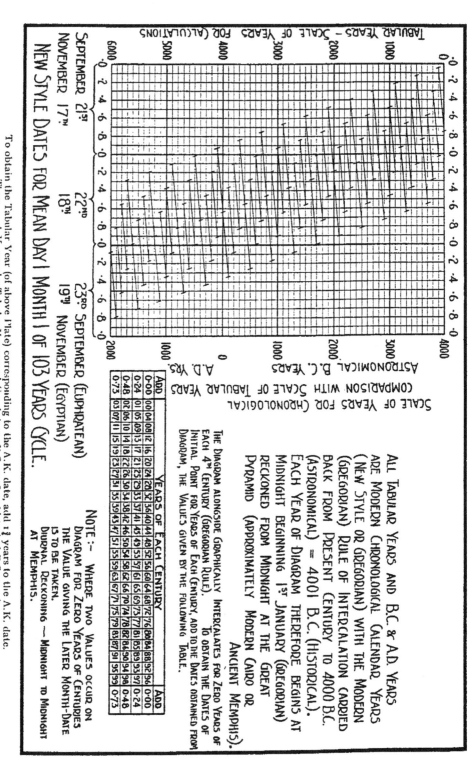

TABULAR YEARS — SCALE OF YEARS FOR (CALCULATIONS

0 · 1000 · 2000 · 3000 · 4000 · 5000 · 6000

ASTRONOMICAL B.C. YEARS. — A.D. YRS.

Scale of Years for (Chronological) Comparison with Scale of Tabular Years

ALL TABULAR YEARS AND B.C. & A.D. YEARS ARE MODERN CHRONOLOGICAL CALENDAR YEARS (NEW STYLE OR GREGORIAN) WITH THE MODERN (GREGORIAN) RULE OF INTERCALATION CARRIED BACK FROM PRESENT CENTURY TO 4000 B.C. (ASTRONOMICAL) = 4001 B.C. (HISTORICAL). EACH YEAR OF DIAGRAM THEREFORE BEGINS AT MIDNIGHT BEGINNING 1ST JANUARY (GREGORIAN) RECKONED FROM MIDNIGHT AT THE GREAT PYRAMID (APPROXIMATELY MODERN CAIRO OR ANCIENT MEMPHIS).

THE DIAGRAM ALONGSIDE GRAPHICALLY INTERCALATES FOR EACH 4TH CENTURY (GREGORIAN RULE). TO OBTAIN THE DATES OF INITIAL POINT FOR YEARS OF EACH CENTURY, ADD TO THE DATES OBTAINED FROM DIAGRAM, THE VALUES GIVEN BY THE FOLLOWING TABLE.

YEARS OF EACH CENTURY

ADD																									ADD
0·00	00	04	08	12	16	20	24	28	32	36	40	44	48	52	56	60	64	68	72	76	80	84	88	92	96	0·00
0·24	01	05	09	13	17	21	25	29	33	37	41	45	49	53	57	61	65	69	73	77	81	85	89	93	97	0·24
0·48	02	06	10	14	18	22	26	30	34	38	42	46	50	54	58	62	66	70	74	78	82	86	90	94	98	0·48
0·73	03	07	11	15	19	23	27	31	35	39	43	47	51	55	59	63	67	71	75	79	83	87	91	95	99	0·73

NOTE:— WHERE TWO VALUES OCCUR ON DIAGRAM FOR ZERO YEARS OF CENTURIES THE VALUE GIVING THE LATER MONTH-DATE IS TO BE TAKEN. DIURNAL RECKONING — MIDNIGHT TO MIDNIGHT AT MEMPHIS.

NEW STYLE DATES FOR MEAN DAY 1 MONTH 1 OF 103 YEARS CYCLE.

SEPTEMBER 21ST	22ND	23RD SEPTEMBER (EUPHRATEAN)
NOVEMBER 17TH	18TH	19TH NOVEMBER (EGYPTIAN)

To obtain the Tabular Year (of above Plate) corresponding to the A.K. date, add 1⅔ years to the A.K. date.

Thus   A.K. 1000⅓ = Tabular Year 1002⅓ (i.e. Astron. B.C. 2998 or historical B.C. 2999).

and   A.K. 1000 = Tabular Year 1001⅔ (i.e. Astron. B.C. 2999 or historical B.C. 3000).

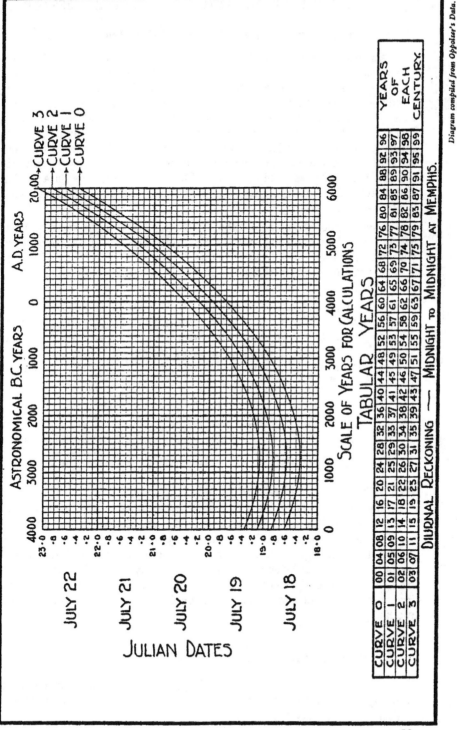

Diagram compiled from Oppolzer's Data.

19

¶ 317.   THE XIITH DYNASTY SIRIUS DATING FIXED.

An interesting example confirming the chronology of Dynasty XII (Table XV) is as follows :—From Table XV, the 7th year of Senusert III $=2082\frac{1}{2}-3\frac{1}{2}$ A.K.[1] The calendar year began in November (Greg.) in 2083 A.K. $=2084\frac{3}{4}$ tabular year of Plates LIX and LX. Now, 2083 A.K. is 23 years after the termination of the preceding 103 years' cycle at 2060 A.K. Hence, from Table III, Day 1, Month I began 0.58 day before the beginning of the mean year of the cycle. From Plate LIX, the beginning of the mean year of the cycle $=17.58$ November (Greg.), there being no addition for tabular year 2084 (as Table of Plate LIX). Combining the data of Table III and Plate LIX, Day 1, Month I, in 2083 A.K. coincided with 17th November (Greg.)—i.e. $17.58-0.58$.

Now in the summer of $2083\frac{3}{4}$ A.K. $=2085\frac{1}{4}$ tabular year of Plate LX, Sirius rose heliacally on 18th July (Julian) $=$ 1st July (Greg.), for the year stated, which was 1916 B.C. (hist.). With Day 1, Month I, at the preceding 17th November (Greg.), the heliacal rising took place on Day 17, Month VIII.

Accordingly we find a record of the 7th year of Senusert III noting the heliacal rising of Sirius on Day 17, Month VIII (¶ 55). This confirms the chronology of Dynasty XII, otherwise astronomically derived from the *Sed hebs*. Why this particular heliacal rising—the first-known recorded heliacal rising in Egypt—was thus particularly recorded at this time is indicated by ¶ 39.

Thus,

Birth of Enoch	..	..	..	..	.. 622 A.K.
Interval of $4\times365\frac{1}{4}$	..	..	..	..	.. $=$1461 solar years.
7th year of Senusert III	..	..	..	..	2083 A.K.

the Hebrew date of the Call of Abram.

The first quarter of the 1461 years' interval—i.e. $365\frac{1}{4}$ years—by ending in 987 A.K., 3 Phœnix cycles from 0 A.K., and at the date of the Epoch of the House of Enoch (Table V, and ¶¶ 37–39 and 313), confirms the intentional chronological connection. The identity established shows that
the period known in later times as the Sothic cycle was known as a cycle of the solar year as early as 622 A.K. (3378 B.C.) as the result of earlier observation, but was not employed as the chronological basis of a vague or shifting calendar year.

¶ 318.   BABYLONIAN CHRONOLOGY.

The resulting new statement of Egyptian history and chronology clears up many hitherto perplexing details in relation to Hebrew and Babylonian

[1] Refer note to Table XV.

history and chronology. The Babylonian Lists are found to be based on the same systems as the Egyptian, both in regard to their fictitious and their original statements. Investigation of the evolution of the Babylonian Lists established an identical original system of chronology based on o A.K. =4000 B.C. (refer Annotations to Tables XVII–XIX). Original system of Babylonian chronology identical with original system of Egyptian chronology.

One special feature of the investigation is the establishing of the duration of the so-called (2nd) Dynasty of Babylon, and of the actual duration of the Supremacy (or Anarchy) of the Aramæans (and Sutu) over Babylon and Assyria (refer Table XIX, at end of this Section). Hitherto obscure historical features cleared up.

Another special feature is that the Lists confirm the datings of Ptolemy's *Royal Canon* wherever Ptolemy shows, in his *Almagest*, that he had astronomical (lunar and solar eclipse) records to fix the regnal years. The exception is where a gap occurs in the eclipse records of Ptolemy's *Almagest*. This is between the reigns of Nabopolassar and Cambyses. The Babylonian Dynastic Tablet and the King List of Berosus both show that Cyrus captured Babylon in 537 B.C., and began his 1st regnal year as " King of Countries " on 1st Nisan (Spring) of 536 B.C., two years later than hitherto accepted from Ptolemy (refer Annotations to Tables XXI and XXVII). Agreement with Ptolemy's astronomical datings. Babylonian chronological lists disagree with Ptolemy for period for which Ptolemy gives no astronomical datings. Lists give Cyrus beginning 536 B.C. Explaining two years' co-regency of Cambyses.

The new data show that the first two years of the eight recorded years of Cambyses were years of co-regency during the 8th and 9th years of Cyrus as " King of Countries." This confirms the six years of Cambyses given by Josephus as years after co-regency, and the seven years of Cyrus given by Xenophon as years prior to co-regency of Cambyses. The six years of Josephus for Cambyses, and the seven years of Xenophon for Cyrus explained.

All this fixes that the reigns from Nebuchadnezzar to Cyrus inclusive are in each case two years later than has hitherto been supposed. This, as will be seen from the synchronisms dealt with in the Tables and Annotations to this Section Ia, brings Babylonian chronology into synchronism with Hebrew chronology. Correction supplied by the Lists affects reigns from Nebuchadnezzar to Cyrus inclusive. This confirmed by Hebrew chronology.

The remaining feature is that a perfect chronological synchronism is established between the so-called 1st Babylonian (Amorite) Dynasty and the XIIth Egyptian Dynasty, and between the Kassite Dynasty of Babylon and the XVIIIth Dynasty of Egypt. This is as shown on Tables XVII and XVIII, respectively. The chronology of the Babylonian period intervening between the period of the latter Table and the known period of Assyrian supremacy—that began under Tiglath-Pileser III—is as shown on Table XIX. The chronology of the Assyrian Supremacy is given on Table XX, and of the Babylonian-Chaldæan supremacy—from Nabopolassar to Nabonidos inclusive —is as given on Table XXI. Synchronisms: 1st Babylonian Dynasty and XIIth Egyptian Dynasty; Kassite Dynasty of Babylon and XVIIIth Dynasty of Egypt.

¶ 319. ABRAHAM, KHAMMURABI, AND SENUSERT III. Synchronisms: Khammurabi the contemporary of Senusert III.

The latter synchronism places Khammurabi of the 1st Dynasty of Babylon as the contemporary of Senusert III of the XIIth Egyptian Dynasty. As Khammurabi is the accepted Amraphel of Genesis xiv, and Independently, Abraham the contemporary of Khammurabi.

since the early chronographers identified Senusert III as Abraham's Pharaoh,[1] the synchronism appears to be complete. Around the reigns of Khammurabi and Senusert III, the known periodic climatic change and resulting famine, in the mountains and deserts North-East and North-West of Babylonia and Assyria, and in Arabia, were driving hordes of nomads into the fertile valleys of the Tigris, Euphrates, and Nile.[2] Hittites from the mountains of Asia Minor were coming into aggressive contact with Babylonia, and their name first appears in the records of the XIIth Dynasty of Egypt.[3] In Egypt, the Hyksos first began to appear in the 6th year of Senusert II, 2063 A.K.

The intensity of the famine, aggravated by immigration, finally affected even Egypt, whose agricultural resources were, and are, dependent upon the Nile inundation. The history of the country shows that at such times attention was directed to the narrow rocky channel at the 1st Cataract. A view of the 1st Cataract locality—looking South—as sketched by Denon during Napoleon's expedition in Egypt, is given in the tail-piece to this Chapter. The Island of Elephantinê is shown in the foreground. Here the river channel, between intervals of clearing, became choked with obstructions —stones, silt, and *sudd*. Famine conditions led to active dredging operations at the 1st Cataract. Such operations were undertaken in the 8th year of Senusert III. The Dynastic chronology, confirmed astronomically, defines the year as 2083½ to 2084½ A.K. (Table XXII and ¶ 317). According to the accepted Hebrew chronology (¶ 39), Abraham was driven by famine in Canaan into Egypt in 2083 to 2084 A.K.[4] Completing the synchronism, Hittites first appeared in Southern Canaan about twenty-five years after Abraham's visit to Egypt (Genesis xiv, 13, compared with Genesis xxiii, 2-20), and after the battle of " four kings with five," in which Amraphel, allied with the Elamites under Chedorlaomer and the Hittites under Tidal, took part.[5]

¶ 320. THE HORSE FIRST APPEARS IN EGYPT, BABYLON, AND SYRIA.

During the period of the Kassite Dynasty, the horse and horse-chariot first appeared in Babylon. The later kings of the Kassite Dynasty held correspondence with the later kings of the XVIIIth Dynasty in Egypt. Accordingly we find the horse and horse-chariot first appearing in Egypt during the XVIIIth Dynasty.

[1]Budge, " History of Egypt," Vol. III, p. 42. Petrie, " History of Egypt," Vol. I, p. 178. Refer also Table XXII at end of this Section, Item I.

[2]Huntingdon, " Royal Geog. Soc.," 1910. Petrie, " Egypt and Israel," pp. 26 and 27. Professor R. A. Macalister, " History of Civilisation in Palestine." Professor J. L. Myres, " Dawn of History," pp. 104, 105.

[3]Professor Garstang, " Land of the Hittites," p. 77, footnote; also Sayce's footnote to p. 324, ibid. Myres, " Dawn of History," pp. 150-152. For connection with Hyksos, refer also Maspero, " Struggle of the Nations," pp. 56, 57, and footnote to p. 52. Budge, " History of Egypt," Vol. III, pp. 136, 137.

[4]Table XXVIII, Annotations A and B, ¶ 39 of this volume, and Oxford Bible, Appendix.

[5]Genesis xiv, 1-12. Refer also Garstang's " Land of the Hittites," pp. 324, 325, Sayce's footnote concerning Tudghul (Tidal) as king of the Hittites, and ally of the Elamite king Chedorlaomer.

In the Book of Genesis, the horse and horse-chariot first appear during the life of Joseph. *(During the life of Joseph in Egypt.)*

The Babylonian astronomical chronology and the Egyptian astronomical chronology both independently place the later Kassites and the later XVIIIth Dynasty Kings of Egypt as contemporaneous (Table XVIII). The chronological synchronism establishes that the earlier kings of the Kassite Dynasty ruled contemporaneously, and, as Sayce has proved, intermarried, with the 1st Babylonian (Amorite) Dynasty, and also claimed falsely to have reigned from the date of the beginning of the 1st Dynasty of Babylon. The same synchronism proves that the Hyksos ruled in Egypt partly contemporaneously with Dynasties XII to XVII. The contemporaneity of Dynasties at this time is noted by Manetho, as quoted by Josephus. The Hyksos, in fact, were for some time supreme, and may have consisted of two contemporaneous dynasties (Dynasties XV and XVI), but did not long survive the XIIth Egyptian Dynasty, and were survived by the XVIIth Egyptian Dynasty, whose Theban kings had raised the standard of revolt. *(Confirmed by astronomical and chronological synchronisms. Earlier Kassites contemporaneous with 1st Dynasty of Babylon. Hyksos partly contemporaneous with Dynasty XII and succeeding Dynasty XVII. These contemporaneous with Dynasties XIII and XIV. Hyksos for a period supreme, but Egyptian Dynasties ruling contemporaneously.)*

There is no evidence, Egyptian or otherwise, to show that the Hyksos introduced the horse and horse-chariot, as has been supposed. The first evidence appears in the XVIIIth Dynasty. Joseph's Pharaoh therefore belongs to the XVIIIth Dynasty. *(No evidence that the Hyksos brought the horse to Egypt.)*

¶ 321. EGYPTIAN RECORDS CONCERNING JOSEPH'S FAMINE.

The most important of the XVIIIth Dynasty kings was Tahutmes III. From his 21st year, when his sole reign began, to his 42nd year inclusive, he was actively engaged on wars in Canaan and Nubia. His conquests extended eastwards to the Euphrates. A gap in his records occurs from his 43rd to 49th years inclusive. In his 50th year we find him active at the 1st Cataract, clearing the obstruction there, and issuing decrees to keep the channel clear. The administrative activity here indicates the usual conditions accompanying famine. The date of the 50th year is $2303\frac{1}{2}$ to $2304\frac{1}{2}$ A.K. The gap in his records of military activities is a period of seven years from $2296\frac{1}{2}$ A.K. to $2303\frac{1}{2}$ A.K. The dated period agrees with the seven years' famine period of Joseph. The dates are identical when we accept the datum of Abraham (¶¶ 39, 317, and 319), and the 430 years of St. Paul from the Call of Abraham to the Exodus (Gal. iii, 17).[1] This gives an interval of 215 years from the Call of Abraham to the entry of Israel into Egypt. This is the period according to St. Paul, and as stated by Josephus.[2] The Hebrew famines from Abraham to Joseph, and the Egyptian famines from Senusert III to Tahutmes III are shown to be in perfect chronological synchronism in Table XXII.[3] For discussion of the actual records and works relating to Joseph's famine, identifying it with the seven years preceding, the 50th year of Tahutmes III, the reader is referred to the Annotations to Table XXII. *(The continuous records of conquests for period from 21st to 42nd year of Tahutmes III. Gap of seven years in records of activity. 50th year record of river improvement at 1st Cataract. Seven years' gap = $2296\frac{1}{2}$–$2303\frac{1}{2}$ A.K. = Hebrew datings for seven years' famine of Joseph. Datings confirm what is the true version of Hebrew chronology.)*

[1] Refer also ¶ 36 and footnote ; and Josephus, "Antiquities," II, xv, 2.
[2] Josephus, "Antiquities," II, xv, 2.
[3] Refer end of this Section.

The Semiti-
cisation of
Egypt from
the time of the
life of Joseph.
The back-
ground of Aten
worship.
The revolt of
the Egyptians
and suppres-
sion of Israel.
Following the conquests of Tahutmes III, Petrie clearly shows that the Egyptians became Semiticised in type, language, art, and institutions.[1] This led to the religious reformation of Amenhotep IV (Akhenaten), and ultimately to the revolt of the Egyptians and the suppression of the Israelites and other Semites in Egypt (refer' Plate LXI and Annotations, and Table XXIII, Annotations).

¶ 322. THE EGYPTIAN DATES FOR THE OPPRESSION AND EXODUS OF ISRAEL.

The over-
lapping of the
last reign of
Dynasty XVIII
and the first
two reigns of
Dynasty XIX.
Ramessu II
appointed co-
regent at the
death of the
last king of
Dynasty XVIII.
Discoveries of recent years in Egypt show that Ramessu II of Dynasty XIX reigned co-regent with his father, Seti I, for eight years. This co-regency dated from the death of Horemheb, the last king of Dynasty XVIII. The overlapping of Dynasties XVIII and XIX implied by this statement is explained by the fact that Horemheb appointed Ramessu I and Seti I in succession as co-regents. This is all as summarised on Plate LXI, and as explained in detail in the Annotations to Plate LXI.

After the death of Seti I, Ramessu II reigned sixty-seven years. His total reign, including co-regency, was therefore seventy-five years. He was followed by his son, Menephtah, who, during his 5th year, appointed his son, Seti II, as co-regent. In this year Menephtah and Seti II defeated the Libyans. The triumphal chants of both kings, Menephtah and Seti II, claim the victory.

From the
beginning of
the co-regency
of Ramessu II
to the date of
the Egyptian
record of the
Exodus is
a period of
eighty years.
One copy of Menephtah's triumphal inscription begins with the date of the battle with the Libyans (Day 3, Month XI = 14th July (Greg.) 1487 B.C. = $2512\frac{3}{4}$ A.K.), but continues with an account of the series of events that followed the battle, later in the same regnal year, $2512\frac{1}{2}$ to $2513\frac{1}{2}$ A.K. The datum for the vague year month dating is given in Table XI Annotations. The inscription ends with a statement that the " seed " (or posterity) of Israel was destroyed.[2] Maspero, Sayce, and Budge agree that this is the Egyptian version of the Exodus of Israel. The reference to Israel follows the statement concerning the pacifying of Canaan after the battle with the Libyans. All the peoples referred to before the name " Israel " occurs are described with the determinatives signifying *men, foreigners,* and *foreign country.* " Israel," however, is described with the determinatives signifying " *men and women,*" and whilst defined as " *foreigners,*" lack the determinative signifying their being in possession of a " *foreign country.*"

From the
beginning of
the reign of
the Pharaoh of
the Opression
—in the Heb-
rew Old Testa-
ment—to the
Exodus is a
period of eighty
years—from
the birth of
Moses to the
end of the
eightieth year
of Moses.
The end of Menephtah's 5th year ($2513\frac{1}{2}$ A.K. = 1486 B.C.) is five years after the death of Ramessu II. The Egyptian Exodus record therefore places the Exodus of Israel eighty years after the beginning of the co-regency of Ramessu II at the death of Horemheb ($2433\frac{1}{2}$ A.K. = 1566 B.C.). This agrees with the age of Moses at the Exodus,[3] eighty years, according to

---

[1]Petrie, " History of Egypt," Vol. III, p. 148. Refer also Sayce, " Higher Criticism and the Monuments," pp. 213–216, and lower half of p. 222.
[2]The Egyptians, like the Assyrians and Babylonians, never admitted disasters to their arms.
[3]Refer Brugsch, " Egypt under the Pharaohs," Revised Edition, p. 318.

Deut. xxix, 5 ; xxxi, 2 ; xxxiv, 7 ; and Exod. vii, 7 ; Moses having been born in the first year (of co-regency) of the Pharaoh of the Oppression (Exod. i, 8–12 ; ii, 1–10).

The Talmud, again, preserving the Jewish tradition, gives the Exodus as five years after the death of the Pharaoh of the Oppression. Naville's excavations on the site of Pithom and Petrie's excavations on the site of Raamses have confirmed that Ramessu II is the Pharaoh of the Oppression. The excavations of the University of Philadelphia Expedition at Beisan in Palestine have disclosed a stela of Ramessu II, stating that " the king had set captive Semites to work on his city of Rameses in Egypt."[1] *The Talmud and recent excavations in the Delta and Palestine confirm that Ramessu II was the Pharaoh of the Oppression and Meneph-tah the Pharaoh of the Exodus.*

As the age of Ramessu II at the time of his death is a matter of importance in relation to the life of Moses and the Exodus, we quote what Sir Gaston Maspero has to say. Maspero states :[2] " The mummy (of Ramessu II) is thin, much shrunken, and light ; the bones are brittle, and the muscles atrophied, as one would expect in the case of a man who had attained the age of a hundred." *Ramessu II died about one hundred years old. The evidence from his mummy.*

¶ 323. THE DATE AND CIRCUMSTANCES OF THE DEATH OF SETI II.

In the year of the Exodus (1486 B.C.=2513½ A.K.), the Hebrew 14th of the 1st Sacred month[3] Nisan ended at sunset of 3rd April (Greg.), when the 15th of Nisan began. In the same year, the Egyptian vague-year Calendar Day 1, Month VIII fell on 13th April (Greg.), by datum of Table XI Annotations. In the latter Egyptian month—the day not mentioned—is dated a shrine of Seti II at Silsileh. The record is dated precisely as Month VIII, Year 2, Seti II, and is the last dated inscription of Seti II. Now, Year 2 of Seti II being Year 6 of Menephtah shows that the shrine was inscribed and set up at the beginning of Year 6 of Menephtah, not many days after the Passover at midnight ending 3rd April (Greg.).

Now, Seti II was the only son of Menephtah, and therefore, according to the account in the Book of the Exodus, he died at midnight ending 3rd April (Greg.) 1486 B.C.=2513½ A.K. It is obvious, then, that the sculptor of the shrine at Silsileh—over 400 miles South of Memphis or Bubastis, where the Pharaoh's court was established at the time of the Exodus—could not have heard the news of the death of the Prince Regent when he inscribed the record in April of that year. We see, then, that Seti II never lived to celebrate the *Seti II, the only son of Menephtah, died at the time of the Exodus of Israel, and during his co-regency.*

---

[1]" The Times," 26th Oct. 1923, p. 11.
[2]" The Struggle of the Nations," p. 428. Refer also, p. 424, and footnotes 3 and 5, and Brugsch, " Egypt under the Pharaohs," Vol. II, pp. 24, 98, 99, and 128, for the data concerning the co-regency of Ramessu II with Seti I, the great age of Ramessu II at his death, and the evidence concerning Menephtah as the Pharaoh of the Exodus ; also Budge, " History of Egypt," Vol. V, pp. 120–132.
The whole subject, from the received standpoint of Egyptian archæology, is very ably discussed by Professor T. Eric Peet in his recent " Egypt and the Old Testament."
Refer also Dr. E. Naville's " The Store-City of Pithom and the Route of the Exodus," " Goshen."
[3]The 1st sacred month, later known as Nisan, was, at the time of the Exodus, called Abib (Exod. xiii, 4).

PLATE LXI.

THE HISTORICAL CONDITIONS IN EGYPT RELATING TO THE CIRCUMSTANCES OF ISRAEL'S OPPRESSION AND EXODUS.

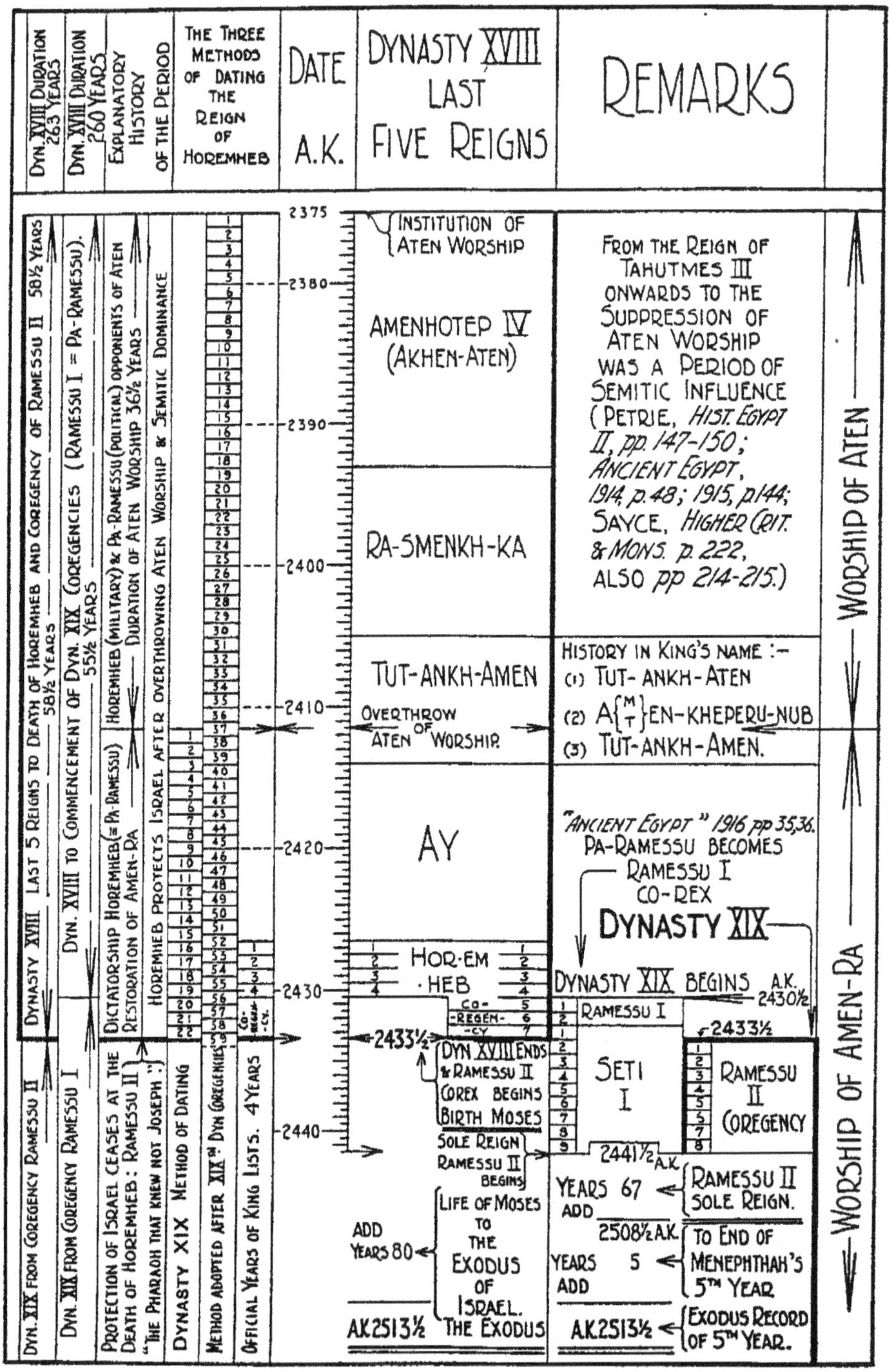

DYN. XVIII DURATION 263 YEARS
DYN. XVIII DURATION 260 YEARS
EXPLANATORY HISTORY OF THE PERIOD
THE THREE METHODS OF DATING THE REIGN OF HOREMHEB
DATE A.K.
DYNASTY XVIII LAST FIVE REIGNS
REMARKS
DYNASTY XVIII LAST 5 REIGNS TO DEATH OF HOREMHEB AND COREGENCY OF RAMESSU II 58½ YEARS
58½ YEARS
DYN. XIX FROM COREGENCY RAMESSU II
DYN. XVIII TO COMMENCEMENT OF DYN. XIX COREGENCIES (RAMESSU I = PA-RAMESSU). 55½ YEARS
DYN. XIX FROM COREGENCY RAMESSU I
HOREMHEB (MILITARY) & PA-RAMESSU (POLITICAL) OPPONENTS OF ATEN
DURATION OF ATEN WORSHIP 36½ YEARS
DICTATORSHIP HOREMHEB (= PA-RAMESSU) RESTORATION OF AMEN-RA
PROTECTION OF ISRAEL CEASES AT THE DEATH OF HOREMHEB: RAMESSU II
"THE PHARAOH THAT KNEW NOT JOSEPH."
HOREMHEB PROTECTS ISRAEL AFTER OVERTHROWING ATEN WORSHIP & SEMITIC DOMINANCE
DYNASTY XIX METHOD OF DATING
METHOD ADOPTED AFTER XIXth DYN (COREGENCIES)
OFFICIAL YEARS OF KING LISTS. 4 YEARS
CO-REGENCY
2375
2380
2390
2400
2410
2420
2430
2440
INSTITUTION OF ATEN WORSHIP
AMENHOTEP IV (AKHEN-ATEN)
RA-SMENKH-KA
TUT-ANKH-AMEN
OVERTHROW OF ATEN WORSHIP
AY
HOR-EM-HEB
CO-REGEN-CY
2433½
DYN XVIII ENDS & RAMESSU II COREX BEGINS BIRTH MOSES
SOLE REIGN RAMESSU II BEGINS
LIFE OF MOSES TO THE EXODUS OF ISRAEL.
ADD YEARS 80
AK 2513½
THE EXODUS
FROM THE REIGN OF TAHUTMES III ONWARDS TO THE SUPPRESSION OF ATEN WORSHIP WAS A PERIOD OF SEMITIC INFLUENCE (PETRIE, HIST. EGYPT II, pp. 147-150; ANCIENT EGYPT, 1914, p. 48; 1915, p. 144; SAYCE, HIGHER CRIT. & MONS. p. 222, ALSO pp 214-215.)
HISTORY IN KING'S NAME :-
(1) TUT-ANKH-ATEN
(2) A{M T}EN-KHEPERU-NUB
(3) TUT-ANKH-AMEN.
"ANCIENT EGYPT" 1916 pp 35, 36.
PA-RAMESSU BECOMES RAMESSU I CO-REX
DYNASTY XIX
DYNASTY XIX BEGINS A.K. 2430½
RAMESSU I
SETI I
2433½
RAMESSU II (COREGENCY)
2441½ A.K.
YEARS 67 ADD
RAMESSU II SOLE REIGN.
2508½ A.K.
YEARS 5 ADD
TO END OF MENEPHTHAH'S 5TH YEAR
AK 2513½
EXODUS RECORD OF 5TH YEAR.
WORSHIP OF ATEN
WORSHIP OF AMEN-RA

ANNOTATIONS TO PLATE LXI.

THE OVERLAPPING OF DYNASTY XVIII WITH DYNASTY XIX CO-REGENCIES.

Outline of the Scheme of Formulation.

The worship of Aten was instituted by Akhen-Aten in his 1st year, 2375 A.K. (Table XIV), and was overthrown at 2411½ A.K., after 36 years and 5 months, by the General Horemheb, who later became Pharaoh (Petrie, "Hist. Egypt," II, 28, 29, 250, 251. Refer also Table XII). Politically associated with Horemheb in overthrowing Aten worship was a high noble, Pa-Ramessu, who, for his services, was created co-regent when Horemheb definitely occupied the throne. A statue of Pa-Ramessu with the name of Horemheb inscribed on the breast and right shoulder gives him the titles of co-regent. Pa-Ramessu is Ramessu I of the Lists ("Ancient Egypt," 1916, pt. I, pp. 35, 36; "Annales du Service des Antiquités de l'Egypte," Tome XIV, Cairo, 1914; G. Legrain, "au Pylône d'Harmhabi à Karnak"). During the reign of Ramessu II the years of Horemheb's reign were dated as beginning from the overthrow of Aten worship at 2411½ A.K. (Petrie). The highest known recorded dating by this method is year 21. The stated total of Africanus for Dynasty XVIII—263 years—shows that Horemheb died 22 years after the overthrow of Aten. This gives the death of Horemheb at 2433½ A.K., whereas the known and astronomically fixed dating for Ramessu I (as Table XIV) beginning Dynasty XIX is 2430½ A.K. This indicates that the last three years of Dynasty XVIII coincided with the first three years of Dynasty XIX. Ramessu I, therefore, reigned as co-regent of Horemheb.

Since Ramessu I reigned not more than 2 years, beginning at 2430½ A.K. (Table XIV), he died a year before Horemheb. This shows that, following the death of Ramessu I at 2432½ A.K., Horemheb appointed Seti I co-regent, a year prior to his own death at 2433½ A.K. Seti I reckoned this as the beginning of his reign, as stated on Table XIV.

At the death of Horemheb at 2433½ A.K., Seti I appointed his son—later known as Ramessu II—co-regent. This co-regency of Ramessu (II) with his father, Seti I, is noted by Brugsch ("Egypt under the Pharaohs," Revised Edition, p. 252), and by Maspero ("Struggle of the Nations," pp. 385, 386). "The Book of the Sothis" is therefore quite correct in placing Ramessu II, followed by Menephtah, after Armaios (Horemheb)—thus ignoring the reigns of Ramessu I and Seti I.

It is not until after the 3rd (sole) year of Horemheb that all trace of Aten worship was swept out of existence (Petrie, "Hist. Egypt," II, 251). This fact is significant, as it was at the end of the 4th (sole) year of Horemheb that the co-regency of Ramessu I began. The rigid suppression of everything associated with Aten worship therefore dates from the rise of the new Dynasty of Ramessides during the reign of Horemheb. This indicates the hatred with which the Ramessides viewed everything associated with Aten worship. They blotted out every possible trace of the former dominance of the Semitic faction in Egypt. With the death of Horemheb, the active oppression of Israel began. Hence that 80 years separate the death of Horemheb and the Egyptian date of the Exodus, and that the like interval of 80 years separates the beginning of Israel's oppression, at the birth of Moses, and the Exodus, according to the narrative of the Book of Exodus.

Now when Horemheb actually ascended the throne in 2426½ A.K., Seti (I), the son of Ramessu (I), received high appointment in the Egyptian army. This would account for Ramessu II—as stated on the Stele of Qubban—receiving the usual Royal honorary appointment in the army at the age of 10. Horemheb was himself the supreme general prior to his actual reign beginning 2426½ A.K. The honorary appointment of Ramessu II, when 10 years old, must be fixed at the latter date. He was, therefore, 17 years old when his co-regency began at 2433½ A.K., and 91 years old at his death at 2508½ A.K. (all as Plate LXI). This confirms Breasted ("Hist. Egypt," p. 462):—

"Finally, having ruled for 67 years, and being over 90 years of age, he passed away, none too soon for the redemption of his empire." (Refer also ¶ 322, quotation from Maspero concerning the mummy of Ramessu II in relation to the question of his age at death.)

The eldest son of Seti I—of name unknown, owing to later erasure by Ramessu II—entered the army at the same time as Ramessu II, but died during the 1st year of Seti I, about the same time as Horemheb (refer Maspero, "Struggle of the Nations," pp. 385, 386). The coincidence is striking, since Ramessu II became co-regent in consequence, and immediately showed his cruelty by his decree condemning to death the male infants of Israel. Brugsch states that "while he (Seti I) actually ruled the land as king, Rameses, his son, as legitimate sovereign, gave authority to all the acts of his father."

Outline of Data confirming the Scheme of Formulation.

The kings of Dynasty XIX ignored all reigns of Dynasty XVIII except Horemheb's, from the time of the institution of Aten worship at 2375 A.K. By a later reckoning of the time of Ramessu II, Horemheb was represented as having reigned 58½ years from the institution of Aten at 2375 A.K. to Horemheb's death at 2433½ A.K. Hence that a record of the time of Ramessu II—the inscription of Mes—refers to a legal decision in the 59th year of Horemheb. This was the last year of Horemheb according to this form of reckoning.

By this form of reckoning, the actual reign of Horemheb began at his alleged 51½ years' duration. Hence the later substitution in the King Lists (version of Africanus) of 51 years for Sethos (*i.e.* Seti I), derived obviously from the known fact of the co-regency of Seti I with Horemheb; the latter being the Armais (or Hermeus) of the Lists, and the former the Sethos of the Lists—represented as two brothers by Manetho (quoted by Josephus, "Contra Apion," I, 26).

By the same form of reckoning, Dynasty XIX began at Horemheb's alleged 55½ years' duration. Hence, as above, that the King Lists (version of Eusebius) give Sethos as reigning 55 years.

Again, the alleged 59th year was the year in which Horemheb died; hence that the version of Manetho's Lists, quoted by Josephus ("Contra Apion," I, 26), gives Sethos as reigning 59 years.

That Horemheb, until his death, protected the Israelites and other Semites in Egypt is preserved in the tradition concerning Hermeus (or Armais)—equated with Danaus (Manetho, as Josephus, "Contra Apion," I, 26)—and Sethos. According to the tradition, Sethos drove Armais out of Egypt. Another form narrates that Danaus fled from Egypt. Manetho identifies Danaus with Armais (Horemheb) as above. But we know that Horemheb died in Egypt.

The fact is that Greek tradition fixed the flight of Danaus from Egypt during the joint reigns of Armais (Horemheb) and Sethos (otherwise called Ægyptus). The identification of Danaus with Armais (Horemheb) is explained by the fact that Horemheb protected the Semites in Egypt from the Ramessides until his death. The Semitic faction, however, had fallen from supremacy with the fall of Aten worship at 2411½ A.K., and large numbers of Semites left Egypt. Thus Greek tradition attaches the arrival of Cecrops in Attica, from Sais in Egypt, to the date 1582 B.C.=2417½—8½ A.K., or six years after the fall of Aten worship. About the same time, Phœnix and Cadmus are represented as leaving Thebes in Egypt, and founding Phœnician colonies in Tyre and Sidon. Since a pedigree supplied by Apollodorus and Euripides connects Danaus genealogically with Egypt and Phœnicia, it would seem that the migrations of Cecrops, Phœnix, Cadmus, and Danaus are all to be referred to the same movement, classified in the Egyptian King Lists of Manetho as the "Phœnician Shepherds" and "Hellenic Shepherds" respectively, and erroneously entered as belonging to the period of Hyksos or "Shepherd" supremacy preceding Dynasty XVIII. Hence that Manetho, as quoted by Josephus ("Contra Apion," I, 14, 15, 26, 27, 32), has confused the three expulsions—the Hyksos at 2170½ A.K., the Semitic "Phœnician and Hellenic Shepherds" from 2411½ to 2433½ A.K., and the Exodus of Israel at 2513½ A.K.

Here, then, in mythology, we have the essence of a true historical narrative. The flight or expulsion of the so-called "Shepherds," who by their migration became "Phœnioian" and "Hellenic Shepherds," was the flight or expulsion of the Semitic faction, which, prior to and during the establishing of Aten worship in Egypt, was the supreme faction at the court of the Aahmessides. Hence that Hecatæus of Abdera, as quoted by "Diodorus Siculus" (I, 27, 46, 55), states:—

"The most distinguished of the expelled foreigners (from Egypt) followed Danaus and Cadmus into Greece, but the greater number were led by Moses into Judæa." Refer also, Num. xiv, 1–4; Neh. ix, 17; Ps. cvi, 26, 27; Ezek. xx, 21–23.

Compare Judges v, 17, with 1 Kings vii, 14; 2 Chron. ii, 14; Ezek. xxvii, 6, 19; Josephus, "Antiquities," iii, 4; all in relation to Dr. Latham's statement in his "Ethnology of Europe" (p. 157).

The data above (both columns) form the basis of the *Old Chronicle's* dating for Dynasty XIX, as proved by the following:—

(Refer Plate XVI, Table E, and ¶¶ 95–97, 138a (3), 214, 250–253, and Table XI Annotations, Cols. 3 and 5.)

Dynasty XIX begins	2412 A.K.=1588 B.C.	Date of Aten worship ending (Plate LXI). This is the date (1588 B.C.) given in modern works for the beginning of Dynasty XVIII. This, of course, omits the Harris Papyrus Interregnum between Dynasties XIX and XX.
Duration	194 years.	
Dynasty XIX ends	2606 A.K.=1394 B.C.	
Interregnum	178 years (references as above, Harris Papyrus, and Table XXIII).	
Dynasty XX begins	2784 A.K.=1216 B.C.	Astronomically fixed by Table XI and Annotations.
Dynasties XX to XXX inclusive ..	868 years, as Africanus for Book III, Manetho's Lists.	
Epoch of Okhos	3652 A.K.=348 B.C.	References as above.

beginning of his 2nd year of co-regency, and that the Silsileh shrine was erected to commemorate the beginning of the Prince Regent's anticipated 2nd year.

The co-regent succeeding was a foreigner. Seti II having been the ruling Pharaoh's only son, we find that after his death the co-regent, prior to the next reign, is given as a foreigner, who took the name " Ramsesupirniri."[1]

The "Sed" period from 46th year of Ramessu II to 1st year of Amenmeses confirms that Seti II never reigned other than as co-regent. The next Egyptian king, Amenmeses, reigned only one year. In this year he celebrated a *Sed heb*. The last *pseudo-Sed heb* celebrated by Ramessu II was in his 46th year.[2] The 1st and sole year of Amenmeses is thirty years later—the interval of the *Sed* period—only by placing Seti II co-regent with his father, as the facts explained have shown.[3]

Chronological summary of Egyptian history relating to the Exodus. A chronological summary of the historical sequence relating to the Exodus of Israel, as derived from Egyptian sources, is given in Table XXIII at the end of this Section (Ia).

¶ 324. JOSHUA'S "WEEK" OF EIGHT DAYS' DURATION.

A chronological revision :— Joshua's "long day" = "two days" reckoned as "one day." Whatever opinion authorities may hold concerning the narrative of Joshua's "long day," it must be admitted that the narrative itself states that the duration of two days in time was reckoned as one day (Joshua x, 13).[4] *In the week of revision :— The duration of eight days was reckoned as one week.* This is confirmed as a chronological fact in Israel's history by Ecclesiasticus xlvi, 4—" Was not one day as long as two ? " To express the matter in another way—one particular week, forty years after the Exodus, was reckoned to be of the duration of eight days.

The effect on chronological calculations:— For all dates prior to 1446 B.C., the apparent 7th day of the week (as normally calculated back from present time) must be reckoned as the 1st day of the week. From the date of this revision (1446 B.C.) all Hebrew weeks have occurred at exact intervals of seven days to the present time. As calculated backwards from the present time, all weeks prior to the revision in 1446 B.C. will have to be corrected to the extent of the day inserted. This may be made clear as follows :—

Let us suppose that Joshua's two days were a 6th and a 7th day of the week in current use until then. The record shows that these two days were reckoned as the 6th day. The day succeeding the revision would normally have been the 1st day of a new week. Owing to the revision, however, the former 1st day of the week had become the 7th day of the week. This has continued until the present time, as the facts will show.

The initial day of the zero year of ancient Calendar Chronology = Day 1, Month 1, 22nd Sept. (Greg.) 4000 B.C. (hist.) = actual first day of the week. When, therefore, we calculate back from the present time, and on the basis of the present week, to 0 A.K., when Universal Calendar Chronology began at the Autumnal Equinoctial Full Moon (¶¶ 297 and 315), midnight beginning 22nd September (Greg.), we find that the latter month dating coincides with the 7th day of the modern Hebrew week. It was, therefore,

[1]Maspero, " Struggle of the Nations," p. 438.
[2]Petrie, " History of Egypt," Vol. III, p. 39.
[3]For the explanation of Ramessu II breaking the continuity of *Sed* periods, in connection with the Phœnix cycle festival of his 27th year, and his celebration of short-period *Sed* festivals thereafter to his 46th year, the reader is referred to Table XI Annotations.
[4]Discussion of this includes also consideration of the question of " the 10 degrees of the sun-dial of Ahaz " (Isaiah xxxviii, 7, 8). Joshua x, 13 gives the additional duration as " about a whole day." Combining Joshua x, 13 and Isaiah xxxviii, 7, 8 gives the two complete days that were reckoned as " One Day " according to Ecclesiasticus xlvi, 4.

the 1st day of the week in use prior to the revision in 1446 B.C. This calculation, and this identity, confirm the Hebrew origin of the week in relation to the year 0 A.K. of ancient Universal Chronology (Gen. i).

The astronomical day began at midnight (Full Moon) of the Autumnal Equinox.

¶ 325. THE REPETITION OF EXODUS WEEK, MONTH, AND SOLAR AND LUNAR YEAR DATINGS AT THE CRUCIFIXION.

What light is thrown upon the identity noted by the statements concerning the week in relation to the Exodus ? As reckoned from the present Hebrew week, the days for the 14th to the 17th, inclusive, of the Hebrew month Nisan, in the year of the Exodus, were, respectively, the 4th to 7th days, inclusive, of the modern Hebrew week, *i.e.* 3rd to 6th April (Greg.), 1486 B.C. Correcting for the revision under Joshua, the 14th to 17th Nisan were respectively the 5th, 6th, 7th, and 1st days of the week at the time of the Exodus.

In the Exodus year—2513½ A.K.=1486 B.C.—the 14th to 17th days, inclusive, of the 1st month (Nisan) = 3rd (Greg.), inclusive, = 5th, 6th, 7th, and 1st days of the week.

The outstanding feature of this identification is that the 16th Nisan in the Exodus year fell on the Hebrew Sabbath, or Seventh day of the week. A remarkable coincidence—due to the revision under Joshua—underlies this identity, since we know from the New Testament that the same identity, 16th Nisan = the Sabbath, occurred in the year of the Crucifixion.

Again, in the Crucifixion year, the 14th to 17th days, inclusive, of the 1st month (Nisan) = 5th, 6th, 7th, and 1st days of the week.

The coincidence, however, becomes still more striking when we observe that the repetition of the day of the week, and the repetition of the lunar phase, both agree after a period of, and occur within $1\frac{3}{4}$ days short of, the exact interval of 1515 solar years from 1486 B.C. to 30 A.D. The precise interval consists of 18,738 lunations, or $1561\frac{1}{2}$ lunar years, and is of the duration of 1515 Julian years less 9.6 days.

Again, at 30½ A.D. = 4028½ A.K., the 14th to 17th days, inclusive, of the 1st month (Nisan) = 5th, 6th, 7th, and 1st days of the week = 4th to 7th April (Greg.), inclusive, exactly 1515 solar years = 1561½ lunar years, from the same Exodus datings.

Should the coincidence noted prove to relate to the Nisan datings of the Crucifixion, the date of the latter should be fixed from the Exodus date as follows :—

Exodus .. .. 2513½ A.K. = 1486 B.C.
Interval 1561½ lunar years .. .. .. = 1515 solar years.

Repetition of Nisan datings .. .. .. 4028½ A.K. = 30¼ A.D.

In both years, 1486 B.C. and 30 A.D., the Sabbath on 16th Nisan was preceded by a day of " holy convocation," the 15th Nisan, which was commanded, after the Exodus, to be a day of rest from servile work. In such case, the Sabbath on 16th Nisan was termed a " high Sabbath."[1]

¶ 326. THE TWO PENTECOSTS—THE EXODUS YEAR AND THE CRUCIFIXION YEAR.

Exodus xvi, 1 narrates that Israel arrived in the Wilderness of Sin on the 15th of the 2nd month. The narrative, by mentioning the date, shows that Day 15, Month II, formed the 1st day datum for the 6th day of verse 5.

The Book of Exodus defines the week in relation to the calendar at Israel's national adoption of the "Sabbath."

[1] Refer John xix, 31. The interval to Pentecost was reckoned from " the morrow after the day of rest" on 15th Nisan—*i.e.* from 16th Nisan inclusive, irrespective of the day of the week upon which 16th Nisan fell—" seven weeks shalt thou number unto thee " (Deut. xvi, 9).
In Lev. xxiii, 15, 16, " Sabbaths" denote " weeks" (Ginsburg).

This definition coincides with the calculated fixing. These six days were the six days of manna and quails (verses 4 and 5), and were, therefore, the six working days of the week (verse 26). Now, by calculation and ¶ 325, Day 15, Month II of 1486 B.C. was the 1st day of the week. This, as shown, is confirmed by the stated position of the week for the year 1486 B.C. in the Book of the Exodus.

The law given on Pentecost, which fell on the Sabbath, 24th May (Greg.) in the Exodus year, 1486 B.C. = 2513¼ A.K. Again, the Jews of the period of the 2nd Temple held that the Law was given to Moses on the 6th of the month Sivan (Month III). The date is that of the Feast of Pentecost. In the year of the Exodus 6th Sivan fell, by calculation, on a Sabbath. The first six days following the giving of the Law should, therefore, be the six working days of the week. In Exodus xxiv the cloud covered Mount Sinai during the six days that followed the giving of the Law in Month III (Sivan). " The seventh day He called unto Moses out of the midst of the cloud." Here the six working days of the week, by calculation, agree with the six days of the cloud on Mount Sinai, confirming that Pentecost was the day upon which the Law was delivered to Moses. This explanation of the six days and the seventh day has its counterpart in the narrative of Genesis i.

The 1st Pentecost of the old Covenant, and the 1st Pentecost of the new Covenant. Chapters xx to xxiii of Exodus describe the events of the day upon which the Law was given, and xxiv, 4-15, the events of the following day. Comparison with Acts, Chapters ii and iii, for the day of the Descent of the Holy Ghost, and Chapter iv for the day following, shows that the events of the two days in Exodus prefigured the events of the two days in Acts (refer note p. 299).

¶ 327. THE DAY OF SALVATION—IN THE EXODUS YEAR AND IN THE CRUCIFIXION YEAR.

The Exodus flight began after midnight, 15th Nisan = 4th April (Greg.) 1486 B.C. = 2513¼ A.K.—on the 6th day of the week.

The route and the easy stages of marching agree with the Israelites travelling " by day and night." In Israel's history there is no account of the Sabbath being held as a day of rest until Exodus xvi, 30, when it is commanded and observed. The flight of Israel from Rameses began after midnight of the 15th of Nisan (Numbers xxxiii, 3), 4th April (Greg.) 1486 B.C., and on the 6th day of the week, according to our astronomical fixing and ¶ 325. If the narratives of the Books of Exodus and Numbers be followed *rigorously* there is only one route possible. This is the route, fixed by Sir Hanbury Brown,[1] along the Wady Tumilat, and explained and adopted by him upon scriptural, topographical, and archæological grounds (refer Plate LXIII, ¶ 356).

[1] " The Land of Goshen." The route discussed is practically the same as that suggested by the celebrated French Abbé Moigno, founder and editor of *Cosmos les Mondes*; by the French engineer, M. Lecointre, in his " La Campagne de Moise pour la Sortie d'Egypte" (1882); and by Linant, Naville, Dawson, and Hull, all reliable authorities.

Concerning the same general route, as the only possible route answering to that described in the Books of Exodus and Numbers, refer Budge, " History of Egypt," Vol. V, pp. 128-132, as to the data collected by Dr. Naville, and discussed by Naville, Sir William Dawson, and Professor Hull in this relation.

The reader must bear in mind what MM. de Lesseps and Lecointre, and Sir Hanbury Brown —all the highest authorities on the engineering and topographical aspects of the problem—have shown, that the Gulf of Suez extended originally up to, and including, the Bitter Lakes and Lake Timsah. Hence the Hebrew designation " the sea of reeds," translated " the Red Sea." The extension of the Red Sea at the time of the Exodus, and the route of the Exodus, are as shown on Plate LXIII. The Israelites crossed over the narrow neck of the original extension of the Gulf of Suez between the existing Bitter Lakes and Lake Timsah.

The sites identified for Rameses, Succoth, and Pi-hahiroth give easy stages—considerably less than a day's march in each case—for a large number of men, women, and children. The total distance from Rameses, of the three marches, is 31 miles, averaging 10⅓ miles per march (Plate LXIII). The easy stages explain the statement in Exodus xiii, 21, that the Israelites travelled " by day and night." Three such marches " by day and night," with two encampments, obviously did not occupy three days. The Egyptians overtook them encamping beside Pi-hahiroth. This was before the evening (comparing Exodus xiv, 9 and 10 with 19 and 20). Obviously, then, the three marches, not being possible in one day and night, and too short for three days and three nights in the circumstances of travelling in haste " by day and night," must have occupied two days.

In such case, Exodus xiv, 19, 20, 24, in fixing the crossing of the " Sea of Reeds " by Israel as taking place during the darkness of the early morning of 17th Nisan, also fixes the later pursuit of the Egyptians and their destruction before the dawn (Exodus xiv, 24 and 27). " Thus," says Exodus xiv, 30, " the Lord saved Israel " ; xv, 2, " The Lord . . . is become my salvation " ; and xv, 13, " Thou in thy mercy hast led forth the people which thou hast redeemed." This 17th Nisan, by calculation, is the first day of the week, the 6th April (Greg.) 1486 B.C.

In the year of our Lord's Crucifixion, the 17th of Nisan is again given as a Day of Salvation. Before the dawn of this day—another first day of the week (Sunday)—our Lord rose from the dead. In 30 A.D. the 17th Nisan fell on the first day of the week (Sunday), 7th April (Greg.), 1515 solar years or 1561½ lunar years from the same day in 1486 B.C.

¶ 328. THE GREAT PYRAMID DEFINES AND FIXES A HEBREW SACRED PERIOD.

The Exodus of Israel from Egypt began, as we have seen, from midnight 15th Nisan=6th day of the week, 4th April (Greg.) 2513½ A.K. (1486 B.C.). An interval of 1515 solar years, equalling 1561½ lunar years, elapsed, and again midnight 15th Nisan=the 6th day of the week (Friday), 5th April (Greg.) 4028½ A.K. (30 A.D.).

The April (Greg.) datings fix the years precisely to the second decimal place as 2513.53 and 4028.53 A.K., respectively. Both dates are given precisely by the Great Pyramid's astronomical and geometrical chronology, and are established by its astronomical data as intentionally representing the years 1486 B.C. and 30 A.D. respectively. The former dating, that of the Exodus of Israel, is indicated by the axis of the Entrance Passage cutting the floor of the 1st Ascending Passage at 2513.5554695 A.K. (Plates XLI, Fig. G and XLII, Fig. A). The second dating is given as the commencement of the Grand Gallery at 4028.531789 A.K. (Plates XLI, Fig. K and XLII, Fig. A). The decimals, in both cases, fix the respective datings as later than the Vernal Equinox.

Side notes (right margin):

Three short marches, " by day and night "—with two rest intervals—from midnight 15th Nisan to evening beginning 17th Nisan.

The crossing of " the Sea of Reeds " between midnight and dawn of 17th Nisan.

The Egyptians destroyed before the dawn of 17th Nisan, 6th April (Greg.), the 1st day of the week.

Proclaimed as the Day of Salvation.

The Day of Salvation repeated at the Resurrection on 17th Nisan, in the year of the Crucifixion, on the 1st day of the week.

In 30 A.D. 17th Nisan fell on the 1st day of the week (Sunday), 5th April (Greg.), exactly 1515 solar years = 1561½ lunar years from the Exodus date.

The 15th Nisan of the Exodus year, 1486 B.C. = 2513½ A.K., and of the year 30 A.D. = 4028½ A.K., defines the dates precisely as 2513.53 A.K. and 4028.53 A.K.

The date 2513.5554695 A.K. defined at the junction of the Entrance and Ascending Passages, and the date 4028.531789 A.K. defined at the beginning of the Grand Gallery in the Great Pyramid.

The Pyramid's astronomical data define datings as 1486 B.C. and 30 A.D. respectively.

Egyptian
astronomical
datings define
1486 B.C. as
2513¼ A.K.,
and as the date
of the Exodus.

No question of
accidental
coincidence.

In this case there can be no question of the Hebrews forging a system of chronology to agree with the datings of the Pyramid's chronology. The Egyptian astronomical records and datings define the Exodus date as 2513¼ A.K., and independently as 1486 B.C. Nor can there be any question of accidental coincidence. Accidental coincidence is a mathematical impossibility, when even a few only of all the innumerable related factors are taken into consideration.

¶ 329. THE INTENTION OF THE PYRAMID'S PASSAGE SYMBOLISM.

The ancient
Egyptians
defined the
Pyramid's
Grand Gallery
as symbolic of
the Epoch of
the Saviour of
the human
race.

The 1st
Ascending
Passage :—
the Egyptian
" Way of
Truth in dark-
ness "=St.
Paul's " yoke
of the Law."

The Grand
Gallery :—
The Egyptian
" Way of
Truth in
light "=St.
Paul's " new
and living
way."

Modern re-
search limits
the Crucifixion
year to 29 A.D.
to 30 A.D.

New data
define the
date as 7th
April 30 A.D.
Pyramid's
Grand Gallery
dating defines
7th April 30
A.D.

When we come to discuss the ancient Egyptian evidence, it will be seen that Egyptian sacred literature identifies the beginning of the Great Pyramid's Grand Gallery as symbolic of the Epoch of the Saviour of the human race. The same evidence, as will be shown, identifies the 1st Ascending Passage as symbolic of the Way of Truth in darkness, and the Grand Gallery of the Way of Truth in light. Similarly, St. Paul speaks of the period from the Exodus year to the Crucifixion year as the period of " the yoke of the Law " —referring to the Law as " our schoolmaster until Christ "—and of the Christian Dispensation " as the new and living way."

Having regard to the fact that modern research has limited the date of the Crucifixion to the years 29 or 30 A.D.,[1] the relation between the Pyramid's symbolism and the Egyptian symbolism on the one hand and the Biblical symbolism on the other is too clear to be disregarded. All the evidence— sacred and secular—relating to the chronology of Christ's Life, as discussed in Section II of this Chapter, attaches the Crucifixion to Friday, 15th Nisan, 7th April (Julian) =5th April (Gregorian) of A.D. 30. This dating and the Pyramid dating (4028.531789 A.P.) both appeared in the first edition of this work. The latter dating, however, had not then been reduced to its equivalent Julian month dating of A.D. 30, since the precise time of the preceding Autumnal Equinox had not been calculated. As now determined, the data are as follows :—Autumnal Equinox 4028 A.P. =25th Sept. (Julian) 29 A.D., 7.45 a.m. at Jerusalem ; Autumnal Equinoctial year=365.2424 days ; 4028.531789 A.P. =7th April (Julian) 30 A.D., 1.20 p.m. at Jerusalem, at which time our Lord was on the Cross.

¶ 330. FROM THE EXODUS OF ISRAEL TO ALEXANDER THE GREAT.

Egyptian
chronology
1215 to 525
B.C.

Beginning of
Dynasty XX
to Persian
conquest.

Synchronises
with Baby-
onian chrono-
logy in rela-
tion to Israel's

The chronology of the Egyptian period from the beginning of Dynasty XX (1215 B.C., as astronomically fixed) to the Persian conquest of Egypt (525 B.C., as astronomically fixed) is as stated in Table XXIV at the end of this Section (Ia). The astronomical and chronological references fixing this statement of the chronology are given in the accompanying Annotations. The outstanding feature of this statement is that it synchronises with Babylonian and Assyrian chronology in relation to essential historical

[1] " Enc. Brit." (11th Edit.), Vol. III, pp. 890d and 891a.

events in Israel's history. This enables us to declare, with a degree of definitiveness hitherto impossible, as to the true periods in Israel's history—

   (1) From the Exodus to the founding of Solomon's Temple ;

   (2) From the founding of Solomon's Temple to its destruction by Nebuchadnezzar ; and

   (3) From the destruction of Jerusalem and the Temple by Nebuchadnezzar to the founding of the Second Temple.

Confirms Biblical chronological statements of intervals between the Exodus, founding of the 1st Temple, destruction of the 1st Temple, and founding of the 2nd Temple.

Interval (1) is fixed as 479 years, the 1st Temple being founded at the commencement of the 480th year from the Exodus. This confirms the statement of 1 Kings vi, 1 (refer also ¶¶ 36 and 321, and footnote to ¶ 36). The date of the founding of Solomon's Temple is, therefore, 2992½ A.K. =1007 B.C. This fixes that the dedication of the Temple (when the Shekinah entered the Temple) occurred precisely at 3000 A.K. =1000 B.C.

Statement of 480th year in 1 Kings vi, 1 confirmed.

Dedication of the 1st Temple 3000 A.K. =1000 B.C.

Interval (2) is fixed as 423 years, Jerusalem being destroyed by Nebuchadnezzar at the date 3415½ A.K.=584 B.C. This agrees with the Babylonian and Medo-Persian data explained in ¶ 318. The period and dates are independently confirmed by the synchronising of the reigns of the Kings of Judah and Israel given in the Annotations to Table XXV. The Babylonian and Egyptian chronological datings therefore confirm the chronological statements of the Hebrew Books of Kings and Chronicles, as elucidated by the synchronistic statement noted. The resulting chronological statement of the Kings of Israel and Judah is given in Table XXV, and the outstanding dates in the history of the Kings of Israel and Judah are as given in Table XXVI, both at the end of this Section.

Destruction of the 1st Temple 3415½ A.K. =584 B.C.

The chronology of the Kings of Israel and Judah fixed.

Interval (3) is fixed as of the duration of 64½ years, thus giving the founding of the 2nd Temple precisely at 3480 A.K.= 520 B.C. in the 2nd year of Darius (I) Hystaspes. This interval, fixed by the data discussed in ¶ 318, is confirmed by the Hebrew data (refer also Tables XXV, XXVIII, and XXX, and Annotations). The historical connection is completed by the statement of Medo-Persian chronology from Cyrus to Alexander the Great. This is as given in Table XXVII at the end of this Section. Essential details concerning this tabulation are given in the Annotations to Tables XXI and XXVII.

Founding of the 2nd Temple 3480 A.K. =520 B.C., in the 2nd year of Darius (I) Hystaspes.

¶ 331. THE ARTAXERXES OF EZRA AND NEHEMIAH.

Ezekiel gives the date of the departure of the Shekinah from the 1st Temple as 5½ years before the destruction of the Temple by Nebuchadnezzar. This is as shown on Table XXX. From the departure of the Shekinah to the founding of the 2nd Temple, in the 2nd year of Darius I (¶ 330), is therefore a period of 70 years. This is the 70 years' period of Divine Indignation noted by Zechariah (i, 1 and 2) as ending in the 2nd year of Darius I. Agreeing with this, the prophet Haggai (i, 1–12) narrates that the Divine Command to build the 2nd Temple was given on Day 1, (Sacred) Month VI—22nd August (Greg.) 520 B.C., a month prior to the beginning of 3480 A.K.—of the 2nd year of Darius. From this fact, every system of

The Shekinah left the 1st Temple at 3410 A.K. =590 B.C., when the 70 years' divine indignation began.

The latter period ended at 3480 A.K. =520 B.C., in the 2nd year of Darius I.

The divine
command to
build the
2nd Temple
then given—
22nd August
(Greg.) 520
B.C.

Jewish
Rabbinical
schemes of
chronology
begin Daniel's
70 " Hebdo-
mads " from
the latter date.

Jews of the
2nd Century
B.C. onward
identified the
Artaxerxes
of Ezra vii
and Nehemiah
with Darius (I)
Hystaspes.

The import-
ance of the
identity in
relation to
Old Testament
criticism.

Meyer and
Anstey on the
name
" Artaxerxes."

Ezra vi, 14
reads " Darius,
even Arta-
xerxes," not
" Darius and
Artaxerxes,"
as translated.

The identity
completely
solves all
the supposed
problems of
Ezra and
Nehemiah.

The
" Artaxerxes "
of Ezra v, 24
onwards, and
of Nehemiah
i-xi, is
Darius (I)
Hystaspes.

Jewish Rabbinical chronology and prophecy interpretation, from the middle of the 2nd Century B.C. to the present time, dates the commencement of the Command of Daniel's prophecy of 70 weeks (or Hebdomads—literally periods of 7 undefined units) upon the basis of Zechariah i, 7 and 12, and Haggai i, 1-12, thus dating the chronological commencement of the " 70 weeks " from the 2nd year of Darius I.

Understanding of the fact noted leads us to the discovery of a fact of equal importance. This is that the Jewish Rabbis, from the 2nd Century B.C. onwards, identified the Artaxerxes of Ezra vii and of Nehemiah with Darius (I) Hystaspes. This discovery clears up all the hitherto *supposed* discrepancies in Ezra and Nehemiah, and confirms two important statements of two writers who are leading authorities on their respective subjects. Thus Professor E. Meyer[1]—the leading authority on Medo-Persian history, customs, and institutions—states that the name " Artaxerxes " could not be adopted by or given to a king until he had *established* himself in his kingdom ; and the Rev. Dr. Martin Anstey[2] has independently pointed out that " Artaxerxes " is the equivalent of " Great Shah," or the equivalent of the modern name " Emperor," and also, that Ezra vi, 14 reads in the Hebrew " according to the commandment of Cyrus and Darius, *even* Artaxerxes, king of Persia." These few facts alter the whole structure of modern criticism in relation to the Books of Ezra and Nehemiah.

For, when we come to examine all the details in Ezra and Nehemiah, we find the context completely confirming the identity. In Ezra, the identity " Artaxerxes = Darius I " holds from vi, 14 onwards. Again, when we compare the List of Priests and Levites in Nehemiah x (concerning the 20th year of " Artaxerxes ") with the List of Priests and Levites under Zerubbabel in the " 1st year " of Cyrus (Nehemiah xii)—an interval of just over 30 years —we find that the " Artaxerxes " of Nehemiah, Chapters i-xi inclusive, cannot possibly be later than Darius I, since the majority of Priests and Levites of the earlier List were still alive at the time of the later List. Now the first recognised historical Artaxerxes is Artaxerxes (I) Longimanus, whose 20th year is 57 years later than the 20th year of Darius I, and 89 years later than the " 1st year " of Cyrus, according to Hebrew reckoning of the regnal years of Cyrus (refer note on Table XXX). The context of the Books of Ezra and Nehemiah therefore confirms the Jewish Rabbinical identity that the " Artaxerxes " of Nehemiah and of Ezra vi onwards = Darius (I) Hystaspes.[3]

¶ 332.   THE BASES AND PRINCIPLES OF JEWISH CHRONO-LOGICAL FORGERIES.

In the preceding Chapter we saw that all the difficulties in relation to Egyptian chronology had been created by the efforts of the Egyptian com-

---

[1] " Enc. Brit." (11th Edit.), Vol. II, p. 661, " Artaxerxes."
[2] " The Romance of Bible Chronology," p. 244 and context.
[3] A complete discussion of this identity bristles with side issues, such as those relating to the identities indicated by the Elephantiné Papyri, Josephus, and the Rabbinical statements. Some of these are cleared up in the present volume. The whole matter, however, will be discussed in its entirety in the second volume of this work.

pilers of the King Lists. We saw that such efforts had been directed to formulating fictitious systems of chronology that would synchronise certain periods—or alleged periods—of Egyptian history with certain astronomically and geometrically defined periods of the Great Pyramid's chronology, held to relate prophetically to periods of civilisation in the world's history. *Egyptian Dynastic chronology compiled to force an agreement between Egyptian history and certain traditional Egyptian prophecies held to relate to astronomically defined dates in the Great Pyramid's chronology.*

In the same way, we find, from the identity established in ¶ 330 and from the Rabbinical data from which the identity was confirmed, that Jewish Rabbinical chronology has undergone a similar process of fictitious evolution. The original chronological basis was the original Hebrew chronology of ¶ 330. In the original this ended in 3480 A.K., at the founding of the 2nd Temple, in the 2nd year of Darius I. The prophecy basis of evolution is Daniel's prophecy of 70 weeks (Daniel ix, 24–27). The constant prophetic datum throughout the evolutionary process is nominally the 2nd year of Darius I. The excuse for a long succession of fictitious chronological identities and prophetical applications was the identity Darius I=Artaxerxes (Ezra vi, et seq., and Nehemiah). *Jewish Rabbinical fictitious schemes of chronology were similarly compiled to force agreement between Jewish history and the chronologically defined prophecies of the Old Testament.*

Two principles governed the application to Jewish history contemporary with the application— *Basis upon which fictitious systems were built was the original Hebrew chronology.*

(1) A contemporary succession of happenings, apparently similar in nature to those defined in Daniel's prophecy for the 70th week, was deemed sufficient to justify the selection of a unit for Daniel's Hebdomad, that would chronologically fit the current historical happenings ; and *Attempts to enforce Daniel's 70 weeks' prophecy.*

(2) The Rabbinical selection of a unit for the Hebdomad as applied to current time, and the framing of a Jewish national policy to enforce the prophecy fulfilment at the time defined by the Hebdomad unit selected. *Explanation of Jewish history, 2nd Century B.C. to 2nd Century A.D. Method I :— Event suggests forgery. Method II :— Forgery suggests event.*

The application of these two principles explains—in fact, *is*—Jewish history from the middle of the 2nd Century B.C. to the middle of the 2nd Century A.D.

Referring to the days since John the Baptist, our Lord, in Matthew xi, 12, refers to the historical effects of such attempts to enforce fulfilment of prophecy —" the kingdom of heaven suffereth violence and the violent take it by force." Wherefore He said to the Jews (Matthew xxi, 43), " The kingdom of God shall be taken from you, and given unto a nation bringing forth the fruits thereof." *Our Lord's reference to the Jewish attempts to enforce fulfilment of prophecy in His own day.*

¶ 333. THE SEQUENCE STAGES OF JEWISH CHRONOLOGICAL FORGERIES.

In the various Jewish Rabbinical interpretations of Daniel's 70 weeks, the week was understood to imply an interval of 7 units of time. The unit of time or " day " was variously understood to be— *Rabbinical interpretations of Daniel's 70 weeks :— The " day " unit =(a) N lunar months ; (b) A lunar year ; or (c) A solar year.*

(a) A period of so many lunar months ;
(b) A period of one lunar year ; or
(c) A period of one solar year.

In the histori-
cal applications
N ranged from
9 to 18 lunar
months re-
spectively at
time of
Judas Macca-
bæus and
Jewish war,
66-70 A.D.

The Book of
Daniel in
existence long
prior to the
Epoch of
Antiochus
Epiphanes.

A comparative
statement of
the various
stages in the
evolution of
Jewish
fictitious
systems of
chronology
from original
Hebrew
chronology.

Table XXVIII.

Although
earlier periods
of the original
Hebrew
chronology
were tampered
with, the
fictitious
systems were
arranged to
end on the true
dates according
to the original
Hebrew
chronology.

The fictitious
systems con-
firm the ori-
ginal system.

The fictitious
derivation
of the modern
Jewish system
of chronology,
with Jewish
year 5685,
beginning
29th September
1924 A.D.

The suspicious
omission of
the one value
for the unit of
the week that
best agrees
with Old and
New Testa-
ments'
numerical
symbolism.

The number 14.

Rabbinical
interpretation
accorded most
weight to "12"
as symbolic of
"Govern-
mental perfec-
tion," in rela-
tion to the
Messianic
kingdom.

Cases (b) and (c) could have no alternatives; case (a) had alternative units ranging from 9 lunar months to 18 lunar months. The 9 lunar months' unit was employed in the prophecy application to Antiochus Epiphanes and Judas Maccabæus, and to the first king of the Asmonæan Dynasty of Judæa. The 18 lunar months' unit was applied to the Jewish war period—66-70 A.D.—by one school of Rabbis, and appears in Josephus. This is all as explained in the Annotations to Table XXVIII, together with solar year equivalents for the variously applied units for case (a) above. Particular attention is directed to the evidence concerning the application to the period of Antiochus Epiphanes. This indicates pretty clearly that the prophecies of Daniel were in existence long prior to 168 B.C.

For a representative statement of the evolution of the Jewish Rabbinical systems of chronology—on the principles outlined above—the reader is referred to Table XXVIII at the end of this Section. Columns (1) to (7) inclusive show, for the system there indicated, that all original Hebrew dates prior to the 2nd year of Darius I could be altered to conform with the system adopted. They also show, however, that the actual dates identified as beginning and ending the period to which the 70 weeks' prophecy was applied were, in both cases, the actual A.K. dates of the original Hebrew chronology. In other words, elucidation of the fictitious construction of the Rabbinical systems shown in Columns (2) to (7) inclusive, confirm that the chronology of Column (1)—derived from the Old Testament—is the original Hebrew chronology. This, as we have seen in ¶¶ 312-322, is identical with the Pyramid's astronomically defined chronology, and with the original Egyptian and Babylonian systems of chronology.

An interesting explanation of the short Rabbinical chronology and of the modern Jewish system of chronology is given in Columns (8) and (9) of Table XXVIII. Both systems, when carefully compared with the statements of Columns (1) to (7), will be seen to confirm the original Hebrew chronology.

¶ 334. A RABBINICAL "OMISSION."

Another matter of importance concerns an important omission in the succession of units adopted by the Jews as defining the "day" of Daniel's "week" or Hebdomad. From the standpoint of Hebrew numerical symbolism, the number 14—equally with the number 12—was the most likely number, within the limits of 9 and 18 adopted (¶ 333), to be selected to define the number of lunar months of the "day" unit. To the Hebrew, 12 was the number of "governmental perfection," and 14 denoted *emphasis* in relation to progressive stages of "spiritual perfection." To the Hebrew, the Messianic kingdom was "governmental perfection." Hence the fact that the majority of Rabbinical interpretations of Daniel's 70 weeks are concerned with "day" units of 12 lunar months, or of 12 divisions of the solar year. The true Hebrew, however, realised—what the post-exilic Jew, in general, failed to realise—that the initial stage in the prophesied cycle of the Messiah was to be effected by "Sacrifice," and that the Messiah is prefigured as the "Lamb."

Now in each day of the week of the Feast of Tabernacles 14 lambs were *Omitted that initial stage of the prophecy relates to Sacrifice.* sacrificed. Here the week, and the day unit of the week, are associated with 14 lambs and with sacrifice. The significance of this, in relation to the *Messiah prefigured as " The Lamb."* Messiah and to the Messianic time units, was known to the Hebrew of the New Testament. Thus Matthew i, 17 gives as follows :—

14 lambs sacrificed daily during the Feast of Tabernacles

Abraham to David	..	..	..	=14 generations.
David to the Jewish Exile	..	..	=14 generations.
The Jewish Exile to Christ	..	..	=14 generations.

The Messianic time unit.

¶ 335. " DESPISED AND REJECTED."

Now Daniel ix, 25 and 26 states that " from the commandment to restore *The datum of Daniel's 70 weeks.* and to build Jerusalem unto Messiah the Prince " shall be 7+62=69 weeks. Only one *Divine Command* is referred to,[1] and this is given at the end of the *The command to build.* 70 years' Divine Indignation (¶ 331). The command is dated in the 2nd *Only one Divine command referred to, that of 2nd Darius I, 520 B.C. =3480 A.K.* year of Darius I, *i.e.* in 520 B.C.=3480 A.K., Pyramid chronology. The Hebrew date is also 3480 A.K. (Table XXVIII).

Daniel continues that the Messiah " shall be cut off " " after " the *The Messiah to be " cut off " after 69 weeks.* 7+62=69 weeks. The statement agrees with the other statements of the Old Testament concerning " Sacrifice "—" but not for Himself," says *A prophecy of sacrifice.* Daniel. The Jews, we know, accepted every " Messiah " but Christ. Every " Messiah " but Christ claimed to lead by physical prowess. Christ led by *The Hebrew sacrificial lamb prefigures the sacrifice of the " Lamb of God."* service and sacrifice, and claimed to be the " lamb " of prophecy. This is the first phase of the Messiah-cycle of the Old Testament prophecy, pre-figured by the 14 lambs sacrificed each day of the week from the Feast of *The 14 lambs sacrificed daily during the week of the Feast of Taber-nacles adopted in the New Testament as prefiguring Christ.* Tabernacles. Hence that John i, 14 speaks of Christ as follows : " The Word was made flesh and dwelt (Greek—" tabernacled ") among us (and we beheld His glory, the glory as of the only begotten son of the Father) full of grace and truth."

Hence the significance of the Jewish Rabbinical omission of 14 as applied *The significant omission of 14 by the Jews as the unit of Daniel's 70 weeks.* to the " day " unit of Daniel's 70 weeks.

¶ 336. THE MESSIANIC 69 WEEKS' PERIOD.

Let us adopt 14 lunations—as the Jews did for every number but 14 *69 " weeks " of 14 lunations per " day "* from 9 to 18—for the " day " unit of the week of Daniel. " Unto Messiah the Prince " was to be a period of 69 weeks. Sixty-nine weeks of 14 luna-*=6762 luna-tions =546.7205 solar years.* tions per " day "=6762 lunations=546.7205 solar years=546 Julian years +259.336 days. Dated from the Divine Command at 3480 A.K. (520 B.C.), *Period ex-tended from Divine com-mand date (520 B.C.) to 1st year of Christ's ministry in 28 A.D.* this interval terminates in the first half of the summer of 28 A.D. (*i.e.* 4026½ A.K.). Now, whatever opinion is followed as to the chronology of Christ's life, one fact is certain. This is that His ministry began not later than

[1]Apart from this, the statements of 1 Esdras iv, 43, 47, 53, 63 ; v, 2, 6, declare that Darius, in Nisan of his 2nd year (the Spring of 520 B.C.) gave Zerobabel letters and a thousand horsemen to protect his party, " that they should come from Babylonia to *build the city* . . . to build Jerusalem and the Temple." Compare Ezra iv, 21 continuously to vi, 15 (referring ¶ 331 *re* " Darius even Artaxerxes" in vi, 14) ; and Haggai i, 1-15, particularly comparing 1 Esdras above with Haggai i, 4.

28 A.D., and terminated not earlier than 29 A.D., or later than 30 A.D. (refer ¶¶ 328, 329). The calculation noted, therefore, shows why the Jews omitted 14 lunations from their theories concerning the value of Daniel's time units for the 70 weeks. It also shows that Daniel's prophecy—as interpreted by the unit harmonising with the Old Testament allegorical type of the Sacrifice of the Lamb—was fulfilled by the Ministry of our Lord.

Confirmed by known range of datings for Christ's Ministry.

This shows why the Jews, who rejected Christ, rejected the unit of 14 lunations.

Again, Daniel's prophecy (ix, 25, 26) states that " after the 7+62=69 weeks shall Messiah be cut off, but not for Himself." Taken literally, and in conjunction with verse 27, there is no statement concerning Messiah being " cut off " at 69½ weeks. It is merely " after " 69 weeks. Now the 69 " weeks " ended in the summer of 28 A.D. Our Lord was crucified certainly in the spring of 29 A.D. or 30 A.D. ; no other year is possible. The prophecy of Daniel ix, 25 and 26 was therefore fulfilled by the ministry and death of our Lord; and by the adoption of the one unit of time prefigured by the Old Testament, and ignored by the Jews.

¶ 337. THE WEEK OF "LIVING WITNESSES."

No one prior to Eusebius identified the ceasing of " the sacrifice and oblation " with the " cutting off " of Messiah ; nor, prior to him, did anyone identify the duration of Christ's ministry with the exact duration of the initial half of the 70th week.

The mystery of the 70th week and the emphasis concerning a terminal period of " one week."

The covenant of the week.

The New Testament and the week of " living witnesses."

The early Christian Church of the 1st century.

The scattering abroad of the power of the holy people.

Daniel *nowhere* refers to a bisection of the 70th week. He refers in ix, 27 to a period of " one week " during which " He shall confirm the covenant with many." As pointed out by the best Hebrew scholars, the " He " referred to is the Messiah. The covenant is therefore the New Testament. This could only be brought into effect by the ministration and death of the Testator—Jesus Christ Himself. The " one week " of verse 27 can only apply to a week of " living witnesses "—the early Christian Church of the 1st century A.D.—prior to the schisms of the 2nd century, and prior to its " scattering " abroad at the beginning of that century. The latter phase seems to be portrayed in Daniel xii, 7 as " the scattering of the power of the holy people."

The one week and its longer duration.

In the mid-period of the early Christian Church falls the destruction of Jerusalem and the " ceasing of the sacrifice and oblation."

The " one week " of verse 27 is obviously a longer period than the unit week of the 69 weeks prior to 28 A.D. If Hebrew prophetic units follow the Pyramid system of units, as the Hebrew chronology follows the Pyramid chronology, then the lengthened unit should be ten times the initial period unit. The initial period unit is a week-unit of 7×14 lunations $=7.92348$ solar years. The lengthened unit should therefore be 79.2348 solar years. $=7 \times 140$ lunations.

Now the 69 weeks ended in the summer of 28 A.D. The " one week " of verse 27 should end 79.2348 solar years later, towards the end of 107 A.D. or near the beginning of 108 A.D. This falls within the reign of Trajan, in whose reign died St. John, the writer of the Apocalypse, and the last survivor of the " living witnesses " (see Rev. i, 2 and 13).

Now Daniel ix, 27 states that " in the *midst of* (*i.e.* not the *bisection* of) the week He shall cause *the sacrifice and oblation* to cease, and for the over-spreading of abominations He shall make it (Jerusalem) desolate........" Our Lord Himself shows[1] that the latter refers to the Roman siege and destruction of Jerusalem and the Temple. The exact *bisection* of the " one week " of 79.2348 solar years from the end of the 69 weeks in the summer of 28 A.D. falls in the spring of 68 A.D. The Jewish war began in the spring of 66 A.D., and Jerusalem and the Temple were destroyed in the summer of 70 A.D., when the " sacrifice and oblation " ceased. The " sacrifice and oblation " therefore ceased " *in the midst of* " the week of " living witnesses."

This confirms that the terminal " one week " was ten times the duration of each of the 69 weeks.

We cannot fail to see, however, that the 70 weeks were also fulfilled precisely as 70 weeks of 14 lunations per day. With this application, the 70th week extended from 28½ A.D. to 36½ A.D.—from the first year of our Lord's ministry to the martyrdom of Stephen, or possibly the conversion of Saul of Tarsus (*Enc. Brit.*, 11th Edit., Vol. III, p. 893, second column). Our Lord's Crucifixion *in the course of* this 70th week, by annulling the daily sacrifice of the Law, thereby prefigured the literal ceasing of the Daily Sacrifice *in the course of* the longer 70th week, reckoned from the same date of commencement as the shorter 70th week, but ten times longer in duration. This, in fact, seems to be implied by the significant fact that Daniel ix does not *specifically* identify the " one week " of verse 27 as belonging to the units of the 70 weeks of verses 24 and 25, and the first half of verse 26. That " one week," by its significant emphasis, appears to stand alone, and yet, as we have seen, it is related to the 69 weeks as a 70th week of ten times longer duration.

The significant emphasis of Daniel ix, 27. The " one week " as related to the 70 weeks and the 69 weeks.

Now we have seen the striking repetition of week-day and lunar month datings in the Exodus year and in the Crucifixion year (¶¶ 325–327). We have also seen that the repetition applies to 30 A.D., when the Exodus year solar datings are also repeated, as is specifically indicated by the Pyramid (¶¶ 328 and 329). We find this repetition continuing in relation to 30 A.D. and 70 A.D. For their unbelief Israel were left to wander 40 years in the wilderness of Sinai—from the Exodus to the entry into Canaan. Following the Crucifixion, 40 years intervened from the date-repeating year 30 A.D. to the destruction of Jerusalem and the Temple in 70 A.D.

Repetitions of week-days and days of the month and luni-solar year. The 40 years succeeding the Exodus of Israel. The 40 years succeeding the Exodus of Christ.

Again, in Isaiah vii, 8, a period of 65 years is allocated for the breaking-up of the ten-tribed Kingdom of Israel. From the destruction of Jerusalem in 70 A.D. to the last Jewish war that ended the fearful rebellion of the pseudo-Messiah Bar Cochab in 135 A.D.—when the Jews were finally forbidden to enter Jerusalem, on penalty of death—is, again, an interval of 65 years.

The 65 years' breaking of Ephraim-Israel. The 65 years breaking of Judah-Israel.

---

[1]Compare in parallel columns, as follows :—

(a)	(b)	(c)
Luke xxi, 5–7	with Mark xiii, 1–4	with Matthew xxiv, 1–3 ;
„ 8–19	„ „ 5–13	„ „ 4–14 ;
„ 20	„ „ 14	„ „ 15.

Comparison of the latter verse of each Gospel effects the identity intended by Jesus. Then, Luke xxi, 21 onwards, with Mark xiii, 15 onwards, with Matthew xxiv, 16 onwards.

TABLE XI.

(A) DATED LIST OF KNOWN PHŒNIX CYCLES (Basis ¶ 314).

As the recurrence of the Phœnix cycle depended upon the ancient fixed calendar and its system of intercalation, the years of the Phœnix system of chronology are stated as "Anno Kalendarii," or abbreviated "A.K."

1. 6½ cycles of 329 years end in reign of last Hyksos king, 31½ years before Dynasty XVIII began   ..   2138½ A.K.=1861 B.C.
   Interval of one cycle   ..   329 years .. 329 years.
2. 7½ cycles of 329 years end in 27th year of Ramessu II (Dynasty XIX)   ..   2467½ A.K.=1532 B.C.
   Interval of one cycle   ..   329 years .. 329 years.
3. 8½ cycles of 329 years end in 12th year of Ramessu III (Dynasty XX)   ..   2796½ A.K.=1203 B.C.
   Interval of one cycle   ..   329 years .. 329 years.
4. 9½ cycles of 329 years end in 22nd year of Uasarkon II (Dynasty XXII)   ..   3125½ A.K.= 874 B.C.
   Interval of one cycle   ..   329 years .. 329 years.
5. 10½ cycles of 329 years end in 25th year of Amasis II (Dynasty XXVI)   ..   3454½ A.K.= 545 B.C.

(B) THE FICTITIOUS CHRONOLOGY OF THE EGYPTIAN KING LISTS BASED ON ERRONEOUS PERIOD OF THE PHŒNIX CYCLE (Refer ¶¶ 38, 39, 59, 105, 106, 317 and Table XV Annotations (D)).

Africanus.

3rd year[1] of Senusert I, of Dynasty XII, at   ..   2325 years of system.
(refer Table XV.)
Add 2 nominal Solar cycles of 1521½ years   ..   3043 years.

Total duration of Dynasties (alleged)   ..   ..   5368 years, omitting Interregnum (including Interregnum gives reign of Amasis II)

Africanus.
Book I,   added Dynastic totals   ..   2283 years.
Book II, added Dynastic totals   ..   2217 years.
Book III, added Dynastic totals   ..   868 years.
_____
5368 years

3rd year of Senusert I (Sesostris), when the Calendar began in Mid-November
Add 1 nominal Egyptian Solar cycle (refer ¶¶ 59, 105 and 106)   ..   ..   2325 years' duration of system.
Last Hyksos king (Dynasty XVI) revised the Calendar 31 years prior to Dynasty XVIII, at alleged   1521 years.
_____
3846 years' duration of system.

Duration of Hyksos Dynasty after Calendar alteration   ..   ..   31 years
Dynasty XVII, erroneously added by Africanus as succeeding Dynasty XVI   ..   151 years } 445 yrs.
Dynasty XVIII, as stated by Africanus   ..   ..   263 years
Dynasty XIX, as stated by Africanus   ..   ..   209 years.
Book III, Dynasties XX to XXXI inclusive, as added from Africanus   ..   868 years.

445 years.
55 years Africanus for Sethos.
_____
500 years of alleged Phœnix Cycle from Hyksos Calendar alteration to 1st year of Ramessu II (refer ¶ 38).

1 nominal Egyptian Solar cycle (refer ¶¶ 59, 105 and 106)   ..   ..   1522 years.   1522 years.
End of reigns of human kings prior to Alexander the Great, when the Calendar again began in Mid-November (but refer previous identity with Amasis II, Table XV Annotations (D)) 5 ..   5368 years' duration of system.

[1] The original Sesostris of Tradition was Senusert III (refer Table XV Annotations (D). All the kings called Senusert in Dynasty XII were later identified as Sesostris. Hence Senusert I was supposed to have been the original Sesostris.

The Sed heb of the 3rd year of Senusert I was confused with the cycle of 1461 years that ended in the 7th year of Senusert III (the real Sesostris). The latter cycle was confused with the Phœnix cycle (¶ 317) and Table XV Annotations (D) as were also the cycles of 1522 years (¶¶ 59, 105 and 106) and 500 years (¶ 38). The 3rd year Sed heb of Senusert I was at 22 years duration of Dynasty XII (Table XVI). Africanus gives the alternative added total to 2309 years (Plate XVI, Table B). Hence the basal 22 years of above statement give the total of 2325 years.

ANNOTATIONS TO TABLE XI.

(Refer also ¶¶ 48—63, 73—75d. 214, and 250—253).

(1)
THE PHŒNIX CYCLE OF THE HYKSOS.
B.C. 1861.

At this date, the last Hyksos' king (Asseth of the Lists) introduced a new year-beginning. Until this date, the *Egyptian Civil Year* had consisted of a calendar year of 360 days intercalated on the 103 years' cycle (¶¶ 31 and 63 and Tables II–IV). An intercalated year of 365 days had existed contemporaneously. Asseth adopted the latter for the Egyptian Civil Year. Obviously his intention was to intercalate the year, thus adopted, to synchronise periodically with the Hyksos' native luni-solar year.

The Egyptian War of Independence intervened before the date of the intended first intercalary year. No intercalations were made during the war. The XVIIIth Egyptian Dynasty therefore received the inheritance of the vague (un-intercalated) year. The Egyptian priests found it a useful adjunct to their policy of State control (¶¶ 123-125), and, while retaining and observing secretly the known ancient cycles, put a curse on any king who should dispense with the vague year.

In 1861 B.C., the Phœnix Cycle ended at 2138¼ A.K. Asseth celebrated the 1st year of the new cycle by beginning Day I Month I of the Egyptian Calendar coincident with the day of the *astronomical* new moon nearest the Autumnal Equinox 2139 A.K. Day 1 Month I in B.C. 1861, therefore=30th Sept. (Julian)=14 Sept. (Greg.), thus cancelling the ancient November Agricultural year until then in use in Egypt.

Day 1 Month I=30 Sept. (Julian) in B.C. 1861 forms the basis for all XVIII Dyn. vague calendar datings and until the 27th year of Ramessu II, B.C. 1532.

The initial 31 years (as Table XIB) being required to complete the alleged cycles of 1522 and 500 years, confirms the astronomical Phœnix dating as 31 years prior to Dyn. XVIII beginning. Dyn. XVII is known as contemporaneous with Hyksos.

(2)
THE PHŒNIX CYCLE OF RAMESSU II.
B.C. 1532.

The vanity of Ramessu II had led him to adopt the name of the legendary Sesostris (Maspero "Struggle Nations" p. 426), originally Senusert III. At the new Phœnix date, in the 27th year of Ramessu II, Ramessu adjusted the Calendar to make the heliacal rising of Sirius occur on Day 1 Month I. The identity, thus effected, is noted in inscriptions at Medinet Habu and in the Ramesseum. Adopting his 27th year as an epoch for a series of *pseudo*-Sed Hebs at short intervals, Ramessu II celebrated *pseudo*-Sed Hebs—or 'End festivals'—in his 30th, 33rd, 34th, 36th, 37th, 40th, and 46th regnal years.

The purpose of this series of festivals was to legalise a corresponding series of experimental Calendar intercalations devised to ensure that a heliacal rising of Sirius would occur again on Day 1 Month I at the next Phœnix date 2796¼ A.K. or B.C. 1203. Here we see the first fictitious chronological scheme in operation, and its motive. The scheme was obviously devised to represent that the 1461 years' cycle, that ended in the 7th year Senusert III, had repeated itself in B.C. 1203; that the 7th year of Senusert III, as alleged, was therefore 2664 B.C., and that the Phœnix cycle was a cycle of 1461 years. The evidence also seems to indicate the desire of Ramessu II to appear as the original Sesostris.

A complaint concerning the confusion arising from the revision effected by Ramessu II, appears in the Anastasi Papyrus IV, of the time of Menephtah.

The datings of Ramessu II and the Hyksos Epoch are independently fixed (1) by the astronomical datings of Dyn. XVIII (Table XIV Annotations). (2) By the Sed Hebs of Table XVI.

Refer next columns for resulting vague year datum.

(3)
THE PHŒNIX CYCLE OF RAMESSU III.
B.C. 1203.

The Calendar revision of Ramessu II (Column 2) was completed at his last *pseudo*-Sed Heb in his 46th year, B.C. 1513. The final experimental adjustment, made in this year, placed Day 1 Month I coincident with 4th Oct. (Jul.) =20th Sept. (Greg.) to ensure that the slip back of the vague year, in the 310 years to the next Phœnix date at B.C. 1203, would bring Day 1 Month I into coincidence with the heliacal rising of Sirius in that year.

From 1513 B.C. the vague year remained undisturbed until the Phœnix date 874 B.C., the 22nd year of Uasarkon II. At the intermediate recurrence of the Phœnix date, in B.C. 1203, vague Day 1 Month I fell on 19th July (Julian), which is the date of the heliacal rising of Sirius in that year. The identity therefore occurred as Ramessu II had arranged it should occur.

At the Temple of Medinet Habu, the heliacal rising of Sirius on Day 1 Month I is noted on work of the 12th year Ramessu III, which fixes that 12th year as 1203 B.C., and therefore the accession of Set-Nekht, the first King of Dyn. XX (who reigned 1 year) at B.C. 1215. Manetho's 868 years for Book III then gives, from the latter date, 2784¼ A.K.=B.C. 1215, the Epoch of Okhos as 3652¼ A.K.=B.C. 347, which is correct (¶ 214).

The 12th year dating of Ramessu III for the heliacal rising of Sirius was formerly suggested tentatively as a Sothic cycle prior to A.D. 139 (Rec. Past. 2nd Ser. Vol. VI. pp. 2, 3, and 6). Similarly the 27th year Ramessu II was originally adopted by Mahler (*Ibid.*, p. 148) as a Sothic cycle prior to A.D. 139, the Sirius datum of Censorinus.

Refer Column 5 for associated data confirming.

(4)
THE PHŒNIX CYCLE OF UASARKON II.
B.C. 874.

Uasarkon II, in his 22nd year, celebrated the new Phœnix date by instituting a new Epoch for the vague year. He omitted the 1st calendar month (*Mesore*) from the last year of the old cycle, purposely to begin the new cycle with Day 1 Month I at the Vernal Equinox. Actually 29 days were omitted. The alteration placed Thoth—hitherto Month II—as Month I.

The precise extent of alteration was ruled by another requirement. This was that the 2nd Calendar Season should begin at Summer Solstitial full moon, thus forming the precedent for the early Greek Olympic year-beginning. Thus, by the revision, Day 1 Month I=30th Mar. (Julian)=22nd Mar. (Greg.) and Day 1 Month IV=28th June (Julian)=21st June (Greg.); the latter date, in B.C. 874 being full moon date. Hence that Uasarkon II, in his 22nd year celebrated an astronomical festival on Day 1 Month IV and named it a *Sed heb*.

Prior to this year, the vague year datum is the 46th year of Ramessu II, the year of the last *pseudo-Sed heb* of that king (Col. 3). Thus in the 3rd year Uasarkon II (B.C. 893), the high Nile at Thebes is recorded for Day 12 Month V. By calculation this is 11th Sept. (Julian) =3rd Sept. (Greg.) B.C. 893. Col. Ross, quoted by Lockyer, gives corresponding high Nile as generally 1st to 8th Sept. (Greg.), prior to Assouan Dam. The calendar dating therefore agrees on the vague year datum of cols. 2 and 3. But by the usually accepted vague year datum of Censorinus, extended back prior to 874 B.C., the high Nile dating of Uasarkon is a month too early. Such a displacement is unknown for ancient or modern times.

Refer next column for associated data confirming.

(5)
THE PHŒNIX CYCLE OF AMASIS II.
B.C. 545.

Tacitus states that a Phœnix cycle ended in the reign of Amasis II, and that the cycle was confused with the 1461 and 500 years' period. Hence the fictitious systems of Tables XI (B) Plate XVI and Table XV Annotations (D).

The identity is generally associated, in the Lists, with the last year of Amasis II.

By Column 3, Dyn. XX began 2784¼ A.K., and the Egyptian Dynasties ended, 868 years later, at 3652¼ A.K. (as in *Old Chronicle*). The totals of Africanus, adding 868 as above, being placed beginning at 2784¼ A.K., give Amasis II ending at his Phœnix date, 3454¼ A.K. Africanus therefore confirms the 2 Phœnix cycles from 12th year Ramessu III to reign of Amasis II. The *Old Chronicle*, again, gives 1st year Ramessu II (following alleged 55 years of Sethos, as Eusebius) as 2467¼ A.K., and as 1 Phœnix cycle prior to the 12th year Ramessu III, the interval including the *Old Chronicle's* interregnum of 178 years (Plate XVI Table E) and the 1 year of Set-Nekht.

(a) Eusebius also gives 1 Phœnix cycle from 1st year Dyn. XX to 22nd year Dyn. XXII, *in lieu* of 22nd year Uasarkon II of Dyn. XXII.

(b) Again, from the Phœnix date of Uasarkon II, B.C. 874 to the actual end of reign Amasis II at B.C. 525, is an interval of 349 years; and 349 years is the total in Eusebius for Dyn. XXII to Amasis both inclusive.

Eusebius, therefore, represents Dyn. XXII as beginning (a) in 895 B.C., or 308 years after the Phœnix date of Ramessu III; and (b) in 874 B.C. the Phœnix year of Uasarkon II.

The former (a) is the true date of the beginning of the reign of Uasarkon II and the latter (b) is the true date of the 22nd year of Uasarkon II (Column 4). This shows that the version of Eusebius erroneously placed Uasarkon II as the 1st King of Dyn. XXII, or *vice versa*, thus omitting 1st 3 actual reigns prior to Uasarkon II. The known duration of these 1st 3 reigns is 71 years, and the difference between the versions of Eusebius and Africanus for Dyn. XXII is 71 years;

TABLE XII.
DYNASTY XVIII.

True Succession (Petrie).	True Succession of Manetho's Names (Petrie).	Order in Africanus.	Order in Eusebius.	Order in Josephus.	Equivalent Monumental Names.	Highest known mon'l. year.	Josephus. Yrs. Mos.	Petrie's accepted duration. Yrs. Mos.	Petrie's Authorities.
1	Amos or Amosis (I)	1	1	—	Aahmes I	22		25-0	Eusebius from Manetho.
2	Amenophthis	3	3	3	Amenhotep I	—	20-7	20-7	Josephus, Africanus, and Eusebius.
3	Tuthmosis	—	—	(1)	Tahutmes I	9	25-4	25-4	Josephus.
4	Khebros or Khebron	2 and 12	2	2	Tahutmes II, conjointly with Hatshepsut	9	13-0	13-0	Josephus, Africanus, and Eusebius.
5	Amensis	4	—	4	Hatshepsut, co-regent for initial 21 yrs. 9 mths. of Tahutmes III	22	21-9	53-10	Monuments, initial 21 yrs. 9 mths. co-regency with Tahutmes III.
6	Miphris or Misaphris	5	4	5	Tahutmes III	54	12-9		Monuments, Josephus, Africanus, and Eusebius.
7	Misphragmuthosis	6	5	6	Amenhotep II	26	25-10	25-10	Josephus, Africanus, and Eusebius.
8	Tuthmosis	7	6	7	Tahutmes IV	7	9-8	9-10	Josephus, Africanus, and Eusebius.
9	Amenophis	8	7	8	Amenhotep III	36	30-10	30-10	Josephus, Africanus, and Eusebius.
10	Oros	9	8	9	Amenhotep IV (Akhen-Aten)	17	36-5	18-0	Monuments
11	Acherres	10	10	10	Ra-Smenkh-Ka	3	12-1	12-1	Josephus.
12	Rathos	11	11	11	Tut-Ankh-Amen	—	9-0	9-0	Josephus.
13	Akherres	13	11	12	Ay (Kheper-Kheperu-Ari-Maat-Ra)	4	12-5	12-5	Josephus and Africanus.
14	Armais	14	12	14	Hor-em-heb	21	4-1	4-1	Josephus, Africanus, and Eusebius.

233- 9
25

Add for Amosis omitted

| TOTAL | | | | | | | 258- 9 | 259-10 | |

Castor's Total .. .. .. 261 years.
Total of Africanus (stated) .. .. 263 years.
Total of Africanus (added) .. .. 259 years.

The complete statement of Josephus includes Achencherres (III) as 13th king for 12 years 3 months. There is no monumental place for this name. Petrie considers that the entry is a duplication due to Acherres and Ackerres occurring already as 12 years 1 month and 12 years 5 months, respectively.

Inscriptions at the Temple of Serabit in Sinai confirm that Hatshepsut was co-regent with Tahutmes III during the first 22 years of the latter's reign. Apart from this, other evidence determines that the 16th year of Amenhotep III, was the 3rd year of Tahutmes III.
Petrie explains that 36 years for Amenhotep III, as against 30 years 10 months from Josephus, is due to co-regency.
Petrie explains that 36 years 5 months in Josephus for Amenhotep IV is the duration of the Aten worship founded by that king.
Petrie explains that the 21 years of Hor-em-heb are dated from his first year of generalship (semi-independent), but, nevertheless 17 years prior to his actually becoming king.

TABLE XIII.

Dynasty XIX.	Highest Monumental Year.		Book of the Sothis, sole stated names.
Ramessu I	2		
Seti I	9		
Ramessu II	67	.. .. ..	Ramessus (II) .. 68 years
Menephtah (with Seti II co-regent for not more than 4 years)	8	.. .. ..	Amenophis .. 8 years.
Amenmeses	1		
(Si-ptah, and) Tausert	6	.. .. ..	Thouris .. .. 17 years.
Total	93 years, added as complete years ..		.. 93 years.

Africanus' stated totals of Dynasties XII to XIX inclusive (Book II) add as	2222 years.	The Old Chronicle and Eusebius for Dynasty XIX give ..	194 years.
Deduct	101 years.	Deduct	101 years.
Africanus' stated total for Book II	2121 years.	Actual duration, as above ..	93 years.

The Book of Sothis, as above, gives

Ramesses, = Ramessu II, following Armaios, = Hor-em-heb in Dynasty XVIII	68 years, as monuments.
Amenophis, = Menephtah	8 years, as monuments.
Thouris, = Tausert	17 years.
Actual known, and astronomically confirmed, duration of Dynasty XIX	93 years, as above.

To this statement, Africanus has interpolated

Seti I as Sethos	51 years.	
Pseudo-Ramesses	60 years.	Refer Note (2) to Annotations (D) Table XXVIII re 111 years' interpolation.
Total interpolated	111 years.	
Known duration	93 years.	
Added total of Africanus for Dynasty XIX ..	204 years.	

	Josephus, as quoted by Budge, "Book of the Kings," Vol. I.		Highest Monumental Year.	Confirming details from the Lists.
Ramessu I ..	Ramesses (I) ..	1 yr. 4 mths. ..	2 ..	Africanus gives one year.
Seti I ..	..		9 ..	
Ramessu II ..	Armesses Miammi..	66 yrs. 2 mths. ..	67 ..	Book of the Sothis and Eusebius give 68 years.
Menephtah ..	Amenophis ..	19 yrs. 6 mths. ..	8 ..	As Book of the Sothis and Armenian Version of Eusebius.
Ramessu I to Menephtah inclusive	87 years ..	..	86 years. added as complete years.	

TABLE XIV.

CHRONOLOGY OF EGYPTIAN DYNASTIES XVIII AND XIX.

Fixed by Tables XI (and Annotations), XII and XIII and confirmed by Table XIV.

	King.	Date of Reign A.K.	Date of Reign B.C.
	Dynasty XVIII.		
1	Aahmes (Amosis I)	2170½–2195½	1829–1804
2	Amenhotep I	2195½–2216½	1804–1784
3	Tahutmes I	2216½–2231½	1784–1768
4	Tahutmes II conjointly during last 13 years with Queen Hatshepsut	2231½–2254½	1768–1745
5 & 6	Tahutmes III with Hatshepsut during his initial 21¾ years	2254½–2308½	1745–1691
7	Amenhotep II	2308½–2334½	1691–1665
8	Tahutmes IV	2334½–2344	1665–1656
9	Amenhotep III	2344 –2375	1656–1625
10	Akhenaten=Amenhotep IV	2375 –2393	1625–1607
11	Ra-smenkh-ka	2393 –2405	1607–1595
12	Tut-ankh-Amen	2405 –2414	1595–1586
13	Ay	2414 –2426½	1586–1573
14	Hor-em-heb	2426½–2430½	1573–1569
	Dynasty XIX (Refer Plate LXI and Annotations).		
1	Ramessu I	2430½–2432½	1569–1567
2	Seti I	2432½–2441½	1567–1558
3	Ramessu II	2441½–2508½	1558–1491
4	Menephtah with Seti II co-regent 5th to 6th years	2508½–2516½	1491–1483
5	Amenmeses	2516½–2517	1483–1483
6	Si-ptah and Tausert	2517 –2523	1483–1477

ANNOTATIONS TO TABLE XIV.

The chronology is astronomically fixed as follows :—

(1) Dyn. XVIII is fixed as beginning in 2170 A.K., 31¼ years after Day 1 Month 1 of 2139 A.K. by Table XI (A) and (B) and Annotations Column (1).

(2) Dyn. XIX is independently fixed as beginning in 2430 A.K., 37 to 37½ years before the Phoenix dating of the 27th year Ramessu II, by Table XI (A) and Annotations Column (2), and by monumental years of Table XIII.

(3) The dates of commencement of Dyns. XVIII and XIX, being thus astronomically fixed, give the duration of Dyn. XVIII as 260 years, this agreeing with Petrie's independently derived duration of Dyn. XVIII Table XII.

The statement of chronology for Dyn. XVIII, as above, is confirmed by the following identities relating to recorded heliacal risings of Sirius :—

(4) (a) A heliacal rising of Sirius was observed on Day 9 Month XI of 9th year Amenhotep III.=2203¼-2204½ A.K. (Table XIV).

(b) Sirius rose heliacally at Memphis on 18th July (Julian) 2203½ A.K.=1796 B.C.

(c) By Table XI Annotations Column (1), Day 9 Month XI in 1796 B.C. coincided with 19th July (Julian).

Lockyer observes that the early morning ground mists of Egypt might cause a heliacal rising to be observed a day late, as an observation from the darkened interior of a temple could date a heliacal rising a day earlier.

(5) (a) A heliacal rising of Sirius was observed on Day 28 Month XI in the 33rd year Tabutmes III=2286½-2287½ A.K. (Table XIV).

(b) Sirius rose heliacally at Memphis on 18th July (Julian) 2286½ A.K.=1713 B.C. (Plate LX).

(c) By Table XI Annotations Column (1), Day 28 Month XI in 1713 B.C. coincided with 17th July (Julian). Refer Note to (a) above.

(6) (a) By repetitions of the 103 years cycle of Table III, new cycles began at 2163 A.K. and 2266 A.K.

(b) By (4) and (5) above the heliacal risings were observed in years 2203 A.K. and 2286 A.K., respectively 20 and 40 years after the beginning of the 103 years' cycles.

(c) The two intervals—respectively 7305 and 14610 days according to the intercalated 365 days' year of Table III—confirm that the heliacal risings were being observed in relation to the vague year and the securely observed intercalated year. Refer Table XI Annotations Column 1 and ¶¶ 123-125.

The Chronology of Dyn. XVIII, again, is confirmed by the following identities relating to recorded new moon festivals, defined by Tabutmes III as held 17 days after the preceding full moon :—

(7) (a) A festival of the new moon was held on Day 21 Month IX of the 23rd year of Tabutmes III=2276½-2277½ A.K. (Table XIV), given as 17 days after the Full Moon of the Coronation Anniversary on Day 4 Month IX.

(b) By calculation the full moon occurred about midnight 26th April (Julian).

(c) By Table XI Annotations Column (1) Day 4 Month IX coincided with 26th April (Julian), thus confirming the recorded observation, and the fact of the Festival of the New Moon being held 17 days later on Day 21 Month IX.

(8) (a) A Festival of the new moon was held on Day 30 Month VI of the 24th year of Tabutmes III=2277½-2278½ A.K. (Table XIV); being, presumably, as in 7 (a), 17 days after the preceding Full Moon of Day 13 Month VI.

(b) By calculation, the full moon occurred on the evening of 4th February (Julian) so that the Festival of the new moon should have fallen on the evening of 21st February (Julian).

(c) By Table XI Annotations Column (1), Day 13 Month VI began at sunset of 4th February (Julian) and Day 30 Month VI began at sunset of 21st February (Julian).

The same datings, as concerning the placing of the vague calendar year in relation to the seasons, are confirmed by the Syrian harvest datings of Tabutmes III.

The statement of chronology for Dynasty XIX is confirmed by the following identities :—

(9) (a) By the datum of Table XI Annotations, Column (1), Day 1 Month I had receded back to coincidence with the heliacal rising of Sirius on 19th July, 2433½ A.K. =Tab. year 2435½ of Plate LX.

(b) By the chronological and historical data of Plate LXI, the later year, 2433 A.K. began the first year of coregency of Ramessu I, which included the beginning of 2434 A.K.

(c) Later Egyptian tradition, as preserved in the King Lists of Manetho and in the Old Egyptian Chronicle, identified the beginning of a Phoenix cycle with the 1st year of Ramessu II (Table XI Annotations, Col. 5), confusing the identity above with the Phoenix cycle of the 27th year Ramessu II, when the revision of the Calendar (Table XI Annotations, Col. 2) again made Day 1 Month I include the heliacal rising of Sirius.

(10) (a) The short period pseudo-sed hebs of Ramessu II ended in his 46th year, 2486½- 2487½ A.K. (Table XI Annotations Col. 2. and Table XIV).

(b) Resumption of the normal series of Sed hebs, beginning from the 46th year of Ramessu II, would give the first 30 years' Sed heb period ending in 2516½- 2517½ A.K.

(c) The latter date gives the 1st year of Amenmeses (Table XIV) as fixed by the monumental and literary data of Table XIII. There should therefore be a Sed heb record of the 1st year of Amenmeses.

(d) Amenmeses died before the completion of his 1st year, and has left a record of a Sed heb.

TABLE XV.

THE CHRONOLOGY OF DYNASTY XII.

King's Name.	Total Duration of each reign. Years.	Duration of reign prior to Successor's Co-regency. Years.	Dated total period of each reign A.K.[1]	B.C.	Dated period of each reign prior to Successor's Co-regency. A.K.[1]	B.C.
Amenemhat I	30	.. 20	.. $1963\frac{1}{2}$–$1993\frac{1}{2}$ = 2036–2006	..	$1963\frac{1}{2}$–$1983\frac{1}{2}$ = 2036–2016	
Senusert I ..	45	.. 42	.. $1983\frac{1}{2}$–$2028\frac{1}{2}$ = 2016–1971	..	$1983\frac{1}{2}$–$2025\frac{1}{2}$ = 2016–1974	
Amenemhat II	38	.. 32	.. $2025\frac{1}{2}$–$2063\frac{1}{2}$ = 1974–1936	..	$2025\frac{1}{2}$–$2057\frac{1}{2}$ = 1974–1942	
Senusert II ..	19	.. 19	.. $2057\frac{1}{2}$–$2076\frac{1}{2}$ = 1942–1923	..	$2057\frac{1}{2}$–$2076\frac{1}{2}$ = 1942–1923	
Senusert III	38	.. 18	.. $2076\frac{1}{2}$–$2114\frac{1}{2}$ = 1923–1885	..	$2076\frac{1}{2}$–$2094\frac{1}{2}$ = 1923–1905	
Amenemhat III	46	.. 42	.. $2094\frac{1}{2}$–$2140\frac{1}{2}$ = 1905–1859	..	$2094\frac{1}{2}$–$2136\frac{1}{2}$ = 1905–1863	
Amenemhat IV	9	.. 5	.. $2136\frac{1}{2}$–$2145\frac{1}{2}$ = 1863–1854	..	$2136\frac{1}{2}$–$2141\frac{1}{2}$ = 1863–1858	
Sebekneferu ..	4	.. 4	.. $2141\frac{1}{2}$–$2145\frac{1}{2}$ = 1858–1854	..	$2141\frac{1}{2}$–$2145\frac{1}{2}$ = 1858–1854	

Basis:—¶¶ 315 and 316   ..   Deluge Datum   ..   1656 A.K.   Zero for new *Sed hebs*.

Recorded *Sed Hebs*:—   120 years.

1st year Senusert I.	.. ..	$1983\frac{1}{2}$–$1984\frac{1}{2}$ A.K.	1776 A.K. *Sep tep sed heb.*
Add 2 years ..	.. ..	2 2	120 years
3rd year Senusert I, and *Sed heb*		$1985\frac{1}{2}$–$1986\frac{1}{2}$ A.K.	1896 A.K. *Sep tep sed heb.*
Add 30 years ..	. ..	30 30	120 years.
33rd year Senusert I and *Sep tep sed heb*..	.. ..	$2015\frac{1}{2}$–$2016\frac{1}{2}$ A.K.	2016 A.K. *Sep tep sed heb.*

(1) As astronomically fixed, Dynasty XII began at   .. $1963\frac{1}{4}$ A.K.
Eusebius, for Duration of Dynasty XII   ..   ..   182 years.

End of Dynasty XII, as above   ..   ..   .. $2145\frac{1}{2}$ A.K.

(2) In the Appendix II, the short system from Africanus gives as follows:—
Ammenemes (Amenemhat I) begins at ..   ..   1962 A.K.
Africanus, for Ammenemes   ..   ..   ..   16 years.

1978 A.K.
Africanus for remaining years   ..   ..   ..   160 years for Dynasty XII.

"Vague Year" Epoch of last Hyksos king   ..   2138 A.K.   Phœnix Cycle at $2138\frac{1}{4}$ A.K.

(3) 19 cycles of 103 years ..   ..   1957 A.K.
Turin Papyrus, for Dynasty XII[2]   ..   ..   ..   213 years.

Beginning of XVIIIth Dynasty   ..   ..   ..   2170 A.K., as astronomically fixed.

[1] The A.K. datings are not guaranteed within ¼ year. Thus, the 7th year Senusert III, according to the Table, is $2082\frac{1}{4}$–¼ A.K., whereas the Sirius dating (¶ 317) shows that the regnal year extended to $2082\frac{3}{4}$ A.K.
[2] The List of the Turin Papyrus was compiled during late XVIIIth Dynasty, or early XIXth Dynasty. Its data as above by giving Dynasty XII terminating at the fixed astronomical date of Dynasty XVIII beginning confirm the early XIXth Dynasty Lists of Abydos and Sakkarah, which both place the kings of Dynasty XVIII following in succession after the kings of Dynasty XII.

ANNOTATIONS (A) TO TABLE XV.

(1)

THE DURATION OF DYNASTY XII REIGNS AND THEIR CHRONOLOGICAL PLACING.

The reigns and coregencies of the first 4 kings are fixed by their contemporary records to the 3rd year Senusert II. The latest contemporary record of Senusert II is of his 13th year and the Turin Papyrus gives him a reign of 19 years (Petrie, Brugsch, Maspero, Sayce, and Breasted). The duration, then, from Dynasty XII beginning to the death of Senusert II is 113 years, as fixed by Brugsch, Sayce, and Breasted.

No monumental or other evidence exists to show that Senusert III, who succeeded Senusert II, was partly coregent with the latter. In consequence, authorities are agreed that the regnal years of Senusert III, for the earlier portion of his reign, are years of sole rule. This is confirmed by the remarkable astronomical dating of the 7th year Senusert III, (refer ¶ 317) as defined in relation both to B.C. reckoning and the A.K. chronology of Table XV. The latter relationship, again, is confirmed by the evolution of the Dynastic Lists outlined in Annotations (D).

The contemporary records identify the XIIth Dynasty river improvement works at the 1st Cataract with the 8th year of Senusert III (¶¶ 319-321 and Table XXII and Annotations). The records show that to make these works effective the country South of the 1st Cataract was more effectively occupied (the Nubians being driven back or placed under subjection). This is a consequence to be noted also in regard to the similar river improvement works of the XVIIIth Dynasty of Kings.

The records indicate that the Southern activities of Senusert III continued up to his 19th year. Little activity in works or conquest is shown anywhere from the 19th year of Senusert III onwards in this reign, although Senusert III is known to have reigned 20 years longer. This fact suggests that Amenemhat III was associated as coregent in the 19th year of Senusert III. This suggestion receives confirmation from the fact that Amenemhat III, as early as his 2nd year, continued the work of his father. Now Amenemhat III is known to have reigned jointly with his father for an uncertain period. By making the joint rule date from the 19th year of Senusert III, the great irrigation and water storage works of Amenemhat III fall into chronological place as an immediate continuation of the work of Senusert III. (Refer Table XXII and Annotations.)

The last recorded dating of Amenemhat III is of his 46th year. From the monuments we know that his son, Amenemhat IV, reigned jointly with him for an uncertain period. The records of Amenemhat IV, as evidenced in his 5th year, supply an indication as to his first 4 years being jointly with his father. According to the Turin Papyrus, Amenemhat IV reigned 9 years, and was followed by his sister Sebekneferu for 4 years. The fact that the names of Amenemhat III and his daughter Sebekneferu occur at Hawara, while the name of Amenemhat IV is absent points to the 4 years of Sebekneferu having been jointly with the last 4 years of Amenemhat IV. This conclusion is confirmed by the Tablet of Abydos, which gives Amenemhat IV as the last ruler of Dynasty XII.

The resulting arrangement and chronology of Dynasty XII are stated on Table XV; the details obtained as above described, being confirmed as to total and chronological placing by the identities (1), (2), and (3) of Table XV.

For the evidence fixing that Dynasties XIII and XIV were contemporaneous with Dynasty XII and with the Hyksos, refer Annotations (B).

For further evidence fixing that the Hyksos were contemporaneous with Dynasty XII, refer Annotations B., relating to the Hyksos Mathematical Papyrus.

(2)

THE INCURSION OF THE HYKSOS IN RELATION TO DYNASTIES XII AND XVIII.

Table XV, by giving the interval of 25 years between the termination of Dynasty XII and the beginning of Dynasty XVIII, shows that the war of Egyptian independence and the expulsion of the Semitic Hyksos or Shepherd Kings is limited to this interval. The chronological sequence thus disclosed rejects the theory—and it has never been anything but a theory—that the Hyksos entirely dominated the whole of Egypt. During the rule of the XIIth Egyptian Dynasty, the monuments of the period show that Dynasty predominant. Other dynasties—as Annotations (B)—reigned contemporaneously, together with the Semitic Hyksos in the North. Access to the quarries of the South for building and monumental materials, together with the use of waterways, was either permitted to those Dynasties, or could not be prevented.

Referring to the domination of the Hyksos, Queen Hatshepsut of Dynasty XVIII, in a record in the rock cut temple near Beni-Hasan, states:—" There had been *Aamu* in the midst of the Delta and in Hauar (the Avaris of Manetho's account in Josephus), and the foreign hordes of their number had destroyed the ancient works; they reigned ignorant of the god, Ra." This record, while identifying the Hyksos with the *Aamu*—the Egyptian name for Asiatics—clearly limits their territory, in Egypt, to the delta. From this it seems clear enough that the power of these Aamu or Hyksos—except during the initial period of the War of Independence, and prior to that, except for occasional raids and expeditions to execute works within the domains of the contemporaneous Egyptian dynasties—did not extend far South of the Delta.

Now these *Aamu* first began to appear in Egypt in the 6th year of Senusert II, 2063 A.K. Khnem-hotep depicts and records, at Beni-Hasan, his receiving, in the year noted, 37 *Aamu* of *Shu*, whose chief Absha is given the title *heq setu*. The title *heq* (prince) combined with the racial name *Shu* is obviously the derivation (Heq-shu) of the name Hyksos. The deputation of 37 was obviously a detached party from a colony of these Aamu of Shu just settled in the Delta. The title, *heq setu*, applied to the leader Absha, is, moreover, as Petrie has pointed out, identical with the title applied to the Hyksos king Khyan User-en-Ra, whose name occurs below the position of Senusert III, and in a line of Kings parallel with the line of XIIth Dynasty kings, in the Karnak List of Tahutmes III.

Aamu of *Shu* were, therefore, settled in the Delta in the 6th year Senusert II, 2063 A.K. This settlement of the Hyksos in the Delta was, at first, a peaceful process, as is narrated by Manetho. It is not until the records of the reign of Amenemhat III are examined that evidence indicates the Hyksos becoming assertive. In the 2nd year of Amenemhat III trouble in the Delta is first indicated by the reference to an expedition to " open up the way of the *Aamu*," i.e., the Wady Tumilat, the road to the Sinai mines (refer Plate LXIII). The historical indications are completed by the XIIth Dynasty records at the Egyptian mining works in Sinai. These records show that actual hostilities between the Hyksos and the Egyptians did not commence until the end of Dynasty XII. They are dated as late as the 45th year of Amenemhat III, and the 7th year of Amenemhat IV, so that work continued at Sinai until 2144 A.K. = 1856 B.C., 1 year before the end of Dynasty XII. The lack of records, prior to the next dated inscription in Sinai, shows that the mines there lay idle until the reign of Amosis I of Dynasty XVIII.

" In the XIIIth Dynasty they seem to have been temporarily abandoned." Budge, "Hist. Egypt," III, 115.

"After a long period of neglect, during which no expeditions were sent to Sinai, we find offerings made by Aahmes " (1st King Dyn. XVIII after the expulsion of the Hyksos). Petrie, " Researches in Sinai," p. 102.

ANNOTATIONS (B) TO TABLE XV.

DYNASTIES XII AND XIII.

In regard to the order of succession of the kings of Dynasties XIII and XIV the Turin Papyrus List and the List of the Tablet of Karnak are in disagreement. To obtain a basis for succession, Egyptological authorities follow the order of the Turin Papyrus List, and to make the Karnak List agree, reverse the order in which the succession in the latter List is stated. It is asserted that this agrees with the archæological evidence as to sequence of style and workmanship of scarabs, etc. Assertions such as this, however, generally occur when the archæological evidence is most lacking. Thus, in this particular instance, the majority of the Turin Papyrus names are unknown on the monuments or scarabs. Few monuments belong to these kings, and such as do, belong to a small group of kings who can be identified as belonging to Dynasty XIII, but regarding whose relationship and order of succession the evidence is altogether doubtful.

That the Hyksos became aggressive before the end of Dynasty XIII is stated by Breasted (" History of Egypt," p. 214), and by Brugsch (" Egypt under the Pharaohs," Vol. I, p. 186). As Dynasty XIII has been shown to have been contemporary with Dynasty XII, and the date of the Hyksos' aggression identified with the end of the latter dynasty, the statements of Breasted and Brugsch leave little to be desired.

In the Tablet of Karnak, as originally placed on the walls of the Temple chamber, the names of the first three kings of Dynasty XIII appear as Kha-ka-Ra (?); Kha-nefer-Ra (Sebekhotep); and Kha-seshes-Ra (Neferhotep), and were opposite the names of the first three kings of Dynasty XII, Amenemhat I, Senusert I, and Amenemhat II, on the other side of the chamber, thus apparently implying contemporaneity (For data relating to the Karnak List refer Appendix).

The next name in the Karnak List of Dynasty XIII is that of Sekhem-suaz-taui-Ra (Sebekhotep). This king appears opposite the position of Senusert III, and is followed by Sekhem-khu-taui-Ra (Sebekhotep), opposite the position of Amenemhat III.

The next king of the XIIIth Dynasty, according to the succession of the Karnak List, is Sankh-ab-Ra, identified as Ameni-Antef-Amenemhat on a table of offerings at Cairo. In the Turin Papyrus—but in the reverse order of the Karnak List—a monumentally known king Ra-smenkh-ka, identified as Mer-Meshau, occurs between Sekhem-khu-taui-Ra and Sankh-ab-Ra Ameni-Antef-Amenemhat. As the latter, in the Karnak List, was placed opposite Amenemhat IV, in accordance with the scheme of the List indicating contemporaneity, the position of Mer-Meshau should be contemporaneous with Amenemhat III.

Bearing in mind these facts implying contemporaneity, the following parallel series of circumstances are to be observed :—

DYNASTY XII.	DYNASTY XIII.
	(1) KHA-KA-RA........No inscriptions or works.
(1) AMENEMHAT I.	
	(2) KHA-NEFER-RA (SEBEKHOTEP) ⎫ co-regent
(2) SENUSERT I	(3) KHA-SESHES-RA (NEFERHOTEP) ⎭
(1) and (2) above, granite statues at Tanis ..	(2) above, granite statue at Tanis.
(1) and (2) above, works at Karnak	(2) above, sculpture at Karnak.
	(2) and (3) above, cartouches of co-regency at Karnak.
The noble Ameny (or Amenemhat) succeeds as Prince of the Oryx nome in the 18th year of (2) above.	The general Amenemhat (or Ameny) represented as adoring (2) above, at Karnak.
Expeditions of Ameny to Nubia.	

Petrie (" History of Egypt," Vol. I, 10th Ed., p. 172) states that " Amenu (and probably Ameny) was a recognised familiar name for the longer Amenemhat, for royal persons, as it was also in private life at Beni-Hasan."

(2) above, inscription at Aswan	(3) above, inscription at Aswan, and at Sehel.
(2) above, built Temple of Osiris at Abydos ..	(3) above, stele at Abydos, recording work of decorating Temple of Osiris at Abydos. Petrie supposes this to have been a restoration of the Temple.
(3) AMENEMHAT II.	(3) KHA-SESHES-RA (NEFERHOTEP), AS ABOVE.
Sa-Hathor, under (3) above, says he is beloved of the king, and was sent to do the work for the temple of the king at his pyramid, and worked the gold mines in Nubia.	Sa-Hathor appears as son of (3) above, and associated on the throne.

ANNOTATIONS (B) TO TABLE XV—*Continued.*
DYNASTIES XII AND XIII.

Tomb of Sa-Hathor at Abydos	(3) above, stele at Abydos; decorated Temple of Osiris at Abydos.
(3) above, inscriptions at Aswan	(3) above, inscriptions at Aswan and Sehel, mentioning Sa-Hathor.
(3) above, inscriptions near Silsileh	(3) above, cartouche near Silsileh.

It is to be noted that whereas the noble Ameny, or Amenemhat, equates Senusert I with Kha-nefer-Ra Sebekhotep, Sa-Hathor equates Amenemhat II with Kha-seshes-Ra Neferhotep, this being the order of succession according to the Tablet of Karnak.

Of Kha-nefer-Ra Sebekhotep, who was co-regent with Kha-seshes-Ra Neferhotep, are statues of grey granite on the Island of Arqo, above the 3rd Cataract. If his contemporaries, Amenemhat and Sa-Hathor are those of the same name in Dynasty XII, this supplies reason for the statues in this place. Both in XII Dynasty inscriptions are stated to have penetrated into Nubia for gold. This would also explain XIIth and XIIIth Dynasty inscriptions contemporaneously at Aswan, Sehel, and Silsileh.

(4) SENUSERT II.

(4) SEKHEM-SUAZ-TAUI-RA (SEBEKHOTEP).

(5) SENUSERT III.

Under (2) above, Mentuhotep was architect of the Temple of Osiris at Abydos. Petrie states ("History of Egypt," Vol. 1, 10th Ed., p. 167):—"Mentuhotep, the chief architect, was also governor of the east desert, or red country, and a man of almost royal importance."

(4) above, states that he was born of "the divine father Mentuhotep."

Sent-s-senb and Sat-Hathor, daughters of (4) above; (female forms of name).

Senb, son of (4) above (Sa-Hathor under (3) above); (male forms of name).

Statue of Senusert III, by Sekhem-suaz-taui-Ra, at Karnak. (Petrie, "History of Egypt," Vol. I, 10th Ed., p. 184.)

(5) SENUSERT III AS ABOVE ⎫
                          ⎬ co-regent.
(6) AMENEMHAT III   ⎭

(5) SEKHEM-KHU-TAUI-RA (SEBEKHOTEP).

(5) above, rebuilt Temple at Bubastis ..

(5) above, built large hall in temple rebuilt by Senusert III, at Bubastis.

(6) above, recorded Nile levels at Semneh in years 5, 7, 9, 14, 15, 22, 23, 24, 30, 32, 37, 40, 41, and 43 of his reign.

(5) above, recorded Nile levels at Semneh during the first four years of his reign.

For continuity of the above Nile records to be assured, the first four years of Sekhem-khu-taui-Ra, when the Nile levels were recorded, should fall within the period during which Amenemhat III was co-regent with Senusert III. This was during the last 20 years of Senusert III, and therefore, during the first 20 years of Amenemhat III. From this, the Nile level records of the first four years of Sekhem-khu-taui-Ra fall in the four years preceding the first Nile record of Amenemhat III in his 5th year, or in the four years between the 9th year record and the 14th year record of Amenemhat III.

Maspero ("Dawn of Civilisation," p. 527, footnote) states :—"The way in which the monuments of Sebekhotep Sekhem-khu-taui and his papyri are mingled with the monuments of Amenemhat III at Semneh and in the Fayum show that it is difficult to separate him from that monarch."

(6) AMENEMHAT III AS ABOVE.

(6) RA-SMENKH-KA MER-MESHAU.

(6) above, Granite sphinxes at Tanis, with added inscription of Apepa on right shoulder of each.

(6) above, Granite statues at Tanis, with added inscription of Hyksos king Ra-aa-qenen Apepa on right shoulder of each.

This corresponds with what we know, from the Sallier Papyrus I, as to the character of the last Hyksos kings, in their studied and deliberate insult levelled at institutions and treasured possessions of the contemporary native kings of Egypt.

In Semitic allegory the right arm signified the king's power. Thus the Hyksos king's name, inscribed on the right shoulder of each of the statues and sphinxes of the kings of Dynasties XII and XIII, would signify that the Hyksos king considered himself to have thus symbolically set his seal upon the power of his Egyptian contemporaries. As Petrie observes, the usurpation is probably by the same Apepa in both cases.

(7) AMENEMHAT IV.

(7) SANKH-AB-RA AMENI-ANTEF-AMENEMHAT.

The above synchronism of kings of Dynasties XII and XIII, by confirming the order and sequence of Dynasty XIII kings, and their synchronous placing opposite Dynasty XII kings in the Karnak List of Tahutmes III, also establishes that the Karnak List places its Dynasty XIV kings contemporaneous with the kings of Dynasties XII and XIII. For further information relating to the Karnak List and the intention of its representation, the reader is referred to the Appendix.

ANNOTATIONS (C) TO TABLE XV.

(1)
AMENEMHAT III AND THE HYKSOS MATHEMATICAL PAPYRUS.

In Annotations (A) Col. 2, we saw that the Heq-shu (Hyksos) entered Egypt in 2063 A.K.—the 6th year of Senusert II—and first became aggressive in the 2nd year of Amenemhat III, 2095½-6½ A.K. The latter year is the 33rd year from the Epoch of the Hyksos' entry into the Delta. Accordingly we find that the Rhind Mathematical Papyrus mentions Amenemhat III in the 33rd year of the Hyksos king Ra-aa-user Apepa (I). The coincidence of the two 33rd years is striking, but is not in itself an identity. The absolute identity is otherwise fixed, however.

On the back of the Hyksos Mathematical Papyrus is a scribe's note, already dealt with in ¶¶ 61 and 62. This shows that the note was made at the commencement of the 2nd year after an intercalation had been effected in both the 360 days' calendar year and in the 365 days' calendar year. Now a 103 years cycle of Table III ended at 2060 A.K. By Table III, an intercalation in the 360 days' year and in the 365 days' year was effected 34 years later at 2094 A.K. The 1st year, following this intercalation, ended and the 2nd year began at 2095 A.K., when the 33rd year from the Epoch of the Hyksos' entry also began. This again equates the Hyksos' 33rd year with the second half of the 1st year and the first half of the 2nd year of Amenemhat III.

Again, it is from the Calendar cycle of the intercalated year of 360 days that the calendar record of Sirius rising in the 7th year of Senusert III is found to agree with the heliacal rising of Sirius as astronomically fixed by Oppolzer's Calculations (refer ¶ 317). Both the intercalated year of 360 days and the intercalated year of 365 days were in use during the XIIth Dynasty, and the scribe's record on the back of the Hyksos Mathematical Papyrus gives the relative positions of the two years holding for the 2nd year after an intercalation, which 2nd year, by two coincidences that cannot both be accidental, is shown to coincide with year 2 of Amenemhat III. For an additional coincidence giving the same identity, refer to Addendum opposite on Annotations (D).

When we find, therefore, that the record, on the Mathematical Papyrus proper, states that the data were copied by the scribe Aahmes in the 12th month of the 33rd year of the reign of Ra-aa-user Apepa (I) from a copy made under Maat-en-Ra* (Amenemhat III); when we find that this record of a 12th month is followed by a scribe's note on the back of the papyrus, of the positions of Month 1 of the 360 days Calendar (intercalated) in relation to the " 5 days over the year " of the 365 days intercalated Calendar, we necessarily conclude that " Month I " follows " Month XII," and therefore that the 2nd year after the intercalation and year 2 of Amenemhat III, who is mentioned, is followed by or were partly coincident with year 33 of Apepa (I), who is mentioned.

The name of the scribe, Aahmes, again, brings us into immediate contact with the form of name peculiar to the time of the XVIIIth Dynasty. The first signs of Hyksos' aggression in the 2nd year of Amenemhat, when the above record was written, clearly relate to the circumstances that led to the Egyptian War of Independence—about 50 years later.

Manetho, according to the version of Eusebius, gives the Hyksos Dynasty preceding Dynasty XVIII as ruling for 103 years. This is the Calendar Cycle, with which the above data are associated. The cycle ended in 2163 A.K. in the reign of the last king of Dynasty XVII—Kames. Manetho states that the Hyksos were expelled by Alis phragmuthosis, which name as Sayce has shown was derived from the name of Kames, Uaz-Kheper-Ra Kames, through the form Uals'ph'ra-Kamuthosis. (" Anc. Emp. East " p. 36).

* For Amenemhat III and Mathematics in early Greek tradition, refer Table X, p. 103, col. 2.

(2)
THE HYKSOS AGGRESSION IN RELATION TO AMENEMHAT III AND EGYPTIAN WORK IN THE DELTA.

As confirming the data and conclusions of Col. 1, it is a fact, worthy of consideration, that there are no works of Amenemhat III, Amenemhat IV, and Sebekneferu—the last three rulers of Dynasty XII—in the Delta, where the Hyksos were predominant ; whereas buildings and statues of the earlier kings of Dynasty XII occur at Tanis and Bubastis. Certain Sphinxes, however, were discovered by Mariette at Tanis, and these, while inscribed with the name of a Hyksos king Apepa have undoubtedly been proved to be identical in style with, and similar in features to, statues of Amenemhat III. This exclusive usurpation of the work of Amenemhat III—the statues of the earlier XIIth Dynasty kings at Tanis and Bubastis not having been usurped by the Hyksos,—points to a deliberate intention to insult Amenemhat III during the actual life of that king. This intention would correspond with what we know, from the Sallier Papyrus I, concerning the satirical and insulting form of Hyksos humour that precipitated the Egyptian War of Independence.

Now the name "Apepa" is inscribed on the *right* shoulder of each of the sphinxes of Amenemhat III. In the same manner each of the granite statues of the XIIIth or XIVth Dynasty king, Mer-Meshau, contains on the *right* shoulder, an added inscription by a Hyksos king Ra-aa-qenen Apepa.

Mer-Meshau—by the synchronisms of Annotations (B) —was the contemporary of Amenemhat III, during the latter's long reign. From what has been said above, this makes Ra-aa-qenen Apepa the contemporary of both Mer-Meshau and Amenemhat III, and a successor of Ra-aa-user Apepa (I) who was living in the 2nd year of Amenemhat III, i.e., in 2095-2096 A.K.

In Semitic allegory, the right arm signified the king's power. Thus the name of the Hyksos king inscribed on the right shoulder of each of the statues and sphinxes of the kings of Dynasties XII and XIII would signify that the Hyksos king considered himself to have thus symbolically set his seal upon the power of his Egyptian contemporaries.

So close is the connection between the reign of Amenemhat III and the period at which the chiefs of the Hyksos settlers usurped the royal titles of the Egyptian kings that Professor Petrie (" Egypt and Israel," p. 13), in spite of his long chronology, is forced to admit that this occurred " soon after the XIIth Dynasty." Thus Petrie—who identifies the Hyksos settlers as Syro-Mesopotamian intruders, or Babylonian immigrants—states as follows :—

" Another Babylonian of the same age is a king Khenzer, whose name is also found as that of a later Babylonian king, Kinziros, or Yukin-ziru. A well-cut tablet, now in Paris, bears the name of Khenzer along with an Egyptian name which he adopted, Ra-ne-maat-ne-kha (or Ra-en-maat-en-kha). This name is based on the name of one of the most celebrated kings of the XIIth Dynasty, Ra-ne-maat, Amenemhat III. The tablet states that the repairs of temples and provision for the worship were being carried on, and gives the king the usual Egyptian titles. All this points to the Babylonian having come into Egypt while the country was still well ordered, soon after the XIIth Dynasty and shows that he acted as a regular Egyptian king."

The facts must be admitted, however, that up to and including the first year of Amenemhat III, XIIth Dynasty works were executed at Tanis, that the sphinxes of Amenemhat III at Tanis were executed during the peaceful period of Hyksos Settlement in Egypt, and were later usurped by the Hyksos king Apepa ; that no XIIth Dynasty work later than this occurs at Tanis, and that it was from Tanis that the Hyksos king Ra-Apepi, according to the Sallier Papyrus I, addressed his famous insulting ultimatum to Seqenen Ra (III) Tau-aa-qen of Dynasty XVII at Thebes. This precipitated the war that led to the expulsion of the Hyksos under the reign of the latter king's successor Kames, or the 1st king of Dynasty XVIII Aahmes or Amosis I.

ADDENDUM TO ANNOTATIONS (C) AND (D) TO TABLE XV.

THE YEAR DATINGS ON THE RHIND MATHEMATICAL PAPYRUS.

The Hyksos Mathematical Papyrus claims to be copied exactly from a Papyrus written under Amenemhat III. If this is correct, then the data given represents the mathematical rules and formulæ in use for practical everyday problems during the XIIth Dynasty. But the abridged and practical nature of the rules and formulæ given clearly indicate that the XIIth Dynasty papyrus was dealing with data that had been evolved long before the XIIth Dynasty began. This is a conclusion already necessitated by the high mathematical attainments evidenced by the metrology and astronomy of the earlier Dynasties, dealt with in Chapters I and II of this work. It is evident therefore that the Papyrus written under Amenemhat III was itself compiled from earlier sources. This conclusion throws some light upon the conditions attaching to the copying out of the Hyksos Mathematical Papyrus. The scribe copying under the Hyksos king clearly accepted the text of the Amenemhat III Papyrus, merely inserting the month and year of the Hyksos king, and his own name as scribe making the copy. Omitting these from the Hyksos copy, we should have the text of the Amenemhat III copy, with the month and year of the latter, however, omitted.

Now the Hyksos copy states that it was made in month IV, Season of Inundation, in year 33 of the Hyksos king, Ra-aa-user (Apepa I), from a similar roll in antique writing made under Amenemhat III (Dynasty XII). It is generally assumed that this refers to Amenemhat III, preceding the times of Ra-aa-user by so many centuries that the writing of the time of Amenemhat III was already deemed to be "antique." From what has been said above, however, it seems to be clear that the scribe of the Hyksos king merely copied what was dated by a scribe of Amenemhat III, i.e. that the roll was written under Amenemhat III "in the likeness of an ancient writing." An alternative Egyptological opinion, however, is that all the data on the existing copy (The Rhind Mathematical Papyrus) was copied at a considerably later date from the Hyksos copy made from the copy of Amenemhat III.

On a blank space on the Hyksos Mathematical Papyrus there is what appears to be a diary of events and calendric notes. On the same blank space there is a statement of accounts. Peet remarks that Möller suggests both entries as "possibly emanating from the same hand," and that Griffith attributes the former to the scribe who wrote the mathematical sections. The general opinion is that the entry relating to the calendar was made not long after the mathematical sections had been written. A possibility that does not seem to have been suggested is that the calendric notes and statement of accounts were entered on a blank sheet of papyrus before any portion of the mathematical sections were written. This conclusion would not be invalidated even if the opinion is accepted that the Rhind Papyrus is a later copy of all the data on a Hyksos papyrus. The calendric notes are dealt with on Annotations (C), Col. (1), opposite and in ¶¶ 61 and 62. In Annotations (C) it is shown that the calendric data agree with the commencement of 2095 A.K. (i.e. 1905 B.C.). The note, however, is dated in the "11th year" of a king or of an epoch. As the note deals with calendric data, it is not improbable that an epoch is implied by the dating. This suggestion, however, would not amount to much did we not know from a record of Ramesus III that there was a recognised Hyksos Epoch, and that records in the Delta were dated from this epoch as

late as his own reign. The use of such a well-recognised epoch would account for the date being given merely as the "11th year," and for the fact that no king is mentioned in relation. From Annotations (D) we see that such an epoch is fixed at 2083½ A.K. and was observed both by Semites and Egyptians. On page 290 it is shown that Senusert III observed the completion of the cycle, fixing the epoch, by celebrating a festival of the heliacal rising of Sirius at 2083½ A.K. The first calendar year of the new epoch would be the calendar year beginning 2084 A.K. and ending 2085 A.K., and, in consequence, the 11th year would be that beginning 2094 A.K. and ending 2095 A.K. At the latter date, the last five days of the 11th year of the 365 days' calendar year would coincide with the 1st five days of the 12th year of the 360 days' calendar year, as is explained in Annotations (C) opposite, and in ¶¶ 61 and 62. Now, since the note dated in the "11th year" mentions this precise coincidence, that dating confirms that 2084 A.K. began the reckoning of a new epoch.

How does this agree with the dating of the Hyksos Epoch on the Ramessu III record? This record, found at Tanis, formerly a Hyksos town, states that it was inscribed in the reign of Ramessu II and in the 400th year of the Hyksos god "Set-aa-pehti Nubti," i.e. Nubti Set, the powerful. With 2064 A.K. beginning the 1st year of the Hyksos Epoch, the 400th year began at 2483 A.K. and ended at 2484 A.K., thus coinciding with the 42nd or 43rd year of Ramessu II (Table XIV). That the latter date, 2484 A.K., is a Semitic and Pyramid prophetic Epoch (ending 2520 unintercalated calendar years of 360 years = 7 × 360 calendar years, or a week of Great Calendar years) gives significance to the dating of "the Stele of 400 years." It is a date appearing in the Babylonian chronological scheme of Berosus (Annotations A to Tables XVII-XIX, Col. 3, and notes to Col. 2). It is the Pyramid dating for the Floor junction of the Entrance and 1st Ascending Passage (¶¶ 344 and 345). It is the date given by the Talmud for an attempted Exodus of 80,000 men of the tribe of Ephraim 30 years before the actual Exodus. This Talmud account gives the actual Exodus as 5 years after the death of the Pharaoh of the Oppression. As the latter Pharaoh was Ramessu II, who, by Table XIV, died at 2508½ A.K., the date of the Exodus is 2513½ A.K., at the end of the 5th year of Menephtah. This agrees with the 5th year Israelitish Exodus Inscription of Menephtah (Table XXIII) and with the Hebrew date of the Exodus (Annotations A to Table XXVIII) and gives 2483½ A.K. for the abortive exodus of the men of Ephraim.

In "Historical Studies" (1911), in the inserted sheet between pages 20 and 21, Sir Flinders Petrie gives his note on "A Seasonal Date of the Hyksos Period." This refers to the calendric notes on the Hyksos Mathematical Papyrus, and in quoting Dr. Griffith's translation of the Hyksos notes there is a misprint in which the number of the year appears as the Roman numeral II in place of the Arabic numeral 11. On pages 49 and 50 of the first edition of the present work, the dating was adopted as given in the misprint. Attention was drawn to the mistake when Professor T. Eric Peet's recent work, "The Rhind Mathematical Papyrus," was received. The year clearly appears as "year 11" in Plate 7, No. 87, and in the translation on page 129 in that work.

THE EVOLUTION OF FICTITIOUS EGYPTIAN CHRONOLOGY FROM THE ORIGINAL ASTRONOMICAL CHRONOLOGY OF THE ANCIENT EGYPTIANS.

(1) The Enoch-Abram Phœnix Epoch and the 1461 Years' Cycle of Genesis:—

There are two chronological Epochs associated with the House of Enoch. These are:—
(i) The Epoch of origin at 622 A.K. (Table V), and
(ii) The Phœnix Epoch, 365 years later, at 987 A.K. (Table V).

The former Epoch is the date of origin of a prophetic interval of 1461 solar years, observed as follows:—

(a)	The origin of the House of Enoch	622 A.K.
	Sacred Cycle of 4 × 365¼ Solar Years	1461 years.
(b)	Call of Abram (¶¶ 39 and 317, and Tables XXII and XXVIII and Annotations to latter)	2083 A.K.

The Biblical date, as Annotations to Table XXVIII, is given as 2083¼ A.K. This, as Table XV, is the beginning of the 7th year of Senusert III. In his 7th year, Senusert III records a festival of the observation of the heliacal rising of Sirius on Day 17, Month VIII. In ¶ 317, it is shown, by the Calendar rules of Table III and Plate LIX, that Day 17, Month VIII at 2083¼ A.K. coincided with 18th July (Julian) when, by Oppolzer's data of Plate LX, Sirius rose heliacally. That Senusert III recognised that a Sacred period of 1461 *Solar* years ended then, and that the period began at the Epoch of the House of Enoch, 622 A.K. is proved by two facts. These are:—
(i) That this is the first Egyptian reference to the heliacal rising of Sirius, and
(ii) That, in later times, as the following data show, cycles of 1461 years were dated from the 7th year of Senusert III.

(2) The Phœnix Legend relating to Sesostris and its Pyramid Epochs:—

Breasted (in his "History of Egypt," p. 189) specifically identifies Senusert III as the *original* Sesostris of Egyptian legend. He, in fact, names him Sesostris III in preference to Senusert III. Thus, Senusert III is variously styled in the Lists, Sesostris, Sesosis, Sesorthis, Tosorthos, and from his *Suten Bat* name, Kau-Kha-Ra, is named Kankharis or Concharis in the Lists. Egyptian tradition held that the 1st Phœnix cycle is to be referred to his reign (Tacitus *Annales* VI, 28). One form of the tradition, therefore, referred his Epoch back to the primary Epoch of Enoch. Thus the Egyptian version, preserved by Africanus, identifies the Sesostris of tradition with Sesorthis or Tosorthos, placed as the 2nd king of Manetho's Dynasty III, placing him chronologically as follows:—

End of reign of 3rd Dynasty king, Sesorthis (the Epoch of Enoch) ..	622 years
Interval of 15 Phœnix cycles	4935 years.
Termination of Egyptian Chronology at Epoch of Okhos (¶ 253)	5557 years.

Here the Pyramid Epoch 5556.23 A.K. (¶ 249) is confused with the date of the Epoch of Okhos, which is also a Pyramid Epoch, 3652–3 A.K. (¶¶ 250–254).

(3) The Phœnix and Sothic Cycles in the Egyptian "Book of the Sothis":—

In ¶ 379 it is shown that the period of 4935 years (or 15 Phœnix cycles) is a Pyramid chronological interval between two Pyramid Epochs, *i.e.*, between the Epoch 987 A.K. and the Epoch 5922 A.K. This accounts for the interval 4935 years appearing as the date of the 1st year of Amasis II in the List of the Egyptian *Book of the Sothis*, and as terminating 1460 years from the date given by the latter List for the last year of Senusert III. Since a cycle of 1461 years ended in the reign of Senusert III, the theory was formulated that a new cycle of 1461 years began then. The alleged new cycle was then identified with the Sothic Cycle of 1460 years. The statement of the *Book of the Sothis* is therefore as follows:—

Correct summation for the terminal year of Kankharis (= Kha-kau-Ra = Senusert III)—but stated as 3477 Anno Mundi	3476 A.M.
Summation of reigns to 1st year Amasis II	1459 years
1st year of Amasis II as correctly added, but stated as 4936. 15 Phœnix Cycles = the Pyramid period of 4935 years	4935 A.M.

The error of 1 year in the *Book of the Sothis*, in adding the totals occurs first at Kankharis, and was clearly intentional, and for the purpose of representing the 1459 years above as 1460 years. This shows that the item of 4935 years preceded a later interpolated item of 1460 years. Tacitus (*Annales* VI, 28) states that the first Phœnix period was identified with Sesostris (Senusert III) and the last period with Amasis II. He remarks that the Phœnix cycle was confused and identified with the Sothic cycle of 1460 years. This accounts for the above statement in the *Book of the Sothis*.

(4) The Astronomical Epoch of Senusert III and its Displacement in the King Lists:—

As explained in ¶ 310 and note, and Table XXII, the Lamaris of Manetho's Dynasty XII is Senusert III, the real Sesostris of tradition. The Version of Africanus shows that the 1461 years of the Old Testament cycle, item (1) to the left, were erroneously reckoned, in the Version of Africanus, not from the 1st Epoch of Enoch at 622 A.K., but from the 2nd Epoch of Enoch at 987 A.K. = termination of 3 Phœnix cycles (Table V). Thus:—

(a)	2nd Epoch of Enoch			987 A.K.
	Sacred Cycle of 4 × 365¼ Solar years			1461 years.
				2448 A.K. alleged
(b)	Africanus Book I	2308 years.		
Do.	Dyn. XII to 7th year Lamaris (Senusert III)	139 years.		
		2447 years.		

The difference of 1 year is obviously due to the Lists reckoning the 1461 years as vague years, and therefore equal to 1460 Sothic years. This identity confirms our deduction. The observed heliacal rising of Sirius, in the 7th year of Senusert III, was associated with the termination of 1461 Solar years from an Epoch of Enoch, as item (1) to the left, and ¶ 317.

(5) The Phœnix Epoch and the Sothic Cycles of the Fictitious King Lists:—

The above explanation of the origin of the later theory of the Sothic cycle is confirmed by the complete application of the theory in Manetho's King Lists. This application of the theory, as found in the Version of Africanus, is as follows:—

	Alleged A.K. Chronology.
Primary Epoch of Enoch, and alleged end of reign of Sesorthis (Dynasty III) as item (2) to left	622 A.K.
¼ Sothic cycle interval	365 years
Total in Castor's Version of the King Lists to the 1st year of Dynasty V ..	987 A.K.
Sothic cycle interval	1460 years.
Total in Africanus to 7th year Lamaris (Senusert III) as item (4) above ..	2447 A.K.
Sothic cycle interval	1460 years.
Total in Africanus for Dyns. I to XVI incl. with Book I, 2308 years and Dyns. XII to XVI incl. 1599 years. The basal fact of identity is that the last Hyksos king of Dyn. XVI introduced the vague year that governed the Sothic cycle (Table XI, Annotations Col. 1)	3907 A.K.
Sothic cycle interval	1460 years.
Total in Africanus (from his stated totals of Dyns.) from Dyn. I to the reign of Amasis II (actually to his 30th year)	5367 A.K.

The above Summations of Africanus include his 182 years for the Harris Papyrus Interregnum between Dynasties XIX and XX.

The 182 years are obtained from the difference between the stated total of Africanus for Book III (*i.e.*, Dynasties XX to XXXI) and the summation of his stated Dynastic totals *i.e.*, 1050—868 = 182. By indicating the 30th year of Amasis II at 5367 A.K., his 25th year, when the Phœnix cycle ended (Table XI), is indicated as 5362 A.K. The actual date (as Table XI) is 3454¼ A.K. The number of chronological years added to the A.K. reckoning in this version is, therefore, 1907¾ years. This addition relates to the original Egyptian astronomical and calendar chronology. A similar addition or shift, of the extent of 1904 years, in the case of the evolution of the Egyptian fictitious chronology, from the Pyramid's precessional and perihelion chronology was explained in ¶¶ 249 to 254 and Plate XLII b.

In the system tabulated in item (3), to the left, the theory depends upon there having been one Sothic cycle from Senusert III to Amasis II. As in the system tabulated above, however, a cycle preceded Senusert III. The initial cycle of the system of item (3), therefore, began at 2016 A.K., which is the actual date of the cycle of 120 years ending in the 33rd year of Senusert I when a *Sep tep sed heb* was celebrated as shown on Table XV.

The 3 alleged Sothic cycles to Amasis II as Tabulated in this item also form the basis of the Version of Eusebius to Amasis II as in Plate XVI, Table A. In the latter, however, the 3 Sothic cycles form the period from Dynasty I inclusive to Amasis II inclusive; the Harris Papyrus Interregnum being ignored.

Again, at a later date, when Alexander conquered Egypt, the Version preserved by Africanus was adapted to give the period of 5367 years of this item ending at the Epoch of Okhos or at Alexander's Conquest. This was obtained by ignoring the Harris Papyrus Interregnum, the summation of Dynasties then giving 5368 for Books I to III inclusive of Manetho, as shown on Plate XVI, Table C, Col. 5.

TABLE XVI.

THE *SED HEBS* OF DYNASTIES XVIII AND XIX.

Kings in whose reigns *Sed hebs* are recorded.	Recorded year of *Sed heb*.	Date of reign from Table XIV.	Year of *Sed heb* from datum of Ramessu II.	Years' duration of 721 years' cycle. Table IV	Interval in years.
Amenhotep I ..	..	..	.. 2195½-2216 A.K.	.. 2196 A.K.	.. 540	
Tahutmes I ..	..	.. 2216 -2231½ A.K.	.. 2226 A.K	.. 570	.. 30
{ Hatshepsut ..	16th year. }	{ 2231½-2276¼ A.K. }			.. 31
{ Tahutmes III ..	3rd year }	{ 2254½-2308½ A.K. } .. 2257 A.K.	.. 601	
Tahutmes III ..	33rd year.	.. 2254½-2308½ A.K.	.. 2287 A.K.	.. 631	.. 30
Amenhotep II ..	..	.. 2308½-2334½ A.K.	.. 2317 A.K.	.. 661	.. 30
Amenhotep III ..	..	.. 2344 -2375 A.K.	.. 2347 A.K.	.. 691	.. 30
Amenhotep IV ..	..	.. 2375 -2393 A.K.	.. 2377 A.K.	.. 721	.. 30
Tut-ankh-Amen ..	..	.. 2405 -2414 A.K.	.. 2407 A.K.	.. 30	.. 30
Seti I (Dyn. XIX)	..	.. 2432½-2441½ A.K.	.. 2437 A.K.	.. 60	.. 30
Ramessu II ..	..	.. 2441½-2508½ A.K.	.. 2467 A.K.	.. 90	.. 30

THE PERIODS OF THE *SEP TEP SED HEB*
(Basis ¶¶ 315 and 316).

				Datum, Deluge ending ..	1656 A.K.		
Period I ..	..	..	..	4 *Sed hebs* ..	120 years	..	Table IV
					1776 A.K.		
Period II	..	..	..	4 *Sed hebs* ..	120 years.	..	Table IV
					1896 A.K.		
Period III	..	..	..	4 *Sed hebs* ..	120 years.	..	Table IV
					2016 A.K.		
Period IV	..	..	..	4 *Sed hebs* ..	120 years.	..	Table IV
					2136 A K.		
Period V	..	..	..	4 *Sed hebs* ..	121 years	..	Table IV
					2257 A.K		
Period VI	..	..	..	4 *Sed hebs* ..	120 years	..	Table IV
					2377 A.K		
Period I	..	..	..	4 *Sed hebs* ..	120 years.	..	Table IV

This festival was never celebrated (Table XI, Annotations

Cols. 2 and 3) ..   ..   2497 A.K.   Continuity broken

TABLE XVII.

CHRONOLOGICAL TABLE OF THE 1ST DYNASTY OF BABYLON AND THE KASSITE DYNASTY, WITH THEIR ASSYRIAN AND SEA-LAND CONTEMPORARIES.

DYNASTY OF THE SEA-LAND. B.C. 1881 to B.C. 1619. KING.	1ST DYNASTY OF BABYLON. 285 YEARS—B.C. 2035 to 1750. KING.	YEARS OF KING LIST A.	DATE A.K.	DYNASTY OF KASSITES. RECKONED AS 576¾ YEARS IN KING LISTS ALLEGED B.C. 2035 TO TRUE ENDING B.C. 1458. KING.	YEARS OF KING LIST A.	DATE A.K.	ASSYRIAN KINGS. KING.
Alleged duration of 11 reigns, 368 years. Actual duration, 262 years.	Sumu-abu	14	1965–1979.	Alleged beginning of Dynasty.			Ilu-shuma. 1965.
	Sumu-la-ilu.	36	1979–2015.				Irishum (son).
	Zabium.	14	2015–2029.	The late Lists represent Gandash as beginning at what was really the commencement of the 1st Dynasty of Babylon. The dating of Agum II confirms that Gandash was Abeshu's contemporary.			Ikunum (son).
	Abil-sin.	18	2029–2047.				Sharrukin I (son).
	Sin-muballidh.	20	2047–2067.				Puzur-Assur I.
	Khammurabi.	43	2067–2110.				Samsu-Hadad I (son of Enlil-kabi).
Ilu-ma-ilu (A.K. 2118).	Samsu-iluna.	38	2110–2148.	Gandash,†	16	2144–2160. circ.	Ishme-Dagan I (son). circ.
Itti-ili-nibi.	Abeshu.	25	2148–2173.	Agum I (son).	22	2160–2182.	Samsu-Hadad II.
Damki-ilishu.	Ammiditana.	25	2173–2198.	Kashtiliash I (son).	22	2182–2204.	Ishme-Dagan II (son).
Ishkibal.	Ammi-zadoq.	21	2198–2219.	Ushshi*.	9	2204–2213.	Samsu-Hadad III (son).
Shushshi.	Samsu-ditana.	31	2219–2250.	Abirattash (son of K.).	—	(2213–2234.)	Puzur-Assur II.
Gulkishar.				Tashigurumash (son).	—	(2234–2255.)	Enlil-nasir.
24 years after Samsu-ditana. 2274 A.K.				Agum II (son).	—	(2255–2276.)	Nur-ili.
Peshgal-daramash.	Hittites overthrew 1st Dynasty in 2250 A.K., and carried statue of Merodach into Milauni. Agum II brought the statue back. A Babylonian hymn states that Merodach was 24 years with the Hittites. Agum II therefore brought it back to Babylon in 2274 A.K. This confirms that Gandash was the contemporary of Abeshu or Samsu-iluna of 1st Dynasty.			Kadashman-kharbe I	—	(2276–2291.)	Assur-rabi.
Adara-kalama.				Kurigalzu I (son).	—	(2291–2306.)	Assur-nirari.
Akur-ul-ana.				Meli-sipak I (son).	—	(2306–2321.)	Assur-bil-nisi-su.
Melam-kurkura.				Kara-indash I.	—	(2321–2336.)	Assur-nadin-akhi.
Eagamil (A.K. 2380).				Kadashman-Enlil I.		(2336–2351.)	Erba-Hadad.
A.K. 2380. Ulamburiash defeats Ea-gamil and reigns in his stead; vassal to his father Burnaburiash.	Kashtiliash — Agum completes conquest of the Sealand.			Kurigalzu II.		(2351–2365¾.)	Puzur-Assur III.
				[Burnaburiash]	22	2365¾–2387¾.	Assur-Yuballidh.
				Kara-indash II. Kadashman-kharbe II. & Nazibugash.			
				[Kurigalzu III](son of B.).	26	2387¾–2413¾.	Enlil-nirari.

The first king of the Sea-land, Ilu-ma-ilu, attacked Samsu-iluna of the 1st Dynasty of Babylon in the latter's 9th year, 2118 A.K. Again, the last king, Ea-gamil, was overthrown by Ulamburiash, circ. 2380 A.K., during the reign of the latter's father, Burnaburiash of the Kassite Dynasty. The duration of the Dynasty of the Sea-land is, therefore, around 262 years. The stated duration of the Dynasty, in the King Lists, is 368 years. This is 106 years in excess of the actual duration. This excess agrees with the 106 years of the Kassite Dynasty from its first king, Gandash, 2144 A.K., to the date at which the 1st Dynasty of Babylon was overthrown by the Hittites.

The late compilers of the King Lists therefore read that Agum I, not Agum II, restored the statue of Merodach to Babylon, 24 years after the Hittites had captured it at the sack of Babylon in 2250 A.K. (See Note above.) This appeared to give Gandash following Samsu-ditana. Samsu-ditana was therefore moved back 106 years to accommodate Gandash. The 1st Dynasty of Babylon being moved back 106 years with Samsu-ditana, also moved Ilu-ma-ilu—the 1st king of the Sea-land, and the contemporary of Samsu-iluna—back 106 years. The Kassite Dynasty, however, remained *initially* undisturbed, with the last king of the Sea-land, Ea-gamil, remaining undisturbed as the contemporary of Burnaburiash.

In effect, therefore, the revision of the late compilers of the King Lists added 106 years to the Dynasty of the Sea-land, giving 368 years for 11 kings, or 33½ years as the average for 11 successive reigns. Authorities have long seen that this is considerably in excess of the truth. The excess is explained as above.

A troublesome relic of the truth—i.e., that the 1st Dynasty of Babylon began 576¾ years prior to the ending of the Kassite Dynasty—was next interred by making the duration of the Kassite Dynasty 576¾ years. Additional kings—possibly ephemeral chieftains like Ulamburiash and his brother Kashtiliash and the latter's son Agum—were interpolated between Agum II and Burnaburiash.

The latter fiction, however, moved the 1st Dynasty of Babylon, together with the 1st king of the Sea-land, Ilu-ma-ilu, back 179 years farther. This troublesome question was overcome by ignoring the contemporaneity of Ilu-ma-ilu and Samsu-iluna. The Dynasty of the Sea-land—stated as of the duration of 368 years—was placed between the end of the 1st Dynasty of Babylon and the beginning of the Kassite Dynasty, stated as of the duration of 576¾ years. This is the form in which the King Lists of later times present the chronology of the Babylonian Dynasties.

Refer Table XVIII for Egyptian, Hebrew, and Hittite synchronisms confirming the relations and chronology here given.

† A record of Samsu-iluna shows that an invasion of Kassites occurred in Samsu-iluna's 9th year. Again, a record of the 3rd century B.C. claims to be a copy of a record made by Gandash, the Kassite. This states that Gandash claimed Nippur as his Capital, that he conquered Babylon, and rebuilt the temple of Enlil destroyed in the operations. This would appear to be a late version of temporary successes of the Kassites under Gandash against Abeshu, for as Johns states "An obscure record points to a fresh invasion by the Kassites" in the reign of Abeshu.

			Arik-dan-ilu.
Nazi-maruttash	17	2413¾–2430¾.	*Hadad-nirari I.*
Kadashman-turgu. } *Kadashman-Enlil II.* }	13	2430¾–2443¾.	
Kudur-Enlil.	6	2443¾–2449¾.	
Sagarakti-suriash	13	2449¾–2462¾.	*Shalmaneser I (built Calah).*
Kashtiliash II.	8	2462¾–2470¾.	
			Tukulti-Enurta I captures Babylon;
Enlil-nadin-sum	1½	2470¾–2472¼.	} *held Babylon for 7 years;*
Kadashman-Kharbe II.	1½	2472¼–2473¾.	} *vassal kings*
Hadad-sum-iddin.	6	2473¾–2479¾.	} *as opposite.*
			Assur-nazir-pal I.
			Assur-nirari & Nebo-Dan.
Hadad-sum-uzur.	30	2479¾–2509¾.	*Bel-kudur-uzur.*
Meli-sipak II.	15	2509¾–2524¾.	
Merodach-Baladan I.	13	2524¾–2537¾.	*Enurta-Pileser.*
Zamama-sum-iddin.	1	2537¾–2538¾.	*Assur-Dan I.*
Bel-nadin-[akhi]	3	2538¾–2541¾.	*Assur-Dan I continues contemporaneous with first king of next dynasty.* (Refer Table XIX).

KASSITE DYNASTY ENDS. 2541¾ A.K. = B.C. 1458.

NOTES:—

Names indicated thus:—Agum II / Nazimaruttash } are in position as given in the Dynastic Tablets.

Names indicated thus:—*Kadashman-kharbe I* / *Kurigalzu II* } are known from their records as belonging to the positions shown above, e.g., between Agum II and Nazimaruttash } in the example here cited.

Kings whose reigns are directly synchronised by their contemporary records are connected thus:—

Ilu-ma-ilu ——— Samsu-iluna.

and *Kara-indash I* ——— *Assur-bil-nisi-su.*

Kings whose reigns are synchronised from recorded data, other than in records mentioning the direct contemporaneity of the reigns, are connected thus:—

Abeshu — — — — Gandash

Dates enclosed in brackets thus:—(........) are derived by averaging between known dates and for a known number of reigns.

* Ushshi occurs here in the King Lists. Agum II does not mention him in his own genealogy, because Ushshi was not his ancestor. The genealogical isolation of Ushshi may—or may not—be related to the fact that a contemporary, Shu-Ushshi, is 5th king of the Dynasty of the Sealand.

TABLE XVIII.

THE CONTEMPORANEITY OF THE DYNASTY OF HYKSOS, AND OF DYNASTIES XII AND XVIII, IN SUCCESSION, IN EGYPT, WITH THE 1ST DYNASTY OF BABYLON AND THE DYNASTY OF KASSITES, DURING THE PERIOD OF THE RISE AND ESTABLISHING OF THE HITTITE EMPIRE.

HITTITE KINGS.	ISRAELITE CONNECTIONS.	HYKSOS' DYNASTY.	Dynasty XII in Egypt. 182 years. From B.C. 2036 to 1854.		1st Dynasty of Babylon. 285 years. From B.C. 2035 to 1750	
			All as in Table XIV.	Date A.K.	Reigns from Table XVII.	Date A.K.
			Amenemhat I..	1963½–1993½	Sumu-abi	1965 –1979
			Senusert I ..	1983½–2028½	Sumu-la-ilu ..	1979 –2015
					Zabium	2015 –2029
			Amenemhat II	2025½–2063½	Abil-sin	2029 –2047
		1st Hyksos King, Apepa I, 2063 A.K.	Senusert II ..	2057½–2076½	Sin-muballidh ..	2047 –2067
Dudkhalia I (Tid'al of Gen. xiv). The contemporary of Senusert III in Egypt, and of Khammurabi (Amraphel) in Babylon. In both reigns occur 1st references to Hittites. Hittites first appear in Southern Canaan between Abraham's visit to Egypt and Sarah's death. (Gen. xiii, 18, xiv, 13, compared with Gen. xxiii, 2–20.)	Abraham 2082–4 A.K. Chaldaea to Egypt and back to Canaan.		Senusert III ..	2076½–2114½	Khammurabi ..	2067 –2110
			Amenemhat III	2094½–2140½	Samsu-iluna ..	2110 –2148
			Amenemhat IV	2136½–2145½		
	REFER TABLE XXII	Hyksos expelled from Egypt 2170 A.K.	Sebek-neferu ..	2141½–2145½	Abeshu	2148 –2173
		Hyksos expelled from Avaris 2172 A.K.	Aahmes I ..	2170½–2195½	Ammi-ditana ..	2173 –2198
			Amenhotep I..	2195½–2216	Ammi-zadoq ..	2198 –2219
			Tahutmes I ..	2216 –2231½		
			Tahutmes II ..	2231½–2254½	Samsu-ditana ..	2219 –2250
			Tahutmes III..	2254½–2308½	KASSITE DYNASTY BECOMES SUPREME. (Table XVII.)	
Hattusil I.	Joseph's Famine. 2296½–2303½ A.K. The Horse, introduced by the Kassites into Babylon, first appears in general use in Western Asia and Egypt. (Gen. xli 43, l 9.)	DYNASTY XVIII IN EGYPT. 260 years B.C. 1829 to 1569. TABLE XIV.	Amenhotep II .	2308½–2334½	Kara-indash I .	(2321 –2336)
			Tahutmes IV ..	2334½–2344		
Subbi-luliuma, his son. (Contemporary Amenhotep III to *circ.* Ra-smenkh-ka).			Amenhotep III	2344 –2375	Kadashman-Enlil I	(2336 –2351)
	From around 2250 A.K. (1750 B.C.) the Kassites, from the Western Mountains of Elam, introduce the horse-known vaguely during the 1st Dynasty of Babylon as "the ass of the mountains." Hence that the horse comes simultaneously into general use— (1) In Babylon during the Kassite supremacy—from around 2250 A.K. (2) Amongst the Hittites in Asia Minor, Syria, and Mitanni. (3) In Egypt during the XVIIIth Dynasty, and (4) Is first referred to in the Book of Genesis during the official life of Joseph in Egypt, 2300 A.K., during the reign of Tahutmes III.				Kurigalzu II .	(2351–2365¾)
			Amenhotep IV.	2375 –2393	Burnaburiash ..	2365¾–2387¾
			Ra-smenkh-ka	2393 –2405		
			Tut-ankh-Amen	2405 –2414	Kuri-galzu III ..	2387¾–2413¾
Mursil, his son. (Contemporary Tut-ankh-Amen to Seti I.)			Ay	2414 –2426½	Nazi-maruttash .	2413¾–2430¾
			Hor-em-heb ..	2426½–2430½		
			Ramessu I ..	2430½–2432½	Kadashman-Turgu	2430¾–2443¾
			Seti I	2432½–2441½		
		DYNASTY XIX IN EGYPT. 93 years. B.C. 1569 to 1476. TABLE XIV.	Ramessu II ..	2441½–2508½	Kudur-Enlil ..	2443¾–2449¾
					Sagarakti-Suriash	2449¾–2462¾
					Kashtiliash II ..	2462¾–2470¾
					ASSYRIANS CAPTURE BABYLON.	
					Enlil-nadin-sum..	2470¾–2472¾
Mutallu, his son; Hattusil II, his brother; Dudkhalia II, successor. (All contemporary with Ramessu II.)					Kadashman-Kharbe II	2472¾–2473¾
					Hadad-sum-iddin	2473¾–2479¾
					Hadad-sum-uzur .	2479¾–2509¾
			Menephtah ..	2508½–2516½	Meli-sipak II ..	2509¾–2524¾
Arnuanta, his son.	EXODUS OF ISRAEL. 2513½ A.K.		Amenmeses ..	2516½–2517½		
			Si-ptah and Tausert ..	2517 –2523		
Asia-Minor invaded from Europe, *circ.* 1500 B.C.	REFER TABLE XXIII AND PLATE LXI.				Merodach-Baladan I	2524¾–2537¾
			DYNASTY ENDS B.C. 1476.		Zamama-sum-iddin	2537¾–2538¾
					Bel-nadin-[akhi] .	2538¾–2541¾
Decline of Hittites during Rise of Aramaean Kingdom. (Damascus to Mesopotamia.) Refer Table XIX.			Anarchy and famine in Egypt followed by Invasion of Canaanites expelled from Syria by Israelites under Joshua. Refer Table XXIII.		Dynasty ends, and Dynasty II of Isin begins, 1458 B.C. Refer Table XIX.	

Dates enclosed in brackets thus (......) are derived by averaging from the known total duration of the Dynasty, and the fixed dates of known reigns, as Note to Table XVII.

Kings whose reigns are synchronised by their contemporary records are connected thus :—Amenhotep IV ______ Burnaburvas II.

ANNOTATIONS (A) TO TABLES XVII–XIX.

BABYLONIAN DYNASTIC SCHEMES (*PRE*-MEDO-PERSIAN) COMPLETED TO NABONIDOS.

(1) DYNASTIC DATES CORRECT FROM B.C. 2035 to B.C. 537.

	Dynasty.	Years	Date A.K.	Date B.C.
	Zero Epoch of System ..		0	4000
	Prior to Deluge (alleged) .. (as Berosus.)	[34,091]		
			1553½[4]	2446
I	8 Kings of Isin (I) .. (Prior to Dyn. II as Annotations B)	126½		
			1680[1]	2320
II	11 Kings of Babylon ..	285		
			1965	2035
III	11 (Contemporaries II & IV)			
IV	36 Kassite Kings ..	576⅝		
			2541⅝	1458
V	11 Kings of Isin (II) ..	132⅞		
			2674½	1325
VI	3 Kings of the Sea ..	21 5/12		
			2695 11/12	1304
VII	3 Kings of Bâzi ..	20 1/12		
			2716	1284
VIII	1 Elamite King ..	6		
			2722	1278
IX	31 Kings of Babylon ..	[546⅝]		
			3268⅝	731
X	21 Kings of Babylon ..	194⅜		
	Fall of Nabonidos ..		3463	537
	136 Kings, Total Years ..	1,909½		

Abstract :—	Years	
Gods before Deluge (as Berosus)	34,091	Note :—In A.K. column 11/12 reckoned as 1 year.
Kings after Deluge ..	1909	
Alleged Total years prior to Cyrus	36,000 (Total of Berosus.)	

(2) DYNASTIC DATES CORRECT FROM B.C. 2035 to B.C. 537.

	Dynasty	Years	Date A.K.	Date B.C.
	Zero Epoch of System ..		0	4000
	Prior to Deluge (alleged)	[34,091]		
			1554[1]	2446
I	8 Kings of Ur .. .. (As Annotations B)	117		
			1671	2329
II	11 Kings of Babylon ..	294		
			1965	2035
III	11 (Contemporaries II & IV)			
IV	36 As Col. 1	576⅝		
			2541⅝	1455
V	11 do.	132⅞		
			2674½	1325
VI	3 do.	21 5/12		
			2695 11/12	1304
VII	3 do.	20 1/12		
			2716	1284
VIII	1 do.	6		
			2722	1278
IX	31 do.	[546⅝]		
			3268⅝	731
X	21 do.	194⅜		
	Fall of Nabonidos ..		3463	537
	136 Kings, Total Years ..	1909		

Abstract :—	Years	
Gods before Deluge (as Berosus)	34,091	Note :—In A.K. column 11/12 reckoned as 1 year.
Kings after Deluge ..	1,909	
Alleged Total Years prior to Cyrus	36,000 (Total of Berosus.)	

THE SCHEME OF THE PTOLEMAIC PERIOD. THE BABYLONIAN DYNASTIC SCHEME OF THE CHALDÆAN PRIEST, BEROSUS.

(3) DYNASTIC DATES SUBSTANTIALLY CORRECT from end of Assyrian 7 years in Babylon, 2478 A.K.

	Dynasty.	Years	Date A.K.	Date B.C.
*	Zero Epoch of System ..		0	4000
I	86 Chaldæans for .. derived from 86⅛ Cycles of the Saros ..	34,091 =		
			1554[1]	2446
II	8 Medes	224		
			1778	2222
III	11 Chaldæans	248		
			2026	1974
IV	49 Chaldæans .. .. (Refer Table XVII *re* 2478 A.K.)	458		
			2484	1516
V	9 Arabians (7 years' error)	245		
			2729	1271
VI	45 Chaldæans	526		
			3255	745
VII	8 Assyrians	121		
			3376	624
VIII	6 Chaldæans	87		
	Fall of Nabonidos ..		3463	537
	136 Kings, Total Years ..	1,909		

Abstract as Columns 1 and 2.

With the exception of the 7 years' error for his Dyn. V placing, Berosus is correct in his datings from end of Assyrian 7 years' rule over Babylon (Table XVIII) to Nabonidos—as notes below.

MEDO-PERSIAN ARRANGEMENT OF THE BABYLONIAN DYNASTIC SCHEMES.

(4) DYNASTIC DATES 1 YEAR TOO LATE FROM B.C. 1324 to B.C. 536 (latter correct).

	Dynasty.	Years	Date A.K.	Date B.C.
	Zero Epoch of System ..		0	4000
	Prior to Deluge (alleged) (As Gods of *Old Egyptian Chronicle*).	[34,201]		
			1140	2860
I	"[8] Kings of Babylon after the Deluge"	[224]		
			1364	2636
II	11 as Col. 2	294		
			1658	2342
III	11 Kings of the Sea ..	368		
			2026	1974
IV	36 as Cols. 1 and 2 ..	576⅝		
			2602⅝	1397
V	11 Kings of Isin (II) ..	72⅞		
			2675½	1324
VI	3 as Cols. 1 and 2	21 5/12		
			2696 11/12	1303
VII	3 do.	20 1/12		
			2717	1283
VIII	1 do.	6		
			2723	1277
IX	31 do.	[546⅝]		
			3269⅝	730
X	21 do.	194⅜		
	1st year of Cyrus ..		3464	536
	136 Kings, Years { as *Old Egyptian Chronicle*	2,324 years		

(Dyns. II–IX: 2,100 years.)

Abstract :—	Years	
Gods before Deluge as *Old Egyptian Chronicle*	34,201	Note :—In A.K. column 11/12 reckoned as 1 year.
Kings after Deluge ..	2,324	
Total Years prior to Cyrus as *Old Egyptian Chronicle*	36,525	

(5) DYNASTIC DATES 1 YEAR TOO LATE FROM B.C. 1324 to B.C. 536 (latter correct).

	Dynasty.	Years	Date A.K.	Date B.C.
	Zero Epoch of System ..		0	4000
	Prior to Deluge (alleged) .. (as Berosus)	[34,091]		
			1030	2970
I	"[8] Kings of Babylon after the Deluge"	[334]		
			1364	2636
II	11 as Cols. 2 and 4 ..	294		
			1658	2342
III	11 as Col. 4	368		
			2026	1974
IV	36 as Cols. 1, 2, and 4 ..	576⅝		
			2602⅝	1397
V	11 as Col. 4	72⅞		
			2675½	1324
VI	3 as Cols. 1, 2, and 4	21 5/12		
			2696 11/12	1303
VII	3 do.	20 1/12		
			2717	1283
VIII	1 do.	6		
			2723	1277
IX	31 do.	[546⅝]		
			3269⅝	730
X	21 do.	194⅜		
	1st year of Cyrus ..		3464	536
	136 Kings, ⅔ of 3652 = ..	2,434 years		

(Dyns. II–IX: 2,100 years.)

Abstract :—	Years	
Gods before Deluge as Berosus ..	34,091	Note :—In A.K. column 11/12 reckoned as 1 year.
Kings after Deluge ..	2,434	
Total Years prior to Cyrus as *Old Egyptian Chronicle*	36,525	

ESSENTIAL DETAIL FOR COLUMNS 1 AND 2. 1ST DYN. OF BABYLON (DYN. II OF LISTS). According to the Fictitious Chronological Systems applying to dates prior to B.C. 2035.

	King.	(a) Years	(a) Date A.K.	(b) Years	(b) Date A.K.
			1680[1]		1671
1	Sumu-abu	14		14	
			1694		1685
2	Sumu-la-ilu	36		36	
			1730		1721
3	Zabium	14		14	
			1744		1735
4	Abil-sin	18		18	
			1762		1753
5	Sin-muballidh	20		20	
			1782		1773
6	Khammurabi	43		55	
			1825[2]		1828
7	Samsu-iluna	38		35	
			1863		1863
8	Abeshu	25		25	
			1888		1888
9	Ammiditana	25		25	
			1913		1913
10	Ammizadoq	21		21	
			1934		1934
11	Samsu-ditana	31		31	
			1965		1965
	Column (1) Total ..	285			
	Column (2) Total			294	

(Columns (a) and (b): Alternative Summation of the Dynastic Tablets.)

Dyn. IX duration is derived from comparison with col. 3 (136 kings for 1909 years in the three cases), and is confirmed by application in cols. 4 and 5, with different basal summations for the fictitious systems. The initial date, 2446, B.C. is derived from col. 3.

The equivalent A.K. reckoning is confirmed as follows:

[1] 1680 = Egyptian date in List of Suidas. 1680 years of 360 days = 1656 solar years = Hebrew Deluge dating. 1680 = ⅔ × 2520; 1656 = ⅔ × 2484. For 2484 refer col. 3. For 2484 as a Pyramid and Hebrew Dating refer ¶¶ 344, 345.

[2] By data (a) to left, Khammurabi ended at 1825 A.K. = ½ × 3650; 3650 being total of Castor's Egyptian gods and kings.

[3] The latter version of Castor is as follows:—

Egyptian Gods for	1550 years = 86 Chaldæan cycles of the Saros.	
Egyptian Kings for	2100 years (refer cols. 4 and 5).	
Total	3650 years.	

[4] From [3] above, the 1554 A.K. dating of Berosus is 86⅛ cycles of the Chaldæan Saros; this explaining the origin of the 86 Chaldæans in the alleged Dyn. I of Berosus (col. 3). For the precise significance of 1554 or 1553½ A.K. = 2446 B.C. refer col. 3 notes.

Dyn. VIII (Berosus)—The 6 Chaldæans are Nabopolassar to Nabonidos inclusive as Table XXI.

Dyn. VII (Berosus)—The 8 Assyrians are Tiglath-Pileser III to Assur-etilllans inclusive as Tables XX and XXI (and Annotations to latter). Tiglath-Pileser III's accession is B.C. 745 (Table XX). This is the B.C. datum for column 3. The resulting scheme gives the basal Dyn. II of Berosus beginning in 2446 B.C. The significance attached to this date is explained as follows:—Prof. G. Forbes (*Hist. Astron.*, *p.* 9) states:—"It is said that the (Chinese) Emperor Chueni (2513 B.C.) saw 5 planets in conjunction the same day that the sun and moon were in conjunction. This is discussed by Father Martin (MSS. of de Lisle), also by M. Desvignolles (Mem. Acad. Berlin, Vol. iii, p. 193), and by M. Kirch (*ibid.* vol. v, p. 19), who both found that Mars, Jupiter, Saturn, and Mercury were all between the 11th and 18th degrees of Pisces, all visible together in the evening on February 28th, 2446 B.C., while on the same day the sun and moon were in conjunction at 9 a.m., and that on March 1st the moon was in conjunction with the other four planets."

Cols. 4 and 5 largely explain their construction when studied in relation to Cols. 1–3.

In Col. 4, 1140 A.K. is the termination of the Dynasty of Enosh (Table V) at the 38th *Sed* festival.

In Col. 5, 1030 A.K. is the termination of 10 Calendar Cycles of 103 years (Tables II and III).

1658 A.K., common to Cols. 4 and 5, is 2 years after the Hebrew Deluge dating, 1656 A.K., and is therefore the date of the birth of Arphaxad. (Genesis xi, 10).

In Cols. 4 and 5, Dyn. IV begins at 2026 A.K., as in case of Dyn. IV of Berosus (col. 3).

Again, in the 17th year Sin-muballidh, Isin was captured (contemporary record). Rightly or wrongly, in later times, this was reckoned as the end of the 1st Dyn. of Isin. The alleged 17th year,—by lower column 1, (a) data to left,—began 1778 A.K. = 2222 B.C. Berosus (Col. 3) gives the Dynasty (of Sin-muballidh) beginning at 1778 A.K. = 2222 B.C.

Again,—by lower Column 1, (b) data to left—the 17th year Sin-muballidh = 1769 A.K. = 2231 B.C. This dating is explained by the following quotation from Sir Henry Rawlinson (in Canon Rawlinson's *Herodotus* I, 353) relating to the traditional founding of Babylon:—

"Age of Semiramis, or date of siege of Troy (according to Hellanicus)	1229	B.C.
Babylon built before that time	1002	years.
—(See Steph. Byz. *ad voc.* Βαβυλών	2231	B.C.
"Era of Ariphon at Athens	826	B.C.
Duration of Assyrian Monarchy	1460	years.*
	2286	B.C.
Deduct reign of Belus	55	years.
Era of Ninus, according to Ctesias	2231	B.C."

* This is the Egyptian Sothic Cycle period.

ANNOTATIONS (B) TO TABLES XVII–XIX.

The original Babylonian Chronology of the Dynasties of Ur and Isin (I): showing that the Dynasty of Ur ruled for 117 years prior to the 1st Dynasty of Babylon beginning, as Annotations (A), Column 2, Dynasty I, and that the 1st Dynasty of Babylon began after the Dynasty of Isin (I) had ruled for 126½ years, as Annotations (A), Column 1, Dynasty I.

The 8 kings of Annotations (A) Column, 1, Dynasty I, are Ishbi-Urra to Bursin II inclusive, with Gungunu added. The 8 kings of Annotations (A), Column 2, Dynasty I, are the 5 kings of Ur, with Ishme-Dagan, Libit-Ishtar and Gungunu added as below.

DYNASTY OF UR.
Duration 117 Years.
A.K. 1848–1965 = B.C. 2152–2035.

1848 A.K.	Dynasty began.
18 yrs.	Ur-Engur
1866 A.K.	Annexes Erech, Larsa, Lagash, and Nippur.
57 yrs.	Dungi, his son; his last year, 58th (contemp. record). (Sacked Babylon during his reign.)
1923 A.K.	
9 yrs.	Bursin I, his son.
	Libit-Ishtar overthrew Bursin I.
1932 A.K. ←	
9 yrs.	Gimil-sin II, his son, vassal of Gungunu.
1941	
21 yrs.	Ibi-sin, his son, carried captive to Ansban by Elamites in his 25th year.
1965 A.K.	Invasion of Kudur-Nankundhi.

PATESIS OF LAGASH.

Ur-Bau.
Ur-Gar.
Gudea, son-in-law of Ur-Bau (circ. 1850 A.K., B.C. 2150).
Ur-Ningirsa, his son.

KINGS CLAIMING TO BE OVERLORDS OF UR.

Ishme-Dagan.

Libit-Ishtar.

←Cause. — Gungunu — Effect→

"King of Sumer and Akkad," "King of Larsa," "King of Ur."

DYNASTY OF ISIN (I).
126½ years prior to 1st Dynasty of Babylon, but total duration 225½ years.
A.K. 1838½–2064 = B.C. 2161–1936.

Dynasty began	1838½ A.K.
Ishbi-Urra[1]	32 yrs
	1870½ A.K
Gimil-Ilishu, his son	10 yrs.
	1880½ A.K
Idin-Dagan, his son	21 yrs.
	1901½ A.K.
Ishme-Dagan, his son	20 yrs.
	1921½ A.K.
Libit-Ishtar, his son / Family ends. ..	11 yrs.
Gungunu overthrew Libit-Ishtar. →	1932½ A.K.
Vassal of Gungunu / Ur-Enurta / New family begins ..	28 yrs.
	1960½ A.K.
Bursin II, his son (for obvious succession refer Dyn. of Ur. Bursin I).	21 yrs
	1981½ A.K.
Iter-Pisha, his son	5 yrs.
	1986½ A.K.
Urri-Imitti, his brother ..	7 yrs.
	1993½ A.K.
[........]	½ yr.
	1994 A.K.
Enlil-Bani	24 yrs.
	2018 A.K.
Zambia	3 yrs
	2021 A.K.
[........]	5 yrs
	2026 A.K.
[........]	4 yrs
	2030 A.K.
Sin-Magir	11 yrs.
	2041 A.K.
Damki-Ilishu I	23
Isin captured	2064 A.K.

Isin captured, as recorded, at the end of the 17th year of Sin-muballiah.

THE 1st DYNASTY OF BABYLON.

This Dynasty began as result of the Elamite Invasion of Kudur-Nankundhi I overthrowing the Dynasty of Ur. The 1st Dynasty of Babylon began in the 5th year of Bursin II of the Dynasty of Isin, *i.e.* in the 127th year (126½ years duration) of the Dynasty of Isin (Annotations A) .. .. 1965 A.K.

Sumu-abu	14 yrs.
	1979 A.K.
Sumu-la-ilu	36 yrs.
	2015 A.K.
Zabium	14 yrs.
	2029 A.K
Abil-sin	18 yrs
	2047 A.K.
Sin-muballidh	20
	2067 A.K
Khammurabi	43 yrs.
	2110 A.K.

Dynasty continues as Tables XVII and XVIII.

KINGS OF ELAM.

Kudur-nankundhi .. (1965 A.K.)

Lila-irtash.

Simti-shilkhak.

Kudur-mabug .. (2023 A.K.)

Kudur-laghamar (Chedorlaomer.) .. Circ. (2088 A.K.).

ELAMITE RULERS CLAIMING S. BABYLONIA.

Warad-sin, son of Kudur-mabug .. (2023 A.K.).

Rimsin, brother of Warad-sin.

[1] The same general principle of evolution was adopted in the formulation of all the schemes of Dynastic Chronology in the ancient East. When a Dynasty A ended before a contemporaneous Dynasty B ended, the 1st king of Dynasty B, ultimately, in the Lists was presented as the successor of the last king of Dynasty A. This happened in the case of the 1st Dynasty of Babylon and the Kassites. It happened in the case of the 1st Dynasty of Babylon, and the Dynasty of the Sea It occurred, again, in the case of the Dynasty of the Sea and the Kassites. This is all as shown clearly on Table XVII when studied in relation to the notes thereon and the Annotations (A) to (C).

Hence that the Babylonian Dynastic List represents the Dynasty of Isin (I) beginning after the Dynasty of Ur, and with Ishbi-Urra succeeding Ibi-Sin.

Synchronisms indicated by connecting lines as in Tables XVII and XVIII and notes to same

THE ORIGINAL BABYLONIAN SCHEMES OF DYNASTIC CHRONOLOGY.

Scheme from 2344 B.C. to 537 B.C.		Scheme from 2231 B.C. to 537 B.C.	
Hebrew Deluge Date	1656 A.K.	Traditional Founding of Babylon, as Annotations (A), notes to Cols. 4 and 5 ..	1768½ A.K.
The Dynasty of Kish:— "After the Flood," Queen Azag-bau "strengthened the foundation of Kish," and reigned "100 years" Her 7 Successors reigned 92 years.	192 yrs.	Dynasty of Akkad:— Sargon I and his Successors, 12 kings in all alleged, for the alleged duration of 197 years.	197 yrs.
Dyn. of Ur began	1848 A.K.		
Dyn. of Ur duration	117		
Elamite Invasion of Kudur-nankundhi	1965 A.K.	Elamite Invasion of Kudur-nankundhi	1965 A.K.
1st Dyn. of Babylon followed by Supremacy of Kassites.	576¾	1st Dyn. of Babylon followed by Supremacy of Kassites.	576¾
Dyn. of Isin (II) began ..	2541¾ A.K.	Dyn. of Isin (II) began ..	2541¾ A.K.
Remaining Dyns. as Annotations (A), Cols. 1 and 2.	921¼	Remaining Dyns. as Annotations (A), Cols. 1 and 2.	921¼
Fall of Nabonidos	3463 A.K.	Fall of Nabonidos	3463 A.K.

THE SEQUENCE ESTABLISHING THE CHRONOLOGICAL ARRANGEMENT OF TABLES XVII, XVIII, AND XIX.

TABLE XIX.—The arrangement is fixed by datings of Dynasties V to X inclusive of Annotations (A), Columns 1 and 2, and is confirmed by the resulting date for Nabonassar agreeing with the known, astronomically fixed date for Nabonassar, and also by the resulting chronology of Tables XVII and XVIII bringing Babylonian and Assyrian chronology precisely into synchronism with the astronomically fixed chronology of the Hebrews and Egyptians.

TABLE XVII.—The arrangement is fixed by the data of Table XIX, and by the historical synchronisms established in Table XVII itself, as independently effected by the data and synchronisms established in these Annotations (B). These all show that the 1st Dynasty of Babylon began at 1965 A.K. = 2035 B.C., and that the rule of the Kassites came to an end 576¾ years later, at 2541¾ A.K. = 1458 B.C. Refer also Annotations (D).

TABLE XVIII.—The known historical synchronisms as set out in this Table, by agreeing in precise detail with the three independently fixed systems of astronomical chronology—the Hebrew, Egyptian, and Babylonian—confirm that all three systems of chronology are correct. The chronological basis of Tables XVII, and XIX is confirmed, as a known chronological basis, by the comparative analysis of the chronological statement of late Babylonian and Assyrian times, as set forth in Annotations (C) to these Tables.

The authorities for the Data compressed into analytic form in these Annotations are the various well-known works of Professors L. W. King, R. W. Rogers, and H. Radau, Drs. H. R. Hall, and C. H. W. Johns, with the new 1st volume of "The Cambridge Ancient History."

THE CHRONOLOGY CONFIRMED BY AN ASTRONOMICAL DATUM:—

(1) By Table XVI a *Sep tep sed heb* (480 years from Datum at 1656 A.K.) was celebrated at 2136 A.K.

(2) By Table XVII the 27th year of Samsu-iluna began at 2136 A.K.

(3) A record of Samsu-iluna states that "a great dedication for the New Year Festival" was observed in the 27th year.

ANNOTATIONS (C) TO TABLES XVII-XIX.

THE EXPLANATION OF LATE ASSYRIAN AND BABYLONIAN CHRONOLOGICAL STATEMENTS.

[To face p. 314 following. (Bl.

KHAMMURABI, ABRAHAM, AND SENUSERT III, IN RELATION TO THE HITTITES AND HYKSOS.

Khammurabi was the 6th king of the so-called 1st Dynasty of Babylon (refer Table XVIII and Annotations (B)). He warred with the Elamites until his 11th year. From his 11th year to his 30th year was a period of peace between Khammurabi and the Elamites in Babylonia. Until his 30th year Khammurabi was nominally vassal of Elam. In his 30th year, he, however, threw off the Elamite yoke, and was completely victorious against the Elamites in Babylonia in the following year. (Refer King, "Hist. Babylon," p. 153 et seq.; Cambridge Anc. Hist., Vol. I, pp. 487-488; Hall, "Anc. Hist. Near East," p. 196; Rogers, "Hist. Bab. and Assyr.," Vol. I, p. 368 et seq.; Johns, "Anc. Bab." p. 78.)

The period from the 11th to the 30th years of Khammurabi is therefore the only period in which Khammurabi could be in alliance with Elam. From Table XVII this period is dated at 2077 to 2096 A.K. Now from Genesis, xiv, 1-5 and the narrative of Abraham's life to xvi, 3 and 16, in relation to xii, 4 and 5, the invasion of Chedorlaomer, king of Elam, and his vassals, Amraphel (Khammurabi), Arioch, and Tidal (king of Goyyim or Hittites)—refer ¶ 319 —into Canaan occurred between 2084 and 2093 A.K. These two limiting dates both fall within the dated period, of Khammurabi's reign, during which the alliance was possible. But we can more closely date the invasion than this. Genesis, xiv, 2-5, states that the 5 kings in Canaan served Chedorlaomer for 12 years, rebelled in the 13th, and were attacked by Chedorlaomer in the 14th year. Now Chedorlaomer could not be free to extend his dominion to Canaan when Khammurabi was disputing with the Elamites in Babylonia. The 12 years' service could not begin, therefore, until Khammurabi's 11th year or later. The earliest dated period for the 12 years is therefore 2077 to 2089 A.K. The 13th year was therefore 2089-2090 A.K. at earliest, and the 14th year, the year of the battle, 2090-2091 A.K. at earliest. Being probably in the Spring, "when kings go forth to battle," the date is 2090½ A.K. at earliest. By the data of Genesis the latest date is the Spring prior to 2093 A.K., and therefore 2092½ A.K. Again, by the fact, that Khammurabi's resistance to the Elamites in Babylonia continued to his 11th year, we may date the beginning of the 12 years' service a year later at the Spring, 2078½ A.K., and "the battle of 4 kings with 5" at 2091½ A.K., at the commencement of the 14th year. The narrative of Genesis and its chronology is therefore seen to agree as precisely with the Babylonian data and chronology as they do with the Egyptian data and chronology.

Now Hittites took part in this battle, and it is after the date of this battle that Hittites are described as first dwelling in Southern Canaan (¶ 319). In the year of the battle Amorites dwelt " in the plain of Mamre " (Gen., xiv, 13). In the year of Sarah's death Hittites dwelt there (Gen. xxiii, 2, 8, 10, 17, 19). Sarah died 62 years after the Call of Abraham at 2083½ A.K., by Gen. xii, 4; xvii, 17; xxiii, 1. The date of Sarah's death is, therefore, 2145½ A.K., 54 years after the "battle of 4 kings with 5." Hittites, therefore, first appeared in Southern Canaan between 2091½ and 2145½ A.K. Now this identification and this dating are important since Maspero (" Struggle of the Nations " p 57) attributes the swarming of the Hyksos into Egypt to the pressure of Hittites coming into Canaan. Sayce, in a footnote to Maspero's statement, remarks that " the Hyksos invasion has been regarded as a natural result of the Elamite Conquest, by Maspero, Lenormant, Meyer, Hommel, and Naville." By Annotations (B), the Elamite Invasion of Babylonia took place in 1965 A.K. By Annotations (A) to Table XV, the Hyksos first entered Egypt in the 6th year of Senusert II, at 2063 A.K. This agrees with the dating above, giving the period of Elamite domination over Southern Canaan as beginning in 2077 to 2078 A.K. The first Hyksos migration obviously was effected by reason of the threatening dominance of Elam. The complicated race movements at this time primarily originated, however, as a result of the recurrence of the periodic famine cycle that affected territories successively from the mountains of Elam and Asia Minor down into Egypt (refer ¶ 319). This again equates the famine of Abraham (2083½ A.K.) and the river improvement and famine relief works of Senusert III in 2084 A.K. (refer ¶ 319 and Table XXII), with the race movements central to the reign of Khammurabi.

As a result of the data discussed in the preceding paragraphs, Budge considers that the Hyksos invasion of Egypt was contemporaneous with the times of Khammurabi. Regarding these times he states :—
" The Elamite and Kassite pressure from the East caused an emigration from Babylonia and her dependencies westwards and southwards, and the people thus dispossessed drove before them the nomadic tribes on the North-East of Egypt " (" Hist. Egypt," Vol. III, pp. 136-137).

Regarding the same movement, Maspero states (p. 56) that " An impulse once given, it needed but little to accelerate or increase the movement ; a collision with one horde reacted on its neighbours, who either displaced or carried others with them, and the whole multitude, gathering momentum as they went, were precipitated in the direction first given."

The Hyksos, the first of this stream to arrive on the borders of Egypt, immediately fortified the Eastern frontier of the Delta. Manetho, as quoted by Josephus (Contra Apion I, 14) attributes this work to the first Hyksos king, giving as reason that " he regarded with suspicion the increasing power of the Assyrians."

" In this statement," says Budge, " we seem to have a reflection of solid historical fact, for the Assyrians here referred to are, no doubt, those who were dwellers in Mesopotamia, and who were subjects of the viceroys of the kingdom afterwards called Assyria, which they ruled on behalf of their overlords, the kings of Babylon, i.e., Khammurabi and his immediate successors. The dwellers in Syria and Palestine joined with the nomadic tribes of the Eastern Desert, and fled to Egypt for safety, and it needed little foresight to see that they might easily be pursued thither by the victorious armies of Assyria and Babylon.' (" Hist. Egypt," III, 135.)

Similarly, in footnote to Maspero, p. 52, Sayce states " Manetho here speaks of Assyrians ; this is an error which is to be explained by the imperfect state of historical knowledge in Greece at the time of the Macedonian supremacy......read Chaldæans where Manetho has written Assyrians. In Herodotus ' Assyria ' is the regular term for ' Babylonia ' and Babylonia is termed ' the land of the Assyrians.' "

The reason for the fortifying of the frontier of the Delta by the Hyksos is clearly given by the narrative of Genesis xiv. Chedorlaomer and his vassals, including Khammurabi (Amraphel) had penetrated Southern Canaan as far South as the Dead Sea. This was too close for the Hyksos who had settled in the Delta. As shown in Annotations (C) to Table XV, the 1st king of the Hyksos, Apepa I, reckoned his reign from the date of the first entry of the Hyksos in 2063 A.K. and his 33rd year was the 2nd year of Amenemhat III, i.e., 2095½ A.K. Apepa I's date therefore agrees with the statement of Manetho as related to the invasion of Chedorlaomer and his Babylonian and Hittite allies at 2091½ A.K.

The facts relating to the earlier migrations into Egypt prior to the campaign of Chedorlaomer into Southern Canaan would account for the facility with which Abram and his servitors—journeying from far " Ur of the Chaldees," captured by the Elamites 118 years previously, —passed through Haran in Mesopotamia and through Canaan, into Egypt in time of famine, all as an apparently rational sequence of movement. The date (2083 A.K.) of his journey falls within the period of 19 years' peace between Khammurabi and the Elamites in Southern Babylonia, later identified as the " land of the Chaldæans." It falls also within the 12 years' servitude of the kings of Southern Canaan under Chedorlaomer.

Although not represented as belonging to a horde of migrating people moving towards Egypt, nevertheless Abram's party moved contemporaneously with such a movement. Naturally the normal rate of movement of the migrating hordes would be accelerated by the famine in Canaan, the severity of which must of necessity have been intensified by the sudden large excess of population projected into Canaan by the first waves of the migratory movement.

We find, therefore, that Babylonian Chronology and the records of Khammurabi relating to the circumstances of the invasion of Chedorlaomer into Southern Canaan confirm that the Journey of Abram happened in 2083 to 2084 A.K. Similarly we find that the Egyptian chronology and the records of Senusert III independently confirm the date (2084 A.K.) and circumstances of Abram's entry into Egypt (Tables XV and XXII and ¶¶ 317 and 319). The following statements of Petrie and Budge, concerning Senusert III, are therefore significant. Petrie (" Hist. Egypt " I 178) states " The name of this king in the Greek Lists, Lakheres, is quite accounted for by the corruption of X into ʌ, by the omission of the top ; thus altering Kha-kau-ra, or Khakeres, into Lakheres." Budge states, " Lachares (Lakheres) must be identified with the Nachares of the Christian chronographers in whose reign the patriarch Abraham is said to have come into Egypt " (" Hist. Egypt," III, 42.)

TABLE XIX.

THE TRUE CHRONOLOGY OF THE BABYLONIAN DYNASTIC TABLET FROM B.C. 1458 TO B.C. 731. 2ND DYNASTY OF ISIN TO 2ND DYNASTY OF BABYLON INCLUSIVE.

	BABYLONIA.		DATE A.K.	ASSYRIA.	MESOPOTAMIA.
	2nd DYNASTY OF ISIN. 132½ Years. B.C. 1458 to 1325.				Aramaeans, Sutu, etc.
1.	Merodach-[shâpik-zêrim] ..	18 years ..	2541¾ – 2559¾.	Assur-Dan I.	ARAMAIC KINGDOM OF MESOPOTAMIA. (Judges iii, 8).
2.	.. ..	6 years ..	2559¾ – 2565¾.	Mutagil-Nusku (his son).	
3.	.. ..				
4.	.. ..				
5.	.. ..				
6.	Nebuchadnezzar I.	— ..	— – 2652¾.	Assur-ris-isi (his son).	Assur-ris-isi occupied Mesopotamia to check incursions of Aramaeans.
7.	Enlil-nadin-pal				
8.	Merodach-nadin-akhi ..	22 years ..	2630¾ – 2651¾.	Tiglath-Pileser I. (his son).	Tiglath-Pileser I checks incursions of Aramaeans, and drives them out of Pitru (the Pethor of Numbers xxii, 5) and across the Euphrates.
9.	Merodach-shâpik-zêr-mâti ..	1½ years ..	2652¾ – 2654¼.	Assur-bil-kala (his son).	ARAMAEANS RECAPTURE PITRU LATER IN SAME REIGN.
	[Hadad-Baladan (Usurper) reign ignored by Lists as Contemporary]		——		In the reign of Hadad-Baladan, Aramaeans plundered cities of Akkad, and Sutu raided Babylonia, carrying off plunder of Sumer and Akkad.
10.	Merodach-zêr-[........] ..	12 years ..	2654¼ – 2666¼.	Samsi-Hadad (his brother).	
11.	Nabu-shum-libur	8 years ..	2666¼ – 2674¼.	Assur-nazir-pal II (his son).	
	DYNASTY ENDS.				
	DYNASTY OF THE SEA-COAST (PERSIAN GULF). 21½ years. B.C. 1325 to 1304.				Aramaeans swarm into Babylonia and Assyria, accompanied by swarms of Sutu.
1.	Simmash-shipak	18 years ..	2674¼ – 2692¼.		The Chaldaeans, a kindred people to the Aramaeans, coming from the North-East of Arabia, swarmed over Southern Babylonia.
2.	Ea-mukin-zari	½ year ..	2692¼ – 2692¾.		
3.	Kassu-nadin-ak	3 years ..	2692¾ – 2695¾.		
	DYNASTY ENDS.				PERIOD OF DETERMINING PHASE OF ABOVE MOVEMENTS, 2650 to 2716 A.K.
	DYNASTY OF BIT BAZI. 20¼ years. B.C. 1304 to 1284.				ASSYRIA WAS FIRST WIPED OUT OF
1.	Ea-Ulmas-sakin-sumu ..	17 years ..	2695¾ – 2712¾.		EXISTENCE, THUS ACCOUNTING FOR THE
2.	Ninip-kudur-uzur I ..	3 years ..	2712¾ – 2715¾.		
3.	Silanim-Suqamuna ..	¼ year ..	2715¾ – 2716.		
	DYNASTY ENDS.				LONG GAP IN ASSYRIAN HISTORY FROM
	DYNASTY OF ELAM. 6 years. B.C. 1284 to 1278.				ASSUR-NAZIR-PAL II TO TIGLATH-PILESER II
	An Elamite	6 years ..	2716 – 2722.	OMINOUS GAP	2670 to 3010 A.K.
	DYNASTY ENDS.				

2nd DYNASTY OF BABYLON. 31 KINGS FOR 546¼ YEARS.
B.C. 1278 to 731.
12 INITIAL NAMES OMITTED FROM THE LIST.

No.	Name	Years	Dates
1.	...		2722 – (2742).
2.	...		(2742 – 2762).
3.	...		(2762 – 2782).
4.	...		(2782 – 2802).
5.	...		(2802 – 2822).
6.	...		(2822 – 2843).
7.	...		(2843 – 2863).
8.	...		(2863 – 2883).
9.	...		(2883 – 2903).
10.	...		(2903) – (2923½).
11.	7th year Eclipse Record		(2923½) – (2942).
12.	(Ninip-kudur-uzur II)	2 years	(2942 – 2944).
13.	Nebo-kin-abli	36 years	(2944 – 2980).
14.	Ninip-kudur-uzur III	½ year	(2980 – 2980½).
15.	...		(2980½ – 2995).
16.	...		(2995 – 3010).
17.	...		(3010 – 3025).
18.	...		(3025 – 3040).
19.	...		(3040 – 3055).
20.	Samas-mudammiq		(3055 – 3070).
21.	Nebo-sum-iskin		(3070 – 3089)
22.	Nebo-Baladan	31 years	(3089 – 3120).
23.	Merodach-zakir-sumi		(3120 – 3143).
24.	Merodach-baladhsu-iqbi		(3143 – 3165).
25.	Bau-akhi-iddin		(3165 – 3187).
26.	[Erba-Merodach]		(3187 – 3209).
27.	Nebo-sum-iskun		(3209 – 3231).
28.	...		(3231 – 3252½).
29.	Nabonassar (B.C. 747)	14 years	3252½ – 3266⅔.
30.	Nebo-nadin-suma	2 years	3266⅔ – 3268⅓.
31.	Nebo-sum-yukin	1 month	3268⅓ – 3268¼.

DYNASTY INDICATED AS ENDING B.C. 731.

IN ASSYRIAN HISTORY.

FOR CHRONOLOGY OF THE FOLLOWING ASSYRIAN REIGNS refer Annotations (D) to Table XXVI

(ASSYRIAN EPONYM CANON BEGINS)

Tiglath-Pileser II.

Assur-Dan II (his son).

Hadad-nirari II (his son).

Tukulti-Enurta II (his son).
Assur-nazir-pal III (his son).

Shalmaneser II (his son), captures Babylon.

Assur-danin-pal (his son).
Samsi-Hadad II (his brother).
Hadad-nirari III (his son)
Shalmeneser III.
Assur-Dan III.
Assur-Nirari.
Pulu = Tiglath-pileser III.
(B.C. 745 to 727).

PERIOD OF SUPREMACY OF ARAMAEAN-CHALDAEAN-SUTU CONFEDERATION OF TRIBES IN BABYLONIA AND ASSYRIA.

Thus, Winckler and King state:—

"We have no trustworthy information as to Assyria or Babylon" at this time.

"......concerning the history of the period information is still lacking."

"......Mesopotamia and Babylonia were at this time the object of the third of the Semitic migrations....the Aramaean....This period covers the above mentioned devastation of Babylonia by the Sutu; and we must also include the advance into Babylonia of the Aramaean tribes which afterwards settled there."

"......With Aslur-nazir-pal (III), who reigned from 885 to 860 B.C., our sources of information once more become abundant...."

"The later Assyria of Ashurnazirpal and Shalmaneser II had (quite a different population, influenced in some degree by the Aramaean immigration.....The wars of aggrandisement were waged by Assyria with a standing Army—that is, with an army of mercenaries.....composed of heterogeneous elements....""

Dates enclosed in brackets thus (.....) are derived by averaging from the known total duration of the Dynasty, and the fixed dates of known reigns, as Note to Table XVII.
Kings whose reigns are synchronised by their contemporary records are connected thus:—Nebuchadnezzar I.   Assur-ris-isi.

TABLE XX.

THE CHRONOLOGY OF THE PERIOD OF ASSYRIAN SUPREMACY.

ALL DATES ARE ASTRONOMICALLY FIXED DATES FROM THE ASSYRIAN CHRONICLE, THE BABYLON-IAN CHRONICLE, THE ASSYRIAN EPONYM CANON, AND FROM THE ANNALS OF SARGON, ETC.; DATES BEING FIXED FROM SOLAR AND LUNAR ECLIPSE RECORDS AND AN UNBROKEN ENUMERATION OF EVERY YEAR FROM ASSUR-DAN III TO ESARHADDON INCLUSIVE (771–668 B.C.).

FOR THE FOLLOWING DATES, NO SINGLE DATUM—CHRONOLOGICAL OR ASTRONOMICAL—HAS BEEN OBTAINED FROM PTOLEMY'S ALMAGEST, NOR FROM HIS DATED CANON OF REIGNS. THE CHRONOLOGY IS FIXED ASTRONOMICALLY ENTIRELY FROM THE BABYLONIAN AND ASSYRIAN RECORDS. THIS IS THE RECEIVED CHRONOLOGY AS STATED WITHIN THE DATED LIMITS OF THE TABLE. THE JULIAN MONTH DATINGS HAVE BEEN SPECIALLY CALCULATED FOR THIS TABLE.

Assyrian king and Julian month dates of Accession and death	"Accession Year" beginning March–April B.C.	"First Year" beginning March–April B.C.	Double Dating for "First Year" beginning March–April B.C.	"First Year" beginning March–April B.C.	"Accession Year" beginning March–April B.C.	Babylonian king and Julian month dates of Accession and death
Tiglath–pileser III Accession 13th Iyyar =11th May, 745 B.C. Death in Tebet= January, 726 B.C.	745	744	743	747	—	Nabonassar.
				733	—	Nadinu.
				731	—	Suma-yukin.
				731	—	Yukin-zira.
				728	729	Tiglath-Pileser III.
Shalmaneser Accession 25 Tebet= 23rd Jan., 726 B.C. Death in Tebet= January, 721 B.C.	727	726	Nil	726	727	Shalmaneser.
Sargon Accession 12 Tebet= 15th Jan., 721 B.C. Death in Ab=Aug., 705 B.C.	722	721	719	721	721	Merodach-baladan. Accession Nisan= March, 721 B.C.
				709	710	Sargon.
Sennacherib Accession 12 Ab= 15th August, 705 B.C. Death 20 Tebet= 22nd January, 680	705	704	Nil	704	705	Sennacherib.
				Nil	703	Merodach-zaki-sumi.
				Nil	703	Merodach-baladan. a soldier of Khabi.
For Synchronisation of Assyrian and Biblical (O.T.) accounts concerning Sennacherib, refer Table XXVI Annotations (C).				702	703	Bel-ebus.
				699	700	Assur-nadin-sum-a.
				693	694	Nergal-yusezib. Captured 7 Tisri= 24th Sept., 693 B.C.
				692	693	Musezib-Merodach. Captured 1 Kisleu= 2nd Dec., 689 B.C.
				688	689	Sennacherib.
Esarhaddon Accession 8 Sivan= 6th June. 680 B.C. Death 10th March-esvan=25th October 668 B.C.	681	680	Nil	679	680	Esarhaddon.
Assur-bani-pal (20 years' reign as Assur-bani-pal).	668	667	Nil	667	668	Saul-suma-yukina (20 years' reign).
Kandalanu (=Assur-bani-pal for additional 22 years'		[647]		[647]		Kandalanu (=Assur-bani-pal for 22 years in Babylon).
Assur-etillani		[625]	ASSYRIAN SUPREMACY ENDS	[625]		NABOPOLASSAR with whom Babylon-ian-Chaldaean Supremacy begins.

DATES BRACKETTED THUS [ ] ARE OBTAINED FROM STATED DURATIONS OF REIGNS ONLY.

ANNOTATIONS TO TABLE XX.

THE "ACCESSION YEAR" AND THE "FIRST YEAR."

At the time of the 1st Dynasty of Babylon (Khammurabi) the method of applying year-names to the regnal years of the king was introduced. The regnal year began on the 1st of Nisan, "when each king of Babylon celebrated the Feast of the New Year's Day, and taking the hands of his god in the temple, thus became the adopted son of the deity and himself divine" (C. H. W. Johns, "Anc. Babylonia," p. 5—refer also ¶ ¶ 34 to 40 of this volume).

During the Kassite Dynasty of Babylon an improved method of reckoning the regnal years of the kings was introduced. At this time, "If a king died in the 20th year of his reign, he was reckoned to have reigned 20 years. The remainder of that year was called the 'beginning' of his successor's reign; but the earliest full year after that First of Nisan, which fell next after his accession, was called his 'first year.' It is usual to call the fraction of a year, which fell after his accession, his 'accession year' to distinguish it from his 'first year'." (C. H. W. Johns, Ibid, p. 7).

It is of importance to observe that this practice—as followed by successive kings and their scribes in dating *current* regnal years—was followed by all kings down to the Medo-Persians inclusive. Thus Darius I Hystaspes has his 'accession year' and his 'first year,' the earliest dating of the latter being 1st Nisan (Mar.-April), and the earliest dating of the former in Sebat (Jan.-Feb.), following news of the death of Cambyses in Syria reaching Babylon in December or January; since the last dating of Cambyses at Babylon is Tebet (Dec. or Jan.) of his 8th and last year. These particular datings, as shown in Annotations to Table XXVII, prove that the first year of Darius I began spring, B.C. 521—the end of the 8th year of Cambyses, who had died 7 months previously in returning to quell the rebellion of the usurper Bardis. This is an item of extreme importance, not only in relation to Medo-Persian history, but in relation to Hebrew history. For this reason the matter is mentioned here to emphasize the importance of accession year and first year datings.

In chronicling the reigns of kings and the duration of Dynasties, however, the chronological scribes of the Babylonians frequently gave the precise duration of reigns from accession to death; the total for the Dynasty being the summation of all such reigns as thus defined.

THE DATES IN PTOLEMY'S CANON OF BABYLONIAN KINGS.

The Assyrian Eponym Canon gives the Accession Year of Esarhaddon as identical with the last year of Sennacherib, which began in March, 681 B.C.; whereas the Babylonian Chronicle gives the Accession year of Esarhaddon in the year following. The reason for the difference is as is explained by the Babylonian Chronicle, that from the death of Sennacherib on 20th Tebet (22nd Jan., 680 B.C.) to the 2nd Adar (3rd March, 680 B.C.) was a period of insurrection in Assyria. Esarhaddon was then absent on an expedition to Armenia, and was saluted by his soldiers as king on 12th Iyyar (12th May) 680 B.C.

As the Babylonian Chronicle states, Esarhaddon did not ascend the throne until 8th Sivan following, *i.e.* on 6th June, 680 B.C.

The above is of importance as explaining why Ptolemy gives 680 B.C. as the 1st year of Esarhaddon. In all other cases Ptolemy's dates for the commencement of the Babylonian reigns are as stated in the column of "First Years," in Table XX. The actual facts are that the Babylonians reckoned 679 B.C. as the 1st year of Esarhaddon, and that the Assyrians reckoned 680 B.C. as the 1st year. Thus the Babylonians have the same dates for the last year of Sennacherib and for the last year of Esarhaddon as the Assyrians had, but they termed the last year of Esarhaddon the 12th year, whereas the Assyrians termed it the 13th year.

The difference in enumeration is due to the Assyrians reckoning the 69 days between the death of Sennacherib and the commencement of the Assyrian New Year (1st Nisan) on 1st April, 680 B.C., as the Accession Year of Esarhaddon; and to the Babylonians reckoning the Accession Year of Esarhaddon from 1st April, 680 B.C., because Esarhaddon did not formally ascend the throne until 12th May, 680 B.C.

Actually, then, there is no difference between the two statements of Esarhaddon's reign, since both the Babylonians and Assyrians inform us that Esarhaddon reigned a few months less than 13 whole years. Ptolemy is, therefore, quite correct in placing Esarhaddon as reigning 13 years, from spring of 680 B.C. to spring of 667 B.C., when the 1st year of Assurbanipal began in Assyria, and the 1st year of his brother, Saul-suma-yukina, began in Babylon.

The Canon of Ptolemy is, therefore, correct as a statement of the beginning of the 1st years of all kings who reigned in Babylon from Nabonassar to Saul-suma-yukina.

TABLE XXI.

THE CHRONOLOGICAL DATA FIXING THE CHRONOLOGY OF THE BABYLONIAN–CHALDÆAN MONARCHY, NABOPOLASSAR TO NABONIDOS INCLUSIVE.

(1)
THE CHRONOLOGY OF THE XTH DYNASTY OF THE DYNASTIC TABLET OF THE BABYLONIANS.
Actually stated as 194½ years from 3268½ A.K. (B.C. 731) to 3463 A.K. (B.C. 537) the overthrow of Nabonidos.

		A.K.		B.C.	
	Compare Table XX (1st years) ..	3268½	=	731	
1	Yukin-zira				3 years.
2	Tiglath-Pileser III	3271½	=	728	2 years.
3	Shalmaneser	3273½	=	726	5 years.
4	Merodach-baladan	3278½	=	721	12 years.
5	Sargon	3290½	=	709	5 years.
6	Sennacherib	3295½	=	704	2 years.
7	Merodach-zaki-sumi				
8	Merodach-baladan, a soldier of Khabi ..	3297½	=	702	
9	Bel-ebus				3 years.
10	Assur-nadin-suma	3300½	=	699	6 years.
11	Nergal-yusezib	3306½	=	693	1 year.
12	Musezib-Merodach	3307½	=	692	4 years.
(6a)	Sennacherib	3311½	=	688	8 years.
13	Esarhaddon	3319½	=	680	13 years.
14	Saul-sum-yukina	3332½	=	667	20 years.
15	Kandalanu	3352½	=	647	22 years.
16	Nabopolassar, Babylonian vassal under Assur-etililani of Assyria .. .	3374½	=	625	2 years.
		3376½	=	623	
	Nabopolassar, independent king of Babylon				21 years.
17	Nebuchadnezzar	3397½	=	602	43 years.
18	Amil-marduk (Evil-Merodach)	3440½	=	559	2 years.
19	Nergal-sherezer	3442½	=	557	4 years.
20	Labashi-marduk during last year ..	3446½	=	553	
21	Nabonidos				17 years.
	1st year Cyrus begins	3463½	=	536	
	Nabonidos overthrown Summer of 537 B.C.				

(2)
THE CHRONOLOGY OF BEROSUS
His 8 Assyrians from Tiglath-Pileser III to Assur-etililani inclusive, followed by his 6 Chaldæans from Nabopolassar to Nabonidos inclusive.

		B.C.
	Compare Table XX (1st years) and Annotations re Esarhaddon ..	744
1	Tiglath-Pileser III	
		726
2	Shalmaneser	
		721
3	Sargon	
		704
4	Sennacherib	
		680
5	Esarhaddon	
		667
6	Assurbanipal	
		647
7	(Do.) as Kandalanu	
		625
8	Assur-etililani	
		623
1	Nabopolassar	
		602
2	Nebuchadnezzar	
		559
3	Amil-Marduk	
		557
4	Nergal-sherezer	
5	Labashi-marduk	
		553
6	Nabonidos	
		536

THE 8 ASSYRIANS OF BEROSUS FOR 121 YEARS, B.C. 744 TO 623.

THE 6 CHALDÆANS OF BEROSUS FOR 87 YEARS. B.C. 623 TO 536.

Comparison of Tables XX and XXI fixes that 1st year Cyrus, according to the Babylonian Lists, and the List of Berosus, began in Spring, B.C. 536. This confirms the general indication of Annotations to Tables XVII to XIX. Refer Annotations (opposite) to Table XXI.

ANNOTATIONS TO TABLE XXI.

Table XXI establishes the date of Cyrus independent of the data of Table XVII Annotations A. The beginning of the reign of Cyrus is given by Ptolemy as 538 B.C. Ptolemy gives no astronomical data to confirm this as he does in the case of Nabopolassar and Cambyses. Between the 5th year of Nabopolassar and the 7th year of Cambyses, Ptolemy gives no astronomical data. Dual datings, such as those of Table XX, and overlapping datings due to coregencies would in consequence, confuse the chronological statement of Ptolemy. Because Ptolemy is correct in all cases where he has had astronomical datings to check his chronological statement, does not mean that he is right where he has had no such astronomical statements. He is certainly wrong in the statement of the period from Nabopolassar to Cyrus inclusive, as the comparative statement of Table XXI shows.

Table XXI Col. (1) shows that Nabopolassar had a double system of datings, as Tiglath-Pileser III and Sargon. Col. (2) compared with Ptolemy's List confirms this. Nabopolassar had an earlier system of dating from the beginning of his reign as the Babylonian viceroy of Assyria under Assur-etillani. The dating of the 5th year of Nabopolassar in Ptolemy's *Almagest*—recording the eclipse observed in that year at Babylon—belongs to this earlier method of dating. The records of the later years of Nabopolassar, when the yoke of Assyria had been definitely shaken off, date from the assertion of Nabopolassar's independence in 623 B.C. His recorded 21 years of rule are dated from this datum (623 B.C.) as a Babylonian Epoch.

Basing on the dates given by Ptolemy for Nabopolassar and Cyrus, historians, without paying much critical attention to the question, have considered that the last two dynasties of Berosus—8 Assyrians for 121 years, followed by 6 Chaldæans for 87 years to Cyrus—necessarily should begin at Nabonassar (717 B.C.) as Table XX and end at 539 B.C.; the latter being the supposed date of the overthrow of Nabonidos prior to the Spring of 538 B.C., the supposed beginning of the 1st year of Cyrus.

But if Berosus had dated from Nabonassar he would have stated "Babylonians" and not "Assyrians" as he has done. Moreover, there are 8 Assyrians from Tiglath-Pileser III to Assur-etililani, inclusive (as Table XXI Col. 2) whereas there are 19 kings of Babylon from Nabonassar inclusive, prior to Nabopolassar, as in right-hand column of Table XX.

THE ESSENTIAL FACTS ARE :—

I (1) THAT BEROSUS GIVES 8 ASSYRIANS FOR 121 YEARS

(2) THAT THE 1ST OF THESE IS TIGLATH-PILESER AND THE LAST ASSUR-ETILLANI.

(3) THAT THE ASTRONOMICALLY FIXED BEGINNING OF THE 1ST YEAR OF TIGLATH-PILESER IS SPRING B.C. 744.

(4) THAT, IN CONSEQUENCE, THE 121 YEARS ENDED AT SPRING, B.C. 623.

(5) THAT THE RULE IN BABYLON THEN PASSED FROM ASSUR-ETILILANI TO NABOPOLASSAR, THE FOUNDER OF THE BABYLONIAN-CHALDÆAN MONARCHY.

II (1) THAT BEROSUS GIVES 6 CHALDÆANS FOR 87 YEARS.

(2) THAT THE 6 CHALDÆANS ARE NABOPOLASSAR TO NABONIDOS INCLUSIVE.

(3) THAT CYRUS THEREFORE BEGAN HIS 1ST YEAR IN SPRING, B.C. 536.

II (1) THAT THE BABYLONIAN DYNASTIC TABLET GIVES 194½ YEARS FROM YUKIN-ZIRA TO OVERTHROW OF NABONIDOS.

(2) THAT YUKIN-ZIRA'S 1ST YEAR, ASTRONOMICALLY FIXED, BEGAN IN SPRING, B.C. 731.

(3) THAT NABONIDOS, THEREFORE, WAS OVERTHROWN IN SUMMER, B.C. 537.

(4) THAT, IN CONSEQUENCE, 1ST YEAR CYRUS BEGAN SPRING, B.C. 536.

The Certain Facts are :—

(1) That the records and other data from native sources fix the 1st year of Cyrus as beginning Spring, B.C. 536.

(2) That the known duration of the reign of Cyrus is 9 yrs. —from records of Cyrus and Ptolemy's Canon of Kings.

(3) That Strassmeier's Babylonian Eclipse record mentions a lunar eclipse on 14th Tammuz in 7th year Cambyses : this being the lunar eclipse of 16th July (Julian) B.C. 523, and 14th Tammuz agreeing with 16th July (Julian) in this year.

(4) That Ptolemy's List (*Almagest*) of Chaldæan Eclipses gives the same eclipse in the 7th year of Cambyses as occurring on 28th Phamenoth of the Egyptian vague year calendar ; the Egyptian month date agreeing with 16th July (Julian) in B.C. 523.

(5) That the 1st year Cambyses, according to the regnal year reckoning adopted for the eclipse record, began in Spring, B.C. 529, 7 years after the 1st year of Cyrus began in Spring, B.C. 536, according to the data of the Dynastic Tablet of Babylon and the data of Berosus.

(6) That, agreeing with this, Xenophon states that Cyrus reigned 7 years.

(7) That, therefore, the 8th and 9th years of the reign of Cyrus coincided with the same 7th year of Cambyses as the 1st and 2nd years of Cambyses as co-rex, according to the reckoning followed in dating the Eclipse record.

(8) That Herodotus confirms this by stating that Cyrus appointed Cambyses co-rex.

(9) That the dated records of Cambyses, according to the reckoning followed in the Eclipse record, go down to the end of his 8th year.

(10) That, accordingly, the sole years of Cambyses after the death of Cyrus were 6 years to the end of his 8th year by the former reckoning.

(11) That confirming this, Josephus gives 6 years as the duration of the reign of Cambyses and that the statement of 6 years for the reign of Cambyses occurs on the Hammamat inscriptions in Egypt of the Persian noble Ataiuhi, who lived during his reign, in Persia, and—being taken as a youth to Egypt after the Persian Conquest—lived afterwards in Egypt.

(12) That the latter method of dating was in use is proved by the fact that Cyrus, dying in the Spring of B.C. 527, caused a record inscribed as beginning his 10th year to be altered, after his death, to the 1st year of Cambyses. This record—on one of the Egibi tablets at Babylon—was formerly read as the "11th year Cambyses," until Prof. E. Meyer explained the matter as above.

(13) That, prior to his conquest of Babylon, Cyrus had reigned successively as king of Ansan, and then as king of Persia, Herodotus giving his total reign (including over Babylon) as 29 years, and Severus, and the Ecclesiastical authorities generally, as 31 years; again indicating the two years co-regency of Cambyses.

Thus the reign is made up as follows :—

Cyrus over Ansan & Persia   22 yrs.
Cyrus, sole reign, Babylon   7 yrs as Xenophon } Known
                                                   } total
    Total sole reign   29 yrs. as Herodotus } reign
Cyrus, with Cambyses co-rex   2 yrs.   } 9 yrs.

Cyrus, total reign   31 yrs. as Severus and others. According to this, the total reign of Cyrus (Ansan-Persia) began in Spring, B.C. 558.

(14) That Julius Africanus states that the 20th year of Artaxerxes Longimanus fell in the 115th year of the reign of Cyrus in Persia (Ansan-Persia) and that also fell in the 4th year of Olympiad 83.
Now 4th year Olv. 83=
          Midsummer, B.C. 445—444= 115th year.
             Add 114—114   114 deduct

Hence 1st yr. Cyrus (Ansan-Persia)= Midsummer, B.C. 559—558= 1st year, this including Spring of B.C. 558, when the total reign of Cyrus began as (13) above.

TABLE XXII.

SYNCHRONISTIC NARRATIVES OF THE BOOK OF GENESIS AND THE RECORDS OF THE XIIth AND XVIIIth EGYPTIAN DYNASTIES.

THE CHRONOLOGICAL SEQUENCE OF THE THREE FAMINES IN THE *BOOK OF GENESIS*.	Years from Call of Abram.	Years from beginning of 8th Year Senusert III.	CONTEMPORANEOUS EGYPTIAN FAMINE RELIEF WORKS, AND EGYPTIAN CONQUESTS TO EFFECT AND RESTORE THE RIVER IMPROVEMENT WORKS BETWEEN THE 1st AND 3rd CATARACTS.
(1) Abram, 75 years old (Gen. XII, 4). Call of Abram. Abram journeys from Mesopotamia into Canaan, and, finding famine in Canaan, continues his journey into Egypt.	0	0=2083½ A.K. (Table XV).	8th year Senusert III (Dyn. XII). Senusert III in this year subdued Nubia, found the canal at the 1st cataract choked, and cleared it. } I.
I. Abram's Famine. Christian chronographers state that this was during the reign of Nacheres=Lacheres=Senusert III (Dyn. XII). (Budge, *Hist. Egypt*, III, 42).			
(2) Abraham 100 years old (Gen. XXI, 5). Birth of Isaac.	25		
(3) Isaac, 60 years old (Gen. XXV, 26). Birth of Jacob and Esau	85	58=2141½ A.K. (Table XV). 72=2155½ A.K. to	River improvement works continued and extended under Amenemhat III, and records of high Nile kept at the Cataracts to Year 5 of Amenemhat IV.
(4) Death of Abraham, 175 years old (Gen. XXV, 7).	100	111=2194½ A.K.	During the war of independence against the Hyksos, and during the Northern wars of Amosis I (Dyn. XVIII) the river improvement works at and above the 1st Cataract fell into the hands of the Nubians.
Famine in Canaan, some time after the death of Abraham (Gen. XXVI, 15-18), and some time			Inscription of Baba at El Kab during Dyn. XVII (war of independence) refers to a famine of many years, obviously owing to low inundation resulting from river not having been kept clear of obstructions at the Cataracts. } II.

II.
Isaac's Famine.

prior to the 40th year of Esau (XXVI, 34), causes Isaac to sojourn in Gerar, amongst the Philistines (XXVI, 1).

Gen. XXVI, 2 :—"Go not down into Egypt"; obviously because Egypt was then barely settled after expulsion of the Hyksos.

112=2195½ A.K. .. (Table XIV).

Beginning of 1st year Amenhotep I (Dyn. XVIII). At the beginning of his reign, Amenhotep I subdued Nubia between the 1st and 2nd Cataracts.

(5) Esau 40 years old, some time after the famine (Gen. XXVI, 34) 125

135=2218½ A.K. .. (Table XIV)

Middle of 3rd year of Tahutmes I.
Inscription of Tahutmes I at 1st Cataract stated :—"Year 3, Month IX, his Majesty commanded to clear this canal after he had found it filled with stones, so that no boat could pass up." Breasted states that in this year Tahutmes I effected the "reorganisation and thorough pacification of the country" between the 1st and 3rd Cataracts.

III.
Joseph's Famine.

(6) Joseph's SEVEN YEARS' FAMINE began 213

2296½ A.K. ..

Jacob, 130 years old, enters Egypt, 2 years after the Seven Years' Famine began. (Gen. XLV, 6—XLVI, 5) 215

2298½ A.K. ..

Joseph's SEVEN YEARS' FAMINE ended 220

220=2303½ A.K. ..

III.

Table XIV.

Beginning of 50th year Tahutmes III Campaign in Nubia. Inscription of Tahutmes III at 1st Cataract (Schel) states :—"Year 50, Day 22, Month IX, under the majesty of Men-kheper-Ra (Tahutmes III), his majesty commanded to cut this canal, after he had found it choked with stones, so that no vessel crossed over it.—The fishers of Elephantine are to dredge this canal every year."

ANNOTATIONS TO TABLE XXII.

THE EGYPTIAN RECORD OF JOSEPH'S FAMINE.

The significance has not hitherto been appreciated of two notable records that date and monumentalize the famine conditions of the period preceding the 50th year of Tahutmes III. We can best follow the facts of this by knowing the history of the famine records from the date of their being inscribed to the present time.

In the year following the 7 years' famine that is, in the 50th year of Tahutmes III, this great king sailed up the Nile to the First Cataract to inspect the river-jam that had with-held from Egypt the necessary volume of water and alluvial deposits of the inundation period, during the years of famine. He punished those responsible and he cut a new canal through the silted barrage, and set up a record of this achievement on the adjacent Island of Sehel.

The record states :—

" Year 50, Day 22, Month IX, under the majesty of king Men-kepher-Ra (Tahutmes III), his majesty commanded to cut this canal, after he had found it choked with stones so that no vessel crossed over it...........The fishers of Elephantinê are to dredge this canal every year."

The date of the record is the 24th of April (Greg.) in B.C. 1696.

The king also, at this time, revived the worship of the local gods of the First Cataract, and raised statues to them and rebuilt their temples and shrines. The object of these activities was to give the priests of the First Cataract gods an interest in keeping the canal clear of obstructions.

Now the record quoted was set up by Tahutmes III on the Island of Sehel. On the same island the king set up a longer record containing all the facts concerning the famine, its causes—as he wished the inhabitants of the locality to believe them—and its duration. The record gives us a wonderful insight into the methods of the great king. It is a record of a remarkable piece of statecraft. The narrative was obviously written to impress the local inhabitants of the period and during succeeding generations. It was dated in the same 50th year of the king. It states that in the 7 preceding years Egypt had experienced a disastrous famine ; that the famine was due to the obstruction at the First Cataract : and that this occurred and the Nile's waters were withheld when the local inhabitants failed to worship the local Nile gods of the cataract. The famine, then, was represented as resulting from the anger of the local gods.

The narrative continued by stating that the king restored the worship of the local Nile gods, rebuilt their shrines and temples, and gave gifts of land and produce to the local priests. All this was obviously to give the priest-hood power to render, and interest in making, effective the decree of Tahutmes' separate inscription that " The fishers of Elephantinê are to dredge this canal every year."

This great famine record of Tahutmes III was carved upon wood. The record referred to Tahutmes III in terms of his Golden Horus name, Zoser-kha-u-sekhem-pehti. This is analogous to the Christian name of modern times. In the course of many centuries, rot and abrasion in the wood of the plaque rendered parts of the inscription illegible. All that remained legible of the Golden Horus name of Tahutmes III were the initial hieroglyphs reading ZOSER.

This famine record again was dated in the 50th year of Tahutmes III, when this king visited and restored the river improvement works and the temples to the local deities at the First Cataract—that is, at Sehel and Elephantinê.

The 50th year was written on the wood plaque of the famine inscription thus ⊓⊓ reading " 50.
⊓ ⊓ ⊓

The vertical legs of the five inverted U's were cut across the hard figuring of the wood. Rot and abrasion in the softer material running along the grain parallel to the natural alignment of the figuring of the wood rotted out and removed four of the five heads joining the vertical legs of the inverted U's. So that the inscription read as

|⏐⏐⏐
⊓⏐⏐⏐⏐   which reads as " 18."

Now at the time of the Ptolemies, in the 3rd century B.C., another famine devastated Egypt. The temples and shrines at the First Cataract had fallen into ruin. Its priests were poor and of little account in Egypt. Seeing their opportunity in the circumstances of the famine, and seizing it, the priests of the Cataract brought forth the dilapidated wooden plaque of Tahutmes III. Finding it too decayed to confirm the moral of the tale they had to tell the Pharaoh of their day, they carved a copy of it upon stone. To give this copy the appearance of antiquity, they included in this copy a reference to the wooden plaque, and the statement that the stone copy was ordered additional to perpetuate the record. By artificial processes of abrasion, weathering, and colouring, they gave the late copy the appearance of great age. This stone copy, however, merely states that the record is of a king whose Golden Horus name was Zoser, and that it was set up in his 18th year. They presented the record, and its dilapidated wooden original to the Pharaoh of the period. Their tale and its confirming forgery were successful, as witness the magnificent Ptolemaic temples in the locality of the First Cataract, extant to the present time.

Egyptological authorities admit that the style of hieroglyph on the stone inscription, and other matters of style, belong to the Ptolemaic period, around the 3rd century B.C. They assert, however, that the Zoser referred to was a king of the 3rd Dynasty. No other king, however, prior to Tahutmes III, of Dynasty XVIII, had a *Golden Horus name* including or commencing with Zoser, or consisting of Zoser. At the same time authorities admit that the customs and institutions and other facts of the Ptolemaic record belong to the times of the XVIIIth Dynasty, and to no earlier period of Egyptian history. We have felt justified therefore in presenting the history of the record in the manner and sequence given. Without doubt the Ptolemaic record is what it claims to be, a copy of an earlier record upon wood, describing the 7 years' famine under Tahutmes III, Joseph's pharaoh, and in his 50th year, the year when Tahutmes visited the First Cataract, cleared it, and set up the buildings and restored the legislation referred to in the record, which year was the year following the 7 years' famine of Joseph.

The reign of Tahutmes III is therefore identified with the coming of Jacob and his sons into Egypt. These were not the only Semites in Egypt at this time. The records of the military campaigns of Tahutmes III tell us of vast numbers of kindred Semitic peoples led as captives, hostages and tribute—as Joseph was led—into Egypt. Such captives were selected for their beauty and comeliness, and for their princely and aristocratic lineage and bearing. They were married into the princely and aristocratic families of Egypt, even as Joseph married the daughter of Potiphar, priest and prince of Heliopolis. The elevation of Joseph to his princely office marked the beginning of other Israelites and kindred Semites in Egypt attaining high official appointments under Tahutmes III and his immediate successors.

ANNOTATIONS TO TABLES XXII AND XXIII.

THE RISE AND FALL OF THE SEMITES IN EGYPT.

The intermarriage of the Israelites with the kindred Semitic peoples in Egypt, and with the Egyptians, accounts for the vast number of the children of Israel at the Exodus. and for the statement in the Book of Exodus, that, besides the 600,000 men, apart from women and children, " a mixed company also went up with them " out of Egypt.

As Prof. Sayce points out in his " Higher Criticism and the Monuments," when, after Joseph had interpreted Pharaoh's dream, the people proclaimed him *abrikku*, a seer, the word here used in Genesis, is neither Hebrew nor Egyptian. It is an ancient Babylonian word that was employed in correspondence Tablets between Babylon and Egypt during the XVIIIth Dynasty, and not before that Dynasty. The people who proclaimed Joseph *abrikku*, could only have been a people from the banks of the Euphrates ; kindred Semitic peoples who had been led to Egypt as captives in conquest or as tribute during the reign of Tahutmes III.

Tahutmes III died 5 years after Joseph's famine ended. The history of succeeding reigns presents us with a picture of peaceful penetration. Semites in increasing numbers attain to the highest official appointments in the Egyptian Empire. Intermarriage Semiticizes the Egyptian nobility, until, in the 3rd reign after Joseph's pharaoh, the history of the reign—that of Amenhotep III—is the history of Semitic Supremacy in Egypt.

Thus Prof. Petrie states :—

" The striking change in the physiognomy and ideal type of the upper classes in the latter part of the XVIIIth Dynasty points to a strong foreign infusion. In place of the bold, active faces of earlier times, there is a peculiar delicacy ; a gentle smile, and a small, gracefully-curved nose are characteristic of the upper classes in the time of Amenhotep III [1] . . . . Being of such a winning type, it is no wonder that they were taken into Egyptian families . . . . No wonder that, after a few generations, we find Semitic words, idioms, and thoughts transfused throughout Egyptian literature. No nation could be proof against such influence. . . . . In language, as is well known, Egypt became Semiticised."

This was the state of affairs under Amenhotep III, less than a century after Jacob's entry. How matters developed in the next reign forms one of the outstanding themes of discussion in Egyptological works. The new king, Amenhotep IV, himself partly Semitic on his mother's side, made a drastic change in the official religion of Egypt. He overthrew the worship of Amen-ra, Osiris, and other Egyptian deities. The new religion set up in place of these was essentially monotheistic. It was Semitic in its origin and in all its ideas, forms and ceremonies. The One God was worshipped in the form of Aten or Aton..possibly the Egyptian form of the Semitic name Adon, Lord. The symbol of His beneficent Presence and work was the Solar Disc without other form of visible attribute. We may view its formulation as a conception to be compared with the idea of God held by Abraham s father, Terah, and by such other Semites as had not been influenced by the Revelation to Abraham. But then we know that the

Israelites themselves between the time of Joseph and until the Revelations to Moses, possessed a poor conception of God as compared with that revealed in the Books of the later Law.

Whilst, therefore, Aten worship may have been a debased form of the worship of the God of Abraham, Isaac, and Jacob, we must not forget the possibility of the visible attribute of the One God, as seen in His work, being held out to the Egyptians as something tangible, to their priest-ridden understanding, of what the One God could mean to them. As to this, let the matter be explained by the French Egyptologist, M. Moret. This great authority on Egyptian religion states concerning the new Semitic form of worship in Egypt under Amenhotep IV, or as he called himself, Khounaten (*i.e.*, Akhen-aten) :—

" The king's desire," says M. Moret, " seems to have been this : to direct the adoration of the Egyptians towards a god who would not be the artificial creator of a priest-hood peculiar to one town, or exclusively national in character, but towards a god incarnating a force in nature, and therefore able to be universally understood and revered. . . . . "

" . . . . It is, perhaps, the first time in the history of the world that we see a king calling to the strangers, Semites and Nubians, his newly conquered subjects, to come and worship, side by side, with his own people, Aton, the Father of All. For the first time, religion is regarded as a *bond* which *binds* together men of different race, language, and colour. The god of Khounaton does not distinguish between Egyptians and Barbarians. All men are equally his sons and should be considered as brothers."

" . . . . Khounaton made him god of the Egyptian Empire at a very opportune moment, when Egypt, extending her conquests beyond her frontiers, incorporates new subjects in Syria and Nubia."

" From this point of view, the attempt of Amenophis (Amenhotep) IV was something more than a political reaction against the encroaching ambition of the high-priests of Amon. . . . . "

" . . . . In the hymn of El-Amarna, there is expressed with sublime elevation, a feeling of gratitude for a God who is a universal Providence, who extends His care not only to men of diverse races but to animals and plants, a feeling of fraternity with the humblest being in Nature, who, endowed with life, may join in giving forth praise to his Creator."

The reign of the pharaoh who established this Semitic form of worship marked the summit of Semitic supremacy in Egypt. His well-meant religious reform was the means of the downfall of Semitic power in Egypt. During the course of his reign of 16 years, the priestly intrigues of the followers of the powerful Egyptian cult of the god Amen-ra, formerly supreme, centred around the representative of a hitherto obscure family. This sinister figure in Egyptian politics was a certain Pa-Ramessu, who about 50 years later, as Ramessu I. the grandfather of Ramessu II, was associated as coregent with the last king of Dynasty XVIII. (Refer Plate LXI and Annotations.)

[1] The type here described by Petrie is the true Semitic type prior to the Roman Dispersion of the Jews. Sir Gardner Wilkinson (Anc. Egyptians, Vol. II, 197-198) draws attention to this fact. Holman Hunt, in his visit to Palestine for his type of Christ, observed that the descendents of Jews there, who had never left Palestine, were, during the 19th Century, of the same Semitic type described by Petrie and Wilkinson. Refer the prediction of the change in the Prophecies of Isaiah (III, 9 ; LXV, 15) and Jeremiah (XXIV, 9).

TABLE XXIII.

THE CHRONOLOGICAL SEQUENCE OF EVENTS INCLUDING THE EXODUS OF ISRAEL.

(Chronological and Historical Data derived from Egyptian Sources entirely).

	Dates as Table XIV.
(1) 21st year of Ramessu II, treaty with the Hittites	1538 B.C.
Sayce states:—	
"The way had been prepared by the Hittites for the Israelitish conquest of Canaan."	
(2) Beginning of 5th year of Menephtah .. .. .. 2nd half of April (Greg.)	1487 B.C.
After 2 generations of Egyptians unskilled in warfare, as Maspero states:—	
"The standing army had almost melted away ; the regiments of archers and charioteers were no longer effective."	
(3) 5th year of Menephtah. Great victory against the Libyans .. .. .. 14th July (Greg.)	1487 B.C.
Menephtah's Song of Triumph states:—	
"The archers of His Majesty made havoc of the barbarians for six hours."	
Budge states:—	
"It is little short of marvellous that this mighty confederation of Libyans and their allies was vanquished by Menephtah's army."	
(4) End of 5th year of Menephtah. Exodus of Israel .. .. .. 4th April (Greg.)	1486 B.C.
(a) According to the Hebrew account, the pursuing Egyptian army was destroyed.	
"For this have I raised thee (Menephtah) up, for to show in thee My power, AND THAT MY NAME MAY BE DECLARED THROUGHOUT ALL THE EARTH." Exod. ix, 16.	Inferred reference to the Libyan battle and the miraculous sequence noted under (2) and (3) above.
(b) The Israelitish stele of Menephtah's 5th year states:—	
"The Israelites are swept off, his seed is no more." (Naville's translation).	
(5) 8th year of Menephtah. Shasu of Adima are received into Egypt and settled by Menephtah's governor at Pithom in the Crown Lands of Goshen, formerly occupied by the Israelites	1483 B.C.

DYNASTY XIX.

(6) End of XIXth Dynasty, 9½ years after the Exodus of Israel .. .. 1477 B.C.

Maspero states:—

"Egypt had set out....for the conquest of the world, and fortune had at first smiled upon her enterprise....Neither the triumphs of Ramses II, nor the victory of Menephtah had been able to restore her prestige....Now her own territory itself was threatened, and her own well-being was in question; she was compelled to consider, not how to rule other tribes, great or small, but how to keep her own possessions intact and ndependent; in short, her very existence was at stake."

THE INTERREGNUM:

(7) The Harris Papyrus written under Ramessu III of Dynasty XX narrates that:—

"Anarchy prevailed, and that the land had had no chief ruler 'for very many years'."

A long period of anarchy of uncertain duration.

(8) The Harris Papyrus continues that there "came a period after that of years of want and misery."

A period of famine of uncertain duration.

(9) And states that, these conditions continuing,

"Arsu the Syrian made himself prince over them."

We have here probably, a record concerning the doings of one of those Canaanites who were driven out of Canaan during the troublous times of the Judges in Israel.

A period of Syrian domination of uncertain duration.

(10) The Harris Papyrus continues its narrative by stating that Arsu was finally overthrown by Set-Nekht, the father of Ramessu III, under whom the narrative of the Papyrus was written.

The XXth Dynasty was founded by Set-Nekht .. .. 1216 B.C.

(11) Regarding the state of the Egyptian army at the beginning of Dynasty XX, Maspero states:—("Struggle of the Nations," p. 457)

"The military institutions of the country had become totally disorganised after the death of Menephtah, and that part of the community responsible for furnishing the army with recruits had become so weakened in the late troubles, that they were in a worse condition than before the 1st Libyan invasion," in the 5th year of Menephtah.

THE INTERREGNUM:

Total duration by astronomical chronology, 261 years;

according to the Old Egyptian Chronicle, 178 years;

according to Africanus, 182 years;

obviously longer than these two statements, since the Old Chronicle gives 101 years excess, and Africanus 111 years excess in Dynasty XIX.

TABLE XXIV.

FROM THE HARRIS PAPYRUS INTERREGNUM TO THE PERSIAN CONQUEST OF EGYPT. B.C. 1216 TO B.C. 525.

	Reign. Years.	A.K. B.C. 2784=1216	B.C. 1216
Dynasty XX at Thebes.			
1. Setnekht	I	2785=1215	Astronomically fixed by data of Table XI and Annotations Cols. 3 and 5.
2. Ramessu III	31	2816=1184	
3. Ramessu IV	6	2822=1178	
4. Ramessu V	4	2826=1174	
5. Ramessu VI } Order of reigns			The total duration of Dynasties XX–XXI inclusive.
6. Ramessu VII } doubtful;			Years
7. Ramessu VIII } duration			As Astronomically fixed = 219
8. Ramessu IX } (35+xl yrs.			As King Lists (Version Africanus) = 249
9. Ramessu X			As Sir W. M. F. Petrie = 251
10. Ramessu XI¹	27		As Prof. J. H. Breasted = 255
Priest Kings at Thebes.			
11. Her-heru / Pai-ankh			Duration of individual reigns uncertain owing to possible varying Supremacy Tanis and Thebes.
12. Pai-nezem I		11. Nes-ba-tuta	
Men-kheper-ra		13. Pa-seb-khanu I	Dyn. XXI at Tanis.
14. Amen-em-Apt		14. Amen-em-Apt	
Pai-nezem II		15. Sa-Amen	
Pasebkhanu		16. Pa-seb-khanu II	
Tat-kheperu-ra			B.C. 967

Astronomically fixed and dated interval. Dyns. XX to XXI inclusive. 249 years.

	Total Reign. Years.	Duration of Reign prior to Successor's Coregency.	Date of Reign prior to Successor's Coregency. A.K. B.C.	
NOTE:— The regnal years are not guaranteed in all cases as correct within half-year, as refer half-year correction to Summation of Dyn.				
17. *Sheshanq I	21	21	3033=967	
18. Uasarkon I	36	29	3054=946	UASARKON II Astronomically fixed. Table XI, Annotations 4 & 5.
19. Takerat I	25	21	3083=917	
20. Uasarkon II	28	23	3104=896	
21. Sheshanq II	0	0	3127=873	
22. Takerat II	25	25	3127=873	TAKERAT II Astronomically fixed by Annotations A, II. to the right.
23. Sheshanq III	52	52	3152=848	
24. Panay	4	2	3204=796	
25. Sheshanq IV	37	37	3206=794	
Total (actually 209½) =	210		3243=757 Actually ended at 3242½ A.K.=757 B.C.	

Dynasty XXII "at Bubastis."

ANNOTATIONS TO TABLE XXIV.

A.—THE ASTRONOMICAL DATA:—

I. The astronomical datings of Ramessu III and Uasarkon II are fixed by Table XI and Annotations.

II. The astronomical dating of Takerat II's 15th year is fixed as follows:—

(1) By Table XXIV the 15th year of Takerat II began in 859 B.C.

(2) In 859 B.C. a full moon occurred on 15th March (Julian) = Egyptian Day 25 Month XII (Mesore) of the vague or shifting year calendar.

(3) The record of Takerat II's 15th year states that on this particular Day 25 Month XII (i.e., the precise day of full moon) "heaven did not eat the moon" (Budge, "Hist. Egypt," VI, p. 90).

(4) The record obviously states that on the day of Full Moon an eclipse of the moon did not take place. Calculations show that an eclipse did not take place. It is of importance to remember that an eclipse of the moon can only take place at full moon. Hence the importance of the identity of the succeeded day with the full moon.

III. The astronomical dating of Taharqa's 1st year is fixed as follows:—

(1) Uasarkon II celebrated a *sed heb* or *end festival* at the end of the Phœnix cycle that fell in his 22nd year (874 B.C.), Table XI and Annotations.

(2) Taharqa, having reigned as a powerful coregent for many years, determined to assert his own supremacy at a *Sed heb* so as to appear divinely appointed as dominant ruler of the land.

(3) Taharqa, therefore, reckoned 6 *Sed* periods, or 180 years from Uasarkon II's *Sed heb* in 874 B.C. This gave the date 694 B.C.

(4) Taharqa, therefore, began his reign as sole ruler in 694 B.C., and celebrated a *Sed heb* at his coronation (Petrie, "Hist. Egypt," III, 301).

(5) By the annals of Assurbanipal and the astronomically fixed datings of Assurbanipal, the death of Taharqa is fixed in 667 B.C.

B.—THE PROBLEM OF THE REIGN OF PSAMTEK I AND ITS SOLUTION.

The facts relating to this are as follow:—

(1) Psamtek I, in an Apis record, claims that his reign began immediately following the death of Taharqa in 667 B.C., and supplies good reasons for his claim.

(2) The records of Dynasty XXVI show conclusively that Psamtek I's reign ended in 609 B.C.

(3) This gives 58 years' duration for the reign of Psamtek I.

(4) The recorded duration of the reign of Psamtek I is 54 years.

(5) If the records supplying the above data are all true records there is only one possible explanation of the facts. This is that Psamtek I reigned 54 years only out of the 58 years that intervened between the commencement of his reign and the termination of his reign. In other words, at some date after the commencement of his reign, Psamtek I was deposed, or failed to act as king during a period of 4 years.

(6) This presentation of the facts and the solution offered find confirmation from the narrative of Herodotus (Bk. II, Chs. 151 and 152). Psamtek I was deposed and banished. He returned with Carian and Ionian mercenaries (the Lydians of Gyges mentioned by Assurbanipal) and recovered his kingdom.

C.—THE RESULTING STATEMENT OF THE SEQUENCE OF HISTORICAL EVENTS:—

(1) The priests of Memphis buried an Apis in the Serapeum, dated in 24th year Taharqa, B.C. 671.

(2) In the 25th year of Taharqa, Esarhaddon defeated Taharqa, and captured Memphis in June 670 B.C.; Taharqa retiring on Thebes.

(3) Esarhaddon departed and Taharqa recaptured Memphis in his 26th year, B.C. 669. In this year, according to Psamtek I's record, an Apis was born.

(4) The record of Psamtek I, by its data, fixes the ceremonial inauguration of the Apis at Memphis in the 27th year Taharqa, late in B.C. 668 or early in B.C. 667.

(5) Hearing of the Assyrian reverses in Egypt, Esarhaddon advanced against Egypt but died on the march in October, 668 B.C.

Chronological Table

Dyn. XXV, Tanis.	Years.	A.K.	B.C.
26. Pedubasht ..	23	3243½=757	3265½-731
27. Uasarkon III ..	14	3275½-724	
(1st 4 years coregent.)			

Dynasty XXIV.

Tafnekht I .. Piankhi I

	Years.	A.K.	B.C.	3275½=724
28. Bakenranef	6	3281½=718	3275½=724	
Kashta.				

Dynasty XXV of Ethiopians.

Reign of Taharga Astronomically fixed Table XXIV, Annulations A, III.

	Years.	A.K.	B.C.
Tafnekht II			3281½=718
Nekau-ba.			
29. Sabaka	12		3293½=706
30. Sabataka	12		3305½=694
31. Taharka	27		3332½=667
Nekau I.			
32. Tanutamen	6		3338½=661

ASSYRIAN SUPREMACY 667-654 B.C.

Refer Annotations.

33.	Psamtek I 2 his 1st and 2nd year	3332½=667
	4 Years' Exile	3334½=665
	Psamtek I 52 his 3rd to 54th yrs.	3338½=661

Tanutamen overthrown in 661 B.C. by Assurbanipal.

The total period, Psamtek I to Psamtek III, is fixed by a continuous series of reliable contemporary records—Apis stele, etc. For complete list of same refer Petrie, "History Egypt," III, 339. For the explanation of the Apis record of Psamtek I —connecting the reigns of Psamtek I and Taharka—refer Annotations to this Table.

Dynasty XXVI.

34.	Nekau II	16	3390½=609
35.	Psamtek II	5	3406½=593
36.	Uah-ab-ra	19	3411½=588
37.	Amasis II	44	3430½=569
38.	Psamtek III a few months.		3474¾=525

The Persian Conquest of Egypt by Cambyses.

---

(6) The Tartan (general) of the Assyrian army continued the campaign, and was joined by a second army under the Rabshakeh from Nineveh. Taharqa's army was defeated early in 667 B.C., at Karbanit; the Assyrians capturing Memphis. Taharqa fled to Thebes, followed by the Assyrians. Still early in 667 B.C., Thebes was captured; Taharqa retiring up the Nile.

(7) During the Assyrian advance, the Assyrians intercepted messages between the Delta princes and Taharqa. The messages disclosed a plan of revolt which the Assyrians immediately took effective steps to thwart.

(8) Assurbanipal states that Taharqa continued his flight to Ethiopia and died there; the Assyrian operations in the meanwhile being completed during the first half of 667 B.C.

(9) In the same year, 667 B.C., Psamtek I was appointed king of Athribis. When, therefore, Psamtek I, in his Apis record, gives his reign as following immediately after the reign of Taharqa, he is dating from his appointment as king of Athribis in the Delta. What he does not tell us is that he was compelled, a year or so later, to flee into the marshes and abroad into Syria for 4 years; that these 4 years were not reckoned as regnal years; and that to hide the gap in his reign the life of the Apis was reckoned as 4 years less than it actually was.

(10) On the death of Taharqa, in 667 B.C., Tanutamen became king of Ethiopia. The 1st year of Tanutamen is therefore the 1st year of Psamtek I. A record of Tanutamen's 3rd year at Luxor indicates that his rule included Thebes in 665-664 B.C.

(11) The annals of Assurbanipal confirm the Dream Stele of Tanutamen, and the traditions relating to Nekau, the father of Psamtek. Tanutamen advanced from Thebes against the Egyptian princes of the Delta and the Assyrian garrison in Memphis. Memphis was besieged and captured. Nekau I, the father of Psamtek was killed in the siege. Psamtek I and the other Delta princes retired into the marshes. By appearing to adopt the dictatorship of Nekau I, Psamtek I was banished from the Delta marshes by the other princes. Apparently Psamtek I was for continuing the conflict, for after his banishment, the other princes of the Delta left the marshes and submitted to Tanutamen.

(12) The annals of Assurbanipal relate that upon receipt of the news of the Assyrian reverses in Egypt, a fresh expedition was organised against Egypt. Thebes was captured and pillaged. Tanutamen was decisively overthrown, and Psamtek I—obviously with the Assyrian army—restored as viceroy of Egypt under Assurbanipal. The Assyrian data fix the date as 661 B.C.

(13) Now 665 B.C. is the earliest date for Tanutamen's 3rd year dating appearing at Thebes. This dating too is the earliest evidence of Tanutamen at Thebes. The date fixes the time of his invasion of Egypt and the banishment of Psamtek I.

(14) With 665 B.C. as the date of Tanutamen, and 661 B.C. as the date of his reinstatement by the Assyrians, the 4 years' difference between his apparent 58 years and the 54 years he claims is accounted for. 661 B.C. is, therefore, identified with the resumption of Psamtek I's broken reign. His 3rd year—postponed for 4 years of banishment—began in 661 B.C.

(15) In the annals of Assurbanipal, the next Assyrian expedition is against Tyre. Following the account of the subjection of Tyre, Assurbanipal states that Gyges, king of Lydia, applied to him for assistance against the invading Cimmerians; but that, after having tendered his submission to the Assyrian king, he (Gyges)—apparently having dealt successfully with the Cimmerians—sent "his forces to the aid of Psammitichus (Psamtek I) of Egypt, who had thrown off the yoke of my dominion."

(16) The first dating of Psamtek I at Thebes is of his 9th year, 655 to 654 B.C., this indicating that by 654 B.C. Psamtek I had established himself as king of all Egypt.

' The king, formerly supposed to be Ramessu X, is now known to be Si-ptah of Dynasty XIX (H. R. Hall, "Anc. Hist. Near East," p. 389, footnote 2). The last Ramessu of Dynasty XX is therefore Ramessu XI, instead of Ramessu XII as formerly supposed.

* Here we have 38 kings in dominant succession—the number in Manetho (Version Eusebius) for Dynasties XX to XXVI inclusive.

* Sheshang I, originally a powerful chief of Libyan mercenaries under the XXIst Dynasty—and descended from a long line of Libyan chiefs, who had settled at Heracleopolis early in the XXIst Dynasty—became petty king in the Delta, by extending his rule over Bubastis, before he actually became king of all Egypt in 967 B.C. (refer Breasted's Records IV. 788 and footnote C; also his "Hist. Egypt," p. 557).

TABLE XXV.

CHRONOLOGY OF THE KINGDOMS OF JUDAH AND ISRAEL, FROM THE DIVISION IN THE KINGDOM TO THE DESTRUCTION OF JERUSALEM BY NEBUCHADNEZZAR, B.C. 970 TO B.C. 584.

KINGS OF JUDAH.	A.K.
Rehoboam (Annotations (C) Table XXVIII)	3029½ to 3046½.
Abijah	3046½ to 3049½.
Asa	3049½ to 3090½.
Jehosophat	3090½ to 3115½.
Jehoram, pro-rex	3106½ to 3108½.
Jehoram, co-rex 1st to 4th years ..	3111½ to 3115½.
Jehoram, 5th to 8th years	3115½ to 3119½.
Ahaziah, co-rex	3117½ to 3118½.
Ahaziah	3118½ to 3119½.
Athaliah	3119½ to 3126.
Joash	3125½ to 3165½.
Amaziah	3165½ to 3194½.
Azariah	3194½ to 3246½.
Jotham	3246½ to 3262½.
Ahaz	3261½ to 3277½.
Hezekiah	3276½ to 3305½.
Manassah	3305½ to 3360½.
Amon	3360½ to 3362½.
Josiah	3362½ to 3393½.
Jehoiakim	3393½ to 3404½.
Jehoiachin	3404½ to 3404½.
Zedekiah	3405½ to 3415½.

KINGS OF ISRAEL.	A.K.	
Jeroboam (Annotations (C) Table XXVIII)	3029½ to 3051½.	
Nabab	3050½ to 3052½.	
Baasha	3051½ to 3075½.	
Elah	3074½ to 3076½.	
Zimri	3075½ to 3076½.	
Omri	3075½ to 3087½.	
Ahab	3086½ to 3108½.	
Ahaziah, co-rex	3106½ to 3108½.	
Joram	3107½ to 3119½.	
Jehu	3119½ to 3147½.	
Jehoahaz	3147½ to 3164½.	
Jehoash, co-rex	3161½ to 3163½.	
Jehoash	3163½ to 3179½.	
Jeroboam II, co-rex	3168½ to 3179½	
Jeroboam II	3179½ to 3220½	A.K. 3168½ to 3220½. including the 6 months, and 1 month of Zechariah and Shallum respectively
Interregnum from 27th to 38th Azariah ..		
Zechariah in 38th Azariah		
Shallum in 39th Azariah		
Menahem	3233½ to 3243½.	
Pekahiah	3243½ to 3245½.	
Pekah	3245½ to 3265½.	
8 years Interregnum	3265½ to 3273½.	
Hoshea	3273½ to 3282½.	

NOTE:—In cases where the terminal regnal year of a king is stated as identical with the initial year of his successor, the statement is according to the records.

ANNOTATIONS TO TABLE XXV.

KINGS OF JUDAH.

REHOBOAM (I Kings, xi, 43; xii, 1; xiv, 21)
(II Chron., ix, 31; x, 1; xii, 13)
Table XXVIII Annotations (C) Death of Solomon .. 3029½ A.K.
Rehoboam .. .. 17 years

ABIJAH began in 18th Jeroboam .. .. 3046½ A.K.
(I Kings, xvii, 2; II Chron., xiii, 1, 2) .. 3 years

ASA began in 20th Jeroboam .. .. 3049½ A.K.
(*i.e.*, towards the end of the 20th year)
(I Kings, xv, 9, 10; II Chron., xvi, 13) .. 41 years

JEHOSOPHAT began 4th Ahab .. .. 3090½ A.K.
(*i.e.*, towards the end of the 4th year)
(I Kings, xxii, 41, 42; II Ch., xvii, 1; xx, 31) 25 years

3115½ A.K.

JEHORAM of Judah Pro-rex, 17th and 18th years Jehosophat (II Kings iii, 1; i, 17) Refer JORAM of Israel .. .. .. — 3100½ A.K. 2 years 3108½ A.K.

JEHORAM of Judah Co-rex began to reign 8 years in 5th Joram of Israel = 22nd Jehosophat (II Kings, viii, 16-17; II Chron., xxi, 5) as Jehosophat died at 3115½ A.K. (as above). Jehoram reigned his first 4 years co-rex — 3111½ A.K. 4 years 3115½ A.K.

JEHORAM alone for remaining 4 years of his 8 years from coregency — 4 years
(Died early in regnal year beginning 3118½) — 3119½ A.K.
AHAZIAH co-rex during his father's illness (II Chron., xxi, 18, 19, and II Kings, ix, 29) beginning in 11th year Joram of Israel .. — 3117½ A.K.
AHAZIAH alone began 12th Joram of Israel (II Kings, viii, 25) and reigned 1 year (II Kings, viii, 26; II Chron., xxii, 2) — 3118½ A.K. 1 year 3119½ A.K.

As a descendent of the house of Omri on his mother's side he was "a son of 42 years" in descent from the house of Omri when he began to reign in 3117½. Thus Omri began 3075½ II Chron. xxii, 2 — 42 years Ahaziah Co-rex — 3117½	His actual age when he began his sole reign on 12th year Joram was 22 years as II Kings viii, 25, 26.

ATHALIAH reigned 6 years after her son Ahaziah was slain. II Kings, xi, 1, 3, 4, 21; xii, 1; II Chron., xxii, 11, 12; xxiii, 1; xxiv, 1 — 3119½ A.K. 6 years 3125½ A.K.

JOASH began in 7th Jehu (3125½) and reigned 40 years. II Kings, xii, 1; II Ch., xxiv, 1 — 40 years 3165½ A.K.

AMAZIAH began (end of) 2nd sole year Jehoash of Israel and reigned 29 years, living 15 years after the death of Jehoash of Israel (II Kings, xiv, 1, 2, 17; II Chr., xxv, 1, 25) — 29 years 3194½ A.K.

AZARIAH began in 27th year of Jeroboam II Co-rex (3194½), II Kings, xv, 1, and reigned 52 years (II Kings, xv, 2; II Chron., xxvi, 3) — 52 years 3246½ A.K.

JOTHAM began at beginning 2nd year Pekah of Israel (see Pekah) and reigned 16 years (II Kings, xv., 32 and 33), II Chron., xxvii, 1, 8 — 16 years 3262½ A.K.

AHAZ began (Co-rex) in 17th year Pekah of Israel and reigned 16 years (II Kings, xvi, 1; II Chron., xxviii, 1) .. .. — 3261½ A.K. 16 years 3277½ A.K.

HEZEKIAH began in 3rd Hoshea of Israel and reigned 29 years (II Kings, xviii, 1, 2). That it was late in the 3rd year Hoshea, and therefore 3276½ A.K., is proved by the next records. — 3276½ A.K.
4th Hezekiah began 3279½
7th Hoshea began 3279½ (II Kings, xviii, 9) — 29 years
6th Hezekiah began 3281½
9th Hoshea began 3281½ (II K., xviii, 10) — 3305½ A.K.

MANASSEH reigned .. .. 55 years
(II Kings, xxi, 1; II Chron., xxxiii, 1) — 3360½ A.K.

AMON reigned .. .. 2 years
(II Kings, xxi, 19; II Chron., xxxiii, 21) — 3362½ A.K.

JOSIAH reigned .. .. 31 years
including Jehoahaz, 3 months
(II Kings, xxii, 1; xxiii, 31; II Chron., xxxiv, 1; xxxvi, 2) — 3393½ A.K.

JEHOIAKIM reigned .. .. 11 years
(II Kings, xxiii, 36; II Chron., xxxvi, 5) — 3404½ A.K.

JEHOIACHIN, 3 months in Spring of 8th year Nebuchadnezzar = 3404½ A.K. (II Kings, xxiv, 8-12; II Chron., xxxvi, 9). Nebuchadnezzar deposed him and "*at the return of the year*," II Chron., xxxvi, 10, took him to Babylon and placed Zedekiah on the throne (verses 10-11) .. .. — "at the return of the year." 3405½ A.K.

ZEDEKIAH reigned .. .. 11 years
(II Kings, xxiv, 18; II Chron., xxxvi, 11)
Refer Table XXX. — 3416½ A.K.

KINGS OF ISRAEL.

JEROBOAM (I Kings, xii, 2, 3, 20; xiv, 20).
Table XXVIII Annotations (C) Death of Solomon 3029½ A.K.
Jeroboam .. .. 22 years
3051½

NADAB began in 2nd Asa .. .. .. 3050½ A.K.
(I Kings, xv, 25) 2
3052½ A.K.

BAASHA began in 3rd Asa .. .. .. 3051½ A.K.
I Kings, xv, 33 24
3075½ A.K.

ELAH began to reign 2 years in 26th Asa .. 3074½ A.K.
Slain in 27th Asa (I Kings, xvi, 8-10) .. 3075½ A.K.

ZIMRI (7 days) 27th Asa (I Kings, xvi, 15) .. 3075½ A.K.

OMRI began 27th Asa (I Kings, xvi, 15-22).. 3075½ A.K.
Reigned 12 years (I Kings, xvi, 23) .. 12 years
(I Kings, xvi, 29) .. .. 3087½ A.K.

AHAB began 38th Asa (I Kings, xvi, 29) .. 3086½ A.K.
(I Kings, xvi, 29) .. .. 22 years
(Died early in regnal year beginning 3107½) 3108½ A.K.

AHAZIAH began Co-rex in the 17th year Jehosophat (I Kings, xxii, 51) — 3106½ A.K. 2 years
Died soon after Ahab, early in regnal year beginning 3107½ (II Kings, i, 1-17 — 3108½ A.K.

JORAM began 18th Jehosophat (II Kings, iv, 1) in the 2nd year Jehoram of Judah Pro-rex (II Kings, i, 17) — 3107½ A.K. 12 years 3119½ A.K.

JEHU anointed king slays Ahaziah of Judah (3119½) and Joram of Israel (3119½). Reign. II Kings, ix; x, 36 — 28 years 3147½ A.K.

JEHOAHAZ began in 23rd Joash (3147½) and reigned 17 years. II Kings, xiii, 1. (Died early in the 17th regnal year beginning 3163½) — 17 years 3164½ A.K.

JEHOASH began in 37th Joash of Judah (3161½). Co-rex for 2 years (II Kings xiii, 10) — 3161½ A.K. 2 3163½ A.K.

JEHOASH began alone. 16 years. (II Kings, xiii, 10). This gives the end of his 2nd (sole) year as 3165½ A.K., when Amaziah of Judah began (II Kings, xiv, 1). Amaziah reigned 29 years (II Kings, xiv, 2 and II Chron., xxv, 1) His reign ended at 3194½ A.K. 15 years after the reign of Jehoash of Israel ended in 3179½ A.K. — 16 years 3179½ A.K.

JEROBOAM II Co-rex from 3168½ to 3179½ A.K. since Azariah of Judah began at 3194½ in 27th year Jeroboam II (I Kings, xv, 1) — 3168½ A.K. 11 3179½ A.K.

JEROBOAM II began alone in 15th year (3179½) of Amaziah of Judah (II Kings, xiv, 23) and reigned 41 years to beginning 27th year Azariah of Judah .. .. — 41 years 3220½ A.K.
Interregnum (shown by the next records) between 27th year and 38th year Azariah of Judah.

ZECHARIAH in 38th Azariah of Judah
II Kings, xv, 8.

SHALLUM in 39th Azariah of Judah.
II Kings, xv, 10-13.

MENAHEM reigned 10 years from 39th to 50th Azariah of Judah. (II Kings, xv, 17, 23). He began therefore late in 39th and ended early in 50th Azariah. This fixes his reign as 3233½ to 3243½ A.K. — 3233½ A.K. 10 years 3243½ A.K.

PEKAHIAH reigned 2 years from beginning 50th to beginning 52nd of Azariah of Judah (II Kings, xv, 23, 27) .. .. .. — 2 years 3245½ A.K.

PEKAH began with his 1st year coinciding with 52nd year Azariah of Judah, and his 2nd year with 1st year Jotham of Judah; and reigned 20 years (II Kings, xv, 27 and 32) — 20 years 3265½ A.K.

PERIOD OF ANARCHY beginning in the 20th year (3265½) from the commencement of the reign of Jotham of Israel and ending at Hoshea becoming king in 12th year Ahaz. (II Kings, xv, 30 and xvii, 1); both years inclusive, *i.e.*, to late in 12th Ahaz, 3273½ A.K. Anarchy caused by Hoshea slaying Pekah, and continued until Hoshea established himself.

HOSHEA began late 12th year Ahaz of Israel (3273½ A.K.) and reigned 9 years (II Kings, xvii, 1). — 3273½ A.K. 9 years

Samaria Captured .. .. 3282½ A.K.

TABLE XXVI.

OUTSTANDING DATES RELATING TO THE HISTORY OF THE KINGS OF JUDAH AND ISRAEL (Table XXV).

A.K.   B.C.

The Disruption. Solomon's Kingdom split into the separate kingdoms of Judah (and Benjamin) under Rehoboam, and Ephraim-Israel (the 10-tribed kingdom) under Jeroboam, after death of Solomon.   (Refer Annotations (C) to Table XXVIII). $3029\frac{1}{2}=970$

Invasion of Judah by Sheshanq I (Shishak), 1st king of XXIInd (Bubastite) Dynasty of Egypt, in his 1st year, (the 5th year of Rehoboam), to establish his claim in having seized the throne of Egypt from the XXIst (Tanite) Dynasty, the allies of Solomon and Rehoboam. (Annotations (A) Table XXVI.) $3033\frac{1}{2}=966$

Omri founded the new Israelitish Capital of Samaria in his 7th year (I Kings, xvi, 23, 24) .. ..$3081\frac{1}{2}=918$

Shalmaneser II of Assyria claims that he invaded Syria in his 6th year (which was the 21st year of Ahab) defeating Ben Hadad of Damascus, and his 12 allies, including Ahab. (Annotations (B) Table XXVI.) $3106\frac{1}{2}=893$

Shalmaneser II of Assyria claims that he invaded Syria, in his 18th year, defeating Hazael of Damascus, and later in the same year, collecting tribute from Jehu, who had just seized the throne of Israel. (Annotations (B) Table XXVI.) $3118\frac{1}{2}=881$ $3119\frac{1}{2}=880$

Pulu—who later usurped the Assyrian throne as Tiglath-pileser III—while acting as viceroy and commander-in-chief of Assur-dan III of Assyria collected tribute from Azariah of Judah, and Menahem of Israel.   This was during the campaign (to Hadrach) of the 7th year of Assur-dan III (The Assyrian Chronicle). This campaign was later claimed by Pulu, when he became Tiglath-pileser III (Annotations B to Table XXVI).   Pestilence, insurrection, and anarchy in Assyria from the 7th year Assur-dan III onwards to the accession of Pulu as Tiglath-pileser III, prevented further tribute being collected until the reigns of Ahaz of Judah, Pekah and Hoshea of Israel, and Resin of Damascus. $3234\frac{1}{2}=765$

The Important Prophetical Date of the vith chapter of Isaiah " in the year that king Uzziah (Azariah) died "= 3246 A.K. (Table XXV). The Vision of the Lord of Hosts and the Prophecy relating to the blindness of the Jews until " the whole land be utterly desolate": " a tenth " to " return " and to be " eaten " ; " the holy seed shall be the substance thereof." The prophecy clearly refers to the Saviour coming from an unbelieving people,—a remnant of whom were to be returned until this was effected ; after which " the land to be utterly desolate." The prophecy is referred to seven times in the New Testament—Matt., xiii, 14 ; Mark, iv, 12 ; Luke, viii, 10 ; John, xii, 40 ; Acts, xxviii, 26, 27 ; Rom., xi, 8. From the date of the prophecy, 3246 A.K., to the final dispersion of the Jews, 4134 A.K.= 135¾ A.D. (Table XXVIII Annotations (F) VIII) is an interval of 888 years. Now according to prophetic symbolism as elucidated within recent generations, 888 is the number symbolic of the Christ, as 666 is the number symbolic of Antichrist. Refer ¶ 338 concerning the connected numerical relations.† $3246 = 754$

The 1st year of Ahaz was the last year of Jotham (Table XXV)= $3261\frac{1}{2}-2\frac{1}{4}$ A.K.

After the death of Jotham, Ahaz offered up pagan sacrifices, and following $3262\frac{1}{4}$ A.K. this was attacked by Rezin of Damascus and Pekah of Israel. Ahaz   to suffered two successive disasters but successfully resisted Rezin of $3263\frac{1}{4}$ A.K. Damascus when the latter besieged him in Jerusalem.

Ahaz next sent messengers to Tiglath-pileser with tribute (which tribute $3263\frac{3}{4}$ A.K. Tiglath-pileser mentions in his records), asking for Assyrian help   to against Rezin and Pekah. $3264\frac{1}{4}$ A.K.

Tiglath-pileser answered the call of Ahaz by investing and capturing $3264\frac{3}{4}$ A.K. Damascus. Ahaz then visited the Assyrian king at Damascus. (Refer   to II Kings, xvi, 1-20 ; II Chron., xxviii, 1-27). $3265\frac{1}{4}$ A.K.

Events that occurred within the 4 years' interval from Accession of Ahaz of Judah, to death of Pekah of Israel. $3261\frac{1}{4}=738$ to   to $3265\frac{1}{4}=734$

As a result of the intrigues of Ahaz, Tiglath-pileser deposed Pekah of Israel, and appointed Hoshea as Assyrian governor of Samaria. Hoshea immediately removed Pekah by assassinating him. $3265\frac{1}{4}=734$

Tiglath-pileser died in January, 726 B.C.=$3273\frac{1}{4}$ A.K. (as Table XX). Hoshea hearing of this, immediately claimed the throne of Israel, $3273\frac{1}{4}$ A.K. (as Table XXV), but gave tribute to Shalmaneser, when the latter appeared against him (II Kings, xvii, 3). $3273\frac{1}{4}=726$

Hoshea then began to rely upon " So, king of Egypt," to whom he sent messengers. Obviously relying upon the strength of the Egyptian behind him, Hoshea omitted to send the annual tribute to Assyria as he had previously done " year by year " (II Kings, xvii, 4). The latter reference to tribute may refer to the years of Hoshea's governorship prior to the death of Tiglath-pileser. In any case, Hoshea was shut up in prison by Shalmaneser, some time between his accession to the throne and the commencement of the siege of Samaria. $3273\frac{1}{2}=726$ to   to $3277\frac{1}{2}=722$

Some time after Hoshea was imprisoned, Shalmaneser began the siege of Samaria which lasted for 3 complete years (II Kings, xviii, 10). That the siege began in the reign of Shalmaneser is stated by II Kings, xviii, 9. The Assyrian data confirming this are given in Annotations (C). Sargon, however, late in his own reign, by dating from his coregency with Shalmaneser, endeavoured to show that the siege began in his own reign. He also obscured the fact that the siege lasted for 3 years.

Although not precisely stated, the narrative sequence of II Kings, xvii, 3-5, seems to imply that Hoshea was imprisoned by the Assyrians in Samaria, under an Assyrian garrison there ; that, in consequence, Samaria rose in revolt and overpowered the Assyrian garrison ; and that the siege was undertaken by Shalmaneser to punish Samaria for the revolt. The Annals of Sargon, in the light of Annotations (C), clearly show that Sargon, acting for Shalmaneser, in 722 B.C., captured Samaria, deposed Hoshea, since Sargon states " my general over them I appointed." In 720 B.C., however, Sargon is still troubled by Samaria. The record is unfortunately broken, but what there is tells us that Sibe (Sabaka) came to the aid of Samaria and was defeated by Sargon at the battle of Raphia (in B.C. 720). $3279\frac{1}{2}=720$ to   to $3282\frac{1}{2}=717$

For the data and events relating to the fall of Jerusalem refer Table XXX.

† The year (754 B.C.) of Isaiah's prophecy concerning the Saviour in relation to the desolation of the land was the initial year of Roman official historical reckoning, A.U.C. The Final dispersion of the Jews (¶ ¶ 337 and 338 and Table XXVIII Annotations (F) VIII) was effected by the Romans in A.D. 135, in A.U.C. 888 ; and 888 is the number symbolic of the Messiah.

ANNOTATIONS (A) TO TABLE XXVI.

EGYPTIAN SYNCHRONISMS WITH KINGS OF ISRAEL AND JUDAH.

The Invasion of Shishak:—

Comparison of the chronological statements of Tables XXIV and XXV with Annotations (C) to Table XXVIII shows that Solomon was the contemporary of Sa-Amen and later of Pa-Seb-Khanu II of the XXIst Egyptian Dynasty at Tanis (Table XXIV). I Kings, iii, 1, states that Solomon at the beginning of his reign married the daughter of the Egyptian king. The Egyptian king referred to can have been no other than Sa-Amen. Solomon began to build the Temple at the beginning of his 4th year=2992½ A.K. (I Kings, vi, 1, and Annotations (C) to Table XXVIII). He completed the Temple at 2999½ A.K. (I Kings, vi, 38) and completed his own house at 3012½ A.K. (I Kings, vii, 1; ix, 1, 10). Some time before the latter date the Egyptian king (obviously Sa-Amen) had captured Gezer, had burnt it and presented its site to his daughter, Solomon's wife (I Kings, ix, 16). Solomon rebuilt the city as part of his scheme of operations in storing materials and housing workmen and soldiers, and in organising communications during the building of the Temple (I Kings, xi, 15-25). The date of the destruction of Gezer by Sa-Amen lies between 2992½ and 2999½ A.K., and obviously about 2994 A.K., to accord with the sequence of operations.

When, therefore, towards the end of Solomon's reign, Jeroboam fled from Solomon, he did not risk seeking sanctuary at the Court of the Tanites, who were allied to Solomon. Jeroboam fled to the Court of a new Dynasty at Bubastis, founded by Sheshanq I (Table XXIV). This occurred not long before the death of Solomon and before Sheshanq (the Shishak of I Kings, xi, 40) was king of *All* Egypt. For this Sheshanq, originally a powerful chief of Libyan merceneries under the XXIst (Tanitic) Dynasty—and descended from a long line of Libyan chiefs who had settled at Heracleopolis early in the XXIst Dynasty—became an independent king in the Delta, by seizing Bubastis, before he actually became king of all Egypt in 967 B.C. (refer Breasted *Records*, IV, 785, and footnote c; also his "Hist. Egypt," p. 527). A careful examination of all the historical facts will be found to show that the death of Solomon, the return of Jeroboam, and the resulting division of his hitherto powerful kingdom were all factors that formulated the schemes and decided the actions of Sheshanq I in seizing the throne of all Egypt. This is confirmed by the chronology relating to Sheshanq I, which chronology has been established entirely from astronomical data and altogether independently of the data now under consideration.

For, as the reader will observe, Sheshanq, having awaited the result of Jeroboam's bid for the kingship over the 10 tribes of Israel, and probably having awaited the death of the Tanite king, invaded Judah (I Kings, xiv, 25, 26; II Chron., xii, 2) in the 5th year of Rehoboam. From Table XXV, the 5th year of Rehoboam began at 3033½ A.K. and from Table XXIV, the reign of Sheshanq I, as king of All Egypt began at 3033 A.K. These two independently established datings confirm the above conclusion relating to the sequence of motives and actions. It is clear that Sheshanq I took advantage of the dissension in the Empire established by Solomon, by taking the kingship of All Egypt from the Tanite Dynasty that had favoured Solomon, and that he immediately hastened to establish his right to the throne by attacking Solomon's son, Rehoboam.

Sheshanq I records his invasion in work belonging to his 21st year and claims to have invaded Israel also. From the date of Sheshanq's work, authorities have inferred that his invasion of Judah was not many years before his 21st year. The astronomical chronology, however, fixes the facts as above.

It is interesting to read what Dr. H. R. Hall states ("Anc. Hist. Near East," p. 439). "Here again we see that the Egyptian did not strike till he could be fairly sure of victory. Solomon had been too powerful for any attack to be made upon him: but no sooner was he dead, and the tyranny, weakness, and unpopularity of Rehoboam made manifest, than the plans of the Pharaoh who had taken Gaza were resumed by his Bubastite successor." The reference to Gaza here does not relate to a previous expedition against Judah or Israel. The statement refers to Dr. Hall's theory as to Gaza having been captured from the Philistines by Solomon's Egyptian contemporary.

Note:—The reader will observe, from the examples cited on this sheet of Annotations, that the Books of Kings and Chronicles, having been originally written up at the end of a king's reign, mention contemporaneous rulers as kings, even when dealing with events preceding their accession to sole rule.

Zerah the "Ethiopian" Invades Judah:—

The invasion of Zerah, the "Ethiopian" (mentioned in II Chron., xiv, 9-15) happened after the first 10 years of Asa (xiv, 1) and before the 15th year of Asa (xv. 10) *i.e.*, between 3059½ A.K. and 3064½ A.K. (by Table XXV). This synchronises with the reign of Uasarkon I, 3054 to 3083 A.K. (Table XXIV). The account in II Chron., states that the invading army consisted of Libyans and Ethiopians (xvi, 8). Petrie reasonably concludes that Zerah is Uasarkon I. Uasarkon I, however, was of Libyan extraction. This would account for the Libyans in the invading army, but not for Uasarkon I being described as "Zerah, the Ethiopian." The connection is to be explained by the recently discovered fact that the "Ethiopian kings (of the later XXVth Dynasty and their Predecessor Piankhi I) were themselves of Libyan Descent" (Peet, "Egypt and O. T." p. 169). Zerah was therefore, in all probability, a Libyan ruler of Ethiopia (and vassal or ally of Uasarkon I) acting for Uasarkon, the Libyan king of Egypt as leader of the combined army of Sudani mercenaries and Libyans. This better explains the facts, for as Peet states, "It is absolutely impossible to get Zerah out of Osorkon (Uasarkon)." (p. 164.) It is to be observed that the narrative in II Chron. neither terms Zerah "king of Ethiopia," nor "king of Egypt"—merely "the Ethiopian."

So, "King of Egypt" and Hoshea:—

During the reign of Shalmaneser (Table XX) 726 to 721 B.C.=3273½ to 3278½ A.K., Hoshea of Israel became vassal of Assyria but conspired with So, king of Egypt (Annotations (C)). Now Sabaka, the Ethiopian noble (of Libyan extraction as above) was commander-in-chief (Petrie, "Egypt and Israel," p. 76) during the reign of Kashta (Table XXIV), and later became king of Egypt. "So," the contemporary of Hoshea and Shalmaneser, therefore, belongs to the period when Sabaka was commander-in-chief of Kashta or Piankhi. From this, Petrie, Hall, and the majority of *archæological* authorities now conclude that So, or Seve, is Sabaka, prior to his being king. Petrie states that, as Beth sheba is also Beth shua in Hebrew, Shaba(ka) or Saba(ka) is Shua(ka) or abbreviated Shua or Sua in Hebrew—"So" being merely the rendering in the *Authorised Version* for "Sua."

Peet, on the other hand, gives what appear to be equally good reasons for concluding that So or Sua was "one of those numerous petty dynasts who ruled in the Egyptian Delta during the years which elapsed between Piankhi's Conquest of Egypt and Shabaka's establishing himself on the Egyptian throne." ("Egypt and O. T." p. 173.)

Taharqa, Viceroy in 14th year of Hezekiah.

This identity follows from II Kings, xviii, 13; xix, 8 and 9, and Annotations (C), and agrees with Taharqa's own statement concerning his having been appointed viceroy at the age of 20 or soon after. (Petrie, "Hist. Egypt," III, p. 296.) Now Taharqa was the younger brother of Sabaka and the uncle of Sabataka, and since Sabaka had been viceroy and commander-in-chief under Kashta and previously under Piankhi I (Table XXIV) we see, clearly enough, that these relations, and the age of Taharqa at the beginning of his coregency, fit the narrative of II Kings, xviii, 13; xix, 8 and 9, already confirmed by the identities of Annotations (C).

Josiah Slain in Action against Nekau II:—

II Kings, xxiii, 29-35; II Chron., xxxv, 20-24. Nekau II became king at 3390½ A.K.=609 B.C. (Table XXIV), in the 15th (2nd reckoning) year of Nabopolassar (Table XXI), and therefore a year after the fall of Nineveh, according to the recently deciphered inscription of Nabopolassar. 4 years later, at the beginning of Nekau's 5th and Nabopolassar's 18th year, 3393½ A.K.=606 B.C., we find Nekau II.—obviously anticipating the rise of Babylon,—endeavouring to capture Carchemish from the weakened Assyrian Empire. The later compiled "Annals" of Nabopolassar represent this and similar Egyptian efforts as having been projected to assist Assyria. But this interpretation is unlikely in view of the fact that Psamtek I had but lately thrown off the Assyrian yoke. Nekau II, at 3393½ A.K., was clearly seizing what he deemed to be a strategical advantage in the hopes of being able to restore the boundaries of the Egyptian Empire as they had stood in the days of Tahutmes III of the XVIIIth Dynasty. Josiah opposed him, was defeated and slain. Nekau II, in turn, was defeated 3 years later in 603 B.C., at Carchemish, by Nebuchadnezzar.

ANNOTATIONS (B) TO TABLE XXVI.

FACTS IGNORED IN THE ASSYRIAN EPONYM LISTS.

THE CONTEMPORARIES OF TIGLATH-PILESER III.

The beginning of the 9th century B.C. is identified with the rise of the Assyrian kingdom under Assur-nazir-pal. With him begins a succession of 5 kings, the records of whose reigns show a steady increase in the power of Assyria. Following this succession is " a period of strange, almost inexplicable, decline. Of the next three reigns we have no single royal inscription, and are confined to the brief notes of the Eponym Lists. From these we learn too little to enable us to follow the decline of Assyrian fortunes, but we gain here and there a glimpse of it, and see also not less vividly the growth of a strong northern power which should vex Assyrian kings for centuries." (Rogers, " Hist. Bab. and Assyr." II, p. 100.)

To appreciate the significance of the statement quoted, it is necessary to remember that the Assyrian Eponym Lists, as we know them, were compiled as a statement of a continuous succession of years, at a date considerably later than the three reigns identified with the decline of Assyrian power. Some mystery obviously attaches to these three reigns. They belong to what appears to have been a period of decline. There are no contemporary records. The only data relating to the three reigns are data compiled at a much later date and ostensibly from the annual records of the Eponyms. It is important to bear the latter fact in mind in considering what follows :—

Now whereas the genealogy of the preceding five kings is known with certainty, no data exist to show what relationship, if any, held between the three succeeding kings, Shalmaneser III, Assur-dan III, and Assur-nirari II, and their predecessors. The important fact is that the actual records of Tiglath-pileser III, who succeeded Assur-nirari II, claim conquests in Syria, dates of which belong to the reigns of Assur-dan III and Assur-nirari II. Now in the Assyrian Chronicle (the notes of the Eponym Lists mentioned by Rogers) there are only two campaigns to Syria in the reigns noted. These are dated in the years 765 and 755 B.C., *i.e.*, 3234½ to 3235½ and 3244½ to 3245½ A.K. respectively. The former date falls in the 2nd year Menahem of Israel=41st year Azariah of Judah. Now II Kings, xv, 19, 20 refers to Menahem giving tribute to Pul. Pulu was the original name of the Assyrian king prior to his adoption of the name Tiglath-pileser, after the death of Assur-nirari II. Therefore since Tiglath-pileser III states that he received tribute from Menahem and Azariah it is obvious that he is referring to his acting for Assur-dan III in 765 B.C. I Chron. v, 26, therefore refers to Pul and Tiglath-pileser as two successive names of one and the same person. II Kings, xv, 19 refers to him as Pul during the reign of Menahem of Israel, in the year 765 B.C., and verse 29 of the same chapter refers to him as Tiglath-pileser, during the reign of Pekah, which ended at 3265½ A.K., or, more precisely, in the course of the year 735 B.C., which was the 9th year of Tiglath-pileser, according to his second method of dating (Table XX). The sequence of names in II Kings, xv, therefore agrees with the facts relating to Tiglath-pileser III.

Now, in the fragmentary inscription of Tiglath-pileser III, mentioning Menahem and Resin of Syria, the statement is followed by the words " In my 9th year." We now see that Tiglath-pileser III is historically relating previous events in Syria—in which he was concerned— with the events of his 9th year, when he deposed Pekah and set up Hoshea as governor. Tiglath-pileser's exact statement is, " Pekaha their king......Asui (Hoshea) I appointed over them......" Therefore II Kings, xv, 29, 30, in narrating concerning Tiglath-pileser taking Israel into captivity in the days of Pekah, states that Hoshea slew Pekah, and reigned in his stead. The two statements are in agreement, both concerning the sequence of events and concerning the date.

The matter as elucidated above explains why the inscriptions of Tiglath-pileser III mention Azariah and Ahaz, of Judah, Menahem, Pekah, and Hoshea of Israel and Resin of Damascus as his contemporaries.

THE CONTEMPORARIES OF SHALMANESER II.

As relating to the preceding column, the following identities show that a gap of 39 or 40 years occurred between the Assyrian succession of 5 predominant kings and the succession of 3 " declining " reigns. This explains that " the inexplicable decline " occurred within the gap of 39 or 40 years, which was ignored in the later compilation of Eponym Lists, precisely as the longer gap in Assyrian history was ignored by Sargon, Sennacherib, and Assurbanipal (Annotations (C) to Tables XVII-XIX).

Table XXV and Annotations show that Ahab died early in his 22nd year. The 3 years of truce between Benhadad of Syria and Ahab of Israel were, therefore, the 19th, 20th, and 21st years of Ahab, since Ahab was slain when he broke the truce by attacking Benhadad as I Kings, xxii, narrates. Now Shalmaneser II, the son and successor of Assur-nazir-pal in Assyria, has recorded on the Kurkh monolith that Ahab of Israel was one of 12 kings, allies of Ben Hadad of Syria in Shalmaneser's 6th year. Shalmaneser states that he defeated them and gives a list of his captures. The alliance of Ahab with Syria can only belong to one or other of the 3 years of truce. The truce was not made because of fear of Assyria (I Kings, xx, 1-34), but because of Israel defeating Syria. The truce was most likely broken because of disagreement between the allies after the Assyrian invasion of Shalmaneser's 6th year. This would identify the 6th year of Shalmaneser with the 3rd year of the truce and therefore with the 21st year of Ahab=3106½-3107½ A.K.

The invasion would be timed to coincide with the Syrian harvest, *i.e.*, " at the return of the year, at the time when kings go forth to battle," (II Sam., xi, 1 ; I Chron., xx, 1) obviously to collect tribute from the approaching harvest. This is confirmed by the Kouyunjik obelisk of Shalmaneser II. This records that in each year the king set forth on his campaigns by crossing the Euphrates in flood, *i.e.*, in the spring. The statement occurs in this inscription concerning the campaign of the 6th year, mentioned above The defeat of Benhadad and his allies, including Ahab, therefore occurred not later than the summer at 3106½ A.K. =893 B.C., in the 6th year of Shalmaneser II. The reign of Shalmaneser II therefore began at 3101½ A.K.= 898 B.C., whereas the date alleged by the Assyrian Eponym Lists is 858 B.C.—40 years later. Modern authorities give his reign as beginning in 860 or 859 B.C. The synchronism of Shalmaneser II with the kings of Israel and Damascus he mentions can be confirmed by other data than as given above. In the record of his 18th year—beginning at 3118½ A.K. by datum above—Shalmaneser defeated Hazael of Syria. (Bull Inscription of Shalmaneser.) In describing the siege of Damascus that followed, Shalmaneser continues with the statement that " In those days I collected tribute from Jehu of Israel."

Now II Kings, viii, 7-15 relates concerning the death of Benhadad of Syria and the succession of his son Hazael. Verse 28 then relates that Joram of Israel was wounded in battle against Hazael of Syria. This explains why Israel did not support Hazael. Whilst Joram was recovering from his wounds he was slain by Jehu at 3119½ A.K. (Table XXV and Annotations.) This accounts for Shalmaneser, towards the end of his 18th year, ending at 3119½ A.K., collecting tribute from Jehu, during the siege of Damascus. If he had collected it earlier in the same year, he would have collected it from Joram.

The resulting chronology of the Assyrian Kings, following the Supremacy of the Aramæan Confederation and prior to the Kings of Table XX, is as follows :—

Tiglath-pileser II	..	..	circ. 990 B.C.
Assur-dan II	..	..	circ. 970 B.C.
Hadad-nirari II	..	..	949—928 B.C.
Assur-nazir-pal	..	..	928—922 B.C.
Tukulti-Enurta II	..	..	922—898 B.C.
Shalmaneser II	..	..	898—863 B.C.
Assur-danin-pal	..	..	863—861 B.C.

Samsi-Hadad II	..	..	861—850 B.C.
Hadad-nirari III	..	..	850—821 B.C.
Gap ignored by later Eponym Lists	..	..	39 years.
Shalmaneser III	..	..	782—773 B.C.
Assur-dan III	..	..	773—755 B.C.
Assur-nirari	..	..	755—745 B.C.

ANNOTATIONS (C) TO TABLE XXVI.

Sargon and Sennacherib fix the dates of Hezekiah's Reign.

An important detail relating to the reign of Sargon of Assyria is the double dating of his records. The Assyrian Eponym Lists give his 1st year as beginning in 721 B.C., and alternatively in 719 B.C. (Table XX). Similarly in the Annals of Sargon, his Ashdod Expedition is dated in his 11th year, and on his Ashdod Inscription (Kouyunjik Cylinder) it is dated in his 9th year. Comparison of the two inscriptions shows that it is the same expedition that is described and dated. The regnal year referred to extended from 1st Nisan 711 B.C. to 1st Nisan 710 B.C.=3288½-3289½ A.K. Reference to Table XXV shows this coincided with the 13th year Hezekiah. Now Sargon narrates concerning this year that Azuri of Ashdod revolted after refusing to pay tribute to Assyria. Sargon states that he "wreaked vengeance" and deposed Azuri and appointed Azuri's brother, Achimite, as governor of Ashdod. This obviously occupied the first part of the year. Then he states that the Hittites set an Ionian in Ashdod, as king there. Sargon hearing of this, rapidly mobilised his army in Assyria, and without taking time to collect his baggage again advanced against Ashdod. The Ionian fled, before his approach, into Egypt to the frontier of Ethiopia. Meanwhile Sargon besieged Ashdod and eventually captured it. Sargon's next move seems to have been a threat to Egypt and Ethiopia, since he states that the king of Ethiopia delivered up to him the fugitive Ionian of Ashdod. Sennacherib's records show that Mitinti was made king over Ashdod, and Sennacherib, late in his own reign refers only to Mitinti. Sennacherib in the account of his campaign against Hezekiah states that he defeated the Ethiopian army of Sabaka. The importance of this will be seen in what follows.

The whole series of events clearly occupied the extent of the one regnal year of Sargon to the beginning of the "14th year of Hezekiah" when—the Ashdod affair having been satisfactorily settled for the Assyrians—Sargon's son, Sennacherib, as Tartan (or commander-in-chief) "came up against all the fenced cities of Judah and took them." (Isaiah, xxxvi, 1; II Kings, xviii, 13.) Isaiah, xx, 1, therefore, in referring to the Ashdod siege states "In the year that Tartan came unto Ashdod (when Sargon the King of Assyria sent him) and fought against it and took it." Had this been the year in which the Tartan came against Judah, Isaiah would have said so. The Ashdod expedition and siege belong to the second half of Hezekiah's 13th year and the invasion of Judah to the early part of Hezekiah's 14th year. Now it is in this year that 185,000 of the host of Sennacherib, (as Tartan of Sargon) died in one night as stated in II Kings, xix, 35, and Isaiah, xxxvii, 36. Accounts from other sources attribute the disaster to pestilence (Josephus, *Antiq.*, x, i, 4) and this seems to have been the explanation adopted by the Assyrians since they left Syria and Judæa alone after this date. The account given by the Egyptians to Herodotus (ii, 141) states that in the night mice gnawed the bowstrings of Sennacherib's army, and that in consequence, the Assyrians took flight in the morning.

In the same year, however, Sargon became active against Merodach-baladan of Babylon and overthrew him in the Autumn. Sargon, then, entered Babylon in the winter of 710 B.C., still in the 14th year of Hezekiah. Now it is important to observe that Merodach-baladan ceased to reign in the autumn of 710 B.C., and that he sent presents to Hezekiah before this (I Kings, xx, 12) during the year of Hezekiah's sickness. The latter is fixed as the 14th year of Hezekiah by II Kings, xx, 1-12, since it is given in verse 6 as 15 years before the death of Hezekiah, who reigned 29 years. It is also dated as succeeding the invasion of Sennacherib, and after the disaster to his host. The latter event is therefore dated by the 2nd Book of Kings and by Isaiah as prior to the actual reign of Sennacherib. The Annals of Sargon have shown that Sennacherib's invasion belongs to 711 B.C. for the siege of Ashdod, and to 710 B.C. for the invasion of Judah and the disaster to the Assyrians. Sennacherib correctly claimed this and other expeditions of Sargon's reign as his, without, however, stating they belonged to the period of his co-regency with Sargon. For this reason, obviously, Sennacherib's records do not date his various expeditions. It is clear, therefore, that the dated Assyrian records fix the 14th year of Hezekiah as beginning 1st Nisan, 710 B.C.=3289½ A.K., and his 1st year as beginning 1st Nisan, 723 B.C.=3276½ A.K. as independently obtained from the Books of Kings and Chronicles (Table XXV). This is an important matter as is shown in the next column.

Shalmaneser and Sargon and the Siege of Samaria.

As derived from the data of the preceding column, three facts have to be emphasized. These are (1) that the record of the Kouyunjik Cylinder, drafted between 710 B.C. and 706 B.C., gives the 1st year of Sargon as beginning 1st Nisan, 719 B.C.; (2) that later the Annals of Sargon, drafted not earlier than 705 B.C., give the 1st year of Sargon as beginning 1st Nisan, 721 B.C.; and (3) that the Assyrian Eponym Lists, as we now have them, were compiled at a date considerably later and give, in different lists, the two alternative datings of Sargon for the beginning of his 1st year. Having regard to the sequence of evolution and compilation we may conclude that the late complete Eponym Lists derived their data for the earlier beginning of Sargon's reign from Sargon's own inscriptions.

Again, when we find the sole authority for the death of Shalmaneser in Tebet (January), 721 B.C., to be the Babylonian Chronicle,—certainly compiled not earlier than the last year of Esarhaddon, 680 B.C., and known only from a copy of the 22nd year of Darius, 500 B.C.—we may conclude that the data relating to Shalmaneser and Sargon in the Babylonian Chronicle are from the same sources as those from which the complete Assyrian Eponym Lists derived their data.

We are therefore introduced to the probability that Shalmaneser did not die in Tebet, 721 B.C., but that his death in this month, on an unknown day of the month, prior to the 12th Tebet, was inferred from the fact that Sargon was appointed coregent on 12th Tebet (15th January), 721 B.C., and began to reckon his 1st year as coregent from 1st Nisan, 721 B.C. This would account for Sargon, when he began his 1st year sole reign at 1st Nisan 719 B.C., proudly adopting the dating of his sole reign until lack of novelty robbed it of its precedence; that, in consequence, to record to posterity his victorious career back to include his years of coregency, he resumed, late in his reign, his original reckoning from the beginning of his 1st year of coregency at 1st Nisan, 721 B.C. The sequence outlined seems to be confirmed by the fact that no monuments or inscriptions of Shalmaneser are extant. Sargon would certainly have destroyed his predecessor's monuments had his intention been to claim his conquests.

The probability inferred from the Assyrian records is reduced to a matter of certainty by the Old Testament records. By the data of the preceding column, the 9th sole year Sargon=13th year Hezekiah beginning 1st Nisan, 711 B.C. Now II Kings, xviii, 9, 10, dates the Siege of Samaria as beginning at the commencement of Hezekiah's 4th year, in Spring, 720 B.C., which is the year preceding the 1st sole year of Sargon. II Kings, xviii, 9, therefore states that it was "Shalmaneser" who "came up against Samaria and besieged it." Verse 10 then states that Samaria was taken "at the end of three years," at the end of "the 6th year of Hezekiah,"=3282½ A.K.=717 B.C. It does not say that Shalmaneser took the city, for Shalmaneser had been dead 2 years, as we now see. It merely states that "*they* took it," thus implying that it was taken by the generals of the Assyrian king.

Now it is essential to read carefully II Kings, xvii and xviii and the Annals of Sargon. II Kings, xvii, 3, states that some time prior to the siege of Samaria, Shalmaneser came up against Hoshea and Hoshea became his servant and gave him presents. Verse 4 then states that Hoshea ceased to send tribute as he had done "year by year" and that Shalmaneser found Hoshea conspiring with So (Sabaka), king of Egypt. This was before Sabaka's sole reign, when he was coregent and commander-in-chief of Kashta, the Ethiopian king (refer Annotations A to Table XXVI. Verse 4, continuing, states that Shalmaneser shut Hoshea up in prison. Verse 5 then states that after this Shalmaneser came up "throughout all the land" and that Samaria was besieged for three years, *i.e.*, from Spring, 720, to Spring, 717 B.C.

In his *Annals*, Sargon claims that he besieged and captured Samaria in the accession year of his coregency (not stated as such). This was in Spring, 721 B.C., and prior to 1st Nisan, 721 B.C., when his 1st year coregency began. He was therefore acting for Shalmaneser in connection with the events of II Kings, xvii, 4. Sargon claims that he took 27,280 persons into captivity at this time from Samaria. He also claims that he immediately transplanted other conquered peoples into Samaria. In his 2nd year from coregency (1st Nisan, 720, to 1st Nisan, 719 B.C.) he, however, still mentions Samaria as in revolt in relation to the advance of Sebeck (Sabaka). This still fits the facts of II Kings, xvii, 4. Sargon claims that at this time he defeated Sabaka at the battle of Raphia. What he said further concerning Samaria is unfortunately broken off. That Samaria, however, was still being besieged and had not yet received its transplanted peoples, is confirmed by Sargon's

(*Continued at foot of Col. 1.*)

(*Column 2 continued.*)

record of his 7th year from coregency (1st Nisan, 715 to 1st Nisan, 714 B.C.) stating that Samaria did not receive the transplanted people until that year. It is clear, therefore, that Sargon's *Annals* gloss over the fact that Samaria troubled him from 721 to 717 B.C.

TABLE XXVII.

A—MEDO-PERSIAN KINGS—CYRUS TO DARIUS III.

	Reckoned whole years of reign from 1st year inclusive.	Date of Beginning of 1st year at 1st Nisan Spring of B.C.	A.K.
1 Cyrus (additional 2 years Cambyses co-rex.)	7	536	3463½
2 Cambyses (including Bardis—7 months and Accession of } Darius)	8	529	3470½
3 Bardis (Usurper as above)	$\frac{7}{12}$	522	3477½
4 Darius (I) Hystaspes (including Nebuchadnezzar III } Usurper)	36	521	3478½
5 Xerxes I }			
6 Artabanus 7 months ignored }	21	485	3514½
7 Artaxerxes (I) Longimanus, 40 years)			
8 Xerxes II .. .. 2 months }	41	464	3535½
9 Sogdianus .. .. .. 7 months)			
10 Darius (II) Nothus	19	423	3576½
11 Artaxerxes (II) Memnon	46	404	3595½
12 Artaxerxes (III) Okhos	21	358	3641½
13 Arses	2	337	3662½
14 Darius (III) Codomannus	5	335	3664½
Battle of Arbela	October	331	3669
Death of Darius III	July	330	3669½

B—THE 2ND YEARS EMPLOYED IN JEWISH CHRONOLOGICAL FORGERIES.
(TABLE XXVIII AND ANNOTATIONS; AND ¶¶ 330-333)

2nd Year Darius (I) Hystaspes	..	..	..	..	..	..	3479½–3480½ A.K.
Do. Artaxerxes I	..	..	..	..	..	..	3536½–3537½ A.K.
Do. Darius II ..	..	..	..	..	..	..	3577½–3578½ A.K.
Do. Artaxerxes II	..	..	..	..	..	..	3596½–3597½ A.K.
Do. Artaxerxes III	..	..	..	..	..	..	3642½–3643½ A.K.
Do. Darius III ..	..	..	..	..	..	..	3665½–3666½ A.K.

BASES OF RABBINICAL IDENTITIES (REAL AND FICTITIOUS):—

Haggai i, 1-12; Zech. i, 1 and 12, and Ezek. xl, 1 (as Table XXX note opposite 13th year of captivity); also Ezra vi, 14, which reads in the Hebrew, " DARIUS *even* ARTAXERXES "—the implied identity holding from Ezra vi, 14, onwards, and synchronising with Nehemiah, Chs. vi to xi inclusive

JEWISH APPLICATION OF IDENTITIES TO DANIEL IX, 2, and 24-27.

ANNOTATIONS TO TABLE XXVII.

I.—Cyrus, Cambyses, and Darius (I) Hystaspes :—

(1) The beginning of the reign of Cyrus in Ansan-Persia. and, again, in Babylon, and the beginning of the coregency of Cambyses, and also of his sole reign are as fixed by Table XXI and Annotations.

(2) By Table XXI Annotations Col. (2), the first year of Cyrus (Ansan-Persia) began at 1st Nisan (Spring) of B.C. 558.

(3) Herodotus (I, 214 ; III, 66, 67 ; IV, 4) gives, from the latter date, Cyrus 29 years, Cambyses (including the usurper, pseudo-Smerdis or Bardis) 8 years, and Darius, 36 years. Total 73 years. By Table XX Annotations, these years all begin from the spring month Nisan, beginning the regnal years, from the " first year " inclusive of each reign.

(4) Herodotus VII 1-4 narrates that Darius died in the 5th year after the Battle of Marathon, definitely fixed as Oct. 490 B.C. Dating from this fixed point, the 1st year is Oct. 490 B.C.—Oct. 489 B.C. and the 5th year Oct. 486 B.C. to Oct. 485 B.C. The latter year included spring 485 B.C. ending the 73 years of Herodotus as (2) and (3) above. The 36 years of Darius, therefore, ended at the 1st of Nisan, B.C. 485.

(5) By the data of Herodotus, the 1st year of Darius I began at 1st Nisan, B.C. 521, this, as Herodotus states, being the termination of the 8 years of Cambyses. The 8 years of Cambyses, therefore, began at 1st Nisan, B.C. 529, as Table XX Annotations Col. 2.

(6) This is confirmed by the two Babylonian eclipse records of the reign of Darius I quoted by Ptolemy. These determine (a) that the 20th regnal year of Darius began between 19th Nov., B.C. 503 and 19th Nov., B.C. 502 and his 1st year, therefore, between 19th Nov., 522 and 19th Nov., 521 B.C. ; and (b) that the 31st regnal year began sometime between 25th April, 492 and 25th April, 491 B.C. and his 1st year, therefore, between 25th April. 522 and 25th April, 521 B.C. Combining (a) and (b) Darius began his 1st year between 19th Nov. (Julian) B.C. 522 and 25th April (Julian) B.C. 521. His 1st year, therefore, began at 1st Nisan (spring) B.C. 521, by Table XX Annotations.

(7) The Babylonian Egibi Tablets begin the 1st year Darius with the 1st Nisan dating.

II.—The Combined Narrative of Darius (Behistun Insc.) and Herodotus :—

(1) Less than a month before the beginning of the 8th year of Cambyses (Oppert and Maspero give the 12th month *Adar*) and when Cambyses was absent in Egypt, Bardis revolted (Feb.-March, 522 B.C.). The accession year of Bardis is the 7th year Cambyses (inscription of Darius).

(2) Cambyses hearing of the revolt set out from Egypt to overthrow Bardis (according to Herodotus).

(3) Bardis was enthroned (late May or early June, according to Oppert and Maspero, from datings of Darius).

(4) Cambyses advancing through Syria intercepted the heralds of Bardis, and received news of the enthronement of Bardis. The narrative and circumstances attach the date to Aug., 522 B.C.

(5) Cambyses, in a rage, violently mounted his horse and accidentally wounded himself. He lingered for over three weeks after his accident and died (Herodotus). This would be late August or early September, 522 B.C. Agreeing with this, Herodotus states that at his death, Cambyses had reigned 7 years, 5 months, obviously beginning 1st Nisan (Mar.-April) 529 B.C. Darius merely narrates that Cambyses, " killing himself, died," Darius, however, did not know this until many months later.

(6) Meanwhile, prior to receiving the news of the death of Cambyses, Darius slew Bardis in Media. The narrative of Darius gives Bardis a reign of 7 months from the time of his revolt, *i.e.*, from March to September inclusive, 522 B.C. Herodotus states that Bardis was discovered to be a usurper in the 8th month of his rule and was slain by Darius. This would give death of Bardis, early Oct., 522 B.C.

(7) Accordingly, the last dating of Bardis is 1st Tisri (Sept. or Oct.), 522 B.C.

(8) News of the death of Cambyses had still not come to Babylon, for the resumed datings of the 8th year of Cambyses continued to be recorded in Babylon to 11th Tebet (Dec., 522 B.C., or Jan., 521 B.C.).

(9) The 11th Tebet dating is the last dating of the reign of Cambyses. News of his death had come to Babylon by the beginning of B.C. 521, for we find the next dating (at Abu-habba) to be of the " Accession Year " of Darius, and in the month Sebat (Jan. or Feb., B.C. 521).

(10) The next dating (Egibi Tablet at Babylon) is 1st Nisan, 1st year Darius (*i.e.*, beginning the 1st regnal year March-April, 521 B.C.).

III.—The Overthrow of Nebuchadnezzar III (Usurper) :—

(1) During 521 B.C., the 1st year of Darius I, Babylon revolted under Nebuchadnezzar III. The earliest dating of the latter's Accession year is 20th Chisleu (early Dec., 521 B.C.).

(2) The 1st year Nebuchadnezzar III beginning 1st Nisan, 520 B.C., is, therefore, the 2nd year of Darius I. The last dating of Nebuchadnezzar III is of his 2nd year—month not stated. This was the 3rd year of Darius I, *i.e.* Nisan, 519 to Nisan, 518 B.C.

(3) Herodotus (III, 150) states that the Babylonians had been preparing for the siege from the time they had heard of the death of Cambyses : and that when Darius became king, they revolted. This was obviously after the 1st Nisan dating of Darius I's 1st year (March-April, 521 B.C.) recorded at Babylon. The Babylonian inscription of Nebuchadnezzar III in December, 521 B.C. (1) above, shows that the revolt took place before the latter date. The dating cannot belong to 522 B.C., since the last record of Cambyses at Babylon belongs to December, 522 B.C. to January, 521 B.C.

(4) Herodotus (III, 151) states that when news of the revolt reached Darius he immediately collected all his forces. marched on Babylon, besieged it, and captured it in the 21st month of the siege (III, 153-158). The Behistun inscription of Darius, as Oppert has shown (1st series *Records of the Past*, VII, 94, 99 notes) confirms the long siege of Babylon mentioned by Herodotus.

(5) Combining the evidence from Herodotus and the inscriptions, the siege obviously began in the second half of 521 B.C.—in the 1st year of Darius I—and ended in the first half of 519 B.C.—in the 3rd year of Darius I—or as Marquart has calculated, in May, 519 B.C.

IV.—The Errors in the Narrative of Herodotus :—

(1) In stating that the 8 full years of Cambyses were from the death of Cyrus.

(2) In stating that the 7 months' revolt of the *pseudo*-Smerdis (Bardis) occupied the 7 months that elapsed between the death of Cambyses, and the beginning of the 1st year of Darius I.

The chronological elucidation here given is of importance in relation to the questions of Old Testament chronology, and Jewish (Rabbinical) chronological forgeries (Table XXVIII and Annotations).

ANNOTATIONS (A) TO TABLE XXVIII.

THE ORIGINAL HEBREW CHRONOLOGY.

I—THE EPOCH OF ABRAHAM, ACCORDING TO THE GENEALOGIES OF GENESIS.

Date A.K.

Genesis v, 3-28 ; vii, 11 ; viii, 13 (as in Calendar Chronology of Table V) Adamic
Dynasties to Hebrew Date of Deluge Ending   1656

Genesis xi, 10—Arphaxad born 2 years after the Deluge   1658

,,   xi, 12—Arphaxad, age 35, begat Salah   1693

,,   xi, 14—Salah,   ,, 30,   ., Heber   1723

,,   xi, 16—Heber,   ,, 34, ,, Peleg   1757

,,   xi, 18—Peleg,   ,, 30, ,, Reu 1787

,,   xi, 20—Reu,   ,, 32, ,, Serug   1819

,,   xi, 22—Serug,   ,, 30, ., Nahor   1849

,,   xi, 24—Nahor,   ,, 29, ,, Terah   1878

,,   xi. 32 } The Epoch { The Duration of the Dynasty of Terah, until the }
,,   xii, 4 } of the   { death of Terah, the father of Abram, 205 years }   2083
       Call of Abram. { Abram then, 75 years old, leaves Mesopotamia }
                      { and enters Canaan }

Refer ¶¶ 30, 317, 379, and Table XXII for Egyptian Chronological data confirming ;
¶ 319 and Table XVIII for Babylonian Chronological data confirming. ....

Thus, the " Oxford Bible " Appendix, p. 35, states, " Adding the results......we have
the date......of Abraham's Call, according to the Hebrew, 2083."

The data relating to the Exodus show that the Epoch began at 2083½ A.K.

II—THE CHRONOLOGICAL INTERVAL BETWEEN THE CALL OF ABRAM AND ISRAEL'S ENTRY
INTO EGYPT.

Call of Abram   ..   ..   Abram 75 years old   ..   2083½ A.K.
       Add   ..   25 years   ..   25 years.

Birth of Isaac   ..   ..   Abram 100 years old   ..   2108½ A K.   Gen. xxi, 5.
       Add   ..   00 years   ..   60 years.

Birth of Jacob   ..   ..   Isaac 60 years old   ..   2168½ A.K.   Gen. xxv, 26.
       Add   ..   130 years.   ..   130 years.

Israel enter Egypt ..   ..   Jacob 130 years old.   ..   2298½ A.K.   Gen. xlvii, 9.

Refer ¶¶ 320 and 321 and Tables XVIII and XXII and Annotations for the Babylonian
and Egyptian data confirming.

III—"THE SOJOURNING" OF THOSE ISRAELITES, "WHO DWELT IN EGYPT," (refer
Annotations (B) IV and V) ENDED AT THE CHRONOLOGICAL DATE, 430 YEARS
FROM THE EPOCH OF THE CALL OF ABRAM :—Exod. xii, 40.

St. Paul (Gal. iii, 16, 17) and Josephus (*Antiq.* II, xv, 2)
relating to Exod. xii, 40 (Epochal years).   Josephus (*Antiq.* II, xv, 2.

Epoch of Call of Abram (I and II   Jacob enters Egypt (II above)   2298½ A.K.
above)   ..   ..   ..   2083½ A.K.

Exod. xii, 40 according to Paul   Josephus   ..   ..   ..   215 years.
and Josephus   ..   ..   430 years.

The Exodus Date   ..   2513½ A.K.   The Exodus Date   ..   2513½ A.K.

Refer ¶¶ 322 and 323, Plate LXI (and Annotations), and Tables XIV, XVIII, and XXIII
(and Annotations) for the Egyptian and Babylonian data confirming.

THE ORIGINAL HEBREW CHRONOLOGY AND THE EVOLUTION OF THE JEWISH RABBINICAL SYSTEMS OF CHRONOLOGY FROM THE ORIGINAL HEBREW.

TABLE XXX

		Original Hebrew	Ante-Josephan	
		(1)	(2)	(3)
	Dynasty of Adam began ..	0 A.K	0	0
	Interval	1878	1878	1878
	Dynasty of Terah began ..	1878 A.K	1878	1878
	Duration Dynasty of Terah	205½	145½	145½
	Abraham 75 Years Old ..	2083½ A.K	2023½	2023½*
	Interval	430	430	430
	The Exodus..	2513½ A.K.	2453½	2453½
	Interval	479	590	590
	1st Temple Founded	2992½ A.K.	3043½	3043½
	Interval	7½	7½	7½
	The Shekinah comes to the Temple	3000 A.K.	3051	3051
	The Shekinah Period	410	410	410
	The Shekinah departs from the Temple..	3410 A.K	3461	3461
70 Years Divine Indignation.	Interval	5½	5½	5½
	Destruction of the 1st Temple	3415½ A.K	3466½	3466½
	Interval	64½	70	70
Divine Command	2nd Year Darius (I) Hystaspes 2nd Temple Founded } B.C. 520	3480 A.K.	3536½	3536½
	Interval	57	↓	↓
163 Years' Precession of Darius I in Rabbinical Fictitious Systems.	2nd Year Artaxerxes I (B.C. 463)	3537 A.K.	3536½ A.K.	3536½ A.K
	Interval	41 →	Add ← 70 weeks (with day-unit of 9 Lunar months) =356½ Solar years	← Add 69 weeks of Lunar years) =468½ Solar years
	2nd Year Darius II (B.C. 422)	3578 A.K.		
	Interval	19 →		
	2nd Year Artaxerxes II (B.C. 403)	3597 A.K.		
	Interval	46 →		
	2nd Year Artaxerxes III (B.C. 357)	3643 A.K.		
	Interval	249½ →		
241½ Years' Period of Pseudo-Messiahs and Jewish Political attempts to set up a Messianic Kingdom.	Asmonean Kingdom began (B.C. 107)	3892½ A.K.	3893 A.K	
	Interval	104		
	Rebellion of Theudas (B.C. 3)	3996½ A.K	→ Col. 10.	
	Interval	8½		
	Judas of Galilee (A.D. 6) ..	4005 A.K.	→ Col. 3.	4005 A.K.
	Interval	48½		
	Egyptian Messiah (A.D. 55)	4053½ A.K.	→ Col. 4	
	Interval	11		
	Jewish War begins (A.D. 66)	4064½ A.K.	→ Cols. 5 and 6.	
	Interval	66		
	Bar Cochab Rebellion (A.D. 132½)	4130½ A.K.	→ Col. 7.	
	Duration	3½		
	End of Rebellion (A.D. 135¾)	4134 A.K.	→ Cols. 8 and 9.	
	Interval	1789		
	Autumnal Equinox of the Current Year (A.D. 1924¾)	5923 A.K.	→ Cols. 8 and 9.	
	For true intervals refer Annotations (A) and (C), and Tables XXV and XXX	PRESENT	DATE COMPARED WITH	

NOTE TO COLUMN (1).
For the first attempt to apply the 70 weeks' prophecy to Jewish history prior to any manipulation of the Original Hebrew Chronology, refer Annotations (E) I, *re* Judas Maccabæus and Antiochus Epiphanes.
For the last attempt on the same basis refer Annotations (E) III, *re* Herod the Great.

NOTE TO COLUMNS (2) AND (3).
This system is a necessary stage in the Evolution of the Systems seen in Josephus, the Talmud and the *Seder Haddoroth*.

Thus Sir Isaac Newton ("Chron. of Anc. Kingdoms Amended," p. 357) states correctly, regarding the manipulations of the Jews, but incorrectly regarding the 1st year of Cyrus as the basis of these manipulations:—
"Some of them took Herod for the Messiah, and hence were called Herodians."
"They seem to have grounded their opinion on the 70 weeks, which they reckoned from the 1st year of Cyrus (I). But afterwards, in applying the prophecy to Theudas, and Judas of Galilee, and at length to Bar Cochab, they seem to have shortened the reign of the Kingdom of Persia."

BASES OF EVOLUTION—DARIUS I = "DARIUS EVEN ARTAXERXES" ¶ 331, AND EZRA VI 14, AND DANIEL'S PROPHECY RELATING TO 69 WEEKS & A 70TH WEEK (DAN. IX).

Josephus System I	Josephus System II	Contemporary System III	Post-Josephan	Talmudic System I	Talmudic System II	Intermediate between (8) & (9)
(4)	(5)	(6)	(7)	(8)	(9)	(10)
0	0	0	0	0	0	0
1878	1878	1878	1878	1878	1878	1878
1878	1878	1878	1878	1878	1878	1878
145	205½	205½	205	145	145½	145
2023*	2083½	2083½	2083	2023*	2023½*	2023*
430	430	430	430	425	425	425
2453	2513½	2513½	2513	2448	2448½	2448
590	590	590	590	480	480	591
3043	3103½	3103½	3103	2928	2928½	3039
		7½				
		3111				
470½	410	410	470½	410	410	410
		3521				
		5½				
3513½	3513½	3526½	3573½	3338	3338½	3449
64½	64½	70	70	64½	70	64½
3578	3578	3596½	3643½	3402½	3408½	3513½
Kings "Eclipsed" by successive "Precessions" of Darius I omitted from Jewish Reckoning (see Newton below).						
3578 A.K. ←	3578 A.K ←	3596½ A.K ←	3643½ A.K. ←	Add 70 weeks of Solar years =490	Interval to Mid 70th week in Solar years =488½	Add 69 weeks of Solar years =483
Add 70 weeks of Lunar years =475½ Solar years	Interval to Mid 70th week in Solar years =486½	Add 69 weeks of Lunar years =468½	Interval to Mid 70th week in Solar years =486½	3892½ A.K.	3895	3996½ A.K.
4053½ A.K	4064½ A.K	4065 A.K.	4130 A.K.	238 Years Precession of Terminal Date Present Jewish Chronology =3892½	← Col. 1.	
← Col. 1.				3½		
← Col. 1.						
← Col. 1.	238 Years Purposely Omitted (Cols. 8 and 9).			3896 =	3896 Jewish Year begins	
				1789	1789	
← Col. 1.	Omission Continued.			5685 =	5685 Jewish Year begins 29th Sept., 1924 A.D.	
DATE BY CURRENT JEWISH YEAR.						

In 363 A.D. the Jews adopted the 19 years' cycle; adopting 205 cycles or 3895 years as ending at Autumnal Equinox, 135¾ A.D. = 4134 A.K. and counting the next year as year 3896 thus:

NOTE TO COLUMNS (4) AND (5).
For the Actual 70 weeks' units employed in formulating the Chronology followed by Josephus refer Annotations (F) VII
For the various intervals of *Josephus* refer Annotations (D)

NOTE that all initial and terminal dates for the application of Daniel's 70 weeks in columns 2 to 7—on the basis 'Artaxerxes' = Darius—are the true Hebrew A.K. dates of column 1, and that the initial date is always the correct A.K. date of the 2nd year of an Artaxerxes or a Darius.

COLUMNS (8) AND (9) represent the derivation of the Modern Jewish System of Chronology. Thus Jewish Year 5685 begins on 29th Sep., 1924 A.D. = 5923 A.K.

COLUMN (8) is the Chronology of the *Seder Haddoroth*, but with 70 weeks of Solar years (490) between alleged 3402½ as 2nd Darius I, and the end of Bar Cochab's Rebellion at 135¾ A.D (alleged 3892½).

The single thick stepped line indicates the Jewish Precession of the 2nd year of Darius I.
The double thick stepped line indicates the Jewish Precession of the various alleged beginnings of the Messianic Kingdom.
This elucidation of the "Artaxerxes" Problem shows how Modern Criticism, in relation to the Books of Ezra and Nehemiah, has been misled by Jewish Fictions of the 1st Centuries B.C. and A.D.
*The Talmud, *Seder Haddoroth* and Josephus agree that Dynasty of Terah ended at 2083½ A.K.

(To face p. 348.

ANNOTATIONS (B) TO TABLE XXVIII.
THE ORIGINAL HEBREW CHRONOLOGY.

IV—THE PROMISE (Gen. xv, 13-14)	THE FULFILMENT (Exod. vi, 3-6)	
" Know of a surety that THY SEED	"And I appeared unto Abraham, unto Isaac and unto Jacob.	BIRTH
	"And I have also established My Covenant with them to give them the land of Canaan,	OF
		ISAAC,
(1) shall be a stranger in a land that is not theirs and	*the land of their pilgrimage* *wherein they were strangers* and	2108½ A.K.
(2) shall serve them } 400 years."	I have also heard the *groaning* of the Child- ren of Israel whom the Egyptians keep in bondage.	400 yrs.
(3) and they shall afflict them	And I have remembered My Covenant."	2508½ A.K.
" And also that nation whom they shall serve WILL I JUDGE (*i.e.*, after the 400 yrs.)	" I will rid you of their bondage, and I will redeem you with an outstretched arm and *with great judgments*."	Death of Ramessu II (Tables XIV and XXIII).
"and AFTERWARD shall they come out with great substance."	"and I *will bring you out* from under the burdens of the Egyptians."	2513½ A.K. EXODUS.

Exodus ii, 23-25. "And it came to pass in the process of time that the king of Egypt (*i.e.*, the oppressor) died......their cry came up to God by reason of the bondage, and God heard their groaning, and God remembered His Covenant......" Refer Plate LXI.

V—THE PROMISE (Gen. xv, 13-16) THE FULFILMENT IN THE PRIESTLY TRIBE, LEVI.
(Continued in Verse 16). (Gen. xlvii, 11 and Joshua xiv, 1, 2).

Isaac, "the seed" stranger and sojourner in Canaan,
Jacob, his son, do. do. in Canaan and Goshen.
Levi, his son, do. do. in Canaan and Goshen.

"But in the fourth gene- 1st Generation Kohath, his son, do. do. in Canaan and Goshen
ration they shall come (Gen. xlvii, 11, states Kohath
hither again, for the entered Egypt with Jacob).
iniquity of the Amor- 2nd Generation Amran, his son, do. do. in Goshen.
ites is not *yet* full." 3rd Generation Aaron, his son, do. do. in Goshen and Sinai.
4th Generation Eleazar, his son, entered Canaan, and distributed
by lot to the tribes of Israel, their in-
heritance in the land of Canaan
(Joshua xiv, 1, 2).

VI—THE DATA OF JOSEPHUS CONFIRM THE HEBREW DATE FOR CALL OF ABRAM :—

Call of Abram (I above) 2083½ A.K.
Interval by Josephus
(*Ant.* VIII, iii, 1) 1020 years.

Josephus for alleged 4th
year Solomon .. 3103½ A.K.

Josephus (*Ant.* VIII, iii, 1) states the latter as 3102. The annotations to right by proving that the system followed by Josephus gave 430 years, Call of Abram to Exodus, and alleged 590 years, Exodus to 4th year of Solomon, show that the alleged total interval of the system is 1020 years, ending at alleged date 3103 A.K. above.

The Book of Judges contains the following statement of periods of servitude—not in succession—undergone by Israel

			years.
Mesopotamia	(iii.	8)	8
Moab	.. (iii, 14)		18
Canaan	.. (iv,	3)	20
Midian	.. (vi,	1)	7
Ammon	.. (x,	8)	18
Philistines	(xiii,	1)	40
			——
Total of all oppression			
periods	.. ..		111

The Jews of the 2nd century B.C., as data and reasons of Table XXVIII, added the 111 years to the 479 years, obtaining as follows :—

Period of I Kings, vi, 1 = 479 yrs.
Interpolated servitudes = 111 yrs.
          ——
          590 yrs.

I Kings vi, 1, in giving the 2nd month of Solomon's 4th year as the 2nd month of the 480th year from the Exodus—*i.e.*, 479 years— includes the 111 years in the 479 years. That this is correct is confirmed by the Egyptian and Babylonian synchronisms.

Josephus, generally 1 to 6 years different in two independent state- ments gives this as 592 years (*Antiq.* VII. iii, 1).

The 430 and 592 of Josephus give 1022 years, but Josephus (*Antiq.* VIII, iii, 1) gives this as 1020 years, thus confirming 590 years above.

ANNOTATIONS (C) TO TABLE XXVIII.

THE ORIGINAL HEBREW CHRONOLOGY.

THE SOLUTION OF THE PERIOD OF JUDGES CONFIRMING THE 480TH YEAR OF I KINGS, vi, 1.

The Hebrew principle of " retrospective " totals in Judges.

		Years
1. Israel in the wilderness..		40
2. Then, Joshua's conquests, death of Joshua, sometime after which Shushan of Mesopotamia oppressed Israel for 8 years, until Othniel delivered Israel " and the land had rest." (Judges iii, 8-11.)	Total 40	
3. Then Moab oppressed Israel for 18 years, Ehud delivered Israel, " and the land had rest." (iii, 14-30.)	Total 80	

Ehud died before the above period ended and was succeeded by Shamgar, whose judgeship extended from period 3 into period 4, including the Philistine oppression of period 4. (iii, 31 ; v, 6 ; compare latter with iv, 17-13, Jael overlapping Shamgar and Deborah.)

4. Shamgar continued as above, and died. Before his death Jabin and Sisera oppressed Israel. The oppression continued for 20 years (iv, 3). Deborah and Barak delivered Israel (iv, 4 ; v, 31) " and the land had rest " (v, 31).	Total 40	
5. In this period, Midian oppressed Israel for 7 years. Gideon delivered Israel (vi-viii), " and the country was in quietness in the days of Gideon " (viii, 28).	Total 40	
6. The usurpation of Abimelech (ix). Slain after 3 years	..	3
7. The Judgeship of Tola (x, 1, 2)		23
8. The Judgeship of Jair (x, 3-5)		22
9. The oppression of Ammon (x, 6 ; xi, 33) 18 years (x, 8)		18

Retrospective narrative of Jephthah : xi, 12-28. Total 300 years of verse 26.   Total 306

10. Judgeship of Jephthah (xii, 7).. ..	..	6
11. Judgeship of Ibzan (xii, 8-10)		7
12. Judgeship of Elon (xii, 11-12).. ..	..	10
13. Judgeship of Abdon (xii, 13, 14) ..		8

14. Philistine oppression. (xiii, 1) 40 years. This period included the Judgeship of Samson (xv, 20 and xvi, 31) " he judged Israel in the days of the Philistines twenty years " xv, 20. The period also covered the Judgeship of Eli (40 years as I Samuel iv, 18) since Eli died during the Philistine oppression, and as a result of it—the carrying off of the ark of God. After the death of Eli, the Philistine oppression was broken under Samuel " So the Philistines were subdued and they came no more...... all the days of Samuel." I Samuel, vii, 13, 14.   ..   40

15. After being returned by the Philistines the ark continued to remain at Kirjath-jearim during the Judgeship of Samuel, 20 years (I Samuel, vii, 2). And continued remaining until David (II Samuel, vi) at the end of 450 years of Acts xiii, 20.   ..   20

16. Saul, king (Acts xiii, 21)	..	40
17. David, king. II Samuel, v, 4 ; I Kings, ii, 11	..	40
18. 4th year Solomon began. Founding of Temple. I Kings, vi, 1	..	3
	Total	480

Actually 479 years as Annotations (B) VI. The only possible overlap is Jephthah with Ammon oppression. 1st year Jephthah = 18th year oppression. Hence 479 years total and 305 years to Jephthah.

FERRAR FENTON'S TRANSLATION—IN MODERN ENGLISH—OF PAUL'S SERMON AT ANTIOCH. ACTS xiii, 16-23.

The Hebrew Principle of " Retrospective " totals used by St. Paul.

" Men of Israel and those that reverence God, listen. The God of this people Israel chose our forefathers and raised up the nation during their residence in the land of Egypt, and with a high arm He led them out of it. And for the space of about 40 years he endured their behaviour in the desert.

" about the space of 450 years." Afterwards when he had conquered seven nations in the land of Canaan, He entrusted them with the possession of their country.

" And contemporary with these events, He gave them judges until the end of Samuel the prophet. And when they demanded a kingdom, then God gave them Saul, the son of Kish, a man of the tribe of Benjamin, for the period of 40 years."

Here we must observe that the period of Israel being " entrusted with possession of their kingdom " extends to the date at which God gave the promise of the everlasting kingdom to David (II Samuel, vii, 16) St. Paul therefore continues (as F.F., v).

" And when He had removed him (Saul), He raised up David for them into the kingdom : and, giving evidence before him, He said, DAVID THE SON OF JESSE I HAVE FOUND A MAN AFTER MY OWN HEART, WHO WILL EXECUTE ALL MY PURPOSES.* From this race God has, according to promise, brought to Israel a Saviour—Jesus."
* I Samuel, xiii, 14.
Emphasis in capitals as F.F.

The approximation implied by St. Paul's words applies to events,; not to the period of 450 years. The latter period is a fixed period of 15 Sed hebs from the Israelitish Exodus Epoch. The Sed heb was anciently associated with the king receiving the gift of Divine Right from the Shekinah or Tabernacle Presence of the Lord (¶¶ 34 to 38). This theme of Divine Right is the whole subject of St. Paul's discourse. The implication is that the Promise of the Everlasting Kingdom was given to David, 15 Sed heb periods or 450 years after the Exodus. Hence with Exodus at 2513½ A.K., this Promise was given at 2963½ A.K. The associated chronology resulting from the parallel column is as follows :—

	2909½ A.K.
Saul (Acts xiii, 21)	40 years
	2949½ A.K.
David at Hebron (I Kings, ii, 11)	7 years
	2956½ A.K.
David at Jerusalem (I Kings, ii, 11)	33 years
	2989½ A.K.
Solomon (I Kings, xi, 43)	40
The Division of the Kingdom (Table XXV) and Annotations	3029½ A.K.

The Temple was founded in 4th year Solomon, the 480th year from Exodus, another Sed heb, the 16th from the Exodus. This confirms the ruling feature giving the Promise of the Everlasting Kingdom to David in 2963½ A.K.

II Samuel, vii narrates that the promise was made to David some time after he was king over all Israel ; but before Miphibosheth, son of Jonathan, stood before David, when, as stated, Miphibosheth had a young son, (II Samuel, ix, 12). Miphibosheth, however, was only 5 years old when Saul and Jonathan were slain, and when David began to reign at Hebron at 2949½ A.K. (II Samuel, iv, 4). Miphibosheth was therefore 19 years old in 2963½ A.K., the date of the Promise of the Everlasting Kingdom, and could therefore have had a young son, when he stood before David shortly after this date.

(Refer Note (2) to Annotations D re 111 years' interpolation in period of Judges and Egyptian Dynasty XIX.)

ANNOTATIONS (D) TO TABLE XXVIII.

THE CHRONOLOGICAL SYSTEMS OF JOSEPHUS (ABSTRACTED).

THE PRINCIPAL EPOCHS OF JOSEPHUS.	The Two Systems of Chronology followed by Josephus. Essential datum of Formulation of both Systems that Destruction of Jerusalem by Nebuchadnezzar = 3513½. *Antiq.* X, viii, 5. (1)	(2)
Deluge (Josephus gives in error as 1556).	1656	1656
Birth of Terah	1878	1878
Call of Abram { (1) Terah dies 205 at Call of Abram, when Abram 75. Gen. xi, 32; xii, 4. (2) Terah aged (70+75) at Call of Abram, when Abram 75. Gen. xi, 26; xii, 4.	2083½	2023
NOTE:—Gen. xi, 26 does not say that Abram was born when Terah was 70 (*Antiq.* I, vi, 5 and *Talmud*). But Gen. xi, 32 and xii, 4 show that the Dynasty of Terah ended after 205 years' duration at death of Terah, Abram's father, when Abram, 75 years old (Gen. xii, 4) left Mesopotamia. The two systems in Josephus give the two alternatives as above.		
Exodus, 430 years after Call of Abram, Annotations A and B, and *Antiq.* II, xv, 2	3513½	2453
David, King at Hebron (based on date for Founding Temple as Josephus)	3060	3000
Solomon becomes king (based on date for Founding Temple as Josephus)	3100	3040
Founding of Temple in 4th year Solomon. (479+111)=590 years after Exodus alleged. (I Kings vi, 1)+111[a] years' oppressions in Judges. Refer Annotations B and C.	3103	3043
Destruction of Jerusalem by Nebuchadnezzar (*Antiq.* X, viii, 5)	3513½	3513½
Interval 69½ weeks of 18 Lunations per "day"		
Destruction of Jerusalem by Titus	4222	4222

[a] Alexandrian Jews in period 1st Century, B.C. to 1st Century, A.D. responsible for altering Manetho's text for Egyptian Dynasty XIX. (Refer Table XIII and Annotations B and C to Table XXVIII.)

Table XIII shows that Manetho's Dynasty XIX was originally stated by him as 93 years: and that a late redactor added details to increase the duration of the Dynasty by 111 years. Now this is the Exodus Dynasty and here we find its beginning has been pushed back 111 years, the exact interval that the Jews of the 1st Century, B.C. interpolated into the period of the Judges. (Refer Table XXVIII, Cols. 2 and 10, and Annotations B and C.) This shows either that a redactor of Manetho, in the 1st Century, B.C. or A.D., was an Alexandrian Jew, or that he was influenced by the fictions circulating among the Alexandrian Jews.

I.—THE FOUNDING OF SOLOMON'S TEMPLE. STATED 3102.

Evidence of System (1) in *Antiq.* VIII, iii, 1.

(a) Call of Abram	2083½	actual date.
Interval of Josephus	1020	
Josephus states 3102.	3103½	as Column 1.
(b) Exodus	2513½	actual date.
Interval of Josephus	592	
Josephus states 3102.	3105½	
Actual System	2513½	actual date.
590 years of System	590	
Date of System (1)	3103½	
(c) Deluge	1656	actual date.
Interval of Josephus	1440	(units obviously lost).
7 years short of total of System	3096	

II.—THE DESTRUCTION OF JERUSALEM BY NEBUCHADNEZZAR. STATED 3513½.

Evidence of System (2) in *Antiq.* X, viii, 5.

(a) Deluge (as error of Josephus)	1556	
Interval of Josephus	1957	
Josephus states 3513½.	3513	as Columns 1 and 2.
(b) Exodus (as System 2)	2453	
Interval of Josephus	1062½	
2 years' excess over Systems due to his 592 years for 590 years of Systems	3515½	
(c) End reign of David, but stated erroneously by Josephus as date of building of Temple .. } ..	3040	
Interval of Josephus	476½	
Josephus states as 3513½. Additional year's error over (b) above due to same detail as gives 3102 for 3103 of System (1) .. .. } ..	3516½	

III.—ROMAN DESTRUCTION OF JERUSALEM, 4222.

Evidence of System (2) in *Wars* VI, x, 1.

(a) Destruction of Jerusalem by Nebuchadnezzar	=	3513½	stated.
Interval of Josephus = 2177—1468½	=	708½	
The date of the late System		4222	
69½ weeks of lunations from 3513½ (see Table XXVIII, Columns 4, 5 and 10).			
(b) Founding of Solomon's Temple (as System 2)	=	3043[1]	
Stated by Josephus as interval after David	=	1179	
The date of the late System as above	=	4222	

[1] NOTE:—3043 years are 2 Egyptian nominal solar cycles, or 1 period associated with the Hindoo *Kali Yug* .. .. } $= \frac{36525}{12}$

ANNOTATIONS (E) TO TABLE XXVIII.

THE EVOLUTION OF JEWISH CHRONOLOGY FROM THE ORIGINAL HEBREW CHRONOLOGY.

I—THE MACCABÆAN THEORY—168-165 B.C. :—

(Refer Josephus *Antiq.* XII, v, 3—vii, 7).

In 168 B.C. Antiochus Epiphanes captured and destroyed Jerusalem, profaned the sanctuary, and forbade the daily sacrifice. In 165 B.C. Judas Maccabæus—the deliverer—defeated the forces of Antiochus Epiphanes, and on 25th *Chisleu* cleansed the sanctuary. The latter date is 3835½ A.K., or December 165 B.C. The sequence of historical events was hailed by the Jews as confirming Daniel's prophecies. The purely Jewish national conception of the promised Messianic Kingdom was believed to be in process of fulfilment. The prophecy of 70 weeks was applied as follows :—

Day-unit of Hebdomad (=week) taken as 9 Lunar months.
Hebdomad (week) = 7×9 Lunar months.
69 weeks = 69×7×9 Lunations = 351½ Solar years.
Dating from the Divine Command to build 2nd Temple,

2nd year Darius I..	3480	A.K. = 520 B.C.
69 weeks (as above) ..	351½	years
Desolation of Antiochus Epiphanes =	3831½	A.K. = 168 B.C.
The 70th week		years
End of 70 weeks	3836½	A.K. = 163 B.C.

Daniel ix, 25, 26, was read in conjunction with Daniel xii, 11 and 12 as giving 1290 and 1335 literal days during which "the daily sacrifice shall be taken away and the abomination that maketh desolate set up." This gave 3½ to 3¾ years from desolation to cleansing, thus :—

Desolation of Antiochus Epiphanes =	3831½	A.K. = 168 B.C.
1290 to 1335 days (maximum) .. =	3¾	years
Cleansing of Sanctuary by Judas ..	3835½	A.K. = 165 B.C.

From the apparent identity fictitiously presented by the Jews, and proclaimed by Josephus, critics have deemed that the Book of Daniel was not written until after Judas Maccabæus had cleansed the sanctuary. Such critics claim that Daniel was written to hearten the followers of the Maccabees. If this had been the case, a better unit value, than the 9 lunar months adopted, would have been selected,—7, 12, or 14. But 9 as a Hebrew unit would carry little weight in Judæa. Obviously the prophecy existed long before Antiochus Epiphanes. The recurrence of circumstances similar to those predicted by Daniel led to the identity. Hence the unit was accepted as it appeared to fit. The prophecy did actually hearten the Jews to accomplish under Judas the defeat of Antiochus and to effect the cleansing of the sanctuary.

II—THE THEORY OF THE ASMONÆAN DYNASTY :—B.C. 107.

9 Lunar months having been adopted in Maccabæan times as the unit of the Hebdomad or week, this theory was retained until it could be no longer applied. It was still retained at the beginning of the 1st century B.C. The retention, however,—when it was seen that the Maccabees failed to establish the Messianic Kingdom—made necessary the adoption of a later date than 3480 A.K., for the 2nd year of Darius I, when the Divine Command was given to build the 2nd Temple.

On the basis of the identity "Darius *even* Artaxerxes," Darius I was identified as Darius I = Artaxerxes I. This actually amounted to omitting the reigns of Darius I, Xerxes I and Artabanus from history. The years omitted in the application of this theory were thus 57 years. The 2nd year of Darius I was therefore brought forward 57 years to the

2nd year of Artaxerxes I = ..	3536½	A.K. = 463 B.C.
Add 70 weeks (9 lunations = 1 day)	356½	years
Asmonæan Kingdom of Judæa began	3893	A.K. = 107 B.C.

Thus, in 107 B.C., the Judæan princes of the Asmonæan Dynasty, descended from the Maccabees, set up a new kingdom of Judæa, with Aristobulus I as the first king in 107 B.C. Here the theory makes Jewish history; whereas in the Maccabæan theory history first suggested the theory.

III—THE THEORY OF THE HERODIANS -B.C. 37.

With the failure and fall of the Asmonæan Dynasty, the Asmonæan theory of the 70 weeks was discredited, together with the precession of Darius I into identity with Artaxerxes I. The true date for the 2nd year of Darius I was reverted to and a new theory of the 70 weeks adopted. The day-unit was taken as the value of the Solar year. Thus,

Divine Command 2nd yr. Darius I =	3480	A.K. = 520 B.C.
69 weeks = 7×69 Solar years .. =	483	years (Solar)
Herod, by procuring the execution of Antigonus, becomes King of Judea	3963	A.K. = 37 B.C.

According to Daniel's prophecy Messiah was to come after 69 weeks. The Herodians therefore adopted the above theory with Herod as the Messiah. The fact is noted by Sir Isaac Newton as quoted in note on Table XXVIII.

IV—THE REBELLION OF THEUDAS, B.C. 3 :—

The failure of Herod and his death necessitated a new effort. Herod died in the Spring of B.C. 3. There immediately arose a new *pseudo*-Messiah in the person of the first Theudas (B.C. 3). This is not the Theudas of Josephus (*Ant.* XX, v, 1) who was the second *pseudo*-Messiah of that name, but the Theudas of Acts v, 36, 37, who lived before Judas of Galilee (verse 37). To show that this Theudas was the Messiah, the Hebrew chronology prior to Darius I was readjusted to give the statement of Col. 10, Table XXVIII, without altering the true A.K. date for Theudas at B.C. 3.

This statement partly formed the basis of the later systems of Josephus and the Talmud. Thus,

2nd year Darius I.. .. .. =	3513½	A.K. alleged.
69 weeks of *Solar* years .. .. =	483	years
Death of Herod and rise of Theudas	3996½	A.K. = 3 B.C.

By 69½ weeks ending at 4000 A.K., there was added weight to the claim, as it appeared as a confirmation of the Jewish tradition of the House of Elias giving 4000 years to Messiah.

V—THE REBELLION OF JUDAS OF GALILEE, A.D. 6.

With the failure of Theudas, a new *pseudo*-Messiah, Judas of Galilee (A.D. 6), entered the field of Jewish politics. His claim was based on a reversion to the fictitious identity, Darius I = Artaxerxes I, and the adoption of 69 weeks of lunar years. Thus, as Table XXVIII, Col. 3 :—

2nd year Artaxerxes I .. .. =	3536½	A.K. = 463 B.C.
69 weeks of lunar years .. .. =	468½	solar years
Rebellion of Judas of Galilee .. =	4005	A.K. = 6 A.D.

For the fate of this rebellion refer Acts v, 36, 37, and Josephus, *Wars*, II, viii, 1; *Ant.*, XX, v, 2.

VI—THE EGYPTIAN *Pseudo*-MESSIAH—A.D. 55.

The claim of this imposter was clearly based on the prophesy of Hosea, xi, 1, repeated in Matthew ii, 15, as "out of Egypt have I called My Son." His rebellion and overthrow are described by Josephus, *Antiq.*, XX, viii, 6. Reference to the rebellion occurs in Acts xxi, 38.

The late date, A.D. 55, for the termination of Daniel's period of 70 weeks, necessitated a late date for the beginning of the period. It was represented that the 2nd year of Darius I was really the 2nd year of Darius II. Thus, as Table XXVIII, Col. 4.

2nd year Darius II .. .. =	3578	A.K. = 422 B.C.
70 weeks of lunar years .. .. =	475½	solar years
Rebellion of Egyptian Messiah ..	4053½	A.K. = 55 A.D.

The date of the rebellion was therefore fixed by the alleged interpretation of the prophecy.

It should be observed that Systems I, II, III, V, and VI all admit the true A.K. dates for the actual years adopted for the systems and that System IV admits the true A.K date for the actual terminal years. This confirms the original Hebrew Chronology of Table XXVIII, Col. 1, when studied in relation to Systems I and III above

ANNOTATIONS (F) TO TABLE XXVIII.

THE EVOLUTION OF JEWISH CHRONOLOGY FROM THE ORIGINAL HEBREW CHRONOLOGY.

VII—THE JEWISH WAR, A.D. 66-70:—

(a) The next Jewish system still retained the fictitious datum of System VI—*i.e.*, that 2nd year Darius I=2nd year Darius II, 3578 A.K. This system, however, adopted solar years for the lunar years of System VI, as follows (Table XXVIII, Col. 5):—

2nd year Darius II   ..   .. 3578 A.K.=422 B.C.
Mid-70th week=69$\frac{1}{4}$ weeks solar = 486$\frac{1}{4}$ solar years

Jewish War began   ..   .. 4064$\frac{1}{4}$ A.K.= 66$\frac{1}{4}$ A.D.

(b) An alternative system, however, instead of stressing the mid-70th week element of Daniel's prophecy, laid stress upon the Messiah coming after 69 weeks, and adopted the lunar year as unit. In accepting the latter, the 2nd year of Darius II was too early. The system, therefore, passed on to Artaxerxes II, following the precedent of Systems II, III, and V, that Darius=Artaxerxes. Thus (as Table XXIII, Col. 6) the system stands as follows:—

2nd year Artaxerxes II   ..   .. 3596$\frac{1}{4}$ A.K.=404 B.C.
69 weeks of lunar years   ..   ..= 468$\frac{1}{4}$ solar years

1st year *Jewish War*   ..   .. 4065 A.K.= 66$\frac{1}{4}$ A.D.

The two systems obviously combined to represent that the rising projected for A.D. 66 had Divine Sanction. The result of the Jewish War, by the destruction of Jerusalem and the Temple in A.D. 70, certainly brought fulfilment of Daniel's prophecy, but not according to the exposition of the prophecy as formulated to incite the Jews to begin the War. (Refer ¶ 394).

(c) The alleged Hebrew chronology formulated to form the basis of System VII (a) above, as in Table XXVIII, Cols. 4 and 5, is the framework of all the Chronological statements of Josephus, in *Wars*, and *Antiquities*. The date of the Destruction of Jerusalem by Nebuchadnezzar, as given by Josephus—*Antiq.* X, viii. 5—is therefore 3513$\frac{1}{4}$, as Table XXVIII, Cols. 4 and 5. He then adopted the true interval of 64$\frac{1}{4}$ years to the 2nd year Darius I, as in System VII (a) above. Josephus knew however that the interval from 2nd year Darius I to the Jewish War as given by Systems VII (a) and (b) was too short. He therefore made the interval too long. He adopted the whole period of the 70 weeks of Daniel, with a day-unit of 16 lunar months. This gave the 70 weeks period of the duration of 634 solar years, the system being as follows:—

2nd year Darius II (alleged I)   .. 3578 A.K.=422 B.C.
70 weeks of 16 lunations per day   634 solar years

Alleged date of Jewish War begin-)
ning 66$\frac{1}{4}$ A.D. as *Antiquities* } 4212 A.K.
Summations=   )

(d) Now Josephus wrote his *Wars* some time before his *Antiquities*. His chronology in *Wars* is slightly different from his chronology in *Antiquities*. In *Wars* he adopted a system similar to that of Table XXVIII, Col. 10, with 2nd year Darius I at alleged date 3513$\frac{1}{4}$, as in the System IV in Vogue in B.C. 3*. This system in *Wars* was employed in connection with 69$\frac{1}{4}$ weeks of day-units of 18 lunar months. Thus, alleged 2nd year Darius I =3513$\frac{1}{4}$
69$\frac{1}{4}$ weeks of 18 lunations per day= 708 solar years

Stated in *Wars*, VI, x, 1 (708$\frac{1}{4}$ yrs.))
as the date of the Destruction of } 4221$\frac{1}{4}$
the City and the Temple by   )
Titus, A.D. 70$\frac{1}{4}$ ..

The 708$\frac{1}{4}$ years are stated as from Babylonian destruction of Jerusalem, but compare Table XXVIII, Cols. 5 and 10.

Here Josephus gives a true rendering of Daniel's prophecy (ix, 24-27). The people of the prince to come were to destroy the city and the sanctuary and to make the sacrifice to cease in the midst of the 70th week. This was actually effected by the soldiers of Titus, without his orders.

A most significant feature in Josephus is that he gives no details of summations of reigns for the period Cyrus to Alexander the Great. This shows the weakness that Josephus experienced in presenting his case, since in all other cases—and having regard to the fact of his time, and that his chronological data are presented in narrative form rather than in tabular form—his chronological statements are very good indeed.

* The System is the transition stage between the System of Columns 5 and the System of Column 10, Table XXVIII.

VIII—THE REBELLION OF BAR COCHAB, A.D. 132$\frac{1}{4}$-135$\frac{1}{4}$.

(a) Following the decisive defeat of the Jews by the Romans in A.D. 70, there is no evidence of any political manoeuvring to set up an alleged Messianic Kingdom until A.D. 132. The date again indicates the chronological interpretation of Daniel's 70 weeks. In the new system we have a reversion to the Darius-Artaxerxes identity and to the mid-70th week interpretation. The late date of A.D. 132 required an additional precession of Darius I into identity with Artaxerxes III. The 2nd year of the latter king required the 70 weeks to be in day-units of solar years. Thus—

2nd year Artaxerxes III ..   ..=3643$\frac{1}{4}$ A.K.=346 B.C.
Mid-70th week=69$\frac{1}{4}$ weeks of yrs= 486$\frac{1}{4}$

                              4130 A.K.=131$\frac{1}{4}$ A.D.

The Rebellion of Bar Cochab therefore began in the following Spring, 4130$\frac{1}{4}$ A.K.=132$\frac{1}{4}$ A.D. Bar Cochab proclaimed himself the Messiah and was accepted by the Rabbi Aquiba. He raised the standard of revolt in Judæa, and flouted the Romans. The Romans were forced to send their best generals against him, and actually, after 3$\frac{1}{2}$ years —the half-week—fulfilled the false interpretation by utterly annihilating the forces of Bar Cochab at the end of the alleged 70 week period in 135 A.D. The Encyclop. Brit. states that 580,000 Jews were killed in the actual fighting " besides the incalculable number who succumbed to famine, disease, and fire." So that we may reckon that over a million Jews met their death as a result of this Jewish forgery for political ends. The result was that the Romans forbade the Jews to enter Jerusalem on pain of death.

(b) After the fall of Bar Cochab, the date seems to have been represented as the date of Messiah—reckoned as 69 weeks of lunar years from the 2nd year of Darius III, since we find Darius III to be the last stage of precession for Darius I. Thus—

2nd year Darius III   ..   ..=3665$\frac{1}{4}$ A.K.=334 B.C.
69 weeks of lunar years .. ..= 468$\frac{1}{4}$ solar years

End of Bar Cochab's Rebellion = 4134 A.K.=135$\frac{1}{4}$ A.D.

(c) The compilers of the *Seder Haddoroth*, however, adopted an entirely new method of fictitious chronology. While adopting the 70 weeks of solar years (490 solar years) they maintained that the date for this period ending was 3892$\frac{1}{4}$ A.K. Now this date actually fell in 107 B.C., when the Asmonæan Kingdom began (System II). This fact notwithstanding, the compilers of the *Seder Haddoroth* placed the rebellion of Bar Cochab as beginning at 3892$\frac{1}{4}$, the latter being therefore the *Seder Haddoroth* date for 132$\frac{1}{4}$ A.D. The Old Testament System of the *Seder Haddoroth* is therefore as stated in Table XXVIII, Col. 8. The manner of its evolution—to explain its 70 weeks' interpretation— is obvious when compared with Col. 1 and the intermediate systems of the other columns. Thus—

Alleged 2nd year Darius I   ..   ..=3402$\frac{1}{4}$ Jewish year
70 weeks of solar years ..   ..   ..= 490

Alleged date for ..   ..   132$\frac{1}{4}$ A.D.=3892$\frac{1}{4}$ Jewish year
Add   ..   ..   .. 1792$\frac{1}{4}$=1792$\frac{1}{4}$

                             1924$\frac{1}{4}$ A.D.=5684$\frac{1}{4}$ Jewish year

This explains why the Jewish year 5685 begins on 29th September of the current year 1924 A.D.

How the present Jewish luni-solar calendar cycle was adapted to fit the system of fictitious chronology thus explained is shown on Table XXVIII below Cols. 8 to 10.

It is significant that none of the Jewish systems ceased employing the correct A.K. dating, for the time current with the system, until after the Crucifixion of our Lord (refer Systems VII (c) and (d) and VIII (b) above).

SECTION IB.—THE MESSIANIC AGE OF THE ANCIENT PROPHECIES.

¶ 338. MESSIANIC TIME-UNITS IN ISRAEL'S HISTORY.

The harmony of the Four Gospels and early accounts from reliable external sources concerning the chronology of our Lord's life and Passion.

In Section II of this Chapter all the evidences, both from the Gospels and from external sources, are discussed in their relation to the chronology of our Lord's life and the harmony of the Four Gospels. A study of this discussion will convince the reader that modern opinion concerning the supposed lack of harmony in the accounts of the Gospels is not due to any discrepancy in the narrations of the Gospels, nor, indeed, in early accredited accounts from external sources. It will be seen that the supposed lack of harmony is due entirely to a modern misconception regarding the chronological starting-point of the Roman A.U.C. year in the early accounts from sources external to the New Testament.

The discussion shows that all the accounts referred to are in complete agreement when it is understood—

The Nativity at Feast of Tabernacles, 4 B.C.

(1) That Christ was born in 4 B.C.=3996 A.K., at the Feast of Tabernacles, 15th Tisri (7th Sacred month), =6th October (Julian), =4th October (Greg.);

The baptism about Feast of Tabernacles 27 A.D.

(2) That Christ was 30 years old and was baptised in the autumn of 27 A.D. =4026 A.K., about the time of the Feast of Tabernacles, which fell, in that year, on 3rd October (Greg.), a *Sunday*;

Duration of the ministry, 2½ years.

(3) That Christ's ministry extended over an interval of 2½ years, the narrative of John's Gospel being continuous—without any gap in continuity of time or incident—from the 1st Passover (28 A.D.) of ii, 23 and iv, 45 to the 2nd Passover (29 A.D.) of vi, 4.

The Crucifixion at the Passover of 30 A.D.

(4) That the Gospels date the Crucifixion on the 15th Nisan of His 33rd year, and on a *Friday*, 5th April (Greg.) 30 A.D.=4028½ A.K., and His Resurrection on *Sunday*, 17th Nisan=7th April (Greg.); this explaining the significance of the repetition of Exodus week-day, month, and year datings in 30 A.D., and the emphatically indicated fixing of this date in the Pyramid.

The ministry of 918 days.

(5) That the interval of His ministry, nominally from *Sunday*, 3rd October (Greg.) 27 A.D. to *Sunday*, 7th April (Greg.) 30 A.D. inclusive, is a period of 918 days; and

(6) That an important distinction, affecting two aspects of our Lord's Passion, is to be drawn between His Resurrection " on the third day " and " the three days and three nights " " in the heart of the earth."

As throwing additional light upon the repetitions of datings relating to the Exodus of Israel from Egypt and the Exodus of Christ, we give the following :—

I. From beginning of o A.K. (4000 B.C.) at midnight
beginning 22nd September (Greg.) to the *deliverance*
of Israel at the crossing of the Sea of Reeds, on 17th } =918,050 days.
Nisan, 6th April (Greg.), 2513½ A.K. (1486 B.C.) ..
$\frac{1}{1000}$th part of this interval .. .. =918 days.
                                                   (+1 hour).

II. Duration of Christ's ministry to His Resurrection on 5th } =918 days.
April (Greg.), 4028½ A.K. (30 A.D.) .. .. ..

The Messianic time-units in relation to aspects of Israel's history prefiguring and typifying the cycle of Christ's Passion.

Again, as ¶ 337 :—

A.K.

III. The breaking of Ephraim (¶ 337),[1]   ⌐3216=784 B.C. ⌐
Isaiah vii, 8.   { 65 years |

Mid-date of Siege of Samaria   .. ⌐3281=719 B.C. |
Interval   .. ..   788 years   } =918 years.

                                         ⌐4069=70¾ A.D. |
The breaking of Judah (¶ 337)   .. { 65 years |
                                       ⌐4134=135¾A.D.⌐

For the relation between the above prophetic chronology and the context of Isaiah vii, 8, compare the latter with verse 14, *et seq*. The reason for the mid-date of the Siege of Samaria satisfying the above conditions will appear in due course. In the meantime, the reader should refer to Table XXX for the mid-date of Nebuchadnezzar's Siege of Jerusalem.

It should also be observed that the duration of Christ's life—from the Feast of Tabernacles, 4 B.C., to the Passover, 30 A.D. =33½ lunar years (precisely) =32½ solar years, or half the time-interval of 65 years connected with the breaking of Ephraim, and later with the breaking of Judah (¶ 337). *The duration of our Lord's life: 33½ lunar years =32½ solar years.*

Again, by ¶¶ 331 and 336, Daniel's period of 69 weeks to Messiah terminates on 1st Sivan, Friday, 12th May (Greg.) 28 A.D. In Section II of this Chapter it is shown that our Lord, at this time, came from Galilee to Jerusalem (John v, 1) for the Feast of Pentecost on 6th Sivan, Wednesday, 17th May (Greg.) 28 A.D. The data establishing this will be seen to be very definite. If the date fulfils the prophecy, our Lord arrived on the 6th day of the week (Friday) 1st Sivan. John v, 1–18 states that Jesus, on His arrival, cured the impotent man at the pool of Bethesda. The Jews complained of the man carrying his bed on the Sabbath day. Obviously, then, the Sabbath began at sunset of our Lord's day of arrival—Friday. Thus John does not say " the same day was the Sabbath," but " *on* the same day was the Sabbath." *Daniel's 69 weeks fulfilled to the day.*

[1]The 65 years of Isaiah vii, 8. This period is generally reckoned as beginning from the year of the prophecy (as, see Guinness, "Approaching End of the Age," pp. 412, 413). From Ahaz, inclusive, to the fall of Samaria and the utter extinction of Israel is 21 years. Israel was literally broken completely at the fall of Samaria. The 65 years' period, therefore, should end then. Thus interpreted, the Messianic significance of Isaiah's words stands out related to the prophetic chronology as above stated.

For the relations between the events described by Sargon for 722 B.C., and the events of the date above given, refer Table XXVI, Annotations C.

¶ 339. THE 153 FISHES.

Now, when we study closely the references to numbers, and the numerical values of periods, in the Old Testament, and also in the New Testament, we find many striking identities. To take a simple case, we find that 6 is connected with *work* in relation to the world (Gen. i). In the same way, the period of our Lord's ministry (" work ")—918 days, as ¶ 338—consists of 6 periods of 153 days. Hence the significance of John xxi, 11, " Simon Peter went and drew the net to land full of great fishes, 153," when compared with Matt. xiii, 47, " The kingdom of heaven is like unto a net, that was cast into the sea, and gathered of every kind "; Luke v, 10, " From henceforth thou shalt catch men "; and Matt. iv, 19, " Follow me, and I will make you fishers of men."

The entire symbolism goes back to the multitudinousness of seed promised to Abraham through the Messiah. Thus in sequence, Gen. xii, 3, " in thee shall all families of the earth be blest "; Gen. xv, 5, " Look . . . tell the stars, if thou be able to number them, . . . so shall thy seed be "; Gen. xvi, 10, " I will multiply thy seed exceedingly, that it shall not be numbered for multitude "; Gen. xvii, 4, " A father of a multitude of nations "; Gen. xlviii, 16, " Let them grow into a multitude in the midst of the earth," or, as the margin rendering is, " as fishes do increase." The symbolism begins in specified detail with Gen. xii, 3, and ends with Rev. vii, 9.

The connection of the symbolism of " the fishes " as referring to " multitudinousness of seed " is unmistakable. In Hebrew, the root common to both words is " *dag*." Thus Gesenius states regarding the Hebrew *dagah* " to cover (like the Arab *daga*, to cover over), this verb is applied to *multitude and plenty* covering over everything (similarly in Arabic). Thus it is once found as a verb, *to be multiplied, to be increased*, Gen. xlviii, 16. Hence *dag*, . . . a fish (so-called from being so prolific . . .)."

¶ 340. THE SYMBOLISM OF THE GOSPEL AGE.

In Section II of this Chapter, it is shown that an ancient prophecy declared that the sign of the promised Messiah's coming was to be the conjunction of the planets Saturn and Jupiter in the zodiacal sign Pisces (the Fishes). It is also shown that four distinct conjunctions in Pisces as defined occurred between the summer of 7 B.C. and the summer of 6 B.C. It is shown that this series of conjunctions, ending 2½ years before the Nativity in the autumn of 4 B.C., is an explanation of the statement of Herod concerning the possible age of the Messiah as " two years old and under according to the time which he had carefully learned of the wise men " (Matt. ii, 16).

The zodiacal sign of the Fishes, therefore, is symbolically and prophetically related to the promise of the *multitudinousness of seed* through the

Messiah, and hence is related to the New Testament symbol of the Fishes.[1] "The fish" the secret emblem of early Christians. This explains why the early Christians, under the Roman persecutions, had the symbol of the fish engraven on their rings and sculptured on their tombs, as is seen in the catacombs of Rome. It was the secret symbol of the persecuted Church.

The duration of Christ's ministry, 6 periods of 153 days—the number of fishes in John xxi, 11—therefore symbolised the 6 periods of work—*ministry* —preparatory to the Resurrection. To spread the Gospel, He chose His 12 disciples, the number here indicating " governmental " or " administrative perfection " (¶ 334)—prefigured by the 12 tribes of Israel under David and Solomon. Extension of the symbolism of the Fishes to the *Gospel age* should, therefore, be related to $12 \times 153 = 1836$. This is the measurement of the length of the roof of the Grand Gallery of the Great Pyramid, as geometrically obtained, and shown on Plate XLIIa. The Grand Gallery, by its increased height, therefore, fittingly symbolises the Gospel age, " the New and Living Way " of St. Paul.

Side note: 153 fishes. Ministry 6×153 days. 12 disciples. 12×153 symbolic of Gospel Age =1836. Roof length of Great Pyramid's Grand Gallery. Symbol of "the New and Living Way" of St. Paul.

The date given by the commencement of the Grand Gallery (Plate XLIa, Fig. K, Plate XLIIa, and ¶¶ 328 and 329) is the date of the Crucifixion (¶ 338), 4028.53 A.K. = 30¼ A.D. The date given by the horizontal from the Queen's Chamber floor level is 3996.09 A.K. = the autumn of 4 B.C., the date of the Nativity. This is as shown on Plate XLIa, Fig. L. That the Queen's Chamber floor level was known to give the date of the Messiah's birth, and the Grand Gallery commencement the date of His Resurrection, will be proved from the ancient Egyptian records relating to the Pyramid. The evidence from this source will be seen to be both emphatic and convincing.

Side note: Beginning of Gallery gives Crucifixion date 30¼ A.D. Queen's Chamber floor level gives Nativity date 4 B.C. Egyptian literary traditions confirm the two identities.

¶ 341. DANIEL'S PROPHECY KNOWN THOUSANDS OF YEARS BEFORE DANIEL.

Now the exact date of the giving of the *Divine Command* to build, in the 2nd year of Darius is Day 1, Month VI = 22nd August (Greg.) 520 B.C. (¶ 331). The Great Pyramid gives exactly the same date, within a week. The above dating gives 3479.91 A.K., and the Pyramid 3479.89275 A.K. The symbolical and geometrical features defining the latter date are as follows :—

Side note: 29,220 years— the Divine period of the Egyptian King Lists relates to a cycle defined in the Pyramid.

The Old and New Testaments have been seen to define the Messiah and His Kingdom in allegorical terms relating to the Pyramid symbolism (¶ 268 and footnote). An outstanding feature of the Great Pyramid's exterior is the 35th course and its axis (Plate XVI, Fig. C ; Plate XLIIa, Fig. A ; and ¶¶ 97–101). The circuit of the Pyramid along this axis is 29,219.3972 P" (Plate XVI, Fig. C, and ¶ 101) = 80×365.242465. In Plate XVI, Table A, we saw that this number (as 29,220) formed the fictitious basis of the Egyptian chronology of the Divine and human Dynasties of Egypt.

Side note: 29,220 lunations ending at Great Step dating began in 520 B.C. =3480 A.K., the 2nd year of Darius I.

[1] Refer ¶ 288 concerning " the Cord " of the " bound fishes " in relation to Pisces, and connect with " the cord " of Deuteronomy xxxii, 8 and 9, as relating to the multitude of seed promised Abraham (¶ 196a).

This is a Pyramid dating for the commencement of Daniel's 70 weeks.

69 weeks to Messiah give 1st year of Christ's ministry, which began at 4026 A.K.

Outstanding features of the Great Pyramid's interior are the Grand Gallery and the Great Step. The Great Step marks the structural end of the Grand Gallery floor. The Great Step also lies in the central vertical plane of the Pyramid, vertically below the apex—in the Old and New Testaments, symbolic of the Messiah as "head and chief corner-stone" (¶ 268 and footnote). The structural beginning of the Grand Gallery, again, defines the Crucifixion date precisely (¶¶ 328, 329, 338). The first year of Christ's ministry is defined by Daniel's 69 weeks (¶¶ 334–336). The basal time-unit of this definition is the lunation, and 29,219.3972 lunations—the numerical value of the 35th course axis circuit—extend from the commencement of the 70 weeks to the Pyramid's dating for the Great Step.

Otherwise expressed, this is as follows :—

The Great Step dating is   ..   ..   ..   5842.33979 A.K.
(Plates XLb, Figs. C and F, and XLIIa.)
Deduct 29219.3972 lunations   ..   .. = 2362.44704 solar years.

The resulting date   ..   ..   ..   3479.89275 A.K.,

the date of the commencement of Daniel's 70 weeks.

From this date 1530 years—or ten times the numerical value symbolising labour in connection with the forming of the Messianic kingdom—end at 5556 A.K., the Pyramid date defined by the Rhomboid of Displacement as the beginning of the period of civilisation to which the Pyramid's Message was designed to apply.

The period of Daniel's prophecy and the period of Christ's ministry are thus connected with the Pyramid's astronomical chronology.

Now the symbolism of the 35th course axis and the numerical value of the circuit of that axis, supplying the above relation, are intimately connected in their relation to the Pyramid's external geometry with the displacement value of 286.1 P″ (¶¶ 148, 199, and 200). In the Pyramid's interior, the latter value is the connecting geometrical link between the external and internal systems of geometrical representation (¶ 259). As the measure of the side of the Rhomboid of Displacement it defines the Grand Gallery height in relation to the Precessional circuit, and the displacement of the Passage system in relation to the Pyramid's central vertical plane (Plates XLb, Fig. C and XXIV respectively). The same rhomboid defines the commencement of the period to which the Pyramid's Message was designed to apply (¶¶ 249–254). This initial date is given as 5556.23 A.K. (¶ 249). This is the date at which the Precessional rate attained the value indicated by the sum of the base diagonals and by the Precessional circuit. The interval between the date thus defined and the spring of Christ's first year of ministry is 1530 years, ten times the number of fishes drawn in the net, to symbolise Christ's work in building up the Kingdom of Heaven (John xxi, 11). Here we have another instance of 10 as a multiple, as in the case observed in ¶ 337.

Daniel's prophecy known thousands of years before Daniel.

The outstanding fact derived from the series of identities noted scarcely needs to be pointed out to the reader. It is clearly evident that, not only was Daniel's prophecy written long prior to Antiochus Epiphanes and Judas Maccabæus, but from early Egyptian tradition in relation to Pyramid prophecy that the prophecy itself was in existence thousands of years before the Book of Daniel was written. Daniel merely received a confirmatory repetition adapted to suit the age to which his prophecies were intended to apply.

¶ 342. THE TWO MODERN SCHOOLS RELATING TO HEBREW
              PROPHECY.

As bearing upon the important issue raised, it is scarcely necessary, in *The two modern schools of exposition.* these days, to inform the general reader that there are two modern schools of exposition relating to Old and New Testament apocalyptic literature. *(I) Declares Hebrew prophecy written after events represented as predicted.* There is the modern critical school, whose essential datum is the postulating of the theory that a " prophecy " never preceded the central events it claimed to predict ; that it was issued to raise the hopes of the despondent sufferers under persecution, the " prophecy " being phrased to predict the contemporary events as belonging to the dark hours preceding the glorious dawn of a new and brighter day.

The other school, to which we have referred, accepts the apocalyptic *(II) Declares Hebrew prophecy to be what it claimed to be—* books of the Old and New Testaments as being what they claim to be, and on this datum applies the various prophecies to history in the manner the *divinely inspired prescience relating* prophecies themselves indicate they should be applied. Important con- *to events remotely* tributors to the expositions of the latter school have appeared in the persons *ahead of the* of Sir Isaac Newton, Professor Birks of Cambridge, and Dr. Grattan Guinness.[1] *promulgation of the prophecy.* The work [2] of the last-named authority represents the last word on the subject as understood up to the year 1878 A.D.   It is still the standard textbook on the subject.

¶ 343. " THE TIMES OF THE GENTILES."

The reader is advised to consult Dr. Guinness's work for the data establish- *Our Lord defines " the Times of the Gentiles " as a long historical period.* ing—from the Old and New Testaments—that the " Times of the Gentiles," to which our Lord referred in Luke xxi, 24, comprise a chronological period of prophetic time, of the duration of 2520 years.   The evidence relating to this *Modern interpretation establishes duration as 2520 years* has been accumulating for several centuries, but was first reduced to systematic editing by Dr. Guinness.   Guinness may be said to have done *=7 " times "* for the scientific study of prophecy what Euclid did for geometry. *=7 × 360.*

From the work referred to, the reader will find that the " time, times and *Guinness's systematic work.* a half " of Daniel vii, 25 and xii, 7, and Revelation xii, 14, and the 42 months of Revelation xi, 2 and xiii, 5, and the 1260 days of Revelation xi, 3 and *The books of Daniel and Revelation define 3½* xii, 6, all relate to the half-period of the Times of the Gentiles.   The latter whole period is known as the Seven Times of Hebrew Prophecy, *i.e.* 7 times *" times " as 1260 symbolic " days," and hence the 7* 360 years, a week of great years, or 2520 years.   According to modern interpretation, as Guinness explains, the years may be solar, calendar, or *" times " as 2520 symbolic days.* lunar years.

Now this interpretation of the Seven Times of Hebrew Prophecy, as con- *The " year-day " theory comparatively modern.* sisting of 2520 years, is comparatively modern, and due to a prolonged study of the evidence.   No evidence exists to show that any Jew or Israelite of *Not adopted by Jew or Israelite in ancient times.* ancient times ever recognised the period to be of the duration here stated.

[1] In the opinion of the present writer, no list of names, however short—representative of notable contributors to prophecy investigation—is complete without that of his esteemed collaborator, the late Dr. H. Aldersmith. [D. D.]

[2] " The Approaching End of the Age " ; also " Light for the Last Days."

Jews deemed the " time " = 1 century and 3½ times = 350 years.
The Jews themselves supposed the " time " to refer to a century, and the 3½ " times " of Daniel to be 350 years. This fact—at first sight detrimental

But the " year-day " theory confirmed by symbolism of Old Testament.
to the " year-day " theory—proves, upon examination of the evidence, to supply an additional argument in favour of the inspirational value of the " year-day " identity. In the first place, the " year-day " identity appears in the Old Testament—in Numbers, xiv, 34 and Ezekiel iv, 4 and 6—as a

The " time, times and a half " = 3½ times = 1260.
Divinely established identity, relating to prophetic symbolism. When, therefore, we find the Jews defining Daniel's " time, times and a half " as

Daniel xii, 7–12 :— 1260 days, 1290 days, 1335 days, symbolise 1260 years, 1290 years, 1335 years.
3½ times—with the " time " = 100 years—and Daniel's prophecy in Chapter xii following the " time, times and a half " of verse 7, with the 1290 days of verse 11, and the 1335 days of verse 12, it seems obvious that the " year-day " identity in Numbers and Ezekiel better fits the case. For with the " year-day " identity, the 1335 and 1290 days of Daniel become respectively 1335

The 1260 days in Revelation symbolise 1260 years.
and 1290 years. Hence the 3½ times, i.e. 3½ × 360 = 1260 days, become 1260 years ; thus agreeing with the parallel prophecies in the Book of Revelation, which mention both the " time, times and a half " (xii, 14) and the 1260 " days " (xi, 3 ; xii, 6).

¶ 344. THE PYRAMID'S PASSAGE JUNCTION DATE.

Great Pyramid represents periods of 1260 and 2520 years, solar and calendar.
Confirming all that Guinness and others have established concerning the sacred period of 2520 years, we find that the Pyramid clearly represents the periods of 1260 solar years and 2520 solar years ; and, independently, the period of 2520 calendar years of 360 days each.

2520 calendar years = 2483.83 solar years.
The period of 2520 calendar years = 2483.83 solar years, and the Junction

Passage Junction date = 2483.77997 A.K.
of the Entrance and first Ascending Passage floor lines of the Great Pyramid is at 2483.7799726 A.P., or A.K. (Plate XLIa, Fig. G and Plate XLIIa, Fig. A). Now, as stated in ¶ 318, and shown in Tables XVII, XVIII, and

The date given by Berosus for the capture of Babylon by Tukulti-Enurta I of Assyria.
XIX and Annotations, the Babylonian bases of fictitious chronology were derived from the Egyptians, whose systems were derived from the Pyramid system of chronology (Plate XVI and ¶¶ 92–99, 212–217, 250–254, and 262). An identity confirming this, and indicating a derivation from the Pyramid's

Confirms Egyptian origin of Babylonian chronological systems.
2520 years' period, is given by the King List of the Babylonian Priest, Berosus. This gives the reign of Cyrus beginning at 3463½ A.K. = 536 B.C. (as Tables XXI and XXVII and Annotations, and Annotations to Table XVII), and the capture of Babylon by Tukulti-Enurta I at 2484 A.K. = 1516 B.C. (Tables XVII and XVIII). The actual date of the latter event—as Table XVII—is 2470¾ A.K. = 1529 B.C. The dating of Berosus is the termination of 2520 calendar years from the Pyramid's o A.K. dating at Autumnal Equinox, 4000 B.C.

An abortive Exodus of Israel dated by Talmud at 2483½.
Again, Jewish tradition in the Talmud preserves the tradition of an attempted enforcement of the Exodus by the men of Ephraim 30 years before the actual Exodus. The date of the actual Exodus, according to Egyptian

Call of Abraham 2083½ A.K.
and Hebrew chronology, is 2513½ A.K. (¶¶ 322 and 323), and is given by the Pyramid chronology (¶ 328). The date of the abortive Exodus, 30 years

previously, is therefore 2483½ A.K., and is given by the Pyramid chronology as the termination of 2520 calendar years from o A.K. The Pyramid origin of the dating and tradition is obvious.

The date is also 400 years from the Call of Abraham. For the chrono- logical and prophetic significance of this, refer Gen. xv, 13. The latter, however, refers to a period of 400 years concerning Abraham's " seed." From the birth of Isaac—Abraham's " seed"—at 2108½ A.K., the 400 years end at 2508½ A.K., the date of the death of Ramessu II (Table XI and Plate LXI). Gen. xv, 14 states that God would judge the oppressors of Israel after the termination of 400 years. For recognition of the fulfilment of this, refer Exod. ii, 23–25, for the death of the Pharaoh of the Oppression, in relation to the promise of Gen. xv, 13, 14, and Exod. iii, 7–9, 16–22 ; iv. 23 ; and vi, 2–8 (particularly verses 4 and 5, as intentionally referring to the fulfilment of Gen. xv, 13 and 14). The chronological elucidation of this period in relation to the associated period of 430 years, and as bearing upon the 480 years of 1 Kings vi, i, is given in Table XXVIII, Annotations.

[Marginal note:] From latter date 400 years of Abraham's " seed " (Gen. xv, 13) end at 2483½ A.K. But birth of Isaac = 2108½ A.K. 400 years of Abraham's " seed " from latter date end at 2508½ A.K., the death of Ramessu II ; confirming prophecy in relation to the appointed time, and promise of judgment of oppressors.

¶ 345. THE " SEVEN TIMES " SYMBOLISM AND THE DELUGE DATING.

Plate LXII indicates how clearly the Pyramid's geometrical system of chronology defines the periods of 2520 and 1260 solar years.[1] In ¶ 344, 2520 calendar years' duration from o A.K. was seen to be given by the floor junction of the Entrance and Ascending Passages. Plate LXII, Fig. B, shows how the junction of the chronological roof line of the Entrance Passage and the chronological floor line of the Ascending Passage defines the termina- tion of 2520 solar years from o A.K. (or A.P.). The exact interval defined by the geometrical construction shown gives the date 2519.9453458 A.K.— 20 days short of the completion of 2520 solar years.

[Marginal note:] Junction of roof and floor lines of Entrance Passage with floor line of Ascending Passage employed to represent 2520 years, calendar and solar, from 0 A.K. Plate LXII.

In Plate LXII, Fig. A, the half-periods of 1260 solar years are represented as forming the diameters of the circles drawn to define the half-periods. The lower horizontal tangent drawn from the second of these circles from o A.K. on the Entrance floor datum, cuts the chronological line of the Ascending Passage at the date 1655.878875 A.K., defining the year of the Hebrew deluge (¶ 313). The same construction, on the Ascending floor datum, gives the same date on the Entrance Passage floor line as is shown on Fig. A. Again, ⅔rds of 2520 calendar years = ⅔rds of 2483.83 solar years = 1655.88 solar years, giving the above Pyramid dating for the year of the Hebrew deluge.

[Marginal note:] The definition of the 1260 solar years, by 1260 inches' diameter circles supplies the geometrical dating of the deluge = ⅔rds of 2520 calendar years.

It will also be observed that 1260 A.K. is given by the geometrical relations of the Entrance Doorway. The horizontal cutting the floor line of the Entrance Passage at this date is defined by the intersection of the Entrance Passage roof line and the geometrical face slope of the Pyramid. The actual dating thus defined is 1259.7600257 A.K. Although this is taken as

[Marginal note:] The geometry of the Entrance Doorway in relation to 1260 A.K.

[1] For the astronomical significance of these periods refer Section III, ¶ 494.

an intentional indication when considered in connection with the other data, the dating lacks the element of definitive precision hitherto seen to be associated with astronomical and chronological values supplied by the Pyramid's geometrical system.

¶ 346. THE PYRAMID'S SACRED CHRONOLOGY OF "THE SEVEN TIMES."

The Pyramid's chronology of " the seven times " confirms the sacred chronological period of 1 Kings vi, 1. 4 "Sep tep sed " periods – 480 years.

The Pyramid's chronology of " the seven times " defines the initial 7 times from 0 A.K. ; the date of the Dedication of Solomon's Temple ; the date of the founding of the 2nd Temple ; and the terminal 7 times ending at 6000 A.K.

We have suggested (in ¶ 36 and footnote, and in ¶¶ 321 and 330) that the periods indicated by the 480th year of 1 Kings vi, 1, and the 450 years of Acts xiii, 17–23, relate to the *Sed* periods of 30 years from the Exodus. This is confirmed by the data of Table XXVIII, Annotations, which independently fix the various details of summation for the 450 and 480 years' intervals. The Exodus year is now seen to have been adopted as a historical epoch. From the Pyramid data relating to the initial period of 2520 years, ending at 2520 A.K., we now see—as indicated on the Plate LXII, Fig. A—that the latter dating formed an epoch of prophetical chronology. Thus 480 years— 16 *Sed* periods, or 4 *Sep tep sed* periods (¶ 34)—from the prophetic epoch 2520 A.K., ended at 3000 A.K. A further period of 480 years from the latter date ended at 3480 A.K.

These dates are, respectively, the date of the Dedication of the 1st Temple, 3000 A.K. (¶ 330 and Tables XXVI and XXVIII),when the Shekinah came to the Temple, and the date of the Divine Command to build the 2nd Temple, 3480 A.K. (¶¶ 330 and 331, and Table XXVIII), when the 70 years of Divine Indignation ended. In the Pyramid, the 3000 A.K. dating is given by the intersection of the Descending Passage roof line and the Pyramid base line ; and the 3480 A.K. dating by the 35th course axis circuit in lunations, from the Great Step dating, as explained in ¶ 341.

The chronological descending distance from the Great Step vertical to the central vertical of Subterranean Chamber = 230.388786 P″, = King's Chamber height.

This central vertical geometrically indicates the vertical tangent to the Pyramid's terminal 1260 circle ; and by this relation defines 6000 A.K. ; also independently defined by the centre of the Granite Leaf.

Reference to Plate LXII, Fig. A and Plate LXIV shows that the terminal 1260 circle of the Descending Passage, ending at 6000 A.K., passes through the exact centre of the Subterranean Chamber. In other words, the South vertical tangent[1] of the terminal Descending 1260 circle, marks the central vertical axis of the Subterranean Chamber. The resulting passage slope distance from the Great Step vertical is 230.420072 P″. This shows that the intended central axis is 230.388786 P″ measured along the passage slope— *i.e.* a distance equal to the height of the King's Chamber (¶ 310a)—South of the Great Step vertical. With the latter value, the resulting geometrical value for the horizontal distance from the sloping floor end of the Descending Passage (at 5504.611740 A.P., or A.K., on Plate XLIIa) to the centre of the Subterranean Chamber is 509.297168 P″. Petrie's corresponding measured distance, stated by him in round numbers of British inches is 509 B″—*i.e.* the middle of the Chamber as defined by Petrie's 346 and 672 B″ respectively, for the North and South sides.

[1]Not shown on Plate LXII ; the feature described has only been noticed since the block for the plate was made. Refer Plate LXIV.

THE GREAT PYRAMID'S CHRONOGRAPH OF SACRED ASTRONOMICAL CYCLES.

FIG. A.

FIG. B.

DETAIL OF JUNCTION OF PASSAGES

KEY DIAGRAM

The 6000 A.P., or A.K., dating is therefore defined by the centre of the Granite Leaf in the Antechamber, and by the centre of the Subterranean Chamber in relation to the terminal Seven Times.

The Universal Law of Divine Harmony.
It is not suggested that the Hebrews knew of these relations. It is suggested, by the Pyramid's indications, that the relationship is the result of the same Divine Harmony already indicated by the Pyramid as constituting the Natural Law governing the Earth and its orbit, in dimensions and motion, and in variations of dimension and motion.

¶ 347. THE "SEVEN TIMES" SYNCHRONISM.

The prophetic element in Egyptian tradition derived from the Great Pyramid.

Hebrew prophecy independently derived.

Both systems identical.

The 6000 years of Hebrew prophecy defined by the Pyramid.

Unlike the evidence from Egyptian sources in relation to Egyptian traditions of Pyramid prophecies, the evidence from the Old and New Testaments indicates that Hebrew prophecy—while synchronising with Pyramid prophecy—was altogether independently derived. Both systems—Hebrew and Pyramid—relate to a period of six millenaries.[1] Both systems emphasise that the central date of this period forms a definite epoch central to all the chronological periods of God's creation as relating to the application of His Law to mankind. In both cases, again, the dates are the same in relation to modern chronology.

An initial period of 2520 solar years from 0 A.K. = 4000 B.C., and a terminal period of 2520 years ending at 6000 A.K. = 2001¾ A.D.

The Pyramid, as shown on Plate LXII, Fig. A, represents an initial sacred cycle of 2520 years from 0 A.K. = 4000 B.C., and a terminal sacred cycle of 2520 years ending at 6000 A.K. = 2001¾ A.D. The latter dating is defined by the vertical passing through the centre of the Granite Leaf in the Antechamber. The Pyramid, again, indicates the bisection of the sacred period at 1260 years.

The 2520 years' period in Hebrew prophecy. Interpretation unknown until modern times.

The Old and New Testaments, as explained in ¶ 343, refer to a period of 7 times, and to a half-period of 3½ times, otherwise expressed as 2520 and 1260 "days" respectively. But no Hebrew or Jew has left any record that these periods were regarded as referring to periods of 2520 and 1260 years. The latter identification was not made until comparatively recent times.

Another matter established by modern prophecy exposition is that the period of 7 times is defined as having stages of chronological beginnings and corresponding stages of chronological endings. Thus Guinness ("Approaching End of the Age") states :—

Chronological steps, initial and terminal, relating to the period.

"The majestic movements of Providence and of history demand time; empires do not rise and fall in a day ; and the omniscient God takes note of the comparatively insignificant *beginning* of a mighty movement as well as of its climax. . . . Hence the propriety of indicating various dates of rise and fall " (p. 372).

"Now, if ' seven times ' be the appointed duration of the ' Times of the Gentiles,' we may expect to find, after an interval of 2520 years from this *Jewish captivity era*, a corresponding ' time of the end,' a period of similar decline and

---

[1] Preceding the " Sabbath of rest for the people of God," the seventh millenary (Heb. iv, 1-11, and 2 Pet., iii, 8).

fall, overthrow and decadence, of the last form or forms of *Gentile ruling power*, ushering in the close of the dispensation, the restoration of Israel, and the kingdom of the Messiah the Son of David " (p. 354).

¶ 348. MODERN INTERPRETATION OF PROPHECY.

A brief outline of modern prophecy interpretation is as follows :—

Our Lord, in Luke xxi, 24, refers to the period of the "Times of the Gentiles" in relation to the time prophecies of Daniel. This gives His authority for Daniel's prophecy and for the 7 times and 3½ times as applied to Judah's history. He describes the period as the duration of Gentile dominion over Jerusalem. Daniel ii, 38 identifies the beginning of Gentile domination of Jerusalem with the reign of Nebuchadnezzar. The 1st Captivity of Judah was effected by Nebuchadnezzar in his first year as co-rex, and included Daniel as captive. This, then, forms the first step of the series of chronological steps introducing the Seven Times of the Gentiles.

With these facts as basis, Dr. Grattan Guinness, in 1878 A.D., predicted a great epoch for Jerusalem and the Jews in connection with the year 1917 A.D. This fact, and its fulfilment, were noted by the late Right Rev. C. G. Handley Moule, D.D. (Lord Bishop of Durham), in an address on 8th June 1919.[1]

(marginal notes) Our Lord accepts Daniel's prophecy. The "Seven Times" of the Gentiles over Jerusalem, earliest chronological step-epoch = 1st year of Nebuchadnezzar as co-rex; the date of 1st Captivity of Judah (including Daniel). On this basis Gentile domination should end in 1917 A.D. This predicted by Dr. Grattan Guinness in 1878 A.D.

[1]Published as a pamphlet by Charles J. Thynne, 28 Whitefriars Street, London, E.C. 4. If this pamphlet is out of print it should be reprinted.
In the course of his address, the Right Rev. Dr. Moule referred, gracefully and tactfully, to the fact that the Books of Daniel and the Revelation of St. John have been explained by certain theological scholars as being, not inspired writings, but "hortatory rhapsodies," respectively "given to cheer sufferers under Antiochus Epiphanes" and "to cheer the victims of Nero or Domitian"; and reminded us that "forty years ago, in 1878, Guinness wrote that they who should see 1917 would probably see a great epoch for Jerusalem. The year came, and Allenby, *reverently victorious*, walked as liberator through the Jaffa Gate."
Continuing, he stated : "About three years ago, an old friend wrote to me, asking whether I did not agree with him that the consummation of an age was coming. He named to me, as what had quickened his own thoughts, a modest but valuable little book, 'The Nearness of Our Lord's Return,' by the Rev. R. W. B. Moore. The personality of my friend was significant. His experiences and life-work would not suggest precisely the student of prophecy. We were contemporaries at Cambridge long ago. He became Fellow of his great College. Then for more than thirty years he was a distinguished public schoolmaster; a layman all the while. But the conditions of our mighty time, taken along with a sober statement of the case for expectation on predictive lines, led this friend of mine to write as he did to me. I think it was significant.
"Rightly he used the phrase 'The consummation of an age.'"
The whole address should be obtained by the reader who is interested in the subject. It is a concise and masterly summary of the "year-day" interpretation of the time indications of Old and New Testament prophecy, and of the fulfilment of prophecy on this interpretation in times past and now current. The book referred to as by the Rev. R. W. B. Moore is published by R. Scott, Roxburghe House, Paternoster Row, E.C.
An important conclusion by Dr. Guinness, in his "Approaching End of the Age," pp. 473, 474, written in 1878, and bearing upon the above, is as follows : "We have noted various indications in the conditions of Palestine and of Israel, and in the political events of our own day, which seem to indicate that the cleansing of the sanctuary and the restoration of Israel are not distant. When these shall take place, when the Moslems, now driven out of Bulgaria, shall be driven also out of Syria, when the nations of Europe, *actuated it may be by mutual distrust and political jealousy*, or it may be by higher motives, shall conspire to reinstate the Jews in the land of their forefathers, *then* the last warning bell will have rung; then the last of the unfulfilled predictions of Scripture as to events prior to the great crisis, will have received its accomplishment; then the second advent of Israel's rejected Messiah to reign in conjunction with His glorified saints as King over all the earth, will be *close* at hand; then the mystery of God will be all but finished, and the manifestation of Christ immediate........THE DESTRUCTION OF THE POWER AND INDEPENDENCE OF THE OTTOMAN EMPIRE SHOULD BE AS A TRUMPET BLAST TO CHRISTENDOM, PROCLAIMING THAT THE DAY OF CHRIST IS AT HAND."
The emphasis in capitals is in the original—46 years ago.

The Lord
Bishop of
Durham (in
1919) directs
attention to
the fulfilment.
The identity
fixes that the
last " time "
of the seven
Gentile times
began in
1557 A.D.
The Pyramid's
displacement
factor defines
the period to
which its
Message was
designed to
apply, be-
ginning in the
first half of
December
1557 A.D.
The Pyramid,
therefore,
defines the
end of the
seven Gentile
times in first
half December
1917 A.D.
Allenby
delivered
Jerusalem.
Since then our
Lord's words
concerning
events succeed-
ing the
deliverance
of Jerusalem
have been
fulfilled by
current events.

Daniel xii, 4, referring to the " times of the Gentiles," declares that the interpretation was to be " sealed up " " even to the time of the end." A similar statement is made by the Rainbow Angel in Revelation x, 4 (refer ¶ 196d). Now the Pyramid chronology system geometrically indicates a similar period of enlightenment defined by Daniel as " the time of the end " (¶¶ 249 and 266). The Pyramid's intention in this relation was seen to be confirmed by Egyptian literary tradition (¶¶ 250–254, 262, and 267). The initial date for the Pyramid's time of the end was seen to be less than a month prior to the beginning of 1558 A.D. The date falls in the first half of December (Greg.) 1557 A.D., and since Daniel's " time," according to modern interpretations, is a period of 360 years, " the time of the end " should extend from the first half of December 1557 A.D. to the first half of December 1917 A.D. Is it merely a coincidence that the army of Lord Allenby delivered Jerusalem from the desolating Turk on the 11th December 1917 A.D. ? The Bishop of Durham in that year thought not, and many will be inclined to agree with him. The Jew is at liberty to return to Jerusalem ; he is at liberty to evolve his own form of government. Gentile domination in Jerusalem has been broken. A period of trouble there, as elsewhere, is shaping—not to the end that many fear—but to the end which Christ foretold would succeed the deliverance of Jerusalem (Luke xxi, 24–28).

It is no coincidence. Christ pictured the conditions in the world that would follow the deliverance of Jerusalem. Jerusalem has been delivered and the conditions pictured are with us.

¶ 349. THE PYRAMID'S " SEVENTH TIME."

Daniel's
" seventh
time " = 1557
A.D. to 1917
A.D.
The Pyramid's
astronomically
defined
" seventh
time " =
5556.23 A.K.
(December
1557 A.D.) to
5916.23 A.K.
(December
1917 A.D.).
Hence the
" seven
times " of
Gentile
dominion
began at
3396.23 A.K.
= December
604 B.C., in
the 1st year of
Nebuchad-
nezzar (co-
rex) ; the
year of Judah's
1st captivity
(Daniel).
Elucidation of
Hebrew
prophecy has
depended upon
modern in-
terpretation ;

The latter conclusion, however, is confirmed by other data. The Pyramid's " time of the end " is indicated as beginning at 5556.23 A.K. This was seen to agree with the historical conditions for the chronological fixing of Daniel's " time of the end " as applied to the seven times of Gentile dominion over Jerusalem. The Pyramid, therefore, defined the date of the termination of the seven times of Gentile dominion as (5556.23 + 360) = 5916.23 A.K. = December 1917 A.D. Seven times (2520 solar years), ending at the latter date, began at 3396.23 A.K. = December 604 B.C. This falls in the 1st year of Nebuchadnezzar, co-rex. In this year Nebuchadnezzar led the first contingent of Judah captive (Tables XXI and XXX). The prophet Daniel was included in this captivity, and informed Nebuchadnezzar that he was the first of the kings of the Gentile dominion of Nebuchadnezzar's dream.

Ancient history and modern history, therefore, confirm the chronological symbolism of Hebrew and Pyramid prophecy. Both Daniel's prophecy and the Pyramid's prophecy fix the period of their interpretation between December 1557 and December 1917. The interpretation of Daniel's prophecy has depended upon modern exposition of prophecy within the time limits defined. The Pyramid's interpretation has depended upon the development of modern gravitational astronomy and mathematics within the same dated limits. To emphasise the intention of this definition and its relation, thus indicated, to the all-embracing Divine Harmony of the Pyramid's Universal Natural Law, the basis of representation is again the Pyramid's displacement value of 286.1 P″. This necessarily follows from the fact that the Rhomboid of Displacement — of side 286.1 P″—defines 5556.23 A.K. =December 1557 A.D. as the beginning of the Pyramid's " time of the end " (Plate XL, Fig. C and ¶¶ 236, 249–254, 262, and 266).

¶ 350. THE LAW OF THE DISPLACEMENT FACTOR.

The Pyramid's displacement value (286.1 P″) has, therefore, proved the key-value to the precise representation of the following :—

(1) The hollowing-in feature of the reflecting surfaces " to prevent diffusion of the reflected light and to stabilise the reflected rays under the influence of variable surface refractions due to heat radiations " (¶¶ 11, 18, and 19) ; for the purpose of defining the principal points of the solar year as astronomically defined, and of the solar year as defined by the phenomena of the seasons (¶¶ 1, 12–24) ; and for the additional purpose of defining the relation of the latter to the prophetical or sacred calendar (¶¶ 15, 25, 63, and 315).

(2) The definition of the exact values of—

    (a) The Sidereal year,
    (b) The Anomalistic year, and
    (c) The Solar year (¶¶ 148–154).

(3) The definition of the exact mean sun distance (¶¶ 157–159).
(4) The definition of the Law of Gravitation in relation to the earth and its orbit (¶¶ 157–159).
(5) The definition of the exact limits of variation in the eccentricity of the Earth's orbit (¶¶ 157–159).
(6) The definition of the exact formula for the annual rate of Precession (¶¶ 234–236 and 243).
(7) The definition of the exact formula for the annual rate of change in the Longitude of Perihelion, by means of the Gallery height, defined by the displacement factor (¶¶ 244–248).
(8) The definition of the year beginning the period for which the Pyramid's Message was designed to apply, and in which the knowledge necessary for its understanding would be discovered ; also thus defining the beginning of Daniel's " time of the end " (¶¶ 248–254, 262, and 266).
(9) The definition of the (same) year as ending a period of 1530 years—numerically ten times the number of fishes symbolising the gathering in of mankind for the Kingdom of Heaven—from the 1st year of the Messiah's ministry (¶¶ 338–341).
(10) The definition of the apex Pyramid—symbolic of the Messiah in Old and New Testament symbolism (¶ 268 and footnote), as related—

    (a) To the Pyramid's external orbital features,
    (b) To the Pyramid's internal passage chronology—astronomical and prophetical, and
    (c) To the Great Step dating and the Rhomboid of Displacement (Plate XXIV ; Plate XXV, Figs. A₁ and A₂ ; Plate XLb, Fig. C ; and ¶¶ 196, 199, 200, and 329).

The symbolism clearly conveyed by the ten categories is —

I. By (10) in relation to the previous nine, that " In Christ are hid all the treasures of wisdom and knowledge " (Col. ii, 3), and that by Christ, God " created all things " (Eph. iii, 9) ; " the world was made by Him, and knew Him not " (John i, 10).

II. By (1) in relation to the succeeding nine that " God is Light " (1 John i, 5) and " God is Love " (iv, 8) ; that Christ is " the Light of the World," who, by His displacement—Daniel's " cutting-off " of the Messiah, " the Light shining in darkness " (John i, 5)—neutralised in Himself the effect of sin—the breaking of Divine Law—by restoring the Light, that, to man, is the essence of Divine Love ; the stabilising of the refracted rays.

Margin note: The displacement factor symbolises the Creator's special sacrifice for mankind—the Messiah's " cutting off, but not for Himself." The stabilising of the refracted rays. " The Light of the world." The one Universal Law of Divine Love.

The displacement, therefore, symbolises God's special sacrifice for mankind. " Herein is love, not that we loved Him, but that He loved us, and sent His Son to be the propitiation for our sins " (1 John iv, 10). God did not meet us half-way. He came to us.

¶ 351. THE LAW AND ITS NUMERICAL RELATIONS.

Margin note: The significance of the ten categories relating to the displacement factor. Comprised in one including category expressive of the function of the displacement factor. The Ten Commandments of the Law and the single including commandment of Christ.

All the related features of the Pyramid's purpose and the outlines of its Message are comprised under the above ten categories. These ten categories of representation are essential to define fully that purpose and message. At the same time, the single displacement value indicates that the ten separate categories of representation merely depict different aspects or applications of a single governing law. Similarly, the Ten Commandments of the Mosaic Law are all comprised under the single command of our Lord " That ye love one another, as I have loved you."[1] The single Universal Law defined by the Pyramid is the One Law of the Universe—the Law of Divine Love, the source of all energy, spiritual and material. This is the whole theme of 1 John iv.

Margin note: The Law of Divine Harmony—Love. Significance of Pyramid's and orbit's decimal system. Ten units = one higher unit.

Hence the significance of the Pyramid's decimal system. All its units have subdivisions of 10; 10 units comprise a single higher unit. Thus Pythagoras—who derived his knowledge from the Egyptian priests, whose knowledge, in turn, had been derived from the Pyramid—proclaimed, as associated with his heliocentric planetary theory, that " ten is the perfect number," and that " all things are numbers " (¶¶ 129–134 and Table X).

Margin note: Explanation of the Pythagorean theory, derived from Egypt, relating to number in Creation.

Again, the numerical value of the Pyramid and Hebrew " 7 times " =7 × 360 = 2520, whilst representing a week of calendar years (or great years), is also the least common multiple of all numbers from 1 to 10 inclusive.[2]

---

[1] John xv, 12 and John xiii, 34 ; refer also John xiv, 14–21 ; 1 John iii, 11 ; iv, 21 ; 2 John 4–6 ; 1 Thess. iv, 9.

[2] The number 10, as we have seen in Chapters III and IV, is the basis of the numerical relations of the solar system. The number 7, however, is the basis of the numerical relations in the scientific subdivisions or particular " kingdoms " of nature, e.g. the " Periodic Law" of Chemistry; the Chemical Law of Matter. Matter in " dissociation," however, brings us into the kingdom that comprises the reservoir of Matter—the kingdom of Energy, or perhaps we should say, the Universe of Energy, as distinct from the Universe of Matter. The Laws in this new Universe cannot be expressed by Newton's Laws, but the latter and the former can both be expressed by Einstein's

Plate LXII shows that the Pyramid's scalar or sacred chronology defined two such periods. The two periods total 5040 years, or 14 "Times" (refer ¶¶ 334–336). Now, in regard to the latter number, Mr. James Gow, in his "History of Greek Mathematics," makes a significant statement. "It is certain," he says, "that Pythagoras considered number to be the basis of creation,"[1] and again, with reference to "the (Greek) philosopher who sought in numbers to find the plan on which the Creator worked," states, "Plato, *Legg*, 737 E, 738 A, says that 5040 has 59 divisions including all the numbers from 1 to 10."[2]

The "seven" times, the L.C.M. of all numbers 1 to 10.
The Pyramid's 14 "times."
Plato's statement in relation to, same as derived from Egypt.

In the sacred number 2520 we have, therefore, the specifically defined value 7 as related to chronologic prophecy, and the underlying creative scalar radix 10. The sum of the two relates to the other sacred number, 153 (¶¶ 338–341), since the sum of all numbers from 1 to 17 inclusive is 153. Refer also category (9) of ¶ 350.

7 and 10 in relation to creative numerical harmony.
Symbolised by summation 7–10.
Numbers 1 to 17 add 153.

Again, in the Pyramid's base circuit, the unit for the year value is 100 P″. Hence, since the King's Chamber floor level—as distinct from the Precessional circuit level—is 1700 P″ above the base, its numerical value, in terms of the external unit, is 17. Hence the significance attaching to the selection of 17 Sothic cycles = 24,837 years, in the compilation of the mythical Divine Dynasties of Manetho (Plate XVI, Table A), as derived from the Great Pyramid's geometrical measures.

"The fishes of Christ."
The unit 17 and the King's Chamber level.
17 Sothic cycles = duration of Egyptian Divine Dynasties.

¶ 352. MESSIANIC PROPHECIES IN ANCIENT EGYPT.

Now, M. Alexandre Moret in his "Gods and Kings of Egypt,"[3] clearly shows that an ancient prophecy was current in Egypt, from the earliest times, proclaiming the coming of a saviour of the human race. All the sacred imagery identified later with the New Testament accounts, an accurate forecast of the purpose of the Messiah's coming, the manner of His death, the rites of the Lord's Last Supper,[4] and, in fact, innumerable details of our Lord's

Early prediction promising the coming of Messiah.
His mission proclaimed.
The Saviour of mankind.
The manner of His death.

Law of Relativity. How many reservoir Universes there may be we cannot know, nor how many proto-laws of relativity, until we come to the One Source and One Law-Origin that includes, maintains, and governs all Universes and all their controlling Laws.

[1] P. 68.

[2] P. 72. For Plato's relations with Egypt in the 4th century B.C., refer Table X.

[3] Refer Section III, ¶¶ 498–498d. For the complete data in Moret's work refer his chapters on "The Passion of Osiris," "Immortality and Retribution," and "The Mysteries of Isis."

[4] Refer Section III, ¶ 498b; and Moret, Ibid., p. 72. Refer also, Budge, "The Gods of the Egyptians," Vol. I, p. 34 *et seq.* Here Unas, the last king of Dynasty V (Sakkarah and Abusir Pyramids) is quoted as "eating the gods"; and as Budge says (p. 38), "in eating them he also ate their words of power and their spirits." Unas says (p. 39) that "he hath eaten the knowledge of every god, and his existence and the duration of his life are eternal and everlasting . . . the seat of the heart of Unas shall be among the living upon this earth for ever and ever." Compare this with Christ's words in John vi, 48–58 : " Except ye eat the flesh of the Son of man, and drink His blood, ye have no life in you : Whoso eateth My flesh and drinketh My blood, hath eternal life " (verses 53 and 54). But the whole chapter should be read. Did we not know the *spiritual* meaning of the words we might deem that Christ was referring to the form of the pagan human sacrifice, that was actually a ceremonial perversion of the promised sacrifice. To what extent the statement of Unas is derived from the *spiritual* promise, from the pagan interpretation of this, or both, cannot be said. As Budge says (p. 32). " The beliefs which were conceived by the Egyptians in their lowest states of civilisation were mingled with those which reveal the existence of high spiritual conceptions."

Now the epoch of Unas is not many years after the epoch of the Great Pyramid builders.

The rites of the Sacrament. Predicted details of His life and teaching. life and teaching were proclaimed in Egypt for thousands of years before His actual Advent. This can all be established, by reference to Moret's work, as giving additional significance to the words of Zacharias in Luke i, 68–70 :—

Such predictions referred to by Zacharias (Luke i, 68-70).
> " Blessed be the Lord God of Israel; for He hath visited and redeemed His people, and hath raised up an horn of salvation for us in the house of His servant David ; as He spake by the mouth of His holy prophets, which have been *since the world began.*"

The reason for Rationalist belief in the " myth " of our Lord. Egyptian priests invented the late fable that the Messiah had come as Osiris. The evidence from Egyptian sources, and from other ancient sources, has hitherto formed the basal data for the Rationalist presentation of the so-called " myth " of our Lord Jesus Christ. The Great Pyramid—and the Egyptian traditions relating to its Message—now enable us to review the whole of the data in a true perspective.

As in the case of the Pyramid chronology, and the Egyptian King Lists' fictitious presentation of this as applied to Egyptian history, so in the case of the promised Messiah, the Egyptians claimed that He had already come in the person of their god Osiris.[1]

In this connection the reader is referred also to ¶¶ 447 and 451, Section II, of this Chapter.

¶ 353. ANCIENT EGYPTIAN BELIEF IN THE PYRAMID'S MESSIANIC SYMBOLISM.

Egyptian religious texts identify Osiris as Messiah and that His mission is symbolised by the Great Pyramid. Mr. Marsham Adams—in the work[2] to which we have already referred (¶¶ 108, 109, and 245)—shows that the imagery of the Egyptian religious texts identifies the Pyramid's Grand Gallery as symbolising the New Way of " Truth in Light," opened up by the Passion of Osiris, and the Queen's Chamber as associated with his female counterpart—variously goddess-mother and goddess-wife—Isis. Hence that Isis is referred to as " Queen of the Pyramid " (¶ 26) and " the Mistress of the commencement of the year " ;

Osiris and Isis in Egyptian interpretation of Pyramid symbolism. Grand Gallery —the new way opened up by the Passion of Osiris. Osiris by association, in this case, being Lord of the Pyramid and Master of the year. Reference to Plate XLI, Figs. K, L, and M, and Plates XLIIa and XLIII, and ¶¶ 325, 328, and 339–341 will indicate the importance of this identification ; particularly in relation to the geometry of the year-circle shown on the Plates to which reference has been made.

The Queen's Chamber— the Chamber of Isis, the divine Mother —" the Chamber of the New Birth." According to Marsham Adams, the Egyptians recognised the Queen's Chamber to symbolise " the place of ' Isis, the divine Mother, the Queen of the Pyramid,' as an ancient papyrus calls her ; corresponding to the place where the soul receives its second birth."[3] Thus the Queen's Chamber is identified by Adams from the Egyptian texts as " The Chamber of the New Birth," and the horizontal passage " from " the Queen's Chamber as

The threshold of the Grand Gallery " the Crossing of the Pure Waters of Life." " the Path of the coming forth of the Regenerate Soul " ; the threshold of the Grand Gallery, and of the Queen's Chamber Passage, being " the Crossing of the Pure Waters of Life."

---

[1]Moret, " Gods and Kings of Egypt," pp. 71, 72.
[2]" The Book of the Master."   [3]Ibid., p. 116.

Having regard to the fact that the date of the Nativity is given by the level of the Queen's Chamber, and the date of the Crucifixion and Resurrection of our Lord by the commencement of the Grand Gallery (¶¶ 328, 338, and 340), the identity between the symbolised datings of our Lord's life and the Pyramid symbolism, as attached to the traditional Messiah of the Egyptian texts, cannot be accidental.

Egyptian interpretation of symbolism as applied to our Lord, confirmed by Pyramid Queen's Chamber and Grand Gallery datings for the Nativity and Crucifixion, 4 B.C. and 30 A.D. respectively.

¶ 354. THE EGYPTIAN "LIGHT OF THE SECOND BIRTH."

Quoting from the "Book of the Dead," Marsham Adams continues[1] :— "'I am Yesterday,' says Osiris in the 64th Chapter, said to be almost coeval with the founder of the (Pyramid) building. . . . 'I am the Dawn,' he continues, 'the Light of the Second Birth, the Mystery of the Soul. . . .'" Referring, again, to the Great Pyramid, the same author states[2] :—" In another papyrus (we read) : ' The God of the Universe is in *the light above the firmament ; and His symbols are upon the earth.*'" Comparing this with Jeremiah xxxii, 18–20, quoted in ¶ 268 in relation to the Great Pyramid as "The Lights " and " Revelation-Measures," we see that Adams makes the identity complete.

Egyptians proclaimed Osiris as " the Light of the Second Birth." " The God of the Universe," and " the Light." " His symbols upon the Earth." Compare Jeremiah's signs and wonders " of God in Egypt. The Pyramid " the Lights," " Revelation-Measures."

Continuing with his synchronistic comparison of the symbolism of the "Book of the Dead " and the symbolic features of the Pyramid's Passage System, Adams shows that the 1st Ascending Passage and the Grand Gallery jointly form " the Double Hall of Truth "; the former, symbolising St. Paul's way of " the Yoke of the Law," being " the Way of Truth in Darkness "; and the latter, symbolising St. Paul's " New and Living Way," being " the Way of Truth in Light," and " the Luminous Chamber of the Orbit " (refer ¶¶ 244–249).

The " Book of the Dead " identifies the two Ascending Passages as " the Double Hall of Truth." (1) " Truth in Darkness," (2) " Truth in Light "; St. Paul's (1) " Yoke of the Law," (2) " New and Living Way."

¶ 355. THE GATE OF THE WAY OF ASCENT.

When we come to consider the Entrance Passage and the Descending Passage, the meaning and intention of the structural and mathematical symbolism are very clear. The Entrance Passage descends from its Entrance Doorway, continuing in descent towards the natural rock. The Ascending Passage, however, provides a new direction before descent accelerates[3] below and beyond the " influence " of the Pyramid's masonry courses. Before the " natural " rock is reached, descent has to pass through the " influence lines " of the 1st Ascending Passage. The beginning of this passage was hidden by the limestone ceiling block dislodged at the time of the operations of Al Mamoun's workmen (¶¶ 191 and 203). Access to this passage was sealed by the granite plugs before the building had been raised many courses (¶ 208). The " influence lines " and the change of direction

Entrance and Descending Passage angle symbolises acceleration in descent. The " influence lines " of the hidden 1st Ascending Passage. Spiritual " influence " symbolised as opening out a new way and changing direction from constrained descent to constrained ascent. The Divine purpose indicated by chronological relations.

---

[1]" The Book of the Master," p. 160.   [2]Ibid., p. 143.
[3]Acceleration in descent is suggested by the angle of descent. The angle of repose for hard limestone, well dressed, on hard limestone, well dressed, is 21° (from relationship $\mu=\tan a$, μ being coefficient of friction=0.38, as Kempe's " Engineers' Year Book," 1923, p. 121, and a angle of repose, therefore 21°).
The Descending Passage angle is 26° 18' 9".63.

The seven
times.

are related to the dates of the *Seven Times*, 2520 solar, and 2520 calendar years, from the epoch of Scalar chronology, and to the date of the Exodus (¶¶ 328 and 344–346).

Access to the
way of ascent
hidden from
the beginning.
The spiritual
means of
access pro-
vided from the
beginning.
Confirmed by
the literary
tradition of
the Egyptians.

From a physical point of view, access to the 1st Ascending Passage and the Grand Gallery was impossible, through the granite plugs, when the existence of the access way was hidden by the limestone lintel. The "Book of the Dead," according to Marsham Adams, refers to the symbolism of the limestone lintel and the granite plugs, as the "Hidden Lintel of Justice" and "the Gate of the Hill," *i.e.* Ascent. Access by initiation and guidance was possible. Thus, as quoted by Adams, the adept cries : "I have come through the Hidden Lintel, I have come like the Sun through the Gate of the Festival,"[1] *i.e.* the festival of the *Seven Times*, in solar years chronologically defined at the roof junction of the Passages (¶¶ 344–346).

¶ 356. THE PASSAGE OF THE HIDDEN LINTEL.

The "cul-de-
sac" of the pre-
elected route
of the Exodus
becomes the
highway of
Israel's
salvation.
The symbolism
of the granite
plug.
"The
inhabitants
of Palestina
. . . shall be
as still as a
stone ; till
thy people
pass over."

Such is the ancient Egyptian interpretation of the Pyramid's symbolism applying to the Exodus of Israel. In the case of Israel's Exodus, the appointed access to the Land of Promise was hidden. The obvious route seemed easy, yet annihilation lay hidden at its end. Such is the symbolism of the Descending Passage. "God led them not the way of the land of the Philistines, although that was near . . . but God led the people about through the way of the wilderness of the Red Sea. . . . Pharaoh will say . . . they are entangled in the land, the wilderness hath shut them in. . . . And Moses said unto the people, Fear ye not, stand still, and see the salvation of the Lord. . . . Thou stretchedst out Thy right hand, the earth swallowed them (the Egyptians). Thou in Thy mercy hast led forth the people which Thou hast redeemed : Thou hast guided them in Thy strength unto Thy holy habitation. The people shall hear and be afraid : sorrow shall take hold on the inhabitants of Palestina . . . by the greatness of Thine arm they shall be *as still as a stone* ; till Thy people pass over, which Thou hast purchased" (Exod. xiii, 17 to xv, 16).

Israel's
apparent
"cul-de-sac"
geographically
located by the
Great Pyramid
and indicated
as the pre-
elected high-
way of salva-
tion—Pi-
hahiroth to
Bethlehem.

Referring to Plate LXIII, the reader will see the significance of the above. Here the angle of the Ascending Passage projected from the Great Pyramid as true bearing from the East—or, to be precise, as the azimuth North of East—is directed across the Israelitish passage of the "sea of reeds" straight to Bethlehem, the place of the Nativity.[2]

¶ 357. THE PYRAMID'S MATHEMATICALLY DEFINED NEGATIVE SYMBOLISM.

The symbolism
of the two
alternatives at
the Exodus.

The alternative to the salvation of Israel at the crossing of "the sea" and the giving of the Law, was by "way of the land of the Philistines"

---

[1] "The Book of the Master," p. 171.

[2] The scientific reader who cares to check the bearing on the latter place should find it exact. If he can correct it to the site of Gethsemane, Calvary, or, preferably, the tomb of the Resurrection, the parallel circumstances of the Exodus of Israel and the Exodus of our Lord would be fittingly symbolised.

PLATE LXIII.

THE ROUTE OF THE EXODUS.

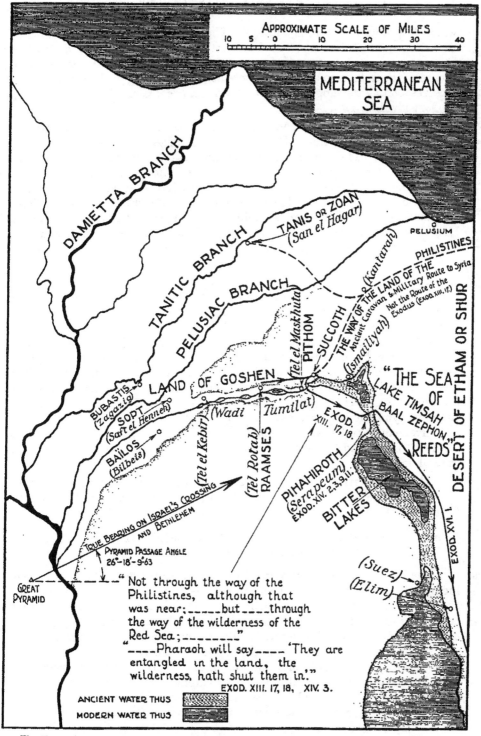

The Extension of the Gulf of Suez shown is from Sir Hanbury Brown's "Map of Goshen." In view of Sir Gaston Maspero's theory of the Exodus Route, it was surprising to find that his map ("Dawn of Civilisation," p. 349) shows the Extension above given.

The apparently obvious way meant return to, and continuance in " bondage," under the negative law of oppression —the way of " descent."

The Pyramid's Descending Passage symbolism of " upside-down-ness "—the inversion of the conditions of spiritual man.

Descent also symbolises negation.

Passing from positive influence to negative influence below the base level.

The two laws in opposition.

The symbolism of accelerated descent, impact, and enforced change of direction.

The negative symbolism of the Subterranean Chamber.

The representation of the Egyptian religious texts relating to the negative symbolism of the Subterranean Chamber.

The hall of Chaos, and annihilation.

The Pyramid's geometrical definition of negative and positive areas of influence.

which " was near " (Exod. xiii, 17). The remainder of this verse explains that the result of this course would be a return to bondage, the way of descent. Descent continued meant an increase in everything negative to spiritual progress ; or to turn to a parallel symbolism, a spreading of the roots without a corresponding development of the branches (refer Gen. xlix, 22, in relation to Gen. xlviii, 4, 11, 14–21).

Fittingly, then, the chronological base line of the Descending Passage symbolism is the roof line. It is this line that defines the points 2500, 2520, and 3000 A.K. The roof line is thus mathematically defined as the negative floor—thus symbolising the inversion of the conditions of spiritual man. Thus defined, the Descending Passage continues into a larger field of negative symbolism. Its continued descent is negative. Its passing below the base level is negative, passing from the influence of the realm of Divine Love and its Law of mutual Love, into the complete influence of the realm of spiritual negation, and its Law of mutual distrust, natural passion, and internecine strife.

Thus the passage continues to its abrupt end, where accelerated descent meets with the impact of the narrow doorway leading to the Subterranean Chamber (Plate LXIV). In the latter, again, the symbolism is entirely negative. The ceiling is smooth—symbolic of the negative floor—and the actual floor rough, like a miniature quarry, or the inverted ceiling of a natural cavern—symbolic of the negative ceiling. Thus, one ancient Egyptian religious picture depicts a chamber with madmen inverted, walking like flies on its ceiling, and beating in their heads with axes, the blades of which are held towards them (all negative symbols). The Descending Passage is therefore symbolic of " upside-downness " in relation to spiritual progress ; the Subterranean Chamber symbolising the hall of Chaos, the only exit from which is the " Dead-End " Passage ending in the natural rock—symbolic of annihilation.

The mathematical symbolism of negative and positive is clearly indicated in relation to the square aroura and the rectangular arouræ of Plate XLIIa (Fig. A).

¶ 358.   THE RHOMBOID OF DISPLACEMENT IN RELATION TO THE DESCENDING PASSAGE.

The symbolism of accelerated descent ending in arresting shock and schism, and the evolution of chaos in a new direction.

The over-shadowing of spiritual conditions influences material conditons relating to the spiritual in man.

The Descending Passage symbolism of accelerated descent and of arrest-ing impact at the doorway to the horizontal rock passage very plainly conveys the intention. It clearly symbolises a sudden arresting shock effecting rupture or schism to permit of the continuing of the fragments along the new direction, and in the narrower and shallower passage. The change of direc-tion, from descending to horizontal progression, clearly relates to a change, not necessarily in spiritual conditions, but in the material relations immediately affecting those spiritual conditions. The emphasis of the material aspect of the symbolism is conveyed by the fact of the symbolism occurring in the natural rock and in connection with the Descending Passage *in* the natural rock. Thus the Descending Passage and the natural rock symbolism relate Descent :— Spiritual in to the spiritual in man subordinate to the material in man, as the Pyramid man sub-ordinate to and its internal symbolism relate to the material in man subordinate to material in man. the spiritual *external to* man (by a process of spiritual " induction," implied Ascent :— in I Peter ii, 4–6). Material in man sub-ordinate to the spiritual external to man.

Now the Pyramid's astronomical and geometrical indications have shown The symbolised influence of us, in conjunction with the Grand Gallery's structural symbolism, the clear the Grand Gallery intention of defining the creation of a " field of influence " in the history of rhomboid of displacement. mankind (¶¶ 249 and 262–266). The initial date of this " field of influence " is defined in relation to the Pyramid's displacement factor (¶ 350 (8)). This, we saw, symbolises the " influence " of the Messiah, who " purchased " The influence of the Messiah (refer Exod. xv, 16, quoted in ¶ 356) the right to exercise this " influence " purchased by his " displace- by this " displacement,"[1] Daniel's " cutting off " (¶¶ 335 and 336 and Dan. ment." ix, 26). The Gallery symbolism indicates the intention of the creation of the The influence exerted to " field of influence." The symbolic and astronomical indications depict the hasten God's purpose in hastening[2] of man's material development to effect God's purpose, through relation to man. Christ, in relation to spiritual development. In the scientific sense, the The Pyramid's symbolism creation of a new " field of influence " brings into being " a high Potential " defines its relative to the former " field." A " high Potential " in the former " field " purpose in terms of has a disturbing influence on the media or entities in the former " field " modern science. until they become attuned to the new " field." This disturbing effect leads " The field of influence." to the breaking-up of old coalitions or groupings—temporary chaos—until The creation readjustment is effected as the result of experimental groupings. When the of " higher potential." regrouping process is complete, the new " field " is a field of equilibrium, and its controlling units are " attuned."

Now, the creation of the symbolised " field of influence " is not depicted The process of readjustment. as upsetting spiritual equilibrium in the realm symbolised by the Grand The new Gallery during the period of the creation of the " field," *i.e.* following equilibrium. the defined interval of 1530 years (¶ 350, category 9). This confirms the Becoming " attuned." symbolism here as relating to the Elected Spiritual Groupings then existing The purpose of Christ's in the world—already attuned to receive a higher " Potential."[3] In the atonement. Descending Passage, however, the symbolism indicates arresting shock, rupture, or schism, and change of direction—chaos and blind following of the " line of least resistance," in the only direction possible—as the initial date of " the field of influence," overhead in the Grand Gallery, is about to be passed under. The symbolical indications are that the approach towards the overshadowing of the " field of influence " of the rhomboid of displacement in the Grand Gallery is signalised by the disturbing effect of this approach upon the symbolism of the Descending Passage.

---

[1] The roof of the Ascending Passage, at the Crucifixion dating, is raised 286.1 P″ vertically—the value of the Displacement Factor applied in an *upward* direction and in " 6 " overlapping stages, symbolic of " work " done in the process of " raising " (Plate XXXII). Refer John xii, 32; I Cor. vi, 14; 2 Cor. iv, 14; Acts ii, 24, 32; iii, 15, 26; v, 30, 31; xiii, 30–37. Refer also Plates XLb (Fig. C) and XLIIa, for the rhomboid of displacement.

[2] Daniel xii, 4 defines the process in operation at " the time of the end " in the following words: " Many shall run to and fro, and knowledge shall be increased."

[3] Refer I Cor. vi, 14, " will raise us up by His own Power."

¶ 359. THE SYMBOLISM OF ARRESTING SHOCK AND SCHISM.

The datings of the symbolism of descent arrested by shock and schism.

The Descending Passage datings associated with the symbolism of arresting shock and schism are as given on Plate LXIV. The datings of the vertical through the following three points are as follows :—

The initial period of the Reformation in Europe.

				A.K.	A.D.	
Descending floor ending	..	..	..	5504.61174,	1506	The initial period
Descending axis ending	..	..	..	5516.30455,	1518	of the Reforma-
Descending roof ending	..	..	..	5527.99736,	1529	tion in Europe.

The unbiassed historical aspect of the Reformation in relation to the symbolism. History and Pyramid symbolism agree.

Anyone reading an *unbiassed historical* account of the conditions leading to and shaping the Reformation in Europe cannot but admit that the symbolism and the historical phase of the period thus defined by the Pyramid's chronology completely agree. It is needless to discuss the rights and wrongs of the matter. What we have to deal with is an historical fact. As such, the conditions symbolised in the Pyramid occurred as the symbolism indicates they should occur, and at the dates defined.

The influence of intuition in sensing the symbolical index of historical changes. Pyramid's symbolism at the time of the Reformation.

Elsewhere (¶¶ 265, 266, and 358) we have referred to the scientific aspect of the creation of the " field of influence." It was suggested that minds attuned to working along lines synchronising with the lines of the created " field " could transmute ideas from the latter into terms tangible to themselves and others of their time. We have also shown that Egyptian symbolism (¶ 357) adopted and pictured the " upside-downness " symbolised by the Descending Passage and Subterranean Chamber. In this connection, it is of interest to find that " an apocalyptic pamphlet of 1508 shows on its cover the Church upside-down. . . ."[1] A few lines lower, the same authority quotes from Lindsay as follows : " It was into this mass of seething discontent that the spark of religious protest fell—the one thing needed to fire the train and kindle the social conflagration."

¶ 360. THE ARRESTING OF DESCENT AT THE EXPENSE OF HIGH POTENTIAL.

" The scattering of the power "; the spreading or distributing of spiritual energy, accompanied by " the publishing of the Gospel among all nations." The arresting of Descent followed by the lowering of high Potential.

The joint symbolism of the Grand Gallery and the Descending Passage indicates that the arrested Descent in the latter is effected at the expense of an ultimate lowering[2] of the Spiritual " Potential " in the former. The symbolised effect, however, is indicated as due to the spreading or distributing of spiritual energy throughout the world, the final acceleration of " the scattering of the power of the Holy people " (Dan. xii, 7). Thus St. Paul (2 Thess. ii, 3) states—

" That time shall not come except there come a falling away first " ;

---

[1] Enc. Brit. (11th Edit.), Vol. XXIII, p. 10.
[2] The same idea of lowering one to be the means of raising up another is contained in Romans xi, 11-15.

PLATE LXIV.

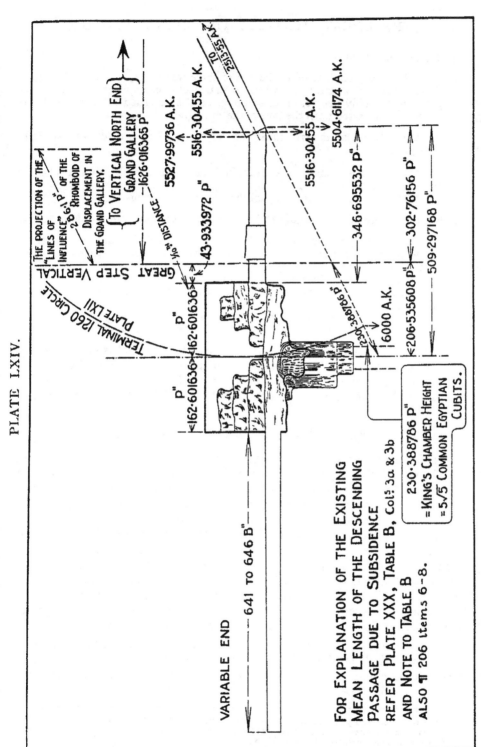

"That time shall not come except there come a falling away first."

"Scattering of the power" accomplished at end of seven times of Gentile dominion, in December 1917 A.D.

and Daniel (xii, 6–9)—

> "How long shall it be to the end of these wonders ? . . . it shall be for a time, times and a half,[1] and when he shall have accomplished to scatter the power of the holy people, all these things shall be finished . . . the words are closed up and sealed until the time of the end" (refer ¶¶ 347–349).

Parallel predictions are those of our Lord. His disciples ask Him (Mark xiii)—

> "Tell us, when shall these things be ? and what shall be the sign when all these things shall be fulfilled ? . . .
> "The Gospel must first be published among all nations."[2]

Following which our Lord places:—
(1) Deliverance of Jerusalem.

(2) Distress amongst nations and perplexity.

(3) Men fearful of the portents.

(4) His own Advent.

Luke xxi, 24, here adds a detail of Christ's answer to that given by Mark xiii—

> ". . . and Jerusalem shall be trodden down of the Gentiles until the times of the Gentiles be fulfilled . . . and there shall be signs . . . upon the earth distress of nations, with perplexity . . . Men's hearts failing them for fear, and for looking after those things which are coming on the earth. . . .
> "And then shall they see the Son of man coming in a cloud with power and great glory.
> "And when these things begin to come to pass, then look up, and lift up your heads ; for your redemption draweth nigh" (refer ¶¶ 268–270).

The hopeful promise in the signs.

Grand Gallery symbolism of lowered potential.

The "falling away" or lowering of Spiritual Potential is symbolised by the overlapping descent, in *seven* stages, of the South end wall of the Grand Gallery, bringing the Gallery roof down to the level of the roof of the low passage to the Antechamber (Plates XXXVa, XXXVI, XLIII, and LVIII).

¶ 361. THE REDEMPTION OF MAN'S LOST FACULTY.

Chaos, then Redemption.

Man's dominion according to the Covenant.

Man's privileges lapse as result of his breaking the Covenant.

God's pre-established clause relating to the redemption prior to the creation of man.

Hence His early promise of renewal.

This all confirms that Chaos must precede Redemption. For the full significance of this in relation to the Pyramid's symbolism, the reader is referred to ¶¶ 255, 256, and 268–270. The "contract" symbolism inferred in ¶¶ 255 and 256 relates properly to the Covenant concerning the free-will relationship of man to God (Gen. ii, 17), whereby man should retain the Spirit of God and have complete dominion "over the earth" (Gen. i, 26). By breaking the Covenant man lost his complete dominion "over the earth" (Gen. iii, 17–19), and forfeited his right to retain the Spirit of God. Nevertheless, God, in His foreknowledge, had already the means prepared for the redemption of man's forfeited inheritance—"the Lamb[3] slain from the foundation of the world" (Rev. xiii, 8)—and hence gave His promise of the renewal of the Covenant in Gen. iii, 15 (compare Rom. xvi, 20).

Confirmed to Abraham.

"Confirmed for one week to many by Christ."

The promise was "confirmed" (Gal. iii, 17) to Abraham (Gen. xii, 3)— "in thee shall all families of the Earth be blessed." All that this blessing means to mankind is contained in the words of St. Peter concerning Jesus Christ (Acts iii, 21)—

---

[1] The terminal 1260 years of the 7 times of the Gentiles. Refer ¶¶ 343 and 344.
[2] Clearly accompanying "the scattering of the power of the holy people."
[3] "By whom God created all things," Eph. iii, 9.

" Whom the heaven must receive until the times of restitution of all things, which God hath spoken by the mouth of all His holy prophets since the world began."

St. Paul (Rom. viii, 21–23)—

" . . . the creature itself also shall be delivered from the bondage of corruption into the glorious liberty of the children of God. For we know that the whole creation groaneth and travaileth until now. And not only they, but we ourselves also, which have the first-fruits of the Spirit, even we ourselves groan within ourselves, waiting for the adoption, *to wit*, the redemption of our body."

Here we have the promise of the restoration or redemption of the lost faculty (¶¶ 164, 255, 256, 350, and 351)—complete dominion over the earth. This promise, viewed in light of modern science (refer ¶ 270), gives a new significance to Christ's own promise concerning faith moving mountains (Matt. xvii, 20).

¶ 362. THE GAP IN THE HARMONY OF CREATION.

All this clearly relates to the spiritual control of the realm of energy that forms the reservoir of the realm of matter. Man's spirit emanates from the Spirit of God. The Spirit of God is the source of all energy ; and energy is the reservoir of matter. Hence that our Lord could walk on the waters, rebuke the spirit of the storm, and calm the storm by so rebuking ; hence that He could pass untouched, unfelt, through the crowd lusting for His destruction. The Spirit that God has given man, man may retain. The condition is simple. Man must first obey the command of Christ, " love one another." This is the Law of God's Universe of Spirit, Energy, and Matter ; all three but varying expressions of the one Divine Energy, Love.

Man may choose to obey his natural impulse—man's predatory law of " the survival of the fittest." This law came into force as the result of man breaking the Covenant. Hence the penalty, already waived, however, if man but chooses to accept God's love. For " God is Love," and nothing may retain His Spirit unless by accepting Christ, His Principle of Love. For " the wages (penalty) of sin (non-love) is death (withdrawal of the Spirit) ; but the gift of God is eternal life "—retention of His Divine Spirit.

To the normal man, this may sound all so wearily threadbare, after centuries of reiteration. But the truth is constant, and lives by reiteration ; whereas falsehood varies and dies. For, consider all God's visible science, it is all wonderful ; it shows marvellous love for the things created. The scientist can see reflected in the created work the Creator's glorious love for His labour. The further science adventures beyond the contaminated matter immediately environing man, the smoother is God's Law seen in operation. The nearer man's physical environment—his forfeited dominion— is examined, the less harmonious is God's Law as seen in operation. For there is a gap in the continuity of God's harmony of Creation, and the gap is man. Man should be the earth terminal for receiving, conveying, and distributing the spiritual energy throughout man's intended dominion, the earth. But man has lost the faculty, having forfeited it.

¶ 363. THE RESTITUTION OF ALL THINGS.

Therefore, as Professor Soddy has stated: "After a hand-to-mouth existence, civilisation has come in for, and has learned how to *spend*, an inheritance it can never hope to restore."

" . . . reaps what it has not sown, and exhausts, so far, without replenishing." Or, as St. Paul has stated: "The whole of creation groaneth and travaileth . . . waiting for the adoption, *to wit*, the redemption of our body."

Christ, by His " displacement," has neutralised in Himself the " displacement " effected by man. By so doing He has " purchased " our " redemption," and is shortly coming to put His kingdom in order.

Such is the earnest message of the Old and New Testaments from Genesis to Revelation. Such is the earnest message of the Pyramid's portrayal of God's science delivered in terms of man's science, as understood in modern times—defined by the Pyramid, and by the Scriptures, as " the time of the end." The closing epoch of the latter period the Scriptures describe as " the consummation," that is, the period preceding or including the final " times of the restitution of all things." St. Paul has declared that " that time shall not come except there come a falling away first." This is defined by the Pyramid's symbolism of the Gallery roof overlapping downwards to the low roof of the Passage to the Antechamber. The symbolism of lowered potential extends inwards to the King's Chamber, and chronologically includes the period of current and immediate future history. The symbolism therefore relates to the period of current history as the period of " the consummation," and, for this reason, is worthy of serious consideration.

SECTION IC.—" THE CONSUMMATION."

¶ 364. THE COMPLETE " DISPLACEMENT " CYCLE.

In the preceding Section Ib we have seen that the Pyramid " displacement " value, in successive outstanding phases of representation, symbolises :

(a) Man's displacement,[1] whereby man lost his inheritance, *i.e.* dominion   Man's dis-
over the Earth ;   placement
                                                                              " separation."

(b) Christ's displacement to restore the spiritual conditions whereby   Christ's dis-
man should regain his inheritance ; and   placement
                                                                        " reconcilia-
                                                                        tion."

(c) The displacement from the existing conditions to higher conditions   The final
to effect the complete " restitution of all things."   displacement
                                                                        " restitution."

The last phase was seen to be concerned with the Scriptural period of   The termina-
" the Consummation."   This period was seen to be related to current history,   tion of the
and to be symbolised by the Antechamber and King's Chamber and their   cycle in rela-
                                                                        tion to the
connecting passages (¶ 363).   King's Cham-
                                                                        ber symbolism.

The significance of all this is clearly illustrated by the plan of these   Traversing of
passages and chambers shown on Plate XXXVb.   Here the reader will see   the displace-
                                                                        ment distance
that the axis of the whole Pyramid passage system is displaced 286.1022 P"   within the
eastwards from the central North to South vertical plane of the Pyramid.   Pyramid first
                                                                        possible in the
The latter plane passes directly in front of the empty coffer in the King's   King's Cham-
Chamber.   At no point within the Pyramid masonry, and along the Entrance   ber.
                                                                        The " restitu-
and 1st Ascending Passages and Grand Gallery, can one deviate far from the   tion " symbol-
                                                                        ised as effected
plane of displacement until the King's Chamber is reached.   At no point   by traversing
                                                                        the displace-
                                                                        ment distance
                                                                        in the King's
                                                                        Chamber,
[1]Man's displacement (a) was "foreknown" to God before the Creation of the World.   There-   reaching a
fore Christ and His " displacement " (b) were pre-elected, to effect (c) the " restitution."   This   point in front of
pre-election is a manifestation of the Love of God.   It is the First Principle—including all other   the coffer—the
Principles of His processes of Creation—of the Creation of the Universe in relation to man.   symbol of " the
                                                                        Open Tomb."
St. Paul, in Ephesians iii, 10, implies it was the purpose of the Creator to hide His complete
foreknowledge, and the Alpha and Omega of His design, from the heavenly powers—His spiritual
servants operating as free-will agents in His work of Creation ; that it was His purpose progressively
to reveal the extent of His foreknowledge and design, obviously to neutralise the effects of the free-
will tendencies of His spiritual agents, and to teach His agents by the Revelation.   Hence Paul
declared that it was the object of his own mission " to make all men see what is the fellowship
of the mystery, which from the beginning of the world hath been hid in God, WHO CREATED
ALL THINGS BY JESUS CHRIST ;
" To the intent that now UNTO THE PRINCIPALITIES AND POWERS IN HEAVENLY
PLACES might be known by the Church the manifold wisdom of God,
" According to the eternal purpose which He purposed in Christ Jesus our Lord ; . . .
" . . . Of whom the whole family in heaven and earth is named. . . . " (Eph. iii, 9–15).
" The stone which the builders rejected, the same is become the head of the corner ; this is
the Lord's doing and it is marvellous in our eyes " (Ps. cxviii, 22 and Matt. xxi, 42).
This central theme of Creation—the pre-elected " displacement " of Jesus Christ—has been
seen to form the harmonic theme upon which all laws—spiritual and material—of man's universe
have been formulated.   This is the message conveyed by the Pyramid's " displacement " factor.
It is the message given by the Old and New Testaments, and crystallised again by St. Paul in
the words, " In whom (Christ) are hid all the treasures of wisdom and knowledge " (Col. ii, 3).

within the Pyramid masonry can the true central North to South vertical plane be reached until the King's Chamber is entered. Here a change of direction occurs. Advancing along the Chamber one is able to stand in the vertical plane hitherto unattainable. In the position thus reached one is standing directly in front of the coffer—the symbol of " the open tomb."

¶ 365. EGYPTIAN RELIGIOUS TEXTS ON THE SYMBOLISM OF THE KING'S CHAMBER.

Ancient Egyptian religious texts concerning the prophetic symbolism of the King's Chamber.

Its Messianic predictive indications adopted as applied to Osiris.

The final mystery symbolised by the King's Chamber.

The mystery of the change.

The Resurrection symbolism.

" Restitution " to be effected by the promised Messiah of Ancient Egyptian prophecy.

The agreement between the prophetic indications of the Old and New Testaments and the symbolism of the Pyramid—particularly in relation to the restoration of the " displacement " symbolised in the King's Chamber—is confirmed by the Pyramid imagery of the Egyptian " Book of the Dead." Thus, concerning the features of the promised Messiah's Passion, as applied to Osiris in the " Book of the Dead," and identified with the symbolism of the King's Chamber, Marsham Adams writes as follows :—[1]

" Then comes the final mystery (associated with the symbolism of the King's Chamber) when the tomb is opened and the body is raised in immortality. ' Hail thou, my Father of Light,' we read in the Chapter (cliv) which tells us how the body of the Holy One shall not see corruption. ' I come having this my flesh freed from decay ; I am whole as my Father, the self-begotten God, whose image is in the incorruptible body. Do thou establish me. Do thou perfect me as the Master of the Grave. This,' so the chapter proceeds, ' is the mystery of the change, in the body, of the life that comes from the destruction of life.' And as we read, we cannot but recall the words of the Apostle : ' Behold, I show you a mystery, for the dead shall be raised incorruptible and we shall be changed.' So, too, in the final chapter of this book we hear the resurrection proclaimed as with a trumpet blast, as in the innermost Chamber of the House (i.e. the Great Pyramid) we find the Open Tomb. ' I have opened the doors,' exclaims the Osiris-soul, now glorious in the house of Light, and united indissolubly with the Creator. . . . ' I have opened the doors. . . . Well is the Great One who is in the coffin. For all the dead shall have passages made to Him through their embalming,' when their body in the flesh shall be raised in incorruption."

Breasted on Ancient Egyptian (Pre-Israelitish) Messianism.

In such manner has the Pyramid's allegory been applied by the Egyptians to their god Osiris, as the Pyramid's chronology has been applied to their King Lists and the fictitious history of Egypt. This is the true explanation of what Professor Breasted has observed concerning " Messianism (in Egypt) nearly a thousand years before its appearance among the Hebrews." [2]

¶ 366. "THE BOOK OF THE DEAD" AND ITS "MYSTERY OF THE OPEN TOMB."

The significance of the King's Chamber as the Chamber of Orientation in Egyptian religious imagery.

The final chapter of the " Book of the Dead," according to Marsham Adams, relates to the King's Chamber and its orientation. This confirms the significance which we attach to the change of direction on entering the

[1] " The Book of the Master," pp. 186, 187.
[2] " Development of Religion and Thought in Ancient Egypt," p. 212.

King's Chamber (¶ 364). In Egyptian imagery, Osiris, the god of the dead, The plane of "displacement" in relation to the "open coffer."
is associated with " the West " and is the " god who came from the West,"
that is, into the East. In the Great Pyramid, the vertical North to South
plane of the apex is the vertical plane of Divine Harmony, the apex being
the symbol of the Messiah (¶¶ 268 and 350 (10)). The central vertical plane
of the Pyramid's symbolism of human history is 286.1 P″ eastwards, and the
" Open Tomb " in the King's Chamber is just slightly westwards from the
vertical plane of Divine Harmony.

Read in conjunction with Hebrew prophetic and ancient Egyptian
religious imagery, the indication of the symbolism would seem to be as
follows :—

Rising from the Open Tomb and stepping towards the East, the Resur- The symbolism of the King's Chamber and the Messianic restitution.
rected One stands in the vertical plane of Divine Harmony. Having appeared
in the plane of mankind's history, and in the flesh of man, and having suffered
death as man, the Messiah, in His resurrection, potentially restored mankind The Egyptian conception of Osiris and "the West" as related to the promised Messiah and the symbolism of the "displacement."
to the plane of Divine Harmony. In order to effect the complete restitution
of mankind and his dominion, and to prepare mankind for the change,[1]
through alternations of order and chaos in ascending degrees of intensity,
it was proclaimed that He would eventually return at an " appointed time "
to hasten the completion of His work. This return, *in the Pyramid's symbolism*, is symbolised as a coming " from the West." Hence the traditional
location of Osiris, and the tradition concerning his " coming from the West,"
i.e. into the East, *in terms of Pyramid symbolism.*

In all essential features, the ancient Egyptian prophecy concerning the Ancient Hebrew, Egyptian, and Pyramid symbolism in agreement.
Messiah, the Hebrew Old and New Testament prophecies relating to Him,
and the Pyramid's symbolism are in complete agreement. Hence the
significance of the following statement [2] by Marsham Adams, concerning the
final chapter of the Egyptian " Book of the Dead " :—

> " One chapter and one chamber yet remain—the Chapter of Orientation The King's Chamber, "the Mystery of the Open Tomb," and the triumph over death and the grave in the Egyptian "Book of the Dead."
> and the Chamber of the Grand Orient (*i.e.* the King's Chamber) beneath the
> Secret Places of the Most High (*i.e.* the Chambers of Construction). . . . Again
> and again is celebrated the Mystery of the Open Tomb . . . the resurrection
> of Osiris-Ra, the Uncreated Light. Four times is that Gospel of ancient Egypt
> proclaimed in the chapter which bears the title of the Orient. ' The tortoise
> dies ; Ra lives ! ' Death is swallowed in Light ; God lives for evermore. ' O
> Amen, Amen,' so continues that chapter of mystery, ' Amen, who art in heaven,
> give thy face to the body of thy Son. Make him well in Hades. It is finished.'[3]
> Thus ends the strange and solemn dirge of Egypt."

¶ 367. THE SYMBOLISM OF THE FLOOR PLANE OF THE KING'S CHAMBER.

From all the related factors discussed, one thing is becoming increasingly The symbolism of the chronological plane of the "consummation" and "restitution."
evident. This is that, according to ancient Egyptian tradition, the Pyramid's

[1]" I go to prepare a place for you."
[2]" The House of the Hidden Places," pp. 245, 246.
[3]Compare John xix, 30.

symbolism presents the horizontal plane of the floor from the Great Step to the King's Chamber as defining the *chronological* plane of what Hebrew prophecy describes as " the consummation of the age " and " the times of the restitution of all things." The date given by the point at which the chronological floor line of the Grand Gallery produced intersects this horizontal plane should therefore be a definite beginning for the terminal period. This point is geometrically defined as a period of 1000 lunations from the Great Step dating (¶ 234 and Plate LXVa and b). The latter dating is midnight ending 25th January 1844 A.D. (¶¶ 237 and 242), giving the former dating as 2nd December 1924 A.D. If the symbolic indications have been read correctly—and the ancient Egyptian traditional interpretation and Scripture prophecy have seemed to confirm the reading—then the period immediately succeeding 2nd December 1924 is indicated as a period relating to an accelera- tion towards " the consummation of the age."

The Pyramid's chronological plane indicating the dating of the current year is also defined by its level—and the numerical value of that level in terms of the Pyramid's external unit—as symbolising the uniting of the two scales of the material universe, 10 and 7 (¶ 351). This fittingly symbolises the period of " the restitution of all things," the restoration of man's forfeited " dominion over the earth," and the restoration to the plane of Divine Harmony. That it will pain and perplex man to be submitted to the process of restoration ; that it will hurt and perplex those furthest from God's Harmony ; that, in consequence, the process will appear a hurtling to destruc- tion—are all affirmed by the predictions of our Lord. Such apparent tragedies were related by Him as the signs of His " preparation." For this reason He forewarned His servants, " and when these things begin to come to pass, then look up, and lift up your heads ; for your redemption draweth nigh " (Luke xxi, 28).

¶ 368. AN ENLARGED SCALE SYMBOLISM OF THE " CON-SUMMATION."

Hebrew prophecy, however, in the Old and New Testaments, defines that the " consummation " is to be effected prior to 6000 A.K.=2001 A.D. The Pyramid chronology gives the latter dating at the centre of the Granite Leaf in the Antechamber (¶¶ 229-247 and Plates XXXVI, XLb, XLIIa, and LXVa). The symbolism, however, extends beyond this, through the Antechamber and the 2nd Low Passage, into the King's Chamber. This continuation of the symbolism, we have seen, is particularly indicated as relating to the " consummation " (¶¶ 364-366). It seems certain, then, that the scale of chronological representation relating to the Antechamber and King's Chamber, and their connected passages, is not the same as that of the general scalar chronology system ending at the centre of the Granite Leaf.

Now a change of scale implies a purpose for the change. Such purpose can only be related to the circumstances of the period to which the Pyramid's message was designed to apply. Such circumstances, then, should be defined by the symbolism of the new scale of chronological representation as applied to the chambers here. The circumstances are symbolised as related to the period of the "consummation." The symbolic indications define that they apply to a period prior to 6000 A.K. By extending beyond the latter date, they define that the symbolism is represented to a larger scale than that of the general scalar chronology system.

¶ 369. THE UNIT VALUE OF THE NEW SCALE.

The enlarged scale of representation, therefore, requires a new time value for the unit of measure. The Pyramid inch unit of measure must, however, remain the unit of representation. The time value for the Pyramid inch in the new representation seems to be indicated by the tradition preserved by the religious texts of the ancient Egyptians. These texts (¶¶ 365 and 366) associate the King's Chamber and its connected Passage and Antechamber with the final mystery of the promised Messiah. The latter, we saw, was falsely claimed by the Egyptians as having lived and died in the person of their god, Osiris, the "Lord of the Year," and the "Lord of the Pyramid" (¶¶ 26, 353, and 354). The complete geometry of the King's Chamber and Antechamber is entirely related to the year circle on the scale of one Pyramid inch to a day. This scale would represent the whole symbolism from the Great Step to the King's Chamber South wall as applying to a period of less than 1½ years, which is obviously too short a period. In the Osirian texts, however, we have the formula "one day counts for a month" (¶ 60), the month in this case being the calendar month of 30 days.

It appears certain, therefore, that this is the scale that should apply to the symbolism the Egyptians identified as relating to the final mystery of Osiris, but which, in the original ancient prophecy, was identified as symbolising the final mystery of the long-predicted Messiah "awaited since the Creation of the World" (¶ 352).

The time value for the Pyramid inch, as a horizontal measurement on the King's Chamber floor level, should be a calendar month of 30 days.

¶ 370. THE GEOMETRY OF THE ENLARGED SCALE CHRONO-
      LOGICAL SYMBOLISM.

The next step in relation to the new large scale chronological representation is to find the zero of the new scale, and its chronological connection with the original or general scalar chronology system. The primary geometrical necessity is that the zero date of the new scale must be related—by a co-ordinate connection—to the same date on the general scalar chronology system, and that the new zero on the general scalar line must be defined by a perpendicular to that line, as in the case of 0 A.K.

Now, St. Paul defines the period of the "consummation" as preceded by a "falling away" (¶ 360). The latter, we saw, is symbolised by the overlapping descent of the Gallery at its South wall (¶ 360). The termination of this feature—at the Entrance Doorway of the 1st Low Passage, leading to the Antechamber—is appropriately the commencement of the symbolism of the period of the " consummation."

The geometrical data defining the commencement of the 1st Low Passage are as given on Plate LXVb. From this it will be seen that the basal data are confirmed by the resulting check data; the latter emphasising the intention. This, as we have had frequent occasion to point out, is the Pyramid's method of defining its basal data as intentional. In this case, the perpendicular DF from the general scalar chronology line ACV defines the zero date, at F, of the new chronological representation as 25758.24925 days from midnight (Pyramid time) ending 25th January 1844 A.D. Here 25758.24925 is half the side of a square of area equal to the area of the quadrant of a circle of 365242.465 circumference. The latter circle, in days, represents 1000 years, this symbolically indicating that the associated measurement relates to the Millenium of Messianic prophecy, and to the ushering in of the epoch of chaos preceding the Messianic 1000 years. The date thus defined as ushering in the period of chaos is the zero date for the Entrance Doorway to the 1st Low Passage, the point F on Plate LXVa. As calculated from the astronomically defined dating for the Great Step, the dating for the commencement of chaos is 5th August 1914. The precise time indicated is 3.54 a.m. (Greenwich Mean Time) of 5th August, or 4 hrs. 54 mins. after the expiry of Great Britain's ultimatum to Germany. It marks the first day of Britain's entry into the Great European War.

¶ 371. THE SYMBOLISM OF THE PERIOD OF CHAOS AND ITS SHORTENING.

Resulting from the geometry of Plates XXXVb (and Addendum), XLIII, and LXVa, the sum of the lengths of the 1st Low Passage preceding the Antechamber and of the 2nd Low Passage leading from the Antechamber is 153.00 P″. This is as shown on Plate LXVb, item IId. Now, as explained (in ¶¶ 338–341 and 351) the number 153, when indicated in connection with Messianic symbolism, relates to Christ's elect, their trials, and their mission in being prepared for and in preparing for the " restitution." A period of chaos had to precede the " restitution " (¶¶ 360 and 363). Such a condition of chaos is symbolised by the stooping progress necessary in the two Low Passages.[1] These are symbolised as relating to a single historical phase of chaos by the associated measure of 153 P. inches, representing 153 calendar months of 30 days; the Antechamber being defined as inserted to symbolise a truce, or temporary cessation of the chaos, until some purpose, indicated by its symbolism, is served. As the geometrical measures and indications fixing the measures and datings of these passages cannot possibly be subjective to any mere *theory* of prophecy fulfilment, it should be a matter of importance

---

[1]Refer ¶ 354, where the 1st Ascending Passage, of greater height vertically, and of slightly greater height perpendicularly, than the horizontal passages, was seen to be symbolic of the period and conditions of progress under " the Yoke of the Law."

to find the initial date indicated for the truce in chaos symbolised by the Antechamber.

Now the date geometrically defined at point F (Plate LXVa) for the beginning of the 1st Passage of Chaos is the 5th August 1914 (G.M.T., 3.54 a.m.). The defined geometrical length of the Passage is 51.956349 P″ (Plate LXVb). This indicates a period of 51.956349 months of 30 days, ending at 8.28 p.m. (G.M.T.), 10th November 1918—14 hrs. 32 mins. before the Armistice ending the Great European War. The date indicated is that of the termination of the German Empire. This officially ended at the abdication of the Kaiser on 9th November, and was made effective by his flight to Holland on 10th November, and by the acceptance of the Armistice terms on 11th November 1918.[1]

Period of Chaos defined as beginning at 5th August 1914, "cut short" by the "truce" symbolism at 10th November 1918.

The 1st day of Britain's entry into the War to the date of the termination of the German Empire.

¶ 372. THE PRINCIPAL DATINGS OF THE ENLARGED SCALE SYMBOLISM.

The complete list of datings for the Low Passages, Antechamber, and King's Chamber, resulting from the geometry of Plates XXXVb (Addendum), XLIII, and LXVa, is stated on Table XXIX, and facing the latter, on Plate LXVc. Although the zero dating for the large scale chronology system is certainly intended to be the 5th August 1914, dating for the 1st Low Passage Doorway, the carrying back of the horizontal floor line to the Great Step has been supposed to indicate *a retrospective application.* The scale has, therefore, been applied backwards to the Great Step, the dating for the latter, *on the enlarged scale of representation,* being 8 hrs. 35 mins. a.m. (G.M.T.), 2nd August 1909.

Principal datings in order :— "Retrospective"; "Great Step" 2nd August 1909. "Zero dating" :— Low Passage Entrance Door, 5th August 1914. Low Passage ends 10th November 1918, when Antechamber "truce in chaos" symbolism begins.

Since the Antechamber has been seen to symbolise a period of " truce in chaos "—beginning 10th November 1918—the dating for the termination of this symbolism should be a matter of importance to the reader. The date is 4 a.m. (G.M.T.), 29th May 1928 A.D. At the point defining this date the 2nd Low Passage begins, symbolising the termination of the enforced " truce in chaos." The symbolism, thereafter indicated by the extent of the 2nd Low Passage, defines the resumption of chaos from 29th May 1928 A.D. to 16th September 1936 A.D.

Antechamber "truce in chaos" ends 29th May 1928, when Low Passage symbolism is resumed, until the dating 16th September 1936, at threshold of King's Chamber.

The latter dating, at the threshold of the King's Chamber, is within a week of 5935 A.K. Reference to Table XXX and Plate LXVI shows that this important dating is 2520 solar years from the date of Jeremiah's prophecy from prison at the central date of Nebuchadnezzar's siege of Jerusalem,

The latter dating is 5935 A.K., the termination of the final chronological stage of the Seven Times of Gentile domination, from the date of Jeremiah's prophecy concerning the rule of Christ as King of Israel.

---

[1]" The Times," Tuesday, 12/11/1918—" Diary of the War " :—
   "Nov. 7. Bavarian Republic proclaimed.
    Nov. 9. Foch received German Envoys.
            Abdication of Kaiser.
            Chancellor Prince Max resigned.
            Berlin revolution.
    Nov. 10. Kaiser's flight to Holland.
            British at Mons.
    Nov. 11. Armistice terms accepted."

PLATE LXVa.

THE GEOMETRICAL RELATIONS OF THE GREAT STEP AND THE FIRST LOW PASSAGE TO THE ANTECHAMBER.

THE NUMERICAL RELATIONS OF THE GEOMETRICAL FEATURES IN PLATE LXVa.

I. GIVEN GEOMETRICAL DATA. p"

(a) PRECESSIONAL CIRCUIT LEVEL   1702·5924907

DEDUCT STEP $\Big\{ \dfrac{286·102256}{4\times10^9} \times 6000^2 \Big\}$ 2·5749199

CO-ORDINATE VALUE

IN PRECESSIONAL FORMULA AS ¶234

LEVEL OF TOP OF STEP   1700·0175708

PLATE XI.b,FIG.C., LEVEL OF FOOT OF STEP 1664·1914217

STEP HEIGHT AB   35·8261491

(b) AD = $n+a$ = 25×SIDE OF AROURA SQUARE

    PYD. SOLAR YEAR VALUE

    = $\dfrac{25\times103·032997\ p''}{365·242465}$ = 70·5236972

REPRESENTING 70·5236972 PYD. SOLAR YEARS

OR 25×103·032997 DAYS

= 2575·824925 DAYS = ½ SIDE SQUARE,

¼ AREA OF CIRCLE 365·242·465 DAYS CIRC.ᴿᶜᵉ OR 1000 YEARS.

(e) RESULTING BF = m = 60·960165 p"

    = 61·037 B"

FROM STRUCTURAL & MEASURED DATA } 61·010 B"

    REFER ¶211d

II. RESULTING GEOMETRICAL CHECK DATA.

(a) ED = a = 2·5231298 p"

REPRESENTING 2·5231298 PYD. SOLAR YEARS

OR 921·554142 DAYS

4 TIMES KING'S CHAMBER HEIGHT

= 921·554142 p"

(4 × 230·3887855 p") REFER ¶310a & PLATE LXIV

(b) AC = y = 80·8510460 p"

REPRESENTING 80·8510460 PYD. SOLAR YEARS

OR 29530·235 DAYS

WHEREAS 1000 LUNAR MONTHS

= 29530·588 DAYS

(c) AE = n = 68·0005674 p"

REPRESENTING 68·0005674 PYD. SOLAR YEARS

OR 24836·694858 DAYS

WHEREAS MANETHO'S EGYPTIAN DIVINE DYNASTIES

= 24836 YEARS REFER PLATE XVI TABLE A

(d) RESULTING SUM OF TWO LOW PASSAGES:—

    1ˢᵗ LOW PASSAGE 51·956349 p"

    2ⁿᵈ LOW PASSAGE 101·046327 p"

    153·002676 p"

    REFER ¶¶ 338-341 & 351

TABLE XXIX.

THE PYRAMID'S ASTRONOMICALLY DEFINED DATINGS FROM THE GREAT STEP TO THE KING'S CHAMBER.

Reference Letters, Plates XXXVa & XXXVb.	Distances from Face of Great Step.	Distances from 1st Low Passage Entrance Door.	Equivalent Date (A.D.). Time stated in terms of Greenwich Mean Time.		Description of Structural Point.
	P″.	P″.	Hour.	Date.	
B.	0.0	— 60.960165	8·35 a.m.	2nd Aug., 1909.	Face of Great Step and Central Vertical Axis of Pyramid and Queen's Chamber.
—	39.418249	— 21.541916	9·43 p.m.	27th Oct., 1912.	Overhang of South Wall overlapping of Grand Gallery.
—	43.933972	— 17.027193	8·19 a.m.	12th March, 1913.	Vertical to North Wall of Subterranean Chamber. (Plate LXIV).
—	49.000000	— 11.960165	4·41 a.m.	11th Aug., 1913.	Vertical to drop in floor of Subterranean Chamber. (Plate LXIV).
F.	60.960165	± 0.000000	3·54 A.M.	5th AUG. 1914.	Entrance Doorway to 1st Low Passage to Antechamber.
R.	103.032997	+ 42.072832	8·20 a.m.	18th Jany., 1918.	Vertical to South Wall of Queen's Chamber. (Plate XXXVb).
K.	112.916514	+ 51.956349	8.28 P.M.	10th NOV., 1918.	End of 1st Low Passage at North Wall of Antechamber.
L.	126.143804	+ 65.183639	4·7 p.m.	12th Dec., 1919.	Limestone floor of Antechamber ends. Granite floor begins.
—	133.233124	+ 72.272959	8·26 a.m.	11th July, 1920.	Face of 1 inch deep Boss on North Face of Granite Leaf.
—	134.233124	+ 73.272959	8·26 a.m.	10th Aug., 1920.	Countersunk North Face of Granite Leaf.
—	141.336942	+ 80.376777	11·11 a.m.	12th March, 1921.	Centre of Granite Leaf as defined by Boss Face and South Face of Leaf.
—	141.836942	+ 80.876777	11·11 a.m.	27th March, 1921.	Centre of Granite Leaf as defined by countersunk North Face and South Face of Leaf.
—	149.440760	+ 88.480595	1·56 p.m.	10th Nov., 1921.	South Face of Granite Leaf.
—	171.046657	+110.086492	6·10 p.m.	20th Aug., 1923.	Centre of Antechamber.
—	177.660302	+116.700137	4 a.m.	6th March, 1924.	Centre of Granite Floor of Antechamber.
—	206.535608	+145.575443	10·13 a.m.	20th July, 1926.	Vertical to centre of Subterranean Chamber. (Plate LXIV).
M.	229.176801	+168.216636	3·53 P.M.	29th MAY, 1928.	South Wall of Antechamber, 2nd Low Passage begins.
N.	330.223128	+269.262963	1·14 A.M.	16th SEPT., 1936.	2nd Low Passage ends on Threshold of King's Chamber.
—	369.137244	+308.177079	11·28 a.m.	27th Nov., 1939.	Vertical to South Wall of Subterranean Chamber. (Plate LXIV).
—	433.256125	+372.295960	1 a.m.	4th March, 1945.	Centre of King's Chamber.
P.	536.289122	+475.328957	0·45 A.M.	20th AUG., 1953.	South Wall of King's Chamber.
—	1010 to 1015	+949 to 954	July, 1992 to Dec., 1992.		Vertical to termination of "Dead End" Passage from Subterranean Chamber. (Plate LXIV).

TABLE OF EVENTS THAT OCCURRED ON THE INDEX DATINGS OF THE SPECIAL CHRONOLOGY SYSTEM.

2nd August 1909.—The Czar of Russia, after visit to Cherbourg on 31st July and conference with the French President, met King Edward and inspected the Fleet at Cowes. On 3rd August, meeting of Imperial Colonial Defence Conference.

27th–28th October 1912.—The Battle of Lüle Burgas began. This was the decisive battle of the 1st Balkan War. "Britannica Year Book" says, re this date, "'Turkey in Europe' had ceased to exist."

12th March 1913.—Austro-Russian crisis. Agreement arrived at on the 11th to commence demobilisation on the 12th of forces concentrated on frontier.

10th August 1913.—Treaty of Bucharest, ending 2nd Balkan War. Mr. J. L. Garvin ("These Eventful Years," Vol. I.) says: "They had made Armageddon inevitable at a second and not distant remove . . . within a year the world was in flames."

4th–5th August 1914.—Great Britain's entry into the Great War.

31st January 1917.—German decision re unrestricted submarine warfare communicated to the United States of America; bringing the U.S.A. into the Great War on 5th–6th April 1917. Germany's "methodical" madness precipitates her downfall.

18th January 1918.—The Bolsheviks, after demanding a Republic of Soviets, dissolved the Russian Constituent Assembly.

"The Times" summed up the situation in the words, "Bolshevik Autocracy Supreme."

This date is defined by the Pyramid's symbolism as an epoch of Jewish destiny.

10th–11th November 1918.—Flight of Kaiser and German acceptance of Armistice terms. The Great War ends.

12th December 1919.—First conference of Powers (Great Britain, U.S.A., France, and Italy at Downing Street) to consider the post-war crisis in its wider international sense; defined by "The Times" as the first sign of "Realities" forming the basis of consideration.

11th July 1920.[1]—Allies final terms (Treaty of Sèvres) forwarded to Turkey in form of an ultimatum for *immediate* acceptance (Spa).

10th August 1920.—Turkish Treaty signed at Sèvres, on anniversary of the Treaty of Bucharest (1913, see above). Ottoman Empire reduced from 613,500 sq. miles in 1914 to 175,000 sq. miles.

Russo-Polish crisis. Labour "Council of Action" in conference (forenoon) with Premier re Labour threat to call a national strike if Allies support Poland. Premier's statement (afternoon) in House of Commons.

12th March 1921.—Conference on Turkish question at St. James's Palace. Modifications in Treaty of Sèvres communicated to Greek and Turkish delegates. Also separate Italian-Turkish agreement; Italy withdrawing from Anatolia.

10th–11th November 1921.[1]—Terms of agreement arrived at between British Cabinet and Irish delegates drafted in form of a Cabinet Note and sent to the Ulster leaders. This note formed the basis of the Irish Settlement.

This is also the end of the period of the abnormal labour and commercial depression that began in the summer of 1920; the terminal dating of the Granite Leaf, and the eve of the important Washington Conference on Armaments.

6th March 1922.—"The Times" (7th March)—"*Egypt under the New Order.*"

"The Sultan of Egypt presided over the first Council of his new Cabinet. . . . It is noteworthy that the British financial advisor was absent. . . . This is the first occasion on record since the advisorship was created . . . in 1883."

23rd January 1923.—Lord Curzon's ultimatum to the Turks re the Mosul Question (Lausanne Conference).

20th–21st August 1923.—Franco-British crisis re Ruhr question and Reparations. French Note (Poincarè Government), replying to Lord Curzon's firm Note, delivered at the British Embassy, Paris, 9 a.m., 21st August.

12th December 1923.—Re Dawes' Enquiry and Reparations. United States Government adopts British Proposal and takes first steps in setting up of Dawes' Enquiry Committee. "The Times" defines this as "A New Beginning."

5th–6th March 1924.—The Caliph (late Sultan) and his son compelled to leave Turkey. The whole House of Othman expelled by 7th March. The definite termination of the Ottoman Empire.

29th May 1924.—Papal Bull published inviting all Catholics to travel to Rome in "Holy Year" (1925) to obtain indulgences for their sins.

"The Times" of 31st May, re "New Tangier (International) Regime," notes the departure on 29th May 1924 of the last British diplomatic representative and the arrival of the new Italian Minister, and draws attention to the importance Italy attaches to Tangier.

2nd December 1924.—A dating of the Pyramid's General Chronology System, indicated as an important epoch (p. 384). The continuation of the General Chronology floor-line, 286 P. inches, the Pyramid's Displacement Factor, from the point defining this date, gives a point on the North Wall of the King's Chamber.

During 1924 a Labour Government displaced the Baldwin Conservative Government for 286 whole days, exclusive of the dates of handing over. The new Parliament met for the first time on 2nd December 1924.

The same date was that of the signing of the Trade Treaty between Britain and Germany.

17th April 1925.—New French Cabinet (Painlevé Ministry—Briand and Caillaux), following the fall of the Herriot (Socialist) ministry, completed and presented to the President of the Republic.

---

[1] To pass under the Granite Leaf (consisting of an upper and a lower stone) one has to adopt a stooping attitude; this implying, in the symbolism, the infliction of a double "yoke" or burden. The fact that the Granite Leaf is wholly internal to the Antechamber seems to imply that the symbolism relates to "domestic" trouble, in addition to concurrent world instability—evidenced by the initial Turkish datings, the terminal Irish dating, and the subsequent Disarmament Conference. The Granite Leaf period—11th July 1920 to 10th November 1921—coincides with the duration of the intense crisis of the Irish problem, and covers the period of abnormal labour depression that followed the post-war "boom."

An important annual dating, 11th–12th December (dependent on Leap Year):—

    11th December 1917—Jerusalem delivered from Gentile domination.
    12th December 1919—"Realities," as in above Table.
    12th December 1923—"A New Beginning," as in above Table.

The 11th–12th December is a Displacement Factor dating, being 286 days from the following Autumnal Equinox. The Great Pyramid's astronomical chronograph defines the Autumnal Equinox as a zero dating. The reader will find the full significance of this developed and elaborated in Booklets Nos. 1, 2, and 3 of "Talks on the Great Pyramid."

Attention is directed to the significance attaching to the number of datings that coincide with important Turkish events, and also to the fact that the Russian, German, and Austro-Hungarian Empires (remnants of the Eastern and Western branches of the Roman Empire—Lord Bryce, "Holy Roman Empire"), and the Turkish Ottoman Empire fell in the course of the Great War or as the direct result of post-war crises.

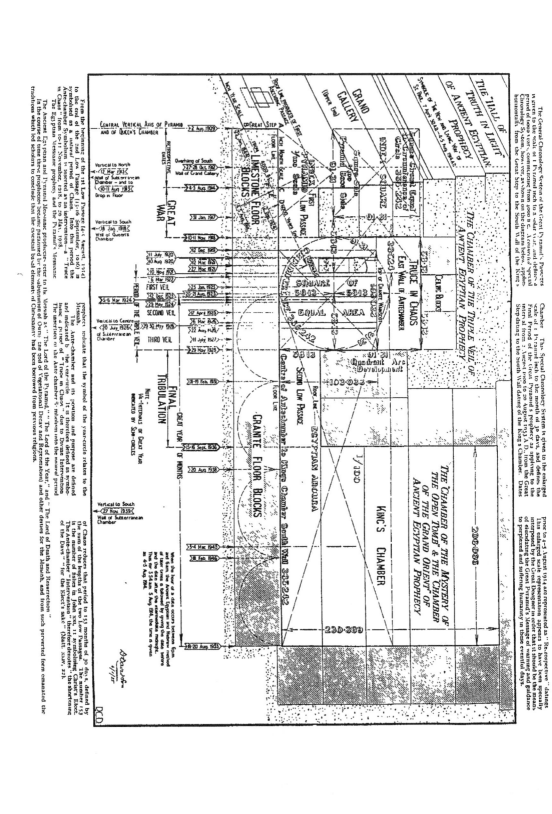

PLATE LXVc.

[To face Table XXIX, p. 392.

TABLE XXX.

THE CHRONOLOGY OF JUDAH'S CAPTIVITIES, AND THE INITIAL STAGES OF THE PERIOD OF GENTILE DOMINATION OVER JERUSALEM.

THE INITIAL PHASE OF THE SEVEN TIMES OF THE GENTILES.

A.K.	B.C.	Regnal Years beginning Nisan		
		Nabopolassar / Nebuchadnezzar	Nebuchadnezzar	Jehoiakim
3393				
1396	604	Nabopolassar 20th year	Nebuchadnezzar 1st year co-rex	Jehoiakim 3rd year
1397	603	21st year	2nd year co-rex	4th year
	602		co rex	5th year
1398	601	Nebuchadnezzar 1st year		6th year
	600	2nd year		7th year
3403	596	7th year	Ezekiel's Captivity Epoch. →	11th year
3404	595	8th year	JEHOIACHIN.	1st year of Captivity
3405	591	9th year	Zedekiah 1st year	2nd year
	594		2nd year	
3409	593	13th year	5th year	6th year
	590			
3412	587	16th year	8th year	9th year
3413	586	17th year	9th year	10th year
3414	585	18th year	10th year	11th year
3415	584	19th year	11th year	11th year
3416	583	20th year		13th year
3417	582			
3428	581	32nd year		13th year
3439	571	43rd year		36th year
3440	561	EVIL MERODACH 1st year		37th year of Captivity
3441	560			
3442	559			
	558			

With the fall of the Assyrian Empire, Nabopolassar became "King of Countries." Hence when Nebuchadnezzar became co-rex, he became "King of Babylon" (refer Dan. i, 1), as in the case of Cyrus, and Cambyses, co-rex.

Jerusalem besieged, and Daniel carried unto captivity (Dan. i, 1), 3rd year of Jehoiakim.

THE FIRST CAPTIVITY OF JUDAH. 70 years' desolation (Jer. xxv, 11, 12; and II Chron. xxxvi, 21-23) date from beginning of 1st year of Nebuchadnezzar, co-rex, 3395½ A.K., to beginning of Hebrew "1st year" of Cyrus the Persian, 3465½ A.K.*

Nabopolassar died before the completion of a regnal year.

In accordance with Babylonian and Assyrian custom in such cases, the last year of { Jeremiah xxv, 1, terms the accession year of
Nabopolassar was the accession year of Nebuchadnezzar. The 1st year of { Nebuchadnezzar the 1st year of that king;
Nebuchadnezzar was reckoned from the following Nisan. { = 4th year of Jehoiakim.

> * The Hebrew reckoning of chronology—from the Book of Daniel—in relation to the Medo-Persian Conquest of Babylon, places Daniel's "Darius the Mede" for the "1st year of the known reign of Cyrus as "King of Countries," i.e., from the Spring (3465½ A.K.) following the Capture of Babylon by the Medes and Persians. Hence 1st year (Hebrew reckoning) and year Cyrus (Persian reckoning).
> To explain the apparent complication of an otherwise obscure "Darius the Mede," consider a modern analogy.
> An observer with the Staff of the King of Serbia at the closing stages of the Great War might date all the outstanding historical events, terminating the War, dated from the Spring following the latter's capture of Babylon as stating the regnal years of "Darius the Mede" under the new conditions.

Jehoiakim reigned 11 years.

JEHOIACHIN REIGNED THREE MONTHS, "in the 8th year of Nebuchadnezzar," II Kings xxiv, 12. THE (2nd) GREAT CAPTIVITY OF JUDAH.

The 1st year of "our captivity" in Ezekiel { Refer also II Kings xxv, 27, for the same reckoning.
reckoned from the month Nisan. { Ezekiel i, 2; and xl, 1, 25th year of Captivity = 14th year after city smitten.

Zedekiah's reign began "at the return of the year" following the Great Captivity, II Chron. xxvi, 9 and 10. Refer also II Kings xxiv, 3-17, and compare Jeremiah xxvii, 1. II Kings, xxiv, 8-12 shows the presence of Nebuchadnezzar at Jerusalem.

Comparison with II Chron. xxvi, 9 and 10 shows that after Nebuchadnezzar had returned to Babylon "he sent for" the dethroned Jehoiachin at the beginning of Zedekiah's 1st year.

The beginning of the 70 years' Divine Indignation (Zech. i, 12):
The Shekinah departed from the Temple in the 6th month of the 6th year of the Captivity (Ezekiel viii, 1; ix, 1-8).

Jerusalem besieged by Nebuchadnezzar in his 17th year, siege beginning in the 10th month of the 9th year of Zedekiah (Jer xxix, 1), the 10th year of the Great Captivity. Siege lasted for 18 months.

Mid-date { Jeremiah in prison (10th year Zedekiah=18th Nebuchadnezzar; Jer xxxii, 1) prophesies.
of the { His prophecy relating to the returning of Israel and Judah from Captivity, the restoration of Jerusalem, and the dawn of
siege. { the Age of Righteousness under Christ as the King of all Israel (Jer. xxxv, 12-19).

The City broken up on Day 9 month IV, 11th year Zedekiah (II Kings xxv, 3 and 4, and Jeremiah xxxix, 2).
The Temple and Jerusalem burnt on Day 7, Month V (II Kings xxv, 8; refer also Jeremiah xxxix, 8), 19th year Nebuchadnezzar.
Ezekiel (xxxiii, 21) defines the year when the city was "smitten" as "the 11th year of our Captivity."
THE 3rd AND LAST CAPTIVITY OF JUDAH.

Ezekiel reckoned this year as the 2nd year after "city smitten," since year 1 of "city smitten" is year 12 of "our captivity"; adding 13 to both reckonings, we get, year 14 after the "city smitten" =year 25 of "our captivity." (See below).

Day 10, Month I, Ezekiel's vision of the Millenial Temple (Ezekiel xl), 600 years, exactly, to Palm Sunday in Crucifixion year. In the 25th year of our captivity.....in the 14th year after the city was smitten." (Ezekiel xl, 1).
Both reckonings include in their respective first years—reckoned from Day 1, Month I—the determining events of these years

Last year of Nebuchadnezzar, from his dated records

1st year of Amil-Marduk (Evil Merodach)=37th year of the Captivity of Jehoiachin (II Kings xxv, 27).

Jehoiachin released on Day 27, Month XII (II Kings xxv, 27).

Heavy black line signifies a gap in statement of continuity in years

TABLE XXXI.

	LUKE xxi, 5-7.	MARK xiii, 1-4.	MATTHEW xxiv, 1-3.
A.D. 30. A.D. 70.	And as some spake of the temple, how it was adorned with goodly stones and offerings. He said, as for these things which ye behold, the days will come, in which there shall not be left here one stone upon another, that shall not be thrown down.	And as He went forth out of the temple, one of His disciples saith unto Him, Master, behold, what manner of stones and what manner of buildings? And Jesus said unto him, Seest thou these great buildings? There shall not be left here one stone upon another, that shall not be thrown down.	And Jesus went out from the temple, and was going on His way: and His disciples came to him to show Him the buildings of the temple. But He answered and said unto them, See ye not all these things? Verily I say unto you, There shall not be left here one stone upon another, that shall not be thrown down.
	And they asked Him, saying Master, when therefore shall these things be? and what shall be the sign when these things are about to come to pass?	And as He sat on the Mount of Olives over against the temple, Peter and James and John and Andrew asked him privately, Tell us when shall these things be? and what shall be the sign when these things are all about to be accomplished?	And as He sat on the Mount of Olives, the disciples came unto Him privately, saying When shall these things be? and what shall be the sign of Thy coming, and of the consummation of the age?
	(Verses 8 to 19 concerning the things to happen till the end.)	(Verses 5 to 13 concerning the things to happen till the end.)	(Verses 4 to 14 concerning the things to happen till the end.)
	Verses 9 to 12. *But the end is not immediately.* Then said He unto them,	*Verses 8 to 13.* *But the end is not yet.*	*But the end is not yet.*
A.D. 30 to A.D. 1936.	Nation shall rise against nation, and kingdom against kingdom: and there shall be great earthquakes, and in divers places famines and pestilences; and there shall be terrors and great signs from heaven.	For nation shall rise against nation, and kingdom against kingdom: there shall be earthquakes in divers places: there shall be famines: these things are the beginning of travail.	For nation shall rise against nation, and kingdom against kingdom: and there shall be famines and earthquakes in divers places. But all these things are the beginning of travail.
A.D. 30 to 135.	But before all these things they shall lay their hands on you.	They shall deliver you up to councils.	Then shall they deliver you up unto tribulation....
A.D. 30 to A.D. 1936.		And the gospel must first be preached unto all nations.... He that endureth to the end, the same shall be saved.	And this gospel of the kingdom shall be preached in the whole world for a testimony unto the nations: and then shall the end come.
A.D. 70.	*V. 20.—But when ye see Jerusalem compassed with armies, then know that her desolation is at hand.*	*V. 14.—But when ye see the abomination of desolation standing where he ought not—(let him that readeth understand—*	*V. 15.—When therefore ye see the abomination of desolation, which was spoken of by Daniel the prophet, standing in a holy place—(let him that readeth understand.*
	Then let them which are in Judæa flee unto the mountains; and let them which are in the midst of her depart out; and let not them that are in the country enter therein.	*Then let them that are in Judæa flee unto the mountains: and let him that is on the housetop, not go down, nor enter in, to take anything out of his house; and let him that is in the field not return back to take his cloke.*	*Then let them that are in Judæa flee unto the mountains: let him that is upon the top not go down to take out the things that are in his house: let him that is in the field not return back to take his cloke.*
	For these are the days of vengeance, that all things that are written may be fulfilled.		
A.D. 70 to 1936.	*Woe unto them that are with child and to them which give such in those days.*	*But woe unto them that are with child and to them that give suck in those days.*	*But woe unto them that are with child and to them that give such in those days.*
A.D. 70 to 1936.	*For there shall be great distress upon the land, and wrath unto this people.*	*For those days shall be tribulation, such as there has not been the like from the beginning of the creation which God created until now, and never shall be.*	*For then shall be great tribulation such as hath not been from the beginning of the world until now, no nor ever shall be.*
A.D. 1918 to 1936.	*And they shall fall by the edge of the sword, and shall be led captive unto all the nations....until the times of the Gentiles be fulfilled.*	*And except the Lord had shortened the days, no flesh would have been saved; but for those sake, whom he chose,*	*And except those days had been shortened, no flesh would have been saved: but for the elect's sake*
A.D. 1918 to 1936.		*He shortened the days.*	*those days shall be shortened.*
A.D. 1918 to 1936.	And there shall be signs in sun, moon, and stars; and upon the earth distress of nations, in perplexity for the roaring of the sea and the billows; men fainting for fear, and for expectation of the things which are coming on the world; for the powers of the heavens shall be shaken.	But in those days, *after that tribulation, the sun shall be darkened, and the moon shall not give her light, and the stars shall be falling from heaven, and the powers that are in the heavens shall be shaken.*	*But immediately, after the tribulation* of those days, the sun shall be darkened, and the moon shall not give her light, and the stars shall fall from heaven, and the powers of the heavens shall be shaken: and then shall appear the sign of the Son of man in heaven; and then shall all the tribes of the earth mourn.
Prior to 16th Sept., 1936 A.D.	And then shall they see the Son of man coming in a cloud with power and great glory.	And then shall they see the Son of man coming in clouds with great power and glory.	And they shall see the Son of man coming on the clouds of heaven with power and great glory.

* "The tribulation" commenced at the Roman siege, while "tribulation of those days" must refer to its end.

In the above, our Lord was referring to Daniel's prophecies concerning the long period of desolation to be visited upon Jerusalem (Dan. xii, 11), concerning the final period of great tribulation (Dan. xii, 1; "a time of trouble such as never was since there was a nation even to that same time, and at that time thy people shall be delivered (Luke xxi, 5-7, and concerning the resurrection and restitution (Dan. xii, 2; 3, 13). He began with the events then imminent, the destruction of Jerusalem and the Temple (Luke xxi, 5-24; ...). He then sketched, in a few words (Luke xvi, second half of verse 27, and verse 24, compared with Mark xiii, 15 and 26 the nature of the events to happen between A.D. 70 and the "time of restitution." This is the portion of the narrative in which occurs the shortening of the days. The latter expression is applied in relation to a period of tribulation "such as hath not been from the beginning of the world until now, no nor ever shall be," clearly defining the same period of tribulation denoted in Dan. xii, 1.

When we remember that both Daniel and our Lord are referring specifically to the tribulation of the Jews, which began at A.D. 70, and has been extended, for the Jews, to the present time, we see clearly that our Lord, in referring to the shortening of the days, defines this as applying to the culminating phase of the tribulation on the Jews. Therefore, having made this identification, He follows with the statement, "immediately after the tribulation of these days...........then shall appear the sign of the Son of Man........"

PLATE LXVI.

THE SEVEN TIMES (2520 YEARS) OF GENTILE DOMINATION IN RELATION TO JERUSALEM

THEIR SUCCESSIVE STAGES OF BEGINNING ♦ THEIR SUCCESSIVE STAGES OF ENDING

THE LAST TIME (i.e. 360 YEARS)

Dec. 1197 A.D. — Dec. 1557 A.D.

SUCCESSIVE STAGES OF ENDING ... SUCCESSIVE STAGES OF BEGINNING

EPACT OF 75 SOLAR YEARS. — 3½ TIMES (LUNAR) = 1260 LUNAR YEARS — 3½ TIMES (LUNAR) = 1260 LUNAR YEARS — REFER TABLE XXX

MAXIMUM PERIOD FOR DANIEL'S 1335 YEARS = 1260 LUNAR + 75 SOLAR — SINCE 2520 SOLAR = 2520 LUNAR + 75 SOLAR — 630 LUNAR YEARS — 630 LUNAR YEARS

THE PERIOD OF THE CONSUMMATION

(b) "The Gospel of the kingdom shall be preached in the whole world for a testimony unto all nations ♦ then shall the end come" (TABLE XXXI)

(a) "Nation shall rise against nation ♦ kingdom against kingdom ... the beginning of travail. Then shall they deliver you up into tribulation" (Tribulation continues)(TABLE LXXI)

(c) "When ye see Jerusalem compassed with armies (the abomination spoken of by Daniel) her desolation is at hand" (TABLE XXXI)

(d) "They (the Jews) shall fall by the sword ♦ be led captive into all nations ... until the times of the Gentiles be fulfilled — then shall be great tribulation such as hath not been etc." TABLE XXXI

TRIBULATION

IV Continued

DANIEL'S "TIME OF THE END" "The words are closed up and sealed until the time of the End" DAN XII. 9.

CHRIST SAID — (MATT. XXI. 43-44) "The kingdom of God shall be taken from you (the Jews) and given to a Nation bringing forth the fruits thereof (i.e. (b) above — The Spreading of the Gospel) and whosoever shall fall upon this stone shall be broken: but on whomsoever it shall fall it will grind him to powder" (REFER DAN IX.)

THE HISTORICAL PERIOD OF THE RELEASING OF THE SCRIPTURES FOR GENERAL USE. THE PERIOD OF PROPHECY INTERPRETATION AND THE SPREADING OF THE GOSPEL TO ALL NATIONS.

"Bringing forth the Fruits"

THE 3½ TIMES OF A — BELOW THE PERIOD OF "THE SCATTERING OF THE POWER OF THE HOLY PEOPLE" (A—BELOW)

(g) "Then shall they see the Son of Man coming" (TABLE XXXI)

(e) "Except those days had been shortened no flesh could have been saved; but for the elect's sake those days shall be shortened" (TABLE XXXI)

(f) "But in those days, after that tribulation ... distress of nations, perplexity" (TABLE XXXI)

THE PROCESS OF ACCOMPLISHING (A—BELOW)

VI ♦ VIII Continued

A "How long shall it be to the end of these wonders? ... for a time, times ♦ a half (i.e. 3½ times or 1260 years — here lunar reckoning as above) and when he hath accomplished to scatter the power of the holy people, all these things shall be finished." DAN XII. 6 ♦ 7

VI — "And for the overspreading of abomination"

VII "He shall make it desolate."

VIII "Even until the consummation, that determined shall be poured upon the desolate."

IV "And unto the end of the war desolations are determined."

III "And the people of the prince that shall come shall destroy the city ♦ the sanctuary ♦ the end thereof shall be with a flood."

II "from commandment to rebuild Jerusalem unto Messiah = 7 + 62 weeks; ♦ after (7+)62 = 69 weeks shall Messiah be cut off"

I "70 weeks are determined upon thy people ♦ upon thy holy city, to finish the transgression, ♦ to make reconciliation for iniquity, ♦ to bring in everlasting righteousness, ♦ to seal up the vision ♦ prophecy, ♦ to anoint the Most Holy"

THE "ONE WEEK" OF 140 LUNATIONS/DAY

69 WEEKS OF 14 LUNATIONS PER DAY

REFER ¶ 334

70 YEARS DIVINE INDIGNATION

REFER ¶ 331 ♦ TABLE XXX

DANIEL'S PROPHECY OF THE SEVENTY WEEKS DAN IX. 24-27 REFER ¶¶ 331-337

VI — "And he shall confirm the covenant with many for ONE WEEK and in the midst or one week he shall cause the sacrifice ♦ oblation to cease"

D "Blessed is he that watcheth, ♦ cometh to the 1335 Days (i.e. years as above). But go thou thy way (Daniel) till the end be; for thou shalt rest ♦ stand in thy lot at the End of the Days." DAN XII. 12 ♦ 13

B ♦ C Continued

AS IN THE CASE OF LUNAR RECKONING ABOVE ♦ THE EPACT OF 75 SOLAR YEARS, THE 1290 YEARS = 1260 LUNAR + 30 SOLAR YEARS FOR THE MAXIMUM PERIOD.

C "there shall be 1290 Days" i.e. 1290 Years.

B "What shall be the end ♦ WEEK OF LIVING WITNESSES of these things? ... from the time (period) that the daily sacrifice shall be taken away ♦ the abomination that maketh desolate set up" DAN XII. 8 ♦ 11.

REFER ¶ 337

70 WEEKS OF 14 LUNATIONS PER DAY 69 + 7 = 14 LUNAR MONTHS

70 WEEKS OF 14 LUNATIONS PER DAY CRUCIFIXION "in midst of the week" i.e. CAUSE OF 70TH WEEK PREFIGURES THE LITERAL CEASING OF DAILY SACRIFICE IN THE MIDST OF THE 70TH WEEK OF 140 LUNATIONS PER DAY.

BASIS OF THE "YEAR — DAY" PRINCIPLE OF INTERPRETATION RELATING TO THE PROPHETIC PERIODS 1260, 1290, 1335, ♦ 2520 "DAYS" AND 2300 "EVENING-MORNINGS"

NUMBERS XIV. 34.—"Even 40 Days, each day for a year ... even 40 years" EZEKIEL IV. 4 ♦ 6 et seq. "Each day for a year" REFER ¶ 343

PHASE OF ENDING — EARLIEST BEGINNING — 2300 "EVENING - MORNING" YEARS ¶ 375 — LATEST BEGINNING — 2300 "EVENING - MORNING" YEARS ¶ 375 — PHASE OF BEGINNING

PERIOD OF CLEANSING SANCTUARY DAN VIII.

DATING OF END JOHN'S CHAPTER.

ANTIOCHUS EPIPHANES IN THE SYRIAN DIVISION OF ALEXANDER'S KINGDOM (BY DESOLATING THE TEMPLE AND CAUSING THE DAILY SACRIFICE TO CEASE IN MACCABEAN TIMES) IS PROPHETICALLY DEPICTED AS PREFIGURING THE LATER ROMAN AND MOSLEM DESOLATIONS. DAN VIII. 9-14, 23-25. PERIOD DAN VIII. 13,14

4-FOLD PARTITIONING OF THE KINGDOM OF ALEXANDER THE GREAT. DAN VIII. 8, 21, 22.

EPOCH OF GREEKS PLATE LXIII.

3415 A.K. This prophecy (Jer. xxxv, 12–19) relates to the return and reunion of Israel and Judah from captivity, the restoration of Jerusalem, and the dawn of the Millenial Age of Righteousness under Christ, as King of All-Israel. The date 5935 A.K. (1936¾ A.D.) is, therefore, the terminal date of the period of fulfilment of the Times of the Gentiles (¶¶ 342–349). The various stages of beginning and ending of the Times of the Gentiles are as shown on Plate LXVI.

¶ 373. THE PRINCIPAL HISTORICAL FEATURES IN THE FULFILMENT OF PROPHECY.

The diagrammatic representation of Plate LXVI in conjunction with Tables XXIX, XXX, and XXXI, should be carefully studied by the reader in relation to the following :— *The prophetic periods in history :—*

(1) The progressive stages in the rise of Babylon and the fall of Judah and Jerusalem at the commencement of the Times of the Gentiles (refer Guinness, quoted in ¶ 347). *(1) Progressive stages of beginning.*

(2) The progressive stages in the evolution of the modern period of chaos, and the downfall of the Empires of modern Continental Europe and Asia Minor—the Western Imperial Powers, Germany, Austria-Hungary, and Russia, claiming representation of ancient Rome, and the Eastern Moslem Ottoman Empire of the Khaliphate—at the termination of the Times of the Gentiles (refer Guinness, quoted in ¶ 347). *(2) Corresponding progressive stages of ending.*

(3) The mid-date of the period of the Times of the Gentiles, reckoned in lunar years,[1] as defining the date of the abomination (the wooden mosque of Omar, built on the site of the Temple) set up by Omar in the spring of 639 A.D., following his capture of Jerusalem and conquest of Syria in 638 A.D.[2] *(3) The mid-date of Gentile Times in Lunar reckoning applies to Moslem domination in Palestine.*

(4) The Departure of the Shekinah, the 70 years' Divine Indignation, the 70 weeks of Daniel's prophecy, and the Life of our Lord. *(4) The 70 weeks of Daniel and their chronological relations.*

(5) The period of 2300 (Dan. viii, 13, 14) to intervene between a determining period in the destinies of the kingdoms of Medo-Persia and Greco-Macedonia, beginning with an epoch inferred, but not defined, in Daniel, and ending at the date of the partitioning of the Empire of Alexander, "the first king" of Dan. viii, 21. *(5) Daniel's prophecy of 2300 "evening-mornings."*

---

[1] Lunar years are employed by the Moslems in their chronological reckoning. It is a striking fact that the lunar year 1335 of Moslem reckoning coincided with 1917 A.D., when Jerusalem was delivered. Refer Dan. xii, 12 and 13, relating to 1335. The real prophetical fulfilment of the 1335 years, as defined by the Pyramid and the solar reckoning of the Seven Times, shown on Plate LXVI, relates to the date 5935 A.K., or 1936¾ A.D.

[2] Ferrar Fenton, in his "Bible in Modern English," correctly establishes, from the context, that Dan. xii, 11, refers, not to an initial year in which "the daily sacrifice shall be taken away and the abomination that maketh desolate set up," but to an initial PERIOD of abominations and desolations beginning with the "taking away of the daily sacrifice," i.e. by the Romans in 70 A.D., and ending with the setting up of a continuous (or daily) abomination, i.e. the wooden mosque of Omar, in 639 A.D. The end of the PERIOD, at 639¼ A.D. is, therefore, the initial date for the commencement of the 1290 "years" of Dan. xii, 11. This rendering, as shown on Plate LXVI, gives the 1290 "years" ending at 1891¼, this date being therefore defined as commencing the historical period "when all these things shall be finished."

The reader's attention is here directed to the fact that the difference between 2520 solar years and 2520 lunar years is 75 solar years, that this difference or Epact must not be treated otherwise than as solar years, and that this Epact of 75, added to 1260, gives Daniel's 1335 (Dan. xii, 12), whether the 1260 years are taken as lunar or solar.

¶ 374. DANIEL'S 2300 " EVENING-MORNINGS."

Now the last period is described as 2300 " evening-mornings," whereas all other prophetic time units in Daniel are " days." The latter, we saw, have historical application both as lunar years and as solar years. The distinctive designation in the case of the 2300 " evening-mornings " must relate to a particular application, since the " evening-morning " is still the designation of the " day." The difference implied clearly concerns the point at which the unit begins and ends. " Evening," as applied symbolically to the year, can only relate to the winter half of the *solar* year, *i.e.* the half of the year beginning at the Autumnal Equinox, and ending at the Vernal Equinox. " Morning," similarly applied, defines the Summer half of the *solar* year; *i.e.* from the Vernal Equinox to the Autumnal Equinox.[1]

Each year of Daniel's period here considered must not only be a solar year, but must begin at an Autumnal Equinox. The period of 2300 years, therefore, begins at an Autumnal Equinox and ends at an Autumnal Equinox.

Another factor to be considered is one noted by Dr. Guinness. He states :[2]

" Let it be remembered that all great movements have almost imperceptible commencements, just as great rivers spring from little brooks. Israel's restoration and the destruction of Mohammedan rule, *i.e.* ' the cleansing of the sanctuary,' are not events to be accomplished in a day or in a year, any more than the overthrow of the city and temple and national existence of the Jewish people was accomplished in a day or in a year."

And again :[3]

" It is evident that the 2300 years of the cleansing of the sanctuary cycle indicate, not so much a closing year, as a closing era, not so much a point as a process. . . . Thus the expression ' unto 2300 years, then shall the sanctuary be cleansed,' seems to mean, then shall the cleansing process begin, not then come to an end."

¶ 375. THE PYRAMID'S 2300 " EVENING-MORNINGS."

The period of 2300 years, like the period of 2520 years, then, has stages of beginning and stages of ending. Now, the last date for the completion of the cleansing of the sanctuary is the official prophetic dating for the beginning of Christ's Millenium, 6000 A.K. This date, like the terminal date of the period of 2300 years, is an Autumnal Equinoctial date. This identity is in itself striking.

A period of 2300 solar years ending at the Autumnal Equinox of 6000 A.K. began at the Autumnal Equinox of 3700 A.K. = 300 B.C. The latter date, again, is the date of the final partitioning of the Macedonian

---

[1]Confirming this, Mr. R. H. Charles, in his " Book of Enoch," p. 59, footnote, states :—
" The Hebrews divided the year into two seasons, embracing Spring and Summer, and embracing Autumn and Winter (Gen. viii, 22 ; Is. xviii, 6 ; Zech. xiv, 8)."
[2]" Approaching End of the Age," p. 433.
[3]" Light for the Last Days," p. 309.

Empire, following the decisive battle of Ipsus (in Phrygia) in 301 B.C. As the result of this battle, the Empire of Alexander was, in 300 B.C., definitely divided into—

(a) The Syrian kingdom of the Seleucidæ ;
(b) The Macedonian kingdom of Cassander ;
(c) The Egyptian kingdom of Ptolemy ; and
(d) The Kingdom of Lysimachus, comprising Thrace, with Bithynia, and the rest of Asia Minor.

Hence, when Dan. viii, 21, 22, concerning the prophecy of 2300 " evening-mornings," states that " four kingdoms shall stand up out of the nation (Grecia) " after its first king (Alexander)—referring to the first dominant king succeeding the domination of Medo-Persia—we see clearly that the event described is the final partitioning of Alexander's Empire in 300 B.C.

The latter fourfold division given as an initial phase of the period in Daniel.

This date, therefore, is the final date for the commencement of the 2300 Autumnal Equinoctial years, as 6000 A.K. is the final date for the termination of the period. In the Pyramid's enlarged scale chronology, however, the final date represented for the symbolism within the Pyramid masonry is the dating for the South wall of the King's Chamber, 20th August 1953 A.D. The latter date is a month prior to the Autumnal Equinox defining 5952 A.K. Now, 2300 solar years ending at 5952 A.K. began at the Autumnal Equinox of 3652 A.K. =348 B.C., the Egyptian Epoch of Okhos.

The Autumnal Equinox of the last year indicated by the King's Chamber datings is 5952 A.K., or 2300 solar years from 3652 A.K. =348 B.C., the Egyptian Epoch of Okhos.

This explains why Egyptian tradition, derived from Pyramid prophecy, associated the rise of Alexander with the Epoch of Okhos, and why the Egyptians manipulated Pyramid chronology to terminate at that date (¶¶ 250–254 and 262). From this fact, it seems clear that Egyptian tradition had originally retained two epochs of the Pyramid's prophetic chronology, the epoch 3652 A.K. and the epoch 5556 A.K. ; the two epochs being confused when the fictitious system of Egyptian chronology was formulated to place 5556 years of *Anno Kalendarii* reckoning as terminating at 3652 A.K.

This application satisfies the initial phase of the period as defined in Daniel. It also indicates that 3652 A.K. was a Pyramid prophetic epoch adopted by the Egyptians.

The epoch for the initial beginning of the 2300 Autumnal Equinoctial years is monumentalised in the Great Pyramid's 35th course axis (Plate XLIIa), and in the Egyptian rectangular *aroura* (Plate XIII). That Egyptian tradition had preserved some fragment of fact relating to the Pyramid's monumentalisation of the " evening-morning " Autumnal Equinoctial symbolism, and identity is proclaimed by the fact that uncertainty prevailed as to whether the Epoch of Okhos should be reckoned as " 15 or 16 years before Alexander's coming into Egypt " in 332 B.C., that is to say, whether the Autumnal Equinox in question was that of 348 B.C. or that of 347 B.C. (3652 or 3653 A.K.).

The epoch proclaimed by the Pyramid's 35th course axis and by the rectangular " aroura."

¶ 376. THE PURPOSE OF THE TRUCE IN CHAOS.

The matter, however, that most immediately concerns us is the fulfilment of prophecy as related to current time. In terms of Pyramid symbolism, this falls within the period defined by the Antechamber and its datings.

Current time and the " truce in chaos." 1918 to 1928

The Antechamber, we saw, symbolises a period of " truce in chaos." The period of this " truce " is defined as extending from 10th November 1918 A.D. to 29th May 1928 A.D., when, as the symbolism proclaims, the restraint upon chaos is to be removed. What is the purpose of this emphatically defined intervention ?

The removal of the restraint upon chaos.
Ignorance concerning obligations.

In ¶¶ 255 and 256 it was suggested that man having failed in his duties towards his Creator, and having ceased to play the part that had been allotted to him in the scheme of Creation, an opportunity would eventually be afforded him to learn of his error and to amend his ways before pressure[1] was brought to bear to force him to fulfil his obligations. It did not follow that he would avail himself of this opportunity, but admonishment, and chastisement immediately following, bring the most ignorant and unwilling creditor to a realisation of his indebtedness.

Opportunity afforded to know, followed by compulsion.
Compulsion in relation to chaos.
The symbolism of the Antechamber geometry as defining the projection of the purpose of God in relation to His measures of compulsion.

The Great Pyramid's chronological symbolism indicates precisely this sequence onwards from its clearly defined date of the Crucifixion. From the symbolised date of the Crucifixion, the Grand Gallery—symbolising the Gospel Age—extends to the symbolised date of the doorway of the 1st Low Passage to the Antechamber. At this date, 4th–5th August 1914, the Great Tribulation of Chaos began. Man's artificial fabric of civilisation collapsed, and mankind was too stunned by the shock to realise the true significance of the catastrophe. Here, then, the Antechamber symbolises the reason for its insertion. By its insertion, the continuity of chaos—dated as extending from 4th–5th August 1914 to 16th September 1936 A.D.—is symbolised as being broken—by Divine intervention—between the 10th–11th November 1918 and the 29th of May 1928 A.D. The break or " truce in chaos " is, therefore, symbolised as a period of realisation, the final opportunity for man to learn of his error and the futility of his patchwork " reconstructions," prior to the final phase of " compulsion " being resumed. The " compulsion " here is not symbolised as " an act of God," but as the consequence of God permitting man's artificial " law "—substituted for His Divine Law—to run its complete and natural course in effecting the collapse of civilisation ; Divine Reconstruction being symbolised as forthcoming when the better part of mankind has learned the lesson intended, and has asked, at a time appointed in God's foreknowledge, for His intervention.[2]

---

[1] " Pressure " is a relative term here. Many similar terms in the Old Testament are also relative terms in the sense here signified. Therefore, God has been erroneously conceived as an unjust God. To save the human race, God purposes to pour out His love upon man to raise him to his proper status in Creation. To man's varying degrees of non-love, the process of Divine Outpouring will be experienced as an agony of correspondingly varying degrees of compulsion. Where love is totally lacking, destruction is the specified result ; there being no injustice in the destruction of that which is useless, and which, if not destroyed, would bring destruction upon the whole race. Where love is latent, God's process is to nurture love *in* application, to teach love by charity, and to stabilise love by sacrifice. This is the meaning of the indications of God's hand in the shaping of the course of the chaos period under the symbol " 153."

[2] Quoted from " Public Opinion," 15th February 1924 :—

THE PREVAILING DISCONTENT.

" These years have shaken us into a prevailing and prevalent discontent. Discontent is everywhere, and I welcome it. I scarcely ever meet anybody who is enjoying the comfort of an

¶ 377. THE CHAMBER OF THE TRIPLE VEIL.

This interpretation of the Antechamber's symbolism is confirmed by the Pyramid tradition preserved in the Egyptian religious texts. Thus, according to Marsham Adams, the Egyptian "Book of the Dead" defines the Great Pyramid Antechamber as the *Chamber of the Triple Veil*.[1] The symbolism implies that the Antechamber is the place of the Screen before the Pyramid's symbolic "Holy of Holies," the King's Chamber. Here we have an analogy with the "Veil in the Temple" of Jerusalem. This, at the Crucifixion, was "rent in twain" (Matt. xxvii, 51), symbolising that its epoch had departed, that a further revelation was given; and that it was the purpose of God, by so revealing Himself, ultimately, at His appointed time, to destroy the *veil* before the face of all people.[2]

The Egyptian "Book of the Dead" defines the Antechamber as "the Chamber of the Triple Veil," and, in a form of imagery identical with that belonging to the Hebrew Scriptures, defines the Chamber as symbolising the period of the unveiling of God's purpose in relation to Man.

Entering the Antechamber, and stooping to pass in an enforced attitude of obeisance below the Granite Leaf, the adept of the Egyptian texts, but now become a Master, would find himself standing between the wall-grooves of the 1st Veil or Screen. Before him he would see, in all, three such successive pairs of wall-grooves—three in the East wainscot (refer Plate LVII), and three opposite grooves in the West wainscot—symbolising the positions of the three successive Veils or Screens. The last Veil or Screen he would see ending at the Doorway of the 2nd Low Passage, and by its removal, would see revealed that Doorway to the Innermost Chamber. Passing through the three successive Veils or Screens, the Master—of the Egyptian texts—would traverse in an enforced stooping attitude the Passage symbolising the Final Humiliation, and then, upon entering the King's Chamber, acclaim, in the words quoted by Adams:

"I have opened the doors. . . . Well is the Great One who is in the coffin. For all the dead shall have passages made to Him."

The imagery of the texts, as applied by Adams, clearly reveals that the Antechamber of the Great Pyramid symbolises the period of the unveiling of God's purpose in relation to the destiny of mankind.

undisturbed and thornless repose. There is something about just now which forbids it. Nobody seems at rest," said the late Dr. Jowett in one of his last sermons reported in the 'Sunday School Chronicle.'

"It affects men as well as women, women as well as men. It is in the garret, in the mansion, in the cottage. It is among masters, among workmen, it is among people who piled up no end of money in the war—because, at any rate, they are afraid to lose it—and among those who lost all the money they had. It worries the serious, it disturbs the frivolous; for frivolity, as I found out pretty early in my ministry, can be a very theatrical disguise for hiding the disquietude and discomfort of the spirit.

"Everybody discontented; some people feeling the need of a God; other people hurrying away to strange shrines and to ghostly things. A conscience roused and sharpened to finer discernment. Sorrow in every street, and in all those sorrow-stricken homes they are groping for comfort. It is favourable to Jesus. It is a people made ready, prepared for Him."

[1] "The House of the Hidden Places," Plate appended.

[2] Refer Is. xxv, 7, 8; 2 Cor. iii, 13–18; Heb. vi, 19, 20, and context; ix, 3, in relation to the whole chapter.

Refer also Heb. x, 20, Christ's Passion opening "the veil" to the "new and living way," symbolised by the Grand Gallery.

¶ 378. THE ANTECHAMBER MID-DATING AND THE PHŒNIX CYCLE.

The initial dating of the progressive unveiling of the Divine purpose in relation to man at the time of the end.

The Antechamber mid-date, 20th August 1923 A.D., the termination of 18 Phœnix cycles at 5922 A.K.

The Antechamber mid-dating is the initial epoch of a terminal period of 365 months, and is separated from the 365 years of the House of Enoch by 15 Phœnix cycles, or 4935 years.

The geometry of the Antechamber, we have seen, relates to the unveiling symbolism of the Chamber of the Triple Veil. Thus, referring to Plate XLIII, we see that the whole geometrical symbolism, from the Great Step to the King's Chamber, is based upon the central vertical line of the Antechamber as datum. The date defined by this central line is 20th August 1923 (Table XXIX). The symbolism implies that the significance attaching to this date, in relation to past history, should be revealed by the passage of the events symbolised by the 1st Screen of the Triple Veil, and in relation to immediately future history, by what is symbolised by the two remaining Screens of the Triple Veil that intervene between 1924 and 1928 A.D. As the symbolism of the Triple Veil—the three pairs of opposite grooves—may be a matter of chronological importance, what is deemed to be the definition of their geometrical dimensions and datings is given in Section III of this Chapter, ¶ 497a (refer also to Plate LXVc).

The central date, 20th August 1923, then, as symbolised, implies the prophetic indication of an epoch relating to the unveiling of God's purpose. This agrees with what was inferred from the Antechamber's symbolism of Divine Intervention creating a " truce in chaos," and by thus agreeing, defines the purpose of the intervention (¶ 376). The central date of this period of " truce in chaos " is, therefore, emphasised as an outstanding epoch in the Pyramid's prophetic chronology. The date is a month prior to the termination of 5922 years of *Anno Kalendarii* reckoning, or of 18 Phœnix cycles of 329 years (¶¶ 33 (1b), 38).

The latter interval a period of fictitious Egyptian chronology derived from tradition of Pyramid prophecy.

Now we saw that the Phœnix cycle derived its name from " the cycle of the House of Enoch or Hanok," and that this derivation attaches to the termination of 3 Phœnix cycles, or 987 years of *Anno Kalendarii* reckoning (¶ 38). 987 A.K. was seen to be the dating in the Book of Genesis for the translation of Enoch (Table V and ¶ 38). The date was the termination of 365 years of the House of Enoch, beginning from 622 A.K. (¶ 37 and Table V). In a similar manner the Phœnix date defining the centre of the Antechamber is indicated as beginning a period of 365 calendar months. These two periods, the 365 years of Enoch and the 365 months of the Antechamber symbolism, are separated by 15 Phœnix cycles, or 4935 years. Now, 4935 years is the duration of a prophetic period of Egyptian fictitious chronology derived from a former knowledge of the Pyramid's prophetic chronology (Table XV, Annotations (D), item 3).

¶ 379. THE EVOLUTION OF EGYPTIAN FICTITIOUS CHRONOLOGY FROM THE PYRAMID'S PROPHETICAL CHRONOLOGY.

(Refer Table XV, Annotations (D).)

The facts proclaiming that the central dating of the Great Pyramid's Antechamber was recognised, in remote times, as defining an outstanding Epoch of Pyramid prophecy are as follows :—

(1) THE PYRAMID'S PHŒNIX CYCLES AND EPOCHS :—

The Pyramid's chronological period ending at 5922 A.K. is defined as comprising—

(a) An initial interval of three Phœnix cycles defined by the Book of Genesis as ending at the translation of Enoch (¶¶ 38 and 317) ... **987**

(b) A terminal interval of fifteen Phœnix cycles from the date given for the translation of Enoch to the central dating of the Antechamber **4935**

Interval to central dating of Antechamber **5922**

Years.

Pyramid chronology :—
A.K.
Enoch 987
Interval 4935
Ante-
chamber 5922

(2) THE PHŒNIX PERIODS OF THE EGYPTIAN KING LISTS :—

These two intervals are given by the fictitious chronologies of the Egyptian King Lists as—

Years.

(a) An initial interval in the King List preserved by Castor (from the beginning of Dyn. I to the 1st year of Dyn. V) **987**
(Appendix and Table XV, Annotations (D), item 5.)

(b) A terminal interval in the List of the Egyptian Book of the Sothis, ending in the 1st year of Amasis II, whose reign ends the List of this Book **4935**
(Appendix and Table XV, Annotations (D), item 3.)

Interval to central dating of Antechamber.. .. .. .. **5922**

Egyptian
fictitious
chronology :—
A.K.
Dyns.I-IV 987
Book
of the
Sothis to ⎬4935
Amasis
II.
5922

(3) THE PYRAMID'S THREE CYCLES OF 1461 SOLAR YEARS :—

The excuse for the fictitious extension of the Egyptian system in Annotations (D) to Table XV, hinges upon a matter of Pyramid tradition. The system in item (5) of these Annotations is a system of three Sothic cycles to the reign of Amasis II. This is also the basis of the system in the Version of Eusebius to the reign of Amasis II, as Plate XVI, Table A. Explanation of the three Sothic cycles is as follows :—

The origin of
the Egyptian
fictitious
system :—
A.K.
622
1461 ⎰ to
⎱ 2083
3000
2922 ⎰ to
⎱ 5922

Three cycles
of 1461 years.

(a) There is the original prophetic cycle of 1461 solar years from 622 A.K. to 2083 A.K., Enoch to Abraham.

(b) *The Central Date* of the Great Pyramid's prophetic, scalar, and astronomical chronology systems, defined at the base level of the Pyramid, is .. .. **3000 A.K.**
Add two prophetic cycles of 1461 years .. .. .. **2922 years.**

(c) *The Central Date* of the Great Pyramid's Antechamber chronology .. .. **5922 A.K.**
(Refer also Plate XLIIa for 1461 A.P. and 4383 A.P.)

(4) THE NUMERICAL SYMBOLISM OF THE CHRONOLOGICAL INDICATIONS :—

A further striking feature of the mid-date of the Antechamber—and its associated cycles—is the following significant sequence of periods :—

(a) House of Enoch .. .. **365 solar years.**

(b) Interval of fifteen Phœnix cycles .. .. .. **4935 solar years.**

(c) Centre of Antechamber to end of King's Chamber .. **365 months.**

Numerical
relations :—
Defined period
of 4935 years
preceded by
365 years, and
succeeded by
365 months.

The sequence begins at

<table>
<tr><td></td><td colspan="2"></td></tr>
</table>

The sequence begins at
(d) Primary Epoch, House of Enoch .. .. .. 622 A.K.
and ends at
(e) The Cleansing of the Sanctuary dating of the King's
    Chamber .. .. 5952 A.K.

(f) Initial date .. .. 622 A.K.
    Sanctuary Cleansing cycle .. .. 2300 years.

    Two prophetic cycles of 1461 solar years .. .. 2922 A.K.

(g) Pyramid Epoch and Egyptian Epoch of Okhos .. 3652 A.K.
    Sanctuary Cleansing cycle .. .. 2300 years.

    Pyramid's Sanctuary Cleansing date at South Wall of
    King's Chamber .. .. 5952 A.K.

(h) Daniel's 2300 " evening-mornings " as an initial cycle 2300 A.K.
    Interval of a second cycle .. .. 2300 years.

                                                         4600 A.K.
    Daniel's 1335 " days " as " evening-morning " years   1335 years.

    Dating of Entrance Doorway to King's Chamber .. 5935 A.K.

Refer Plate LXVI for the 1335 years based on the lunar reckoning, ending at the same date, 5935 A.K.

¶ 380. THE SYMBOLISM OF GEOMETRICAL TRANSLATION.

These facts of chronology, real and fictitious, all combine to prove the importance attached by the identities established, and by the Pyramid symbolism, to the mid-dating of the Antechamber.

Until the measurer reaches this point in the Antechamber he is not in a position to define the geometrical relationship that exists between the Antechamber and the distance traversed from the Great Step to reach the Antechamber. Here, however, the geometry, centred upon this point, as represented on Plate XLIII, and evolved from this mid-point of the Antechamber as origin, symbolically indicates that a predetermined date is reached in the destiny of mankind, and in the unveiling of God's purpose in relation to mankind.

Examining the matter further (Plate XLIII), we find that the defined geometry of the year circle in the Antechamber is translated, or reduced, into the form of direct rectilinear measurement connecting *retrospectively* with the Great Step, and prophetically with the King's Chamber. Not only is this the case, but within the Antechamber the year-circle measures of circumference and circular area are translated, or reduced, into the form of

Marginal notes:

Initially defined date:—
622 A.K.
2300 cycle.

2922 A.K.

2 cycles of 1461 years.

Epoch of Okhos:—
3652 A.K.
2300 cycle.

5952 A.K.

The Pyramid's erminal dating in the King's Chamber.

Summation of Daniel's cycles:—
2300 A.K.
2300 years.

4600 A.K.
1335 years.

5935 A.K.

Pyramid's initial dating in the King's Chamber.

The same by lunar reckoning.

The mid-date of the Antechamber is geometrically symbolised as the chronological viewpoint of history revealed in its true perspective as the fulfilment of prophecy.

The mid-date of the Antechamber's granite-defined square of equal area and its initial and terminal datings are symbolised as defining a the rectilinear and surface measures of the square of area equal to the year-circle area. This translation begins at the commencement of the Granite Floor (dating 12th December 1919 A.D., Table XXIX), is central to the centre of the square of equal area (dating 6th March 1924 A.D., Table XXIX), and, within the Antechamber, terminates, or reaches the climax of its symbolised intention at the Doorway to the 2nd Low Passage, the Passage of Chaos resumed (dating 29th May 1928 A.D., Table XXIX). The same features of translation extend to the King's Chamber, and, in fact, govern every dimension, linear and superficial, of that Chamber.

period identified with the translation or reduction from the exact terms of a certain scheme of first principles into certain dependent terms derived from that scheme, but derived for application on other lines than those intended in the primary scheme.

¶ 381. THE YOKE OF INDUSTRIAL SCIENCE.

This predominant symbolism of the translated measures is the most significant feature of the Chambers here. It clearly relates to a dual application. The clue to the dual application of the translation effected lies in the purpose for which the translated measures were originally derived, and in the manner in which they were originally applied. The translated measures (Plates XLIII and XXXVb) are all indicated as defining the geometrical derivation of the three ancient Civil Scales of measurement, figured on Plate XV, as derived from the Sacred Scale. In ¶¶ 84, 88, and 116, we saw that this Civil System was formulated in the period of a former civilisation—prior to Egyptian Dynastic history. Its formulation was seen to indicate a state of society in which the uncultured many were organised to carry out highly skilled work under the intermittent direction of a cultured few (¶ 116).

The symbolism of translation. Indication of a dual application. The translated measures define the three Ancient Scales of Civil Measures derived from the Sacred Scale. Ancient purpose to organise mass production of highly skilled work by semi-skilled labour.

These Civil Scales of measurement were found to be in use in Egypt prior to the commencement of Egyptian Dynastic history. The period, therefore, in which the translated measures were applied for the purpose of organising the labour of the unskilled or semi-skilled multitude, for mass production on a large scale, is the closing period of the former civilisation that ended with the Dynasty of the House of Noah. The Pyramid's large scale chronology indicates, by the symbolic application of the ancient translated measures, the recurrence of these conditions [1] generally, from the primary chronological dating of the Great Step, 1844 A.D., but in accentuated form from the special dating of the Great Step, 1909 A.D. The former clearly defines the beginning of the modern epoch of industrial development, and the latter, the date of the epoch of its consummation, the modern disastrous epoch of Armaments (refer ¶¶ 269, 270, in relation to ¶¶ 163–166 and 255 and 256).

Application belongs to the declining days of Adamic civilisation. A similar application of "rule-of-thumb" methods, derived from precise science adopted in modern industrial science. Application culminates in similar disastrous consequences. The modern slavery of armament competition and scientific warfare.

---

[1] Another parallel between the days of Noah and the period of the " consummation " is given by our Lord in Matt. xxiv, 37:

" As the days of Noah were, so shall also the coming of the Son of man be. For as in the days that were before the flood they were eating and drinking, marrying and giving in marriage, until the day that Noah entered into the ark,

" And knew not until the flood came, and took them all away: so shall also the coming of the Son of man be."

Here refer Genesis vi, 11: " The earth was corrupt before God, and the earth was filled with violence."

¶ 382. THE SYMBOLISM OF THE PROCESS LEADING TO RESTI-TUTION.

The symbolism of Divine Intervention, effecting a "Truce in Chaos" from 10th November 1918 to 29th May 1928, defines the diverting of the forces of destruction to bring the nations under the dominion of Christ.

An important feature of the symbolism, however, relates to the indication of Divine Intervention (¶¶ 371 and 372). It is the structural insertion of this indication that defines the period of "Truce in Chaos"—10th November 1918 A.D. to 29th May 1928 A.D.—and at the same time defines the system of "translated measures" (¶¶ 380 and 381) governing the symbolism from the Great Step to the King's Chamber. This dual aspect of the feature noted clearly symbolises that the process of Divine Intervention relates to the employment of the forces of destruction in such manner and sequence of evolution as will bring the nations of this world under the dominion of the Kingdom of Christ.[1]

The symbolism also defines the concurrent revealing of God's purpose. Man's "chaos" controlled and directed by the creation of a "shock-absorbing" process to prepare mankind for the coming restitution.

At the same time the clear indication of intervention defines the dual purpose seen in the symbolism of the "translated measures." The manner in which these are indicated clearly symbolises the concurrent revealing of God's purpose. The symbolism shows that this is effected by the translation of a finite element of God's precise science into terms of man's empirical science, and that modern civilisation has debased this Divine science and has diverted it into the channels of destruction. This and the detailed features of the symbolism also define the effecting of God's purpose by the creation of a "shock-absorbing" process, to control the forces of destruction, and to redirect the channels of man's science into concurrence with the streams of Divine energy actuating God's science. That this "shock-absorbing" process is related to our Lord's Passion is the central theme of the progressive sequence of prophecy from the Book of Genesis to the Book of Revelation. Hence it was that our Lord proclaimed to His Elect "when these things begin to come to pass, then look up, and lift up your heads; for your redemption draweth nigh." The unveiling implication is that the very projection of the "shock-absorbing" process into the chaotic vortex of civilisation will appear of a nature, and be expressed as a process, equally disastrous in its initial and crucial stages, to those for whose benefit the process is projected.

¶ 383. THE "SHORTENING" OF THE PERIOD OF CHAOS.

Symbolism of the two Low Passages relates, not to two separate periods of chaos but to a single period of chaos shortened by the insertion of the Antechamber "truce in chaos" indication.

The significance of the whole symbolism lies in the fact, not that the Antechamber "truce" intervenes between the end of a first period of chaos and the beginning of a second period of chaos, but that the "truce" is defined as inserted to shorten what otherwise would have been a single period of chaos extending from 5th August 1914 to 16th September 1936.[2] Instead of being indicated as a single Low Passage 269.260165 P″ long, from the Grand Gallery to the King's Chamber, the Low Passage is indicated separated into two portions, together totalling 153 P″ long (¶ 371). The numerical value thus resulting from the Great Intervention symbolised, defines the "shortening"

[1] Refer concluding paragraph of ¶ 270.
[2] The late Lord Fisher stoutly maintained that the sudden cessation of the Great European War was the result of Divine Intervention.

of the period of chaos, as effected for the purpose of the " restitution " *This insertion reduces the total period of chaos to 153 calendar months.*
(¶¶ 338–341, 351, and 371). The period of " Intervention " is represented by
the diameter of the year circle, *i.e.* the length of the Antechamber, 116.26 P"
—the latter circle being the symbol of the " Lord of the Pyramid " and
" the Lord of the Year," the promised Messiah of ancient prophecy (¶¶ 26,
353, 354, 365, 366, and 369). In this connection the reader is also referred
to the symbolism of the year circle in Plates XLIa and b, XLIIa, and XLIII.

Viewed in relation to Hebrew prophecy in the Old and New Testaments, *153, being the numerical symbol of the elect, defines the shortening as effected for " the elect's sake," as promised by Christ concerning the world's greatest tribulation.*
the Divine Intervention is symbolised as effected by our Lord Jesus Christ.
Speaking of such a period, our Lord, in Matt. xxiv, 21, 22, refers to " great
tribulation, such as was not since the beginning of the world to this time, no,
nor ever shall be. And except those days should be shortened, there should
no flesh be saved ; but for the elect's sake[1] those days shall be shortened."
Refer also Mark xiii, 19, 20, and particularly Luke xxi, 23, 24.

¶ 384. CHRIST'S PROMISE OF THE " SHORTENING."

Our Lord's words, as quoted in Matthew and Mark, seem to indicate, *The sequence of our Lord's prediction :— Jerusalem, as it then stood, to be destroyed and to remain a desolation " until the times of the Gentiles be fulfilled."*
at first sight, a reference to the period of the Roman destruction of Jerusalem
in 70 A.D. The synchronistic comparisons in Table XXXI of the narratives
of Matthew and Mark with the narrative of Luke establishes quite a different
interpretation. Comparison shows that in Luke xxi the second half of
verse 23 and the whole of verse 24 apply to the description of Matt. xxiv, 21
and 22, and Mark xiii, 19 and 20. This establishes that the latter two
references apply to the whole period from the destruction of Jerusalem in
70 A.D. " until the times of the Gentiles be fulfilled."

Reference to Table XXXI will show that " the shortening of the days " *During this period of desolation, the Jews to be led captive into all nations— outcasts.*
applies to the final phase of tribulation. Our Lord was here referring to
Daniel's prophecies concerning the long period of desolation to be visited upon
Jerusalem (Dan. xii, 11), concerning the final period of great tribulation *The culmination of this period of tribulation upon the Jews to be the final greatest tribulation referred to by Daniel as related to the ending of the times of the Gentiles.*
(Dan. xii, 1 and 7), and concerning the resurrection and restitution (Dan. xii,
2–4, 12, 13). He began with the events then imminent, the destruction of
Jerusalem and the Temple (Luke xxi, 5–7, 20–24 in relation to Dan. ix, 26, 27),
and then sketched, in a few words (Luke xxi, second half of verse 23 and 24,
compared with Matt. xxiv, 21 and 22, and with Mark xiii, 19 and 20), the
nature of the events to happen between 70 A.D. and the " times of the
restitution." This is the portion of the narrative in which the reference to *The days of this tribulation to be shortened for the elect's sake.*
" the shortening of the days " occurs. The latter expression is applied in
relation to a period of tribulation. Our Lord defines that this period of
tribulation is that predicted by Daniel (xii, 1) as preceding the " restitution." *Following the period in which the days of tribulation are shortened " the Son of man comes."*
Dan. xii, 6–13 describes the period as following immediately the termination
of the second half-period (1260 years) of the 7 times (refer ¶¶ 342–349 and
Plate LXVI), and our Lord (in Matt. xxiv, 29 and 30) describes His coming
as " immediately after the tribulation of those days " ; the said " tribulation "

[1] Hence the significance of 153 in the Pyramid's symbolism of tribulation, shortened purposely by the insertion of the Antechamber to effect this.

being that in which " for the elect's sake those days shall be shortened." Reference to ¶¶ 348, 349, and 360 will show that the " shortening of the days " must apply to the final period of chaos—during which Jerusalem was to be delivered—and therefore to the period including and succeeding 1917 A.D.

¶ 385. 4TH AUGUST 70 A.D. AND 4TH AUGUST 1914 A.D.

The Roman destruction of Jerusalem and the Temple on 4th August 70 A.D., as ushering in the period " for the overspreading of abominations" to " make desolate," is represented by our Lord as prefiguring the commencement of World Chaos on 4th August 1914 A.D.

In this connection it is interesting to recall that many students of prophecy have held that our Lord intended to present the Roman destruction of Jerusalem and the Temple as prefiguring the Chaos of the Final Tribulation. The beginning of His prophetic outline relates to the destruction of the Temple (Matt. xxiv, 2). The destruction of the Temple by the Romans happened on the 10th of the Jewish month Ab,[1] in 70 A.D. This began the period " for the overspreading of abominations " to " make desolate " (Dan. ix, 27), thus fulfilling Dan. ix, 26, that " the people of the prince that shall come shall destroy the city and the sanctuary ; and the end thereof shall be with a flood, and unto the end of the war desolations are determined." Here " the war " referred to relates to the whole period of Gentile domination until " the Consummation " (verse 27).

Now the 10th of Ab[1] in 70 A.D. began at sunset of 3rd August (Greg.) and ended at sunset of 4th August (Greg.), on which date the Temple was destroyed by the Romans in 70 A.D. The 4th of August (Greg.) 70 A.D., therefore, began the period of desolations, thus prefiguring, by 1844 solar years, the beginning of the period of World Chaos on 4th August (Greg.) 1914 A.D.

¶ 386. THE SIGNIFICANCE OF THE ANTECHAMBER'S ANNIVERSARY DATINGS.

The daily sacrifice ceased 12th July (Greg.) 70 A.D., preceding Jerusalem's desolation.

Great War Peace treaty ratified 12th July (Greg.) 1919 A.D. preceding European " Peace " desolations.

The type of the apparent " failure " cf the great sacrifice.

Dan. ix, 27, however—to which our Lord refers—defines the date at which " He shall cause the sacrifice and oblation to cease " as the beginning of the period " for the overspreading of abominations." At the Roman siege of Jerusalem the daily sacrifice ceased on the 17th of the Jewish month Tammuz of 70 A.D.[2] This date began at sunset of 12th July (Greg.) 70 A.D., 1849 years before the 12th of July (Greg.) 1919 A.D., when the fateful " Peace " treaty was ratified. Surely the conditions attaching to the sequence from the two dates are analogous, when, under the modern conditions, we hear on all sides the query " Has Christ's Church failed ? " (refer ¶¶ 351 and 352).

Readers will remember that it took the world some time to realise the disastrous effect of the " Peace " treaty of 1919. As if to emphasise the

---

[1] Josephus, " Wars of the Jews," VI, iv, 5.
It is a remarkable fact that it was not due to Titus or any order from Vespasian that the Temple was destroyed. It was accomplished by the troops of Titus (Josephus, " Wars," VI, iv, 5 and 6) on their own initiative, thus fulfilling the prediction to the letter—" the *people* of the prince that shall come."
[2] Josephus, " Wars of the Jews," VI, ii, 1.

futility of the " Peace " treaty, the Granite Leaf, by its initial and terminal The face of the granite boss index measure, 11th July (Greg.) 1920 A.D. the leap year true first anniversary of the Peace treaty ratification.
datings, seems to direct attention to the first anniversary of the ratification
of the Peace treaty and to the third anniversary of the overthrow of the
German Empire. The occurrence of these two outstanding anniversary
datings—in view of the precise geometrical data from which they have been
derived—can scarcely be deemed to be accidental. The same anniversary
symbolism is indicated by the Granite floor beginning; its dating, 12th
December 1919, being the anniversary of the deliverance of Jerusalem in 1917.

The Pyramid's chronology, following an astronomical reckoning of years, The significance of the anniversary symbolism— delayed action. Confirming this, the Antechamber defines three principal anniversary datings all relating to outstanding dates of the Great War.
does not define anniversary datings by the Gregorian Leap Year cycle.
From 12th July 1919 to 12th July 1920 are 366 days, whereas the solar year
is 365.24+ days; whence the face of the 1-inch projecting Boss on the
Granite Leaf of the Pyramid's Antechamber defines the 11th July 1920 A.D.
the true first anniversary of the ratification of the " Peace " treaty (Table
XXIX). Similarly, the South face of the Granite Leaf defines the 10th of
November 1921 A.D. the true anniversary of the end of the German Empire,
as defined by the dating of the Antechamber Entrance Doorway. The
Granite Leaf, compelling a stooping attitude to pass under, therefore
symbolises the yoke of the after-effects of the Great War, the yoke being
defined as related to the anniversary of the ratification of the " Peace "
treaty and the anniversary of the end of the German Empire.

The Boss depth, again, as forming the 1-inch index measure to the The significant symbolism of the Granite Leaf and the Boss index measure.
geometry of the Antechamber, proclaims the Boss and its dating as forming
the index to the chronological symbolism of the Antechamber—defining the
period and conditions of " Truce in Chaos," all as following in sequence from
the conditions enforced by the " Peace " treaty.

¶ 387. THE PROPHETIC SYMBOLISM AND THE BRITISH RACE.

The depth of the Boss on the Granite Leaf defines the 30 days' month The dated symbolism of the yoke of the Granite Leaf coincides with the period of intensified chaos in Ireland. The Boss dating the anniversary of the Battle of the Boyne 230 years previously, i.e. 55th Daniel's prophetic period of 2300 years.
from 11th July 1920 to 10th August 1920. As this depth forms the index to
the Antechamber geometry and its chronological symbolism, we see that its
datings form the index to the events relating to those datings. In our own
land, the 10th of August 1920 ushered in a period of intensified chaos in
Ireland; the dating of the Boss face being also the true anniversary of another
event whose commemoration is related to strife in Ireland—the Battle of the
Boyne.[1] The connection with Pyramid symbolism and chronology may not,
at first sight, be apparent. The date of the Battle of the Boyne—11th July
(Greg.) 1690 A.D.—however, marks the final phase of the Reformation's
political effect upon Great Britain, if not the final phase in relation to Ireland.

[1] The actual date of the Battle of the Boyne is 1st July (Julian) = 11th July (Greg.) " not
12th, as Lecky says, ' Hist. of Ireland,' III, p. 427," Enc. Brit. (11th Edit.), IV, p. 356.
Reference to the daily and weekly newspapers dealing with the fateful week-end of 10th to
12th July 1920 will show how the inflaming of Irish passion was more deliberately provoked than
usual, at this time, by what Mr. A. M. Thompson described, at the time, as the " ancient feuds
and grudges " that " are annually revived as part of a deliberate policy to prevent reconciliation
between fellow-inhabitants of the island." This is neither intended to blame nor to excuse one
party or the other, but as a sanely judged allusion to a fact of recent history.

The dated emergence from the yoke of the Granite Leaf gives the date of the Irish agreement.
The initial date of Ireland's final phase of the disturbance produced by this great movement coincides with the Boss dating of the Granite Leaf. The date is 11th July (Greg.) 1920 A.D., 230 years—$\frac{1}{10}$th of the scriptural sanctuary cleansing period of 2300 years (Dan. viii, 14 and 26)—later than the Battle of the Boyne.

As previously noted, the anniversary feature of the Granite Leaf's chronological symbolism is emphasised by the fact that we find its terminal dating (given by the South face) indicates the third anniversary of the fall of the German Empire. The dating is 10th November 1921 A.D. In our own affairs the date marked a definite stage in the settlement of the Irish Question. On this particular day (5 p.m.) the terms of agreement between the British Cabinet and the Irish Delegates[1] were drafted in the form of a Cabinet Note and sent to the Ulster leaders. This Note formed the basis of the terms of the Irish Settlement signed on 13th December 1921.

The same dating as related to the work and deals of the Washington Conference. The dawn of a new ethical epoch in the history of the English-speaking peoples. The failure of the Conference and its triumph.
The day and the event are strangely related to another event whose significance lies in the immediate future. The following day drew attention to the New World, and the Armistice Commemoration there attended by the delegates of the First World Conference to shock the atmosphere of " Truce in Chaos " with a Christian-like proposal. The next day, again—the 12th November 1921—brought the eve of the Washington Conference with its projection of high ideals. Hope thereafter soared high—so high, indeed, that Mr. Thomas Hardy was moved to declare " the omens now seem favourable." Such, in fact, is a crisp definition of the symbolism of the passing from under the shadow[2] of the Granite Leaf. That this was truly a passing from under the shadow for the nations responsible for the projection of the high ideals of the Conference is becoming increasingly clear. Not, however, from under the shadow of trial and perplexity, but from under the sinister shadow of the moral darkness of responsibility for the continuance of chaos.

The creation of a new element of order in the chaotic orbit of world destiny.
Generations of English-speaking peoples yet unborn will look back upon the Washington Conference as upon the dawn of a brighter moral day for their race. They will see that it marks a new ethical epoch in the history of the English-speaking peoples; not as an epoch to be immediately identified with the determination of decisive issues, but as an epoch that saw the creation of an element of order in the still chaotic orbit of world destiny.

The attempt to institute an era of peace frustrated. English-speaking peoples drawn closer together. A stabilising process in a world of instability.
Such, we interpret, is the significance of the noblest failure in history since the accursed age of Armaments had its dawn. For whatever the significance may be to the British Race, the immediate effect upon the world was a shattering of its highest hope. For Christ's law of mutual love, as the single effective factor operative in the overthrow of chaos, failed to prevail in the international heart of man. Magnanimity, as always amongst men, was mistaken for weakness. Weakness, mistaking its signs of disintegration for strength, reverted to the annihilating law of man and the big

---

[1] " The Daily Mail," November 11, 1921.
[2] At the same date Dr. Macnamara said: " We have been passing constantly under the shadow in 1921."

battalions. Yet that magnanimity did prevail as a factor still to show its influence is to us a certainty. For the two great English-speaking peoples were drawn closer together in a bond of understanding and human sympathy in those twelve weeks than in as many decades previously. Sympathy began with the British gesture to Ireland, and was cemented by the joint British-American gesture to the world. This, to us, is the meaning of the Granite Leaf symbolism—the passing out of a race from under the yoke of misunderstanding, intolerance, and suspicion, inherited and resuscitated from the intolerant period of the Reformation.

¶ 388. THE STONE KINGDOM AND THE KINGDOMS OF THE GENTILE IMAGE.

At this stage of our study it is well for us to remember an important utterance of our Saviour. To the Jews he said: " The Kingdom of God shall be taken from you and given unto *a nation* bringing forth *the fruits* thereof. And whosoever shall fall upon this stone shall be broken, but on whomsoever it shall fall it shall grind him to powder " (Matt. xxi, 42–44). Here, again, our Lord is basing His teaching upon, and formulating His predictive statements in terms of the now despised prophecies of Daniel. He is referring to Daniel's prophecy relating to the Image of Nebuchadnezzar's dream and the Stone Kingdom (Dan. ii, 44). Daniel said to Nebuchadnezzar " thou art this head of gold." Daniel here identifies Nebuchadnezzar as the first king to hold dominion during the prophetic period of the 2520 years of the times of the Gentiles. *[Christ confirms a prophecy of Daniel. The Kingdom taken from the Jews. The new Stone Kingdom to bring forth the fruits of God's Kingdom. The powers of the Gentile Image to be broken in falling upon the Stone Kingdom.]*

Students of prophecy have been generally agreed that the final phase but one of the Gentile Image relates to the partitioned kingdoms of the Roman Empire. Modern historians agree that the German and Austrian Empires and the Russian Empire, respectively, represented the modern phases of the Western and Eastern Empires of Rome.[1] The imperial heads of the respective modern Empires claimed as much. All three have fallen, as Daniel prophesied they would; for, as Daniel said, " the great God hath made known to the king what shall come to pass hereafter : and the dream is certain and the interpretation thereof is sure." The Western elements have fallen in fighting against the Eastern, and the Eastern against the Western. Hence the significance of the iron and clay " the kingdom shall be divided . . . they shall not cleave one to another, even as iron is not mixed with clay." *[The duration of the Kingdoms of the Image 2520 years from Nebuchadnezzar. The modern representatives of these kingdoms identified by modern prophecy exposition and by modern historians. The Empires of Germany, Austria, and Russia.]*

¶ 389. THE PYRAMID DEFINES THE STONE KINGDOM AND ITS EPOCH.

But what of the prophetic kingdom of stone ? However we may deem this kingdom to be nearly or remotely related to the Church of Christ, it is clear that the phase of the Stone Kingdom of Daniel ii, contemporary with *[The Stone Kingdom a literal kingdom.]*

[1] Refer Bryce's " Holy Roman Empire."

the " iron and clay " elements of the Gentile kingdoms, is as distinctly intended to represent a literal kingdom on the Earth as the kingdoms of the
Gentile Image are defined as literal kingdoms on the Earth.   Gentile dominion
over Jerusalem was to cease at a definite phase of the termination of the
Seven Times of the Gentiles (¶¶ 348 and 349, Plate LXVI, and Luke xxi, 24).
Such a definite phase of termination, occurred in the Autumn of 1917 A.D.
(¶ 348), and in December of that year Jerusalem was delivered by the British
forces.

Now, in Daniel's prophecy of the Gentile Image, the Stone Kingdom is
the constant opponent of the final kingdoms (" the feet ") of the Fourth
Element (" the legs of iron ") of the Image.   Historically, the succession of
the Four Elements is from East to West, from Babylon (the head) to Western
Europe (the feet).   Britain—geographically placed as " the stone " lying
at " the feet of the image "—has been the opponent of a long series of aggressive powers rising in Western Europe.   Power after power—from Spain in
the reign of Elizabeth to Germany in the reign of George V—has fallen in
attempting to overthrow Britain, thus seemingly proclaiming the tendencies
of the Stone Kingdom to grow into " a great mountain filling the whole
earth " (Dan. ii, 35).   This is no merely chimerical theory of imperialism,
but a fact of identity derived from a co-ordinated comparison of circumstances,
historically and chronologically fulfilled by the rise and development of the
British Empire and its daughter nation, the United States of America.

The prophecies of Daniel (ii, 37–40 ; vii, 3–28 ; viii, 20, 21) specifically
name the first three Gentile Powers to dominate the Holy Land—Babylon,
Medo-Persia, and Greco-Macedonia.   The fourth Power, as described by Daniel
(ii, 40–42 ; vii, 7, 23, 24) precisely fits the Empire of Rome.   The division
of the Roman Empire into the Eastern and Western Empires is predicted
by Daniel ii, 41.   The division of these into the medieval and modern States
of Europe is defined by Daniel ii, 34 and 42–44, and vii, 7 and 20.   As the
prophecy and history relate to a geographical precession of empires and
kingdoms from Babylon (the head) to Western Europe (the feet), it is clear
that " the feet " relate to the medieval and modern kingdoms of Western
Europe.   Geographically, Britain is " the Stone Kingdom " lying at the
" feet " of the image.   The aggressive Western European Powers began
with Spain in the reign of Elizabeth.   Elizabeth's reign began in 1558 A.D.,
and the epoch of the Pyramid's message is defined as beginning less than a
month prior to 1558 A.D. (¶ 349).   This message is indicated as extended
to the period 1558 A.D. to 2045 A.D. (¶¶ 236, 249–254, 262, and 266), these
initial and terminal datings being respectively—

(a) The date at which the Precessional rate is defined by the *sum of the
Pyramid's base diagonals* ;
(b) The date (2045 A.D.) at which the Longitude of Perihelion is defined
by the *sum of the Pyramid's base angles* (refer Plate LXVII).

These two geometrical relations completely define the form and dimensions of the Great Pyramid.   The Pyramid, again, is the Scriptural symbol

of the Stone Kingdom (¶ 268 and footnote). The Pyramid's message is therefore defined as extended to the Stone Kingdom between the years 1558 A.D. and 2045 A.D. (refer ¶¶ 249–254 and 262–268 as to the Pyramid's message and European civilisation). The history of the British race from the former date answers precisely to the predicted history of the Stone Kingdom, thus directing attention to the significance of Daniel ii, 44 : " And in the days of these kings shall the God of Heaven set up a kingdom, which shall never be destroyed : and the kingdom shall not be left to other people, but it shall break in pieces and consume all these kingdoms and it shall stand for ever."

How the astronomical, chronological, and geometrical symbolism of the Pyramid defines Britain as the Stone Kingdom beginning its functions at 1558 A.D.

¶ 390. THE MISSION OF A FALLIBLE RACE.

It would be a long matter to follow up the scriptural reasons given for this implied Divine selection of a race, which, if more worthy of the honour than some races, is nevertheless as unworthy as most of any Divine preference. It will suffice to refer the reader to the reason given by our Lord. Referring to the Stone Kingdom, He defined this as " a nation " to supplant the Jews and to " bring forth the fruits of the Kingdom of God." This promise we must read in conjunction with another statement of our Lord that " this Gospel of the Kingdom shall be preached in all the world for a witness unto all nations ; then shall the end come " (Matt. xxiv, 14). Clearly, then, the nation which by its acts and decisions has enabled the latter element of prophecy to be fulfilled, must be the nation " bringing forth the fruits," and therefore the " stone kingdom " of prophecy. Again we find the history of the propagation of the Gospel in foreign lands synchronous with, and dependent upon, the colonising efforts of the British Race.

The Stone Kingdom—supplanting the Jews—" to bring forth the fruits," by opening up the world, so that " this Gospel of the Kingdom shall be preached in all the world for a witness unto all nations."

This mission fulfilled by the British Race, alone of all races.

This strange question of the Divine selection of a fallible race has its ante-type in the Divine selection of humble fishermen and tax-gatherers— long ignorant of the purpose of their selection—to be the first witnesses of the Gospel of the Kingdom. They saw and heard, and failed fully to understand, until their Master's mission was accomplished. Then they remembered, and understood His Gospel. This Gospel concerns the whole of humanity. Humanity has failed to understand the literal meaning and truth of this Gospel. Humanity has learned or heard the Word without understanding its literal significance. Humanity, however, had perforce to know, even if it has failed to understand. The *emphasis* of our Lord is *directed to* this *knowing.* The implication is that understanding will dawn with the hastening of God's purpose, and that this, in cause and effect, *is* God's purpose.

Parallel between selection of the disciples and selection of the Stone Kingdom.

The mission of the Stone Kingdom to proclaim to all humanity the coming extension of God's Kingdom.

Christ's emphasis directed to humanity knowing of His purpose.

The implication that understanding will come when His purpose is effected.

¶ 391. THE MYSTICAL BODY OF CHRIST AND HIS BRIDE.

Hence the significance of the promise to Abraham, " in thee shall all families of the Earth be blessed." This is explained by the fact that the relationship holding between Christ and His disciples—prior to His Ascension

The Abrahamic promise extended to the Earth.

Spiritual
Israel, the
Body of Christ;
literal Israel,
the Bride of
Christ.
Restitution to
be effected in
the world
through the
restoration of
literal outcast
Israel.—has, in many senses, a parallel in the relationship holding between the Saints of Christ (the spiritual Israel—Gal. iii, 7–29) and the Stone Kingdom, prior to the coming literal Ascension of the Spiritual Israel (Matt. xxiv, 29–31 ; 1 Cor. xv, 51–53). This, again, explains the mystery of the relation between the material and the spiritual in the Kingdom of Heaven upon Earth. Spiritual Israel is Christ's mystical Body (1 Cor. xii, 12–31 ; Col. i, 18) ; literal Israel—the " divorced wife of Jehovah " in Hosea—purified is to become the Bride of Christ. " I will betroth thee (Israel) unto me for ever . . . *and I will sow her unto me in the Earth* " (Hos. ii, 19–23) ; or (Rev. xxi, 9–14) " Come hither, I will show thee the Bride, the Lamb's wife . . . the holy Jerusalem, descending out of Heaven from God . . . and names written thereon, which are the names of the twelve tribes of the children of Israel."

The promised
world inherit-
ance of Israel
relates chiefly
to Israel's
position after
the Messianic
restoration.Now the many promises to Israel in the Old Testament, concerning the material inheritance of that nation, define the Israel of the then remotely future age as occupying a definite strategic position in the world, and fulfilling certain missions.[1]   The complete specification of Israel's position

[1]THE PROMISES TO ISRAEL.

(1) The promises concerning the extent of Israel's dominion, and concerning the possession of the desolate heritages (Deut. xxxii, 7–9, 29).
   Concerning Christ's raising up of Israel to possess the desolate heritages, refer " My Magazine," May 1922, pp. 493–498, as partly quoted below.
(2) The promise of irrigation schemes and cultivation of desert places (Is. xli, 18–22).
(3) The promise concerning Israel's mission to free the slaves and to remove oppression (Is. lviii, 6).
(4) The promise concerning Israel's restoration of the ancient places (Is. lviii, 12 ; lxi, 4).
(5) The promise that Israel were to become " a nation and a company of nations " (Gen. xvii, 6 ; xviii, 18 ; xlviii, 16, 19).
(6) The promise that Israel were to become "the chief of the nations " (Deut. vii, 6). God's reason for this and His purpose (Is. xliii, 21).
(7) Israel to possess maritime power (Ps. lxxxix, 25, 27).
(8) Israel to possess the " gate of his enemies " (Gen. xxii, 17, 18).
(9) Israel to be, when necessary, the leading military power, invincible (Jer. li, 19, 21 ; Exod. xxiii, 27 ; Is. liv, 17).
(10) Israel to be the leading mercantile power (Num. xxiv, 7 ; Is. lx, 9; refer Delitzsch, footnote to ¶ 393).
(11) Israel's symbols to be the lion and unicorn, or the bull (Num. xxiv, 8, 9; xxiii, 22 and 24).
(12) Israel " to bring forth the fruits " (Gen. xlix, 22).
(13) Israel as the " stone kingdom " to stand for ever (Matt. xxi, 42–44 ; Dan. ii, 44).
(14) Israel to be given " the heritage of the heathen " (Ps. cxi, 5, 6).
(15) The Sabbath " to be a sign between Himself and the children of Israel, for ever, for a perpetual covenant " (Exod. xxxi, 16, 17).
(16) Israel to place the Jews back in Palestine (Jer. iii, 18).
(17) Israel to be known by another name, and to repudiate with scorn identity with the same race as the Jews (Is. lxv, 15).
(18) God's dealings with Israel to baffle the opinions of the critic (Is. xxix, 14 ; Jer. xxiii, 1, 2).

The article, ' The Mighty Multitude of People,' in " My Magazine "—referred to above—states as follows :—

   " The most wonderful thing about the world is that through all ages until modern times the population of the greater part of it remained quite small.   Then the white people began to increase rapidly.   If we want to understand the world we live in we cannot do better than think about this very curious thing.
   " The world became solid and inhabitable ages since—ages measured in years so many that we cannot grasp their magnitude.   Think of our own homeland, for ages uninhabited. . . .
   " How large was that population two hundred years ago, just yesterday in history ? It is very difficult to make an estimate, but certainly the number was very small.   A hundred

and missions, of course, extends to Israel in the Messianic Age. But the prophecies make it plain that the inheritance was to come by the forming of the preliminary phase of the Stone Kingdom, and in progressively cumulative stages of spiritual and material experience leading up to Israel's final restoration. Such progressively cumulative stages—marred, it is true, by many elements of mercenary selfishness [1]—have all been traversed in the process of formation of the British Empire and the United States of America. This agrees with the progressively cumulative development of the Stone Kingdom, and shows that in some wonderful way Divine Providence has employed a race to build up the Nuclear Kingdom to form the *material* basis for the restoration of all-Israel; both that section of Israel known as the Jews (Judah-Israel), and that larger section of Ephraim-Israel—the 10-tribed kingdom—lost to historical research for twenty-five centuries (refer Matt. x, 5-7). This explains a phase of the "shock-absorbing" process in operation [2] as defined by the Pyramid symbolism in ¶ 382, for Israel are defined as God's "battle-axe and weapons of war to break in pieces the nations" (Jer. li, 20), and this, too, is the function of the Stone Kingdom (Dan. ii, 44, and Matt. xxi, 43, 44)—God's controlled forces of armament employed against the armament of the forces of destruction.

But the inheritance to come in cumulative stages, in forming the literal Stone Kingdom, to lead up to the Messianic fulfilment. Thus defined, the promised inheritance is held by the English-speaking peoples. Their possession of the inheritance for the purpose of Israel's restoration. God's "shock-absorbing" process in the material as in the spiritual. Divinely controlled forces of armament to balance the power of the destructive forces of armament.

¶ 392. THE MESSIANIC ABSORPTION AND EXPANSION OF THE EXISTING STONE KINGDOM.

Are, then, the peoples of the British Race, however unworthy they may be, the custodians of the *material* destinies of the nucleus of God's Kingdom on Earth? If so, the message of the Great Pyramid should be primarily directed to the British Race (¶ 389). No nation, other than Britain, entered the Great War on the 5th August 1914 A.D. This is the date defined by the Pyramid as the commencement of the period of chaos for the people concerned. The

The Pyramid's special Antechamber chronological symbolism confirms the Pyramid's general chronological symbolism.

and sixty years ago the entire population of what we now call the United Kingdom was only about ten million people.
"But after that the British peoples grew so rapidly that in another 160 years—a brief flash of time as compared with all that had gone before—the ten millions grew to the forty-seven millions we have to-day. Let us set it out.
"In all the ages from the beginning of the earth down to 1760 the British Isles gained only ten million people.
"Then, in only a hundred and sixty years more, thirty-seven million more people were added.
"*That is so wonderful as to seem miraculous if we think about it.*
"And here is another thing just as wonderful. What we now call the United States of America was almost uninhabited down to quite recent times. A few tribes of Indians roamed its rich surface, but so few arts had they that they made a very poor living and often suffered from privation. Then white settlers arrived from Europe, who knew how to cultivate the land and use tools. The population grew, but still it remained small as we count populations to-day.
"... In 1840, about the time the railway came into the world, the United States had only seventeen million people. In 1870 this number had grown to thirty-nine millions. To-day the population is over a hundred millions. *America has grown from seventeen to one hundred and six millions in only eighty-two years, and has gained almost all her people in the last hundred years.*"
[1] Even His disciples had their Judas, and this Judas had his price.
[2] Our Conservative Premier, Mr. Baldwin, defined the British race as "the shock-absorber of the world." This was defined in relation to world chaos. The same, however, applies to the absorption of the Jew. But it is God's purpose that this should be so.

Both indicate the Pyramid's message extended to the British Race as the Stone Kingdom of prophecy.
same fact seems to be proclaimed by the application of the Granite Leaf datings to the remote origin and recent development of our trouble in Ireland (¶ 387), and to the symbolic definition of a new focussing of Christian ideals by the English-speaking peoples in the chaotic vortex of world conditions produced by the fetish of armaments.

Until its absorption by the Messianic Stone Kingdom, the British Race is destined to hold the power and perform the functions of the Stone Kingdom. The process of absorption, by elimination of offensive and iniquitous elements.
The complete Pyramid, again, is the symbol of the Stone Kingdom in perfection. The state of perfection thus symbolised (¶ 268, footnote) defines the perfect Messianic state of the Stone Kingdom—the Union of the Body of Christ (¶ 391), spiritual Israel, with the Bride, the purified and restored literal Israel. Until that event transpires, the British Race, it would seem, are destined to hold the power of the Stone Kingdom—which, from the time of its first inception, " shall never be destroyed " and " shall not be left for other people," but " shall stand for ever." Nevertheless our Lord has said that at His return He " shall send forth His angels, and they shall gather out of His kingdom all things that offend and them which do iniquity " (Matt. xiii, 41).

Jeremiah's prophecy relating to the Messianic restoration and increase of Israel. The peace of God.
Of this return of our Lord, Jeremiah has prophesied as follows :—

" Woe be unto the pastors that destroy and scatter the sheep of My pasture ! saith the Lord.

" . . . Behold I will visit upon you the evils of your doings, saith the Lord.

" And I will gather the remnant of my flock out of all the countries whither I have driven them, and will bring them again to their folds ; and they shall be fruitful and increase.

" . . . I will raise unto David a righteous Branch and a King shall reign and prosper, and shall execute judgment and justice in the earth.

" In His days Judah shall be saved, and Israel shall dwell safely ; and this is His name whereby He shall be called, THE LORD OUR RIGHTEOUSNESS " (Jer. xxiii, 1–6).

¶ 393. THE CURRENT FUNCTION OF THE EXISTING STONE KINGDOM.

Successive stages relating to the deliverance of Jerusalem to precede Christ's advent as King of Israel. The first stage accomplished in 1917 A.D.
According to both the Old and New Testament promises, the coming of " THE LORD OUR RIGHTEOUSNESS " was not to be long delayed after Jerusalem had been freed from the yoke of Gentile domination. The period of Seven Times of the Gentile domination over Jerusalem had successive stages of beginning, and has, therefore, corresponding successive stages of ending (Plate LXVI). The first stage of termination fell in 1917 A.D., and was fulfilled by the deliverance of Jerusalem from the desolating rule of the Turkish Empire. That Jerusalem had successive phases of overthrowing implies that it is to have successive phases of deliverance.

The accomplishing of this stage by the British forces at the time predicted indicates that the British Race is now reckoned amongst the kingdoms of the Gentile image.
Now if the British Race is not the Race of the prophetic Stone Kingdom, then Jerusalem is still under Gentile domination. But we have seen that the British Race stands in the prophesied position of the Stone Kingdom, and that this identity proclaims that the British Race—in the British Empire and United States of America—forms the nucleus for the ingathering of the House of Israel and the House of Judah (the Jews). According to the

prophecies, the House of Judah is to " walk to " the House of Israel to return to the Land.[1] We see, then, the apparent anomaly of the Jews walking to a so-called Gentile Power, possessing the mandate to rule and to restore Judah to Palestine. The function of the Stone Kingdom—the bringing forth of the fruits of the Kingdom of God—and the performance of this function by the British Race in over a century of its history explain the difficulty. The apparent anomaly is explained as the result of God's hand in co-ordinating the free-will efforts of man—the fertile and the apparently futile alike—to effect His predetermined purpose.

Let it be granted at once that the Mandate is neither operating smoothly nor effectively, according to the standards whereby human patience can gauge results. Such initial sequence in the most fruitful of world policies has always been an enigmatical factor in the history of the British Race. The impelling motive is a vaguely conceived sense of Divine purpose. Human factors, thus induced to operate from many different standpoints, have had their various opposing tendencies eliminated by mutual abrasion, and too often have had their best efforts initially thwarted by the grosser elements that are attracted by the prospect of easy material gain.

¶ 394. A WORLD LESSON IN ISRAEL'S HISTORY.

The whole history of Israel relates to a people who believed in the *material* aspects of the Divine promises given to them, and by thus *partially* believing, seeking by their own *material* efforts to shape and accomplish the high purposes of God. This is the whole story behind the Rabbinical manipulation of the 70 weeks' prophecy of Daniel and the attendant schemes of fictitious chronology evolved from time to time to give authority to the various political schemes projected. This is the whole story of the breaking and scattering of the Jewish people. Jewish efforts to fulfil the Jewish interpretations of prophecy accomplished the very overthrow of the Jewish people, predicted in the prophecies from the foreknowledge of God.

Something of the same nature lies at the back of the Zionist troubles in Palestine. According to the prophecies, both Judah and Israel are to be returned to Palestine—not the whole race, but *representative* elements of them (Jer. iii, 14)—not at any time appointed by themselves or conditioned by themselves or others, but at a time appointed by God, and entirely conditioned by Him. Religious organisations exist to further and promote this

[1] Even the great German commentator, Dr. Delitzsch, saw that Isaiah's prophecy, concerning the later Divinely authorised return of Judah and Israel (Is. lx), describes the return as taking place from an insular and maritime kingdom, situated off the Western coasts of Europe. In his annotation on Isaiah lx, he states :—

"The prophet here turns his eye to the sea. . . . The faith of the distant lands of the West is now beginning to work. These things thus flying along like clouds and doves are ships, with those of Tarshish FROM THE FARTHEST EXTREMITIES OF THE EUROPEAN INSULAR QUARTERS OF THE GLOBE AT THEIR HEAD—*i.e.* acting as the leaders of the fleet which is sailing to Zion, AND BRINGING ZION'S CHILDREN FROM AFAR."

In the same connection, Delitzsch cites Isaiah lix, 19, " So shall they fear the name of the Lord from the West."

element and other elements of God's purpose, but unless these organisations submit themselves to Divine conditioning their projects can only meet with failure.

The specified conditions attached to Israel's return and God's reasons for restoring Israel, and for the means adopted in effecting the restoration.

In the case of the restoration of all Israel this conditioning is defined as a very simple matter. Thus Ezekiel (xxxvi, 33–38), in outlining that God will accomplish the cleansing of Israel from their sins, the inhabiting of the desolate land, and the increasing of the race, and that His reason for so doing is that the heathen should know the Lord by His works, announces the single condition (verse 37) :—

"Thus saith the Lord God; I will yet for this be enquired of by the house of Israel, to do it for them."

¶ 395. THE CONDITIONS OF DELIVERANCE FROM THE FINAL TRIBULATION.

Both the Bible prophecies and the Pyramid's symbolic prophecy define that the final phase of chaos will compel Israel to pray God to deliver them from their greatest tribulation; and, as a result of this prayer, that deliverance comes in 1936 A.D.

Read in relation to the other prophecies concerning Israel's final tribulation, we see from Ezekiel that God has appointed the means whereby Israel in her agony of tribulation will be brought as a nation to call upon God in terms of our Lord's prayer—" Thy Kingdom come, Thy will be done in earth, as it is in heaven." In appointing the means, He has appointed the time. The time is defined as the time of the last trouble ending in 1936 A.D. This, in the Bible, is defined as the terminal date of the Seven Gentile Times, 2520 years after Jeremiah's prophecy of Christ's Second Coming [1] in Power. This, in the Pyramid, is defined as the terminal date of the second portion of the period of chaos, beginning 29th May 1928 and ending at 16th September 1936 A.D.

The British Race, as the Stone Kingdom, comes under the final tribulation, as indicated in the Pyramid prophecy.

The same condition of deliverance— national prayer —and its certainty of compulsion, are indicated as applying to the British Race.

It is essential, in this connection, that we should remember the prophetically defined function of the British Race. The Pyramid defines its message and the period of chaos as relating to the British Race (¶¶ 385–390). The British Race—by virtue of their possessing the functions of the Stone Kingdom —are to be instrumental in effecting the material elements of God's purpose as defined by the prophecies. The condition attaching to the prophecy of Ezekiel xxxvi, 33–38, therefore, applies to the British Race as the condition whereby success is to be assured. Israel's tribulation is to fall upon the British Race to compel that race to call upon the Lord " to do it for them." This is the whole message of the Pyramid and its purpose. It will carry

[1] There are two phases connected with our Lord's Coming or " Presence." The date of the first phase is defined as unknown, indeterminate (Matt. xxiv, 37–44; Mark xiii, 32–37). This phase relates to the visible manifestation of His " Presence " to gather His saints. The second phase relates to His visible descent with His saints upon the final phase of the confederation of Gentile kingdoms gathered against Jerusalem, and His judgment of the world thereafter (Jude, verses 14 and 15). This is the Coming to complete and perfect the Stone Kingdom, by the union of the Spiritual Israel and the Literal Israel, the union of the Body of Christ (His Saints) and the Bride (Literal Israel). The destruction of the final phase of the Gentile confederation is thus effected by the spiritual Stone Kingdom in Christ coming to purify and possess; even—so the allegory runs in the Old and New Testaments—as a loving husband at the repentant call of his divorced wife answers by forgiving, and in forgiving, by his love, cleanses, and possesses anew in love reciprocated.

conviction to many when this purpose is confirmed. Not to save the many from the time of trouble, but to guide them to the Light that will deliver them from out of the trouble at its zenith.

¶ 396. THE FINAL DESTRUCTION OF THE POWER OF THE GENTILE IMAGE.

The historical phase upon which are concentrated all the prophecies of the Old and New Testaments in relation to the Consummation is the final gathering of all nations against Jerusalem. This confederation of nations is prophetically specified as gathered together by a single Northern Power, or by a Dictator or Prince dominating a single Northern Power. Now, whereas the various prophecies always relate to the same general sequence of events, and to parallel conditions associated with these events, the name of the single Northern Power is not always the same. Generally the name is symbolic of the geographical location of the Power. In Revelation xiii and xix, 19 this Power is indicated as the final phase of " the beast," to which are attached the " kings of the earth and their armies " ; the designation in this case being symbolic of the nature of the Power as relating to its glory lying in strength of armament, and its physical ability to destroy.

The scriptural description of the final phase of the Gentile image.

The Gentile confederation gathered against Jerusalem.

The leading Power defined in geographical terms, and in terms symbolic of its nature.

Thus in Daniel xi, 40–45, xii, 1–3 it is the last civil power representing " the King of the North " ; in Isaiah xiv, 4–25, xxi, 4–9, lxvi, 15–19, and Micah v it is the last civil power representing (geographically) " Assyria " (*i.e.* the power in the North) ; in Ezekiel xxxviii and xxxix it is a final civil power under the symbolic " Gog, leader of Rosh,[1] Meshech, and Tubal," with " Gomer, and all his bands ; the house of Togarmah of the *North quarters*, and all his bands ; and many people with thee." All these relate to locations North of Armenia. In Rosh, Meshech, and Tubal we may see the origin of the modern names Russia, Moscow, and Tobolsk. The " gathering of all nations " against Jerusalem at the Consummation is also prophetically described in Zechariah xii and xiv, and in Joel iii.

Russia, under the control of a Dictator, or of a Power acting under a Dictator, is specifically defined as the principal territorial source of the final confederation of the kingdoms of the Gentile power.

Synchronistic comparison of these various prophecies as to details and sequence shows that the final official and representative return of Israel and Judah is defined as taking place *after* the destruction of Gog and all his hosts. Refer Ezekiel xxxix, 25, concerning the return of " the whole house of Israel " after the destruction of Gog. A partial and unofficial return is shown thereby to have taken place prior to Gog's onslaught. That this partial return relates chiefly to Judah (the Jews) is clearly stated in Zechariah, chapter xii. The representative nature of the final official return is indicated by Jeremiah iii, 14, in relation to iii, 18, by the type of Jehovah's " Bride." " . . . I am married unto you : and I will take you one of a city, and two of a family, and I will bring you to Zion. . . . In those days the house of Judah shall walk TO the house of Israel, and they shall come together out of the land of

This confederation completely destroyed at the last siege of Jerusalem.

Following this deliverance, the official representative return of Israel and Judah is defined as taking place.

[1]This is the literal rendering, as see " Companion Bible " on Ezekiel xxxviii, 2 and xxxix, 1.

the North [1] into the land that I have given for an inheritance unto your fathers."

¶ 397. BRITAIN AND RUSSIA IN PROPHECY.

The prophecies imply a partial and unofficial return—of the Jews — under the protection of the Stone Kingdom, prior to the final tribulation.

Prior, then, to the final—or official and representative—return of Israel, and before the preceding culminating phase of the Last Tribulation, the prophecies very clearly picture a partial and unofficial return under the protection of a state that must be the Stone Kingdom (Ezek. xxxviii, 13). This protecting kingdom is described as the " King of the South " in the prophecy of Daniel xi, 40 to xii, 13. The prophecy relates to the " time of the end " and to " the time of trouble " of *Daniel's people* (*i.e.* the Jews). The occasion of the trouble is the overwhelming onslaught of " the King of the North," whose invasion is opposed by " the King of the South." For over a century students of prophecy have seen that the event is defined as following Judah's partial return (Zech. xii), but prior to the Divinely authorised representative return of " the whole house of Israel " (Ezek. xxxix, 25–29). The Gog of Ezekiel xxxviii is therefore identified with the " king of the North " of Daniel xi, 40.

The two final opponents :— Daniel's final " King of the North " = Ezekiel's Gog = Russia. Daniel's final " King of the South " = Ezekiel's " merchants of Tarshish and all the young lions thereof " = Daniel's Stone Kingdom = the British Race. Armageddon and our Lord's return.

For over a century reliable exponents of prophecy have identified Ezekiel's Gog with Russia and with Daniel's " King of the North," and have identified Ezekiel's opponent of Gog—*i.e.* the " merchants of Tarshish [2] with all the young lions thereof "—with the British Race, as Daniel's " King of the South." Thus, between 1830 and 1850, such eminent exponents of prophecy as Professor Birks of Cambridge and the respective authors of " The Kings of the East " and " Armageddon " foresaw, from the prophecies, that a confederation of the British Race would become the opponent of a confederation of European hegemonies under a Russian dictatorship, or under a dictatorship controlling Russia ; these two opposing confederations, at the time of our Lord's return, facing each other on a broad front, with the Valley of Megiddo in Palestine as the location of the principal strategic flank.[3]

Ezekiel defines warfare of modern proportions.

That the Final War is a war of modern proportions is clearly indicated by Ezekiel xxxix, 9, 12, 14—the weapons to supply fuel for seven years, and the burials in the locality of Megiddo to occupy seven months (refer also verses 14 and 15 as to the process of cleansing continuing).

[1]There is no equivalent for " North-West " in Hebrew. Hence, when some prophecies speak of a return " from the West " " in the ships of Tarshish " and others from the " North," the two designations combine to define the return as from the North-West.

[2]Refer footnote to ¶ 393 as to Dr. Delitzsch's identification of the " ships of Tarshish."

[3]The military situation thus defined by Ezekiel appears to be the final phase of a long series of operations described in Daniel xi, 40–45, in which the " king of the South " is initially defeated. Daniel xi, 44 indicates reasons for the withdrawal of the forces of the " king of the North " into the North and East. However this may be related to the time in question, the event of Daniel xi, 44 is certainly both prior to Israel's Divinely authorised return in Ezekiel xxxvii and xxxix, 25, and prior to the overthrow of Gog in Ezekiel xxxviii. The last event, *i.e.* the overthrow of Gog, is clearly identical with the events of the second half of verse 45 in Daniel xi, and in Daniel xii, 1, and the events of Zechariah xii. By a careful reading of all the chapters of Ezekiel, the reader will find that the chapters and order of his prophecies do not necessarily follow always in chronological sequence, either in relation to Ezekiel's life or in relation to the prophetical narratives.

¶ 398. A SEVENTY-EIGHT YEARS' OLD INTERPRETATION IN COURSE OF FULFILMENT.

In 1846—long before Britain had any connection with Egypt—Professor Birks wrote concerning the Final Opposition as follows :— *The prophecy interpretation of Professor Birks defines the then future political situation as it is now shaping towards tangible fulfilment.*

"Hence we have a strong presumption that *one* mighty leader will hereafter group under his banner the western tribes of Europe, the power of Russia, and the districts held long before by the King of the North. This chieftain, whether a Russian Emperor or a second Napoleon more successful in his Eastward warfare, would fulfil every condition which the vision of Daniel suggests, and which the words of Ezekiel seem evidently to require. . . ."

"Egypt alone seems too feeble to undertake any serious resistance to a confederacy so vast and mighty. . . . That the same power which holds the vast southern Empire of India may then also have possession of Egypt, and from thence push against the inroads of his northern adversary, it would be rash to expect with confidence, but the conjecture is not unreasonable. The course of events and the necessities of commerce appear more and more to be grouping together India, Egypt, and Britain. . . . When, therefore, all the continent shall be gathered under one head, as King of the North, it seems not improbable that the maritime Empire of Britain may be the rival power, and that its acquisition of Egypt will give to it the prophetic character of the King of the South" ("Two Later Visions of Daniel," pp. 333, 334).

Elsewhere the same writer stated, in the same work, that—

"The great leader of the North will overflow and pass on to the South to crush the power which has assailed him. The description answers exactly to the words of Ezekiel, where he predicts the march of Gog against the land of Israel."

¶ 399. AN INTERPRETATION—THIRTY YEARS AGO—IN COURSE OF FULFILMENT.

In a remarkable paper read before "The Prophecy Investigation Society," London, on 21st November 1893, the late Dr. Aldersmith stated as follows :— *Dr. Aldersmith's prophecy interpretation defines the Great European War, the end of the Turkish Empire, the deliverance of Jerusalem, and the moulding of Russia to take her place as the Gog of Ezekiel—the opponent of the British Race in the final phase of chaos.*

"Very many changes may be expected during the coming war-woe, now so imminent on the nations of Europe. The Turkish Empire ('the second woe,'[1] as I think it is) must cease before Russia can take her place as the Gog of Ezekiel, or the Assyrian, and the third or last woe. 'The times of the Gentiles' referred to by our Lord, will also have to be fulfilled, and Jerusalem will then be no longer trodden down by Gentile feet.

"Now we find a certain people referred to in Ezekiel xxxviii as 'the merchants of Tarshish, with all the young lions thereof.' Who are these? Let anyone consult Mr. Chamberlain's book, 'The Time of the End'; or 'Palestine Repeopled,' by the Rev. J. Neil; or the Rev. T. R. Birks' works, and he will have no doubt that Great Britain, or rather Greater Britain, is intended; for we may certainly expect our colonies to help in such an emergency. The British Empire undoubtedly will have to withstand Russia and her allies over the final settlement of the Eastern Question, which has always been a matter between Russia and Great Britain, as the parties most interested. Ezekiel says 'The Lions oppose.' Curious, that the term 'lions' is used here—the symbol of the

[1] Rev. ix, 12 ; xi, 14. Refer also quotation from Guinness, ending footnote to ¶ 348.

British Empire—and they say, ' Art thou come to take a spoil ? ' which surely means defiance.

"Again Isaiah informs us that the Jews, ' with their silver and gold with them,' are to be replaced in Palestine by ' the ships of Tarshish ' (Is. lx, 9), viz. Great Britain's ships. If, on the other hand, we consult Jeremiah iii, 18, we find the House of Judah, or the Jews, are to walk ' TO ' the house of Israel to be replaced in Palestine. Jeremiah's words are : ' In those days the House of Judah shall walk to the House of Israel, and they shall come together out of the Land of the North to the land that I gave for an inheritance to your fathers.'

"If you care to look more carefully into this matter, you will find that both ' The Speaker's Commentary ' and the ' Cambridge Bible ' say the word is ' walk TO,' not ' walk WITH,' the House of Israel. In fact, ' The Speaker's Commentary ' says : ' The right translation of the preposition is important, "THEY SHALL WALK *TO* THE HOUSE OF ISRAEL " ' . . . ISRAEL is represented as the first to REPENT, and JUDAH must go to her, in order that they may come together back to the Holy Land ; divided no longer into JEWS and ISRAELITES, but merged into one people."

¶ 400. THE HAVEN OF REFUGE FOR ISRAEL AND JUDAH.

The remnant of the 10 tribes of Israel already gathered into the Stone Kingdom by the time the Jews are finally driven into that haven of refuge for Israel.

The phase of Russia depicted as in opposition to the British Race, as the Stone Kingdom is still future.

The implied sequence of events leading to this phase analogous to the events of the French Revolution extending to the major part of Europe.

A consequent reaction against Jewish part in Russian Bolshevist " régime," driving Continental Jews to seek British protection.

The prophecies clearly indicate that literal Israel—the people of the 10 tribes—must already, unknown to the world, have been gathered into the nucleus of the Stone Kingdom [1] by the time that certain predicted circumstances drive the Jews from the kingdoms of the Gentile Image to walk to [2] the haven of refuge of the house of Israel. This haven of refuge we have seen to be the nucleus of the Stone Kingdom. The latter we have seen to be prophetically defined in chronological time, geographical location, sequence of historical events, and moral, commercial, and strategical development, as identical with the power or powers of the British Race. Opposed to this race, the prophecies depict a confederation of European and near Eastern peoples under the domination of a dictatorship exercised upon or through a still future phase of the Russian peoples. Related to the sequence of events leading up to the formation of this phase—which sequence is analogous to the successive revolutionary phases that established the Empire of Napoleon, but which is now outlined on a vaster scale as extending to the major portion of Continental Europe—are the predicted conditions leading up to the expulsion or withdrawal of the multitudes of Jews remaining in Continental Europe. This points to a phase of " anti-Semite " revolution following the Jewish epoch in Russia identified with the Bolshevist régime. Britain's recent part in gathering the refugees from Bolshevist Russia proclaims what Britain's part will be in " gathering in " the Jewish refugees from an anti-Semitic Europe. This part of Britain is the prophesied rôle of the " ships of Tarshish " (¶ 393 and note).

[1] " . . . I will sift the ' house of Israel ' among all the nations, like as corn is sifted in a sieve, yet shall not the least grain fall upon the earth " (Amos ix, 9).
" My God will cast them (10-tribed Israel) away, because they did not hearken unto Him ; and they shall be wanderers among the nations " (Hosea ix, 17).
" Hear the word of the Lord, O ye nations, and declare it in *the isles afar off*, and say, He that scattereth Israel will gather him and keep him " (Jer. xxxi, 10).
Refer Delitzsch, quoted in footnote to ¶ 393.
[2] Refer ¶ 396, as to Judah " walking to " Israel prior to their joint representative return.

¶ 401. A MODERN JEWISH EPOCH PROPHESIED.

The Russian Question, then, is prophetically related to the expulsion or withdrawal of the Jews from Europe, and their return to Palestine in " the ships of Tarshish," " their silver and their gold with them," as Isaiah says. Now everything in history and prophecy is related in cause and effect. The epoch of this Russian Question, as related to the Jewish Question, is the epoch of the establishment of the Bolshevist régime in Russia. This date is indicated in the Pyramid as the chronological turning-point in the history of the Jews.

The Pyramid's special chronology system defines the turning point in the history of the Jews as the date of the establishing of the Bolshevist " régime " in Russia ; 18th January 1918, five weeks after the deliverance of Jerusalem.

The Pyramid's dating for this tragic time in the history of the Jews is the dating of the South Wall of the Queen's Chamber. This, as shown on Plate XXXVb, occurs at the date defined by point R in the 1st Low Passage leading to the Antechamber. As indicated on Table XXIX, the date is 18th January 1918 A.D.—little more than a month after the deliverance of Jerusalem. On this date, according to " The Times," 22nd January 1918, the Bolsheviks, after demanding a Republic of Soviets, dissolved the Russian Constituent Assembly. On the same day the British Ambassador, Sir George Buchanan, arrived in London from Petrograd. " The Times " correspondent, writing from Petrograd two days later, defined the situation in the words " Bolshevist Autocracy Supreme."

Again, in " The Times " of 19th January 1918, a remarkable article, headed " Russia's Annus Mirabilis "—dated 13th January 1918—thus designates the Russian Julian-year that began 13th January 1917 and ended 13th January 1918—a year of two revolutions.

The fateful second revolution in Russia broke out in October 1917— a date as fateful as the event it witnessed. For, as prophetically and chronologically confirming what history has told us concerning the interwoven but antagonistic destinies of Russia, Turkey, and Judah, the 1335th lunar year of Turkish reckoning terminated on 17th October 1917 A.D. In this same remarkable year of Russia's downfall to Bolshevism, Jerusalem was delivered.

The interwoven destinies of Russia, Turkey, and the Jews.

The " Second (Turkish) Woe "[1] ended, then, at the completion of the 1335th lunar year, at the same time as the " Third (Russian) Woe " began to shape itself. Judah's period of transition lies between the two " Woes."

The shaping of the elements of the Third Woe, and the transition of Judah.

---

[1] It may be that the passing of the Turkish Empire is only a phase of the passing of Turkey, in which case Turkey may either exist to complete the final phase of the Second Woe, or to be embodied in the confederation associated with the Third Woe.

Now the reader cannot fail to have seen the symbolical importance the Pyramid's chronology attaches to the Great Step dating. This is midnight ending 25th January 1844, and is 391 years from the date of the rise of the Ottoman Empire, *i.e.* the capture of Constantinople in 1453 A.D. According to modern prophecy interpretation, the mystical " Euphrates " of prophecy and the Second Woe of Revelation relate to the Ottoman Empire. In Revelation xiv, 12–21 the Second Woe and the mystical " Euphrates " are mentioned in connection with a period of " an hour, and a day, and a month, and a year." On the year-day identity, neglecting the hour, this reduces to 1 + 30 + 360 = 391, thus indicating the 391 years of Ottoman power to 1844 A.D. In the latter year, in March 1844, a decree of religious toleration was forced from the Sultan of Turkey.

The Step dating is also 2520 lunar years (*i.e.* the 7 Gentile Times), or 2445 solar years from the death of Nabopolassar and the accession of Nebuchadnezzar (refer Table XXX).

Does anything further need to be added to explain why the turning-point of Judah's history is given by the Pyramid chronology as ending on the day that witnessed the dissolution of the Russian Constituent Assembly by the Bolsheviks?

¶ 402.   THE SYMBOLISM OF JEWISH DIVERGENCE UNDER THE LAW ANNULLED.

Queen's Chamber and Passage symbolism and datings relate prophetically to Jewish history as the Antechamber and Passages, and their symbolism and datings relate to the destinies of Israel, the Stone Kingdom, and the British Race.

We see, then, that the Queen's Chamber datings relate to Jewish history, precisely as the Low Passage and Antechamber datings were seen to relate to the destinies of Israel, the Stone Kingdom, and the British race.   A moment's consideration upon the part of the reader will show how appropriately the Queen's Chamber and its horizontal Passage of Access symbolise the history of the Jews.   The roof level of the Queen's Chamber horizontal Passage is the level of the termination of the 1st Ascending Passage roof. The dating of the latter is the date of the Crucifixion (¶ 328).   Hence, since the 1st Ascending Passage symbolises the ascending way of " the Yoke of the Law " (¶ 329), the horizontal Passage to the Queen's Chamber clearly

The horizontal Low Passage to Queen's Chamber symbolises Judah remaining under the Law and without spiritual progress after the date of the Crucifixion as defined by Grand Gallery commencement.

symbolises continuance under the " Yoke of the Law," but without *ascent*, and by continuously increasing divergence from the " New and Living Way." This symbolism, therefore, clearly applies to the Jews, and to the Jews only, after the Crucifixion (Plate XXXIX).

The symbolism of stepping down as implying the degradation of the Jews prior to their being brought to realise Christ as their Saviour.

Again, as the horizontal Passage approaches the Queen's Chamber, there is a sudden step *down* in the floor (Plate XXXIX).   This step down brings the horizontal Passage floor to the level of the Queen's Chamber floor. According to ancient Egyptian interpretation—derived from Pyramid tradition—the Queen's Chamber symbolises the place of " second birth " (¶¶ 353 and 354).   In the Pyramid's geometrical chronology the level of the Queen's Chamber floor (¶ 340)—symbolised as reached by a sudden stepping down or descent on the part of the Jews—is the level defining the date of the Nativity.   This all seems to symbolise the degrading of the Jews until they come to a sudden realisation of what the Life of Christ, from His Birth to His Death, means to them.

¶ 403.   THE TURNING-POINT IN THE JEWISH DEGRADATION.

The Jewish part in the triumph of Bolshevism 18th January 1918 A.D. Dating given by the symbolism of Judah's turning-point in the Queen's Chamber.

Thus debased, the symbolism indicates that a turning-point in the destiny of the Jews is reached at the triumph of Bolshevism on the 18th of January 1918 A.D.   Reference to Plate XXXVb shows the significance of this dating, which occurs at the point R.   Groping, without " Light," along the South Wall of the Queen's Chamber—from R to Z on Plate XXXVb— the outcast *in the horizontal plane of debasement* is guided, unknown to himself, towards the central vertical plane of Restitution.   The limit of his progress in this direction from the turning-point R is the distance RZ.   This distance, as shown on Plate XXXVb, is equal to the distance RN, which defines the date of the threshold of the King's Chamber as 16th September 1936 A.D.

This, again, is the prophesied date of the union of Israel and Judah at the return of Christ, with His Saints, as King of All-Israel (¶¶ 372 and 379 (4h), and Plate LXVI).

The symbolism therefore indicates that the geometrically defined square RNTZ (Plate XXXVb) connecting, in plan, the structurally (and geometrically) defined Queen's Chamber and King's Chamber, relates to the effecting of the apparently impossible. The symbolism defines the process as of God, and by means not realised by man as operating to attain any tangible result, let alone God's pre-elected plan (refer ¶¶ 390 and 393). As in the case of the Granite Plugs, symbolising the ascent of Israel through impossible physical conditions (¶¶ 355 and 356), so in the case considered, the geometrical square RNTZ, connecting, in plan, the Queen's Chamber and the King's Chamber, symbolises God again effecting the translation of Judah from the lower plane of debasement to the higher plane of the Consummation and Restitution.

Marginal note: Divine guidance symbolised as afforded on the lower spiritual plane to bring Judah into the scheme of Restitution. The geometrical square connecting the plan of the Queen's Chamber with the plan of the King's Chamber. This symbolises and dates the divinely effected union of Israel and Judah at the King's Chamber threshold dating, 16th September 1936 A.D.—2520 years from Jeremiah's prophecy concerning the coming of the Lord our Righteousness to effect this union.

¶ 404. THE ALPHA AND OMEGA OF GOD'S PURPOSE.

Now, in ¶¶ 334–337 we saw the importance of the numeral 14 in relation to the chronological placing of Christ's birth, ministry, and sacrifice. Both the numeral itself and our Lord's life were rejected by the Jews as factors relating to the fulfilment of Daniel's prophecy of the 70 weeks. Yet it was precisely those factors that fulfilled the 70 weeks' prophecy.

Marginal note: The Jews and Christ in relation to the 70 weeks' prophecy. The rejection of the prophetic 14. Isaac on the altar prefigures Christ on the Cross. Isaac 14 years old.

Likewise the Jews failed to see the significance of Abraham's trial of faith. They failed to see that Isaac on the altar was intended to prefigure the Sacrifice of Christ, that the substitution of the ram symbolised that God Himself had pre-elected the Sacrifice, and that the pre-elected One was not Isaac, but a still future Redeemer to come of Abraham's " seed." Hence we find from the chronological relations—as confirmed by the text of Genesis xxii, 1–9[1]—that Isaac was 14 years old at the time, the numeral again prefiguring the chronological relations that proclaim Christ " the Lamb of God." Thus :

Twelve times 153 .. ..=1836² A.K. (¶¶ 334 and 340).		
The Displacement defining God's Sacrifice .. 286 (¶ 350).		
Isaac on the Altar when 14 years old.. .. 2122 A.K.		
Interval .. .. 1906½ years.		
Christ on the Cross .. .. .. 4028½ A.K. { Commencement of Grand Gallery.		
The same interval .. .. 1906½ years.		
Judah looks upon " Me whom they have pierced " (Zech. xii, 10) at the final deliverance of Jerusalem .. .. .. } 5935 A.K. { Threshold of King's Chamber.		

Marginal note: The chronological chain of prophecy :—

A.K.
12 × 153 = 1836
Displacement } 286
Isaac sacrifice } 2122
Interval 1906¼
Christ sacrifice } 4028¼
Interval 1906¼
Zech. xii 10 } 5935.

[1]Genesis xxii, 5 distinguishes between the age of Isaac " the lad " and the age of the " two young men " accompanying Abraham and his son. Isaac was not of sufficient age to be termed " young man." Yet he was old enough to carry the faggots for his own intended sacrifice. This agrees with Isaac being 14 years old at the time, as indicated by the chronological identity prefiguring Christ's Sacrifice.

[2]In ¶¶ 239–241 it was shown that the Pyramid's " score " dating is 1856 A.K.—defining the *Alcyone* alignment at that date (2144 B.C.)—and that *Alcyone* in ancient times was the star of

"I would not, brethren," said St. Paul (Rom. xi, 25), "have you ignorant of this mystery, lest ye be wise in your own conceits, that a *hardening in part* hath befallen Israel, until the *fulness of the Gentiles be come in.*"

This "fulness of the Gentiles" can only relate to the terminal phases of "the Times of the Gentiles" (Plate LXVI). These terminal phases extend from 12th December 1917 to 16th September 1936 A.D. Jerusalem was delivered by the British forces on the former date, and according to the Scriptural prophecies and the chronological symbolism of the Pyramid, is to be finally delivered from its greatest tribulation at the latter date by the Coming of Christ with Power and great Glory. This is the last siege of Zechariah xii, where (in verse 10) it is stated that the Jews "shall look upon Me whom they have pierced, and they shall mourn for Him . . . as one that is in bitterness for his firstborn."

This, then, is the significance of the Queen's Chamber, and its symbolism of the second birth, as relating to the Birth of Christ—"The King of the Jews"—His Crucifixion by the Jews, and His Return to be mourned by the Jews as one mourns for "his firstborn."

¶ 405. THE DEFINITE PERIOD AND PURPOSE OF THE PYRAMID'S MESSAGE.

The Message of the Pyramid, then, cannot be deemed to be extended to enlighten the Jews prior to their being enlightened by Christ Himself. The destiny of the Jews, however, is indicated as interwoven with the destiny of the British Race. The Message of the Pyramid, as proclaimed by its Antechamber and connected Low Passage datings and symbolism, is extended to the British Race. It may be that this Message has yet to be developed and translated into more acceptable form. It may be that the Message is to have its greatest period of application when its dated warnings draw attention to the fact that the Message is true. The significance of identities that are past has little influence on human impulse or inertia. Identities that are predicted weight with their full significance those that are most affected by the identities when they occur. The Scriptural and Pyramid prophetic indications here relate primarily to the British Race, and will weigh most heavily in their fulfilment upon the British Race. The Scriptural

"the foundation." Owing to this identity, tradition obviously connected the epoch of the Pyramid's building with the "score" dating, and with the *Alcyone* alignment.

In the above statement of prophetical chronology we have a date, 1836 A.K., 20 years earlier than the "score" dating at 1856 A.K. Obviously, Egyptian tradition held that 1836 A.K. defined the date of the Pyramid's founding, since the Egyptian priests told Herodotus that the actual building of the Great Pyramid occupied 20 years ("Herodotus," II, 124).

For present purposes it is immaterial whether the tradition is correct or not as identifying the epoch of the Pyramid's building. What is important is that the tradition connects two Pyramid epochs, the "score" dating at 1856 A.K.=2144 B.C., and the prophetical dating 1836 A.K. =2164 B.C., relating to the chronological statement prefiguring the Sacrifice of the Messiah. The latter dating is midway between Sir John Herschel's date, 2160 B.C., and Professor Piazzi Smyth's date, 2170 B.C., for the *Alpha Draconis* alignment at Entrance Passage altitude. As a period, the interval of 1836 years is defined by the length of the roof of the Grand Gallery, symbolising the "New and Living Way" of the Elect in Christ (Plate XLIIa and ¶ 340). The number symbolising the Elect is 153 (¶¶ 339, 340, 351, and 371), and 1836=12×153, 12 being the factor symbolising "governmental perfection" in Hebrew prophetic symbolism (¶¶ 334 and 340).

and Pyramid prophecies indicate the British Race as the haven for fugitive Jews (¶ 393 and footnote, and ¶ 391 footnote, items 16 and 17). The majority of the British Race will scorn and repudiate the allotted rôle, but they are destined to fulfil it. It is part of the Pyramid's Message to proclaim this.

The Scriptural prophecies, again, indicate that the Final Tribulation is to fall heavily alike upon the Jews and on those who receive and protect them. This, too, is confirmed by the Pyramid chronology, and its prophetic symbolism. To bring them out of this affliction, Scriptural prophecy proclaims " I will yet be enquired of by the house of Israel to do it for them " (¶¶ 394 and 395). This proclamation of prophecy was seen to apply equally to the British Race, as the nucleus of the Stone Kingdom (¶ 395), and was seen to be confirmed by the Pyramid (¶¶ 387 and 403). The Pyramid's Message, therefore, proclaims to the British Race that in its hour of darkest peril it will be compelled to call upon the God of Israel to deliver it. The same message is conveyed by Isaiah in relation to the Pyramid, and as confirming its Divine Message. Isaiah's message (xix, 14–25) clearly refers to the days when Egypt shall fall to the power of the King of the North (Russia and her confederates), and being delivered by the advance of the King of the South (Britain, her colonies, and the U.S.A.), shall participate in the blessings incidental to Israel's restoration. This message, as already quoted, reads as follows (verses 19 and 20) :—

The British Race, Israel, and the Jews to be compelled to ask God to deliver them in their time of trouble. Isaiah's Message proclaims the purpose of the Great Pyramid.

> " In that day shall there be an altar to the LORD in the midst of the land of Egypt, and a pillar at the border thereof to the LORD.
> " And it shall be for a sign and for a witness unto the LORD of hosts in the land of Egypt : for they shall cry unto the LORD because of the oppressors, and he shall send them a saviour, and a great one, and he shall deliver them."

SECTION I.—SUMMARY AND CONCLUSIONS.

(A) THE PROBABILITIES OF THE CO-ORDINATION.

¶ 406. GENESIS AND REVELATION.

The new evidence relating to the first eleven chapters of Genesis leads to conclusions altogether unexpected.
One outstanding and significant result of our investigations has been the demonstration of the inadequate nature of modern exposition and criticism concerning the first eleven chapters of Genesis. A similar limitation of understanding has been seen to apply to modern study of the Old Testament generally, but in no such degree as marks the study of Genesis, and, in particular, the study of the first eleven chapters of Genesis.

It is truly startling to find that these eleven chapters of the First Book of the Pentateuch comprise something distinctly different from anything hitherto known to exist, or imagined as existing, in any form of literature, sacred or profane. That the narrative of these chapters is a statement of a chronological succession of historical facts cannot now be doubted. But when we realise, as we must realise from the facts now elucidated, that we are only at the beginning of the study concerning what the narrative really means, it behoves us to be cautious before we make any positive assertion.

The First Book of Genesis presented as a vision of past history, as the Book of Revelation is presented as a vision of future history.
The first eleven chapters of Genesis comprise what Ferrar Fenton, in his " Bible in Modern English," rightly designates " The First Book of Genesis." It seems to be certain—from the new evidence—that this First Book of Genesis describes a vision of past history, as the Book of Revelation describes a vision of future history. In both cases the method of presenting the vision is conformable to the age in which the vision was given and translated into narrative form.

The former the Prologue, the latter the Epilogue to the history of the seed of Abraham.
The First Book of Genesis is therefore the Prologue to the history of Abraham and his seed. The history of Abraham's seed follows successively through the historical narratives of the Old and New Testaments, up to the Apostolic Age. Following the Prologue of Genesis, this history begins with the promise of the New Testament, and ends with its coming into effect after the death of the Testator, Jesus Christ. The Book of Revelation, then, forms a fitting Epilogue to the history of Abraham's " seed." It is a vision of the complete fulfilment, in the future, of the Promise to Abraham —" in thy seed shall all families of the earth be blessed "—and of the manner in which this fulfilment would be effected.

¶ 407. THE CONCENTRATED NARRATIVE FORM OF THE FIRST BOOK OF GENESIS.

The vision of six days portrays the events of six periods of creation.
Beginning with the narration of a vision of six consecutive days, the First Book of Genesis compresses, in epic form, the events of six long successive

periods of a finite stage of God's Creation.[1] This finite stage of Creation is defined as applying to the organisation of the Earth in the form in which it is known to us. Previous finite stages of God's infinite process of Creation are mentioned in the first verse of Genesis. Here it is stated literally that " by headships[2] (by an indefinite series of stages or categories of processes ?) God created that which produced the (visible) heavens, and that which produced the earth." Here everything that preceded, in the indefinite past, the final phase of the earth's material development, is included in this single initial verse of Genesis. Again, everything relating to the final phase of the earth's material development—each event of six long active creative periods —is compressed into the narrative of a vision of six days.

Passing to the Book of the Generations of Adam, we find this is similarly compressed in Chapter V of Genesis. Here a complete dynasty is presented as the founder of the dynasty, and the total duration of the dynasty is presented as the life of its founder. Thus originated in this remote period the constitutional formulæ " the king is dead, long live the king," and " the king never dies, he only demises the throne." The king was not deemed to be dead until the direct line of his dynasty ceased. Successive heads of the house possessed the same name. The headship and name continued from successor to successor. *(margin: The successive dynasties of the Adamic race are presented as successive generations from the first Adam.)*

A similar compression is frequently met with in the Books relating to Israel's history, when non-essential genealogical items are mentioned. Thus, in Numbers xxxii, 40, " Moses gave Gilead unto Machir,[3] the son of Manasseh; and he dwelt therein." Machir, here, clearly means " the House of Machir." This is the sense in which the names of the antediluvian patriarchs are used in the Book of the Generations of Adam (Gen. v). *(margin: The same method of presentation adopted in non-essential genealogical details of Israel's history.)*

The fact of the genealogical compression in the First Book of Genesis, however, could not have been proved to demonstration otherwise than by the discovery of the significant ending of a dynasty always in the last year *(margin: This method of presentation, in the First Book of Genesis, is demonstrated by the cyclic datings, and the significance attaching to these.)*

[1]It is every bit as marvellous to suppose the creation of this wonderful world and all its entities and kingdoms in sixty million years as it is to suppose its creation in six literal days. The marvel lies in the fact of creation, not in the time in which it was effected.

What we are concerned with, however, is the meaning of the narrative intended by the text of Genesis. Does it mean a literal day or a long period ? Does it mean a generation when it mentions a generation, or does it mean thereby a dynastic succession of generations ? If we can prove, in the latter case, that the second alternative was intended, then we have proved the fact of a literary form of presentation in the Book of Genesis that was adopted for early religious plays, and that later formed the basis of presentation of the drama. Thus a historical play is necessarily performed as a series of historical acts in one night. This, however, is merely an illustration, for, as we have seen, the same literary form of compression has been adopted in prophecy or in the narratives describing visions.

The first chapter of Genesis is clearly the narrative of a vision in the first instance, since it is obvious that the narrator was not present when the events he describes occurred. The narrator obviously was speaking or writing in language that described something he saw. This is evident from the graphical virility of the narrative. What he saw was clearly seen in a vision picturing the events of six days, or in a vision extending over six days. In the visions described in the later Books of the Old Testament and in the Book of Revelation, spiritual beings are represented as explaining each successive act of the vision. The presence of a spiritual being of this nature is implied by the concluding words of the description of the events of each day of creation.

[2]Plural and indefinite.

[3]Gen. l, 23: " And Joseph saw Ephraim's children of the third generation; the children also of Machir, the son of Manasseh, were brought up on Joseph's knees."

of a calendar cycle (Table V and ¶¶ 37–40 and 313). The known fact, from archæological sources, that the continuity of kingship, or the official ending of the kingship, was effected in the terminal year of a calendar cycle—which was seen to have been derived from a former stage of civilisation—directed attention to this question, and indicated that the race with which this civilisation originated was to be identified with the race of the First Book of Genesis.

¶ 408. THE OUTLINE OF ADAMIC HISTORY.

The hypothesis suggested by the new evidence.

Although it is impossible to make any definite assertion, certain broad outlines of a tangible history seem to be suggested by the narrative of the First Book of Genesis, when considered in relation to the new evidence. Adopting the hypothesis thus suggested, the resulting outline of history, as it seems to be presented, may be stated tentatively as follows :—

The election of the first Adam the final process of the active stages of the Earth's creation.

Passive and objective law and order attained.

" God rested."

The First Book of Genesis describes the special creative selection or election of the First Adam and his seed—the Adamic race. The selection is described as the final and objective process of the six finite " active " stages of the Earth's creation. With the completion of this final process a definite " passive " and objective stage of law and order was attained in relation to the Earth and man. Man, provided with his special faculties, was placed in supreme dominion on the Earth, to adjust himself to the passive working of the Laws of God as translated into visible effect in man's dominion. The beginning of this passive operation of God's Laws, as a result of the active creative work of the six " days " of the vision of Earth's creation, is described as God resting upon the " seventh day."

The fall of the first Adam.

The Divine tuition of the Adamic race.

Its migration into the East.

The Adamic world isolated from the external world of the Gentiles.

The destruction of the Adamic civilisation.

The Divine tuition of the First Adam is described as the form in which the Divine election of Adam was made manifest after his failure to retain his place in God's created scheme. Driven out from the realm of his first dominion, he was forced to migrate eastwards.[1] In the new realm in which he was forced to settle, the conditions were such that he could sustain himself only by the most arduous labour.[2] Here is pictured the existence and development of the Adamic race in an isolated world of its own,[3] shut off by natural barriers from the external world, and therefore remote from the general races

[1]Since it was from the East he was prevented from returning (Gen. iii, 24).

[2]Gen. iii, 17–19, 23 compared with viii, 21 and 22.

[3]This shutting off of the Adamic world or " Earth " from the general races of mankind is indicated by Genesis iv, 14–16. Cain says: " Behold, Thou hast driven me out this day from *the face of the earth* ; and from Thy face shall I be hid ; and I shall be a fugitive and a vagabond *in the earth* . . . and Cain went out from *the presence of the Lord*, and dwelt *in the land of Nod*, on the *East of Eden*."

Here the Divine tuition of the Adamic race is implied by " *the presence of the Lord* " (the Shekinah of Israel's tabernacle and temple) in the Adamic world, translated as " the face of the earth." Cain's enforced migration from the latter into the external " Earth " is represented as his being expelled from " the presence of the Lord." Cain's journey to the East side of Eden indicates that he travelled from the East to a land between the Adamic " Earth " and Eden, which latter is located by Genesis ii, 8–14 as West from Asshur (the city, and not Assyria as the A.V. rendering gives), and as including the upper reaches of the Euphrates, and also of the Tigris (Hiddekel). The Adamic " Earth " was, therefore, a land-locked area somewhere East of the Tigris.

of mankind. The narrative traces the history of the Elect race from the divinely foreknown fall of the First Adam to the divinely foreknown failure of his race, and to the consequent destruction of the race. The personal family of Noah, alone of the isolated land-locked world of the Adamic race, was saved from the catastrophe that visited the whole race, destroying all its creatures and engulfing its civilisation, with all its possessions and works.

One remarkable feature, implied rather than directly stated, concerns *Intercourse be-tween the* the relations between the external world and the world of the Adamic race. *Adamic world and the* The barriers of isolation, although hindering intercourse with the external *Gentile world.* world, did not prevent murderers from being expelled. Intermarriages with *The cause and effect of the* the external world, at first limited to outcasts and renegades (Gen. iv, 16), *failure of the Adamic race.* finally became the custom. Wives were taken from the races of the external world (Gen. vi, 2),[1] resulting in a raising of the physical standard and the lowering of the spiritual standard (vi, 4, 5). Spiritual control gave place to physical violence (vi, 11). Man's law of the survival of the fittest (for succumbing to which Cain had been expelled) now spread throughout the Adamic world; " violence filled the earth . . . for all flesh had corrupted his way upon the earth."

¶ 409. THE JUDGING OF THE DYNASTIES.

Here the narrative of the First Book of Genesis presents us with a very *The judgment of the Adamic* significant statement concerning an outstanding feature of the times depicted. *dynasties in relation to the* The conclusions derived from the genealogies of Genesis (Table V), and from *calendar and cyclic festivals.* the related calendar cycles of Tables II to IV, have shown that the dynasties of the Adamic world were judged as to their fitness at the termination of

---

[1] In Hebrew sacred literature, " the sons of God " is a term applied (1) to the Heavenly Host (Job i, 6; xxxviii, 7); (2) to the Adamic race—implied by Christ as the "Last Adam" restoring the seed of the First Adam; (3) to the perfect Israel (Hosea i, 10); and (4) in the New Testa-ment, to the Elect in Christ (1 John iii, 1). Late tradition confused the applications (1) and (2) in relation to the narrative of Genesis vi, 1–4. This gave rise to the popular tradition that the " fallen angels," or a class of spiritual beings designated the " Watchers " in the apocryphal elements of the Book of Enoch—under the temptation of the " fallen angels "—took unto them-selves wives of " the daughters of men." There is nothing, however, in any of the canonical Books of the Old or New Testaments representing that any spiritual being other than man, and other than by being born in the flesh of man, can partake of the actual physical nature of man. These Books certainly represent that certain spiritual beings can appear to the eyes of man, temporarily, in the *semblance* of man's bodily structure, for the purpose of impressing the human recipient of a message with the actuality of the message thus delivered. The appearance, however, is never represented as being in the actual physical state of man.

If the designation " the sons of God " in Genesis vi, 2 is actually intended to apply to fallen " heavenly beings," the narrative can only mean that such spirits took possession—*i.e.* " spirit-possession "—of the souls of men of the Adamic race, that the latter had first to submit themselves *willingly* to being " spirit-possessed," or " demon-possessed," and having submitted, were compelled by the lust of the spirits possessing them to seek wives of the daughters of the gentile races. This sequence is quite in accordance with the teaching of the Old and New Testaments, and is confirmed as an intermediate stage of interpretation by comparison of Genesis vi, 1–4 and iv, 19–24 with Enoch vi, 1 to vii, 6, and viii, 1. Thus, in Genesis iv, 22–24 it is Tubal-cain who is represented as the founder of the brass and iron industries, and the inventor of weapons of war (refer ¶ 415 and notes); whereas in Enoch viii, 1 it is Azâzêl, a chief of "the Watchers," who " taught men to make swords, and knives, and shields, and coats of mail, and made known to them metals and the art of working them . . ." For both accounts to agree with Hebrew beliefs, an intermediate stage of narrative is necessary. In this intermediate narrative, Tubal-cain's inventive genius would be represented as the result of his having submitted himself to "demon-possession" by Azâzêl (refer to Lev. xix, 31; xx, 6; Deut. xviii, 11).

The Seat of Judgment the Shrine of the Shekinah.
The Divine Oracle.
The decree openly signified.
calendar cycles, and of outstanding intercalary periods, such as those occurring at intervals of 30 and 120 years, and 97, 103, and 329 years. The manner in which the ritual—attending the celebration of periods thus ending—was followed in ancient Egypt, although in a corrupted form, has indicated what the tradition was concerning the Adamic judgment. Tradition held that the Seat of Judgment was the Shrine of the Shekinah. Here the postulant for continuity of Divine Right of Kingship presented himself—and his selected co-regent—at a calendar festival, before the Presence Form of the Deity. As in the operation of Urim and Thummin—the Divine Oracle of the Hebrews, connected with the Ark of the Covenant and the High Priest's breastplate —the fitness or otherwise of the king to continue was openly signified. The dynasties of Genesis are, therefore, always given as ending at a calendar festival or cyclic festival. The direct line of the dynasty had come to an end prior to the festival, or, alternatively, the Divine Right had been withheld from the dynasty at the particular calendar festival recorded.

This explanation throws a flood of light upon such expressions in Genesis as " Enoch walked with God 300 years (*i.e.* 10 calendar periods of 30 years) after he begat Methuselah " (v, 22). Enoch's dynasty ended, not because it was corrupt, but, as verse 24 states: " Enoch walked with God: and he was not; for God took him."

A flood of light thrown upon hitherto inexplicable statements.
We see, also, that the beginning of the dynasty of Methuselah formed a new epoch, which ended at the termination of three Phœnix cycles in 987 A.K. (Table V). Then, again, what significance do we now see in the following statements:—

" Noah was a just man, and perfect IN HIS GENERATIONS, and Noah WALKED WITH GOD " (vi, 9);

" Cain went out from THE PRESENCE OF THE LORD, and dwelt in the land of Nod, on the East of Eden " (iv, 16).

¶ 410. THE LOSS OF THE SPIRITUAL FACULTIES.

The last judgment period of the Adamic race.
The last "Sep tep sed heb" coincided with the year of the Deluge.
The significance of the 120 years of Genesis vi, 3.
The significant statement noted (¶ 409) in Genesis concerns the 120 years of vi, 3. This is the period of the ancient Egyptian *Sep tep sed heb*, or 4 Sed periods of 30 years. In accordance with the narrative of Genesis v, this period was seen to end at the Deluge. The calendar epoch for the Deluge chronology began at the birth of Noah, 1056 A.K. (Table V). From this epoch the calendar period of 601 years (Table IV) ended at the completion of the Deluge at 1656 A.K., thus ending the five 120 years' cycles; the fifth and last repetition, in accordance with Table IV, being a period of 121 years. The last period began 121 years before the completion of the Deluge, and therefore 120 years[1] before the beginning of the Deluge at 1655 A.K., in the 600th year of Noah.

The Adamic race represented as having lost its power of controlling flesh by having become flesh.
This explains the significance of the last 120 years' period of Genesis vi, 3, in the light of the statement that " My Spirit shall not always strive with man, for that he ALSO is flesh; yet his days shall be 120 years." Here the

[1] In this relation refer to ¶¶ 196b–196d.

emphasis relates to the Adamic race having partaken of the physical nature of the races external to the Adamic world or "Earth." By having partaken of this nature the Adamic race had still further debased and subverted its special spiritual faculties. It had lost the power of controlling "flesh" by having become "flesh," and by thus losing, had still further lost the power of its spiritual dominion over the Earth and all the physical kingdoms and entities of the Earth.

The narrative concerning our Lord—as the "Last Adam"—rebuking the *spirit* of the storm, and by so rebuking, calming the *storm*, describes the illustration by our Lord, to the seed of the "First Adam," of one application of the special spiritual faculties operative in the power of spiritual dominion over the Earth. Here, again, it is illustrated that the Prologue (the First Book of Genesis) describes the means whereby the spiritual power was *forfeited*, that the history of Israel from Abraham to Christ describes the means whereby the spiritual power was *redeemed*, and that the Epilogue (Revelation) describes the means whereby the original *Gift* will be restored to be " a blessing to all families of the earth."

[margin note: Our Lord's calming of the storm considered as bearing upon the question of the lost power of the seed of Adam.]

¶ 411. THE PHYSICAL CHARACTERISTICS OF THE ADAMIC "WORLD."

The narrative of the First Book of Genesis clearly implies that the Adamic " world " was a sterile mountain-encircled basin, or system of basins, situated some considerable distance East of the River Tigris.[1] The only locality satisfying these conditions—within the historical period—is that of the mountain-encircled and land-locked system of basins lying in Eastern Turkestan and Tibet. These territories comprise an earthquake area that is still very active, and are characterised by a continuous change in physical features and conditions, due principally to dessication, on a large scale, and at a rate practically unknown elsewhere on the earth. The latter phenomenon forms one of the outstanding branches of investigation still of special interest and attraction to the geologist, who specialises in phenomenal changes of this nature. With this phenomenal factor governing the conditions of change in the physical conditions of Eastern Turkestan, it may well be that the inundation of this locality, ascribed to the later tertiary period, actually occurred within the historical period. That this interpretation of the existing physical evidences is probably correct seems to be indicated by the peculiar locations in which have been found " belts of dead poplars, patches of dead and moribund tamarisks, and vast expanses of withered reeds " and " ripple-marks of aqueous origin."[2] In any case, it is extraordinary that in following the

[margin note: A sterile mountain-enclosed basin East of the Tigris. Identified with Eastern Turkestan and Tibet. The physical characteristics of the latter confirming the identity. The existing physical evidences of the Deluge described in Genesis.]

[1] ¶ 408, and footnotes to same.
[2] The "Enc. Brit." (11th Edit.), Vol. XXVII, pp. 422, 423, Art. "East Turkestan," states:—
" . . . Though it is in reality an elevated plateau . . . it is nevertheless a depression when compared with the girdle of mountains which surround it on every side except the East, and even on that side it is shut in by the crumbling remains of a once mighty mountain system, the Pe-shan. . . .
" The mountain ranges which shut off East Turkestan from the rest of the world rank among the loftiest and most difficult in Asia, and indeed in the world. . . .
" . . . During the later tertiary period all the desert regions would appear to have been covered by an Asian Mediterranean or, at all events, by vast fresh-water lakes, a conclusion

indications of the literary evidences we have found a locality where the topographical and geological conditions are precisely those that these literary indications have led us to expect.

¶ 412. CHINESE RECORDS AND THE DELUGE OF GENESIS.

Subsidence and earthquake movements as related to the former submerged lakes of Eastern Turkestan and Tibet.
    Now it seems obvious that earthquake movements produced the effect described as " the breaking up of the fountains of the great deep " (Gen. vii, 11).[1]   Here we have the description of the collapsing of the crust of the earth that roofed over the great submerged lakes of Eastern Turkestan and Tibet. Such conditions cannot have failed to extend in their effect—to a minor, but nevertheless disastrous, extent—into China.   The magnitude of the earthquake wave resulting from the collapse of the submerged lakes must have been felt very appreciably as far as the coasts of China, and the ultimate result would be the inundation of the land by a tidal wave.   The overflow from the great central basins of Eastern Turkestan and Tibet was bound to swell to an abnormal extent the flow of the Hwang-ho.

Records concerning the effects of these movements upon China.
    It is not surprising, therefore, to find that the Chinese records describe precisely this sequence of events and this geographical location.   The dated period in which this Deluge is placed by the Chinese Shu-King includes the date of the Deluge of Genesis.[2]   The dates of the Shu-King, as will be seen, are also based on the calendar datum and cycles of the First Book of Genesis.

which seems to be warranted by the existence of salt-stained depressions of a lacustrine character ; by traces of former lacustrine shore lines, more or less parallel and concentric ; by discoveries of vast quantities of fresh-water mollusc shells, the existence of belts of dead poplars, patches of dead and moribund tamarisks, and vast expanses of withered reeds, all these crowning the tops of the jardangs, never found in the wind-scooped furrows ; the presence of ripple-marks of aqueous origin on the leeward side of the clay terraces and in other wind-sheltered situations ; and, in fact, by the general conformation, contour lines, and shapes of the deserts as a whole.   From the statements of older travellers, like the Venetian Marco Polo (13th Century) and the Chinese pilgrim, Hsüan Tsang (7th Century), as well as from other data, it is perfectly evident, not only that this country is suffering from a progressive dessication, but that the sands have actually swallowed up cultivated areas within the historical period."

[1] The narrative also refers, of course, to a coincident phenomenal downpouring of rain, implied as a result of the same exceptional conditions producing, or caused by, the general earthquake shock.

[2] The Deluge date of Genesis, 2345-2344 B.C., falls within the reign of the Chinese King Yaou, who reigned, according to the Shu-King, from 2356 B.C. to 2254 B.C. (W. G. Old, " The Shu-King," Appendix, pp. 301, 302).   Chinese records accordingly identify a great deluge within this reign.   In the Shu-King (*ibid.*, Section V) Yu, the Chinese engineer and administrator, is represented addressing the Emperor Yaou as follows :—
    " When the floods were lifted to the heavens, spreading far and wide, surrounding the hills and submerging the mounds, so that the common people were bewildered and dismayed . . . I drained off the nine channels, directing them into the *Four Seas* ; I dug out ditches and canals and brought them into the rivers."
    In a footnote to Book II, Section I, Mr Old states : " Wang-hwang, the historian, says that ' formerly the heavens rained down incessantly, the wind blowing from the North-East, and the ocean, overflowing the land, submerged the country, and obliterated the course of the *Nine Rivers* ' ; and in this he has the support of Li-taou-yuen. Tsae-chin, the commentator of the Shu-King, who wrote in the beginning of the 13th Century A.D., gives the names of the eight streams which, together with the Hwang-Ho, formed the ' Nine Rivers ' . . . they are all to be found between latitude 37° and 39° North, to the East of Peking, and appear to have formed a confluent with the Ho not far from the Coast."
    The " overflowing " of the sea would be the natural consequence of the earthquake wave inferred above as resulting from the collapse of the submerged lakes in the interior.   Yu also refers to years of work in clearing and draining the valleys and ravines in the mountains of the interior.

The Chinese Noah — the Fu-hi of Chinese mythology — is not only mentioned in relation to the Deluge, but in connection with his selection of the animals by " sevens " (Gen. vii, 2), in connection with his sacrifice after the Deluge of certain of the animals saved with him (Gen. viii, 20), and in connection with the rainbow covenant of Genesis ix, 8–17 (¶ 196b). The Chinese date for the epoch of Fu-hi is the date in Genesis for the epoch of the House of Noah (¶ 313). *Chinese traditions concerning the Deluge of Genesis and its sequel.*

¶ 413. THE TRADITIONAL "WORLD" OF THE CHALDÆANS.

The Chinese tradition relating to Fu-hi states that he made his appearance on " the mountains of Chin " after the Deluge (¶ 196b). In light of the data co-ordinated in relation, this statement can be considered as historically valid, and as indicating that the last representative of the House of Noah, after his preservation, appeared on the mountains in the West of China. This is quite in accordance with the narrative of Genesis. For, as Ferrar Fenton has shown in his translation of the First Book of Genesis, " the compound Hebrew word ' Ararat ' means simply and literally ' the Peaks of the High Hills.' " *Chinese tradition concerning Noah and the mountains of Tibet and Eastern Turkestan. The Ararat of Genesis.*

Apart from this identification, however, it is a well-known fact that race migrations carry with them the designations of outstanding topographical features of the land of origin, or the designations of national or ideal sites, and mythological cities and realms relating to religious beliefs. In the latter case there is the well-known example of the " Asgard " of the Norse, which ideal place-name accompanied them in all their migrations. It seems obvious, therefore, if the general topographical name " Ararat " was identified with the specific topographical feature connected with the preservation of Noah, that subsequent migration of the race would carry the place-name with it. This would account for the story of the Noachian Deluge being traditionally connected with Ararat in Armenia. *Place-names and race migrations. The migration of the place-name "Ararat."*

However this may be, the question is definitely settled by Genesis xi, 2. This describes that after the Deluge " as they journeyed FROM THE EAST,[1] that they found a plain in the land of Shinar; and they dwelt there." The remnants of the Adamic race are therefore depicted as migrating from the East into the valleys of the Euphrates and Tigris. Here, then, in the literary and pictorial traditions of the races inhabiting this district, we should expect to find some indication pointing to the topographical features that constituted the barriers of the land of the original Adamic race. In consequence, we find that the traditional world, as represented by the Chaldæans, was described as contained within a basin, engirdled by high mountain ranges, deemed, in the later Chaldæan beliefs, to be the pillars supporting the sky.[2] *The migration of the Adamic survivors into Chaldæa from the East. The traditional world of the Chaldæans a representation of the former world of the Adamic race.*

---

[1]The traditional identification with Ararat in Armenia accounts for the insertion of the marginal alternative " eastwards."

[2]Maspero, " Dawn of Civilisation," p. 543.

Maspero here gives a diagram of Jensen's reconstruction of the Chaldæan " world," and remarks on its similarity to the Egyptian " world." He states : " The earth, which forms the lower part or floor " of the world " is something like an overturned boat in appearance, and

¶ 414. THE GEOGRAPHICAL DISTRIBUTION OF THE WHITE RACE.

The new world of the Noahitic race amongst the Gentiles.

The narrative of Genesis x clearly states that after the Flood in the Adamic " world " Noah and his sons and their descendants migrated from the East into new territories, henceforth to be identified as the New World of the Noahitic race. The narrative states further that the nations already living in this New World were territorially subdivided, according to " the families of the sons of Noah." The concluding statement is that " these are the families of the sons of Noah, after their generations, in their nations : and by these were the nations divided in the earth after the flood." Ferrar Fenton's rendering of Genesis x, 31 and 32, in Modern English, is even more clearly definitive : " These are the sons of Shem, by their tribes and in their languages *in their countries*, AMONG THE HEATHEN." " The above were the families of the sons of Noah and their descendants by tribes. From them they spread themselves AMONGST THE NATIONS ON THE EARTH AFTER THE FLOOD."[1]

The concentrated "mental idiom " of the First Book of Genesis is analogous to the expressive phraseology of modern science and technology, which compresses the subject-matter of generations of experience and research into a single comprehensive expression.

In formulating our conclusions concerning the precise meaning of this tenth chapter of Genesis, it is clear that we must bear in mind the governing feature of the narrative of the First Book of Genesis. In this we have been brought into contact with the use of an ancient form of mental idiom, the chief characteristic of which was the compression of matters of complex detail, concerning a former civilisation, into a succession of expressive ideas. It is not precisely allegory, as we understand the use of allegory : it is rather the substitution of a complete idea for a complex narrative explanatory of the complete idea. The analogous application in modern times would be the substitution of the root word of a sentence—that best expresses the central idea of the sentence—for the whole sentence. This analogy is defective, however, chiefly for the reason that nowadays the complete historical and philosophical significance of root words is largely problematical. This, however, was not the case at the time the First Book of Genesis was written. The mental idiom of the First Book of Genesis (that now

hollow underneath, not like one of the narrow skiffs in use among other races, but a kufa, or kind of semicircular boat such as the tribes of the lower Euphrates have made use of from the earliest antiquity down to our time. The earth rises gradually from the extremities to the centre. . . ."

In other words, the basin of the " world " is depicted as possessing a domed floor, comprising the inhabited land surface. The domed floor—or bottom of the basin—is represented as terraced on its outer surface, and as forming the roof of a vast subterranean cavern covering over the submerged waters of " the great deep." There is, therefore, an annular channel forming the lowest level of the floor of the basin, and contained between the domed centre of the floor and the sides of the basin formed by the encircling mountain ranges. This annular channel, or circular valley, in Maspero's reproduction of Jensen's reconstruction, is represented as containing the seas surrounding the dry land dome. This is obviously an addition to the original conception derived from the tradition of the Adamic " world," and is what one would expect from the race receiving this tradition and applying it to their own geographical conditions, since they were acquainted with the Persian Gulf and the Indian Ocean to the South and East, with the Red Sea and Mediterranean on the West, and with the Black Sea and Caspian Sea on the North.

In the same manner the Egyptians adopted the traditional conception of the Adamic " world " to the geographical conditions surrounding Egypt (refer Maspero's diagram, ibid., p. 16).

[1] In this relation the F. F. rendering of Genesis xi, 1–9 should also be read, as it gives a *literal* rendering conveying a distinctly different impression from that obtained from the A.V. It must be admitted, however, that Fenton too frequently seems to take liberties with the original.

seems to us to partake of the nature of an allegory) was the mental idiom of the times, and formed what we might term the current intellectual atmosphere in which ideas were circulated and exchanged. In such case the phraseology of the First Book of Genesis has its counterpart in the phraseology and symbology of modern science and technology, in which the meanings attached to words and single ideas, more frequently than not, express, when employed in simple combinations, the equivalent of volumes of descriptive matter relating to generations of experience and research.

It is not surprising, therefore, to find, as it was discovered in the first instance by Professor Sayce, that the tenth chapter of Genesis is not an " ethnological table " but a " descriptive chart of Hebrew geography, the various cities and countries of the known world being arranged in it genealogically in accordance with Semitic idiom. . . ."[1]

The idiom of the First Book of Genesis describes in genealogical terms the geographical distribution of the remnants of the Adamic race.

Sayce's conclusions in this relation are significant. For, as he continues, " We are not to look, then, to the tenth chapter of Genesis for a scientific division of mankind into their several races. We are not to demand from it that simple and primitive division according to colour. . . . As a matter of fact, all the tribes and nations mentioned in the chapter belonged to the white race. Even the negroes are not referred to, though they were well known to the Egyptians, and the black-skinned Nubians are carefully excluded from the descendants of Cush."[2]

The resulting identity equates the Adamic race with the white race.

The whole context of the First Book of Genesis—studied in the light of the new evidence, and considered in relation to the origin and the physical and ethical characteristics of the white race—confirms Sayce's conclusions. The restless energy and the " spiritual " stamina—as distinct from purely *bestial* stamina—characteristic of the white race, their dominating influence over other races, and their so-called " conquest " of nature and of nature's science and elements, all indicate their retention, to a certain extent, of the power—not yet entirely latent—and the faculties—not yet completely atrophied—attributed in the First Book of Genesis to the founder of the Adamic race, and, in a lesser degree, to the Adamic race.

Characteristics of the white race that confirm the identity.

¶ 415. THE EARLIEST ADAMIC COLONIES IN THE GENTILE WORLD.

This brings us to the consideration of another question. Cain was exiled from the Adamic " world." The narrative of Genesis also implies that renegades married into the nations of the external " world " and lived there, since this is necessarily the initial stage in the sequence of events that led up to wives being brought from the external world into the Adamic world. The families of such as remained in the external world were not, otherwise than partially, as in China, affected by the Deluge that destroyed the Adamic world. Such families were " Gentilised," but were, nevertheless, partly

Renegade adventurers into the world of the Gentiles.

The Gentilised families of such not generally affected by the Deluge.

---

[1] " Higher Criticism and the Monuments " (6th Edit.), p. 119
[2] Ibid., p. 120. The whole context of pp. 119–123 should be read in this relation.

descended from the Adamic white race. Their stock, in all probability, still exists to-day, and should be capable of identification by their proficiency in the arts and methods of the white race, and by their possession of the dominant and " spiritual " characteristics of the white race.

The Cainite colonies in the Gentile world, before the Flood occurred in the Adamic world.

Adamic culture first introduced amongst the Gentiles.

The Adamic colonists become industrial feudal lords.

But we are not concerned with this highly hypothetical question, further than to direct attention to the relationship holding between the Cainites and other Adamic renegades on the one hand, and the Gentile races on the other hand. Now, it is a remarkable fact that the First Book of Genesis makes no reference to the details of the civilisation in the Adamic world. In dealing with the descendants of Cain, who brought the influence of Adamic culture[1] into the world of the Gentiles, Enoch, the son of Cain, is mentioned as building a city, Jubal—the traditional inventor of music—is mentioned in relation to the harp and the organ, and Tubal-cain as " an instructor of every artificer in brass and iron." It is important to know what is signified by " instructor." The literal meaning of the word thus translated is " stimulator." The alternative sense implied by " stimulator " has suggested " whetter," and, possibly for this reason, Ferrar Fenton has translated " improver of every work in copper and iron," *i.e.* improving by whetting. This, however, seems to be a very free rendering. Hebrew tradition, generally, associated the invention of iron and copper work—in the Gentile world—with Tubal-cain. He was something more than an improver. He was the first organiser of the industry, and also the " stimulator " (to be interpreted literally either as " the feeder " or as the " quickener " or " hastener ") of those engaged upon the work of his inventions. The whole context seems to define Tubal-cain as the overlord and taskmaster of the industry he had introduced into the Gentile world.[2] In light of other data elucidated in this volume, this seems to be the correct rendering.[3]

The Cainite colony responsible for the reduction of the Adamic primary system of measures to the secondary (rule-of-thumb) system for Gentile use.

For, as we have seen in Chapter II of this volume, the highly scientific and accurate system of measurements of the Adamic race, when introduced into the external world, was reduced to an accurate but rule-of-thumb

[1]Refer ¶ 41, as relating to the sudden beginning and rapid development of an already highly developed art.

[2]In this relation refer ¶ 45 concerning the subject races being prevented from using, and from thus becoming skilled in, the use of metal tools, and, by inference, metal weapons.

[3]The " Enc. Brit." (11th Edit.), Vol. XVI, p. 122, states: " This narrative clearly intends to account for the origin of the various arts as they existed in the narrator's time ; . . .

" . . . An ancient poem (Gen. iv, 23, 24) is connected with this genealogy :—

> ' Adah and Zillah, hear my voice ;
> Ye wives of Lamech, give ear unto my speech.
> I slay a man for a wound,
> A young man for a stroke ;
> For Cain's vengeance is sevenfold,
> But Lamech's seventyfold and seven.'

In view of the connexion, the poem is interpreted as expressing Lamech's exultation at the advantage he expects to derive from Tubal-cain's new invention ; the worker in bronze will forge for him new and formidable weapons, so that he will be able to take signal vengeance for the least injury."

That the above rendering is clearly the correct rendering is seen by comparison of Genesis iv, 15 with iv, 24. The A.V. rendering of verse 23 in light of the comparison is incorrect. The marginal rendering agrees better with the context. The passage refers to what Lamech foresees himself capable of doing, and is not a reference to anything he has done.

system of equivalents. We now see that this introduction was effected prior to the Noachian Deluge. This accounts for the existence of the derived system amongst the pre-dynastic Egyptians,[1] and elsewhere throughout the ancient East, long prior to the construction of the Pyramids of Gizeh. It was stated (¶ 116), as indicated by the metrological and archæological evidence, that " the secondary (or derived) system was obviously formulated at a time when the uncultured many were organised to carry out highly skilled work under the intermittent direction of a cultured few." Mackenzie, in his " Ancient Man in Britain "—quoted extensively in the first chapter of this volume—shows that from the earliest times, under conditions practically amounting to slavery, mining operations, smelting, and metal working were carried on by a subordinate race under a sparsely distributed dominant and cultured race. Such operations were conducted in Spain, Portugal, and Britain, in order to export the products to the East, and may well have been conducted elsewhere at the same time. Under such conditions, we can understand Tubal-cain being a " stimulator of every artificer in brass and iron." In other words, Tubal-cain seems to have been a feudal lord of industry, possessing slaves who were workers in the finished products of brass and iron. As, however, the name Tubal-cain, as in the case of the direct Adamic line of genealogies, probably relates to the house or dynasty[2] of Tubal-cain, we must modify the conclusion in light of this identification. This would represent the dynasty of Tubal-cain as ruling over an enslaved race employed to work the metals brought from the slave mines and smelting works of Western Europe, the operations of which, and the transport of the products of which, were under the direction and organisation of other renegade families of the Adamic race. Here we are presented with an early historical picture of the adventures and cupidity of the restless wanderers of the white race—the forerunners, by millenaries, of the Spanish conquistadores and of such great English seamen as Drake and Hawkins, who by their daring and activities inaugurated the epoch of Britain's expansion overseas, and thus set in motion the long series of efforts that, under the guiding hand of Providence, have presented the world with the greatest Empire it has ever seen.

The earliest instance of the organisation of mass production by semi-skilled or un-skilled labour.

The earliest industrial slaves in Western Europe.

The mining colonies in Portugal, Spain, and Britain.

The territorial isolation of the various processes of a single industry to prevent the subordinate races from using the weapons manufactured against their Adamic over-lords.

The history of the Adamic colonists analogous to the history of the Spanish and English adventurers of the Elizabethan period.

¶ 416. THE PARTICIPATION OF THE GENTILES.

The evidence concerning the primary system of measures and other related data indicated that these had originated with a lost civilisation of the ancient East (¶¶ 113–116). This lost civilisation was seen to be identical with the civilisation of the Adamic race of the First Book of Genesis (¶¶ 312–317). What we have since learned, in addition to this identity, is that the colonising of the sea-boards along the maritime trading routes of the ancient Gentile world was effected by Adamic renegades long prior to the cataclysm

Renegade colonies of the Adamic race respon-sible for founding the original basis of the high civilisations of the Ancient East.

[1] For some such reason as that now advanced, Piazzi Smyth defined the 20.63 B" cubit of this derived system " the Cainite cubit."

[2] This is not denied by the poetic boast of Lamech—inferred as such in the preceding note. For Tubal-cain, the son of Lamech, the father of the house of Lamech, could still have been the one who introduced the industry into the Gentile world, and who first organised it on the basis afterwards developed by the dynasty of Tubal-cain.

that destroyed the civilisation of the Adamic world.   We have also seen that this cataclysm did not affect the Gentile world—except, perhaps, locally—and that the Adamic colonies in the Gentile world built up the basis of civilisation in the countries bordering the Persian Gulf, the Indian Ocean, the Red Sea, and the Mediterranean, prior to the migration from the East of the surviving Noahitic branch of the Adamic race.

The Adamic race is the white race.
The implied function of the white race and its destiny as related to the Abrahamic promise.
The Pyramid's displacement factor and a universal law of relativity.

What we have also learned in addition is that the Adamic race is the white race, and that the cultural civilisation of the world from the earliest times has been due to the white race.   What we do not know is the extent to which the stock of the white race has influenced the stock of other races, or of all races.   The scriptural promise of redemption, by its being extended to " all families of the earth " in the days of Abraham, seems to imply that the white race has influenced, to some extent, the stock of all other races, and that, in consequence, by having become " also flesh," and thereby having lowered its spiritual " potential," it has also raised the spiritual " potential " of " all flesh."   This would go far towards explaining the mystery of the foreknowledge of God as related to His permitting a sequence of events—represented as according with promises and predictions indited in His Name—that from the beginning presupposed (and, in fact, asserted) the pre-election of a Saviour before there was either the active necessity to save or the entities to save.   Here, again, we seem to be presented with an application of the enigmatical displacement factor (discussed in ¶¶ 350, 358–364) that has been seen to govern the numerical relations of a universal law of relativity, ranging, in its application, from man's universe of spiritual energy into man's universe of material energy.   The graphical representation of this displacement factor, and of all it signifies, has been seen to constitute the one essential theme of the message of the Great Pyramid.

¶ 417. THE DATE OF THE PYRAMID'S CONSTRUCTION.

The Great Pyramid built as a message from the Adamic white race to the present white race.
The message expressed in terms of the modern science of the white race.

Now, all the co-ordinated evidences discussed in this volume have shown that the Great Pyramid was built at the instigation of, and under the direction of an architect or engineer belonging to the race of the lost civilisation of the ancient East.   This fact now identifies the architect or engineer of this lost civilisation as belonging to the Adamic race.   It was shown that the metrologically and geometrically indicated data of the Great Pyramid proclaim the object of its design and construction, which was seen to be expressed in the form of a graphical message from the civilisation of the past to a civilisation of the future ; and now to be interpreted as a message from a former civilisation of the white race to the present civilisation of the white race. The message is proclaimed in terms of natural science, and is, therefore, a message from scientists to scientists, or to such as understand the terms of natural science.

The latitude and longitude were selected as the particular latitude and longitude essential for defining completely the application of the data constituting the message (¶ 46).   Here we have an indication of the dispatch of an expedition from an already settled and organised community to effect A special expedition a prolonged settlement in Egypt. A scientific expedition for the purpose organised by the Adamic mentioned, it need hardly be pointed out, does not correspond to the type of race for the purpose of the predatory expedition organised by the Adamic renegades. All the evidence Pyramid's construction discussed points to a single conclusion. This is that the expedition was in Egypt. planned by and executed from the parent body of the Adamic race, or the According to the data of survivors of that race. There is nothing in the narrative of Genesis, nor Genesis and the Pyramid elsewhere in the Books of the Old Testament, justifying the once popular this expedition may have been assumption that an ancient monument now extant must of necessity be dated dispatched any time between as post-diluvian. Nor yet is there anything to justify the modern alternative 3500 B.C. and 2000 B.C. assumption that the Book of Genesis is not a true historical account. This, we consider, has been settled by the new evidence. So far as the evidence from the Old Testament is concerned, the Pyramid may have been built at any time between 3500 B.C. and 2000 B.C. The Pyramid's own astronomical data indicate that it may have been built at any time between the two precisely dated years 3434 B.C.[1] and 2144 B.C. (¶¶ 239–242 and Plate XLIb, Fig. N).

¶ 418. EGYPTOLOGICAL DATINGS.

Recent Egyptological schools of chronology would agree to a date The archæological evidences from ranging from 3100 to 2700 B.C., but the evidence upon which these dates Egyptological sources indi- are based is altogether too obscure to form a trustworthy datum for cate the prob- chronology. In any case, the resulting hypothesis is entirely discounted by able date of the Pyramid's the reliable astronomical evidence co-ordinated in the first chapter of this construction as between 3100 volume, and in the chronological tables and annotations of this chapter. and 2700 B.C.

[1]The Coptic tradition of Masoudi's Arabic MS. relating to the Great Pyramid's construction and the purpose of its construction has been partly quoted in ¶ 111. We have seen that the essential statements in this tradition have been confirmed by the geometrical, metrological, astronomical, and prophetical data supplied by the Great Pyramid. The MS. tradition states, as quoted in ¶ 111, that the Pyramid was built "before the Flood." The portion not quoted states further that it was built as the result of a vision, in which the Flood was predicted. The date of the vision is given as 300 years before the Flood. If we can suppose that this part of the tradition came from the same ancient Egyptian source as the other items discussed, then we can accept the date 2640 B.C. as the approximate date of the Pyramid's founding, according to an Egyptian tradition that has proved reliable in other essential respects. Now the astronomical datings given by the Pyramid's Entrance (Plate XLIa, Fig. H) range from 1345½ A.K. to 1407½ A.K., or 2654 B.C. to 2592 B.C. These may, or may not, relate to the period of the Pyramid's construction. They show, however, the probable origin of the Coptic tradition.
A similar tradition is mentioned by Josephus in "Antiq.," I, ii, 3, and by the pseudo-Hermes (as quoted by Cedrenus). According to both these writers the work was executed before the Flood, by the Sethites according to Josephus, and by Enoch according to "Hermes." The statement of Josephus is worth quoting: "They (the Sethites) also were the inventors of that peculiar sort of wisdom which is concerned with the heavenly bodies and their order. And that their inventions might not be lost before they were sufficiently known, upon Adam's prediction that the world was to be destroyed . . . they made two pillars . . . [one in brick ; one in stone] . . . they inscribed their discoveries on them both . . . to exhibit these discoveries to mankind ; . . . Now this (the pillar of stone) remains in the land of Siriad unto this day." This tradition (by Table V datings) would give the date of the Pyramid's construction by the dynasty of Sheth as not later than 2958 B.C. The tradition according to "Hermes" would give the construction by the dynasty of Enoch within the period 3378 B.C. to 3013 B.C. These traditions are not referred to as providing any reliable data, but for the purpose of indicating how, even at a time when the Flood was supposed to have covered the whole earth, tradition associated the building of the Great Pyramid with antediluvian times, and with the preservation of antediluvian science relating to astronomy, and the necessity for this science being passed on to the future.

The possibility that these dates may be too early.

On the other hand, the remotely early dates of Petrie's school of chronology[1] are based chiefly upon the totals of Manetho's King Lists—which have been proved to be fictitious by the co-ordinations of Plate XVI and ¶¶ 92-99, 108, 109, and 250-254—and which, it is claimed, are confirmed by the application of a theory of the vague year and the Sothic cycle, a theory which is now seen to be impossible of application prior to the XVIIIth Dynasty (Plate IX, ¶¶ 48-63, 312-317, Annotations to Table XI, and Annotations to Table XV).

The early Egyptian system of short chronology. This agrees with the date 2144 B.C. for the Pyramid's construction. The system, however, may have been formulated to effect this identification.

It must be admitted that prolonged investigation of the purely archæological data relating to the period intervening between the IIIrd and the XIIth Egyptian Dynasties, as these data are presented, fails to afford evidence of a satisfactory nature that can account for a shorter interval than 700 years. This, however, may be due to the unconsciously dominating influence of the fixed theories of Egyptian chronology held by the excavators and collectors of the data relating to this period, and by those who have sifted and arranged the data for presentation in textual and tabulated co-relation. Other fixed theories were held by certain schools of Egyptians long prior to Manetho. One early Egyptian theory of this nature formed what was an Egyptian scheme of short chronology. According to this, the VIth Egyptian Dynasty was contemporaneous with the XIIth Dynasty, and the IVth Dynasty with the Vth Dynasty. This agrees with the 2144 B.C. date for the construction of the Great Pyramid. The arrangement, however, of dynasties may have been dictated by a tradition that the astronomically defined dating 2144 B.C. of the Pyramid related to the date of construction. For this reason, the pre-Manethon Egyptian theory mentioned has been relegated to the Appendix.[2]

The archæological evidence apparently confirming the short system of Ancient Egyptian chronology. The relative importance of the date of the Pyramid's construction. The two modern schools of Egyptological chronology differ to the extent of 1500 years for early periods.

It is, nevertheless, startling to find, when we come to test this short chronology system of the Egyptians in light of the purely monumental data relating to Dynasties IV and V, and Dynasties VI and XII, that the tomb inscriptions referring to kings of the former two dynasties, and the comparative sequence of events and dated festivals recorded in the latter two dynasties, afford very extensive evidence in support of the theory. The conclusions derived from the new evidence relating to the Adamic civilisation, however, show that, so far as concerns the scope of the present volume, the question of the date of the Pyramid's construction is not a matter that need concern us. The narrative of Genesis, the Pyramid's own astronomical datings, and the archæological evidence of modern Egyptology, all indicate the possibility of the Pyramid's construction as early as the period lying between 3500 and 2700 B.C. Modern archæological opinion denies the possibility of any later

[1] The archæological indications discussed in relation to primitive astronomy in ¶¶ 282-284 show that dynastic history in Egypt cannot have commenced prior to 3500 B.C. at the earliest.

Again, any references in Euphratean or Egyptian records to the Noachian Deluge—as distinct from the mythological texts dealing with the primordial chaos—or to the Egyptian story of the Destruction of Mankind, must have originated, and must have been inscribed at a date later than 2343 B.C. The Xth Dynasty papyrus, discussed in ¶ 28, is therefore later than this date, and, in consequence, the Xth Dynasty cannot be placed earlier than 2200 B.C., i.e. 1500 years later than Petrie's date for the Xth Dynasty beginning. This agrees with the astronomical datings of the XIIth Dynasty.

[2] Appendix II, Table LXVI, and Annotations.

date, and emphatically denies the possibility of a date as late as 2144 B.C.
Archæologists, however, have been frequently proved wrong in their dates,
their errors amounting to 1000 years and more concerning periods of history
prior to 2000 B.C. As matters stand at present, the two outstanding schools
of Egyptological chronology differ to the extent of 1500 years concerning
dates in the period under consideration. To the plain man, unacquainted
with the state of the evidence that renders such a condition of things possible,
it will appear that a matter of an additional five and a half centuries' error
may be easily possible. He may believe that the date of the Pyramid's
construction is 2144 B.C., and he may yet be shown to be correct in his belief ;
but until the date can be reliably proved by contemporary records of an
astronomical nature, similar to those definitely fixing the chronology of
the period from Dynasty XII to the Christian era, the plain fact, that must
be realised, is that the date of the Pyramid's construction cannot be fixed
with certainty. The irony of the existing archæological circumstances is
that the two outstanding Egyptological schools of astronomical chronology
differ in regard to the application of certain calendar principles that did not
apply within the period regarding which the rival schools differ. This is
clearly proved by Plate IX and context, and Tables XI–XVI and Annotations.

The assumptions forming the bases of both schools of chronology shown in this volume to be impossible. ¶

¶ 419. A QUESTION OF PROBABILITY.

What has been advanced (in ¶¶ 406–418) as a hypothesis concerning the
Adamic race and its culture as related to the design and construction of the
Pyramid has been shown to be confirmed in many of the essential features
formulating the hypothesis. From this it would appear that the hypothesis
satisfies the conditions better than previous hypotheses advanced in this
connection. It certainly satisfies many different categories of conditions
hitherto deemed to be irreconcilable, which is surely the ultimate test of any
theory. But the hypothesis as a whole—it must be admitted—still stands as
a co-ordination of direct and circumstantial evidences—unevenly interrelated
—and stronger in probabilities than in well-attested facts. Let it be emphatically declared that this statement is made concerning the co-ordination and
not concerning the several independent factors and essential features comprising the co-ordination. The majority of these must be deemed to be established by direct evidence as facts, that, co-ordinated in the light of data not
yet discussed in the present relation, may yield a perfect solution, which,
nevertheless, we believe will be found to be not far removed from the lines
of the present hypothesis.

The clear distinction to be drawn between the co-related probabilities and the co-related facts discussed in the original co-ordination of historical documents and archæological evidences discussed in this volume.

Again, in laying stress upon the purely probable nature of the hypothesis,
it must be emphasised that, in doing so, the above statement must not be
understood as applying to the direct evidence supplied by the Great Pyramid
nor yet to the certain identities establishing the actuality of its message and
the purpose of its message. The hypothesis as a whole has been advanced
merely as a tentative solution that may lead ultimately, under investigation,
to a perfect solution that will bridge, in a historical sense, the gap between

the lost civilisation of the past and the present civilisation ; that will account satisfactorily for the motives that dictated the construction of the Great Pyramid ; and that will explain the nature and origin of the restless spiritual energy of the white race as related to the clear indications in the Great Pyramid's message concerning the redemption of a lost spiritual faculty.

(B) THE FACTS OF THE CO-ORDINATION.

¶ 420. GENESIS, A TRUE BASIS OF HISTORY.

The history of the Adamic race and of the origin of Israel. The Book of Genesis is a true statement of the history of the Adamic race and of the origin of the people of Israel. Whilst different opinions may be advanced concerning the idiomatic significance to be attached to certain features of its narrative, this general statement cannot be shaken. The first eleven chapters consist of an earlier document, or the surviving fragments of earlier documents, dealing with the history of the Adamic race.

The internal evidence relating to an advanced knowledge of astronomy in the Adamic age. The narrative, as it stands, proves that the Adamic race had made great advances in astronomy, and knew accurately the value of the solar year. This is proved by the fact that the various dynasties are given as ending officially in every case in the last year of an intercalary period, or in the last year of a cycle dependent upon or related to an extremely accurate intercalary cycle of 103 solar years.

The astronomical chronology of the Adamic world and the calendar festivals were introduced into the Gentile world prior to the Deluge in the Adamic world, thus explaining a continuity of tradition not necessarily due to Adamic survivors. The bare facts concerning these cycles and their periods, and the ceremonial aspect of the festivals identified with the terminal years of such periods, became known to the ancient nations of the Gentile world long before the cataclysm occurred that destroyed the Adamic civilisation. When, therefore, the Deluge destroyed the Adamic race, the continuity of the succession of chronological festivals in the Gentile world did not depend upon the tradition brought over by the survivors of the Adamic race. This explains why the Chinese literary records not only give Chinese dynastic epochs that are identical with dynastic epochs of the Book of Genesis, but also give, as Chinese dynastic epochs, certain Adamic calendar and cycle datings that are not given in the Book of Genesis. The same explanation

The Chinese, Babylonians, and Egyptians all have two main chronological epochs, the zero epoch of Adam and the epoch of the Deluge ending. The latter epoch was adopted as the universal epoch for the Sed heb period. accounts for the fact that although Egyptian chronology, after the date of the Deluge, continued to be based on the succession of 103 years' cycles from the original zero epoch of Adam, the calendar festivals relating to the *Sed* periods and the *Sep tep sed* periods (30 and 120 years respectively) were based on the epoch chronologically defined as the termination of the Adamic Deluge. The adoption of the latter basis was clearly due to the influence of the survivors of the Adamic race who spread themselves abroad amongst the Gentile nations after the Flood. The universal adoption of this basis—at least by the Chinese, Egyptians, and Babylonians—gives us some indication of the dominating personalities of the few Adamic survivors, and the influence anything derived from the Adamic civilisation had upon the institutions of the Gentile nations.

The retention of the original Adamic chronology by the Hebrews, Egyptians, and Babylonians, and the adoption of the Deluge epoch as a new datum for the 30 and 120 years' periods by the Egyptians and Babylonians, enable us to establish precisely the original Adamic chronology in relation to our modern chronological epochs and their connected astronomical and historical data. Similarly, the independent histories of Egypt and Babylon can now be synchronised perfectly at all points of contact with the history of Israel from Abraham to Moses, from Moses to Solomon, from Solomon to Zedekiah, and from Zedekiah to Christ. The records of the Chinese,[1] Babylonians,[2] Egyptians, and Hebrews all prove independently that the zero epoch (o A.K.) of Adamic chronology is 4000 B.C., and that the date of the termination of the Adamic Deluge is 1656 A.K. =2344 B.C.

[margin note:] The records of the Chinese, Babylonians, Egyptians, and Hebrews all independently prove that the zero epoch of the Adamic race = 0 A.K. =4000 B.C., and that the epoch of the termination of the Adamic Deluge =1656 A.K. =2344 B.C.

¶ 421. THE EGYPTIAN DATING OF ISRAEL'S HISTORY.

The retention by the ancient Egyptians of the original astronomical chronology of the A'damic civilisation has been proved by the original chronology of the Egyptian King Lists and independently by the calendar

[1] The Chinese data consist of the following :—
I. As proving that o A.K. =4000 B.C.

    (a) The epoch of Fu-hi (the Chinese Noah) is given as 2944 B.C., which date by the Hebrew and Egyptian data is the date of the beginning of the dynasty of Noah at 1056 A.K.

    (b) The epoch of the dynasty of Yaou is given as 2356 B.C. which, according to the Adamic chronology, is 1644 A.K. This is the last year of the 15th Phoenix cycle from o A.K. =4000 B.C., and therefore the year in which the Phoenix festival was celebrated that saw the inauguration of the dynasty of Yaou.

II. As proving that 1656 A.K. =2344 B.C., and that this date was the epoch of the Adamic Deluge ending, and of the beginning of a new reckoning of 30 years' periods as in Egypt and Babylon.

    (a) The Chinese records represent that the Deluge occurred during the dynasty of Yaou, dated as 2356 B.C. (I (b) above) to 2254 B.C., i.e. 1644 A.K. to 1746 A.K. respectively.

    (b) The termination of the dynasty of Yaou at 1746 A.K. is 90 years or 3 Sed heb periods from 1656 A.K. This indicates that the dynasty of Yaou was officially recorded at the Sed festival, as having terminated. It is confirmed, therefore, that as amongst the Egyptians the date of the Deluge ending was reckoned as an epoch of Sed hebs amongst the Chinese. The Sed period is, therefore, the origin of the 60 years' (or double Sed heb) period still employed, or employed until recently, in Chinese chronology.

[2] The Babylonian evidence confirming the Egyptian and Chinese epoch for the new Sed heb reckoning, as the epoch of the Adamic Deluge ending, is given in the bottom right-hand corner of Annotations (B) to Tables XVII–XIX.
It will also be observed (Annotations (B)) that the official date for the termination of the dynasty of Ur, and the beginning of the 1st Dynasty of Babylon at 1965 A.K., is 309 years or 3 primary cycles of 103 years from the date of the Deluge ending 1656 A.K.
The beginning of the dynasty of Akkad (Annotations (B)) was, however, represented as the official beginning of that dynasty at a Sed heb festival based on the Phoenix epoch of Enoch, 987 A.K. It was derived as follows :—

Phoenix epoch of Enoch	987 A.K.
7 cycles of 103 years =1 great cycle of 6 Sep tep sed periods ..	721 years.
	1708 A.K.
2 Sed heb periods	60 years.
Alleged official beginning of dynasty of Akkad	1768 A.K.

This date was later adopted as the epoch of the founding of Babylon, i.e. 2331–2332 A.K. (refer Annotations (A) to Tables XVII–XIX lower right-hand corner).

The ancient Egyptian records, independently of any other evidence, fix the Adamic and B.C. dates and the precise historical circumstances of the events relating to the principal points of contact between Egypt and Israel, from Senusert III and Abraham to Darius Hystaspes and Ezra.

and astronomical datings of the contemporary Egyptian records. These have established the precise dates of Egyptian history from the beginning of the XIIth Egyptian Dynasty to Alexander the Great. More remarkable still, however, is the accurate manner in which the contemporary Egyptian records define the dates and essential events relating to the outstanding points of contact between Egypt and Israel. It is no exaggeration to state that the exact chronology of the Old Testament, in terms of the Adamic system of astronomical chronology, can be established from Egyptian sources alone. Nor is it any exaggeration to say that the precise dates of contact between Israel and Egypt, in all cases, can be *fixed independently* from Egyptian records.

The Egyptian dated records of Abraham's and Joseph's famines, the death of the firstborn son of the Pharaoh of the Exodus, and the Exodus.

The year of Abraham's entry into Egypt is fixed by the date of the Egyptian record of the famine relief work undertaken in Egypt in that year. The dated period of the seven years' famine of Joseph is given by the contemporary Egyptian records. The precise date of the death of the " firstborn son " of the Pharaoh of the Exodus, and the precise date of the Exodus, are again given by the contemporary Egyptian records. In all cases, the accompanying narratives supplied by the related Egyptian records of the various periods concerned supply a living historical context, and the narratives of the Books of Genesis and Exodus fall naturally into their place in the story as essential parts of an animated whole.

The Egyptian dated outline of Israel's history from 2083½ A.K. =1916 B.C. to 3480 A.K. =520 B.C.

If, therefore, we may suppose, for the time being, that the narratives of the Books of Genesis and Exodus contain no references to their being connected with any single chronological scheme, we can nevertheless determine from the Egyptian data the chronological scale in relation to which the events that are recorded in these Books actually happened. Treating, therefore, the narratives concerning (a) Abraham, (b) Joseph, and (c) the Exodus, as the description of events that are not presented as chronologically connected, the three independent narratives are fixed by the Egyptian astronomical datings as follows :—

	A.K.	B.C.
(a) From the call of Abraham to Abraham entering Egypt..	$\begin{cases} 2083\frac{1}{2} \\ 2084\frac{1}{2} \end{cases}$	$=1916$ $=1915$

(Table XV, Annotations (D) (1), Table XVIII, and Annotations (D), and Table XXII.)

(b) Israel enter Egypt	$2298\frac{1}{2}=1701$

(Table XXII and Annotations.)

(c) The Exodus of Israel from Egypt	$2513\frac{1}{4}=1486$

(Table XXIII and Annotations.)

Later narratives of the Old Testament, similarly treated, and chronologically defined by the Egyptian data, establish the following dates :—

	A.K.	B.C.
(d) The founding of Solomon's Temple	$2992\frac{1}{2}$	$=1707$

(By data of Annotations (A) to Table XXVI.)

(e) The dedication of Solomon's Temple	3000	$=1000$

(By data of Annotations (A) to Table XXVI.)

The chronological synchronisms with later Babylonian history also determine :—

	A.K.	B.C.
(f) The date of the destruction of Jerusalem by Nebuchadnezzar (Table XXX)	3416=	584
(By data of Egyptian Table XXIV synchronising with data of Babylonian Tables XXI and XXVII.)		
(g) The founding of the 2nd Temple in Jerusalem, in the 2nd year of Darius I. (Table XXVIII)	3480=	520
(By data of Egyptian Table XXIV agreeing with data of Medo-Persian Table XXVII.)		

¶ 422. THE BABYLONIAN DATING OF ISRAEL'S HISTORY.

The retention by the ancient Babylonians of the original astronomical chronology of the Adamic civilisation has been proved by the original chronological formulation of the Babylonian Dynastic Tablets. This has been independently confirmed by the very considerable amount of information, derived from this chronological formulation, concerning the cyclic and calendar dates of the Adamic chronology. Additional confirmatory evidence has been supplied by the astronomical datings. These, however, in the earlier periods, do not occur as contemporary records in such profusion as in Egypt. This may be due, not so much to the fact of the records not having been unearthed, as to the fact of the calendar basis upon which they have been framed being so far imperfectly understood, if understood at all. A very definite hint concerning this is supplied by the data of Annotations (B) to Tables XVII–XIX. This seems to indicate that the datum and the method of intercalation followed at the time of the 1st Dynasty of Babylon were identical with the datum and intercalary rules relating to the 103 years' cycle adopted by the Egyptians. The only difference seems to have consisted of the two different month dates for the beginning of the calendar year, as indicated on Plate LIX.

The ancient Babylonian records, independently of any other evidence, fix the Adamic and B.C. dates and the precise historical circumstances of the events relating to the principal points of contact between Babylon and Israel from Khammurabi (Amraphel) and Abraham to Darius Hystaspes and Ezra.

If it can be definitely confirmed by independent data that the autumnal equinoctial basis was adopted by the 1st Dynasty of Babylon, then it should be possible to fix the datings of the recorded information relating to the observations of the planet Venus towards the end of the 1st Dynasty of Babylon ; unless, of course, the festivals were regulated by a secretly observed calendar, and the observations of Venus dated with reference to a luni-solar year calendar.

The early Babylonian observation of the planet Venus.

Apart from this question, however, the Babylonian chronology is quite sufficiently established by the astronomical data already known. As in the case of the Egyptian records, the contemporary Babylonian records fix the precise dates of contact between Israel and Babylon. The year of Abraham's journey into Canaan and Egypt is fixed by the date determined from the Babylonian records for Chedorlaomer's expedition into Canaan (Annotation (D) and Tables XVII–XIX). The date agrees with the

The Babylonian date for Chedorlaomer's and Khammurabi's expedition into Canaan fixes, independently of other evidence, the A.K. and B.C. date of Abraham's journey.

Egyptian date for the year of the events relating to Abraham's migration. Again, the records of correspondence between the Kassite kings of Babylon —the dates of whose reigns are known from the Babylonian data—and the kings of Egypt of the XVIIIth Dynasty, confirm the Egyptian date for Israel's entry into Egypt.

Babylonian chronology fixes the beginning and ending of Israel's relations with Babylon.   In addition, the Babylonian data fix the precise dates for the last years of the kingdom of Judah. These dates synchronise with the later years of Egyptian history according to the statement of the original Adamic chronology. Altogether, the complete synchronism confirms the Egyptian datings for the events in Israel's history as given in ¶ 421; and, in addition, fixes the date of the destruction of Jerusalem by Nebuchadnezzar as 3416 A.K. =584 B.C., and the date of the founding of the 2nd Temple at Jerusalem in the 2nd year of Darius I as 3480 A.K.=520 B.C.

¶ 423.   THE ASTRONOMICAL DATING OF THE CALL OF ABRAHAM.

The cyclic datings of the Adamic chronology that governed the durations of Adamic dynasties extend to the date of the call of Abraham.   Investigation of the chronological basis of the Book of Genesis establishes the fact that the statement of dynasties, as unit items of essential genealogical detail, ceases at Abraham. This quite accords with the fact that the Old Testament is the history of the man Abraham and his " seed." From Abraham onwards the generation has become the unit item of *essential* genealogical detail. When *non-essential* genealogical detail is dealt with, the narrative frequently gives evidence of reversion to the original system. This was seen in the case of the house of Machir (¶ 407).

The dynasty of Terah ended at the death of Terah, the father of Abraham. It was recorded as officially ending at the date of the call of Abraham, the Divine selection of the new dynasty. Now, had the 205 years of the dynasty of Terah been intended to be understood as the duration of the life of Abraham's father, the sequence of the narrative would have been altogether different. Had such been the intention, can we imagine the narrative intentionally giving Abraham as born when Terah was 130 years old, and then following with the intentional relation of Sarah's laughter at the prediction of Abraham having a son when he was 100 years old ?

The cycle of 1461 solar years from the epoch of Enoch to the epoch of Abraham.   If, on the other hand, the facts concerning the intention of the narrative are as we have given them, then the official termination of the dynasty of Terah, and the official beginning of the independent dynasty of Abraham should, in accordance with the ruling feature of the preceding portion of the narrative, be defined by the termination of a calendar cycle. It is actually given as occurring at the end of a cycle of 1461 solar years that began at the epoch of Enoch 622 A.K.

The termination of the same cycle celebrated by Senusert III in Egypt.   The termination of the same cycle was celebrated in the 7th year of Senusert III of the XIIth Egyptian Dynasty. This 7th year of Senusert III was not fixed by this identity. The independent astronomical fixing was seen to be confirmed by the identity, and the identification with Abraham's cycle was confirmed by the historical relations concerning Abraham's journey into Egypt and concerning the 8th year of Senusert III. The date of the call of Abraham, as given by the Old Testament in terms of Adamic chronology, was therefore seen to be identical with the date of the call of Abraham as derived from the Egyptian chronology.

The Adamic chronology datings by the three independent lines of investigation, the Book of Genesis, the Egyptian records, and the Babylonian records respectively, are therefore identical. This, however, did not fix independently from the Old Testament sources the equivalent B.C. date for the Adamic date thus independently derived from Genesis. This was seen to be given by the chronological details of the later Books of the Old Testament. The B.C. date thus obtained was seen to be identical with the B.C. date obtained from Egyptian sources, and independently from Babylonian sources. *The Adamic datings of Israel's history by Babylonian, Egyptian, and Hebrew records are identical in all three cases; the Babylonian and Egyptian records fix the corresponding B.C. datings.*

¶ 424. THE HEBREW SYSTEM OF RETROSPECTIVE TOTALS.

It is only when we come to the matter of expressing the Adamic datings of early Hebrew history in terms of B.C. years, that we find how much we have still to learn concerning early Hebrew methods of thought and representation. The question forms one of the many factors relating to *ancient* Hebrew mental idiom that must eventually revolutionise the whole basis of textual criticism of the Old Testament. Much passes for textual criticism that is merely the result of inexperience in the practical affairs of everyday life in all ages. But when this inexperience extends to matters concerning forms of thought dealing with phases of everyday life that do not now exist, and have ceased to exist for countless centuries, it must be apparent that the conclusions advanced in such cases as the results of textual criticism can have little or no basis in fact. *Ancient Hebrew mental idiom and the problem of Old Testament chronology. Textual criticism in relation to Hebrew mental idiom.*

In this volume we are dealing only with the chronological aspects of this form of criticism, and will confine ourselves within these limits. For over twenty-two centuries heated controversies have centred upon the statements concerning the 430 years of Exodus xii, 40 and the 480th year of 1 Kings vi, 1. Jewish opinion has remained unaltered concerning the former, but for its own purposes—explained at length in ¶¶ 331–335 and Annotations (E) and (F) of Table XXIX—Jewish forgery has occasioned the controversies centred upon the period of 480 years. *The problems of the 430 years of Exodus xii, 40 and the 480th year of 1 Kings vi, 1.*

In the matter of the period of 430 years, the Samaritan and Septuagint Versions of the Pentateuch have each, in their own way, striven to amend the text to express the meaning of the related passage as the Hebrews understood it. Both emendations have only succeeded in accentuating a difficulty, and in perpetuating the belief in a difficulty that does not really exist in the original as it was understood by the early Hebrews. Precisely as the year 1924 is now understood as 1924 "Anno Domini," so to the early Hebrews the 430 years dating for the Exodus was understood as relating to 430 years of the era of Abraham. Similarly, the 480th year of 1 Kings vi, 1 was understood as describing the 480th year of the era of the deliverance *The true solution of the two chronological problems.*

of Israel from bondage. The 480th year is now confirmed by the summation of Column (1) Annotations (C) to Table XXVIII. That the Exodus date was reckoned as a new epoch is confirmed by the nature of the details of this enumeration. Thus items 1 to 5 inclusive are each 40 or 80 years, and altogether total 240 years, or two periods of the *Sep tep sed* interval, covering half the period of the chronological statement. Again, the short period items, until the 40 years' periods or multiples of 4 years are resumed, total the cycle of 103 years (*i.e.* items 6 to 13 inclusive).

Thus, in spite of the fact that the post-exode Israelitish calendar was a luni-solar calendar, we find, nevertheless, reliable evidence indicating that something of the nature of the Adamic system of intercalations was used contemporaneously to define periods identified with a definite sequence of historical happenings. This is the apparent background of the Hebrew system of retrospective totals seen in application in Annotations (A, III), (B), and (C) to Table XXVIII.

The resulting B.C. dates for Israel's history agree with the B.C. dates derived from the Babylonian and Egyptian records. The elucidation of this Hebrew system of retrospective totals solves the problem of the Hebrew chronology from Abraham to Zedekiah. The resulting B.C. datings for the Adamic datings in Israel's history confirm, in all cases to the year, the B.C. and Adamic datings given independently by the Egyptian and Babylonian records.

¶ 425. MESSIANISM AND THE GREAT PYRAMID.

The cyclic datings of Adamic chronology are seen to be continued by the Hebrew prophetic books as governing events in the future. This identity confirms the independent conclusions of Grattan Guinness's school of prophecy interpretation. Investigation of the prophetical books of the Old and New Testaments next establishes the fact that astronomical cycles and periods, related to the astronomical system of the Adamic chronology, are represented as governing the stated sequence and periods of historical events in the future. This identification is seen to confirm the conclusions, relating to prophetical cycles, advanced by the school of interpretation concerning Hebrew apocalyptic literature; now identified in modern times with the name of the late Dr. Grattan Guinness.

The early appearance of Messianic prophecies in Egypt. Egyptian literature associates Messianic prophecy with the Great Pyramid. Hebrew sacred literature allegorises the Messianic kingdom in the form of a Pyramid. A thorough investigation of this question has shown that the various prophecies, relating to the Messiah and the Restitution, belong not only to the books of the Old Testament, but also to the early Adamic literature circulating in the ancient East. Thus, in ancient Egypt, archæologists were surprised at finding " Messianism 1000 years before the Hebrews." Now, it is in Egypt that the Messianic literature, or the religious imagery derived from early Messianic texts, universally identifies the symbolism of Messianism with the Great Pyramid. Confirming this association of prophetic idea and symbolism as essentially having originated with the Adamic race, the books of the Old and New Testaments represent the *Union* of the two bodies (spiritual Israel and literal Israel), comprising the Messianic kingdom under one head, Christ, by the type of a Pyramid of which the " head-stone " (apex-stone), also designated " the chief corner-stone," symbolises the Christ.

It is not surprising, therefore, to find Jeremiah referring to certain "signs and wonders" set up in Egypt as a consequence of the will of God, and to find him referring to these as extant in his own day. Nor have we far to seek for the single structure which Isaiah defines as "a pillar in the midst of the land of Egypt"—*i.e.* in the centre of the quadrant of the Delta —and also as "an altar at the border thereof"—*i.e.* on the elevated plateau of Gizeh that marks the border of the desert and the limit of the cultivated land (refer to Plate III). Isaiah describes it as a "pillar . . . and an altar to the Lord of Hosts," and associates its purpose with a then remotely future stage of the world's history when tribulation should prevail to such an extent as to require the intervention of the Lord.

Jeremiah and Isaiah identify the structural embodiment of the Messianic Pyramid as the Great Pyramid of Gizeh.

All the general indications therefore define that the design and construction of the Great Pyramid are to be traced to the religion of the Adamic race. It is only after the construction of the Great Pyramid that we find the purest form of monotheism and the highest conception of the promised Messiah in Egypt. These are almost precisely identical with the form and conception later presented in the books of the Old and New Testaments. It has been shown, however, that the two presentations have operated as the result of two independent spiritual impulses or series of spiritual impulses, commonly known as the process of progressive revelation.

The Great Pyramid's construction organised by the Adamic race.

¶ 426. THE PYRAMID'S LAW OF RELATIVITY.

A thorough examination of the constructional features of the Great Pyramid's exterior proved that these features defined the design as concerned with the monumentalisation of the annual occurrences of the Adamic astronomical and calendar year, and with the complete representation of the dimensions and motions of the Earth and its orbit, and of the changes in these dimensions and motions. In other words, the Pyramid was found— by its representation of a simple geometrical co-ordination of Earth measurement and the value of the solar year—to indicate, in such simple geometrical form, a Universal Law of Gravitation, defining the Earth, its orbit, and their motions, and the changes in these motions in precise and accurate terms of Earth-time and Earth-distance measurement. This representation was seen to give the astronomical equivalent of the Adamic age for the modern astronomical definition of the laws of gravitation, either as expressed by Newton, or as now revised by Einstein.

The Great Pyramid is a graphical representation of a universal law of relativity geometrically expressed.

This representation defines the Earth and its orbit in dimensions and motions and the variations in these dimensions and motions all in precise terms of modern gravitational astronomy.

This representation and the intention of this representation were confirmed by the literary records and traditions of the Egyptians. From these it was also seen that the single linear measurement and the single angular measurement, defining the shape and dimensions of the Pyramid, supplied the essential basis of the Adamic dynamical astronomy, relating (1) to precession, and the variations and mathematical epochs of precession; and (2) to the change in the longitude of perihelion, the variations in the rate of change, and the epochs necessary for the mathematical expression of the factors defining the change. The latter representation was seen to be

The representation confirmed as intentional by details of Egyptian literary traditions relating to the Great Pyramid.

PLATE LXVII.

Fig. A.

Terminal Epoch of Pyramid's Orbital Chronology defined by
SUM OF BASE ANGLES
of Pyramid Section = 103°·42'·286
= Longitude of Perihelion in 2045 A.D.
(¶¶ 212, 247, 249)

35th Course Axis, Square Circuit (HJKL)
= 8·3652·42·465.

Base Square Circuit (DEFG) = 36524·2465.

Structural Base Circuit
(DₐHₐENₐFQₒGₐT) = 36525·647·1536.

Internal Geometrical Base
Octag: Circuit (DUEVFW6X)
= 36525·99/317.

X is intersection
of DT and GS produced.

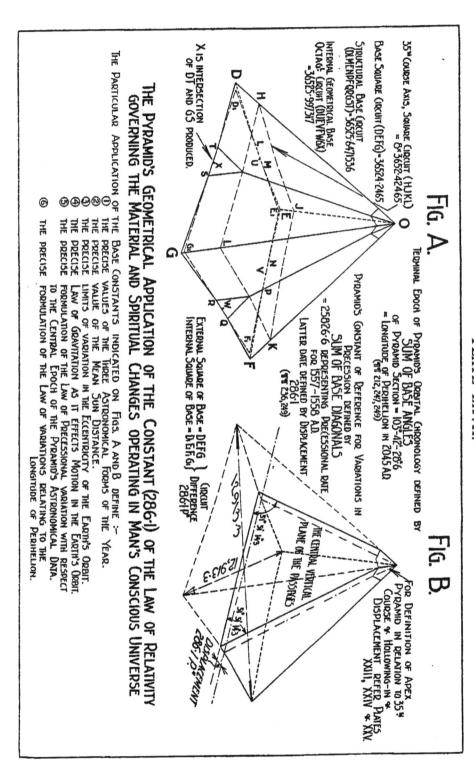

Pyramid's Constant of Reference for Variations in
Precession defined by
SUM OF BASE DIAGONALS
= 25026·6 representing Precessional Rate
for 1557–1558 A.D.
Latter date defined by Displacement
2861·
(¶¶ 236, 249)

External Square of Base = DEFG } Circuit
Internal Square of Base = DₐEₐFₐGₐ} Difference
2861·p²

Fig. B.

For Definition of Apex
Pyramid in relation to 35th
Course & Hollowing-in &
Displacement refer Plates
XXII, XXIV & XXV.

The Central Vertical
Plane of the Passages

Displacement 2861·p

THE PYRAMID'S GEOMETRICAL APPLICATION OF THE CONSTANT (286·I) OF THE LAW OF RELATIVITY GOVERNING THE MATERIAL AND SPIRITUAL CHANGES OPERATING IN MAN'S CONSCIOUS UNIVERSE

The Particular Application of the Base Constants indicated on Figs. A and B define :—

① The precise values of the three Astronomical Forms of the Year.
② The precise value of the Mean Sun Distance.
③ The precise limits of Variation in the Eccentricity of the Earth's Orbit.
④ The precise Law of Gravitation as it effects Motion in the Earth's Orbit.
⑤ The precise Formulation of the Law of Precessional Variation with respect to the Central Epoch of the Pyramid's Astronomical Data.
⑥ The precise Formulation of the Law of Variations relating to the Longitude of Perihelion.

(1).

THE GREAT PYRAMID'S BASE CIRCUIT AND ITS SCALE.

I. The literary records of the ancient Egyptians state that the various Egyptian systems of measures related to a geometrical representation of the value of the solar year in days and of other related mathematical functions. The actual measurements of the ancient Egyptians, when examined, confirm this (refer to Chapter II).

The examination of the Egyptian measures proves that the basal unit of the geometrical representation was a unit of 1.0011 British inches.

II. The records of the ancient Egyptians state that the dimensions of the Great Pyramid were of the linear and angular values given on Plate LXVII, geometrically defining the value of the year in days and other related mathematical functions (refer to Chapter II).

The same records define that the Great Pyramid's unit of linear measure was of the value of 1.0011 British inches.

III. The actual measurements of the Great Pyramid—determined from Sir William M. F. Petrie's reliable survey—show that the dimensions of the Great Pyramid were of the linear and angular values given on Plate LXVII as geometrically defining the value of the year in days and other related mathematical functions (refer to Chapters II and III).

These dimensions are all in units of 1.0011 British inches; this fixing that 1 Pyramid inch = 1.0011 British inches.

IV. The records of the ancient Egyptians—by their data concerning the mathematical functions of the representation—define the adopted mean value of the solar year as 365.24465 days, and as the mean value of a long succession of accurate calendar cycles. This is an extremely accurate mean value when considered as applying to the long period indicated by the data mentioned.

The Great Pyramid's base side, in Pyramid inches, when divided by 25, gives the above value; and

The one 10-millionth part of the Earth's polar radius divided by 25 gives 1.0011 British inches, the value of the Pyramid inch.

V. The calendar cycles defining the ancient Egyptian and Pyramid's mean value of the solar year are cycles indicated in the Hebrew Book of Genesis (Chapters I and VI), and the Pyramid's base side consists of 365.242465 Hebrew sacred cubits.

The Hebrew sacred cubit consists of 25 Pyramid inches, and divides 10 million times into the Earth's polar radius.

(2).

THE GRAVITATIONAL ASTRONOMY OF THE PYRAMID'S EXTERIOR.

In the horizontal plane of the Pyramid's base, DEFG, let two horizontal lines be drawn outwards from each corner of the Pyramid's base, such as the corner G, and in each case perpendicular to the structural base lines, such as GS and GR. There will then be eight horizontal perpendiculars, two from each of the corners, D, E, F, and G. Each base side will therefore have two *approximately* parallel horizontal perpendiculars, one from each of the corners defining the base side. Not being truly parallel—owing to the two perpendiculars meet at a point (Fig. A)—the two perpendiculars will meet at a point. The four points, thus defined from the North, East, South, and West base sides respectively, lie, in each case, truly North, East, South, and West respectively from the centre of the Pyramid's base square. The four points also lie on the circumference of a circle, the centre of which is the centre of the Pyramid's base square.

This scale geometrically defines, precisely to a scale of one 25-millionth, an essential function of the law of gravitation in relation to the Earth's orbit.

The circle thus defined to scale is what we have termed the Earth's "speed circle." The radius of the latter circle is equal to the major axis of the Earth's orbit. The radius of the circle defined by the Pyramid's base is one 25-millionth part of the latter astronomical dimension. Then, since the Pyramid inch is the one 25-millionth part of the Earth's polar radius, the two scales of geometrical representation on a common decimal basis are seen to be intentionally related (refer to Chapter III).

The three geometrical base circuits of the Pyramid, as indicated on Fig. A, respectively define the accurate values of the solar or tropical year, the sidereal year, and the anomalistic (or orbital) year in days (refer to Chapter III).

The ascertainable date at which the annual rate of precession was defined by the sum of the Pyramid's diagonals is 1558 A.D. This is 286 years prior to the central precessional epoch, defined by the geometrical ephemeris of the Pyramid's Passage system as 1844 A.D. Confirming the intention, the Passage system is displaced 286.1 P', as shown on Fig. B (refer to Chapter III).

Similarly, the sum of the base angles of the Pyramid's section gives the longitude of perihelion for 2045 A.D., terminating a period of ⅛th of 36,534 years from the date at which the longitude of perihelion was 0° (refer to Chapter IV).

(3).

THE GREAT PYRAMID'S PRINCIPLE OF RELATIVITY.

The texts of the ancient Egyptian Messianic prophecy identify the Great Pyramid as a symbolic representation of Messianic prophecy.

The literary traditions descended from the ancient Egyptians state that the Great Pyramid contains records relating to astronomical cycles, chronology, and prophecy.

The Hebrew Messianic prophecies are identical in sequence with the ancient Egyptian Messianic prophecies, and refer to the Messiah and His Kingdom in terms of a Pyramid allegory in which the Messiah is the apex-stone, and His kingdom is the "Stone Kingdom."

The geometrical representation of the Great Pyramid's Passage system defines a complete and accurate system of astronomical chronology in terms of modern astronomical chronology. Its principal structural features are identified as relating to allegorical features in the ancient Egyptian and Hebrew Messianic prophecies.

In all of these various relations the Pyramid's "displacement factor" (286.1) is constantly indicated as the essential factor relating to *change* in physical and spiritual conditions. By means of this factor, the variations in precession and the rates of precession, in the change in the longitude of perihelion and the rate of change of the latter, and in the eccentricity of the Earth's orbit, are all given by the Pyramid's Passage ephemeris as precisely and accurately as modern astronomy requires. The same displacement factor is employed to define the accurate value of the tropical year and the accurate value of the anomalistic year, as values that depend upon a change affecting the orbit in relation to the sidereal year, whose precise value is given by the *structural* circuit of the Pyramid's base.

When the Messianic prophecies of the ancient Egyptians and Hebrews are read in relation to the structural and geometrical allegory of the Pyramid's Passage system, the displacement value is also found to apply, intentionally, in the representation, as relating to spiritual changes taking place in history and in relation to time as defined by the Pyramid's astronomical system. The corresponding Pyramid dates are, in all cases, dates that define the outstanding changes relating to the Christian fulfilment of Messianic prophecy in history.

The manner in which all three sources combine to explain the significance of the displacement factor is confirmed by the manner in which the explanation has been fulfilled in time, place, and circumstance. The Great Pyramid defines, in scientific terms, that "in Christ are hid all the treasures of wisdom and knowledge," that by Him God "created all things," and that "the world was made by Him, and knew Him not" (¶350 *et seq.*).

completely indicated in relation to the two factors above mentioned—by the outstanding displacement factor of the Great Pyramid.

This displacement factor is expressed as a geometrical function of the solar year in terms of standard Earth-distance measurement. It defines the extent of hollowing-in of the Pyramid's base sides, and the eccentric displacement of the Pyramid's Passage system. At the same time its applications indicate its intentional representation as the mathematical factor governing the physical changes in the Earth's solar system.

A summary of the data establishing this intention is given by Plate LXVII and Annotations. Comparison of the mathematical relations of this displacement factor with the symbolism of the Pyramid's exterior, as read in the light of Hebrew and Egyptian Pyramid symbolism, establishes the intentional representation of this displacement factor, as illustrative of the governing principle of the laws of the Creator in man's spiritual and physical

dominions. This application was seen to express the existing displacement of man from the harmony of God's creation. It was seen to be expressive of the Messiah's displacement to effect the bridging of the gap,[1] and by means of this bridging to build up the spiritual part of the Messianic kingdom, that the building up of the latter should shape the destinies of the material part. The final feature of the applications was accordingly seen to express, as effected by the preceding phase—the final complete union of the two parts of the Messianic kingdom, and the final displacement of man from his existing state of spiritual and physical being into that state of spiritual and physical being that will complete the harmony of God's creation. This application of the displacement factor was dealt with in ¶¶ 350, 351, and 364 (and footnote).

¶ 427. THE SYMBOLISM OF DIVINE TUITION.

The geometry of the displacement factor was seen to be connected in all its applications with the geometry of the Apex Pyramid. The latter was defined by the Pyramid's geometrical relations—viewed in the light of the Bible's Pyramid allegory—as symbolic of the "stone which the builders rejected," that formed the ideal type, the model of the whole design. This

reference to the rejection of the ideal model by "the builders" has a two-fold application. This twofold application gives us something of the nature of a tangible reason for the circumstances relating to the original displace-

ment of man. One application refers to the heavenly host of God's spiritual beings who acted as His spiritual agents, actively co-operating with Him,

as the Head, in the work of creation. This spiritual body bears the same relation to God as the spiritual Israel—the Church—bears to its Head, Christ. The other application refers to the literal Israel as God's chosen agents on Earth to assist in the work of Christ in building up the Kingdom of Heaven on Earth. In this application, Peter, in Acts iv, 11, informs the

[1] Refer to Section II, Table XXXVIII.

Jews that " This (Christ) is the stone which was set at nought by you builders (the Jews), which is become the head of the corner." Peter, therefore, in addressing his 1st Epistle-to those of the dispersed peoples of literal[1] Israel, who through Christ had become of the body of spiritual Israel, refers to such, not as " builders," but as " living stones " of whom " are *built* up a spiritual house."

The whole of 1 Peter ii should be read in relation to the first two verses of Chapter i, and in relation to Hosea i, 9, 10 and ii, 23, and as intentionally indicating that by Christ the " building " has been taken out of the hands of man, and that literal Israel can take their part in the building of this *spiritual* house, the body of Christ, only by entering into that body in the spirit, and becoming not " builders " but " living " elements of whom the body is " built up." *The Messianic law of humility. The former " builders " must become humble elements of the building, as foreordained by God.*

Paul, in Ephesians iii, refers to this new process in Christ as an object-lesson to the heavenly host of God's spiritual agents of creation, obviously in order to teach them something concerning His eternal purpose that has been hidden[2] from them, and which they had failed to discover for themselves in their participation in the scheme of creation, or, as Paul expresses the matter— *The application of Christ's law of humility in the building and establishing of the Messianic kingdom to constitute an object-lesson to the creative builders of the heavenly host.*

"To the intent that now UNTO THE PRINCIPALITIES AND POWERS IN HEAVENLY PLACES might be known by the Church the manifold wisdom of God.

" According to His eternal purpose which He purposed in Christ Jesus our Lord. . . . Of whom the whole family in heaven and earth is named." *Christ the perfect mode of God's creation.*

And as Paul states in Colossians ii, 3 and Ephesians iii, 9—

" In whom are hid all the treasures of wisdom and knowledge."
" The mystery, which from the beginning of the world hath been hid in God, WHO CREATED ALL THINGS BY JESUS CHRIST." *The Apex Pyramid the model of the whole Pyramid.*

¶ 428. CHRIST THE IDEAL MODEL OF GOD'S CREATION.

All this obviously relates to Christ being the ideal model of God's creation,[3] as typified by the Apex Pyramid, or by the headstone and chief

---

[1]The 1st Epistle of Peter is clearly addressed to Israelites of the ten tribes " scattered throughout Pontus, Galatia, Cappadocia, Asia, and Bithynia " (1 Pet. i, 1). This is confirmed by the words in which Peter addresses these " dispersed " strangers in 1 Pet. ii, 9, 10. The words of verse 10 in particular settle the question : " Which in time past were not a people, but are now the people of God : which had not obtained mercy, but now have obtained mercy." These words, taken from Hosea (i, 9, 10 ; and ii, 23), were addressed only to ten-tribed Israel.

[2]Concerning " the Son of Man," the Book of Enoch (xlviii, 6) states : " For this reason has He been chosen and hidden before Him (God) before the creation of the world. . . ."
As is stated in ¶¶ 498–498e, the Egyptian Osiris usurped the attributes and functions of the promised Messiah of early Egyptian prophecy. This accounts for the *original* source of the appellation applied to Osiris—" the Hidden One."

[3]The Messiah was the Architypal Man. Thus, of Christ, the Messiah, it is written : " All things were created by Him and for Him ; and He is before all things, and by Him all things consist " (Col. i, 16 and 17). " Who verily was foreordained before the foundation of the world " (1 Pet. i, 20). Long before man or the higher animals appeared on earth, lower organisms were forming and developing on lines and principles foreshadowing the higher organism, man. Through all the species of organic life the same underlying scheme is progressively apparent, and the same

God's scheme of creation— as relating to Christ—not fully disclosed to His spiritual agents ; the purpose being that when God eventually corrected the free-will tendencies of His agents, both in Heaven and in Earth, they should, by the lesson, be brought fully into harmony of operation in God's creation by realising the magnitude of Divine love as expressed in the highest form of sacrifice.

corner-stone of the Pyramid allegory of the Old and New Testaments. This clearly implies that the ideal type, Christ, was not adhered to in the developing, by God's spiritual agents, of certain details of creation relating to the Earth and man. This implication necessarily suggests further that the intention of the sacred writings is concerned with the indication of a displacement that occurred in the spiritual conditioning of the heavenly hosts (Jude, verse 6) prior to or coincident with the final stage of Earth creation—man ; and that, as a result of this heavenly displacement, the displacement of man followed, more or less, as a natural consequence.

The tendency of free-will in operation being to deviate from principles of operation that have to be taken on faith, the spiritual agents of creation deviated from God's principle (Christ) in certain details of creation relating to Man. This is expressed as " the rejection " of " the apex-stone " by " the builders."

The sacred writings further define that both displacements had been eternally foreknown by God to be the necessary consequences of the operation of free-will in His scheme of creation ; that, nevertheless, this operation of free-will was known by Him in His supreme wisdom to form the essential element in the created state of spiritual being for the reception and emanation of Divine love ; and that, as a consequence of this eternal foreknowledge, He had already—before the processes of active creation began—appointed that he Himself should suffer to effect the reconciliation, to illustrate to His created beings in Heaven and Earth the highest form of the outpouring of Divine love from the highest state of spiritual being in which Divine love had been received from the Father. God, therefore, cut off from Himself the One Fundamental Essence of His Creation, the Highest Creative Expression of Himself, who is the Fountain Source of Love. By projecting this Spiritual Essence of His own Eternal Being, as Christ—not into the high spiritual realms where the displacement in creation had been first effected, but into the lowest spiritual realm of Earth's creation—He set in action the foreordained cycle of events, that, reacting upwards from the lowest spiritual realms to the highest, would restore the free-will balance of love in all God's creation.

The eternal purpose of God in Christ is to instruct all His spiritual beings in the acquirement of perfect unity in love by means of implicit faith in the perfection of His providence.

In this relation we must realise that the sacred writings represent God as conditioning the revealing of Himself, and of His eternal attributes, to the spiritual state of each realm of His creation. Do unto others as you

principles are seen to apply that culminate in the structure of man, who, according to Genesis i, 26 and 27, was made in " the image of God," which " Image " is that of Christ " who is the image of the INVISIBLE God, the firstborn of every creature " (Col. i, 15). The Psalmist, therefore, in Psalm cxxxix, 14–16 (A.V.), sings : " I am fearfully and wonderfully made : marvellous are Thy works ; and that my soul knoweth right well. My substance was not hid from Thee when I was made in secret, and curiously wrought in the lowest parts of the Earth. Thine eyes did see my substance, yet being unperfect ; and in Thy book all my members were written, which in continuance were fashioned (or, what days they should be fashioned) when as yet there was none of them." Similarly " Bereshith Rabbah," Chapter I, states that " Six things preceded the creation of the world. Some of them were created ; some existed as ideals, as part of the thought of the Creator, to emerge, created in the future ; so that their real being (noumena) was in existence, although ages should pass before their appearance as phenomena." " Of the name of the Messiah, who is the subject of the whole of Psalm xxii, it is written (verse 17), ' His name existeth eternally.' R. Ababah Bar Rabbi Zengirah says : ' Also repentance, the coming back of the sinner to his God, existed in ideal, before the creation of the world ; as it is written (Ps. xc), " Before the mountains were brought forth,"—from that very hour Thou turnedst man to contrition, saying, ' Return ye children of men.' ' "
(Edwin Collins. " The Wisdom of Israel," p 24.) In a footnote here Mr. Collins adds that " ' contrition ' is the *correct* translation of *dakka*, which the A.V. erroneously renders in this verse ' destruction,' a rendering entirely inconsistent with the context and not warranted by the etymology of the word."

would have others do unto you, and so will God deal with you. If the spiritual state of being demands " an eye for an eye and a tooth for a tooth," then God reveals Himself to that state in His stern form as the God of justice and rectitude. This is the form in which He reveals Himself most frequently in the Old Testament to Israel. In this form—and under the name, Jahveh or Jehovah—the Hebrews deemed it to be calamitous even to pronounce His name. The sequence relating to all this is the background of our Lord's teaching : to pray to be forgiven, as we forgive others.

¶ 429. THE NAMES OF GOD—ELOHIM AND JAHVEH.

In the Old Testament God, the Creator, appears under two names, Elohim and Jahveh (Jehovah). Similarly, in the early period of Egyptian dynastic history, the one God appears under the two aspects, Heru-ur and Set. These two aspects were later separated to form the Egyptian pagan deities, the elder Horus and Set. In the original Egyptian monotheism, however, Heru-ur was the eternally beneficent aspect of the Creator, and Set was the aspect associated with judgment, correction, punishment, and death. The hieroglyphic representation consisted of the face of Heru-ur and the face of Set being depicted as two aspects of one being.

The Hebrew names of the two aspects of the Creator —Elohim and Jahveh. The early Egyptian names—Heru-ur and Set ; two aspects of the one being.

It would appear, therefore, that the sacred writings represent aspects of God as the Creator of mankind's universe, to be symbolically duplicated in His creation. Thus we have the two bodies, the spiritual Israel (the Body of Christ) and the literal Israel (the Bride of Christ), represented as becoming one body by the " Marriage of the Lamb." It is significant, therefore, to find that the name Elohim is plural, and that it defines the whole unity of the Godhead as expressed by the perfect operation of His spiritual agents of creation. As, however, the displacement from perfection was foreknown to the creator (Elohim), His aspect as Jahveh is defined by Genesis ii, 7, as already active in the " forming " of man. " And Jahveh-Elohim formed man dust from the ground." The name Jahveh here, in light of the later chapters of Genesis, and the Old Testament generally, is clearly necessary to the scheme of the Book of Genesis, according to which scheme the first eleven chapters form the Prologue to the history of Abraham and his seed. Thereafter, in the Old Testament, Jahveh is represented as the aspect of the Creator presented to Israel under the Law. " And *Elohim* spake all these words, saying, I am *Jahveh* thy *Elohim* that brought thee out from the land of Egypt, from the house of slaves. There shall not be to thee other *Elohim* before My face " (Exod. xx, 1–3).[1]

The symbolism of two bodies in unity applied individually to elements departing from the harmony of unity. The symbolisms of restoration to unity.

Elohim and Jahveh in the Genesis narrative of creation.

[1] Textual critics believe that the two different names belong to two rival accounts of creation, one account attributing the creation to *Elohim*, and the other account attributing it to *Jahveh*. The narrative of creation in Genesis—as we now have it—is accordingly stated to be a composite narrative. This is the basal theory of textual criticism as extended to the books of the Old Testament. Whenever the name *Elohim* occurs, the narrative containing it is said to belong to an original Elohistic document, and when the name *Jahveh* occurs, the connected narrative is explained as belonging to an original Jahvistic document.

¶ 430. THE NAME JAHVEH PRESUPPOSES CHRIST.

The revelation of Jahveh in creation presupposes the fall of Man, and is the revealed corrective aspect of God preparatory to the revelation of the aspect of God as Christ. The result of the displacement in the heavenly realms and the displacement in man's spiritual realm overcome by our Lord's displacement.

As "*Elohim*" comprises *Jahveh*, so does *Jahveh* comprise the Potential *Messiah*. Our Lord therefore said, "I and my Father are ONE," "Before Abraham was I AM," these expressions being clearly related to the words of *Elohim* in Exod. iii, 14. "I AM THAT I AM—Thou shalt say unto the Children of Israel, I AM hath sent me unto you." This identity, when considered in the light of the rejection, by "the builders," of Christ as the ideal type of man's creation, indicates that the intention is to define that the "displacement" in the harmony of creation (Jude, verse 6) took place in connection with the creation of man, and that God had already made provision for this. Under the type of the serpent, in the 3rd Chapter of Genesis, the "displacement" in the heavenly realms of creation is represented as responsible for the "displacement" of man from his first estate.[1]

Under the type of the "seed of the woman" Christ is promised as the perfect Adam, who will overcome, by His sufferings in man's spiritual and material states of being, the "displacement," not only in man's created realm, but also in the high spiritual realms where "displacement" first occurred.

Our Lord's conquest over death. His subsequent operations in the heavenly realms. The final concentration of the forces of Christ. The spiritual realm of man the scene of the final conflict. The spiritual conflict has its coincident counterpart in a final material conflict on the Earth.

The Resurrected and Ascended Christ is, therefore, described in the New Testament as proceeding directly from this victory over death in man's spiritual realm to prepare the heavenly realms for the complete restitution. He is described as overcoming the spiritual powers of darkness in the heavenly realms of light; as driving out evil from the higher to the lower realms of spiritual being. His final victory is proclaimed as to be achieved in the spiritual environment of the Earth and over the spiritual powers of darkness driven by Him into the realms of man's spiritual being. This final enforced concentration of the spiritual powers of evil in the spiritual environment of the Earth is described as responsible for the evil predicted as dominating the Earth prior to our Lord's Second Coming. Our Lord warned His elect to

---

[1] In the Book of the Wisdom of Solomon (i, 12–ii, 23 and 24) it is stated: "God made not death: neither hath He pleasure in the destruction of the living. . . . For God created man to be immortal, and made him to be an image of His own eternity. Nevertheless through envy of the devil came death into the world." So in Enoch lxix, 11: "For man was created exactly like the Angels to the intent that he should continue righteous and pure, and death, which destroys everything, could not have taken hold of him, but through this their knowledge they are perishing, and through this power (of knowledge) it (death) is consuming me."

In Enoch lxix it is Gadreel, the Satan, "who has taught the children of men all the blows of death, and he led astray Eve." In Revelation xx, 2 we have the statement: "The dragon, that old serpent, which is the Devil, and Satan." This, together with the passages above quoted, throws light upon the identity of the serpent of Genesis iii. We must, therefore, understand the words of Genesis iii, 15—"I will put enmity between thee and the woman, and between thy seed and her seed; it shall bruise thy head and thou shalt bruise his heel"—as addressed to Satan, who in the form of a serpent is depicted as having "led astray Eve."

Thus even in the texts and representations of the Egyptians and Babylonians, the spirit of evil is depicted in the form of a serpent, dragon, or crocodile. In Egypt, the child-God Horus, "the seed," is portrayed as standing upon the head of a crocodile, and as bruising serpents in his hands.

The reader interested should refer to the account of the Babylonian Tablet concerning "The Revolt in Heaven," Rec. Past (1st Ser.), Vol. VII, p. 127, and see what the translator, H. Fox Talbot, has to say concerning its relation to the references in Job xxxviii, Jude 6, and Rev. xii, 3.

look for signs of this domination as the signs indicative of the nearness of His literal presence.

In all the early monotheistic literatures of the ancient East dealing with the establishing of the Messianic kingdom the essential features, concerning this overcoming of the spiritual powers of darkness in " high places," are either implied or stated. As this is a prominent aspect of the Great Pyramid's allegory, it is of importance to review the nature of the data that have been employed in the formulation of the allegory.

The parallel indication in Pyramid Messianism.

¶ 431. THE PYRAMID'S LAW RELATING TO PHYSICAL CHANGES.

The Passage system of the Great Pyramid and its Chambers are defined as related to the geometry of the Pyramid's exterior. The geometrical indications establishing this are simple angular and linear functions of the geometry of a circle representing, in terms of Earth standard units of linear measurement, the value of the solar year. The resulting lengths and other dimensions of the Passages and Chambers are identical with the corresponding measured distances of modern times.

The mathematical relations of the Pyramid's exterior and interior. The gravitational geometry of the Passage system.

Examination of the geometrical data of the Passage system further establishes the fact that these data constitute an accurate graphical or geometrical representation of the law or laws of gravitational astronomy. Elucidation of this feature supplies us with precisely accurate formulæ relating to precession and the change in the longitude of perihelion. These formulæ agree exactly with the modern formulæ, and define every point in the geometrical scale of the Passages as representing in each case a specific known year as related to modern astronomical time. The data derived from the formulæ are confirmed by various independent astronomical data also geometrically indicated. The check data, generally, relate to the total angle of precession and the longitude of perihelion for a known modern year as related to an ascertainable ancient year.

The Pyramid's astronomical ephemeris accurately defines every year, within a period of close on 7000 years, in relation to modern astronomical time. The astronomical data agree precisely with modern astronomical data.

In all of these derived data, the important factors governing astronomical changes and variations are in all cases represented as mathematical functions of the single factor we have found operating throughout, and have defined as the displacement factor (286.1). A climax is reached in the application of this factor when it defines—

The law of the displacement factor (286.1) relating to physical changes.

(1) That all changes bear a significant mathematical relationship when expressed with reference to an Epochal Period of 286.1 years, beginning in December 1557 A.D. and ending at midnight terminating 25th January 1844 A.D. ;

(2) That the beginning of the Epochal Period is indicated as the beginning of the period to which the Pyramid's Message is addressed ; and

(3) That the same date of commencement is indicated as the beginning of the 7th repetition of a period of 360 years, this 7th repetition ending in December 1917 A.D. ; this repetition and this date of

The definition of the epoch to which the Pyramid's Message is addressed. The initial date defined is coincident with the initial date of Daniel's " time of the end." The deliverance of Jerusalem in prophecy and in history.

its termination being defined by the Old Testament as relating to "*the time* of the end" in which the prophecies were to be elucidated, and at the termination of which—December 1917 A.D.—Jerusalem was to witness the first phase of its deliverance from Gentile domination.

Here, again, the displacement factor is defined as operating, not only in astronomical and historical changes, but as operating in a sense that indicates a spiritual significance.

¶ 432. PYRAMID, EGYPTIAN, AND HEBREW MESSIANISM.

The ancient Egyptian allegorical prophecy of the Messianic kingdom, defined as relating to the structural and geometrical allegory of the Pyramid and the Pyramid allegory of the Old and New Testaments relating to the Messianic kingdom, are both confirmed in detail by the elucidation of the Pyramid's geometry and its astronomical chronology.

The application of the displacement factor last dealt with was seen to confirm the ancient Egyptian traditions and religious imagery that identified the Great Pyramid with the elucidation of prophecy and with the establishing of the Messianic kingdom. It was also shown to confirm the Pyramid allegory of the Old and New Testaments and the astronomical periods of the Hebrew prophecies, giving the dates of the various stages of history that were predicted as related to the establishing of the Messianic kingdom.

Examination of the religious texts of ancient Egypt dealing with the prophetical allegory of the Great Pyramid then showed that certain features of the Pyramid's Passage system and Chambers were depicted as defining specific events in Messianic history. The astronomical datings of the Pyramid's Passage chronology fixed the chronological relations of the events thus specified, and certain identities resulted. These identities established the following :—

The three independent sources of data establish that the prophecies relating to the evolution of the Messianic kingdom give a true dated prediction of outstanding historical events concerning Israel, Christ, and His Church up to modern times. The three sources agree concerning events in the immediate future, as relating to the coming literal presence of our Lord.

(1) That the earliest Messianic prophecies of the dynastic Egyptians were the Messianic prophecies of the Great Pyramid ;

(2) That the prophecies of the Great Pyramid are identical with the prophecies of the Old and New Testaments, as expressed in relation to chronological scale, and nature and sequence of events ;

(3) That the events thus dated and defined as to occur up to modern times have occurred at the dates defined, and in the nature and sequence of events defined ;

(4) That events predicted as to happen in the future are predicted in the same precise chronological sequence by the two independent sets of data ; and

(5) That such sequence of future events, defined by the two sets of data as to precede the literal presence of the Messiah, are represented as occurring between the current year and the 16th of September 1936 A.D.

¶ 433. THE FIXED CHRONOGRAPH OF HISTORY.

Principal features of the identities obtained :—

Outstanding identities obtained from the independent sets of data are the following :—

(1) (a) The common astronomical chronology of the Hebrews, Egyptians, and Babylonians defines that the Adamic Deluge occurred from 1655–1656 A.K.=2345–2344 B.C. *The fixed date of the Adamic Deluge and its relation to chronological law.*

(b) The Pyramid's astronomical chronology defines the date 1655.8 A.K., =2344 B.C., in relation to the Hebrew prophetic cycle of 2520 years.

(2) (a) The astronomical chronology of the Hebrews and Egyptians defines that the Deluge began on 31st October (Greg.), All Hallow's Eve, and officially terminated on 5th November of the following year. *The precise day of the Deluge beginning fixed, and its relation to chronological law.*

(b) The Great Pyramid's noon reflexion phenomena annually defined the anniversary of the former date on one or other of the days, 31st October to 2nd November (Greg.), the exact month date being dependent upon the relationship of the Gregorian Calendar year to the Solar year. This definition belongs to the law relating to changes, and was therefore prophetic rather than retrospective.

(3) (a) The astronomical chronology of the Hebrews and Egyptians defines the precise date of the Exodus as 2513½ A.K.=1486 B.C. *The precise date of the Exodus fixed and its relation to chronological law.*

(b) The astronomical chronology of the Pyramid defines the date 2513½ A.K. =1486 B.C., as related cyclically to 2520 calendar years and 2520 solar years from 0 A.K., and also to the Deluge date, and symbolically represents the date thus given as defining a new epoch in history in relation to the establishing of the Messianic kingdom.

(4) (a) Hebrew prophecy defines the date of the Divine Decree to build the 2nd Temple, 3480 A.K.=520 B.C., as the date of the commencement of a prophetic period whose termination would be identified with the presence of the Messiah in the early summer of 28 A.D. *The Divine Decree to build the 2nd Temple. Its date fixed in terms of chronological law.*

(b) The Pyramid's astronomical chronology defines the date 3480 A.K. =520 B.C., and the manner in which this is defined indicates that this date was understood in Pyramid times as a definite epoch relating to the Messiah and the purpose of His Coming.

(5) (a) The evidences from the New Testament and from secular sources establish that our Lord was born 3996 A.K.=4 B.C., that His Ministry began *The fixed dates of the Nativity and Crucifixion and their relation to the chronological law defined by the Great Pyramid.*

$$4026 \text{ A.K.}=27\tfrac{3}{4} \text{ A.D.,}$$

and that he was crucified

$$4028\tfrac{1}{2} \text{ A.K.}=30\tfrac{1}{4} \text{ A.D.};$$

the latter two datings confirming the prophecy mentioned in (4) above.

(b) The imagery of the Egyptian religious texts relating to the symbolism of the Passages and Chambers of the Great Pyramid, indicate that the floor level of the Queen's Chamber and the beginning of the Grand Gallery symbolise the respective dates of the Birth and Passion of the Messiah, the dates of the level and point thus indicated being given by the Pyramid's astronomical chronology as 3996 A.K.=4 B.C. and 4028½ A.K.=30¼ A.D. respectively.

(6) (a) The chronological data of the ancient Egyptian traditions relating to the Pyramid and the Messianic kingdom indicate that the date 5556–5557 A.K.=1557¾–1558¾ A.D. relates prophetically to the epoch of a new stage of European civilisation preparatory to the establishing of the Messianic kingdom. *The final historical period preparatory to the Messianic kingdom. This final period defined as beginning December 1557 A.D.*

(b) The Old Testament prophecies indicate that the same date 5556¼ A.K. =December 1557 A.D. relates to the beginning of "the time (360 years) of the end," during which "time" the prophecies were to be elucidated and the nucleus of the Stone kingdom (symbolised by the Pyramid) was to be formed. *The prophetic "time of the end" December 1557 A.D. to December 1917 A.D.*

(c) The Great Pyramid's chronology and symbolism indicate, by means of the displacement factor, that the date 5556.23 A.K.=December 1557 A.D. relates to the beginning of the period of civilisation to which the Pyramid's Message is addressed, and to the fact that during this period the purpose of God concerning the Messianic kingdom will be accelerated to a rapid historical climax.

(d) The historical evolution of the British race since 1557–1558 A.D. indicates that all the promises concerning the material development of the nucleus of the Stone kingdom have been fulfilled in the British race, that the purpose of this rapid material development has been to accelerate the selection of the spiritual elements of the spiritual counterpart, and that the ultimate purpose is to effect the ingathering of literal Israel (the Bride of Prophecy) preparatory to the Coming of Christ

PLATE LXVIII.

OBVERSE.   REVERSE.

THE ORIGINAL SEAL OF THE UNITED STATES OF AMERICA,
SHOWING OBVERSE & REVERSE.

" This device of the Great Seal was adopted by Act of the Continental Congress on 20th June 1782, and re-adopted by the new Congress 15th September 1789. The Act provided for an *obverse* and a *reverse*, as set forth in this plate ; the *reverse* is not used. This is a plate of the first and original Seal, which, by use, has been worn out."

[The authors are indebted to Mrs. A. Rowlett and Messrs. Robert Banks & Son, Publishers, London, for the above data.]

and His Saints (the Bridegroom of Prophecy) for the union prophetically described as " the Marriage of the Lamb."

(e) A factor in this rapid acceleration of material development has been the separation of the great daughter nation of the British race—the United States of America—from the company of nations forming the Federation of Greater Britain. That this separation has been for the purpose of strengthening the potential power of the material Stone kingdom seems clearly to be indicated by one of those significant evidences of the hand of God so frequently seen in history when sought. For, as if to declare that the apparent separation constitutes in the scheme of God a binding link of His purpose, the Great Seal of the United States of America on its reverse side represents the Pyramid—as the symbol of the Stone kingdom—with the Apex Stone—symbolic of Christ, " the headstone of the corner "—suspended under the eye of Providence axially over the centre of the structure thus represented as incomplete without it.

This is as illustrated on Plate LXVIII.

¶ 434. THE FUNCTION OF THE BRITISH RACE.

The concluding identity of ¶ 433 explains why, under the hand of God, *The destined function of the United States of America in relation to British history.* circumstances so mysteriously operated in the events of the Great War; in the first instance, to cause the United States of America to stand aloof from European affairs; and in the final instance, to throw their whole weight into the scale on the side of the nation from which they had separated. Had it not been for this separation, would this influence have proved as great as it did prove?—in other words, would North America, under British rule, have been the power it now is? In the case alternative to separation, would such influence have been exerted in the right way and at the right moment? The fact remains that the war could not have been terminated at the time it was terminated without the weight of the United States of America being thrown into the balance at the date and in the manner it was given.

Now what is the significance of this? The chronological symbolism of the *The date of the Great War period defined by the Pyramid.* Great Pyramid defines the first day of Greater Britain's entry into the Great War as 4th–5th August 1914 A.D., and it defines the day upon which the rapid sequence of events brought the War to a close, 10th–11th November 1918 A.D.

Related to the events occurring between these two dates, it defines the *Greater Britain, the United States of America, and the final settlement of the Jewish question.* definite establishing of Bolshevist autocracy on 18th January 1918 A.D. as an event closely connected with the final tribulations of the Jews. These several events and indications, when viewed in relation to Biblical prophecy, clearly show what Britain's part is in God's scheme, what the part of the United States is, and what relation this allocation of responsibility bears to the question of the Jew.

The material destiny of the British race relates to the overthrowing of *The connected destinies of Greater Britain and the United States and their relative responsibilities in the material part of God's scheme.* the physical forces of oppression and chaos. The portion of Greater Britain is to bear the initial shock of the conflict. In past history, until the recent war, it had been Britain's destiny to carry such burdens alone. Now the destiny of the United States is made manifest. Isolated from the old world of traditions and traditional jealousies and suspicions, she stands as a reservoir of energy to be thrown into the scale when and where most required and opportune; one with the peoples of Greater Britain, under the hand of God, to break oppression and to remove every yoke, "the battle-axe of God" and "the armoury of His indignation."

¶ 435. THE SHORTENING OF THE PERIOD OF CHAOS AND ITS OBJECT.

This is no glorification of war or conquest. There is no glory therein, *The enigma of British history: Circumstances dictate decision. Each decision provided for. Provision renders decision effective.* but to glorify God by preventing oppression; nor is there need to incite to the accomplishment of arms, or the necessity to forearm. God has ordained a certain race for a specific purpose, and God will render effective the carrying out of that purpose. In light of the facts we have related, this is indeed a certainty. Circumstances have compelled, and are compelling, the British race to fulfil its divinely appointed mission.

The overwhelming burden borne by Greater Britain.

The new provision : the United States of America.

The European War terminated at the time appointed for it to terminate only as result of this new provision. The defined alternative circumstances.

Circumstances have rendered the burden greater than Britain can bear alone ; but other circumstances, under the hand of God, have been shaped to supply the deficiency. This was seen in the recent war. The object of these circumstances being then brought into operation was obviously to terminate the war at the date God had determined in His foreknowledge it should be terminated to effect His purpose. The Great Pyramid defines the period following the Great European War as a period of " truce in chaos," purposely imposed by God in what otherwise would have been a war of annihilation, defined by the Pyramid as extending from 4th–5th August 1914 to 16th September 1936 A.D.

Our Lord's prediction concerning the sudden ending of the War, and the purpose of this sudden ending.

The Pyramid's symbol of the elect in relation to " the truce in chaos."

The final tribulation and the Message of the Great Pyramid concerning the period from 29th May 1928 A.D. to 16th September 1936 A.D.

Our Lord predicted the imposing of such a truce before His Second Coming. He referred to this truce as " a shortening of the days for the elect's sake," and to the fact that without the " shortening " " no flesh would have been saved." In His enacting of the circumstances of the miraculous draft of fishes He indicated His elect as prefigured under the number " 153." The indication of the number 153 in relation to the work of preparation for the Messianic kingdom occurs frequently in the Great Pyramid. It occurs in the case of the indication of the period of chaos defined as beginning on 4th–5th August 1914. By the insertion of the period of " truce in chaos," the Pyramid indicates that the scale of months of 30 days, applying to this representation, is " shortened " in its application to the period of chaos to a total of 153 months. The remaining portion of chaos is indicated as extending from 29th May 1928 to 16th September 1936 A.D. The significant fact in this relation is that the United States were operative in thus " shortening the days for the elect's sake." From the evidence already discussed in this Chapter this would imply that they have yet to bear their part, jointly with Greater Britain, in the events leading up to the final restoration of Israel. This is defined as the final and direst phase of the Great Tribulation, and, whether the United States come into the vortex of chaos early or late, we must be assured that when they do come they will come at a time appointed by God and directed by circumstances. However this may be, it is declared in the prophecies that all the forces of " God's armament " are to be compelled by the circumstances of their tribulation to call upon God to do it for them. When they have been thus compelled to call upon God at His appointed time, He will send them a Saviour, and a great one, and He will deliver them. This is promised in the prophecy of Isaiah concerning the Pyramid and its purpose, and from this we may be sure, viewing the question from every standpoint in which we have considered these matters, that the

The object of the Pyramid's Message.

object of the Pyramid's Message was to proclaim this same Jesus as the Deliverer and the Saviour of Men, to announce the dated circumstances relating to His Coming, and to prepare men by means of its Message— whether they believe it or not in the first instance—to adapt themselves spiritually to the circumstances of His Coming when the fact of the Message becomes to them a matter of certainty.

ADDENDUM TO THE CONCLUSIONS CONCERNING THE SPECIAL CHRONOLOGY SYSTEM.

Particular attention is directed to the fact that a clear distinction must be drawn between the intention underlying the representation of the Great Pyramid's General Chronology System and the intention underlying the representation of its Special Chronology System. The former was intended to be studied and its significance (as relating to astronomical and historical changes *in the past*) understood during the period that is defined by the Special Chronology System. The indications of the latter system, however, were clearly intended to form an index to current events in our " tragic epoch," and to be a guide, jointly with the prophecies of the Old and New Testaments, to each successive phase of development within this period. *The distinction between the General Chronology System and the Special Chronology System. The intention of the latter.*

The present writer is quite conscious of the fact that he has carried his investigation of the data beyond the scope of presentation as thus defined. He has, however, tried to make it plain that the object of prophecy (divinely revealed) is not to disclose to man the events of history in a manner to be understood in detail of time, place, and circumstance, before these events do happen, but to forewarn and to give a general indication of guidance when the events begin to happen ; and, when the events have actually occurred, to show that they did happen as they were predicted to happen from the foreknowledge of God. This is very clearly stated by our Lord. He tells us to " watch," to study the predictive indications, and implies that we must not jump to conclusions concerning predictive data that, whilst precisely correct, are utterly beyond our comprehension until they are completely demonstrated by their fulfilment. *The object of prophecy divinely revealed.*

It surely must be obvious to the reader that it has never been the purpose of God to rob man of his free-will and the cumulative experience of the experimental efforts of free-will in mankind's history. One way to have robbed man of his free-will and of this experience would have been to make the prophecy relating to man's experimental efforts a simple predictive narrative defining clearly to man's comprehension every phase of success and failure from origin to climax in man's history. Could anything be more disheartening than to imagine mankind in the past proceeding with its efforts in face of the certain predictive knowledge of history as we now know it ? Show us our mistakes in the minutest detail before we make them and life is robbed of its every value. The fact of the foreknowledge of God necessarily implies that such foreknowledge is not revealed to man until the events foreknown have been fulfilled. Divinely revealed prophecy is therefore an enigma until history provides the exposition by fulfilment. Prophecy, therefore, is the means whereby God indicates His foreknowledge to man, and such is the purpose of prophecy. Otherwise the certainty of predictive knowledge would, paradoxically, cause man to alter the sequence of events predicted. *What a perfect exposition of prophecy would mean for mankind.*

The predictive
indications
relating to
the immediate
future.
The writer had all this in mind in carrying his investigations, relating to the Special Chronology System and its predictive indications, to what appeared to him to be a logical conclusion. He had intended to explain something of this in the course of the text dealing with the matter, but found it difficult to do so without breaking the sequence of presentation.

The inter-
pretation
advanced in
the present
chapter
concerning
these.
Let it therefore be clearly understood that where anything of an assertive nature occurs in the text of this chapter concerning the Special Chronology System and its indications relating to the immediate future, such appearance of assertion is due entirely to the manner of presentation rather than to any special conviction of the writer. Let it also be clearly understood that this statement applies not to the clear definition of intention concerning the Special Chronology System and the purpose and application of its predictive indications, but solely to the interpretation advanced *by the writer* as explaining these predictive indications. The latter interpretation has been advanced as a preliminary basis for the study of others more qualified than the writer is to deal with this matter.

What is
deemed to be
certain.
What is certain to the writer is that by the 16th of September 1936 A.D. there will be no question of doubt, criticism, or theory concerning this matter. Both the Pyramid and the Bible define that certain important events are to happen prior to that date, and that prophecy will have fulfilled its purpose by that date. The Pyramid defines that these events are to happen between 29th May 1928 A.D. and 16th September 1936 A.D.[1]

What is
deemed to be
uncertain.
Divinely
revealed
prophecy and
expositions
relating to
the same.
For this reason the writer has included the conclusions concerning this under his " Facts of Co-ordination." What is uncertain is the precise sequence of the events predicted in Biblical prophecy as to happen within this period. All expositors of Biblical prophecy have been partly right and partly wrong in dealing with the interpretation of the predictive indications relating to events future to them but now past. The error is always seen to lie in the exposition, never in the Biblical prophecy. From the point of view of the scholastic theologian this is an assertion. From the co-ordination of data discussed in this volume it is deemed to be a statement of fact. The writer, however, does not wish to appear dogmatic. He has found that positive results can be derived from the elimination of negative issues ; and, for this reason, welcomes criticism concerning any or all of the lines of co-ordination upon which he has based the conclusion stated in this chapter.

[1]The Special Chronology System of the Great Pyramid was not developed by the writer until the spring of 1921. As early as 1915 the late Dr. Aldersmith had already elucidated the Biblical datings of Table XXX in the precise form in which that Table is now given. From this Dr. Aldersmith defined the terminal date of the Great Tribulation as 1936.

SECTION II.—THE CHRONOLOGY OF OUR LORD'S LIFE AND THE
HARMONY OF THE GOSPELS.[1]

¶ 436. THE INDEPENDENT NATURE OF THE SCRIPTURAL AND HISTORICAL EVIDENCES.

We now proceed to the discussion of the chronology of our Lord's Life *The scriptural and historical* and the harmony of the Gospels. During the progress of our discussion *evidences are studied in* we shall compare the scriptural evidence with the historical evidence derived *related sequence as* from secular sources, and it will become apparent to the careful reader that *they come naturally* the inferences to be drawn from both sets of evidence are identical and lead *under review.* to the same conclusions. At the same time, he will note that in no case is *But the two sets of evi-* the scriptural evidence[2] necessarily used to fill up a gap in the historical *dence can be separated from* evidence,[3] nor is it ever necessary to strengthen the historical evidence, or to *the text to supply inde-* maintain its sequence, by making use of evidence derived from scriptural *pendently the same con-* sources. *clusions.*

The dates for the Nativity, Baptism, and Crucifixion derived from the data and evidence contained in the Old and New Testaments coincide with the dates obtained by an investigation of secular history. Furthermore, these same dates agree with those contained in Sections IA and IB of this Chapter, which, the reader will remember, were obtained by an examination of the prophetic books of the Old Testament.

[1] This section was written originally by the late Dr. Aldersmith to form a separate work, from data independently compiled by the joint authors, and co-ordinated by Dr. Aldersmith to embody the essential features of what appeared to be the basal and irrefutable arguments of both sets of independent data. All the astronomical calculations and Tables XXXV–XXXVIII were prepared by the present writer.

Owing to the importance of the co-ordination, it was deemed advisable to have the form of presentation revised by a competent and independent third party. This section has therefore been re-edited by Mr. J. Clemishaw in its now existing form. The discussions concerning the course of Abia (¶ 446), and relating to the " three days and three nights " (¶¶ 481–489), and the precise hours of the Crucifixion and death of our Lord (¶¶ 488 and 489), together with Tables XXXV, XXXVII, and XXXVIII, have been written up since Dr. Aldersmith's death.—[D. D.]

[2] The essential framework of the scriptural evidence is—

    (a) The chronological significance of " two years old and under according to the time which Herod had carefully learned of the wise men."
    (b) The data concerning the duration of our Lord's Life and the duration of His Ministry.
    (c) The data concerning the day of the week and the day of the month of the Crucifixion.

[3] The essential framework of the historical evidence is—

    (a) The co-ordinated evidences concerning the duration of our Lord's Life.
    (b) The co-ordinated evidences relating to the year in which His Ministry began.
    (c) The co-ordinated evidences relating to the year of His Crucifixion.

The date of the death of Herod, although taken as the starting-point of our chronological enquiry, depends upon a co-ordination of scriptural and historical evidences. It was deemed necessary to adopt this date as a starting-point, as it forms a datum common to the two sets of evidence.

The relation between the co-ordination in the present Section and the prophetic indications discussed in Section I.

It is of the utmost importance that the reader should bear in mind that this present section was originally written as a separate work, and that the elucidation of the prophetic books followed as a direct consequence of the dates and conclusions established by the investigation of those sacred and secular evidences which we are now about to consider.

¶ 437. THE STATEMENT OF THE PROBLEM.

The eight essential points of the problem.

The points we have to determine by reference to the evidence contained in the Old and New Testaments are as follows:—

(a) At what hour of the day was the Passover lamb killed on the 14th Nisan?

(b) At what hour of the day did the first day of unleavened bread begin?

(c) Whether the expression " between the two evenings " is an instant of time or a period of the day, and if it be an instant of time, at what hour of the day did this occur?

(d) The age of our Lord at His Baptism.

(e) The duration of His Ministry, whether $2\frac{1}{2}$ or $3\frac{1}{2}$ years. This depends upon the explanation of the feast of John v, 1–18.

(f) The date of the Crucifixion of our Lord, whether the 14th or 15th Nisan.

(g) The day of the week of the Crucifixion and of the Resurrection.

(h) The distinction, if any, between " three days and three nights " and " rose again on the third day."

Date of Nativity certainly in period 7 B.C. to 4 B.C.; Crucifixion certainly in period 29 A.D. to 33 A.D.

With these limits fixed and the eight essentials known, the problem can be solved.

Then, as it is known with certainty that our Lord was born in the period 7 B.C. to 4 B.C. inclusive, and crucified in the period 29 A.D. to 33 A.D. (now reduced by modern analysis to 29 A.D. to 30 A.D.), the date of the Crucifixion can be settled by the calculation of the week-days and new moons of Nisan in conjunction, (f) and (g). This, in conjunction with (a), (b), and (c), fixes the day of the week, the day of the month, and the year of the Crucifixion. Item (e) then fixes the date of the Baptism, and item (d) the date of the Nativity.

SECTION IIA.—THE DATE OF THE NATIVITY.

¶ 438. JOSEPHUS ON THE DATE OF HEROD'S ACCESSION.

Let us now examine the evidences that enable us to fix the date of the Nativity from secular sources, at the same time combining the deductions thus obtained with those drawn from scriptural history. The reader will do well to consult Table XXXII[1] in order to obtain a clear idea of the relationship that holds between the various styles of chronology employed. *The various styles of chronology encountered in the scriptural evidences and in the evidences from secular sources.*

Our first essential date is the year of the death of Herod the Great. Herod was proclaimed king by the Romans on the 184th Olympiad.[2] The Olympiad was a period of four years, the end of which was celebrated by the games commencing the next period. The first Olympiad was from $3223\frac{3}{4}$ A.K. to $3227\frac{3}{4}$ A.K., that is, 776 B.C. to 772 B.C., reckoning from midsummer to midsummer. The end of the 184th Olympiad was, therefore, $3959\frac{3}{4}$ A.K., at midsummer in 40 B.C., or in the year 714 A.U.C. But the years of Herod's reign, as given by Josephus, do not date from the time he was proclaimed king, but refer to his actual reign after the death of Antigonus, which occurred in the autumn of 37 B.C.[3] *The importance of the date of the death of Herod the Great. Herod proclaimed King by Romans in 40 B.C. The actual reign of Herod, following the death of Antigonus, began in 37 B.C.*

Josephus frequently assures us that over three years passed between the formal proclamation of Herod by the Romans and his actual obtaining of the kingdom upon the taking of Jerusalem and the death of Antigonus.

¶ 439. JOSEPHUS ON THE DATE OF HEROD'S DEATH.

Now Josephus counts his year from Nisan to Nisan, and Smith and Wieseler have shown that he would have counted the portion of Herod's first year before Nisan as one whole year.[4] He states that Herod reigned for 34 years after the death of Antigonus, and since his second year of actual reign commenced at Nisan 36 B.C., it is obvious that his 34th year of actual reign terminated at Nisan 3 B.C., in the latter part of 750 A.U.C., or $3996\frac{1}{2}$ A.K. It is also known that Herod died shortly before a Passover. *The Hebrew custom of dating accession years as whole years. The chronological statements of Josephus give the death of Herod as preceding the Passover of 3 B.C.*

[1] At the end of this Section, IIA.

[2] Josephus, "Ant.," XIV, 14, 5.

[3] Josephus ("Ant.," XIV, 16, 1–4, and XV, 1, 2) states that the death of Antigonus occurred in the 185th Olympiad, while Marcus Agrippa and Caninius Gallus were consuls at Rome. Smith says this consulship coincided with 717 A.U.C. Since 1 A.U.C. $=3246\frac{1}{4}$ A.K. to $3247\frac{1}{4}$ A.K. $=$ spring 753 B.C. to spring 752 B.C., then 717 A.U.C. $=$ spring 37 B.C. to spring 36 B.C. Antigonus was captured in June or July 37 B.C., taken captive to Antioch, and executed there. This would be late in 3962 A.K., or early in 3963 A.K., in the autumn of 37 B.C.

[4] This is in accordance with the Jewish and Israelitish custom seen in operation in the data of Table XXV and Annotations.

It is sometimes stated that Herod's death occurred in 4 B.C. Let us, therefore, examine the question from another standpoint to see if we can obtain confirmatory evidence of the date of 3 B.C., which we have deduced from the history of Josephus.

¶ 440. THE LUNAR ECLIPSE IN JOSEPHUS.

The lunar eclipse mentioned occurred 12th–13th March (Julian) 4 B.C., 749 A.U.C., prior to the beginning of 750 A.U.C. on 21st April 4 B.C.

The records of an eclipse of the moon, preserved by Josephus, will afford us the materials for our investigation. He states[1] that Herod " burnt the other Matthias," and adds " that very night there was an eclipse of the moon." There was no eclipse of the moon visible at Jerusalem in the early part of 3 B.C., and Wurm's calculations (which we have verified) give 12th–13th March (Julian) 4 B.C. for this eclipse.[2] Since the A.U.C. year began on the 21st April, the corresponding A.U.C. dating for this period of 4 B.C. is 749.

¶ 441. HEROD'S FUNERAL IN RELATION TO THE TWO PASSOVERS, 4 B.C. AND 3 B.C.

The narrative of Josephus gives the death of Herod as considerably over a month prior to the following Passover ; whereas the eclipse of 4 B.C., when Herod was alive, was less than a month prior to the following Passover.

Now the feast of the Passover in 4 B.C. occurred on the 10th of April (Julian), that is to say, barely a month after the eclipse. Consider the account by Josephus of what took place in the interval between the death of Herod and the following Passover. " They prepared for the funeral," " the body was carried on a golden bier," " behind marched the whole army." This march was from Jericho to Herodium, a march which, according to a competent authority,[3] must have taken 25 days. Then Archelaus continued his mourning till the seventh day. Allowing for the funeral preparations, we have thus an interval of about 5 weeks between the death of Herod and the end of the mourning of Archelaus. Then we read of feasts and rioting occurring upon the approach of the feast of the Passover, and a " regiment of armed men " being sent to suppress the rioters.[4] All this requires time, and we shall probably be justified in considering that an interval of 2 or 3 weeks elapsed between the end of the mourning and the feast of the Passover.

¶ 442. THE DEATH OF HEROD IN JANUARY 3 B.C.

The eclipse record of Josephus confirms his chronological statements that Herod died not long before the Passover of 3 B.C.

Since the death of Herod, therefore, preceded the Passover by considerably more than a month, and since the eclipse in 4 B.C. preceded the Passover by barely one month, it is obvious that Herod did not die in the spring of 4 B.C. This is further confirmed by Josephus' narrative of what occurred

[1] Josephus, " Ant.," XVII. 6, 7, and 8, in his description of the last period of Herod's life.
[2] Refer to Table XXXVI. This eclipse is supposed to have been in 750 A.U.C. by those (as Wieseler) who did not realise the fact that the A.U.C. year commenced on the 21st April.
[3] Whiston's Josephus, " Ant.," XVII, 8, 3, footnote. The distance from Jericho to Herodium was 200 stadia, and the text implies a daily march of 8 stadia.
[4] Josephus, " Ant.," XVII, 9, 1–3.

during the rest of Herod's life after he burnt the priest on the day of the eclipse. His life up to the time of his death is fully and completely described, and anyone can see that the events narrated must have occupied many months.

This proves that Herod died in 3 B.C., and the narrative shows that his death must have taken place 7 or 8 weeks before the Passover. In 3 B.C. the date of the Passover on the 15th Nisan was 31st March (Julian), thus placing the time of his death in the month Sebat—January to February—or, at the very latest, early in the following month Adar— late February.

This is confirmed again by the narrative of events between the eclipse and the death of Herod.

The Jewish Megillath Taanith states that the death of Herod occurred on the 1st of the month Sebat, which, in 3 B.C., fell on 18th January (Julian), 8 weeks and 3 days before the Passover. The probabilities are that this date is correct, and we therefore consider it established that Herod died in 3 B.C., 8 weeks and 3 days before the Passover of that year. If, on the other hand, the date referred to 4 B.C., it would give the death of Herod as occurring 2½ months before the eclipse on 15th Ve-Adar (the inter-calary month), when Herod was still alive.

The Jewish Megillath Taanith dates the death of Herod on 1st Sebat, confirming that the eclipse in 4 B.C. was 10 months prior to Herod's death in 3 B.C.

¶ 443. THE GENERAL EVIDENCE CONCERNING THE TIME OF THE NATIVITY.

Let us now consider the scriptural evidence relating to the time of the Nativity. It would appear, from the narrative of Matthew ii, that no long period of time elapsed between the Nativity and the return from Egypt. In this interval Joseph and Mary returned from Bethlehem to Nazareth, they went into Egypt, and the slaughter of the children and the death of Herod took place. It is significant that St. Luke entirely omits the journey into Egypt, thus indicating that only a short time elapsed between their leaving Nazareth (before our Lord was born) and returning there after their sojourn in Egypt. According to Luke (ii, 21–24, 39) Mary fulfilled her 7+35 days of purification and went to Jerusalem. If, as we propose to demonstrate, Christ was born soon after the Autumnal Equinox of 4 B.C., Mary would have gone up to the Temple about the middle of November. This agrees with the time required for the events which occurred between the Nativity and the death of Herod.

The short interval between the Nativity and the return from Egypt after the death of Herod in 3 B.C. indicates the date of the Nativity as falling in 4 B.C.

¶ 444. THE GOVERNORSHIP OF QUIRINIUS.

Luke's statement that Christ was born when Quirinius was governor of Syria, and his description of the census that then took place, has been much criticised and derided by modern critics. It is said that Quirinius' governorship of Syria was several years after 4 B.C., and that Cæsar Augustus never issued any decree regarding the census of the Roman world.

Modern criticism concerning Luke's statement.

The first governorship of Quirinius included 4 B.C. to 1 B.C. The question of the governorship of Quirinius has been cleared up by Zumpt. Alford says:[1] "Zumpt, by arguments too long to be reproduced here, but very striking and satisfactory, fixes the time of his *first* governorship at from 4 B.C. to 1 B.C. . . . Justin Martyr three times distinctly asserts that our Lord was born under Quirinius, and appeals to the *register* then made. . . . We conclude, then, that an ἀπογραφὴ or enrolment[2] of names with a view to ascertain the population of the empire was commanded and put into force at this time."

¶ 445. THE SYSTEM OF ENROLMENT INAUGURATED BY AUGUSTUS.

Indications show that the enrolment was arranged to be made at the beginning of the civil year in the case of Syria, and to coincide with the Feast of Tabernacles in October, between vintage and ploughing, when "the Word became flesh and tabernacled amongst us." It is obvious that the Greek " πᾶσαν τὴν οἰκουμένην " refers to the inhabitants of the Roman Empire, and not to " all the world," as translated in the Authorised Version. It is important to decide at what time this enrolment or census would be likely to take place. We know that the Romans always endeavoured to avoid disturbing the Jewish feasts, laws, and customs, when applying their imperial decrees to the province of Syria. This decree would necessarily be identified with the civil year of the province, which commenced in Tisri, in our September or October. This month would be the most convenient for taking a census of the people, as it came between the vintage and the season of ploughing and sowing. It is probable, then, that the census was taken in the month of Tisri,[3] and that the Nativity was at the time of the Feast of Tabernacles, that is, the 15th Tisri, in the seventh sacred month, when, therefore, " The Word became flesh and *tabernacled*

---

[1] "Greek Testament," Vol. I, pp. 455, 456.

[2] Sir William Ramsay says: " We now know that there was in the Roman empire a system of census taking regularly every fourteen years, and that the system was inaugurated by the Emperor Augustus . . . it was preceded by a proclamation issued by the Governor of the province . . . directing that every person should repair to his place of origin, his proper home, to be counted there . . . that knowledge has come to us within the last twenty years. . . . Augustus, then, formed this great plan of world survey and world registration . . . and in the course of doing this, all that he succeeded in doing was to bring about the fulfilment of a prophecy. The Saviour must be born in Bethlehem."—(" The Trustworthiness of the New Testament," *Bible League Quarterly*, July 1915.)
Sir William Ramsay, arguing from the date he assigns to the census, places the date of the Nativity earlier than 4 B.C., and refers to two inscriptions that have been found at Antioch. The first referred to was copied at Antioch in 1912 A.D., concerning P. Sulpicius Quirinius, and is " said to date " between 10 and 7 B.C.; and Sir William Ramsay says concerning the second inscription found: " A year or more before 6 B.C. it (Antioch) paid Quirinius the compliment of electing him as an honorary magistrate. . . . It is also a crowning step in the proof that the story in Luke ii, 1–3 is correct, for it exhibits to us Quirinius as engaged in the war, and therefore as Governor of Syria before 6 B.C. . . . Every circumstance narrated by Luke has been conclusively proved to be natural and probable. The circumstances are those which ordinarily accompanied a Roman census, and Quirinius was in office *about that time for several years*. Thus Quirinius and Servilius were governing the two adjacent provinces, Syria-Cilicia and Galatia, *around the year* 6 *B.C.* when the first census was made" (the italics are ours).—(" The Bearing of Recent Discovery on the Trustworthiness of the New Testament," pp. 285, 293, 300.)
As it is stated that Quirinius was governor " around the year 6 B.C.," we see no proof that the census was in 6 or 8 B.C. (as stated by some). When all the other indications show that the census was in 4 B.C., they also show that the governorship of Quirinius included that date " around the year 6 B.C."

[3] Additional evidence of the census having actually been taken is furnished by Justin Martyr, Augustine, and Chrysostom, who all refer to the register containing the entry of the Nativity as in existence at Rome in their time, and available for inspection.

amongst us " (John i, 14). This would explain the statement that the inn at Bethlehem was full, the crowding being due to the Feast of Tabernacles, and not merely to the enrolment.[1]

In this year, 4 B.C., the 15th Tisri, or the day of the Feast of Tabernacles, fell on a Saturday,[2] that is to say, on the Sabbath, or the seventh day of the week in the seventh sacred month. The feast-day falling on the Sabbath would make that Sabbath a " High Day," or double Sabbath. Thus the Sabbath following the Crucifixion, on Friday, the 15th Nisan, was a double Sabbath (John xix, 31).[3]

¶ 446. THE DATING OF THE COURSE OF ABIA CONFIRMS THE NATIVITY DATE.

The statement in Luke (i, 5) that Zacharias was " a priest of the course of Abia," will furnish the material for another line of investigation, as the birth of Christ occurred fifteen months later. The courses would naturally follow the numerical order of precedence defined for the divisions of the sons of Aaron. In 1 Chron. xxiv we find that the sons of Aaron are divided into 24 orders for " the governors of the Sanctuary," and these orders are defined according to lot and numerical precedence, that of Abijah (Abia) being defined as the eighth. The question as to whether the courses were of equal length, and when the first course began, is settled by two parallel references in 1 Chron. xxvii, 1–15 and 1 Kings iv, 7, where the duties of the twelve captains that served the king and of the twelve officers of his household are defined. Here we see that each captain and each officer had one month of duty, and that the first course of the captains was for the first month (Nisan) of the year.

(margin: Abijah, the 8th course of the 24 courses of the sons of Aaron. The 24 courses began from 1st Nisan—each course for half a month.)

Similarly, then, for the 24 courses of the temple we have 24 courses of half a month each, with course 1 in the first half of Nisan. The course of Abia, the 8th, would therefore fall in the second half of month IV (Tammuz).

(margin: The course of Abijah fell in second half of the month Tammuz.)

In 5 B.C. 1st Nisan began at sunset 9th March (Julian). From this date to the sunset beginning 15th Tammuz (when the course of Abia began) was an interval of 103 days, bringing us to sunset 21st June (Julian), and the

(margin: This fixes Tebet as the month for the events of Luke i, 26–36.)

---

[1]Colonel G. Mackinlay remarks : " Jerusalem was crowded three times a year at the great feasts. . . . Bethlehem, only six miles distant, would also be crowded at those times. Enrolment by itself would not of necessity cause overcrowding. . . . This crowding would be far more likely to happen if the enrolment took place at one of the feasts . . . the crowding at the inn, therefore, points to the probability that the Feast of Tabernacles was at hand. . . . All male Jews were obliged to come to the Feast of Tabernacles, which is at Jerusalem. To this it is replied : Palestine is a small country : so small that any Jew could easily be present at the temple at Jerusalem long before the close of the eight days of the feast. . . . The northern Israelites at this period of the Nativity were of the two tribes, not of the ten. Consequently, after enrolment all would be near Jerusalem because the districts apportioned to Judah and Benjamin were surrounding the city." " The Date of the Nativity was 8 B.C.," pp. 5, 23.

[2]Refer Table XXXVI.

[3]Clinton says : " The Nativity was not more than eighteen months before the death of Herod, nor less than five or six. The death of Herod was either in the spring of 4 B.C. or in the spring of 3 B.C." Sir Robert Anderson states (The Coming Prince) that Zumpt's discoveries respecting the census of Quirinius enable us, adopting Clinton's datum, to assign the death of Herod to the month Adar of 3 B.C., and the Nativity to the autumn of 4 B.C.

In 5 B.C.
Tebet ended
29th December
(Greg.) and
279 days in-
tervened to
the date of
the Nativity.
4th October
(Greg.) 4 B.C.

course of Abia ended at sunset beginning 1st Ab, that is, 5th July (Julian). The narrative of Luke i, 5–23, therefore, falls within the period 19th June (Greg.) to 3rd July (Greg.), with verse 23 ending at the beginning of month V (Ab). The five months of verse 24 are therefore from early in month V (Ab) to early in month X (Tebet). The sixth month of verses 26 and 36 began early in the tenth month of the year. The beginning of the period preceding the Nativity is clearly in month X (Tebet), which ended at 29th December (Greg.) in 5 B.C. From the latter day to the day of the Nativity, assumed as 4th October (Greg.) in 4 B.C.,[1] is a period of 279 days. This confirms our hypothesis that the Nativity occurred at the Feast of Tabernacles in 4 B.C.

¶ 447. THE SCRIPTURAL INDICATIONS OF AN ASTRONOMICAL DATUM.

Further evidence is afforded by the statement (Matt. ii, 14) that Herod slew all the male children from two years old and under, "according to the time which he had carefully learned of the wise men." The fact that all the male children under two years of age were slain obviously indicates that the Magi were ignorant of the precise date of the Messiah's birth, but they knew, or had reason to suppose, that it had occurred within the last two years. We cannot doubt that they were following some written or traditional prediction, a prediction referring to some general warning that was to be followed by a definite sign. It is clear that this warning had occurred two years previously, and it was this warning that had caused the Magi to look for the sign "His star in the East." What, then, was this warning? As we know that the Magi were great observers of the heavens, it is highly probable that any warning of this nature foretold in their prophecies would be of an astronomical character. Let us, therefore, search the astronomical records of this epoch for any extraordinary phenomena that were visible at this time.

¶ 448. THE ASTRONOMICAL INDICATIONS OF THE DATUM OF THE MAGI.

Smith states:[2] "Kepler finds a conjunction of Jupiter and Saturn in the sign Pisces in 747 A.U.C., and again in the spring of the next year with the planet Mars added."[3]

Thus four conjunctions occurred in the sign Pisces as follows:—

1st Conjunction, Saturn and Jupiter	..	3992¾ A.K. = May 7 B.C.
2nd ,, ,, ,, ,,	..	3993 A.K. = Oct. 7 B.C.
3rd ,, ,, ,, ,,	..	3993¼ A.K. = Dec. 7 B.C.
4th ,, Saturn, Jupiter, and Mars		3993½ A.K. = Spring 6 B.C.

[1]Refer Table XXXVI. 4th October (Greg.) in 4 B.C. is equivalent to 15th Tisri.
[2]" Dict. Bible," Vol. VIII, p. 1072.
[3]The " Enc. Brit.," 11th Edit., Vol. III, p. 888, gives three conjunctions of Jupiter and Saturn in 7 B.C., May, October, and December.

We have thus a very extraordinary series of celestial phenomena taking place within the short period of nine months that ended two and a half years before the beginning of 3996 A.K. in 4 B.C., or two and a half years before the date we have assumed as that of the birth of Jesus Christ. If the prophecy of the Magi foretold these conjunctions, and, furthermore, foretold that the birth of the Messiah would be at the beginning of the year, then the occurrence of these conjunctions would have caused them to await the second and final sign, "His star in the East," and would have indicated to them that the birth would occur at the beginning of some year soon after the Autumnal Equinox 3994 A.K. The actual appearance of the star which led them to Bethlehem in 3996 A.K. = 4 B.C. would have shown that the Nativity might have occurred at the beginning of any of the years 3994, 3995, or 3996 A.K., that is to say, within a period of two years. If we, then, can show that such a conjunction of Jupiter and Saturn in Pisces was associated with the birth of the Messiah, we shall have given good reason for believing that the prophecy of the Magi foretold that the Messiah would be born at the beginning of the year. Thus they were able to tell Herod that the child had been born within a period of two years.

These astronomical indications, occurring as the scriptural data lead us to expect, confirm that a prediction, known to the Magi, defined the birth of the Messiah as occurring about the autumn year-beginning following the completion of the indications.

Following the completion of the heralding indications the Magi awaited the predicted final sign, the appearance of "His star in the East."

¶ 449. THE EVIDENCE RELATING TO THE PREDICTION OF THE CONJUNCTIONS.

The "Encyclopædia Britannica" states :[1]

"It is a curious coincidence that a medieval Jew, R. Abarbanel (Abrabanel), records that the conjunction of these particular planets in this particular constellation was to be a sign of the Messiah's coming. It is just conceivable that his statement may ultimately depend on some such ancient tradition as may have been known to the Chaldæan Magi."

A Jewish tradition relating to the conjunctions of Jupiter and Saturn in Pisces being the heralding sign of the imminence of the Messiah.

It is important to note that this statement was made by a Jew. Had it been made by a Christian, or even by a Pagan, one could suppose that some early Christian writers associated the Nativity with the conjunctions, but it is hardly conceivable that a Jew would accept this identification from Christian sources, and associate it with the birth of the Messiah he was still awaiting. Since the early Christians did not make this identification and the later Jews did, it is surely a legitimate conclusion that we are dealing with a prophecy that had endured for many ages among the Jewish people, and was in existence long before the Nativity. We may conclude also that the series of conjunctions led the Magi to look for the star of the Messiah,[2] and that the interval, containing two Autumnal Equinoxes, between the completion of the series and the appearance of the star, led the Magi in 4 B.C.

The fact of the existence of the tradition among the Jews in medieval times—obviously not derived from any early Christian tradition—leads to the inference that the actual conjunctions were accepted by the Magi as heralding the birth of the Messiah.

[1] 11th Edit., Vol. III, p. 888.
[2] "The Jews in an ancient book of theirs ('Zohar') say more than once that when Messiah shall be revealed, a bright and shining star shall arise in the East" ("Gill's Commentary").
"The false Christ, who under Adrian (from 132-135 A.D.) took up arms for the last terrible struggle with Rome, gave himself out as the Messiah whom Balaam had foretold, and assumed the name of Barchocab, or the son of the star" (R. C. Trench).

to give the age of the infant Christ as "two years" "or under, according to the time." Here we have further confirmation of our theory that the birth of the Messiah occurred in the year 4 B.C.

¶ 450. THE ALTERNATIVE MONTH DATINGS OF THE NATIVITY.

We have now examined the question of the date of the Nativity from several different angles, and the result of our investigation has been a clear indication that Christ was born at the Feast of Tabernacles in the year 4 B.C. As the reader is, of course, aware, many other dates and many other years have been suggested and supported with some show of proof. It will not be unprofitable to examine a few of these suggested dates to see if they will withstand the test of our investigation.

Let us first examine the traditional date of 25th December. If Christ had been born on 25th December 4 B.C., Mary's period of purification alone would have extended beyond the death of Herod, which, according to our earlier investigation, and according to the Megillath Taanith, occurred on 18th January 3 B.C. This fact alone renders it historically impossible that our Lord was born on 25th December, and this conclusion is confirmed by many other circumstances. At the time of the Nativity the shepherds were in the open country, keeping watch over their flocks by night. It was not the custom to keep the flocks in the open later than the end of October, and certainly they would not have been in the open on a winter night. Again, it is hardly likely that Mary, in her delicate condition, would have travelled to Bethlehem in mid-winter. On the other hand, the flight to Egypt could not have taken place in summer, as well-authenticated records establish the fact that the earliest time for attempting this journey, otherwise than by sea, was October or November. As the death of Herod occurred in January 4 B.C., the flight to Egypt could not have been in the spring. All these general indications lead us to our former conclusion that the Nativity must be dated in September or October.

¶ 451. THE ORIGIN OF CHRISTMAS.

It may be of interest to the reader briefly to recapitulate the well-known facts concerning the festival known as Christmas. The 25th December, which originally coincided with the Winter Solstice, was observed by the pagans as Natalis Invicti Solis, the birthday of the unconquerable sun. No such festival as Christmas was known in the Christian Church until the 3rd century, when the Roman Church established 25th December as the festival of the Nativity. But centuries before that time a festival was observed by the pagans on that day, and this same festival can be identified in Egypt as early as 2000 B.C. It is obvious, therefore, that the festival of Christmas is a survival of paganism, probably adopted by the Roman Church at a time when many converts from paganism were being received into the fold, and it was thought advisable to sanctify a pagan festival which many of the converts were accustomed to celebrate, and probably would have continued to celebrate, whether the Church had sanctioned it or not.

¶ 452. THE IMPOSSIBILITY OF THE SUGGESTED DATES.

The statement we have already discussed, that Zacharias was a priest of the course of Abia, has led other investigators to other conclusions. Many have based their calculations upon the statement in the Talmud that the Temple was destroyed by Titus on the 9th Ab 70 A.D., and the fact that Josephus, writing of the same event, mentions that the course of Jehoiarib had just commenced.

Working on this basis Wieseler determines the time for Zacharias as October 748 A.U.C., and the Nativity for January. But this January is 3 B.C., only a week or two before the death of Herod, which is clearly impossible.

Wieseler's Nativity date January 3 B.C. is only a week or two before the death of Herod.

Other calculations have resulted in the Nativity being dated back to 6 or 8 B.C. Grattan Guinness put it in 6 B.C., but he dates the death of Herod in 4 B.C., between the eclipse of the moon and the Passover, which, as we have shown, is impossible. He also puts the Baptism in 26 A.D., that is to say, more than a year before the 15th year of the joint rule of Tiberius commenced. This is done in order to make 33½ years from the Nativity to the Crucifixion, the date of which he gives as 29 A.D. This date also, as we shall show later, is incorrect.

Since at his baptism our Lord was not over thirty years of age in the 15th year of Cæsar (Table XXXIII), any earlier date than 4 B.C. for the Nativity is impossible.

TABLE XXXII.

THE FOUR DIFFERENT YEARS EMPLOYED FOR CHRONOLOGICAL RECKONING.

ASTRO-NOMICAL ANNO KALEN-DARII.	A. U. C.	DIONYSIAN.	MODERN CHRONO-LOGY.	HISTORICAL NOTES.
	April 21. (Julian.) A.U.C.		January 1. B.C. 5.	
September 23 (Gregorian) A.K. 3995.	749.			
	April 21. A.U.C. 750.		January 1. B.C. 4.	JOSEPHUS:— Eclipse, March 13 (Julian); Passover, April 11 (Julian). A.U.C. 749. THE NATIVITY (Tisri), B.C. 4=A.K. 3996=A.U.C. 750.
September 23 A.K. 3996.				
	April 21. A.U.C. 751.		January 1. B.C. 3.	Death of Herod (1st Sebat=18 Jany. Jul.) B.C. 3=A.K. 3996½=A.U.C. 750,) in his 37th year after being proclaimed king by the Romans on the 184th Olympiad, A.U.C. 714=A.K. 3959½=B.C. 40. NOTE:—Beginning of 1st Olympic year=A.K. 3223¾= midsummer, B.C. 776. A.U.C. commenced A.K. 3246½=April 21, B.C. 753.
September 23 A.K. 3997.				
	April 21. A.U.C. 752.		January 1. B.C. 2.	The NATIVITY ..A.K. 3996 =autumn B.C. 4. Add .. .. 30 years. The BAPTISM ..A.K. 4026 =autumn A.D. 27½ Add for Ministry.. 2½ years. The CRUCIFIXION ..A.K. 4028½= spring A.D. 30¼.
September 23 A.K. 3998.			January 1. B.C. 1.	
	April 21. A.U.C. 753.			
September 23 A.K. 3999.			January 1. A.D. 1.	The year reckoning of modern chronology commences three months in advance of the Dionysian Era; nearly four months in advance of A.U.C. time; and nine months in advance of the original astronomical year reckoning, A.K.
	April 21. A.U.C. 754.	March 25 (Julian). THE YEAR OF OUR LORD 1.	..............*	* False Dionysian date of the Nativity, December 25 (Julian).
September 23 A.K. 4000.			January 1. A.D. 2.	
	April 21. A.U.C. 755.	March 25. DIONYSIAN A.D. 2.		
September 23 A.K. 4001.			Ending December 31 Julian or Gregorian according to computation adopted.	
Ending at Autumnal Equinox.	Ending April 20 (Julian).	Ending March 24 (Julian).		NOTE:—September 23 beginning A.K. 4000 terminates 4000 years. Thus middle of A.K. 4000=A.K. 4000½= termination of 4000½ yrs.

SECTION IIB.—THE DURATION OF OUR LORD'S MINISTRY.

¶ 453. THE POINTS FOR INVESTIGATION.

A minute examination of all the available evidence will be necessary in order to enable us to determine the duration of our Lord's ministry and the day of His Crucifixion. Our examination will comprise the following points :—

(1) The date of the 15th year of Tiberius Cæsar.

(2) The scriptural evidence concerning the age of our Lord at His Baptism.

The six essential points of the investigation.

(3) The scriptural evidence concerning the length of His ministry.

(4) The evidence of ancient writers giving 782 A.U.C. as the year of the Crucifixion.

(5) Astronomical evidence bearing upon the Jewish calendar.

(6) The scriptural evidence concerning the day of the month and the day of the week on which the Crucifixion took place.

(1) THE 15TH YEAR OF TIBERIUS CÆSAR.

¶ 454. THE PROVINCIAL AND THE OFFICIAL METHODS OF RECKONING.

St. Luke (iii, 1) states that John the Baptist began his preaching in the 15th year of the reign of Tiberius Cæsar. For a short period, from 16th January 13 A.D. to 19th August 14 A.D., Tiberius was joint emperor with Augustus, assuming the supreme power on the death of Augustus, which occurred on the latter date. Two methods of reckoning the reign of Tiberius were in existence : the provincial method, which counted both the time of the joint-reign and the time of the sole-reign ; and the official method, which counted only the time of the sole-reign. It is obviously of supreme importance to determine which of these methods was used by St. Luke in dating the beginning of John the Baptist's ministry in the 15th year of Tiberius Cæsar.

The provincial method of reckoning the rule of Tiberius as beginning 16th January 13 A.D.

The official (Roman) method of reckoning the sole-reign of Tiberius from 19th August 14 A.D.

¶ 455. THE PROBABILITY THAT LUKE FOLLOWED THE PROVINCIAL RECKONING.

Let us assume, as a working hypothesis, that St. Luke, being a provincial, and writing in a province for provincials, would employ the provincial method of reckoning. (The reader should now refer to Tables XXXIII and XXXIV, where he will find a comparison of the two methods of reckoning,

If the provincial reckoning was followed by Luke, this places the preaching of John the Baptist in 27 A.D.

TABLE XXXIII.

THE REIGN OF TIBERIUS CÆSAR, ACCORDING TO PROVINCIAL AND OFFICIAL RECKONINGS.

REGARDING THE JOINT-REIGN RECKONING IN THE PROVINCES:—

From 16th January, A.D. 13 (*Enc. Brit.*), Tiberius "had bestowed upon him *the same authority as the Emperor himself possessed over the provinces.*" (*Lyman's Roman Emperors.*) "There is good ground to believe that St. Luke dates the year of the reign of Tiberius from his association with Augustus as joint Emperor, in A.U.C. 765, a method of computation which certainly existed, and would be especially likely to prevail *in the provinces.*" (Dean Farrar.)

REGARDING THE OFFICIAL RECKONING OF THE SOLE REIGN, FROM THE DEATH OF AUGUSTUS:—

Augustus "died on the 19th of August, A.D. 14" (*Enc. Brit.*) "The same report that announced the death of Augustus, proclaimed Tiberius in possession of *the supreme power.*" (Tacitus, *Annales*).

THE PROVINCIAL METHOD OF RECKONING. THE JOINT-REIGN.

1st Year, 16th January	A.D. 13 to A.D. 14	= 765–766 A.U.C.
2nd Year, ...	A.D. 14 to A.D. 15	= 766–767 A.U.C.
3rd Year, ...	A.D. 15 to A.D. 16	= 767–768 A.U.C.
4th Year, ...	A.D. 16 to A.D. 17	= 768–769 A.U.C.
14th Year, ...	A.D. 26 to A.D. 27	= 778–779 A.U.C.
*15th Year, ...	A.D. 27 to A.D. 28	= 779–780 A.U.C.
16th Year, ...	A.D. 28 to A.D. 29	= 780–781 A.U.C.
17th Year, ...	A.D. 29 to A.D. 30	= 781–782 A.U.C.
†18th Year, ...	A.D. 30 to A.D. 31	= 782–783 A.U.C.

THE OFFICIAL METHOD OF RECKONING. THE SOLE-REIGN.

1st Year, 19th August,	A.D. 14 to A.D. 15	= 767–768 A.U.C.
2nd Year, ...	A.D. 15 to A.D. 16	= 768–769 A.U.C.
3rd Year, ...	A.D. 16 to A.D. 17	= 769–770 A.U.C.
13th Year, ...	A.D. 26 to A.D. 27	= 779–780 A.U.C.
14th Year, ...	A.D. 27 to A.D. 28	= 780–781 A.U.C.
†15th Year, ...	A.D. 28 to A.D. 29	= 781–782 A.U.C.
§16th Year, ...	A.D. 29 to A.D. 30	= 782–783 A.U.C.

* If the Baptism of our Lord was in the 15th joint reign, it was in Autumn, A.D. 27, A.U.C. 780.

† The 28th joint reign includes Nisan A.D. 30, A.U.C. 782. Hippolytus states that the Crucifixion occurred in the 18th year of Tiberius. If A.D. 30-31 is the highest dating for the Crucifixion, the reckoning of Hippolytus cannot refer to the sole reign but to the 18th joint year of Tiberius. This places the Crucifixion in A.D. 30.

† If the Baptism had been in the 15th sole year, it would have been in the Autumn of A.D. 29, A.U.C. 782.

§ The 16th sole year includes Nisan A.D. 30, A.U.C. 782. Julius Africanus states that the Crucifixion occurred in the 16th year of Tiberius. If A.D. 29 is the lowest date for the Crucifixion, this cannot refer to the 16th year joint which ended at 16th January A.D. 29. Africanus therefore refers to the 16th sole year, which ended at 19th Aug. A.D. 30. This places the Crucifixion in A.D. 30.

IT IS IMPORTANT TO OBSERVE THAT THE A.U.C. YEAR BEGAN FROM 21st April (Julian).

IT IS ALSO OF IMPORTANCE TO NOTE THAT THE ANCIENT AUTHORITIES NEVER MADE THE MISTAKE OF BEGINNING THE A.U.C. YEAR FROM ANY OTHER DATE IN THE YEAR; AND THAT MODERN AUTHORITIES HAVE MADE, AND STILL DO MAKE, THE MISTAKE OF BEGINNING THE A.U.C. YEAR FROM 1st JANUARY (Julian). THIS MISTAKE IS THE PIVOT UPON WHICH ELUCIDATION OF THE WHOLE MATTER HINGES.

TABLE XXXIV.

THE 15th YEAR OF TIBERIUS CÆSAR IN TERMS OF THE FOUR DIFFERENT YEAR-RECKONINGS.

Modern chronology, commencing January 1st (Greg.).

Dionysian   ,,   ,,   March 25th (Jul.).

A.U.C. year ,,   ,,   April 21st (Jul.).

Anno Kalendarii   ,,   September 22-24 (Greg.).

Joint rule of Tiberius ,,   January 16, A.D. 13.
15th year   ,,   ,,   ,, A.D. 27.

Sole reign of Tiberius ,,   August 19, A.D. 14.
15th year   ,,   ,,   ,, A.D. 28.

1st year of A.U.C. reckoning, A.K. 3246½, B.C. 753.

   A.U.C. 779 commenced April 21 (Jul.) A.K. 4024½.
                     A.D. 26½.

1st Olympic year, A.K. 3223½, B.C. 776.

FOR DETAILS CONCERNING THE
CHRONOLOGICAL SEQUENCE OF EVENTS
REFER TABLE XXXV.

15th year from beginning of *joint* rule of Tiberius commenced Jan. 16, A.U.C. 779.

John came preaching, A.K. 4025½, A.U.C. 779-780, A.D. 27½.

THE BAPTISM, A.K. 4026, A.D. 27½, A.U.C. 780, Autumn.

THE FIRST PASSOVER, Feast-day, 15th Nisan, A.U.C. 780, March 30 (Jul.), A.K. 4026½, A.D. 28½.

15th year of *sole* reign of Tiberius commenced Aug. 19, A.D. 28.

THE SECOND PASSOVER, Feast-day, 15th Nisan, A.U.C. 781, Monday, April 18 (Jul.), A.K., 4027½, A.D. 29½.

Entry into Jerusalem, 10th Nisan, Palm Sunday, April 2 (Jul.)
THE THIRD PASSOVER, 15th Nisan, THE CRUCIFIXION, Friday, April 7 (Jul.), A.K. 4028½, A.D. 30½, on the Feast-day, A.U.C. 782.

The Nativity, A.K. 3996 B.C. 4
                      30 years

The Baptism, A.K. 4026, A.D. 27½
3 Passovers in
  Ministry   2½ years

CRUCIFIXION, A.K. 4028½, A.D. 30½,
in the 18th year from commencement of *joint* rule, and
16th year of *sole* reign of Tiberius Cæsar.

|To face p. 474.

and a *précis* of the evidence bearing on the matter.) That this is a justifiable assumption is shown by the fact that, in the Old Testament, the first year of Cyrus is reckoned from his joint-reign with Darius the Mede, and the nine years of his reign are computed by all chroniclers from the joint-reign and not from the sole-reign. The result of adopting this hypothesis is to place the date of the baptism of our Lord in the year 27 A.D. Let us leave it at this for the moment and proceed to the consideration of the next point.

If Luke followed the official reckoning, this places the preaching of John the Baptist between autumn 28 A.D. and autumn 29 A.D.

(2) THE DATE OF THE BAPTISM OF JESUS CHRIST.

¶ 456. THE EVIDENCE OF THE GOSPELS.

From the narrative of Matthew (iii, 3) it would appear certain that a period of some months must have elapsed from the first appearance of John to the Baptism of our Lord, and Luke (iii, 23) informs us that Christ was about thirty years of age when He was baptised. If Christ was born in the month Tisri, 4 B.C., He was about thirty years old in the autumn of 27 A.D., 4026 A.K., 780 A.U.C. This means that John must have started preaching in the spring of that year (27 A.D., 779–780 A.U.C.), which was in the 15th year of the joint-reign. If, however, we date the Baptism from the sole-reign, the details of the narrative cannot be made to adjust themselves. The years of the sole-reign did not begin until the 19th August 14 A.D., so that, in this case, John could not have appeared before the 19th August 28 A.D. Even if he had commenced his teaching immediately there would not have remained sufficient time for the events mentioned in Matthew (iii, 3) to take place between this date and the autumn Baptism. But, as it is highly improbable that he would have begun his ministry at this late season of the year, we are forced to postpone the beginning of his preaching until the spring of 29 A.D. This means that Christ would not have been baptised until the summer of 29 A.D., when he would have been nearly thirty-two years of age, and the Crucifixion would have been in 32 or 33 A.D., years that are impossible, as we hope to prove later. We therefore regard it as established that the 15th year of Tiberius Cæsar alluded to by Luke is the 15th year of the joint-reign, that is, from the 16th January 27 A.D. to the 16th January 28 A.D., and that the baptism of our Lord took place in the autumn of 27 A.D.[1]

Adopting the provincial reckoning of Tiberius places the Baptism in 27 A.D., our Lord being thirty years old in the autumn of that year.

Adopting the official reckoning, however, would place the Baptism in the autumn of 29 A.D., when our Lord was thirty-two years old.

Since Luke states that Jesus was "about thirty" at his Baptism Luke obviously follows the provincial reckoning.

The date of the Nativity being autumn 4 B.C., the gospels give the date of the Baptism as autumn 27 A.D.

---

[1] We desire, once again, to stress the fact that the A.U.C. year began on the 21st April (Julian). Modern chronologers, in dealing with the life of our Lord, have supposed that the A.U.C. year corresponded with the A.D. year now used, commencing on the 1st January. This has been the cause of many serious errors in calculating the date of the Baptism by the A.U.C. year; events that occurred towards the close of 780 A.U.C. having been placed in its beginning, and the Baptism antedated by nine months, and made to occur before the 15th year of Tiberius even commenced. Thus we find, in Smith's "Dictionary of the Bible": "Born in the *beginning* of 750 A.U.C. (or the *end* of 749) Jesus would be thirty in the *beginning* of 780 A.U.C. (27 A.D.). Creswell is probably right in placing the Baptism of our Lord in the *beginning* of this year (27 A.D.), and the first Passover during His ministry would be that of the same year;' Wieseler places the Baptism later in the spring or summer of the same year" (Vol. I, p. 1074; our italics). It is obvious that 750 A.U.C. is supposed to have commenced in January 4 B.C. This is shown by the words "or in the end of 749," which were added so as to include the previous 25th December.

(3) The Length of the Ministry.

¶ 457. THE PROBLEM OF THE PASSOVERS.

The scriptural evidence concerning the length of our Lord's ministry, and the scriptural evidence of the date of His Crucifixion, are so interwoven that it is not possible to discuss them separately. In fixing the year of the Crucifixion it is essential to determine whether the duration of the ministry
was two and a half years or three and a half. This period of three and a half years has been adopted by many writers as a consequence of the error in computing the A.U.C. year, to which we have just alluded. It is of the utmost importance to observe that the beginning of the Roman year was after the Passover, thus the Passover in 27 A.D. was on the 10th April, and therefore in 779 A.U.C. ; and the Passover in 780 A.U.C., the first after the Baptism, was at the close of that year, on the 29th March 28 A.D. This
error in supposing that the A.U.C. year corresponded with the A.D. year is responsible for the assumption that there were four Passovers between the Baptism and the Crucifixion. It is quite certain that the first Passover of our Lord's ministry was in 780 A.U.C. Owing, however, to the error noted,
authorities have placed the first Passover in the first quarter of 780 A.U.C., which actually ended on 21st April 28 A.D., the Baptism being in the autumn of 27 A.D., in the same A.U.C. year, 780. It is obvious, therefore, that only three Passovers could possibly have occurred between the Baptism in the autumn of 27 A.D. and the final Passover in the spring of 30 A.D.[1]

¶ 458. THE UNDEFINED FEAST IN JOHN'S GOSPEL.

There is no evidence in any of the gospels that our Lord's ministry included more than three Passovers. John is the witness as to their number, and the first Passover after the Baptism is mentioned in Chapter ii, 13, 23. In Chapter v, 1 we read that there was a " feast of the Jews, and Jesus went up to Jerusalem." It is important to decide if this feast was a Passover. If the reader will consult the parallel tabulation of the narratives of the

---

[1]If our Lord had been crucified in 29¾ A.D., and His ministry had lasted three and a half years, His baptism would have been in 25¾ A.D., that is to say, a year and a quarter before the 15th year of the joint-reign of Tiberius Cæsar. If His ministry had lasted two and a half years, His baptism would have been in 26¾ A.D., still some months before the 15th year of the joint-reign commenced in January 27 A.D. If, therefore, our Lord was born in 4 B.C., the Crucifixion cannot have been in 29 A.D. The view that the ministry only lasted eighteen months is negatived by the fact that John mentions three Passovers after the Baptism.

Dr. Grattan Guinness dates the Nativity in 6 B.C. in order to get 33½ years to 29 A.D. This involves two errors : the dating of the Nativity two and a half years before the proved date of the death of Herod in 3 B.C., and dating the Baptism at least a year before the 15th year of the joint-reign of Tiberius.

Further confirmation of the date of 780 A.U.C. (28 A.D.) for the first Passover of the ministry is afforded by the following passage (John ii, 20) : " The Jews therefore said, forty and six years was this temple in building, and wilt thou rear it up in three days." This refers to the rebuilding by Herod, which was begun in 734 A.U.C. If 46 years be added to 734 we get 780 A.U.C. This Passover is mentioned in John ii, 13, 23.

four gospels (Table XXXV) he will observe that in every case the Gospel of St. John supplies the gaps in the narratives of the other three, prior to the events of Holy Week, without covering any of the ground traversed by the others. (There is one significant exception to this statement, which will be considered later.) This feature of St. John's gospel leads us to conclude that it was intended to supply only what the other gospels had omitted concerning the essential details of the ministry of Jesus between the time of His baptism and His triumphal entry into Jerusalem.

If, then, this undefined feast was a Passover, we are forced to conclude that John has omitted the events of a whole year between Chapter iv and Chapter v, and this in a case where the other three gospels do not supply the events of the period omitted. That this is not the case is apparent from the fact that, at the time of this undefined feast, John the Baptist was still " witnessing " (John v, 32), and from the fact, the one significant exception referred to above, that John begins the next chapter with the feeding of the five thousand, an event that is recorded in all the other gospels. This breaking of the general rule of St. John's gospel enables us to determine the succession of events and to synchronise the narratives of the four gospels at this particular point. The space of time that elapsed between the undefined feast and the feeding of the five thousand is filled by the events described in the other gospels, the imprisonment and death of John the Baptist, and there is no place for the hypothetical lost year that has to be accounted for if the undefined feast was a Passover.[1]

(margin) Elucidation of this purpose shows that the undefined feast was not a Passover. The chronological connection between John's gospel and the three gospels concerning the events between the first Passover and the second Passover.

¶ 459. THE UNDEFINED FEAST IDENTIFIED BY CONTEXT. (TABLE XXXV.)

We are told that this undefined feast occurred before the imprisonment of John the Baptist. Immediately after the first Passover (John iii and iv) Jesus went to Galilee, passing through Judæa and Samaria, and after reaching Galilee He returned to Jerusalem for this particular feast. On His way up to Galilee, whilst passing through Samaria, He drew upon the state of the crops for a parable, " The fields . . . are white already to harvest." It is evident, therefore, that the time of the harvest was approaching, and that He passed through Samaria between the Passover and Pentecost.

(margin) After the first Passover Jesus, during His journey to Galilee, drew upon the signs of an early harvest for a parable.

Let us now consider the events that took place after this undefined feast. We are informed that He returned into Galilee after He had heard of the imprisonment of John the Baptist (Matt. iv, 12). Luke (Chapters iv and vi) tells us that He came to Nazareth and read in the synagogue " on

(margin) Soon after His arrival in Galilee He made a rapid return journey to Jerusalem for the undefined feast.

---

[1] Alford (" Greek Testament," Vol. I, pp. 740, 741) discussing this matter says: " We cannot with any probability gather what feast it was. . . . It can hardly have been a Passover, both on account of the omission of the article before ἑορτή, and because, if so, we should have an interval of a whole year between this chapter and the next, which is not probable."

Dean Farrar (" Life of Christ," Excursus VIII) says : " Now the feast here mentioned could hardly be the Passover or the Feast of Tabernacles, because, as we have seen, St. John, when he mentions those feasts, mentions them by name. . . . If this were the Passover St. John would omit a whole year of our Lord's ministry without a word."

A fortnight after His return to Galilee His disciples plucked the ears of corn to eat.
the sabbath day," and that, proceeding to Capernaum, " He taught them on the sabbath days." " He preached in the synagogues of Galilee," and then, still in Galilee, " on the second sabbath after the first, that He went through the corn-fields ; and His disciples plucked the ears of corn, and did eat, rubbing them in their hands."

The sequence proves that the undefined feast was the first Pentecost of our Lord's ministry.
Thus we have a period of two weeks clearly defined between His coming into Galilee after the undefined feast and His disciples plucking the ears of corn. It is clear, therefore, that Jesus visited Jerusalem for this feast between the time when He passed through Samaria and drew His parable from the ripening harvest, and the time when His disciples plucked the ears of corn in Galilee. This seems to indicate, not only that Christ went to Jerusalem for the first Passover of His ministry, but that He also went there in the same first year, at the time of First-fruits, that is, Pentecost, or the time of the Feast of Weeks. It would appear, therefore, that the feast of John v, 1 was the Feast of Pentecost in the first year of our Lord's ministry.[1]

¶ 460. THE GOSPEL OF JOHN DEFINES A TWO AND A HALF YEARS' MINISTRY.

The object of John's gospel. John's precise definition of the principal feasts of our Lord's ministry.
We have already drawn attention to the fact that the Gospel of St. John supplies all the chronological details not supplied by the other gospels, and have indicated our opinion that the intention of the Gospel of St. John was to link up and harmonise the narratives of the other three gospels. The remarkable precision of St. John in defining all the important feasts is strong confirmation of this hypothesis, and it appears obvious that St. John's object in repeating, in Chapter vi, events that were already related by the other gospels, was to synchronise these events with the second Passover, which, he says, was at hand shortly after the events recorded in Chapter vi. By this means we are enabled to determine the time of the year when occurred the events narrated by the three gospels, prior to the events of Chapter vi of the fourth gospel.

By defining three Passovers only, John states that the duration of our Lord's ministry was two and a half years ; thus agreeing with the Baptism at 27¾ A.D. and the Crucifixion at 30¼. A.D.
The second Passover mentioned by St. John is in Chapter vi, 4, and prior to the final Passover ; he also mentions two other feasts, the Feast of Tabernacles (vii, 2, 14, 37) and the Feast of Dedication, when it was winter (x, 22). As the third and final Passover then followed (xi, 55, xii, 1), the evidence is conclusive that the ministry lasted only two and a half years. This duration of the ministry agrees with the date of the Baptism in the autumn of 27 A.D. and the Crucifixion in 30 A.D.

[1]John iv, 35 : " Say not ye, There are yet four months and then cometh harvest ? " cannot mean that this was spoken four months before the harvest, for the verse concludes with the words, " the fields . . . are already white to harvest." " There are yet four months and then cometh harvest " may have been some proverb or popular saying then current in Palestine, concerning the interval between the end of the cold season and the time of the harvest ; that is, from February to May inclusive. Our Lord appears to be drawing His parable from the evident signs of an early harvest.

TABLE XXXV.

THE DURATION OF OUR LORD'S MINISTRY FROM THE NARRATIVE SEQUENCE OF THE FOUR GOSPELS.

I.—FROM THE PREACHING OF JOHN THE BAPTIST TO THE FIRST PASSOVER.

	Incidents.	Town.	Locality.	Matthew.	Mark.	Luke.	John.
months	The Ministry of John the Baptist to The Baptism of our Lord.	Bethabara	East of S. E. Corner of Galilee, and East of Jordan.	iii, 1 to iii, 17.	i, 1 to i, 8.	iii, 1 to iii, 22.	i, 6 to i, 15.
months	Call of the first disciples	do.	do.	.. ..	.. ..	.. ..	i, 19-51.
	Jesus in Galilee	Cana, Capernaum.	Galilee.	.. ..	.. ..	.. ..	ii, 1-12.
	The 1st Passover of our Lord's Ministry..	Jerusalem.	Judæa.	.. ..	.. ..	.. ..	ii, 13, to iii, 21.

II. FROM THE FIRST PASSOVER TO THE SECOND PASSOVER.

	Incidents.	Town.	Locality.	Matthew.	Mark.	Luke.	John.
	The disciples of Jesus baptise in Judæa ..	.. .. ..	Judæa	.. ..	.. ..	.. ..	iv, 1.
	Journey through Samaria. Our Lord's Parable drawn from the state of the crops around Samaria, "white already to harvest" (John iv, 35).	.. .. ..	Samaria.	.. ..	.. ..	.. ..	to iv, 42.
From the first Passover to the ripening of the corn; about 1 month.	Our Lord in Galilee	Cana.	Galilee.	.. ..	.. ..	.. ..	iv, 43-54
	Rapid return of our Lord to Jerusalem for a "Feast of the Jews." He arrived on the eve of the Sabbath and restored the impotent man. The next series of incidents shows that His coming was for the Feast of Pentecost, and that He arrived and came hurriedly to His Temple on the Sabbath preceding Pentecost. This hurried coming fulfilled Malachi iii, 1, and Daniel ix, 25, for which refer ¶ 338. Obviously for this reason, Matthew, Mark, and Luke all begin their narratives of our Lord's Ministry from this time.	Jerusalem.	Judæa.	.. ..	.. ..	.. ..	v, 1 to v, 47.
	Imprisonment of John the Baptist ..	.. .. ..	.. ..	iv, 12 and 17.	i, 14 and 15.	.. ..	
	Our Lord returned to Galilee THE FIRST SABBATH (Luke iv, 16). He preached in the Synagogue at Nazareth.	Nazareth	Galilee. ..	.. ..	vi, 1.	iv, 15-30.	
	Journey in Galilee	Capernaum	Galilee. Galilee.	iv, 13, to viii, 17; viii, 1-4;	i, 16 to	iv, 31 to	
	"THE SECOND SABBATH AFTER THE FIRST" (Luke vi, 1). The disciples pluck the ears of corn.	Capernaum	Galilee. Galilee.	ix, 1-17. xii, 1-8.	ii, 22. ii, 23-28.	v, 39. vi, 1-5.	
	For the remainder of the year, to the 2nd Passover, our Lord confined His teaching and work to Galilee and the shores of the Sea of Galilee.	.. .. ..	Galilee and Sea of Galilee.	Refer Oxford Bible Appendix, pp. 64 and 65.			
	The 2nd Passover nigh (John vi, 4).. ..		The East Coast of Galilee.	.. ..	.. ..	.. ..	vi, 4.
	The feeding of the five thousand	Bethsaida.	The East Coast of Galilee.	xiv, 13-21.	vi, 30-44.	ix, 12-17.	vi, 5-13
	THE 2nd PASSOVER. Our Lord's discourse—obviously at the Passover—on Himself as the true Passover, "the bread which I give is My flesh," "I am the living bread which came down from Heaven," "I am that bread of life." (Refer Table XXXVII.)	.. .. ..		xiv, 34.	.. ..	.. ..	vi, 26-70

III. FROM THE SECOND PASSOVER TO THE THIRD PASSOVER.

Incidents.	Town.	Locality.	Matthew.	Mark.	Luke.	John.
For incidents in sequence refer Oxford Bible Appendix, p. 65 ..	.. .. ..	.. ..	xv, 1, to xviii, 35.	vii, 1, to ix, 45.	ix, 22, to ix, 56.	
The Feast of the Tabernacles..	Jerusalem.	.. ..	.. ..	.. ..	.. ..	vii, 2-10.
Refer Oxford Bible Appendix, p. 65		.. ..	.. ..	.. ..	.. ..	vii, 1 to x, 11.
Refer Oxford Bible Appendix, p. 65	.. .. ..	.. ..	xii, 22 to xii, 45.	.. ..	x, 1 to xiii, 17.	
The Feast of Dedication	Jerusalem.	.. ..	.. ..	.. ..	.. ..	x, 22-40.
The Message to Herod	.. .. ..	.. ..	.. ..	.. ..	xiii, 31-33.	
Refer Oxford Bible Appendix, pp. 65 and 66 ..	.. .. ..	.. ..	xix, 1 to xx, 34.	x, 1 to x 52.	xiii, 23 to xix, 28.	xi, 1 to xi, 54.
The Events of Holy Week: Refer Oxford Bible Appendix, p. 66	.. .. ..	.. ..	xxvi, 6-13. xxi, 1-46. xxii, 1-46. xxiii, 13-33. xxiv, 1-51. xxv, 1-46 xxvi, 3-16.	xiv, 3-9, xi, 1-33. xii, 1-12. xii, 13-37. xii, 41-44. xiii, 1-37. xiv, 1-11.	xix, 29-48, xx, 1-19. xx, 20-44. xxi, 1-4. xxi, 5-36. xxii, 1-6.	xii, 1-9. xii, 12-19. xii, 20-36.
THE 3rd (and last) PASSOVER	.. .. ..	.. ..	xxvi, 17, et seq.	xiv, 12, et seq.	xxii, 7, et seq.	xiii, 1, et seq.

[To face p. 478

¶ 461. THE SIGNIFICANCE OF OUR LORD'S MESSAGE TO HEROD.

The significance of the "THIRD" day, the "THIRD" year, and, by inference, the "THIRD" month, in connection with our Lord's ministry and sacrifice, should be carefully considered. On the "third day" the earth brought forth fruitfulness (Gen. i, 9–13); on the "third day" Isaac was laid on the altar (Gen. xxii, 4), a prophetic type of our Lord's sacrifice; on the "third day" Christ rose again, after He had been crucified in the "third year" of His ministry, which was the thirty-third year of His life.

After the Feast of Dedication at the end of 29 A.D., our Lord, early in 30 A.D., sent His message to Herod. Referring to the months Sebat, Adar, and Nisan, under the type of "days," as "to-day," "to-morrow," and "the third day," He predicts His being "perfected" on the "third day," i.e. in the month Nisan.

The significance of this "third day" as a type of our Lord's "third year" of ministry, and of the "third day" when He was resurrected, is apparent when we consider the terms of our Lord's message to Herod (Luke xiii, 32). This message was given after the Feast of Dedication, and some months before the final Passover (Table XXXV). This Feast of Dedication, only mentioned by St. John, and another example of the intention of his gospel, began at sunset 17th December (Julian) 29 A.D. and ended at sunset 18th December (Julian). Our Lord's message to Herod was some time after this, and yet some months before the Crucifixion. He said, "Behold, I cast out devils and perform cures *to-day and to-morrow*, and the *third day* I am perfected." With the prophetic type of a day for a year, and a day for a month, the interpretation is that "to-day" was the current month Sebat, 24th January to 23rd February 30 A.D.; "to-morrow" was the month Adar, the twelfth month, 23rd February to 24th March; and "the third day" was the first month of the year, the month Nisan, 24th March to 23rd April 30 A.D. These last two and a half months of our Lord's ministry were thus typified by Him as symbolic of the first, second, and third years of His ministry, and of the first, second, and third days from His Crucifixion to His Resurrection.

The type, however, also prefigures His Resurrection on the third day, and by the analogy with the third month, shows that the type extended to His years of ministry. The analogy sequence:— (1) Third year; (2) Third month; (3) Third day; and all of His 33rd year. The third year is possible only with a two and a half years' ministry.

(4) THE EVIDENCE OF ANCIENT WRITERS CONCERNING THE YEAR OF THE CRUCIFIXION.

¶ 462. THE CRUCIFIXION IN 782 A.U.C.

We now propose to examine the evidence of the ancient writers and historians concerning the year of the Crucifixion. The years that are usually given by modern authorities are 29 A.D. and 30 A.D., but the Crucifixion has been placed in every year from 29 A.D. to 33 A.D. As the B.C. and A.D. reckoning was not used before the 6th century, and even then not universally, all the ancient writers refer to the A.U.C. year, and all the ancient writers refer to the final Passover in the same astronomical year, 4028 A.K., in the spring of that year; that is, at the end of 782 A.U.C. But while this A.U.C. year is generally admitted, commentators have fallen into the common error of supposing that the

782 A.U.C. began after the Passover of 29 A.D. and ended after the Passover of 30 A.D. Modern authorities generally fall into the error of beginning the A.U.C. year from 1st January instead of 21st April.

A.D. year corresponds with the A.U.C. year, and that they both began on the 1st January.

Thus Browne ("Ordo Sæc.") says: "The consular date assigned, almost with one consent, by the Latin fathers is the year of the two Gemini, 782 A.U.C., 29 A.D."; and the writer in the "Encyclopædia Britannica" does not even refer to the A.U.C. year, but sums up as follows: "Thus 29 A.D. is the year, the 18th of March is the day to which Christian tradition (whatever value, much or little, be ascribed to it) seems to point."

Now, 782 A.U.C. does *not* correspond with 29 A.D. by modern chronology. It does almost correspond with 29 A.D. by Dionysian reckoning,[1] as there is only rather less than a month's difference between the beginning of the A.U.C. year and the Dionysian year. But this month's difference is sufficient to render it impossible to date the Crucifixion both in 782 A.U.C. and in 29 A.D., as the Passover of 29 A.D. occurred before 782 A.U.C. began.

Commentators who accept or support the year 29 A.D. have made the mistake of supposing that the Passover took place in the beginning of the A.U.C. year, when undoubtedly it occurred at its close. The alternative dates for the Passover in 29 A.D. (18th March and 17th April) were in 781 A.U.C., and, by both Dionysian and modern chronology, the Passover in 782 A.U.C. was on 6th April 30¼ A.D., 4028½ A.K.

¶ 463. A MATTER OF SIMPLE ARITHMETIC.

The year 30 A.D. for the Crucifixion tallies with the year 4 B.C. for the Nativity. It is an astonishing thing that many learned men who accept the date of 4 B.C. for the Nativity can suppose that the Crucifixion occurred in 29 A.D. This is merely a matter of arithmetic. It must be remembered that there is no such year as 0 B.C. in historical reckoning, consequently, when B.C. years are added to A.D. years one year must be deducted from the total.[2] Also, the months must be taken into account. With B.C. dates we are reckoning backwards, consequently, October 4 B.C. must not be calculated as 4¾ B.C. From October 4 B.C. to March or April 29 A.D. is only 31½ years, but many writers have added as follows :—

The Nativity ..	..	..	..	October 4 B.C.
The Crucifixion ..	..	..	..	March 29 A.D.

32½ years.

on the understanding that there are 33 years from October 4 B.C. to October 29 A.D. But, as we have shown, this period must have one year deducted, making it only 31½ years.

[1] Refer to Table XXXIV.
[2] This can be seen at a glance by reference to Table XXXII, Column 4.

¶ 464. HIPPOLYTUS AND THE CORRECT DATES FOR THE NATIVITY AND CRUCIFIXION.

We now quote two striking statements of Hippolytus, as confirming that our Lord was crucified in 30 A.D. In his Commentary of Daniel, Hippolytus states :

(1) That Christ was crucified in His 33rd year.
(2) That He was crucified in the 18th year of Tiberius.

These two statements are in perfect agreement, each with the other, and with the Nativity in 4 B.C. and the Crucifixion in 30 A.D. If Christ was born in the autumn of 4 B.C. and crucified in the spring of 30 A.D., He was then in His 33rd year. Furthermore, the 18th year of the joint reign of Tiberius (refer to Table XXXIII) began on the 16th January 30 A.D. Reference to Table XXXIII will show that Julius Africanus also dates the Crucifixion in 30 A.D.[1]

The data of Hippolytus— with the independent data of Africanus— are both given in Table XXXIII.

Both Hippolytus and Africanus state that the Crucifixion occurred in 30 A.D.

Hippolytus also states that the Nativity was in 4 B.C.

(5) ASTRONOMICAL EVIDENCE.

¶ 465. THE HEBREW LUNI-SOLAR YEAR AND CALENDAR.

The discussion of Aramaic calendar datings by Professor Sayce, Dr. Knobel, and others, and the comparison of these with Assyrian calendar datings, has established the fact that the luni-solar year and calendar of the Jews in the centuries before the Christian era were identical with the Assyro-Babylonian year and calendar. The year and calendar which the Jews had followed for centuries prior to the Babylonian captivity were identical with the year and calendar which they found in use in Babylon during their captivity there. The reason for this identity is, as has been shown in Table XIX and Annotations, that the Babylonians and Assyrians of that date owed many of their institutions to a long succession of invasions and occupations over several centuries by hordes of Aramaic nomads. In consequence of the same contact we find that the Aramaic calendar was derived from the Assyrian calendar. The language of the Jews at the time in question was Aramaic, and their luni-solar year and its method of intercalation and its calendar were Aramaic. The Aramaic year, intercalation, and calendar were the Jewish year, intercalation, and calendar (refer to ¶ 491e). Comparison of all the known dated records shows that the full moon of the month Nisan never preceded the vernal equinox. Sir Robert Anderson has also shown, from the Mishna, that the same fixed rule applied to the early Jewish calendar.

The luni-solar calendar of the early Hebrews, early Jews, Arameans, and Assyro-Babylonians was identical.

The full moon of the first month Nisan (or Abib) never preceded the vernal equinox.

[1] The " Encyclopædia Britannica " (11th Edit., Vol. III, p. 891) gives the latest date assigned to the Crucifixion by any authority as 33 A.D., and rejects this as too late, and not authorised by a single Christian authority before the 4th century. Eusebius obtained this date from a statement made by a pagan chronicler, Phlegon (in the time of Hadrian), who notes in 32–33 A.D. an earthquake in Bithynia, and a total eclipse of the sun at " the sixth hour of the day." Eusebius supposed the earthquake to be that of the Crucifixion, and the eclipse to be the cause of the darkness " at the sixth hour." But the eclipse referred to by Phlegon cannot possibly be connected with the Crucifixion, as no total eclipse occurred in 32–33 A.D. in the months of March or April.

The above
identity has
governed the
Jewish calen-
dar in all
organised
Jewish com-
munities to
the present
time.

There is neither scriptural nor archæological authority for the later Talmudic practice requiring the crescent of the new moon of Nisan to be observed and recorded by witnesses at Jerusalem before the month of Nisan could be deemed to commence. Nevertheless, in effect, the year as determined by the older rules did not materially differ from the year as fixed by the witnesses of the first visible crescent of the moon of Nisan, for in all times, and in all countries following the Hebrew calendar and year, the months were so arranged in the luni-solar year as to commence at the *visible* new moon, and not at the astronomical new moon, which is *invisible*. Invariably, then, we find that the full moon of Nisan fell on the 14th Nisan. This identity holds prior to the Babylonian captivity, from the Babylonian captivity to the 2nd century A.D., the Talmudic year of the witnesses notwithstanding, and from the 4th century A.D., with the present revised Jewish calendar. The modern calendar differs but little from the older calendar, except that the rules applying to the modern Jewish calendar are slightly more complicated for the purpose of avoiding certain festivals falling upon days of the week that are deemed to be incompatible.

¶ 466. THE EARLIEST CHRISTIAN TRADITION.

Christian
tradition, from
the earliest
times, has
maintained
that the full
moon of Nisan
must not pre-
cede the vernal
equinox.

When we remember that the first Christian community at Jerusalem was not scattered abroad until the 2nd century A.D., we have good grounds for beginning our investigations concerning Christian traditions in that century. At that time, we know, full moon of Nisan fell upon the 14th Nisan. The " Encyclopædia Britannica " states :

In this
feature they
agreed with
the Jewish
practice.

> " So early as the 2nd century of our era, great disputes had arisen among the Christians respecting the proper time of celebrating Easter, which governs all other movable feasts. The Jews celebrated their Passover on the 14th day of the *first month ;* that is to say, the lunar month of which the 14th day either falls in, or next follows, the day of the vernal equinox. Most Christian sects agree that Easter should be celebrated on a Sunday. Others followed the example of the Jews, and adhered to the 14th of the moon. . . . In order to terminate dissensions . . . the Council of Nicæa, which was held in the year 325, ordained that the celebration of Easter should thenceforth always take place on the Sunday which immediately follows the full moon that happened upon, or next after, the day of the vernal equinox. . . ."[1]
>
> " . . . it follows that the paschal full moon, or the 14th of the paschal moon, cannot happen before the 21st of March, and that Easter in consequence cannot happen before the 22nd of March."[2]

The point to be observed in the above is that the dispute among the Christians of the 2nd century A.D. was not about the equinoctial limit for the paschal moon, but whether Easter should be on the Sunday following the 14th day of the vernal equinoctial paschal moon or actually on the 15th day of the *moon*. In the earliest times, all are agreed, Jews and Christians alike, that the paschal full moon must not be earlier than the day of the vernal equinox.

[1] 11th Edit., Vol. IV, p. 992.   [2] Ibid., p. 997.

¶ 467. THE EFFECT OF THE FINAL JEWISH DISPERSION.

From 132 to 135 A.D., the Jews in Judæa were in revolt against the Romans. In this disastrous war 580,000 Jews were slain, and considerably more than a million died as a result of fire, pestilence, and famine. During the war the Jews under the false Messiah, Barcochab, cruelly persecuted the remnant of the first Christian community in Judæa. The community was scattered abroad to complete the second phase of Christian witnessing (refer Daniel xii, 7). The significance of this is seen by reference to the features of Isaiah's prophecy in the year 754 B.C. (the Roman epoch of A.U.C. reckoning) as dealt with in Table XXVI and note to same, and as related to the data discussed in ¶¶ 337 and 338, and Table XXVIII, Annotations (F) VIII. *The signifi-cance of the final dispersion of the Chris-tians and Jews from the Holy Land.*

Up to this date—135 A.D. or 888 A.U.C.—the compilation of the Jewish calendar was permitted only in Judæa.[1] Between 70 A.D. and 135 A.D. the rule of the Palestinian rabbis—requiring the 1st of Nisan to be fixed by the records of witnesses observing the first visible crescent of the moon of Nisan—seems to have applied in the governing of the calendar. This, as we have seen, made little or no difference in the beginning of Nisan, as compared with former times ; nor did it affect the vernal equinoctial limit.

After 135 A.D., however, and until 363 A.D., the various scattered Jewish communities along the coasts and in the adjacent lands of the Mediterranean, and in Arabia, Persia, etc., were without central authority as to the fixing of the calendar. The least learned of such communities seem, indeed, to have possessed nothing of the nature even of a rule-of-thumb method to guide them in the observance of the luni-solar year and their sacred festivals. Thus the " Encyclopædia Britannica " states : *After the dis-persion, and prior to 363 A.D., isolated Jewish communities were without central author-ity as to the fixing of the calendar, and sometimes, through error, allowed the full moon of Nisan to occur before the vernal equinox;*

> " Christian controversialists from Anatolius of Laodicæa (277 A.D.) onwards accused the Jews of disregarding the (Christian) equinoctial limit, and of some-times placing the paschal full moon before it."

There would have been no basis for such accusation against the Jews unless the Christian controversialists had evidence from Jewish sources that the Jews of the period had departed from an original practice.

¶ 468. THE REVISED JEWISH CALENDAR.

So long as the Rabbinical authorities had been able to maintain a central authority in Palestine, just so long had they refused to promulgate any rules concerning the fixing of the ecclesiastical year. As a result the dispersion in 135 A.D. brought confusion in regard to the ruling of the calendar. To correct this confusion the Jewish rabbis at length were persuaded that the old dictum could not be applied to scattered communities that did not recognise a central authority in the Holy Land. They were ultimately *The Jewish luni-solar calendar re-organised to conform to the needs of the dispersion.*

[1] Berakot, IX, 1-5 (Cambridge University Edition).

compelled, in 363 A.D., to frame a luni-solar calendar cycle based on the Metonic cycle of 19 years. The system of chronology adopted to conform to this arrangement—or *vice versa*, the arrangement to conform to the chronology—was the system we have discussed in Table XXVIII, Cols. 8 and 9, and Annotations (F) VIII to this Table.

One item stands out prominently in the revised calendar. The calendar cycle is framed with regard to the vernal equinoctial limit, as in the original calendar. However we may accuse the Jews of losing the spirit of their laws and prophecies, we can never have occasion to accuse them of violating the letter of their laws and traditions. No race on earth has clung so tenaciously to the strict letter and form of their laws and traditions. In a matter of their calendar, can we deem it likely they would conform to the vernal equinoctial limit as the ruling datum for their luni-solar year merely because the Christians were governed by this datum? It is far more likely that they would frame a system with the object of confounding the basis of the Christian ecclesiastical year. When we remember the fierce controversies between Jews and Christians in these early centuries, and at the time when the Jews were re-establishing their ecclesiastical year, we are inclined to think that had the Jews had any excuse, based upon Jewish practice at the time of our Lord, to place the paschal full moon before the vernal equinox, they would have done so without the slightest hesitation. That they did not do so, we may conclude, was because they were shackled by law, tradition, and custom.

That this matter may be made plain, we again quote the " Encyclopædia Britannica," which states that the revised Jewish calendar was framed " in order that the Passover, the 15th day of Nisan, may be kept at its proper season, which is the full moon of the vernal equinox, or that which takes place after the sun has entered the sign Aries."[1] The sign Aries here referred to must not be confused with the zodiacal sign of that name. The reference is to the sun at the vernal equinox entering upon a space of 30° that originally coincided with the zodiacal sign Aries. The term as used in modern astronomy is, therefore, anomalous (refer ¶ 311). It is purely a supposititious sign, defined only by its geometrical extent from the equinoctial colure. The statement quoted merely means that the full moon of Nisan cannot precede the vernal equinox.

¶ 469. ASTRONOMY IN THE BIBLE AND ASTRONOMY IN THE TALMUD.

The Talmud is possibly the only commentary on the Bible that denies astronomy a place in fixing the year. The Talmud restricts the exercise of authority in the matter of the year to the rabbis in Jerusalem, and to the accident of a remote witness's observation. It is clear that the object was to maintain the priests as sole arbiters in this matter; it certainly does not

[1]Vol. IV, p. 1000.

mean that the priests themselves ever allowed any witness's observation to determine the month of Nisan in such fashion as would place the full moon of Nisan anticipating the day of the vernal equinox. The dictum was not so much to govern the priesthood in their determination of the year's beginning, as to prevent other than the priests at Jerusalem from exercising an authority which the latter deemed it essential should be theirs alone. In this, then, as in so many other matters, the Talmud's circulating of the dictum on the plea that the priests were interpreting the wishes of God in making it less possible for the Jews to worship the sun, moon, and stars, was a hypocritical subterfuge cloaking the real determining purpose.

In the Bible itself there is no such dictum. Rather do we find in the first chapter of Genesis that God " made two great lights," and " the stars also," " to divide the day from the night," and to " be for signs, and for seasons, and for days, and years." Is it likely, then, that the beginning of the year of the Hebrews should have been dependent upon the uncertain date of the ripening of the crops, as so many have urged ? Is this the meaning of Exodus xiii, 10, concerning the Passover, " thou shalt therefore keep this ordinance in *His season* from year to year " ? If, then, the luni-solar year was fixed by " the two great lights," the sun and moon, in relation to the spring and lunar month Nisan, it seems clear that the relation must have been one holding in regard to the day of the vernal equinox and the full moon of Nisan. This relation would have been an anomaly had it permitted the full moon of Nisan in one year to succeed the vernal equinox, and in another year to precede it. *No such dictum exists in the Bible. The Old Testament dictates an astronomical definition of the year and its seasons and states that the Passover was to be observed in " His season."*

All this tends to confirm what we deem to have been established already, that the full moon of Nisan during scriptural times, as in the modern Jewish calendar, never preceded the day of the vernal equinox. To this must be added the rule, holding in all the ancient countries of the East where the luni-solar year was in use, that the 1st day of Nisan was the day of observed new moon, and not the day of astronomical (invisible) new moon. This means that, in general, sunset beginning 1st Nisan was a day later than astronomical new moon. *The priests, however, themselves observed the astronomical fixing of the seasons. Consequently the full moon of Nisan was never permitted to precede the vernal equinox.*

As we believe the evidence shows that 30 A.D. is the year of the Crucifixion, and as it has been a matter of debate as to whether the 14th Nisan or 15th Nisan was the day of the Crucifixion, further research should settle the latter point, and also the question as to the day of the week.

¶ 470. THE FIXING OF NISAN IN THE YEAR OF THE CRUCIFIXION.

Some writers have objected to the year 30 A.D. on the ground that the 14th Nisan (dating from the astronomical new moon) was on a Wednesday. This undoubted fact, however, does not disprove the date 30 A.D., but absolutely confirms it. In ancient times, as we have explained, the month was so arranged that the first day of the month was the day of the observed *The 1st day of Nisan began at sunset of the day following astronomical new moon (which is invisible).*

new moon, and not of the invisible astronomical new moon. We think we have made this matter plain above, but in this connection again quote the "Encyclopædia Britannica"[1]: "In earlier Jewish times all months were reckoned to begin at the first sunset when the new moon was visible."

The Jews' 1st of Nisan in the year of the Crucifixion was, therefore, one day after the astronomical new moon that preceded the full moon first after the vernal equinox.

The assumption that the 15th Nisan was on a Friday brings us down to one year. According to the "Encyclopædia Britannica" the only possible year on which Thursday was on the 14th and Friday on the 15th Nisan, from 28 A.D. to 33 A.D. inclusive, is 30 A.D. The "Encyclopædia Britannica" also gives 18th March as the 14th Nisan in 29 A.D., and on a Friday, by the Jews' observed new moon. The latter dating is, however, clearly impossible, for the many reasons already dealt with, but chiefly for the reason that the 15th of Nisan would have fallen several days *before* the vernal equinox. The "Encyclopædia Britannica" rightly gives the alternative date for the 14th Nisan in 29 A.D., 17th April (Julian), which was a Sunday. This is the correct date of the Passover in 29 A.D., as the intercalary month Ve-Adar must have come in that year. It is very evident why the correct month dating has been ignored; because it did not fit in with Thursday or Friday for the Crucifixion in 29 A.D., the assumed Passover in 782 A.U.C.

With regard to the other years historically impossible, by consulting Table XXXVI it will be seen that in 28 A.D. the 15th Nisan was on 30th March (Julian), a Tuesday. The year 33 A.D. is excluded on historical grounds—as shown—but the 14th of Nisan was on 3rd April (Julian), a Friday, on the same day of the week as in 29 A.D., had it been possible to adopt the March date, prior to the vernal equinox.

As in the case of the scriptural and historical considerations, we are again left with 30 A.D. as the only possible year for the day of the Crucifixion to agree with a Thursday or Friday, by the Jews' observed new moon following the vernal equinox, in the series of years from 28 A.D. to 33 A.D. inclusive.

In the adopted year, 30 A.D., if the Crucifixion took place on Thursday, 14th Nisan or alternatively, on Friday, 15th Nisan, then 1st Nisan began a day after astronomical new moon.

¶ 471. THE EGYPTIAN CALENDAR MONTH TRADITIONAL DATINGS FOR THE CRUCIFIXION.

The "Encyclopædia Britannica" says: "The earliest known calculations by Basilidian Gnostics, quoted in Clem. Alex., *Strom.*, I, 147, gave alternative dates, Phamenoth 25, Pharmuthi 25, Pharmuthi 19."[2]

From what we know concerning the Gnostics and their preference for the then discarded institutions and superstitions of the ancient Egyptians

[1]Vol. III, p. 890.   [2]Vol. III, p. 891.

TABLE XXXVI.

TABLE OF CALENDAR DATES FOR ASCERTAINING NEW TESTAMENT CHRONOLOGY.

Tabular Year, as in Plates LIX and LX.	Historical Year.	Date of Astronomical New Moon preceding 1st Nisan.		1st NISAN. Sunset to Sunset.			14th NISAN. Sunset to Sunset.					15th NISAN. Sunset to Sunset.					15th TISRI. Sunset to Sunset.				
		Julian.	Gregorian.	Julian.	Gregorian.	Day of Week.	Fixed Alexandran Calendar.	Vague Egyptian Calendar.	Julian.	Gregorian.	Day of Week.	Fixed Alexandran Calendar.	Vague Egyptian Calendar.	Julian.	Gregorian.	Day of Week.	Fixed Alexandran Calendar.	Vague Egyptian Calendar.	Julian.	Gregorian.	Day of Week.
3996.*	B.C. 5.*	March 8·34.	March 6·34.	March 9-10.	March 7-8.	Thurs.-Frid.	Phamen. 27.	Pharmu. 2.	March 22-23.	March 20-21.	Wedns.-Thurs.	Phamen. 28.	Pharmu. 3.	March 23-24.	March 21-22.	Thurs.-Frid.	Phamen. 28.	Pharmu. 3.	Sept. 16-17.	Sept. 14-15.	Sat.-Sun.
3997.	B.C. 4.†	March 27·24.	March 25·24.	March 28-29.	March 26-27.	Wedns.-Thurs.	Pharmu. 16.	Pharmu. 21.	April 10-11.	April 8-9.	Tues.-Wedns.	Pharmu. 17.	Pharmu. 22.	April 11-12.	April 9-10.	Wedns.-Thurs.	Pharmu. 17.	Pharmu. 22.	Octob. 5-6.	Octob. 3-4.	Frid.-Sat.
3998.	B.C. 3.	March 16·61.	March 14·61.	March 17-18.	March 15-16.	Sun.-Mon.	Pharmu. 5.	Pharmu. 10.	March 30-31.	March 28-29.	Sat.-Sun.	Pharmu. 6.	Pharmu. 11.	Mar. 31 Apl. 1.	March 29-30.	Sun.-Mon.	Pharmu. 6.	Pharmu. 11.	Sept. 24-25.	Sept. 22-23.	Tues.-Wedns.
4027.	A.D. 27.	March 26·08.	March 24·08.	March 27-28.	March 25-26.	Thurs.-Frid.	Pharmu. 15.	Pharmu. 27.	April 9-10.	April 7-8.	Wedns.-Thurs.	Pharmu. 16.	Pharmu. 28.	April 10-11.	April 8-9.	Thurs.-Frid.	Pharmu. 16.	Pharmu. 28.	Octob. 4-5.	Octob. 2-3.	Sat.-Sun.
4028.*	A.D. 28.*	March 14·45.	March 12·45.	March 15-16.	March 13-14.	Mon.-Tues.	Pharmu. 3.	Pharmu. 16.	March 28-29.	March 26-27.	Sun.-Mon.	Pharmu. 4.	Pharmu. 17.	March 29-30.	March 27-28.	Mon.-Tues.	Pharmu. 4.	Pharmu. 17.	Sept. 22-23.	Sept. 20-21.	Wedns.-Thurs.
4029.†	A.D. 29.†	April 2·35.	March 31·35.	April 3-4.	April 1-2.	Sun.-Mon.	Pharmu. 22.	Pakhon. 5.	April 16-17.	April 14-15.	Sat.-Sun.	Pharmu. 23.	Pakhon. 6.	April 17-18.	April 15-16.	Sun.-Mon.	Pharmu. 23.	Pakhon. 6.	Octob. 11-12.	Octob. 9-10.	Tues.-Wed.
4030.	A.D. 30.	March 22·73.	March 20·73.	March 23-24.	March 21-22.	Thurs.-Frid.	Pharmu. 11.	Pharmu. 24.	April 5-6.	April 3-4.	Wedns.-Thurs.	Pharmu. 12.	Pharmu. 25.	April 6-7.	April 4-5.	Thurs.-Frid.	Pharmu. 12.	Pharmu. 25.	Sep. 30 Oct. 1.	Sept. 28-29.	Sat.-Sun.
4031.	A.D. 31.	March 12·08.	March 10·08.	March 13-14.	March 11-12.	Tues.-Wedns.	Pharmu. 1.	Pharmu. 14.	March 26-27.	March 24-25.	Mon.-Tues.	Pharmu. 2.	Pharmu. 15.	March 27-28.	March 25-26.	Tues.-Wed.	Pharmu. 2.	Pharmu. 15.	Sept. 20-21.	Sept. 18-19.	Thurs.-Frid.
4032.*†	A.D. 32.*†	March 30·98.	March 28·98.	Mar. 31 Apl. 1.	March 29-30.	Mon.-Tues.	Pharmu. 19.	Pakhon. 3.	April 13-14.	April 11-12.	Sun.-Mon.	Pharmu. 20.	Pakhon. 4.	April 14-15.	April 12-13.	Mon.-Tues.	Pharmu. 20.	Pakhon. 4.	Octob. 8-9.	Octob. 6-7.	Wedns.-Thurs.
4033.	A.D. 33.	March 19·35.	March 17·35.	March 20-21.	March 18-19.	Frid.-Sat.	Pharmu. 8.	Pharmu. 22.	April 2-3.	Mar. 31 Apl. 1.	Thurs.-Frid.	Pharmu. 9.	Pharmu. 23.	April 3-4.	April 1-2.	Frid.-Sat.	Pharmu. 9.	Pharmu. 23.	Sept. 27-28.	Sept. 25-26.	Sun.-Mon.

EXPLANATORY NOTES:—(1) (*)=LEAP YEAR.
(2) Astronomical New Moon Dates stated in Jerusalem Time.
(3) Abbreviations for Names of Egyptian Months:—
   (a) Phamen. =Phamenoth.
   (b) Pharmu. =Pharmuthi.
   (c) Pakhon. =Pakhon.
(4) (†)=Years containing the Intercalary Month Ve-Adar.

Tabular years in first column are merely obtained by adding 4000 to A.D. years. They are not the years of any Scriptural or Historical Chronology, but they are useful for distinguishing Leap Year in relation to B.C. years, as in Plates LIX and LX.

For Gnostic Christian Egyptian Calendar alternative datings of Crucifixion, see Encyclopaedia Britannica, (11th Edit.) Vol. III, p. 891.

It is more likely that Gnostic dates are Vague Calendar Dates, rather than Alexandrian fixed Calendar Dates. If therefore these dates agree with 14-15 Nisan for A.D. 30, it is likely the agreement will be found in the Column of Vague Calendar Dates. This is discussed in ¶ 471 and Annotations to ¶ 471.

Lunar Eclipses of B.C. 4 recorded by Josephus, *Antiq.* XVII, vi. 4, " that very night there was an eclipse of the moon. 13th Ve-Adar=12-13 March (Jul.)=10-11 March (Greg.) Astro. Full Moon at 12·47 March (Jul.)=10·47 Mar. (Greg.) Ideler gives Eclipse as beginning at 1h. 48m. and ending at 4h. 11m. (from midnight) of March 13th (Julian), and therefore falling 13th Ve-Adar, and not in 14th Ve-Adar, the date of Astronomical Full Moon.

[To face p. 486.

—which institutions and superstitions they wove into their own peculiar conceptions of Christianity—we may be sure that their Egyptian months of reference belonged to the Egyptian vague or unintercalated year of 365 days. In Table XXXVI are given the Egyptian month datings corresponding to the 14th and 15th Nisan for years 27 to 33 A.D. inclusive, as these month datings are given by the fixed Alexandrian (Julian) calendar, and by the vague Egyptian calendar for the years stated. From this it will be seen that of three alternative Gnostic datings from the " Encyclopædia Britannica " none of them agree with either calendar for any of the years 28, 29, 31, 32, and 33 A.D. In 30 A.D., however, it will be noted that the stated date of 25 Pharmuthi of the vague year calendar fell on Friday, 7th April, the 15th Nisan for that year.

One gives the true dating of the current Egyptian vague year for 30 A.D.

Now we have shown in Table XI Annotations, Col. 4, that the Egyptian king Uasarkon II altered the beginning of the calendar year from the former beginning at 1st Mesore to a beginning at 1st Thoth, which remained as the first month of the year until the vague year was finally discarded some time about the 4th century A.D. We showed that Uasarkon effected his alteration for a certain astronomical purpose, by omitting what should have been the current month Mesore. The King List of Manetho (Version of Africanus) by its totals for Dynasties XIX to XXXI inclusive—ignoring the Harris Papyrus interregnum—shows that the late Alexandrian schools of theoretical chronographers were aware of the alteration previously effected. One or other of the Alexandrian cults endeavoured to restore the original calendar, ignoring the change, and considering the alleged Sothic cycle of 1460 years to end as they believed it should have ended. In addition to all this, there were two Alexandrian theories as to the extent of the omission from the calendar. One held that the omission had been one of a month of 30 days only ; another held that the omission included the terminal epact of 5 days, as well as the 30 days of Mesore. The effect of the first theory would have been that Pharmuthi 25 should be Phamenoth 25 for the 15th Nisan in 30 A.D. Hence the latter alternative Gnostic dating for the 15th Nisan. The second theory, however, does not account for the third alternative dating. The facts relating to the Alexandrian theories mentioned are given in the Annotations on next page.

Another gives the true dating for 30 A.D. according to the vague year calendar, restored to its original Mesore month beginning.

Another chronological revision, with a known attendant blunder, accounts for this third alternative Gnostic dating. In 46 B.C. Julius Cæsar instituted the Julian calendar and method of intercalation. The same method of intercalation was adopted for the fixed Alexandrian Egyptian calendar. The Julian intercalation was at first, in error, made at the end of every three years, instead of, as intended, every four. The error was discovered at the time of Augustus and correction was made for it at the end of 36 years.[1] In the case, however, with which we are dealing, we have to consider that the dating is the result of a Gnostic calculation. If this calculation was made with reference to the vague Egyptian calendar, and on the presumption

The third Gnostic dating gives the true dating for 30 A.D. according to the Gnostic calculations based on the original erroneous intercalations of the Julian calendar from the time of Julius Cæsar.

[1] " Enc. Brit.," Vol. IV, p. 991.

THE SOTHIC CYCLE THEORIES OF THE ALEXANDRIANS, THAT FORMED THE BASES OF THE BASILIDIAN GNOSTIC CALCULATIONS FIXING THE CRUCIFIXION DATE AS FRIDAY, 7TH APRIL, A.D. 30.

The latitude datum for the observing of successive heliacal risings of Sirius in Egypt was the town of Men-neferu (Memphis). In late Egyptian times the identification was lost and Men-neferu, Grecianised as " Menophres " was supposed to be the name of a king. Some time prior to the 4th Century A.D., " Menophres " was identified as the name of the last king of Manetho's List of the XVIIIth Dynasty. In the version of Eusebius this name occurs as Menophis and Ammenophis. In the version of Africanus it is Amenophath. The three names are intended for the same king, actually Menephtah, duplicated from Dynasty XIX. This Meno-phis, then, as identified with the supposed Menophres, was believed, in the early centuries A.D., to be the king in whose reign the last Sothic cycle began. The epoch of this sup-posed cycle was therefore defined as the Era of Menophres. From the supposed identification with Menophis, alleged last king of Dynasty XVIII, the Era of Menophres was reckoned as the last year of Dynasty XVIII. In the 1st Century A.D., the number of years from the Era of Meno-phres to the death of Augustus in A.D. 14 was reckoned up from the version of Africanus. The summation of dynastic totals in Book III was reckoned as ending at Alexander's conquest of Egypt in 332 B.C. From 332 B.C. to 14 A.D. there are 345 years, and with one year for the last year of the alleged Menophres= Menophis, the summation to the death of Augustus is as follows :—

Last year Menophres= Menophis .. .. = 1 year.
Duration of Dynasty XIX (Africanus stated) 209 years.
 Book III   ,,   ,, 1050 years.

Alleged Era of Menophres to Alexander, B.C. 332 1260 years.
 B.C. 332 to death of Augustus in A.D. 14 .. 345 years.

Added total from " Era of Menophres " to death of Augustus .. .. .. 1605 years.

This summation of Manetho's totals, as preserved by Africanus, shows clearly enough that the summation of 1605 years, later adopted by Theon of Alexandria, ended at the *death* of Augustus in 14 A.D. It is a period of no chrono-logical importance except for the fact that some unknown writer of the 1st or 2nd century A.D. seems to have ad-vertised the period as the interval between Menophres and " the end of Augustus." Some time during the 3rd century A.D., however, the opinion prevailed amongst the Alexandrians that there was no interregnum between Dynasty XIX and Dynasty XX. The prevailing opinion, however, was applied differently by three separate Alexan-drian Schools. The different applications were as follows :
(1) One school held correctly that Uasarkon II had omitted a month from the calendar in his year of revision. (This is the basis of the month datings of the Cruci-fixion referred to in ¶ 471.) As shown in Table XI Annotations, Col. 4, the omission was exactly 29 days and not 30 days as reckoned by this school of Alexandrians. They held that as a result of the 30 days' omission, the 1460 years' Sothic Cycle should end 4 × 30= 120 years later than its apparent ending at 139 to 143 A.D., and therefore at 259 to 263 A.D.

(2) Another School held that the Epact of 5 days was omitted in addition to the month of 30 days in the year of revision. As a result of this, they reckoned that the Sothic cycle should end 4 × 35= 140 years later than its apparent ending at 139 to 143 A.D., and therefore at 279 to 283 A.D. This is proved by the data in the next column.

(3) A third School held that no month had been omitted, and in consequence, that the Sothic Cycle, ending apparently at 139 to 143 A.D., had commenced 1460 years previously at 1322-1318 B.C.

With the Lists of Manetho (Version of Africanus) as basis, the Alexandrian school of chronologers—referred to as the 2nd School in the preceding column—not only deleted the interregnum between Dynasty XIX and Dynasty XX, but, knowing that Dynasty XIX kings had been duplicated in the List of Dynasty XVIII, omitted the 209 years of Dynasty XIX as comprising the inter-polated period. Their summation was therefore as follows :—

Manetho, Book I (Africanus—stated)= .. 2308 years.
 ,, Book II (,, —added)= .. 2218 years.
                                                           4526 years.
Deduct for Dynasty XIX .. .. .. 209 years.

End of Dynasty XVIII = Menophis = Menophres 4317 years.
1 Sothic Cycle .. .. 1460 years.

Alleged Alexandrian date for 284 A.D. .. 5777

Now until 284 A.D., the chronology followed by the Christians of Alexandria gave 284 A.D. as year 5787 of the World. As noted by the Encyclopædia Britannica (11th Ed., Vol. vi, pp. 314, 316) in that year, 284 A.D., the Alexandrians altered the date to 5777 A.M. This is the total obtained from the summation of Manetho and the Sothic Cycle based on the alleged Epoch of Menophres= Menophis. This also explains why the Era of Augustus ended in 283 A.D., and why the Era of Diocletian, known afterwards as the Era of Martyrs, began in the 2nd year of Diocletian, 284 A.D.—the alleged 1st year of a new Sothic Cycle, according to the system of the 2nd School of Column (1).

At a later date, the followers of the 3rd School of Column (1) resuscitated the earlier statement, based on the tabulation in Column (1) opposite, that 1605 years separated the Era of Menophres and the death of Augustus. The statement was re-edited to explain that it was " the ceasing of Augustus " or " the end of Augustus," implying the end of the Era of Augustus and the beginning of the Era of Diocletian in 284 A.D. This is the meaning of Theon's statement, in the 4th Century A.D., that " there intervened between Menophres and the end (ceasing) of Augustus a period of 1605 years." The Alexandrian Greek text is as quoted by Torr, " Memphis and Mycenæ," p. 56, note d. Theon adopting the datum of Censorinus that the Sothic Cycle of 1460 years began in 1322 B.C., and ended in 139 A.D., obtained 145 years from 139 A.D. to 284 A.D., and therefore, 1605 years to the Era of Dio-cletian in 284 A.D.

Now, by Table XIII, the first three reigns of Dynasty XIX, ending with Menephtah—identified as " Menophres " by the Alexandrians —total the first 87 years of Dynasty XIX. Africanus gives the total duration of the Dynasty as 209 years stated. The difference is 122 years for the alleged duration of Dynasty XIX according to the following Alexandrian system based on the revised datum of the 1605 years above.

Alleged Era of Menophres .. .. .. 1322 B.C.
Alleged duration of Dynasty XIX after Menephtah= Men-ophres.. .. .. = 122 years.
Africanus, Book III, reckoned by Alexandrians as ending at Alexander's Conquest, 332 B.C. 868 years. } 1460 years.
B.C. 332 to A.D. 139 .. .. 470 years. }

Alleged Sothic Cycle, B.C. 1322 to A.D. 139 .. .. .. = 1460 yrs. ending 139 A.D.

These facts concerning the Alexandrian theories of chronology—together with the Gnostic theory relating to the Julian intercalations mentioned in ¶ 471—formed the bases of the three sets of Gnostic calculations (mentioned in ¶ 471) that, when examined, each define the Crucifixion of our Lord as having occurred on Friday, 7th April (Julian), A.D. 30.

that the erroneous intercalation in the Julian calendar had continued to 30 A.D., there would have been 6 intercalary days' total in excess in the presumed Julian synchronous calendar, so that the actual date of 7th April (Julian) for 15th Nisan in 30 A.D. would have been 1st April (Julian), this agreeing with the 19th Pharmuthi of the vague Egyptian calendar in 30 A.D. As this is the dating of the third Gnostic alternative, and since the other two alternate datings, as explained, agree for 7th April (Julian) 30 A.D., on the basis of the Alexandrian theories concerning the Egyptian calendar, and in one case with the facts, we conclude that the Gnostics knew that the Crucifixion occurred on 7th April (Julian) 30 A.D.

SECTION IIc.—THE MONTH-DAY AND THE WEEK-DAY OF THE CRUCIFIXION.

¶ 472. THE ESSENTIAL FEATURES OF THE PROBLEM.

Was the Crucifixion on Thursday or Friday? Although we have already given clear and definite reasons for our conclusion that the Crucifixion took place in 30 A.D., nevertheless the final proof of this dating depends upon the fixing of the month-day and the week-day of the Crucifixion.

Was it on the 14th Nisan or the 15th Nisan? Apart altogether from the question of the year, the day of the Crucifixion is a problem in itself, which resolves itself into two alternatives, viz.:

(a) Whether the Crucifixion was on a Thursday or on a Friday.
(b) Whether the Crucifixion was on the 14th or 15th Nisan.

In 30 A.D. the 15th Nisan coincided with Friday.

If the scriptural evidence defines that the Crucifixion occurred on the sixth day of the week (Friday) and also that it occurred on the 15th Nisan, the previous indications from scriptural and historical sources fixing 30 A.D. as the year of the Crucifixion are confirmed. As we have seen from the astronomical evidence, the fixing and arrangement of the calendar determined that the full moon of Nisan should fall on the 14th of the month. This means that the preceding 1st Nisan was one day later than the astronomical new moon. Now, in 30 A.D. the astronomical new moon for Nisan occurred on 22.74th March (Julian) or 20.74th March (Greg.) by Jerusalem time. This was at 5 hrs. 23 min. in the afternoon of 22nd March (Julian), less than an hour before sunset. Hence the 1st Nisan, 30 A.D., began at sunset, 23rd March (Julian), and the 14th Nisan began at sunset, Wednesday, 5th April (Julian), and ended at sunset, Thursday, 6th April (Julian), on the fifth day of the week. It would appear, therefore, that the Crucifixion must be dated Friday, 15th Nisan, 30 A.D. If all the scriptural evidence agrees with this identity, this agreement, combined with all the other evidence we have adduced in support of 30 A.D., must definitely establish that 30 A.D. is the year of the Crucifixion. The scriptural evidence at our disposal for the purpose of this discussion is very full and complete, and the guiding rule of our investigation must be that no single detail in the narrative of any one gospel shall disagree with a parallel detail in the narrative of any other gospel.

¶ 473. THE TIME OF OUR LORD'S LAST SUPPER.

Tables XXXVII and XXXVIII confirm the statements of the following text. Let the reader now make a careful study of Tables XXXVII and XXXVIII, for all the scriptural evidence has been embodied in these tables, and the discussion in the text will be confined to matters explanatory of, or extraneous to, the tables, and statements will be made that can only be confirmed by reference to these tables.

TABLE XXXVII.

THE PASSOVERS OF THE EXODUS AND CRUCIFIXION YEARS

(For the days of the Week in the Exodus Year refer ¶¶ 324–327).

3RD APRIL (GREG.)	ENDS →	← BEGINS	4TH APRIL (GREG.)	1486 B.C.
NOON SUN-SET		MID-NIGHT	SUN-RISE	NO
FIFTH DAY OF THE WEEK →		THE SIXTH DAY OF THE HEBREW WEEK		(CONTIN
14TH NISAN (ABIB) ENDS →← BEGINS		15TH NISAN (ABIB) 1486 B.C.	→ 15TH NISAN (CONTIN	

The Passover Lamb to be kept " until the 14th day of the same (1st) month (Nisan, or Abib)..

Exod. xii, 6,   ...kill it in the evening " (Hebrew " between the two evenings ").

Exod. xii, 7,   The sprinkling of the door and lintel with the blood of the lamb.

Exod. xii, 8, " eat the flesh in that night....*and unleavened bread*." Exod. xii, 11, " with *your* loins girded, your shoes on your feet, and your staff in your hand....eat it in haste : IT IS THE LORD'S PASSOVER."

"At midnight the Lord smote all the first-born in Egypt." Exod. xii, 29.

(midnight)

Exod. xii, 12, " For I will PASS through the land of Egypt this night and will smite.."

Exod. xii, 42, " It is a night to be much observed unto the Lord for bringing them out from the land of Egypt."

Deut. xvi, 1, " for in the month Abib (Nisan) the Lord thy God brought thee forth out of Egypt by *night* : " this referring to the cause producing the effect.

Exod. xii, 41, " the selfsame day that all the hosts of the Lord we land of Egypt."

Numbers xxxiii, 3, " and they Rameses in the 1st month, on the 1st month ; on THE MORN PASSOVER the children of Isra an high hand IN THE SIGH Egyptians."

Exod. xii, 13,   " The BLOOD shall be to you for a TOKEN upon the houses where ye are : and when I see the blood I will (THE BLOOD A TOKEN).   PASS OVER you."

NOON   SUN-SET   THE FIRST STAGE OF ISRAEL'S SALVATION.   SUN-RISE   NO

Exodus xii, 21, " Take a lamb...and KILL THE PASSOVER."

Exod. xii, 22,   " Strike the lintel and the two side posts with the blood."

(midnight)

Exodus xii, 22, " None of you shall go out of his house *until the morning*."

xii, 23, " when He seeth the blood upon the lintel and on the two side posts the Lord will PASS OVER the door."

Exod. xiii, 3-4, " and Moses people, Remember this day, in wh from Egypt......*there shall no l* eaten. This day came ye out in (Nisan)."

Exod. xii, 26-27, " And it shall come to pass, when your children shall say unto you, What mean ye by this service ? That ye shall say,

IT IS THE SACRIFICE OF THE LORD'S PASSOVER."

xii, 24, " Ye shall observe this thing (*i.e.*, as verses 21-23) for an ordinance........for ever."

Levit. xxiii, 5,   " In the 14th day of the 1st month *between the two evenings* is the Lord's Passover."

Deut. xvi, 6,   Passover lamb sacrificed at " *the going down of the sun*."

Exod. xii, 18,   " In the 1st month on the 14th day of the month at even (*i.e.*, dusk) ye shall eat unleavened bread, until the 21st day of the month at even (dusk)."

Levit. xxiii, 5, clearly refers to the sacrifice of the Passover ; the killing of the lamb. Note the rapid sequence of Exod. xii, 6-13. Killing and sprinkling on 14th Nisan ; eating and being preserved by the blood on 15th Nisan.

(midnight)

Exod. xii, 30-33, Pharaoh calls Moses and Aaron by night and bids them take Israel out of Egypt.

Israel carry their dough befor (Ex. xii, 34).

Exod. xii, 39, " and they bak which they brought out of Egyp

The commemoration of this Temple, and of New Testament the Talmud, the *Chagigah*, co afternoon of 15th Nisan.

Levit. xxiii, 6, " And on the 15th day of the same month is the FEAST OF UNLEAVENED BREAD unto the Lord : seven d unleavened bread." Compare with Exodus xii, 8—the flesh of the Passover lamb sacrificed prior to the sunset beginning 15th Nisan, unleavened bread " in that night." Compare also the ordinance concerning the 2nd Passover, for those not able to keep the first, sacrificed " between the two evenings " of 14th day, 2nd month, and eaten thereafter with unleavened bread (Numbers ix, 11).

The eating of the 2nd Passover therefore commemorates the giving of quails on the evening beginning the 15th day of the 2nd mo 1-15), and manna on the morning following.

Quails, the 2nd Passover supper)............and............(manna, " bread to eat " (Exod. xvi, 15), the type of the 1st bakin 1st Passover.

Note that the 6 days of quails and manna in Month II are 6 week days, and that the 7th day (following) is the 1st instituted Sa history. Refer ¶ 326.

Numbers, xxviii, 16-18, " The 14th day of the 1st month (Nisan), is the Passover of the Lord. And in the 15th day of this month is seven days shall unleavened bread be eaten. In the 1st day (*i.e.*, 15th Nisan) shall be an holy convocation : ye shall do no manner o A SABBATH or rest day.

Compare above with Exodus xii, 18, above (under 14th Nisan) and Deut. xvi, 6, showing that " the Passover of the Lord " in Nu refers to the whole festival of " the sacrifice of the Lord's Passover " (Exod. xii, 21-24 above) which began with the " killing of t lamb) " on 14th Nisan, and prior to sunset beginning 15th Nisan.

The Hebrew interval known as " BE-TWEEN THE TWO EVEN-INGS," defined by 1 Kings, xxii, 35, 36, as preceding SUN."

"The king (Ahab)....in his chariot....died *between the two evenings* ;....and there went a proclamation throughout the whole host about *the going down of the sun*."

" THE GOING DOWN OF THE SUN."

The Hebrew day consisted of " evening-morning " or " night and day." Thus 14th Nisan began with the commencement of " evening " (night or darkness). This " evening " (darkness) ended at dawn of 14th Nisan. The " morning " (daylight) of 14th Nisan extended from sunrise to sunset ; when the " evening " (darkness) of 15th Nisan began. Noon of 14th Nisan therefore lay midway " between the two evenings," *i.e.*, between dawn ending the " evening " of 14th Nisan and sunset beginning the " evening " of 15th Nisan. Noon of 14th Nisan is therefore " between the two evenings " ; which hour is followed by " the going down of the sun," during the afternoon.

"And the 1st day of unleavened bread, when they KILLED (SACRIFICED) THE PASSOVER, His disciples said unto Him, Where wilt Thou that we go and prepare that Thou mayest EAT THE PASSOVER."

Compare Leviticus xxiii, 5; Deut. xvi, 6; Exodus xii, 18; and Numbers xxviii, 16 above, in relation to Levit. xxiii, 6 and Exod. xii, 21-24.

"they made ready the Passover."

"Now the FEAST OF UN-LEAVENED BREAD drew nigh WHICH IS CALLED THE PASSOVER."

The Passover lamb of the priests was selected on 10th Nisan (Exod. xii, 13) and was sacrificed by them on the afternoon of 14th Nisan. The appointed Lamb—"the lamb of God" (John i 29) "slain from the foundation of the world" (Rev. xiii, 8)—for that year was "Christ our Passover." He came up to Jerusalem on 10th Nisan, but was rejected by the priests, but was accepted by God as His Spiritual Sacrifice. On this day (John x,ii 23-33) Jesus said "The hour is come, that the Son of man should be glorified....Now is my soul troubled ; and what shall I say ? Father, save me from this hour : ....Father, glorify Thy Name. Then came there a voice from Heaven, saying, I have both glorified it, and will glorify it again.....Jesus answered and said, This voice came not because of me, BUT FOR YOUR SAKES....And I, if I be lifted up from the earth will draw all men unto me. This He said, signifying what death He should die."

Jesus was accepted by God as His Spiritual Sacrifice, as "Christ our Passover" (I Cor. v, 7). Had He, therefore, been crucified on 14th Nisan, when the literal Passover was sacrificed, the spiritual and the literal sacrifices would have been confused. Christ was the true Spiritual Sacrifice from the foundation of the world. The Sacrifice of the Passover lamb was a literal enactment typifying this Spiritual Sacrifice. Hence that "the blood of the lamb was a token" of the Great Passover, and hence the tokens of our Lord's Last Supper.

"And in the evening He cometh with the twelve."

Mark xiv, 17, "And in the evening He cometh with the twelve."

Mark xiv, 22-24, "And as they did eat, Jesus took bread, and blessed, and brake it, and gave it to them, and said, Take, eat : THIS IS MY BODY. And He took the cup, and when He had given thanks, He gave it to them ; and they all drank of it. And He said unto them, THIS IS MY BLOOD OF THE NEW TESTAMENT, which IS SHED FOR MANY."

THE BLOOD A TOKEN. (Refer Ex. xii, 13 above.)

After which our Lord said (John xvi, 33 ; xvii, 1-4) "I have overcome the world."

"Father, THE HOUR is come : Glorify Thy Son, that Thy Son also may glorify Thee : As Thou hast given Him power over all flesh, that He should give eternal life to as many as Thou hast given Him.. I have finished the work which Thou gavest me to do."

THE BREAD—THE BODY OF CHRIST. (Refer ¶ 391.)

SPIRITUAL ISRAEL THE MYSTICAL BODY OF CHRIST.
"THE CHURCH WHICH IS HIS BODY." Refer I Cor. xii, 12-31 ; Col. i, 18 ; Hence I Cor. x, 16-17, "The bread which we break, is it not the communion of the body of Christ ? For we being many are one bread, and one body : for we are all partakers of that one bread." Or as R.V. margin, "We who are many, are ONE LOAF, one body."

But there are two Bodies. There is also.. "THE BRIDE"—LITERAL ISRAEL—(¶ 321). "For thy Maker is thine husband.......thy Redeemer the Holy One of Israel.......For the Lord hath called thee (Israel) as a woman...." Isa. liv, 5, 6.

"I will show thee the bride, the Lamb's wife ......the names of the twelve tribes of the children of Israel." Rev. xxi, 9-12.

There being two symbolical "bodies "—the Spiritual Israel (Christ's Body) and Literal Israel, the Lamb's Bride—and one "loaf" symbolising the Spiritual Israel, another "loaf" should symbolise the literal Israel. Hence the significance of the two loaves of fine flour brought as a wave offering at the Feast of Pentecost (Levit. xxiii, 17) seven weeks after the predetermined day of the Resurrection of the body of our Lord, "the first-fruits of the grave." (Refer ¶ 326.)

THE FIRST STAGE OF MANKIND'S SALVATION.

THE PASSING OVER OF DEATH FROM MANKIND.

OUR LORD'S MIDNIGHT AGONY IN GETHSEMANE.

" Father, if Thou be willing, remove this cup from me : nevertheless, not my will, but Thine, be done. ..and being in an agony ....His sweat was as it were great drops of blood falling down to the ground." Luke xxii, 42-44.

Judas betrays our Lord to the priests. Luke xxii, 47-54.

(midnight)

As the events of the night of the 15th Nisan in the Exodus year shaped the circumstances that determined the Exodus after dawn of the 15th of Nisan, so do the events of the night of the 15th Nisan in the Crucifixion year shape the events that followed after dawn.

"THY WILL BE DONE." Luke xxii, 42.

Our Lord's midnight prayer answered by the betrayal of Judas, by our Lord being led, during dark, " to Caiaphas, the high priest, where the Scribes and Elders were assembled," who answered " He is guilty of death." Matt. xxvi, 57-66. The result of His trial after dawn was predetermined by the circumstances before dawn.

As there are two "loaves" symbolising the two "bodies " (of the preceding annotations), so there are two Passovers (as under the Exodus institutions above). There is a Second Passover for those not able to partake of the First. The 2nd Passover commemorated the first day of manna and quails (refer ¶326). Our Lord deals with this fully in John vi, 26-65, " I am the bread which came down from heaven.....I am that bread of Life. Your fathers did eat manna in the wilderness, and are dead. This is the bread which cometh down from heaven, that a man may eat thereof, and not die. I am the living bread.......the bread that I will give is my flesh, which I will give for the life of the world."

Then, concerning the significance of the 2nd Passover, our Lord, between His Resurrection and Ascension, held a 2nd Feast with His disciples, when they drew the miraculous draft of 153 fishes, symbolising the Church (¶¶ 339, 340, 350, 351). John xxi, 9, "as soon then as they were come to land, they saw a fire of coals there, and FISH laid thereon, and bread. Jesus saith unto them, BRING OF THE FISH WHICH YOU HAVE NOW CAUGHT. Simon Peter........drew the net to land full of great fishes, 153........Jesus saith........Come and dine........Jesus then cometh, and taketh bread, and giveth them, and fish likewise." Observe the two lots of Fish as in the case of the two Loaves."

THE FEAST-DAY that was a memorial of the baking of the unleavened dough in the first journey after leaving Rameges. Exod. xii, 39, above.

Then was celebrated the actual ritual of the FEAST OF UNLEAVENED BREAD. It is this Feast that John xiii, 1-2, defines as "the feast of the Passover," since he states that our Lord's Supper was ended, and Jesus was washing His disciples' feet " before the feast of the Passover." Hence that John xiii, 26-30, relating to the conclusion of the Supper on the evening beginning 15th Nisan, and as concerning our Lord telling Judas to proceed "quickly " with his work of betrayal states " For some thought, because Judas had the bag, that Jesus had said unto him, Buy those things that we have need of against the FEAST....and it was night," i.e., prior to midnight of 15th Nisan. The FEAST therefore relates to a FEAST during the daytime of 15th Nisan.

Literal Israel being typified by one of the two loaves of Levit. xxiii, 17 (as preceding annotations to the left), so the Exodus of Israel on the 15th of Nisan (6th day of the week) prefigured the Exodus of our Lord on the 15th of Nisan (6th day of the week). Luke ix, 31, therefore, states concerning our Lord's transfiguration, and the appearance of Moses and Elias, that the latter " spake of His decease (Greek—Exodus) which he should accomplish at Jerusalem."

As, at dawn of the 15th of Nisan, Israel began their Great Exodus, so, " as soon as it was day " on the 15th of Nisan," the elders....chief priests and scribes.....led Him into their council "—the first stage of His Exodus. He was then led before Pilate. " It was the preparation (i.e., the day before the Sabbath of the Passover (i.e., signifying that the Sabbath following was a particular Sabbath, " a high "Sabbath "), and about the 6th hour " (i.e., 9 a.m. to 12 noon). John xix, 14.

" And they took Jesus and led Him away. And He bearing His cross went forth......" (John xix, 16-17), even as, 1515 years previously Israel's " going forth" had been prefigured by Israel's going forth with their unleavened dough " bound.....upon their shoulders." The first feast of the Exodus—the feast of the baked unleavened dough—prefigured, on the day and at the hour, the crucifixion of our Lord, " the bread of life " ; " my flesh."

* Hence John xix, 31.

"THE FIRST DAY OF UNLEAVENED BREAD,
when they killed (sacrificed) the Passover," Mark xiv, 12.
(above, quoted in full under 14th Nisan).

Compare with Levit. xxiii, 5 and 6 above ; Exod. xii, 18 (verses 7-27 ; 51) above ; and with Numbers xxiii, 5 above.

14TH NISAN	ENDS →	← BEGINS	15TH NISAN A.D. 30	15TH NISAN (CONTINUES)
DAY OF THE WEEK	→	←	THE SIXTH DAY OF THE HEBREW WEEK	(CONTINUES)
MON	SUN-SET	MID-NIGHT	SUN-RISE	NOON

4TH APRIL (GREG.)   ENDS → ← BEGINS   5TH APRIL (GREG.)   A.D. 30.

---

om Notes on Ch. xxiii, Leviticus, by the Rev. C. D. Ginsberg, LL.D., in Vol. I, "Old Test. Commentary for English Readers," Edited by Charles John Ellicot, D.D., Lord Bishop of Gloucester.

rse 5 :—" In the fourteenth day of the first month." is called Abib in the Pentateuch (Exod. xiii, 4, xt. xvi, 1), and Nisan in the later books of Scripture ther, iii, 7)...... All handicraftsmen, the tailors, barbers and laundresses, were obliged to k either from morning or from noon, according to the different places in Palestine. Leaven was mid-day, and it had to be burned in the forenoon. desisting from and burning the leaven was thus Two desecrated cakes of thanksgiving offerings a bench in the Temple ; as long as they were thus the people ate leaven. When one of them was abstained from eating but did not burn it ; but

when the other was taken away all the people began burning the leaven." It was on this day that every Israelite who was not infirm, ceremoniously defiled, uncircumcised, or beyond 15 miles from the walls of Jerusalem, had to appear before the Lord in the Holy City, with an offering in proportion to his means (Exod. xxiii, 15 ; Deut. xvi, 16, 17). Those who came from the country were gratuitously accommodated by the inhabitants with the necessary apartments (Luke xvii, 10-12 ; Matt. xxvi, 18), and the guests in acknowledgment of the hospitality they received left to their hosts the skins of the paschal lambs, and the vessels which they used in their religious ceremonies. Josephus, who was an eye-witness to the fact, tells us that at the Passover, in the reign of Nero, there were 2,700,000 people, when 256,500

lambs were sacrificed. Most of the Jews must therefore have encamped in tents without the walls of the city, as the Mohammedan pilgrims now do at Mecca. It was for this reason that the Romans took great precaution, using both force and conciliatory measures, during festivals (Matt. xxvi, 5 ; Luke xiii, 1).

Note to verse 5 : " At Even ; " or, in the evening, as the A. V. renders this phrase in the parallel passage (Exod. xii, 6), literally denotes " between the two evenings " ....The paschal lamb in the evening sacrifice began to be killed and the blood sprinkled at 12-30 p.m. This is more in harmony with the fact that the large number of sacrifices on this day could only be offered up in the longer period of time.

TABLE XXXVIII.

NOTE.—In comparing the Gregorian month datings for 1486 B.C. and 30 A.D., it must be remembered that the Gregorian rule of intercalation causes the Gregorian month datings to oscillate generally within a range of a day before or after the fixed dates of the true solar year.

THE EVENTS LEADING UP TO AND INCLUDING THE EXODUS OF ISRAEL ARE REPRESENTED BY THE SACRED NARRATIVE AS PREFIGURING THE EVENTS LEADING UP TO AND INCLUDING THE EXODUS ("decease" Greek = Exodus, Luke ix, 31) OF OUR LORD.

(Refer Table XXXVII and ¶¶ 325-328).

For the days of the week in the Exodus Year refer ¶¶ 324, 325.

| A.D. 30 CRUCIFIXION YEAR | | | EXODUS YEAR 1486 B.C. | | |
GREGORIAN MONTH DATES	DAYS OF THE WEEK / HEBREW MONTH DATES		HEBREW MONTH DATES / DAYS OF THE WEEK		GREGORIAN MONTH DATES
30TH MARCH	7TH DAY	9TH NISAN	9TH NISAN	7TH DAY	30TH MARCH
31ST MARCH	1ST DAY	10TH NISAN	10TH NISAN	1ST DAY	30TH MARCH
	2ND DAY	11TH NISAN	11TH NISAN	2ND DAY	31ST MARCH
1ST APRIL	1ST DAY	12TH NISAN	11TH NISAN	3RD DAY	31ST MARCH
2ND APRIL	2ND DAY	13TH NISAN	12TH NISAN	3RD DAY	1ST APRIL
3RD APRIL	4TH DAY	14TH NISAN	13TH NISAN	4TH DAY	2ND APRIL
	3RD DAY	15TH NISAN	14TH NISAN	3RD DAY	3RD APRIL

Sunset beginning 9th Nisan { "JESUS, 6 DAYS BEFORE THE PASSOVER, CAME TO BETHANY," John xii, 1.

The anointing of the "Lamb of God" (John xii, 3-9) "for My Burial," Matt. xxvi, 12; John xii, 7. In Matt. xxvi, 3-13, and Mark xiv, 3-9, this event does not come in chronological order, as it does in John xii, 1-9.

THE TRIUMPHAL ENTRY INTO JERUSALEM (PALM SUNDAY), ON THE NEXT DAY (10th Nisan), John xii, 12

OUR LORD AS THE "LAMB OF GOD," ACCEPTED BY GOD AS HIS SACRIFICE. John xii, 27-33.

"In the 10th day of this month (Nisan=Abib) they shall take to them every man a LAMB,....a lamb for an house;....keep it up until the 14th day of the same month......kill it in the evening" (i.e., "between the two evenings" =noon and after, as see Table XXXVII). Exod. xii, 3-6.

Matt. xxi, 18-22, and Mark xi, 12-19 give the narrative concerning the "morrow" following 10th Nisan.

Matt. xxi, 23-xxvi, 5, and Mark xi, 20-xiv, 2, give the narrative concerning the 2nd "morrow" after 10th Nisan.

The definition of the day is given by Mark xi, 20 in relation to xi, 12.

On the afternoon of this day (Matt. xxvi, 2 and Mark xiv, 1) Jesus said "after two days is the feast of the Passover and the Son of Man is betrayed TO BE crucified"; 2 days to intervene and to be followed by the Betrayal. (Refer also Mark x, 32-34).

In His statement quoted above, our Lord equates the time of His betrayal with the time of the feast of the Passover.

Here the fact is emphasised that God's Sacrifice of His Son—the Lamb of God—consisted of His having permitted His Son to be betrayed by one of our Lord's own disciples. The betrayal was possible only by our Lord's isolation "in the heart of the earth" for "three days and three nights." The isolation ended at the Resurrection.

"In the heart of the earth" denotes, not burial, but completeness of isolation. The "spiritual body" of "natural man" exists in this state, whether encased in the flesh, or released at death. This state is the "unseen world" of the New Testament writers, who thus understood the Hades of the Greeks. Death makes no difference to the spiritual state. For "three days and three nights" our Lord was "cut off"—isolated—in that state; half the period in the flesh, and half the period in death. Refer Eph. iv, 9; I Peter iii, 19; Luke xxiii, 43.

The Feast of Unleavened Bread. The Sacrifice of the Lord's Passover. Both prefigured the principal aspects of the purpose of our Lord's Sacrifice. Both began from noon of the 14th of Nisan.

At noon of 14th Nisan, leaven was put away. (Ginsberg, note on Table XXXVII.) The putting away of leaven signified the purpose of the Messiah in becoming "the Last Adam" to "purge from the seed of the First Adam" the leaven of malice and wickedness," in preparation for the receiving of "the unleavened bread of sincerity and truth." I Cor. v, 7-8, and xv, 44-58.

To become fully and effectively the last Adam our Lord had of necessity to be "cut off," or isolated from His supremely high spiritual state. He descended—when still in the flesh—into the realm of the spiritual body of the seed of the First Adam. This prefigured by the putting away of leaven at noon of 14th Nisan. The 14th of Nisan of the Crucifixion year was, therefore, appropriately the first day of the "three days and three nights in the heart of the earth," i.e., our Lord's complete spiritual descent (isolation), as the Last Adam, to purge the leaven from the spiritual state of the seed of the First Adam. This explains the significance of one aspect of the enactment of our Lord's Last Supper on the evening following the noon at which leaven was put away. He gave His disciples the symbolic offering of the "unleavened bread of sincerity and truth"; the bread, "My flesh"; thereby signifying that thereafter they were "partakers of one Body" (refer Table XXXVII) from which "the old leaven" had been purged (I Cor. v, 7-8.)

The following noon of 15th Nisan witnessed His death upon the Cross, typified 1515 years earlier by the first feast of the Exodus, made from the baked unleavened dough.

The killing of the Passover lamb began after noon of 14th Nisan (Refer Table XXXVII & Ginsberg note.)

The "Sacrifice of the Lord's Passover" extended the full 24 hours over noon of 15th Nisan. As the selection of the Paschal lamb by the priests on the 10th Nisan prefigured God's acceptance of His Son as the appointed Sacrifice (God's Sacrifice—as refer column opposite at 10th Nisan—so the "cutting-off" of the life of the lamb by the priests on the afternoon of 14th Nisan prefigured the spiritual "cutting off" of our Lord on the 14th Nisan, the first of the "three days and three nights in the heart of the earth."

Again, the sprinkling of the blood of the lamb as a "token" and the eating of the Paschal Supper on the afternoon and evening respectively of 14th-15th Nisan prefigured the giving of the wine to His disciples and the spiritual significance of the enactment—as a "token" of His blood to preserve from death; and the eating of the "token" of His Body. The Passing over of the angel of death at midnight of 15th Nisan at the Exodus, again, prefigured the midnight agony of our Lord's spiritually bridging the gap between man's spiritual state and the high spiritual realms from which He Himself had been "cut off"; thus affecting the "Passing over" of death from mankind.

His going forth to Pilate and forth from Pilate with His Cross was the first journey of His Exodus. The second journey of His Exodus began at His death, when spiritually He passed into the cul-de-sac of the wilderness that shut Him off from life. At the anniversary of the crossing of the Sea of Reeds—and at the dawn of the same day of the week, day of the month and day of the year (1515)—the Last Adam burst the partition of death that had been imposed on the seed of the First Adam. This ended our Lord's Cycle of "three days and three nights in the heart of the earth."

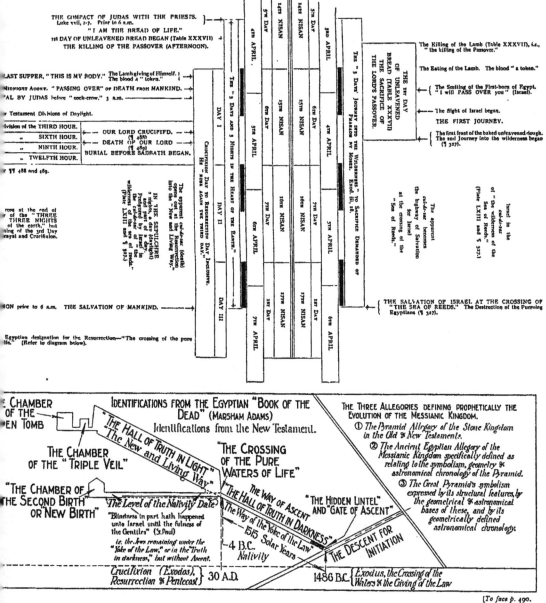

THE COMPACT OF JUDAS WITH THE PRIESTS. }
Luke xxii, 1-7. Prior to 6 a.m.
"I AM THE BREAD OF LIFE."
1st DAY OF UNLEAVENED BREAD BEGAN (Table XXXVII)
THE KILLING OF THE PASSOVER (AFTERNOON).

LAST SUPPER, "THIS IS MY BODY." The Lamb giving of Himself. }
The blood a "token." {
MIDNIGHT AGONY. "PASSING OVER" of DEATH from MANKIND.
"AL BY JUDAS before "cock-crow." 3 a.m.

Testament Divisions of Daylight.
vision of the THIRD HOUR.
"   "   SIXTH HOUR.   OUR LORD CRUCIFIED.
"   "   NINTH HOUR.   DEATH OF OUR LORD
"   "   TWELFTH HOUR.   BURIAL BEFORE SABBATH BEGAN.

¶¶ 488 and 489.

rose at the end of
of the "THREE
THREE NIGHTS
of the earth," but
ning of the 3rd Day
trayal and Crucifixion.

ON prior to 6 a.m.   THE SALVATION OF MANKIND.

Egyptian designation for the Resurrection—"The crossing of the pure
life." (Refer to diagram below).

CRUCIFIXION DAY to RESURRECTION DAY INCLUSIVE.
He "ROSE AGAIN THE THIRD DAY."

DAY I
DAY II
DAY III

Ten "3 Days and 3 Nights in the Heart of the Earth."

IN THE SEPULCHRE
"3 nights, a day (daylight)
and part of a day (at
Passover), in the
wilderness of the sea of
reeds." (Plate LXIII and ¶ 327.)

The apparent cul-de-sac (death)
opens out, at the Resurrection,
into the "New and Living Way."

CRUCIFIXION DAY to RESURRECTION DAY INCLUSIVE.

5TH DAY
4TH APRIL
14TH NISAN
5TH APRIL
3RD APRIL
6TH DAY
15TH NISAN
4TH APRIL
7TH DAY
16TH NISAN
5TH APRIL
1ST DAY
17TH NISAN
6TH APRIL

THE "3 DAYS' JOURNEY INTO THE WILDERNESS" TO SACRIFICE DEMANDED OF PHARAOH BY MOSES. Exod. iii, 18.

THE 1ST DAY
OF UNLEAVENED
BREAD (TABLE XXXVII)
THE SACRIFICE OF
THE LORD'S PASSOVER.

The Killing of the Lamb (Table XXXVII), i.e.,
"the killing of the Passover."

The Eating of the Lamb. The blood "a token."

{ The Smiting of the First-born of Egypt.
"I will PASS OVER you" (Israel).

The flight of Israel began.
THE FIRST JOURNEY.

{ The first feast of the baked unleavened dough.
The 2nd Journey into the wilderness began
(¶ 327).

The apparent
cul-de-sac
becomes
the highway of Salvation
for Israel
at the crossing of the
"Sea of Reeds."

Israel is in the
cul-de-sac
of "the wilderness of the
Sea of Reeds,"
(Plate LXIII and ¶ 327.)

{ THE SALVATION OF ISRAEL AT THE CROSSING OF
"THE SEA OF REEDS." The Destruction of the Pursuing
Egyptians (¶ 327).

CHAMBER
OF THE
EN TOMB

IDENTIFICATIONS FROM THE EGYPTIAN "BOOK OF THE
DEAD" (MARSHAM ADAMS)
Identifications from the New Testament.

THE THREE ALLEGORIES DEFINING PROPHETICALLY THE
EVOLUTION OF THE MESSIANIC KINGDOM.
① The Pyramid Allegory of the Stone Kingdom
in the Old & New Testaments.
② The Ancient Egyptian Allegory of the
Messianic Kingdom specifically defined as
relating to the symbolism, geometry &
astronomical chronology of the Pyramid.
③ The Great Pyramid's symbolism
expressed by its structural features, by
the geometrical & astronomical
bases of these, and by its
geometrically defined
astronomical chronology.

THE HALL OF TRUTH IN LIGHT
The New and Living Way

THE CHAMBER
OF THE "TRIPLE VEIL"

"THE CROSSING
OF THE PURE
WATERS OF LIFE"

"THE CHAMBER OF
THE SECOND BIRTH"
OR "NEW BIRTH"

The Level of the Nativity Date

"Blindness in part hath happened
unto Israel until the fulness of
the Gentiles" (St. Paul)

i.e. the Jews remaining under the
"Yoke of the Law," or in the "Truth
in darkness," but without Ascent.

Crucifixion (Exodus),
Resurrection & Pentecost } 30 A.D.

THE WAY OF ASCENT
THE HALL OF TRUTH IN DARKNESS
The Way of the Yoke of the Law
1515 Solar Years
-4 B.C.
Nativity

"THE HIDDEN LINTEL"
AND "GATE OF ASCENT"

THE DESCENT FOR
INITIATION

1486 B.C. { Exodus, the Crossing of the
Waters & the Giving of the Law

[To face p. 490.

The paschal lamb was killed during the afternoon of the 14th Nisan. Two references establish this conclusion, " between the two evenings " and " the going down of the sun." As the year in Hebrew is defined as " winter-summer," and the day as " evening-morning," it appears obvious that the expression " between the two evenings " can only refer to the hour of noon, or the point of time midway between the two evenings. This is confirmed by the parallel reference to " the going down of the sun," obviously, as explained on Table XXXVII, defining the period between noon and sunset, during which period the paschal lambs were killed.[1]

The paschal lamb could be slain any time after noon of 14th Nisan, and prior to sunset beginning 15th Nisan.

The lamb was eaten during the night of the 15th Nisan, and everything tends to show that the Last Supper of our Lord was the paschal supper on this night. If we compare the details of this supper with the instructions in Exodus concerning the paschal supper, it will be seen that they agree precisely, and that the eating of the flesh of the lamb in the first paschal supper is the ante-type of the eating of the bread at the Last Supper of our Lord. The blood of the lamb is given as a token of the Old Testament ; the wine is given as a token of the New Testament. This is the impression that we obtain from the narrative of St. Mark when we consider it in relation to the instructions in Exodus ; and we hope to show that the other gospels agree with this conclusion, and that their harmony on this important point confirms the impression thus derived in every essential feature.

The paschal supper was eaten after sunset beginning 15th Nisan.

The co-ordinated details of Tables XXXVII and XXXVIII prove that our Lord's Last Supper was the paschal supper.

¶ 474. THE " TWO SABBATHS " OF THE CRUCIFIXION PASSOVER.

It is necessary at this point to examine the contention that the Crucifixion was on Thursday, the 14th Nisan. Ferrar Fenton (" The Complete Bible in Modern English ") remarks that John xx, 1 reads, " Now on the first day following the sabbaths," and that the plural word " Sabbaths " proves that two Sabbaths occurred together in the Jewish calendar. He therefore concludes that the Crucifixion took place on Thursday, 17th March 29 A.D.

John's gospel states that two " Sabbaths," i.e. two " days of rest," preceded the Resurrection.

It is difficult to see how this invalidates our previous conclusion. If the Crucifixion was on a Friday—the feast day—the 15th Nisan, the text is quite correct in saying " following the sabbaths," for, in such case, Friday and Saturday were both Sabbaths. Friday, the first day of the feast, would be deemed a Sabbath (Num. xxviii, 18), and Saturday was the normal Sabbath of the week.[2]

These were the feast day of " rest " decreed for the 15th Nisan, and the normal week day of rest—the seventh day of the week—on the 16th Nisan.

The distinction between these two Sabbaths, the one a feast day and a day of holy convocation—and therefore a day of rest—and the other the normal Sabbath of the week, is an important factor in establishing the harmony of the four gospels. The first three gospels distinctly state that our

The three gospels clearly state that our Lord's Last Supper was the paschal supper on the 15th Nisan, on the same day of the month as that on which the feast was held, when " rest " was decreed.

[1] See Dr. Ginsberg's note in Table XXXVII.

[2] Apart from all other considerations, Ferrar Fenton's date of 17th March is quite untenable. Firstly, the 17th of March is a pre-equinoctial date; and secondly (assuming a pre-equinoctial dating to be permissible), in 29 A.D. the 14th Nisan would have fallen on Friday the 18th March.

Lord partook of the paschal supper with His disciples on the night before the Crucifixion; and, according to all three accounts, the Last Supper must have been eaten on Thursday evening, 6th April (Julian), that is to say, the evening beginning the 15th Nisan. But many have concluded that the Gospel according to St. John is at utter variance with the other three gospels in this respect, and consider that, according to St. John, the Crucifixion was on the 14th Nisan, some hours before the lambs were killed, and that the Last Supper was taken on a day in advance of the true time.

¶ 475. THE FEAST DAY FOLLOWING THE LAST SUPPER.

Jesus washes His disciples' feet after the supper and before the feast.

The evidence concerning the need for haste after the supper, to buy any goods necessary for the feast following, prior to the beginning of the decreed day of " rest " on the same 15th Nisan.

The definition of the rest decreed for feast days, and of feast days that were entirely days of rest, as compared with the normal weekly day of rest.

Now St. John tells us (xiii) that Jesus washed His disciples' feet during supper before the Feast of the Passover, and later on He said to Judas, " That thou doest, do quickly." But some of the disciples thought that Jesus meant " Buy what things we have need of for the feast," because Judas was carrying a bag or wallet. This supposition on the part of some of the disciples can only be accounted for by assuming that the day following the Last Supper was a feast day.[1] Many references in the Books of Exodus, Leviticus, and Deuteronomy establish the fact that such feast days were regarded as days of holy convocation, on which *servile* work was forbidden. Such days were " rest " days, and therefore " Sabbaths."[2] In the case of one particular feast, the Day of Atonement, it is decreed that this feast shall be observed as an ordinary Sabbath, on which all manner of work is forbidden, but the instructions regarding the other feasts are not so clear and definite. Thus, for the seven days of unleavened bread, we read: " In the first day (15th Nisan) ye shall have a holy convocation; ye shall do no servile work " (Lev. xxiii, 7). Here we seem to have the definition of a holy convocation *in* the day, and the legitimate assumption is that no servile work was to be done during the period of the holy convocation. The distinction between these two feasts, the Day of Atonement and the Passover, is clearly seen in the 23rd Chapter of the Book of Leviticus. Whether the *intention* was to define the whole of the 15th Nisan as a day of holy convocation or not, the apparent looseness of the definition would afford the Rabbis of the period an excuse for adopting, if they so desired, the restricted period. Probably a difference concerning this point formed one of the many outstanding issues between the Pharisees and the Sadducees.

¶ 476. THE BETRAYAL ON 15TH NISAN.

The washing of the disciples' feet and the going forth of Judas on the evening of 15th Nisan are events that are defined in the gospels as preceding a rest day that began on the 15th Nisan, and that was known colloquially as the feast day.

However this may be, it is certain that the 15th Nisan contained a period of holy convocation of undefined duration. Now the washing of the disciples' feet would undoubtedly have been accounted servile work, but probably would not have been condemned before midnight, when the actual hour of the Passover anniversary began. Similarly, the Pharisees

---

[1]Our Lord was apparently warning Judas to hasten if he wished to receive the money he had been promised by the priests (Mark xiv, 11).
[2]The seventh day of the week was called the " Sabbath " only because it was a day of " rest."

and Sadducees could complete their bargain with Judas by paying him his price before midnight;[1] after that hour they would be breaking the law concerning the holy convocation. If, then, we may conclude that the period of holy convocation commenced at midnight, we see the reason for the disciples' assumption that Judas was being sent out in haste to buy provisions for the feast. But this only holds if we accept the 15th Nisan as the day of the Crucifixion, and the evening of the 15th Nisan for the Last Supper. If the Last Supper had taken place on the evening of the 14th Nisan, there would have been no need for haste, as the disciples supposed, for the purchases could have been made on the following morning, or at any time during the day. The betrayal was, therefore, on the 15th Nisan, following the interval of two clear days predicted by our Lord on the afternoon of the 12th Nisan (Table XXXVIII). The two days defined the interval prior to the Feast of the Passover, at which our Lord said He was to be betrayed.

[Margin note: If the Last Supper had been on the evening of 14th Nisan, there would have been no need for the haste deemed to be necessary for buying goods for the feast. These could have been purchased in the following day-time of 14th Nisan.]

Again, towards the end of the same day, the 15th Nisan, Joseph of Arimathea took the body of our Lord from the cross and laid it in the sepulchre. St. Luke states (xxiii, 54–56): "And that day was the preparation, and the sabbath drew on." The women who followed His body to the sepulchre hastened with their preparation of spices and ointments, "and rested the sabbath day according to the commandment." The preparation was the day before the sabbath, and therefore the sixth day of the week.[2]

[Margin note: "The preparation" is the day before the normal Sabbath of the week.]

---

[1] Therefore Jesus said to Judas before midnight, "That thou doest, do quickly" (John xiii, 27). The compact with the priests and their "promise to give Judas money" was prior to the 1st day of unleavened bread, which began at noon of 14th Nisan (Mark xiv, 10–12). Judas departed before midnight of 15th Nisan to receive the money.

[2] The "preparation of the Passover," referred to in John xix, 14, merely means that in the year in question the feast day fell on the sixth day of the week, and therefore on the "preparation" (refer Mark xv, 42). Sir Robert Anderson ("The Coming Prince") says: "But does not St. John expressly state that it was 'the preparation of the Passover,' and must not this necessarily mean the 14th of Nisan? The plain answer is that not a single passage has been cited from writings either sacred or profane in which that day is so described; whereas, among the Jews, 'the preparation' was the common name for the day before the Sabbath, and is used by all the Evangelists."
Mark (xv, 42) clearly states that the day of the Crucifixion "was the PREPARATION, that is, THE DAY BEFORE THE SABBATH." In this statement it is obvious there is no reference to the preparation in connection with the Passover. It simply defines that every sixth day of the week was the Preparation. When, as in the Crucifixion year, the Preparation was also a day of holy convocation, and therefore a day of rest or a Sabbath, the gospels show that work of necessity was permitted in the late afternoon—called the "even" in Mark xv, 42—preceding sunset beginning the Sabbath of the week. The gospels therefore emphasise that this afternoon was the afternoon of the Preparation in stating that Joseph of Arimathea took the body from the cross on the late afternoon of the day of holy convocation that occurred on 15th Nisan.
Again, malefactors were condemned to carry their own crosses. Jesus, therefore, began His Exodus journey by carrying His cross on the morning of 15th Nisan (John xix, 16–17). When a substitute was necessary, no free Jew could take the burden. It was transferred to the shoulders of Simon of Cyrene (N. Africa). Simon, from his name, was probably a gentilised Israelite.
The Rev. Dr. E. H. Plumptre states concerning "the Preparation" as follows:—
"Here the answer lies on the surface. That name (*Paraskeué*) was given to the day of the week, our Friday, the day before the Sabbath, and had absolutely nothing to do with any preparation for the Passover. The gospels show this beyond the shadow of a doubt (Mark xv, 42; Matt. xxvii, 62; Luke xxiii, 54). If any confirmation were wanted it may be found in the fact that the name is applied in a Graeco-Roman decree quoted by Josephus ("Ant.," XVI, 6, 2) to the week day which answers to our Friday. Even the phrase which seems most to suggest a different view, the 'preparation of the Passover' in John xix, 14, does not mean more, on any strict interpretation, than the 'Passover Friday,' the Friday in the Passover week, and coming, therefore,

¶ 477. THE EATING OF THE PASSOVER BY THE PRIESTS.

The ceremonial defilement that would have been incurred by the priests in entering the prætorium prior to their "eating the Passover." Anderson's explanation:— That the "Passover" here refers to the feast in the daytime of 15th Nisan.

Many commentators have founded their assumption that, according to St. John, the Crucifixion took place on the 14th Nisan, on the statement in that gospel (xviii, 28) that the priests "themselves entered not into the palace, that they might not be defiled, but might eat the Passover." This is supposed to prove that the lambs had not been killed before the trial, and that, according to St. John, the trial was on the 14th Nisan. This argument, however, is built upon false premises. Sir Robert Anderson says: "These writers, one and all, confound the paschal supper with the festival which followed it, and to which it lent its name. The supper was a memorial of the redemption of the firstborn of Israel on the night before the Exodus; the feast was the anniversary of their deliverance from the house of bondage. The supper was not a part of the feast . . . in the same way that the Feast of Weeks came to be commonly designated Pentecost, the Feast of Unleavened Bread was popularly called the Passover. That title was common to the supper and the feast, and included both; but the intelligent Jew would never confound the two; and if he spoke emphatically of the *feast* of the Passover, he would thereby mark the festival to the exclusion of the supper."[1]

¶ 478. THE PASCHAL SUPPER AND THE "FEAST" OF THE PASSOVER.

The first day of unleavened bread and the day of "the sacrifice of the Lord's Passover" were identical. Both began noon of 14th Nisan (Table XXXVIII). The "feast" of unleavened bread, however, was on 15th Nisan.

The distinction between the paschal supper and the feast is clearly shown in Leviticus (xxiii, 4–6): "These are the set feasts of the Lord, even holy convocations. . . . In the first month, on the fourteenth day of the month at even, is the Lord's Passover. And on the fifteenth day of the same month is the feast of unleavened bread."[2] The term "Passover" was undoubtedly used for both the supper and the feast.[3] This feast day was the 15th Nisan, following the paschal supper, and if this fact be borne in mind the supposed lack of harmony in the Gospel of St. John vanishes. Chapter xiii begins with the Last Supper on Thursday evening. Then follows the disciples' assumption that Judas was being sent to " buy what

---

before a Sabbath more solemn than others (John xix, 31). It may be noted further that the term *Paraskeué* was adopted by the Church, Western as well as Eastern, as a synonym for the *Dies Veneris*, or Friday."—(" New Testament Commentary for English Readers," Vol. I, p. 560.)

With regard to " that Sabbath " being " a high day," this means that a Sabbath followed the day of the Crucifixion, which was the day of the feast of unleavened bread, also a Sabbath according to the law. Hence " that Sabbath," the ordinary weekly Sabbath, was a High Sabbath, a double Sabbath, and it was also the 16th Nisan, when the wave offering of the first sheaf was made.

[1]" The Coming Prince," 10th Edit., pp. 108–118. This subject is fully explained here, and ends with " The midnight agony in Gethsemane was thus the great antitype of that midnight scene in Egypt when the destroying angel flashed through the land. And as His death was the fulfilment of His people's deliverance, so it took place upon the anniversary of ' that selfsame day that the Lord did bring the children of Israel out of the land of Egypt by their armies ' (Exod. xii, 51)."

[2]See also Numbers xxviii, 16, 17 and Exodus xii, 14–17.

[3]Luke xxii, 1. " Now the feast of unleavened bread drew nigh, which is called the Passover." Josephus, " Ant.," XVII, 90, 3, " Now upon the approach of that feast of unleavened bread . . . which feast is called the Passover."

things we have need of for the feast," showing that the feast day, on which The paschal lamb was eaten on the evening beginning the 15th Nisan. our Lord was crucified, followed the Last Supper. Hence "the Passover" in John refers to the Feast of the Passover, and not to the paschal supper.

Further evidence on this point is afforded by the passage in John xviii, 39. The "feast" was eaten in the daytime of the 15th Nisan. Pilate said: "Ye have a custom that I should release unto you one at the passover." On what day was this prisoner released? St. Mark (xv, 6) Barabbas was released at the "feast." says, "Now at the *feast* he used to release unto them one prisoner"; St. Matthew (xxvii, 15), "Now at the *feast* the governor was wont to release Our Lord was therefore crucified at the "feast" on 15th Nisan. unto the multitude one prisoner"; and according to the narrative of St. Luke, "Release unto us Barabbas" was said on the day of the Crucifixion. The four gospels are therefore in agreement. The prisoner, then, was released on the feast day. St. John's gospel thus agrees with the other three gospels in stating that the Crucifixion was on the feast day when the prisoner was released, and it is evident that St. John followed a common custom in using the word "Passover" when referring to the Passover feast.[1]

¶ 479. OUR LORD ACCEPTED AS "THE LAMB OF GOD." (TABLES XXXVII AND XXXVIII.)

If we accept the dating of the 15th Nisan 30 A.D. for the Crucifixion, Our Lord's coming to Jerusalem on 10th Nisan (Palm Sunday) as the "Lamb of God" fulfilled the prophecy of Zechariah and fulfilled the prophetic enactments attached to this day 1515 years before. we see the fulfilment of Zechariah's prophecy, " Rejoice greatly, O daughter of Zion ; shout, O daughter of Jerusalem : behold, thy king cometh unto thee ; he is just and having salvation ; lowly, and riding upon an ass, even upon a colt, the foal of an ass." In 30 A.D. Palm Sunday was on the 10th Nisan, and this is the day when the paschal lambs were selected.[2] To fulfil the type of the prophecy it was essential that our Lord should come to Jerusalem as "The Lamb," for acceptance or rejection, on the 10th day of Nisan. In the series of years from 28 A.D. to 33 A.D. there is only one The Christian tradition of Palm Sunday identifies the Crucifixion year as 30 A.D. year in which the 10th Nisan fell on a Sunday and the 15th Nisan on a Friday, that is 30 A.D. In 29 A.D. the 10th Nisan was on a Wednesday, or, if the incorrect Passover dating in March be accepted, it would have been on a Monday.

¶ 480. THE DAYS IN THE SEPULCHRE.

But one point yet remains to be considered : the time our Lord's body Sequence :— 14th Nisan Noon The Lamb slain. Sunset 15th Nisan The Last Supper The Betrayal The Crucifixion Burial. Sunset 16th Nisan. remained in the sepulchre. The lambs were killed before the sunset that ushered in the 15th Nisan. The supper was taken that same evening, on the 15th Nisan, and our Lord was crucified on the following day, but still on the 15th Nisan. As the priests feared the people, they did not take our Lord on the feast day when many people were abroad, but on the night before.

[1]For the precise significance of this feast refer to Table XXXVII, extreme right-hand column.
[2]Exodus xii : " In the tenth day of this month (Nisan) they shall take to them every man a lamb. . . . Ye shall keep it up until the fourteenth day of the same month . . . kill it at even . . . and this day (the 15th Nisan) shall be unto you for a memorial, and ye shall keep it a feast unto the Lord."

The sequence of events is as follows :—

Crucifixion and burial on 15th Nisan.

15th Nisan .. Day I in Sepulchre .. Christ crucified and buried before sunset, the sixth day of the week.

Resurrection on 17th Nisan on the first day of the week, and the third day from His Crucifixion.

16th Nisan .. Day II in Sepulchre .. ending at sunset on Saturday, the seventh day of the week, a High Sabbath.

17th Nisan .. Day III in Sepulchre .. Christ rose early on the first day of the week.

Conclusion :— Our Lord was crucified on Friday, 15th Nisan 30 A.D.

It is thus apparent that if the Crucifixion was on a Friday it was on the 15th Nisan, the feast day. We deem that we have proved that it could not have been in 29 A.D., with a two and a half years' ministry, and consider it established that the date of the Crucifixion was Friday the 15th Nisan 30 A.D., 782 A.U.C., 4028½ A.K.

¶ 481.   "IN THE HEART OF THE EARTH."

The declaration of our Lord concerning His isolation in natural man's spiritual state, defined as Hades, for " three days and three nights."

There is, however, a passage relied on by those who say the Crucifixion was on a Thursday. Our Lord said (Matt. xii, 40) : " For as Jonas was three days and three nights in the whale's belly ; so shall the Son of man be three days and three nights in the heart of the earth." Alford says : " Jonah himself calls the belly of the sea monster ' the belly of Hades ' ... the type is not of our *Lord's body* being deposited in the tomb of Joseph of Arimathea, for neither could that be called ' the heart of the earth,' nor could it be said that ' the Son of man ' was there during that time ; but of our Lord's *personal descent into the place of departed souls* (see Eph. iv, 9 ; 1 Peter iii, 19 ; Luke xxiii, 43)."[1]

One thing is clearly obvious : " the heart of the earth " signifies " Hades." With this identification assured, the strict meaning of the passage depends upon what our Lord and the New Testament writers implied by *Hades.* We propose to advance evidence to show, from the New Testament—[2]

What we must prove to be the significance of this spiritual isolation of our Lord.

(1) That our Lord *in the flesh* could be, and was, spiritually isolated— " cut off "—in the spiritual state of Hades from the day upon which the 1st day of unleavened bread began, " when the Passover was sacrificed " (14th Nisan), until the hour of His death upon the cross.

(2) That thereafter He continued " cut off " in the spiritual state of Hades, in the state of death, until His Resurrection on the morning of 17th Nisan.

(3) That the period during which He was " cut off " in Hades was therefore " three days and three nights."

---

[1]" Greek Testament," Vol. I, p. 133.

[2]This evidence has been compiled and the conclusions drawn from it have been formulated since the death of Dr. Aldersmith. The fact is mentioned to limit responsibility for what, very possibly, may be the basis of much controversy.—[D. D.]

¶ 482. THE COMPACT OF JUDAS.

It is not altogether clear, from the narratives of the gospels, precisely *The time of the* at what hour of the 14th Nisan this spiritual isolation of our Lord began. *compact of Judas and its* The same uncertainty extends to the time of the negotiations of Judas with *relation to the beginning* the priests to arrange the details concerning our Lord's betrayal. It is *of our Lord's spiritual* certain, however, from Mark xiv, 10–12, that these negotiations—when Judas *isolation.* was promised the money (verse 11)—were conducted before noon of 14th Nisan, since from noon of that day until sunset the priests were fully occupied in killing the paschal lambs (refer to Table XXXVII). The forenoon of the 14th of Nisan was also a busy time for the priests in preparing for the Passover. This seems to indicate that Judas, at the request of the priests, had hurried to an emergency meeting in the early morning of the 14th of Nisan before their activities of the day began.

Apparently, then, the negotiations for our Lord's betrayal, by one of *Table* His own disciples, began what our Lord had always previously referred to *XXXVIII gives* as His " time "[1]—*i.e.* the time of His spiritual isolation. For it seems to *of events* be obvious that the compact could not be effected in relation to what was *covering the* God's sacrifice of His Son until the time arrived that God had appointed. *period of our* The compact of Judas, therefore, appears, at first sight, to be related to the *isolation—* initial phase of God's sacrifice in permitting His Son to be " cut off " or *" three days* isolated from the spiritual conditions in which the compact could not possibly *and three* have been made. This possible conclusion, however, will be seen to require *nights."* modification, but not to such an extent as will alter the definitive fixing of the three days and three nights.

The sequence of the Great Sacrifice, tentatively adopted as covering the entire period of the " three days and three nights " spiritually in Hades, is given in comparative form in Table XXXVIII.

¶ 483. THE TYPE OF THE PUTTING AWAY OF LEAVEN.

On the other hand, the unleavened bread as a type of a particular aspect *The first day* of our Lord's Passion (1 Cor. v, 7 and 8) seems to define that His spiritual *of unleavened* isolation—to effect the purpose of this particular aspect—began at noon *first day of* of the 14th Nisan, when leaven was put away (as see Ginsberg's note quoted *our Lord's* on Table XXXVII). In any case it is certain that His spiritual isolation *" three days* began many hours before His actual betrayal by Judas—as distinct from *nights."* the compact of Judas. It certainly began before His midnight agony in the garden of Gethsemane. The testamentary aspect of the Last Supper also required that His isolation began before the Supper. This being the case, His spiritual isolation may be deemed to have taken effect at latest from noon of 14th Nisan, when the paschal lambs began to be slain, and when leaven was put away.

Either time of beginning can fit the requirements of " three days and

---

[1]In this relation refer John vii, 2–8 concerning our Lord's reference to the Feast of Tabernacles that preceded His Crucifixion.

Oriental custom relating to a part of a day or a part of a night being expressed as a whole day or a whole night respectively. three nights." For, as Alford says: " In the Jerusalem Talmud (cited by Lightfoot) it is said ' that a day and a night together make up a νυχθήμερον, and that any part of such a period is counted as a whole.' "[1] There is, however, an obvious effort here to effect an identification that does not really exist. There is no doubt that the expression " three days and three nights " intentionally defines three distinctive periods of daylight and three distinctive periods of night. In such case, as the oriental custom is (the Talmud citation being another application to the day as a whole) the initial part of a period of daylight—less than 12 hours—and the terminal part of a period of night—less than 12 hours—would fit the expression. Thus $2\frac{1}{2}$ days and $2\frac{1}{2}$ nights—the half-day initial and the half-night terminal—would have been defined as " three days and three nights."

Not applicable to the interval from the Crucifixion to the Resurrection. The expression, however, cannot be made to apply to the time from our Lord's death to the Resurrection. This interval was $1\frac{1}{2}$ days and 2 nights, or possibly $1\frac{1}{2}$ nights, as He rose " early on the first day of the week " (Mark xvi, 9) and before sunrise (verse 2).

¶ 484. THE SPIRITUAL STATE OF NATURAL MAN.
(1 Cor. xv, 40–56.)

Natural man and Hades. " There is a natural body and there is a spiritual body " (1 Cor. xv, 44). The spiritual body of natural man is defined as belonging to the world of the unseen, the Hades of the Greeks. This is the sense in which " Hades " is used in the New Testament.

Spiritual man and the spiritual realms of Christ.

Death makes no difference to the spiritual state. On the other hand, the spiritual body of spiritual man in Christ belongs to the spiritual realms of Christ. Paul therefore refers to " your members which are on earth," clearly implying that the members of the spiritual body in Christ are already in the spiritual realms of Christ. Death makes no difference to the spiritual state. " Where thy treasure is there will thy heart be also." The heart of natural man is not in the realms of Christ, but is in the realms of the unseen world—the Hades of the Greeks as understood by the New Testament writers. Collectively this unseen world of the spiritual body of natural man is therefore " the heart of the earth."

The birth of natural man.

The re-birth of spiritual man.

The conditions for the latter were created by our Lord's sacrifice. Every person born into the world is born a " natural " man. According to our Lord's teaching, this means that the spiritual body of natural man, on coming into the Earth, is already in natural man's " unseen world "— " in the heart of the earth." For the spiritual body to enter the spiritual realms of Christ it is essential that it should be " re-born " into those spiritual realms. The means whereby this regeneration in natural man is effected is by the spiritual body, while it is still in the flesh, being received into the " body of Christ " (refer Table XXXVII and ¶¶ 268 (and note) and 391). The process neither consists of ritual nor initiation, but is an actual phase of spiritual evolution, resulting from a life of faith in the efficacy of Christ's sacrifice. This sacrifice was, in reality, a great active process in

[1] " Greek Testament," Vol. I, p. 153.

God's creative work. It was the active process of creating a bridge to span the gap effected by man in the harmony of God's creation. In comparison with this active creative process all normal processes of life—reproduction, historical developments, epoch-making discoveries and inventions—are merely the mechanically passive processes of age-long Natural Law.

¶ 485. THE SIGNIFICANCE OF THE PUTTING AWAY OF LEAVEN.

The Great Sacrifice came into operation by our Lord being " cut off " *The putting away of leaven at noon of 14th Nisan prefigured " the cutting off of Messiah "—the spiritual isolation of our Lord.* from His own supremely high spiritual realms ; not at His birth, in the flesh, nor yet at His baptism, but on the first day of unleavened bread in the last year of His ministry. The dough of the Exodus—prepared without leaven —prefigured the necessity for, and the day of, this " bread from heaven " coming into operation. This is why the first day of unleavened bread *Two aspects of our Lord's Passion prefigured by the unleavened dough and by the eating of the Passover lamb.* (Table XXXVII) is coincident with the full 24 hours' period of " the sacrifice of the Lord's Passover." In the Crucifixion year this began on the day of the compact of Judas and extended to the Crucifixion. Leavened bread was being put away at noon of the 14th Nisan, after the compact, and un-leavened bread began to be eaten after noon, when the killing of the paschal lambs began. This significance of the unleavened bread, as prefiguring a major aspect of our Lord's Passion, is clearly explained by St. Paul in I Cor. v, 7, 8 in relation to " Christ our Passover." From this we see the significance of our Lord's own words at the Last Supper. This was truly the eating of the Passover on the evening following the beginning of the first day of unleavened bread, and therefore on the evening ending Thursday, but beginning the 15th Nisan in 30 A.D.

Because of His being " cut off " " in the heart of the earth " during *Our Lord's Last Supper enacted His complete descent into man's spiritual state, to be able, in that state, to signify that thereafter His followers could partake of one spiritual body—the new spiritual state of man created by Christ.* the period of " the sacrifice of the Lord's Passover," our Lord could enact the giving of His spiritual body to His disciples, who were then spiritually in " the heart of the earth " in which our Lord was also then isolated. There-fore He gave them the " tokens "—the bread, " My Flesh " ; the wine, " My Blood of the New Testament," or New Covenant. Here we have the Testator giving to His disciples the " tokens " of His last Will and Testament, thereby signifying that thereafter they were " partakers of One Body " (refer Table XXXVIII) from which " the old leaven " had been " purged " (I Cor. v, 7, 8).

¶ 486. THE TOKENS OF THE LAST SUPPER AND THE PASSING-OVER OF DEATH.

Then followed the great passing-over of death from mankind—the *The midnight agony of our Lord, the " passing-over " of death from mankind, prefigured by the angel of death " pass-ing-over " Israel in Egypt.* midnight agony in the garden of Gethsemane—prefigured 1515 years before on the same day of the week, month, and year by the passing-over of the angel of death. In both cases the " blood " was the " token " of the passing-over that was to take place at midnight to deliver, in the one case,

Israel from the bondage of the Egyptians, and in the other case, mankind from the bondage of sin and death (refer Table XXXVII). The sequence in relation to our Lord's Passover signifies that this again was possible only by His having been " cut off."

The betrayal after midnight of the first day of unleavened bread, and therefore on the 15th Nisan. Following His agony was the active betrayal by Judas. This was after the midnight of 15th Nisan, which is clearly shown by the narrative of the gospels as given in sequence on Table XXXVIII. On the afternoon of 12th Nisan our Lord said : " *After* two days is the feast of the Passover and the Son of man is *betrayed* TO BE crucified " (Matt. xxvi, 2). The parallel phrase in Mark xiv, 1—concerning the same date—equates the " feast of the Passover " with " the feast of unleavened bread." The statement of our Lord therefore defines that from the afternoon of 12th Nisan two days were to intervene *prior to* His betrayal. This means that His betrayal was to follow the afternoon of 14th Nisan, and therefore to occur some time during the 15th Nisan. The narrative of the betrayal fixes the hour as between midnight and dawn, obviously of 15th Nisan. Now it is the betrayal that is thus dated and not the Crucifixion. Our Lord's Last Supper preceded this betrayal, and therefore occurred in the evening beginning 15th Nisan.

¶ 487. THE PARABLE ENACTED AT THE EXODUS.

Abraham's trial of faith enacted to indicate that God Himself had provided the Great Sacrifice. The trial of Abraham's faith, by his being asked to offer up his son in sacrifice, was a parable enacted to show to Abraham, and his seed after him, that God Himself had provided the sacrifice necessary. This was indicated by the ram being provided *in lieu* of Isaac. The intention of this enactment was seen to be confirmed by the chronological relations (¶ 404).

The negotiations of Pharaoh, again, prefigure by their results that the " three days " journey of isolation to sacrifice was not to be performed by Israel, but by Christ in being sacrificed Himself. Similarly, the events leading up to the Exodus of Israel from Egypt followed a sequence that prefigured the purpose of God in relation to His appointed sacrifice. Moses was instructed to demand of Pharaoh permission for Israel to proceed a three days' journey into the wilderness to sacrifice. Here, again, we have a parable enacted to instruct the future Israel in the ways of God. As in the case of Abraham's sacrifice, the demand was not permitted by God to be satisfied. God " hardened Pharaoh's heart." Pharaoh, therefore, did not let Israel go. The voluntary efforts of Israel and Pharaoh were thus indicated as subordinated to the will of God to prefigure, by the sequence, the unalterable nature of God's purpose that, as had been predetermined before the Creation, was to be effected by the sacrifice of His Son.

The three days' journey into the *cul de sac* (Plate LXIII and Table XXXVIII) of the wilderness of isolation—to be cut off—for the purpose of Israel offering up a sacrifice was not, therefore, permitted. Israel was brought out of bondage by other means. Israel's salvation was " purchased " by the sacrifice of " the lamb slain from the foundation of the world " (Exod. xiv, 30 ; and xv, 13, 16, in relation to Rev. xiii, 8).

All this prefigured that the "three days' journey" of isolation for the Great Sacrifice was not to be performed by Israel as a nation. The demand, and the sequence resulting from the refusal of the demand, were enacted as a parable to a later Israel. This people was ultimately to know that the "three days'" isolation for the sacrifice was to constitute the spiritual isolation of the Messiah. They were to see that this isolation formed the final phase of the Messiah being "cut off," "but not for Himself" (Dan. ix, 26).

This spiritual "cutting off" of the Messiah was necessary to make God's sacrifice an actual sacrifice—and not merely a nominal sacrifice. As a result of this, Christ became completely and effectively the Last Adam; to take the shock within Himself of the agony of reconciliation, thus creating for the seed of the fallen First Adam, the potentiality of redemption and salvation (refer I Cor. xv, 45–58). *The feature of our Lord's Passion that made God's sacrifice of His Son an actual sacrifice.*

¶ 488. THE HOUR AND DURATION OF THE CRUCIFIXION.

Now there is the important matter of the time of the Crucifixion. Mark (xv, 25) states that Christ was crucified at the third hour. John (xix, 13–18) states that He was not yet crucified, but was brought forth by Pilate to be shown to the Jews "about the sixth hour." To those unacquainted with Palestinian usage relating to the periods of the day in New Testament times, this appears to be a contradiction. There is, however, no contradiction. It was possible for our Lord to be crucified at the end of the period known as the time of the "third hour," and yet to be brought forth by Pilate shortly before the beginning of the period known as the time of the "sixth hour." This can best be understood by an outline of the divisions of the day in New Testament times. *Explanation of the fact that our Lord was crucified towards the end of the period of the third hour, shortly before the period of the sixth hour of the day began.*

THE DIVISIONS OF THE NIGHT.	THE DIVISIONS OF DAYLIGHT.
About	About
The 1st watch (the evening watch) .. 6 to 9 p.m.	The third hour.. 6 to 9 a.m.
The 2nd watch, known as the midnight watch. 9 to 12 midnight.	The sixth hour.. 9 to 12 noon.
The 3rd watch (cock-crow) .. .. 12 to 3 a.m.	The ninth hour.. 12 to 3 p.m.
The 4th watch (the morning watch) .. 3 to 6 a.m.	The twelfth hour 3 to 6 p.m.[1]

The divisions of the night and the divisions of the day.

Thus the midnight watch was the period of three hours ending at midnight; and the morning watch the period of three hours ending at sunrise. Similarly, the "third hour" was an abbreviated designation for the three

---

[1] Nevertheless, when a specific hour is spoken of, as in Matthew xx, 6 and 9, where the eleventh hour is mentioned, that specific hour is intended; in this case about 5 p.m. to 6 p.m.

In the example here given (Matt. xx, 1–16), the working day of labourers in the vineyard is given, from sunrise to sunset. Comparison of verse 1 with verses 3, 5, and 6—the householder going out in the early morning to hire labourers, and again at the third hour, sixth hour, ninth hour, and eleventh hour—shows that the times intended were the specific hours, about 6 a.m. (early morning), 9 a.m. (the precise time of the specific third hour), noon (the precise time of the specific sixth hour), 3 p.m. (the precise time of the specific ninth hour), and 5 p.m. (the precise time of the specific eleventh hour). The last hour is identified by the fact that the labourers hired at that hour worked one hour only (verse 12), to sunset. Twelve hours were reckoned between sunrise and sunset irrespective of the time of the year.

hours' interval ending three temporal hours after sunrise, *i.e.* ending about 9 a.m.

Our Lord was therefore exhibited by Pilate to the Jews before 9 a.m., when it was getting towards or "'about the sixth hour" interval of the day, as stated by John, and was crucified, still before 9 a.m., towards the end of "the third hour" interval of the day, as stated by Mark.

¶ 489. THE IRONY OF THE JEWS' FEAST.

The divisions of the day indicate that our Lord was crucified shortly before 9 a.m., that darkness continued from 9 a.m. to noon, and that our Lord died about noon, at the end of the first day of unleavened bread, that prefigured His first day of spiritual isolation.

Our Lord being crucified in the "third hour" and "about the sixth hour," has shown that the three hours' intervals of daylight are intended in the gospel narratives. The "third hour" interval ended about 9 a.m., when the three hours' period of the "sixth hour" interval began. When, therefore, Mark (xv, 25 and 33) states that our Lord was crucified in the "third hour," and that "when the sixth hour was come, there was darkness over the whole land until the ninth hour," and again, in verses 34–38, that He died "at the ninth hour," the narrative defines that the whole period during which Christ was on the Cross until His death was three hours, and that His agony was veiled by the darkness during this time. It also tells us that our Lord died, not at 3 p.m., as has been commonly supposed, but at the hour of noon, when the first day of unleavened bread terminated; and at which hour the Jews were celebrating their joyful feast commemorating the first baking from the unleavened dough carried on their shoulders on the morning of the Exodus out of Egypt.

The first journey of Israel's Exodus prefigures the first journey of Christ's Exodus.

By the irony of circumstances they had created the Jews were then joyfully celebrating a feast that had been instituted to prefigure the last hours of their Saviour on the Cross, on which, by their instigation and desire, He had been crucified that very morning. His carrying forth of the Cross in the morning, prior to its being given to Simon of Cyrene, was prefigured by the Israelites at the Exodus carrying forth the unleavened dough bound on their shoulders (refer Tables XXXVII and XXXVIII). The remaining parallel circumstances whereby the events of the Exodus of Israel prefigured the events of the *Exodos* of our Lord are tabulated on Tables XXXVII and XXXVIII, and have been dealt with in ¶¶ 324, 325.

¶ 490. THE IMPORTANCE OF THE SECULAR EVIDENCE.

The reasons given for so much attention having been directed to evidence from secular sources.

It is possible that the student of Scripture, who believes in the absolute reliability of Holy Writ, may take exception to our having directed our readers' attention to evidence that is derived from secular sources, and may consider that it was unnecessary to devote so much space to the discussion of this secular evidence. We believe that many Christian readers find it difficult to realise the requirements of other readers who have not the faith in the Scriptures possessed by the Christian, and are somewhat selfish in ignoring their demands for extraneous evidence. This work has been written, primarily, for the benefit of the reader who does not, and who cannot believe, but who earnestly desires to believe, if it be possible; and secondarily, in order to afford to the believing Christian that satisfaction and enlightenment that may be derived from the synchronisation of sacred and secular history. For this reason, therefore, in fixing the chronology of our Lord's life, considerable attention has been given to secular evidence, and it has been our object to show that the sacred and secular historians are nowhere at variance, and that the evidence from both sources is in perfect harmony and synchronism.

TABLE XXXIX.   (Refer ¶ 491).

(A).

The Gregorian Calendar Year Dates for 1st July of the Julian Calendar Year from Tab. Year o (*i.e.*, Astro. B.C. 4000) to Tab. Year 5999 (*i.e.*, A.D. 1999).

Can be used to find the Gregorian month dates corresponding to the Julian month dates from 1st March (Julian) and 31st December (Julian) inclusive.

Tabular Years of Plate LIX (inclusive).	0	1000	2000	3000	4000	5000
0– 99	May 30	June 7	June 14	June 22	June 29	July 7
100–199	May 31	June 8	June 15	June 23	June 30	July 8
200–299	June 1	June 8	June 16	June 23	July 1	July 8
300–399	June 2	June 9	June 17	June 24	July 2	July 9
400–499	June 2	June 10	June 17	June 25	July 2	July 10
500–599	June 3	June 11	June 18	June 26	July 3	July 11
600–699	June 4	June 11	June 19	June 26	July 4	July 11
700–799	June 5	June 12	June 20	June 27	July 5	July 12
800–899	June 5	June 13	June 20	June 28	July 5	July 13
900–999	June 6	June 14	June 21	June 29	July 6	July 14

(B).

The Gregorian Calendar Year Dates for 1st February of the Julian Calendar Year from Tab. Year 1 (*i.e.*, Astro. B.C. 3999) to Tab. Year 6000 (*i.e.*, A.D. 2000).

Can be used to find the Gregorian month dates corresponding to the Julian month dates from 1st January (Julian) inclusive to 1st March (Julian) exclusive.

Tabular Years of Plate LIX (inclusive).	0	1000	2000	3000	4000	5000
1– 100	Dec. 31*	Jany. 8	Jany. 15	Jany. 23	Jany. 30	Feby. 7
101– 200	Jany. 1	Jany. 9	Jany. 16	Jany. 24	Jany. 31	Feby. 8
201– 300	Jany. 2	Jany. 9	Jany. 17	Jany. 24	Feby. 1	Feby. 8
301– 400	Jany. 3	Jany. 10	Jany. 18	Jany. 25	Feby. 2	Feby. 9
401– 500	Jany. 3	Jany. 11	Jany. 18	Jany. 26	Feby. 2	Feby. 10
501– 600	Jany. 4	Jany. 12	Jany. 19	Jany. 27	Feby. 3	Feby. 11
601– 700	Jany. 5	Jany. 12	Jany. 20	Jany. 27	Feby. 4	Feby. 11
701– 800	Jany. 6	Jany. 13	Jany. 21	Jany. 28	Feby. 5	Feby. 12
801– 900	Jany. 6	Jany. 14	Jany. 21	Jany. 29	Feby. 5	Feby. 13
901–1000	Jany. 7	Jany. 15	Jany. 22	Jany. 30	Feby. 6	Feby. 14

* 31st Dec. (Greg.) is here the last day of the Gregorian Tabular Years o to 99 inclusive, but coincident with 1st Feby. (Julian) of the Julian Tabular Years 1 to 100 inclusive.

TABLE XL.   (Refer to ¶ 491).

PERPETUAL CALENDAR FOR TABULAR YEARS IN PLATES LIX AND LX (for both Old (Julian) and New Style (Gregorian) Intercalations). Giving Data from which the day of the week, for any day of any month of any year, can be determined.

(A).
Old Style (Julian) Centuries.
Leap Years in *Italics*.

0	—	—	*400*	*300*	*200*	100
700	*600*	*500*	*1100*	*1000*	*900*	*800*
1400	*1300*	*1200*	*1800*	*1700*	*1600*	*1500*
2100	*2000*	*1900*	*2500*	*2400*	*2300*	*2200*
2800	*2700*	*2600*	*3200*	*3100*	*3000*	*2900*
3500	*3400*	*3300*	*3900*	*3800*	*3700*	*3600*
4200	*4100*	*4000*	*4600*	*4500*	*4400*	*4300*
4900	*4800*	*4700*	*5300*	*5200*	*5100*	*5000*
5600	*5500*	*5400*	*6000*	*5900*	*5800*	*5700*
6300	*6200*	*6100*	*6700*	*6600*	*6500*	*6400*
0	1	2	3	4	5	6

Factors.

(C).
Years in each Century.
Old Style and New Style
Intercalations.
Leap Years in *Italics*.

00	01	02	03	—	*04*	05
06	07	—	*08*	09	10	11
—	*12*	13	14	15	—	*16*
17	18	19	—	*20*	21	22
23	—	*24*	25	26	27	—
28	29	30	31	—	*32*	33
34	35	—	*36*	37	38	39
—	*40*	41	42	43	—	*44*
45	46	47	—	*48*	49	50
51	—	*52*	53	54	55	—
56	57	58	59	—	*60*	61
62	63	—	*64*	65	66	67
—	*68*	69	70	71	—	*72*
73	74	75	—	*76*	77	78
79	—	*80*	81	82	83	—
84	85	86	87	—	*88*	89
90	91	—	*92*	93	94	95
—	*96*	97	98	99	—	—
0	1	2	3	4	5	6

Factors.

(B).
New Style (Gregorian)
Centuries.
Leap Years in *Italics*.

0	—	—	—
400	300	200	100
800	700	600	500
1200	1100	1000	900
1600	1500	1400	1300
2000	1900	1800	1700
2400	2300	2200	2100
2800	2700	2600	2500
3200	3100	3000	2900
3600	3500	3400	3300
4000	3900	3800	3700
4400	4300	4200	4100
4800	4700	4600	4500
5200	5100	5000	4900
5600	5500	5400	5300
6000	5900	5800	5700
6400	6300	6200	6100
6800	6700	6600	6500
0	1	3	5

Factors.

Months.   Factors for Leap Years are given in *Italics*.

	Jan.	Feb.	Mar.	Apr.	May	June	July	Aug.	Sep.	Oct.	Nov.	Dec.		
Old Style Factors (Julian).	2	5	5	1	3	6	1	4	0	2	5	0	Old Style Factors (Julian).	(d)
Do. do. Leap Years.	*1*	*4*	5	1	3	6	1	4	0	2	5	0	Do. do. Leap Years	
New Style Factors (Gregorian).	6	2	2	5	0	3	5	1	4	6	2	4	New Style Factors (Gregorian).	(e)
Do. do. Leap Years.	*5*	*1*	2	5	0	3	5	1	4	6	2	4	Do. do. Leap Years	

RULE :—$\dfrac{\text{Day of the Month} + \text{Month Factor} + \text{Century Factor} + \text{Year Factor.}}{7}$

For remainder 0, the day is Sunday.
For remainder 1, the day is Monday.
For remainder 2, the day is Tuesday.
For remainder 3, the day is Wednesday.
For remainder 4, the day is Thursday.
For remainder 5, the day is Friday.
For remainder 6, the day is Saturday.

If the total of the factors is less than 7, treat the total as the remainder.

TABLE XLI. (Refer to ¶ 491).

(A) THE LATER EGYPTIAN CALENDAR (365 days' Vague Year).

Name of Season.	From	To	Thoth I	Paophi II	Hathor III	Khoiak IV	Tybi V	Mekhir VI	Phaun-ruoth VII	Phar-muthi VIII	Pakhon IX	Paoni X	Epephi XI	Mesore XII	Epag. Days
Shat or Akhet = Season of Sowing		To I Thoth	365	335	305	275	245	215	185	155	125	95	65	35	5
		III Paophi	30	365	335	305	275	245	215	185	155	125	95	65	35
		III Hathor	60	30	365	335	305	275	245	215	185	155	125	95	65
		IV Khoiak	90	60	30	365	335	305	275	245	215	185	155	125	95
Pert = Season of Growing		V Tybi	120	90	60	30	365	335	305	275	245	215	185	155	125
		VI Mekhir	150	120	90	60	30	365	335	305	275	245	215	185	155
		VII Phamenoth	180	150	120	90	60	30	365	335	305	275	245	215	185
		VIII Pharmuthi	210	180	150	120	90	60	30	365	335	305	275	245	215
Shem = Season of Inundation		IX Pakhon	240	210	180	150	120	90	60	30	365	335	305	275	245
		X Paoni	270	240	210	180	150	120	90	60	30	365	335	305	275
		XI Epephi	300	270	240	210	180	150	120	90	60	30	365	335	305
		XII Mesore	330	300	270	240	210	180	150	120	90	60	30	365	335
Epagomenal Days (5 days over)			360	330	300	270	240	210	180	150	120	90	60	30	365

NOTE:—The month name identifications hold only for the period 875 B.C. to the 3rd Century A.D. Without the month name identifications this Calendar applies to Table III and Plate LIX. In such case, when an intercalary month intervenes between the two month datings, add 30 days to the total stated in (A).

(B) THE EARLY CHALDÆAN AND THE EARLY EGYPTIAN CALENDAR (360 days' year).

Egyptian Name of Season.	From	To	I	II	III	IV	V	VI	VII	VIII	IX	X	XI	XII
Shat or Akhet = Season of Sowing		To Month I	360	330	300	270	240	210	180	150	120	90	60	30
		Month II	30	360	330	300	270	240	210	180	150	120	90	60
		Month III	60	30	360	330	300	270	240	210	180	150	120	90
		Month IV	90	60	30	360	330	300	270	240	210	180	150	120
Pert = Season of Growing		Month V	120	90	60	30	360	330	300	270	240	210	180	150
		Month VI	150	120	90	60	30	360	330	300	270	240	210	180
		Month VII	180	150	120	90	60	30	360	330	300	270	240	210
		Month VIII	210	180	150	120	90	60	30	360	330	300	270	240
Shem = Season of Inundation		Month IX	240	210	180	150	120	90	60	30	360	330	300	270
		Month X	270	240	210	180	150	120	90	60	30	360	330	300
		Month XI	300	270	240	210	180	150	120	90	60	30	360	330
		Month XII	330	300	270	240	210	180	150	120	90	60	30	360

This Calendar applies to Table III and Plate LIX. When an intercalary month intervenes between the two month datings add 30 days to the total stated in (B).

(C) THE MODERN CALENDAR: OLD (JULIAN) OR NEW (GREGORIAN) STYLES.

From	To	Jan.	Feb.	Mar.	Apr.	May	June	July	Aug.	Sept.	Oct.	Nov.	Dec.
	To January	365	334	306	275	245	214	184	153	122	92	61	31
	February	31	365	337	306	276	245	215	184	153	123	92	62
	March	59	28	365	334	304	273	243	212	181	151	120	90
	April	90	59	31	365	335	304	274	243	212	182	151	121
	May	120	89	61	30	365	334	304	273	242	212	181	151
	June	151	120	92	61	31	365	335	304	273	243	212	182
	July	181	150	122	91	61	30	365	334	303	273	242	212
	August	212	181	153	122	92	61	31	365	334	304	273	243
	September	243	212	184	153	123	92	62	31	365	335	304	274
	October	273	242	214	183	153	122	92	61	30	365	334	304
	November	304	273	245	214	184	153	123	92	61	31	365	335
	December	334	303	275	244	214	183	153	122	91	61	30	365

EXCEPTION:—IN LEAP YEAR If the last day of February comes between the two dates, add 1 to the number of days obtained from the Table.

TABLE XLII. (Refer ¶ 491a).

ARAMAIC AND ASSYRIAN LUNAR CALENDAR; ALSO HEBREW SACRED CALENDAR.

THE LUNAR CALENDAR :—

Days in Month	30	29	30	29	30	29	30	29	30	29	30	29
From	Nisan	Iyyar	Sivan	Tammuz	Ab	Elul	Tisri	Marchesvan	Chisleu	Tebet	Sebat	Adar
To Nisan	354	324	295	265	236	206	177	147	118	88	59	29
Iyyar	30	354	325	295	266	236	207	177	148	118	89	59
Sivan	59	29	354	324	295	265	236	206	177	147	118	88
Tammuz	89	59	30	354	325	295	266	236	207	177	148	118
Ab	118	88	59	29	354	324	295	265	236	206	177	147
Elul	148	118	89	59	30	354	325	295	266	236	207	177
Tisri	177	147	118	88	59	29	354	324	295	265	236	206
Marchesvan	207	177	148	118	89	59	30	354	325	295	266	236
Chisleu	236	206	177	147	118	88	59	29	354	324	295	265
Tebet	266	236	207	177	148	118	89	59	30	354	325	295
Sebat	295	265	236	206	177	147	118	88	59	29	354	324
Adar	325	295	266	236	207	177	148	118	89	59	30	354

GENERAL RULE. TO FIND 1st NISAN :—Find Julian date of astronomical new moon nearest to the Vernal Equinox of the year considered (days being reckoned from midnight to midnight). Place 1st Nisan as beginning at sunset of Julian day following. If 15th Nisan coincides with or succeeds the date of the Vernal Equinox the placing of 1st Nisan is correct. If 15th Nisan precedes the date of the Vernal Equinox the placing is wrong, and the Intercalary month Ve-Adar must be placed between Adar and Nisan. In such case repeat the process for 1st Nisan relatively to the next later astronomical new moon.

It is to be noted that the days for the Lunar Calendar are reckoned from sunset to sunset.

NOTE :—If Ve-Adar intervenes, in an Intercalary Year, add 29 or alternatively 30 days to the number of days obtained from above.

The Calendar position of the astronomical new moon will indicate which alternative is necessary.

Hebrew Sacred Calendar Month Nos.	Hebrew Civil Calendar Month Nos.	Aramaic name of Month.	Assyrian name of Month.
I	VII	Nisan	Ni'sannu.
II	VIII	Iyyar	Airu
III	IX	Sivan	'Sivanu
IV	X	Tammuz	Duzu
V	XI	Ab	Abu
VI	XII	Elul	Ululu
VII	I	Tisri	Tasritu
VIII	II	Marchesvan	Arakh-samna (" the 8th month ").
IX	III	Chisleu	Cisilivu
X	IV	Tebet	Dharbitu
XI	V	Sebat	Sabahu
XII	VI	Adar	Addaru
(Intercalary)	(Intercalary)	Adar (Ve-adar)	(Arakh-makru) ("the Incidental month").

NOTE :—In addition to the Lunar Calendar above, there was, both in Babylonia and Assyria, an Astrological Calendar consisting of 12 months of 30 days each—the old Calendric year of 360 days. It is relative to the months of this Astrological Calendar that certain Astrological formulæ on the inscriptions associate new and full moons and eclipses with dates that are entirely out of place in the Lunar Calendar. Each of the months of the Astrological Calendar had the same names as the equivalent Lunar Calendar months, the names of which were, in fact, derived from the month names of the old Chaldæan 360 days'-year Calendar.

TABLE XLIII. (Refer ¶ 491a).

FOR JULIAN YEARS AND DATES REFERRED TO SAME.

Leap Year Cycles. in each Century.	Julian Years in each Century. All Zero Years of Centuries are Leap Years, Year 00 below.			
	Leap Year. (a).	1st Ordinary Year. (b).	2nd Ordinary Year. (c).	3rd Ordinary Year. (d).
Cycle I	00	01	02	03
Cycle II	04	05	06	07
Cycle III	08	09	10	11
Cycle IV	12	13	14	15
Cycle V	16	17	18	19
Cycle VI	20	21	22	23
Cycle VII	24	25	26	27
Cycle VIII	28	29	30	31
Cycle IX	32	33	34	35
Cycle X	36	37	38	39
Cycle XI	40	41	42	43
Cycle XII	44	45	46	47
Cycle XIII	48	49	50	51
Cycle XIV	52	53	54	55
Cycle XV	56	57	58	59
Cycle XVI	60	61	62	63
Cycle XVII	64	65	66	67
Cycle XVIII	68	69	70	71
Cycle XIX	72	73	74	75
Cycle XX	76	77	78	79
Cycle XXI	80	81	82	83
Cycle XXII	84	85	86	87
Cycle XXIII	88	89	90	91
Cycle XXIV	92	93	94	95
Cycle XXV	96	97	98	99

Note :—In the following Rules " mnb " = " midnight beginning."

RULE   I. Number of days from Mnb 1st Jany. (Julian) Tab. Year 0 to mnb 1st Jany. (Julian) of any Tab. Year (a)—of any century—=number of Tab. Years × $365\frac{1}{4}$.

RULE II. Number of days from mnb 1st Jany. (Julian) Tab. Year 0 to mnb 1st Jany. (Julian) of any Tab. Year (b)—of any century—=(number of Tab. Years × $365\frac{1}{4}$) $+\frac{3}{4}$.

RULE III. Number of days from mnb 1st Jany. (Julian) Tab. Year 0 to mnb 1st Jany. (Julian) of any Tab. Year (c)—of any century—=(number of Tab. Years × $365\frac{1}{4}$) $+\frac{1}{2}$.

RULE IV. Number of days from mnb 1st Jany. (Julian) Tab. Year 0 to mnb 1st Jany. (Julian) of any Tab. Year (d)—of any century—=(number of Tab. Years × $365\frac{1}{4}$) $+\frac{1}{4}$.

RULE V. Number of days from mnb 1st Jany. (Julian) Tab. Year 0 to mnb of any day of any Julian month of any Tab. Year =number of days obtained from Rules I to IV inclusive, and added thereto the number of days obtained from Table XLI (C).

Note :—If the terminal date falls on or after 1st March—or on Feby. 29—in a Leap Year (a) add one day to the number of days stated in Table XLI (C).

RULE   VI. If the terminal month date is a Gregorian date, convert to Julian by means of Table XXXIX (A), and then apply Rules I to V inclusive.

RULE VII. For the number of days between any two dates of any two years, treat as two separate calculations from Tab. Year 0 Jany. 1st (Julian), and deduct the separate totals. The formulæ need not be worked out as separate totals of days ; but the formula for the earlier year can be subtracted from the formula for the later year, to give the required interval in Julian Years, days, and fraction of a day.

RULE VIII. For the number of days from the P.M.T. instant of Autumnal Equinoctial Full Moon B.C. (Hist.) 4000 (=mnb 24 Oct. Julian, or mnb 22 Sept. Gregorian, of Tabular Year 1), apply Rules V to VII and then deduct 662 days.

RULE   IX. G.M.T. =Greenwich Mean Time ; P.M.T.=Pyramid Mean Time ; B.M.T.=Babylon Mean Time.
P.M.T. = G.M.T. + 2 hrs. 4 mins. 31.9 secs., or = G.M.T. + 0.0865 day.
G.M.T. = P.M.T. — 2 hrs. 4 mins. 31.9 secs., or = P.M.T. — 0.0865 day.
B.M.T. = G.M.T. + 2 hrs. 57 mins. 56 secs., or = G.M.T. + 0.1236 day.
G.M.T. = B.M.T. — 2 hrs. 57 mins. 56 secs., or = B.M.T. — 0.1236 day.
B.M.T. = P.M.T. + 0 hrs. 53 mins. 24 secs., or = P.M.T. + 0.0371 day.
P.M.T. = B.M.T. — 0 hrs. 53 mins. 24 secs., or = B.M.T. — 0.0371 day.

Derived from Great Pyramid Longitude=31°-7′-57″, E. of Greenwich.
Babylon Longitude=44°-29′ E. of Greenwich.

For Jerusalem Mean Time (J.M.T.) :—
J.M.T. = G.M.T. + 2 hrs. 20 mins. 56 secs., or = G.M.T. + 0.0999 day.
J.M.T. = P.M.T. + 0 hrs. 16 mins. 24 secs., or = P.M.T. + 0.0134 day.

Derived from Jerusalem Longitude=35°-14′ E. of Greenwich.

TABLE XLIV. (Refer ¶ 491a).

FOR CALCULATING DATES OF ASTRONOMICAL NEW AND FULL MOONS AND ECLIPSES;
CHRONOLOGICAL JULIAN DATINGS OBTAINED BY COMPARISON WITH DATA DERIVED
ACCORDING TO TABLES XLI (C) AND XLIII AND RULES FOR SAME.

(A). The Lunations of the Lunar Year.

Number of Completed Lunations	Number of Days
1	29.530586
2	59.061176
3	88.591764
4	118.122352
5	147.652940
6	177.183528
7	206.714116
8	236.244704
9	265.775292
10	295.305880
11	324.836468
12	354.367056

(B). Chronological Comparison of Julian Years and Lunations.

Number of Completed Lunations	Number of Julian Years, and number of days over (+) or under (—).
13	1 J.Y. + 18.647644 d.
25	2 J.Y. + 7.764700 d.
38	3 J.Y. + 26.412344 d.
50	4 J.Y. + 15.529400 d.
62	5 J.Y. + 4.646456 d.
75	6 J.Y. + 23.294100 d.
87	7 J.Y. + 12.411156 d.
99	8 J.Y. + 1.528212 d.
112	9 J.Y. + 20.175856 d.
124	10 J.Y. + 9.292912 d.
137	11 J.Y. + 27.940556 d.
149	12 J.Y. + 17.057612 d.
161	13 J.Y. + 6.174668 d
174	14 J.Y. + 24.822312 d.
186	15 J.Y. + 13.939368 d.
198	16 J.Y. + 3.056424 d.
211	17 J.Y. + 21.704068 d.
223	18 J.Y. + 10.821124 d.
236	19 J.Y. + 29.468768 d.
248	20 J.Y. + 18.585824 d.
260	21 J.Y. + 7.702880 d.
273	22 J.Y. + 26.350524 d.
285	23 J.Y. + 15.467580 d.
297	24 J.Y. + 4.584636 d.
310	25 J.Y. + 23.232280 d.
322	26 J.Y. + 12.349336 d.
334	27 J.Y. + 1.466392 d.
347	28 J.Y. + 20.114036 d.
358	29 J.Y. — 20.299496 d.

Which last completed gives the unit chronological Eclipse Period (Eclipses occurring alternately at opposite nodes).
NOTE :—Note that the last line is (—) days, whereas all the others are (+) days.

(C). Lesser Chronological Eclipse Periods.

Number of Cycles Completed.	Number of Julian Years, and number of days under.	Number of Completed Lunations.
1	29 J.Y.— 20.299496 d.	358
2	58 J.Y.— 40.598992 d.	716
3	87 J.Y.— 60.898488 d.	1074
4	116 J.Y.— 81.197984 d.	1432
5	145 J.Y.—101.497480 d.	1790
6	174 J.Y.—121.796976 d.	2148
7	203 J.Y.—142.096472 d.	2506
8	232 J.Y.—162.096472 d.	2864
9	261 J.Y.—182.695464 d.	3222
10	290 J.Y.—202.994960 d.	3580
11	319 J.Y.—223.294456 d.	3938
12	348 J.Y.—243.593952 d.	4296
13	377 J.Y.—263.893448 d.	4654
14	406 J.Y.—284.192944 d.	5012
15	435 J.Y.—304.492440 d.	5370
16	464 J.Y.—324.791936 d.	5728
17	493 J.Y.—345.091432 d.	6086
18	521 J.Y.— 0.140928 d.	6444

NOTE :—Note that all the periods of days stated above are (—), and are therefore to be understood as deductions from the stated periods of Julian Years.

(D). Greater Chronological Eclipse Periods.

Number of Cycles Completed.	Number of Julian Years, and number of days under.	Number of Completed Lunations.
1	521 J.Y.—0.140928 d.	6444
2	1042 J.Y.—0.281856 d.	12888
3	1563 J.Y.—0.422784 d.	19332
4	2084 J.Y.—0.563712 d.	25776
5	2605 J.Y.—0.704640 d.	32220
6	3126 J.Y.—0.845568 d.	38664
7	3647 J.Y.—0.986496 d.	45108
8	4168 J.Y.—1.127424 d.	51552
9	4689 J.Y.—1.268352 d.	57996
10	5210 J.Y.—1.409280 d.	64440
11	5731 J.Y.—1.550208 d.	70884
12	6252 J.Y.—1.691136 d.	77324

NOTE :—Note that all the periods of days stated above are (—), and are to be understood as deductions from the stated periods of Julian Years.

ASTRONOMICAL FULL MOON DATES. RULE I. To find number of days from *mnb 1st Jany. (Julian) Tab. Year o to the instant of Astronomical Full Moon occurring in any other Tab. Year following, add as follows :—

(1)	..	.. Constant =	1 Julian Year +297.1238 days.	
(2)	..	.. From D =	???? Julian Years —	? days.
(3)	..	.. From C =	??? Julian Years —	? days.
(4)	..	.. From B =	?? Julian Years +	? days.
(5)	..	.. From A =		? days.

TOTAL .. = ???? Julian Years + ? days P.M.T.

Then, number of days required = (???? Julian Years × 365¼ days) + ? days. For comparison with Data from Table XLIII.

ASTRONOMICAL NEW MOON DATES. RULE II :—To find, as above, but for an astronomical new moon, ascertain nearest full moon date, before or after, and add or subtract respectively 14.765 days.

LUNAR AND SOLAR ECLIPSE DATES. RULE III. LUNAR ECLIPSES :—From any astronomical full moon date (Rule I) at which a Lunar Eclipse occurred, to find a later or previous astronomical full moon date at which a Lunar Eclipse occurred on the Cycle of 29 J.Y. less 20.299496 days.

Obtain, from (C) and (D) only, the interval in Jul. Years and odd days, and add or subtract from total number of Julian Years and odd days which give the basal astronomical full moon Eclipse Date.

Comparison with Data obtained from Table XLIII, Rules I to IX, will give the Julian or Gregorian Date of the astronomical Full Moon at which the required Lunar Eclipse occurred.

If the interval, in Cycles of 29 J.Y. less 20.299496 days, between the two dates considered, is an even number of Cycles, the Eclipse occurs at the same node in both cases; if the number of Cycles is odd, the Eclipses occur at the opposite nodes from each other.

(D) gives even numbers of Cycles of 29 J.Y., &c. days, so that as to whether the number of Cycles is odd or even, is determined from the number of the Cycle extracted from (C) to form, by adding to the number extracted in (D), the total interval between the two Eclipses. This determining number for the node is supplied by the 1st left-hand Column of (C).

RULE IV. Solar Eclipses :—As in Rule III, but substitute " astronomical new moon " for " astronomical full moon," and " Solar Eclipse " for " Lunar Eclipse."

* mnb = " midnight beginning."

SECTION III.—DETAILS CONCERNING PLATES.

¶ 491. PLATE LIX. JULIAN AND GREGORIAN MONTH DATES.

Accessory tables and rules. Simple arithmetic only necessary. Certain simple tables and rules are necessary to enable the general reader to check the calculations that have been based on Plate LIX in conjunction with Tables II, III, and IV. By the inclusion of the new tables and rules it will be found that nothing further than simple arithmetic is necessary to follow and check the essential chronological calculations of this work.

Table XXXIX (A) Gregorian month dates for 1st July (Julian). Table XXXIX (A) gives the month dates of the Gregorian Calendar year corresponding to the 1st of July of the Julian Calendar year from Tabular year 0 of Plate LIX to Tabular year 5999 of Plate LIX, i.e. from astronomical 4000 B.C. to 1999 A.D.

Table XXXIX (B) Gregorian month dates for 1st February (Julian). Table XXXIX (B) gives the month dates of the Gregorian Calendar year corresponding to the 1st of February of the Julian Calendar year from Tabular year 1 of Plate LIX to Tabular year 6000 of Plate LIX, i.e. from astronomical 3999 B.C. to 2000 A.D.

Gregorian month dates for any Julian dates. Julian and Gregorian Leap Years. From these two tables, in conjunction with Table XLI (C), the Gregorian date corresponding to any Julian date within the period stated can be instantly obtained. Julian Leap Years, in which February had 29 days, can be obtained from Table XL (A) and (C). Gregorian Leap Years, in which February had 29 days, can be obtained from Table XL (B) and (C).

Table XL. The day of the week—4000 B.C. to 2800 A.D. Table XL gives data from which can be obtained the day of the week for any day of any month of any year within the period 4000 B.C. (astro.) to 2800 A.D. The process of calculation consists in merely adding the several factors for the day of the month, the month, the century, and the year, and then dividing by 7. The remainder indicates the day of the week required.

Table XLI. Ancient Egyptian and Euphratean Calendars and the modern Calendar. The number of days from the day of one month to the same day of a later month. Table XLI gives the number of days from a certain time of a particular day of one month to the same time of the same particular day of any later month within the range of the Calendar year. This is given in (A) for the early Egyptian intercalated 365 days' Calendar year of Table III and for the later Egyptian unintercalated or vague Calendar year of 365 days; in (B) for the early intercalated 360 days' Calendar year of Table III; and in (C) for the modern Calendar of 365 days, intercalated according to the Julian or Gregorian rules.

Experience necessary to teach method of using tables A full explanation as to the use of these and the other tables and their rules could be given, but the reader will find that it is only the experience of making mistakes, and finding the reason for the mistakes, that will teach him the structural basis of the tables and rules, and give that facility with which precise and rapid calculations can be made.

Typical examples worked out to introduce the reader to the method of using the tables The best introduction to this practical application will be found in the typical examples worked out, with the aid of the various tables, in ¶¶ 491b, c, and d, and 492. In working out similar cases the reader should be constantly on the alert to guard against overlooking the matter of Leap Year, and similar intercalations in the case of the early Egyptian intercalated Calendar year of 360 days, and the Hebrew, Aramaic, and Assyrian Luni-solar Calendar year.

¶ 491a. LUNI-SOLAR DATINGS AND CALCULATIONS.

To fix the Calendar months of the Hebrew, Aramaic, and Assyrian Lunar year for any particular Tabular year of Plate LIX and Tables XXXIX and XL, it is first necessary to fix the Julian month date for the new moon of the month Nisan. *Fixing the Julian month dates of the Luni-solar Calendar months for any particular year.*

Table XLII gives the Lunar Calendar, and the days from one month to any other month as in Table XLI, together with the general rule relating to the fixing of the 1st of Nisan by the new moon, and the rule concerning intercalation. *Table XLII. The Julian month dates of new and full moons.*

The time of astronomical new and full moons in terms of the number of days and fraction of a day after midnight beginning 1st January (Julian) of the particular Julian Tabular year (of Table XXXIX) in which they occurred, or will occur, can be determined by following in succession the rules of Tables XLIII and XLIV. *Tables XLIII and XLIV.*

It is always better first to determine the number of days and the fraction of a day after midnight beginning 1st January at which the new moon of Nisan occurred. Then, by fixing from rule of Table XLII the Julian date for 1st Nisan, obtain the exact placing of the whole Lunar Calendar for the particular Tabular year. The new and full moons for the year can then be obtained in terms of both the Julian Calendar of Table XLI and the Lunar Calendar of Table XLII. *The fixing of the 1st of Nisan.*

In fixing the 1st of Nisan it will be found necessary to obtain the Gregorian month dating as well as the Julian month dating, since it is from the former that the test for the Vernal Equinoctial limit for the full moon of Nisan can best be applied. *The Vernal Equinoctial limit for full moon of Nisan.*

The effect of lunar acceleration and of tidal retardation of the Earth's rotation does not seriously alter the time of new and full moons required for chronological purposes. The exact amounts of acceleration and retardation respectively, in any case, are still uncertain, but their total effect, expressed as altering the time of a new or full moon in 4000 B.C. is considerably less than 1 day. For this reason the modern value of the lunation has been adopted in Table XLIV. *The comparative effect of lunar acceleration and tidal retardation of the Earth's rotation for chronological purposes.*

The chronological zero full moon beginning 0 A.K. (4000 B.C. (hist.) = Tabular year 1) when taken as occurring precisely at midnight beginning (P.M.T.)[1] 22nd September (Greg.) = 24th October (Julian) is 0·3738 of a day earlier than is given by the modern lunation value of Table XLIV. The latter value, of course, is the mean value during the year, and is applied in the calculations as the mean value throughout. The slight difference obtained cannot therefore be taken as evidence either against the identity of absolute full moon with midnight on the Pyramid meridian, or as indicative of the precise total effect due to lunar acceleration and tidal retardation. *The application of the mean value of the lunation for modern times.*

The determination of the precise time in hours, minutes, and seconds for every calculation of a lunation requires the ordinary mathematical processes of advanced astronomy. Such precision is, however, unnecessary for chronological purposes, since in no case would the refinement of calculation alter the date of a new or full moon as fixed by Tables XLIII and XLIV. The same remark applies to the time of lunar and solar eclipses derived from the data of these tables. It is to be observed, however, that the mathematical processes of astronomy are necessary for the precise determination of the latitude and longitude on the Earth's surface relating to the observation of eclipses. *The limitations of the lunar tables from the precise astronomical standpoint. The determination of lunar and solar eclipse dates.*

¶ 491b. THE LUNAR ECLIPSE OF THE SEVENTH YEAR OF CAMBYSES. EXAMPLE OF CALCULATIONS—STAGE I.

The Babylonian Tablet discovered by Father Strassmeier records a partial lunar eclipse at Babylon in the 7th year of the Persian King Cambyses (refer to Annotations, Table XXI, Col. 2). The Tablet states that the eclipse occurred on the 14th day of the month Tammuz. This eclipse is also mentioned by Ptolemy (reference as *The data of the Babylonian Tablet. Ptolemy's data in the "Almagest."*

---

[1] P.M.T. = Pyramid mean time.

above) in the *Almagest*, and is again identified with the 7th year of Cambyses. The time, according to Ptolemy, was 1 hour before midnight at Babylon. Ptolemy, however, gives the Egyptian month dating. This will be investigated shortly.

Data of modern calculations. Sir Isaac Newton, Pingré, Oppolzer, Newcomb, and other authorities, have all fixed 16th July (Julian) 523 B.C. (hist.) as the date of the eclipse noted. This is independently confirmed from our tables.

First stage of calculation by tables. I. To find, in the first instance, if 16th July (Julian) 523 B.C. (hist.) is a full-moon date.

By Plate LIX (hist.) 523 B.C.=(astro.) 522 B.C.=T.Y. 3478.

By Table XLIII, T.Y. 3478=year (c) of Julian Leap Year Cycle.

By Table XLIII, Rule III—

mnb.[1] 1st January T.Y. 0 to mnb.
    1st January T.Y. 3478   ..=3478 Julian years.+ $\frac{1}{2}$ day.
Table XLI, mnb. 1st January to
    mnb. 1st July T.Y. 3478   ..=   +181 days.
mnb. 1st July to mnb. 16th July
    T.Y. 3478 ..   .. ..=   + 15 ,,

mnb. 1st January T.Y. 0 to mnb.
    16th July T.Y. 3478 ..   ..=3478 Julian years.+196$\frac{1}{2}$ days.

For the identity required the full moon should fall between mnb. 16th July and mnb. 17th July of T.Y. 3478, or at the duration of 3478 Julian years 196$\frac{1}{2}$ days to 197$\frac{1}{2}$ days from mnb. 1st January T.Y. 0.

The time by the tables of the full moon at which the eclipse occurred. From Table XLIV, Rule I, for full moon, we have—

(1) Constant ..   ..   1 Julian year +297.124 days P.M.T.
(2) From (D) ..   ..   3126 Julian years— 0.846 day.
(3) ,,   (C)   348   ,,   ,, —243.594 days.
(4) ,,   (B)   3   ,,   ,, ÷ 26.412 ,,
(5) ,,   (A) ..   ..   +118.122 ,,

Adding algebraically .. 3478 Julian years+197.218 days P.M.T.
Deduct period to mnb.
    16th July T.Y. 3478   3478 ,,   ,, +196.5   days.

Full moon after mnb. 16th July T.Y. 3478 = 0.718 day P.M.T.
Reducing to Babylonian time (Table XLIII,
    Rule IX) add ..   .. 0.037 ,,

    0.755 day B.M.T.[2]

This fraction represents—

        18 hrs. 7 mins. after mnb. 16th July (hist.) 523 B.C.

or

        6 hrs. 7 mins. in the afternoon of 16th July 523 B.C.

Our Tables therefore give full moon as occurring 4 hrs. 53 mins. before the eclipse was seen at Babylon. The time indicated by the tables is, of course, approximate, but is sufficient to show so far as examined that the data of the tables are in agreement with the essential astronomical data.

[1] mnb.=midnight beginning.   [2] B.M.T.=Babylonian Mean Time.

¶ 491c. EXAMPLE OF CALCULATIONS—STAGE II.

II. To confirm that a lunar eclipse occurred on the day of the full moon determined.
Second stage of calculation by tables.

If a series of cycles of the 29 Julian years less 20 days (as Table XLIV (C))—the unit chronological eclipse period—from 16th July T.Y. 3478 give a recent full-moon date at which a lunar eclipse occurred, the eclipse date, 16th July 523 B.C., is confirmed by the tables.

From ¶ 491b take	3478 Julian years	+197.218 days.
By Rule III, Table XLIV (D), add ..	2084 ,, ,,	— 0.564 day.
By Rule III, Table XLIV (C)[1], add ..	319 ,, ,,	—223.294 days.
Adding algebraically	5881 Julian years	— 26.640 days.
=5880	,, ,,	+338.610 ,,

To find the Julian month dating corresponding to above—

By Rule III, Table XLIII, T.Y. 5880=year (a) of the Leap Year Cycle. Hence—

mnb. 1st January T.Y. 0 to mnb. 1st
    January T.Y. 5880 .. ..=5880 Julian years+ 0 days.
By Table XLI (C) mnb. 1st January
    to mnb. 1st December .. ..=   +334 ,,
    Add for T.Y. 5880 being a
        Leap Year .. ..   + 1 day.
mnb. 1st December to mnb. 4th
    December .. ..=   + 3 days.

Total mnb. 1st January T.Y. 0 to
    mnb. 4th December T.Y. 5880 ..=5880 Julian years+338 days.

Now T.Y. 5880 is 1880 A.D. (by Plate LX).

Comparison of the two totals above therefore shows that full moon fell on 4th December (Julian) 1880 A.D. at 0·610 of a day after midnight (P.M.T.).

By Table XXXIX (A), in 1880 A.D.=5880 T.Y., 1st July (Julian)=13th July (Greg.), and therefore 1st December (Julian)=13th December (Greg.), and 4th December (Julian)=16th December (Greg.).
The tables indicate that a lunar eclipse occurred at the full moon of Stage I of the calculation.

Hence 4.61 December (Julian)=16.61 December (Greg.) P.M.T.

By Table XLIII, Rule IX, deduct 0.087 to obtain G.M.T.

16.523 December (Greg.) G.M.T.

According to the tables, then, full moon occurred at 12.33 p.m. (G.M.T.) of 16th December (Greg.) 1880 A.D.

From the " Nautical Almanac " or " Whitaker's " for 1880, a total lunar eclipse occurred on 16th December at 3 hrs. 39 mins. afternoon, or 3 hrs. 6 mins. after the time of the full moon obtained from our tables. Our tables, therefore, confirm the lunar eclipse of 16th July (Julian) 523 B.C. (hist.).

[1]The determining number of cycle 11 in Table XLIV (C) indicates that the lunar eclipse of 16th July (Julian) 523 B.C. occurred at the opposite node from the lunar eclipse of 16th December (Greg.) 1880 A.D.

¶ 491d. EXAMPLE OF CALCULATIONS—STAGE III.

Third stage of calculation by tables.

III. To confirm by our tables that the Lunar Eclipse of the 7th year of Cambyses fell on 14th Tammuz as stated by the contemporary Babylonian Tablet.

From Table XLII, General Rule, we have to find, in the first instance, the Julian date of astronomical new moon nearest the Vernal Equinox.

By the process of Calculation I (in ¶ 491b) mnb. 1st January T.Y. o to a full moon in T.Y. 3478 .. .. = 3478 Julian years + 79.096 days.

To obtain succeeding astronomical new moon add .. ..   + 14.765 „

3478 Julian years + 93.861 days.

From Calculation I (¶ 491b) deduct interval mnb. 1st January T.Y. o to mnb. 1st January T.Y. 3478 .. .. ..   3478 „   „ + 0.5 day.

Time of astronomical new moon after mnb. 1st January T.Y. 3478 .. .. .. =   93.361 days.

To find the Julian and Gregorian month dates corresponding to the time thus defined—

From Table XLI (C) mnb. 1st January (Julian) to mnb. 1st April (Julian) .. .. = 90 days.
                                                 Add .. .. 3 „

From mnb. 1st January (Julian) to mnb. 4th April (Julian) = 93 days.

By Table XXXIX (A) for T.Y. 3478—

                1st July (Julian) = 25th June (Greg.).

Therefore

                1st April (Julian) = 26th March (Greg.).
        Add 3   3

                4th April (Julian) = 29th March (Greg.).

By the tables, therefore, astronomical new moon occurred at

                4.361 April (Julian) P.M.T.
                = 29.361 March (Greg.) P.M.T.

If the preceding full moon was the full moon of Nisan, the full moon of Nisan would have fallen before the Vernal Equinox, contrary to the rule of Table XLII. The astronomical new moon of 29.361 March (Greg.) was, therefore, the astronomical new moon datum for the 1st of Nisan (by General Rule of Table XLII). This gives the 1st of Nisan beginning at sunset of the Julian day following, i.e. sunset of 30th March (Greg.) or 5th April (Julian).

The calculation by the tables gives the same Babylonian month dating for the lunar eclipse as is stated on the Babylonian Tablet.

From Table XLII—   .
Sunset beginning 1st Nisan to sunset beginning 1st Tammuz = 89 days.
                                Add .. .. .. 13 „

Sunset beginning 1st Nisan to sunset beginning 14th Tammuz = 102 days.

TABLE XLV. (Refer Annotations to Table XI).

THE JULIAN MONTH DATES, FOR DAY 1 MONTH 1 OF THE EGYPTIAN VAGUE YEAR FROM THE YEAR IN WHICH IT WAS FIRST ESTABLISHED (HIST. B.C. 1861) TO THE 3RD CENTURY A.D., WHEN IT WAS FINALLY DISCARDED.

Tabular Years of Plate LX	4200	4100	4000	3900	3800	3700	3600	3500	3400	3300	3200	3100	3000	2900	2800	2700	2600	2500	2400	2300	2200	2100	Tabular Years of Plate LX
0–3	July 4	July 29	Aug. 23	Sept. 17	Oct. 12	Nov. 6	Dec. 1	Dec. 26	Jany. 20	Feb. 14	Mar. 11	May 4	May 29	June 23	July 18	Aug. 12	Sept. 6	Oct. 1	July 27	Aug. 21	Sept. 15		0–3
4–7	3	28	22	16	11	5	Nov. 30	25	19	13	10	3	28	22	17	11	5	Sept. 30	26	20	14		4–7
8–11	2	27	21	15	10	4	29	24	18	12	9	2	27	21	16	10	4	29	25	19	13		8–11
12–15	1	26	20	14	9	3	28	23	17	11	8	1	26	20	15	9	3	28	24	18	12		12–15
16–19	June 30	25	19	13	8	2	27	22	16	10	7	April 30	25	19	14	8	2	27	23	17	11		16–19
20–23	29	24	18	12	7	1	26	21	15	9	6	29	24	18	13	7	1	26	22	16	10		20–23
24–27	28	23	17	11	6	Oct. 31	25	20	14	8	5	28[4]	23	17	12	6	Aug. 31	25	21	15	9		24–27
28–31	27	22	16	10	5	30	24	19	13	7	4	27	22	16	11	5	30	24	20	14	8		28–31
32–35	26	21	15	9	4	29	23	18	12	6	3	26	21	15	10	4	29	23	19	13	7		32–35
36–39	25	20	14	8	3	28	22	17	11	5	2	25	20	14	9	3	28	22	18	12	6		36–39
40–43	24	19	13	7	2	27	21	16	10	4	1	24	19	13	8	2	27	21	17	11	5	Sept. 30[1]	40–43
44–47	23	18	12	6	1	26	20	15	9	3	Feb. 28*	23	18	12	7	1	26	20	16	10	4	29	44–47
48–51	22	17	11	5	Sept. 30	25	19	14	8	2	27	22	17	11	6	July 31	25	19	15	9	3	28	48–51
52–55	21	16	10	4	29	24	18	13	7	1	26	21	16	10	5	30	24	18	14	8	2	27	52–55
56–59	20	15	9	3	28	23	17	12	6	Jany. 31	25	20	15	9	4	29	23	17	13	7	1	26	56–59
60–63	19	14	8	2	27	22	16	11	5	30	24	19	14	8	3	28	22	16	12	6	Aug. 31	25	60–63
64–67	18	13	7	1	26	21	15	10	4	29	23	18	13	7	2	27	21	15	11	5	30	24	64–67
68–71	17	12	6	Aug. 31	25	20	14	9	3	28	22	17	12	6	1	26	20	14	10[2]	4	29	23	68–71
72–75	16	11	5	30	24	19	13	8	2	27	21	16	11	5	June 30	25	19	13		3	28	22	72–75
76–79	15	10	4	29	23	18	12	7	1	26	20	15	10	4	29	24	18	12		2	27	21	76–79
80–83	14	9	3	28	22	17	11	6	Dec. 31	25	19	14	9	3	28	23	17	11		1	26	20	80–83
84–87	13	8	2	27	21	16	10	5	30	24	18	13	8	2	27	22	16	10		July 31	25	19	84–87
88–91	12	7	1	26	20	15	9	4	29	23	17	12	7	1	26	21	15	9	Oct. 4[3]	30	24	18	88–91
92–95	11	6	July 31	25	19	14	8	3	28	22	16	11	6	May 31	25	20	14	8	3	29	23	17	92–95
96–99	10	5	30	24	18	13	7	2	27	21	15	10	5	30	24	19	13	7	2	28	22	16	96–99
Tabular Years of Plate LX	4200	4100	4000	3900	3800	3700	3600	3500	3400	3300	3200	3100	3000	2900	2800	2700	2600	2500	2400	2300	2200	2100	Tabular Years of Plate LX

[1] Began in Tab. Year 2140 at 2139 A.K. (Refer Annotations to Table XI, Column 1).
[2] Ended in Tab. Year 2469 at 2467½ A.K. (Refer Annotations to Table XI, Columns 2 and 3).
[3] Began, after final adjustment, in Tab. Year 2488 at 2487 A.K. (Refer Annotations to Table XI, Columns 2 and 3).
[4] Began, after adjustment, in Tab. Year 3127 at 3125½ A.K. (Refer Annotations to Table XI, Column 4).

* 29th Feby. in Tab. Year 3244.

[To face p. 515.]

From Table XLI (C)—

    Sunset of 5th April (Julian) to sunset of 5th July (Julian) ..= 91 days.
              Add   ..   ..   ..   11 ,,

    Sunset of 5th April (Julian) to sunset of 16th July (Julian) ..=102 days.

The identity derived above shows that the tables give the 14th of Tammuz beginning at sunset of 16th July (Julian) in 523 B.C. As the eclipse observed at Babylon is stated to have occurred (central) about 11 p.m., 16th July (Julian) in that year, the tables are therefore seen to confirm the record of the 7th year of Cambyses.

¶ 491e. THE RULE CONCERNING THE VERNAL EQUINOCTIAL LIMIT.

The example given confirms the placing of the Aramaic and Assyrian lunar calendar of Table XLII, and the rule concerning the Vernal Equinoctial limit for the full moon of Nisan. Every known dating from Aramaic, Assyrian, and Babylonian sources confirms this. Now the Aramæans derived their calendar month names from Assyria during their period of predominance there (Table XIX). Their rule concerning intercalation and the Vernal Equinoctial limit was derived from the same source. The fact that the Jews adopted the Aramaic lunar month names confirms the inference already derived (¶ 465), that they conformed to the universal rule concerning the Vernal Equinoctial limit. This fact being established renders the date 29 A.D. for the Crucifixion impossible, and confirms that the only possible year for the Crucifixion is 30 A.D. (¶ 470).

The full moon of Nisan could not precede the Vernal Equinox in the luni-solar Calendar year of the Hebrews, Aramæans, Babylonians, and Assyrians. This fact confirms that the Crucifixion was in 30 A.D. and not in 29 A.D.

¶ 492. PLATE LX. EXAMPLE OF CALCULATIONS—STAGE IV.

From the examples already given in the text of this Chapter, and in the Annotations to Tables XI and XIV, the reader can readily find the method of using Plate LX. To enable the reader to check the recorded month dates of the heliacal rising of Sirius during the period in which the vague year was solely employed for *civil* reckoning, Table XLV has been added. This gives the complete history of the placing of the vague year calendar, and the history of its various adjustments from the time of its institution (1861 B.C.) until the 3rd century A.D., when it was finally discarded.

Plate LX and Table XLV. The history of the Egyptian vague year calendar from its institution in 1861 B.C. to the 3rd century A.D.

As an example of the use of this table, let us complete our investigation of the previous example of ¶¶ 491b–491d.

Ptolemy states that the lunar eclipse—11 p.m. 16th July (Julian) 523 B.C.— occurred in the evening beginning the 18th of the Egyptian month Phamenoth, which was the VIIth month of the vague year at that time (Table XLI (A)).

Ptolemy's Egyptian vague year calendar dating for the eclipse of the 7th year of Cambyses confirmed by the table.

Now, by the previous example, 523 B.C.=Tab. year 3478.

By Table XLV, in Tab. year 3478, Day 1 Month I fell on 1st January (Julian). Since the Egyptian days began at sunset, Day 1 Month I began on 31st December.

By Table XLI (A)—

    Midnight Day 1 Month I to midnight Day 1 Month VII=180 days.
            Add   17   17 ,,

    Midnight Day 1 Month I to midnight Day 18 Month VII=197 days.

By Table XLI (C)—

        mnb. 1st January to mnb. 1st July =181 days.
           Add   16   16 ,,

        mnb. 1st January to mnb. 17th July=197 days.

The eclipse occurred 1 hour before midnight and on 16th July.

The above identity confirms that 1 hour before midnight beginning 17th July fell in the evening beginning 18th Phamenoth (Month VII), as is stated by Ptolemy.

¶ 493. PLATE LXI AND ITS, SCALE OF CHRONOLOGY.

The application of Plate LXI.

The Plate is amply explained in ¶¶ 322 and 323, and in Annotations to Plate LXI and Annotations to Tables XXII and XXIII. Its scale of chronology is fixed by the data of Tables XI (and Annotations), XIV (and Annotations), XXII (and Annotations), XXIII and XXVIII (and Annotations A and B).

The short-period "Sed hebs" of Ramessu II adopted for purpose of experimental intercalation to fix the vague year beginning, for a particular year, at a required place in the Sothic year.

One fact relating to the chronology of Dynasty XIX requires emphasising. This concerns the pseudo-*Sed heb* periods of Ramessu II (refer Annotations to Table XI). The *Sed heb* period was actually 30 years. Ramessu II, for the purpose of altering the vague year to a required position for a given year, celebrated short-period *Sed hebs*, generally at 3 years' intervals. The short periods were for the purpose of experimental intercalation and readjustment necessitated by observations taken to make the intercalations conform to the intention of the Calendar revision.

The zero year for the short-period "Sed hebs" was the 27th year of Ramessu II; the year in which a new Phœnix cycle began.

The fact that *Sed heb* means "the tail festival" or "the end festival" indicates that the 1st pseudo-*Sed heb* in the 30th year of Ramessu II ended a pseudo-*Sed heb* period, the initial date of which formed the zero datum for the series of pseudo-*Sed hebs*. The 2nd pseudo-*Sed heb* was celebrated in the 33rd year of Ramessu II, thus indicating that the zero chronological datum of the series fell in the 27th year of Ramessu II. The identification shows clearly that the zero datum adopted was that of the Phœnix cycle festival of the observation of the heliacal rising of Sirius in the 27th year of Ramessu II. The last pseudo-*Sed heb* was celebrated in the 46th year of Ramessu II.

The intention of the calendar revision by Ramessu II at this time.

The experimental observations and readjustment of the intercalations on the basis of the risings of Sirius, therefore, covered a period of 19 years. Within this period 7 pseudo-*Sed hebs* were celebrated. These clearly define 6 calendar adjustments as a result of experimental observations, and a final (7th) adjustment at the end of 19 years. This would leave Day 1 Month I of the vague year in such a position in the Sothic year as to ensure its coincidence with the day upon which the heliacal rising would be observed in the terminal year of the current Phœnix cycle of 329 years.

The significance attaching to the numerical value of the various intervals of intercalation.

It should be noted that the observations beginning with the 27th year as zero, and recorded for the 30th, 33rd, 34th, 36th, 37th, 40th, and 46th years, give intervals of 1, 2, 3, 4, 6, 9, 10, 12, 13, 16, and 19 years—by selection of recorded years. There are 5 intervals of 3 years, 3 intervals of 4 years, 4 intervals of 6 years, 2 intervals of 9 years, 3 intervals of 10 years, 1 interval of 12 years, 2 intervals of 16 years, and 1 interval of 19 years. Observations of the heliacal rising of Sirius at the beginning and ending of all such periods would enable the day of the heliacal rising of Sirius at the end of the current cycle to be accurately forecasted. This could be effected by the summation of selected combinations of the various periods expressed in days, and could be confirmed by similar summations of other selected combinations.

The Phœnix cycle of 329 years fictitiously adjusted to appear ending as if it had always been celebrated as a cycle of 1460 Sothic years.

The initial experimental period of 19 years left 310 vague years to complete the Phœnix cycle by Day 1 Month I falling upon the day in which Sirius rose heliacally. The cycle thus "faked" to terminate at an apparent ending of the vague year cycle was intended to be adopted as the termination, not of 329 years from Ramessu II Sesostris, but of 1460 Sothic years from Ramessu II Sesostris.

The vanity of Ramessu II explained.

As Petrie observes : " It was only the vanity of Ramessu II—the man who is shown worshipping himself—that appropriated this festival (the Sed heb) to the glorifying of his reign." It was a vanity, however, that impelled him to identify himself with the legendary conqueror Sesostris, and so to disorganise the calendar as to ensure his being identified with the original Sesostris, in whose 7th year a cycle of 1461 solar years terminated (refer to ¶ 317 and Annotations D¹ to Table XV).

¶ 494. PLATE LXII. LUNI-SOLAR CYCLES.

This Plate is fully explained in ¶¶ 344–347. The astronomical significance of *The Pyramid* the periods of 1260 and 2520 solar years has not, however, been explained. With the *and Hebrew* modern value of the solar year and the modern value of the lunar month, 1260 solar *of 1260 and* years are ½ day in excess of 15,584 lunar months, or 1298⅔ lunar years. The period *years are luni-* of 1260 solar years, therefore, forms a cycle of the luni-solar year. The Pyramid's *solar cycles.* chronological representation of this period (Plate LXII) as an initial cycle from the Autumnal Equinox full moon of 4000 B.C. (0 A.K.) indicates the intention of representing the period as a luni-solar cycle.

Another sacred luni-solar cycle is the cycle of 1040 solar years discovered by the *De Cheseaux's* Swiss astronomer, De Cheseaux.² With the values of modern times, 12,863 lunar *luni-solar cycle* months are 1 hr. 34 mins. in excess of 1040 solar years. De Cheseaux showed *years.* that the 1040 years' luni-solar cycle was the difference between the sacred cycle of *The Pyramid* 1260 years and the sacred cycle of 2300 years (¶¶ 374–379 and Plate LXVI). This *sacred cycle* confirms that Daniel's 2300 "evening-mornings" relate to solar years only, and to *years is a luni-* solar years beginning at the Autumnal Equinox (¶ 374). The same connection *solar cycle* defines that the *primary* chronological application of the 1260 and 2520 years, as in *cycles of 1040* the Pyramid's chronology of Plate LXII, is to solar years beginning at the Autumnal *and 1260 solar* Equinox, or at the Autumnal Equinoctial lunar year beginning. *years.*

De Cheseaux's discovery showed that the sacred period of 2300 solar years was also a luni-solar cycle. With the modern values, 2300 solar years are only 10 hrs. 9½ mins. in excess of 28,447 lunar months. When we remember that the Pyramid's astronomical data and its message are addressed to modern times, and that the Pyramid's axial epoch for processional references is 1844 A.D., we see the possibility of the accurate values of the 1040 years', 1260 years', 2300 years', and 2520 years' luni-solar cycles being represented in relation to some such particular epoch.

¶ 495. PLATE LXIII. THE PYRAMID'S PASSAGE BEARING ON THE CROSSING OF "THE SEA OF REEDS."

This Plate is discussed in ¶ 327 (and note) and ¶ 356. In the same connection *The original* the reader should refer to Table XXXVIII. The Pyramid's indication of the true *discovery of* bearing on Bethlehem had already been shown by Messrs. Edgar in their "Great *the Pyramid's geometrical*

¹It should be explained how Lamaris, as in Annotations (D), items 4 and 5 to Table XV, *bearing on* came to be identified, in the example there given, with Senusert III. Senusert III = Lakheres, *Bethlehem.* Lachares, and Nachares (Annotations D, Col. 2 (foot) to Tables XVII–XIX). In the example *the same bear-* under consideration Lamaris was equated with Lachares. As the example is from the Version of *ing indicating* Africanus, this can be seen from comparison of the known sequence of XIIth Dynasty kings with *the point at* the sequence as given by the Version of Africanus. *crossed "the sea of reeds,"*

Known Sequence.	Sequence in Africanus.
Amenemhat I.	Ammenemes.
Senusert I.	Sesonchosis.
Amenemhat II.	Ammanemes.
Senusert II.	Sesostris.
Senusert III.	Lamaris.
Amenemhat III.	Ammeres.
Amenemhat IV.	Amenemes.
Sebek neferu-Ra.	Skemiophris.

as fixed by Sir Hanbury Brown.

The Suten-Bat name of Amenemhat III = Maat-en-Ra or En-Maat-Ra transliterated as Ammeres. (A'-maa'-Ra.)

²"Mémoires posthumes de M. de Cheseaux," 1754, discussed by Dr. Grattan Guinness, "Approaching End of the Age," pp. 400–404.

Other indications confirming.

Pyramid Passages," Vol. I. It was not deemed by the present authors to be an absolutely reliable geometrical indication in itself—from the point of view of definitive intention. When Plate LXIII was drawn, however, it was seen that the same geometrical bearing pointed out the precise location of the crossing of "the sea of reeds" as fixed by Sir Hanbury Brown in his "Land of Goshen." Having regard to the scriptural identity relating to the parallel circumstances and dates of the Exodus of Israel and the *Exodos* of our Lord as indicated by the Old and New Testaments, and by the Great Pyramid's chronological prophecy—as expressed in comparative form in Table XXXVIII and diagram—the geometrical indication of the crossing of "the sea of reeds" was adopted as confirming the Edgars' theory.

The intention of the same bearing confirmed by the symbolism and dating of the Exodus in the Pyramid's Entrance Passage.

The geometrical definition of the bearing explained.

The axis of the Pyramid's Entrance Passage also gives the date of Israel's Exodus and the crossing of "the sea of reeds" as the turning-point in the evolution of the Messianic kingdom, from descent to ascent. The way of ascent, however, is indicated as gained through an impenetrable obstruction. This symbolism precisely fits the conditions of the crossing of "the sea of reeds" at the location indicated by the Pyramid's passage angle bearing. By "passage angle," the general reader must here clearly understand that this, in the particular case under discussion, applies to a development of the Pyramid's passage section into the horizontal plane, and with the central axis from base to apex of the section lying from the Pyramid towards the north. In other words, the Pyramid's passage angle is here indicated as an oriented function of the Pyramid's geometry transferred into the plane tangential to the Earth's surface at the Great Pyramid.

The Exodus and the crossing of the waters of "the sea of reeds."

The Crucifixion and the Resurrection.

"The crossing of the pure waters of life."

The attention of the reader is here directed to the diagram on Table XXXVIII. This shows that the ancient Egyptian designation for the beginning of the Pyramid's Grand Gallery, which gives the date and symbolism of the Crucifixion and Resurrection, confirms the analogy emphasised by the Old and New Testaments as holding between the events of the Exodus and the events of our Lord's Passion. "The crossing of the pure waters of life," as descriptive of the Resurrection, confirms that the latter was prefigured by Israel's crossing of the waters of "the sea of reeds."

¶ 495a. THE LAND OF GOSHEN AND THE ROUTE OF THE EXODUS.

Hebrew "Goshen" =LXX and Coptic "Gesem" =Egyptian "Kesem" =medieval "Gesse."

In the "acme" of Arabia.

Pi-Sopt in Goshen identified with Saft-el-Henneh.

The reader will find many interesting evidences relating to the identification of Goshen in Sir Hanbury Brown's "Land of Goshen."

In Egyptian the name is "Kesem." In the LXX and Coptic translations of the Bible, "Goshen" is translated "Gesem." Both give "Gesem" as in the *nome* of Arabia. In medieval times the name is "Gesse," and is identified as North of Suez. The hieroglyphic texts identify Kesem as a *district*, and a *city* in which stood the Temple of Sopt, the god of the Arabian *nome*. Dr. Naville's excavations identified the modern site of Saft-el-Henneh (Plate LXIII) as the site of the ancient Pi-Sopt, the *religious* capital of the Arabian *nome*.

Pithom = Tel el Maskhuta.

Rameses = Tel Rotab.

The first stage of the Exodus route along Wadi Tumilat.

The problem of the provisioning of Israel in Sinai. Sinai, from long prior to 2000 B.C. to present time, not able to support more than 5000 people.

Similarly Naville's excavations at the site known as Tel el Maskhuta (Plate LXIII) and Petrie's excavations at the site known as Tel Rotab (Plate LXIII) identified these places respectively as the ancient sites of Pithom and Rameses. Other sites have been suggested by other authorities for Pithom and Rameses, but the identifications upon which these depend ignore the narrative of the Book of Exodus relating to the route of the Exodus. There certainly appears to have been more than one town-name in the Delta containing the name "Rameses," but not specifically designated "Ramessu" or "Rameses." The fact remains, however, that, by adopting the narrative of the book of Exodus, the Egyptological data agree in placing the first stage of the Exodus route in the Wadi Tumilat (Plate LXIII). With this, Sir Ernest Budge agrees, although, as his concluding remark quoted below seems to show, he obviously dislikes identifying himself with the belief in the southern trend of the Exodus route after the crossing of "the sea of reeds." The reason for this is obvious. The wilderness route necessitated the miraculous provisioning of the hosts of Israel. For, as Sir William M. F. Petrie states in his "Researches in Sinai" and "Egypt and Israel," the evidences from the time of the VIth Egyptian Dynasty up to the present time, show that, within the period thus defined, Sinai could not support more than 5000 inhabitants.[1]

Budge's statement, to which we have referred, is as follows :—

"Taken together, the known facts about the land of Goshen and the land of Rameses indicate that the passage of the "Red Sea" was not made either as far north as any portion of Lake Menzeleh or as far south as Suez, and that whatever water was crossed by them, be it lake or be it sea, was situated at no great distance from the eastern part of the Wâdî Tûmîlât. . . ."

"The narrative of the Book of Exodus calls the water which the Israelites crossed 'Yam Suph,' i.e. the 'sea of reeds,' a name which they would never have given to the sea in general ; and there is no doubt that they called the water by that name because it was of great extent and because it contained reeds. . . . The present writer, who has gone over the routes proposed both by M. Naville and Sir William Dawson, thinks that, if the matter is to be considered from a practical standpoint, the only possible way for the Israelites to escape quickly into the Etham desert was by a passage across Lake Timsah. On their route after they had crossed he offers no opinion."[2]

¶ 495b. GOSHEN AT THE TIME OF MENEPHTAH.

The following statement by Sir Hanbury Brown is of more than ordinary significance, in the light of the fact that Menephtah's battle with the Libyans, referred to in the statement, is now proved to have taken place eight or nine months only before the Exodus (Table XXIII).

"The contemporary records of the hieroglyphics show that, at the time when the Hebrews came and settled in Goshen, it was not an organised province occupied by an *agricultural* population. It was part of the marsh land called the 'Water of Ra.' It could therefore be given by the king to foreigners without disturbing the native population."

"The same hieroglyphic documents record that in this land—the land of the Water of Ra—Baïlos was situated. Now Baïlos of the hieroglyphics is Bilbeis of to-day. These documents further state, in narrating how King Merenptah (Menephtah) fought a battle against foreign invasion near Baïlos, that the country round it 'was not cultivated, but was left as pasture for cattle, because of the strangers. It was abandoned since the time of the ancestors.' Whether this is a reference to its occupation by the Israelites or not, the passage proves that the district was used for pasturage and not for cultivation, and that consequently it had been in the hands of the wandering shepherds of Asia."[3]

¶ 495c. THE PROBLEM OF LAKE MENZELEH AND THE EARLIEST SUEZ CANAL.

One other matter relating to the topographical evidences remains to be dealt with in this connection. This concerns the omission of Lake Menzeleh on Plate LXIII

[1]It has been argued that this fact confirms the contention that Israel at the Exodus did not number more than 5000. In the formulation of the theory relating to the 5000 of Israel, many of the numerical references to the actual statements of fighting men have had to be ignored. The theory is based on the fact that " alaf " translated 1000, also means " family," " group," or " tent." On this basis the numbers are reduced to 5000.

But one cannot read Exodus xii, 37 and 38 as signifying " about 600 tents on foot that were *men*, beside children. And a mixed multitude went up also with them." Of course we quite clearly understand that the theory presupposes that the text has been corrupted by the supposed successive re-editing of an early composition, derived from several original documents. Did not this opinion form the background of the presentation of the theory, there would have been no basis for its formulation. The theory admittedly does not account for the numbers of the Levites (Num. iii) nor for the number of the first-born. The theory at first sight appears plausible enough, but a close scrutiny of the books of Exodus, Numbers, etc., fails to justify it on many other points than those admitted to be at variance with the theory. The male Levites between the ages of 30 and 50 years, numbered by Moses and Aaron in the 2nd year in the wilderness (Num. iv), alone total 8580, or 3580 more than the supposed total of all the fighting men of Israel.

[2]" Hist. Egypt," Vol. V, pp. 130–131.
[3]" The Land of Goshen," pp. 29 and 30.

Mediterranean end of the Isthmus has lowered and the Red Sea end has risen since then. (compare with Plate III). The engineering and topographical authorities responsible for the reconstruction of the map of the time of the Exodus (refer note to ¶ 327) explain that the evidences indicate that the Mediterranean end of the Isthmus of Suez has subsided and the Red Sea end has risen since the time in question.

The nature of "the sea of reeds." The Red Sea end had already risen considerably even at the date of the Exodus. The former sea-water had at that time become a shallow, reedy, fresh-water "estuary," fed intermittently by the shallow flood branch of the Nile that flowed through the Wadi Tumilat.

How the rising of the land and the choking of discharge of the Nile into the Red Sea had produced "the sea of reeds." Formerly—at an uncertain date prior to the Exodus—it would have been possible to navigate from the Nile into the Red Sea, along the Wadi Tumilat branch. Before the time of the Exodus the density of reeds—incidental to the rising of the land producing fresh-water shallows, and giving the name "the sea of reeds" to these shallows—had rendered navigation impossible. To open up a navigable communication between the Nile and the Red Sea, Seti I commenced a canal. Work on this was A XIXth Dynasty canal cut to restore the original natural navigable communication between the Mediterranean and the Red Sea—via the Nile. continued by Ramessu II. The canal was cut to join the Nile near Zagazig, and its course towards the Gulf of Suez followed the course of the existing Freshwater Canal ; the latter, in fact, being largely a utilised portion of the ancient canal. It was in navigable use at the time of Darius I, having either been completed by the latter king, or else, as is more likely, re-opened by him.

¶ 495d. TWO OPINIONS CONCERNING THE DEATH OF THE PHARAOH OF THE EXODUS.

Synopsis of the Egyptian data relating to the Exodus of Israel. The Egyptian data relating to the Exodus of Israel has proved the following :—

(1) That the Exodus occurred at the end of the 5th or the beginning of the 6th year of Menephtah, about the time of the death of his only son and co-regent Seti II.

(2) That after the Exodus—Seti II being dead—the co-regency passed to a foreigner, a Syrian.

(3) That the land of Goshen, having been vacated by the Israelites, was free for settlement, and that such settlement was effected by other nomads in the 8th year of Menephtah.

The data represent the Pharaoh of the Exodus living 3 years after the Exodus. (4) That the disaster to the flower of the Egyptian army and nobility at the crossing of "the sea of reeds" was so overwhelming that Egypt succumbed to disorganisation and anarchy 9½ years later.

This probability foreseen by Rawlinson prior to the discovery of definite evidence. The Egyptian evidence necessarily presupposes that Menephtah lived 3 years after the Exodus, and therefore that he had not entered "the sea of reeds" with his pursuing hosts. This is contrary to the popular opinion concerning the meaning and intention of the narrative of Exodus. Now it is a remarkable fact that long before the evidence summarised above came to light, Professor G. Rawlinson[1] had deduced from the behaviour[2] of Menephtah at the battle against the Libyans in his 5th year The 5th and 6th years of Menephtah identified by Bunsen, Lenormant, and Sayce— that he had not the courage to enter the "sea of reeds" with his chariots, that the Exodus occurred soon after his 5th year, and that he lived until his 8th year.

It is also remarkable that Bunsen, over 40 years before the discovery of the Egyptian record giving the date of the Exodus, stated that "the Exodus must have taken place in the first 5 or 6 years of Menephtah."

as the years relating to the events concerned with the Exodus—respectively 40, 30, and 14 years before the discovery of the Exodus record of Menephtah's 5th or 6th year. Lenormant, 30 years, and Sayce, 14 years before the discovery of the Exodus record, placed the Exodus "soon after the Libyan invasion in the 5th year." These various authorities all held that Menephtah had reigned *at least* 8 years.

If, therefore, popular opinion is correct in interpreting the Book of Exodus as describing that the Pharaoh was drowned with his hosts, the Egyptian evidence

[1] "Ancient Egypt," pp. 264 and 265.
[2] For which refer to Maspero's "Struggle of the Nations," pp. 433 and 434.

must be deemed to differ in representing the Pharaoh as living three years longer. Of course, it is always possible that in such an event the fact of the drowning of the Pharaoh was hidden from the Egyptians for three years. But this explanation can scarcely hold. The real explanation is that the Book of Exodus does not say that the alleged Pharaoh was drowned. The popular opinion concerning the reading of the text is based on the unconsciously adopted supposition that modern conditions applying to the military employment of the horse held at the ancient time in question.

Popular opinion concerning the Book of Exodus and the alleged drowning of the Pharaoh. The Book of Exodus does not state that the Pharaoh was drowned.

¶ 495e. "THE HORSE AND HIS RIDER."

The actual fact is that no Egyptian ever learned to ride a horse. The horse was used exclusively for the chariot. The chariot had the usual single pole, to which two horses were yoked. The "rider "[1] was the charioteer.

The facts concerning the "riding" of horses in ancient Egypt.

The real reason why Menephtah did not lead his charioteers into action against the Libyans, and later against Israel, was simply because he was too old (over 60 years of age) for the necessary activity. When we remember the construction of the chariot of the period, the wonder is that younger men could maintain their balance in such a vehicle, the body of which was a mere platform fixed on a single shaft, the whole being fitted to the axle of the two wheels without any contrivance equivalent to the springs of any modern vehicle. As Maspero states:

Menephtah too old to lead his chariotry in action. The facts concerning the Egyptian chariot and charioteers.

> " The chariot itself was very liable to upset, the slightest cause being sufficient to over-turn it. Even when moving at a slow pace, the least inequality in the ground shook it terribly, and when driven at full speed it was only by a miracle of skill that the occupants could maintain their equilibrium. At such times the charioteer would stand astride of the front panels, keeping his right foot only inside the vehicle, and planting the other firmly on the pole, so as to lessen the jolting, and to secure a wider base on which to balance himself. To carry all this into practice long education was necessary, for which there were special schools of instruction, and those who were destined to enter the army were sent to these schools when little more than children . . . the chariotry, in fact, like the cavalry of the present day, was the aristocratic branch of the army, in which the royal princes, together with the nobles and their sons, enlisted."[2]

Maspero's authoritative statement.

¶ 495f. "I HAVE GOTTEN ME HONOUR UPON PHARAOH."

From the statement in the Song of Moses (Exod. xv, 19, A.V.) that " the horse of Pharaoh went in with his chariots and with his horsemen into the sea," it might be concluded that Menephtah entered " the sea " mounted upon his horse, and therefore that the Pharaoh was drowned with " his chosen captains." " The horse of Pharaoh," however, as the context shows, is merely an expression analogous to the modern phrase " horse and foot." In the passage quoted, it will be seen there is

Pharaoh's chariotry went into the "sea," his captains, horsemen, and horses were drowned ; but nothing is stated concerning Pharaoh personally.

[1] The Hebrew word translated " rider " is of similar meaning to the Egyptian word for " charioteer," which Chabas translated " rider."

Maspero states, not in connection with the narrative of the Book of Exodus, but in describing the organisation of the Egyptian army during the XVIIIth and XIXth Dynasties, that

> " No Egyptian ever willingly trusted himself to the back of a horse, and it was only in the thick of a battle when his chariot was broken, and there seemed no other way of escaping from the mêlée, that a warrior would venture to mount one of his steeds. There appear, however, to have been here and there a few horsemen who acted as couriers or aides-de-camp ; they used neither saddle-cloth nor stirrups, but were provided with reins with which to guide their animals, and their seat on horseback was even less secure than the footing of the driver in the chariot " (" Struggle of the Nations," p. 218).

This statement throws considerable light upon the narrative of the Book of Exodus. For Exodus xiv, 23–25 states that " The Lord . . . took off their chariot wheels, that they drove them heavily ; so that the Egyptians said : ' Let us flee from the face of Israel.' " Obviously, as Rawlinson has pictured the scene, " The chariot wheels sank into the soft ooze, the horses slipped and floundered ; all was disorder and confusion." In this chaos, the charioteers would each mount one of their horses to flee from the waters, so that, as the Song of Moses (Exod. xv, 1) narrates, " The horse and his rider hath He thrown into the sea."

[2] " Struggle of the Nations," p. 218.

no other mention of " horses." " Horse "—signifying the plural—" chariots," and " horsemen," therefore, completely define the composition of the chariotry. The statement therefore means that " Pharaoh's chariotry went into the sea." This, as we have seen, is confirmed by the Egyptian evidence. Again, elsewhere, in the Song of Moses (Exod. xv, 4–5, R.V.) we have—

" Pharaoh's chariots and his hosts hath He cast into the sea ; and his chosen captains are sunk in the sea of weeds. The deeps cover them : they went down into the depths like a stone."

The miserable and lonely last three years of Menephtah's reign. " I have gotten me honour upon Pharaoh." Here there is no mention of Pharaoh being " sunk," but only of " his chosen captains," his " chariots," and his " hosts." Thus, by leaving the Pharaoh of the Oppression with the crumbling remnants of his power, and to bemoan the loss of his only son, were the words of Exodus xiv, 18, ix, 16 fulfilled—

" And the Egyptians shall know that I am the Lord, when I have gotten Me honour upon Pharaoh, upon his chariots and upon his horsemen."

" That my name may be declared throughout all the earth." " For this have I raised thee (Menephtah) up, for to show in thee My power, AND THAT MY NAME MAY BE DECLARED THROUGHOUT ALL THE EARTH."

How the prediction has been fulfilled in the 3409 years of Israel's history. One wonders, indeed, if any event in history, with the single exception of the history of the life and death of our Lord, has been so extensively " declared throughout all the earth," and during a period of such prolonged duration, as this description of the Exodus of a people then historically, politically, and ethnologically so obscure and insignificant. No one can deny that, at the time the narrative was written, the Israelites were numbered amongst the minor and insignificant nations of the ancient world. Nor can it be denied that the news of their Exodus from Egypt has been " declared throughout all the earth " together with the Name of " the Lord God of the Hebrews," all precisely as predicted by the Book of Exodus. This is one of the many " coincidences " of fulfilment for which the Sacred Books of this " peculiar people " are singularly and remarkably famous.

A warning to ambitious rulers and oppressors in every age and clime. But the words quoted above contain more than this. They are intended clearly to imply that the Pharaoh has been " raised up " by the God of the Hebrews—for the sequence of which refer to Table XXIII—for the purpose of showing, by the extent of his fall, the puny and ephemeral nature of the greatest kingly power when measured against the Power of this Almighty God.

¶ 496. PLATE LXIV. THE GEOMETRICAL DATA OF THE ROCK-CUT PASSAGES AND CHAMBER.

The natural rock-cut portion of the Pyramid's Passage and Chamber System. Subsidence effects in the natural rock were necessarily of a different nature from subsidence effects in the Pyramid's masonry mass. This question has been fully dealt with in ¶¶ 176, 177, 186–194, 206, 207, and 211. Greater horizontal and vertical local differences due to subsidence must be expected in the natural rock definition of the Subterranean Chamber and its horizontal passages than, for instance, Effect of subsidence movements upon same. in the masonry mass defining the King's Chamber and Antechamber and their horizontal passages. This is due to the fact that, in natural rock movements, local adjustments, due to high concentration of subsidence effect from a wide area of Buckling of strata naturally produces greater local diminution in passage lengths and greater vertical differences locally than in built masonry passages of Pyramid. movement, take place as the result of plastic flow in a larger mass of rock than is possible in built-up masonry. Owing to this, a subsidence in the rock strata may lower the strata, say, to the general extent of 20 inches, and yet, owing to local buckling in the strata, may leave within a short distance one section of strata 5 inches higher, and another section 5 inches lower, than the general extent of subsidence.

In the case under consideration, the buckling of the strata would also considerably shorten in a horizontal direction the particular section of strata in which the buckling took place. The general evidence of Plate XXXI indicates the probability of the shortening of the " Dead-end " Passage from the Subterranean Chamber by such buckling of the strata in which the Passage has been cut. Plate XLIIa—by the square aroura geometrically connecting the Queen's Chamber and the Subterranean Chamber and " Dead-end " Passage—indicates the intention of defining the termination of the " Dead-end " Passage by the half side of the square aroura, 1030 P″ horizontally from the Pyramid's centre. Plate LXIV indicates that the existing extreme end of the " Dead-end " Passage is 1015 P″ horizontally from the Pyramid's centre. These data indicate the extreme probability of the distance having been shortened 15 P″ by buckling ; the extent of diminution in length representing 1½ per cent. only of the original length. Evidence of this buckling effect exists in the data given on Plate XXX, relating to the existing and original geometrical position, horizontally, of the point E. Correction for the point E, by the geometrical datum of Plate XXX, has largely eliminated the amount of compression to be taken into account in defining the horizontal distance from the centre of the Pyramid (or Great Step Vertical) to the centre of the Subterranean Chamber. In this connection it may be of interest to the reader to have his attention directed to the fact that the geometrical definition of the centre of this chamber, as shown on Plate LXIV, was seen to result directly from the geometrical datum of Plate XXX when co-ordinated with the data of Plate LXII. The identity was not observed until the block for Plate LXII had been made. Plate LXIV had, in consequence, to be added to show this. The fact is mentioned in note to ⁋ 346.

The probable effect of such upon the Subterranean Chamber and its "Dead-end" Passage.

The termination of the " Dead-end " Passage and the roof of the Subterranean Chamber defined by the square aroura of Plate XLIIa.

Existing evidences confirming this.

A significant sequence of induction, deduction, and unexpected confirming data.

⁋ 497. PLATES LXVa, b, AND c. THE SPECIAL CHRONOLOGY SYSTEM.

In Plate LXVa the horizontal measurements given are derived from the geometrical definition of the Antechamber and King's Chamber measurements shown on Plate XLIII. The primary necessity of Plates LXVa and b were to define the horizontal distance m=BF, from the Great Step to the Entrance Doorway of the 1st Low Passage, in terms of the Pyramid's linear functions of the year-circle geometry. The data fulfilling this requirement, and the data confirming the intention of this, are given on Plate LXVb, under Categories of data, I and II respectively. The mathematical reader's attention is directed, in particular, to the fact that the geometrical data I (a) and (b) are confirmed, to the 6th decimal place of an inch, by the independent geometrical check datum II (a). Having regard to the fact that both these data are independent data of the geometry of the year-circle, it cannot be said that the coincidence is accidental, especially when the identity thus effected is the means of indicating that the datings of the Pyramid's astronomical chronology for the beginning and ending of the 1st Low Passage into the Antechamber are respectively the first day and the last day of Britain's participation in the Great European War. Evidently there is something here that we cannot and may not understand. It is, however, something that is clearly indicated as intentionally defining and dating what it appears to define and date. The resulting datings of the Antechamber and King's Chamber and their connecting low passages are given on Plate LXVc and in Table XXIX.

The principal geometrical features of the special chronology system, and the definition of intention.

Two independent functions of the geometry of the year-circle, one basal and the other confirmatory, define the intention emphatically to the 6th decimal place of the unit of representation.

These gave the dating of the initial and terminal days of the Great European War in terms of the Pyramid's astronomical chronology and in terms of modern astronomical chronology.

⁋ 497a. THE PILASTER AND WALL GROOVE DATINGS.

Certain dates appear on Plate LXVc that are not given on Table XXIX, nor by the data of Plates LXVa and b. These are the dates defined by the Wall Pilasters and by the Wall Grooves between the Pilasters in the Antechamber. These dates were considered to be indicated as follows :—

The time unit value of the Pyramid inch representation in the horizontal from the Great Step to the South Wall of the King's Chamber was indicated as a calendar month of 30 days (⁋ 369). From Plates XLIII and LXVa, the distance from the North Wall of the Antechamber to the South Face of the Granite Leaf—36.5242465

The geometrical basis of the pilaster and wall groove datings are given tentatively.

The supposed geometrical basis.

P ″—therefore represents 36.5242465 calendar months, or 3 solar years. From this it was seen—

(1) That the centre of each pilaster also bisected the over-all distance of two adjacent grooves into two lengths each representing 2 solar years ; the distance of one groove width and a half pilaster width being, therefore, 24.349498 P″.

(2) That the centre of the first pilaster bisected the granite floor length of the Antechamber, which, by Plate XLIII and Addendum to Plate XXXV is 103.032997 P″ ; the distance of two groove widths and 1½ pilaster widths being, therefore, ½ of 103.032997 P″=51.5164985 P″.

(3) That, by Plate XLIII and Addendum to Plate XXXV, the distance from the south face of the Granite Leaf to the south end of the Antechamber is (116.2608746—36.5242465) P″ or 79.736628 P″.

One pilaster width = 5.635005 P″.

One groove width = 21.531995 P″.

These agree closely with the measured widths.

Deducting the sum of the distances derived in (1) and (2) from the distance derived in (3), gave the distance from the south face of the Granite Leaf to the near edge of the 1st Wall Groove as 3.870632 P″. Again, subtracting 3 times the distance of (1) from the sum of the distances in (1) and (2) gives ½-width of pilaster as 2.8175025 P″, or one pilaster width as 5.635005 P″. This by (1) gives groove width as 21.531995 P″.

Not certain that the measures were intended to give specific datings.

The signifi-cance of the Antechamber as "the Chamber of the Triple Veil" rather than "of the Three Veils."

The distances thus obtained agree very closely with the actually measured distances, and have therefore been adopted *tentatively*.

It is not, however, certain that the three grooves were intended to be geometrically defined or to supply dates for the series of events or circumstances which the symbolism of the grooves seem to indicate. The ancient Egyptian prophetic allegory relating to the Antechamber symbolism defines this under the type of the Chamber of the Triple Veil, as concerned with the unveiling of God's purpose within the period represented by the Antechamber as a whole. There is a clear distinction to be drawn between the symbolism of a "Triple Veil" and a symbolism of *Three Veils*. The Pyramid's Antechamber symbolism relates, not to "Three Veils," but to a "Triple Veil."

¶ 498. PLATE LXVI. HORUS-SET ORIGINALLY TWO ASPECTS OF THE ONE GOD.

The graphical representation of Hebrew prophecy and Pyramid prophecy and their historical fulfilment, in terms of gravitational chron-ology. The Egyptian Pyramid alle-gory of the Messianic prophecy.

This plate—when studied in relation to Tables XXX, XXXI, XXXVII, XXXVIII, and Plates XLIIa and b, LXII, and LXVc—gives a complete graphical representation of Hebrew prophecy and of Pyramid prophecy and their historical fulfilment in terms of gravitational chronology. By this historical fulfilment confirming the Pyramid's dated allegory relating to the Messianic prophecies of the ancient Egyptians, con-siderable light is thrown upon many obscure features of Egyptian religion of various periods.

Horus and Set originally the positive and negative aspects of the one God. Posi-tive relating to perfection, and negative to imperfection in Creation.

Light and darkness.

We have already dealt with the question of Horus (Ḥeru-ur) and Set having been originally the names in early Egypt designating two different aspects of the One God[1] (¶ 429 *et seq.*). Ḥeru-ur was the aspect seen in the perfection of the Creator's work ; the aspect in which were revealed the promise and intention of giving Eternal Life to mankind. Set was the aspect presented to man under the condemnation of death, and as looking in temporal judgment upon mankind. Horus was the aspect looking upon light ; Set the aspect looking upon darkness.[2]

[1] Refer Budge, "Gods of the Egyptians," Vol. I, 138–146, 466–467.
[2] Budge (ibid., p. 466) states the original form of the name Horus was "Ḥeru, *i.e.* ' he who is above,' or ' that which is above.' It appears, however, that at a very early period this con-ception of Ḥeru was partly lost sight of, and, whether as a result of the different views held by certain early schools of thought, or whether due to the similarity in sound between the name

It cannot now be denied, in the light of the identity holding between the three systems of Messianic prophecy—that of the ancient Egyptians, that of the Pyramid's Symbolism, and that of the Old and New Testaments—that Ḥeru-ur was the ancient Egyptian designation for the aspect of the Creator revealing the promise of the Messiah. To the Egyptians of this early period, the Messiah was the " Hidden One " in Ḥeru-ur. The kings of the early Egyptian Dynasties had therefore Horus names and Set names, Horus-Set, and Golden Horus names much as we now have Christian names. It is not until the end of the Vth Dynasty that " Son of Ra " names appear.

Now the organisers of the construction of the Great Pyramid appear to have come into Egypt during the reign of Seneferu, the last king of Dynasty III. Certainly no long interval of time separated Seneferu and Khufu (Dynasty IV), since the wife of the former was living during the reign of the latter, when the Great Pyramid was being completed. It is interesting, therefore, to find that the purely Egyptian religious practices were suppressed during the latter's reign, that Seneferu is the first king appearing with a Golden Horus name, and that Khufu, in spite of the suppression of the native Egyptian religion or religions, possessed both a Horus name and a Golden Horus name. Budge states that " the general meaning of the latter name, when applied to the king, is that he is of, or like, the gold of Horus, *i.e.* he is of the same substance as Horus." Here we seem to have the first indication in Egypt of the essential element of the Messianic promise.[1]

¶ 498a. THE CREATOR AS SPIRITUALLY SEEN BY MAN IN " LIGHT " AND IN " DARKNESS."

At the time of the Vth Dynasty, Osiris, the original agricultural god of the primitive Nile Valley, had already been recognised as the god of the Dead. At the same time, however, Horus was still recognised as the Creator possessing the two aspects, Ḥeru-ur and Set.[2] This is clear from one remarkable passage in the Vth Dynasty Pyramid texts. In the text of Unas, last king of Dynasty V, it is stated of the dead king: " Unas standeth up and is Horus ; Unas sitteth down and is Set," reminding one of the words in Daniel xii, 13 : " But go thou (Daniel) thy way till the end be ; for thou shalt rest (*i.e.* in the grave), and stand (*i.e.* in resurrection) in thy lot at the end of the days." Now we have already seen the dead Unas depicted as performing a ceremony identical in every feature described with the Christian sacrament (¶ 352 and notes). This identification, brought into relation with the Horus-Set ritual of Unas, indicates that we are certainly dealing with a ceremony that

' Ḥeru ' and the word for ' face,' Ḥer or Ḥrâ, the idea which became associated with the god Ḥeru was that he represented the face of heaven, *i.e.* the face of the head of an otherwise unknown and invisible God."

(P. 467) : " Ḥeru-ur, *i.e.* ' Horus the Elder,' or the ' aged ' . . . originally . . . represented a phase or aspect of Horus, the face of heaven, and it was he who was the twin god of Set ; Ḥeru-ur was the face by day and Set the face by night."

[1]Budge (ibid., pp. 138 and 154–155) states :
" If literary compositions belonging to the first three Dynasties are ever brought to light from the tombs of Egypt, we shall probably find that the idea of the oneness of God is expressed with just as much force and certainty as it is under the following dynasties. . . ."
" . . . The Egyptians, after the IVth Dynasty, were the victims of conservatism and conventionality ; . . . the decay which set in after the IVth Dynasty, and which stifled the development of painting and sculpture, also attacked the religion of the country, and the noble conception of monotheism, with its cult of the unseen, was unable to compete with the worship of symbols, which could be seen and handled, until the time when Osiris was recognised as the One God, who was also the giver of Eternal Life. . . . The general outline, however, of their religion is clear enough, and it shows us that they possessed a good, practical form of monotheism and a belief in immortality which were already extremely ancient even in the days when the Pyramids were built."

[2]Budge states : " In the Pyramid Texts (Dyns. V and VI) we find Set associated very closely with Horus, and he always appears in them in the character of a god who is a friend and helper of the dead."

The Egyptian text of Unas and the Hebrew text of Daniel. was based on the early Egyptian Messianic prophecy. Set is the aspect of the One God revealed in " Truth in Darkness," and Horus the aspect of the One God revealed in " Truth in Light " (¶¶ 329, 353, and 354, and Diagram on Table XXXVIII), or in " the New and Living Way " of St. Paul's teaching.

The Egyptian God Osiris gradually usurped the attributes of the original Set, who then became simply the Egyptian god of spiritual darkness and the arch-fiend of the Egyptian Underworld.   Set, as understood by the Egyptians, obviously originally represented the aspect later usurped fully by Osiris, as the judge of the dead. Osiris, by displacing Set, made it necessary for the devising of a rôle for Set in the Underworld of the Egyptians. The Egyptian Osiris robbed the Egyptian Set of his benevolent attributes and left Set simply to perform the rôle of chastiser, that led ultimately to Set being identified as Set-Typhon, the opponent of the Egyptian Horus, and the enemy of Osiris. In this form, Set-Typhon was the arch-fiend of the Egyptian Underworld. The text of Unas belongs to a period of transition. For, whereas Set is not therein represented as the arch-fiend of later times, but as an Underworld aspect of Horus, Osiris, nevertheless, appears as the god of the Dead. That difficulty was experienced in reconciling the conceptions of Set and Osiris, in the Underworld, is shown by the combined conception Osiris-Set—in place of the original Horus-Set—having been apparently formulated during the early period of the XIXth Dynasty under Seti I., when Ramessu II, the oppressor of Israel, acted as co-regent.

¶ 498b. RECONSTRUCTION OF THE OUTLINE OF THE ORIGINAL EGYPTIAN MESSIANIC PROPHECY.

The Egyptian god Osiris next usurped the attributes of the original aspect Ḥeru-ur.   The Egyptian Osiris, not content with usurping the attributes of the original Set aspect of Horus, also displaced completely the original Horus, by usurping the attributes of the Ḥeru-ur aspect. The original agricultural god was thus finally identified as the original " One God, who was also the giver of Eternal Life." In this form many of the Messianic attributes were enshrined in Osiris, but some difficulties

Osiris was therefore ultimately adopted by the Egyptians as representing " the One God the giver of Eternal life."   seem to have led to the creating of " the younger Horus " as the son of Osiris, to conquer the serpent that, tradition held, had slain Osiris.

Osiris stepped into the place of the Messiah of ancient Egyptian prophecy, " the younger Horus."   The Osiris of late Egyptian times is, however, essentially represented as the Messiah of the ancient prophecy. It is with this aspect of Osiris that M. Moret deals in his " Kings and Gods of Egypt."

The details of the narrative of the ancient Messianic prophecy that were applied to the Osirian myth. The annunciation of the Lord of all. The benefactor of the world. The ruler.   To Osiris was relegated " The task of disciplining turbulent humanity. Osiris was the teacher awaited since the Creation of the world.[1] When he was born, ' a voice proclaimed that the lord of all things had come upon earth.' A certain Pamyles of Thebes received an ' annunciation ' of the glad tidings . . . he heard a voice ' which commanded him to proclaim that Osiris, the great king, the benefactor of the whole world, had just been born.' . . . It was imperative that a ruler[2] should come."[3]

As indicative of a derived feature of the original Messianic prophecy of ancient Egypt relating to the predicted token of the New Testament in our Lord's Last Supper we quote the following from Moret :—

The prediction of the elements of our Lord's Last Supper.
> " Osiris pressed the grapes, DRANK THE FIRST CUP OF WINE, and, where the land was unsuited to the culture of the vine, ' he taught the people how to make a fermented drink from barley.' Henceforward, men ceased to feed on one another, and with cannibalism endemic warfare disappeared."[4]

Partaking of the Body and the Blood.   The emphasis is ours, and the barley element is obviously due to the dogmatists who preferred another element to wine. The sequence of the giving of the token of the blood of the Messiah and the ceasing of cannibalism is significant. Clearly the original Egyptian Messianic prophecy contained a prediction relating to the New

[1]Compare Luke i, 70 ; John ix, 39 ; 2 Cor. v, 15-21 ; Rom. viii, 22.
[2]Compare Luke i, the whole chapter.
[3]Moret, ": Kings and Gods of Egypt," pp. 71. 72.
[4]Ibid., p. 72.

Testament doctrine concerning " partaking of the body of the Messiah, and drinking His blood."   This explains why the dead king Unas, not long after the construction of the Great Pyramid, is referred to as " eating the gods " and " their words of power and their spirits " (refer to ¶ 352, note).

¶ 498c. THE EVOLUTION OF THE OSIRIAN MYTH.

All this indicates the lines along which the evolution of the idea of Osiris had proceeded.   The original conception had held that " the teacher awaited since the creation of the world " had not yet been manifested on earth.   The vegetation myth of the corn god Osiris had existed prior to its absorption of the borrowed element of " the awaited teacher."   This early form had not pictured Osiris as other than an allegorical personification of the vegetational phenomena of the seasons.   Osiris, at that time, had not been represented as a god who had taken human form and had lived on earth.   This serves to show that the religious ceremonies, from which the early vegetational Osirian cult had borrowed, had centred around and illustrated the conception of the life purpose, not of a " teacher who had already lived and died, but of a predicted, long-hoped-for, and awaited teacher," whose coming was, in some mysterious manner, to end in His sacrifice and bring about the regeneration of mankind.

The picture presented of Osiris, as a god who had been manifested in Egypt, and had died there, belongs to a later period of Egyptian history.   Egyptian tradition, at the time of the XVIIIth Dynasty, held that the tomb of the 1st Dynasty king Zer—whose name was misread as " Khent " (a name of Osiris as " god of the dead ")—was actually the tomb of Osiris.   Zer was, therefore, represented as having been the incarnation of the god Osiris.

Marginal notes: Indications that the prophecy preceded the identification with Osiri the original corn-god of the primitive Nile valley. The prophecy related not to a Saviour who had come, but to a Saviour who was to come. The Osirian myth of late times represented that the Saviour of gods and men had already come in the person of Osiris. Osiris had therefore to receive a definite incarnation. In XVIIIth Dynasty times he was identified with Zer, a king of the 1st Dynasty.

¶ 498d. THE CEREMONY OF RENEWAL AND THE SED HEB.

In the earlier ceremonies of the composite Osiris—*i.e.* the corn god with the added attributes of the promised " Teacher "—the rebirth of the god was enacted by the passing of an effigy of the dead Osiris through the skin of a bull, or some other animal sacred to Set, the evil spirit of the Egyptians at the time of this phase of the Osirian cult.[1]   Even as early as the time of the 1st Dynasty, the tablets of the period picture this element as an essential item of the ceremonies performed at the renewal of the kingship at the Sed festival (refer to ¶¶ 34–40 in relation to Annotations (c) to Table XXVIII).   Other tablets of the same period picture the king, thus renewed, dancing or running before the supposed Presence-form of a particular god in the shrine.   The ceremony of dancing and running was not, however, confined at that date to the *Sed* festival, although the ceremony was always performed before the supposed Presence-form in the shrine.   The nature of the *Sed* Festival or Festival of

Marginal notes: The pagan Osirian enactment of the rebirth. A physical process substituted for an original spiritual allegorical enactment. The king, renewed, dances and runs before the supposed Presence-form of a particular god in the shrine.

[1] At a still later period the skin of the beast is replaced by a wooden cow, variously interpreted as the cow of Isis-Sothis, or as Nouit, " the goddess cow of the heavens."   M. Moret states that " even to-day, in India, when a man has been contaminated by contact with infidels, he believes he can be reborn, purified, if he passes through a golden cow in order to simulate birth" (" Kings and Gods of Egypt," p. 86).

The sequence of evolution is as follows :—

(a) Ḥeru (Horus) was the name of the Creator in His aspect revealing the promise of the Saviour and regenerator of men (¶¶ 498 and 498a).

(b) This aspect, " Ḥeru," was confused with " Face " " Hera " and identified with the visible heavens (¶ 498 and note).

(c) " Het-Ḥeru," "the House of Horus "—originally the spiritual heavens was identified with the visible heavens, and with a specific part thereof (¶ 29).

(d) " Het-Ḥeru " was later personified as the goddess Hathor (¶ 29), and as the sky goddess was " the cow goddess," and the earliest form of Hathor is associated with the " cow goddess," the passing of the effigy through the skin of the cow (or other beast) enacted the rebirth (or the second or new Messianic birth) revealed in the Ḥeru aspect of the Creator.

The golden cow of the tradition in India may have been derived originally from some tradition relating to the signification of the " Golden Horus name."

This element borrowed from the original ceremony of renewal.

Renewal indicates, however, that the ceremony of dancing before the shrine must have originated in connection with the ritual of the Festival of Renewal.

¶ 498e. THE ANCIENT ANTICIPATORY PASSION PLAY.

The original Passion Play depicted all the elements of the original Messianic prophecy.

The Passion, the purging of evil from the flesh ; the burial, the passing through the cycle of death ; the resurrection, the inauguration of the new cycle of rebirth.

All the various elements clearly indicate the nature of the belief from which they originated and developed.   They picture the enacting of an *anticipatory* " Passion Play."   The underlying conception is clearly concerned with a belief in an " awaited teacher," who, by His Passion, was to purge the flesh of mankind of its evils ; by His burial, to pass through the cycle of death that evil, and the knowledge of evil, had brought to mankind ; and, by so doing, to inaugurate a new cycle of rebirth, to be resurrected, having overcome the mysterious processes that had withheld from man the Divine Gift of regeneration.

The various forms of the Passion Play at different periods of Egyptian history.

This ancient belief, woven into the ceremonies of the expanded conception of Osiris, is presented to us by the Osirian texts of the various periods of Egyptian history.   It is presented, however, only in the form in which the belief was accepted by the Egyptians at the time that each particular text was indited or inscribed.   The belief itself was universal and not alone the exclusive possession of the Egyptian Osirian or any other Egyptian cult.   For, as M. Moret remarks : " As far back as the ancient (Egyptian) Empire, we see that all the gods receive the rites of the Osirian cult."[1]

The Passion Play as pictured by the tablets of the earliest dynasties, and the representation of the supposed Presence-form (in the shrine) of an un-named God.

As a matter of fact, the earliest Dynastic tablets in no case identify the supposed Presence-form in the shrine as that of any particular god or goddess of any of the Egyptian cults, although the majority of these deities are referred to in other equally ancient records.   They merely define by hieroglyphic symbol that the attributes of the supposed Presence-form are the attributes that were later usurped by Osiris and other gods invested with the functions and attributes of the long " awaited teacher."

[1] " Gods and Kings of Egypt," p. 90.

APPENDIX I
THE EGYPTIAN KING LISTS

TABLE XLVI.

The King List of Manetho

Africanus heads this—"The Egyptian Dynasties after the Deluge"

BOOK I

DYNASTY I AT THIS

	Africanus Version	Years		Eusebius Version	Years		Armenian Version Eusebius	Years
1	Menes	62		Menes	60		Menes	30
2	Athothis	57		Athothis	27		Athothis	25 and 27
3	Kenkenes	31		Kenkenes	39		Kenkenes	39
4	Uenephes	23		Uenephes	42		Uenephes	42
5	Usaphais	20		Usaphais	20		Usaphais	20
6	Miebis	26		Niebais	26		Niebais	20
7	Semempses	18		Mempses	18		Mempses	18
8	Bieneches	26		Vibethis	26		Vibestes	26
	Added Total	263		Added Total	258		Added Total	276 and 226
	Stated Total	253		Stated Total	252		Stated Total	252

DYNASTY II AT THIS

	Africanus	Years		Eusebius	Years		Armenian Eusebius	Years
1	Boethos	38		Bochos			Bochus	
2	Kaiechos	39		Choos			Cechous	
3	Binothris	47		Biophis			Biophis	
4	Tlas	17						
5	Sethenes	41						
6	Chaires	17						
7	Nephercheres	25						
8	Sesochris	48		Sesochris	48		Sesochris	48
9	Chenneres	30						
	Added & Stated Total	302		Stated Total	297		Stated Total	297

DYNASTY III AT MEMPHIS

	Africanus	Years		Eusebius	Years		Armenian Eusebius	Years
1	Necherophes	28		Necherochis			Necherochis	
2	Tosorthos	29		Sesorthos			Sesorthos	
3	Tyreis	7						
4	Mesochris	17						
5	Soyphis	16						
6	Tosertasis	19						
7	Aches	42						
8	Sephuris	30						
9	Kerpheres	26						
	Added & Stated Total	214		Stated Total	198		Stated Total	197

DYNASTY IV AT MEMPHIS

	Africanus	Years		Eusebius	Years		Armenian Eusebius	Years
1	Soris	29		Suphis			Suphis	
2	Suphis I.	63						
3	Suphis II.	66						
4	Menkheres	63						
5	Ratoises	25						
6	Bicheris	22						
7	Sebercheres	7						
8	Thamphthis	9						
	Added Total	274						
	Stated Total	277		Stated Total	248		Stated Total	248

Eusebius gives "17 kings for 448 years"

DYNASTY V AT ELEPHANTINE

	Africanus	Years		Eusebius	Years		Armenian Version Eusebius	Years
1	Usercheres	28		Othois			Othius	
2	Sephres	13						
3	Nephercheres	20						
4	Sisires	7		Phiops			Phiops	
5	Cheres	20		27 others			27 others	
6	Rathures	44						
7	Menkheres	9						
8	Tatcheres	44						
9	Onnos	33						
	Added Total	248						
	Stated Total	218						

Eusebius states "31 kings for - years"

DYNASTY VI AT MEMPHIS

	Africanus	Years		Eusebius	Years		Armenian Eusebius	Years
1	Othoes	30		Othoes	30		Othius	
2	Phios	53		Phius	53			
3	Methusuphis	7		Methusuphis	7			
4	Phiops	100		Phiops	95?			
5	Menthesuphis	1		Menthesuphis	1			
6	Nitokris	12		Nitokris	12		Nitokris	
	Added Total	203		Stated Total	203			
	Stated Total	203		Stated Total	203			

@ T 198A * Petrie "Hist. Egy." I. 99.

DYNASTY VII AT MEMPHIS

Africanus	Eusebius	Armenian
70 Kings in 70 days	5 Kings in 75 days	5 Kings in 75 years

DYNASTY VIII AT MEMPHIS

Africanus	Eusebius	Armenian
27 Kings in 146 years	5 Kings in 100 years	9 (others) Kings in 100 years

DYNASTY IX AT HERAKLEOPOLIS

Africanus		Eusebius		Armenian	
Akhthoes		Akhthoes		Akhthoes	
18 others		3 others		3 others	
Stated Total	409	Stated Total	100	Stated Total	100

DYNASTY X AT HERAKLEOPOLIS

Africanus	Eusebius	Armenian
19 Kings in 185 years	19 Kings in 185 years	19 Kings in 185 years

DYNASTY XI AT THEBES

Africanus	Eusebius	Armenian
16 Kings in 43 years	16 Kings in 43 years	16 Kings in 43 years
Ammenemes 16 years	Ammenemes 16 years	Ammenemes 16 years

TOTAL YEARS BOOK I

Africanus Book I	Eusebius	Armenian Version
Stated Book I	Various alternative summations	Various alternative summations
Cory — 2308	1842 * 1848	1800 * 1882
Bunsen — 2500		
Added various totals by alternative additions		

Combined 1841, 1847, 1916, 1917, 1922, * 1923.

TABLE XLVII.

THE KING LIST OF MANETHO

BOOK II

DYNASTY XII AT THEBES

	VERSION AFRICANUS	YEARS	VERSION EUSEBIUS	YEARS	ARMENIAN VERSION EUSEBIUS	YEARS
1	Sesonchosis	46	Sesonchosis	46	Sesonchosis	46
2	Ammanemes	38	Ammanemes	38	Ammanemes	38
3	Sesostris	48	Sesostris	48	Sesostris	48
4	Lamaris	8	Lamaris	8	Lampares	8
5	Ammeres	8				
6	Ammenemes	8		42		42
7	Skemiophris	4				
	Added Total } 160		Added Total } 182		Added Total } 182	
	Stated Total }		Stated Total } 245		Stated Total } 245	

DYNASTY XIII AT THEBES

60 Kings in 453 years · 60 Kings in 453 years · 60 Kings in 453 years

DYNASTY XIV AT XOIS

76 Kings in 184 years · 76 Kings in 184 years · 76 Kings in 484 years

DYNASTY XV

	PHOENICIANS OR CANAANITES (SHEPHERDS)	
6 Theban Kings	6 Theban Kings	6 Theban Kings
Stated Total 284	Stated Total 250	Stated Total 250

DYNASTY XVI

32 Grecian Shepherds for 518 years. · 5 Theban Kings for 190 years · 5 Theban Kings for 190 years

DYNASTY XVII

43 Shepherd Kings & 43 Theban Kings reigned together for 151 years.

VERSION AFRICANUS	YEARS	VERSION EUSEBIUS	YEARS	ARMENIAN VERSION EUSEBIUS	YEARS
Saites	19	Saites	19	Saites	19
Bnon	44	Bnon	40	Bnon	40
Pachnan	61	Apophis	14	Apophis	14
Staan	50	Archles	30	Archles	30
Archles	49	Stated & Added Total 103		Stated & Added Total 103	
Aphobis	61				
Stated & Added Total 284					

DYNASTY XVIII AT THEBES

	VERSION AFRICANUS	YEARS	VERSION EUSEBIUS	YEARS	ARMENIAN VERSION EUSEBIUS	YEARS
1	Amos	25	Amosis	25	Amoses	25
2	Khebros	13	Khebron	13	Chebron	13
3	Amenophthis	21	Ammenophis	21	Amophis	21
4	Amensis	22	Miphres	12	Miphres	12
5	Misaphris	13	Misphragmuthosis	26	Misphragmuthosis	26
6	Misphragmuthosis	26	Tuthmosis	9	Tuthmosis	9
7	Tuthmosis	9	Amenophis	31	Amenophis	31
8	Amenophis	31	Oros	36	Orus	28
9	Oros	37	Achencherses	16	Achencheres	16
10	Acherres	32				
11	Rathos	6	Acherres	8	Anchenres	8
12	Acherres	12	Cherres	15	Cheres	15
13	Acherres	12	Armais	5	Armais	5
14	Armesses	5	Rameses	68	Rameses	68
15	Rameses	1	Menophis	40	Menophis	40
16	Amenophath	19				
	Added Totals 259		Added Totals 325		Added Total 317	
	Stated Total 263		Stated Total 348		Stated Total 318	

DYNASTY XIX AT THEBES

	VERSION AFRICANUS	YEARS	VERSION EUSEBIUS	YEARS	ARMENIAN VERSION EUSEBIUS	YEARS
1	Sethos	51	Sethus	55	Sethos	55
2	Dadakes	61	Rampses	66	Rampses	66
3	Ammenephthes	20	Ammenephthis	40	Amenephthis	8
4	Rameses	60				
5	Ammenemnes	5	Ammenemes	26	Ammenemes	26
6	Thuoris	7	Thuoris	7	Thuoris	7
	Added Total 204		Added and Stated Total 194		Added Total 162	
	Stated Total 209				Stated Total 194	

TOTAL YEARS BOOK II

AFRICANUS		EUSEBIUS		EUSEBIUS, ARMENIAN VERSION	
Stated Total 2121		Added Stated Totals } 1967		Added Stated Totals } 2267	
Added Stated Totals } 2222					
Summation of Primary Added Totals } 2213		By Alternative Additions } 1879, 1881, 1904, 1942, 1944.		Summation of Added Totals } 2141	
By Alternative Additions } 2217, 2218, 2236, 2243.					

TABLE XLVIII.

THE KING LIST OF MANETHO

BOOK III

	VERSION AFRICANUS	YEARS	VERSION EUSEBIUS	YEARS	ARMENIAN VERSION EUSEBIUS	YEARS
	DYNASTY XX AT THEBES 12 KINGS IN 135 YEARS		**DYNASTY XX AT THEBES** 12 KINGS IN 178 YEARS		12 KINGS IN 172 YEARS	
	DYNASTY XXI AT TANIS		**DYNASTY XXI AT TANIS**			
1	SMENDES	26	SMENDES	26	SMENDES	26
2	PSUSENNES	46	PSUSENNES	41	PSUSENNES	41
3	NEPHERCHERES	4	NEPHERCHERES	4	NEPHERCHERES	4
4	AMENOPHTHIS	9	AMENOPHTHIS	9	AMENOPHTHIS	9
5	OSOCHOR	6	OSOCHOR	6	OSOCHOR	6
6	PSINACHES	9	PSINACHES	9	PSINACHES	9
7	PSUSENNES	14	PSUSENNES	35	PSUSENNES	35
	ADDED TOTAL	114	ADDED AND STATED TOTAL	130	ADDED AND STATED TOTAL	130
	STATED TOTAL	130				
	DYNASTY XXII AT BUBASTIS					
1	SESONCHIS	21	SESONCHOSIS	21	SESONCHOSIS	21
2	OSORTHON	15	OSORTHON	15	OSORTHON	15
3	TAKELOTHIS	25				
		13	TAKELOTHIS	13	TAKELOTHIS	13
		42				
	ADDED TOTAL	116	ADDED AND STATED TOTAL	49	ADDED AND STATED TOTAL	49
	STATED TOTAL	120				
	DYNASTY XXIII AT TANIS		**DYNASTY XXIII AT TANIS**			
1	PETUBASTES	40	PETUBASTIS	25	PETUBASTIS	25
2	OSORCHO	9	OSORTHON	10	OSORTHON	10
3	PSAMMUS	10	PSAMMUS	9	PSAMMUS	9
4	ZET	31				
	ADDED TOTAL	89	ADDED AND STATED TOTAL	44	ADDED AND STATED TOTAL	44
	STATED TOTAL					
	DYNASTY XXIV BOCCHORIS 44 YEARS		**DYNASTY XXIV** BOCCHORIS 44 YEARS		BOCCHORIS 44 YEARS	
	DYNASTY XXV		**DYNASTY XXV**			
1	SABAKON	8	SABAKON	12	SABAKON	12
2	SEBICHOS	14	SEBICHOS	12	SEBICHOS	12
3	TARKOS	18	TARAKOS	20	TARAKOS	20
	ADDED AND STATED TOTAL	40	ADDED AND STATED TOTAL	44	ADDED AND STATED TOTAL	44
	DYNASTY XXVI AT SAIS					
1	STEPHINATES	7	AMMERIS	12 OR 18	AMMERES	18
2	NECHEPSOS	6	STEPHINATHIS	7	STEPHINATHS	7
3	NECHAO	8	NECHAO I	6 OR 8	NECHAOS I	6 OR 8
4	PSAMMETICHOS	54	PSAMMETICHOS	44	PSAMMETICHOS	44
5	NECHAO II	6	NECHAO II	6	NECHAO II	6
6	PSAMMUTHIS	6	PSAMMUTHIS II	17	NECHAUS II	17
7	UAPHRIS	19	VAPHRIS	25	VAPHRIS	25
8	AMOSIS	44	AMOSIS		AMOSIS	
9	PSAMMECHERITES	1/2				
	ADDED AND STATED TOTAL	150 1/2	ADDED TOTAL	163	ADDED AND TOTALS 155 OR 163 OR 167	163
			STATED TOTAL		STATED TOTAL	

	VERSION AFRICANUS	YEARS	VERSION EUSEBIUS	YEARS	ARMENIAN VERSION EUSEBIUS	YEARS
			DYNASTY XXVII		**DYNASTY XXVII**	
1	CAMBYSES	6	CAMBYSES	3	CAMBYSES	3
2	DARIUS HYSTASPES	36	MAGOI	3/4	MAGOI	3/4
3	XERXES THE GREAT	21	DARIUS	36	DARIUS	36
4	ARTABANUS	7 1/2	XERXES	21	XERXES	21
5	ARTAXERXES	41	ARTAXERXES (41)	40	ARTAXERXES	40
6	XERXES II	2 1/2	XERXES II	3/4	XERXES II	3/4
7	SOGDIANUS	7 1/2	SOGDIANUS	3/4	SOGDIANUS	3/4
8	DARIUS XERXES	19	DARIUS XERXES	19	DARIUS XERXES	19
	ADDED AND STATED TOTAL	124 1/2	ADDED AND STATED TOTAL (BUDGE)	120 1/2 121 1/2	ADDED AND STATED TOTAL	120 1/2
	AMYRTAEUS 6 YEARS		**DYNASTY XXVIII AT SAIS** AMYRTAEUS 6 YEARS		AMYRTAEUS 6 YEARS	
			DYNASTY XXIX AT MENDES		**DYNASTY XXIX AT MENDES**	
1	NEPHERITES	6	NEPHERITES	3	NEPHERITES	3
2	ACHORIS	13	ACHORIS	13	ACHORIS	13
3	PSAMMUTHIS	1	PSAMMUTHIS	1	PSAMMUTHIS	1
4	NEPHERITES	1/2	MUTHIS	1	MUTHES	1
			NEPHERITES	1/2	NEPHERITES	1/2
	ADDED AND STATED TOTAL	20 1/2	ADDED AND STATED TOTAL	21 1/2	ADDED AND STATED TOTAL	21 1/2
			DYNASTY XXX AT SEBENNYTUS		**DYNASTY XXX AT SEBENNYTUS**	
1	NECTANEBES	18	NECTANEBIS	10	NECTANEBIS	10
2	TEOS	2	TEOS	2	TEOS	2
3	NEKTANEBOS	18	NECTANEBOS	8	NECTANEBOS	8
	ADDED AND STATED TOTAL	38	ADDED AND STATED TOTAL	20	ADDED AND STATED TOTAL	20
			DYNASTY XXXI		**DYNASTY XXXI**	
1	OCHUS	2	OCHUS	6	OCHUS	6
2	ARSES	3	ARSES	4	ARSES	4
3	DARIUS	4	DARIUS	6	DARIUS	6
	ADDED AND STATED TOTAL	9	ADDED AND STATED TOTAL	16	ADDED AND STATED TOTAL	16

TOTAL YEARS BOOK III

	AFRICANUS		EUSEBIUS		EUSEBIUS, ARMENIAN VERSION	
STATED Book I	1050	ADDED STATED TOTALS	835%	ADDED STATED TOTALS	831%
ADDED STATED TOTALS	868%				
BY ALTERNATIVE ADDITIONS	{848% 852% 864%}	BY ALTERNATIVE ADDITIONS	{836% 840% 841%}	BY ALTERNATIVE ADDITIONS	{831% 835% 839%}

BUDGE (BK KINGS 1 pLXXIII)
80% OR 803% BY HAVING
DYN. XXIV AS AFRICANUS.
THIS BASIS OF HERODOTUS (OUR PLATE XVI)

TABLE XLIX.

THE OLD EGYPTIAN CHRONICLE.

" Among the Egyptians there is a certain tablet called the Old Chronicle, containing 30 Dynasties in 113 Descents, during the long period of 36,525 years. The first series of princes was that of the Auritæ; the second was that of the Mestræans; the third of Egyptians."

				Years.	Years.
Hephæstus (or Vulcan)					
Helius (or the Sun)			..	30,000	
Kronus (or Saturn), and the other 12 gods			..	3,984	
8 demigods			..	217	
				————	34,201
15 generations of the Cynic circle			..	443	

Dynasties—

						Years.	Years.
XVI. Tanites		8 kings or dynasties			..	190	
XVII. Memphites ..	4	,, ,, ,,			..	103	
XVIII. Memphites ..	14	,, ,, ,,			..	348	
XIX. Diospolites (or Thebans)	5	,, ,, ,,			..	194	
[Interregnum ..	..	.. .. ..			..	178]	
XX. Diospolites (or Thebans)	8	kings or dynasties			..	228	
XXI. Tanites	6	,, ,, ,,			..	121	
XXII. Tanites	3	,, ,, ,,			..	48	
XXIII. Diospolites (or Thebans)	2	,, ,, ,,			..	19	
XXIV. Saites	3	,, ,, ,,			..	44	
XXV. Ethiopians ..	3	,, ,, ,,			..	44	
XXVI. Memphites ..	7	,, ,, ,,			..	177	
XXVII. Persians	5	,, ,, ,,			..	124	
XXVIII.						[6]	
XXIX. Tanites		,, ,, ,,			..	39	
XXX. A Tanite	1	,, ,, ,,			..	18	
		69 kings or dynasties			..	2,324	2,324
							36,525

" Embracing in all 30 Dynasties, and amounting to 36,525 years."
From Syncellus' " Chron." 51, and Eusebius' " Chron." 6.

Syncellus remarks : " The period of the 113 generations, described by Manetho in his three volumes, comprises a sum-total of 3555 years."

TABLE L.

THE TABLE OF ERATOSTHENES.

	Years.	A.M.		Years..	A.M.
1. Menes	62	2900	20. Apappos	100	3469
2. Athothes	59	2962	21. Ekheskosokaras ..	1	3569
3. Athothes	32	3021	22. Nitokris	6	3570
4. Diabies	19	3053	23. Myrtaios	22	3576
5. Pemphos	18	3072	24. Thyosimares ..	12	3598
6. Toegar (Momkeiri) ..	79	3090	25. Thinillos	8	3610
7. Stoichos	6	3169	26. Semphroukrates	18	3618
8. Gosormies	30	3175	27. Khouther ..	7	3636
9. Mares	26	3205	28. Meures	12	3643
10. Anoyphis	20	3231	29. Khomaiphtha ..	11	3655
11. Sirios	18	3251	30. Soikyniosokhos ..	60	3666
12. Chnubos Gneuros ..	22	3269	31. Peteathyres ..	16	3726
13. Rauosis	13	3291	32. Ammenemes ..	26	3742
14. Biyris	10	3304	33. Stammenemes ..	23	3768
15. Saophis I	29	3314	34. Sistosikhermes ..	55	3791
16. Saophis II	27	3343	35. Maris	43	3846
17. Moschares	31	3370	36. Siphoas	5	3889
18. Mousthis	33	3401	37. Phrouron ..	19	3894
19. Pammes	35	3434	38. Amouthartaios ..	63	3913–3976.

38 kings in 1076 years.

TABLE LI.

JOSEPHUS.

DYNASTY XV OF SHEPHERDS.

		Years.
1. Salatis	..	19
2. Beon	..	44
3. Apachnas ..	..	$36\frac{7}{12}$
4. Apophis	..	61
5. Jannas	..	$50\frac{1}{12}$
6. Assis	..	$49\frac{1}{2}$

6 kings in $259\frac{2}{3}$ years.

DYNASTY XIX.

		Years.
Sethosis	..	59
Rampses	..	66
Amenophis	..	..
Sethos	..	..

DYNASTY XVIII AT THEBES.

		Years.
1. Tethmosis ..	..	$25\frac{1}{4}$
2. Chebron ..	..	13
3. Amenophis ..	..	$20\frac{7}{12}$
4. Amessis ..	..	$21\frac{1}{4}$
5. Mephres ..	..	$12\frac{3}{4}$
6. Mephramuthosis	..	$25\frac{5}{6}$
7. Thmosis ..	..	$9\frac{3}{4}$
8. Amenophis ..	..	$30\frac{5}{6}$
9. Orus	..	$36\frac{5}{12}$
10. Acencheres I ..	..	$12\frac{1}{12}$
11. Rathotis ..	..	9
12. Acencheres II ..	..	$12\frac{5}{12}$
13. Acencheres III	..	$12\frac{1}{4}$
14. Armais	..	$4\frac{1}{12}$
15. Ramesses ..	..	$1\frac{1}{3}$
16. Armesses Miammi ..		$66\frac{1}{4}$
17. Amenophis ..	..	$19\frac{1}{2}$

17 kings in 333 years.

TABLE LII.

CASTOR'S RECKONING.

Gods.				Years.
Hephæstus	..	..	..	680
Sol Hephæsti Fil.	..	..	..	77
(Agatho-dæmon and Cronus) }	..	..	..	420
Osinosiris	..	..	..	28
Orus Stoliarchus	..	..	..	28
Typhon	..	..	..	45

Demigods.				
Anubis	..	..	..	83
Apion (Hercules)	..	..	..	77
(6 demigods	..	..	..	140)
Colliguntur Deorum regna	..	..	..	1550
Ecynii (P. I. E. Cynici)	..	..	..	2100
				3650

Hæc finis de primo tomo Manethonis habens annos 2100.

				Kings.	Years.
i. Mineus (Menes) and 7 descendants	..			8	253
ii. (Bœthus and) 8 others	..	..		9	302
iii. Necherocheus (Necherophes) and 8 others	..			9	214
iv. (Soris and) 17 others	..	..		18	214
(error	..	..			3)
v. (Userkheres and) 21 others	..	..		22	258
vi. Othœs and 7 others	..	..		8	203
viii. 14 others	..	..		14	140
ix. 20 others	..	..		20	409
(x), xi. 7 others	..	..		7	204
Totals	..	..		115	2200

				Years.
xii. Diospolites	..	..		(15)9
xiii. Bubastites	..	..		153
xiv. Tanites	..	..		184
xv. Sebennites	..	..		224
xvi. Memphites	..	..		318
xvii. Heliopolites	..	..		221
xviii. Hermopolites	..	..		26(1)
Total	..	..		1520

Usque ad 17 mann. potestatem scribitur tomus habens 1520 annos.

TABLE LIII.

THE BOOK OF THE SOTHIS.

	Years.	A.M.		Years.	A.M.
1. Mestraim (Menes) ..	35	2776	44. Khenkheres	26	4015
2. Kurodes ..	63	2811	45. Akherres	8	4041
3. Aristarkhos	34	2874	46. Armaios	9	4049
4. Spanios	36	2908	47. Ramesses	68	4058
5. .... }	72	2944	48. Amenophis	8	4126
6. .... }			49. Thuoris	17	4134
7. Osiropis	23	3016	50. Nekhepsos	19	4151
8. Sesonkhosis	49	3039	51. Psammuthis	13	4170
9. Amenemes	29	3088	52.	4	4183
10. Amasis	2	3117	53. Kertos .. .. 16(20)		4187
11. Akesephthres ..	13	3119	54. Rampsis	45	4207
12. Ankhoreus	9	3132	55. Amenses (Ammenemes)	26	4252
13. Armiyses	4	3141	56. Okhuras	14	4278
14. Khamois	12	3145	57. Amendes	27	4292
15. Miamus	14	3157	58. Thuoris	50	4319
16. Amesesis	65	3171	59. Athothis (Phusanos)	28	4369
17. Uses	50	3236	60. Kenkenes	39	4397
18. Rameses	29	3286	61. Uennephis .. .. 32(42)		4436
19. Ramessomenes ..	15	3315	62. Susakeim	34	4478
20. Usimare	31	3330	63. Psuenos	25	4512
21. Ramesseseos	23	3361	64. Ammenophis ..	9	4537
22. Ramessameno ..	19	3384	65. Nepherkheres ..	6	4546
23. Ramesse Iubasse ..	39	3403	66. Saites	15	4552
24. Ramesse Uaphru ..	29	3442	67. Psinakhes	9	4567
25. Konkharis[1]	5	3471	68. Petubastes	44	4576
26. Silites	19	3477	69. Osorthon	9	4620
27. Baion	44	3496	70. Psammos	10	4629
28. Apakhnas	36	3540	71. Konkharis	21	4639
29. Aphophis	61	3576	72. Osorthon	15	4660
30. Sethos	50	3637	73. Takalophis	13	4675
31. Kertos	29	3687	74. Bokkhoris	44	4688
32. Asseth[2]	20	3716	75. Sabakon, the Ethiopian	12	4732
33. Amosis (Tethmosis) ..	26	3736	76. Sebekhon	12	4744
34. Khebron	13	3762	77. Tarakes	20	4756
35. Anemphis	15	3775	78. Amaes	38	4776
36. Amenses	11	3790	79. Stephinathes ..	27	4814
37. Misphragmuthosis ..	16	3801	80. Nekhepsos	13	4841
38. Misphres	23	3817	81. Nekhao I	8	4854
39. Touthmosis	39	3640	82. Psamitikhos	14	4862
40. Amenophthis	34	3879	83. Nekhao II Pharao ..	9	4876
41. Oros	48	3913	84. Psamuthis	17	4885
42. Akhenkheres ..	25	3961	85. Uaphris	34	4902
43. Athoris	29	3986	86. Amosis	50	4936

[1] " 700 years of 25 kings of the cycle in Manetho called Cynic end with the 5th year of this king."
[2] " This king added the 5 Epagomenæ, and in his time they say the Egyptian year was reckoned as 365 days, having before his time counted only 360. In his time the heifer was made a god and called Apis."

TABLE LIV.

DYNASTY.	TABLET OF ABYDOS.	TABLET OF SAKKARAH.	DYNASTY.	TABLET OF ABYDOS.	TABLET OF SAKKARAH.
I.	1. Mena 2. Teta 3. Atta 4. Ata 5. Hesepti 6. Merbap 7. Semenptah (?) 8. Kebh	1. Merbapen 2. Kebhu	VI. (cont.)	39. Merenra- 　　　Mehtiemsaf 40. Neterkara 41. Menkara	
			VII.	42. Neferkara 43. Neferkara-Neby 44. Zedkara-Shema	
II.	9. Bezau 10. Ka-kau 11. Baneteren 12. Uaznes 13. Senda	3. Neter-bau 4. Kakau 5. Baneteru 6. Uaznes 7. Send 8. Neferkara 9. Sekru-neferka 10. Zefa . . .	VIII.	45. Neferkara-Khendu 46. Hermeren 47. Sneferka 48. Nekara 49. Neferkara Telulu 50. Herneferka 51. Neferkara 　　　Pepysenb 52. Sneferka Onnu	
III.	14. Zazay 15. Nebka 16. Zesersa 17. Teta 18. Sezes 19. Neferkara 20. Sneferu	11. Beby 12. Nebkara 13. Zeser 14. Zeserteta 15. Huni 16. Sneferu		53. . . . ikaura 54. Neferkaura 55 Herneferka 56. Neferarikara	
			XI.	57. Nebhaptra 58. Sankhkara	37. Nebhaptra 38. Sankhkara
IV.	21. Khufu 22. Razedf 23. Khafra 24. Menkaura 25. Shepseskaf	17. Khufuf 18. Razedf 19. Khaufra 20. Menkaura 21. (Broken) 22. ,, 23. ,, 24. ,,	XII.	59. Shetepabra 60. Kheperkara 61. Nubkaura 62. Khakheperra 63. Khakaura 64. Maatenra 65. Maatkherura	39. Shetepabra 40. Kheperkara 41. Nubkara 42. Khakheperra 43. Khakara 44. Maatenra 45. Maatkherura 46. Sebekkara
V.	26. Userkaf 27. Sahura 28. Kakaa 29. Neferfra 30. Ra en user 31. Menkauhor 32. Zedkara 33. Unas	25. Userkaf 26. Sahura 27. Neferarikara 28. Shepseskara 29. Khaneferra 30. Menkahor 31. Zedkara 32. Unas	[XVIII.	66. Nebpehtira 67. Zeserkara 68. Aakheperkara 69. Aakheperenra 70. Menkheperra 71. Aakheperura 72. Menkheperura 73. Nebmaatra 74. Zeserkheperura- 　　　setepenra	47. Nebpehra 48. Zeserkara 49. (Aakheperkara) 50. (Aakheperenra) 51. (Menkheperra) 52. (Aakheperura) 53. (Menkheperura) 54. Neb(maatra) 55. . . . setepenra
VI.	34. Teta 35. Userkara 36. Meryra 37. Merenra 38. Neferkara	33. Teta 34. Pepy (I) . 35. Merenra 36. Neferkara 　　　(Pepy II)	XIX.	75. Menpehtira 76. Menmaatra	56. Men(pehtira) 57. Men(maatra) 58. (Usermaatra)- 　　　setepenra

PLATE LXIX.

TABLET OF KARNAK

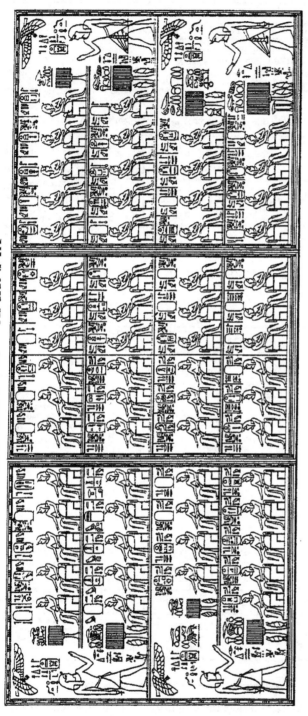

· INDEX REFERENCE TO TABLET OF KARNAK ·

AC ≈ IONG.

PLATE LXX.

DIAGRAMMATIC KEY TO THE LIST OF KARNAK

THIS LIST WAS FORMERLY IN THE HALL OF ANCESTORS AT KARNAK,
ARRANGED AS INDICATED BELOW, BUT IS NOW IN THE LOUVRE.
AS GENERALLY INDICATED AND EXPLAINED IN EGYPTOLOGICAL WORKS,
LITTLE CONCEPTION OF THE ORIGINAL ARRANGEMENT, AS ON
THE WALLS OF THE HALL OF ANCESTORS CAN BE OBTAINED BY
THE READER.

TWO ROWS OF ANCESTORS A TO H, & a TO h FACING TAHUTMES AT M.

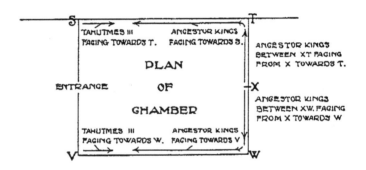

TAHUTMES III.
(DYN. XVIII.) IN
POSITION M, FACING
ANCESTORS A···H & a···h.

TAHUTMES III.
(DYN. XVIII.) IN
POSITION N, FACING
ANCESTORS B···H, & a···h.

A & B = KINGS OF DYN. III.
G, D, E = KINGS OF DYN. V.
F, G, H.= ARE ERASED.
a, b, c, d, e. = ANTEFS &
   MENTUHOTEPS (XI)
f, g & h = KINGS OF DYN. VI.
B, G, D, E, F, G = KINGS OF
   DYN. XII.
H = ANTEF KING.
a = KING OF DYN. XII.
b, c, d = KINGS OF DYN. XVII.
e, f, g = Do. OF DYN. XI (LATER
   ANTEFS & MENTUHOTEPS)
h. NAME ERASED.

TWO ROWS OF ANCESTORS B TO H, & a TO h, FACING TAHUTMES AT N.

DIAGRAMMATIC ELEVATION OF WALL ST, AND HALF WALL TX.

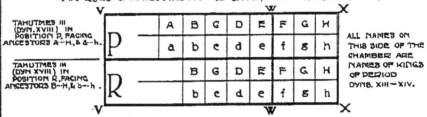

TWO ROWS OF ANCESTORS A TO H, & a TO h, FACING TAHUTMES AT P.

TAHUTMES III
(DYN. XVIII) IN
POSITION P, FACING
ANCESTORS A···H, & a···h.

TAHUTMES III
(DYN XVIII) IN
POSITION R, FACING
ANCESTORS B···H, & b···h.

ALL NAMES ON
THIS SIDE OF THE
CHAMBER ARE
NAMES OF KINGS
OF PERIOD
DYNS. XIII — XIV.

TWO ROWS OF ANCESTORS B TO H, & b TO h, FACING TAHUTMES AT R.

DIAGRAMMATIC ELEVATION OF WALL VW, & HALF WALL WX.

TABLE LV.

KINGS ON KARNAK LIST—(SEE DIAGRAMMATIC KEY).

LIST ON HALF-CHAMBER S, T, X—KINGS OF DYNASTIES III, V, VI, XI, XII, AND XVII.

Ref. Letters	A	B	C	D	E	F	G	H
M List King Name	Nefer-ka-Ra.	Seneferu.	Sabu-Ra.	An.	Assa.	(Erased)	(Erased)	[Sekhem ?]-smen-taui-ka ?
Manetho's Dynasty	Dyn. III Preceding Seneferu.	Dyn. III Last king.	Dyn. V 2nd king.	Dyn. V 6th king.	Dyn. V 8th king.	....	....	
Ref. Letters	a	b	c	d	e	f	g	h
M List King Name	(Erased) (Antef ? or Mentuhotep ?)	Antef (king).	Antef (king).	Men(tuhotep).	Antef (prince).	Teta.	Pepy.	Mer-en-Ra.
Manetho's Dynasty	Dyn. XI ?	Dyn. XI	Dyn. XI	Dyn. XI	Dyn. XI	Dyn. VI 1st king.	Dyn. VI 2nd king.	Dyn. VI 3rd king.
Ref. Letters	A	B	C	D	E	F	G	H
N List King Name		Sehetep-Ab-Ra.	Nub-Kau-Ra.	(Erased)	(Erased)	Maa-Kheru-Ra.	Sebek-neferu-Ra.	Antef (king).
Manetho's Dynasty		Dyn. XII Amen-em-hat I.	Dyn. XII Amen-em-hat II.	....	....	Dyn. XII Amen-en-hat IV.	Dyn. XII (Skemiophris).	Dyn. XI ?
Ref. Letters	a	b	c	d	e	f	g	h
N List King Name	Kheper-ka-Ra.	Seqenen-Ra Taa-aa-Qen (III).	Sekhent-Neb-Ra.	User-en-Ra (Khian).	Nub-Kheper-Ra.	Neb-Kheru-Ra.	Senefer-ka-Ra.	....
Manetho's Dynasty	Dyn. XII Senusert 1.	Dyn. XVII (Thebes).	Dyn. XVII (Thebes).	Dyn. XVII (Hyksos).	Dyn. XI ? Antef (V ?).	Dyn. XI Mentuhotep (III ?).	Dyn. XI Antef (VI ?).	Dyn. XI ?

LIST ON HALF-CHAMBER V, W, X—ALL KINGS OF DYNASTIES XIII AND XIV.

Ref. Letters	A	B	C	D	E	F	G	H
P List King Name	Kha-ka-Ra ?	Kha-nefer-Ra (Sebekhotep).	Kha-seshes-Ra	Sekhem-suaz-taui-Ra ? (Sebekhotep).	Sekhem-khu-taui-Ra (Sebekhotep).	Sankh-Ab-Ra (Ameni-Antef-Amen-em-hat).	Suaz-en-Ra.	...ka.
Ref. Letters	a	b	c	d	e	f	g	h
P List King Name	(Erased)	Mer-Sekhem-Ra.	Mer-Kau Ra (Sebekhotep).	Ses-User-Taui-Ra.	....Ra.	Senefer-Ra.	Kha-(hotep ?)-Ra (Sebekhotep ?).	Kha-Ankh-Ra (Sebekhotep).
Ref. Letters	A	B	C	D	E	F	G	H
R List King Name		....Uah-Khau-Ra.	Suah-en-Ra.	Mer-Hotep-Ra.	Khu-taui-Ra.	(Erased)	(Erased)	Sekhem-uaz-kau-Ra (Sebekemsaf).
Ref. Letters	a	b	c	d	e	f	g	h
R List King Name	....Ra.	....Ra.	Senefer-Ra.	Suaz-en-Ra.	Za....Ra.	(Erased)	(Erased)	(Erased)

APPENDIX II

DATA RELATING TO THE EVOLUTION OF FICTITIOUS SYSTEMS OF CHRONOLOGY IN THE KING LISTS OF THE ANCIENT EGYPTIANS

TABLE LVI.

THE EVIDENCE CONCERNING AN INTERPOLATION OF 1000 YEARS IN THE EGYPTIAN KING LISTS.

A.

Old Chronicle.	Book of the Sothis as stated.	Origin of Book of the Sothis.
Dynasty XVI began (alleged) .. 1772 A.K. (Refer ¶ 95 and Table LXIV.)	Menes began (alleged) .. .. 2776 A.M.	Menes began (alleged) .. 2776 A.M.
Interval .. .. 695 years.	Interval for 23 kings .. .. 695 years.	Interval for 23 *Sed hebs* 691 years.
Stated 1st year of Ramessu II Sesostris .. .. .. 2467 A.K.	Stated 1st year of Konkharis Sesostris (Kha-kau-ra Senusert III) .. 3471 A.M.	3467 A.M.
Actual *Sed heb* of Ramessu II (Table XI) or 7½ actual Phœnix periods of 329 years .. .. ..(2467½ years)	For confusion of Ramessu II Sesostris and Senusert III Sesostris refer Table XI Annotations, Table XV Annotations (D) and ¶ 493. (Refer also to Table LXII.)	Deduct interpolated "Phœnix" period of .. 1000 years (¶ 38). Actual *Sed heb* of Ramessu II (Phœnix 2467½) .. .. .. 2467 A.K. (Table XI)

B.

	CASTOR.		SUIDAS.		EUSEBIUS. Plate XVI.
	Years.	Totals.	Years.	Totals.	
GODS. Hephaistos ..	680		§ 1680		
Other gods ..	570	1250	570	2250	
DEMI-GODS. Anubis ..	83 *217		83 *217		BOOK I. Kings .. 1842 years (Table C, Col. 8)
Other demi-gods ..	300		300		BOOK II. Kings .. 1967 years (Table C, Col. 8)
					3809 years.
COLLIGUNTOR DEORUM REGNA ..		1550		2550	BOOK III. Kings .. 841½ years (Table C, Col. 8)
ECYNII (PIE CYNICI) ..		‖ 2100		‖ 2100	
TOTAL ..		3650 years.		4650 years.	(1000 Years' Interpolation) 4650½ years (¶ 99)

* Compare with Manetho's 1217 in C.   § Refer Annotations (A) to Tables XVII–XIX, Cols. 1 and 2, Note 1.
‖ Refer to 2100 years in Cols. 4 and 5, Annotations (A) to Tables XVII–XIX.

TABLE LVI—*continued.*

C.

MANETHO'S DIVINE DYNASTIES :—VERSION I.

		Years.	Totals.
GODS.	Hephaistos ..	9000	
	4 other gods ..	2626	11626 = diameter of circle of 36525 circumference.
DEMI-GODS.	Typhon ..	359	
	9 demi-gods ..	858	*1217 whereas $\dfrac{3652.5}{3} = 1217.5$.

TOTAL FOR GODS AND DEMI-GODS, 12843 years.

* Refer B, indicating 1000 years' interpolation.

Otherwise added :—

				Years.	
Hephaistos	..	..	..		9000 years.
4 other gods	..	..		2626	
Typhon	..	..		359	2985 years†
9 demi-gods	..	..			858 years.
					12843 years.

† Refer D for 2984 and alternative 2984.

D.

OLD CHRONICLE ALTERNATIVE VERSIONS.

									Stated Version.	Alternative Version.	
GODS.	Hephaistos	..	..	..	..	..	..	..	30000 years	30000 years	
	Other gods	..	..	..	..	..	..	..	†3984 years	†2984 years	} 1000 years' interpolation indicated.
DEMI-GODS.	8 demi-gods	..	..	..	..	..	..	..	*217 years	*1217 years	}
	15 generations of the Cynic cycle ..	..	..						443 years (¶¶ 94 and 95) ..	443 years	
	Dynasty XVI to Dynasty XIX inclusive ..	..							835 years	835 years	} 1456 years
	INTERREGNUM	..	..	..					178 years	178 years	}
	Dynasty XX to Dynasty XXX inclusive ..	..							868 years	868 years	.. 2324 years.
	TOTAL	..	..	..					36525 years.	36525 years.	

* Refer B and C.   † Refer C.

TABLE LVII.

EVIDENCE OF THE 1000 YEARS' INTERPOLATION IN THE VERSION OF MANETHO'S KING LISTS PRESERVED BY EUSEBIUS.

A.

BOOK I (Eusebius) ...	1853 years.	*2329 years.	2329 years.	2325 years.
BOOK II (Eusebius) ...	1932 years.			1456 years. 1460 years.
Dynasty XX begins (Ramessu III) at ...	↑3785 years.			↑3785 years. 3785 years.
BOOK III (Africanus and Old Chronicle) ...	868 years.	2324 years.		868 years. 868 years.
	4653 years.	*4653 years.		*4653 years. 4653 years.

* 1000 years' interpolation in Scheme of Original Old Chronicle (¶ 95) and 1001 years in Scheme of Table LVIII (A).
↑ 1001 years' interpolation in earlier Scheme of Table LVIII (A) following.

B.

EUSEBIUS, BOOK I.

Dynasty.	Years.	Years' duration of scheme.
I ...	258	0 to 258.
II ...	*302	258 to 560.
III ...	198	560 to 758.
IV ...	448 }	758 to 1206.
V ...	—	
VI ...	203	1206 to 1409.
VII ...	↑—	
VIII ...	100	1409 to 1509.
(To mid-VIIIth Dyn. = 1 Sothic cycle.)		
IX ...	100	1509 to 1609.
X (Mid-Xth Dyn. =1702. Plate XVI.)	185	1609 to 1794.
XI ...	43	1794 to 1837.
Ammenemes ...	16.	1837 to 1853.
BOOK I	1853 years.	

EUSEBIUS, BOOK II.

Dynasty.	Years.	Years' duration of scheme.
XII ...	182	1853 to 2035.
XIII ...	453	2035 to 2488.
XIV ...	184	2488 to 2672.
XV ...	250	2672 to 2922 = 2 Sothic cycles.
XVI ...	190	2922 to 3112.
XVII ...	103	3112 to 3215.
XVIII ...	376	3215 to 3591.
XIX ...	194	3591 to 3785.
BOOK II	1932 years.	

* 302 years from Africanus, in place of 297 years in Eusebius.
↑ 75 days' total as stated by Manetho is not entered, as it is of no importance as a summation.

TABLE LVIII,

THE EARLIER SYSTEM FROM WHICH THE SCHEME OF TABLE LVII ORIGINATED.

A.

(Dynasties IV, V, and XIII of Table LVII (A) omitted).

BOOK I.				BOOK II.				SUMMATION.	
Dynasty I	..	258 years.		Dynasty XII	..	182 years.			
Dynasty II	..	302 years.		Dynasty XIV	..	184 years.			
Dynasty III	..	198 years.		Dynasty XV	..	250 years.		BOOK I	=1305 years.
Dynasty VI	..	203 years.		Dynasty XVI	..	190 years.		BOOK II	=1479 years.
Dynasty IX	..	100 years.		Dynasty XVII	..	103 years.			2784 years,† (Old Chron. 2784 A.K.)
Dynasty X	..	185 years.		Dynasty XVIII	..	376 years.		BOOK III =	868 years.
Dynasty XI	..	43 years.		Dynasty XIX	..	194 years.			3652 years. (Old Chron. 3652 A.K.)
Amenemes	..	16 years.							
BOOK I	..	1305 years.		BOOK II	..	1479 years.			

† Refer Table LVII (A) preceding for 1001 years' Interpolation.

B.

Earlier Version of Manetho.			The Scheme of the Old Chronicle from which the earlier Version of Manetho was derived.	
Dynasty I began	.. 0 A.K.		Old Chronicle chronology of human kings begins ..	0 A.K.
3rd year Senusert I (Dyn. XII), and *Sed* festival at founding of Temple of Heliopolis, alleged date (*i.e.*, 1st 23 years of Dyn. XII = 1305 + 23 = 1328 A.K.)*	1328 A.K.		15 generations of the Cynic cycle began ..	1328 A.K.
Dynasty XX began (as true chronology Table XXIV) ..	2784 A.K.		Dynasty XX began (Table XXIV) ..	2784 A.K.
Reign of 1st king, Seti-nekht (as true chronology Table XXIV)	1 year.		Reign of Seti-nekht (Table XXIV) ..	1 year.
Reign of Ramessu III begins (as true chronology Table XXIV)	2785 A.K.		Reign of Ramessu III begins (Table XXIV) ..	2785 A.K.
For middle of 12th year Ramessu III, add ..	11¼ years.		For middle of 12th year Ramessu III, add ..	11¼ years.
12th year Ramessu III, and heliacal rising of Sirius on Day 1, Month I	2796¼ A.K.		12th year Ramessu III, and heliacal rising of Sirius on Day 1, Month I ..	2796¼ A.K.
=8¼ cycles of 329 years. (Table XI)			=8¼ cycles of 329 years. (Table XI)	
Dynasties end (Epoch of Okhos) ¶¶ 214, 250-254..	3652 A.K.		Dynasties end (Epoch of Okhos) ¶¶ 214, 250-254..	3652 A.K.

* The 3rd year of Senusert III was the 23rd year of Dynasty XII.

TABLE LIX.

SYSTEMS INDICATED BY THE VERSION OF AFRICANUS.

A.

(I)

AFRICANUS.

BOOK I	2303 years.
BOOK II	2213 years.
	4516 years.
Dynasty XX ..	135 years.
2 × 2325½ = ...	4651 years. See below, and ¶ 99.

Half above summation ..	2325½ years.
BOOK I, to beginning of Dynasty XII	2303 years.
For reign of Amenemhat I, add, from monuments ..	20 years.
	2323 years.
For middle of 3rd year Senusert I (year of a *Sed heb*) add	2½ years.
	2325½ years.

(II)

AFRICANUS.

BOOK I	2283 years.
BOOK II	2217 years.
BOOK III	868 years.
TOTAL ..	5368 years.

From Column (I)

1st year Menes to 3rd year Senusert I	2325½ years.
3rd year Senusert I to end of Dynasties = 2 solar cycles of 1521½ years	3043 years.
	5368½ years.

whereas above total is 5368 years.

B.

Africanus, Book I	2303 less 309* = 1994 years.
Africanus, Book II ..	2213 .. .. 2213 years.
	4516 less 309* = 4207 years.

1st year, Silites (Hyksos king) ..	3477 A.M. acc. to Bk. of Sothis.
Half Sothic cycle = Half 1460 years..	730 years.
1st year, Rampsis (III)..	4207 A.M. acc. to Bk. of Sothis.
Half Sothic cycle = Half 1460 years..	730 years.
1st year, Amosis (II), stated as "4936," for	4937 A.M.

(15 × 329) = 15 Phœnix Cycles = 4935 years.

* Africanus and Castor for Dynasty IX	= 409 years.
Eusebius for Dynasty IX	= 100 years.
Difference = 3 cycles of 103 years	= 309 years.

TABLE LX.

THE ORIGINAL CHRONOLOGY BASIS OF THE FICTITIOUS ELEMENTS IN THE KING LISTS.

(Refer to ¶ 493, Table XV Annotations (D) and Table XI Annotations).

A.

From Table LIX (B), Dynasty XII, as alleged, began at ... 1994 years of system.
For beginning of 3rd year of Senusert I =23rd year of Dynasty, as proved, add ... 22 years.

Actual date of 23rd year Senusert I =2016 A.K. (Table XV) ... 2016 years of system.
Deduct 2 cycles of 120 years ... 240 years.

Book of the Sothis date for Menes, 2776 A.M., less 1000 years interpolated ... 1776 years of system (Table XV).
Add 23 Sed heb periods evidenced by the Book of the Sothis, Old Chronicle, and the difference between the versions
of Africanus and Eusebius* ... † 691 years.

23 Sed heb periods end in astronomically fixed 27th year of Ramessu II ... 2467 A.K.

* Plate XVI, Table C, Cols. 4 and 8.   † By Table IV, 23 Sed hebs=721—30=691 years.

B.

As above, with ... 1776 A.K.   add 1000 years interpolated ... 2776 A.M. Book of the Sothis date for 1st year Menes.
Add 23 Sed hebs ... 691 yrs.   add Book of the Sothis 695 years ... 695 years.

27th year Ramessu II... 2467 A.K.   add 1000 years interpolated 3467 ... 3471 A.M. 1st year Konkharis, as Sesostris.
Add 2 Phoenix cycles 658 yrs.   658 ... §654 years. Book of the Sothis to last year Ramessu (II).

22nd year Uasarkon II 3125 A.K. ... add 1000 years interpolated 4125 ... 4125 A.M., last year Ramessu (II) according to the Book of the Sothis.

§ The interval of the Book of the Sothis between the 1st year of Konkharis as Sesostris, and the last year of Ramessu II Sesostris is 654 years, as above, and this period of 654 years
is given by Dexippos (apud Syncellum, p. 334) as the duration of the Phoenix cycle.

C.

THE NUMERICAL BASES OF THE BOOK OF THE SOTHIS SYSTEM.

(Confirming the conclusions of ¶ 493.)

		ORIGIN OF CONCEPTION.
IDENTITY I.	Menes.	
	(a) 23 names intervening between Menes and Konkharis (as Sesostris) ...	} 23 Sed hebs for 691 years.
	(b) 23 names from Konkharis (as Sesostris) to Ramesses (II) (as Sesostris) ...	
IDENTITY II.	(a) 15 names, Amasis to Ramesse Uaphru inclusive, prior to Konkharis (as Sesostris) ... Konkharis, followed by names of 6 Hyksos kings	} 15 generations of the Old Chronicle derived from 15 half-cycles of $164\frac{1}{3}$ years=$2467\frac{1}{3}$ A.K., the 27th year of Ramessu II.
	(b) 15 names, Amosis to Ramesses (as Sesostris) inclusive ...	

TABLE LXI.

THE CONFUSION OF THE SOTHIC CYCLE WITH THE PHŒNIX CYCLE. (Refer to ¶ 493).

	Version of Eusebius.	Version of Africanus.
BOOK I	1842 years.	2293 years.
BOOK II	1967 years.	2222 years.
Total duration to end of Dynasty XIX	3809 years.	4515 years.
Deduct, for Dynasty XIX ..	194 years.	209 years.
Duration to beginning of Dynasty XIX, Ramessu I } from monuments, Seti I } Table XIII	3615 years.	4306 years.
	2 years. Sethos (from Africanus)	51 years.
	9 years.	
Duration to beginning of next king, Ramessu II	3626 years.	4357 years.
Add, for middle of 27th year of Ramessu II	26.5 years. (Table XI).	26.5 years. (Table XI).
Total duration to 27th year of Ramessu II	3652.5 years, = 2.5 Sothic cycles in vague years.	4383.5 years, whereas 3 Sothic cycles = 4383 vague years.

In which 27th year a festival was held celebrating the termination of 7½ actual periods of the Phœnix cycle of 329 years (Table XI).

TABLE LXII.

THE SYSTEM OF "THE BOOK OF THE SOTHIS." (Refer also to Table LVI A).

1st king, Mestraïm (Menes), began ..	2776 Anno Mundi, as stated.	
Details of the reigns of the 25 kings add as 700 years. } Interval of "700 years of 25 kings of the Cycle in Manetho called Cynic (i.e., Sothic) end in the 5th (the last) year of this king. (Konkharis)" ..	700 years .. as stated.	
25th king, Konkharis,* ends ..	3476 Anno Mundi, but stated as 3477 Anno Mundi.	
Added details of reigns stated, from the end of Konkharis to the beginning of the reign of Amasis II	1459 years .. .. .. 1459 years.	
1st year of Amasis II	4935 Anno Mundi, but stated as 4936 Anno Mundi.	
15 Cycles of 329 years	4935 years, as added total to Amasis II.	

Konkharis ends .. 3476 A.M., as added.	Konkharis* ends .. 3476 A.M., as added.	1 Sothic cycle 1460 years.
Add 1 Sothic cycle 1460 years.	Add half Sothic cycle.. 730 years.	4 Cycles of 329 years 1316 years.
1st year Amasis II.. 4936 A.M.	1st year Ramessu III.. 4206 A.M. (4207, stated).	Beginning of reign of Mestraïm (Menes) } 2776 Anno Mundi.

* Konkharis= Kha-kau-ra (Senusert III), the original Sesostris. (Annotations D to Table XV. Refer also ¶¶ 39, 317, and 493.)

TABLE LXIII.

THE DEVELOPMENT OF THE SOTHIC CYCLE THEORY.

Book I (as Africanus) .. .. 2303 years.

Add for 3rd year Senusert I (Sesostris)=23rd year of Dynasty XII .. .. 22½ years, for middle of the year.

Radius of circle of circumference 14610=2325⅓ .. .. 2325⅓ years.   Duration of kings in Old Chronicle=2324 years.

Add 1 Sothic cycle .. .. 1461 vague years, or 1460 Sothic years.

3786⅔ vague years, or 3785⅓ Sothic years (refer to Table LVII A).

Add ½ Sothic cycle .. .. .. 730⅔ vague years, or 730 Sothic years.

4517 vague years.

Book I (Dynasties I to XI inclusive, and Ammenemes) .. .. 2303 years, as Africanus.

Book II (Dynasties XII to XIX inclusive) .. .. .. 2213 years, as Africanus.

Alleged beginning of Dynasty XX, omitting Interregnum, at .. 4516 years .. 4516

Add for Seti-nekht, 1st king of Dynasty XX .. .. 1 year 135 years, as Africanus for Dynasty XX.

Alleged 1st year of Ramessu III at .. .. .. 4517 years   4651 = 2 × 2325⅓ = radius of circle of circumference 29220.

"15 generations of the Cynic cycle" .. .. .. 443 years (¶¶ 94 and 95) .. 443 years.

Dynasty XVI to Dynasty XIX inclusive .. .. 835 years .. .. .. 835 years.

Interregnum between Dynasty XIX and Dynasty XX .. 178 years, as Old Chronicle, or 182 years, as Africanus.

Duration from 1st year Menes to 1st year Ramessu III (Dyn. XX) 1456 years .. .. 1460 years, the theoretical period of the Sothic cycle.

TABLE LXIV.

A CHRONOLOGICAL SYSTEM COMBINING THE ORIGINAL ASTRONOMICAL CHRONOLOGY AND THE FICTITIOUS SOTHIC CYCLE CHRONOLOGY.

	I.		II.
Manetho's Divine Dynasties, Scheme I (Plate XVI, Table A)	12843 years	(Plate XVI, Table A)	13900 years, Scheme II.
Old Chronicle, 15 generations for 438.5* years from 1328.5 A.K. end at	1767 A.K.	Book of the Sothis	700 years.
10 Sothic Cycles	14610 vague years	=	14600 Sothic years.

* 15 generations of $\dfrac{1461}{50}$ vague years = 438.3 vague years.

Manetho's Divine Dynasties, Scheme I, for 12843 years prior to Calendar Reckoning.

Calendar reckoning began ..	o A.K.	
Egyptian Dynastic reckoning began ..	1329 A.K.	(¶¶ 94 and 95).
Add 15 generations of the Cynic (Sothic) cycle	438 years.	(*i.e.*, 15 generations of $\dfrac{1460}{50}$ Sothic yrs.)
Old Chronicle's Dynasty XVI began ..	1767 A.K.	=14610 years from beginning of Divine Dynasties.
Add for Old Chronicle's Dynasty XVI..	190 years,	as Version of Eusebius.
Old Chronicle's Dynasty XVII began ..	1957 A.K.,	=19 cycles of 103 years (Table III).
Add for Old Chronicle's Dynasty XVII	103 years,	as Version of Eusebius.
Old Chronicle's Dynasty XVIII began ..	2060 A.K.,	=20 cycles of 103 years (Table III).
Add for Old Chronicle's Dynasty XVIII	348 years,	as Version of Eusebius.
Old Chronicle's Dynasty XIX began ..	2408 A.K.	
Add for Old Chronicle's Dynasty XIX..	194 years,	as Version of Eusebius.
Old Chronicle's Interregnum began ..	2602 A.K.	
Add for Old Chronicle's Interregnum ..	182 years,	as Version of Africanus.
Old Chronicle's Dynasty XX began (correct date)	2784 A.K.,	as Table XXIV.
Add Old Chronicle's Dynasties XX to XXX inclusive	868 years,	as Africanus for Dynasties XX to XXXI inclusive
2 Sothic cycles from o A.K. = 3652.5 Sothic years	3652 A.K.,	as Tables LVIII and LXV also ¶¶ 214, 250-254.

Africanus, 1050 years, Book III. Plate XVI Tables B and C.

Former placing of scheme of Old Chronicle for beginning of Dynasty XIX	2412 A.K.	
Stated 1st king, Sethosis (Seti I), as in Eusebius.. ..	55 years.	
Alleged 1st year Ramessu II .. (7½ cycles of 329 years = 2467½ years)	2467 A.K. (Tables LVI A and LX.)	
But actual date of Phœnix cycle ending in 27th year Ramessu II =2467½ A.K. (Tables XI, LX, and, by context, Table LXI.)		
New placing of scheme of Old Chronicle for beginning of Dynasty XIX	2408 A.K., as Table.	
Stated 1st king, Sethosis (Seti I), as Manetho quoted by Josephus .. .. .. :.	59 years.	
Alleged 1st year of Ramessu II (as above)	2467 A.K. (Tables LVI A and LX.)	

TABLE LXV.

THE CHRONOLOGY SYSTEM OF THE IIIRD BOOK OF MANETHO (AFRICANUS) COMBINING THE ORIGINAL AND SOTHIC SYSTEMS OF CHRONOLOGY.

Dynasty XX, as in Old Chronicle System,
  began (true date by Table XXIV)   2784   A.K.
  Add for Africanus' Dynasty XX ..   135   years.

Dynasty XXI began   2919   A.K.
  Add for Africanus' Dynasty XXI ..   130   years.

Dynasty XXII began   3049   A.K.
  Add for Africanus' Dynasty XXII ..   120   years.

Dynasty XXIII began   3169   A.K.
  Add for Africanus' Dynasty XXIII, 3
  known kings   58   years.   (3 kings only stated by Eusebius.)

Africanus' unknown "king," Zet, began   3227   A.K. =1767 A.K. + 1460 (see Table LXIV).
  Add for otherwise unknown "king,"
  Zet, interpolated in Africanus   Petrie states "No explanation of this
  (¶ 138a)..   31   years.   name has been given." (But refer to
                                                   ¶ 138a).

Dynasty XXIV began   3258   A.K.
  Add for Africanus' Dynasty XXIV ..   6   years.

Dynasty XXV began   3264   A.K.
  Add for Africanus' Dynasty XXV ..   40   years.

Dynasty XXVI began   3304   A.K.
  Add for Africanus' Dynasty XXVI ..   150½   years.

Dynasty XXVII began   ..   ..   3454¼   A.K. =10¼ cycles of 329 years; Phœnix cycle
                                                 of Amasis II.*
  Add for Africanus' Dynasty XXVII..   124¼   years.

Dynasty XXVIII began   ..   ..   3578⅜   A.K.
  Add for Africanus' Dynasty XXVIII   6   years.

Dynasty XXIX began   ..   ..   3584⅜   A.K.
  Add for Africanus' Dynasty XXIX ..   20¼   years.

Dynasty XXX began ..   ..   ..   3605¼   A.K.   3605 A.K. =35 cycles of 103 years, and
                                                  date of many cycles ending, as men-
                                                  tioned in ¶ 33, item II, a to d.
  Add for Africanus' Dynasty XXX ..   38   years.

Dynasty XXXI began ..   ..   ..   3643¼   A.K.
  Add for Africanus' Dynasty XXXI..   9   years.

Dynasty XXXI ended ..   ..   ..   3652¼   A.K.   (as Table LXIV and references there.)

* Here the cycle is given as ending with the reign of Amasis II. The A.K. date is correct for the cycle, but this is for the
25th year of Amasis II (Table XI and Annotations Col. 5).

Manetho's Divine Dynasties, Scheme I (Plate XVI,
  Table A and Table LXIV)   ..   ..   12843 years.
Old Chronicle's 15 generations for
  438½ years end at   ..   1767 A.K.   1767 years.
                                                          14610 years = 10 Sothic cycles.
  Add 1 Sothic cycle   ..   ..   1460 Sothic years   1461 vague years.

Interpolated king, "Zet," (un-
  known) begins at   ..   3227 A.K., or   ..   ..   16071 years = 11 Sothic cycles.

TABLE LXVI.

THE CYCLICAL BASES OF THE EGYPTIAN THEORY RELATING TO THE ANCIENT EGYPTIAN SHORT CHRONOLOGY SYSTEM.

(In ¶ 418 it is explained that this Short Chronology System was advanced only as an alternative theory of Chronology as opposed to the theory of the Long Chronology of the Lists, for Dynasties prior to Dynasty XI. The Later Lists, as given by Manetho contain elements of both systems.)

I.

Item	Value
Demi-gods for (Table LVI, C, and D), 15 generations of Cynic cycle ..	1217 years.
Deluge began (by Table V) ..	438 Sothic years.* / 1655 A.K. ‡
Africanus' Dynasty II ..	303 years.
Table III, 19 cycles of 103 years ..	1957 A.K.
Old Chronicle and Eusebius for Dynasty XVII ..	103 years.
Table III, 20 cycles of 103 years; Old Chronicle and Eusebius for Dynasty XVIII ..	2060 A.K. / 348 years.
Table LXIV Old Chronicle and Eusebius for Dynasty XIX ..	2408 A.K. / 194 years.
Table LXIV Africanus, Interregnum ..	2602 A.K. / 182 years.
Table XXIV, Dynasty XX began / Old Chronicle and Africanus, Book III ..	2784 A.K. / 868 years.
Epoch of Okhos ..	3652 A.K.

* Refer to Table LXIV.

II.

Item	Value
Demi-gods for ..	1217 years.
15 generations of Cynic cycle ..	438 Vague years.*
Deluge ended (Table V) Africanus' Dynasty I ..	1656 A.K.‡ / 263 years.
Africanus' Dynasty XI ..	1919 A.K. / 43 years.
(Refer to Table XV) Africanus, AMMENEMES ..	1962 A.K. / 16 years. / 1978 A.K.
Africanus' Dynasty XII ..	160 years.
6½ cycles of 329 years (2138½ years) ..	2138 A.K.
Africanus Dynasty XVIII ..	259 years.
Africanus' Dynasty XIX ..	209 years.
Old Chronicle date / Old Chronicle Interregnum ..	2606 A.K.‡ / 178 years.†
Table XXIV, Dynasty XX began / Africanus and Old Chronicle, Book III ..	2784 A.K. / 868 years.†
(348 B.C. by Plate XVI, Table F and ¶¶ 214, 250-254) ..	3652 A.K.‡

III.

Item	Value
Demi-gods for ..	1217 years.
15 generations of Cynic cycle ..	438 Vague years.*
Deluge ended (Table V) Eusebius' Dynasty I ..	1656 A.K.‡ / 258 years.
Eusebius' Dynasty XI ..	1914 A.K. / 43 years.
Table III 19 cycles of 103 years ..	1957 A.K.
Turin Papyrus for Dynasty XII ..	213 years.
Dynasty XVIII began, as Table XIV (true date) ..	2170 A.K.
Table XII, Dynasty XVIII ..	260 years (Petrie)
Table XIV (true date) ..	2430 A.K.
Table XIII, Dynasty XIX ..	93 years.
Table XIV (true date) / True Interregnum (Table XXIII) ..	2523 A.K. / 261 years.
Table XXIV, Dyn. XX began (true date) (Africanus, Book III) ..	2784 A.K. / 868 years.
..	3652 A.K.

† 2606 A.K. fixed as Old Chronicle's statement by data following in same column.

THE SHORT CHRONOLOGY OF THE ARMENIAN VERSION OF EUSEBIUS.

Item	Value
Deluge ended (Table V) / Armenian Version of Eusebius for Dynasty I (stated total) ..	1656 A.K. / 226 years.
Armenian Version of Eusebius for Dynasty XI (stated total) ..	1882 A.K. / 43 years.
Armenian Version of Eusebius for Dynasty XII (stated total) ..	1925 A.K. / 245 years.
Dynasty XVIII began, as Table XIV ..	2170 A.K.

‡ The Sed heb period of Table IV Series No. (1):

Item	Value	
Birth of Noah (Table V) / Add, for beginning of 600th year ..	1656 A.K. / 599 years.	= Chinese Epoch of Fo-hi (¶ 315) = 2944 B.C. (Historical).
deduct ..	= 599 years.	
600th year of Noah, Deluge began ..	1655 A.K.	= 2345 B.C.
601st year of Noah, Deluge ended ..	1656 A.K.	= 2344 B.C.

ANNOTATIONS TO TABLE LXVI.

A PRE-MANETHON THEORY RELATING TO CO-EQUAL ANTIQUITY OF EARLY DYNASTIC CAPITALS.

THIS (*i.e.*, Abydos). (Thinites).	MEMPHIS. (Memphites).	ELEPHANTINE.	HERAKLEOPOLIS.	THEBES. (Thebans).	Later Origins.	
					XOIS.	AVARIS (Hyksos).
Dyn. I	Dyn. III					
Dyn. II	Dyn. IV	Dyn. V	Dyn. IX	Dyn. XI		
	Dyn. VI			Dyn. XII	Dyn. XIV	Dyn. XV
	Dyn. VII		Dyn. X	Dyn. XIII		
	Dyn. VIII			Dyn. XVII		Dyn. XVI

Compare with the parallel rows and dynastic groupings of the Karnak List (Table LV).

Thus, commenting on the Dynastic Lists extracted by him from the Egyptian History of Manetho, Eusebius states :—

"If the quantity of time covered by the Kings is in excess we must remember, in the first instance, that there were at one and the same time several kings in Egypt, *for we are told that the Thinites and Memphites reigned simultaneously, AND OTHERS ALSO.* Moreover, some seemed to have reigned in one place, some in another, each Dynasty being confined to its own Canton, so that several kings did not reign successively, but different kings reigned at the same time in different places." (Euseb. *Chron., Can.,* i, 20, sect. 3).

It is significant that Eusebius did not make this statement on his own authority. Obviously he is referring to some passage or other in Manetho's work, or to some literary tradition in existence concerning the basis of the Ancient System of Egyptian short chronology.

XIIth Dynasty records claim that the Temple of Heliopolis was founded by Senusert I of Dynasty XII, and that Senusert I erected an obelisk at this Temple in the year of a cycle of 120 years ending. Pliny states that Pepy I of Dynasty VI erected an obelisk at Heliopolis, and a record of Pepy I mentions that a festival of 120 years was celebrated in his reign. The statement of Pliny indicates that the Egyptian source, from which the statement was derived, identified the 120 years' festival of Pepy I with the 120 years' festival of Senusert I, thus making Dynasty VI and Dynasty XII contemporaneous.

A striking fact that would tend to confirm this School of Egyptian Chronology in its theory is that the general sequence of events relating to expeditions, the routes and objectives of these expeditions, quarrying and mining, and the general development of art is strikingly similar in the two dynasties.

Again, inscriptions of Dynasty V appear to refer to the last king of Dynasty III and the kings of Dynasty IV in succession as contemporaneous with the kings of Dynasty V. This evidence was obviously adopted as confirming the theory.

Another feature that would be deemed to confirm the theory, is that the sequence of dynastic succession presented by the theory gives no gaps between the various periods during which the mines and quarries in Sinai were worked by the Egyptian kings from the Ist Dynasty to the XIXth Dynasty inclusive, excepting during the period of two decades covered by the Egyptian War of Independence against the Hyksos. Nor by the theory is there any break in the worship and in the continuation of the evolution of religious ideas concerning the great gods of the Egyptians. There is a representation of continuous development in Egyptian ideas in every phase of Egyptian life.

The supposed contemporaneousness of Dynasties VII and VIII in succession with Dynasties XII and XVII in succession, and with Dynasty X, would be deemed to be confirmed by the fact that Asiatic invaders entered Egypt and that similar conditions due to the invasion occurred within the three respective periods.

Altogether it is quite a good theory when closely examined from every reliable archæological and chronological standpoint. Had it been advanced in this form about a century ago, the chronological systems of Egyptian archæology, and the scientific principles upon which archæological excavations have been carried out, might have developed upon lines distinctly different from those now established.

The real origin of the theory seems to have been related to the fact that the 30 years' and 120 years' festival periods, at the time of the XIIth and XVIIIth Dynasties, were based on the year of the Adamic Deluge Ending (1656 A.K. =2344 B.C.). We know, however, that the same festival periods, prior to 1656 A.K., were based on the Zero Epoch (0 A.K. = 4000 A.K.) of Adamic astronomical chronology (Table V). We also know that the Adamic Deluge was confined to the territory (or "world") of the Adamic race, and did not affect Egypt. The chronological theory, however, obviously presupposes that the Adamic Deluge affected Egypt. At any rate it presupposes that the 30 years' festivals originated at 2344 B.C. Since these festivals were celebrated by the kings of the Ist Egyptian Dynasty, the theory places the Ist Dynasty as beginning at this date of the Adamic Deluge ending. For this reason the 30 human dynasties of the King Lists of the Egyptian priest, Manetho, as preserved by Africanus, are described as "The Egyptian Dynasties after the Deluge." A similar formulation of the Babylonian chronology has been shown in Annotations (A) and (B) to Tables XVII-XIX.

Another short system of Egyptian chronology—shorter even than that we are considering—is implied by the interval of 23 Sed hebs or 691 years deemed to have intervened between the *Sed heb* of Mena, and the *Sed heb* of Ramessu II's 27th year. (Tables LVIA, LX, LXII, and LXIV.) The datum of the latter system is 1776 A.K., the date at which was celebrated the first festival of 120 years from the Deluge date 1656 A.K. By this system, 1776 A.K. is *nominally* the 1st year of Mena.

Manetho (Africanus) gives the reign of Mena as 62 years. By the former system Mena began at 1656 and ended at 1718 A.K., and by the latter, began at 1776 and ended at 1838 A.K. Now Josephus was thoroughly acquainted with Manetho's history. His extracts are the only actual extracts—apart from the Lists of Kings—from Manetho's text. Josephus states that Solomon became king at 3100 or alternatively 3040 *Anno Mundi* (refer Annotations D to Table XXVIII), and that "the interval "—between Menes (Mena) and Solomon was "more than 1300 years." (Antiq. VIII, vi, 2.) Obviously Josephus referred to 1718 A.K. for the end of the reign of Mena since that date (reckoned as *Anno Mundi*, by Josephus) is 1382 years and 1322 years respectively prior to his alternative dates for the beginning of Solomon's reign.

Josephus also adds an interesting commentary from Manetho on the period of the Hyksos. Referring to the expulsion of the Hyksos, Josephus quotes Manetho as stating :—

"That the kings of the Thebais (Dynasty XVII) *and of the other parts of Egypt,* made an insurrection against the Shepherds (Hyksos of Dynasty XVI), and that there a terrible and long war was made between them." This reference to kings of "the other parts of Egypt" as ruling at the same time as kings of Thebes (Dynasty XVII) can only be to kings of Dynasties XIII or XIV. This element of contemporaneity has already been proved by Table XV and Annotations A to D in relation to Table XIV and Annotations. At the same time, we must not fail to observe that this contemporaneity was held by the Egyptian compilers of the short chronology to extend to Dynasties VII and VIII.

TABLE LXVII.

THE PHŒNIX CHRONOLOGY OF THE KING LISTS. (Refer to Table XI Annotations, Col. 5).

A.

Dynasty XX began at .. .. 2784 years.
Intrpolation by Eusebius .. .. .. 1000 years.

Alleged beginning of Dynasty XX .. 3784 years = 11¼ Phœnix cycles. .. 3785½ A.K. = 3785 years. — Table LVII for Dynasties I to XIX inclusive.
Dynasties XX and XXI (Eusebius) .. 308 years
Add for 22nd year of Dynasty XXII .. 21 years = 1 Phœnix cycle. .. 329 years

Alleged 22nd year of Dynasty XXII .. 4113 years = 12¼ Phœnix cycles. .. 4113½ A.K. = 4113 years. — Eusebius, for Dynasties XX to XXVI inclusive. Added totals of Dynasties (Table XLVIII).
One Phœnix cycle .. .. .. 329 years = 1 Phœnix cycle. .. 329 years .. 657 years

Alleged termination Amasis II (4441½). (Dyn. XXVI ending 4442) .. 4442 years .. 4441½ A.K. = 13½ Phœnix cycles .. 4442 years. — 3 Phœnix cycles or 987 years in excess of true date (Table XI). Refer to Annotations D, items 4 and 5, to Table XV.

B.

Dynasty XXVI ends with Persian Conquest of Egypt (Table XXIV) .. 525 B.C. — Africanus gives total duration of Dynasty XXII as .. .. 120 years.
Duration of Dynasties XXII to XXVI, as Eusebius .. 349 years. — Eusebius .. .. .. 49 years.
Difference .. .. .. 71 years.
Dynasty XXII began, according to Eusebius, at .. .. 874 B.C. — which is the duration given by Breasted for the first three reigns of Dynasty XXII.
which is the astronomically fixed date of the 22nd year of Uasarkon II of Dynasty XXII. (Tables XI and XXIV).

C.

Old Chronicle and List of Africanus give Dynasty XX commencing with Set-nekht at .. .. 2784 A.K. = 1216 B.C., as astronomically fixed. (Tables XI and XXIV.)

Version of Africanus, Dynasty XX, stated total .. 135 years.
Version of Africanus, Dynasty XXI, added total .. 114 years.

Total duration of Dynasties XX and XXI .. 249 years = 249 years.

According to Version of Africanus, Dynasty XXII began at .. .. 3033 A.K. = 967 B.C.
First three kings (as Breasted)=Difference between Africanus and Eusebius .. 71 years. = 71 years.

Fourth reign, Uasarkon II, began at .. .. .. 3104 A.K. = 896 B.C.
For middle of 22nd year .. .. .. 21½ years. 21½ years.

22nd year of Uasarkon II, Phœnix cycle ends .. 3125½ A.K. = 874 B.C., as astronomically fixed.

D.

INITIAL DIFFERENCE	AFRICANUS.	EUSEBIUS.
		12 years.*
Dynasty XX	135 years stated	178 years stated.
Dynasty XXI	114 years added	130 years stated.
Dynasty XXII	120 years stated	49 years stated.
TOTAL	369 years.	369 years.

First three kings, Dynasty XXII .. 71 years, commencing 967 B.C. — Termination of which begins Africanus and Eusebius alternative commencement of Dynasty.
To 22nd year inclusive of Uasarkon II .. 22 years.
Eusebius' duration for Dynasty XXII .. 49 years. — Added duration of Dynasty as Africanus,
Difference to Africanus' 116 years .. 67 years. = 116 years.
Actual duration of Dynasty XXII .. 209 years, ending at 758 B.C.
But actually .. .. 209½ years, ending at 757 B.C. as Table XXIV.

* Due to Phœnix cycle beginning in 12th year of Ramessu IIII (Table XI), and 1 year of Set-nekht beginning Dynasty (Table XXIV).

INDEX

OF AUTHORS AND AUTHORITIES REFERRED TO IN THE TEXT.

GENERAL INDEX.

Roman numerals refer to Plates, and to Tables when the word " Table " is inserted before the numeral.

The names of Kings and Deities included in this Index are those referred to in the Text. Names of Kings and Deities contained in Dynastic Lists and Tables, and in Annotations thereto, are not included.

CPSIA information can be obtained
at www.ICGtesting.com
Printed in the USA
LVHW061909050321
680706LV00010B/573

9 781169 367821